# Tolley's Taxwise I 2016/17

## Income Tax (including International issues)
## National Insurance
## Corporation Tax
## Capital Gains Tax
## Stamp Duty
## VAT

**Authors:**

**Rebecca Benneyworth MBE FCA BSc**

**David Heaton FCA CTA of Baker Tilly**

**Lynne Poyser BMedSc (Hons) ATT CTA**

**Philip Rutherford LLB CTA**

**Cheryl Scott ex HMRC**

**Andrew Tall FCA, CTA**

**Julie Ward CTA**

**Contributors from Francis Clark LLP**

**General Editor:**

**Rebecca Benneyworth MBE FCA BSc**

Tolley®

**Members of the LexisNexis Group worldwide**

| | |
|---|---|
| United Kingdom | RELX (UK) Limited, trading as LexisNexis, 1-3 Strand, London WC2N 5JR |
| Argentina | LexisNexis Argentina, Buenos Aires |
| Australia | LexisNexis Butterworths, Chatswood, New South Wales |
| Austria | LexisNexis Verlag ARD Orac GmbH & Co KG, Vienna |
| Benelux | LexisNexis Benelux, Amsterdam |
| Canada | LexisNexis Canada, Markham, Ontario |
| China | LexisNexis China, Beijing and Shanghai |
| France | LexisNexis SA, Paris |
| Germany | LexisNexis Deutschland GmbH, Munster |
| Hong Kong | LexisNexis Hong Kong, Hong Kong |
| India | LexisNexis India, New Delhi |
| Italy | Giuffrè Editore, Milan |
| Japan | LexisNexis Japan, Tokyo |
| Malaysia | Malayan Law Journal Sdn Bhd, Kuala Lumpur |
| New Zealand | LexisNexis NZ Ltd, Wellington |
| Singapore | LexisNexis Singapore, Singapore |
| South Africa | LexisNexis Butterworths, Durban |
| USA | LexisNexis, Dayton, Ohio |




Published by LexisNexis


A CIP Catalogue record for this book is available from the British Library.

ISBN for this volume: 9780754552796

Printed and bound by CPI Group (UK) Ltd, Croydon, CR0 4YY

Visit LexisNexis Butterworths at www.lexisnexis.co.uk

# About this book

For over 30 years Tolley's Taxwise I has provided practitioners with a practical means of keeping up to date with changing legislation by way of worked examples. The publication is updated annually to show the changes introduced by the Finance Acts.

The publication is useful as a manual for staff and practitioners giving guidance as to the layout of computations and notes explaining both the law and practice relating to taxation issues. In addition, the worked examples provide a comprehensive study aid to students of taxation, allowing the testing of theoretical knowledge on practical examples of a style that could well form the basis of an examination question for professional qualifications.

## COVERAGE

A selection of taxation examples based on the legislation current for 2016/17, complete with annotated solutions.

The examples are preceded by a summary commencing on page (xix) of the main provisions of Finance Act 2016, which received Royal Assent on 15 September 2016. Where appropriate, the examples also reflect announcements or include comments about future changes which will be included in subsequent Finance Bills.

The book is not an exhaustive work of reference but it shows the treatment of all the points that are most likely to be encountered.

The contents list starting on page (v) shows the broad coverage of each example. In addition, there is a general index at the back of the book to assist in the location of specific points.

## GENERAL EDITOR:

**Rebecca Benneyworth** MBE FCA BSc (Hons)

## THE AUTHORS

**Rebecca Benneyworth** MBE FCA BSc is a lecturer and writer on a variety of taxes. Rebecca is former editor of Tax Adviser magazine and consultant editor for a number of tax publications. She is Chair of the Tax Faculty of the ICAEW, and a prolific lecturer on the CPD circuit. Winner of the HMRC External Engagement awards in 2011, she is involved in all aspects of tax affecting small businesses, their owners and their advisers. She is also a volunteer for charities advising the elderly on their tax affairs, and educating young people on financial literacy and the tax system.

**David Heaton** FCA CTA is a former Partner at Baker Tilly who has been advising employers and their employees on their tax & NI liabilities for over 25 years. He is now an independent tax consultant. His clients have ranged from global companies with complex cross-border NI issues to one-man consultancy businesses caught by the 'IR35' rules. He works as a national specialist across all sectors of business.

**Lynne Poyser** BMedSc (Hons) ATT CTA is the in-house writer of the Personal Tax module of TolleyGuidance. An expert in personal taxation with over 15 years' experience, Lynne joined Tolley from BDO, where she worked in the private client team and the national tax training department, having previously worked for Grant Thornton and Arthur Andersen. Lynne has written for Taxation magazine, Tax Adviser magazine and is a tutor for Tolley Exam Training. She is also the current Chairman of the London branch of ATT and CIOT.

**Philip Rutherford** LLB CTA is the Senior Tax Director for Molson Coors Europe, where he has overall responsibility for tax across Europe. Phil is also a member of the Chartered Institute of Tax. Prior to Molson Coors, Phil worked and trained with KPMG, gaining both ATT and CTA qualifications. Phil specialised in tax investigations working in both the fields of direct and indirect tax. He also writes for TolleyGuidance, LexisNexis PSL, Tiley and Collison, Tolley Capital Gains Tax and has written a number of Tax Digests.

**Andrew Tall** FCA, CTA has over a decade's experience in "Group A" accountancy firms as a corporation tax specialist focusing on owner-managed businesses. At Simmons Gainsford LLP he advises clients on corporate tax matters including interactions with owner-manager tax issues, corporate restructuring, enquiries, research and development tax credits, capital allowances and taxation of companies in Administration and Liquidation. Andrew is also a volunteer for the Tax Faculty of the Institute of Chartered Accountants of England and Wales (ICAEW). Here he volunteers on the Small and Medium Enterprise committee and the Enquiries and Appeals committee.

**Julie Ward** CTA has worked on Taxwise every year since 2003-04. She has over 20 years experience in tax and has worked for a number of large London firms including PricewaterhouseCoopers. Julie currently works for The Tax Hut Ltd and specialises in owner managed businesses.

## COMPANION PUBLICATION

Tolley's Taxwise II 2016-17 (covering Inheritance Tax and Taxation of Trusts and Estates).

# Contents

# Abbreviations

| | |
|---|---|
| AMV | actual market value |
| art | Article |
| ATCA | Advance Thin Capitalisation Agreement |
| CAA 2001 | Capital Allowances Act 2001 |
| Cf. | compare |
| CFC | Controlled foreign company |
| CGT | Capital gains tax |
| CGTA 1979 | Capital Gains Tax Act 1979 |
| CIR | Commissioners of Inland Revenue ('the Board') |
| CIS | Construction Industry Scheme |
| CRCA | Commissioners for Revenue and Customs Act |
| CT | Corporation tax |
| CTA 2009 | Corporation tax Act 2009 |
| CTA 2010 | Corporation tax Act 2010 |
| CTSA | Corporation tax self-assessment |
| CTT | Capital transfer tax |
| CUP | Comparable uncontrolled price |
| EC | European Communities |
| ECJ | European Court of Justice |
| EEC | European Economic Community |
| EFRBS | Employer-financed Retirement Benefits Scheme |
| EU | European Union |
| Ex D | Exchequer Division |
| FA | Finance Act |
| F (No 2) A | Finance (No 2) Act |
| FII | Franked investment income |
| FOIA 2000 | Freedom of Information Act 2000 |
| FY | Financial year |
| HC(I) | High Court (Ireland) |
| HL | House of Lords |
| HMRC | Her Majesty's Revenue and Customs |
| ICTA | Income and Corporation Taxes Act 1988 |
| IHT | Inheritance tax |
| IHTA 1984 | Inheritance Tax Act 1984 |
| ISAs | individual savings accounts |

| | |
|---|---|
| ITA 2007 | Income Tax Act 2007 |
| ITEPA 2003 | Income Tax (Earnings and Pensions) Act 2003 |
| ITTOIA 2005 | Income Tax (Trading and Other Income) Act 2005 |
| IUMV | initial unrestricted market value |
| LIVR | Limited information value report |
| MSCs | managed service companies |
| MSCP | managed service company provider |
| NIC | National insurance contribution |
| NMW | National minimum wage |
| pa | per annum |
| PEPs | personal equity plans |
| PIDs | property income distributions |
| pm | per month |
| POA | Payments on account |
| POCA 2002 | Proceeds of Crime Act 2002 |
| QCBs | qualifying corporate bonds |
| RBPA | Renovation of Business Premises in disadvantaged Area |
| s | Section |
| SA | Self-assessment |
| Sch | Schedule |
| SE | Societas Europaea |
| SED | Seafarers' earnings deduction |
| SI | Statutory instrument |
| SIPPs | self-invested personal pensions |
| SSCBA 1992 | Social Security Contributions and Benefits Act 1992 |
| SP | Revenue Statement of Practice |
| Sp C | Special Commissioners |
| TCGA 1992 | Taxation of Chargeable Gains Act 1992 |
| TIOPA 2010 | Taxation (International and Other Provisions) Act 2010 |
| TMA 1970 | Taxes Management Act 1970 |
| UAP | Upper accruals point |
| UEL | Upper earnings limit |
| VAT | Value added tax |
| VATA 1994 | Value Added Tax Act 1994 |

# Rates and allowances

## PERSONAL TAX RATES

(1) Income tax is chargeable on taxable income, ie that part of income which remains after all allowable deductions, including personal allowances, have been made.

The rates of tax for 2016/17 are:

| | *Taxable income* £ | *Rate* | *Dividend rate* |
|---|---|---|---|
| Basic rate | 0–32,000 | 20% | 7.5% |
| Higher rate | 32,001–150,000 | 40% | 32.5% |
| Additional rate | 150,001+ | 45% | 38.1% |
| | | | |
| Starting rate for savings | 0–5,000 | 0% | |
| Savings nil rate band (basic rate taxpayers) | 0–1,000 | 0% | |
| Savings nil rate band (higher rate taxpayers) | 0–500 | 0% | |
| | | | |
| Dividend nil rate band | 0–5,000 | | 0% |

The rates of tax for 2015/16 were:

| | *Taxable income* £ | *Rate* | *Dividend rate* |
|---|---|---|---|
| Basic rate | 0–31,785 | 20% | 10% |
| Higher rate | 31,786–150,000 | 40% | 32.5% |
| Additional rate | 150,001+ | 45% | 37.5% |
| | | | |
| Starting rate for savings | 0–5,000 | 0% | |

As savings income is taxed after non-savings income (and before dividend income), the starting rate for savings applies only to the extent that the taxable income from non-savings sources does not exceed the starting rate band.

The savings nil rate band (2016/17 onwards) applies after the starting rate for savings (should the latter be appropriate). The amount of the savings nil rate band, called the savings allowance, depends on the taxpayer's marginal rate. Basic rate taxpayers have a savings allowance of £1,000 and higher rate taxpayers have a savings allowance of £500. Additional rate taxpayers cannot benefit.

The dividend nil rate band (2016/17 onwards) applies to the first £5,000 of dividend income.

If the starting rate for savings or the savings nil rate band is applicable, it forms part of the basic rate band, not an addition to it.

(2) Discretionary and accumulation and maintenance trusts are charged on non-dividend income at a single rate, called 'the trust rate', which is 45% for both 2016/17 and 2015/16. A standard rate band of £1,000 applies to the first slice of income chargeable at the trust rate. Trustees of other trusts are generally liable at the basic rate of 20%, though the trust rate applies to specified types of income.

The rate of tax for discretionary and accumulation and maintenance trusts on dividend income, called 'the dividend trust rate', is 38.1% for 2016/17 and 37.5% for 2015/16. Trustees of other trusts generally pay tax on dividend income at the dividend rates.

Trusts for vulnerable people can elect to be taxable as if the income of the trust were the income of the beneficiary.

(3) Personal allowances for 2016/17 and 2015/16 are:

| | *2016/17* | *2015/16* |
|---|---|---|
| | £ | £ |
| Personal allowance: | 11,000 | 10,600 |
| Reduced by £1 for every £2 by which income exceeds | 100,000 | 100,000 |
| Born before 6 April 1938 | 11,000 | 10,660 |
| Excess allowance over basic amount of | | 10,600 |
| reduced by £1 for every £2 by which income exceeds | | 27,000 |
| Married couple's allowance (tax saving thereon 10%)† | | |
| Elder born before 6 April 1935 | 8,355 | 8,355 |
| Excess allowance over basic amount of | 3,220 | 3,220 |
| reduced by £1 for every £2 by which income exceeds | 27,700 | 27,700 |
| Transferable marriage allowance †† | 1,100 | 1,060 |

† Reduced in tax year of marriage by 1/12th for each complete month (running from 6th day of one month to 5th day of next) in that year prior to the date of marriage

†† From 6 April 2015 an individual can to elect to 'transfer' 10% of his personal allowance to his spouse or civil partner. Rather than increasing the amount of the transferee's personal allowance, relief will be given via a tax reduction at 20%. The transferee's personal allowance is reduced by the amount 'transferred'. To be able to make the election neither party can be an additional rate taxpayer nor claim married couple's allowance.

| | *2016/17* | *2015/16* |
|---|---|---|
| | £ | £ |
| Blind person's allowance | 2,290 | 2,290 |

(4) Tax credits for 2016/17 and 2015/16 are:

| ***Credit element*** | ***Annual amount*** | |
|---|---|---|
| | *2016/17* | *2015/16* |
| | £ | £ |
| Family element of CTC | 545 | 545 |
| Child element of CTC | 2,780 | 2,780 |
| Disability element of CTC[1.] | 3,140 | 3,140 |
| Severe disability element of CTC[1.] | 1,275 | 1,275 |
| Basic element of WTC | 1,960 | 1,960 |
| Couple's or lone parent element of WTC | 2,010 | 2,010 |
| 30 hour element of WTC | 810 | 810 |
| Disability element of WTC[2.] | 2,970 | 2,970 |
| Severe disability element of WTC[2.] | 1,275 | 1,275 |
| For both WTC and CTC | | |
| – income threshold | 6,420 | 6,420 |

| *Credit element* | *Annual amount* | |
|---|---|---|
| | *2016/17* | *2015/16* |
| – withdrawal rate | 41% | 41% |
| – first threshold (those entitled to CTC only) | 16,105 | 16,105 |
| Income disregard – increases | 2,500 | 5,000 |
| Income disregard – decreases | 2,500 | 2,500 |
| Childcare element | | |
| Percentage of eligible costs | 70% | 70% |
| Maximum eligible costs (weekly) | | |
| – one child | 175 | 175 |
| – two or more children | 300 | 300 |

Footnotes

1. The disability element of CTC is paid for each child for whom a disability living allowance (DLA) is due or if the child is registered blind. If the higher care component of DLA is due then the severe disability element is paid.
2. If both claimants in a joint claim are disabled then the award will include two elements per couple.

## TAXATION OF DIRECTORS AND OTHERS IN RESPECT OF CARS

### CAR BENEFIT CHARGES

Car benefits charge is based on $CO_2$ emissions and ranges from 5% to 37% of list price (for details see **Example B4**). For tax years prior to 2015/16, the maximum was 35%.

The percentages for cars without a $CO_2$ emissions figure for 2016/17 is 16%, 27% or 37% of list price depending on engine size. For 2015/16 and prior years different percentages applied depending on whether the car was registered on or after 1 January 1998 or before 1 January 1998.

The percentage for electric cars is 7% for 2016/17 and 5% for 2015/16. For tax years 2010/11 to 2014/15 the percentage was 0%.

List prices are increased by 3% for diesel cars, but not so as to exceed the 37% maximum.

The list price is reduced by up to £5,000 in respect of a capital contribution from the employee.

For cars 15 years old or more at end of tax year with a market value of £15,000 or more, market value is substituted for list price if higher.

The benefit is reduced proportionately if the car is not available for part of the year.

### CAR FUEL BENEFIT SCALES

Car fuel benefit is calculated using the same $CO_2$-based percentage rates as are used for calculating car benefits, and applying those percentage rates to the following set of figures:

| | 2016/17 | 2015/16 |
|---|---|---|
| Basis figure | £22,200 | £22,100 |

## VAN BENEFITS

Benefits for vans weighing up to 3,500 kg are as follows:

| | 2016/17 | 2015/16 |
|---|---|---|
| Benefit for van with significant private use (which emits $CO_2$) | £3,170 | £3,150 |
| Benefit for van with significant private use (which does not emit $CO_2$) | £634 | £630 |
| Additional fuel scale charge for unrestricted private use | £598 | £594 |

## TAX-FREE HMRC APPROVED MILEAGE RATES FOR BUSINESS USE OF OWN TRANSPORT

Approved rates for 2016/17 and 2015/16 for income tax are as follows:

| | *First 10,000 business miles* | *Additional business miles* |
|---|---|---|
| Cars and vans | 45p | 25p |
| Motor cycles | 24p | 24p |
| Bicycles | 20p | 20p |
| Passenger payments, car or van only, per passenger | 5p | 5p |

## CLASS 1 NATIONAL INSURANCE CONTRIBUTIONS

National insurance contribution rates for 2016/17 are as follows (with 2015/16 figures in brackets where different):

| | |
|---|---|
| **Class 1 contributions** | |
| Lower earnings limit: | £112 a week |
| Earnings threshold (employers): | £156 a week |
| Earnings threshold (employees): | £155 |
| Upper earnings limit (employees only): | £827 (£815) a week |
| Employees | |
| 12% of weekly earnings between | £155 and £827 (£815) |
| Reduced rate for married women and widows with valid certificate of election | 5.85% on weekly earnings as above |
| For both categories of employees an additional 2% is chargeable on the balance of earnings over £827 (£815) per week. | |
| Employers | 13.8% on all earnings over £156 (£148) per week |
| Employment allowance | £3,000 (£2,000) |

Employees do not pay national insurance contributions if they are under 16 or over state pension age. Employers' contributions are payable.

From 6 April 2015, employers are not required to pay Class 1 contributions for employees under 21 years of age as long as the earnings do not exceed the upper earnings limit. From 6 April 2016 this is extended to apprentices under the age of 25.

The employment allowance is offset against he employers' Class 1 contributions. Only one company in a group can claim the employment allowance. Excluded employers include

## CONTRACTED OUT EMPLOYEE

Contracting out was abolished from 6 April 2016 following the introduction of the single tier pension.

In 2015/16, the reduction in contributions, which applied to weekly earnings from £155 (£156 for employers) to £770 is:

| | *Salary related schemes* |
|---|---|
| Employees | 1.4% |
| Employers | 3.4% |

In 2015/16 employees also received these rebates on earnings between £112 and £155 a week, on which they do not pay contributions. Employers receive these rebates on earnings between £112 and £156.

## OTHER NATIONAL INSURANCE CONTRIBUTIONS

| | | |
|---|---|---|
| **Employers' Class 1A and Class 1B contributions** | 13.8% | |
| **Class 2 contributions** | | |
| Self-employed flat rate | £2.80 | a week |
| Small profits threshold | £5,965 | a year |
| **Class 3 contributions** | | |
| Voluntary contributions | £14.10 | a week |
| **Class 4 contributions** | | |
| 9% of profits between | £8,060 and £43,000 (£42,385) | |
| and 2% of all profits above £43,000 (£42,385). | | |

## CAPITAL GAINS TAX

Total net gains of individuals for 2016/17 and 2015/16 not exceeding £11,100 are exempt.

In 2016/17, taxpayers with gains above the annual exempt amount pay CGT at:

| | *Upper rate gains* | *All other gains* |
|---|---|---|
| Gains falling within the unused income tax basic rate band | 28% | 20% |
| Gains falling within the higher rate and additional rate band | 18% | 10% |

Upper rate gains are those made in respect of residential properties (whether in the UK or overseas) and carried interest.

In 2015/16 taxpayers were taxed at 18% on any part of the net gains falling within the unused basic rate band and 28% on the balance (if any). Losses and the annual exempt amount can be set off against gains in the manner most favourable.

All gains to which investors relief (from 2016/17 onwards) and entrepreneurs' relief applies are taxed at 10%.

Personal representatives are entitled to the same annual exemption as individuals for the year of death and the next two years. Gains not covered by the exemption are taxed at 28% or 20% in 2016/17 onwards depending on the type of the gain. For 2015/16 and previous years gains were taxed at 28%.

Gains of trusts in which the settlor retains an interest are taxed as the settlor's gains. For other trusts, the trustees are entitled to an annual exemption of £5,550 in 2016/17 and 2015/16, divided equally between trusts created by the same settlor, subject to a minimum exemption of £1,110 for each trust. Gains in excess of the exemption are taxed at 28% or 20% in 2016/17 onwards for both discretionary trusts (including accumulation and maintenance trusts) and other trusts, depending on the type of the gain. For 2015/16 and previous years gains were taxed at 28%.

**Entrepreneurs' relief limit – lifetime qualifying gains**

| | |
|---|---|
| 2016/17 & 2015/16 | £10 million |

**Investors' relief limit – lifetime qualifying gains**

| | |
|---|---|
| 2016/17 | £10 million |

## CAPITAL GAINS TAX ACTUARIAL TABLE FOR LEASES (TCGA 1992 SCH 8)

| *Years* | *Percentage* | *Years* | *Percentage* |
|---|---|---|---|
| 50 (or more) | 100.000 | 24 | 79.622 |
| 49 | 99.657 | 23 | 78.055 |
| 48 | 99.289 | 22 | 76.399 |
| 47 | 98.902 | 21 | 74.635 |
| 46 | 98.490 | 20 | 72.770 |
| 45 | 98.059 | 19 | 70.791 |
| 44 | 97.595 | 18 | 68.697 |
| 43 | 97.107 | 17 | 66.470 |
| 42 | 96.593 | 16 | 64.116 |
| 41 | 96.041 | 15 | 61.617 |
| 40 | 95.457 | 14 | 58.971 |
| 39 | 94.842 | 13 | 56.167 |
| 38 | 94.189 | 12 | 53.191 |
| 37 | 93.497 | 11 | 50.038 |
| 36 | 92.761 | 10 | 46.695 |
| 35 | 91.981 | 9 | 43.154 |
| 34 | 91.156 | 8 | 39.399 |
| 33 | 90.280 | 7 | 35.414 |
| 32 | 89.354 | 6 | 31.195 |
| 31 | 88.371 | 5 | 26.722 |
| 30 | 87.330 | 4 | 21.983 |
| 29 | 86.226 | 3 | 16.959 |
| 28 | 85.053 | 2 | 11.629 |
| 27 | 83.816 | 1 | 5.983 |
| 26 | 82.496 | 0 | 0 |
| 25 | 81.100 | | |

If the duration of the lease is not an exact number of years, find the percentage for the number of whole years and add to it for each extra month one-twelfth of the difference between that percentage and the next higher percentage (counting an odd 14 days or more as one month).

## CORPORATION TAX RATES

| *Financial years (ie beginning 1 April)* | *2012* | *2013* | *2014* | *2015* | *2016* |
|---|---|---|---|---|---|
| Corporation tax full rate (%) | 24 | 23 | 21 | 20 | 20 |
| Small profits rate (%) | 20 | 20 | 20 | N/A | N/A |
| Marginal relief limits (£000's) | | | | | |
| Lower | 300 | 300 | 300 | N/A | N/A |

| *Financial years* | *2012* | *2013* | *2014* | *2015* | *2016* |
| --- | --- | --- | --- | --- | --- |
| Higher | 1,500 | 1,500 | 1,500 | N/A | N/A |
| Marginal relief calculation | | | | | |
| (M – P) × I/P × fraction | 1/100 | 3/400 | 1/400 | N/A | N/A |
| Effective marginal rate (%) | 25 | 23.75 | 21.25 | N/A | N/A |
| Ring fence profits – full rate (%) | 30 | 30 | 30 | 30 | 30 |
| Ring fence profits – small profits rate (%) | 19 | 19 | 19 | 19 | 19 |
| Ring fence fraction | 11/400 | 11/400 | 11/400 | 11/400 | 11/400 |

A diverted profits tax of 25% was introduced on 1 April 2015. This is an anti-avoidance regime which applies to multinational companies.

## ANNUAL TAX ON ENVELOPED DWELLINGS (ATED)

| *Property value* | *2016/17* | *2015/16* | *2014/15* |
| --- | --- | --- | --- |
| £500,000 or less | Nil | Nil | Nil |
| £500,001 to £1,000,000 | £3,500 | Nil | Nil |
| £1,000,001 to £2,000,000 | £7,000 | £7,000 | Nil |
| £2,000,001 to £5,000,000 | £23,350 | £23,350 | £15,400 |
| £5,000,001 to £10,000,000 | £54,450 | £54,450 | £35,900 |
| £10,000,001 to £20,000,000 | £109,050 | £109,050 | £71,850 |
| £20,000,001 and above | £218,200 | £218,200 | £143,750 |

The property value is taken at the valuation date. For properties within the annual tax on enveloped dwellings regime when it was introduced on 1 April 2013, the valuation date was 1 April 2012. A revaluation exercise must be undertaken every five years, so the next valuation date is 1 April 2017.

A capital gains tax charge applies when a property within the annual tax on enveloped dwellings is subject to disposal. A tax rate of 28% applies to the gain.

## STAMP DUTY LAND TAX (SDLT) ON RESIDENTIAL PROPERTY

| *Effective date* | *Consideration* | *Rate* | *Rate on additional residential properties* |
| --- | --- | --- | --- |
| From 1 April 2016 | Up to £125,000 | Nil | 3% |
| | £125,001–£250,000 | 2% | 5% |
| | £250,001–£925,000 | 5% | 8% |
| | £925,001–£1,500,000 | 10% | 13% |
| | £1,500,001+ | 12% | 15% |
| From 4 December 2014 to 31 March 2016 | Up to £125,000 | Nil | |
| | £125,001–£250,000 | 2% | |
| | £250,001–£925,000 | 5% | |
| | £925,001–£1,500,000 | 10% | |
| | £1,500,001+ | 12% | |
| From 22 March 2012 to 3 December 2014 | Up to £125,000 | Nil | |
| | £125,001–£250,000 | 1% | |
| | £250,001–£500,000 | 3% | |
| | £500,001–£1,000,000 | 4% | |
| | £1,000,001–£2,000,000 | 5% | |

| *Effective date* | *Consideration* | *Rate* | *Rate on additional residential properties* |
|---|---|---|---|
| | £2,000,001+ | 7% | |
| From 6 April 2011 to 21 March 2012 | Up to £125,000 | Nil | |
| | £125,001–£250,000 | 1% | |
| | £250,001–£500,000 | 3% | |
| | £500,001–£1,000,000 | 4% | |
| | £1,000,001+ | 5% | |

From 4 December 2014 the rates of SDLT for residential property apply progressively in bands rather than the slab regime which applied prior to that date. From 1 April 2016 a supplementary percentage of 3% applies to purchases of additional residential properties. The supplementary percentage does not apply to purchases costing less than £40,000. If there is a period of overlap in the ownership of a main residence, the supplementary percentage can be refunded if the first residence is sold within 36 months of the second main residence purchase.

If the residential property is acquired by a non-natural person (eg a company) the rate of SDLT which applies is:

| *Effective date* | *Consideration* | *Rate* | *Rate on additional residential properties* |
|---|---|---|---|
| From 1 April 2016 | Up to £125,000 | Nil | 3% |
| | £125,001–£250,000 | 2% | 5% |
| | £250,001–£500,000 | 5% | 8% |
| | £500,001+ * | 15% | 15% |
| From 4 December 2014 to 31 March 2016 | Up to £125,000 | Nil | |
| | £125,001–£250,000 | 2% | |
| | £250,001–£500,000 | 5% | |
| | £500,001+ * | 15% | |
| From 20 March 2014 to 3 December 2014 | Up to £125,000 | Nil | |
| | £125,001–£250,000 | 1% | |
| | £250,001–£500,000 | 3% | |
| | £500,001+ | 15% | |
| From 22 March 2012 to 19 March 2013 | Up to £125,000 | Nil | |
| | £125,001–£250,000 | 1% | |
| | £250,001–£500,000 | 3% | |
| | £500,001–£1,000,000 | 4% | |
| | £1,000,001–£2,000,000 | 5% | |
| | £2,000,001+ | 15% | |

*Although the banding system applies for residential property from 4 December 2014, this is not extended to non-natural persons. If a residential property is acquired by a non-natural person for more than £500,000, the entire consideration is chargeable at 15%.

## STAMP DUTY LAND TAX (SDLT) ON RESIDENTIAL PROPERTY

| *Effective date* | *Consideration* | *Rate* |
|---|---|---|
| From 17 March 2016 | Up to £125,000 | Nil |
| | £125,001–£250,000 | 2% |
| | £250,001+ | 5% |

| *Effective date* | *Consideration* | *Rate* |
|---|---|---|
| Up to 16 March 2016 | Up to £125,000 | Nil |
| | £125,001–£250,000 | 1% |
| | £250,001–£500,000 | 3% |
| | £500,001+ | 4% |

From 17 March 2016 the rates of SDLT for residential and non-residential property apply progressively in bands rather than the slab regime which applied prior to that date.

## SDLT ON LEASES

| *Residential property* | | *Non-residential property* | |
|---|---|---|---|
| **From 17 March 2016** | | | |
| *Net present value of rent* | *Rate* | *Net present value of rent* | *Rate* |
| Up to £125,000 | Nil | Up to £150,000 | Nil |
| £125,001+ | 1% | £150,001 to £5,000,000 | 1% |
| | | £5,000,001+ | 2% |
| **Up to 16 March 2016** | | | |
| *Net present value of rent* | *Rate* | *Net present value of rent* | *Rate* |
| Up to £125,000 | Nil | Up to £150,000 | Nil |
| £125,001+ | 1% | £150,001+ | 1% |

## LAND AND BUILDINGS TRANSACTION TAX

From 1 April 2015, SDLT no longer applies in Scotland. Instead land and buildings transaction tax (LBTT) applies.

| *Residential property* | | *Non-residential property* | |
|---|---|---|---|
| Consideration | Rate | Consideration | Rate |
| Up to £145,000 | Nil | Up to £150,000 | Nil |
| £145,001–£250,000 | 2% | £150,001–£350,000 | 3% |
| £250,001–£325,000 | 5% | £350,001+ | 4.5% |
| £325,001–£750,000 | 10% | | |
| £750,001+ | 12% | | |

As for SDLT, the LBTT on residential property is applied in bands, whereas the LBTT on non-residential property is applied on a slab method.

Residential leases are generally exempt from LBTT. Non-residential leases are subject to the same thresholds and rates as for SDLT: where the net present value is up to £150,000 the tax is nil and 1% is charged over £150,000.

## STAMP DUTY

| | |
|---|---|
| Shares put into depository receipts or put into duty free clearance systems | 1.5% |
| Purchase of own shares by company | 0.5% |
| Transfers of stock or marketable securities | 0.5% |
| Takeovers, mergers, demergers, schemes of reconstruction and amalgamation (except where no real change of ownership | 0.5% |

Stamp duty is rounded up to the nearest £5. Where the consideration is less than £1,000 the instrument is exempt.

## VAT

The VAT rates are as follows:

| VAT rate | From 4 January 2011 | From 1 January 2010 to 3 January 2011 |
|---|---|---|
| Standard rate | 20% | 17.5% |
| Reduced rate | 5% | 5% |

The VAT registration limits are:

| Period | Taxable supplies |
|---|---|
| 1 April 2016 to 31 March 2017 | £83,000 |
| 1 April 2015 to 31 March 2016 | £82,000 |
| 1 April 2014 to 31 March 2015 | £81,000 |
| 1 April 2013 to 31 March 2014 | £79,000 |
| 1 April 2012 to 31 March 2013 | £77,000 |
| 1 April 2011 to 31 March 2012 | £73,000 |

Registration is required if taxable supplies exceeded these limits in the last 12 months or are expected to exceed these limits in the next 30 days.

Although, even if this test is met, registration is not required if the taxable supplies in the next 12 months are not expected to exceed:

| Period | Taxable supplies |
|---|---|
| 1 April 2016 to 31 March 2017 | £81,000 |
| 1 April 2015 to 31 March 2016 | £80,000 |
| 1 April 2014 to 31 March 2015 | £79,000 |
| 1 April 2013 to 31 March 2014 | £77,000 |
| 1 April 2012 to 31 March 2013 | £75,000 |
| 1 April 2011 to 31 March 2012 | £71,000 |

The above are also the deregistration thresholds for those periods.

The partial exemption de minimis limits for reclaiming all input tax on supplies are if the input tax attributable to exempt supplies either:

- averages £625 per month or less; or
- accounts for 50% of all input tax.

Taxable persons with taxable supplies of £150,000 or less are eligible to use the flat rate scheme rather than the VAT rates shown above. The flat rate used depends on the category of business:

| | *Flat rate (taxable supplies from 4 January 2011)* | *Flat rate (taxable supplies between 1 January 2010 and 3 January 2011)* |
|---|---|---|
| Accountancy or book-keeping | 14.5% | 13% |
| Advertising | 11% | 10% |
| Agricultural services | 11% | 10% |
| Any other activity not listed elsewhere | 12% | 10.5% |
| Architect | 14.5% | 13% |
| Boarding or care of animals | 12% | 10.5% |

| | *Flat rate (taxable supplies from 4 January 2011)* | *Flat rate (taxable supplies between 1 January 2010 and 3 January 2011)* |
|---|---|---|
| Business services that are not listed elsewhere | 12% | 10.5% |
| Catering services, including restaurants and takeaways | 12.5% | 11% |
| Civil and structural engineer or surveyor | 14.5% | 13% |
| Computer and IT consultancy or data processing | 14.5% | 13% |
| Computer repair services | 10.5% | 9.5% |
| Dealing in waste or scrap | 10.5% | 9.5% |
| Entertainment or journalism | 12.5% | 11% |
| Estate agency and property management services | 12% | 10.5% |
| Farming or agriculture not listed elsewhere | 6.5% | 6% |
| Film, radio, television or video production | 13% | 11.5% |
| Financial services | 13.5% | 12% |
| Forestry or fishing | 10.5% | 9.5% |
| General building or construction services | 9.5% | 8.5% |
| Hairdressing or other beauty treatment services | 13% | 11.5% |
| Hiring or renting goods | 9.5% | 8.5% |
| Hotel or accommodation | 10.5% | 9.5% |
| Investigation or security | 12% | 10.5% |
| Labour-only building or construction services | 14.5% | 13% |
| Laundry or dry-cleaning services | 12% | 10.5% |
| Lawyer or legal services | 14.5% | 13% |
| Library, archive, museum or other cultural activity | 9.5% | 8.5% |
| Management consultancy | 14% | 12.5% |
| Manufactured fabricated metal products | 10.5% | 9.5% |
| Manufacturing food | 9% | 8% |
| Manufacturing not listed elsewhere | 9.5% | 8.5% |
| Manufacturing yarn, textiles or clothing | 9% | 8% |
| Membership organisation | 8% | 7% |
| Mining or quarrying | 10% | 9% |
| Packaging | 9% | 8% |
| Photography | 11% | 10% |
| Post Offices | 5% | 4.5% |
| Printing | 8.5% | 7.5% |
| Publishing | 11% | 10% |
| Pubs | 6.5% | 6% |
| Real estate activity not listed elsewhere | 14% | 12.5% |
| Repairing personal or household goods | 10% | 9% |
| Repairing vehicles | 8.5% | 7.5% |
| Retailing food, confectionary, tobacco, newspapers or children's clothes | 4% | 3.5% |
| Retailing pharmaceuticals, medical goods, cosmetics or toiletries | 8% | 7% |
| Retailing not listed elsewhere | 7.5% | 6.5% |
| Retailing vehicles or fuel | 6.5% | 6% |
| Secretarial services | 13% | 11.5% |
| Social work | 11% | 10% |

| | *Flat rate (taxable supplies from 4 January 2011)* | *Flat rate (taxable supplies between 1 January 2010 and 3 January 2011)* |
|---|---|---|
| Sport or recreation | 8.5% | 7.5% |
| Transport or storage, couriers, freight, removals and taxis | 10% | 9% |
| Travel agency | 10.5% | 9.5% |
| Veterinary medicine | 11% | 10% |
| Wholesaling agricultural products | 8% | 7% |
| Wholesaling food | 7.5% | 6.5% |
| Wholesaling not listed elsewhere | 8.5% | 7.5% |

Taxable persons can use the flat rate scheme until the taxable supplies are £230,000 or more.

## FINANCE ACT 2016 MEASURES RELEVANT TO THIS PUBLICATION

| *Section in FA 2016* | *Description of measures* | *Example* |
|---|---|---|
| *1* | Income tax rates are unchanged for 2016–17. | |
| *2* | For 2017-18 the basic rate limit is to be £33,500. The basic rate limit for 2016-17 is unchanged at £32,000. | |
| *3* | For 2017–18, the standard personal allowance is set at £11,500. The government has set an objective to raise the personal allowance to £12,500 by the end of this parliament. | |
| *4* | This clause introduces a new Personal Savings Allowance for individuals. The allowance exempts savings income (such as interest). The amount of the allowance is dependent upon an individual's tax rate:<br>Basic rate = £1,000<br>Higher rate = £500<br>Additional rate = no allowance<br>The allowance is in addition to the 0% starting rate for savings which was introduced in 2014. From 6 April 2016 banks, building societies and National Savings ceased to deduct income tax at source from interest paid to customers. | A5 |
| *5 and Sch 1* | The taxation of dividends has been reformed for 2016-17 onwards. The dividend tax credit has been abolished. Instead a new dividend allowance of £5,000 has been introduced and dividends above this limit are taxed:<br>Basic rate = 7.5%<br>Higher rate = 32.5%<br>Additional rate = 38.1% | |
| *6* | As part of the devolution of Scotland, the structure / names of the income tax rates are being changed. The changes are expected to take effect from 2017-18 onwards. | |
| *7* | This change to the benefits wording is to ensure that a "fair bargain" does not apply where there are specific charging rules. | |
| *8* | From 2019–20, the appropriate percentage for calculating car benefit is to be 16% for cars with CO2 emissions of 50g/km and lower; 19% for cars with emissions greater than 50g/km but no greater than 75g/km; and 22% for cars with emissions greater than 75g/km but less than 95g/km, rising for greater emissions to a maximum of 37% for cars with emissions of 180g/km or more. The appropriate percentages for cars without a CO2 emissions figure are to be 23%, 34% and 37%, depending on cylinder capacity. | B4 |
| *9* | The appropriate percentages for cars which cannot produce emissions under any circumstances are 9% for 2017-18 and 13% for 2018-19. | B4 |
| *10* | The diesel 3% supplement was due to be abolished from 6 April 2016. It will now be retained for 2016-17 and subsequent years. Further provisions to remove the diesel supplement are expected to be made in a future finance bill for 2021-22 onwards. | B4 |
| *11* | Last year saw the introduction of benefit charges for zero-emission vans. The charge is being phased in as a percentage of the normal van benefit. This section introduces a more gradual phase in period. | B2 |
| *12 and Sch 2* | Following consultation, from 6 April 2017, income from sporting testimonials and benefit matches for employed sports persons will be liable to income tax and national insurance. This is subject to an exemption of £100,000 provided the event is not contractual or customary. | |
| *13* | The trivial benefits exemption replaces a concessionary practice and applies for income tax, national insurance and P11D reporting. Benefits costing less than £50 are exempt provided:<br>• not cash or vouchers<br>• not pursuant to a salary sacrifice scheme or any other contractual obligations<br>• not in recognition of the employee's services.<br>• if the employer is a close company, the total trivial benefits to a director (or other office-holder and their family or household) does not exceed the annual cap of £300. | B2 |

| *Section in FA 2016* | *Description of measures* | *Example* |
|---|---|---|
| *14* | This clause is designed to restrict tax relief on travel and subsistence for individuals who are working through an employment intermediary (agency, umbrella or personal service company). Where it applies, the legislation treats each engagement as a separate employment for travel purposes. This makes each workplace "permanent" rather than "temporary" resulting in any home to work travel being "ordinary commuting costs" and hence not allowable. The legislation also allows for the recovery of PAYE debts in the event of any fraudulent representations. | N2 |
| *15* | Voluntary payrolling of benefits in kind is extended to include vouchers and credit tokens. | |
| *16 & Sch 3* | Schedule 3 makes some minor changes to employee share schemes. They are largely technical and corrective and include a new anti-avoidance measure and a "reasonable excuse" for certain tax-advantaged plans. | |
| *17 & Sch 3* | This is intended to clarify the tax treatment of Restricted Stock Units (a non-tax advantaged scheme) paid to internationally mobile employees. From 6 April 2016, tax will arise under Chapter 5 relating to securities options, rather than earnings. This change will impact on all future events irrespective of the date on which the units were acquired. | |
| *18* | The clause amends the "disguised remuneration" rules in ITEPA 2003 part 7a. The amendments are designed to:<br>• Clarify the operation of the rules,<br>• Counter certain tax avoidance arrangements,<br>• Withdraw transitional relief where settlement with HMRC has not been reached by 31 March 2017.<br>Further changes have already been announced for inclusion in the Finance Bill 2017 following consultation. | |
| *19 & Sch 4* | As announced last year, the standard lifetime allowance is reduced from £1.25 million to £1 million from 6 April 2016. Similar to previous reductions in the lifetime allowance new "protections" have been introduced. | A6 |
| *20* | A technical change to replace legislation following the introduction of the single tier state pension. | |
| *21* | A technical change designed to reduce administration on dependant's pensions schemes. | |
| *22 & Sch 5* | Various minor changes are introduced from the date of Royal Assent to ensure the pension rules operate as intended following the introduction of pension flexibility. | |
| *24* | The simplified expenses provisions in ITTOIA 2005 ss 94H to 94I are amended to include partnership's business use of home. | C3 |
| *25* | Following consultation, the existing framework for averaging fluctuating profits over two years has been retained and an additional option of averaging over five years added for self-employed farmers etc. | C14 |
| *26* | Last year, changes were made to the taxation of residential property income. The changes restrict the deductions for finance costs in calculating property profits and instead allow a basic rate reduction in calculating tax liability. The rules are being phased in from 2017-18 onwards. This clause makes a number of minor adjustments including confirming that individual beneficiaries of deceased estates are entitled to the basic rate tax reduction. | |
| *27* | This clause gives the power to make further regulations that will allow Individual Savings Accounts (ISA) to retain their tax-advantaged status following the death of the account holder. | N7 |
| *28* | All energy generating activities, including the production of gas or other fuel, are excluded from the tax-advantaged venture capital schemes from 6 April 2016. The tax-advantaged schemes are EIS, SEIS and VCT. | N7 |
| *29 - 30* | Minor technical change to EIS and VCT accounting periods used in meeting qualifying tests. The change is being made retrospectively with the right to elect to dis-apply. | |

| *Section in FA 2016* | *Description of measures* | *Example* |
|---|---|---|
| *32* | New income tax relief in ITA 2007 s 412A for bad debts on peer-to-peer loans (P2P). Relief for qualifying bad debts are given:<br>• Automatically against interest received from other loans on the same P2P platform in the same tax year,<br>• Sideways relief against interest from other P2P platforms in the same tax year,<br>• Carry-forward relief against eligible P2P loans in the next four tax years. | |
| *33 - 35* | These sections have been introduced following consultation and address HMRC's fears that low rates of capital gains tax and increases in dividend taxation could lead to increases in unacceptable tax avoidance such as phonenixism and moneyboxing by:<br>• Making the existing transaction in securities (TIS) rules have wider application,<br>• Simplifying the process HMRC have to follow to counter a tax advantage under TIS, and<br>• Introducing new TAARs. | J4 |
| *36 - 38* | Rules aimed at investment managers to determine when "rewards" should be taxed as income or as chargeable gains. | |
| *39 & Sch 6* | The rules on deduction of tax at source have been amended such that banks, building societies and National Savings are no longer required to deducted tax at source from interest paid to customers. | |
| *40 - 43* | The rules on deduction of tax when paying royalties to a connected party abroad are tightened. From 17 March 2016 anti-treaty shopping provisions have been inserted. From 28 June 2016 the class of royalties caught is widened, a new UK source rule is introduced and consequential amendments to the diverted profits rules. | |
| *44* | For the financial year 2017 to the main rate of corporation tax is 19%. | |
| *45* | For the financial year 2019 the main rate of corporation tax is 17%. | |
| *46* | Vaccine Research Relief is abolished as planned on 31.3.2017. | |
| *47* | This is a consequential change to the wording used in the state aid cap caused by changes in research and development (R&D) relief. | |
| *48 & Sch 7* | The loan relationship rules are amended for changes in accounting standards such as FRS 102. | |
| *49* | To mirror the increase in the rate of dividend taxation (FA 2016 s 5) the rate of tax charged under CTA 2010 s 455 on loans to participators is increased to 32.5%. | |
| *50* | A new exemption from the s 455 loans to participators rules for charities where the loan is only applied for charitable purposes. | |
| *51 - 52* | These sections seek to counter arrangements using bodies such as partnerships or LLPs to transfer assets in ways that aim to bring the assets into the intangible fixed asset regime. New rules apply from 25 November 2015. | |
| *53 & Sch 8* | New corporation tax relief for qualifying orchestral concerts. | |
| *54* | Minor changes to television tax relief. | |
| *63 & Sch 9* | Changes to the patent box legislation to ensure compliance with the new international framework developed by the OECD including a new R&D fraction. | I5 |
| *65 & sch 10* | From 1 January 2017, these rules seek to counter hybrid mismatch arrangements by typically multinational enterprises. The mismatch can involve either double deductions for the same expense or deductions for an expense without any corresponding receipt being taxed. The new rules apply from 1 January 2017. | |
| *67* | Closure of a tax avoidance scheme involving receiving non-taxable income in return for taking on liabilities under a lease that give rise to tax deductible amounts. | |
| *68* | Enhanced capital allowances are available for expenditure on plant and machinery for use in designated assisted areas within enterprises zones for eight years from the date the area is designated. | |

| *Section in FA 2016* | *Description of measures* | *Example* |
|---|---|---|
| *69* | Strengthening of the existing anti-avoidance rules in CAA 2001 ss 213-218 to counter schemes reported to HMRC that seek to reduce disposal value for capital allowances purposes. | |
| *70* | New statutory rules to ensure the value of trading income received in non-monetary form is taxable in full as trading income. | |
| *71 - 73* | From 1st / 6th April 2016 replacement furniture relief is introduced and the legislation on replacement and alteration of trade tools/wear and tear allowance repealed. | D2 |
| *74* | Definition of transfer pricing guidelines updated to incorporate Profit Shifting (BEPS) final report published by the OECD in 2015. | |
| *75 - 81* | New income and corporation tax charges for non-residents with a trade of dealing in or developing land in the UK. | |
| *82 & Schs 11 - 12* | The rates of capital gains tax on disposal of an interest in residential property and capital carried interest have been retained at current rates (18% / 28%). The rates for "other" gains have been reduced to 10% and 20%. | L1 |
| *83 - 85* | Last year saw a tightening of the rules on entrepreneurs' relief. These sections contain some relaxations of the new rules back dated to their introduction to mitigate their affects in a number of commercial situations. | L5 |
| *86 & Sch 14* | Investors' relief applies a 10% CGT rate on qualifying gains up to a lifetime limit of £10 million. This is a separate relief to Entrepreneurs relief. There is no minimum percentage shareholding (ER = 5%) but shares have to be held for three years (ER = 1 year) | L5 |
| *87* | Introduction of a lifetime limit of £100,000 for exempt gains under Employee Shareholder Agreements entered into after 16 March 2016. | |
| *88* | Anti-avoidance to prevent Employee Shareholder schemes being used by investment fund managers for disguised fees or carried interest. | |
| *89* | Minor changes to the taxation of UK residential property by non-resident rules. The changes are mainly backdated to 5 April 2015 when the rules were first introduced. The changes are to ensure there is neither double-counting nor under-counting (this change only applies from 26 November 2015). | |
| *90* | Relaxation (made optional) of the requirement to file a NRCGT return where the disposal is on a no gain / no loss basis and or arm's length lease is granted to an unconnected party for no premium. | |
| *91* | Capital gains tax has been added to the Provisional Collection of Taxes Act 1968. This allows temporary statutory force to resolutions of the House of Commons that renew, vary or abolish certain taxes and duties. The principal practical application of this is to allow the government to collect taxes on a provisional basis between budget day and the coming into operation of the Finance Act. | |
| *97 - 120* | Part 6 of the FA 2016 introduces the new apprenticeship levy which will be charged to employers to fund new apprenticeships. | |
| *122 - 123* | These provisions seek to tackle online vat fraud and avoidance. They give HMRC powers to compulsorily register an overseas business and direct they appoint a VAT representative; plus joint and several liability for online marketplaces. | |
| *126* | Reform of the tax calculation on non-residential and mixed used properties from 17 March 2016. Tax is now calculated on the portion of the consideration which falls within each rate band. | |
| *127* | An additional 3% charge for purchases of dwellings (residential properties). The charge applies to individuals who already own other dwellings (and not replacing a main residence) and purchases by non-individuals. | D6 |
| *155 - 157* | These sections make procedural changes to the operation of the GAAR and introduce a 60% penalty for those using arrangements caught by GAAR. | N6 |
| *158 & Sch 18* | This is a new regime of warnings and escalating sanctions for those who persistently engage in tax avoidance schemes. | N6 |
| *159* | Tightening of the promoters of tax avoidance scheme (POTAS) legislation. | N6 |

| *Section in FA 2016* | *Description of measures* | *Example* |
|---|---|---|
| *160 & Sch 19* | Requirement for qualifying entities (large companies etc) to publish a tax strategy and introduction of a "special measures" regime to target large businesses that HMRC regard as persistently undertaking aggressive tax planning, or who refuse to engage with HMRC in a transparent manner. | |
| *161 – 165 & Schs 20, 21 & 22* | Following consultation, these clauses have been introduced to tackle offshore tax evasion and therefore relate to errors involving an offshore matter or offshore transfer.<br>From dates to be appointed:<br>• The penalties for inaccuracies (FA 2007 Sch 24), late notification (FA 2008 Sch 41) and late returns (FA 2009 Sch 55) are amended to increase the minimum penalties. The legislation also provides circumstances where a taxpayer must provide additional information to obtain the maximum penalty reduction.<br>• A new asset-based penalty is introduced for deliberate offshore inaccuracies and failures where the PLR exceeds £25,000.<br>• New criminal offences for inaccuracies, late notification and late returns where tax relates to offshore income, assets or activities.<br>From 6 April 2016<br>• New civil penalties for enablers of offshore tax evasion,<br>• Publication of details of deliberate tax defaulters and their enablers. | G3 |
| *166 & Sch 23* | For 2016/17 onwards HMRC can issue an assessment (a "simple assessment") of an individual's income or capital gains tax liability without the taxpayer submitting a self-assessment. This is intended to be used where HMRC believe they already have all the information they need to calculate a taxpayer's liability | |
| *167* | Following HMRC's defeat in the Higgs case this clause ensures a four year time limit is in place for self-assessment tax returns in the future. | |
| *168* | HMRC can withdraw a notice to file a self-assessment tax return in relation to 2014/15 onwards if they consider it is no longer necessary. | |
| *169-171* | These clauses aim to ensure that where HMRC is party to a tax-related debt anywhere in the UK the rates of interest charged are those contained in tax legislation. Clause 171 also ensures this applies to national insurance debts. | |
| *175 - 176* | These extend HMRC's existing data gathering powers in FA 2011 Sch 23. They currently apply to "merchant acquirers" such as credit card companies. This extension will extend the list of "data-holders" to enable HMRC to collect data from third party providers of electronic stored-value payment services – so called "digital wallets" (eg companies like eBay, PayPal, Airbnb etc) and business intermediaries. HMRC are trying to "future proof" the legislation to include emerging new data sources of a similar type. | |
| *179 – 181 & Sch 24* | These provisions have been introduced to comply with EU obligations and relate to the collection, publication and disclosure of data on state aid tax reliefs and other tax advantages. | |
| *183 - 188* | These provisions put the Office of Tax Simplification on a statutory footing and make provision for its governance and operations. | |

# Income tax, tax credits and national insurance – personal tax

# Question

Christopher Thackery, aged 50, lives in Kent with his wife Helen, aged 39, and their son, Mark, aged 14. Their respective incomes are as follows:

## Christopher Thackery:

| | | £ |
|---|---|---|
| (i) | Salary as a sales representative for year ending 5 April 2017<br>(tax deducted under PAYE £5,388) | 33,340 |
| (ii) | Bonus based on the company profits for the accounting year to: | |
| | 31 March 2015 (paid 1 June 2016) | 4,600 |
| | 31 March 2016 (paid 1 June 2017) | 4,750 |
| (iii) | Investment income | *Year ended 5 April 2017* £ |
| | Dividends received from UK companies | 1,890 |
| | Interest received from Midwest Bank | 1,220 |
| | National Savings Bank interest (Easy Access Savings) | 1,600 |
| | Interest on National Savings Certificates | 815 |
| | Interest arising on overseas bank accounts | 180 |
| | Rental income | 4,930 |

## Helen Thackery:

| | | |
|---|---|---|
| (i) | Profits from hairdressing business operated since 2002 | |
| | Year to 31.7.2016 | 10,445 |
| | Year to 31.7.2017 | 8,500 |
| (ii) | Building society interest – amount received in year ended 5.4.2017 | 915 |

## Mark Thackery:

Mark has a building society account, the source of capital being gifts from his father. The interest for the year ended 5 April 2017 was £24. He also has dividends of £360 on shares given to him by his grandfather.

## Outgoings year ended 5 April 2017

Christopher paid mortgage interest of £4,320 on a home loan of £84,000. He also paid £3,000 interest on a loan to buy the rented property, which had been let throughout the year at a full rent. The couple do not incur any childcare costs and Helen is nominated as the main carer of Mark.

(i) Compute the income tax due (or repayable) for each family member for the year 2016/17. Comment separately on the availability of child benefit based on Helen and Christopher's 2016/17 income.

(ii) State the tax treatment and reduction in liability arising if Christopher Thackery paid £1,600 net in 2016/17 into a personal pension plan, and compare that treatment with a similar contribution by Helen Thackery.

(iii) Compare the effect on Christopher's tax position in (ii) if his bonus was £66,300 instead of £4,600. Assume that the tax deducted under PAYE was £29,056.

Ignore foreign taxation.

# Answer

## (i) Income Tax Computations 2016/17

### Christopher Thackery

| | | | | £ | £ |
|---|---|---|---|---|---|
| *Non-savings income:* | | | | | |
| Salary | | | | 33,340 | |
| Bonus (paid 1 June 2016) | | | | 4,600 | 37,940 |
| Rental income (4,930 less interest paid 3,000) | | | | | 1,930 |
| | | | | | 39,870 |
| *Non-dividend savings income* | | | | | |
| National Savings Bank | | | | 1,600 | |
| Midwest Bank interest | | | | 1,220 | |
| Foreign bank interest | | | | 180 | 3,000 |
| *Dividend income* | | | | | |
| UK dividends received | | | | | 1,890 |
| | | | | | 44,760 |
| Personal allowance | | | | | 11,000 |
| Taxable income | | | | | 33,760 |
| Tax thereon: On non-savings income | | | | | |
| Basic rate | 28,870 | @ | 20% | 5,774 | |
| On savings income other than dividends | | | | | |
| Nil rate | 500 | @ | 0% | — | |
| Lower rate | 2,500 | @ | 20% | 500 | |
| On dividend income | | | | | |
| Nil rate | 1,890 | @ | 0% | 0 | |
| | 33,760 | | | | |
| Tax liability | | | | | 6,274 |
| *Less*: Tax deducted under PAYE | | | | | 5,388 |
| Tax due | | | | | 886 |

### Helen Thackery

| | £ |
|---|---|
| Business profits (yr ended 31 July 2016) | 10,445 |
| Building society interest | 915 |
| | 11,360 |
| Personal allowance | 11,000 |
| Taxable income | 360 |
| Tax thereon: @ savings starting rate 0% | 0 |

### Child benefit

As the recipient of the higher income, Mark would be liable to withdrawal of child benefit in 2016/17 if his income exceeded the limit of £50,000. His income for this purpose is the net adjusted income for tax purposes, which is £44,760, so no high income child benefit charge will apply in 2016/17.

### Mark Thackery

Mark's building society interest of £24 and dividend is covered by his personal allowance, so he has no income tax liability. Although the source of the bank interest was funds gifted by his father, this is not taxable on Christopher as it is less than £100.

## (ii) Payment of a personal pension premium

Christopher Thackery's personal pension premium of £1,600 is net of basic rate tax. The gross premium is therefore £2,000. Providing the payment is within the limits allowed, no tax relief is withdrawn from such a payment even if the payer has no tax liability. Relief is available on the amount up to the individual's earnings for the year, although amounts paid in excess of the annual allowance will be subject to a tax charge. For someone like Christopher who would be liable to higher rate tax were it not for the dividend nil rate band, the extra relief over and above the basic rate tax retained at source is given by extending the basic rate limit by the amount of the premium, so that in Christopher's case the revised limit is £34,000. The position would therefore be as follows:

| | | | | | |
|---|---|---|---|---|---|
| | | £ | | | £ |
| Taxable income as in (i) | | | | | 33,760 |
| Tax thereon: | On non-savings income | | | | |
| | Basic rate | 28,870 | @ | 20% | 5,774 |
| | On non-dividend savings income | | | | |
| | Nil rate | 1,000 | @ | 0% | — |
| | Lower rate | 2,000 | @ | 20% | 400 |
| | On dividend income | | | | |
| | Nil rate | 1,890 | @ | 0% | — |
| | | 33,760 | | | 6,174 |
| *Less*: Tax deducted as before | | | | | 5,388 |
| Tax due | | | | | 786 |

Thus the effect of paying a pension premium of £2,000 gross, £1,600 net, is to give relief of:

| | |
|---|---|
| Reduction of tax due (886 – 786) | 100 |
| Tax relief given by deduction from premium | 400 |
| | £500 |

The relief is less than 40% because the effect of increasing the basic rate band by £2,000 in this case is to provide an additional £500 of savings nil rate band, as Christopher is now a basic rate taxpayer, even allowing for the dividend nil rate band. The changes to the structure of taxation of both savings income and dividends in 2016 are marked here. Without the dividend nil rate band, Christopher would be a higher rate taxpayer on his dividend income, and the dividend income could potentially have saved him (32.5% - 7.5%) + 20% = 45%.

Helen Thackery would also pay the premium of £2,000 net of basic rate tax. She would be restricted to a maximum premium of £3,600 (gross) or 100% of her relevant earnings. Since she is not a higher rate taxpayer the premium would not affect her tax liability and she would retain the £200 deducted at source. #TableB

(iii)

If Christopher's bonus was £66300 instead of £4,600 this is sufficient to increase his income above £100,000 and push him into the band of income where his personal allowances will be abated (see **explanatory note 6**). Payment of a pension contribution in this band of income is particularly tax efficient, as the contribution reduces the income for the purposes of abatement, thus providing additional tax relief on the premium.

| | | | | £ | £ |
|---|---|---|---|---|---|
| *Non-savings income:* | | | | | |
| Salary | | | | 33,340 | |
| Bonus (paid 1 June 2016) | | | | 66,300 | 99,640 |
| Rental income (4,930 less interest paid 3,000) | | | | | 1,930 |
| | | | | | 101,570 |
| *Non-dividend savings income* | | | | | |
| National Savings Bank | | | | 1,600 | |
| Midwest Bank interest | | | | 1,220 | |
| Foreign bank interest | | | | 180 | 3,000 |
| *Dividend income* | | | | | |
| UK dividends received | | | | | 1,890 |
| | | | | | 106,460 |
| Personal allowance | | | | 11,000 | |
| Reduced by: | | | | | |
| Income | | 106,460 | | | |
| Personal allowance income limit | | 100,000 | | | |
| One half of excess of | | 6,460 | | 3,230 | 7,770 |
| Taxable income | | | | | 98,690 |
| Tax thereon: On non-savings income | | | | | |
| Basic rate | 32,000 | | @ 20% | 6,400 | |
| Higher rate | 61,800 | | @ 40% | 24,720 | |
| On savings income other than dividends | | | | | |
| Nil rate | 500 | | @ 0% | — | |
| Higher rate | 2,500 | | @ 40% | 1,000 | |
| On dividend income | | | | | |
| Nil rate | 1,890 | | @ 0% | — | |
| | 98,690 | | | | |
| Tax liability | | | | | 32,120 |
| *Less*: Tax deducted – under PAYE | | | | | 29,056 |
| Tax due | | | | | 3,064 |

Payment of pension contribution of £1,600 net

| | £ | | £ |
|---|---|---|---|
| Total income as above | | | 106,460 |
| Personal allowance | | 11,000 | |
| Reduced by: | | | |
| Income | 106,460 | | |
| Less pension contribution (gross) | 2,000 | | |
| | 104,460 | | |
| Personal allowance income limit | 100,000 | | |
| One half of excess of | 4,460 | 2,230 | 8,770 |
| Taxable income | | | 97,690 |
| Tax thereon: On non-savings income | | | |

| | | | | |
|---|---|---|---|---|
| | | | £ | £ |
| Basic rate | 34,000 @ | 20% | | 6,800 |
| Higher rate | 58,800 @ | 40% | | 23,520 |
| On non-dividend savings income | | | | |
| Nil rate | 500 @ | 0% | | — |
| Higher rate | 2,500 @ | 40% | | 1,000 |
| On dividend income | | | | |
| Nil rate | 1,890 @ | 0% | | — |
| | 97,690 | | | 31,320 |
| *Less*: Tax deducted | | | | 29,056 |
| Tax due | | | | 2,264 |

Thus the effect of paying a pension premium of £2,000 gross, £1,600 net, is to give relief of:

| | |
|---|---|
| Reduction of tax due (3,064 – 2,264) | 800 |
| Tax relief given by deduction from premium | 400 |
| | £1,200 |

At this level of income, payment of the pension premium will have no impact on the high income child benefit charge, as the higher income exceeds £60,000 so the child benefit is removed in full. In the marginal band of income between £50,000 and £60,000, however, the gross amount of the pension contribution is deducted from the net income for child benefit purposes, so for some taxpayers additional relief will be available through the reduction in the child benefit charge. Strictly the tax liability should include the high income child benefit charge, but the question has no details as to whether an election not to receive the child benefit has been made, so the tax effect cannot be calculated here.

## Explanatory Notes

*Scope of income tax charge*

(1) Income tax is charged broadly on the world income of UK residents, subject to certain deductions for earnings abroad and for individuals who are not domiciled in the UK (see **Examples F1–F7** for international aspects including the UK taxation of non-residents and non-domiciliaries). The UK excludes the Channel Islands and the Isle of Man.

The Scotland Act 2012 / FA 2014 s 289 provide for a Scottish rate of income tax (SRIT) which is levied on Scottish taxpayers who have each of the general rates of income tax reduced by 10%, allowing the Scottish Parliament to impose either more or less than 10% to replace it. From April 2017, the Scottish Government will also be free to set the higher and additional rate thresholds, but not the personal allowance. Although there is a single Scottish rate, the structure gives rise to basic, higher and additional rates once added into the tax computation. The Scottish rate applies to the non savings income of Scottish taxpayers. For guidance on Scottish taxpayer status see https://www.gov.uk/government/publications/scottish-rate-of-income-tax-technical-guidance-on-scottish-taxpayer-status. HMRC has issued "S" PAYE codes as part of the normal 2016 tax cycle. The Scottish parliament is expected to announce the rate of SRIT for 2017/18 and the relevant thresholds in autumn 2016.

Certain aspects of UK tax are affected by the provisions of the European Union, EU law taking precedence over UK law. The EU treaty limits the right of member states to impose taxes, and requires that the laws of member states do not discriminate against members of other states. Furthermore the UK tax legislation must be compatible with the European Convention on Human Rights and the Human Rights Act 1998.

Businesses may pay their taxes in euros, although liabilities will still be calculated in sterling and under- or overpayments may arise because of exchange rate fluctuations before payments are actually credited by the tax authorities. SI 1998/3177 prevents unintended tax consequences arising in the UK as a result of the adoption of the euro by other EU states.

*Taxable income*

(2) An individual's income for tax purposes is called his total income (ITA 2007 s 23). It is the sum of all income of that person computed in accordance with the provisions of the Income Tax Acts. In addition to provisions within the Income Tax Act 2007 trading and other income (eg property) is computed under the Income Tax (Trading and Other Income) Act 2005 (ITTOIA 2005). Each source of income is known as a 'component' of total income. Under the legislation qualifying expenses can be deducted from income in arriving at the taxable amount.

Earnings and pensions are taxed in accordance with the Income Tax (Earnings and Pensions) Act 2003 (ITEPA 2003).

After totalling all components of income, certain payments are deducted to arrive at total income, namely allowable interest (see **explanatory note 14**). Where relevant, trading losses are also deducted. **Part (ii)** of the Example illustrates that retirement annuity premiums reduce earnings, and thus total income, whereas personal pension contributions do not. Gift aid donations to charity or to registered community amateur sports clubs do not reduce total income, relief being given in the same way as for personal pension contributions, but see **Example A3 explanatory note 3** for the special personal pension contributions and gift aid rules in relation to age allowance and **Example A5 part (f)** for the different treatment of personal pension contributions and gift aid donations for top slicing relief on life insurance policies. See also **Example A2.**

**Part (iii)** of the Example illustrates the effect of personal pension contributions on the abatement of personal allowances for taxpayers with net adjusted income in excess of £100,000. See **explanatory note 4.**

*Income exempt from tax*

(3) Certain income is exempt from tax, the principal items being as follows:

(i) Interest and bonuses on National Savings Certificates.

(ii) Income from Individual Savings Accounts plus Junior ISA's and Child Trust Funds.

(iii) Terminal bonuses on Save As You Earn (SAYE) contracts.

(iv) Prizes (including Premium Bond prizes) and bettings winnings.

(v) The stipulated capital element of a purchased life annuity.

(vi) Statutory redundancy payments (and certain other payments on termination of employment).

(vii) Educational grants and scholarships.

(viii) Maintenance payments.

(ix) Qualifying sickness and unemployment insurance payments (such as benefits paid from permanent health insurance policies, income protection insurance, mortgage payment protection insurance, and insurance to meet loan repayments or domestic bills).

(x) Damages and compensation for personal injury (whether received as a lump sum or by periodic payments).

(xi) Some state benefits, including universal credit, bereavement support payments, wounds and disability pensions, war widows' pensions, personal independence payment, disability living allowance, attendance allowance, income support (except to the unemployed and to strikers), tax credits, housing benefit, pensioners' Christmas bonus, pensioners' winter allowance and pension credits (see **Example B2 explanatory note 1** for details of taxable state benefits).

(xii) The government on occasion seeks to exempt non-resident competitors from income tax arising on particular sporting activities. For example, the Glasgow 2014 Commonwealth Games and 2015 London Anniversary Games.

(xiii) Adoption allowances.

Tax is not normally payable on cashbacks and rebated commissions received by someone as an ordinary retail customer (see HMRC Statement of Practice 4/97).

*Charging income to tax*

(4) The tax year runs from 6 April to 5 April. Income is taxed on a 'current year basis', which means that the taxable income is always that of the tax year (except for business income, for which the taxable income is normally the profits of the accounting year ending in the tax year).

Employment earnings are charged to tax when they are received (or when remitted to the UK for certain non-domiciled individuals, see **Example F1**), regardless of the year in which they were earned. Christopher's bonus received in June 2016 is thus charged in 2016/17, even though it was earned in the previous tax year.

(5) In working out how much tax is payable, certain payments, eg pension premiums (see **explanatory note 12**), donations to charity (see **explanatory note 13**), and currently allowable interest payments under headings (i) to (vi) in **explanatory note 14**, qualify for tax relief at the taxpayer's highest tax rate, although in the case of personal pension premiums the minimum tax saving is the tax of 20% deducted from the premium, as illustrated in **part (ii)** of the Example in relation to Helen Thackery. Patent royalties are also paid net of basic rate tax (except where paid by one company to another – see **Example A5 part (a)**), but in this case the relief may not be retained by a non-taxpayer (see **explanatory note 13**). Certain qualifying investments, such as under the Enterprise Investment Scheme or Venture Capital Trust Scheme (see **Example N7**) or to Social Enterprises, give relief at 30% of the investment, and the Seed EIS scheme gives relief at 50%, irrespective of the investor's marginal rate of tax. Qualifying investments in Community Development Finance Institutions give relief at 5% of the investment for up to five years (see **Example N7**).

(6) As well as being able to save tax on certain payments, taxpayers may claim various tax allowances. For details see **Example A3**.

In addition, a family unit or a single person may be able to claim tax credits or universal credit. These are payable if the claimant(s) have low income or a child. For details see **Example A7**.

*Rates of tax*

(7) For 2016/17, on income other than savings income, tax is payable at the basic rate of 20% on the first £32,000 and the higher rate of 40% on income up to £150,000. Above that a rate of 45% applies – this is known as the additional rate.

Different rates apply to savings income, the main items of which are dividend income, interest from banks and building societies, interest on company debentures and government stocks, the income element of a purchased life annuity (see **Example A4 explanatory note 3**) and accrued income charges on the sale/purchase of interest-bearing securities (see **Example A5**) (ITA 2007 ss 8 and 9). Savings income is taxed as the next slice of income (except for termination payments – see **Example B5 explanatory note 9**. Dividends are treated as the top slice of income. Tax is payable on savings income other than dividends at the savings starting rate of 0% until the £5,000 limit is used (the savings rate limit) then at the basic rate of 20% on income up to the basic rate limit of £32,000, at 40% up to taxable income of £150,000, and 45% thereafter. The savings starting rate only applies to the extent that taxable non-savings income does not exceed the £5,000 limit. In addition, there is a savings nil rate band which attaches to the first £1 of taxable savings income in excess of the savings starting rate band, making it available to taxpayers with higher non savings income. The nil rate band is of variable size, depending on whether the taxpayer's income exceeds the basic rate limit or the higher rate limit. The amount for taxpayers with income below the basic rate limit is £1,000, and £500 for those with income above this limit. The amount is nil for those with income over £150,000. See **Example A5**.

Dividend income also carries a nil rate band of £5,000, which attaches to the first £1 of taxable dividend. After this, dividend income is taxed at the dividend ordinary rate of 7½% on income up to the basic rate limit, the dividend upper rate of 32½% and the dividend additional rate of 38.1% .

The rates on dividends and other savings income apply not only to UK income but also to foreign savings income (except for income charged to tax on a remittances basis, to which the normal non-savings income rates apply – see **Example A5**). Relief is available for foreign tax deducted. The savings income rates do not apply to other investment income, such as rents or to annuities (other than purchased life annuities), or to other taxable income even if the underlying source is savings income (see **Example A2 part (b)**).

Tax is no longer deducted from UK building society and bank interest received. For details see **Example A5**.

The self-employed pay Class 2 & 4 national insurance contributions. Class 2 are flat rate and class 4 are based on their profits. Both are collected via self-assessment along with income tax. Class 2 is due to be abolished from April 2018.

*Taxation of the family*

(8) Income and capital gains of a married couple are taxed on each of them separately. Each is entitled to a personal allowance and annual exemption. The age-related married couple's allowance goes to the husband, unless an election is made to transfer all or half of it to the wife. In any event, any unused tax saving may be transferred to the other spouse if income is too low to use it. For the detailed provisions see **Example A3**.

Although still called the married couple's allowance, the allowance is also available to members of a registered civil partnership provided that at least one of the partners was born before 6 April 1935. For couples married on or after 5 December 2005 and for all civil partners, the higher of the two incomes will be used to determine the allowance (as opposed to that of the husband for couples married before that time).

Although not relevant in this case (Christopher would be liable to higher rate tax were it not for the dividend nil rate band) from 6 April 2015 married couples / civil partners not liable at higher rate can transfer up to 10% of their personal allowance (£1,100 for 2016/17) to their partner.

By contrast entitlement to tax credits is dependent upon the total income of the couple computed in accordance with the rules for tax credits. For the detailed provisions see **Example A7**.

(9) A person is liable to the high income child benefit charge if they or their partner are entitled to child benefit for any week in the year, and their own income is more than £50,000 and greater than that of their partner. At income of £60,000 the child benefit is clawed back in full by the charge, and taper applies for income between £50,000 and £60,000. The income for this purpose is the net adjusted income, as for the abatement of personal allowances (see **explanatory note 6**). **Example A2** deals with high income child benefit charge in detail.

(10) The income of unmarried children under 18 is treated as the parent's, if it derives from funds transferred to the child or settled on the child by the parent. There are certain exceptions, including income of up to £100 a year, which covers Mark's building society interest in this Example. For further details see **Example A2**.

*Personal pension premiums*

(11) UK residents under 75 may pay contributions to buy themselves a pension. The detailed provisions are in **Example A6**. Generally speaking pension contributions are paid net of basic rate tax , including stakeholder pension premiums, and higher rate relief where relevant is given in the payer's self-assessment or coding notice. The extra higher rate relief is given by extending the basic rate band by the amount of the payment, as shown in **Part (ii)** of the Example for Christopher Thackery. There is also an impact where the personal allowance has been abated for net adjusted income of more than £100,000 illustrated by **Part (iii)** of the Example. Where income exceeds £150,000 the annual allowance may be less.

(For further details, see **Example A6.**)

National insurance contributions are not deducted in calculating earnings for pension contribution purposes (FA 2004 s 189(2)), and pension scheme payments (either under personal, stakeholder, retirement annuity or occupational schemes) are not deducted in calculating earnings or profits on which national insurance contributions are calculated (SSCBA 1992 Sch 2 para 3).

*Position of non-taxpayers in relation to tax relief deducted from payments*

(12) The tax deducted from personal pension premiums may be retained by both taxpayers and non-taxpayers.

Where tax has been deducted at source from gift aid donations to charity then the taxpayer needs to have paid sufficient tax to cover the amount deducted. The tax paid for this purpose includes income tax, non-repayable tax credits on dividends and capital gains tax (see **Example N4**).

*Allowable interest*

(13) A loan taken out to buy a life annuity, secured on the borrower's only or main residence (often known as an equity release scheme) before 6 April 2000 by someone aged 65 or over qualifies for tax relief. The relief was originally given at the then basic rate of 23% on the first £30,000 of a qualifying loan. Relief for such loans remains available (under the Mortgage Interest Relief At Source (MIRAS) scheme where appropriate) for loans taken out before 9 March 1999 (or for which a written offer had been made before that date), providing the property was the borrower's main residence immediately before that date. Despite the reduction in the basic rate to 20%, relief for home annuity loans continues at 23% (ICTA 1988 s 353(1AA)). If the taxpayer leaves the property, eg to move into a nursing home, or remortgages the property, or moves to a different property, the relief will continue so long as the loan or replacement is still outstanding (ICTA 1988 s 365). Relief is not available on any other home loans. There was a consultation on removing this relief, by 2019, but the proposals were rejected.

Relief at the payer's marginal rate is available for interest on loans under the following headings.

(i) Loans to buy plant or machinery, for example an office machine, for use in a partnership or in one's employment (ITA 2007 s 390). Relief in this case is restricted to interest payable not later than three years after the end of the tax year in which the loan was made. Where there is part private use, relief is restricted to the business proportion of the interest. Employees cannot claim relief for plant and machinery unless it is *necessarily* provided for use in their employment (ITA 2007 s 390 and CAA 2001 s 36).

(ii) Loans to buy shares in or lend money to a close company that is a trading or property investment company, providing the borrower either owns more than 5% of the ordinary share capital, or owns some share capital and has worked for the greater part of his time in the management or conduct of the company in the period since obtaining the loan to the time the interest is paid (ITA 2007 s 392). From 6 April 2014, the rules are extended to companies resident in the European Economic Area provided they would be 'close' if they were resident in the UK. The loan interest does not qualify for relief if either income tax relief or capital gains deferral relief has been given in respect of the shares under the enterprise investment scheme (see **Example N6**).

(iii) Loans to a partner to buy an interest in a partnership or to lend money to it, providing the borrower is still a partner when the interest is paid and providing he is not a limited partner or a partner in an investment limited liability partnership (see **Example C12**) (ITA 2007 s 398).

(iv) Loans to personal representatives to pay inheritance tax on a deceased person's personal property (ie property other than freehold land and buildings), in respect of interest paid within one year from the making of the loan (ITA 2007 s 403).

(v) Loans for the purchase of shares in unquoted employee-controlled trading companies by their full-time employees or spouses (ITA 2007 s 396). From 6 April 2014, the rules are extended to include companies resident in the European Economic Area.

(vi) Loans to acquire a share or shares in a co-operative (ITA 2007 s 401).

In no circumstances can bank overdraft interest be deducted from *total* income, no matter for what purpose the overdraft is used. Relief is only available for bank overdraft interest where it is paid in connection with a business and is thus deductible as a business expense under the trading rules (see **Example C12 explanatory note 9**) or where it relates to let property. F(2)A 2015 s 24 introduces a restriction on the deduction of finance costs relating to let residential properties from 6 April 2017. The restriction provides for a tax reduction for such costs by reference to the basic rate. The restriction will be phrased in and take full effect in 2020/21. (see **Example D2**).

Where the claim for allowable interest relates to trading purposes then if the interest cannot be offset within the tax year it may be added to trading losses carried forward (see **Example E1**) or included in a terminal loss claim (see **Example E3**) (ITA 2007 s 88).

However, interest available for relief under this category is included in the income tax reliefs cap applying from 2013/14 onwards. Under the cap, the total amount set off against total income relating to losses (including trading losses of the year and carried back under ITA 2007 ss 64 and 72) is restricted to £50,000 in the year of set-off, or 25% of the taxpayers' gross income, if greater. Trading losses unrelieved as a result of the cap are carried forwards and set off against future profits of the same trade, to which the cap does not apply. See **Example E1.**

*Self assessment*

(14) Around one third of taxpayers are technically required to 'self-assess' the amount of income tax and capital gains tax payable, although HMRC will still work out the tax if the taxpayer wants them to, providing returns are sent in early enough or filed via the Internet. Most taxpayers, however, account for their tax under PAYE. HMRC issue assessments themselves in some circumstances, including where tax is due on savings income, and where they discover that tax has been underpaid because the taxpayer has failed to disclose relevant information.

If Christopher Thackery receives a self-assessment tax return, then he is required to compute his 'tax due for 2016/17 before payments on account'. This will be the tax liability less tax deducted at source (ie PAYE tax, tax deducted by banks and building societies etc and dividend tax credits).

All taxpayers affected by the high income child benefit charge are within self assessment, even if they request the charge to be collected through their PAYE code, unless they have elected not to receive child benefit. If they have elected not to receive child benefit, they will need to review their income each year, to establish whether the election should be withdrawn retrospectively. The time limit is 12 months after the due filing date for the tax return for the year concerned.

In Christopher Thackery's case, the tax due arises because the rental income and savings income have been received without deduction of tax. The actual liability will always be slightly different from the exact figure because of the rounding of allowances and rates under the PAYE system.

Because of the nature of Christopher's income in **Part (ii)** no payments on account will have been made. Provided Christopher files his tax return by 31 October 2017, or electronically by 30 December 2017 HMRC will collect the amount due by way of an adjustment to his PAYE code number in 2018/19 (see **Example B1 explanatory note 13**). If the return is filed too late for a coding adjustment, the tax due must be paid by 31 January 2018. In **Part (iii)** his income is sufficient to trigger both a payment of tax and payments on account, unless his tax code has been adjusted to reflect the reduced personal allowance available. All taxpayers with income of over £100,000 are required to make a tax return each year. For detailed notes on self-assessment see **Example G2.**

# Question

(a) Mr Victor, a married man aged 55, has the following income for 2016/17:

| | £ |
|---|---|
| Non-savings income (gross) | 43,975 |
| Dividend | 10,600 |

His two children, Arthur aged 23 and Brian aged 15, are beneficiaries under a relevant property trust set up by Mr Victor in 2002, under which the children are entitled to the income at age 18. The trust's investments comprise interest-bearing securities. In 2016/17 the income of the trust was £4,000, the trustees paying £2,000 gross in respect of each of the children and deducting tax therefrom at the appropriate rate. Brian has no other income. Arthur is a post graduate student at university and in addition to the trust income he has vacation earnings of £800 (from which no tax has been deducted) and a research grant.

Mrs Victor does not work, her only income being savings income of £1,810 . She received child benefit payments of £1,076 in respect of Brian during 2016/17.

Show the tax position of Mr Victor and his children for 2016/17.

(b) Outline:

(i) the broad principles of the income tax treatment of trusts;

(ii) tax-effective transfers by parents to their infant children;

(iii) tax planning possibilities for husband and wife.

(c) Set out the tax treatment relating to:

(i) financial support to adopters;

(ii) receipts from foster care.

# Answer

## (a) Mr Victor and his children – Income tax computations 2016/17

Arthur's income from the trust is his in his own right and tax will have been deducted by the trustees at the basic rate of 20%. Brian's income will be treated as his father's income, taxable not as savings income but as miscellaneous income (ITTOIA s 629). The trustees will have deducted tax at 45% (see **part (b)(i) note 4** of the Example). The tax position is therefore as follows:

### Mr Victor

| | | | | £ |
|---|---|---|---|---|
| Non-savings income, including Brian's income from the trust | | | | 45,975 |
| Dividends | | | | 10,600 |
| | | | | 56,575 |
| Personal allowance | | | | 11,000 |
| Taxable income | | | | 45,575 |
| Tax thereon: | | | | |
| On non-savings income | 32,000 | @ | 20% | 6,400 |
| | 2,975 | @ | 40% | 1,190 |
| On dividend income | 5,000 | @ | 0% | — |
| | 5,600 | @ | 32½% | 1,820 |
| | 45,575 | | | |
| Tax liability | | | | 9,410 |
| *Add:* High income child benefit charge (see note below) | | | | 699 |
| *Less:* Tax deducted by trustees | | | | 900 |
| Tax payable | | | | 9,209 |

### Brian

Brian has no taxable income, his only income being treated as his father's under the parental settlement rules, since he is under 18 and unmarried.

### Arthur

Arthur's trust income is not treated as his father's because he is over 18.

His research grant is exempt from tax. His trust income of £2,000 plus his vacation earnings of £800 are below his personal allowance of £11,000 so he can recover from HMRC the tax of £400 deducted from the trust income.

### Child Benefit charge

Mr Victor has the higher income of the couple, and as a married man living with his wife is therefore liable to the high income child benefit charge for 2016/17. As his income is between £50,000 and £60,000, he falls into the taper band, so the charge is calculated as follows:

| | £ |
|---|---|
| Income | |
| Mr Victor (as above) | 56,575 |
| *Less*: Threshold | 50,000 |
| | 6,575 |
| Taper is 1% for each £100 over the threshold, so | 65% |
| Taper applied to child benefit amount of £1,076 | £699 |

## (b)

### (i) *Tax treatment of trusts*

The tax treatment of trusts is dealt with in detail in the companion to this book, **Tolley's Taxwise II 2016/17**. The broad principles are as follows:

(1) The settlor remains liable for income tax on the trust income if he or his spouse/civil partner has retained an interest in the settlement or where the settlement transfers income but not capital. Spouse/civil partner does not include a future, former or separated spouse/civil partner or the settlor's widow(er) or surviving civil partner (ITTOIA 2005 s 624).

These provisions do not apply to annual payments made for commercial reasons in connection with an individual's business. There are also exceptions for outright gifts between spouses/civil partners, and for various arrangements made on separation or divorce. There is no charge on the settlor to the extent that the trust income is given to charity (see **Example N4 explanatory note 5**).

All income treated as the settlor's income under ITTOIA 2005 s 624 is charged to tax in accordance with whichever provisions of the Income Tax Acts as would have applied had the income arisen directly to the settlor. So savings income of the trust is taxed as savings income of the settlor.

(2) Even if a settlement is of capital in which the settlor does not retain an interest, if income of the settlement is paid to or for the benefit of an unmarried child of the settlor who is under 18, it is treated as the settlor's income, subject to the exceptions in **part (b)(ii)** of the Example (ITTOIA 2005 ss 626–627). The tax deducted by the trustees from the payment counts as tax paid by the settlor (ITA 2007 s 494(3)). If the settlor has to pay any further tax he is entitled to recover it from the trustees, or from the person who received the income (ITTOIA 2005 s 646), (but see **part (b)(ii)** of the Example). The income charged as the settlor's income under ITTOIA 2005 s 629 is treated as miscellaneous income and it does not count as savings income. This applies even if the income is derived from dividends, because such income comes from the general pool of income in the trust.

(3) Where someone has an interest in possession in a trust, ie the right to income (usually a life interest), the trustees are liable to tax at the dividend ordinary rate of 7.5%% on dividend income, the lower rate of 20% on savings income and at the basic rate on other trust income (without any deduction for their expenses) and they deduct tax at the appropriate rate from income payments to the life tenant. Non-taxpaying beneficiaries can claim repayment of the tax deducted.

(4) Where the trust is a relevant property trust, the trustees are liable to tax at the trust dividend rate of 38.1% on dividend income and at 45% on other income, after deducting trust expenses (ITTOIA 2005 s 568). The first £1,000 of relevant property trust income is instead liable at the rates set out at 3 above, that is dividends 7.5%%, savings income 20%, non-savings income 20% (FA 2005 s 14). The £1,000 will be shared if the settlor set up other trusts, subject to a minimum amount of £200. Even though tax on dividends is paid at 38.1%, the trustees deduct tax at 45% on payments to beneficiaries (and non-taxpaying beneficiaries may claim repayment of the tax deducted).

(5) Special rules apply by election, where the trust has a vulnerable beneficiary. In order to qualify the beneficiary must be entitled to all of the income and the property must be held for the vulnerable beneficiary absolutely. If the beneficiary qualifies as a minor he/she must be absolutely entitled to the

property at 18. A vulnerable person is either a disabled person who is incapable of administering their affairs by reason of a mental disorder, or a person in receipt of attendance allowance, or disability living allowance (higher or middle rate), or a minor (under 18) where one or both parents have died. The election enables the tax liability of the trust to be computed using the tax rates and allowances applicable to the vulnerable beneficiary. The treatment extends to capital gains tax.

For full details see **Tolley's Taxwise II 2016/17**.

## (ii) *Tax-effective transfers by parents to infant children*

Children are taxpayers in their own right, no matter how young they are, and they are entitled to the personal allowance against their income. This does not apply to certain income from their parents, as indicated in (i) above. The following items are not caught by the parental settlement rules:

(1) Income deriving from funds provided by the parent if it is less than £100 a year. The £100 income limit applies separately to each parent.

(2) Junior ISA's to which the parents can contribute up to the limit of £4,080 in 2016/17 . Similarly, those children who have Child Trust funds can receive contributions of up to £4,080 in 2016/17 from parents.

(3) Children's Bonds for children under 16. The maximum holding per child is £3,000 in the current issue plus earlier issues of the Bonds. All interest and bonuses are tax-free, but no further returns are earned after the child's 21st birthday.

(4) Premiums of up to £270 a year on a qualifying friendly society life assurance policy for a child under 18. The returns under the policy are exempt from tax, but friendly societies are not able to reclaim dividend tax credits.

(5) Contributions of up to £3,600 a year to a personal pension policy on behalf of a child, such contributions being paid net of basic rate tax, which is retained whether or not the child is a taxpayer. The contributions would probably be exempt from inheritance tax under the rules for regular gifts out of income (inheritance tax is dealt with in detail in the companion to this book, **Tolley's Taxwise II 2016/17**). The child cannot draw pension benefits from the fund until he/she reaches the minimum retirement age currently 55.

Income arising on bare trusts created by parents in favour of their children under 18 on or after 9 March 1999, and income from funds added to existing trusts on or after that date is taxed as income of the parent, unless covered by the £100 limit dealt with above.

In **part (a)** of the Example the effect of Brian's trust income of £2,000 being treated as Mr Victor's income is to increase Mr Victor's income liable to high income child benefit charge. As stated in (i) note 2, the settlor has the right to recover from the trustees any additional tax payable by him. ITTOIA 2005 s 619A states that the settlement income is regarded as the top slice of the settlor's income. This is, however, overridden by ITA 2007 s 16 requiring savings income to be treated as the top slice of income. Although the settlement income is in fact savings income, it is not treated as such in Mr Victor's hands.

In fact, the inclusion of the trust income increases his overall tax liability by £1,015 (50.7%), because the trust income is charged to tax at 40%, costing £800, and it also increases the taper of child benefit by an additional 20% (£2000/£100 %) costing roughly £215. Mr Victor is entitled to treat the tax at 45% deducted by the trustees from the trust income (£900) as paid by him (**see (i) note 2**).

Bare trusts created under a parent's will are still effective, and also bare trusts created by other relatives, although it is not possible to make a reciprocal arrangement for someone to create a trust for his relative's children and for the relative to do the same for his children. A disadvantage of bare trusts is that the child cannot be prevented from having the property put into his own legal ownership at age 18.

Bare trusts created by parents are still effective for capital gains purposes, so that it is possible to use such trusts to acquire investments for children that produce capital growth rather than income.

It is possible for a child of any age (those who have a Child Trust Fund can convert it to an ISA) to have a Junior ISA but it will be administered by an adult with parental responsibility until the child reaches the age of 16. The parent is not taxable on the income arising in respect of contributions made by him. No withdrawals will be possible until the child reaches the age of 18.

### (iii) *Tax planning for married couples and civil partners*

As far as capital gains tax is concerned, each member of a couple is entitled to the annual capital gains tax exemption. Losses of one may, however, not be set against gains of the other. Transfers of assets between them in tax years when they are living together for all or part of the year are made on a no loss/no gain basis. See **Example L1**.

It may be sensible for a couple to rearrange their affairs in order to obtain the maximum benefit from being taxed separately, for example if one party has insufficient income to use his/her personal allowance. Although not relevant in this question, it is also possible for married couples / civil partners not liable to higher rate tax to transfer up to 10% of their personal allowance (£1,100 for 2016/17) to their partner.

It is not possible for one party to give the other the right to part of his/her income without transferring the capital, but outright transfers of capital, with no right for the transferring party to control the capital or derive a benefit from it, are tax effective (ITTOIA 2005 s 624). (The fact that the individual who gave the asset away later gets it back on the other's death, or as a gift, does not make the transfer ineffective providing the initial gift was not made with any express or implied stipulation as to what the receiving individual could do with it.) An attempt by two directors owning all the shares in a company to increase their wives' income by issuing them with preference shares (for which the wives paid a nominal amount) carrying rights to 30% of the profits but no voting rights nor rights to participate in surplus assets was treated as an income settlement, and thus ineffective in *Young v Pearce, Young v Scrutton* (1996).

In Tax Bulletin 64 (April 2003) HMRC issued further guidance on the settlements legislation and how they felt it could apply to individuals and businesses in non-trust situations. They listed factors they would consider in deciding whether the settlements legislation should be applied:

- A main earner draws a low salary leading to enhanced dividends paid to shareholders who are family members.
- Disproportionately large returns on capital investments.
- Different classes of shares enabling payment of dividends only to shareholders paying lower rates of tax.
- Waiver of dividends to enable higher dividends to be paid to those liable at lower rates of tax.
- Income being transferred from a person making most of the business profits to a friend or family member who pays a lower rate of tax.

Common situations which HMRC felt could invoke the settlement rules were:

- Shares are issued that carry only restricted rights.
- Shares are gifted that carry only restricted rights.
- Income of a company is derived mainly from a single employee but shares are held by others.
- A share in a partnership is gifted or transferred at below market value.
- Dividend waivers occur.
- Dividends are only paid on certain classes of shares.
- Dividends are paid to a settlor's minor children.

HMRC confirms that ITTOIA 2005 s 624 will not apply if there is no 'bounty' or if the gift is to a spouse/civil partner and is an outright gift which is not wholly, or substantially, a right to income, eg a gift of shares in a quoted company.

The Tax Bulletin article gives various examples of where HMRC considers that the settlements legislation will apply. Their view was originally upheld in the case of *Jones v Garnett* where shares were held by husband and wife and the main earner (Mr Jones) drew a salary below the going rate for the work he had done. As a result the dividend paid to Mrs Jones was deemed to arise from the 'bounty' created by the failure to draw a salary at the going rate. Therefore, under ICTA 1988 s 660A (now ITTOIA 2005 s 624), that dividend income was taxable on Mr Jones. The Court of Appeal disagreed with the HMRC view and held that there was no bounty provided when Mrs Jones acquired her share in the company. The House of Lords unanimously dismissed HMRC's appeal in July 2007. They held that while the arrangements constituted a settlement, the exemption for outright gifts between spouses/civil partners applied (ITTOIA 2005 s 626). Consequently, Mrs Jones was taxable on the dividends she received even though most of the profit was as a result of Mr Jones's efforts. Following the Lords decision, HMRC announced that they intend to legislate to 'reverse' the decision. Although a consultation document setting out proposed new legislation addressing this problem was issued in December 2007, this was widely criticised, and concern was expressed as to how the proposed legislation would apply in practice. Budget 2009 announced that the legislation was not to be implemented at present. It is possible that this could be re-introduced in the future. Where capital transfers are made, and the property consists of mortgaged property, one point that needs watching is that if the liability to pay the mortgage is taken over by the transferee, stamp duty land tax may be payable.

Spouses and civil partners normally own joint property as 'joint tenants', which means each has equal rights over the property and when one dies it goes automatically to the other. The joint tenancy can, however, be severed and replaced by a 'tenancy in common' in which the share of each is separate, and may be unequal, and may be disposed of in lifetime or on death as the individual wishes. Where property is in joint names, it is deemed to be owned equally for income tax purposes unless it is actually owned in some different proportions and a joint declaration is made to that effect (ITA 2007 s 836). Declarations apply to income arising on or after the date of the declaration. For a declaration to be valid, notice must be given to HMRC (on Form 17) within the period of sixty days beginning with the date of the declaration. The form only covers the assets listed on it. Any new assets must be covered by a separate form. Tax Bulletin 63 (February 2003) makes it clear that normally bank and building society joint accounts are held in such a way that each owner is equally entitled to the whole account. Form 17 can only be used for these accounts if the parties have formally changed the legal basis on which the account is held.

The provisions of ITA 2007 s 836 deeming joint ownership do not apply if the property is shares in a close company. Instead the income from the shares must be divided between husband and wife in accordance with their actual ownership rights in the shares.

The deemed equal ownership is not relevant for capital gains purposes. The actual underlying beneficial ownership determines the capital gains treatment (see **Example L1 part** (a)).

## (c)

### (i) *Financial support to adopters*

Where a family receives financial support from a local authority or adoption agency the amount received is free of income tax under ITTOIA 2005 s 744.

### (ii) *Foster carers (ITTOIA 2005 part 7 chapter 2)*

A standard tax exemption applies to foster carers which, together with an optional simplified method of computing taxable profits for those foster carers whose income exceeds the exempt amount provides a simple basis for calculating taxable income.

The exempt limit is the sum of

- £10,000, per residence, per full tax year (s 808), plus
- £200 per week for a child aged under 11, and £250 per week for a child aged 11 or older (s 811).

Where a foster carer's gross receipts exceed the above limits, then, instead of computing their business profits using the normal rules, they can elect to deem their profit as being the excess of gross receipts from foster care over the exempt limits. The election must be made by the first anniversary of the 31 January after the year of assessment, or such longer period as HMRC may allow (s 818). (There is statutory provision for the deadline to be extended if there is a late adjustment to the profits from the provision of foster care (s 819).) A carer who is exempt or using the simplified method of computing profits is not entitled to capital allowances (s 826). No balancing charge or balancing allowance arises when they become exempt or elect to go into the simplified scheme. If the foster carer goes back to using the normal method of computing profits he or she can claim capital allowances on assets still held at the start of that period, including assets purchased during the periods when he or she was exempt or using the simplified scheme (ss 824–827).

If a taxpayer ceases to trade as a foster carer whilst within the exempt limit, then any overlap relief due on cessation is given as a loss (s 828).

## Explanatory Notes

*High income child benefit charge*

(1) The high income child benefit charge removes child benefit from households where at least one partner has income of more than £50,000.

The charge is a taper applied to the child benefit payable in the year, with 100% taper applying at income of £60,000. Between these limits the taper is calculated as follows:

$$\frac{\text{Net adjusted income} - £50,000}{£100}\%$$

rounding the percentage down to the next whole number.

The net adjusted income for this purpose is after deducting losses, gift aid payments (gross) and the gross amount of pension contributions paid. This is the same amount as that used for abatement of personal allowances in the case of income over £100,000 and for elderly taxpayers in receipt of age related allowances. See **Example A1 (iii)** for an illustration of the former, and **Example A3** for an illustration of the latter.

(2) The liability to high income child benefit charge is based on a household where the individual lives with a partner. The definition of partner includes civil partners, and couples living together as husband and wife or civil partners. The same criteria will be used for the child benefit charge as is used for the purpose of tax credits. Where one member of the couple is entitled to child benefit for a week in the year, then the partner with the higher income is liable to the charge if their net relevant income exceeds £50,000.

There is an associated liability to notify chargeability by 5 October after the relevant tax year – so for 2016/17 by 5 October 2017.

(3) There are practical difficulties associated with computing and reporting the charge where the couple do not share financial information, and particularly when both are late completing their tax returns.

It will be possible to ask HMRC in writing whether the partner's income is higher or lower than a stated amount (providing sufficient details of the partner for HMRC to identify them). However, if at the point of the request, the partner's income for 2016/17 has not yet been finalised, then HMRC will only confirm on the basis of the latest information available to them. This would seem to indicate that the income of the partner should be re-confirmed after the end of January, and any amendments made to the client's tax return where necessary.

(4) Where a couple know that they will be losing their full entitlement to child benefit as at least one partner has income of more than £60,000, it is possible to elect not to receive child benefit. Once an election is made it will remain in force until withdrawn.

It is important to be aware that making an initial claim to child benefit also secures the right of the recipient to protected status for state pension purposes, so a couple with high income should still make a claim to child benefit on the arrival of their first child, and then make an election not to receive it, so that the mother's pension rights remain protected.

Where an election not to receive child benefit is made and it subsequently transpires that neither parent has income of more than £60,000 the election can be retrospectively withdrawn and the child benefit will be paid in full.

(5) Child benefit charge is part of the tax charge on an individual, so will give rise to payments on account in the same way as additional tax. When it was first introduced it only applied for one-quarter of the year meaning that the impact was particularly large when the tax payment fell due for the second (full) year. This is also true if a baby is born late in the tax year.

(6) In the February 2015 issue of Tax Adviser Rebecca Benneyworth explains a practical issue of the high income child benefit charge. Where a taxpayer has elected not to receive child benefit (on the basis they expect their annual income to be above £60,000) and after the end of the tax year (when preparing their tax return) it is found that their income was below £60,000 but above £50,000 then there is a partial entitlement to child benefit. A revocation of the election not to receive the benefit is necessary. However, this is a binary choice, the child benefit will be paid in full for the relevant year and the taxpayer is then in the position of owing a partial high income child benefit charge.

See www.taxadvisermagazine.com/article/out-pocket.

# Question

(a) In April 2016, Elise and Tim Jensen had their second child and she won £200,000 on the lottery. The lottery win has been placed in a fixed deposit in Elise's name. Elise has agreed a two year career break and when she returns to work the couple wish to buy an old property. At that time, Tim will cease employment and renovate their new property whilst doing the school / nursery runs. Their expected gross income is:

| | 2016/17 | | 2017/18 | | 2018/19 | |
|---|---|---|---|---|---|---|
| | Elise | Tim | Elise | Tim | Elise | Tim |
| | £ | £ | £ | £ | £ | £ |
| Employment income | 9,960 | 40,000 | 0 | 41,000 | 11,000 | 11,600 |
| Savings interest | 5,000 | 0 | 5,000 | 0 | 5,000 | 0 |

Comment on whether they should claim marriage allowance.

(b) John Brown, who was born on 6 June 1936, married Ann Old (born 4 January 1942), on 10 May 2016. Their incomes for 2016/17 are as follows:

| | | | |
|---|---|---|---|
| John Brown: | Pension | 16,800 | |
| | Building society interest | 11,000 | £27,800 |
| Ann Old: | Pension | 19,000 | |
| | Dividends | 12,000 | £31,000 |

Calculate the income tax payable by each of them for 2016/17.

(c) John and Jane Stone were divorced in 1987. Since that time John (who has remarried) has paid maintenance of £3,500 pa to Jane (who has not remarried). They were both born in 1936. Their income in 2016/17 is as follows:

| | *John* | *Jane* |
|---|---|---|
| | £ | £ |
| Pension | 33,715 | 10,830 |
| Building society interest (amounts received) | 3,100 | 300 |
| Dividends (amounts received) | 6,500 | 950 |

Compute the net tax payable by or repayable to John and Jane for 2016/17.

(d) D Partid died on 10 June 2016. He was born in 1937. His income for the period from 6 April 2016 to the date of his death was as follows:

| | |
|---|---|
| State pension | £3,500 |
| Dividends | £2,000 |
| Building society interest credited | £1,000 |

He left a widow aged 45 and a child aged ten. Mrs Partid, income for the year amounted to:

Salary per P60 £13,120 (PAYE deducted £424)

Building society interest of £2,000.

Show the tax position of Mr and Mrs Partid for 2016/17.

(e) Julia Jones, a single lady, will reach retirement age on 6 January 2017. She is then entitled to a state pension of £120 per week. She will continue to work for at least one year at a salary of £62,000 pa. She has savings income of £3,000 pa gross but no other pension provision.

Set out the tax liability (using 2016/17 allowances and rates throughout) arising on the state pension on the assumption that Julia:

(i) Takes the pension of £155.00 per week from 6 January 2017.

(ii) Defers her pension for one year, ceasing employment on 5 January 2018 when she will receive a pension of £164 per week.

(iii) Indicate what would happen if Julia died before she took her deferred pension.

# Answer

## (a) Elise and Tim Jensen: whether they should claim marriage allowance

*2016/17*

Without an election Elise would pay no tax as her earnings are below the personal allowance and her savings are covered by the 0% savings rate.

*Elise income tax liability 2016/17 if claim marriage allowance*

| | | £ | | £ |
|---|---|---|---|---|
| Non-savings income | | | | |
| | Salary | | | 9,960 |
| Savings income | | | | |
| | Interest | | | 5,000 |
| | | | | 14,960 |
| | | | 11,000 | |
| | | | (1,100) | |
| | | | | 9,900 |
| Taxable income | | | | 5,060 |
| Tax thereon: Non-savings income | | | | |
| | Basic rate 60 | @ 20% | 12 | |
| | On savings income other than dividends | | | |
| | Savings rate 5,000 | @ 0% | 0 | |
| | 5,060 | | | |
| Tax liability | | | | 12 |

### Notes

(1) If Elise's earnings related to the first part of the tax year, PAYE was probably deducted at source and would need to be reclaimed.

By making the election Tim will receive a tax reduction of £220 (£1,100 @ 20%) giving an overall saving of £208 (£220 - £12). The claim can be made during the year and relief included in Tim's PAYE code.

*2017/18*

The personal allowance for 2017/18 has been set at £11,500. Elise is not using her full personal allowance and the claim for marriage allowance made in 2016/17 will automatically continue to this subsequent year enabling Tim to receive a tax reduction of £230 (£1,150 @ 20%).

*2018/19*

The personal allowance for 2018/19 has been not yet been set, so we will assume that it continues at the rate of £11,500. Elise and Tim expect to earn £11,000 and £11,600. If the election is allowed to continue, £1,150 of Elise's personal allowance will be transferred to Tim as a tax reduction and he will then pay no tax. Most of the transferred allowance will be wasted. Elise would also then only have a personal allowance of £10,350 (£11,500 - £1,150) and hence would have to pay tax of £130 (£11,000 - £10,350 @ 20%).

By withdrawing the election, Tim would pay no tax as his personal allowance covers his income in full. Elise would also pay no tax. The saving by withdrawing the election is therefore £130. The claim to withdraw the election needs to be made between 6 April 2017 and 5 April 2018, and will take effect from 6 April 2018.

See **Explanatory note (2)** for full details.

## (b) Tax position of John Brown and Ann Old for 2015/16

### John Brown

| | | | | | £ | £ |
|---|---|---|---|---|---|---|
| Pension | | | | | 16,800 | |
| Building society interest | | | | | 11,000 | 27,800 |
| Personal allowance | | | | | | (11,000) |
| Taxable income | | | | | | 16,800 |
| Tax thereon: | | | | | | |
| On non-savings income | 5,800 | @ | 20% | 1,160 | | |
| On savings income | 11,000 | @ | 0% | | | |
| | 10,000 | @ | 20% | 2,000 | | |
| Tax payable | | | | | | 3,160 |

### Ann Old

| | | | | | £ | £ |
|---|---|---|---|---|---|---|
| Pension | | | | | 19,000 | |
| Dividends | | | | | 12,000 | 31,000 |
| Personal allowance | | | | | | (11,000) |
| Taxable income | | | | | | 20,000 |
| Tax thereon: | | | | | | |
| On non-savings income | 8,000 | @ | 20% | 1,600 | | |
| On dividends | 5,000 | @ | 0% | | | |
| | 7,000 | @ | 7.5% | 525 | | 2,125 |
| *Less*: Married couple's allowance (born before 6.4.1935 and elder aged 75+) | | | | | 8,355 | |
| Reduced by ½ × (31,000 – 27,700) | | | | | 1,650 | |
| | | | | | 6,705 | |
| *Less*: 1/12th of £6,705 | | | | | 559 | |
| | | | | | 6,146 | |
| Tax saving at 10% | | | | | | 615 |
| Tax payable | | | | | | 1,510 |

### Notes

(i) Only claimant's income affects married couple's allowance, even if it is given by reason of other spouse's/civil partner's age.

(ii) The married couple's allowance is reduced by half the excess of the claimant's income over £27,700, before being reduced by 1/12th for each tax month before the date of marriage.

(iii) Tax would be saved if income-producing assets were transferred from the claimant to the other spouse/civil partner to avoid the claimant's allowances being affected by the income limit. However, this should be done carefully as the other spouse/civil partner might end up with more income in the year and so would be the individual entitled to the allowance. This is less of an issue for couples who *married* before 5 December 2005 (see **note (iv)** below). See also **explanatory note 4**.

(iv) If the marriage had taken place in May 2006 instead of May 2016 then married couple's age allowance would be given to the husband. Thus, John would receive the tax saving which would have been calculated as follows:

| | |
|---|---|
| Married couples allowance | 8,355 |
| Reduced by ½ × (27,800 – 27,700) | 50 |
| | 8,305 |
| Tax saving @ 10% | 831 |

This is a difference of £216 in married couple's allowance.

The difference can be explained by the fact that a full-year's married couple allowance is available rather than merely 11/12ths (worth an additional £559 at 10%), and the taper is reduced because John's income is lower.

## (c) Net tax payable by or repayable to John and Jane Stone for 2016/17

### John Stone

| | £ | | | £ |
|---|---|---|---|---|
| Pension | | | | 33,715 |
| Building society interest | | | | 3,100 |
| Dividends | | | | 6,500 |
| | | | | 43,315 |
| Personal allowance | | | | 11,000 |
| Taxable income | | | | 32,315 |
| Tax payable thereon: | | | | |
| On non-savings income | 22,715 | @ | 20% | 4,543 |
| On savings income | 500 | @ | 20% | — |
| | 2,600 | @ | 20% | 520 |
| On dividends | 5,000 | @ | 0% | — |
| | 1,185 | @ | 7½% | 89 |
| | 315 | @ | 32½% | 102 |
| | 32,315 | | | 5,254 |
| *Less*: Married couple's age allowance (basic amount – see **note (i)**) | 3,220 | | | |
| Relief for maintenance to former wife (see **note (ii)**) | 3,220 | | | |
| | 6,440 | @ | 10% | 644 |
| Tax payable | | | | 4,610 |

### Jane Stone

| | | Income |
|---|---|---|
| | | £ |
| Pension | | 10,830 |
| Building society interest | | 300 |
| Dividends | | 950 |
| | | 12,080 |
| Personal allowance | | 11,000 |
| Taxable income | | 1,080 |
| Tax payable thereon: | | |
| On savings income | 130 @ 0% | — |
| On dividends | 950 @ 0% | — |
| Tax due | | — |

### Notes

(i) John is born before 6 April 1938, but his income is too high for him to benefit from the full married couples allowance. He is, however, entitled to the basic married couple's allowance of £3,220 regardless of his income (see**explanatory note 3**.

(ii) Maintenance received is not taxable. Maintenance relief is only available for payers who satisfy the relevant conditions (see **explanatory notes 5** and **6**) and one of the parties to the marriage was born before 6 April 1935. The relief is 10% of maintenance paid to a maximum of 10% of £3,220.

## (d) Tax position of Mr and Mrs Partid for 2016/17

### Mr Partid

| | Income |
|---|---|
| | £ |
| State pension | 3,500 |
| Building society interest | 1,000 |
| Dividends | 2,000 |
| | 6,500 |
| Personal allowance | (11,000) |
| Tax due | — |

Personal representatives will notify HMRC that married couple's allowance of £8,355 is to be transferred to the widow.

## Mrs Partid

| | £ | | | £ |
|---|---|---|---|---|
| Total income | | | | 15,120 |
| Personal allowance | | | | 11,000 |
| Taxable income | | | | 4,120 |
| Tax thereon: Non-savings income | | | | |
| 2,120 @ 20% | 424 | | | |
| Savings income | | | | |
| 2,000 @ 0% | 0 | | | 424 |
| *Less:* Married couple's age allowance (transferred from husband) | 8,355 | @ | 10% | 836 |
| Tax due | | | | NIL |
| Tax deducted at source | | | | 424 |
| Tax repayable | | | | 424 |

Mrs Partid may also be entitled to tax credits or universal credits after the death of her husband. She should notify the Tax credits Office within 1 month of her husband's death to secure her claim.

## (e) Deferral of state pension

### (i) Tax liability on state pension – commencing 2016/17

Julia has income of (£62,000 + £3,000) £65,000 before drawing her state pension and is therefore a 40% taxpayer. Her tax liability on state pension is

| | |
|---|---|
| State pension – | |
| 13 weeks @ £155 = £2,015 @ 40% = | £806 |
| *2017/18* | |
| Julia will have other income of at least (£46,500 (9/12 of £62,000) + £3,000) in 2017/18 and is still a higher rate taxpayer | |
| Liability on state pension | |
| 52 weeks @ £155 = £8,060 @ 40% = | £3,224 |
| *2018/19* | |
| Assuming Julia ceased paid employment in January 2018 her liability in 2018/19 is | |
| | £ |
| State pension | 8,060 |
| Savings income | 3,000 |
| | 11,060 |
| Personal allowance | (11,000) |
| Taxable | 60 |
| Tax on savings income at 0% | NIL |

### (ii) Deferral for one year

If Julia defers her state pension then her liability on pension becomes

| | |
|---|---|
| *2017/18* | |
| State pension (income as in (i) **above**) | £ |
| 13 weeks @ £164 = £2,132 @ 40% = | 853 |

*2017/18 and 2018/19*

| | £ |
|---|---|
| State pension | 8,528 |
| Savings income | 3,000 |
| | 11,528 |
| Personal allowance | (11,000) |
| Taxable | 528 |
| Tax on savings income at 0% | NIL |

## (iii) Death

If Julia dies after deferring her state pension, but before opting to take the lump sum or increased pension, no amount would be payable to her estate as she is single. (See **note (c)** below.)

## Notes

(a) The Pensions Act 2004 amended Schedule 5 to the Social Security Contributions and Benefits Act 1992 (SSCBA 1992) with effect from 5 April 2005 to increase the subsequent pension payable following deferment and also to enable the deferred pension to be taken as a lump sum with no increase in state pension. State pension includes Basic Pension, SERPS, S2P and Graduated Pensions (SSCBA 1991 Sch 5 para A1). However, for those taking their state pension from 6 April 2016 there is no option of a cash lump sum, and the pension payable is the new single tier state pension, payable at a rate of £155 per week.

The state pension rules change for those reaching retirement age from April 2016 onwards. This is:

Men born on or after 6 April 1951 and

Women born on or after 6 April 1953.

For those born before the above dates, deferral must be for a minimum period of five weeks and gives an uprating of pension of 1% for each five weeks of deferral (10.4% pa uplift) (SSCBA 1992 Sch 5 para 2A).

Those born after the above dates qualify for the new state pension where deferral must be for a minimum period of nine weeks and gives an uprating of pension of 1% for each nine weeks of deferral (5.8% pa uplift) and there is no option of a lump sum. www.gov.uk/new-state-pension/eligibility.

It will often be more advantageous also to defer taking the state pension until the first day of the new tax year so that it benefits from the reduced other income – as in Julia's case; the pension is further enhanced by the additional deferral.

(b) The lump sum available under the old scheme is not treated as income but is taxed at a flat rate based upon taxable income (excluding the lump sum) for the year (F(No2)A 2005 s 7).

If total income (excluding lump sum) for 2015/16 is:

| | | |
|---|---|---|
| Nil | the rate is | 0% |
| £1 to £31,785 | the rate is | 20% |
| £31,786 to £150,000 | the rate is | 40% |
| £150,001 upward | the rate is | 45% |

(c) If a state pension is deferred and the taxpayer dies before opting to take a lump sum or enhanced pension then the benefits are lost unless there is a surviving spouse or civil partner. If the deceased taxpayer had a spouse or civil partner then, provided the period of deferment is at least twelve months, the surviving spouse (partner) may elect to receive a lump sum based upon basic state pension plus one-half of the additional pension deferred (SSCBA 1992 Sch 5 para 3C). Alternatively, the surviving spouse (partner) may take an enhanced pension of an amount equal to the increase the deceased would have been entitled to had deferment ceased on the date of death. This applies after five weeks of deferment.

(d) Deferral will reduce a claimant's income for the purpose of drawing benefits or council tax benefit. However, when the increased pension is drawn entitlement to such benefits may be reduced. To mitigate the effects of taking a lump sum the amount received (net of tax) is disregarded in calculating such benefits.

# Explanatory Notes

*Personal allowances*

(1) UK resident taxpayers are entitled to a basic personal allowance unless this has been forgone in favour of a claim to the remittance basis by non-domiciled taxpayers (see **Example F4**). The basic personal allowance is abated when the adjusted net income of the taxpayer exceeds £100,000. In arriving at the income for this purpose, the total income is reduced by loss relief claims and the gross amount of both pension contributions paid and gift aid payment made and treated as made during the year. The personal allowance is then reduced by £1 for each £2 that the adjusted net income exceeds the income limit of £100,000, until it is withdrawn completely at adjusted net income of £122,000.

The personal allowance and blind person's relief, where relevant, reduce statutory income and save tax at the payer's highest tax rate. Married couple's allowance and maintenance relief for the over 65s save tax at 10% for 2016/17. The tax saving is given by reducing the tax payable by the appropriate amount. See Example B1for the way this is done through the PAYE system.

*Transferable tax allowance for married couples and civil partners (known as Marriage Allowance)*

(2) FA 2014 introduced ITA 2007 s 55A – 55E with effect from 6 April 2015. From this date, a spouse or civil partner who is not liable to income tax above the basic rate can transfer one tenth of their personal allowance to their spouse /civil partner, provided the recipient is also not liable to income tax above the basic rate. Where an individual or their spouse is entitled to the married couple's allowance (born before 6 April 1935 – see Ann Old above) they are not entitled to marriage allowance.

The marriage allowance can normally be claimed if all the following apply:

(a) The individuals are married or in a civil partnership,

(b) The transferor's annual income is below the basic rate threshold after the transfer of the allowance (2016/17 £43,000)

(c) The recipient's annual income is below the basic rate threshold (2016/17 = £43,000)

(d) Both parties were born on or after 6 April 1935.

Note that the transfer is only likely to benefit a couple where the transferor has income (other than interest income of up to £6,000 which would be covered by the savings starting rate band and the personal savings allowance) of an amount below the personal allowance, or dividend income taxed at 7.5%.

If an individual is entitled to a personal allowance but is not a UK resident for the tax year, they must have hypothetical income before they can surrender to their spouse / civil partner.

The marriage allowance is given to the recipient as a tax reduction at the basic rate of income tax. An individual cannot have more than one tax reduction or election for a tax year.

An election will normally automatically continue for subsequent tax years unless it is withdrawn or the conditions are breached. If the election is made after the end of the tax year to which it relates, the election only applies to that year, but the couple must still be married or civil partners at the date of the claim. Otherwise, the transferor can only withdraw their election with effect from the tax year following the tax year in which they make the withdrawal. However, the transferor has the option to withdraw their election with effect from the tax year that their marriage or civil partnership comes to a legal end. An election also becomes ineffective and does not continue for subsequent years where the recipient does not obtain a tax reduction.

To make a claim see www.gov.uk/marriage-allowance

*Age-related allowances*

(3) The married couple's allowance is no longer available unless at least one spouse or civil partner was born before 6 April 1935. Where available, the allowance is given as a reduction of tax payable, rather than as a deduction from taxable income, and saves tax at 10%. For 2016/17 the allowance is £8,355. The allowance is reduced if the claimant's total income is over £27,700, the reduction being equal to half of the excess over £27,700, but not so as to reduce the allowance below a basic allowance of £3,220 (ITA 2007 ss 36 and 37). See **explanatory note 1** for the definition of total income.

For marriages before 5 December 2005, the allowance was always given in the first instance to the husband. A married woman is, however, entitled as of right to half the basic allowance, ie £1,610, if she makes a claim (on Form 18) to that effect. Alternatively the couple may jointly claim for the *whole* of the basic allowance of £3,220 to be given to the wife. In either case, the claim must be made *before* the beginning of the relevant tax year, ie before 6 April 2016 for 2016/17 (except in the year of marriage, when the claim may be made within that tax year). The allowance will then be allocated in the chosen way until the claim is withdrawn, or where a joint claim has been made for the whole of the basic allowance to go to the wife, until the husband makes a fresh claim for half of that amount. The withdrawal or husband's claim must also be made before the beginning of the tax year for which the revised allocation is to take effect (ITA 2007 s 47).

The husband is entitled to any extra allowance over the basic £3,220, and it is his income level that determines how much of the extra allowance is available.

Civil partners are also allowed married couples allowance provided that at least one partner was born before 6 April 1935. For such couples, the allowance is initially allocated to the partner with the higher total income in the year. This allocation also applies to married couples whose marriage is on or after 5 December 2005 (ITA 2007 s 46).

A husband and wife who got married before 5 December 2005 can elect for the new rules to apply. The election must be made jointly, before the start of the first year to which it is to apply and it cannot be withdrawn.

If the tax payable by either spouse/civil partner is too low to use the tax saving to which he/she is entitled on the married couple's allowance, that spouse/civil partner may notify HMRC (on the tax return or on Form 575) that the excess is to be transferred to the other spouse/civil partner (s 47). The time limit for making the claim is four years from the end of the tax year.

Where there are other deductions from tax payable, the married couple's allowance is treated as the last deduction (except for double taxation relief on foreign income) (ITA 2007 s 27), thus maximising the amount that is available to be transferred to the other spouse/civil partner.

Allowing a wife to claim half of the basic married couple's allowance by right gives greater equity, although more than four fifths of the allowance still goes to the husband unless he agrees for the wife to claim a further £1,610.

In addition, although where a husband claims the allowance, any unused tax relief may be transferred to the wife, relief for the basic allowance would be given earlier by making the advance claim to transfer it if it was known that the husband would not be paying enough tax to use it.

It should be noted that a claim to transfer half or all of married couple's allowance to the spouse/civil partner prior to the start of the tax year may save tax if the transferor is likely to have unused non-repayable tax credits on dividends. The increase in the transferor's taxable income because of the transfer of allowances may enable the dividend credits to be used, with the transferee using the transferred allowance against his/her own liability.

*Married couple's allowance – year of marriage/entering into a civil partnership*

(4) The married couple's allowance is available to those born before 6 April 1935 irrespective of the date of marriage or civil partnership.

In the year of marriage or registration, the allowance is reduced by 1/12th for each complete tax month (ending on the 5th) before the wedding/registration date (ITA 2007 s 54).

Where a party's income is sufficiently above the income limit for the married couple's allowance to be affected the income restriction is applied first, and the resulting allowance is then reduced according to the date of marriage/registration, as shown in **part (b)** of the Example.

*Year of separation – married couple's allowance and maintenance payments*

(5) For a couple one or both of whom was born before 6 April 1935, the married couple's allowance is given in full in the tax year of separation, but it is not available in later tax years except where someone born before 6 April 1935 remarries or enters into a civil partnership (or a younger person marries or enters into a civil partnership with a person who *was* born before 6 April 1935).

(6) All maintenance payments are exempt from tax in the hands of the recipient and they are received in full without tax being deducted (ITTOIA 2005 s 727). Where either of a separated or divorced couple was born before 6 April 1935 the payer may claim a deduction from his/her tax liability at 10% on up to £3,220 of maintenance paid to the spouse/civil partner (either for the recipient's own maintenance or for the benefit of a child under 21) (ITA 2007 s 453). Relief is not available if payments are expressed to be payable direct to a child, even though actually paid to the wife (*Billingham v John* 1997). The maintenance relief is not increased where there is more than one ex-spouse/civil partner receiving maintenance.

The full maintenance relief is given in the year of separation, as well as the married couple's allowance. Payments due after the recipient remarries do not qualify for relief. If the payer remarries or enters into a civil partnership he/she will still be entitled to maintenance relief as well as any married couple's allowance.

The above provisions also apply to maintenance paid under court orders and written agreements the proper law of which is that of a part of a European Community member state, or a member state of the European Free Trade area forming part of the European Economic Area. For a list of the relevant countries see HMRC Manual, Relief Instructions Re 1190 (ITA 2007 s 453).

No relief is available for payments which are voluntary and not made under a legal obligation.

*Age-related allowances in year of death*

(7) Married couple's allowance, where available, is given to the husband unless a claim has been made for all or half of the basic allowance to go to the wife. The full allowance is available in the year of death of either husband or wife.

The surviving spouse may have transferred to him/her any part of the allowance claimed by the other spouse that the other's income is too low to use, providing the personal representatives notify HMRC accordingly (ITA 2007 s 51).

All the allowances available to a wife in the year of her husband's death are available against *any* of her income for the full tax year.

(See **explanatory note 4** above for civil partners and marriages after 4 December 2005.)

*Dealing with the deceased's estate*

(8) When someone dies, the tax position of the deceased for the year of death must be dealt with by the personal representatives, who also have a tax liability in respect of transactions carried out by them in completing the administration of the estate. Under self-assessment, the normal time limit for enquiring into a tax return is twelve months from the date the return is filed (see **Example G2 explanatory note 14**). To minimise delays in winding up estates and trusts, and in distributing estate or trust property, HMRC will, on request, issue

tax returns before the end of the tax year of death, or of winding up an estate or trust, and will give early confirmation if they do not intend to enquire into the return. For more on the taxation of the deceased's estate, see **Tolleys Taxwise II 2016/17**.

The personal representatives will not usually be able to settle the deceased's tax liabilities until probate is obtained. The deceased's tax district should be asked to arrange for the HMRC Accounts Office not to issue any further Statements of Account in the meantime. Under FA 2009 sch 53 section 12, interest on tax falling due after death will not start to run until thirty days after the grant of probate.

HMRC has a specialist bereavement unit, which deals with all aspects of the deceased's estate available on 0300 200 3300. Also see www.gov.uk/after-a-death.

(9) For further provisions on taxation of spouses and civil partners see **Example A2**.

*Retirement age*

(10) The retirement age for women born after 5 April 1950 will rise through the period April 2010 to November 2018 from 60 to 65. From December 2018 the state pension age for both men and women will increase from 65 to reach 66 by October 2020. From 2026 to 2028 state pension age for both men and women is proposed to increase to 67 and from 2044 to 2046 to 68. There are also plans to review (and probably increase) the state pension age based on life expectancy every five years with the next review being expected in 2017. There is a state pension age calculator available from the Direct Gov site at http://pensions.direct.gov.uk/en/state-pension-age-calculator/home.asp and a state pension age timetable www.gov.uk/government/uploads/system/uploads/attachment_data/file/310231/spa-timetable.pdf.

*National insurance contributions*

(11) Julia Jones will not be required to pay Class 1 primary (employee) national insurance contributions on any earnings after she reaches pensionable age. However, her employer will continue to be liable to pay secondary (employer) contributions on her earnings.

# Question

(a) Doreen, a widow since 1997, was born on 18 August 1939. Her income in the year ended 5 April 2017 consisted of:

| | £ |
|---|---|
| Retirement pension | 7,870 |
| Building society interest | 2,934 |
| 3½% War Loan interest (£2,000 of the stock was sold March 2017) | 105 |
| National Savings Bank interest | 85 |
| Purchased life annuity (gross amount, including agreed capital element £632) | 790 |
| Dividends received from UK companies | 700 |

Doreen's grandchildren, James aged 17 (still at school) and Bertha aged 15, have lived with her and been maintained by her since their parents were killed in an aeroplane crash in 2005. They have an interest in a discretionary trust set up by the wills of their parents and during 2016/17 the trustees paid the sum of £990 to help with an educational trip abroad for Bertha. Bertha does not have any other sources of income.

Calculate the amount of Doreen's and Bertha's income tax repayments for 2016/17.

(b) In 2016/17 John, a single man aged 60, has pension income of £7,780 (no tax deducted under PAYE). He also has building society interest of £8,720. He made a gift aid payment to the local church amounting to £400.

Calculate John's income tax position for 2016/17.

(c) Nigel, a widower aged 50, makes a single gift aid donation to a registered community amateur sports club of £800 in 2016/17. Show the tax saving arising from the payment if Nigel's income is:

| | *(i)* | *(ii)* | *(iii)* |
|---|---|---|---|
| | £ | £ | £ |
| Salary | 43,975 | 23,975 | 23,975 |
| Building society interest | 3,000 | 21,000 | 11,000 |
| Dividends | 1,000 | 3,000 | 13,000 |
| | 47,975 | 47,975 | 47,975 |

(d) Alan, a single man aged 35 has income from self-employment as a solicitor of £110,000 in 2016/17. He made a one off pension contribution of £5,000 (gross) in the year, and normally makes a donation to charity at some point, although he has not got around to it this year. Prepare a computation of his tax liability for 2016/17, and advise him regarding both his pension contribution and donations to charity, assuming that the 2016/17 tax year has just ended.

# Answer

## (a) Doreen – Income tax repayment 2016/17

| | | | | Income | Income tax paid |
|---|---|---|---|---|---|
| | £ | | | £ | £ |
| *Non-savings income* | | | | | |
| Retirement pension | | | | 7,870 | |
| *Savings income* | | | | | |
| Building society interest | 2,934 | | | | |
| 3½% War Loan interest (see **explanatory note 1**) | 105 | | | | |
| National Savings Bank interest | 85 | | | | |
| Income element of annuity (see **explanatory note 3**) | 158 | | | 3,282 | 32 |
| *Dividend income* | | | | 700 | |
| Net total income | | | | 11,852 | 32 |
| Personal allowance | | | | 11,000 | |
| Taxable income | | | | 852 | |
| Income tax thereon (see **explanatory note 5**): | | | | | |
| On non-dividend savings income | 152 | @ | 0% | 0 | |
| On dividends | 700 | @ | 0% | 0 | |
| | | | | 0 | |
| Tax payable | | | | | 0 |
| Repayment due | | | | | 32 |

## Bertha – Income tax repayment 2016/17

| | Income | Income tax paid |
|---|---|---|
| | £ | £ |
| *Non-savings income* | | |
| Income from discretionary trust (see **explanatory note 4**) | | |
| (990 + (45/55) 810) | 1,800 | 810 |
| Personal allowance | | |
| (£11,000, but restricted to income) | 1,800 | |
| | – | |
| Tax repayable | | 810 |

Doreen may also be entitled to tax credits or universal credits in respect of the children, given her income level. For more information about tax credits and entitlement to them see **Example A7**.

## (b) John – income tax position 2016/17

| | Income |
|---|---|
| | £ |
| *Non-savings income* | |
| Pension | 7,780 |

| | | | Income |
|---|---|---|---|
| | | | £ |
| *Savings income other than dividends* | | | |
| Building society interest (6,976 + 1,744) | | | 8,720 |
| | | | 16,500 |
| Personal allowance | | | 11,000 |
| Taxable income | | | 5,500 |
| Income tax thereon: | 5,000 | @ 0% | 0 |
| | 500 | @ 0% | 0 |
| | 5,500 | | |

## Note:

As tax chargeable of £100 equals the tax of £100 retained on the charitable gift (400 net + 100 tax @ 20% = £500 gross), the repayment is not restricted.

## (c) Nigel – tax relief on gift aid donation 2016/17

Nigel is a higher rate taxpayer, so his basic rate threshold is increased from £32,000 to £33,000 as a result of the gift aid payment of £800 net, £1,000 gross. Where a higher rate taxpayer has income from a number of sources, the effect of extending the basic rate band is to give relief at 20% plus the marginal rate otherwise chargeable on the slice of income that moves below the basic rate threshold as a result of the extension.

The position in Nigel's case is therefore as follows:

| | | | | | (i) | (ii) | (iii) |
|---|---|---|---|---|---|---|---|
| | | | | | £ | £ | £ |
| Salary | | | | | 43,975 | 23,975 | 23,975 |
| Building society interest | | | | | 3,000 | 21,000 | 11,000 |
| Dividends | | | | | 1,000 | 3,000 | 13,000 |
| | | | | | 47,975 | 47,975 | 47,975 |
| Personal allowance | | | | | 11,000 | 11,000 | 11,000 |
| Taxable income | | | | | 36,975 | 36,975 | 36,975 |
| *Tax due without gift* | | | | | | | |
| Non-savings income: | | | | | | | |
| 32,000 / | 12,975 / | 12,975 | @ | 20% | 6,400 | 2,595 | 2,595 |
| 975 / | – / | – | @ | 40% | 390 | – | – |
| Savings income: | | | | | | | |
| 500 / | 500 / | 500 | @ | 0% | – | – | – |
| – / | 18,525 / | 10,500 | @ | 20% | – | 3,705 | 2,100 |
| 2,500 / | 1,975 / | – | @ | 40% | 1,000 | 790 | – |
| Dividends: | | | | | | | |
| 1,000 / | 3,000 / | 5,000 | @ | 0% | – | – | – |
| – / | – / | 3,025 | @ | 7½% | – | – | 227 |
| | | 4,590 | @ | 32½% | | | 1,617 |
| 36,975 | 36,975 | 36,975 | | | 7,790 | 7,090 | 6,539 |
| *Tax due with gift* | | | | | | | |
| Non-savings income: | | | | | | | |
| 32,975 / | 12,975 / | 12,975 | @ | 20% | 6,595 | 2,595 | 2,595 |

| | | | | | (i) £ | (ii) £ | (iii) £ |
|---|---|---|---|---|---|---|---|
| Savings income: | | | | | | | |
| 500 / | 500 / | 500 | @ | 0% | – | – | – |
| – / | 19,525 / | 10,500 | @ | 20% | – | 3,905 | 2,100 |
| 2,500 / | 975 / | – | @ | 40% | 1,000 | 390 | – |
| Dividends: | | | | | | | |
| 1,000 / | 3,000 / | 5,000 | @ | 0% | – | – | – |
| – / | – / | 4,025 | @ | 7½% | – | – | 302 |
| – / | – / | 3,975 | @ | 32½% | – | – | 1,292 |
| 36,975 | 36,975 | 36,975 | | | 7,595 | 6,890 | 6,289 |
| Saving of higher rate/upper rate tax | | | | | 195 | 200 | 250 |
| Basic rate tax retained out of gift aid payment | | | | | 200 | 200 | 200 |
| Tax saving | | | | | 395 | 400 | 450 |

This represents a tax saving of (i) 39.5%, (ii) 40% and (iii) 45.0%.

This is because the income that has moved below the basic rate threshold is:

(i) Salary of £975, giving tax saving of 19.5% + 20% = 39.5% (The savings nil rate band replaces the additional savings income which would otherwise have been taxed at basic rate)

(ii) Building society interest of £1,000, giving tax saving of 20% + 20% = 40%

(iii) Dividends, giving tax saving of 20% + 25%(32.5% - 7.5%) = 45.0%

## (d) Alan – Income tax liability 2016/17

| | | | £ | £ |
|---|---|---|---|---|
| Profits | | | | 110,000 |
| Personal allowance | | | 11,000 | |
| Reduced by ½ × ((110,000 – 5000) – 100,000) | | | (2,500) | 8,500 |
| Taxable income | | | | 101,500 |
| Tax thereon: | | | | |
| On non-savings income | 37,000 @ | 20% | | 7,400 |
| | 64,500 @ | 40% | | 25,800 |
| | 101,500 | | | 33,200 |
| Basic rate tax retained out of pension payment | | | | 1,000 |
| Tax liability | | | | 34,200 |

Alan's options, now that the tax year has ended, are limited to making a donation to charity which can be carried back to the previous year, reducing the net adjusted income taken into account for the purpose of abatement of the personal allowance, producing a substantial tax saving. The maximum saving is made with a donation of £4,000 net, but this may be more than Alan wishes to donate. For illustrative purposes, a donation of £800 (£1,000 gross) is considered.

| | £ | £ |
|---|---|---|
| Profits | | 110,000 |
| Personal allowance | 11,000 | |
| Reduced by ½ × ((110,000 – 6000) – 100,000) | (2,000) | 9,000 |
| Taxable income | | 101,000 |

| | | | | |
|---|---|---|---|---|
| Tax thereon: | | | | |
| On non-savings income | 38,000 | @ | 20% | 7,557 |
| | 63,000 | @ | 40% | 25,200 |
| | 101,000 | | | 32,800 |
| Saving of higher rate tax | | | | 400 |
| Basic rate tax retained out of gift aid payment | | | | 200 |
| Additional tax saving | | | | 600 |

The tax saved by the additional donation of £800 is 60% of the gross gift, accounted for by the reduction in abatement of personal allowance at a rate of £1 for each £2 reduction in income, so there is an additional £500 of personal allowance, accounting for the further reduction in of £200.

Although payment of pension contributions can mitigate the effect of the reduction in allowances, these must be paid during the tax year concerned, so as Alan is planning retrospectively only a gift aid donation and related carry back claim can affect his availability of personal allowances in 2016/17.

## Explanatory Notes

*Interest on Government Stocks and National Savings Bank accounts*

(1) Interest on 3½% War Loan has always been paid gross (half yearly in June and December). By selling some of her stock in March 2017, Doreen effectively received three months' interest (ie from December 2016) as part of her capital proceeds. There are 'accrued income scheme' provisions to treat such amounts that accrue on any marketable securities other than shares as income. The provisions do not, however, apply where the nominal value of all securities held does not exceed £5,000. This exception applies in Doreen's case, since £105 represents interest on £3,000 stock (£2,000 of which has now been sold), so the provisions would not apply to her March 2017 sale. For details of the scheme see **Example A5**.

(2) Interest on National Savings Bank accounts has also always been received in full without tax being deducted. For details see **Example A5**.

*Purchased life annuities*

(3) When a life annuity is purchased for a lump sum, part of the annual payment is deemed to be a return of the capital and is not taxable. The rate of tax deducted at source on the income element is the lower rate of 20%. The capital element is determined by HMRC, with the usual rights of appeal (ITTOIA 2005 s 717 Part 6 Chapter 7). Doreen will receive a cash sum of £758, being £158 income less £32 tax = £126 plus £632 capital.

*Income from a discretionary trust*

(4) The payment towards Bertha's educational trip counts as her income and since it is paid from a discretionary trust its value is after tax of 45% not 20% (ITA 2007 s 493 – see **Example A2 part (b)(i) note 4**). An income tax repayment claim can be made on behalf of Bertha to recover the £810 tax deducted since her income is covered by her personal allowance. See **explanatory note 12** below as to why vulnerable trust treatment does not apply.

*Order of deductions*

(5) A taxpayer may offset allowances and reliefs against income of different descriptions in the most advantageous order unless the legislation provides otherwise (ITA 2007 s 23). As far as tax rates are concerned, the legislation provides that savings income is to be treated as the slice of income above the non savings income, and that dividend income is to be treated as the slice above savings income. (ITA 2007 s 12). As the savings starting and nil rates applies only to savings income, the most advantageous way of offsetting the personal allowance will normally be first against non-savings income, then savings income, then dividend income which is taxed at 7.5% in the basic rate band. Married couple's allowance, where

available, is given as a reduction of tax payable rather than being offset against income. Any surplus married couple's allowance may be transferred to a spouse/civil partner. The legislation provides for the allowance to be treated as the last deduction, except for double taxation relief on foreign income, thus maximising the unused amount available to be transferred (ITA 2007 s 47 – see **Example A3 explanatory note 2**).

*Restriction of basic personal allowance for high income individuals*

(6) When an individual's net income (after deducting gross gifts to charities and personal pension contributions) exceeds £100,000 the personal allowance is restricted. It is reduced by £1 for each £2 of net income aver the £100,000 limit, with the allowance reducing to nil at net adjusted income of £122,000. The tax rate remains 40%.

*Repayment claims*

(7) Repayments arise where tax is deducted at source from some income and other income is too low to utilise available allowances. HMRC will also refund overpaid tax before the end of the relevant tax year in certain circumstances (see www.gov.uk/claim-tax-refund/overview). Form P50 is used to claim tax back when a taxpayer has stopped employed work, P50Z, P53Z & P55 relate to pensions and form R40 is the traditional annual repayment claim form, but since the changes to the taxation of interest in 2016, repayment claims are rare. HMRC also have online / telephone methods to claim refunds. Some repayment claims may be made outside the self-assessment system. HMRC do not require the claims to be supported by tax vouchers, although they may call for extra information if they cannot calculate the repayment from the information shown on the claim form.

Where someone is taxed under PAYE, an overpayment of £10 or less is not repaid unless a specific claim is made. It will usually be dealt with by a coding adjustment in the following year (SP 6/95). (For detailed notes on PAYE see **Example B1**.)

(8) Nigel is a higher rate taxpayer. A higher rate taxpayer with mainly PAYE income making regular fixed donations or pension contributions could ask HMRC to include the relief in their PAYE code. Or they could ask to be brought within self-assessment and file annual tax returns.

(9) Although special tax treatment is available for trusts with vulnerable beneficiaries these rules cannot apply to Bertha or James in **part (a)**.

In order to claim special treatment the beneficiary must be a disabled person or a relevant minor. A disabled person is a taxpayer who is incapable of administering his/her own property by reason of a mental disorder or a person in receipt of attendance allowance or disability living allowance (higher or middle rate). A relevant minor is a person under 18 where one or both of the parents have died. Bertha and James are therefore relevant minors. In addition the trust must also qualify. To do so the property must be held for the benefit of the vulnerable person absolutely. The beneficiary must be entitled to all of the income, and where the beneficiary is a minor they must be entitled to the property at 18. In the case of Bertha and James the trust is a relevant property trust and therefore does not qualify.

Where special treatment is claimed, available by election, the tax liability of the trust is computed in the normal way. The trustees then make a claim to reduce that liability to the amount due treating the trust income and capital gains as being the income or gains of the vulnerable beneficiary computed by adding those amounts to the actual income and gains of the beneficiary. The increase in the liability of the individual is the trusts tax liability. See **Tolley's Taxwise II 2016/17** for a computation of such a claim.

# Question

(a) Outline the sources of income chargeable to tax as savings and other income, indicate how income tax is charged on savings income.

(b) Briefly set out the basic principles of the Accrued Income Scheme giving details of:

(i) securities affected by the scheme;

(ii) persons affected by the scheme;

(iii) how the accrued income scheme works.

(c) Interest on 8½% Treasury Stock is paid half yearly on 25 January and 25 July, the stock going ex-dividend on 18 January and 18 July.

Mr Pinter bought £100,000 nominal stock ex-dividend for settlement on 21 January 2017. He sold the stock cum-dividend for settlement 11 June 2017.

Show the accrued income adjustments arising from these transactions.

(d) In December 2011 Joe Friend, who is a widower, retired from his employment. He received a tax free lump sum of £100,000 and a pension of £14,900 per annum. PAYE deducted at source for 2016/17 amounts to £2,260. He immediately invested £20,000 in a single premium insurance company bond with a life of five years and another £20,000 in a similar bond but with a life of ten years. For both bonds the compound growth had been 15% pa for the first two years and nil since. Joe has taken annual withdrawals of 5% of the initial investment in each bond. In 2016/17 Joe's other income was the state retirement pension of £7,400 and building society interest of £2,000.

Calculate Joe's tax liability on the gain arising in 2016/17.

(e) Show what the position in (d) above would have been if Joe Friend's taxable income after allowances had been £31,600 including dividend income of £2,000.

(f) Show the effect on the position in (e) if, after receiving the proceeds from the five year bond, Joe had made a gift aid donation to charity of £1,600 in February 2017.

(g) State the impact on the calculation of the gain if Jo had been non UK resident for part of the policy term.

# Answer

## (a) Income assessable

Under ITTOIA 2005 Part 4 interest and investment income is chargeable to income tax as either savings income or dividend income on the income paid in the fiscal year. Savings income (defined by ITA 2007, s 18) includes:

| | |
|---|---|
| Chapter 2 | Interest |
| Chapter 7 | Purchased life annuities |
| Chapter 8 | Profits from deeply discounted securities |
| Chapter 9 | Gains from contracts for life assurance (to the extent chargeable on an individual or personal representatives) |

In addition, the savings rates also apply to accrued income chargeable under ITA Part 12, Chapter 2.

Dividend income includes (per ITA 2007, s 19):

| | |
|---|---|
| Chapter 3 | Dividends – UK companies |
| Chapter 4 | Dividends – non-UK companies |
| Chapter 5 | Stock dividends |
| Chapter 6 | Release of a loan to a participator in a close company |

In addition tax is charged as non-savings income by Part 5 of ITTOIA 2005 on:

| | |
|---|---|
| Chapter 2 | Receipts from intellectual property |
| Chapter 3 | Films and sound recordings |
| Chapter 4 | Telecommunication rights |
| Chapter 5 | Settlements |
| Chapter 6 | Income from estates |
| Chapter 7 | Annual payments |
| Chapter 8 | Income not otherwise charged to tax |

Employment income, employment related annuities (retirement annuities) and pensions are chargeable under the Income Tax (Earnings and Pensions) Act 2003 (ITEPA 2003) as non-savings income (see **Examples B1–B7**).

Trading income is charged as non-savings income under ITTOIA 2005 Part 2, and property income under ITTOIA 2005 Part 3.

The other parts of ITTOIA 2005 deal with:

| | |
|---|---|
| Part 6 | Exempt income |
| Part 7 | Rent-a-room and foster carers |
| Part 8 | Special rules for foreign income |
| Part 9 | Partnerships |

Tax is chargeable on the sum of income from all sources liable to UK tax subject to allowable deductions and reliefs.

### Self-assessment

See **Examples G1** and **G2** for self-assessment.

## Tax rates

For 2016/17 the rate of tax on income up to the basic rate limit (£32,000) is 20% on non-savings income, 20% on savings income other than dividends and 7½% on dividends, the rates applicable to income above that limit being 40% and 32½% on dividend income until income exceeds the additional rate threshold (£150,000) when the rates become 45% and 38.1% for dividends. However, where taxable non-savings income is less than £5,000, a starting rate of 0% applies to savings income within that band (treating it, as usual, as the next slice of income). These rates apply to both UK and foreign savings income, except for any foreign income that is taxed on a remittances basis, to which the non-savings tax rates apply.

However, from 6 April 2016 there are also two nil rate bands in addition to the rates shown above. There is a £5,000 dividend nil rate band, which commences at the first £1 of taxable dividend. The nil rate band effectively reduces the basic rate band availability if it falls within the basic rate band. So a taxpayer with a salary of £8,000 and £36,000 of dividends would pay no tax on the salary and £3,000 of the dividend, as they fall within the personal allowance. The next £5,000 comprises the dividend nil rate band, leaving £27,000 taxable at 7½%. The balance of the dividend (£1,000) is taxed at 32½%.

There is also a savings nil rate band, which starts at the first £1 of taxable savings income above the savings starting rate band. This band varies according to the level of income of the taxpayer. If the total income is within the basic rate band, the personal savings allowance (the amount of the nil rate band for savings) is £1,000. Where the total income exceeds the relevant basic rate band this drops to £500, and it is zero for taxpayers with income of more than £150,000.

## Deduction of tax at source

Until 6 April 2016, tax was deducted at source from most sources of savings and other income, the rate of tax deducted from interest, royalties and annual payments being the basic rate of 20%. However, from 6 April 2016 the requirement for some deposit takers (banks and building societies) to deduct basic rate at source has been abolished, as has the requirement to deduct tax from interest on government securities. This more closely aligns with the tax treatment of interest through the personal savings allowance, which gives rise to a band of savings income taxed at 0%.

Prior to 6 April 2016, tax was not deducted at source from:

- most National Savings interest (see **explanatory note 4**),
- interest on all gilt edged securities (other than bearer gilts) acquired on or after 6 April 1998 is paid gross, unless the holder applies to receive it net (ITA 2007 s 892), Those already holding stocks on 6 April 1998 are treated as having applied for net payment, but may apply at any time for gross payment,
- interest on 3½% War Loan,
- interest on bearer gilts (ITA 2007 s 893 and s 1024),
- from interest, patent royalties and annuities paid by a company to another company that the paying company reasonably believes to be liable to corporation tax on the amount received or is an EU company,
- copyright royalties unless they are paid to non-residents (see **explanatory note 7**),
- payments by and to local authorities.

Finance Act 2013 extended the scope of tax deduction to all interest. The range of people to whom companies and local authorities may pay such amounts gross includes bodies exempt from tax, such as charities, pension funds, and those managing ISAs, TESSAs and PEPs (ITA 2007 s 930 onwards). See **explanatory note 9** re special provisions for royalty payments by companies to certain recipients entitled to double tax relief. Retirement annuities and other employment-related annuities have been brought within the PAYE scheme from 6 April 2007. (FA 2004 Sch 36 para 43 and FA 2005 Sch 10 paras 60, 61(a), 64(2).) Prior to this, such annuities were paid net of basic rate tax (or gross where the annuitant was a non-taxpayer and completed a form R89).

Company debenture interest is paid net of tax except when paid to another company etc as indicated above or where the debenture stock is a listed security (see later in this note).

There is a general requirement in ITA 2007 s 874 to deduct tax at source from interest paid to a non-resident, subject to any express provisions to the contrary. There are such express provisions for certain bank and building society interest (see **(iv) above**), and exemption from tax is sometimes provided under a double tax agreement. See **Example F3** for further details.

Interest on all quoted eurobonds is paid gross to both individuals and companies (ITA 2007 s 882). A quoted eurobond is any interest-bearing security issued by a company that is listed on a recognised stock exchange. 'Company' for this purpose includes a building society, so that building society permanent interest-bearing shares (see **Example K2 explanatory note 1**) are within the definition of eurobond.

Where a taxpayer is not ordinarily resident in the UK (see below) tax is not deducted on UK government stocks. Nor is tax deducted where the recipient is exempt from tax, such as interest paid to UK charities (exempt under ITA 2007 s 532). ITA 2007 s 597 gives HMRC power to make specific regulations relating to the deduction of tax on government stocks that are not within the gross payment provisions.

Under FA 2005 s 51 returns from alternative finance arrangements are to be treated as interest for the purposes of ITTOIA 2005. This will include returns from arrangements that do not involve the receipt or payment of interest in adherence with Shari'a law. Such agreements and returns are economically equivalent to conventional banking product interest. However, they were not previously taxed as interest. Under this legislation the profit is taxed as savings income.

### Interest on late paid debts

Under the Late Payment of Commercial Debts (Interest) Act 1998 statutory interest is payable where payment is delayed on certain contracts for the supply of goods or services. Such interest is not annual interest and is brought into tax as a trading receipt under ITTOIA 2005. The interest is paid gross and will normally be an allowable deduction for trading concerns. Similar tax treatment applies to interest payable under the terms of a trading contract. In the case of a company interest is included in the loan relationships regime. If interest for late payment is received by an individual other than in the course of business then it will be taxable at the savings rate (either 0% or 20%, depending on the amount of non-savings income).

### Remittance basis

Where a taxpayer is not domiciled in the UK, then they may claim under ITA 2007 s 809B to be liable to tax on a remittance basis in respect of income and gains arising abroad. If the remittance basis is successfully claimed then tax will be due on the full amount received in the UK within the tax year without deductions.

However, the availability of the remittance basis was significantly curtailed from 2008/09 with further changes each year thereafter. For more details of the remittance basis see **Example F4**.

### (b)

The accrued income scheme was originally introduced as an anti-avoidance measure to prevent the process known as 'bond-washing'. 'Bond-washing' was a practice whereby holders of securities (such as government stocks or corporate bonds) would dispose of their stocks immediately prior to the date on which interest became payable. The price obtained for the security included the 'accrued interest' on the stock, but the profit on the security was taxed under the capital gains rules rather than being treated as income (as it would have been had the interest actually been received).

This practice was particularly prevalent at a time when CGT rates were lower than those applying to income tax. It also allowed taxpayers to use capital gains tax exemptions and reliefs against profits which would otherwise have been treated as income.

The accrued income scheme provisions are in Income Tax Act 2007 (ITA 2007) Part 12. They set out how to compute accrued interest on a sale or purchase of stocks and bonds.

### (i) Securities affected by the scheme (ITA 2007 s 619)

The accrued income scheme applies to interest-bearing marketable stocks and bonds including:

- British Government securities ('gilts');
- building society permanent interest bearing shares (PIBS);
- local authority bonds; and
- company debentures and loan stock.

The scheme does not apply to ordinary or preference shares in a company, units in a unit trust, bank deposits or National Savings Certificates.

### (ii) Persons affected by the scheme

The accrued income scheme does not apply to companies (ITA 2007 s 5). Any profits made by companies on the sale and acquisition of securities are dealt with under the 'loan relationships' rules (see **Example K2**).

The scheme applies to individuals, trusts and estates. However the vesting of securities in personal representatives on a person's death is not subject to the accrued income scheme provisions (ITA 2007 s 620(2)(a)), nor is a transfer to a legatee by the personal representatives in the interest period in which death occurs (ITA 2007 s 636).

Individuals are not caught by the accrued income scheme if the nominal value of their total holdings does not exceed £5,000 at any time in both:

- the tax year in which the next interest date falls; and
- the previous tax year.

(ITA 2007 s 639).

Individuals are not caught by the scheme if they are not resident in the UK (ITA 2007 s 643).

For individuals who are resident in the UK but are not UK domiciled, the scheme only applies to UK securities (ITA 2007 s 644).

The scheme does not apply to traders in securities, for whom these transactions represent trading profits (ITA 2007 s 642).

### (iii) How the accrued income scheme works

To make the required tax adjustments under the accrued income scheme it is necessary to determine whether a sale or purchase was 'cum-dividend' or 'ex-dividend'. The term 'cum' means 'with' and 'ex' means 'without', therefore a transaction with the right to the next dividend is 'cum-dividend' and a deal without the right to the next dividend is 'ex-dividend'.

It is common practice to use the terms 'ex-div' and 'cum-div' even though the return on the investment is in fact interest and perhaps the terms 'ex interest' and 'cum interest' would be more appropriate. The HMRC guidance on this area uses the terms 'ex-div' and 'cum-div'.

All stocks will have an ex-div date. Most stocks pay interest every six months (although some pay annually and some pay quarterly). If an investor holds stock at the ex-div date, the investor will be entitled to receive the next interest payment, even if the investor disposes of the stock before the actual date on which the interest is paid. There may be a few weeks between the ex-div date and the date on which the interest is physically paid.

Once the ex-div date has passed, the market price for the stock will go down. This is because a purchaser will not thereafter have a right to the net interest payment and will therefore offer a lower amount to purchase the stock.

The price of the stock will vary for many reasons, one of which is that the purchase price will or will not include the right to the next interest payment. A transaction cum-div will be priced to include the right to receive the next interest payment in full even though the stock will have been owned for less than the full interest period.

All securities have a 'nominal value'. This is the value on which interest payments are calculated. The nominal value is also the value at which the stocks will be redeemed. However, the 'nominal value' is unlikely to be the same as the market value of the stock. All accrued income will be calculated on nominal values. Market values are irrelevant for income tax.

The accrued income scheme calculates the 'accrued interest' every time stock is bought and sold and allocates this interest between buyer and seller. The accrued income is effectively the increase or reduction in the price of the stock depending on whether the stock has been purchased or sold 'cum-div' or 'ex-div'.

In practice, most taxpayers who buy and sell stock will receive a contract note and details of any accrued income will be shown on that contract note.

The way in which the accrued interest scheme works depends on whether:

(a) the taxpayer is the buyer or seller; and

(b) if the stock is being transferred 'cum-div' or 'ex-div'.

There are therefore four possible scenarios:

(1) A person selling stock cum-div.

Selling 'cum-div' means that the buyer will be entitled to the next interest payment. Therefore the price of the stock will be increased by accrued interest. This accrued interest, known as the 'accrued income profit', is taxable on the seller at the time of the next interest payment.

The accrued interest is calculated on a daily basis from the date of the previous interest payment through until the date of settlement based upon the gross interest payable.

It is taxed as 'miscellaneous income' and is entered on an individual's self-assessment tax return at boxes 1 and 3 on page Ai 1 of the Additional Information pages (SA101).

The income is taxed in the tax year in which the next interest date falls. For instance, if the next interest date following settlement is 30 April 2016, the accrued income charge is taxed in 2016/17.

(2) A person selling stock ex-div.

Selling 'ex-div' means that the seller will be entitled to the next interest payment, therefore the price of the stock will be decreased by accrued interest. That amount is known as the 'accrued income loss' and is a deduction from the next interest payment on that security before entering onto the self-assessment tax return.

(3) A person buying stock cum-div.

A purchaser of securities 'cum-div' will be entitled to the full amount of interest payable on the next interest date, therefore the price paid will be increased by the accrued interest. That amount is the 'accrued interest loss' because it represents the return of the investor's own funds when the interest is paid. It is deducted from the amount paid before inclusion in the self-assessment tax return.

(4) A person buying stock ex-div.

When buying 'ex-div' there is no entitlement to the next interest payment therefore the price paid is reduced by the 'accrued interest profit'. That amount is taxed at the date of the next interest payment by inclusion in the self-assessment tax return (boxes 1 and 3 on page Ai 1 of the Additional Information pages (SA101)).

## (c) Mr Pinter – purchase and sale of 8½% Treasury Stock

### Treatment of the purchase for settlement on 21 January 2017

This is a purchase ex-div, therefore the seller will receive the full half-year interest to 25 January 2017 of £4,250. The purchase price will have been reduced to take into account the interest due from 22 January 2017 (the day after the settlement date) and 25 January 2017. This amounts to:

Days from 22 January to 25 January 2017:

$$\frac{4}{365} \times £8,500 = £93.15$$

The seller is entitled to an accrued income loss of £93.15 to reduce his taxable income for 2016/17 (in which the next interest payment date, 25 January, falls) and Mr Pinter will have an accrued income profit on the same amount for that year.

### Treatment of the sale for settlement on 11 June 2017

This is a sale cum-div therefore the buyer will receive the full half-year interest to 25 July 2017. The purchase price will have been increased to take into account the interest due between 26 January and 11 June 2017. This amounts to:

Days from 26 January to 11 June 2017:

$$\frac{137}{365} \times £8,500 = £3,190.41$$

Mr Pinter will have an accrued income profit of £3,190.41 in 2017/18 (in which 25 July 2017 falls) and the buyer is entitled to an accrued income loss of the same amount for that year.

The accrued income loss reduces the taxpayer's savings income, and thus saves a basic rate taxpayer 20%. Accrued income profits are taxed at the savings rate if available (ITA 2007 s 18(3)(d)).

If Mr Pinter is a basic rate taxpayer he will obtain tax relief in 2016/17 at 20% on £93.15 and pay tax in 2017/18 at 20% on £3,190.41. If the other parties are basic rate taxpayers, they will get relief at 20% in each case. If anyone is a higher or additional rate taxpayer then the applicable rate will be 40% or 45% respectively.

## (d) Joe Friend – tax liability on gain on single premium bond in 2016/17

There is no liability on annual withdrawals from single premium bonds providing they do not exceed 5% of the initial investment.

The annual amounts withdrawn are taken into account in calculating the gain when the bond is finally cashed.

Joe Friend therefore has no liability in 2016/17 in relation to the ten year bond which he still holds. The position on the five year bond that matured in December 2016 is as follows:

| | | £ |
|---|---|---|
| 2012/13 | Initial investment in December 2011 | 20,000 |
| | 15% growth in value | 3,000 |
| | | 23,000 |
| | Less 5% of £20,000 withdrawn | (1,000) |
| | | 22,000 |
| 2013/14 | 15% growth | 3,300 |
| | 5% withdrawn | (1,000) |
| | | 24,300 |
| 2014/15 | 0% growth | – |
| | 5% withdrawn | (1,000) |
| | | 23,300 |
| 2015/16 | 0% growth | – |
| | 5% withdrawn | (1,000) |
| | | 22,300 |

| | | |
|---|---|---|
| 2016/17 | 0% growth | – |
| | Value on maturity | 22,300 |
| | Add annual withdrawals (4 × £1,000) | 4,000 |
| | | 26,300 |
| | Less original investment | (20,000) |
| | Profit on bond | 6,300 |

The bond profit is only liable to tax on the excess, if any, at higher rate/additional rate tax less basic rate tax. However, historically a tax charge could arise indirectly if the individual qualified for an age allowance and the addition of the bond income restricted the allowance available.

Joe's income tax position in 2016/17, taking into account the bond profit, is as follows:

| | | £ | Tax |
|---|---|---|---|
| State pension | | 7,400 | |
| Occupational pension | | 14,900 | 2,260 |
| Savings income – building society | | 2,000 | |
| Profit on bond | | 6,300 | |
| | | 30,600 | 2,260 |
| Personal allowance | | 11,000 | |
| Taxable income | | 19,600 | |
| Tax thereon: | | | |
| Non savings: | 11,300 @ 20% | 2,260 | |
| Savings: | 1,000 @ 0% | 0 | |
| | 7,300 @ 20% | 1,460 | |
| | | 3,720 | |
| Less basic rate tax deemed to have been paid on bond profit | | | |
| | £6,300 @ 20% | 1,260 | |
| Tax | | 2,460 | |
| Tax paid at source | | (2,260) | |
| Tax payable | | 200 | |

The tax charge has arisen on £2,000 of interest, with only £1,000 being covered by the personal savings allowance.

A tax charge can also arise for those with income in excess of £100,000, and the effective marginal rate produced is 60%.

Top slicing relief is available to reduce the rate of tax charged on the bond profit as indicated in **(e) below**. This is of no benefit where an allowance is being restricted, because the relief applies only where a different tax rate would apply to the 'appropriate fraction' of the bond profit.

## (e) Joe Friend – tax liability on gain on single premium bond in 2016/17 if taxable income after allowances was £31,600

To the extent that the bond profit falls within the basic rate band tax it is charged at 20%. The tax thereon is covered by the notional credit. The tax payable on the excess is (40 – 20) = 20%. The position is therefore as follows:

| | £ |
|---|---|
| Basic rate threshold | 32,000 |
| Income | 31,600 |

| | | |
|---|---|---|
| Basic rate band remaining | | 400 |
| Bond profit | | 6,300 |
| Bond profit in higher rate band | | 5,900 |
| Tax thereon | @ 20% | 1,180 |
| *Less:* | Top slicing relief (see below) | 320 |
| | | 860 |
| Annual equivalent of bond profit: | | £ |
| 1/5 × 6,300 | | 1,260 |
| Within basic rate band | | 400 |
| Taxed | @ 20% | 860 |

Tax on annual equivalent (860 × 20% =) £172, multiplied by 5 (policy years) = £860, therefore top slicing relief is (1,180 – 860 =) £320.

Tax on income of (31,600 + 6,300 =) £37,900:

| | | | £ |
|---|---|---|---|
| Non-savings income | 29,600 | @ 20% | 5,920 |
| Dividend income | 2,000 | @ 0% | — |
| | 31,600 | | 5,920 |
| Bond profit (part) | 400 | @ 20% | 80 |
| | 32,000 | | |
| Bond profit (balance) | 5,900 | @ 40% | 2,360 |
| | 37,900 | | 8,360 |
| *Less:* Top slicing relief | | | (320) |
| Basic rate tax deemed to have been paid on bond profit | 6,300 | @ 20% | (1,260) |
| Tax payable | | | 6,780 |

Similar principles apply where the taxpayer's top rate of tax in 2016/17 is 45%.

## (f) If Joe Friend made gift aid payment of £1,600 net, £2,000 gross, in February 2017

### With taxable income after allowances of £31,600 as in (e)

The basic rate band of £32,000 is increased by £2,000 to £34,000. The increase does not apply, however, when computing top slicing relief on life insurance bonds, so that the top slicing relief remains at £320 as calculated in (e). The position would therefore be:

| | | | | £ |
|---|---|---|---|---|
| Taxable income after allowances | | | | 31,600 |
| Bond profit | | | | 6,300 |
| Taxable Income | | | | 37,900 |
| Tax thereon: | | | | |
| Non-dividend income | 29,600 | @ 20% | 5,920 | |
| Dividend income | 2,000 | @ 0% | 0 | |
| | 31,600 | | | |
| Bond profit (part) | 2,400 | @ 20% | 480 | |
| | 34,000 | | | |
| Bond profit (balance) | 3,900 | @ 40% | 1,560 | 7,960 |
| *Less:* Top slicing relief as in (b) | 37,900 | | | (320) |
| Basic rate tax deemed to have been paid on bond profit | | | | (1,260) |

| | | £ |
|---|---|---|
| | | 6,380 |
| Amount previously payable as in (b) | | 6,780 |
| Additional tax saving | | 400 |
| Tax treated as deducted from gift aid payment | 2,000 @ 20% | 400 |
| Total saving (effective rate 40%) | | 800 |

### Paying a registered pension scheme premium in place of gift aid

The tax liability on the bond in (e) above could be eliminated by Joe Friend paying an allowable pension premium in 2016/76 of £860 gross, £688 net. For the net cost of £688 the tax of £860 on the bond profit would be eliminated and there would be £860 in a pension fund. Although the treatment of pension payments is the same as for gift aid payments, ie the basic rate band is increased by the gross payment, there is no provision denying that increase when computing top slicing relief.

## (g) If Joe Friend had been non-resident for some time during the policy term

### With taxable income before allowances of (31,600 + 10,000 =) £41,600 as in (b)

Until Finance Act 2013 the only policies which could recognise non residence of the beneficiary in the calculation of the gain on the policy were those issued outside the UK. The period of non residence during the term of the policy excludes a portion of the gain by a pro-rata calculation made in days. Non UK issued policies do not, however, have a deemed basic rate deduction, so tax is due in full on the net gain so calculated. (See **explanatory note 11**).

Finance Act 2013, Sch 8 extended this relief to policies issued in the UK. The change applies to policies taken out on or after 6 April 2013, although an existing policy may be triggered into the new rules by certain changes. The gain is computed by apportioning the gain between the UK resident and non UK resident periods of the policy term.

## (h)

### *(i) Individual Savings Accounts (ISAs)*

(1) ISAs are available to individuals aged 18 or over who are resident in the UK (plus Crown servants working overseas (eg diplomatic or overseas civil service) or their spouse or civil partner). Someone who becomes non-resident may retain the tax-exempt benefits of existing ISAs but no further investments may be made. Joint accounts are not permitted. ISAs are available indefinitely, with no set end date, although there is no statutory minimum period for which the accounts must be held. There is no lifetime limit on the amount invested.

(2) ISAs are available to individuals aged 18 or over who are resident and ordinarily resident in the UK. Someone who becomes non-resident may retain the tax-exempt benefits of existing ISAs but no further investments may be made. Joint accounts are not permitted. ISAs are available indefinitely, with no set end date, although there is no statutory minimum period for which the accounts must be held. There is no lifetime limit on the amount invested.

A person aged 16 or 17 can open a cash ISA, but care must be taken to ensure that the funds to open such an ISA did not originate from the child's parents. In that case the income from the ISA would be taxable on the parent under the settlements provisions if, with other such income, it exceeded £100. If the funds originate from the parents it may be preferable to open a junior ISA (see below). Alternative finance Isa's became available in 2016/17.

(3) The ISA regulations are in SI 1998/1870 as amended. The annual investment in an ISA may be split into two components:

(i) cash;

(ii) stocks and shares.

*Cash*

The following investments qualify for the cash component:

(a) Bank and building society deposit or share accounts (or European equivalent);

(b) Units in a money market fund;

(c) Units in a money market only fund of funds;

(d) Designated National Savings;

(e) Alternative finance arrangements equating to the above.

*Stocks and shares*

Before 30 June 2014, there were strict rules on the qualifying investments for the stocks and shares component of an ISA as follows:

(a) Shares issued in any country and quoted on a recognised stock exchange. From 5 August 2013 this is expanded to enable investment into qualifying SME equity markets by changing the wording of the legislation to 'either officially listed on a recognised stock exchange or in the EEA, admitted to trading on a recognised stock exchange';

(b) Securities with at least five years to run (when acquired by the ISA) issued in any country and quoted on a recognised stock exchange;

(c) Government Securities of UK or European Economic Area countries (or strips thereof) with at least five years to run when acquired by the ISA;

(d) Units in authorised unit trusts or OEICs (open-ended investment companies) which do not hold more than 50% of value of their investments in securities with less than five years to run;

(e) Shares in qualifying investment trusts (again the 50% rule in (d) above applies);

(f) Units or shares in UCITS (undertakings for collective investments in transferable securities), subject to the 50% rule in (**d**);

(g) Depositary interests, including CREST depositary interests;

(h) Bonds issued by multilateral institutions. These are organisations to which core contributions may be reported as official development assistance, eg the United Nations Development Programme or the African Development Fund;

(i) Cash held pending investment.

(j) From 1 July 2015 securities issued by registered societies and securities admitted to trading on a recognised stock exchange in the European Economic Area.

Before 30 June 2014, investments had to pass the 5% test, whereby the investor could not be certain or virtually certain of receiving 95% of the unit purchase price at any time in the following five years. If such guarantees exist, then most units qualified as a component of cash ISA.

Since 1 July 2014 stocks and shares ISA's are permitted to hold cash or cash like investments and certain securities such as retail bonds which have less than 5 years to run to maturity. Since 1 July 2014, subject to the provider's rules, it is potentially possible to transfer a cash ISA to a stocks and shares ISA and vice versa. The concepts of cash ISAs and stocks and shares ISAs have been retained as it is thought investors may wish to keep the two types of investment separate.

(4) For 2016/17 the maximum that can be invested in a ISA is £15,240. This limit can be split between a cash ISA and stocks and shares ISA as the investor wishes. For 2014/15, as new ISA's were introduced part of the way through the tax year, there were two sets of limits on the amounts that could be invested. From 6 April 2014 to 30 June 2014, the maximum investment was £11,880 of which up to £5,940 could be saved in cash. (The whole amount could be invested in stocks and shares if the saver wished.) From 1 July 2014 to 5 April 2015 the limit was £15,000 pa and it could be split between a cash ISA and stocks and shares ISA as the investor wished. Any subscriptions made to an ISA between 6 April 2014 and 30 June 2014 counted against the £15,000 ISA limit.

There is no minimum subscription. Although there is no minimum holding period for the NISA, it is not currently possible to withdraw and reinvest at will. Once the investment in a component reaches the limit for the year, no further investment in the component may be made in that year, regardless of withdrawals. From Autumn 2015 ISA savers are permitted to withdraw and replace money from their cash ISA within a tax year without it counting towards their annual ISA subscription limit for the year.

(5) Savers may hold only one stocks and shares ISA and one cash ISA per year, which may be with different managers. Transfers of the balance of a NISA may be made to another manager during the year. From 1 July 2014 it is possible to make a transfer from a stocks and shares ISA to a cash ISA. The legislation allows for the transfer to be of the whole or part of the balance paid in before 5 April 2014. However, not all ISA providers allow part transfers.

(6) ISAs are free of income tax and capital gains tax, but where ISA investments are in shares, tax credits on dividends are not reclaimable. Where the ISA investment is in securities rather than shares, the 20% tax deducted is reclaimable by the ISA manager. Before 30 June 2014, where interest arose on cash held for reinvestment in a stocks and shares ISA, the account manager had to account for tax at 20% to HMRC (this applied to PEP funds reclassified as ISAs from 6 April 2008). There was, however, no effect on the investor, who was neither treated as having received taxable income nor entitled to a tax refund. From 1 July 2014 there is no requirement to account for tax on interest in a stocks and shares ISA.

If tax relief on a ISA is found to have been wrongly given, HMRC may make an assessment on either the account manager or the investor.

(7) Shares received from savings-related share option schemes and share incentive plans (see **Example N1**) may be transferred within 90 days into the stocks and shares component of the ISA free of capital gains tax, so long as, together with any other investments, they are within the annual subscription limit. This applies even where the shares would not otherwise be qualifying investments (for example, because they are not listed/traded on a recognised stock exchange). There is no separate single company limit, and there is no facility to transfer shares acquired under a public offer or following demutualisation of a building society or insurer. The shares component of a NISA is kept separate from any other holdings of the investor for the purpose of the capital gains rules for matching disposals with acquisitions.

(8) Stakeholder ISAs offer terms that meet minimum criteria for charges, access and terms set by the government. The main terms are:

| | *Cash* | *Shares* |
|---|---|---|
| Charges | None | 1½% for first 10 years of net assets plus stamp duty and dealing charges |
| Access | Withdrawal within 7 days; minimum amount £10 or less | Minimum £500 a year or £50 a month |
| Terms | Interest no lower than 1% below base rate, upward changes to be reflected within one month, no other restrictions | Units/shares to be single priced, and at least 50% to be invested in EU shares/securities |

In addition the product must:

- use plain English;
- not link with any other product (no bundling);
- undertake to maintain the CAT standard for existing customers.

(9) An investor in a ISA can transfer his investment to another manager. The transfer must be of the whole of the current year's subscription and/or the whole or any part of a previous subscription.

*Help to buy ISA*

(10) From 1 December 2015, first-time buyers will be able to save up to £200 a month in a dedicated ISA that the government will top up by 25%, up to a maximum of £3,000. Couples will be able to open an account each if they are buying together, meaning a potential boost of up to £6,000 towards a deposit for a first home.

From 6 April 2017, individuals aged between 18 and 40 will be ablr to save up to £4,000 per annum into a single lifetime ISA and receive a 20% bonus from the Government at the end of the year.

www.gov.uk/government/uploads/system/uploads/attachment_data/file/413899/Help_to_Buy_ISA_Guidance.pdf

www.gov.uk/government/uploads/system/uploads/attachment_data/file/414027/FTB _factographic-_final.pdf

*Surviving spouse or civil partner*

(11) From 6 April 2015 in respect of deaths on or after 3 December 2014, the NISA regulations are amended to provide an additional ISA allowance equal to the value of the deceased person's ISA savings at their date of death. In certain circumstances, this enables the individual who is eligible for the additional allowance to transfer the inherited funds into their own ISA. Finance Act 2016 extends this by allowing the income during the period of administration to be tax free.

## *(ii) Junior ISA (JISA)*

Junior ISAs (JISA) were introduced in November 2011 as follows.

(1) Qualifying children are able to have one cash and one stocks and shares JISA at any time with an overall annual contribution limit of,

| | |
|---|---|
| Tax year 2015/16 & 2016/17 | 4,080 |
| Tax year 2014/15 | |
| 1 July 2014 to 5 April 2015 | 4,000 |
| 5 April 2014 to 30 June 2014 | 3,840 |

See answer (i) 4 above for the increase in the limit during the tax year 2014/15.

(2) Contributions are allocated between cash and stocks and shares as an investor chooses and ability to transfer funds from one type of JISA to another,

(3) Children with a CTF (see (iii) below) were not originally eligible for a JISA, although the original CTF annual investment limit of £1,200 was increased to match the Junior ISA limit.

(4) Originally it was intended that CTFs and JISAs would remain separate and hence it would not be possible to transfer CTFs into JISAs. From April 2015, it is possible to transfer savings from a child trust fund to a JISA.

(5) Returns are tax free – for both child and parents (interest arising on the account will not be taxed on the parents, even if they provided the funds),

(6) Accounts are owned by the child and funds locked in until they turn 18,

(7) From age 16 a child can open and manage a JISA account,

(8) Existence of a JISA will not affect an individual's entitlement to adult NISAs. Therefore from age 16 a child could open both a JISA and an adult NISA, with the JISA contributions not impacting upon the adult NISA subscription limits,

(9) At age 18, JISA accounts become adult NISAs by default, with the funds then being accessible,

(10) There are no government contributions into normal JISA accounts although provision will be made for looked after children,

(11) There is a Sharia-compliant version.

### *(iii) Child Trust Fund*

The arrangements for the Child Trust Fund (CTF) were established by SI 2004/1450, 2422, and 3369, and applied to children born between 1 September 2002 and 2 January 2011. The accounts were designed to encourage savings and included contributions from government. However as part of a package to tackle the UK's budget deficit the government reduced and then ceased contributions. Children born from January 2011 onwards do not qualify for (and their parents are not able to open) a CTF. Accounts set up for eligible children continue to benefit from tax free investment growth and no withdrawals are possible until the child reaches 18. The child's friends and family can continue to contribute up to the annual overall totals set out at (e)1 above (originally £1,200 but now linked to the JISA threshold above) per year. It is also possible to change the type of CTF account (shares vs cash) and or move it to another provider. From April 2015 it is also possible to convert a CFT into a JISA.

## Explanatory Notes

*Interest received by companies*

(1) For companies, all interest payable and receivable, including interest from abroad, is brought into account under loan relationship rules calculating the company's income, together with profits and losses on disposals. The detailed provisions are in **Example K2**. Tax is not deducted from interest paid by a company to a company within the charge to corporation tax or to certain other recipients, or from interest on listed company securities, as indicated in **part (a)** of the Example.

*Basis of assessment*

(2) Income tax is charged on all amounts computed under ITEPA 2003, ITTOIA 2005 and ITA 2007. On interest the amount is the full amount of interest arising in the tax year (ITTOIA 2005 s 370).

(3) Interest 'arises' on the date it is received. In the case of a bank account the interest arises when it is credited to the account. For non-corporate taxpayers there are no adjustments to take account of interest that is merely accruing. Different rules apply to companies (see **Example K2**).

*National Savings investments, ISAs and Junior ISAs*

(4) National Savings and Investments offer a wide range of investments. Income bonds (including guaranteed income bonds) carry interest which has always been paid without deduction of tax monthly. Capital bonds carry guaranteed interest that is credited gross each year. The interest is accumulated until the bond is cashed in, but tax may be charged on the interest when credited. Fixed rate savings bonds pay interest net of tax annually at rates fixed a year at a time, and the bonds can be cashed at any anniversary date without interest penalty. Tax is paid via self assessment or through a codin adjustment.. National Savings

Certificates, which may be fixed-interest or index-linked, carry interest which is accumulated until they are repaid, and the interest is free of all taxation. Premium bonds earn no interest at all, and any prizes are free of all taxation. For children under 16, Children's Bonds are available, under which all interest and bonuses are tax-free. For details see **Example A2 part (b)(ii) note 2.**

(5) Interest on the cash component of Individual Savings Accounts (ISAs), Junior ISAs and Child Trust funds are exempt from tax providing the rules of the schemes are satisfied. For details see **question (h)** above.

*Deduction of tax at source from copyright and patent royalties*

(6) Where copyright royalties are paid, basic rate tax is not deducted at source unless:

(a) the owner's usual place of abode is outside the UK (ITA 2007 s 906) (and even then, tax is not deducted if the royalties are paid to a non-resident professional author);

or

(b) the copyright is held as an investment and the royalties are deemed to be annual payments subject to deduction of tax under ITA 2007 s 902.

Copyright royalties that are paid in full are a normal trading expense. If they are paid net by individuals they are deducted from total income.

(7) The treatment of patent royalties is different from that of copyright royalties. The Income Tax Act 2007 has changed the tax treatment of charges on income (annual payments and patent royalties). The approach is intended to remove many of the complexities in the original legislation. It is now mandatory to deduct income tax at the basic rate (unless covered by ITA 2007 s 902(3)). The tax so deducted is then collected as part of the payer's self-assessment. Relief is now given for annual payments and patent royalties as a deduction in calculating net income.

*Treatment of royalties in computing income*

(8) Where copyright royalties are received by individual authors, composers etc, the income is income of their profession. Royalty receipts from purchased copyrights will be intellectual property charged under ITTOIA 2005 s 579.

(9) The position of patent royalties received by individuals is similar. Where they are received by the inventor, the receipts are taxed as earned income (FA 2004 s 189 new (2A)).

The Tax Law Rewrite project changed the definition of relevant UK earnings. As before and stated above, patent income arising to an individual who devised an invention counts as relevant UK earnings, but the exceptions previously in TA 1988 s 833(5C) and (5E) have been removed. These prevented earned income treatment for patents that had been purchased (ie, held as an investment). A wider range of patent income now potentially qualifies as 'relevant UK earnings'.

*Accrued income scheme*

(10) For sales of interest bearing securities (but not shares), the accrued income provisions of ITA 2007 s 619 onwards apply.

The accrued income provisions prevent income tax being avoided by selling securities just before an interest payment date, thus receiving the interest as part of the capital proceeds. The rules do not apply if the nominal value of all the securities held by an individual in the tax year in which the next interest payment on the securities falls due or in the previous tax year does not exceed £5,000.

*Capital gains tax*

(11) Capital gains tax (CGT) essentially charges tax on the profit made by an investor on the sale of an asset. The disposal of a security could therefore give rise to a CGT charge as well as an accrued income adjustment.

The contract note for the sale and purchase of securities will normally detail the amount of any accrued income. For CGT, exclude any accrued income loss from acquisition cost and add any accrued income profit to acquisition cost as otherwise there will be an element of double counting or double taxation. On sale, deduct any accrued income profit and add any accrued income loss to sale proceeds.

Most securities liable to the accrued income scheme, such as British Government stock, qualifying corporate bonds and building society PIBS, are exempt from CGT, however some securities, such as non-sterling loan stocks, are chargeable to CGT.

*Tax credits and tax treatment of accrued income*

(12) Accrued income profits and losses are taken into account in computing income for tax credits (SI 2002/2006 reg 14(2)(ix)). The profit increases income of the tax year in which the next income payment, after the settlement date, falls. Accrued income loss reduce the interest received on the next interest date. Profits and losses are not netted off unless they relate to the same stock with the same interest payment date.

*Discounted securities*

(13) Taxpayers other than companies are subject to special rules dealing with discounted securities (ITTOIA 2005 ss 427–460). The accrued income scheme does not apply to such securities. The discounted security rules apply where the issue price is lower than the redemption price by more than ½% per year between issue and redemption, or, if that period exceeds 30 years, by more than 15%. Investors are charged to income tax in the tax year of disposal, at savings rate (if available), on the profit. If a loss arises on securities acquired before 27 March 2003 then that loss may be offset against the total income of the year (for trustees against income from discounted securities only) otherwise loss relief is not available (ITTOIA 2005 s 454).

On death there is a deemed disposal at market value with tax charged accordingly. Transfers from the personal representatives to legatees are also deemed disposals with income tax being charged on the estate on the difference between value at death and value at transfer.

*Variable rate securities*

(14) The rules set out above apply to all securities that have interest that is:

- fixed;
- fixed by reference to a published base rate; or
- at a rate fixed by reference to a published index of prices (eg RPI, CPI etc).

If interest is otherwise variable then ITA 2007 s 627 and s 635 apply. These provisions require the transferor to calculate taxable interest in a just and reasonable manner, but no adjustment (in practice, relief) applies for the transferee.

*Non-qualifying policies*

(15) If a policy is not a qualifying policy, the proceeds are free of capital gains tax, but any profit is charged to income tax at the excess, if any, of higher rate/additional rate tax over the basic rate (ITTOIA 2005 s 530) subject to top slicing relief (see **explanatory note 18** below).

The most common form of non-qualifying policy is a single premium bond, as in this Example. In each year (ending on the anniversary of the policy) withdrawals of not more than 5% of the initial investment may be made without attracting a tax liability at that time (to a maximum of 20 years). Any excess over the 5% limit is charged to tax at the excess of higher rate/additional rate tax over the basic rate, amounting to 20% in this Example as indicated in **part (b)**. The 5% limit is, however, a cumulative figure and amounts unused in any year swell the tax-free withdrawal available in a later year. Any annual withdrawals that are not taxed when made are taken into account as part of the profit when the bond matures.

*Top slicing relief*

(16) In calculating the tax on the bond profit, top slicing relief is available (ITTOIA 2005 s 535). The surplus on the bond is divided by the number of complete policy years that the bond has been held (or since the last

chargeable event), and the amount arrived at is treated as the top slice of income to ascertain the tax rate, which is then applied to the full profit.

If there are two chargeable events in one year, top slicing relief is calculated by working out the appropriate fractions for each policy and adding them together to arrive at the amount charged as the top slice of income.

**Part (f)** of the Example shows the effect on top slicing relief of paying gift aid donations and pension premiums. The provision preventing a gift aid donation from reducing income for top slicing purposes is in ITTOIA 2005 s 535(7). See **Examples A6** and **N4** for detailed notes on gift aid payments and pension premiums respectively.

*Allowances withdrawn*

(17) Although in many instances it is possible to cash in a bond when no higher rate/additional rate tax is payable, there is a possible tax charge as a result of the withdrawal of basic personal allowance for those born before 1938 or with income over £100,000. For those with income in excess of £100,000, entitlement to the basic personal allowance is withdrawn at the rate of £1 for every £2 of income over £100,000. The allowance therefore ceases to be available when income exceeds £122,000.

*Losses on single premium bonds*

(18) If there should be a loss on a single premium bond, tax relief is not available, but if such a loss occurs in a year when the taxpayer is chargeable at higher rates and earlier withdrawals have been charged to tax, the lower of the amount of the deficiency on the bond and the total amount previously charged to tax on the bond will be allowed as a deduction in calculating the taxpayer's liability to tax at excess rates. The saving will be at the excess of higher rate/additional rate over basic rate tax for non-dividend income and the excess of the appropriate dividend rate of 7.5%, 32½% , 38.1% (ITTOIA 2005 s 539).

*Dividend income*

(19) Dividend income is normally treated as the top slice of income (ITA 2007 s 16). This is, however, subject to ITTOIA 2005 s 535(4) dealing with giving relief for higher rates of tax on life policy gains, which provides that life gains are taken into account *after* dividend income to compute the relief. Hence in Joe Friend's case in **part (e)** of the Example the life policy gain was taxed as the top slice of the income regardless of how much of the income was dividend income.

*Shares in life policies*

(20) The transfer of shares in life policies between spouses/civil partners living together, is not normally a chargeable event. Consideration should therefore be given to assigning a policy to a lower rate or non-taxpaying spouse prior to any surrender. In any other circumstances where a policy is changed from joint to single names or vice versa it will be treated as a part assignment and therefore subject to the 'chargeable events' rules outlined in this Example. Any gain arising will be taxed on the transferor. No tax charge will be made if the transfer is made for no consideration (ITTOIA 2005 ss 505–514).

*Personal portfolio bonds*

(21) There are anti-avoidance provisions in ITTOIA 2005 ss 515–526 and SI 1999/1029 relating to personal portfolio bonds. Personal portfolio bonds are broadly investment linked or index-linked policies that enable the policyholder to select the underlying investments or index. For policy years, other than the last year, there is an annual taxable gain (yearly charge) amounting to 15% of a deemed gain equal to the total of the premiums paid and the total deemed gains in earlier years, less any taxable amounts withdrawn in earlier years. The yearly charge is taxed in a similar way to the normal chargeable events rules, but top slicing relief is not relevant. The total amount of gains taxed under the yearly provisions is deducted from any gain arising when the policy terminates. If gains arising during the life of a policy are reversed when the policy comes to an end, a compensating deduction will be made from taxable income.

Most bonds taken out before 17 March 1998 are excluded from the provisions, and those who needed to change the terms of the policy to benefit from this exclusion had until the end of the first policy year after

5 April 2000 to do so. Policyholders who were not UK resident on 17 March 1998 will have at least 12 months after becoming resident to make the change.

*Commissions and discounts*

(22) In general, commissions on a policyholder's own policies that would otherwise form part of trading profits or employment income are not taxed if a member of the general public would have received an equivalent amount. S 94/97 and www.hmrc.gov.uk/manuals/eimanual/eim64605.htm.

In relation to a policyholder's own life policies, where commission is received, netted off or invested, the qualifying status of the policy is not affected if commission is paid under a separate commission contract. If a discounted premium is paid, it is the net premium that is taken into account to decide whether the policy qualifies.

In relation to life policy chargeable events, if commission is paid separately, the gain is calculated by reference to the gross premium. Commission invested in the policy counts as part of the premiums paid. Where a premium is paid net of commission, or a discounted premium is paid, the gain is calculated using the amount paid.

FA 2007 introduced anti-avoidance provisions to stop the exploitation of the commission rules. The scheme involved the policyholder taking out a large single premium life policy, typically linked to an interest bearing cash deposit fund. A large proportion of the commission received by the adviser was passed to the policyholder as a tax-free payment. The bond was then cashed when its value returned to the original premium value, ie at the point that there was no chargeable event gain. Thus the actual increase in value, ie the rebated commission, avoided a tax charge.

The legislation only applies where the premiums paid in a year exceed £100,000 and the policy is held for less than three years. Where the provisions apply only the net premium, after any commission rebate, is deducted in computing the chargeable event gain. The provisions apply to individuals and trusts (ITTOIA 2005 s 541A and 541B). The deduction of commission from the premium does not apply if the chargeable event is the death of the policyholder.

The insurer will produce a certificate of chargeable event gains without reference to any rebated or reinvested commission and it will be the responsibility of the taxpayer to compute the taxable chargeable event gain taking into account the commission adjustment if required by this legislation.

Gains on life insurance policies owned by companies are normally taxed as loan relationships after 1.4.08 (FA 2008 s 36 and Sch 13, now in CTA 2009 Part 6 Chapter 11).

*Tax credits*

(23) The profit on a bond is counted as investment income for tax credits. No top slicing relief is available. Assuming that the claimants have used their £300 deduction against other investment income this could mean that a taxpayer, only liable at basic rate, would have a significant withdrawal of tax credits. See **Example A7** for details.

*Non-UK life insurance bonds*

(24) Gains made on foreign life assurance policies are liable to UK income tax if the holder is UK resident when the policy is encashed. There is no notional tax credit available unless the policy has suffered a comparable European Economic Area tax charge (ITTOIA 2005 s 532), or a similar foreign tax charge (ITTOIA 2005 s 534).

Top slicing relief is available (see **explanatory note 18** above).

If the policyholder was resident outside the UK for part of the period since the policy was taken out then the gain is reduced as follows:

$$\text{Gain} \times \frac{\text{No of days non-resident}}{\text{No of days policy held}} = \text{Chargeable Event Gain}$$

(ITTOIA 2005 s 528)

Many overseas bonds are written in jurisdictions with favourable tax regimes, such as the Channel Islands or the Isle of Man. No tax is charged on the income or gains of the policy during its life thus allowing gross roll-up of most income. Note that if the income received has borne a non-repayable withholding tax then the benefit of that tax will be lost.

On encashment the whole of the gain is subject to income tax without any credit. By use of top slicing relief, and careful timing, it may be possible to restrict the tax charge to basic rate only thus saving the higher rate/ additional rate charge that would have applied had the income been chargeable on the taxpayer when it arose.

*ISAs*

(25) The legislation relating to ISAs is contained in ITTOIA 2005 Part 6 Chapter 3 and related regulations. SI 2007/2119 introduced significant changes effective 6 April 2008. Only one cash ISA, and one stocks and shares NSA may be opened per year, and may be with different providers.

(26) For 2012/13 onwards the contribution limits rise according to the Consumer Prices Index (CPI) (as do the limits for JISA and CTF) to the nearest £120 (to make monthly payments easier). For the tax years 2010/11 and 2011/12 the contributions limits were linked to the rise in the RPI.

(27) ISA legislation was simplified by SI 2007/2119 from 6 April 2008, after which the terms 'maxi' and 'mini' ISA ceased to exist. Personal Equity Plans (PEPs) and the stocks and shares component of maxi ISAs became stocks and share ISAs. Tessa Only Individual Savings Accounts (TOISAs), mini ISAs and the cash component of maxi ISAs became cash ISAs. Prior year cash ISAs, including the TOISA element, can be transferred to stocks and shares ISAs in addition to the current year investment limit. All ISA's became NISAs on 1 July 2014.

(28) The annual investments in TESSAs taken out before 6 April 1999 did not affect the ISA limits and the capital (but not interest) from TESSAs maturing after 5 April 1999 could be paid into the cash component of an existing maxi ISA, or into an existing cash mini ISA, or into a separate TESSA only ISA, within six months of maturity. From 6 April 2008 these accounts were reclassified as cash ISAs.

(29) The aim of ISAs is to encourage more people to save. Adult non-taxpayers do not benefit from a cash ISA if their income is below the personal savings allowance, but if they have taxable dividend income, an ISA would be appropriate for them. The capital gains exemption is not relevant to those with modest portfolios whose gains would be covered by the annual exemption.

(30) JISA accounts may therefore be attractive where funds are predominately being provided by parents. For example, JISAs may be considered by those parents wishing to save to fund their child's university education (although they need to be aware that the child obtains access to the account at age 18).

(31) ISAs can be an alternative to a personal pension plan where the ISA investment could be funded by taking income from a company by way of a dividend rather than remuneration, thus saving national insurance contributions (see **Example N5 part (d)**). The advantage is most marked where the taxpayer is a basic rate payer only. Although no tax relief is obtained on the ISA investment, the fund is tax-free (apart from non-repayable dividend tax credits), and withdrawals may be made tax-free and without any restrictions.

(32) Those who are resident in the Channel Islands or Isle of Man are not UK resident for tax purposes. Those employed by the Crown overseas are, however, treated as performing duties in the UK and are eligible to invest in ISAs as are their spouses. If an investor becomes non-resident he may retain the ISA but cannot make any further contributions unless and until he becomes resident again. Account managers should be notified immediately when an account holder dies, as the investments are no longer exempt.

# Question

## A

Summarise the legislation relating to pension contributions giving brief details of the limits on contributions and the options and benefits available on retirement and death.

## B.

Stephen is self-employed. His personal pension contributions are paid annually in March each year to an ongoing pension arrangement. His pension input period (PIP) ends on 6 April each year. The amounts he contributes are determined after a meeting with his financial adviser. His contributions for the last few years have been:

| Tax year | Contribution |
|---|---|
| 2012/13 | £30,000 |
| 2013/14 | £30,000 |
| 2014/15 | £60,000 |
| 2015/16 | £20,000 |

Assuming that his income is expected to be £200,000 in 2016/17, what is the maximum pension contribution he can make in March 2017, without incurring an annual allowance tax charge?

## C.

Dr Jolly is a medical practitioner who is in general practice. He makes his accounts up to 31 December in each year. In the year to 31 December 2016 his profits, adjusted for taxation (except for superannuation payments made) amounted to £112,500. He has other income in 2016/17 of:

| | |
|---|---|
| Bank Interest Received | £1,100 |
| Dividends Received | £5,300 |

He made a donation under Gift Aid to a national charity of £1,000 and paid (net) a pension contribution of £8,000.

Dr Jolly's staff are members of the NHS superannuation scheme. The employer's contribution for the year to 31 December 2016 amounted to £11,900.

As well as receiving NHS income, Dr Jolly is a police surgeon, has a consultancy with a leading engineering firm, undertakes insurance and HGV medical examinations and signs death certificates, passport applications, etc.

Your examination of Dr Jolly's superannuation account within his records provides the following information:

| | | £ | £ |
|---|---|---|---|
| 01.01.16 | Creditors – superannuation due | | 7,468 |
| 31.01.16 | Quarterly payment | 2,965 | |
| 30.04.16 | Quarterly payment | 2,965 | |
| 20.05.16 | Settlement for 2015/16 | 3,983 | |
| 31.07.16 | Quarterly payment | 3,113 | |
| 30.10.16 | Quarterly payment | 3,113 | |
| 31.12.16 | Creditors – superannuation due | 6,221 | |
| | Charged in accounts | | |
| | Employer's Contribution | | 10,424 |
| | Employees' Contribution | | 4,468 |
| | | 22,360 | 22,360 |
| 01.01.17 | Creditors – superannuation due | | 6,221 |
| 31.01.17 | Quarterly payment | 3,113 | |
| 02.04.17 | Settlement for 2016/17 | 3,975 | |
| 30.04.17 | Quarterly payment | 3,113 | |

In May 2017 the NHS scheme administrator informs Dr Jolly that his pension input for the year 2016/17 amounted to £29,950.

You are required to:

(a) adjust the taxable profits for the year ended 31 December 2016 for superannuation paid;

(b) indicate how relief is given for superannuation paid by Dr Jolly; and

(c) compute Dr Jolly's 2016/17 tax liability.

# Answer

## A. Pension contributions

Registered pension schemes operate under the rules introduced by Finance Act 2004 Part 4, Finance Act 2005 Part 5 and related regulations, which came into force on 6 April 2006. The rules were significantly amended by Finance Act 2011 in respect of 2011/12 onwards, and Finance Acts in 2013, 2014, 2015 and 2016 made further amendments. The Taxation of Pensions Act 2014 also introduced new rules on pensions coming into payment and how they may be drawn.

An individual can belong to, or contribute to, as many schemes as they wish at any time (FA 2004 s 188).

The legislation gives tax relief on pension contributions paid to a registered pension scheme in a fiscal year. There are no carry back or carry forward rules, although unused relief from a year can be carried forward (see below). The way in which tax relief is given for contributions made by individuals depends upon the method of payment. This is set out in detail at **explanatory note 6**. In the case of contributions paid by an employer, tax relief will be given in the accounting period in which contributions are paid (FA 2004 s 196(2)).

Tax relief on contributions may be restricted in a number of ways.

Currently, the rate of relief for pension contributions is not affected by the Scottish Rate of Income Tax (SRIT), as the combined UK and Scottish rate is the same as the UK rate outside Scotland. This may change in the future if the Scottish government changes the SRIT without the UK rate changing by the same amount.

### Annual allowance (FA 2004 ss 227 to 238)

The first test compares the 'total pension input' for a pension input period (PIP) with the annual allowance for that year. Until 8 July 2015, the PIP could end at any time in the tax year, but it was then aligned by Finance (No 2) Act 2015 with the end of the tax year at 5 April 2016 by granting a double allowance (£80,000) for the period 6 April 2015 to 8 July 2015, and allowing up to £40,000 from that period to be carried forward to the period 9 July 2015 to 5 April 2016.

The standard annual allowance is £40,000 for 2014/15 onwards (£50,000 for 2011/12 to 2013/14), but unused annual allowance may be carried forward for up to three years, with relief given in the later tax year when the contributions are paid.

The standard allowance is subject to a restriction to £10,000 (known as the 'money purchase annual allowance') for those who access their money purchase pensions flexibly, and those who take certain amounts from defined benefit schemes, from 2015/16 onwards. As with the standard allowance, 2015/16 was split by 9 July 2015, with £20,000 being allowed in the first period and up to £10,000 being available for carry forward into the second period.

For high earners (those with 'adjusted income' over £150,000), from 2016/17 onwards, the annual allowance is variable, subject to a minimum of £10,000: it tapers away by £1 for every £2 of adjusted income above £150,000, so that the annual allowance is £10,000 for anyone with adjusted income of £210,000 or more. Adjusted income is, broadly, taxable income plus any pension contributions made in the year. This prevents employers making large contributions that are disregarded.

If any of the restricted £10,000 remains unused, it may not be carried forward to later tax years.

Where the annual allowance has been exceeded for a tax year, the excess is reported on the additional information pages of the tax return. It is taxed at the taxpayer's marginal rate for that tax year. Under the pre-9 July 2015 rules, when the PIP might end in the middle of a tax year, the annual allowance charge could frequently arise in the tax year following that in which the contribution was paid (a contribution made after the end of a PIP but before the end of the tax year – ie, in the next PIP – was relieved in the tax year when the new PIP ended, so it is possible that the rate of tax relief given and the rate at which it was clawed back could differ. This should not arise for 2016/17 as the PIP has been aligned with the tax year. See **explanatory notes 3 and 4**.

## Total pension input (FA 2004 s 229)

The 'total pension input' is computed for the purpose of the Annual Allowance calculation. This is the sum of the contributions made to pension policies plus the increase in value of defined benefit pensions in the current scheme (preserved or deferred benefits are exempt from the AA regime unless they were accrued in the current PIP, such as by those who change jobs and occupational pension schemes in mid-year with benefits accruing for part of the year in each job). See **explanatory note 2** below as to a definition of the period that is a 'pension input period' and for the method of computing the value of pension input for defined benefit schemes.

If exceptionally an individual has 'total pension input' in excess of their annual allowance then there will be a tax charge on the individual on any amount of pension inputs over the annual allowance (s 227(4)). The rate of tax borne on the tax charge is the taxpayer's marginal income tax rate(s) for the year, treating the excess contribution as if it were his top slice of income. The individual may elect to have the fund trustee pay the tax if the annual allowance charge is at least £2,000 and the contributions have all been paid into the same scheme. If the total pension input exceeds the annual allowance but no single scheme has received inputs above the allowance, the contributor may request that the trustees pay the tax from the fund.

## Maximum tax relief by reference to earnings (FA 2004 ss 186 to 203)

The second test restricts the tax relief for contributions paid by an individual in the fiscal year, to the higher of

- 100% of UK earnings chargeable to tax, or
- £3,600 (provided relief at basic rate is given at source)

(FA 2004 s 190).

The interaction between the two tests means that tax relief is effectively limited to the lower of the annual allowance for the PIP and earnings for the tax year, or if higher, £3,600.

Contributions outside occupational schemes are normally paid net of basic rate tax – the pension provider reclaims the basic rate tax relief from HMRC each quarter.

If contributions are paid in excess of the above limits, the excess amount will be allowed to remain within the pension fund, but the tax relief on it will be repayable (via the self-assessment return), or a refund of contributions may be claimed from the provider, which will automatically adjust the tax relief claimed.

For example, John, who is a self-employed higher rate taxpayer normally earning approximately £70,000 pa, makes a pension contribution of £8,000 pa each year, being equivalent to a gross contribution of £10,000 less tax relief of £2,000. In 2016/17 John's UK earnings unexpectedly only amount to £3,000. He will, therefore, have a tax-deductible premium limited to (£2,880 net + £720 tax =) £3,600, being the maximum allowed to a non-taxpayer.

If he does nothing, the provider will reclaim £2,000 from HMRC when the relief due is limited to just £720. He will therefore have to self-assess the £1,280 of excess tax relief. He may instead claim an 'excess contributions lump sum' of £6,400, less tax relief not due of £1,280, giving £5,120 in net cash, ie, £8,000–£2,880) from the fund without any tax being charged (the provider will correct the tax reclaim in its quarterly return). This is the excess over the figure he was entitled to contribute. (FA 2004, ss 188(2) and 190).

An individual is entitled to tax relief on pension contributions paid in a tax year provided he is a 'relevant' UK individual (s 188(1)). A relevant UK individual is defined in s 189 as an individual who:

- has UK earnings chargeable to UK income tax, or
- was resident in the UK at some time during the tax year, or
- was resident in the UK when he joined the pension scheme and has been resident in the UK during part of the last five years, or
- the individual or his spouse (or civil partner) has earnings from overseas Crown employment subject to UK tax.

The contributions may be paid directly to the pension provider or paid via an employer-sponsored scheme. Relief is also available where the contribution is in the form of a transfer of eligible shares, ie those acquired under a SAYE option scheme or approved share incentive plan (s 195). Such transfers must be made within 90 days of exercising the SAYE option (when the shares are appropriated to the employee). The shares will be treated as a contribution equal to their market value at the date of transfer. Normally contributions are made net of tax and therefore tax relief is given on the grossed up value, subject to the normal limits of 100% of pay or £40,000 (plus unused allowance, if any).

Employer contributions to registered pension schemes are always made gross, as they fall outside the scope of both PAYE (ITEPA 2003, s 308) and NIC (Contributions Regs 2001, SI 2001/1004, Sch 3 Part VI, para 2). This means that there is usually an advantage to substituting employer contributions for employee contributions, since the latter are made out of pay after the deduction of PAYE and NIC – only the tax is recovered by the scheme, while the employee and employer NICs are lost.

Where pension contributions are made by the employer, the full amount paid in the accounting period may be allowed in the employer's income tax or corporation tax calculation, subject to the usual restriction that the payment must have been made 'wholly and exclusively' for the purpose of the trade or as a management expense in an investment business (FA 2004 s 196). (See HMRC manuals at BIM 46001 for further guidance). In order for pension contributions paid to be allowable they must form part of a normal remuneration package. They are not considered as a stand-alone amount. It follows that a salary sacrifice will not prevent or enhance a tax deduction. Contributions will be allowable if the overall salary package is a normal commercial amount.

It is likely that HMRC will disallow any amount identifiable as relating to a non-trade purpose, for example, as part of arrangements to dispose of a business where the payment represents part of the sale proceeds, or of exceptional size. This would be an issue if the employer was not carrying on a trade, eg, a property holding company paying a contribution that amounted to more than a reasonable expense of management. The main focus of disallowance is likely to be in respect of directors who are controlling shareholders or their relatives, and possibly where the salary package has been significantly increased, eg where funds previously taken as dividends are now taken as a pension contribution.

Where, exceptionally, the employer makes special contributions (including those made to correct a funding shortfall) and those contributions are in excess of £500,000 then the special contribution will be spread over two, three or four years. (FA 2004 s 197). (See **part b** as to the calculation of the special contribution and detailed rules on spreading.)

## Lifetime allowance (FA 2004 ss 214–226)

Benefits from money purchase schemes are based upon amounts paid in plus the growth in value of the fund, and the value of the fund is relatively easy to calculate at any time. Defined benefit schemes, in contrast, have benefits based upon age, salary (measured as eg, final, average, last twelve months, last three years, etc) and years of service, so the value of the fund must be calculated using a formula, which (for these purposes, if not in real life) is a simple multiple of 20 times the annual pension entitlement.

The lifetime limit restricts the total pension input which can be accumulated tax-free over a member's lifetime for both types of scheme. The lifetime allowance is a proxy for denying excess tax relief to high earners: in defined benefit schemes it is impossible to limit relief on contributions year-by-year because pension entitlement is enhanced by extra service rather than extra contributions, so the tax relief is given annually (up to the annual allowance) but any excess is recouped out of the fund when benefits crystallise and the fund is worth more than the lifetime allowance.

A fund is not tested during its accumulation period – the period over which contributions are made and funds invested for growth. The member can have as many different funds as he wishes. The lifetime limit only applies when withdrawals are made (known as 'benefit crystallisation events, or BCEs – see below). If the fund value on which a withdrawal is to be made exceeds the lifetime allowance (or the remaining value if there has been a previous withdrawal) there is a tax charge, known as the lifetime allowance charge.

The level of the lifetime allowance varies and recent rates are set out below:

| | £ |
|---|---|
| 2016/17 & 2017/18 | 1,000,000 |
| 2014/15 – 2015/16 | 1,250,000 |
| 2012/13 & 2013/14 | 1,500,000 |
| 2010/11 & 2011/12 | 1,800,000 |

There are various protection schemes under which individuals with pension savings accumulated before the changes to lifetime allowance (that is before April 2012, before April 2014 and before 2016) can elect to retain a higher limit if their funds are higher than the new limit but below the old limit at the relevant date of change.

A more flexible form of protection was included in Finance Act 2014, called Individual Protection 2014 (IP14), which members can elect for up to 5 April 2017.

Contributors with funds of between £1.0m and £1.25m at 5 April 2016 need to consider this again in view of the reduction of the lifetime allowance to £1m at that date. They may apply for Fixed Protection 2016 (FP16), which requires all contributions and salary-related benefit accrual to cease, or Individual Protection 2016 (IP16), which provides a personalised lifetime allowance fixed at the value of the pension funds as at 5 April 2016 but allows further contributions to be made and defined benefits to accrue. Contributors may apply for both FP16 and IP16, which provides protection in case FP16 is lost at some point due to something beyond the contributor's control (eg, FP16 would be lost if the contributor took up employment with an auto-enrolment scheme and he was unable to opt out within the first month).

Elections before IP14 had to be made by 5 April before the limit reduced, but applicants for IP14 were given three years to elect, and because HMRC was not ready in time for the 2016 change, which was not actually legislated until the Finance Act 2016 was passed in autumn 2016, no application deadline was set for FP16 or IP16.

### Benefit crystallisation event (FA 2004 s 216 and Sch 32)

When a withdrawal is made from any fund, other than a transfer to another registered pension scheme or pension splitting, this is known as a 'benefit crystallisation event'. (FA 2004 s 216.)

At that stage the withdrawal is valued and if the withdrawal exceeds the available lifetime allowance then the excess will be subject to a lifetime allowance charge. If the amount to be used is lower than the remaining lifetime allowance, then no tax charge arises but that proportion of the lifetime allowance that has been used will be noted and only the remaining percentage will be available on subsequent benefit crystallisation events (s 219). If a contributor has two pension pots worth £0.5m and £1.5m respectively, and decides to draw from the smaller pot, the £0.5m would not trigger a lifetime allowance charge but would use up 50% of the current lifetime allowance. When the contributor later draws on the larger pot, only 50% of the then-current lifetime allowance (which might be more or less than the 2016–17 value of £1m) would be available against that benefit crystallisation.

Where the amount being used for a benefit crystallisation event exceeds the lifetime allowance then the excess is subject to a lifetime allowance charge (s 215) of:

- 25% if the balance is used to buy a pension or left in the fund for future drawdown (and, in addition, the pension emerging is still taxable as income in the usual way), or
- 55% if taken as a lump sum, or still in the fund and not in drawdown at age 75.

### Pension benefits (FA 2004 ss 164 to 171 and Sch 28 and 29)

Benefits can currently be taken from most pension schemes from age 55 (or earlier in cases of ill-health retirement), depending on the rules of the scheme. The age at which an individual can access their personal pension is expected to be increased from 55 to 57 from April 2028 and thereafter be linked to ten years before the state pension age. Subject to the rules of the pension scheme, which must allow early retirement, there is no requirement for the employee to leave service when starting to draw a pension.

Part of the benefit crystallisation can be taken as a tax-free lump sum, to a maximum of 25% of the fund being crystallised, restricted by the lifetime allowance and the scheme rules. This gives an effective maximum for 2016/17 of 25% × £1 million = £250,000.

In the case of a money purchase scheme, the lump sum is up to 25% of the fund. In the case of a defined benefit scheme, the scheme pension is multiplied by 20, and any entitlement to an additional lump sum (ie, not a lump sum by commutation) added, to give a notional value, 25% of which is the maximum lump sum (FA 2004 Sch 29 para 3(6)). This is adjusted where the member had started to draw an annuity before 6 April 2006.

Where a member of a money purchase scheme uses the fund to buy a scheme pension to which defined benefits rules then apply, shortly before retirement, then the tax-free lump sum is restricted to 25% of the original fund. (FA 2006 Sch 23(22)).

The tax-free lump sum cannot simply be recycled into pension funds (ie, used to pay contributions that attract further tax relief), and any such recycling may constitute an unauthorised payment (see **explanatory note 22** as to the tax consequences). This provision applies even if the pension contribution is made before the lump sum is drawn. It does not apply if all of the following apply:

- the total tax-free cash received in a 12-month period does not exceed 0.75% of the lifetime limit,
- the increase in pension contributions does not exceed 30% of the lump sum,
- the contributions are not more than 30% higher than might have been expected, and
- the recycling is not pre-planned.

(Sch 29 para 3A).

Historically, the balance of the money purchase fund was used to buy a pension for the life of the member (in defined benefit schemes, the scheme provides the pension). This option is still available but there is no longer any obligation to purchase an annuity. Any annuity taken can be written for the joint lives of the member and spouse (including civil partner) and for a term certain not exceeding ten years. The pension may be:

- level;
- increasing (including one-off increases);
- linked (eg to RPI or based upon a with-profits fund);
- with lump sum death benefits.

Where a pension is purchased with a death benefit then the death benefit payable on a death after age 75 will be subject to a tax charge of 55%. There is no tax charge on a lump sum death benefit if the member has not attained the age of 75. The death benefit must represent the difference between the amounts paid in lifetime and the original amount paid for the annuity policy. Such a policy is known as a 'value protected annuity' (though the amount it costs to protect the value reduces the annuity).

When a member elects to take some benefits from his money purchase pension, he need not purchase an annuity. If he decides to draw a pension from the fund it is known as a drawdown fund. A drawdown pension fund is not used to buy an annuity but instead the annuity (income) is paid from the fund. There used to be limits to the amount of income a member could draw in a drawdown pension year, based on the Government Actuary's calculated annuity rate for the member's age:

| | |
|---|---|
| From 27 March 2014 to 5 April 2015 | 150% |
| 6 April 2013 to 26 March 2014 | 125% |
| On or before 5 April 2013 | 100% |

A drawdown pension year was the period of 12 months starting when the individual first became entitled to a drawdown pension and each succeeding period of 12 months (Sch 28 para 9 and 23). Therefore, if a member first became entitled to a drawdown pension on 1 June 2012, the higher maximum drawdown pension of 150% would first have been available for the drawdown pension year starting on 1 June 2014. The percentage related to the amount of annuity the Government Actuary calculates he could purchase with the value of the fund. This was known as 'capped drawdown'. This was recalculated every three years until the member reaches age 75, and then every year thereafter.

Where a member intending to take a drawdown pension could confirm a minimum level of other pension income (from 27 March 2014 £12,000, previously £20,000 per annum) and made no further contributions to pension arrangements, he could draw on the drawdown pension fund without limit. This was known as 'flexible drawdown'.

All withdrawals from drawdown funds are subject to tax as pension income. There is no NIC liability as pensions from registered schemes are exempt.

The old drawdown rules were replaced by a new flexi-access regime from 6 April 2015 under the Taxation of Pensions Act 2014. Those members in capped drawdown arrangements before that date may convert to the new regime, or they may stay under the capped drawdown rules and not be impacted by the £10,000 money purchase annual allowance. Those in flexible drawdown arrangements automatically moved into the new regime.

For those crystallising their pension benefits since 5 April 2015 those with defined contribution pensions can choose how much they withdraw without limit from their fund. 25% of such withdrawals would be free of tax (as now see above – there will still be a lifetime allowance charge if the fund taken into flexi-access drawdown, or taken as a lump sum, exceeds the lifetime allowance) and the balance taxed as the top slice of income. There is no need to formally have a drawdown fund, nor do the limits over maximum annual pension apply to them – they can take funds as and when they choose, subject to paying tax on the taxable pension or lump sum taken at the member's marginal rate. Under typical flexi-access drawdown, the member may take the tax-free cash element and then draw wholly taxable sums by way of a pension thereafter, but there is now an alternative. Instead of taking all the tax-free cash and going into a drawdown arrangement, the member may instead take an uncrystallised fund pension lump sum (UFPLS) with each withdrawal, so that 25% of each withdrawal is treated as part of the tax-free cash and the balance is taxable as income. Those taking a UFPLS thereafter have a money purchase annual allowance of £10,000.

## Death benefits (FA 2004 s 167 and Schs 28 and 29)

The rules after the April 2015 reforms depend principally on whether the member is in a money purchase or defined benefit scheme, the death occurs before or after age 75, and sometimes on whether the benefits have crystallised (ie, benefits have been taken).

- Fund uncrystallised: the whole fund, after testing against the lifetime allowance, can be paid to any beneficiary, tax-free, as a lump sum, annuity or drawdown pension, provided this happens within two years of the scheme administrator being notified of the member's death. After two years, they are taxed at the recipient's marginal rate.
- Fund already in drawdown (ie, crystallised): the whole fund can pass on tax-free to any beneficiary as a lump sum or drawdown pension, and the drawdown fund can be used to buy an annuity at any time. The two-year rule for lump sums also applies.
- Annuity already in payment: any beneficiary can receive payments tax-free including any protected lump sum death benefit. The same two-year rule also applies.

Where a death occurs after age 75:

- Fund uncrystallised: the fund may be paid to any beneficiary, as a lump sum, annuity or drawdown pension, taxed at the recipient's marginal rate, or it may be paid to a trust as a lump sum, subject to a 45% tax charge.
- Fund crystallised: as for uncrystallised fund.
- Annuity already in payment: any beneficiary can receive payments taxed at the recipient's marginal rate, or the fund can be paid to a trust subject to a 45% tax charge.

Any annuities already in payment at 6 April 2015 will be taxed at the recipient dependant's marginal rate.

The payment of a dependant's pension from a defined benefit scheme will be taxed at the dependant's marginal rate, regardless of the age of the scheme member at death.

Under the pre-2015 rules, the whole of the fund, including contributions and growth in value and any insured or uninsured benefits payable on death, could in most cases be paid as a death benefit, with no tax, provided it was before crystallisation, within two years of the pension provider being advised of the death, and the total of all of the deceased's funds did not exceed the lifetime allowance. If the conditions were not met (eg, because the fund was worth more than £1.25m), lump sums were taxable at 55%. If the conditions were met, an annuity or drawdown pension could instead be provided tax-free, but if not they were taxable at 25%. Similar provisions applied to the proceeds of tax-registered overseas pension schemes.

After age 75, the lump sum death benefit was liable to a tax charge at a flat rate of 45%, deducted by the provider, although this changed to the beneficiary's marginal rate from 6 April 2016. However, a drawdown pension could already be provided for dependants on the death of the member, taxable at the beneficiary's marginal rate in the same way as a dependant's pension payable by an occupational scheme.

Any amount in excess of the lifetime allowance is subject to tax of 55% (25% if taken as a pension by a surviving spouse). If a fund is inherited, the amount involved is not counted towards the beneficiary's lifetime allowance.

### Overseas pension schemes (FA 2004 s 150(7))

Payments to recognised overseas pension schemes will also attract tax relief. If payments are not made by way of a deduction from pay (before tax) then the contributions are included on the tax return and full relief given subject to the same restrictions as for UK-based schemes. To check whether a scheme is recognised see https://www.gov.uk/government/publications/list-of-qualifying-recognised-overseas-pension-schemes-qrops.

### Further details

See **explanatory notes 1–13** below for examples of maximum pension contributions, annual allowance charge and lifetime allowance charge. The notes also give more details on how tax relief will be given, transitional provisions, unsecured pension, alternatively secured pensions and term assurance.

**Explanatory notes 14–26** give details of the interactions with other legislation, such as national insurance, losses, divorce and tax credits.

## B.

Stephen's pension contributions in the tax years 2012/13 to 2016/17 will have been tested against the annual allowance and special annual allowance in those years (if relevant). The introduction of the £50,000 (now £40,000) annual allowance in 2011/12 was accompanied by a carry forward of unused relief rule which may provide additional contributions for Stephen in 2012/13 and subsequent years, over and above the £50,000 / £40,000 limits for the year. For this purpose, the annual allowance for the three years preceding the change was deemed to be £50,000, and a computation of unused relief is made. It is essential that the dates of the pension input periods (PIPs) are recorded and allocated to the tax years, as this computation is made against the amounts that were paid in the PIP ending in the tax year, which will frequently differ from the amounts shown on the tax return for the year for all years before 6 April 2016. See **explanatory note 2** for details of how the Pension Input Period is calculated.

| Contribution paid in | PIP ending on | Tax year in which PIP ends | Contribution paid | Unused in period | Cumulative carry forward to 2016/17 |
|---|---|---|---|---|---|
| | | | £ | £ | £ |
| March 2013 | 6.4.13 | 2013/14 | 30,000 | 20,000* | 20,000 |
| March 2014 | 6.4.14 | 2014/15 | 30,000 | 10,000 | 30,000 |
| March 2015 | 6.4.15 | 2015/16 pre-alignment | 60,000 | 20,000† | 30,000† |
| March 2016 | 6.4.16 | 2015/16 post-alignment | 20,000 | –† | 30,000† |

* Although there is £30,000 (net) in unused relief, only relief relating to the three preceding tax years is available, so the £20,000 in relation to 2013/14 must be used up in 2016/17 or it will be lost. Any excess each year over the current annual allowance is set against the oldest available relief.

† The contribution in March 2015 fell into a PIP that ended in 6 April 2015, ie, in 2015/16. That year was split into pre- and post-alignment periods, with an annual allowance in the period to 8 July 2015 of £80,000, so the £60,000 contribution left £20,000 unused. The annual allowance for the post-alignment period to 5 April 2016 was £nil, but Stephen was entitled to carry forward the unused £20,000 from the pre-alignment period, so he was able to use up the whole £80,000 allowance in the tax year 2015/16, leaving just the brought forward unused relief to carry forward.

Technically, Stephen had three PIPs ending in 2015/16, all counting towards the annual allowance – although there were revised limits for 2015/16 only. Stephen's PIPs are:

- PIP ended 6 April 2015 – contribution £60,000
- Period from 7 April 2015 to 8 July 2015 – no contributions made
- Period from 9 July to 5 April 2016 – contribution £20,000

**Explanatory note 3** sets out the special rules for 2015/16 in more detail.

Stephen is also likely to be affected by the tapering of annual allowance in 2016/17. With income of £200,000 before contributions, his annual allowance for 2016/17 will be reduced by £25,000 ((£200,000 – £150,000) ÷ 2) to £15,000. He will, however, still be able to bring forward the unused relief of £30,000 from the past three years and pay up to £45,000 without incurring an annual allowance charge. This is explained in more detail in **Explanatory note 4.**

## C.

### (a) *Dr Jolly adjusted profits of year to 31 December 2016*

| | £ | £ |
|---|---|---|
| Profits before superannuation adjustments | | 112,500 |
| *Add*: Charged in accounts for Dr Jolly | | |
| Employer's contribution | 10,424 | |
| Employee's contribution | 4,468 | 14,892 |
| Net profit for tax purposes | | 127,392 |

### Note

No adjustment is required for staff superannuation provided the amount charged in the accounts is equal to the amount paid in the accounting period (FA 2004 s 196).

### (b) *Relief for superannuation paid*

Dr Jolly is a member of the National Health Service Pension Scheme, which is a registered pension scheme. Relief is, therefore, available for contributions paid within the fiscal year.

In the year 2016/17 the amount paid was:

| | | £ |
|---|---|---|
| 30.04.16 | Quarterly payment | 2,965 |
| 20.05.16 | Settlement for 2015/16 | 3,983 |
| 31.07.16 | Quarterly payment | 3,113 |
| 30.10.16 | Quarterly payment | 3,113 |
| 31.01.17 | Quarterly payment | 3,113 |
| 02.04.17 | Settlement for 2016/17 | 3,975 |
| Claim in 2016/17 tax return (box 3 on page TR4) | | 20,262 |

## (c) *Tax Liability of Dr Jolly for 2016/17*

| | | | £ | |
|---|---|---|---|---|
| Self-employed earnings | | | 127,392 | |
| Bank interest received (1,100 less 500 personal savings allowance) | | | 600 | |
| Dividends | | | 5,300 | |
| | | | 133,292 | |
| Superannuation paid | | | 20,262 | |
| | | | 113,030 | |
| Personal allowance* | | | 10,110 | |
| Taxable income | | | 102,920 | |
| Tax thereon: | | | | |
| Earned income | 32,000 | @ 20% | 6,400 | |
| | 11,250 | @ 20%** | 2,250 | |
| Earned and savings income | 54,370 | @ 40% | 21,748 | |
| Dividends in higher rate band | 5,000 | @ 0% | – | |
| | 300 | @ 32½% | 97 | |
| | 102,920 | | | 30,495 |
| Class 4 national insurance | | | | |
| On 43,000 – 8,060 | @ 9% | | 3,145 | |
| On 127,392 –43,000 | @ 2% | | 1,688 | 4,833 |
| Total Liability | | | | 35,328 |

| | | |
|---|---|---|
| * Adjusted net income for personal allowance restriction | | |
| Net income as above | | 113,030 |
| Less: Gross pension contributions | £8,000 × 100/80 | (10,000) |
| Less: Gross Gift aid donation | £1,000 × 100/80 | (1,250) |
| Adjusted net income – reduces personal allowance by £890 ((101,780 – 100,000) ÷ 2) | | 101,780 |
| ** Basic rate band is extended by: | | |
| Gross pension contributions (paid net) 8,000 × 100/80 | | 10,000 |
| Gross Gift Aid payments 1,000 × 100/80 | | 1,250 |
| | | 11,250 |

## Explanatory Notes

(1) From 6 April 2006 the previous tax provisions relating to occupational and personal pension schemes were replaced by a single scheme for all registered pension schemes. Finance Act 2011 made a number of major changes to the existing pension regime, reducing the annual allowance from 2011/12, the lifetime allowance from 6 April 2012, and removing the requirement to annuitise from 6 April 2011. Further changes have been made by Finance Act 2013, with the reduction of the annual allowance to £40,000, and the lifetime allowance to £1.25 million with effect from April 2014 until April 2016, after which it became £1 million. The Taxation of Pensions Act 2014 introduced new flexibility into how pensions are drawn, while Finance (No 2) Act 2015 and Finance Act 2016 introduced further reforms, in particular to ensure PAYE was due on payments and to relax how death benefits are treated.

Pension providers are able to invest in many types of investment, excluding direct investment in residential property, and certain tangible moveable property where the policy holder can influence investment decisions (FA 2004 Sch 29A). The borrowing limits are restricted, normally to a maximum of 50% of the fund value. The minimum pension age is now 55 (earlier retirement still being permitted on ill health grounds). It is expected that the age at which an individual can access their pension will be increased to 57 from April 2028 and then aligned at ten years before state pension age.

*Pension inputs (FA 2004 s 229)*

(2) A pension input is the amount contributed to a pension policy in a pension input period plus the increase in value of defined pension benefits. Where the amounts contributed are in cash or equivalent they are easily valued. Where the pension scheme provides a defined benefit then the scheme administrator will compute the increase in value of the pension benefits using the formula.

| | |
|---|---|
| (Opening Benefits × 16) + Lump Sum = | X |
| (Closing Benefits × 16) + Lump Sum = | Y |
| Increase | Z |

The opening value of benefits is uprated for inflation each April by applying the CPI increase for the previous September (ie, in the same way as SERPS and S2P pensions are uprated).

The administrator of each fund will produce a figure for each member. Where, exceptionally, the difference is a decrease the amount will be deemed to be nil. Therefore, all positive increases are aggregated with the contributions paid by the member, or others (eg his employer) to the defined contribution fund. The sum is known as 'total pension input'. This is used to test against the annual allowance (see **explanatory note 6** below).

There is no pension input if, before the end of the tax year, the member has died, or taken all of the benefits available from that fund as a result of retirement due to serious ill health.

A 'pension input period' ('PIP') is defined in FA 2004 s 238. A PIP commences for a registered pension scheme when the individual's rights begin to accrue, or in the case of a money purchase scheme, the date of payment of the first premium. The period used to end, until 2016/17, on the date nominated by the scheme administrator, however the period could not exceed one year. This was to allow maximum flexibility to scheme administrators. Typically, the nominated date would be the end of the tax year, or the scheme accounting year end. Each subsequent PIP was for 12-months until all benefits had been provided under the pension arrangements. From April 2011, the default date for the end of the pension input period was 5 April following the date the member joined the scheme. In 2015/16, all PIPs were aligned by bringing existing non-5 April periods to an end by 8 July 2015, granting a double annual allowance for that first part of the year, and creating a new, separate, PIP for the period from 9 July 2015 to 5 April 2016 into which up to £40,000 of unused annual allowance could be brought forward from the pre-alignment period. For 2016/17, all PIPs are aligned with the tax year.

However, for members of schemes before April 2006, the pension input period was usually 6 April rather than 5 April. This produced a one-year misalignment between the tax year for which figures were reported on the tax return, and the pension input period ending in the tax year, which determined whether the annual allowance for the year had been fully utilised. **Part (b)** of the Example illustrates this. If Stephen's pension input period had ended on 5 April rather than 6 April, the amount of unused relief would have been arrived at differently:

| Contribution paid in | PIP ending on | Tax year in which PIP ended | Contribution paid | | Available unused relief |
|---|---|---|---|---|---|
| | | | £ | | £ |
| March 2013 | 5.4.13 | 2012/13 | 30,000 | | 20,000 |
| March 2014 | 5.4.14 | 2013/14 | 40,000 | | 10,000 |
| March 2015 | 5.4.15 | 2014/15 | 60,000 | | (20,000) |
| March 2016 | 5.4.16 | 2015/16 post-alignment | 20,000 | | 20,000 |
| March 2017 | 5.4.17 | 2016/17 | ? | Net total | 30,000 |

So the total premium that might be paid without triggering the annual allowance charge in March 2017 is £70,000 (£40,000 for the year and £30,000 brought forward). In this example, the PIP amounts and the amounts entered on the tax return are identical, whereas in the example above, they were one year out of synchronisation. The pension input periods in 2015/16 will still be adjusted, even though they are already aligned with the tax year, so the PIPs ending in 2015/16 will be the period from 6 April 2015 to 8 July 2015 (no contributions were paid, though, meaning that up to £40,000 of the £80,000 of the annual allowance could be carried forward to the post-alignment period) and that from 9 July 2015 to 5 April 2016. If Stephen had by chance made a contribution already in 2015 – before 8 July, he would in fact have been able to gain up to a further £40,000 in relief. For more information on the special rules for 2015/16 see the Example, and **explanatory note 3**.

Calculation of the pension input amount for defined benefit schemes is more complex, as illustrated in the following example.

**Example**

John is entitled to a pension on 1/60th of final salary plus 3/80ths lump sum. He had 15 years' service as at 6 April 2014, the commencement of the pension input period, and a salary of £48,000 per annum. Assume that CPI increase for the year was 3.1%. By 5 April 2015 his salary had increased to £65,000 per annum. John's pension input for 2014/15 was

| | | £ | £ |
|---|---|---|---|
| Opening value | 15/60ths × £48,000 × 16 | 192,000 | |
| | 45/80ths × £48,000 | 27,000 | 219,000 |
| Add CPI inflation adjustment | 219,000 × 3.1% | | 6,789 |
| | | | 225,789 |
| Closing value | 16/60ths × £65,000 × 16 | 277,333 | |
| | 48/80ths × £65,000 | 39,000 | 316,333 |
| Pension input | | | 90,544 |
| Annual allowance limit 2014/15 | | | (40,000) |
| Excess contribution | | | 50,544 |

John is entitled to obtain tax relief on contributions paid to all schemes to the maximum of his earnings for the year chargeable to UK tax. However, as his contributions exceed £40,000 (the annual allowance permitted for 2014/15) he will attract an annual allowance charge of 40% (his marginal rate of income tax) on the excess unless he has unused relief available in any of the three preceding years. If he has not had a previous substantial pay rise, it is likely that he has available unused relief which will eliminate the tax charge in 2014/15.

Because the calculation of pension inputs cannot be made until after the end of the pension input period John will have to estimate his pension input from the defined benefits scheme to determine the amount he wishes to contribute; this will be an ongoing issue for those wishing to top up their pension arrangements by the payment of AVC's or other freestanding contributions. It is particularly difficult where pay rises are awarded to DB scheme members with effect from 1 April each year: the CPI increase from the previous September will be known in time to perform a check before the end of the tax year, but the calculation of the closing value will not be known until any pay rises are notified, which may be on 31 March. Since most DB scheme members will rely on the scheme administrators to calculate and notify the pension input, they are unlikely to know by 5 April how much they could safely pay in AVCs without triggering an annual allowance charge.

*Alignment of PIPs to the tax year 2015/16*

(3) To facilitate changes to the annual allowance for high earners in 2016/17 (see below) pension input periods needed to be aligned to the tax year. This change was done in 2015/16 as follows:

- All PIPs for members of schemes came to an end on 8 July 2015
- New PIPs commenced on 9 July 2015 which all ran until 5 April 2016

For PIPs ending in the period from 6 April 2015 to 8 July 2015 (known as the pre-alignment period) there was an annual allowance of £80,000. The annual allowance for the post-alignment period – from 9 July 2015 to 5 July 2016 was zero, but the taxpayer could carry forward up to £40,000 of unused relief from the pre-alignment period. This carry forward had to be used before any unused relief from earlier years could be accessed. If unused, it could be carried forward from 2015/16.

For defined benefit schemes with a PIP ending on 5 April each year, the pension input had to be calculated for the whole year, as illustrated above, then time-apportioned to the pre- and post-alignment years for comparison with the transitional annual allowance (see example 'Jill' below).

*Restricted annual allowance from 2016*

(4) The alignment of PIPs to the tax year enables changes to the annual allowance for higher earners, which are restricted by a taper calculation for 2016/17 onwards. Although ostensibly the tapered annual allowance applies to additional rate taxpayers, the definition of a "high income individual" brings in some individuals who are not, in fact liable to income tax at 45%.

**High income individual**

An individual is a high income individual if

- the individual's 'adjusted income' for the year is more than £150,000, and
- the individual's 'threshold income' for the year is more than £150,000 minus the annual allowance amount before taper (so currently £110,000).

'Adjusted income' is the net income at Step 2 in section 23 of ITA 2007, plus:

- relief under s 193(4) or 194(1) FA 2004 deducted in arriving at Step 2 (relating to pension arrangements),
- any deductions made from employment income for that year in respect of pension contributions made under net pay arrangements,
- the total pension input amount for the tax year less any contributions made by the individual as a member of any scheme, and
- taxable lump sums received under pension schemes.

'Threshold income' is the Step 2 net income as before, plus

- salary sacrifice amounts in relation to pension contributions where the agreement was entered into on or after 9 July 2015
- the amount of contribution paid in the year in respect of which the individual is entitled to be given relief under s 192 FA 2004 (relief at source), and
- taxable lump sums as above.

If the individual is affected by these rules, the annual allowance is tapered by 50% of the excess of the adjusted income over the limit of £150,000. Note that the adjusted income includes employer pension contributions, so if these are substantial, this is likely to trigger the limit.

In simple terms, adjusted income is taxable income plus any pension inputs for the year. Threshold income is taxable income without pension inputs. The aim of the rules is to prevent the highest earners from avoiding the 45% tax rate by having their employers make their pension contributions.

**Example**

Stella is the headmistress of a substantial private school. Her salary is £140,000 per annum and she is a member of the school's final salary pension scheme with a PIP ending on 5 April each year. Her calculated pension input amount for 2016/17 is £39,554. She has no other income and no deductions in her tax computations in 2016/17.

| | | £ |
|---|---|---|
| Adjusted income: | | |
| | Salary | 140,000 |
| | Pension input | 39,554 |
| | | 179,554 |

So Stella's adjusted income exceeds the limit. Her threshold income is £140,000 (her salary) so she is a high income individual, and her annual allowance will be tapered.

The annual allowance for 2016/17 is calculated as follows:

| | £ |
|---|---|
| Standard allowance | 40,000 |
| Less (179,554 – 150,000) ÷ 2 | (14,777) |
| Annual allowance limit 2016/17 | 25,223 |

Bearing in mind that her salary level means that she has no personal allowance, Stella has an excess contribution of £14,331 (39,554 – 25,223), on which tax is due at 40% and 45% giving a total tax charge of £5,949 (£10,000 at 40% and £4,331 at 45%).

*Annual allowance – excess contributions (FA 2004 s 227)*

(5) Where 'total pension inputs' are in excess of the annual allowance for the fiscal year, then the excess is subject to the 'annual allowance charge' depending on the member's marginal rate of tax. This is entered on to the self-assessment tax return additional information pages at box 10 on page Ai 4.

**Example**

Jill has been notified by the scheme administrators of her defined benefits pension scheme that, following a substantial pay rise, the 'pension input' for the year 2015/16 was £90,000. Jill had available unused relief brought forward of £15,000, so she faces an annual allowance tax charge. Her income for 2015/16 (after personal allowances) was £45,000, making her a higher rate taxpayer.

When Jill completes her Self-Assessment Tax Return for 2015/16 she will have to enter an annual allowance charge computed as follows:

| | | Pre-alignment | Post-alignment |
|---|---|---|---|
| | £ | £ | £ |
| Time-apportionment | | 94/366 | 272/366 |
| Total pension input | 90,000 | 23,115 | 66,885 |
| Annual allowance 2014/15 | | (23,115) | *(40,000) |
| Brought forward unused relief | 15,000 | — | (15,000) |
| Excess chargeable | | | 11,885 |

* AA for pre-alignment period was £80,000, for post-alignment period was £nil, but up to £40,000 could be carried forward from the pre-alignment period.

As Jill's marginal rate of tax is 40% and the excess contribution does not take her above £150,000, the full amount is taxed at 40%: £4,754.

In 2015/16, although the tax year was split into two for the purposes of the annual allowance, there was only a single annual allowance charge. The comparison of the contributions with the annual allowance was done separately for the pre- and post-alignment periods, but a single annual allowance charge arose if the limit was exceeded. The annual allowance for the year 2015/16 is described in **explanatory note 3**.

*The way tax relief is given (FA 2004 ss 190 to 201)*

(6) The way in which tax relief is granted depends upon the way in which the contributions are paid. All personal pensions give relief at source. Employers' schemes can be trust-based (ie, the contributions are pooled in one fund held by a trustee company) or contract-based (ie, the employer pays the contributions into separate funds for each member).

Employer contributions are always paid gross and do not affect payroll taxes, or the employees' tax returns, except where an annual allowance charge must be self-assessed.

Members' own contributions to contract-based schemes (eg, group personal pensions, NEST, etc) are paid net of basic rate tax, ie, out of net pay (s 192). Relief is therefore granted as follows:

Basic rate – at source (the pension fund reclaims the basic rate tax from HMRC and grosses up any contributions made from net pay by 100/80)

Higher rate – basic rate relief is given at source, and the extra 20% is claimed by way of the self-assessment tax return (or adjusted PAYE coding notice).

Higher rate relief is normally obtained by increasing the basic rate band for income tax by the gross pension contribution (s 192(4)). This effectively increases both the higher rate threshold and the additional rate threshold, albeit only in terms of the collection mechanism rather than total liability. When calculating income for age allowance purposes and restriction of personal allowance for those with income of more than £100,000, the gross pension payment is deducted from income (s 192(5)).

If a member pays a contribution to the employer's trust-based occupational scheme, the contribution is paid to the pension provider gross. Tax relief is effectively given to the member by the net pay scheme (s 193). This means that the gross pension contributions are deducted from earnings for PAYE (but not NI) and relief given by taxing pay net of pension contributions.

Because employer-deducted contributions to trust-based schemes are excluded from earnings, relief for higher rate tax is given automatically. If an employer-deducted contribution cannot be relieved by deduction from earnings (eg, payment made after month 12 payroll has been processed) or where earnings are not liable to PAYE, such as benefits, then the employee makes a claim on the self-assessment tax return, and earnings are reduced by the unrelieved premiums paid.

Retirement annuity premium (RAP) contributions, that is policies effected prior to 1 July 1988, continue to be paid gross unless the policy has been converted by the provider to relief at source (s 194). Relief for premiums paid gross is given by reducing earnings by the pension contributions made when computing total income (s 194(1)). The claim is normally made in the tax return.

A member may contribute up to £2,880 pa in cash to a personal or 'stakeholder' pension (whether under an individual or a group arrangement), with basic rate relief given at source, so the contribution is equivalent to £3,600 pa gross, even if the member has no taxable earnings. The tax relief is given automatically because the pension premium is paid net of the basic rate tax that the provider reclaims from HMRC. There is no recovery of the tax deducted at source.

If contributions in excess of the annual allowance are paid then the excess is clawed back by the 'annual allowance charge' of 40% (or 45%).

Where tax is deducted at source on an amount in excess of £3,600, and earnings are nil (or less than £3,600 pa), then the first £2,880 of the payment will be deemed to be a net pension contribution and the excess will be deemed to be a gross pension payment on which no tax relief is available. Some pension providers will agree to refund any excess premiums paid, provided the refund is claimed within six years of the end of the tax year in which the contributions were made. This is known as a 'refund of excess contributions lump sum' and is an authorised payment by the scheme (FA 2004, Sch 29 para 6) that is not taxable (ITEPA 2003, s 636A). It also does not count as a benefit crystallisation event, nor does it trigger a lifetime allowance test. The following example illustrates how such a situation can occur.

Jack, a self-employed builder, normally makes reasonable profits and pays a net pension contribution of £500 per month by automatic direct debit. His accounts for the year ended 31 January 2016 were affected by a large bad debt and show a tax-adjusted net profit of £2,800. He has no other earnings.

| | |
|---|---|
| Jack is entitled to tax relief in 2015/16 on the higher of | |
| – 100% earnings = | 2,800 |
| – or | 3,600 |
| In 2015/16 Jack has paid pension contributions (net) of | |
| 12 × 500 = | 6,000 |
| Maximum allowable (£3,600 × 80% =) | 2,880 |
| Gross pension contribution (no relief available) | 3,120 |
| Total pension contribution paid by Jack (net) | 6,000 |
| Tax repaid to pension scheme (£3,600 × 20%) | 720 |
| Amount added to Jack's pension scheme | 6,720 |

The pension provider must be informed, as it will have claimed £1,500 in tax relief from HMRC, which must be corrected.

*Lifetime limit (FA 2004 ss 214 to 226)*

(7) When pension benefits, other than State Pensions, are drawn there is a 'benefit crystallisation event'. At that time it is necessary to check the amount of pension funds used against the lifetime limit. If the amount is below the lifetime limit then full benefits can be paid with no additional tax charge. If a previous 'benefit crystallisation event' has used part of the lifetime limit then only the remaining percentage of the limit for the current year can be applied.

**Example of one fund and one crystallisation**

George has a pension fund of £1.75 million and is aged 75 next week. He wishes to take the maximum amount as a lump sum using the balance to buy a pension. The lifetime limit for 2016/17 is £1 million. Ignore transitional rules.

| | £ | £ |
|---|---|---|
| Value of fund | 1.750,000 | |
| Maximum tax-free lump sum | | |
| 25% x £1 million | 250,000 | 250,000 |
| | 1,500,000 | |
| Balance of lifetime limit used to | | |
| buy a pension (75% x 1 million) | 750,000 | |
| Excess | 750,000 | |
| Lifetime allowance charge | | |
| Taken as lump sum – 55% | 412,500 | 337,500 |
| Maximum lump sum | | 587,500 |

If George had not wished to take the excess as a lump sum but instead wished to buy a pension then the tax charge would be as follows:

| | £ |
|---|---|
| Excess of fund | 750,000 |
| Lifetime allowance charge – 25% of £750,000 | (187,500) |
| Available to buy pension | 562,500 |

Effectively the tax charge will be identical as when the pension is taken it will be taxable income liable at say 40% therefore the tax due on the pension will be:

| | £ |
|---|---|
| 40% x £562,500 (assumed pension received) | 225,000 |
| Lifetime allowance charge @ 25% of £750,000 | 187,500 |
| Giving total of | 412,500 |

Thus the total tax collected by HMRC is 55% of £750,000 in each instance.

In practice very few members will have only one fund, or will draw the whole of their fund on one occasion. Where there are multiple withdrawals then the test has to be done each time benefits crystallise. The percentage of the lifetime allowance that has been used is calculated and only the remaining percentage of the later year's lifetime allowance will be available for later benefits.

**Example of two crystallisations**

William had a 'benefit crystallisation event' in 2007/08 using £1 million of his pension funds.

He had a further 'benefit crystallisation event' in 2015/16 using £700,000 of his pension fund. The lifetime allowance limit in 2015/16 was £1,250,000.

| | |
|---|---|
| 2007/08 Lifetime limit | £1.6 million |
| 'Benefits crystallisation event' fund used | £1 million (ie 62.5% of lifetime limit) |

| | £ |
|---|---|
| 2015/16 Lifetime limit | 1,250,000 |
| Deemed used in 2007/08 62.5% x £1.25 million | (781,250) |
| Available lifetime allowance | 468,750 |
| Crystallised 2015/16 | 700,000 |
| Lifetime allowance excess chargeable | 231,250 |

There will be no charge on any other pension funds held until they have a 'benefit crystallisation event'. Then, as the whole 100% of the lifetime allowance has been used, the fund value on crystallisation will be chargeable. Had William chosen to take fixed protection from April 2012, he would have retained the lifetime limit of £1.8 million, and his available lifetime allowance would have been higher, leaving a much smaller tax charge. However, he is out of time to elect for this, and would not have been able to add to his pension fund after 6 April 2012 should he have made the election.

Individual Protection 2014 (IP14) may be beneficial to him, if we assume that the crystallisation is of his remaining pension savings.

IP14 calculates the 'relevant amount' as the sum of A, B, C and D, as follows:

- A is the value of pre-2006 pensions in payment (none in this case)
- B is the value of any pre-2014 benefit crystallisation events: this is £1 million;
- C is the uncrystallised amount in registered pension schemes at 6 April 2014 – which we have assumed is the amount now to be crystallised of £700,000; and
- D is the uncrystallised amount in relieved non-UK pension schemes at 6 April 2014.

So William's relevant amount is £1,000,000 + £700,000 = £1,700,000

IP14 then sets the lifetime allowance for William at £1,500,000 (See explanatory note 7(c)) so the computation would be:

| | |
|---|---|
| 2007/08 Lifetime limit | £1.6 million |
| 'Benefits crystallisation event' fund used | £1 million (ie 62.5% of lifetime limit) |
| 2015/16 Lifetime limit with IP 14 | £1,500,000 |
| Deemed used in 2007/08 62.5% × £1.5 million | (£975,000) |
| Available lifetime allowance | £525,000 |
| Crystallised 2015/16 | £700,000 |
| Lifetime allowance excess chargeable | £175,000 |

**Pensions in payment as at 6 April 2006**

If an individual had a pension in payment as at 6 April 2006 then immediately before the first 'benefit crystallisation event' occurring there is a deemed 'benefit crystallisation event', the amount of the lifetime limit used is

25 × existing annual pension in payment

If the individual had a pre-6 April 2006 income withdrawal then the existing pension is deemed to be 120% of the standard annuity (see **explanatory note 7**) regardless of the amount actually drawn.

If the individual took a tax free lump sum prior to 6 April 2006 then that amount when aggregated with the lump sum to be taken must not exceed 25% of the lifetime allowance.

In practice many individuals with existing vested policies or pensions in payment will use the transitional provisions (see **explanatory note 8** below). Enhanced protection is available if no pension contribution, or increases in benefit rights, occur after 5 April 2006 even if the 'A day value' of the funds was below £1,500,000. This enables the benefits to be taken after 5 April 2006 without consideration of the lifetime allowance. The maximum tax-free lump sum may still be restricted.

*Drawdown pensions (FA 2004 s 165)*

(8) A drawdown pension is currently available from age 55. On commencing drawdown there is a benefit crystallisation event. At that time tax-free cash can be taken up to 25% of the fund. The amount designated

as available to pay the drawdown pension plus the tax-free cash taken is treated as the amount crystallised (s 216(1)(b)1).

The balance of the fund must then be used to pay a pension each year. The pension will be taxable and subject to PAYE. There is no minimum withdrawal and the maximum withdrawal for those who crystallised their pension before 6 April 2015 was 150% (see answer A pension benefits above) of the government standard annuity which could be purchased with the value of the fund. This is calculated when the benefits are first drawn and recalculated every three years thereafter. At age 75 it is recalculated every year. The amount taken can be varied each year. There is no maximum drawdown for those taking their pension benefits from 6 April 2016 onwards, but the amounts drawn as pension are taxed as income on the pensioner. The maximum lump sum at each benefit crystallisation event is 25% of the fund, and any additional amounts drawn will be taxed as pension income of the pensioner.

If the pensioner dies before age 75 and before a pension is bought then the fund can be used:

- to buy a pension for spouse or other dependant, or
- to provide a drawdown pension for spouse.

*Transitional provisions (FA 2004 Sch 36)*

(9) Existing pension rights as at 6 April 2006 could be preserved by using the following provisions from Finance Act 2004. The freezing of the standard lifetime allowance for five years may have implications for those seeking to benefit from transitional relief. Some individuals may consider drawing benefits earlier than previously planned to avoid future growth causing a charge.

**Primary protection (Sch 36 para 7)**

(a) Primary protection is given to any pension member who had a fund valued in excess of £1.5 million as at 6 April 2006. The pension member was required to give notice to HMRC. Notice must have been given by 6 April 2009.

Where notice was given then there will be an enhancement to the lifetime limit. This is calculated as:

$$\frac{\text{Fund value @ 6 April 2006} - \text{£1.5 million}}{\text{£1.5 million}} \times \text{Lifetime Limit}$$

For example if Alison had a fund of £2 million as at 6 April 2006 then the lifetime limit enhancement will have been:

$$\frac{\text{£2 million} - \text{£1.5 million}}{\text{£1.5 million}}$$

= 33⅓% (expressed as a percentage)

Therefore in a later year, say 2010/11, the lifetime limit for Alison would have been the actual limit of £1.8 million × 133⅓% = £2.4 million.

**Enhanced protection (Sch 36 para 12)**

(b) Where a pension fund member had relevant pension arrangements that became registered pension schemes on 6 April 2006 and had ceased active membership of all registered pension schemes then enhanced protection was available from 6 April 2006. There was no minimum fund value to claim enhanced protection.

If the member has **any** pension input then the value of enhanced protection is lost and only primary protection is available. This applies to contributions made or benefits uprating received on or after 6 April 2006.

Where the member has elected for enhanced protection then there will be no lifetime charge when a pension and tax-free lump sum are drawn. The tax-free lump sum is still restricted to 25% (or a lower specified percentage) of the fund value.

If the member makes any contribution, or his benefits are enhanced, or the member wishes to withdraw his notice then enhanced protection may be replaced by primary protection.

**Fixed protection**

(c) When the annual allowance reduced to £1.5 million on 6 April 2012, scheme members were able to register for fixed protection to retain the benefit of the previous limit of £1.8 million. They were required to elect for this in writing by 6 April 2012, and could not make any additional pension contributions after that date, nor could they acquire any additional pension rights. Those scheme members who wished to continue to contribute to a scheme will therefore not have been able to make an election for fixed protection. Members needed to notify their employer not to auto enrol them in a scheme from October 2012 onwards when auto-enrolment started to roll out, as this would compromise their fixed protection election.

A further fixed protection election was available in April 2014 for those who had not previously elected to protect their lifetime limit from reductions. The election must be made by 5 April 2017. This is termed 'fixed protection 2014' or 'FP14' and is similar in effect to the fixed protection described above for the 2012 change. Individual Protection 2014 ('IP14') was introduced by Schedule 6 of the Finance Act 2014, which set the individual's personal lifetime allowance at:

- if the relevant amount was more than £1.5 million (as for William above), the greater of the standard lifetime allowance and £1.5 million; or
- otherwise, the greater of the standard lifetime allowance and the individual's relevant amount.

The calculation of the relevant amount is illustrated above for William (see **Explanatory note 7**). Note that for individual protection, it is not necessary to cease contributions to pension arrangements.

**Valuation of funds at 6 April 2006 for protection**

(d) In order to compute the value of a pension fund as at 6 April 2006 it is necessary to add the value of all uncrystallised funds, ie the monetary value of defined contribution funds, plus the annual rate of pension to which the member is entitled × 20, plus the lump sum to which the member is entitled. To this is added the value of all crystallised pensions, ie, pensions in payment (for this purpose the annual pension is multiplied by 25 to take into account the lump sum already taken) plus an amount equal to the value of benefits that were taken prior to 6 April 2006 wholly or mainly in the form of a tax-free lump sum. Where the taxpayer was making income withdrawals the pension used was the maximum available under the arrangements.

**Retirement before age 50 (Sch 36 paras 21–23)**

(e) If the pension member has the right to draw their pension because of their profession before age 50 (eg sportsmen) then that right is preserved providing it was in place as at 6 April 2006.

**Lump sums (Sch 36 paras 24–36)**

(f) Protection is provided for an accrued right to a lump sum in excess of £375,000 as at 6 April 2006.

This right is preserved by increasing the maximum lump sum accrued as at 6 April 2006 by the pro rata increase in the lifetime limit.

Justin was entitled to a lump sum as at 6 April 2006 of £600,000. He crystallised his pension in 2010/11 when the lifetime limit was £1.8 million. His maximum lump sum was then:

$$\frac{£1.8 \text{ million } (2010/11 \text{ limit})}{£1.5 \text{ million } (2006/07 \text{ limit})} \times £600{,}000 = £720{,}000$$

A further protection was available if under an occupational pension scheme the member was entitled to a lump sum that exceeded 25% of the uncrystallised rights as at 6 April 2006. This protection worked by computing the accrued lump sum as at 6 April 2006 and increasing that figure in line with the increasing lifetime limit as above. To that amount could be added 25% of the value of benefits that had accrued since 6 April 2006. If benefits are transferred from the scheme then protection is lost and only 25% of the fund is available as a lump sum.

*Funded unapproved retirement benefit scheme (FURBS)*

(10) Where contributions to an existing FURBS (funded unapproved retirement benefits scheme before 6 April 2006) have been taxed on the employee and the income and gains of the scheme have been taxed on the trustees *and* no further contributions are added from 6 April 2006 then any amounts paid out as a lump sum will be tax-free.

If contributions are added to the FURBS after 5 April 2006 only the value on 5 April 2006 increased by RPI will be tax-free.

*Unfunded unapproved retirement benefit schemes (UURBS)*

(11) Promised benefits under unfunded pre-2006 unapproved retirement benefit schemes do not constitute a pension input and do not give rise to a benefits in kind charge (because no payments are made into the scheme). When any benefits are drawn they will be taxable as pension income immediately. The employer (or former employer) only obtains tax relief when taxable benefits are paid.

Employer contributions to non-registered pension schemes are not tax deductible until the benefit is paid out to the employee.

*Employer-financed retirement benefit schemes (EFRBS)*

(12) The EFRBS replaced FURBS and UURBS in April 2006. Any contributions to EFRBS are irrelevant to the registered pensions regime introduced on A-day. EFRBS used since April 2011 may trigger tax charges under the disguised remuneration regime introduced as ITEPA 2003, Part 7A.

*Term assurance*

(13) Tax relief for term assurance written under pension rules has been withdrawn. Relief continues on policies taken out before 6 December 2006 provided the sum insured is not increased or the term extended (FA 2007 Sch 18). Where relief is available the premiums will be pension inputs counting towards the annual limit. Because those policies are registered pension schemes the potential proceeds will count towards the lifetime limit. Tax will be charged if the total proceeds plus other pension fund values exceed the lifetime limit (at 55% of the excess).

*Commutation of trivial pensions*

(14) To reduce the possibility of very small pension funds having to buy annuities at poor rates because of the administrative costs involved it has been possible, from 6 April 2006, to withdraw the whole amount on vesting provided this is allowed under the pension scheme's rules. The amount taken in excess of the tax-free sum is treated as pension income and is liable to income tax. Until 6 April 2015 this facility was only available where

– the total value of *all* pensions for that individual was less than £30,000 (from 27 March 2014 previously £18,000),

– the individual was aged at least 60,

– the whole of all funds were withdrawn within a 12-month period,

– all rights were extinguished by the payment from the fund.

In addition small pots to £10,000 (from 27 March 2014, previously £2,000) could be taken as a lump sum regardless of total pension wealth. This applied to up to three (from 27 March 2014 previously two) separate pension pots. All of these rules were updated by the pensions freedoms introduced by the Taxation of Pensions Act 2014 with effect from 6 April 2015 which allows benefits from money purchase arrangements to be taken as and when the pensioner decides (from the minimum pension age), with a tax-free lump sum of 25% and the balance drawn treated as taxable income of the year. The minimum age for both defined contribution and defined benefit schemes was reduced from 6 April 2015 to 55 (or earlier in ill-health cases) instead of 60. Otherwise, the rules for defined benefit schemes continue as described above.

*National insurance contributions*

(15) Registered pension premiums are not deducted from profits for Class 4 national insurance purposes (SSCBA 1992 Sch 2, para 3(2)). Nor do they reduce earnings for employers' and employees' Class 1 contributions (SI 2001/1004 para 24), although an *employer's* pension contributions to an employee's policy do not count as earnings for Class 1 purposes (see **explanatory note 19**).

*Losses*

(16) Where relief for losses is claimed under trade loss relief against general income (ITA 2007 s 64) or early trade loss relief (ITA 2007 s 72), the loss is set against total income, and no set-off order is specified. A s 64/s 72 claim may therefore be regarded for pension purposes as reducing non-trading income in priority to trading income, thus enabling relevant earnings of the claim year to be left at a higher level.

*Contracting out of S2P*

(17) When the state pension was restructured by Social Security Act 1975, introducing the state earnings-related pension scheme (SERPS), employers who already had earnings-related pension schemes in place were permitted to contract out of SERPS, provided the schemes took on the responsibility for paying what the state would have paid as a SERPS addition to the state basic pension, which was known as the contributor's 'protected rights'. Most occupational schemes, which were then nearly all final salary (defined benefit) schemes, provided for a better pension than SERPS, and part of the fund covered the protected rights obligations.

In 1998, contracting out by means of money purchase pension schemes was allowed for the first time, with the members' SERPS rights protected by requiring employers to pay minimum contributions that would suffice to pay the SERPS pension forgone. From 6 April 1998 until 5 April 2012, employers could contract their schemes out of SERPS (which became S2P in 2002 – see **explanatory note 18**) on a basis that was either defined benefit or money purchase.

Unless an employee was already in such a contracted out registered occupational scheme and paying rebated NI contributions, he could elect to contract out on a personal basis, whilst continuing to contribute for a basic retirement pension through NICs. Employees and employers still paid full NICs, but HMRC paid the combined employer/employee contracting-out rebate plus tax relief at the basic rate on the gross equivalent of the employee's share of the rebate to the pension provider after the end of the tax year (see **Example H1 part** (e)(i)).

The fund accumulated with such money purchase rebates was formerly (until abolition in April 2012) known as a protected rights fund. Benefits could be taken from age 60 onwards and had to be drawn by age 75. The fund could normally be commuted for a lump sum and the pension had to include provision for widows'/ widowers' pensions, just like the S2P pension it replaced.

Contracting out in respect of money purchase schemes ceased on 5 April 2012, and the rebate was abolished. Protected rights policies were thereafter treated like any other personal pension. There are now no restrictions on making direct contributions to such policies and members can draw benefits from age 55.

The rebate for contracted out defined benefit schemes, which was never paid into a protected rights policy because the occupational scheme took over the responsibility for paying the earnings-related pension, was reduced from April 2012 and abolished with the introduction of the new single-tier state pension in April

2016. All employees (except for a small number of women married before 11 May 1977 who made an election to reduce their NIC rate and rely on their husbands' NICs for their state pension) and their employers now pay standard rate NICs, with no interaction with the private pension regime.

*Upper accruals point*

(18) As part of state pension restructuring the upper accruals point (UAP) was introduced from 2009/10. This was separate from the upper earnings limit (UEL), which previously marked the limit of accrual of earnings-related benefits under SERPS/S2P. The UEL increased quite significantly in 2009/10 to align with the higher-rate tax threshold. The UAP introduced in 2009/10 and fixed at £40,040 pa was the earnings level above which no further earnings-related pension entitlement accrued, although it did not cap NIC liabilities. The UAP was abolished in April 2016, when the new single-tier state pension was introduced, because the new pension is no longer related to earnings, other than in requiring NICable earnings at the LEL if a year is to qualify towards entitlement.

*Employer contributions*

(19) An employer can contribute to the registered pension plan of an employee. As with employers' contributions to company schemes, the employer's contribution to an employee's registered pension scheme is not treated as the employee's earnings (ITEPA 2003 s 308), nor is it liable to employer's national insurance contributions (Social Security (Contributions) Regulations SI 2001/1004 para 24 and Sch 3 Part VI).

In view of the fact that employers' pension contributions are not liable to national insurance, whereas there is no national insurance saving on an employee's pension contributions, it could be tax-efficient for a salary sacrifice to be made by the employee, and for the employer to pay a pension contribution of the sacrificed amount boosted by the employer's national insurance saving. The cost to the employer would be the same. For example, if a basic rate taxpayer paid £80 a month into his personal pension the gross pension contribution would be £100. If he made a salary sacrifice of £117 per month, his net pay would reduce by the same amount, ie:

| | | | | |
|---|---|---|---|---|
| Gross pay | | | 117 | |
| Tax | @ 20% | 23 | | |
| Class 1 NI | @ 12% | 14 | 37 | £80 |

His employer could then contribute £117 plus the employer's NI of £117 @ 13.8% = £16, giving a gross pension contribution of (117 + 16 =) £133 per month.

This approach is effective at any level of contribution until the tapering rules for higher earners begin to apply. Those whose earnings plus pension contributions (employer plus employee) exceed £150,000 face a reduced annual allowance as described above. However, there is no annual allowance in the NIC exclusion for employer contributions, so even at higher levels of earnings there are potential advantages to sacrificing salary, bonuses or even termination compensation above £30,000 in exchange for extra employer pension contributions.

*Commissions on pension policies*

(20) HMRC issued a statement of practice SP 4/97 on their view of the tax treatment of commission, cashbacks and discounts. As far as pension policies were concerned, care had to be taken to ensure that commission arrangements did not jeopardise the tax approval of the fund (as to which see **explanatory note 23**). The main point is that the commission arrangements had to be under a separate contract. The pension contribution was treated as the net amount paid if the commission was deducted from the contribution or a discounted premium was paid. If the contribution was paid in full and the commission was received separately, tax relief was given on the full amount. A pension scheme's tax approval could be withdrawn if commission paid as a result of transfers between schemes represented an unauthorised payment.

The income position for the recipient of the commission was that it did not count as income if it was received by an ordinary member of the public. Commission passed on to customers by agents or employees of pension providers counted as part of the agent's or employee's income, but there was usually an offsetting expenses deduction. Commission on an employee's own contracts did not count as employment income if it was available on the same basis to the general public. Similar treatment applied by concession to the self-employed.

The question of commissions fell away following the introduction of advisory fees and the outlawing of commissions on pension investments under the Retail Distribution Review on 31 December 2012.

*Transfers between funds*

(21) Someone with a registered pension plan who enters pensionable employment may transfer his pension fund to the new employer's scheme or to another registered scheme, or to a qualifying recognised overseas pension scheme ('QROPS') without tax consequences.

*Mis-sold personal pension plans*

(22) Some employees were wrongly advised to opt out of their employers' schemes and take out personal pension plans funded by their own contributions. Where compensation is received for such wrong advice, the compensation is exempt from tax, although any interest added to the compensation is taxable.

*Unauthorised payments*

(23) Tax is charged at 40% on any unauthorised payments including recycled tax-free lump sums, non-arm's length transactions with a member, or employer (s 208), or on deregistration of the fund by HMRC (s 242). The tax is payable by the member (or employer) or, on deregistration, by the scheme administrator.

Where the total unauthorised payments in any 12-month period exceed 25% of the value of member's rights in the fund a further surcharge of 15% will apply (ss 209–213).

A further penalty known as a 'scheme sanction charge' will be imposed on the administrator at the rate of 40% of the relevant transaction. This applies where a fund borrows more than 50% of the fund value, or makes unauthorised payments (other than benefits in kind chargeable to income tax by FA 2004 s 173). Where the sanction charge applies as well as the unauthorised payment charge then the charge is reduced by the lower of the unauthorised payment charge or 25% of the chargeable figure, giving an effective rate of 15% (ss 239–241).

If Alan's pension fund was valued at £1,000,000 and the administrator made an unauthorised payment of £50,000 to Alan the charges would be:

| | | |
|---|---|---|
| | | £ |
| – On Alan 40% × £50,000 (s 208) | | 20,000 |
| – On the Administrator | | |
| 40% × £50,000 (s 239) | 20,000 | |
| Less tax paid by Alan restricted to | | |
| 25% × £50,000 | 12,500 | 7,500 |
| Effective rate of tax is 55% | | 27,500 |

If the payment had been £251,000 to Alan then there would be a surcharge on Alan of 15% (£5,209) giving a total charge of 70% (ie £251,000 × 70%=) £175,700.

*Pension splitting on divorce*

(24) A pension fund can be split on divorce without affecting the tax-free status of the fund. A divorcing couple will not be *required* to share pensions, but all schemes (whenever they were post-2006 registered or pre-2006 approved) are regarded as including pension sharing provisions. Where the pension is shared, the spouse/civil partner in a pension scheme will get reduced pension rights (a 'pension debit') and rights will be allocated to the other spouse/civil partner (a 'pension credit'). The pension credit received will count towards the lifetime allowance at a benefit crystallisation event. If the pension credit is a pension in payment then that pension will already have been applied against the other party's lifetime allowance. To prevent double counting, the recipient's lifetime allowance will be increased by an appropriate factor to reflect the

value of the pension arising from the pension credit (FA 2004 s 220). The pension credit to the transferee spouse/civil partner must be administered in the same way as for any other registered pension scheme. Benefits may be taken from age 55 with the usual options for a lump sum, drawdown pension etc. The pension splitting legislation applies to all types of pension arrangements other than the state pension.

*Stakeholder pensions*

(25) Stakeholder pensions were introduced in 2001 as a low cost personal pension. For a pension to qualify as a stakeholder pension, the costs must be restricted to 1% of the fund per annum. For those joining from 6 April 2005 the charges can be up to 1.5% of the fund value per year for the first 10 years and 1% thereafter. The investment fund can be chosen by the policyholder or be the default investment. That default may have a lifestyle feature allowing the insurer to move funds into low risk products as retirement approaches (SI 2005/577). The premiums must be able to be started or stopped at will and the minimum premium cannot exceed £20.

Until auto-enrolment was introduced on 1 October 2012 (see (34) below), all employers with five or more employees were required to provide employees with access to a registered stakeholder scheme, except as indicated below. That obligation has been replaced with a requirement to provide a qualifying workplace pension scheme and to automatically enrol workers, but some stakeholder schemes that meet the new criteria remain in operation.

Those who operated a qualifying salary-related occupational scheme that all relevant employees were eligible to join within one year of starting work, and those who offered a group registered pension to all relevant employees which had no exit charges, that was available after no more than thirteen weeks' service and to which the employer contributed at least 3% of earnings, did not have to offer a stakeholder scheme. Relevant employees were all employees employed in the UK except those whose earnings were below the lower earnings limit (£112 per week in 2016/17) at any time in the previous three months, those under 18 or within five years of normal pension age, employees who had been offered membership of an occupational pension scheme and had declined to join, and non-residents without UK net relevant earnings. If employees of non-exempt employers joined a scheme, employers had to deduct the net contributions from net pay if the employee so requested and forward them to the scheme provider by the 19th of the following month.

*Non-cash contributions to schemes*

(26) A provision may be made for contributions to be made not only in cash but by way of transfer of shares received under SAYE share option schemes, approved share incentive plans and approved profit sharing schemes (as to which see **Example N1**). Such transfers must be made within 90 days of exercising the SAYE option or of shares being appropriated to the employee. The shares will be treated as contributions equal to their market value at the date of the transfer. Tax relief will then be given on the contributions in the same way as for cash contributions (with the same annual allowance limits).

*Tax credits*

(27) Income for tax credits is reduced by tax-deductible pension contributions paid by the claimant or partner. The amount of the deduction is the gross allowable premium paid.

*Employer provided pensions – Deductible contributions*

(28) The limit on deductibility of contributions by most trading employers is the requirement that the expenditure be incurred wholly and exclusively for the purpose of the trade. In investment companies, contributions are treated as expenses of management. This will normally mean that all contributions paid in the chargeable period will be deductible (FA 2004 s 196). (See HMRC manuals at BIM 46001 for further guidance.)

In order for pension contributions paid to be allowable against trading profits they must form part of a normal remuneration package. They are not considered as a stand-alone amount. It follows that a salary sacrifice will not prevent a tax deduction. Contributions will be allowable if the overall salary package is a normal commercial amount.

It is likely that HMRC will disallow any amount identifiable as relating to a non-trade purpose, for example as part of arrangements to dispose of a business where the payment represents part of the sale proceeds, or of exceptional size.

The main focus of disallowances is likely to be in respect of directors who are controlling shareholders or their relatives/friends, and where the salary package has been significantly increased, eg, where funds previously taken as dividends are now taken as a pension contribution that makes the remuneration package so disproportionate that HMRC can show that it was not incurred wholly and exclusively for the purposes of the trade.

In the case of Harold and Frank they run a highly profitable trading company. HMRC would normally accept a remuneration package of any amount that could be funded by the efforts of the controlling directors. It follows that a total package that includes a bonus for earlier years, even though paid mainly as a pension, will be a commercial amount incurred 'wholly and exclusively' for the purpose of the trade. It is unlikely that a pension contribution of £550,000 or less would be challenged in this set of circumstances.

Where large contributions are made the relief may be spread. This applies where contributions are made in two consecutive chargeable periods and the amount paid in the current period exceeds 210% of the amount in the previous period. The excess over 110% is known as the 'relevant excess contribution' and is then subject to the following rules (FA 2004 s 197).

| | | | |
|---|---|---|---|
| (1) | If the excess is less than £500,000 | – | no restriction applies. |
| (2) | If the excess is between £500,000 and £999,999 | – | ½ allowed in current period<br>½ allowed in following period. |
| (3) | If the excess is between £1,000,000 and £1,999,999 | – | ⅓ allowed in current period<br>⅓ allowed in next period<br>⅓ allowed in following period. |
| (4) | If the excess is £2,000,000 or more | – | ¼ allowed in current period<br>¼ allowed in each of the following three periods. |

Where the previous and current chargeable periods are not of equal length the amount paid in the previous chargeable period is adjusted by applying the fraction:

$$\text{Contribution in previous period} \times \frac{\text{Days in current chargeable period}}{\text{Days in previous chargeable period.}} = \text{relevant contribution}$$

If the employer ceases trading before relief has been fully given for the spread contributions, the unrelieved contributions are deductible in the period of cessation or spread evenly over the period that starts on the first day of the current chargeable period (ie, the period of actual payment) and ends on the date of cessation (FA 2004 s 198).

*Self-administered schemes*

(29) Employers may use an insurance company to provide a registered pension scheme.

Employers can instead (or also) establish under trust a registered self-administered scheme receiving the pension premiums into a fund under the control of trustees, one of whom must be an appropriately qualified person, referred to as the pensioneer trustee. This may be done in conjunction with an insurance company, actuary or professional trustees.

This gives the employers flexibility over the investment of the fund pending its being required to pay the retirement benefits, but the employer must always remember that the fund is under the control of the trustees and that it must be sufficiently liquid at the right time to provide the retirement benefits.

The insurance company in the first case, and the pensioneer trustee in the second, will structure the scheme and register it with HMRC.

*Self-assessment*

(30) Trustees of registered pension schemes, other than insured schemes, are within the scope of self-assessment, and trustees are required to notify HMRC by 5 October following the tax year if they have a liability to tax and do not receive a return. The same self-assessment rules and time limits apply to trusts as for individuals. Pension fund trustees may complete returns on an accounting year basis and accounts should accompany the return. The return must be filed electronically.

Self-assessment does not apply to scheme administrators (although they may be the same people as the trustees), who have separate responsibility for notifying liability on various chargeable events. HMRC will issue assessments to collect the tax due.

*Pension inputs: annual allowance charge*

(31) To confirm that Dr Jolly is not liable to an annual allowance charge it is necessary to compare total pension inputs with the annual allowance for 2016/17.

| | £ |
|---|---|
| Pension inputs | |
| Defined benefits scheme (NHS) | |
| – per administrator | 29,950 |
| Defined contribution scheme | |
| – own pension (gross) | 10,000 |
| | 39,950 |

As £39,950 is less than the annual allowance for 2016/17 of £40,000 no annual allowance charge is payable.

It should be noted that the pensions input on a defined benefits scheme is calculated by reference to the increase in the benefits accruing: the amount paid into the scheme is irrelevant except for the purposes of the employer's tax deduction. See **explanatory note 5** for details of the calculation. In practice such calculations are undertaken by the pension scheme administrator.

*Relief for contributions paid*

(32) Tax relief is available for contributions paid, restricted to earnings of the year (see **explanatory note 7**). Where contributions are paid net of basic rate tax the basic rate band is extended by the grossed up pension contribution.

Normally contributions to a defined benefits scheme are paid via the employer and the net pay scheme is used to give relief (FA 2004 s 193). However, a GP doctor is self-employed and, therefore, relief cannot be given in that way. Instead the contributions actually paid in the fiscal year are deducted in arriving at taxable income. Relief is claimed on the self-assessment tax return by way of an entry into box 3 on page TR4. No deduction is permitted for any contribution of the taxpayer in computing the Class 4 national insurance contributions, other than in respect of employer contributions paid based on the earnings of the taxpayer's employees.

*Contributions by retired GP's*

(33) Tax relief is only due provided the payer has UK earnings. Because GP's make payments on account in respect of superannuation with a settlement when the annual return is submitted it is possible for payment of the final superannuation contribution to be made in the fiscal year after retirement. Insofar as the contribution exceeds earnings in that year, no relief will be given.

Should the final adjustment be a refund of contributions that should be credited against the actual payments made and an amended tax return filed, normally for the year of retirement.

*Auto-enrolment*

(34) Auto-enrolment started in October 2012 and the concept is very simple: employers are required to enrol staff in a qualifying workplace pension scheme, with a specified minimum rate of contribution, if they are not already in one. However, the implementation is anything but simple and what follows is a brief overview.

All employers with at least 'one worker' are subject to this legislation and non-compliance is subject to penalties. There is no exemption for small employers, but director-only companies have no responsibilities under auto-enrolment. The date that an employer must implement auto enrolment depends on the number of workers employed on 1 April 2012. Small employers (those with fewer than 30 workers) started to fall under the regime from 1 January 2016. Each employer is allocated an individual date of commencement known as their staging date. The staging date for these SMEs will fall between 1 January 2016 and 31 March 2017, determined by their PAYE employer reference number. New employers since April 2012 have a staging date set by reference to the first time they pay a worker. The staging date will fall between 1 May 2017 and 1 February 2018.

The staging date can be checked at http://www.thepensionsregulator.gov.uk/employers/tools/staging-date.aspx by entering the employer's PAYE reference number, although the Pensions Regulator is writing to all small employers at least 12 months before their staging date to ensure that they are aware of their responsibilities.

The staging date is the deadline by which an employer needs to have a qualifying pension scheme in place and be ready to enrol workers. (Although employers can ask to commence auto-enrolment early or to postpone the actual commencement of enrolling by up to three months.) The staging date is a date to work backwards from in terms of an action plan. The Pensions Regulator has published on its website a series of detailed guides to automatic enrolment aimed at employers, trustees, individuals, business advisers and the public sector.

http://www.thepensionsregulator.gov.uk/employers/the-essential-guide-to-automatic-enrolment.aspx

This sets out a number of steps to be followed and a complex step for some will be finding out who they need to enrol and who is allowed to join (opt in) when there is no auto-enrolment obligation (eg, because they do not earn enough). This will require the employer to go through all workers on an individual basis and review their circumstances. Some relevant definitions:

- A worker is 'an employee OR someone who has a contract to perform work or services personally, that is not undertaking the work as part of their own business'.
- Workers are then subdivided by their age and earnings into:
  - Eligible jobholders (who must be auto-enrolled)

    Working or ordinarily working in the UK, and

    Aged 22 to state pension age, and

    Earnings above the earnings triggers which for 2016/17 are:

  - Weekly: £192
  - Fortnightly: £384
  - Four-weekly: £768
  - Monthly: £833
  - Yearly: £10,000
  - Non-eligible jobholders (who are not required to be automatically enrolled but can choose to opt in)

Working or ordinarily working in the UK, and

Aged 16 to 21 or state pension age to 74 with qualifying earnings above the NIC LEL, (entitled to employer contributions) or

Aged 16 to state pension age with earnings above the NIC LEL but below the earnings trigger above (entitled to employer contributions).

- Entitled workers – have the right to join a pension scheme (but no entitlement to employer contributions)

Aged 16 to 74

Working or ordinarily working in the UK and

Earnings below the NIC LEL.

An employee is someone who works under a contract of employment. A director who works as an office holder with no employment contract will not be a 'worker'.

The definition of 'worker' is quite wide and it may be necessary to review the use of any agency workers and any self-employed contractors, for example a cleaner or maintenance person. Categorisation of workers is not a one-off task. It is ongoing and it is necessary to have in place mechanisms to monitor workers' ages / earnings and ensure they are categorised correctly as they cross the 22 / state pension age thresholds and the current earnings triggers. All workers must be informed by the employer of their rights under auto-enrolment.

Under auto-enrolment employers must register online with The Pensions Regulator and complete a declaration of compliance within five months of the staging date. This applies even if they have no employer duties for their workers. Employers also have a legal responsibility to let workers know how the reforms will affect them within certain time limits (including those workers who are not eligible) and any implications in relation to any existing pension schemes.

Once an eligible jobholder has been auto-enrolled he or she can opt out (within the first month) but there are rules to ensure this is not actively encouraged by the employer and every three years an employer has to re-enrol such workers (they can then again opt out). However, those who present a certificate of protection of their personal pension benefits to the employer (signalling that they have taken fixed or enhanced protection for their lifetime allowance) will not be auto-enrolled subsequently. Those with some of the forms of protection mentioned above on the introduction / reduction of the pension lifetime limit will need to opt out as a condition of their protection is no further pension contributions. Where workers opt out, they are treated as if they had never been in the pension scheme (any contributions made will be refunded). After the one month opt-out period, workers are free to leave the scheme at any time (subject to any employer practice's such as notice periods, no further pension contributions will be made).

Once workers have been enrolled, the legislation sets minimum levels of pension contributions for both the workers and the employer which increase in phases.

From 1 October 2012 until 5 April 2018, the minimum contribution is 2% of earnings between the NIC LEL and UEL ('band' earnings), of which the employer must bear at least half. The employee pays 0.8% out of net pay, which the pension scheme tops up to 1% with basic rate tax relief reclaimed from HMRC.

The combined rate then rises to 5% for one year, with the employer paying at least 2% and the employee 2.4% cash plus 0.6% tax relief.

The second planned rise, on 6 April 2019, is to a combined rate of 8%, with the employer paying 3% and the employee 4% plus 1% tax relief.

The worker's pension contributions are deducted from pay via the payroll and an authority to make such a deduction should be correctly documented in any employment contract.

The Pensions Regulator's 'Detailed guidance No 4 – pension schemes' gives guidance on choosing a pension scheme. NEST (the National Employment Savings Trust) is a government-backed online basic pension scheme designed to be the default automatic enrolment scheme for those employers who are of no interest to commercial pension providers because they are too small and likely to be unprofitable. Its key features for employees and employers are set out at http://www.nestpensions.org.uk/schemeweb/NestWeb/public/whatisnest/contents/whatisnest.html. Its use is not compulsory: employers can also set up their own scheme, use their existing scheme (if it qualifies or can be amended to qualify) or appoint other third party pension providers.

The Pensions Regulator has issued a very large volume of advice, some links to which are given above, in addition see websites listed below.

Various tools:
http://www.thepensionsregulator.gov.uk/en/employers

Creating an action plan:
http://www.thepensionsregulator.gov.uk/docs/detailed-guidance-2.pdf

Very long detailed advice aimed at advisers is at: http://www.thepensionsregulator.gov.uk/doc-library/automatic-enrolment-detailed-guidance.aspx#s11496

*Future pension changes*

(35) The government is still consulting on the future of pension saving, with all options being considered. The option of abolishing tax relief on contributions in exchange for tax-free pension income on retirement was considered, but the idea was poorly received and politically too risky. Instead, the government plans to introduce a new scheme intended to be attractive to the majority of savers and open to anyone between the ages of 18 and 40, without the complexity of pensions. This will be a new Lifetime ISA from April 2017 into which anyone will be able to save up to £4,000 per year, topped up by basic rate tax relief to £5,000. The fund will be available for use as a deposit on first home worth up to £450,000 and/or to save for retirement, withdrawal tax-free being an option from age 60. Earlier withdrawal will be subject to a clawback of the tax credit on contributions and a 5% penalty.

*Pension liberation fraud*

(36) Pension liberation fraud is where individuals are encouraged to access their pension savings before they reach retirement. The pension is transferred to a new registered pension scheme and then 'liberated' by the member, resulting in significant tax charges and promoter's fees. To counter this, FA 2014 s 43 introduced additional powers to enable HMRC to detect and prevent the registration of liberation schemes, and to detect and de-register liberation schemes already registered.

# Question

## A.

(a) Outline the basic principles of tax credits, setting out the criteria to be satisfied for eligibility for:

- (i) Working tax credit (WTC).
- (ii) Childcare element of WTC.
- (iii) Child tax credit (CTC).

(b) How is 'income' computed for tax credits?

(c) What changes in circumstances must be reported to HMRC, and by what date?

(d) What is an 'award period', and why are separate calculations required for each 'relevant period' within the award period?

(e) What information must be provided at the end of each fiscal year and how will underpayment/ overpayment of tax credits be dealt with?

## B.

(a) Brian and Angela Smith are married. Brian is self-employed preparing accounts to 31 December each year. Angela is employed. Both usually work more than 30 hours per week. They have one child, Joanna, aged 3. She attends an approved nursery costing £165 per week. Because Angela is pregnant she has increased the time Joanna spends at the nursery and from 5 January 2017 the cost increases to £200 per week. On 1 March 2017 Colin was born. No nursery costs were incurred for Colin in 2016/17. Angela was still on statutory maternity leave at 5 April 2017.

Their income for 2015/16 per their tax returns was:

| | | *Brian* | *Angela* |
|---|---|---|---|
| Self-employment | | 16,490 | |
| Per P60 | | | 22,700 |
| Per P11D | – Car | | 2,160 |
| | – Medical | | 640 |
| Investment income (gross) | | 180 | 520 |

Brian pays £133.33 per month (net) to a personal pension policy and Angela pays £40 (net) per month under gift aid to the local church.

Their income for 2016/17 per their tax returns was:

| | | *Brian* | *Angela* |
|---|---|---|---|
| Self-employment | | | |
| (Accounts y/e 31/12/16) – Loss | | (2,800) | |
| Per P60 | | | 16,100 |
| Per P11D | – Car | | 2,160 |
| | – Medical | | 700 |
| Investment Income (gross) | | 20 | 140 |

Included in Angela's P60 for 2016/17 is Statutory Maternity Pay of £2,326 for 10 weeks and Statutory Sick Pay of £193. Brian will make a claim under ITA 2007 s 64 to carry his loss back to 2015/16.

A renewal claim for tax credits for 2015/16 was filed by Brian and Angela on 30 July 2015 and renewal information provided on 6 July 2016. Notification of increase in nursery costs and the birth of Colin were given on 5 March 2017.

Compute the tax credits payable to Angela or Brian during 2016/17 (the provisional award), and the under/overpayment arising for 2016/17 after calculation of the final award.

(b) Re-compute the position on the assumption that instead of a loss the accounts of Brian for the year ended 31 December 2016 showed a profit of £34,000.

C.

(a) Describe the calculation of income for the self-employed for the purposes of Universal Credit.

# Answer

## A.

### (a) *Basic principles*

Tax credits were introduced as a form of 'negative income tax' with effect from 6 April 2003. The primary legislation is the Tax Credits Act (TCA) 2002 which is supplemented by numerous statutory instruments. The aim of the legislation is to provide help to those on low income who are working and those with children. The method of award is based upon the family unit. The claim is based on joint income of the couple where:

- this is a married couple living together and not permanently separated; or
- a man and a woman living together as husband and wife; or
- a same-sex couple (from 5 December 2005).

If the claimant is a lone parent or someone who is aged 25 or over and working at least 30 hours per week, then the claim is based on the income of that person. Special rules apply to those with a disability which puts them at a disadvantage in getting a job.

An award is made per day. The elements of tax credits are computed by dividing the yearly amount by the number of days in the tax year (SI 2002/2008 regs 6–9) and rounding up to the nearest penny. All days with the same entitlement within the award period are aggregated and are known as a 'relevant period'.

Income is based upon broadly the taxable income of the fiscal year. That is again divided by the number of days in the tax year and applied to the relevant periods.

The first award of tax credits is provisional and is based on the income of the preceding year, ie for 2016/17 the claim is initially based upon the income of 2015/16. The actual income of the award period is then compared with the income of the previous year when the award is finalised. If the income has increased, the income disregard applies to ignore the first element of the increase, only taking into account any additional increase. The income disregard is currently £2,500 (SI 2006/963 reg 4) (The original level of the disregard was £2,500. However, it was increased to £25,000 (to reduce administration) and then knocked back down to £10,000 and then £5,000 (2013/14 to 2015/16) when it was felt it was being used for tax planning). So if the income of 2015/16 used for the provisional award was £12,000, and the actual income for 2016/17 for was £30,000, the increase is £18,000. The first £2,500 of the increase is disregarded, making the income used to finalise the claim £27,500 (£12,000 + (£18,000 – £2,500)). There is also a disregard for income reductions of £2,500 (from 2012/13).

The claim must be made at the time that eligibility arises; an award can only be backdated up to one month prior to the date of submitting a completed claim. Thus to claim tax credits for 2016/17 in full a claim must be made by 6 May 2016. If, for example, a claim was submitted on 2 August 2016 then the award period would commence on 2 July 2016 and only 278 days of credits would be payable for 2016/17.

Protective claims are necessary for any claimants who think that their income for the current year could be low enough to make them qualify. Claims should be made by 6 May in the tax year. Protective or provisional claims could apply to claimants with:

(i) children,

(ii) self-employed income, or

(iii) employment where income may significantly reduce within the fiscal year eg redundancy.

An award in payment at 5 April 2016 will continue to be paid until the renewal pack is returned, or 31 July if earlier, subject to HMRC can send claimants notification that their claim will no longer be automatically renewed unless they make a relevant request within 30 days. Any alteration to existing claims will be backdated to 6 April provided the information is provided by 31 January.

If the forms are not returned or the claim is not renewed online by 31 July then tax credit payments will cease.

If the forms (or online renewal) are not returned by 31 July then increased claims based on the renewal information will only be backdated one month. Furthermore HMRC will institute proceedings to recover tax credit payments made between 6 April and 31 July.

All other claimants will file details of income at the year-end. This will be used to correct the claim to 'actual' and also form the basis of claim for the following year. A return is required by 31 July 2017 for 2016/17. If income is not known at that time an estimate should be used with the return being corrected by the following 31 January ie in the above Example by 31 January 2018.

Any underpaid credit will be paid to the claimant and any overpaid amount is recovered by HMRC. In computing overpayments / underpayments, the first £2,500 increase / reduction in income between the preceding year and the current year is ignored .

Eligibility for tax credits are set out below.

### (i) Working Tax Credit (WTC)

A person is entitled to Working Tax Credit if they are working at the date of claim, or will commence work within seven days and are:

- aged at least 16, and working for not less than 16 hours per week and have a child for whom he is responsible, or
- aged at least 16, working for not less than 16 hours per week, and have a disability that puts him at a disadvantage in getting a job and satisfy either the 'qualifying benefit test' or the special 'fast-track' rules to qualify for a disability element, or
- aged at least 25, and working not less than 30 hours per week, or
- from 6 April 2011, people aged 60 and over qualify for working tax credits if they work at least 16 hours a week (previous limit 30 hours).

Where a couple are responsible for a child, the working hours to qualify for working tax credit are 24 in total for a couple, and one of the couple must work for at least 16 hours a week. For single parents, couples where one is aged over 60, or receives disability element of WTC or is in receipt of carer's allowance or where one of the couple is incapacitated, in hospital or in prison the limit is 16 hours a week.

Work must be expected to continue for at least four weeks, and must be for payment.

In arriving at hours normally worked customary or paid holiday and unpaid time allowed for meals, etc is disregarded.

A person is treated as engaged in qualifying remunerative work for any period during which they are on statutory maternity, paternity or adoption leave providing that they were in qualifying work before they went on leave. This also applies to the self-employed providing that they would have qualified for statutory maternity, paternity or adoption leave if they had been an employee. Any additional non-statutory leave does not count as a period in work eg unpaid additional maternity leave.

In the same way, a person is treated as being in qualifying remunerative work for the first 28 weeks if they are receiving Statutory Sick Pay or various other benefits because of illness. This provision is also applied to the self-employed as appropriate.

The disability element of WTC is paid if the claimant has a physical or mental disability which puts them at a disadvantage in getting a job, eg seeing, hearing, communicating with people, mobility, mental disability, or exhaustion and pain, and satisfies the 'qualifying benefit' test or the special 'fast-track' rules.

There are three 'qualifying benefit' tests. Either the claimant is receiving one of the following:

- Personal independence payment (PIP) or Disability Living Allowance (DLA). PIP replaced DLA for most people aged 16-64 making new claims from 2013. By the end of 2017 most existing DLA claims are expected to be switched to PIP or attendance allowance (those 65 and over).

- Attendance Allowance
- Industrial Injuries Disablement Benefit with Constant Attendance Allowance (CAA)
- War Disablement Pension with CAA or Mobility Supplement
- A vehicle provided under the Invalid Vehicle Scheme

or they must have received one of the following in the previous six months:

- Employment and Support Allowance or Incapacity Benefit
- Income based Jobseeker's Allowance*
- Income Support*
- Council Tax Reduction (replaced Council Tax Benefit in 2013)*
- Housing Benefit*

* This must include a Disability Premium or a Higher Pensioner Premium.

or they have been training for work in the last eight weeks following a period of receiving certain disability benefits.

There is also a set of fast-track rules for those who are finding it hard to stay in work because of a disability. They allow a claimant to qualify for the disability element earlier than under the 'qualifying benefit' tests above.

The Severe Disability element is payable if the claimant is entitled to a Disability Living Allowance (Highest Care Component) or Attendance Allowance (Higher Rate).

For more detail on all these disability elements see "WTC2 Child Tax Credit and Working Tax Credit". www.gov.uk/government/uploads/system/uploads/attachment_data/file/419570/WTC2-2015.pdf

All WTC payments are made by HMRC directly to the claimant.

The annual income threshold is currently £6,420 with credits being reduced by 41p for every £ of income over the threshold. The credits available for 2016/17 are shown in the rates and allowances on page (xii).

## (ii) Childcare element of WTC

A claimant is entitled to claim for childcare if they are eligible for WTC even if, because of taper currently 41%, the amount payable is nil. The claimant(s) must have one or more children and pay for registered or approved childcare. The childcare element is 70% of the amount payable with a maximum cost of £175 per week for one child or £300 per week for two or more children. If the claim is by a couple both partners must work at least 16 hours unless one partner is incapacitated or is an in-patient at a hospital or is in prison.

Payment of this element of WTC is made to the main carer with the Child Tax Credit (CTC).

Approved care is care provided for a child by a registered childminder or an accredited organisation. Childcare can be claimed until the Saturday following the 1 September following a child's 15th birthday, or a further year if the child is disabled.

To compute the average weekly childcare costs one of the following methods is used depending on the method of payment:

- If the charges are for a fixed weekly amount take the weekly amount for the last four weeks and divide by 4;
- If the charges are for a fixed monthly amount multiply that amount by 12 and divide by 52;
- If the charges vary take the amount paid in the last 52 weeks (or the last 12 months) and divide by 52;

- If childcare costs have not yet commenced, or have started in the last 52 weeks then an estimate of the costs for the next 52 weeks (divided by 52) is used;
- If payment of childcare is expected to last for less than 52 weeks then the estimated total is divided by the expected weeks of provision;
- If costs decrease for at least four weeks in a row by £10 per week or more, or childcare ceases, then notification of this change in circumstance is required within one month. The method of calculation of the new average weekly cost is determined by the original method used. If that was the same amount paid weekly then the new average weekly cost is the amount to be paid in the next four weeks divided by 4. In all other cases the new average weekly cost is the estimated amount payable over the next 52 weeks divided by 52 (use the expected number of weeks of payment in both places in the above calculation if provision is for less than 52 weeks);
- If one of the claimants is on statutory maternity, paternity or adoption leave they are still treated as being in work for the purposes of having qualifying childcare costs, but only in respect of any existing children of the family for whom they incur childcare costs. They cannot claim childcare for the new child.

Approved child care means care provided by:

- registered childminders, nurseries and play schemes;
- out-of-hours clubs on school premises run by a school or a local authority;
- childcare schemes run by school governing bodies under the 'extended schools' scheme;
- childcare schemes run by approved providers;
- in England and Scotland certain approved childcare provided in the claimants' home.

A claim cannot be made for childcare provided in the claimants' home by a relative, or for the child's education.

Where childcare is provided in the home of a relative then that relative must also provide care to children who are not related. Thus a relative (eg aunt or grandparent) will not normally be able to qualify for looking after the relative's child in their own home even if they are an approved childcare provider. In order to make a claim the relative would also need to look after a non-related child. (SI 2005/93).

### (iii) Child Tax Credit (CTC)

CTC is paid directly to the main carer, usually the mother. In order to claim CTC it is necessary to be responsible for a child or qualifying young person.

A child is a person who has not attained the age of 16 and they remain a child for tax credit purposes until immediately before the 1 September following their 16th birthday.

A qualifying young person is a person aged under 20 who is either in full-time non-advanced education, approved training or, has ceased full-time education, and has registered for work or training with a qualifying body for work or training in which case, CTC continues for a further 20 weeks after he ceases full-time education.

In 2013, the government started to raise the age of participation in England. This means that pupils now have to stay in education or training until the end of the academic year in which they turn 18.

If a child or young person dies the entitlement ceases eight weeks following death (but not beyond the date when the qualifying young person would have reached age 20).

If the child or qualifying young person has a child of their own, only one claim for CTC can be made in respect of that newborn child. If the intermediate parent is under 16 then the grandparents would claim for both 'children' as no claim by the intermediate parent would be possible. If the intermediate parent was 16 or over then the claim could be made by the parent and the grandparent would not then be able to claim for their 'young person'. This would require the intermediate parent to be supporting the child however. If that was not the case then the grandparent could continue to claim for both providing that the intermediate parent still qualified as a young person.

Being responsible for a child (or qualifying young person) means that the child must normally live with the claimant. If the child lives with more than one potential claimant(s), the claim is to be made by the person or couple having 'main responsibility' for the child. Parties can jointly elect which of them satisfies the main responsibility test. In the absence of such an agreement HMRC make the decision and in order to do so they will ask questions to discover:

- which address does the child give as a contact address, or for mail;
- where the child spends most nights, goes to after school;
- who keeps clothes/toys/belongings:
- who buys their clothes, food, underwear, provides pocket money;
- which is the registered address for healthcare, social worker, health visitor:
- whether there are any court orders determining responsibility.

The various elements of CTC available for 2016/17, are shown in the rates and allowances on page (xii). Most of the credits are tapered in the same way as they are for WTC, ie a reduction of 41p for every £ of income over the threshold. If the claimant is also entitled to WTC the threshold remains at £6,420. Taper will reduce WTC (excluding childcare) before CTC. It then reduces childcare and finally CTC. If the claimant is only entitled to CTC, eg the claimant is not working, or is a student or student nurse, the threshold is £16,105.

The family element of CTC is tapered last and at the same rate 41%. However, it is proposed that the family element may not be available to new claimants where the first child is born after 6 April 2017.

Claimants in receipt of income support or income based jobseeker's allowance are automatically entitled to the maximum amount of WTC and CTC (TCA 2002 s 7 and SI 2002/2008 reg 4).

Claimants in receipt of pension credit who are also responsible for a child will be entitled to the full amount without the taper provisions applying (SI 2003/2170).

## (b) *Income for tax credits*

Income for tax credits is computed for the claimant, or joint claimants, for the fiscal year. The amounts to include or exclude are set out in SI 2002/2006 as amended. The legislation requires the income to be computed in the following manner.

### Step 1

Add together

- Pension income
- Investment income, including chargeable event gains (before top-slicing relief)
- Property income
- Foreign income
- Notional income.

If the result is £300 or less, treat as nil. If the result is more than £300 only the excess is included. The £300 applies on a per claim basis ie the income of a couple is added together and the £300 deducted from the sum.

### Step 2

Add together

- Employment income
- Social Security income
- Student income (ie certain student dependant grants)
- Miscellaneous income.

### Step 3

Add together Steps 1 and 2.

### Step 4

Add trading income to Step 3 or deduct a trading loss of the year from Step 3. This could be the trading loss of a partner.

From the above is deducted

- Gift Aid payments (gross)
- Pension payments (gross).

Where a Gift Aid contribution is carried back by election, then it is deductible for tax credits in the fiscal year of payment.

### Employment Income

Employment income means:

- Any earnings received in the tax year, including any money's worth (see below)
- Any expense payment chargeable to income tax
- Any non-cash voucher, credit token or cash voucher, chargeable to income tax (excluding qualifying childcare vouchers)
- Any termination payment chargeable to income tax

- Any SSP
- Any SMP, SPP or SAP to the extent that it exceeds £100 per week per person (note the rate of SMP for 2016/17 is £139.58 per week)
- Benefit in kind on cars and car fuel and the taxable part of any mileage allowances
- Any amount subject to tax by ITEPA 2003 s 225 (restrictive undertakings)
- Any strike pay.

In calculating the value of a benefit to be included, the higher of the following two figures is used:

(1) The monetary value of the benefit to the employee, or

(2) The cost to the employer of providing it (less any contribution by the employee).

Taxable benefits included in employment income are broadly the cash equivalent of company cars and fuel, taxable expenses payments and mileage allowances, cash and non –cash vouchers and credit tokens and money's worth – broadly, anything that can readily be converted into cash.

Employment income does not include:

- Pension income
- Qualifying removal expenses (under £8,000)
- Payments covered by most ITEPA 2003 expenses claims (travelling costs, professional fees etc)
- Items covered by specific concessions eg staff suggestion schemes
- Deemed earnings under IR 35
- Employer provided childcare vouchers.

From employment income may be deducted:

- Travel expenses
- Fees and subscriptions to professional bodies
- Employee liability insurance
- Entertainers expenses
- Fixed sum deductions
- Personal security assets and services
- Give As You Earn donations
- Allowable expense claims
- Allowable claims for mileage allowance relief (ie where the employer has paid less than the mileage allowance rates).

## Pension Income

This includes pensions paid by

- The Crown

- Annuities under a Retirement Benefit Scheme, Superannuation Scheme, etc, Unapproved Pension Payments
- Lump sums payable where state pension has been deferred
- Taxable lump sums arising from commutation of trivial pension policies.

### Trading Income

This is the profit or loss for the year disregarding averaging. From 6 April 2015, all new claimants for WTC must show that they are trading on a commercial basis and their business is carried on with a view to achieving profits. Those with earnings below a threshold (working hours @ NLW) will be asked to provide evidence of their commercial approach. For new/loss making businesses this evidence could include a business plan.

It was originally proposed that it would be made a legal requirement that a WTC claimant must register for self-assessment and obtain a unique taxpayer reference (UTR) before making a claim to WTC. The legal requirement to obtain a UTR before making a claim has been deferred although new claimants will be advised that they should register.

### Student Income

This means any grant under the Education (Student Support) Regulations 2002 other than

- A grant for a dependent child,
- A grant for books, travel or equipment.

### Investment Income

This is investment income as calculated for income tax but without top-slicing relief for chargeable events.

### Property Income

This is as for income tax (ie excluding non-taxable rent a room income). It is the amount chargeable to tax ie after deduction of losses brought forward (box 38 on SA tax return property pages).

### Foreign Income

This means income arising outside the UK which is **not**

- Employment income
- Trading income
- Investment income.

Foreign income is computed on an income arising basis whether or not remitted. The 10% relief for certain foreign pensions is given.

Foreign income includes any income arising or income that has been excluded from UK liability by a double taxation agreement.

### Notional Income

Notional income means income, which a claimant is treated as having, but which he does not in fact receive.

This includes amounts treated as income under ITTOIA 2005, including:

| | | |
|---|---|---|
| – | s 277 | Premium on rent |
| – | s 409 | Stock dividends |
| – | s 415 | Release of a loan to a participator by a close company |
| – | s 624 | Income rising under a settlement where the settlor retains an interest |
| – | s 629 | Payments to unmarried minor children of the settlor |
| – | s 633 | Sums paid to settlor otherwise than as income |
| – | s 652 | Income from the residue on an estate |
| | ITA 2007 s 628 | Accrued income scheme |
| | FA 2004 s 84 & Sch 15 | Benefit charge on pre-owned assets |

If a claimant has deprived himself of income for the purpose of securing entitlement to, or increasing the amount of, a tax credit he is treated as having that income. This could include dividends not received because of a dividend waiver.

If income would become available to a claimant upon making an application for that income he is treated as having that income.

If a claimant provides a service for less than full value to another person who could afford to pay, then trading income or employment income is deemed to include the full value. This does not apply where the claimant is a volunteer, or is engaged to provide the service by a charitable or voluntary organisation and the Board are satisfied that it is reasonable for the claimant to provide the service free of charge.

### Miscellaneous Income

This includes any other income chargeable not already included above, such as an amount taxable on change of accounting basis.

### (c) *Changes in circumstances*

The tax credits rules require a claimant to notify within one month any changes in

(i) the claiming unit (eg starting to live with a partner or separating from a partner), including being part of a same-sex unit;

(ii) childcare payments where certain reductions in payments occur;

(iii) ceasing to be 'in the UK' (see **explanatory note 4**);

(iv) changes in hours worked where the level decreases below 30, 24 or 16 hours per week;

(v) changes in the number of children eligible for the tax credits within the claiming unit.

Failure to notify can result in a penalty not exceeding £300.

Other changes in circumstances, which would result in an increase in credits, should also be notified within one month because the entitlement to the new element of the claim can only be backdated for this period.

Changes which have to be notified, and which carry the potential £300 penalty, are:

- Date of marriage (if claiming as a single person)
- Date of commencement to live as a couple
- Date ceased to live as a couple (including death)
- Decrease in childcare payments to nil or by £10 a week or more
- Claimant leaves the UK for 8 weeks or more at the beginning of a temporary absence of 52 weeks or less (the period is extended to 12 weeks in circumstances of illness or bereavement)

- Claimant leaves the UK for a period which will be more than 52 weeks
- Partner of claimant returns to the UK after period of absence during which they were treated as not being 'in the UK' (see **explanatory note 4** for more detail on these 'residence rules')
- Birth or death of a child
- Change in the 'main responsibility' for a child
- Child ceases full-time education after 1 September following their 16th birthday
- Changes to the number of working hours.

Other changes in circumstances which should be notified at some time are:

- Increase in childcare of £10 a week or more lasting four weeks in a row
- Changes to entitlement to disability elements.

It is also obviously useful to tell HMRC about changes of employer, address, bank account or childcare provider.

Changes in income can be notified in year, or at the year-end. If there is an increase in excess of the disregard (currently £2,500) over the income of the previous year the tax credit award will be recalculated and an overpayment of tax credits may have to be returned to HMRC.

If income decreases then it is advisable to notify the reduction to HMRC. Subject to the disregard (£2,500) this may increase the tax credits award. The recalculated daily rate is currently paid from the date of notification, but the increase from the previous 6 April to date of notification is not normally paid until the final award notice is issued after notification of actual income for the year. This is to try and avoid substantial overpayments arising where income bounces back up later in the tax year. For example, Sam is made redundant in July. When he notifies (instantly), his tax credits are recalculated for the whole tax year based on the new lower estimate of income plus the disregard, but the increase is only paid in respect of the period from July. The potential overpayment from April to July is withheld to prevent an overpayment if Sam's income increases for any reason. This is common; for example, Sam finds new employment. In such circumstances, the tax credit system can struggle with substantial increases in income (eg back to the previous year level) occurring close to the end of the tax year as there is not sufficient time to collect the overpayment.

Where there is a change in the adult composition of a household and the claimant is late in reporting (except where dishonest), there may be an overpayment on the 'old' claim and a failure to make a 'new' claim. For example, one partner dies and therefore the remaining partner ceases to be entitled on the 'old' joint claim and instead becomes entitled to claim as a 'new' lone parent. In such circumstances the claimant can request (not automatic) 'notional entitlement'. This reduces the overpayment on the old claim by what the claimant would have been entitled to had they claimed promptly in their new capacity. Notional entitlement does not cover the period of one month backdating of new claims. Where a claimant is already repaying an overpayment that arose before the introduction of these rules they can claim notional entitlement but any money already paid over will not be repaid.

HMRC can claw back unpaid overpayment debts on old claims from new tax credit awards (from October 2014). For example, Clare has two children and claimed tax credits as a single parent. In 2016 she forms a new relationship with John. Her single claim ends and they make a joint claim. However, Clare has been overpaid by £1,750 on her former single claim. Under the cross-claim recovery rules HMRC can seek repayment from the new joint claim. Cross-claim recovery can apply in these situations:

(a) A joint ongoing claim can be reduced to recover debts from old single claims of one or both members of the couple,

(b) A single ongoing claim can be reduced to recover debts from an old single claim of the same person, or

(c) A joint ongoing claim can be reduced to recover debts from an old joint claim if the same two people are involved in each claim.

It appears that the cross-claim rules do not apply if the debt arose on an old joint claim and the new claim is made with a different partner. For example, assume Clare above was originally married to Paul and they made a joint claim with the same overpayment arising. The debt owed on Clare and Paul's joint claim could not be clawed back from Clare and John's new claim.

Tax Credits interact with Housing Benefit and Council Tax benefits, so it is necessary to notify the Local Authority of any change in the level of award.

## (d) *Four-week run on*

Any award of WTC may run on for four weeks following the claimant's hours dropping below the 16/24/30 hours per week. The measure is designed to reduce overpayments and to ease the transition from tax credits to benefits. This applies when claimants cease to work or start working fewer hours per week.

Claimants, where entitled, will be eligible to claim income support or Job Seeker's Allowance and other income-related benefits whilst in receipt of the WTC four-week run on. Under social security legislation, WTC will be treated as income for benefit purposes.

## (e) *Award periods and relevant periods*

An award period is normally a fiscal year, however if eligibility first arises in the year, eg on birth of first child, it is the period from the date of eligibility (or one month before date of claim if later) to the end of the fiscal year. If eligibility ceases before the end of the year then the award period ceases on that day.

Within the award period each day is considered separately, however all days with the same entitlement are aggregated and that period is known as a 'relevant period'.

In all instances the average income of the year of claim is used, as computed for tax credits.

The same principle is used to calculate the maximum award for a relevant period although the childcare credit rules are slightly different to allow for the fact that there are weekly, rather than daily, maxima.

## (f) *Year-end procedures*

A claimant is required to provide such information as will enable HMRC to confirm the claim made and to continue payments for the following year.

Where a recomputation applies the renewal information will require a declaration of actual income by 31 July. If actual income is not known estimates must be provided and the form marked to show an estimate has been used. The actual figures must be filed by 31 January following.

If income has reduced by above the disregard amount and additional tax credits are due the amount will be paid directly to the claimants.

If income has increased below the disregard (currently £2,500) no adjustment is made to the income part of the claim for the year under review. The increased income will be used in recomputing the provisional award for the following year, ie the award now being paid.

If income has increased above the disregard the excess is taken into account resulting in an overpayment of credits at the taper rate currently 41% of the excess. The excess payments will be recovered from future tax credit awards wherever possible (see **explanatory note 6**). Otherwise direct payment will be required. The amount is recovered as tax and is due within 30 days of the notice. On application overpayments may be repaid by 12 monthly instalments without interest. TCA 2002 s 37 provides for interest to be charged on overpayments of tax credits but only where the overpayment is attributable to the fraud or neglect of any person. In cases of hardship application may be made to arrange for repayment of the overpayment over a period in excess of 12 months.

TCA 2002 s 29(5) also provides for overpayments to be recovered through the PAYE system. For those earning up to £30,000 the maximum debt that can be recovered via a PAYE code is £3,000 pa. Safeguards apply to prevent excessive deductions from salary through PAYE.

In the case of a joint claim, both members of the family unit are required to sign claim forms and both have to repay any excess, ie there is a joint and several liability (TCA 2002 s 28(4)).

## B.

### (a) *Brian and Angela Smith – Tax Credits Claim 2016/17*

**Initial award based on 2015/16 income**

**Award period**

| | |
|---|---|
| Date of renewal claim | – 30 July 2015 |
| Date of eligibility (made prior to 31 July) | – 6 April 2015 |
| Renewal pack returned | – 6 July 2016 |
| Award period year to 5 April 2017 | (365 days) |
| Relevant period – initially the whole year | (365 days) |

**Initial eligibility**

| | | |
|---|---|---|
| WTC | – | Yes both work full time |
| Childcare | – | Yes |
| CTC | – | Yes for one child |
| Family element | – | Yes |

**Income**

| | | £ | £ |
|---|---|---|---|
| Investment income | | | |
| Brian | | 180 | |
| Angela | | 520 | |
| | | 700 | |
| *Less*: | | 300 | 400 |
| Self-employment | | | |
| Brian | | 16,490 | |
| *Less*: Personal pension | $\left(£1,600 \times \frac{100}{80}\right)$ | 2,000 | 14,490 |
| Employment | | | |
| Angela – P60 | | 22,700 | |
| Car | | 2,160 | |
| | | 24,860 | |
| *Less*: Gift Aid | $\left(£480 \times \frac{100}{80}\right)$ | 600 | 24,260 |
| Base income on PY basis for 2015/16 | | | 39,150 |

### Maximum claim (per day)

| | | | £ | | |
|---|---|---|---|---|---|
| WTC | – Basic | | 5.37 | | |
| | Second adult | | 5.51 | | |
| | 30 hours | | 2.22 | | |
| CTC | – One child | | 7.62 | | |
| | – Family element | | 1.50 | | |
| Relevant period = 365 days × | | | 22.22 | = | 8,110 |
| Childcare, £165 × 70% × 52 | | | | | 6,006 |
| | | | | | 14,116 |
| Restricted by | | | | | |
| | Income | 39,150 | | | |
| | Income threshold | 6,420 | | | |
| 41% × | | 32,730 | | = | 13,419 |
| | | | | | 697 |

Payable at the rate of £13.40 pw (£53.62 per 4 week) to Angela (if required, the first or last payment is adjusted to include rounding).

### Award revised to actual, calculation of final award

Award period year to 5 April 2017 (365 days).

### Relevant periods

| | | | |
|---|---|---|---|
| Changes | – | Childcare from 5 January 2017, but not notified until 5 March 2017, therefore increase claim from 5 February 2017 | |
| | – | Birth of Colin – 1 March 2017 (notified 5 March 2017 ie within 1 month) | |
| 6 April 2016 to 4 February 2017 | | | 305 days |
| 5 February 2017 to 28 February 2017 | | | 24 days |
| 1 March 2017 to 5 April 2017 | | | 36 days |

### Income

| | £ | £ | £ |
|---|---|---|---|
| Investment income | | | |
| Brian | 20 | | |
| Angela | 140 | | |
| | 160 | | |
| *Less*: £300 restricted to | 160 | | – |
| Employment | | | |
| Angela – P60 | 16,100 | | |
| *Less*: SMP 10 weeks @ £100 | 1,000 | | |
| | 15,100 | | |
| Car | 2,160 | | 17,260 |
| *Less*: Trading loss | | 2,800 | |
| Personal pension | | 2,000 | |
| Gift Aid | | 600 | (5,400) |
| Income for tax credits 2016/17 | | | 11,860 |

**Maximum claim (per day)**

| | *6/4/16–4/2/17* | *5/2/17–28/2/17* | *1/3/17–5/4/17* |
|---|---|---|---|
| | £ | £ | £ |
| WTC – Basic | 5.37 | 5.37 | 5.37 |
| Second adult | 5.51 | 5.51 | 5.51 |
| 30 hours | 2.22 | 2.22 | 2.22 |
| CTC – Child | 7.62 | 7.62 | 15.24 |
| – Family element | 1.50 | 1.50 | 1.50 |
| | 22.22 | 22.22 | 29.84 |

× days in relevant period:

| | | | | |
|---|---|---|---|---|
| | | £ | £ | £ |
| | | 6,777 | 533 | 1,074 |
| Childcare (per relevant period): | | | | |
| £165 × 52 × 305/365 × 70% | | 5,019 | | |
| £175/7 = £25 × 24 × 70% | | | 420 | |
| £175/7 = £25 × 36 × 70% | | | | 630 |
| Maximum credits due | £14,453 | 11,796 | 953 | 1,704 |

| | | | | |
|---|---|---|---|---|
| Restricted by | | £ | £ | £ |
| Income £14,360 | | 11,999 | 944 | 1,417 |
| Threshold £6,420 | | 5,365 | 422 | 633 |
| | | 6,634 | 522 | 784 |
| × 41% | £3,255 | 2,720 | 214 | 321 |

**Payment of claim (calculation of under payment)**

| | |
|---|---|
| *– As WTC to worker* | |
| Maximum | £ |
| (5.37 + 5.51 + 2.22) × 365 | 4,782 |
| *Less*: restriction | 3,255 |
| To Brian or Angela per claim | 1,527 |
| *– As WTC and CTC to carer* | |
| Balance of TC (14,453 – 4,782) | 9,671 |
| Paid in year | 697 |
| Payable to Angela | 8,974 |

Angela and Brian's initial award for 2017/18 will be based on 2016/17 income and their circumstances at the time of renewal. It will be necessary to know whether Angela is going back to work after her period of statutory maternity leave because this will determine whether the couple can continue to claim the childcare element. If she does return to work, and incurs childcare costs for both children, a different maximum of £300 per week will apply. If Brian believes that he will make a profit in the year to 31 December 2017 of a similar level, to year ending 31 December 2015 then it would be advisable to notify HMRC of the increased earnings levels so that an overpayment does not arise from 6 April 2018.

(iii) carry forward trade loss relief (ITA 2007 s 83); or

(iv) carry forward where trade transferred to a company (ITA 2007 s 86); or

(v) terminal trade loss relief (ITA 2007 s 90); or

(vi) trade losses treated as CGT loss (ITA 2007 s 71).

(See **Examples E1–E4.**)

(b) Class 4 national insurance contributions – Claim against income liable to Class 4 only (SSCBA 1992 Sch 2 para 3(4)) (see **Example H1**).

(c) Tax Credits – Claim against income of the *couple* or single claimant for year of loss only (SI 2002/2006 reg 3(1)). Any amount not used in this way may be deductible from trading income from the same source of the claimant in subsequent years. Uncommercial losses are not relievable. From 6 April 2015, a self-employed business should be trading on a commercial basis with a view to achieving profits.

Separate schedules will be needed to compute the carried forward amount for each claim.

Where the taxpayer with the loss has had more than one relevant period within the year, it is thought that the loss is restricted by the relevant days of the claims made. Where a loss claim (or gift aid or pension claim) is made a Form TC 825 is completed and filed with HMRC. In circumstances where a couple have parted HMRC will notify the loss to be used in future years, eg Alan lived with Beth until 30 July 2016. They parted, and on 6 February 2017 he moved in with Carol. In 2016/17 Alan had a loss of £14,000. Beth's income (for tax credits) is £17,000 and Carol £10,000.

The income calculation is always for the full fiscal year.

| | *Alan & Beth* | *Alan* | *Alan & Carol* | |
|---|---|---|---|---|
| | £ | £ | £ | |
| Alan | Nil | Nil | Nil | |
| Partner | 17,000 | | 10,000 | |
| *Less:* Loss | 14,000 | – | 10,000 | |
| | 3,000 | | Nil | |
| Days in relevant period | 116 | 190 | 59 | |
| Loss used | | | | |
| (116/365 × 14,000) | 4,449 | Nil | | |
| (59/365 × 10,000) | | | 1,616 | |
| Loss for year | | | | 14,000 |
| Used re Alan and Beth | | | 4,449 | |
| re Alan | | | Nil | |
| re Alan and Carol | | | 1,616 | 6,065 |
| Loss to carry forward | | | | 7,935 |

Loss claims should be made after claims for Gift Aid or pension payments as any excess loss can be carried forward.

*Being 'in the UK' and Temporary Absences*

(4) When computing *income* for tax credits the income tax definitions of Resident and Domicile are used although this is not of much practical relevance since virtually all worldwide income counts for tax credit purposes.

When considering entitlement (ie whether someone can claim tax credits) different rules are relevant. TCA 2002 s 3(3) requires the claimant(s) to be 'in the UK'. This requires physical presence in the UK on the days of entitlement.

The Tax Credits Residence Regulations (SI 2003/654) state that a person shall not be treated as being 'in the UK' if they are not ordinarily resident here, although this does not apply to a Crown servant posted overseas or his partner. HMRC guidance asserts that the definition of ordinarily resident for tax credits is:

"a person is ordinarily resident if they are normally residing in the UK (apart from temporary or occasional absences) and their residence here has been adopted voluntarily and for settled purposes as part of the regular order of their life for the time being."

Certain EC workers are treated as being ordinarily resident, as are certain persons in the UK as a result of compulsion by law. CTC is a family benefit under EC law and some claimants will qualify regardless of the requirements of these regulations.

Persons who are ordinarily resident for tax credit purposes (see HMRC Manual at TCTM 02026-02031) can also be treated as being 'in the UK' for certain periods of temporary absence. This is an absence which is not expected to be for more than 52 weeks in total. In this situation the first 8 weeks of absence are ignored. This is extended to 12 weeks if the absence or continued absence is due to the illness of the claimant or the illness/death of his partner, or his or his partner's child or qualifying young person, or a close relative of his or his partner.

It follows that if a claimant, who is part of a couple, works abroad for a temporary period, then for the first 8 weeks they will still be treated as a couple and a joint tax credit claim will be available. After 8 weeks the partner in the UK must notify the absence of the other (within one month) and the partner remaining in the UK will become a single claimant. This *may* increase the claim as only the UK partner's income will be counted. (If there are no children the claimant remaining in the UK would lose the couple's element of WTC assuming that they were working themselves and therefore entitled to WTC.)

Unfortunately the provision that deems a person as being resident for up to 8 or 12 weeks of absence does not also deem them to be working in the UK. This means that a parent remaining in the UK with children will lose their entitlement to claim childcare credits during that period. This is because the tax credits claim is by a couple, but one member (the parent overseas) is not working in the UK.

On the return of the overseas worker a further notification will be required (within one month) and the claim must revert to a joint claim. If the claimant was not part of a couple the only notification which has to be made is their own lengthy or permanent departure from the UK. When the individual returns to the UK they will have a choice as to whether they make a new claim to tax credits. They will obviously have to do so within one month of qualifying in order to get the maximum entitlement.

*Penalties*

(5) There is a penalty for fraudulently or negligently making incorrect statements etc in connection with tax credit claims, or notifications of changes in circumstances, limited to a maximum of £3,000 per offence.

There is a maximum penalty of £300 initially and £60 per day thereafter for failure to provide information when required.

There is a separate penalty for failure to notify certain changes in circumstances within one month (three months before April 2007):

- Changes in the claiming unit (eg starting to live with a partner or separation), or ceasing to be 'in the UK'.
- Falls in childcare costs to nil or by £10 per week or more for four or more weeks.
- Ceasing to be 'in the UK'.
- Changes in hours worked (decrease below 30, 24 or 16).
- Changes in eligible children.

Any changes in income arising from an enquiry for income tax may have a corresponding effect upon a claim for tax credits. In the same way any agreed alteration of income for tax credits may affect income tax and possibly national insurance.

*Overpayments*

(6) Where HMRC become aware of an overpayment in a year, eg notification of change in circumstances or increase in income, they will automatically recover the amount from the tax credits due to be paid for the remainder of the year. If this causes hardship then the claimant may apply for a top-up payment, however, such amounts will be recovered by becoming an overpayment at the year-end.

To determine 'hardship', HMRC will use the same maximum deduction rates as for year-end recoveries.

For year-end overpayments and in-year overpayments the maximum deduction from future awards of tax credits will be:

| | | |
|---|---|---|
| If claiming maximum WTC/CTC | – | 10% of current tax credit award |
| If claiming family element of CTC only | – | 100% of current tax credit award |
| In all other cases | – | Where current year household income is below £20,000 or before 5 April 2016 - 25% of current tax credit award. |
| | – | Where current year household income is above £20,000 after 6 April 2016 – 50% of current tax credit award. |

From October 2015, HMRC began to recover WTC overpayments from CTC awards and CTC overpayments from WTC awards. Prior to that date, WTC overpayments were only recovered from WTC and CTC overpayments from CTC.

In exceptional circumstances HMRC will not recover an overpayment. This will be where the overpayment was due to an HMRC mistake and the claimant believed that the award was correct. See Code of Practice 26 for further details https://www.gov.uk/government/publications/tax-credits-what-happens-if-youve-been-paid-too-much-cop26.

For joint claims both parties remain liable for overpayments even if they no longer live together. However, HMRC will take into account the circumstances of the individual case in deciding how to take proceedings to recover the overpayment. This can include asking for one former partner to pay all or most of the amount due, or by taking different forms of action against each partner.

*Employer provided childcare vouchers*

(7) An employer can currently provide his employees with childcare vouchers up to certain limits. Qualifying vouchers do not count as income for tax credits and are not liable to income tax or national insurance. (See **Example B2 explanatory note 24** for the conditions attached to the vouchers in order to obtain tax free status.)

Care must be taken when claiming tax credit childcare to ensure that the amount of childcare claimed is net of the cost covered by such vouchers.

Although this appears a generous tax-free perk, as most employers restricted salary by an amount equal to the tax-free voucher provided it results in a very small increase.

| | | £ | £ | £ |
|---|---|---|---|---|
| Before voucher | | | | |
| Childcare | | | 55.00 | |
| Covered by tax credits – 70% | | | 38.50 | |
| Net cost (from net pay) | | | | 16.50 |
| With Voucher | | | | |
| Childcare £55 – £55 voucher | | | Nil | |
| Loss of salary | | | (55.00) | |
| Net of Tax | @ 20% | 11.00 | | |
| NI | @ 12% | 6.60 | 17.60 | |
| | | | (37.40) | |
| *Less* increase in tax credits | | | | |
| £55 (reduction in income) | @ 41% | | 22.55 | (14.85) |
| Difference in net income – Gain | | | | 1.65 |

For 2012/13 onwards 41% taper applies to all income. For 2016/17, at maximum childcare costs, 41% taper applies until a couple's income is as below:

| | | | | | | |
|---|---|---|---|---|---|---|
| | No of Children | 1 | 2 | 3 | 4 | 5 |
| WTC | Basic | 1,960 | 1,960 | 1,960 | 1,960 | 1,960 |
| | Second adult | 2,010 | 2,010 | 2,010 | 2,010 | 2,010 |
| | 30 hours | 810 | 810 | 810 | 810 | 810 |
| CTC | Number of children | 2,780 | 5,560 | 8,340 | 11,120 | 13,900 |
| | Family element | 545 | 545 | 545 | 545 | 545 |
| | Max childcare* | 6,370 | 10,920 | 10,920 | 10,920 | 10,920 |
| | | 14,475 | 21,805 | 24,585 | 27,365 | 30,145 |
| | Taper @ 41% | 35,305 | 53,183 | 59,963 | 66,744 | 73,524 |
| | Plus basic threshold | 6,420 | 6,420 | 6,420 | 6,420 | 6,420 |
| | Maximum income qualifying for tax credits | 41,725* | 59,603 | 66,383 | 73,164 | 79,944 |
| | Maximum income qualifying for tax credits where no childcare cost | 26,188 | 32,969 | 39,749 | 46,530 | 53,310 |
| | *If family unit is a couple both must work at least 16 hours per week | | | | | |

For 2017/18 onwards the above figures will change as it is proposed the family element will not be available where the first child is born after 6 April 2017 and the child element may be restricted to a maximum of two children.

*Marginal rate*

(8) The National Living Wage (NLW) was introduced from 6 April 2016 for those aged 25 and over at £7.20 per hour. Therefore, someone in full-time employment should earn at least £13,104 per annum It is proposed that the NLW will rise to over £9 an hour by 2020.

The marginal tax rate for 2016/17 for a family on tax credits earning in excess of £6,420 is 73%. This is made up of income tax at 20%, NIC at 12% and tax credit withdrawal at 41%.

*Pension contributions*

(9) As shown in question B, Brian's losses and the income disregard (currently £2,500) interact favourably for claimants. Historically the same has been true for one-off pension contributions. However, the reduction in the disregard reduced the scope for future planning in this area.

*Enquiries*

(10) For interaction of tax credits and self-assessment see **Example G6.**

*Reduction in tax credits 2016/17 onwards*

(11) In July 2015 a number of changes were announced that reduce the tax credits available from 6 April 2016 of:

– A freeze for four years for all elements of WTC and CTC except disability elements,

– A reduction in the income threshold of £6,420 to £3,850 (this change was withdrawn and the threshold remains at £6,420),

– An increase in the taper withdrawal rate from 41% to 48% (this change was withdrawn and the rate remains at 41%),

– A reduction in the income disregard from £5,000 to £2,500.

Plus for 2017/18

– For children born after 6 April 2017 child tax credit will be limited to two children,

– For those starting a family after 6 April 2017 the family element may not be available.

As stated above, two of the proposed changes were withdrawn due to public opposition, however the remaining four still achieve the desired result of reducing tax credits. A knock on effect may occur for some with previous overpayments. As stated above where in receipt of "maximum tax credits" the overpayment can only be recovered from an ongoing award at 10%. The numbers qualifying for maximum tax credits may reduce due to the changes and hence some people may find not only has their award reduced but they move into the 25% / 50% recovery band.

*Switch from tax credits to universal credit (UC)*

(12) Universal credit was launched during 2013. It is currently only available in certain areas and circumstances.

It is the government's intention that claimants will move from tax credits to UC. The timetable for implementation has been subject to change and delay. The current estimate is to move claimants by July 2022. Whether a new claimant can claim tax credits or universal credits is determined by their postcode and circumstances. The Low Incomes Tax Reform Group (LITRG) has launched an online tool to help potential claimants check which system is relevant. http://universalcreditinfo.net/

As mentioned above the basis of calculation of UC is very different and claimants could receive significantly different amounts. For those moved from tax credits to UC by HMRC/DWP with no changes in circumstances, the government has promised a form of protection and that the claimant will not get less money. The cuts to tax credits above mean that people are likely to be on lower levels of tax credits at the point they move across to UC. It is expected this protection will gradually reduce over the years if rates of UC increase. If a claimant has a change of circumstances that means they have to move to UC they will not receive any transitional protection.

The existence of savings can affect the UC award. Where savings exceed £6,000, the DWP assume £1 of income for every £250 over the £6,000 threshold. This reduces the potential award available. Where savings exceed £16,000 a claimant may not get any UC. However there are again transitional rules for those moved across by HMRC / DWP from tax credits.

Tax credits are dealt with by HMRC and UC is the responsibility of the DWP. New regulations have been issued to allow tax credit awards to be in-year finalised when a tax credit claimant makes the transition to UC.

# Employment Income

# Question

## A.

Your firm has recently been instructed to act as advisers to a newly incorporated manufacturing company, Byrd Ltd.

Mr Tallis, the managing director of Byrd Ltd, has requested you to write to him summarising the major points in the operation of a Pay As You Earn (PAYE) scheme in order that he can ensure his new part-time accounts assistant is operating the scheme correctly and maintaining the necessary records.

You have established that the staff complement comprises two full-time working directors, one employee earning £8,400 per annum (plus substantial reimbursed expenses), the accounts assistant, who is a new graduate, aged 21, earning £16,000 per annum, an apprentice aged 18 and earning £12,000 plus tuition fees and other course expenses, and several part-time employees, including two students aged 18 and 19, each earning approximately £80 per week.

Write to Mr Tallis setting out the information requested and ensuring that your letter covers the following specific points:

(a) requirements on employees joining and leaving,

(b) records required for operation of PAYE, NI and other employer obligations,

(c) calculation of pay and payment of monies to HMRC, and

(d) end of year returns and forms.

Note: Ignore the requirements of the statutory sick pay, statutory maternity pay, statutory adoption pay, statutory paternity pay and statutory shared parental pay schemes.

## B.

In connection with the HMRC Form P11D explain:

(a) the purpose of this form,

(b) when, by whom, and in respect of whom, it is necessary to complete and submit the form,

(c) the major contents of the form.

Outline the purpose and contents of Form P9D.

# Answer

## A. Operating PAYE

Smith & Co,
Old Street, Newtown.
1 October 2015

Mr Tallis
Managing Director, Byrd Ltd.

Dear Mr Tallis,

As requested I summarise below the major points in the operation of a Pay As You Earn (PAYE) scheme and other payroll responsibilities.

(1) The company must register immediately as a new employer via HMRC's website or by telephone on 0300 200 3211. Basic guidance is now on HMRC's website: https://www.gov.uk/paye-for-employers. The website includes tax and national insurance tables and employers' online help books in PDF and HTML format, together with a link to a collection of downloadable Basic PAYE Tools, which together form an invaluable resource, containing electronic versions of most employer forms, guidance and tables and including calculators, forms to fill in on-screen and step-by-step help for people new to running basic payroll. There is also free very basic payroll software suitable for smaller businesses, or you may wish to invest in a software product which will complete all of the calculations automatically. There is a wide range of software products on the market with a correspondingly wide range of prices, although HMRC publishes a list of accredited products on its website (https://www.gov.uk/payroll-software/paid-for-software), which you should check to ensure that any system you buy meets the minimum requirements. The basic HMRC product does not cover full payroll functionality but it will allow you to input and file online the minimum data necessary to comply with the real-time information requirements. The new company will need to register online to use the Government Gateway so that your software will be able to file the necessary information. You will be sent a single use activation code by normal post as a security measure, and you will not be able to use the Gateway before you have applied the activation code that is sent to you.

The accounts assistant should familiarise himself with the workings of the PAYE and NIC scheme and refer to the employers' guides on the internet on points of difficulty. The guidance available on the internet is updated annually and should be the first source of information rather than older paper versions you may come across, which can become out of date quite quickly. The employers area is signposted from the main HMRC homepage on GOV.UK (https://www.gov.uk/topic/business-tax/paye), and includes a huge range of information for employers, including a diary to remind your staff when routine payroll tasks need to be completed. There are also a series of webinars available to help employers learn about how to operate PAYE (see https://www.gov.uk/government/news/webinars-emails-and-videos-on-employing-people), together with an online e-learning product and a series of short tax information films that HMRC has made available on YouTube. Help for existing employers is available from the helpline on 0300 200 3200. It is possible to obtain PAYE forms online at https://www.gov.uk/government/collections/payroll-publications-for-employers, where they are stored as i-forms (dynamic forms completed on screen) or in PDF format. There is also an internet service for PAYE at https://www.gov.uk/paye-online/using. More details of this are at **(11) below**.

(2) All new employees should be asked for parts 2 and 3 of Form P45 given to them by previous employers or by Jobcentre Plus if they have been drawing jobseeker's allowance. The best help available for those taking on a new employee is on the HMRC employers' website. The item 'Taking on a new employee' is available via the 'Search' function. This sets out how to check that the employee can legally work for you, and what to do with the P45 they present to you. The guidance leads you through each step, including links to advice on software and payroll options you can use to record their pay and tax. For employees who produce Form P45, the information on it counts as new starter information to be submitted to HMRC as part of the RTI system. You will not need to send part 3 of the P45 sent to HMRC – online submission of new starter information through RTI is mandatory for all businesses except a tiny number who are exempt from the RTI re-

quirements. Part 2 should be retained. These procedures must be followed whether or not the employee's pay with you will exceed the tax and national insurance thresholds, so it is particularly important in relation to the part-time employees. Care must be taken to check whether the employee is subject to a student loan repayment deduction. This is shown in Box 5 on Form P45 by the inclusion of the letter Y (see (**10**) below).

The amount of tax to be deducted from each employee is worked out by reference to his or her tax code. HMRC work out the tax code for each employee. For new employees who give you a P45 from their previous employer, you should use the tax code included that form. HMRC will notify you of any changes in employees' codes. The employer is not told how the code is made up. If a code looks wrong, the employee must query the value with HMRC's helpline. The employer cannot change a PAYE code unilaterally.

(3) If a new employee does not produce Form P45, the online guidance on taking on a new employee specifies the action to be taken. You will have to ask them to complete a starter declaration of some kind; there is an optional starter checklist on the HMRC website to collect the basic information you need and to establish which tax code to use. Alternatively, your software may also provide a suitable checklist.

(4) You need to collect certain basic information about every employee, however much he or she earns and however long he or she works for you. You need to send payroll information to HMRC about everyone you employ before or on every payday. This includes those earning under the Lower Earnings Limit, people paid just once a year and any temporary or casual staff. You send the basic information collected at the outset of the employment to HMRC in a Full Payment Submission (FPS) every time you pay the employee, with the details of that payment.

The basic information you must collect and report with every payment is:

- full name;
- gender;
- date of birth;
- full address;
- National Insurance number.

The first FPS you submit for a payment to a new employee must include the date the employment started.

The starter declaration will enable you to decide whether to use a cumulative emergency PAYE code (1100L), a week1/month1 emergency code (1100L W1/M1) or give no allowances, using code 0T, according to which declaration the new employee makes, and to decide whether you need to make student loan deductions.

(5) When an employee for whom a deductions working sheet is in use leaves, you must report their final payment from you in the FPS for that payment, noting their date of leaving in that FPS too. Form P45 must be completed, and the bottom three copies (including part 1A which is the employee's copy) handed to the employee. Your online notification of the final payment of earnings to the employee tells HMRC's computer that the employee no longer works for you so that his tax code can be allocated to any new employer who notifies him as a new starter. If you have to make another payment to the former employee (eg, a delayed bonus), you need to submit an FPS showing the payment, using a 0T tax code, and including his personal details as both a new starter and a leaver on the same return.

(6) On or before each pay day, the details of pay and the tax and employer's and employee's national insurance thereon, together with any student loan deduction (calculated in each case from the tables, or using appropriate computer software) must be recorded on the deductions working sheets or computer equivalent and reported online to HMRC using your RTI software. The accounts assistant will need a summary sheet of the total pay and the total tax and national insurance due. Within fourteen days after the end of each tax month, ie by the 19th (22nd if paid electronically), a cheque for the total amount due for the month must be received by HMRC Accounts Office with an accompanying payslip (supplied by HMRC). Electronic payments do not need to be accompanied by a payslip, although including the correct employer reference number is very important. If your average monthly total payments of PAYE, NIC and student loan deductions for the current year are less than £1,500 you may choose to pay HMRC quarterly rather than monthly. This is easily arranged by phoning the contact centre.

(7) You are entitled to claim an employment allowance unless most of your work is under a public sector outsourcing contract, which seems unlikely. This means that you calculate NIC deductions as normal for employer and employee, but pay to HMRC only the employee deductions and the excess of the calculated employer deductions over £3,000 for the year to date. Where the amount you remit differs from the total tax, NIC and student loan deductions you have made from pay (eg, because you recover some SMP), you must submit an EPS online after the month-end but before the date on which you pay over your deductions so that the HMRC system can register that you should pay a smaller amount than the total of all the FPSs suggest. On occasions, you may have no deductions to remit (eg, because of large SMP payments being recovered) and you should send an EPS (by 19th of the next month) to notify HMRC that you will be paying nothing for that period.

(8) Details of what counts as pay are given in the employers' guides. Broadly it covers all cash payments and also benefits in kind if they can be readily converted into cash. Reimbursed expenses are Generally exempt from tax on the employee provided the employer has a proper system of control over payments. (See **explanatory note 8** below).

Certain amounts will be included in gross pay for national insurance, but not for income tax. These amounts are liable to Class 1 national insurance contributions when paid but are treated as benefits for PAYE and included on Form P11D. See Chapter 5 of CWG2 'Employer's Further Guide to PAYE and NICs' for the detail on these payments.

If your employees contribute to your stakeholder or a personal pension scheme, any contributions you deduct are taken from net pay after tax and NIC. If you make an employer contribution direct to the scheme, you do not need to deduct PAYE tax or account for NICs. If you decide to set up an occupational pension scheme that is not a group personal pension, you will deduct the employees' contributions from gross pay before calculating the PAYE tax charge, but no deduction is allowed for NICs purposes.

(9) At the end of the tax year you will be required to submit year-end declarations electronically to HMRC. This process is now part of the RTI system: when you make your final submission of the tax year, you flag it as such. The P35 used to include six standard questions about your returns, but these have now been removed under the RTI system. If you make your final declaration between 5 and 19 April, you submit an FPS, but after 19 April you submit an EPS. When you submit this end of year information online, you will need to produce a Form P60 for the employee so they have a record of their pay, tax and other deductions for the year, and also one copy for your backup records, unless you wish to use electronic P60 notifications, in which case you must ensure that employees have appropriate facilities for reading the forms. Form P60 must be issued on paper or electronically by 31 May to any employees in post at 5 April (for those who leave your employment between 6 April and 31 May, you may send a copy to their last known address, but you should not send a P60 to anyone who left during the tax year to whom you gave a P45). The electronic process allows employers to complete the information and declarations online, receiving a confirmation of receipt almost immediately.

A Form P11D must be completed for each director and employee showing details of all benefits provided other than anything already included as pay on the deduction working sheets, or in respect of which you have entered into a PAYE settlement agreement with HMRC to settle the tax liability for all relevant employees. The boxes on the form that are relevant for Class 1A national insurance contributions (see (**explanatory note 9**) below) are colour coded. If an employee has left after 5 April, the copy may be sent to his last known address. You are not *required* to give copies to employees who leave *during* the year unless they make a written request, but it would be sensible and helpful to the employee to do so. This could be done either at the time the employee leaves or when issuing copies to other employees at the year-end. There is not currently any plan to require electronic submission of Forms P11D, although HMRC are encouraging use of End of Year Expenses and Benefits online forms.

(10) Class 1A employers' national insurance contributions, at 13.8% (for 2016/17) of the cash equivalent of benefits, are payable annually in arrears on the provision of all taxable benefits that are not subject to Class 1 or Class 1B NICs. The amount due is calculated annually from the P11D entries and is payable to the Accounts Office using the special payslip by 19 July following the end of the tax year (22 July if payment is made electronically, with a modified payment reference explained on the HMRC website). The payment is shown on Form P11D(b) which must be filed with the PAYE tax office by 6 July. Interest is charged from the day after the July due date on any late payment.

When company cars and fuel are first provided to employees, and when cars cease to be available, HMRC must be notified on Form P46 (Car) within 28 days after each quarter to 5 July, 5 October, 5 January and 5 April. An online version of the P46 (Car) may be used to notify changes of company car during a tax year. From April 2016, you can choose to tax the company car benefit through payroll, although you should discuss this with us before making a decision, which applies to each tax year at a time.

(11) Where a student took a student loan as a new borrower after August 1998 then repayment of that loan will be collected by way of a deduction from salary. You are not required to take any action unless you receive a start notice (SL1) from HMRC or a P45 or starter declaration with the student loan box ticked. The first deduction date will be on the next pay date. For new employees 'Y' in box 5 on Form P45 triggers the deduction, as does the student ticking the relevant box on the optional starter declaration when you take him or her on. The repayment is 9% of the excess of earnings over £333 per week (£1,444 per month, or £17,335 per year). Deductions must continue until a stop notice (SL2) is received. Earnings will be the amount computed for national insurance purposes. The limit is different, at £21,000 per year for students **starting** to repay loans in April 2016 (those whose courses started in September 2012 or later), so you should check HMRC's employer guidance in factsheet CSL2 as each new tax year starts and any Employer Bulletins that you are sent by email. You may in due course employ students for whom different thresholds apply because they started their courses and took their loans under different rules.

(12) Some of your employees are under the age of 21. This means that, even if they have earnings above the earnings threshold for NIC (the point at which you begin to have to pay employer NICs), you do not have to pay employer NICs if, on payday, they are still under 21 and their earnings for the week do not exceed the 'upper secondary threshold' (£815 pw this year). If they are paid a bonus that takes their earnings above that limit, the excess is subject to normal rates of employer NICs. Your payroll software will ask for dates of birth and should deal with this automatically. Note that the nil rate of NIC for under-21s only applies to you as the employer: the employees still have to pay contributions if their earnings are above the normal employee threshold.

(13) It is mandatory for all payroll information to be e-filed by all employers under RTI. Employers may also receive Forms such as P6 (coding details) and P9 (code amendments) via secure email. P11Ds can be e-filed, or the online forms used, but neither is mandatory.

(14) Large employers (250+ employees) are obliged to pay PAYE/NI and associated amounts electronically, so you will need to monitor this as your business grows. If any employer pays PAYE/NI electronically, or through the bank, the cleared payment must arrive by the 22nd of the month (or the previous bank working day if the 22nd is a bank holiday or falls on a weekend). All employers are subject to a penalty regime if PAYE, NIC, student loan and CIS deductions are paid late more than once in a tax year. The surcharge rises from 1% of the late payment if it happens twice, three times or four times to 4% if 11 or 12 payments are late. Any payment (including the first payment that is not subject to the 1% charge) made more than six months late attracts a 5% surcharge, and twelve months late a further 5%.

(15) Interest is charged on PAYE, NIC, student loan and CIS deductions that remain outstanding 14 days after the end of the tax month, ie, from 19 October 2016 for payments to employees in the period 6 September to 5 October (22 October if you pay HMRC electronically), except for Class 1A contributions, where interest runs from the due date of payment, ie 19 July 2017 for 2016/17 (again, 22 July if you e-pay). There are also penalties if you are late filing RTI submissions, P11D, P11D(b) or P9D data, or if you deliberately or carelessly provide incorrect information in a P11D, P11D(b) or P9D or in relation to a PAYE return. For student loan deductions there are penalties for fraudulently or negligently making incorrect deductions, or making or receiving incorrect payments. Such interest and penalties are not deductible in computing the tax liabilities of the employer. The penalties for incorrect returns are based on the behaviour giving rise to the inaccuracy, and where errors have been made after taking reasonable care, no penalty is charged. Where an employer fails to take reasonable care the penalty can be up to 30% of the 'potential lost revenue' (ie, tax, NIC, etc underpaid or over-refunded), but the system allows substantial discounts for disclosing the errors to HMRC in full. Penalties for dishonesty are considerably higher. From April 2016, there are likely to be automatic penalties for late filing and late payment of deductions, but you are currently allowed a little leeway in that there is a temporary relaxation for returns made within three days of the statutory filing date.

(16) If your company failed to pay national insurance contributions because you had been fraudulent or negligent, you, as a director of the company, could be held personally liable for the failure if the company becomes

insolvent. It is essential that you make sure that the payroll is properly administered and that all liabilities are paid by the due date.

(17) As you have employees on your payroll, you will be obliged to set up a qualifying workplace pension scheme and automatically enrol your employees, unless they choose to opt out. The start of your obligation is known as your 'staging date', which you can find at http://www.thepensionsregulator.gov.uk/ employers/ staging-date.aspx by inputting your employer PAYE reference. It should be 1 October 2017 for a new business started this year, but you can start earlier if you wish. You are required to make the pension deductions from pay and remit them promptly to the pension provider. For a typical small employer, the employee contributions, which are net of basic rate tax, are deducted from net pay. They do not affect the amount of PAYE or national insurance contributions payable. Employers are obliged to contribute to the scheme, but the payments do not have to be included in the payroll for tax and NI purposes. Until 30 September 2017, your employer contribution must be at least 1% of pay for those employees who qualify. It then rises to 2% for one year, then to 3% from 1 October 2018. Employees must contribute, 1%, 3% and 5% over the same periods. The amounts deducted from employee wages must be paid to the provider not later than the 19th of the following month. If you fail to do so, a report will be sent to the regulatory authority. Persistent offences are likely to result in fines being imposed upon the company.

There are a number of pension scheme providers who will accept small employers into low-cost pension arrangements, such as the National Employment Savings Trust (NEST), and provide simplified documentation and administration, generally online. I recommend that you look carefully as early as possible at the auto-enrolment requirements (see www.tpr.gov.uk) that will follow in the near future.

This is only an outline of the main points of the PAYE scheme, and if there are any points of difficulty I will be happy to discuss them with you.

Yours sincerely,

A N Other

## B. Form P11D

(a) The purpose of Form P11D is to give HMRC details of taxable expenses payments and benefits provided in the tax year to directors or to other employees. There are some very restricted exemptions. The form also enables the employer to compute his liability to Class 1A national insurance on benefits. A copy must be provided to employees and directors to enable them to complete their self-assessment tax returns and, if they wish, to work out their own tax. The form must show not only payments and benefits provided by the employer himself but also by anyone else where the employer has arranged for that other person to provide the payments or benefits. Insignificant private use of assets and services provided to enable an employee to do the job is exempt from tax (and national insurance contributions) and is not included on Forms P11D (ITEPA 2003 s 316). The exemption does not apply to potentially high value items, such as motor vehicles, boats, aircraft, and alterations to living accommodation. The Treasury has the power to issue regulations exempting minor benefits (ITEPA 2003 s 210) and has done so for a small number of such benefits like the provision of welfare counselling. Generally speaking, reimbursed expenses which are genuine business expenses are not reported on form P11D, as they are exempt from tax.

(b) Form P11D must be completed by employers and sent to HMRC, with a copy to the employee/director, by 6 July after the end of the tax year. There are penalties if the forms are submitted late, or if the employer fraudulently or negligently provides incorrect information in the form.

A form has to be completed for each director and for each employee , except those for whom no taxable expenses payments or benefits have been provided, when employers are simply required to confirm to HMRC on Form P11D(b) that all the necessary Forms P11D have been completed and returned. (Form P11D(b) is also used to notify the amount of Class 1A contributions due, as indicated in **part A** of the Example at **explanatory note (9)**). The due date for Form P11D(b) is the same as for Form P11D, ie 6 July following the tax year.

The definition of 'director' includes every director except one who:

(i) earns less than £8,500 per annum, and

(ii) owns not more than 5% of the ordinary share capital of the company, and

(iii) either works full-time or works for a charitable or non-profit making body.

A third party who has provided taxable expenses payments or benefits to an employee or director other than by arrangement with the employer has no obligation to prepare a P11D but must provide details of the cash equivalents to the employee/director by 6 July following the end of the tax year. This does not apply to corporate hospitality unless the provision was in return for services rendered by the employee/director or the provision was directly or indirectly procured by the employer, or by someone connected with him. Nor does it apply to gifts costing not more than £250 in total from the same donor (ITEPA 2003 s 324). Taxable third party benefits not arranged by the employer are subject to a Class 1A national insurance liability that is payable by the provider, who must report them directly. This will be relevant if you provide rewards directly to the staff of retailers who sell your products. You may also decide to pay the tax on awards to your staff. Tips and items included in a Taxed Award Scheme are also excluded from the P11D, although they are taxable. (Under the Taxed Award Scheme the third party is already required to provide information to the employee – see **explanatory note 8**.) The third party does not have to provide information to HMRC unless he is required to complete a return under TMA 1970 s 15 or, as noted, the Class 1A charge arises on third party benefits.

(c) The major contents of Form P11D are details of the provision of cars and car fuel for private use, beneficial loans, relocation expenses, excess mileage allowances for use of the employee's own car (see **Example B4 explanatory note 20**), vans made available for private use, private medical etc treatment and insurance, general expenses allowances for business travel, travelling and subsistence, entertainment, home telephone benefits, subscriptions, services supplied, vouchers and credit cards, assets given or transferred to the director/employee, or placed at his disposal, taxable nursery provision and educational assistance, provision of living accommodation, and income tax paid for a director and not deducted from his wages. Except where tax liability has been settled by the employer under a Taxed Award Scheme or by a PAYE Settlement Agreement (see **explanatory note 9**), all other taxable expenses payments and benefits must also be shown, including payments made on the employee's behalf and not repaid.

Payments include those made by credit card or any other means. HMRC's view is that the figures quoted must include value added tax where appropriate.

Employers must calculate and show on the form the cash equivalent of all the benefits. The amounts reported by the employer do not take into account any reduction for allowable expenses, for which the employee must make his own claims (see below). Employers may obtain from HMRC optional working sheets for living accommodation, cars and fuel, vans, beneficial loans, relocation expenses and mileage allowances. These are also included on the employers' area of the HMRC website.

Except where special valuation rules apply, the cash equivalent of benefits is normally the marginal cost to the employer of providing them, less any amount made good by the employee (if you provide a company car, the law gives a deduction for amounts made good only if they are paid in the tax year, not after the end of the year). Where the employer gives the employee a voucher (other than certain childcare vouchers), the taxable value for the P11D is the price paid by the employer to buy the voucher, which may be at a discount to face value if vouchers are bought in bulk. There are special rules for determining the taxable value of childcare vouchers which make them a tax-advantaged benefit in kind.

If, unusually, an asset given to an employee is worth more second-hand than it cost the employer to buy it, the market value is taxed instead of the cost (eg, if a builder sells a new house to an employee at a discount). If the asset has already been used in the business and has depreciated (eg, a car), the second-hand value is taken as the cash equivalent, unless the '20% rule' has applied – see below. The cash equivalent for cars is based upon the list price of the car and its carbon dioxide emissions figure, and the fuel benefit is calculated by applying the percentage based upon the emissions figure to £22,100 pa. A fixed charge of £3,150 may apply for private use of a company van, with an extra fixed amount of £594 if fuel is provided for any private mileage that is other than insignificant. (See **Example B4** at **explanatory note 18**.)

The provision of living accommodation attracts a charge equivalent to its annual value less any rent paid, plus an additional charge if the cost of the accommodation exceeds £75,000, plus a further charge in respect of running costs if applicable, although this element is limited to 10% of pay. There are proposals to change the calculation of the cash equivalent of this benefit, likely to take effect in 2017.

Where other assets are provided for the employee's use the cash equivalent is 20% of the market value at the time the asset is first provided, proportionately reduced if the asset is also used for business purposes. Where the asset is subsequently given outright to the employee, the taxable value is the original cost less the total of 20% charges, even if market value is less.

A single mobile phone (including a smartphone that incorporates a web browser, but not a portable computer that can be used to make only internet-based calls) can also be provided for the employee tax-free.

The cash equivalent of beneficial loans is the difference between the interest paid by the director/employee, if any, and interest calculated at a rate prescribed by statutory instrument. Loans to buy a residence are within the beneficial loans rules (see **Example J2 explanatory note 5**).

Taxable benefits are liable to Class 1A national insurance and must be shown separately from expenses. For example, if an employer provides private medical insurance for an employee or his family, that is a benefit on which tax and Class 1A national insurance contributions are due. However, if the insurance is to cover medical risks whilst working overseas for the employer, that is an expense not giving rise to a tax or NI liability. If the contract for the purchase of a benefit is made by the employee but paid by the employer, that is a payment made on behalf of the employee liable to Class 1 national insurance contributions (employer's and employee's contributions). It must also be shown on Form P11D and is liable to income tax, but not under PAYE. See **explanatory note 8** re benefits provided under the Taxed Award Scheme.

Payments made to employees in respect of reasonable additional costs incurred as a result of working from home can be exempt from tax and are not reported on Form P11D. Where the amount paid does not exceed £4 per week, no justification is necessary for the payment, provided the employee works from home under arrangements reached with the employer to their mutual convenience. Where the amount paid exceeds this amount, the payment is tax-exempt to the extent that it represents a reimbursement of additional expenses incurred as a result of working from home. This can include additional costs of broadband connection if appropriate. Employers may wish to seek a dispensation in respect of higher payments. Guidance is available in the Employment Income Manual which is the internal guidance available to HMRC staff. The manuals are available on the internet at www.hmrc.gov.uk/manuals/eimanual/index.htm. Paragraph EIM 01472 and the following pages provide plenty of information to support employers on this topic.

## Explanatory Notes

*PAYE codings*

(1) The foregoing covers the main features of the PAYE scheme and the requirements for completing Forms P11D and P9D. The PAYE regulations are in SI 2003/2682. The tax calculation is made using code numbers notified by HMRC on Form P6 or P9(T). The code represents the tax allowances and deductions the employee is entitled to, reduced by amounts needed to cover other adjustments, such as benefits charges for cars and fuel, or to avoid too much income being charged at the basic rate where someone has more than one employment. Codes for higher rate taxpayers are often increased to give higher rate relief for personal pension contributions which benefit only from basic rate relief at source. Where the employee has untaxed income from other sources it is frequently deducted from the employee's allowances to avoid tax having to be accounted for separately on that other income. Inevitably, coding adjustments will often be based on estimates and will not result in the exact amount of tax due being collected, so that year-end adjustments or adjustments to the next year's coding may have to be made. In *Blackburn v Keeling* the Court of Appeal held that a loss likely to arise in 2003/04 could not be included in a 2002/03 code. The taxpayer was a name

in various Lloyd's syndicates and claimed carry-back relief for losses to be declared in May 2003. HMRC can now use the PAYE code to collect tax and Class 2 NIC debts of up to £3,000 by adjusting payroll deductions for any taxpayer. For those whose income is expected to be higher than £30,000 the code may be adjusted by a larger amount, up to £17,000 on a sliding scale for those with incomes of up to £90,000 or above.

(2) The code number is the amount of the allowances less the last digit, so that the code for a single person entitled to the personal allowance of £11,000 is 1100L. Most codes are three numbers followed by a suffix. For example, suffix L denotes single personal allowance, P age-related allowance for someone aged 65 to 74 and Y age-related allowance for someone aged 75 or older.

For 2016/17 a married couple or civil partners, both of whom pay no more than basic rate tax, can elect to transfer £1,100 from one spouse/partner to the other. The L-suffix code is reduced by 110 for the donor (who is given an N-suffix code) and increased by 110 for the donee (who is given an M-suffix code).

The suffixes enable HMRC to implement changes in these allowances by telling employers to adjust the codes by a specified amount. Some codes have a prefix instead of a suffix, eg prefix D which is used to collect higher rates with no allowances and at a flat rate (D0 prescribes 40%, D1 prescribes 45% flat rate), and prefix K which is used to collect tax on an excess of an employee's taxable benefits or a pensioner's state pension over available allowances. The maximum tax deducted from any payment of earnings under K codes is, however, normally restricted to 50% of the payment. Other codes are BR, which means basic rate tax applies, 0T, which means no allowances are available (eg, where HMRC has estimated that an employee will earn more than £122,000 so that no personal allowance is due, or for payments made after termination of employment and the issue of a P45), NT, which means no tax is to be deducted. A code with a T suffix means the code is only to be changed if a specific notification is received from the tax office.

(3) The tax tables work on a cumulative basis, so that the allowances are spread evenly over the tax year, unless for some reason it would be inappropriate for the cumulative basis to apply in a particular case (for example, where a coding is reduced to take account of an increase in a separate source of untaxed income), and to apply the tax tables on a cumulative basis would result in a very large decrease in take-home pay for one particular week/month (for example, where a code is changed late in the tax year). In such cases, the deductions for the remainder of the tax year are made on a non-cumulative or week 1/month 1 basis which means that one week's or month's proportion of the allowances due for the tax year is given against each week's/month's pay. When this basis is used it is shown in the code, eg '810L W1' or '810L M1'. The tax tables make provision for collecting tax at the 45% additional rate for top earners, but where employees have more than one job with total earnings above £150,000 but below that threshold in each job individually, HMRC can issue a D1 code to collect tax at 45% flat rate in one or more of the jobs, so the correct tax will eventually only be collected by self-assessment.

*Employees joining and leaving*

(4) The P45 and alternative starter declaration procedure enables the cumulative basis to be continued from one employment to another where appropriate. Form P45 has a separate part 1A for the employee and the form shows a separate figure for the pay and tax in that employment if it differs from the cumulative figures (ie, if pay from a previous employer is included in the totals). Where a new employee does not produce Form P45, then the employer ask the employee to provide information for starter declaration and to certify

(a) that this is his first job since 6 April and he has not drawn taxable jobseeker's allowance or taxable employment and support allowance or a state or occupational pension, or

(b) that the employment is now his only job but he has had another job since 6 April or has received taxable JSA or ESA(C), but does not receive a pension of any kind, or

(c) that he has another employment or receives a pension.

Before RTI was introduced, the treatment of completed Forms P46 depended on the circumstances. For employees who stated that they received a pension, the forms had to be sent to HMRC and tax deducted at the basic rate (PAYE code BR was normally used). Otherwise, the forms were not sent to HMRC if the employee's earnings did not exceed the NI lower earnings limit (£107 a week for 2012/13).

Under RTI, the personal information for every employee and the details of any payments are reported on an FPS. A deductions working sheet must be prepared in order to record the amount paid, and to account for tax and national insurance contributions as and when pay exceeds the earnings threshold. The starter declaration must collect details of the employee's full name, full current address, date of birth, NI number and gender, together with the start date.

For all employees receiving any payment of earnings, pay and deductions data must be sent online to HMRC in an FPS on or before the date of payment, together with all the standing data. Where employees earn in excess of the tax threshold (£211 per week for 2016/17), tax is deducted on the normal cumulative basis for type (a) cases and on a week 1 or month 1 basis for type (b) cases, using code 1100L W1/M1 until a code number is received. Employees paid between the NIC threshold and the tax threshold will be liable to national insurance contributions, but no tax until the tax threshold is reached.

If the employee does not certify any of the statements on the starter declaration, then the employer deducts tax using code 0T until further instructions are received from HMRC, who should identify the employee as a new starter and issue the appropriate code. National insurance contributions are only operated once the NIC threshold (£156 per week for employers, £155 per week for employees for 2016/17) is reached.

Where an employee is retiring on a pension paid by the employer (ie, not by the pension scheme trustees), the employer used to complete Form P46(Pen) instead of Form P45. Under RTI, this is no longer necessary. Instead, the employer gives the new pensioner a retirement statement (showing the previous employment details up to retirement) and sets an 'occupational pension' indicator on the FPS, noting the annual amount of the pension in that submission. For every future payment of pension, the pension indicator is also set. When the employee becomes a pensioner, a new Payroll ID must be allocated and the change must be flagged on the first FPS (showing both old and new ID numbers). Tax on the pension is then deducted using the existing code but on a week 1/month 1 basis until further instructions are received, but no NI contributions are due.

If the employee retires and starts to draw a pension from a pension trustee or scheme, the employer treats the pensioner as a leaver for RTI purposes, flagging the final payment as such in the final FPS of the employment. Special rules apply if the pension is paid to the dependants or executors of a deceased employee.

If the employer starts to pay a pension to a person who continues in employment (ie, without retiring, or retiring fully), it is necessary to set up a second Payroll ID for the pension payments and to apply code 0T to the new pension payments until HMRC issues the correct code. The old code continues in use for the continuing employment. The first FPS for the pension must set an occupational pension indicator and show the annual pension amount. The indicator must be set for all further pension payments.

*Accounting for PAYE*

(5) Employers do not have to use Basic PAYE Tools supplied by HMRC, and may use their own approved software.

(6) Employers who expect their average total monthly payment for PAYE, national insurance and student loan deductions (and taking into account sub-contractors' deductions for those in the construction industry where appropriate), to be less than £1,500 may pay quarterly, 14 days after 5 July, 5 October, 5 January and 5 April, instead of monthly. Those small employers who pay their employees weekly or monthly but only have to pay quarterly must still submit an FPS with each payment, and for the two out of three months where no remittance is made an EPS must be submitted so that HMRC's system does not expect a cash receipt to match the FPS deductions totals.

*Car and car fuel provision*

(7) The calculation and treatment of benefits in kind for directors and other employees is dealt with in detail in **Example B4**. Where employees are provided with cars and/or fuel, or car/fuel provision is withdrawn, employers have to provide details to HMRC on Form P46(Car) within 28 days after each quarter to 5 July, 5 October, 5 January and 5 April. An online report of company car changes is made in order to correct PAYE codes. The employee may also change the details of his company car through his personal tax account. For company cars and fuel details see **Example B4**.

*Taxed Award Schemes*

(8) Where employers or third parties have entered into a 'Taxed Award Scheme' with HMRC, under which the scheme providers agree to pay the tax on non-cash incentive awards at the relevant rate for the recipients, certificates showing the entries to be made in tax returns are given to employees by scheme providers separately from Forms P11D, and relevant information is also provided separately to HMRC. Class 1 national insurance contributions are payable on the tax paid by scheme providers, but not on the prizes themselves. Where the benefits are provided by a third party, Class 1A rather than Class 1 contributions are payable. Where the employer has not arranged for the awards to be provided, the third party *must* pay both the Class 1A contributions and the associated tax. At the end of the tax year, the employer must submit a form P35(TAS) and forms P440 to HMRC summarising the awards made and tax accounted for. TAS schemes remain outside RTI.

*PAYE Settlement Agreements (PSAs)*

(9) Some employers enter into PAYE settlement agreements (PSAs) with HMRC under which they pay a lump sum to cover the tax liability of their employees on expenses and benefits that are minor or irregular, or where it would be impracticable to apply PAYE (for example where benefits are shared) (ITEPA 2003 ss 703–707). Items covered by the PSA need not be shown in RTI submissions, or on Forms P11D and P9D, nor are they shown on employees' tax returns. Once a PSA has been negotiated with HMRC, it may be renewed annually for later years, subject to adjustment for changed circumstances. The employer's payment under the PSA is due by 19 October (22 October for e-payment) following the end of the tax year. Class 1B national insurance contributions are payable for 2015/16 at 13.8% on the benefits etc taxed under the PSA, to the extent that there would have been a national insurance liability under Class 1 or Class 1A. In addition a Class 1B liability of 13.8% is due on the tax payable under a PSA (SSCBA 1992 s 10A and SI 2001/1004 regs 41, 42). The Class 1B contributions are payable by employers at the same time as they pay the tax on the PSAs.

Items included in a PSA are not part of the income reportable on the employee's self-assessment tax return and the national insurance contributions are not credited to the employee's account.

Interest is charged on overdue tax and Class 1B contributions from 19 October (22 October for e-payers).

*Penalties for late and incorrect employer returns*

(10) Employers need to be fully aware of the requirements of the PAYE scheme, because there are penalties for late filing of FPS and late payment of monthly or quarterly remittances, and interest is charged where the tax and national insurance due for a tax month have not been received by HMRC by the 19th of the following month (or 22nd if paid electronically (SI 2003/2682 reg 82). Interest on Class 1A contributions runs from the day after the 19th July (or 22nd July for e-payers) due date (see **part A note (9)** of the Example). See **explanatory note 9** above re interest on late-paid income tax and Class 1B contributions under PSAs.

The initial penalty for each late Form P11D or Form P9D was and remains up to £300, and there is a further penalty of up to £60 a day if the failure continues.

FA 2009, Sch 55 set out new, harmonised penalties for failure to deliver a return, which included PAYE returns, but the PAYE element of the new regime was superseded by the introduction of RTI.

For 2016/17, penalties will be charged for late submission of FPSs if more than one month's FPSs were late, and late by more than three days. The first default is disregarded (except for those small employers who make one annual payment of earnings), but later defaults attract a penalty that escalates with the number of employees: £100 for 1-9 employees, £200 for 10-49 employees, £300 for 50-249 employees and £400 for large employers with 250-plus staff. Submissions over three months late may attract a tax- and NIC-geared penalty of 5% of the amounts that should have been reported.

The penalties for inaccuracies on returns which lead to a loss of tax (or potential loss of revenue) are geared to the behaviour giving rise to the penalty in accordance with Finance Act 2007, Schedule 24. There is no penalty for mistakes having taken reasonable care, but in other circumstances the penalty will be:

- for inaccuracies arising from carelessness – 30%;

- for inaccuracies arising from dishonesty which is not concealed – 70%;
- for inaccuracies arising from dishonesty with concealment – 100%.

These penalties are subject to reductions when the inaccuracy is disclosed to HMRC voluntarily. In general, penalties for disclosure when the taxpayer is not under threat of discovery are less than those where the disclosure is made after an enquiry commences. The minimum penalties when disclosure has occurred are:

| *Type of behaviour* | *Minimum penalty – unprompted disclosure* | *Minimum penalty – prompted disclosure* |
|---|---|---|
| Careless | 0% | 15% |
| Deliberate understatement | 20% | 35% |
| Deliberate with concealment | 30% | 50% |

HMRC also have power to visit employers' premises to undertake PAYE audits, and as well as the PAYE audit teams they have compliance officers who concentrate particularly on expenses payments and benefits for P11D employees and any international expenses and payments. PAYE audits and the penalty and interest provisions are dealt with in **Example G5**. HMRC compliance checks are dealt with in **Example G6 explanatory note 14.**

*Date when earnings regarded as paid*

(11) ITEPA 2003 s 686 lays down rules to determine when a payment of, or on account of, employment income is to be regarded as being made for the purpose of applying PAYE, so that the definitions of payment for PAYE purposes and receipt for assessment purposes match.

The general rule is that PAYE must be applied at the date income is paid.

Payment is deemed to occur on the earliest of:

(a) the date on which the payment is made;

(b) the date on which an employee becomes entitled without restriction to remuneration;

(c) the date on which sums on account of director's remuneration are credited in the company's records;

(d) the end of a period during which a director's remuneration is determined;

(e) the time when a director's remuneration is determined, if that is after the end of the period to which the remuneration relates.

Any restriction on the right to draw money is ignored.

Under old standard articles of association, directors' remuneration is normally determined by the company in a general meeting. HMRC will therefore treat the date of the annual general meeting at which the accounts are approved as the date of legal entitlement. However, the new model Table A articles under Companies Act 2006 (SI 2008/3229) have changed this long-standing position: directors in all companies that have adopted the new style of articles are entitled to 'such remuneration as the directors determine' and it 'accrues from day to day' unless the directors determine otherwise. Tax law has not been amended to reflect this new position.

*Pay in the form of readily convertible assets and tax avoidance arrangements*

(12) Under provisions in ITEPA 2003 ss 696 and 702 relating to income tax and SI 2001/1004 Schedule 3 relating to national insurance contributions, PAYE tax and Class 1 national insurance contributions must be accounted for when an employee is provided with marketable assets such as stocks and shares, gold bullion, futures and commodities, assets subject to a fiscal warehousing regime, assets that give rise to cash without any action being taken by the employee, assets in the form of debts owed to the employer that have been assigned to the employee, and assets for which trading arrangements exist or are likely to come into existence. The convertible assets provisions apply equally where vouchers and credit tokens are used to

provide the assets, and the legislation has been strengthened to ensure that the vouchers provisions operate as intended. It has also been made explicit that the convertible assets provisions apply to agency workers and to those working for someone in the UK but employed and paid by someone overseas.

Benefits chargeable under the convertible assets provisions are treated as notional pay for PAYE, and the tax and national insurance due is deducted from actual cash payments made either when the notional payment is made or later in the same income tax month. If there is insufficient pay, the employer must still pay over the amount due with his remittance for that month, the payment then being treated as tax paid by the employee (ITEPA 2003 s 710). If the employee does not then make good that amount to the employer within 90 days of the end of the tax year, he is treated for tax purposes as having received further pay of that amount (ITEPA 2003 s 222), such pay being shown on year-end Forms P11D and P9D. Later reimbursement does not cancel the penal tax charge.

PAYE/NI applies where pay is provided in the form of the enhancement of the value of an asset owned by the employee (such as paying premiums to increase the value of an employee-owned life policy).

PAYE/NI also applies where an employee is taxable on the exercise, assignment or release of a share option, or when a risk of forfeiture is lifted, or when shares are converted into shares of a different class, if the shares can be readily realised for cash and the arrangement is not tax-advantaged and registered as such with HMRC. Options exercised under a tax-advantaged scheme are generally not subject to PAYE/NI unless the conditions are not met. The tax provisions are broadly mirrored in the national insurance legislation, with detailed differences. See **Example N1** for further details. Employers and employees can jointly elect for the liability for employer's Class 1 national insurance contributions to be transferred from the employer to the employee, with the amount payable being a deduction from the taxable amount arising on an unapproved share option (see **Example H1 explanatory note 14**).

PAYE must also be applied to notional payments from certain tax avoidance schemes. This applies PAYE from the deemed date of payment to tax avoidance schemes (FA 2006 s 92 and s 94). Similar rules apply for NI where parallel regulations are made.

Where a relevant step is taken under the disguised remuneration provisions in Part 7A of ITEPA 2003, the value of that step is treated as a payment of PAYE income to the employee in question and the employer is required to account for PAYE as if cash had been paid. As with the employment-related security rules, the employer must recover the PAYE liability from the employee within 90 days of the end of the tax year to avoid a further liability on the employee under ITEPA 2003 s 222. Since some of the relevant steps that might be taken do not put cash into the employee's hand, this provision can be punitive and is intended as a deterrent to employers thinking of providing disguised remuneration via a third party such as an employee benefit trust or employer-financed retirement benefits scheme. The value of the relevant step is also treated as earnings for NIC purposes, although there is no deemed payment rule, so there may be no Class 1 liability if the step does not involve actual payment.

*Self-assessment*

(13) Under self-assessment, those who pay all their tax through PAYE are not required to self-assess, although if they wish to do so they may require HMRC to send them a return. The time limit for making this demand is three years from 31 October following the end of the tax year, eg by 31 October 2016 for 2012/13 (ITEPA 2003 s 711). If an employee's return shows an underpayment of less than £3,000, then providing the return is submitted by 30 October (or if filed electronically by 30 December) following the tax year, eg by 30 October 2013 for 2015/16, the underpayment will be dealt with by a PAYE coding adjustment unless the employee wishes to pay it directly. Where there is an overpayment of PAYE tax, those who do not self-assess will still be able to make a repayment claim outside the self-assessment system. See **Example G2** for the position regarding coding claims under self-assessment and HMRC's power to enquire into such claims.

(14) Even if employees do not have to fill in tax returns under self-assessment, they must still keep records relating to their tax liabilities. Records must be retained for 22 months from the end of the tax year, unless the employee is also self-employed or receives rents from property letting, in which case the retention period is five years ten months. If HMRC enquires into the employee's tax affairs, records must be retained until the end of the enquiry if later than the normal period (TMA 1970 s 12B). Relevant records include Forms

P60, P11D or P9D, P45 or P160 and P46(Pen) for pensioners, information to support expenses claims and coding notices. Such records should also be retained for tax credit claims.

*Charitable donations under payroll deduction scheme*

(15) Participating employers may arrange for their employees to have deductions made from their pay for donation to charities of the employee's choice through an agent or agency charity under the Payroll Giving scheme (ITEPA 2003 s 713). The earnings are taken into account net of the deduction for PAYE purposes, so that the figure of pay on the year-end Form P60 is after making the deduction (but the deduction does not reduce earnings for national insurance purposes). The deduction must be made under a scheme authorised by HMRC and subject to regulations made by statutory instrument (SI 1986/2211).

The employer may deduct as an expense against profits any expenses incurred in operating a payroll giving scheme, including payments to an approved agency to meet the agency's expenses in running a scheme (ITTOIA 2005 s 72 and CTA 2009 s 72).

(16) For detailed notes on charitable donations see **Example N4.**

*Miscellaneous points*

(17) Where someone receives employment and support allowance (ESA) based on contributions (known as 'ESA(C)') rather than a means test, the benefit is taxable. For those liable to tax under PAYE (eg, on an occupational pension), tax on the ESA(C) is collected by a coding adjustment. Those not subject to PAYE on other income have tax deducted directly from the benefit by the Department for Work and Pensions under a simplified form of PAYE.

(18) For the detailed provisions on employers' and employees' national insurance contributions, see **Example H1.**

(19) When fixing employees' pay, employers are required to comply with the requirements of the National Minimum Wage Act 1998 and the National Minimum Wage Regulations 1999 (SI 1999/584). There are also various burdens imposed on employers in order to implement aspects of Government policy. As indicated in the Example, employers are required to collect repayments of student loans through PAYE. They will also be required to give paid time off for studying or training to employees satisfying stipulated criteria. Employers who do not have a qualifying workplace pension scheme will be required to set one up by, at the latest, 1 October 2017 (see **Example A6** for details of personal pension schemes). New auto-enrolment rules began to apply from October 2012 onwards, affecting the largest employers first, under which all employers (commercial and domestic) have to enrol their employees in a qualifying workplace pension scheme, albeit with a right for the employee to opt out.

The Scottish rate of income tax introduced from 6 April 2016, has affected employers in England if one of their workers is classed as a Scottish resident. In that event, an 'S' indicator is shown on coding notices and HMRC will notify employers when to start and stop applying the Scottish rate.

(20) Employers may make special PAYE arrangements for foreign national employees (known as tax equalisation) under which the employers meet all or part of the employees' tax and provide a professional adviser to deal with employees' UK tax affairs. A guide to tax equalisation is provided in Revenue Help Sheet HS212.

(21) Special arrangements can also be made with HMRC where an employee working outside the UK is subject to double taxation, both under PAYE and by withholding in the foreign country – see HMRC PAYE Manual PAYE82001.

(22) Where an employee working abroad does not pay income tax on his earnings, but must pay national insurance contributions, special payment arrangements can be made – see HMRC PAYE Manual PAYE82004.

(23) Shares purchased as partnership shares by an employee under an approved Share Incentive Plan are bought out of salary before the deduction of PAYE or NI, the maximum amount being the lower of £1,800 pa or 10% of salary. For full details see **Example N1.**

(24) For details of the employer's responsibility to deduct PAYE on tips and gratuities together with the national insurance liability on such payments, see **Example G5** at **part** (D).

# Question

Honiton is employed by International Megabytes plc, and has a gross salary for 2016/17 of £46,500 before deducting pension contributions to his employer's group pension scheme of 5%. In June 2015 the company seconded him to the Newcastle office so that he could supervise the installation of a new reporting system in that area. It is anticipated that this assignment will last for two years and at the conclusion of that period he will return to work in the head office in Swindon.

During his stay in Newcastle he is living with his wife and youngest child in a company house, which cost £80,000 in 1995 and has an annual value of £700. His two older children are remaining in Swindon with their aunt. The company paid certain of the household bills for the Newcastle house, which for the year ended 5 April 2017 are as follows:

| | £ |
|---|---|
| Electricity | 530 |
| Gas | 710 |
| Gardener | 277 |
| Redecoration | 680 |

The company required Honiton to provide his own furniture at the temporary location. Honiton pays the company £70 per month by way of contribution towards the cost of his accommodation.

The company provides him with a car ($CO_2$ figure 146 grams per kilometre) which had a list price of £18,600 when purchased new in August 2015. He pays for all petrol but is reimbursed by the company for the full amount, including private petrol amounting to £1,765. For the duration of his stay in Newcastle his wife has been provided with a small car ($CO_2$ figure 98 grams per kilometre) bought second hand in February 2012, list price £9,200. Honiton contributes £48 per month towards the provision of this car. His wife pays for all her petrol.

Honiton spends time working away from the office, and has a fully equipped office at home in Newcastle, including a laptop computer costing £1,500 which he uses extensively for work, a smartphone costing £500 used when out on business, and a desk and other furniture in his home office. The company pays for broadband subscription costs on a package which allows unlimited use; the contract is in the company's name and costs £30 per month. The data tariff for the smartphone cost £25 per month; the contract is in the company's name.

Other benefits provided are:

(i) Medical insurance costing £1,480 under a company scheme. This included £300 for additional medical cover for Mr Honiton for periods spent outside the UK on company business. (Mr Honiton received hospital treatment in the UK during the year, for which the insurance company paid £750.)

(ii) Meals in the company's staff dining room. The dining room, which is open to all staff at the Newcastle office, provides subsidised lunches at £1.50 against an estimated cost of £4. On the basis of 240 working days the subsidy is worth £600 in a full year.

(iii) The Newcastle office runs a crèche on site for the children of any of the staff. Honiton's daughter, age 3, attends the crèche twice a week. The cost, which is borne by the company, is £250 per month.

(iv) During the year the company paid Mr Honiton's travelling expenses amounting to £6,750 and reimbursed entertaining incurred by him of £1,560. These amounts relate wholly to company activities.

(v) Mrs Honiton was sent a £50 bouquet of flowers by the company when she came out of hospital after an operation, and every member of staff was given a £30 turkey at Christmas.

In July 2016 Honiton and his family are offered a holiday to Minorca as a prize in the company's productivity increase scheme. The cost of the holiday would have been £2,200, but the family is unable to take up the prize and allows the company to pass it to another employee. The company operates a staff loan scheme at 2% per annum interest. In December 2015 Honiton borrowed £14,733 for personal expenditure. The loan is for a period of five years with no repayment for the first two years. The official rate of interest is 3% from 6 April 2016. Assume the rate remains unchanged for the remainder of 2016/17.

Honiton receives an award of £200 in June 2016 for passing the examinations of the Computer Institute.

(a) Compute the amount taxable as employment income for 2016/17, setting out the amounts on which Class 1 and Class 1A national insurance contributions are payable.

(b) Outline how this would change if IM plc opted to tax all possible benefits in kind through the payroll.

(c) Comment on any differences between Mr Honiton's remuneration for income tax: for Class 1 national insurance purposes.

(d) Outline how Mr Honiton's wife's child benefit entitlement will affect his tax liability.

# Answer

## (a) Honiton – amount assessable as employment income for 2016/17

| | £ | £ | £ |
|---|---|---|---|
| Salary | | 46,500 | |
| *Less*: Pension contributions 5% | | 2,325 | 44,175 |
| Taxable benefits: | | | |
| Provision of living accommodation – | | | |
| Annual value | 700 | | |
| Running expenses (530 + 710 + 277 + 680) | 2,197 | | |
| Additional charge on accommodation costing more than £75,000 | | | |
| (80,000 – 75,000) = £5,000 @ 3% | 150 | | |
| | 3,047 | | |
| *Less*: Contribution | (840) | 2,207 | |
| Provision of car – | | | |
| Car charge 18,600 × 26% | | 4,836 | |
| Fuel scale charge 22,200 × 26% | | 5,772 | |
| Provision of computer, mobile phone and broadband contract | | – | |
| Provision of car for wife – | | | |
| 9,200 × 16% | 1,472 | | |
| *Less*: Contribution (providing this is paid as a condition of the car being available for private use) | (576) | 896 | |
| Medical insurance | 1,480 | | |
| *Less*: re Overseas business trips | (300) | 1,180 | |
| Subsidised canteen | | –* | |
| Access to in-house crèche | | –* | |
| Travel and subsistence | 8,310 | | |
| *Less*: Incurred wholly for company activities | (8,310) | – | |
| Flowers and Christmas turkey | | –† | |
| Interest on beneficial loan of £14,733 @ 3% | 442 | | |
| *Less*: Amount paid (2%) | (272) | 170 | |
| Award for passing Computer Institute exams | | 200 | 15,261 |
| | | | 59,436 |

* Exempt if available to all staff

† Trivial benefit as no more than £50 and non-contractual

## *Class 1 and Class 1A national insurance contributions*

### Class 1 contributions

| | £ | £ |
|---|---|---|
| Salary | 46,500 | |
| Cash award | 200 | |
| | 46,700 | |
| Primary (employee's) contributions | | |
| 12% × (43,000 – 8,060) | 4,192.80 | |
| Plus | | |
| 2% × (46,700 – 43,000) | 74.00 | 4,266.80 |
| Secondary (employer's) contributions | | |
| 13.8% × (46,700 – 8,112) | | 5,325.14 |

### Class 1A (employer's) contributions on taxable benefits

| | £ | £ |
|---|---|---|
| Benefits as above | 15,261 | |
| *Less*: Cash award | 200 | |
| | 15,061 | |
| Contributions due by 19 July 2015 | | |
| 13.8% × 15,061 | | 2,078.42 |

### (b) Payrolling of benefits

The taxable value of the benefits would not be changed if the employer chose to tax them through payroll. Even if IM plc had registered before 6 April 2016 to payroll all possible benefits in kind, the living accommodation and cheap loan benefits would appear on Honiton's P11D, as they cannot yet be included in the payroll. All benefits other than the cash reward for passing the exam would still need to be included in the calculation of IM plc's Class 1A liability on form P11D(b) at the end of the tax year. They would be included in payroll for PAYE purposes, but not for Class 1 NIC purposes.

When IM plc registers the company for payrolling of benefits in kind (PBIK), Honiton's PAYE code should be adjusted to remove the car and private medical benefits, and IM plc should then include one-twelfth of the estimated benefit in each pay period as additional notional gross pay, deducting the same amount from net pay to account for the fact that the value in gross pay was not all provided in cash. This should be adjusted during the year if the estimates change so as to spread the revised balance over the remaining number of pay periods. The value of payrolled benefits in kind appears as a separate field in the RTI FPS, as well as being included in total gross pay, but this should be handled by the payroll software.

### (c) Differences between pay for tax, for national insurance and for tax credits

Pay for national insurance purposes is broadly the same as pay for income tax, but the main difference is that it is taken before deducting the employee's occupational pension contributions and charitable payments under the payroll giving scheme. Employee contributions to personal or stakeholder pension plans are deducted from pay after both PAYE and NIC have been deducted. Payments in kind are excluded from pay for Class 1 national insurance unless they are specifically chargeable under the provisions of SI 2001/1004 reg 25 and Sch 3, and this is so even if the employer elects to tax benefits in kind through the payroll. These charging provisions also cover vouchers which may be exchanged for any of the relevant items. The payments in kind that are specifically treated as if they were cash pay are gilt-edged stock, company loan stock, futures, options, certificates of deposit, units in authorised unit trusts, company shares, marketable assets such as gold or commodities, gemstones and certain alcoholic liquor, and *any* asset (including a voucher) for which trading arrangements exist to enable it to be exchanged for an equivalent amount (see **Example B1 explanatory note 12**). Although excess relocation costs reimbursed are deemed to be payable for Class 1 NIC purposes, they are excluded from PAYE and are reported on form P11D for income tax purposes. If they would have been exempt from income tax if they had fallen below the £8,000 limit, booklet CWG5 states that any such relocation costs above the limit that are in fact taxable should be dealt with as a Class 1A item, rather than Class 1, irrespective of whether the excess represents a benefit in kind or a reimbursement of a personal expense.

HMRC takes the view that payments in kind are to be regarded as pay for Class 1 national insurance purposes if they can be turned into cash by mere surrender, rather than needing to be sold, so premium bonds transferred to an employee would count as pay for Class 1 but the gift of a television set or computer would not – Class 1A would apply instead (see below). Cash vouchers, vouchers exchangeable partly for cash, and nearly all other vouchers count as pay for Class 1, the main exception being qualifying childcare vouchers to the extent that they are tax-free for the employee concerned.

Although payments in kind escape a Class 1 national insurance charge except as indicated above, employers have to pay a separate charge – Class 1A contributions – on virtually all benefits provided to P11D employees that are not charged to PAYE tax and Class 1 contributions (see **explanatory note 24** about the provision of childcare). The amounts chargeable to Class 1A contributions are the amounts of the taxable general earnings that are outside Class 1 and Class 1B liability and are taken from the entries on Forms P11D (or the P11D items that have been payrolled). The charge does not apply if the benefit is *wholly* offset by a matching deduction for tax purposes. Where, however, there is both business and private use, in HMRC's view, Class 1A contributions are payable on the full amount, even though employees are entitled to a deduction for the business proportion for tax purposes. This view was challenged successfully before the First-Tier Tribunal in Antique Buildings Limited (TC00408), where the company won its argument that the Class 1A liability on the provision of a company helicopter for part-time private use should be based on the taxable benefit only, ie after allowance for the business use claim made by the employee, but the decision related to legislation that had already been changed to ensure that the full benefit was subject to the Class 1A charge.

Class 1A contributions are payable annually in arrears, the payment for 2016/17 being due by 19 July 2017 (22 July 2017 for e-payment – HMRC must have cleared funds by that date).

The Class 1A chargeable amount includes the amounts of the car and car fuel benefits that are charged to income tax for employees' private use of *employer-provided* cars. Class 1A contributions are similarly payable on the flat-rate taxable amounts for private use of employer-provided vans and fuel in such vans. No fuel scale charge, and therefore no Class 1A charge, will arise if the employer pays only for business fuel using its advisory fuel rates for company vehicles, or pays for all fuel but recovers private fuel costs by charging the employee the relevant advisory fuel rate.

If an employer provides private fuel for an employee's *own* car or van, Class 1A rather than Class 1 contributions are payable if the employer provides the fuel directly, or pays for it by way of company credit card, agency card, etc, providing the fact that the fuel was being bought on behalf of the employer was explained in advance so that the contract for the purchase is made between the employer (with the employee acting as his agent) and the supplier. If the employee buys the fuel personally and reclaims the cost, Class 1 employer's and employee's contributions are payable on the full amount, except to the extent that records are available to identify the business mileage. Instead of paying for private and business fuel for employees' own cars and vans, it is usually more tax- and NIC-efficient for a business mileage allowance to be paid using HMRC authorised mileage rates (see **explanatory note 20**). If the employer pays for fuel, the employee may make a claim to HMRC for tax relief based on the authorised mileage rate applied to business mileage, but that possibility does not exist for NIC purposes: the employer must apply the mileage rate exclusion in making the weekly or monthly reimbursement.

## (d) Child benefit

Mr Honiton earns between £50,000 and £60,000, so he will suffer an extra tax charge based on a percentage of the child benefit received by his wife for the year: he will pay 1% of the child benefit value for every £100 by which his total income exceeds £50,000.

Mrs Honiton's child benefit entitlement from 6 April 2016 to 5 April 2017 should be (£20.70 + £13.70 + £13.70) × 52 = £2,501.20. For every round £100 by which Mr Honiton's income exceeds £50,000, he will pay £25.01 in a high income child benefit charge under self-assessment, so he will owe £2,350 for 2016/17 (with taxable income of £9,436 over the £50,000 lower limit, he has to repay 94% of the child benefit his wife receives, rounded down to the nearest £1). HMRC may adjust his PAYE code automatically in future years to collect the charge, based on the charge having been incurred for 2015/16. This is unconnected with any decision by IM plc to tax benefits in kind through payroll.

If Mr Honiton's income is certain to rise above £60,000 in future, Mrs Honiton may elect not to receive the child benefit in future years, thereby avoiding the tax charge on her husband while protecting her entitlement to national insurance carer's credits.

## Explanatory Notes

*Chargeable income*

(1) The tax charge under ITEPA 2003 covers earnings from employment and also pensions, both from employers and from the State, and some other social security benefits.

Taxable social security benefits include:

- Bereavement allowance
- Carer's allowance
- Contributory employment & support allowance
- Income support
- Jobseeker's allowance
- Statutory adoption pay }
- Statutory maternity pay } Taxable whether paid through payroll by the employer or paid by the DWP
- Statutory paternity pay (ordinary and additional) }
- Statutory sick pay }
- Statutory shared parental pay }

Non-taxable social security benefits include:

- Long-term incapacity benefit which began before 13 April 1995
- Increases in taxable benefits in respect of a child
- Attendance allowance
- Back to work bonus
- Bereavement payment (nb: not bereavement allowance, which is taxable)
- Child benefit and child's special allowance

- Child and working tax credits
- Council tax benefit
- Disability living allowance
- Guardian's allowance
- Health in pregnancy grant
- Housing benefit
- Income-related (means-tested) employment & support allowance
- Industrial injuries benefit (except industrial death benefit)
- In-work credit, emergency discretion fund payment and emergency fund payment
- Pensioner's Christmas bonus
- Personal Independence Payments
- Return to work credit
- Severe disablement allowance
- Social fund payments
- State maternity allowance
- State pension credits
- Universal credit

(2) Employees are taxed on their earnings, which includes any salary, wage or fee, any gratuity or other profit or benefit of any kind, unless there is a specific exemption (ITEPA 2003 s 62). To be earnings from the employment, the remuneration must be in return for the employee 'acting as or being an employee' (*Hochstrasser v Mayes*, HL 1959). It broadly means something that is a reward for services rendered in the employment, but the case of *Hamblett v Godfrey* (1986) showed that the test is wider, and covered payments made to employees at GCHQ Cheltenham to compensate them for giving up their right to be in a trade union, because the rights were connected with the employer/employee relationship. The related Special Commissioners cases of *Boothe v Bye* and *Wilson v Bye* in 1995 held that payments to retain two directors as employees to the date the company was sold were from their employments. In *White v IRC* SpC 357 in January 2003, housing allowance paid outside the employee's contractual terms was held to be from the employment. (A payment to compensate an employee for loss of rights under a share option scheme on his ceasing to be eligible following a management buy-out was, however, held to be not taxable in *Wilcock v Eve* 1994, although this decision has been overtaken by a change in the law – see ITEPA 2003 Part 7 Chapter 5.)

A payment by the employer for a debt for which the employee is legally responsible (referred to as meeting a pecuniary liability of the employee) counts as pay both for tax and national insurance, but the liabilities are handled differently. Class 1 national insurance contributions are payable at the time of payment through payroll, but tax is not deducted under PAYE (which only applies on payments made directly to the employee or on deemed payments such as those under the disguised remuneration rules) and the payments are reported on Forms P11D and, until 2015/16, P9D at the year-end (see **Example B1 part B**). This rule applies to payments for home telephone bills if the *employee* is the subscriber, unless the employer does no more than meet the cost of business calls excluding rental. It does not apply if the *employer* is the subscriber. In either case there would be a charge on P11D employees (see **explanatory notes 11 and 12**), subject to a claim for a deduction for the cost of the business calls. All employees are classed as P11D employees from 6 April 2016. Where there is no Class 1 charge (ie the employer is the subscriber) there will be a Class 1A charge on the full amount of the bill, unless the telephone is only available for business use. Where the employer meets a pecuniary liability of the employee and Class 1 liability arises, there can be no Class 1A liability, and the amount is reported in a different box on the P11D.

(3) Where employees receive commissions and discounts from their employers, the commissions count as pay even if paid to or passed on to the customer or invested for the customer's benefit. HMRC have, however, stated that where the transaction is at arm's length and is a normal part of the employer's business, the employee will usually be able to claim a deduction under the 'wholly, exclusively and necessarily' expenses rule (see **explanatory note 5**). Commissions on employees' own transactions also count as pay, unless the same commissions are available to the general public. Discounted prices for an employee's own transactions as distinct from commission sacrifices do not normally result in a tax charge, but if the cost to the employer exceeds the price paid, employees are charged to tax on the excess (only P11D employees were charged under this rule before 6 April 2016). 'Cashbacks' as inducements to employees to enter into transactions are not taxable if they are available on the same terms to the general public. For further details see SP 4/97 (updated in 2005).

(4) The charge is on taxable earnings *received* in the tax year (ITEPA 2003 s 15). Earnings are treated as received for income tax purposes on the earliest of the following (s 18):

(a) when actual payment is made of, or on account of, the earnings;

(b) when a person becomes entitled to payment of, or on account of, the earnings

and in the case of directors;

(c) when sums on account of the earnings are credited in the company's accounts or records (whether or not there are any restrictions on the director's right to draw the earnings);

(d) the end of a period, where the earnings for the period are determined before it ends;

(e) the time when the earnings for a period are determined, if that is after the end of the period.

For companies with pre-Companies Act 2006 articles of association, directors' remuneration is normally determined by the company in general meeting unless the shareholders agree on some other occasion to remunerate the directors with certain sums. HMRC therefore usually treat the date of the annual general meeting at which the accounts are approved as the date of legal entitlement. New companies, or companies that have adopted the latest model articles, will normally have a provision in the articles to the effect that directors' remuneration is determined by the directors rather than the shareholders, and accrues from day to day unless otherwise specified. The tax rules used to determine the date of payment of earnings have not been amended to reflect the new Companies Act position, so the five rules set out above still apply.

There are parallel rules to determine when income is deemed to be paid for PAYE (ITEPA 2003 s 686) (see **Example B1 explanatory note 11**).

For NIC purposes, payment is held to take place when the money is put unconditionally at the disposal of the earner (eg, a credit is made to loan account on which the earner can draw).

*Allowable expenses*

(5) Under rules that were in place for many years up to 5 April 2016, certain expenses could be deducted from the earnings to arrive at the taxable pay. FA 2015 inserted new s 289A into ITEPA 2003 to change the rules from 6 April 2016 so that, if an expense is deductible, it is exempt (subject to three conditions – see below).

Under the pre-2016 rules, an employer had to report all expenses as taxable earnings on a P11D, unless a dispensation was held. The employee then had to make a claim for a deduction to ensure that no tax was payable on the expenses. Under the 2016 rules, the new exemption means that the employer need not report the expenses on a P11D, the employee need not make a claim for a deduction, and HMRC need not process unnecessary paperwork when no tax is at stake.

Where a payment is made that is not exempt under the new rules, the employer is expected to process it as taxable pay through the payroll, although HMRC has yet to give guidance on how that is to be done where the taxable expense payment is made to a third party rather than to the earner himself.

The conditions attached to the new rule in s 289A making expenses exempt if they are deductible are that:

- they are calculated and paid or reimbursed in an approved way (eg, reimbursement of actual expenses incurred, or at a rate set out in law or agreed with HMRC);
- they are not paid under salary sacrifice arrangements (eg, where the employee agrees to accept a lower wage in exchange for receiving a tax-free lunch or travel allowance); and
- the employer operates a system of checks to ensure that the expenses have in fact been incurred, and incurred for allowable purposes, and has no reason to suspect that the employee has not incurred the expenses or has not incurred them for an allowable purpose.

If the employer wishes to pay a tax-free round sum subsistence allowance rather than reimburse actual costs, it may adopt flat-rate meal allowances set out in Income Tax (Approved Expenses) Regs 2015, SI 2015/1948, Reg 2(2) (these are not yet reflected in booklets CWG2 or 480) or agree bespoke rates in advance with HMRC, which will remain valid for up to five years.

Under non-statutory HMRC benchmark rules before 6 April 2016:

- A rate of up to £5.00 could be paid for breakfast cost where a worker had left home earlier than usual and before 06:00, and had incurred an expense in buying breakfast away from home after the qualifying journey had started.
- A rate of up to £5.00 could be paid where the worker had been away from his home/normal place of work for a period of at least five hours and had incurred the cost of a meal.
- Where the worker had been away from his home/normal place of work for a period of at least ten hours and had incurred the cost of a meal or meals a rate of £10 would be allowed.
- However, a further rate of up to £15.00 could be paid where the employee had to work later than usual, finished work after 20:00 having worked his normal day and had to buy a meal which he would usually have eaten at home.

The new statutory meal allowance rates from 6 April 2016 follow the same pattern, albeit with slightly different wording and with extra obligations for the employer, such as having the checking regime in place to ensure that the allowances claimed are in respect of qualifying travel and were actually being spent as intended, and not knowing or suspecting that the conditions would not have been met. (ITEPA 2003, s 289A(2)–(4)). Anything exempted from income tax by *s 289A* is also excluded from earnings for NIC purposes (Social Security (Contributions) Regulations 2001, SI 2001/1004, Sch 3 Part VIII para 8A).

The rates were set by regulation in December 2015 so as to give HMRC the power to agree bespoke rates under ITEPA 2003, s 289Bin advance of implementation on 6 April 2016. The standard rates are now expressed, for both income tax and NIC purposes, as an amount that does not exceed:

- £5 where the duration of the qualifying travel in the day is five hours or more;
- £10 where the duration of the qualifying travel in that day is 10 hours or more; or
- £25 where the duration of the qualifying travel in the day is 15 hours or more and is ongoing at 8pm.

A supplementary allowance not exceeding £10 per day may be added to either of the first two allowances where the allowance is paid for a period that is ongoing at 8pm.

Note that the rules allowing a claim for subsistence and mileage allowances were tightened from 6 April 2016 to exclude most workers who supply their services via intermediaries. If they work under a right of supervision, direction or control, or work through a personal service company that falls within the IR35 regime, each assignment is classed as a separate employment, so each new base is likely to be a permanent workplace. Travel and subsistence claims are only possible in respect of temporary workplaces.

The general expenses rule dealing with the deductibility of expenses rather than round sum subsistence payments is in ITEPA 2003 s 336, which provides that if an employee is 'obliged to incur and pay out of earnings . . . qualifying travelling expenses, or any amount (other than qualifying travelling expenses) incurred wholly, exclusively and necessarily in the performance of the duties of the employment' he may claim a deduction for those expenses. For detailed notes on travelling expenses see **Example B6 explanatory note 6**.

For expenses not reimbursed by the employer, it is notoriously difficult to meet the wholly, exclusively and necessarily test and the quite separate requirement that the expenditure must be incurred in the performance of the duties. HMRC's Employment Income Manual acknowledges the problem at paragraph EIM31637: 'because the general rule for employee expenses is extremely restrictive it is tempting to conclude that no expense could ever be deductible'. It later states 'however the rule is intended to permit some deductions' but does not give any indication what they might be.

Numerous taxpayers have failed to obtain a deduction under this section including the appellants in *Fitzpatrick v CIR* and *Smith v Abbott* (1994) which involved journalists buying competitors' newspapers and subsequently the case of *Hinsley v HMRC* (SpC 569) in which an airline pilot was obliged to reimburse his training costs when he left the company's employment.

After the Special Commissioner's decision in favour of HMRC in *Consultant Psychiatrist v Revenue and Customs Commissioners* (SpC 557) 2006, HMRC updated its Employment Income Manual. The case involved a psychiatrist employed by an NHS trust who claimed a deduction under ITEPA 2003 s 336 for training in an area that was desirable for her professional development and necessary for her continuing professional development. Paragraph EIM 32530 was extended to include 'no deduction is due for the costs of continuing professional education (CPE). That is so even if participation in such activities is compulsory, and failure to do so may lead to the employee losing his or her professional qualifications, and/or their job. CPE is not a duty of the employment for the purpose of section 336.' This analysis is simply an incorrect generalisation and does not accord with the Special Commissioner's decision, which was that the claim failed because the employee was not performing any duties under her contract when undergoing the training, a point that turned on the contractual situation of the individual concerned. An exemption would have been due if the work-related training had been funded by the employer (ITEPA 2003 s 250). HMRC has since been challenged successfully in the similar case of *Revenue & Customs Commissioners v Banerjee* ([2010] EWCA Civ 843), where the Commissioners, the High Court and the Court of Appeal found, on the facts, that the taxpayer's attendance at the courses in question was an objectively necessary requirement of the job, rather than something she merely did at her employer's request or undertook to qualify her to do her job or improve her prospects of promotion. It is difficult to see how HMRC can validly claim that attending CPE courses at the direction of an employer, in paid working time, under a contract (whether as a trainee or an employee), is anything other than performing the duties of that employment, but one might expect resistance from HMRC to a claim for a deduction in respect of such courses, given the contents of the manual. The HMRC guidance suggests that the decision in the *Banerjee* case should not be extended any further than training undertaken by an employee employed on a training contract where 'training was an intrinsic contractual duty of the employment', which is usually the case in any professional employment role where CPE/CPD is required.

An employee can claim a deduction for living costs at a temporary workplace (attended for 24 months or less, which is not the whole period of the employment contract), but this does not extend to the costs of spouse/partner or children (ITEPA 2003 ss 336 to 338).

Some expenses that are not covered by the general rule in s 336 are specifically allowed by statute, such as contributions to registered pension schemes, most professional subscriptions that are relevant to the employment (ITEPA 2003 ss 343 and 344), and charitable donations under the payroll giving scheme (ITEPA 2003 ss 713–715).

To avoid unnecessary work, payments by employers in respect of expenses for which the employee could obtain a deduction were not normally treated as pay under the PAYE scheme, so that the employee did not have to make an expenses claim, but there were special rules for those earning £8,500 per annum or more and for directors (see below at **explanatory note 11** onwards). These dispensation rules were abolished at 6 April 2016.

*Provision of living accommodation*

(6) The annual value of accommodation provided for an employee is specifically chargeable to tax (less any rent paid), no matter how little he earns, except where it is provided in the performance of his duties (ITEPA

2003 s 99). This exception does not apply to a director unless he owns not more than 5% of the ordinary share capital and either works full-time or works for a charitable or non-profit making company. If the employer pays the employee's council tax and water charges, the payments count as taxable benefits unless the accommodation is within the s 99 rules for job-related accommodation, in which case the payments escape tax (ITEPA s 314) and also national insurance contributions (SI 2001/1004 Sch 3 Part VIII para 10).

Where the cost of the accommodation provided exceeds £75,000 an additional charge is made, even if the employee escapes the annual value charge by paying rent to cover it. The additional charge is calculated as follows:

((Cost + improvements) – £75,000) @ beneficial loan interest rate at *beginning* of tax year (6 April 2015 – 3% as used in the Example).

If the employee is paying rent in excess of the annual value of the property, the excess reduces the additional charge. Employees exempt from the charge on annual value because the accommodation is job-related are also exempt from the additional charge. (Section 99 disapplies the whole of Chapter 5 of Part 3 of ITEPA 2003 which includes the additional charge.)

Both the charge on annual value and the additional charge are scaled down pro rata if the accommodation is provided for only part of the year, and are also reduced to the extent that part of the property is used exclusively for business.

Annual values for UK properties are based on rateable values, even though domestic rates have been abolished. However, this is only HMRC practice as the legislation strictly assesses the market rent for the first £75,000 of value. Where no annual value is available, or where there is a material change of circumstances, employers should estimate what the annual value would have been under the rating system. Special rules apply in Scotland.

For properties outside the UK the annual value will be the rent that could be obtained for the property let on an annual basis, unfurnished, on the assumption that the landlord meets costs of repairs and insurance and the tenant meets all other costs customarily borne by the tenant (HMRC Manual EIM 11441).

The cost of the provision of services in relation to the accommodation (ie, heating, lighting, cleaning, repairs, maintenance, decoration and the provision of furniture) is chargeable as a benefit in addition to the provision of the accommodation itself. This applies even if the employee is provided with the accommodation in the performance of his duties, although in that case the charge for the provision of services cannot exceed 10% of the employee's emoluments excluding the value of those services (ITEPA 2003 s 315) (see **Example J2 part (C)** for an illustration). This rule only applied to P11D employees and directors before 6 April 2016.

There is specific legislation in ITEPA 2003 ss 64 and 109 which prevents salary sacrifice schemes being used to reduce the tax charge for the provision of living accommodation. The prohibition in s 289A on the exemption of living expenses if there is a salary sacrifice arrangement may also be relevant.

The annual tax on enveloped dwellings (ATED) does not affect any benefit in kind charge. Although it is a cost to the non-natural person who provides the dwelling, the taxable benefit in kind is valued using the basis and formula outlined above. The ATED charge is not an occupier's liability borne by the employer, so it is not a benefit or facility for the employee. There is in any event an exemption under the ATED rules for job-related accommodation provided by an employer carrying on a trade on a commercial basis that uses the enveloped dwelling to accommodate workers.

*Relocation expenses*

(7) When an employee is relocated and his existing home is not within reasonable travelling distance of his new workplace, qualifying removal expenses and benefits are exempt up to a maximum of £8,000 per move so long as (a) the employee does change his residence and (b) they are paid or provided in the period from the date of the job change to the end of the next following tax year (or the end of a later tax year if HMRC grant an extension). Allowable expenses include expenses of disposing of the old property and buying another, removal expenses, providing replacement domestic goods, travelling and subsistence (including temporary accommodation), and bridging loan expenses (ITEPA 2003 Part 4 Chapter 7). A payment to an employee to compensate him for a fall in value when he sells his home does not qualify and is fully taxable.

The company house in Newcastle is Honiton's permanent location for the duration of his assignment, rather than temporary accommodation while he seeks a permanent home, and it does not therefore qualify under the relocation expenses provisions. If Honiton had incurred expenses in moving to the Newcastle house they would have qualified up to the £8,000 limit.

Where an employee sells his home to the employer or to a relocation company on terms that give him the right to share in any later surplus, there would be a taxable benefit if the value of that right plus the amount initially paid to the employee exceeded the open market value of the property.

Employers do not have to operate PAYE on qualifying relocation payments, but qualifying expenses payments and benefits in excess of £8,000, and all non-qualifying expenses and benefits, must be reported on year-end P11D returns. Somewhat unexpectedly, the taxable benefit of the excess over £8,000 is liable to Class 1A national insurance contributions for P11D employees whether the employer provides the qualifying benefit (such as a bridging loan) or reimburses a qualifying cost incurred by the employee in excess of the £8,000 limit. Both PAYE and Class 1 national insurance contributions are payable on non-qualifying expenses reimbursements.

For the capital gains tax treatment where an employee sells his home to a relocation company see **Example L8 explanatory note 14**.

*Employee liability insurance etc*

(8) The cost of employee liability insurance, professional indemnity insurance and work-related uninsured liabilities is not a taxable benefit if paid by the employer and is an allowable expense if paid by the employee (ITEPA 2003 s 346). National insurance contributions are not payable on such benefits provided they are not made available under salary sacrifice arrangements, paid for by way of a round sum allowance or paid to the employee in advance of the expense being incurred. Relief can continue for six years after the year in which the employment ceased (ITEPA 2003 ss 555–564).

*Vouchers*

(9) Cash vouchers are treated as pay and are chargeable to tax (and Class 1 national insurance contributions) at the time of receipt (ITEPA 2003 s 81). Non-cash vouchers (other than certain childcare vouchers – see **explanatory note 24** below) are also treated as pay, but are dealt with by year-end notification on Forms P11D/P9D (except where they are used in connection with the provision of assets that can be readily converted into cash, in which case they are also charged to tax and Class 1 national insurance contributions under PAYE – see **Example B2 explanatory note 12**). Non-cash vouchers cannot currently be taxed under the payrolling option for benefits in kind, but the government announced plans in Budget 2016 to permit this from April 2017.

The benefit is the cost of the voucher plus the cost of the goods and services for which it may be exchanged (ITEPA 2003 s 87). Vouchers are sometimes used in connection with incentive award schemes (see SP 6/85 for the costs to be taken into account and see **Example B2 explanatory note 8** for notes on such schemes). There is a specific exemption for vouchers used to obtain a car parking space (ITEPA 2003 s 266(1)(a)). Class 1 national insurance contributions are charged on most non-cash vouchers, subject to certain exceptions that mainly mirror income tax provisions but also including the permitted value of qualifying childcare vouchers (SI 2001/1004 Sch 3 Part V). For detailed notes on the national insurance position on vouchers see **Example H1 part (B)**. Because childcare vouchers are widely used as a NIC-saving device in salary sacrifice arrangements, the relief has been restricted since April 2011 for new recipients who are higher or additional rate taxpayers and, furthermore, the employer-supported childcare scheme under which vouchers are provided is to be phased out from April 2017, to be replaced by a tax-free childcare scheme that will not be compatible with salary sacrifice arrangements.

*Non-P11D employees – salary sacrifice arrangements etc*

(10) For employees and directors who, before 6 April 2016, were not within the special rules outlined in **note 11** below, the charging rules of ITEPA 2003 did not apply to benefits in kind except where:

(a) A specific amount of salary had been sacrificed for the benefit, in which case under the principle established in *Heaton v Bell* [1969] 2 All ER 70 the amount forgone was taxable (subject to what is said in **note 6** re living accommodation), or

(b) The benefit could be converted into cash, in which case the taxable amount was the second-hand value.

If a non-P11D employee was provided with a benefit in kind that was a service (other than providing living accommodation), rather than goods that could be resold, it will have had no second-hand value and will not have been taxable. These benefits became taxable on all recipients from April 2016 when the £8,500 threshold for P11D employment was abolished.

*P11D employees/directors*

(11) All employees are now subject to the same, normal rules that used to apply to P11D employees. Directors who did not own more than 5% of the ordinary share capital and either worked full-time or worked for a charitable or non-profit making company were subject to the special rules if they earned less than £8,500 per annum. All other directors were included in the normal rules whatever they earned (ITEPA 2003 s 216). The rules separating the low-paid and affording their benefits different treatment were abolished with effect from 6 April 2016, although the old 'P9D' rules were maintained in new statutory provisions for ministers of religion (who are traditionally paid a low stipend) as were special provisions for live-in carers, who might otherwise have become liable in respect of utility and certain other costs in relation to their accommodation.

Earnings for the purpose of the £8,500 rule were calculated inclusive of expenses payments and benefits and *before* deducting any allowable expenses other than employees' contributions to the employer's pension scheme and some other reliefs (former ITEPA 2003 s 218).

The expenses payments made by an employer for his employee are notified annually to HMRC on Form P11D (see **Example B2**). Employers used to be able to ask HMRC to grant a dispensation (notice of nil liability) under ITEPA 2003 s 65 in relation to expenses that would have been allowable under the ITEPA 2003 s 336 'wholly, exclusively and necessarily' rule or other rules allowing deductions from employment income. If the dispensation was granted, the expenses did not have to be shown on the Form P11D, so that they were not treated as pay. Dispensations were most frequently given for travelling and subsistence expenses, professional subscriptions and entertainment. They did not apply to a particular employee if the effect would have been to reduce the employee's earnings below the £8,500 limit. Dispensations were also effective for national insurance contributions. Dispensations became unnecessary from 6 April 2016 when deductible expenses became exempt, meaning employers had nothing to report in respect of them, so they were abolished. A limited range of round sum allowances are still permitted (see above).

Forms P11D do not need to show items covered by a PAYE settlement agreement (see **Example B2 explanatory note 9**), nor details of non-cash incentives under 'Taxed Award Schemes', to which special provisions apply (see **Example B2 explanatory note 8**). No entries are required for mileage allowance payments in respect of non-company vehicles that do not exceed the statutory limits because they are exempt from tax, so there is no need to report them and then claim a deduction (see **explanatory note 20**).

See **Example B2 explanatory note 14** for the record-keeping responsibilities of employees under self-assessment.

(12) Virtually all benefits received by reason of employment are chargeable to tax as earnings, but the employee/director may then make a claim for any expenses incurred 'wholly, exclusively and necessarily' in the performance of his duties. The benefits provisions apply not only to benefits provided to the employee himself, but also benefits to his 'family or household', defined as his spouse/civil partner, children and their spouses/civil partners, parents, and his servants, dependants and guests (ITEPA 2003 s 721(4) and (5)). If Honiton and his family had taken up the offer of the holiday, the cost to his employer would have been reported as a taxable benefit on his P11D.

Benefits consisting of the private use of assets and services used for performing the duties of the employment are, however, exempt, if the private use is insignificant, except for motor vehicles, boats, aircraft and alterations to living accommodation (ITEPA 2003 s 316 – see **Example B2 part B(A)**). Under ITEPA 2003 s 210 HMRC have the power to exempt minor benefits. They have used this power to exempt any private use of hearing aids and other equipment, services or facilities provided to disabled people under the Access to Work Programme or Disability Discrimination Act 1995 to enable them to do their work (but this still does not include the 'excluded benefits' as given in ITEPA 2003 s 316(5) and listed above). Exemptions are also provided for such matters as the lunchtime use of a works bus service, employer-provided pensions advice, and the use of on-site sporting facilities by non-employees of the provider, all of which are trivial but technically taxable.

FA 2016, s 13 added new trivial benefit rules to ITEPA 2003 as s 323A with effect from 6 April 2016. In order to minimise the volume of small amounts reported on P11D, provided a benefit costs less than £50, is not a cash payment or a cash voucher, and is neither contractual nor given in return for some particular service in the employment, a benefit will be exempt. This explains why the bouquet of flowers for Mrs Honiton and the Christmas turkey do not constitute taxable benefits in 2016/17. There is no limit on the number of such gifts that an employer may give, except in the case of directors of close companies and their families, in which case the annual limit is £300.

When the employee shareholder status was introduced by the Growth & Infrastructure Act 2013, it was specifically provided that employers must provide independent legal advice to anyone offered shares in exchange for certain rights. The cost of such provision, by direct provision or reimbursement, is also exempted (ITEPA 2003 s326B).

The effect of the benefits provisions used to be to treat all amounts arising from the P11D employee's or director's employment as taxable (unless they were specifically exempt) and to place the onus of an expenses claim on him. This was mitigated by the provisions for dispensations and PAYE settlement agreements. This Example illustrates many of the provisions. Other points are covered in **Example J2**. The new rules make items provided by the employer either taxable or exempt, so that there is no need to report exempt items and no need for the employee to make a claim.

The employee/director is charged on the 'cash equivalent' of the benefit. This normally means the cost to the employer (including VAT where appropriate in the view of HMRC, whether recovered or not) less any amounts made good by the employee. In the case of *Pepper v Hart*, HL [1993] 1 All ER 42, concerning a schoolmaster who paid reduced fees for his son, it was confirmed that 'cost' for in-house benefits means the additional cost of providing the benefit, ie, its marginal cost, and not a proportion of total costs.

Special rules apply where an asset has been used by an employee before it is given to him (see **explanatory note 21**) and to the calculation of the benefit of cheap loans and private use of cars and vans (see **explanatory notes 26, 13** and **18** respectively).

Virtually the only benefits that escape tax (for employees earning at a rate of £8,500 or more and directors before 6 April 2016, and now for all employees) are:

(a) a single mobile telephone when the contract is in the name of the company (ITEPA 2003 s 319 – see **explanatory note 19**);

(b) free canteen meals and light refreshments (see **explanatory note 23**);

(c) certain computer equipment available to employees generally and first made available before 6 April 2006 (ITEPA 2003 s 320 – see **explanatory note 27**);

(d) employers' contributions to provide for a retirement or death benefit, (except where insuring against insolvency under an unfunded retirement benefits scheme (ITEPA 2003 s 307)) or employers' contributions to a registered pension scheme (ITEPA 2003 s 308);

(e) the provision of a parking space for a car, van, motor cycle or bicycle (or voucher to obtain one) at or near the place of work or reimbursement of an employee's expense in obtaining such a parking space near his work (ITEPA 2003 s 237);

(f) works bus services (ITEPA 2003 s 242) and subsidised public transport (ITEPA 2003 s 243) (see **explanatory note 28**);

(g) provision of cycles and safety equipment for use mainly for travel to work or for business journeys (ITEPA 2003 s 244 – see **explanatory note 29**);

(h) the provision of services or assets to protect the employee from a special security threat, such as from terrorists (ITEPA 2003 s 377);

(i) the provision of crèche facilities to any value, or approved child care or child care vouchers of up to a given limit (ITEPA 2003 ss 270A and 318–318D – see **explanatory note 24**);

(j) certain entertainment and gifts (ITEPA 2003 ss 264 and 265 – see **explanatory note 31**);

(k) stress counselling and outplacement counselling for redundant employees (ITEPA 2003 s 310);

(l) welfare counselling services available to employees generally (SI 2000/2080);

(m) in-house sports facilities (ITEPA 2003 s 261);

(n) the payment or reimbursement by the employer of personal expenses such as newspapers and phone calls up to an average VAT-inclusive amount of £5 a night (£10 if outside the UK) where an employee is away from home overnight on business (ITEPA 2003 s 240); and

(o) certain accessories for company cars relating to disability or personal security (see below).

HMRC has confirmed that no benefit charge arises where an employee uses recreational facilities or canteen facilities on the premises of another employer where the employees of that employer work at the same site and use the same facilities. See also **explanatory notes 8** and **35**. The government began consulting in mid-2016 on proposals to prevent salary sacrifice schemes from reducing the tax and NIC payable where a tax-free benefit is exchanged for a lower salary. The new rules on round sum meal allowances in s 289A already prevent these expenses being paid tax-free if they are part of a salary sacrifice scheme, but it is intended that all tax-free benefits with the exception of pension contributions, childcare vouchers and health-related benefits such as cycle-to-work schemes should be similarly restricted in future.

*Private use of employer-provided cars*

(13) The private use of a car provided by the employer attracts a benefits charge, unless the car qualifies as a 'pool car' under ITEPA 2003 s 167 or as an 'emergency vehicle' under ITEPA 2003 s 248A, or is otherwise not commonly used as a private vehicle and unsuited to private use (such as a Formula 1 racing car, or a hearse). A pool car is one that is used by more than one employee, is not normally garaged at an employee's home, and where the private use, if any, is merely incidental to the business use (see SP 2/96 for HMRC's interpretation of 'incidental private use'). An emergency vehicle is a car made available to a member of the fire, police or ambulance service to enable them to respond quickly to emergencies by taking the vehicle home. Special averaging and banding rules apply to cars used by employees in the motor industry – such as those of salesmen and engineers – see HMRC employment income manual EIM 23650. Motorhomes are classed as cars for these purposes.

The charge for private use of taxable cars is based on the list price, without limit (ITEPA 2003 Part 3 Chapter 6). The value includes accessories supplied with the car (other than mobile phones) and any accessory costing £100 or more that is added later, but not including accessories for disabled employees and, from 6 April 2011, security enhancements such as bullet-proofing necessitated by the nature of the employment. Replacement accessories only increase the taxable value of the car to the extent, if any, that they are superior to the old ones, ie, they cost more than accessories that are equivalent to the old ones.

The list price is the manufacturer's, importer's or distributor's list price of an individual car at the time of first registration (including delivery and VAT, but excluding road tax), not the price actually paid. Cars valued at more than £15,000 and at least 15 years old at the end of the tax year are taxed according to their open market value if more than the list price (so as to tax classic cars at their true value). An employee contribution of up to £5,000 towards the initial cost of a car reduces the cost on which the tax charge is based (ITEPA 2003 s 132).

The charge is a percentage of price graduated according to the level of the car's carbon dioxide emissions (see **Example B4 part (A)** for the relevant percentages).

The taxable benefit covers all benefits connected with the provision of the employer's car, including the London Congestion Charge and a 'cherished number' registration plate, but excluding private fuel (see below) and the provision of a chauffeur (ITEPA 2003 s 239(5)).

Where the employee makes a payment to the employer as a condition of the car being available for private use, this sum reduces the taxable benefit (ITEPA 2003 s 144). From 2014/15, the payment reduces the taxable benefit only if it is made within the tax year of charge, although HMRC has indicated that, by concession, it is likely to accept reimbursement up to the P11D deadline for the year, which is more practical.

Where a car is jointly owned by employer and employee, the car is regarded as having been provided by the employer and the $CO_2$-based scale charge still arises, according to the court in *Christensen v Vasili* [2004] EWHC (Ch) 476 and Upper Tribunal in *GR Solutions v R&CC* (TC01928 and [2012] UKFTT 234).

*Provision of private fuel*

(14) There is a separate additional charge for the provision of private fuel in an employer-provided car, based on the percentage used for the car benefit (see **Example B4**), whether the cost of the fuel is reimbursed or paid directly (ITEPA 2003 ss 149–153).

The fuel charge is not varied according to the level of business mileage. It is not reduced by any contribution made by the employee unless the employee makes good to the employer the whole cost of the fuel for his private use, in which case there is no assessable benefit.

The fuel charge is calculated by applying the percentage applicable to the car benefit to £22,200 (£22,100 for 2016/17). Where free fuel ceases to be provided during the tax year, the benefit is reduced pro rata (unless fuel is again provided later in the same tax year, in which case a full year's charge will apply).

HMRC issues a quarterly table of advisory fuel rates for *company* cars that can be used to charge employees for fuel provided by the employer (eg, by allowing the use of a fuel card) for private miles travelled in the company car, or to reimburse employees for fuel they buy that is used for business miles travelled in the company car. If the employer prefers he may provide evidence of actual costs and substitute them for the advisory rates. Without such evidence any excess payment will be liable to PAYE and Class 1 national insurance contributions (but the fuel scale will not apply). Failure to charge for fuel provided for all private miles in an employer's car will result in the scale charge being applied. The scale charge cannot apply where the employee drives his own car: any fuel provided for private purposes will be taxable on its cost.

*Company cars – advisory fuel rates for company cars from 1 September 2016*

These rates apply to all journeys on or after 1 September 2016 until further notice. As rates are updated quarterly, they appear here: https://www.gov.uk/government/publications/advisory-fuel-rates/advisory-fuel-rates-from-1-march-2016.

| Engine Size | Petrol and petrol hybrids | Diesel | LPG |
|---|---|---|---|
| 1400cc or less | 11p | | 7p |
| 1600cc or less | | 9p | |
| 1401cc to 2000cc | 13p | | 9p |
| 1601cc to 2000cc | | 11p | |
| Over 2000cc | 20p | 13p | 13p |

The rates are acceptable to HMRC for VAT purposes (see **explanatory note 20**), but employees claiming the allowance must provide enough VAT receipts to cover the amounts claimed before the employer may recover the input tax (see further below). For more on the decision whether to accept free fuel or not, see **Example B4(C)**.

*Change of car and periods of unavailability*

(15) Where the car is not available for part of the year, the car charge and fuel charge are reduced proportionately. It is treated as not available for any day if it was not made available until after that day, or ceased to be available before that day, or if it was incapable of being used at all for not less than 30 consecutive days. Where a car is unavailable for less than 30 days, a temporary replacement of similar quality is ignored and the same car is regarded as provided throughout.

Employers have to give HMRC details of the first provision and the cessation of provision of cars and car fuel to employees on the online version of Form P46 (Car). The form must be submitted within 28 days after each quarter to 5 July, 5 October, 5 January and 5 April. These returns are no longer required in practice where an employee's company car is changed during the year, but the option to do so by online notification is available. Details of all car and fuel provision are also required on year-end Forms P11D.

*VAT and national insurance on cars and fuel*

(16) In addition to the income tax charges, the employer has to pay VAT on the provision of fuel for private use. VAT is not payable on the provision of the car itself, even if the employee makes a payment for private use, unless the employer recovers all of the input tax on the acquisition of the car, or leases it from a lessor who reclaimed all the input tax on it, in which case a payment by the employee would attract VAT. Employer's Class 1A national insurance contributions are payable both on the provision of fuel in a car provided by the employer and the provision of the car itself (see **part (B)** of the Example and also **Example H1**). The national insurance charges are based on the income tax cash equivalent figures, taking into account any reduction for any employee contributions for the use of the car.

Unlike the income tax and national insurance charges, the VAT scale charges apply to all employees who are provided with fuel no matter what they earn, and no matter whether the car is owned by the employer or the employee, except where an employee has paid for the fuel in full, including VAT, in which case the output VAT has to be accounted for. The VAT fuel scale charges are shown at the front of the book.

The VAT scale charges are based on the $CO_2$ emissions rating, now using a table starting at 120 g/km to set the emissions bands. The rates were updated in May 2016.

See **explanatory note 19** re VAT on mobile phones.

*Cars or cash*

(17) Because of the increased levels of scale charges for income tax, and the added burden of VAT and national insurance, it is often more cost effective for an employer not to provide fuel for private use. It may also be more effective not to provide a car but to pay the employee for use of his own car using the approved mileage allowance rates (see **explanatory note 20**), although these are updated only rarely. Because the employee will not have the option of claiming for actual costs this method will be most useful in the case of older cars which have high list prices or any cars with high business mileage. In most other cases the facility to claim actual costs against the employer's profits will outweigh any increase in the taxable benefit in kind for the employee.

Some employers may offer employees extra salary in place of private use of the company car and/or fuel. Before 6 April 2016, non-P11D employees could be taxed on the salary forgone if they were allowed to switch at any time between cash pay or company car. P11D employees were, and now all employees are, charged to tax and national insurance on what they actually get, either car or cash (ITEPA 2003 s 119).

*Private use of vans*

(18) A fixed tax charge applies for private use of vans with a laden weight of 3.5 tonnes or less (ITEPA 2003 ss 154–166). The taxable amount is reduced by any payment by the employee for private use.

There is no benefit in kind charge where a van is primarily provided to an employee for business purposes but the employee is permitted to take the vehicle home (ordinary commuting). All other private use of the vehicle must be disallowed. However, the legislation does permit other private use if it is insignificant.

Examples of insignificant use published by HMRC include an employee who:

- takes an old mattress or other rubbish to the tip once or twice a year;
- regularly makes a slight detour to stop at a newsagent on the way to work;
- calls at the dentist on his way home.

Examples of use which is NOT insignificant include an employee who:

- uses the van to do the supermarket shopping each week;
- takes the van away on a week's holiday;
- uses the van outside of work for social activities.

Where the above exemption does not apply the taxable amount is a fixed charge of £3,170 per annum (£3,150 before 6 April 2016) where an employee has exclusive private use of a van. In addition, where fuel is provided for private mileage the charge will be increased by a further £598 to £3,768 (£594 for 2015/16). The taxable benefit is reduced proportionately if the van is not provided for the whole year, or is unavailable for thirty consecutive days or more, or for periods when the van is a shared van.

Where vans are shared between several employees, the fixed charges of £3,170 and £598 are apportioned among the users. It is up to the employer to carry out the apportionment. The calculation for unavailability is done first, then that for shared use, then the reduction for payments for private use.

If a van is accepted as a van for VAT purposes then it will normally be treated in the same way by HMRC for income tax. A twin cab pickup with a net load capacity of more than one tonne will be treated as a van. The addition of a weatherproof top over the loading area is treated as reducing the official payload by 45kg, and the load capacity must not be reduced to below 1 tonne if the vehicle is to be treated as a van rather than a car. Car-derived vans will be treated as cars unless they meet the technical criteria specified by HMRC. A description of such car-derived vans is available on https://www.gov.uk/hmrc-internal-manuals/vat-input-tax/vit50600#IDAUXU1H.

A van charge is reduced proportionately if the vehicle is not available for a period of not less than 30 consecutive days. If a van is provided part way through a year, or available only for part of the year, then again a pro-rata charge applies.

Where the van is made available concurrently to more than one employee for private use by the same employer then the cash equivalent is worked out as if the van was not shared and then that charge is reduced on a just and reasonable basis to apportion the charge between the users.

Where it is a condition of the van being made available for private use that the employee is required to pay for, and does pay for, that use, the cash equivalent is reduced correspondingly.

Vans qualifying as 'pooled' do not result in a benefit on the employees that use them. A van qualifies as pooled using the same tests as for cars if:

- it was not normally kept overnight at or near any of the employees' homes;
- employees' private use was incidental to business use;
- it was in a pool for use by employees or one or more employers and it was used by employees and not used by one them to the exclusion of others.

The fuel benefit applies if any fuel is provided for more than insignificant private use. It will not apply if fuel is made available for business travel only, or the employee is required to make good the cost of private travel and in fact does so.

As for cars, no benefit charge applies for emergency vehicles (fire, police or ambulance vehicles normally fitted with a flashing blue light) where private use is prohibited except on an emergency call out. Electric-powered vans with no tailpipe emissions also attracted no benefit charge until 6 April 2015, when the scale was set at 20% of the conventional van scale (ie, £630). This will rise in stages (40%, 60%, 80%, 90%) until the two are at the same level from 6 April 2022.

*Mobile phones*

(19) The provision of a single mobile phone is not taxable on the employee. The contract must be in the name of the company. However, no charge will be imposed in respect of any mobile phones provided for the employee's use (or the use of members of his family or household) before 6 April 2006 (ITEPA 2003 s 319).

Smartphones, other than portable computers that can make calls only over the internet using VOIP technology, are regarded as mobile phones despite including powerful computer facilities (R&C Brief 02/12).

When the employee has more than one mobile phone on which private calls can be made, he may choose which phone is to be the taxable phone for the year. The benefit in kind is calculated by taking into account the cost of the handset (which is frequently very low or even zero) and the monthly charges from the service provider. The benefit is reduced by deducting any amounts incurred wholly, exclusively and necessarily in the performance of the duties – that is the element relating to business use. However, no deduction is ever possible for the fixed rate airtime charges, which normally provide 'inclusive minutes'. A deduction for business use is only available in respect of minutes billed over and above the standard monthly charge.

Despite the income tax exemption, private use by employees affects the input VAT that employers may recover. HMRC have, however, announced that input VAT may be recovered on the cost of the phones and on standing charges and also on call charges if private use is not permitted. If the employer charges employees for private use, input VAT on calls may be recovered in full but output VAT must be accounted for in the charges to employees. If no charge is made input VAT must be apportioned appropriately.

*Business use of own vehicle, motor cycle or bicycle*

(20) Where an employee uses his own transport for business purposes, he is entitled to relief for the business use and may calculate the deduction by using fixed rates (ITEPA 2003 ss 229–236).

The fixed rates are as follows:

| | | |
|---|---|---|
| Cars and vans: | First 10,000 miles in tax year | 45p per mile |
| | Each additional mile | 25p per mile |
| Motor cycles | | 24p per mile |
| Bicycles | | 20p per mile |

Payments by the employer up to the fixed rates for business mileage using an employee's own transport are not liable to tax. Nor is Class 1 national insurance due on any business mileage allowance up to 45p per mile – there is no 10,000-mile annual limit. They do not need to be reported on P11D and cannot be included in a dispensation (because they are tax-exempt rather than deductible when a claim is made). Any excess is liable to Class 1 national insurance through payroll (but see below) and for tax purposes the excess will be shown on Forms P11D.

If the employer does not pay mileage allowances, or pays less than the fixed rates, the employee may claim an appropriate expenses deduction (mileage allowance relief) in his tax return or submitting a claim (but only for tax, not NICs). Employees may not claim based on actual costs, and the fixed rate cannot be increased by relief for loan interest paid or capital allowances.

If, instead of paying a mileage allowance, the employer reimburses the employee's fuel costs, the reimbursement counts as pay for Class 1 contributions, excluding the business proportion providing this is supported by mileage records. Class 1A rather than Class 1 contributions would be payable if an employer's credit card or agency card was used to buy fuel as agent of the employer, as indicated in **part (B)** of the Example.

In addition to the mileage allowance payment, an employer may also pay up to 5p per passenger per mile free of tax and national insurance for fellow employees carried in the employer's or employee's car or van where the journey constitutes business travel for both driver and passengers. The employee cannot claim any relief if the employer does not pay the passenger rate.

Journeys for which the employer can reimburse the employee must meet the definition of business travel. Extensive guidance on this subject is given by Booklet 490. In broad terms, a journey to a place where the duties of the employment are to be performed is an allowable journey unless that journey is normal (or substantially ordinary) commuting, described as a journey between a permanent workplace and a place which is not a workplace. See **Example B6 explanatory note 6** for more details of allowable travel.

Employers have to pay the VAT scale charges on private fuel provided for employees' own cars. They currently can reclaim the input tax if they reimburse the cost to the employees, and can claim input tax on the fuel element of a mileage allowance, but not on the part of the allowance that is for repairs etc. The advisory rates in **note 14** should be used for this purpose. Following a March 2005 decision by the European courts that ruled that recovery of VAT paid by an employee was illegal, HMRC issued Value Added Tax (Input Tax) (Road Fuel Purchased by Employees) (Order) 2005. This confirms that input tax on fuel purchased by employees on behalf of their employer is recoverable, provided it is used in the business in making taxable supplies and is supported by a VAT receipt. This leaves the financial position for employers unchanged, but adds the administrative requirement for a VAT receipt to be retained, although there is no requirement for any particular VAT receipt to be related to any particular business journey or claim.

If the employer buys the rights to a 'cherished number' registration plate and makes the use available to an employee for his own car (ie, not on a company car), that is taxable as the provision of an employer-owned asset (see below). On a company car, the provision of a personalised number plate is covered by the normal scale charge, and the list price is unaffected by the cost of the right to use the special number, which as a right rather than a physical object is not classed as an accessory.

*Use of employer-provided assets other than cars, vans or living accommodation*

(21) Where an employee has the use of an asset other than a car, van, living accommodation or land, the cash equivalent of the benefit is 20% of the market value of the asset at the time of its first provision plus the full amount of any expense incurred in providing the asset (hence the charge on Honiton for the use of the furniture in the company house). The cash equivalent is reduced proportionately where there is partial business use of the asset, and is also reduced pro rata if the asset is only provided for part of the year. If the ownership of the asset is subsequently transferred to an employee then he is charged to tax at that time on the *higher* of:

(a) The market value of the asset at the time of the transfer of ownership.

(b) The market value at the time of the original provision less the total amounts charged on any employee as benefits under the benefits code of ITEPA 2003 for the use of the asset.

This calculation does not apply to the transfer to an employee at market value of a previously-loaned computer if the computer was first made available to the employee before 6 April 2006 or of a bicycle or cycle safety equipment previously used for qualifying journeys (ITEPA 2003 s 206(6)).

The courts have not been asked to rule on the correct treatment of an asset that is jointly owned by employer and employee, other than motor cars.

*Medical insurance & treatment*

(22) The cost of medical insurance provided by the employer is assessable on directors and employees under the general charging provisions of the benefits code (ITEPA 2003 Part 3 Chapter 10). The cost of any medical treatment paid by the insurance scheme is irrelevant. The measurement of the benefit is *what it cost to buy* that insurance. There is an exception for both tax and national insurance for the cost of medical insurance and/or medical treatment while an employee is working abroad (ITEPA 2003 s 325 and SI 2001/1004 Sch 3 Part VIII).

ITEPA 2003 s 320C, from 6 April 2014, exempts the provision or reimbursement of up to £500 pa of medical treatment to an employee if the treatment has been recommended by certain occupational health services engaged by the employer to help an employee to return to work after sickness absence. The exemption does not apply where the provision is made under salary sacrifice or flexible benefit scheme arrangements.

*Meals and luncheon vouchers*

(23) Employees are not taxed on the benefit of free or subsidised meals if the meals are provided for the staff generally on the employer's own premises or in a canteen located elsewhere (but if a public restaurant was used, there would have to be an area separate from that open to the general public), or where using the canteen situated at the place of employment run by another employer where the facilities are not taxable on that employer's staff. (ITEPA 2003 s 317). Where companies do not have such separate facilities, the provision of meal vouchers is covered by the voucher provisions of ITEPA 2003 s 89 (see **explanatory note**

9). The whole value is taxable and NICable. The same value is treated as pay for Class 1 national insurance contributions. The full cost of the vouchers is allowable as an expense to the employer.

*Child care*

(24) The provision of child care facilities for children aged under 18 is, subject to conditions, fully exempted from the employee benefits charging provisions (ITEPA 2003 s 318). The exemption does not cover supervised activity provided primarily for educational purposes.

The facilities may be provided jointly with other employers, voluntary bodies or local authorities, but each employer must be partly responsible for finance and management. The premises must be registered where required by law, and they cannot be domestic premises. In addition, the exemption covers another employer's staff, who work at the providing employer's premises, when using the childcare facilities.

The exemption does *not* cover cash allowances or paying the employee's child care bills. Such provision for child care expenses is liable to Class 1 national insurance as for tax. A limited exemption applies to the provision of vouchers or the provision by the employer of child care in facilities other than the employer's and in circumstances that meet certain conditions.

For employees who were in receipt of child care benefits before 6 April 2011, an employer may provide tax- and NIC-free vouchers for qualifying child care or a contracted nursery place to a value not exceeding £55 per week. The employer may also pay the voucher administration costs in addition to the £55 without creating a taxable benefit. The vouchers must be accessible to all employees or to all persons working at the location where the scheme operates, except for those earning only the national minimum wage who may be disregarded in certain circumstances. The child only qualifies up to 1 September after its 15th birthday (plus an extra year if it is disabled). Both father and mother can receive vouchers to the value of £55 per week under this provision for the same child, even if they both work for the same employer. See also former booklet IR115 and the former Helpbook E18 (2012) (ITEPA 2003 ss 318–318D). It is currently possible to combine the provision of child care with equivalent salary sacrifice.

For details of tax credits claimable in respect of qualifying child care costs and details of when it is disadvantageous to receive tax-free child care vouchers see **Example A7**.

The tax reliefs for employer-supported childcare changed from April 2011 for new recipients, with the reliefs restricted for higher rate and additional rate taxpayers so that the value of the relief is the same for all taxpayers. For new recipients, the employer must now assess the employee's basic earnings at the start of the tax year or, on an annualised basis, at the time of joining the scheme. After deducting from those annual earnings the single personal allowance, the employer then decides whether the employee would be a basic, higher or additional rate taxpayer for the year. Those assessed to fall into the basic rate may receive £55 of childcare benefit tax- and NI-free, while those in the 40% bracket may receive £28 per week and those in the 45% bracket £25 per week. Any value provided to the employee above those limits must be reported on P11D and, for vouchers, dealt with through payroll, as the excess is subject to Class 1 NI liability.

Employer-supported childcare is to be reformed from April 2017 with new tax-free childcare accounts.

*Examination prizes*

(25) The definition of earnings under the benefits code will catch a cash prize paid at the employer's discretion to an employee. This is also counted as earnings for tax credits. If the payment is in kind then it will be liable to Class 1A national insurance (instead of Class 1) and excluded for tax credits.

*Beneficial loans*

(26) P11D employees who have interest-free or favourable interest rate loans from their employers are taxed on the shortfall of the interest charged compared with the official rate (ITEPA 2003 Part 3 Chapter 7). The official rate is normally fixed for the whole tax year, although there is provision for the rate to be changed if interest rates move significantly during the year. The rate since 6 April 2015 has been 3% (previously 3.25% after 6 April 2014). There is no tax charge on loans made to employees on commercial terms by employers who lend to the general public or if the loan is a qualifying loan for interest relief (see **Example A1 explanatory note 14**). Nor is there any charge if the total of all beneficial loans does not exceed £10,000

at any time in the tax year (£5,000 for 2013/14 and earlier years). If an employee has two or more loans at a beneficial rate, they are aggregated for the purpose of calculating the cash equivalent, except where the loans have separate terms and conditions and one or more of them qualifies to be treated as a public rate loan, in which case that loan may be disregarded.

See **Example J2** for further notes and a detailed illustration of the beneficial loans rules.

*Equipment and facilities provided for the performance of the duties*

(27) Where provision of a computer falls within ITEPA 2003 s 316, no benefit arises. To be exempt under this section private use must not be significant and it must have been provided solely to enable the employee to perform their employment duties. If there is a mixed motive, no exemption is available. Section 316 is widely drafted and would also cover an iPad or broadband use, provided the business needs merit the provision. This exemption will therefore cover the provision and related costs of the home office equipment, laptop computer and tablet, which is regarded as a computer rather than a mobile phone. In establishing whether private use is significant, a qualitative approach is taken, to avoid the need for employers to record the business and private use on a time basis. If the provision is required to enable the employee to perform his duties, then the private use is regarded as insignificant.

Where an employee is taxable on the private use of a computer, the benefit is calculated as in **21 above**, ie, based on 20% of the cost of the computer (including VAT) plus related expenditure, eg, insurance and maintenance. Output VAT on the provision of the computer for private use should also be charged, based on the VAT fraction of the private proportion of the estimated depreciation for the year. Where computer equipment was first made available to employees generally before 6 April 2006 (including members of their family or household), the benefit is chargeable to income tax and Class 1A national insurance only to the extent that the cash equivalent (*before* reduction for business use etc) exceeds £500.

The transfer of ownership of the computer will not give rise to the charge set out in **21 above** provided the employee pays full market value and provided it was first made available before 6 April 2006.

Where the employer also provides broadband internet facilities under a contract in his name, and no breakdown between business and private use is possible, then HMRC accepts that no benefit in kind is chargeable, provided the facility is made available solely for the employee to perform his duties. This obviates the need to monitor business and private use.

*Subsidised transport*

(28) There is no benefit in kind charge on the provision by an employer of a free or low cost works bus service, free or subsidised travel on local public stopping bus services used by employees to travel to or from work, or employer financial or other support for other bus services used for such journeys providing in this latter case that the employees do not obtain the service on more favourable terms than other passengers (ITEPA 2003 s 242). A works bus must have 9 or more passenger seats, be used for qualifying journeys, and must be available to the employees generally. It may be used for limited purposes during a working day without the employees incurring a benefit, eg, to take them shopping in the lunch break.

*Bicycles*

(29) Workplace parking for bicycles and motor cycles is free of tax and national insurance (ITEPA 2003 s 237). Furthermore, an employer may provide a cycle (and safety equipment) for commuting and business journeys (ITEPA 2003 s 244). The offer of cycles and equipment must be available to the employees generally and used mainly for qualifying journeys. Transfer of ownership at market value will not give rise to a tax charge (as set out in **21 above**). Alternatively, an employee may provide his own cycle for business journeys, claiming an allowance of 20p per business mile as indicated in **note 20 above**. If the employer pays less than 20p per business mile the employee may make a tax claim for the shortfall.

To encourage employees to travel to work by cycle, employers were for several years able to provide 'cyclist breakfasts' on designated cycle-to-work days without a tax charge on the employee. This was available even if only part of the employee's journey to work was by bicycle but the relief was abolished from 6 April 2013 as a simplification measure.

*Car sharing arrangements*

(30) Where employees car share and the arrangements break down in exceptional circumstances (eg, the driver is required to return home during working hours because of illness of spouse/children) then the employer may provide transport to take the employees home without a charge to tax.

*Entertaining expenses (including staff entertaining) and gifts*

(31) If an employee receives amounts specifically for entertaining, or is specifically reimbursed for entertaining expenses he has incurred (such as the £1,560 received by Honiton in this Example), those expenses are deductible (and therefore now exempt) in calculating taxable income provided the expenses are disallowable in the employer's computation of taxable income (ITEPA 2003 s 357). They are disallowed in the employer's computation of taxable profit and employers who are trading organisations must tick a box on Form P11D to indicate that this has been done. Employees of charities that are exempt from income and corporation taxes need not meet the disallowance test, although UK-based employees of foreign businesses with no taxable UK presence can often be affected.

If an employee pays entertaining expenses out of his salary or out of a round-sum allowance not specifically earmarked for entertaining, he is assessed on the full salary or allowance and may not claim any deduction, but the employer is allowed to deduct the full salary or allowance paid to the employee in his profit computation.

The benefit arising from entertaining provided to employees by third parties is not charged to tax, unless it has been procured by the employer or it relates to services performed or to be performed in the employment (ITEPA 2003 s 265). Gifts to employees from third parties of up to £250 in a tax year are exempt (ITEPA 2003 s 324), unless they are procured by the employer or relate to services that are part of the employee's normal duties. Section 264 provides that employees are not charged on the benefit of one or more annual parties etc that are open to staff generally, providing the cost to the employer for each person attending (including employees' guests) does not exceed £150 a year (VAT-inclusive). If the total cost per person for all annual functions exceeds £150 the exemption can be claimed on one or more of the functions for which the total cost does not exceed £150. HMRC has been known to argue that a staff function does not qualify under this rule unless it is 'annual' (eg, a 50th anniversary celebration for the business, which by definition only happens once), but this interpretation is more restrictive than the original concession, which was intended to reduce administrative burdens arising from small benefits. For the treatment of entertaining expenses for the employer see **Example C2 explanatory note 7**.

*Scholarships and training courses*

(32) Although income in the form of scholarships and educational grants is exempt from tax for the recipient under ITTOIA 2005 s 776, scholarships awarded to children of employees are assessable on the parent (ITEPA 2003 ss 211–215) unless they are fortuitous awards paid from a trust fund or scheme under which not more than 25% of the total payments relate to employees.

(33) An employee is not taxed on the payment or reimbursement by his employer of the cost of a training course providing it satisfies stipulated criteria (ITEPA 2003 Part 4 Chapter 4). The provisions cover not only directly job-related training but also training in health and safety and to develop leadership skills. As well as the direct costs, the exemption covers learning materials, examination fees and registration of qualifications. Travelling and subsistence expenses are allowed to the same extent as they would be for employment duties.

Where employees are retrained in new work skills when they are about to leave or have left their present jobs, they are not taxed on the benefit of the expenses of retraining which are paid for or reimbursed by the employer, and the employer is able to deduct the cost in calculating taxable profits (ITEPA 2003 s 311).

Employees on full-time and sandwich courses at universities and colleges lasting 1 year or more may be paid a bursary of up to £15,480 a year tax- and NIC-free while they are on the course (Revenue Statement of Practice 4/86 updated 1 September 2007 and SI 2001/1004 Sch 3 Part VII para 12).

*Long service awards*

(34) An employer may make a non-taxable award in kind (or in company shares) to an employee to mark not less than 20 years of service. The award must have a value not exceeding £50 per year of service and tax-free awards cannot be made at intervals of less than 10 years (ITEPA 2003 s 323). Vouchers exchangeable only for goods may be NIC-free if the long service award qualifies as tax-free (SI 2001/1004 Sch 3 Part V para 6) but not if they are vouchers to obtain readily convertible assets or exchangeable for cash.

*Homeworkers' expenses*

(35) Payments by the employer for reasonable additional household expenses incurred in carrying out duties of the employment at home under home-working arrangements are exempt from income tax under ITEPA 2003 s 316A. To minimise the need for record keeping, HMRC has stated that employers can pay up to £4 per week or £18 per month without supporting evidence of the costs the employee has incurred (EIM01476). The rate was £3 per week before 6 April 2012. Payments over and above this amount must be reimbursement of reasonable additional household expenses incurred, which can extend to the payment of broadband contract charges in the name of the employee, provided this is an additional cost that the employee incurred as a result of working from home.

*National insurance*

(36) For detailed notes on national insurance contributions see **Example H1**. For the special rules relating to marketable assets such as gold and commodities see **Example B2 explanatory note 12.**

*Tips and gratuities*

(37) See **Example H1 part (D)** for the tax and national insurance treatment of gratuities.

*Pension provision*

(38) HMRC have confirmed that tax-efficient pension contributions will be relievable by employers as deductible business expenses if the overall remuneration level is reasonable for the work done (BIM46035). If the employee has a pension input of more than £40,000 (£10,000 for those with earnings above £210,000, and an intermediate amount for those with adjusted income between £150,000 and £210,000) and suffers the annual allowance charge on the excess contributions or the excess value of increased pension benefits, the tax charge is payable under self-assessment by the employee, not through payroll or P11D. The employer need not deduct tax from any employer contributions made, nor will any national insurance liability arise.

*Late-night taxis home*

(39) A member of staff who works late and for whom a taxi home is provided is not taxable on the cost of the taxi provided that the late night working conditions are met and the journey is one of no more than 60 in the tax year. The late-night working conditions must all be met for the taxi to be tax free:

- the employee is required to work later than usual, and at least until 9pm;
- this occurs irregularly;
- by the time the employee leaves work public transport has ceased, or it would not be reasonable to expect the employee to use it; and
- the transport is by taxi by road or similar.

For more information about the administration of late-night taxi payments, and the records that HMRC expects employers to keep, see the Employment Income Manual at EIM 21831. Under proposals by the Office of Tax Simplification this relief was to be abolished from April 2012 but the change was abandoned because of the difficulties it would cause to employers and HMRC's policing activities.

# Question

(1) Q works for 007 Support Ltd and normally works at and lives near the company's London site. He was asked to go to a Hereford site for a period of seventeen months from 3 August 2015. He commutes on a weekly basis and 007 Support Ltd reimburses his travel and hotel costs, plus a £4.50 lunch allowance. After a review of the project in August 2016, it is decided that Q is needed at the site for at least another 18 months, but he is also required to spend Monday each week in the Bristol office, travelling there from home and going on from there to his hotel in Hereford. The company continues to pay his weekly commuting expenses and hotel costs, including his laundry bills. Outline the correct treatment of the various expenses for the company.

(2) Ms M who is Q's assistant normally works at the London site but is required to travel to the Hereford site for one day, 18 May 2016. She normally travels into London using her season ticket. She drives directly to Hereford from her flat in Ashford which is a round trip of 436 miles. 007 Support Ltd reimburses the full costs of her day's journey to Hereford. The theoretical round trip from the London office to Hereford is 296 miles, which is significantly less than the actual costs incurred travelling from home. Assuming the company pays her 45p per mile, how much of her expenses claim must be passed through payroll? Explain your reasoning.

(3) S is a freelance investigator who works through his own personal service company, Sceptre Ltd. 007 Support Ltd hires him for a month, working in the Hereford area as Q's assistant, paying him a daily rate and expenses against the submission of an invoice from his company with supporting vouchers for the expenses. He is told that Q is in charge of the project and is entitled to instruct S in how to conduct the tasks he is given. He is required as part of the exercise to travel to a number of places of interest to Q. How should 007 Support Ltd and Sceptre Ltd treat the expenses payments for tax and NIC?

(4) Part of Q's role is to recruit for 007 Support Ltd a number of field agents who work for him across Herefordshire, Gloucestershire and Powys. They are all offered a nominal pay rate of £20 per hour, but they can choose instead to take a lower hourly rate and to have paid instead their daily travel to and from the site tax-free, plus a tax-free subsistence allowance at the HMRC-approved rate of £5 per day. How should 007 Support Ltd deal with the payment of these expenses?

# Answer

(1) The Hereford site initially counts as a temporary workplace, as he is expected to attend there for less than two years. Neither tax nor Class 1 NIC liabilities will therefore arise in relation to the reimbursed costs.

If he uses the train from home to Hereford and back, he can be reimbursed for the tickets with no tax consequences because the costs are exempt. He would be entitled to a deduction for travel between home and a temporary workplace, so ITEPA 2003 s 289A deems the expenses to be exempt.

If he drives his own car, he can claim 45p per mile tax- and NIC-free for the first 10,000 business miles per year. Once his business mileage exceeds 10,000, the tax-free amount reduces to 25p per mile, although the NIC-free rate is still 45p. If the company pays him 45p for mileage above 10,000, the tax is accounted for by reporting the excess for taxation purposes on his P11D.

If he drives the company Aston Martin, he may claim the HMRC advisory fuel rate tax-free for all his commuting mileage.

The lunch allowance falls within the statutory meal allowance set by ITEPA 2003 s 289A and is therefore tax- and NIC-free. The laundry costs are classed as incidental overnight expenses and are tax-free provided they cost no more than £20 per week (ie, £5 per night spent in the hotel).

Once the decision is made to extend his stay beyond 24 months, however, Hereford becomes a permanent workplace at once. When the company continues to pay his hotel, travel and subsistence costs, they will all be taxable and NICable. Anything paid in cash to Q must be payrolled, and the hotel costs (booked and paid for by 007 Support Ltd, and therefore a benefit in kind for Q) must be reported on his P11D or included in the company's PSA.

The position in relation to Bristol depends on whether it can be classed as another permanent workplace. If so, travel between home and Bristol will be classed as ordinary commuting, but between Bristol and Hereford it will be treated as business travel between two permanent workplaces. If it can be treated as a temporary workplace, which seems likely since the arrangement is not planned to last more than 24 months, both legs of the Monday journey will be classed as business travel and the expenses may be treated as exempt.

(2) Hereford is clearly a temporary workplace that Ms M is required to attend in the performance of her duties, so all the costs of travelling between home and the Hereford office are deductible for Ms M and therefore exempt when paid by 007 Support Ltd. The company needs to make no payroll or P11D entries in respect of the expense reimbursement.

If the employer had only reimbursed her for the 296 miles, being the theoretical round trip from her normal office location to Hereford (because she would have had to incur the cost of travelling between Ashford and London anyway), Ms M would have been able to claim a tax deduction via a P87 or her self-assessment return for the additional cost of the journey not originally allowed, ie, 140 miles @ 45p per mile. There would however only be Class 1 NIC relief on the amount actually reimbursed by the employer, and no retrospective NIC relief for the cost she had incurred in excess of the reimbursement.

(3) S works through a personal service company, and he is effectively in disguised employment (ie, within IR35), being explicitly subject to supervision, direction and control by Q in carrying out his duties, even though he is legally employed by Sceptre Ltd and Sceptre is supplying his services under a contract between itself and 007 Support Ltd.

S and Sceptre Ltd therefore fall within the rules that apply to workers whose personal services are supplied via an intermediary. Sceptre Ltd will need to make a calculation under ITEPA 2003 Part 2 Chapter 8 (the IR35 rules) and possibly treat itself as making a payment of earnings on 5 April in respect of this contract. 007 Support Ltd can pay Sceptre's invoices as rendered, without making any deductions, but when Sceptre reimburses or settles S's expense claims, it will need to take care to separate out the costs of travel and subsistence relating to the work at the Hereford office, which must be payrolled, and those related to the other places where he is sent by Q, which should be exempt.

Because the arrangements fall within IR35, ITEPA 2003 s 339A deems the Hereford office to be a permanent workplace, so any costs of commuting between home and that office will be treated as remuneration, with no deduction available. However, any other site to which he is sent, either from Hereford or from home, will count as a temporary workplace, so the mileage costs and any subsistence costs should be exempt from tax and NIC.

(4) Expenses paid under salary sacrifice arrangements no longer qualify for a deduction for income tax (ITEPA 2003, s 289A) or exclusion from earnings for NIC purposes (Contributions Regs 2001, Schedule 3 Part 8 para 1A), so the whole of the sums paid to the agents must be subject to PAYE and NIC through the payroll, whether they opt for the £20 per hour wages take the lower rate and the expense payments. This is so even if they can prove that they have incurred travel and subsistence costs in travelling to a temporary workplace.

## Explanatory Notes

(1) The treatment of employees' travelling expenses (which is accepted generally by HMRC to include subsistence while travelling) is dealt with for income tax purposes in ITEPA 2003 ss 337–342. Relief is given for travelling expenses, that is, amounts necessarily expended on travelling in the performance of the duties of the employment, or other travelling expenses which are attributable to the necessary attendance of the employee at any place in the performance of his duties and are not expenses of ordinary commuting or private travel. Further rules apply to international travel.

With effect from 6 April 2016, with the introduction of s 339A into ITEPA 2003 by FA 2016, workers supplied by intermediaries to provide their personal services to clients, under any kind of supervision, direction or control as to how they work, have to treat each assignment as a separate employment. A similar rule applies to those working through personal service companies within IR35. This means that most new engagements will lead to the intermediary worker ordinarily commuting between home and a new permanent workplace. These rules do not apply to workers who carry out their duties in the end user's home (eg, district nurses, domestic cleaners and carers).

Ordinary commuting broadly means travel from home to the permanent workplace. Private travel means travel between home and a place that is not a workplace, or between two places neither of which is a workplace. A permanent workplace is a workplace that is not a temporary workplace, and a temporary workplace is a workplace the employee attends to perform a task of limited duration or for some other temporary purpose. A workplace is not a temporary workplace if the employee works there continuously for a period of more than 24 months or if the employment itself is only expected to last for all, or almost all, of the period at that workplace.

Note, though, that in certain circumstances an employee may have a temporary workplace even though he only ever attends a single workplace in that employment. In *Michael Williams* (TC02062), the worker in question took on a contract at Heathrow Terminal 5 with the intention that, after 16 months, he would move to the employer construction company's site at Kings Cross. In the event, he moved into a different role at Heathrow until his employment ceased, more than 24 months after it had started. It was held that Heathrow was a temporary workplace until it became clear that he would be staying there for more than 24 months, ie, when he was offered the new contract at Heathrow after 16 months. For the period after the change of intention, Heathrow was a permanent workplace, so his travel and subsistence costs in that period were not deductible.

Where home is a permanent workplace, it is nevertheless still home, so travel between such a home and another permanent workplace (eg, by those who work part-time from home and part-time from an office) is still ordinary commuting, as shown by the decision in *Lewis v Revenue and Customs Commissioners* [2008] STC (SCD) 895.

Work at a particular place is regarded as continuous if the duties of the employment fall to be performed to a significant extent at that place (significant being regarded by HMRC as 40% or more). Site-based employees with no permanent workplace are allowed the cost of travelling to and from home, and subsistence while away, providing the job at the site is expected to and does last for not more than 24 months. As and when it becomes clear that the job will last for more than 24 months, travel and subsistence expenses are taxable from that time. Site-based employees are not allowed relief for subsistence expenses if they have no permanent home, because subsistence expenses must be attributable to the business travel.

Employees are entitled to relief for the full amount of qualifying travelling expenses. The full cost of meals and accommodation while travelling or staying away on business is allowable as part of the cost of travel. Business travel includes travelling on business from home where the journey is to (or from) a temporary workplace, or where the nature of the employment requires the employee to carry out his duties at home (but doing work at home for convenience rather than because of the nature of the job does not turn the home into a workplace). Where a journey has both a business and a private purpose, the expense will be allowed if the journey is substantially for business purposes.

As far as national insurance contributions are concerned, the rules are almost the same as for income tax, except that mileage payments may be made at 45p for every mile without NIC becoming due, whereas for income tax there is a 10,000 mile per year limit in each employment before a lower rate of 25p applies. Contributions will normally be payable only if the employer makes a payment to the employee that exceeds the cost of a business journey.

*Home to work travel expenses - analysis*

(2) It is well established in income tax law that the costs incurred by an employee in travelling from his home to his normal place of work are expenses incurred in placing himself in a position to carry out his employment, not in carrying out the employment itself. Accordingly, any payment by an employer of, or as a contribution towards, any such expenses incurred by the employee is earnings for contribution purposes. In the case of *Warner v Prior* [2003] STC SCD 109 Sp C 353 a supply teacher worked from home and travelled to different schools in the area and claimed the cost of travelling as an expense. It was held that the expense of travel to and from home to the schools was not allowable as 'her secondary place of work at home was dictated by where she lives and not by the requirements of the job itself.' Also in *HP Lewis v HMRC* [2008] Sp C 690 a Revenue officer (L) had worked for many years at HMRC offices within daily commuting distance of her home in Warwickshire. In 2000 she successfully applied for a post in London. She was allowed to work at the London office for two or three days each week, and from her home for two or three days each week. She claimed a deduction for the costs of travelling from Warwickshire to London. HMRC rejected the claim on the basis that this expenditure was 'ordinary commuting', which was not deductible by virtue of ITEPA 2003, s 338. The Special Commissioner upheld HMRC's ruling and dismissed L's appeal. See HMRC Booklets 480 (2016), Chapter 4 and 490, Chapter 3. There are now six exceptions to the rule stated above.

The first arises where the employee is a disabled person for whom training or employment facilities (ie sheltered workshops) are being provided under the Disabled Persons (Employment) Act 1944, s 15. If an employer defrays or contributes towards the expenses which such an employee incurs in travelling from his home to his main place of work, the employer's payments are to be excluded from earnings for contribution purposes. [Social Security (Contributions) Regulations 2001, SI 2001/1004, Sch 3, Part V, para 5(a) and Part X, para 8(b) as amended by Social Security (Contributions) (Amendment No 2) Regs 2010, SI 2010/188; ITEPA 2003, s 246]. See HMRC Booklet 480 (2016), paras 5.21, 11.17, 13.5 and 490, para 8.22. This exception was introduced to bring disabled people in sheltered workshops into line with disabled people in open employment for whom State-provided help with travelling expenses does not count as earnings for contribution purposes. See also HM Revenue and Customs National Insurance Manual NIM06390.

The second exception arises where the employee is temporarily working at some place of work other than his usual place of work, eg at the premises of one of his employer's clients or on detached duty at some branch of the business other than the branch at which he normally works. If the employer pays or contributes towards the expenses which such an employee incurs in travelling from his home to his temporary place of work and, at the outset, the temporary placement is not expected to last for more than 24 months, the employer's payments are to be excluded from earnings for contribution purposes. Before 6 April 2016, there appeared to be some basis in law for a rule that had regard to a temporary workplace. It would have appeared to lie in Smith v Stages [1989] AC 928, [1989] 1 All ER 833, HL (a vicarious liability case) where it was held that an employee who, for a short time has to work for his employer at a different place of work some distance away from his usual place of work will be acting in the course of his employment when travelling from and returning to his ordinary residence if he travels in his employer's time.

From 6 April 2016, the NIC position was moved onto a statutory footing that matches the income tax position.

Where any period of work at a temporary workplace is not expected to exceed 24 months, tax or NICs are not required to be deducted from the payments. However, if the period at the temporary workplace is expected from the outset to exceed 24 months then the favourable treatment will not apply. The employee need not return to the original permanent workplace. The recurrence of temporary employment in manipulation of the 24-month period will not be allowed but travel between employments or offices in the same group of companies will be allowed (see HMRC Booklet 490, Chapter 3 and ITEPA 2003, ss 338, 339, 339A; Social Security (Contributions) Regulations 2001, SI 2001/1004, Schedule 3 Part 8 para 3).

Note that this second exception does not apply, with effect from 6 April 2016, to workers supplied via an intermediary (ie an umbrella company or a personal service company) who are under supervision, direction or control as to how they work. Any IR35 company supplying its owner-director is within the scope of this rule.

The third exception relates to costs incurred on fuel, repairs etc for use in a car made available to the employee in connection with his employment. This exception was extended to company-owned vans with effect from 21 July 2008.

The fourth exception applies when there is a disruption to public transport caused by a strike or some other form of industrial action, or when an employee has worked to 9 pm or later at the request of his employer and this has not happened more than 60 times already in that year so that it does not then form part of the normal pattern of the employment. See Booklets 480 and 490, and HM Revenue and Customs National Insurance Manual NIM06370. This corresponds to the income tax exception set out in ITEPA 2003, ss 245, 248. The exception also applies when travel (including foreign travel) expenses are paid under ITEPA 2003, ss 341, 342, 369–371, 376.

Where the employer (rather than the employee) incurs the expense of the employee's home to work travel by, for example, arranging a taxi on the company account the benefit enjoyed by the employee is a payment in kind and is not earnings for Class 1 purposes although a Class 1A charge arises. Before 6 April 2016, when the distinction between P9D and P11D employees was abolished, the Class 1A charge would have arisen only in respect of P11D employees, but now all employees fall within the benefits code and potentially attract a Class 1A NIC liability. The same comment was applicable to the purchase of, for example, a rail season ticket until 6 April 1999, but that is no longer so because non-cash vouchers were then brought into Class 1 liability.

The fifth exception relates to the travel expenses of unpaid directors of not-for-profit companies, following the introduction of a statutory exemption for expenses previously disregarded under ESC A4. ITEPA 2003, ss 241A, 241B and 340A were inserted by the Enactment of Extra-Statutory Concessions Order 2014, SI 2014/211. Where the director is obliged to incur expenses as the holder of the unpaid employment and they are attributable to the director's necessary attendance 'at any place' in the performance of the duties of the employment, they are also excluded from NICable earnings by SI 2001/1004, Sch 3, Pt VIII, para 3A.

The sixth exception, from 6 April 2016, relates to the travel expenses of local authority members attending official council meetings that became statutorily tax-free by virtue of ITEPA 2003, s 295A (inserted by F(No 2)A 2015, s 29). These also became NIC-free under Contributions Regs 2001, Schedule 3, Part 8, Para 17.

*Site-based employees*

(3) 'Site based' employees such as those in the construction industry or computer support industries often have no normal place of work. They work at various sites consecutively spending weeks or months at each site. The expense of travel in getting from home to site is not incurred in the performance of the duties. These expenses were therefore included in gross pay for tax and NICs until 6 April 1998. The employee was deemed to be travelling to the job, as opposed to the travelling appointment situation, where he is travelling

on the job. If the employee then has to travel between sites it will be treated as travel between two (or more) places of work and is therefore in the course of employment. 'Reasonable' reimbursed travelling expenses between sites will not be liable for tax or NICs.

In a travelling appointment, the employee has to travel as part of his duties. He is travelling on the job rather than to the job, as in the case of a person with a normal place of employment. In such a case, the employment generally commences when the employee leaves home and therefore his travelling expenses are incurred in the performance of the duties of that employment. In these cases, expenses paid should not be included in gross pay for tax or NICs. The expenses of travelling to the boundary of the area of the area of responsibility are liable to tax and NICs if the employee lives outside the area within which he is required to travel as part of his job (see Booklet 490).

When the tax and NIC treatment of travel expenses for intermediary workers was reformed with effect from 6 April 2016, nothing changed the treatment of site-based workers supplied by intermediaries. While FA 2016, s 14 inserted ITEPA 2003, s 339A to deny tax relief to certain supervised intermediary workers for the costs of travelling between home and work, the relief affected was only that previously available for travel to a temporary workplace under ss 338–339. The tax relief for the travel costs of site-based workers (eg, district nurses, meter readers, in-home carers, etc) is given by s 337, which was unaffected. The same applies for the statutory relief from NIC liability.

In the case of offshore oil and gas rig workers, the reimbursement of expenses incurred by those workers in the course of transferring to or from the mainland is disregarded for tax and NIC purposes. This also includes the provision of overnight accommodation in the vicinity of the mainland departure point. See Booklet 480 (2016), para 5.21 and ITEPA 2003, s 305.

*PSCs & intermediary rules*

(4) From 6 April 2016, Finance Act 2016, s 14 inserted ITEPA 2003, s 339A to remove tax relief in respect of travel expenses between home and work (ie, under ss 338–339) for workers supplied by intermediaries, which includes all PSCs that are not managed service companies within ITEPA 2003, Part 2, Ch 9 (albeit with a slightly extended definition – see below). The equivalent changes were introduced into contributions legislation as Social Security (Contributions) Regs 2001, Sch 3, Part 8 para 3ZB.

This provides that, where a worker personally provides services other than in the client's home and those services are provided via an employment intermediary, each engagement is now to be regarded as a separate employment, mirroring the new income tax rules. This severely limits the scope to claim a deduction for home to work travel expenses, although expense deductions will still be available where the duties involve travelling to other temporary workplaces during the course of an engagement (i.e., in the same way as relief would apply to a permanent employee of the client).

For most intermediary workers, this rule does not apply if it is shown that the manner in which the worker provides the services is not subject to (or to the right of) supervision, direction or control by any person, but where the engagement falls within the IR35 rules in ITEPA 2003, Part 2, Chapter 8 and the PSC is not a managed service company, this exclusion does not apply.

Where a PSC is not within Chapter 8 of Part 2 'merely because the circumstances in s 49(1)(c) . . . are not met' (ie, there is no disguised employment, such as where a genuinely self-employed contractor has decided to operate through a limited company) and the company is not a managed service company, para 3ZB does not apply, so home to work travel payments should still be tax-and NIC-free.

For the purpose of both of these tests, the definition of 'managed service company' is extended beyond the meaning given by ITEPA 2003, s 61B to include those PSCs that would be managed service companies if all of the income was not paid out as employment income and therefore disregarded under s 61B(1)(c). The MSC is excluded in both situations because the rules in Chapter 9 of Part 2 already tax and NIC payments that reimburse the costs of travel between home and work.

As with all new legislation, a targeted anti-avoidance rule was included. In determining whether the block on relief for home-to-work travel expenses should apply, no regard is to be had to any arrangements the main purpose, or one of the main purposes, of which is to secure that this rule does not to any extent apply.

In practical terms, the new rules mean that a PSC worker whose engagement falls within IR35 will no longer be able to extract money from his or her company as tax- and NIC-free travel expenses and thereby sidestep the IR35 rules that require PAYE and NIC deductions.

The new rules were clearly aimed at those employment businesses that operated a 'payday-by-payday' tax relief model for expenses and used it to reduce taxable wages to a varying degree each week or month. Employees would be given an 'umbrella' employment contract, under which they would be sent to work at a series of temporary workplaces. This entitled the employer to pay them home-to-work travel expenses tax- and NIC-free if they so chose. However, instead of offering a wage of £500 per week, the employment business would typically employ workers under a contract guaranteeing a net payment and use tax- and NIC-free home-to-work travel expenses to reduce the overall cost of meeting that commitment. This type of salary sacrifice arrangement is no longer effective.

*6 April 2016 reforms to general expenses rules*

(5) Following recommendations from the Office of Tax Simplification, FA 2015 reformed the expenses regime from 6 April 2016 so that dispensations could be abolished, employers no longer needed to report non-taxable expenses on form P11D, and employees no longer needed to make a claim for a deduction. In addition, the £8,500 limit for P11D employment was abolished, along with the P9D, with all employees being brought within the scope of the benefits code. Under the normal ITEPA 2003, s 70 rule, expenses paid by an employer are still deemed to be earnings (now for all employees, irrespective of earnings level), a deduction has typically had to be claimed where the expenses were incurred for an allowable purposes.

In simple terms, under ITEPA 2003, s 289A, any expenses that would qualify for a deduction under the normal rules is now exempt (meaning that they are no longer required on a P11D), except if it is paid under a salary sacrifice arrangement. Those non-qualifying expense payment are simply treated as taxable pay (but subject to PAYE and Class 1 NICs, not P11D reporting). This may be particularly significant to those employers who were paying allowances such as home working expenses of £4 per week tax-free under a salary sacrifice arrangement – that arrangement is no longer effective.

In order to replace the relaxations afforded by dispensations for round sum expense allowances when they were abolished in April 2016, employers were also given the power to pay round sum meal allowances at statutory rates (s 289A) or at bespoke rates explicitly agreed with HMRC for up to five years at a time (s 289B). These are as an alternative to reimbursing actual expenditure.

In order to qualify for the exemption, the employer must operate a checking system and have no reason to suspect that the expenses in question have not been incurred.

The official guidance is that reimbursement of the actual amount spent will fall within the terms of the excluding regulations, as will any part of a round sum allowance which corresponds to an actual, identifiable business expense.

From 6 April 2016, it must fall within the scope of ITEPA 2003, s 289A or s 289B without falling within Reg 22(12) or 22(13) of the Contributions Regs 2001 (which requires it not to exceed the statutory or bespoke rate. The official guidance on NICs in CWG2 (2016), pages 72–74 has not yet caught up with the change in the NIC regulations.

From 6 April 2009 until 5 April 2016, HMRC-specified round sums (so-called 'benchmark scale rates') could be applied in certain circumstances if the employer preferred to use a fixed rate rather than actual expenditure (see EIM05231). As noted, provision was made in ITEPA 2003, s 289B (inserted by FA 2015, s 11) for flat rate expense reimbursement rates to be approved by HMRC for exemption of such expenses from income tax from 6 April 2016, and, as already noted, the NIC regulations were amended so as to adopt the same rules from the same date.

Under the non-statutory HMRC benchmark rules:

- A rate of up to £5.00 could be paid for breakfast cost where a worker left home earlier than usual and before 06:00, and incurred an expense in buying breakfast away from home after the qualifying journey started.

- A rate of up to £5.00 could be paid where the worker had been away from his home/normal place of work for a period of at least five hours and had incurred the cost of a meal.
- Where the worker had been away from his home/normal place of work for a period of at least ten hours and had incurred the cost of a meal or meals, a rate of £10 would be allowed.
- However, a further rate of up to £15.00 could be paid where the employee had to work later than usual, finished work after 20:00 having worked his normal day and had to buy a meal which he would usually have eaten at home.

The new statutory meal allowance rates from 6 April 2016 followed the same pattern, albeit with slightly different wording and with extra obligations for the employer, such as having the checking regime in place to ensure that the allowances claimed were in respect of qualifying travel and were actually being spent as intended, and not knowing or suspecting that the conditions would not have been met – see ITEPA 2003, s 289A(2)-(4). Anything exempted from income tax by s 289A is also excluded from earnings for NIC purposes – see Contributions Regs 2001, Sch 3 Part 8, para 8A.

The rates were set by the Income Tax (Approved Expenses) Regs 2015 as early as 21 December 2015 so as to give HMRC the power to agree bespoke rates in advance of implementation on 6 April 2016. The standard rates are now expressed, for both income tax and NIC purposes, as an amount that does not exceed:

- £5 where the duration of the qualifying travel in the day is five hours or more;
- £10 where the duration of the qualifying travel in that day is 10 hours or more; or
- £25 where the duration of the qualifying travel in the day is 15 hours or more and is ongoing at 8pm.

A supplementary allowance not exceeding £10 per day may be added to either of the first two allowances where the allowance is paid for a period that is ongoing at 8pm.

With the abolition of the P9D, certain low earners could have been disadvantaged. To prevent this in the case of ministers of religion (who are low paid but with benefits in kind) and live-in domestic carers (who could have become liable to tax on ancillary costs associated with their board and lodging), a new statutory regime was created (ITEPA 2003, ss 290–290G, and s 306A) to tax their expenses on the same basis as the old P9D rules.

# Question

(a) Explain the method of calculation of the cash equivalent of the benefit applicable to a motor car owned by a company and made available to an employee to be used both for business and privately.

(b) Set out the method to be used if the vehicle does not have a $CO_2$ emissions figure.

(c) John Hodges is employed by Cecil Ltd. He travels 7,000 business miles and 8,000 private miles per annum in his company car, which he will change in September 2016. His employer has offered John a choice of car from the following pool of cars that are available in the company fleet:

| Car | $CO_2$ emissions figure | Fuel type | Expected list price plus accessories |
|---|---|---|---|
| | g/km | | £ |
| Land Rover Discovery 3.0 | 193 | Diesel | 40,005 |
| VW Passat 1.4 TSI 160 | 124 | Petrol | 24,035 |
| Toyota Hilux twin-cab pickup* | 174 | Diesel | 21,760 |
| Ford C-Max 2.0 | 169 | Petrol | 29,035 |
| Toyota Prius 1.8 | 70 | Petrol hybrid | 25,295 |
| Nissan Leaf 24kw | 0 | Electric | 26,490 |

* Load capacity 1,060kg

Advise John of the amounts on which income tax would be charged in 2016/17 in respect of each car assuming the car was available for the full year from 6 April 2016. Comment on the longer term level of tax liabilities.

(d) Comment on the advisability of Cecil Ltd providing fuel for John to use privately in the company car.

(e) The chairman and major shareholder has recently expressed an intention to buy a second-hand Ferrari Freccia Rossa as his next company car for £60,000. He is aware that it is not very 'green', as its $CO_2$ emissions are 350g/km, but he thinks the company can afford it at such a reasonable price for a luxury car, although he would not buy the same model new because the list price is still £239,000, as it was when the car was first sold. Describe the likely tax and NIC costs if he goes ahead with his plan.

(f) Boris is the office junior and errand boy, normally using his bicycle to make deliveries around town. When the company opens a second office in a nearby town, the chairman recognises that Boris will need to use a car to do his job, so the business buys a small second-hand car and tells Boris to use it when he needs it. He is told to leave the keys on reception when he finishes for the day, but he is allowed to take the car home if he happens to be out on an errand at the end of the working day, which happens two or three times each week. Explain briefly the rules that determine whether the company should report a taxable benefit on Boris's P11D in respect of the use of the car.

# Answer

## (a) Computation of cash equivalent of car benefit

### Carbon dioxide emissions figure

Where a car is provided by an employer to an employee or member of his family or household the cash equivalent of the benefit is based on the published carbon dioxide ($CO_2$) emissions figure (in grams per kilometre) for a given car. That figure is determined by the manufacturer using an EU standard test.

Many aspects affect the emissions figure, including the size and efficiency (state of tune) of the engine, fuel used, transmission (manual, automatic, two- or four-wheel drive) and accessories (eg, air conditioning). Each model variant will have a separate emissions figure. For cars registered from 1 March 2001 the official emissions rating appears on Form V5, the registration document, to which reference should be made or on the internet at www.vca-.gov.uk. For cars registered between 1 January 1998 and 1 March 2001 the official emissions figure can be obtained from the Internet, at carfueldata.direct.gov.uk/search-new-or-used-cars.aspx.

Except at certain special levels, the emissions figure is rounded down to the nearest whole 5 grams below, eg, $CO_2$ emissions figure 187 g/km becomes 185 g/km, and is then converted to a percentage using the HMRC table shown below. Cars are expected to become more environmentally friendly and the scale figures are being progressively reduced.

The maximum percentage to be applied to the list price of the car is now 37% (it was 35% before April 2015). In calculating the benefit, the list price was capped at £80,000 (see **Example B2 explanatory note 13** for detailed notes on the meaning of list price) until 5 April 2011, when the cap was removed.

*Scale charges for petrol cars*

| *$CO_2$ emissions (g/km)* | *Percentage of list price (add 3% for diesel, but cap at 37%)* | | | | |
|---|---|---|---|---|---|
| | 2015–16 | 2016–17 | 2017–18 | 2018–19 | 2019–20 |
| 0 to 50 | 5 | 7 | 9 | 13 | 16 |
| 51-75 | 9 | 11 | 13 | 16 | 19 |
| 76-94 | 13 | 15 | 17 | 19 | 22 |
| 95 | 14 | 16 | 18 | 20 | 23 |
| 100 | 15 | 17 | 19 | 21 | 24 |
| 105 | 16 | 18 | 50 | 22 | 25 |
| 110 | 17 | 19 | 21 | 23 | 26 |
| 115 | 18 | 20 | 22 | 24 | 27 |
| 120 | 19 | 21 | 23 | 25 | 28 |
| 125 | 20 | 22 | 24 | 26 | 29 |
| 130 | 21 | 23 | 25 | 27 | 30 |
| 135 | 22 | 24 | 26 | 28 | 31 |
| 140 | 23 | 25 | 27 | 29 | 32 |
| 145 | 24 | 26 | 28 | 30 | 33 |
| 150 | 25 | 27 | 29 | 31 | 34 |
| 155 | 26 | 28 | 30 | 32 | 35 |
| 160 | 27 | 29 | 31 | 33 | 36 |
| 165 | 28 | 30 | 32 | 34 | 37 |
| 170 | 29 | 31 | 33 | 35 | 37 |
| 175 | 30 | 32 | 34 | 36 | 37 |

*Scale charges for petrol cars*

| *$CO_2$ emissions (g/km)* | *Percentage of list price (add 3% for diesel, but cap at 37%)* | | | | |
|---|---|---|---|---|---|
| 180 | 31 | 33 | 35 | 37 | 37 |
| 185 | 32 | 34 | 36 | 37 | 37 |
| 190 | 33 | 35 | 37 | 37 | 37 |
| 195 | 34 | 36 | 37 | 37 | 37 |
| 200 | 35 | 37 | 37 | 37 | 37 |
| 205 | 36 | 37 | 37 | 37 | 37 |
| 210+ | 37 | 37 | 37 | 37 | 37 |

* The maximum percentage cannot exceed 37% from 6 April 2015 even if the car runs on diesel.

## Special provisions for particular circumstances

Diesel cars have a lower $CO_2$ figure than the equivalent petrol models. To maintain an equitable balance of taxable benefits with petrol vehicles (because diesel drivers would otherwise have much lower taxable benefits than petrol drivers who have very similar company cars), the percentage is currently increased by 3%. This currently applies subject to the maximum of 37%. It was planned in 2014 that the scales would focus on simple $CO_2$ ratings from April 2016 and no diesel surcharge would apply thereafter, but this policy was reversed in Budget 2016, when it was announced that the 3% surcharge would continue until 2021.

The scale on which the benefit is based is to be amended several times over the next three years:

- From 2016/17, the starting point rose to 7% for the lowest band (0 to 50 g/km), 11% for 51 to 75 g/km, and 15% of list price for any car rated from 76 to 94 g/km, and the 3% diesel surcharge remained in place. The maximum percentage of list price to be taxed stayed at 37%.
- From 2017/18, all benefits will rise again, by 2% of list price, albeit with the same 37% cap.
- From 2018/19, the least polluting cars (0–50 g/km) will see their benefit rise by 4% of list price to 13%, those that are currently classed as ultra-low emissions cars (51–75 g/km) by 3% to 16%, and all other cars by 2%. The maximum 37% scale charge will then be reached at emissions of 180 g/km or more, which would have attracted only a 22% scale charge ten years ago.
- From 2019/20, as the law currently stands, every band will see a further rise of 3% of list price, subject to the maximum of 37% (reached at 165g/km).
- The Government has announced plans to keep the $CO_2$ basis for 2020/21 but is to consult on the taxation of ultra-low emissions cars.

Disabled drivers who are required to use an automatic car because of their disability may use the $CO_2$ figure of the equivalent manual car and, where the automatic version is more expensive than the manual, disabled drivers may use the list price of the equivalent manual car (ITEPA 2003 s 124A).

If a normally fuelled car is converted to use gas, the cost of conversion is excluded from list price. However, a car designed to use gas or bi-fuels at manufacture receives no reduction from list price in cases where the car benefit is taxed by reference to the $CO_2$ emissions figure. Such cars used to benefit from a lower % rate but the discounts were withdrawn from 6 April 2011 so that the focus is solely on the actual $CO_2$ emissions rating rather than the fuel type.

Electric cars were exempt until April 2015, when the rate became 5%. There are no special rates for alternatives. Gas cars have a $CO_2$ figure. Bi-fuel cars have two $CO_2$ figures, the lower (invariably the gas figure) being used to calculate the relevant percentage. One other provision applying to alternative fuel cars is that the cost of conversion is disregarded in deciding the list price for bi-fuel gas and petrol cars where conversion is after type-approval.

## Periods of unavailability, older cars, payments by employee etc

A reduction for periods of unavailability of at least 30 consecutive days is available. The list price is reduced by capital contributions made by an employee not exceeding £5,000. Where the car is jointly owned by employer and employee, there is still a scale charge as if the car was provided solely by the employer, although the list price can be reduced by the employee's capital contribution up to £5,000. There are no discounts for business use or for the age of the vehicle. Where the car provided is more than 15 years old at the end of the tax year ('classic' cars) and has a market value exceeding £15,000 then market value is substituted for list price. A maximum figure of £80,000 applied to the list price or market value until 5 April 2011, although this cap has now been abolished.

Where a payment is made by the employee as a condition of the car being made available for private use, this amount is deducted from the computed benefit in kind, provided it is paid to the employer within the tax year or, by concession, by the P11D submission deadline of 6 July. For years up to 5 April 2016, where the employer leased a vehicle to an employee at a leasing rental determined by full open market rates, there was consequently no economic benefit to the employee (he could have leased the car from an independent third party for the same price), which meant no taxable benefit, and therefore there was no need to calculate a $CO_2$ value or make a P11D entry. However, HMRC did not concede this until August 2016, after FA 2016, s 7 had changed the law in ITEPA 2003, s 114 to disregard any such 'fair bargain' arrangements for 2016/17 onwards, and impose the $CO_2$ formula calculation, with a deduction from the formula-based value for employee payments, even if the employee does not benefit economically.

Second cars are charged at the same rate as first cars, even if there is no business use.

### Company vans

Where a company van is made available for private use that is more than insignificant, a flat-rate scale charge applies, which was set at £3,170 for 2016/17. The benefit is not based on the $CO_2$ emissions or fuel type of the van. If free fuel is provided for private motoring in a company van that attracts a scale charge, the flat-rate fuel scale is £598 for 2016/17.

A twin- or double-cab pickup often has an interior that is equivalent to the specification of a car rather than a commercial vehicle, and it may be either a car or a van for these purposes, depending on its payload capacity rather than its actual use. If the vehicle has an official payload capacity of 1,000kg or more, it is treated by rule-of-thumb by HMRC for income tax, NICs and VAT as a van. Any hard-top cover for the load area is treated as weighing 45kg, so the payload capacity must be at least 1,045kg for the vehicle to be treated as a van rather than a car. On the basis that the Toyota Hilux model mentioned has a payload capacity of 1,060kg, it is treated as a van for benefit in kind purposes.

Company vans that have a maximum laden weight of more than 3,500kg are exempt from scale charges provided they are not used mainly privately. Electric vans that run on batteries have a cash equivalent value of 20% of the conventional van benefit, but this is set to rise in stages in future to the same level as the normal van benefit. No fuel benefit charge applies in respect of any electricity paid for by the employer to recharge the van.

## (b) Computation of cash equivalent where $CO_2$ figure is unavailable

Cars registered before 1 January 1998 (presumably now very rare as company cars) do not have a $CO_2$ emissions figure computed to the relevant standard. The percentage of list price for those few cars still provided as company cars is based on engine size, but with no discounts for age, as follows:

| Engine size (cc) | Percentage of car's price taxed |
|---|---|
| 0–1400 | 16% |
| 1401–2000 | 27% |
| 2001 and over | 37% |
| Cars without a cylinder capacity (eg, rotary-engined petrol cars) | 37% (but not electric cars with no emissions) |

These rates will rise to 18%, 29% and 37% for conventional engines from 6 April 2017.

A limited number of cars produced on or after that date will also not have a $CO_2$ figure, eg, kit cars, imports of specialised cars from outside the EU, home-built cars. The percentage to be used is then:

| Engine size (cc) | Percentage of car's price taxed |
|---|---|
| 0–1400 | 16%*† |
| 1401–2000 | 27%* |
| 2001 and over | 37% |
| Cars without a cylinder capacity (eg rotary-engined petrol cars) | 37%† |

* Plus 3% supplement for diesel cars.

† Electrically propelled cars: 7% for 2016/17, then successively 9%, 13%, and 16% for the following tax years.

## (c) John Hodges – cash equivalent of benefits

| List price | | | 2016/17 |
|---|---|---|---|
| | £ | % | £ |
| Land Rover (diesel) | 40,005 | | |
| $CO_2$ figure 203 = 200 | | 37 (max) | 14,802 |
| VW Passat 1.4 TSI 160 | 20,900 | | |
| $CO_2$ figure 124 = 120 | | 21 | 4,389 |
| Toyota Hilux | 21,760 | | |
| Load capacity = 1,060 kg = van | | n/a | 3,170 |
| Ford C-Max 2.0 | 29,035 | | |
| $CO_2$ figure 169=165 | | 30 | 8,711 |
| Toyota Prius 1.8 | 25,295 | | |
| $CO_2$ figure 70 | | 11 | 2,782 |
| Nissan Leaf 24kwh | 26,490 | 7 | 1,854 |

Thus, leaving aside the electric car, which because of its very limited range (around 124 miles on a full charge) is unrealistic for use as a company car for most people, the most expensive traditional car in the schedule (the Land Rover) gives the highest tax charge but the cheapest car (the VW Passat) does not give the lowest tax charge. The lowest taxable benefit for a car that is not range-restricted comes from the Toyota Prius, an electric hybrid with very low emissions. This is even better than the van benefit chargeable for private use of the Toyota twin-cab pickup. The price of the Prius is mid-range. Apart from the Hilux this model is also the only vehicle in the list on which the employer could claim a 100% first-year or enhanced capital allowance if bought new. The threshold for the 100% allowance has now been reduced to 75g/km. The Hilux is the only vehicle on which a VAT-registered employer could reclaim input tax.

Because 'perk cars' have the same charge as business cars, it may be very tax-efficient to provide a perk car, especially where the emissions percentage is low (say 21% or lower). The provision of a car where the percentage is high (say 29% or higher) is unlikely to be cost-effective. The provision of a business car may continue to be tax-effective if the emissions figure is low (and very low emissions should mean high capital allowances) or private miles are high. The provision of an employee's own car and payment of mileage allowances at the HMRC approved rate is likely to be more tax-efficient in the case of older, larger cars where the taxable benefit may exceed the second-hand value of the car. In the case of *Prince Erediauwa* (2010) TC00869, a taxpayer driving a very old but very expensive company car mistakenly thought that it was a pooled car, which would attract no taxable benefit. It was held by the tribunal to be a company car available for his private use, with a taxable benefit of 35% of its high, original list price, and the tax payable for one year was more than the second-hand value of the car.

## (d) Provision of fuel for private use

In most circumstances, the provision of fuel for private use in a company car is not cost-effective because the benefit is an 'all or nothing' charge that will be assessable in full, even if the employee only uses £1 of private fuel which he does not reimburse. *Impact Foiling Ltd and others v Revenue and Customs Commissioners* (SpC 562) 2006 demonstrated the cost of failing to record and check business and private mileage accurately. The two directors in this case were found to have kept inaccurate mileage logs that underestimated private mileage for 2002 to 2004. In January 2005 the company invoiced the directors for the full cost of fuel for the periods, but the Commissioners upheld the fuel benefits as the directors had not made good the cost of private fuel in the relevant year as specifically required by the legislation allowing relief for reimbursement. This requirement was extended to payments as a condition of the car being made available for private use for 2014–15 onwards, closing down the possibility of retrospective reimbursement (although HMRC has indicated that it will, by concession, allow a deduction for payments made before the P11D submission deadline).

Where an electric car is provided with zero emissions, there is no fuel benefit for the provision of recharging facilities by the employer, which may be attractive once practical electric vehicles and enough charging stations become available.

For non-electric cars, an increase in salary to compensate for the employees buying their own fuel for private motoring can cost the employer and employee less than the cost of the fuel purchased. The price of fuel and the advisory fuel scale will alter over the life of the car, but the principle can be illustrated using current figures and rates. In the case of John Hodges he would have a tax charge on a benefit for 2016/17 as follows (annual amounts, pro-rata to actual dates car provided):

| | | |
|---|---|---|
| Land Rover | 22,200 × 37% | £8,214 |
| VW Passat | 22,200 × 21% | £4,662 |
| Toyota Hilux | Van charge | £598 |
| Ford Galaxy | 22,200 × 30% | £6,660 |
| Toyota Prius | 22,200 × 11% | £2,442 |

Cecil Ltd could use the advisory fuel rates for company cars (see **Example B2 explanatory note 14**) or actual costs to calculate how much extra salary, if any, to pay.

Assuming fuel consumption as shown below (official, rather than real world values), and assuming the price of fuel to be 120p per litre = £5.45 per gallon, the position would be:

| | | Actual fuel cost per mile (inc VAT) | Advisory scale rate from 1/09/16 |
|---|---|---|---|
| Land Rover | 35.3 mpg | 15p | 13p |
| VW Passat | 45.6 mpg | 12p | 11p |
| Toyota Hilux | 38.7 mpg | 14p | n/a † |
| Ford C-Max | 34.9 mpg | 16p | 13p |
| Toyota Prius | 70.6 mpg | 8p | 13p |

† Advisory rate not accepted for vans – reimbursement of actual required.

Assuming that John Hodges is a basic rate taxpayer, the salary increase required and overall savings to Cecil Ltd (disregarding VAT) might be:

### If Cecil Ltd provides private fuel for the VW Passat

| | £ | £ |
|---|---|---|
| Fuel cost to Cecil Ltd for 15,000 miles | | |
| 329 gallons @ £5.45 (actual inc VAT) | 1,793 | |
| Class 1A national insurance on fuel charge £4,662 × 13.8% | 643 | 2,436 |
| Cost to John | | |
| Tax charge on £4,662 @ 20% | 932 | |
| *If John buys fuel and charges Cecil Ltd for 7,000 business miles, using advisory fuel scale rates* | | |
| Fuel cost (as above) | 1,793 | |
| *Less*: business use 7,000 miles @ 11p | (770) | |
| Net extra fuel cost to John | 1,023 | |
| *Less*: tax saved as above | (932) | |
| Cost to John – net pay increase needed | 91 | |
| Extra costs for Cecil Ltd | | |
| Gross pay increase by Cecil Ltd: £91 ÷ (100%–(20%+12%)) (allowing for 20% PAYE and 12% primary NICs) | | 134 |
| Employer's NIC on £134 | | 18 |
| Cost of business fuel to Cecil Ltd 7,000 miles @ 11p | | 770 |
| Total company costs if no free fuel given | | 922 |
| Saving to Cecil Ltd by not providing free fuel for private use (£2,436–£922) | | 1,514 |

### If Cecil Ltd provides private fuel for the Toyota Prius

| | £ | £ |
|---|---|---|
| Fuel cost to Cecil Ltd for 15,000 miles | | |
| 212.5 gallons @ £5.45 (actual inc VAT) | 1,158 | |
| Class 1A national insurance on fuel charge £2,442 × 13.8% | 337 | 1,495 |
| Cost to John | | |
| Tax cost on £2,442 @ 20% | 488 | |
| *If John buys fuel and charges Cecil Ltd for 7,000 business miles, using advisory fuel rate* | | |
| Fuel cost (actual, as above) | 1,158 | |
| *Less*: business use reimbursed by Cecil Ltd 7,000 miles @ 13p | (910) | |
| Net cost to John | 248 | |
| *Less*: Tax saved as above | (488) | |
| Net saving for John – no extra salary needed | 240 | |
| Cost of business fuel to Cecil Ltd: 7,000 miles @ 8p | | 560 |
| Saving to Cecil Ltd | | 935 |

The calculations are assumed to be VAT neutral, although in practice it will be necessary to take into account input VAT recovery on the actual cost or advisory rate and scale charges for notional output tax on the supply to the employee. Similar savings would apply to the other cars considered.

If John drove the Toyota Hilux, the tax cost to him of the free fuel would be only £120 (£598 @ 20%). Cecil Ltd would have to buy 388 gallons of diesel, costing around £2,115 (inc VAT), of which around £1,128 (8/15ths) would relate to John's private mileage. Cecil Ltd would also pay only £83 in Class 1A NICs on the provision of the benefit. Since the advisory mileage rates do not apply to vans, John would have to spend the £1,128 personally to escape a scale charge that costs him only £120, so it would clearly make sense for John and Cecil Ltd to keep the benefit in kind of free fuel for private motoring rather than pay personally for private fuel.

## (e) Provision of luxury company car

In the circumstances outlined, the chairman's choice of company car will give rise to a taxable benefit for him of 37% of the £239,000 list price (ie, £88,430), rather than being based on the cost of the car to the company. From 6 April 2015, the maximum $CO_2$ rating rose to the maximum 37%, so his taxable benefit should stay at that level for the next four years. He is also likely to have a taxable benefit of 37% of £22,200 (ie, £8,214) on the provision of fuel for private motoring. If he is a 45% taxpayer, his total income tax liability for 2016/17 on the car with a true market value of £60,000 would therefore be £43,473. In addition, the company would be liable to Class 1A NICs at 13.8% of £96,644, ie, £13,337. This would be repeated each year. In contrast, if the company bought the car and gave it outright to the chairman as a bonus, his one-off tax charge would probably be £27,000 and the company's one-off Class 1A liability would be £8,280. There would then be tax and NICs to pay on any running costs borne by the company in excess of the 45p per mile that the company could pay for the chairman's business mileage.

## (f) Boris

It now does not matter whether Boris earns at least £8,500 including any taxable benefit in respect of the private use of the car, as the P9D/P11D distinction has been abolished, and all employees fall within the benefits code. The benefit will be taxable (on the basis of the car's original list price and $CO_2$ emissions rating) unless he can demonstrate that his use of the car meets the requirements of the pooled car rules in ITEPA s 167, which would mean that no tax charge would arise. If he fails to do so, he will also face a tax charge on the provision of fuel for private use in respect of his commuting between home and the office.

The car will be classed as a pooled car only if five conditions are met:

(i) it is available to, and actually used by, more than one employee;

(ii) it is made available, in the case of each of those employees, by reason of their employment;

(iii) it is not ordinarily used by Boris to the exclusion of the others;

(iv) any private use by Boris is merely incidental to his business use of it; and

(v) it is not normally kept overnight at or near Boris's residence unless it is kept on premises occupied by the company.

Employees may normally take a pooled car home overnight to enable them to leave early on a business journey the following morning, and this may happen up to 60% of the time, although Boris's regular pattern of use of the car suggests that, even if he stays below the 60% threshold, HMRC is likely to regard his travel between home and work as something other than 'merely incidental' to his business travel. It is also not clear that any other employee actually uses the car. In any event, Boris and any other employees who use the car should be required to keep detailed mileage records in order to justify any claim that their use is solely or overwhelmingly for business purposes with only incidental private use.

# Question

(a) Explain the tax treatment of lump sum payments made when an employee takes up employment (sometimes called 'golden hellos').

(b) On 31 December 2016 Gordon Jones retired from his employment with Widgets International plc after 30 years' service, the first 12 of which were at the company's overseas branch. He received a lump sum ex gratia payment of £100,000.

Show how much of the £100,000 is taxable.

(c) Mrs Baines retired from her employment on 31 October 2016 because of a permanent disability. She was awarded an ex gratia lump sum payment of £40,000 on that day.

Show how much of the £40,000 is taxable.

(d) Mrs Juliette Brassington, office manager of T & S Textiles Ltd, was made redundant on 5 September 2016. She received £20,000 as compensation for loss of office. Her season ticket loan of £6,000 was written off and she was also given her company car at its agreed value of £4,000.

Show the amount on which she is taxable in respect of the redundancy package.

(e) Gerry Scattergood was made redundant from Shillingford in February 2017 after many years' service.

After leaving he was paid a lump sum of £40,000 under a settlement agreement which has been accepted by HMRC as compensation for loss of office. He also received £2,000 statutory redundancy pay.

Gerry's taxable salary for 2016/17, before considering the £40,000, amounted to £27,435 above his personal allowance, none of which was savings income and all of which had been taxed through the monthly payroll.

Calculate the tax and NI ultimately payable on the £40,000 termination payment.

How would it differ if Gerry and his former employer agreed in the settlement agreement that the compensation payment would be split, so that £30,000 was payable immediately on signing the agreement and £2,500 was payable quarterly in the following tax year?

(f) Supposing the statutory income of £27,220 of Gerry Scattergood for 2016/17 in **part (e)** had included contributory jobseeker's allowance totalling £600, state how this will have been dealt with for tax purposes.

(g) Alistair Green was made redundant in May 2016. He received statutory redundancy pay of £11,600, enhanced by his employer to £23,200, and rather than asking him to serve his notice period, his employer exercised its discretion under his employment contract to pay him £10,800 in lieu of notice. He was also paid £2,000 in lieu of untaken holiday days, as provided for in his contract. How, if at all, are these payments taxed?

(h) Ali Sadiq is a banker who has earned £140,000 and paid £20,000 into his personal pension scheme. Because he feels he has been subject to discrimination at the bank for some time, he resigns in January 2017, claims constructive dismissal and sues the bank for injury to feelings caused by the discrimination. Assume in previous years he paid a contribution equal to the annual allowance each year into his pension. His compensation payment is calculated at £200,000, but his employer suggests that it can pay the money as an extra employer pension contribution to Felix's pension fund, as the bank need not then deduct PAYE or national insurance contributions. State the tax implications of this proposal.

# Answer

(a) Where a lump sum payment is made to a prospective employee, it is necessary to decide whether the payment is taxable under the general earnings rules as remuneration for future services, or whether it represents compensation for some right or asset given up on taking up the employment, in which case it escapes a general earnings charge. These are essentially questions of fact to be decided by the tribunal, with the usual rights of appeal.

In *Jarrold v Boustead* (1964) a signing-on fee to a rugby football player to compensate him for giving up his amateur status was held not to be taxable. The same applied to an allotment of shares to an accountant to compensate him for giving up his position as senior partner in his own firm and taking on employment as managing director with a former client company (*Pritchard v Arundale* (1971)). But in the case of *Glantre Engineering Ltd v Goodhand* (1983), a payment to the company's accountant when he took on the role of financial director with the small, dynamic but relatively new company was held to be an inducement to take up the employment rather than compensation for leaving his previous employment with a nationally known firm of accountants. Similarly, a payment by Nottingham Forest Football Club to former England Peter Shilton when he was transferred to Southampton FC was held to be an inducement to join Southampton rather than an ex gratia payment on leaving Nottingham Forest (*Shilton v Wilmshurst*, HL (1991)). It is clear therefore that great care needs to be taken when considering the tax treatment of such payments.

Sometimes a lump sum is paid in return for the individual agreeing to restrict his conduct or activities in some way, for example agreeing not to take up employment with a competitor within a certain period of time after leaving (often called a 'golden handcuff'). All payments in respect of such restrictive covenants are taxed as pay (and subject to Class 1 national insurance contribution liability) in the normal way, and the employer is allowed to deduct them as an expense (ITEPA 2003 s 225). If an employee makes such an agreement in return for a non-cash benefit, the value of the benefit still counts as earnings for tax and Class 1A national insurance contributions (ITEPA 2003 s 226). HMRC do not regard s 225 as applying where the only restrictive undertaking additional to those in the contract of employment given by the employee is that he will not pursue an action against the employer concerning the termination of his employment (Statement of Practice SP 3/96).

If an employee is paid a 'signing-on bonus' that is repayable in the event of leaving within a specified period, it will be taxable and NICable when paid, but any repayment should be deductible on leaving early, in the year of repayment, but only for tax purposes and only against other employment income in the year, as ITEPA 2003, s 11 expressly allows for negative earnings but there is no provision for carry-back (*Julian Martin*, [2013] UKUT 0429). There are no NIC provisions for negative earnings that allow any repayment of the original contributions. The NIC position might be protected by making the signing-on bonus a formal loan that is written off in stages, so that the payment does not become earnings for NIC or tax purposes until each tranche is released, but this would also give rise to a reducing deemed loan benefit on the P11D and a Class 1A liability each year until the whole amount has been released.

Employer NIC liabilities in respect of 'golden hellos' or 'golden handcuffs' are ordinary secondary Class 1 liabilities and as such may be covered by the employment allowance.

(b) **Gordon Jones**

HMRC may take the view that Gordon has simply retired, which would mean that the ex gratia payment represents an arrangement to provide a benefit from an employer-financed retirement benefits scheme (EFRBS) and is therefore taxable in full under ITEPA 2003 Part 6 Chapter 2, in which case none of the provisions granting full or partial exemption relating to overseas service (ITEPA 2003 ss 413 and 414) or the £30,000 exemption (ITEPA 2003 s 403(1)) will be available. Normally a tax-free lump sum on retirement can only be paid from a registered pension scheme. However, some terminations of employment of older workers, while really dismissals for redundancy or waning competence, are described as early retirement to save embarrassment for all concerned. HMRC accepts (see EIM15022) that it is necessary to establish the true reason for the termination: if Gordon's departure is in fact a dismissal (eg, for redundancy) rather than a retirement, it could still be possible to treat the payment as falling within s 401, benefiting from both foreign service relief and the £30,000 exemption.

If the payment is not regarded as caught under ITEPA 2003 s 394 (relevant benefits from EFRBS, taxable in full), the position will be as follows:

| | £ |
|---|---|
| Ex gratia sum on retirement – 31 December 2016 | 100,000 |
| *Less:* Exemption under ITEPA 2003 s 403 | 30,000 |
| | 70,000 |
| *Less:* Exemption for overseas service (see **explanatory note 6(c)(ii)**) 12/30ths | 28,000 |
| Taxable part of £100,000 | 42,000 |

No national insurance is due on compensation payments. If the payment is made to Gordon on the day he leaves the employment and before his P45 has been issued, it is taxable under PAYE at the normal rates and reported in the same way as regular pay. If the payment is made after the termination, after the issue of the P45 and after the date of leaving notification on the last FPS, the company is obliged to deduct PAYE using tax code 0T on a non-cumulative (ie, W1/M1) basis. The payment must be reported on an FPS, flagged as a payment after leaving (but showing the original date of leaving). The company should revise the year-to-date figures to include the taxable termination payment (unless the termination payment falls into a later tax year). Gordon will probably have to claim a refund of any additional rate tax deducted.

(c) **Mrs Baines**

Mrs Baines's ex gratia lump sum should be wholly exempt from tax under the 'golden handshake' provisions because it arises through her disability (ITEPA 2003 s 406). Unless the disability was the result of an accident, however, the payment will possibly be regarded as being received under an employer-financed retirement benefits scheme, in which case it will be chargeable to tax in full under ITEPA 2003 Part 6 Chapter 2.

(d) **Mrs Juliette Brassington**

The golden handshake provisions apply both to cash payments and benefits in kind, but only if they are not otherwise chargeable to tax. If an ex gratia payment or benefit represents a reward for past services, it will be charged to tax under the general earnings provisions, in which case national insurance will also be due, Class 1 on the cash and Class 1A on the benefit. If it is not, it may be regarded as a benefit from an EFRBS (see **(b) above**). HMRC have, however, stated that this will not normally apply to a straightforward redundancy package. The season ticket loan write-off is taxable under ITEPA 2003 s 188, so cannot benefit from the £30,000 exemption. Unless the car is regarded as a reward for past services or an EFRBS non-cash benefit, therefore, its value will be exempt from tax under ITEPA 2003 s 403(1), along with the compensation payment of £20,000. In view of the amounts involved it would have been more straightforward if Mrs Brassington had been given a tax-free redundancy payment of £30,000, then allowed to pay off the loan and buy the car from the company at the market value of £4,000. A loan write-off would normally be classed as a payment of earnings for Class 1 NIC purposes, but this case involves a compensation arrangement, so no Class 1 NICs should be due.

(e) **Gerry Scattergood – Tax payable on lump sum termination payment**

| | £ | | £ |
|---|---|---|---|
| Termination payment | | | 40,000 |
| Exempt under ITEPA 2003 s 403(1) | 30,000 | | |
| *Less:* Required to cover statutory redundancy | 2,000 | | (28,000) |
| Taxable portion remaining | | | 12,000 |
| Less unused part of basic rate band (32,000 – 27,435) | | | (4,565) |
| Taxable at the higher rate | | | 7,435 |
| Tax payable: | 4,565 | @ 20% | 913 |

| | | |
|---|---|---|
| £ | | £ |
| 7,435 | @ 40% | 2,974 |
| 12,000 | | £3,887 |

Note that the PAYE deduction would be higher because of the 0T code used and Gerry would have to claim a refund.

The deduction would only ultimately have been correct if Gerry had left in month 12 and received the termination payment before the issue of the P45 and without a 0T code. In February or any earlier month, he would not have received the benefit of all of his annual allowance and basic rate band.

As he was paid after the P45 was issued, code '0T Month 1' would apply, taking no account of allowances or tax already paid. The maximum monthly basic rate band is £2,666.67, and the maximum monthly higher rate band is £9,833.33 (assuming no allowances). Gerry has received a taxable amount of £12,000, so the PAYE tax deduction under code 0T would amount to (2,666.67 @ 20%) 533.33 + (9,333.33 @ 40%) 3,733.33 = £4,266.66. If Gerry earned nothing further later in the year and received no taxable jobseeker's allowance, he could reclaim £379.66.

No NI would be due on a compensation payment as it is not earnings from the employment.

If the settlement agreement had provided for £10,000 of the £40,000 to become payable only three months later, in the next tax year, the PAYE due in February would have been reduced to £400 (£2,000 @ 20%), which would have exactly met his eventual tax liability for the year, avoiding the need for a refund claim. When the £2,500 quarterly instalments were paid in the next tax year, basic rate tax would have been due to be collected under PAYE using code 0T (ie, £2,000 in total), but the ultimate level of tax due would depend on his total income for the year, and some or all of the payment might be covered by his personal allowance, leading to a refund claim.

(f) The jobseeker's allowance of £600 received by Gerry Scattergood, although taxable, will have been paid to him in full by the DWP, and if he was still unemployed at the end of the tax year the benefit office will have worked out his tax position by reference to his coding and sent him any refund due. If he has underpaid tax the underpayment will normally be collected by a coding adjustment for a later year. If he had started work again before the end of the tax year, the benefit office would have refunded any tax overpaid to that point and given him a Form P45U to produce to his new employer. Compensation payments do not prevent an unemployed person getting unemployment credits for national insurance purposes for the period covered by the compensation (provided the person registers at the Jobcentre and looks for work).

(g) Alistair's statutory and enhanced redundancy pay of £23,200 are compensation within s 401, so should be covered by the £30,000 exemption for compensation payments and be free of national insurance liability. The pay of £10,800 in lieu of notice arises from a provision of the employment contract (rather than from a breach of that contract), so it is earnings rather than compensation and is taxable in full and subject to national insurance liability. If it is paid before the issue of the P45 and the notification of a leaving date on an FPS, normal cumulative PAYE and normal national insurance rules apply; if after termination and after the issue of the P45 and reporting of a leaving date on an FPS, PAYE would be deductible using code 0T and national insurance contributions would be charged as if the payment represented one week's earnings. The £2,000 in lieu of untaken holiday days was also provided for in his contract and is treated in the same way as the contractual pay in lieu of notice. No new P45 should be issued, and the payment should be reported on an FPS, flagged as a payment after leaving (but showing the original date of leaving). The company should revise the year-to-date figures to include the taxable payment (unless the termination payment falls into a later tax year).

(h) Ali has already earned £140,000, but has paid out of those earnings pension contributions of £20,000, so any taxable termination payment above £30,000 would take his earnings above £150,000 and be liable to the 45% tax rate. Damages for discrimination are not ordinarily otherwise chargeable to income tax, but the compensation payment made is directly connected with the termination of the employment, so it falls within the scope of ITEPA 2003, s 401.

At first blush, up to £20,000 of the taxable element of the compensation payment (ie, the £40,000 annual contribution limit less the £20,000 contribution already paid) could be converted into an extra employer pension contribution with full tax relief. However, any taxable termination payment *or employer pension contribution* of more than £10,000 would take Ali's 'adjusted income' for pensions annual allowance purposes above £150,000, leading to the annual allowance being tapered down to a minimum of £10,000. If anything more than £10,000 was paid into the pension scheme in the tax year, Ali would have to self-assess an annual allowance charge on the excess at the relevant marginal rate of tax.

However, no national insurance contributions would be due whether the payment was taken as compensation or a special pension contribution of any amount. Since the employer would be paying more than Ali's annual allowance into a single pension scheme in the tax year and the annual allowance charge would be more than £2,000, Ali could elect for the trustees of the pension scheme to meet the tax liability out of the fund, with a corresponding reduction in his ultimate benefit entitlement. The time limit for the election is 31 July of the calendar year after that in which the tax year ends, so Ali would have to make the election by 31 July 2018. However, since the taxable termination payment will be free of NIC liability anyway, there would be no benefit from paying anything via the pension scheme.

If Ali is already over the age of 55, he could immediately start to draw a pension, taking 25% of the fund tax-free as an uncrystallised funds pension lump sum, and paying tax on any other amounts at his marginal rate as and when he draws them in a later tax year, but this advantage would come at the cost of paying 45% tax on the contribution, so any pension contribution should be avoided: the termination payment will take Ali's adjusted income well above £150,000 in any event, so £10,000 of his previous contribution of £20,000 will already be subject to the annual allowance charge.

If the company would agree to deferring Ali's termination until 6 April or later, it could then pay an employer pension contribution in the next tax year, but if it paid compensation of £200,000, of which just £30,000 was tax-free, his adjusted income even without finding another job would be £170,000, again making him a high-income individual for pension purposes. Ali's annual allowance would therefore be tapered to £30,000 (ie, a reduction from £40,000 of £10,000 ([£170,000–£150,000] × ½).

## Explanatory Notes

*Golden handcuffs*

(1) The rules in relation to lump sum payments on commencement of employment are explained in **part (a)** of the Example.

*Termination payments and benefits*

(2) A payment or benefit received in connection with the termination of the holding of an office or employment or any change in its functions or earnings, whether made in pursuance of any legal obligation or not is, if not otherwise chargeable to tax, chargeable to tax under ITEPA 2003 Part 6 Chapter 3. Special rules do, however, apply to the calculation of the taxable amount. P11D benefits cannot be taxed under the P11D rules after termination, as the former employee is then no longer within the benefits code, but the P11D valuation rules are often applied to benefits that are taxable under the Part 6 rules.

Section 403 can apply to a termination payment received in the UK by a taxpayer who is neither resident nor ordinarily resident in the UK in the tax year and who did not perform any UK duties in that year. The exemption and reliefs in **note 6(c)** will apply where appropriate.

(3) Tax is charged in the tax year or years in which payments and benefits arise, after applying the reliefs and exemptions in **note 6** below. The £30,000 exemption is allocated to the earliest payments and benefits received. If both payments and benefits are received in the same tax year, the exemption is used first against cash payments then against benefits. Benefits are valued using the benefits code, or if an asset has appreciated since the employer acquired it, the market value at the relevant time using the 'money's worth' principle (ITEPA 2003 s 415(2)(a)). Where the benefit is a beneficial loan, the taxable amount is treated as interest paid (ITEPA 2003 s 416), so that relief is available if the loan is a qualifying loan (see **Example A1 explanatory note 14**). The £30,000 is only available once in relation to a particular employment, so an

employee who receives £20,000 tax-free as compensation for buying out an enhanced redundancy entitlement can only claim to have £10,000 free of tax when he is actually made redundant several years later (see *Colquhoun* [2010] UKUT431).

(4) The proviso 'This chapter does not apply to any payment chargeable to income tax apart from this Chapter' in ITEPA 2003 s 401(3) is a reminder that a lump sum payment is not automatically exempt from the normal rules of taxing remuneration. The test is broadly whether the lump sum payment arises from *cessation of the employment or duties*, rather than a payment for services already performed or to be performed in the future.

If it can be seen to relate to services already performed (eg, the contract of service provides for a twelve months' employment at £3,000 per month and a lump sum of £64,000 at the cessation of the twelve months' employment) or to services to be performed (eg, the employee is currently paid £20,000 per annum, and he agrees to accept a reduced salary of £15,000 per annum for the next five years in consideration of a lump sum of £20,000 now), the payment will be caught as general earnings and liable to Class 1 national insurance contributions in the normal way.

HMRC have sought to treat enhanced redundancy payments as liable to tax and national insurance contributions in the normal way where the arrangements had become part of the terms of the contract of employment. This was held not to be correct in the case of *Mairs v Haughey* 1993, the House of Lords deciding that the relevant factor was whether the payments were for services rendered by the employees or because their jobs had ceased to exist. It can be argued that the same reasoning should apply to all compensation for loss of office, whether it is contractual or not. It is important, however, that any payment must not be specifically provided for in the employment contract (even if the payment is discretionary), or be part of an established practice on the part of the employer. Such payments could be regarded as made under the terms and conditions of the employment and would be liable to both tax and national insurance. HMRC won the case of *EMI Group Electronics Ltd v Coldicott* in the High Court in 1997 (confirmed by the Court of Appeal in 1999) on the grounds that pay in lieu of notice in that case was a contractual substitution for earnings, whereas in the *Mairs v Haughey* case the payment was a contractual substitution for a redundancy payment. HMRC also won the case of *Richardson v Delaney* in 2001, which related to compensation based on a compromise agreement varying a taxable provision within the contract of employment.

If a contract of employment provides for a payment to be made, or for the employer to have the right to make a payment to determine the contract lawfully, payment made if the notice in the contract is not given to the employee will be treated by HMRC as earnings liable to tax and national insurance. Where the contract does not so provide, or the employer demonstrably chooses not to exercise the right to make a payment in lieu (see *Cerberus Software Ltd v Rowley* [2001] EWCA Civ 497) and the employer requires the employee to leave immediately, he will be in breach of the contract of employment and the payment will represent compensation for that breach. Care should, however, be taken with the consequential employment law implications of the employer failing to honour the terms of the employment contract. See Tax Bulletin 63 February 2003 for HMRC's view on the tax treatment of payments in lieu of notice.

Where there is no obvious right for the employee to claim compensation for a breach of contract, HMRC's view is usually that the payment must be a reward from the employment and therefore taxable earnings. That this is not the correct approach was demonstrated in *Wilson v Clayton* [2004] EWCA Civ 1657, where an employer paid compensation for unfair dismissal that was not legally due under employment protection legislation. HMRC argued that the only possible source was therefore the contract of employment, making the payment taxable as earnings, but the Court of Appeal held that it was indeed a payment of compensation for unfair dismissal, despite the employment tribunal having had no vires to consent to the award. The same mistaken starting point underlay the dispute in *Resolute Management Services Ltd v Revenue and Customs Commissioners* [2008] STC (SCD) 1202. In a company that was always scheduled to close down once its project was complete, an executive resigned voluntarily, abandoning a potential right to a future enhanced redundancy payment, with no right to claim compensation. The board awarded her an *ex gratia* termination payment in lieu of the redundancy payment she might have received had she stayed until the business closed down. HMRC argued that, in the absence of a right to compensation, it must have been a payment of earnings, but the Special Commissioner agreed that the payment was derived directly from the termination and nothing else, so it was nominally taxable under the s 401 rules. (In the event, no tax was due in the UK, because the employee had become resident in the US before the payment was made and the taxing rights fell to the US IRS under the UK-US tax treaty because termination compensation is treated as 'other income' rather than remuneration.)

*Benefits under employer-financed retirement benefits schemes*

(5) Certain payments and benefits received on termination of employment are treated as benefits under an employer-financed retirement benefits scheme rather than being taxed under the provisions of ITEPA 2003 Part 6 Chapter 3. This applies where there are 'arrangements' to provide relevant benefits, so that tax is chargeable under ITEPA 2003 s 394. Before 6 April 2006 schemes were known as unapproved retirement benefits schemes. Now unregistered schemes are known as employer-financed retirement benefits schemes (EFRBS). Generally, the taxation post-6 April 2006 differs in some important ways from the old regime but transitional rules apply for some former unapproved retirement benefits schemes in respect of certain payments on or after that date. The general rule is that relevant benefits received from the 'scheme' will be charged to tax as employment income under ITEPA 2003 s 394. EFRBS transactions may now also fall under the disguised remuneration provisions in ITEPA 2003 Part 7A, but only one tax charge should apply.

The key difference is that the meaning of relevant benefits differs for unapproved schemes.

Generally, a relevant benefit is any pension, lump sum, gratuity or other like benefit given:

(a) on retirement or on death, or

(b) in anticipation of retirement, or

(c) after retirement or death in connection with past service, or

(d) on or in anticipation of or in connection with any change in the nature of the employee's service, or

(e) by virtue of a pension sharing order or provision.

For EFRBS, both cash and non-cash benefits count as 'relevant benefits'.

However, the term 'relevant benefit' does not include benefits provided solely by reason of an employee's disablement or death by accident occurring whilst he or she is in the employer's service, nor benefits provided on ill-health.

In addition, relevant benefits (for EFRBS) do not include:

(i) pension income within Part 9 ITEPA 2003, or

(ii) benefits chargeable under Schedule 34 FA 2004 (relevant non-UK schemes).

There must be a 'scheme' for a charge to arise under the non-approved or employer-financed retirement benefits scheme legislation.

The definition of this term for both schemes is essentially the same and states that it 'includes a deed, agreement, series of agreements or other arrangements' providing for relevant benefits. SP13/91 (withdrawn at 5 April 2006) explained that, in HMRC's view, a scheme may be quite informal. It includes, for example:

- A decision at an employer's meeting.
- A decision by an employee with delegated authority or in accordance with a policy.
- The making of a payment under a plan, pattern, policy, practice or decision-making process or custom.

Although SP13/91 has been withdrawn because of the introduction of the simplified pensions regime, that does not affect HMRC's interpretation of 'scheme'.

If an employer agrees with the employee to provide death-in-service cover, a scheme will exist for these purposes. If the cover is provided by an appropriate life insurance policy, any proceeds paid to the beneficiaries on death are excluded from the definition of relevant benefits, but if the lump sum benefit is instead paid by the employer it will be taxable as a relevant benefit under an EFRBS, although no NI liability should arise as the payment is not earnings and is not deemed to be earnings for NI purposes. Note that death in service cover provided within a registered pension scheme will count towards the lifetime allowance for tax-approved pensions.

Under SI 2006/210 and ITEPA 2003 s 393B, there is no tax charge on the payment of a lump sum by an EFRBS under the rules that were in place before 6 April 2006.

Where the benefits include a beneficial loan, the amount taxable under ITEPA 2003 s 394 in respect of the loan is treated as interest paid (ITEPA 2003 s 399), so that relief is available if the loan is a qualifying loan (see **Example A1 explanatory note 14**).

(Note that the payment by an employer of a contribution to an EFRBS after 6 April 2011 is itself likely to give rise to taxable earnings (with an immediate PAYE and NIC liability – although the latter is questionable if no actual payment or award of unconditional entitlement takes place) under Part 7A of ITEPA, introduced by FA 2011, when the trustees earmark the funds for the benefit of the employee or lend the funds to the employee as an advance on his eventual entitlement.)

*Reliefs and exemptions*

(6) If it can be established that a payment is not otherwise chargeable to tax and therefore falls to be treated under the special rules for lump sum payments, ITEPA 2003 s 403 et seq give certain exemptions and reliefs as follows:

(a) Certain amounts received are wholly exempt from the s 401 provisions, viz:

- Payments and benefits for entering into a restrictive covenant (since caught specifically under ITEPA 2003 s 225, as shown in **part (a)** of the Example).
- Payments made in connection with the employee's death, injury or disability (but these may nevertheless be taxable as EFRBS benefits).
- Benefits under registered pension schemes.

(b) In addition, the first £30,000 of other sums received does not attract tax (any statutory redundancy payments being included in this figure (ITEPA 2003 s 403)).

(c) If part of the service in the employment is performed overseas, then the following rules apply:

(i) *No tax at all is charged* where the foreign service comprises:

- in any case, three-quarters of the whole period of service; or
- the whole of the last ten years, if the service exceeded ten years; or
- if the service exceeded twenty years, half of the period of service including any ten out of the last twenty years (ITEPA 2003 s 413).

(ii) *If the foreign service is not covered under the above provisions* the taxable amount is reduced by the proportion of foreign service to total service (ITEPA 2003 s 414).

(iii) Any lump sum benefits from an overseas pension scheme or a Section 615(3) UK scheme for expatriates working outside the UK are exempt from tax in the same way as other amounts received if **(i) above** applies, and are proportionately chargeable as in (ii) if (i) does not apply (ITEPA 2003 s 395B – formerly Revenue concession A10 – and s 414A).

(iv) Foreign service means that the employee was not resident and not ordinarily resident in the UK or he was entitled to the 100% deduction for non-UK work (eg, in the case of a seafarer).

*Legal costs*

(7) If an employee incurs legal costs in obtaining a termination payment they do not in principle reduce the taxable amount. Where, however, an employer pays an employee's legal costs in obtaining the payment, this would clearly be unfair. Under ESC A81, until 6 April 2011, HMRC would not treat the payment of costs as a taxable benefit if the payment was made by the former employer direct to the employee's solicitor under a specific terms of a compromise agreement following an out of court settlement, or if it was made to the employee under a Court Order. The concession was formally legislated (by SI 2011/1037) from 6 April 2011, creating a new s 413A in ITEPA 2003 to give the same kind of relief, albeit with a slight technical difference in its scope that is unlikely to be significant.

*Way in which tax is collected and reporting requirements*

(8) To the extent that a termination payment exceeds £30,000 it is treated as pay for PAYE purposes. If it is paid before the employee leaves, and is entered on the tax deduction working sheet and Form P45, PAYE is applied in the normal way. If the payment is not made until after the employee has left and been issued with Form P45, and the final payment has been reported as such on an FPS, the payment is still taxed under PAYE, but the employer is required to deduct tax using code 0T on a non-cumulative basis (ie, Week 1/Month1). Note that gains realised from unapproved share option exercises after termination were taxed until 6 April 2012 using code BR rather than 0T, which is how all post-termination payments were taxed until 5 April 2011. Class 1 national insurance is not payable on a compensation payment, but the exercise of an unapproved share option gives rise to deemed earnings for NIC purposes.

Where the taxable amount relates to a benefit rather than a cash payment, tax will not be deducted by the employer.

The employee will pay the whole of the tax on benefits, and any further tax due on cash payments, in his self-assessment, or claim a refund if appropriate. The due date of payment is 31 January after the end of the tax year, eg, 31 January 2018 for 2016/17, and interest on underpaid tax, if relevant, would run from that date. Although making the payment after the employee has left used to defer the payment of tax for a higher rate taxpayer (ie, because code BR was used), it could result in increased payments on account for the following year (perhaps necessitating a claim to reduce them because they resulted from a one-off event), since the balance of tax payable formed part of the tax paid directly rather than through PAYE. The introduction of the 0T W1/M1 code for all post-termination payments will generally mean that recipients will now over-pay PAYE and will need to claim a refund.

As far as the employer is concerned, unless the termination settlement is wholly cash, or the total value of the settlement including benefits is estimated not to exceed £30,000, the Income Tax (PAYE) Regulations 2003 Regs 91–93 and 96 provide that the employer must provide details to HMRC not later than 6 July following the end of the tax year in which the termination settlement was awarded (copies being provided to employees to enable them to complete their tax returns). The details should cover the total value of the settlement, the amounts of cash and the nature of the benefits to be provided and their cash equivalents, indicating which, if any, amounts and benefits are to be provided in later years. No further report needs to be submitted unless, exceptionally, there is a subsequent variation increasing the value of the termination settlement by more than £10,000, in which case a report must be sent to HMRC by 6 July following the tax year of variation. If a report is not submitted because the value is originally estimated not to exceed £30,000, but it subsequently exceeds that amount, a report and employee copy must be provided by 6 July following the tax year in which the value is increased. The employer is theoretically liable to a penalty of up to £300 if he fails to submit a report, plus up to £60 a day from the time the £300 penalty is imposed until the report is submitted. If an incorrect report is submitted the penalty is geared to the lost revenue, according to the behaviour giving rise to the inaccuracy. A mistake having taken reasonable care is not subject to a penalty. See **Example B1 note 10** for more details about the penalties for inaccuracies in returns.

*Top-slicing rules*

(9) Where the income of the year in which a termination payment is received includes dividend or savings income, then although the dividend / savings income is treated as the top slice of income for all other purposes (except in relation to tax charges on life assurance policies and certain payments from settlor-interested trusts), it is taken into account before termination payments (ITA 2007 s 1012).

In **part (e)** of the Example, therefore, if Gerry Scattergood's other taxable income of £27,435 had included dividend income of £10,000, the rates of tax payable by him would have been:

| | | |
|---|---|---|
| On non-savings income | 22,435 | @ 20% |
| On dividend income | 5,000 | @ 0% |
| | 4,565 | @ 7.5% |
| Basic rate band | 32,000 | |
| Higher rate dividend tax | 435 | @ 32.5% |
| | 32,435 | |
| On compensation | 12,000 | @ 40% |

Without the special rule the increase in tax payable would have been:

| | | |
|---|---|---|
| Increase of | £4,565 @ (32.5–7.5)% = | 1,141.25 |
| Less saving of | £4,565 @ (40–20)% = | 913 |
| | | 228 |

Where practicable, the termination of employment should be timed so as to reduce the employee's liability at the higher rate. If the employee's income will fall after he leaves, for example, it would be better to defer some or all of the termination payment to the beginning of a new tax year so that little or none of his employment earnings are included in his income. The mandatory use of the 0T W1/M1 PAYE code may mean that too much tax is deducted at source (any taxable amount of more than £12,500 paid in one month will take the payment into the 45% tax band in that month), but is now unavoidable unless the compensation is agreed to be paid in instalments spread across a tax year so that no additional rate tax becomes payable at the time of payment.

*Jobseeker's allowance (JSA)*

(10) JSA is means-tested after the first six months, rather than being based on past NI contributions paid, and JSA is not payable in any event to those over state pension age.

(11) The receipt of a termination payment does not affect entitlement to non-means-tested JSA (based on national insurance contributions paid) except to the extent that it represents pay in lieu of notice. However, it does affect entitlement to the means-tested allowance (or universal credit) if the claimant then has more than £6,000 capital, and if capital exceeds £16,000 the means-tested allowance is not available.

(12) JSA is chargeable to tax as social security income under Part 10 of ITEPA 2003, as indicated in **part (f)** of the Example. In most cases an overpayment rather than an underpayment will arise, because the amount received is usually less than the available personal allowance. The taxpayer does not get a refund, however, until he starts work again, or until the end of the tax year if he remains unemployed. The claimant hands in his P45 from his last employment when claiming JSA, and the DWP issues a special P45, including previous pay and tax plus JSA, for the employee to hand to a new employer when he comes off benefit.

If employees are on strike, they may be able to claim income support. Employers cannot make tax refunds to employees while they are on strike. (Refunds would normally be due because no wages would be paid to utilise the tax-free pay the employee is entitled to each week.) Even if the strike continues beyond the end of the tax year the employee will not receive any refund from the employer. The employer will give him a statement at the tax year-end showing any refund due for that tax year and the refund will be made by HMRC when his position for the year is finalised.

*Pensions annual allowance charge*

(13) Taxable compensation payments are classed as specific employment income but any taxable compensation payments will not be relevant to testing whether the pensions annual allowance of £40,000 (£50,000 before 6 April 2014) has been exceeded, since this is measured solely by reference to pension inputs (ie,

contributions in money purchase arrangements and increases in entitlement in defined benefit schemes). The taxable compensation payment (ie, the excess over £30,000) is added in to total income to determine the marginal tax rate for the purposes of taxing any excess contributions, or tapering the allowance when adjusted income exceeds £150,000, so termination payments may have an indirect effect on the value of any annual allowance charge payable.

Where contributions to a member's scheme exceed the annual allowance (whether tapered or not) and an annual allowance charge of at least £2,000 becomes payable, FA 2004, ss 237A–237F provide that he may require the trustees to meet the charge out of the fund.

# Question

(a) Mark, who runs a garage business providing vehicle repairs, has written to you asking for advice about the mechanics who work in his garage. They wish to be treated as self-employed, and Mark has asked for your views on whether or not this is possible, the tax implications for him of their being so treated, and the potential risk to him if he treats them as self-employed and subsequently HMRC deems them to be employees.

Prepare brief notes for a meeting with Mark to discuss the matter.

(b) Wanda, a single woman, has recently returned to the UK after working overseas for a number of years. She is undecided whether to accept an offer of full-time employment from a company located near her home, or to set up her own consultancy business using her home as the base for her business.

You have advised her that the rules governing the deductibility of expenses for employees differ from the rules for self-employed persons. Wanda has now asked for a report summarising the position.

Prepare the report for Wanda, covering the basic rules for allowable expenditure, and their application in particular to travelling expenses (both within and outside the UK), subscriptions, and clothing.

(c) Ken Brown is employed as a clerk in the local factory, but has for many years been interested in antiques and he has pursued this as his hobby in most of his spare time.

In order to finance a holiday in the Bahamas, however, Ken had recently started buying and selling antiques for which he charged less than the normal retail price but nevertheless made a reasonable profit. When discussing this with a friend, he was told that he would have to pay income tax on this income as he was in fact carrying on a trade.

Consider whether or not Ken is carrying on a trade, giving your reasons fully and referring to leading cases in this area.

(d) In January, Lily cleared out her loft to make way for a loft extension and decided to sell the large quantity of old clothes, toys, books etc she had accumulated on eBay. This was so successful that in March she set up her own eBay shop. In July, Lily was approached by a friend to sell their old items for a percentage of funds realised, and in August she started to attend markets and car boot sales with a view to buying items for resale.

Review Lily's activity at each of the months mentioned above, and consider whether it constituted trading.

(e) Julian is a freelance web designer. He has a list of client businesses who ask him to update their websites from time to time, but when he has no contracts he finds work through The Geekshop, an IT employment agency that will take him onto its books as a freelancer. Its contracts with its large IT clients and with Julian specify that he need not deliver his services personally, but when he does work for Geekshop's clients he is invariably required to follow their procedures.

Explain the tax and NIC position for Julian when he is paid by The Geekshop for work for its clients.

# Answer

## (a) Notes for meeting with Mark on employed or self-employed status of mechanics

(1) The main distinction between trading income from self-employment taxable by ITTOIA 2005 Part 2 and employment income taxable under ITEPA 2003 is that the former income is generated under contracts for services and the latter from a contract of service or contract of employment (ITEPA 2003 s 4(1)(a)). HMRC have issued factsheets ES/FS1 and ES/FS2 giving very basic guidelines to help in the decision. (A separate publication CIS 349 used to be available for those in the construction industry, but now only much less detailed guidance is available online.) There is also an online tool at https://www.gov.uk/employment-status-indicator to assist in determining employment status in most general cases.

(2) Factors pointing to employment are that the individual works wholly or mainly for one business, that he needs to carry out the work in person, to take orders as to when and how to do it, to work at the premises of those providing the work, or at a place determined by them, and to work directed hours at an hourly, weekly or monthly rate, and that he is paid for overtime, sickness and holidays. Membership of an employer's pension scheme is also a very strong indicator of employee status.

(3) Factors pointing to self-employment are that the individual risks his own capital and bears any losses arising, that he controls whether, how, when and where he does the work, provides his own equipment, is free to employ or subcontract others to do the work he has undertaken, and is required to bear the cost of correcting faulty work.

(4) Normally, no single factor is in itself conclusive in one direction or the other, and all the circumstances need to be taken into account. Nevertheless, two factors pointing towards self-employment are usually highly persuasive (if not determinative of the issue). First and most importantly, the unrestricted right for the person to select a substitute to do the work: a worker who does not have to provide personal service cannot be working under a contract of service. Alternatively, but carrying less weight, there is the lack of mutual obligation between the worker and the person requesting the work that is beyond the scope of the currently agreed project. Every contract involves mutual obligations, but if the nature of those obligations is that the worker is free to work elsewhere at any time, and to take on his own helpers at his own expense so that he can do two tasks at once, and to work how and when he pleases provided the service is delivered to the agreed timescale, the mutual obligations needed for a contract of service will be absent. However, where a contract provides for the use of substitutes and the freedom to arrange delivery of the service as the worker sees fit, these contractual terms have to be genuine and not merely included in a contract in order to mislead the tax authorities. Written evidence, such as contracts, invoices, VAT registration, will have a considerable bearing on the decision, but HMRC may also interview the workers and customers to establish whether the real contracts differ from the paper evidence.

(5) If the mechanics were treated as self-employed, Mark would pay for their services in full and they would be liable for tax and Class 2 and Class 4 self-employed national insurance contributions. If their turnover was high enough they would have to register for VAT, although this would seem unlikely for a typical mechanic acting as a sole trader. Alternatively, they might choose to voluntarily register for VAT.

(6) Applying the general principles outlined above, however, it seems likely that HMRC would be very likely to regard the mechanics as employees. If Mark treats them as self-employed without seeking a ruling in advance, and they are later deemed to be employees, he will be primarily liable for PAYE and national insurance contributions. That amount might not be recoverable, or recoverable in full, from the employee under the PAYE and NIC regulations, especially if the individual is no longer working for Mark. A deduction from taxable profits will normally be allowed for any settlement of the liability by the employer. There would also be penalties based on the tax and NI underpaid if the failure is considered to have occurred through lack of care or deliberate failure, and since April 2010 a formula-based penalty of up to 14% for underpayment of PAYE and NIC (ie, 4% for failure to make all 12 months' remittances, plus 5% for being over six months late and 5% for being over 12 months late). Interest would also be charged at the statutory rate from the 19$^{th}$ of the month after the end of the tax month of payment until the date the liability was settled. If Mark paid his deductions over electronically each month, interest would be calculated from the 22$^{nd}$ rather than

the 19th. There is no deduction available against Mark's profits for the penalties or interest. HMRC would not initiate collection of the tax from the mechanics unless they were held to have known that Mark had wilfully failed to deduct tax.

A case heard by the Special Commissioners (*Demibourne Ltd v HMRC* (2005)) highlighted the difficulties of getting a worker's status wrong. In that case, a worker was treated as self-employed. He was therefore paid gross and he declared his earnings on his self-assessment return (and paid the tax accordingly – no NI was due as he was over state pension age). Subsequently, HMRC queried the worker's status on a PAYE enquiry. They considered that the worker was in fact an employee and raised a determination on the company under SI 2003/2682 reg 80 for the PAYE due but unpaid. By this time it was too late for the worker to reclaim his incorrectly self-assessed tax from HMRC and the employer had no right of recovery from the employee.

The Special Commissioner agreed that the worker was an employee and therefore that the reg 80 determination should be upheld. However, he realised that this would have meant HMRC receiving the tax twice (once from the worker and once from the employer) at the expense of the employer. He suggested that HMRC gave a credit for the tax already accounted for although such a request could not be binding on HMRC. Following the case of Demibourne, HMRC abandoned its long-standing arrangement of allowing an equitable offset of tax paid by individuals while they were treated as self-employed in arriving at the PAYE settlement due. In many cases they requested 100% of any unpaid tax and NI from the employer. The employer had then, to the extent possible, to recover amounts from its employees and the employees had then, to the extent possible, to amend their self-assessments. HMRC was concerned that, once an employer had concluded a contract settlement after a status investigation, it could no longer be liable for the tax that had been offset. However, a worker could legitimately (within the four-year time limit) require a refund of the self-assessed tax, as it had never been due. This never happened in practice (a fact confirmed by HMRC), but the concern about fairness and protecting revenue led to the issue of new regulations.

HMRC has a power to make a direction transferring to the employee the liability for the PAYE not deducted in cases where self-assessment tax has been paid on the earnings. (Reg 72E–72G, SI 2003/2682). This removes the anomaly created by the *Demibourne* decision.

It is also possible (albeit expensive because of court costs) where an employer has met an employee's income tax and NIC obligations by applying the regulations, for the employer to make a claim against the employee in restitution when no recovery is possible under the regulations, because time limits have expired or there are no payments of earnings from which to make deductions. This was illustrated in *McCarthy v McCarthy & Stone plc* [2007] EWCA Civ 664, where a former employer successfully claimed reimbursement of PAYE and employee NIC costs in respect of unapproved share options exercised after retirement.

(7) HMRC used to have at least one person in each of their area offices nominated to deal with questions on an individual's status, although the concept of area offices is now obsolete and the status officers are available in fewer geographical locations. Mark should contact his PAYE office to ask for a ruling from the responsible status officer. It would also be acceptable to use the online ESI tool to arrive at a view on status provided the data input were valid and complete and results were properly documented, by printing and retaining the responses at the conclusion of the test.

(8) Tax and NI contributions are charged on deemed salary when personal services equivalent to a disguised employment are provided through an intermediary such as a partnership or limited company. The rules are usually referred to as 'IR35', so called because of the Budget day press release that introduced the concept. The charge is on the intermediary, therefore the client cannot be liable for the tax and national insurance of the worker where an intermediary is used. Mark could safeguard his position by insisting that his workers can only provide services to him other than as an employee if a partnership or limited company is used as an intermediary, or he could take the mechanics into partnership or an LLP and agree a profit share similar to their employee wages, although this has many ramifications beyond tax and NI and is not a step to be taken without much forethought. There would also be a risk that the workers, if they became salaried members of an LLP with no real variability of remuneration, no capital in the business and no influence over the running of the business, would in any event be deemed to be employed and subject to PAYE and Class 1 NICs without their gaining any employment rights.

**(b)**

To: Wanda
From: A N Adviser 17 October 2016

*Rules governing the deductibility of expenses for employees compared with the rules for self-employed persons*

(1) The main difference in the expenses treatment for employees compared with the self-employed is that employees are allowed to deduct expenses that are wholly, exclusively and necessarily incurred in the performance of the duties of their employment, whereas the self-employed are allowed to deduct expenses that are incurred wholly and exclusively for the purpose of their trade, profession or vocation, without any requirement that the expenses should be necessary.

(2) Dealing first with employees, the general expenses rule is found in ITEPA 2003 s 336, which provides that an employee is allowed to deduct expenses wholly, exclusively and necessarily incurred in the performance of his duties. Sections 337–342 of ITEPA 2003 give relief for certain travelling expenses, with additional provisions for overseas travel in ss 370 to 375.

(3)

(i) Travel expenses are allowed where they are either in the performance of the duties of the employment or for 'necessary attendance' at a temporary workplace (ITEPA 2003 ss 337–340).

The full cost of (a) travelling on business direct from home and (b) associated subsistence expenses is allowed, unless the journey is ordinary commuting to/from your permanent workplace. Fixed mileage allowance payment rates may be used if the travel is in the worker's own vehicle.

If an employee is temporarily sent from the normal workplace to a different workplace for up to 24 months, returning to the normal place of work thereafter, relief is allowed for the related travelling, accommodation and subsistence expenses. This will not apply if the temporary posting is expected to exceed 24 months. If it does in fact exceed or looks as if it will exceed 24 months the expenses are allowable up to the time that fact becomes known.

Workers employed by an intermediary who supplies their personal services to others are treated from 6 April 2016 as having a separate employment for each assignment, unless they are not subject to supervision, direction or control as to how they carry out the work. This means that the location of the work will often be deemed to be a permanent workplace, so commuting expenses will be taxable and NICable if paid by the employer.

(ii) If *part* of the duties of an employment are performed abroad, it is specifically provided by ITEPA 2003 s 370 that travel expenses *paid or reimbursed by the employer* for any journey from any place in the UK to the overseas destination and back again are allowed, providing the duties can only be performed abroad and that the 'wholly and exclusively' rule is satisfied (see s 370(4) and (5)). The provisions of ITEPA 2003 s 338 outlined in (i) above would, however, give relief for the expenses of travelling abroad wholly for business whether the cost was borne by the employer or the employee, and would in addition give relief for subsistence expenses. ITEPA 2003 s 371 also provides relief for up to two journeys a tax year by a spouse and children to visit an employee working abroad for 60 days or more, but this is not relevant in your case. Similarly if *all* the duties of the employment are performed abroad, the employee is entitled to a deduction for the expenses of travelling abroad to take up the appointment and returning to the UK thereafter if the earnings include an amount in respect of such travel (ITEPA 2003 s 370(1)–(3)) ie, they are again paid or reimbursed by the employer. Relief is also allowed for board and lodging expenses in similar circumstances (ITEPA 2003 s 376).

(iii) If *all* the duties of one or more employments are performed abroad and providing the employee is resident in the UK (and domiciled here if the employer is a foreign employer), the employee is entitled to a deduction for the expenses of travelling abroad to take up the appointment, travelling between the appointments, and returning to the UK thereafter. For this relief there is no requirement for the payments first to have been met by the employer (ITEPA 2003 ss 341, 342). The employee is entitled to deduct an appropriate part of the expenses if the travelling is only partly for the purposes of the employment (ITEPA 2003 ss 341(5) and 342(8)).

(iv) Where someone makes a dual purpose visit (eg a business trip combined with a holiday), either in the UK or abroad, this will not deny relief for the expenses providing the journey had to be made in the performance of the duties of the employment. If, however, a deduction is being claimed under ITEPA 2003 s 370 to balance an expenses payment by an employer (as in **(ii) above**), it will be denied if the journey has both a business and a private purpose. The cost of any journey that was specifically private would obviously be disallowed (for example, if an employer required an employee to go to Paris, but the employee went to the South of France on holiday first).

(4) Subscriptions that are payable in order to be able to carry on particular employments, for example, that of an architect, health professional or teacher (ITEPA 2003 s 343), are specifically allowable by statute. This also applies to other professional subscriptions to bodies of persons approved by HMRC, providing the activities of the body are relevant to the employment (ITEPA 2003 s 344).

Subscriptions other than approved professional subscriptions must satisfy the general rule that they be 'wholly, exclusively and necessarily incurred' and very few subscriptions would qualify. A list of subscriptions may be obtained at https://www.gov.uk/government/publications/professional-bodies-approved-for-tax-relief-list-3.

Subscriptions paid for by the employer will also be free of NIC liability unless paid under a salary sacrifice arrangement, or paid as a round-sum allowance, or paid in advance of the expense being incurred (SSCR 2001, Sch 3, Part 10, para 11).

(5) The expense of clothing is not allowed unless it is protective clothing, a performer's costume or a uniform. This is so even if the clothing is worn only at work.

(6) If an employee is required by an employer to work from home, the employee will probably incur extra costs of heating, lighting and telephone charges. Most home expenses would have been incurred anyway (eg, council tax, insurance, telephone rental) so they do not meet the test of being wholly, exclusively and necessarily incurred in the performance of the duties. However, as an administrative concession, HMRC will allow an employer to pay an allowance of £4 per week or £18 per month (in addition to the cost of business telephone calls) tax- and NI-free towards the extra costs of home workers. Any expenses incurred solely for business use, such as the employer having a new broadband connection installed at the home, should still be deductible, but HMRC will sometimes require evidence of business use.

(7) Turning now to the position of the self-employed, the general rule is found in ITTOIA 2005 Chapter 4, which provides that a self-employed person cannot deduct expenses unless they are 'wholly and exclusively laid out or expended for the purposes of the trade, profession or vocation' (s 34), and that the expenditure must be of an income and not a capital nature (s 33).

(8) As far as travelling expenses are concerned, the cost of travel from home to work base is not allowed, and journeys that are partly for business and partly for private purposes are disallowed. There is no distinction between travelling expenses in the UK and abroad, unless the trade, profession or vocation is carried on wholly abroad, in which case the cost of travelling abroad and back again, and between two separate foreign businesses, is allowed, providing the absence is wholly and exclusively for the purpose of performing the functions of one or more of the businesses (ITTOIA 2005 ss 92–94).

Where a self-employed person's sole work base is his home, all business travelling from the home base is allowed, even if there is only one person for whom work is done. But merely doing some of your work at home, even if it is not insignificant, does not enable you to claim the cost of travelling from home to the main work base (see *Samadian v Revenue & Customs Comrs* [2014] UKUT 0013). However, if the self-employed person starts to work full-time for one customer at one distant location for an extended period of time, it is likely that HMRC will deny a deduction for home-to-work travel and subsistence costs, a policy that was supported by the first-tier tribunal in *TD Hanlin v HMRC* (TC01078). In that case, a self-employed CIS contractor who lived in Coventry claimed unsuccessfully the costs of weekly travelling to and from, and living during the week in, Kent, where he had been working on a contract for seven or eight years.

(9) Subscriptions to trade associations, although not usually satisfying the general expenses rule, are allowed providing the association has entered into an agreement with HMRC to pay tax on the excess of their receipts over their allowable expenses. Other subscriptions would need to satisfy the general rule.

(10) As far as clothing is concerned, the self-employed are in no better position than employees, and unless clothing is special or protective clothing the cost is not 'wholly and exclusively' for the purposes of the business.

The position is different for value added tax, because there is no 'wholly and exclusively' requirement. Input tax can be recovered if the clothing is for business purposes, with an apportionment if there is part private use.

(11) As far as home working expenses are concerned, most home expenses for self-employed workers also have a dual purpose, which should mean that they are not deductible, but it is accepted that some proportion of costs can be attributable to the part of the home used as an office. In practice, a deduction may be claimed for the element of mortgage interest or rent, insurance and utilities costs that corresponds to the business use area where that part is wholly and exclusively for business use. This may in practice be a matter of negotiation with HMRC. The cost of a separate business telephone line should be fully deductible. Any part of the home set aside exclusively for business use may attract business rates and may affect the principal private residence exemption for CGT. As a sole trader, Mark could simplify his expense calculation and claim a flat rate for working from home to cover heat, light and insurance (but telephone and internet expenses must be claimed separately), the amount being based on how many hours per month he spends working from home, with a minimum of 25 hours being needed to trigger a claim for a £10 deduction, 51 hours for £18 and 101 hours for £26.

(12) To summarise, although the requirements for expenditure to be allowable in an employment are more stringent than for the self-employed, there are a large number of areas, in particular those dealt with in this report, where the treatment is broadly the same.

## (c)

In order to decide whether activities constitute trading, the starting point is the basic definition of a trade in ITA 2007 s 989, which states that the word trade 'includes any venture in the nature of trade'.

On its own the definition is not very helpful, but it has been given legal interpretation in many cases that have come before the courts.

In 1955 the Royal Commission on the Taxation of Profits and Income established six 'badges of trade', which represent the major considerations to be taken into account in deciding whether or not a trade is being carried on. These were:

(1) The subject matter of the realisation.

(2) The length of the period of ownership.

(3) The frequency or number of similar transactions by the same person.

(4) Supplementary work on or in connection with the property realised.

(5) The circumstances that were responsible for the realisation.

(6) Motive.

Some or all of these would usually be present in trading activities, although the absence of any one or more would not necessarily indicate that a trade was not being carried on. An element of speculation or risk may also indicate a trading venture (see below *re Eclipse Film Partners No 35 LLP*).

In relation to subject matter, it was considered in *CIR v Fraser* (1942) that there were only three reasons for purchasing an article: for own use or consumption, as an investment possibly to yield income, or for resale at a profit, ie, for the purpose of trading. The very nature of some assets will point towards trading rather than investment or own use. In *CIR v Rutledge* (1929), for example, there was an isolated purchase of 1 million rolls of toilet paper. And in *Wisdom v Chamberlain* (1969), concerning the short-term purchase and resale of silver bullion as a hedge against devaluation, it was clear that the asset itself gave the owner no aesthetic pleasure or pride of ownership. In both cases the profits were held to be assessable as trading profits.

A long period of ownership may indicate investment rather than trading. Obviously many assets appreciate in value with the passage of time, and holding assets to realise capital gains rather than buying and selling short-term to realise income has been widespread practice among those liable to income tax at higher rates. A quick sale, on the other hand, may not necessarily indicate trading, for example, when an asset is received as an inheritance and is disposed of shortly afterwards.

An isolated profitable transaction has been held to be trading, as in the case of *CIR v Rutledge* (above). Frequent repetition of transactions obviously constitutes even stronger evidence of trading, and it may be particularly important where the nature of the asset is not such as to be usually regarded as trading stock, eg *Leach v Pogson* (1962), where the taxpayer was held to be trading in establishing and selling driving schools. But there is a prima facie presumption against trading for speculative dealings in securities, and making 200 such transactions in about three years was held not to be trading in *Salt v Chamberlain* (1979).

Where an asset is resold after being processed or worked on in some way, this may indicate trading, eg, buying in bulk and breaking down into smaller saleable units. A leading case in this area is *Cape Brandy Syndicate v CIR* (1921), where a syndicate imported brandy, blended it, re-casked it and resold it.

A need for ready money to meet a sudden emergency would be clear evidence of the absence of a trading motive on the sale of an asset.

The lack of a profit motive is not conclusive evidence against trading (*re Duty on Estate of Incorporated Council of Law Reporting for England and Wales*, 1888). But clearly the existence of a profit motive is a very strong indicator that a trade exists.

In January 2007 HMRC issued a new Internet-based guide (now incorporated into https://www.gov.uk/working-for-yourself/what-counts-as-self-employed) for people who trade online, through classified adverts and car boot sales. This set out six examples of individuals selling and examined whether they were trading. It also listed their nine badges or indicators of trading as follows:

| *Indicators of trading* | *Points to consider* |
|---|---|
| 1. Profit seeking motive | An intention to make a profit supports trading. |
| 2. The number of transactions involved | Systematic and repeated transactions support trade. |
| 3. The nature of the goods sold | Are the goods only capable of being turned to advantage by being sold? Or do they yield income, or give enjoyment though pride of ownership? |
| 4. Existence of similar trading transactions | Was this a one-off transaction or part of a pattern that suggests trading? |
| 5. Changes to the goods | Were the goods repaired, modified or improved to sell them more easily? |
| 6. The way the sale was carried out | Were the goods sold in a way that indicates trading, or to raise cash in an emergency? |
| 7. The source of finance | Was money borrowed to buy the goods? Were any profits to be used to repay the loan? |
| 8. Interval of time between purchase and sale | Goods being traded are usually bought then sold quickly. |
| 9. Method of acquisition of the goods | Goods acquired by an inheritance, or as a gift, are less likely to be the subject of trade. |

Applying these general considerations to the circumstances of Ken Brown's activities, it is clear that he will almost certainly be held to be carrying on a trade.

His original activity of purchasing antiques as a hobby, and presumably owning them for lengthy periods and reselling some of them from time to time, would be regarded as investment rather than trading. Antiques would give him pride and pleasure in their ownership, and their appreciation in value over time would give the opportunity to realise a profit on his investment. But the nature of his activities has changed with the commencement of short-term buying and selling. It was stated in the case of *Hawes v Gardiner* (1957), that what started as a hobby may develop into a trade, and that is almost certainly the case here. Ken's intention of holding for personal enjoyment and investment has changed to frequent buying and selling short-term to make an immediate profit.

As a result of the change of Ken's hobby to a trade, there is also a liability to Class 2 national insurance. Ken must notify the change before 31 January after the end of the tax year by submitting CWF1 to HMRC's National Insurance Contributions & Employer Office at Newcastle upon Tyne, by calling the helpline on 0300 200 3505 or registering via the online CWF1. Failure to notify before 31 January following the end of the tax year of commencement will result in a penalty geared to the lost contributions and the behaviour leading to the failure (SI 2001/1004 reg 87A) in line with the direct tax changes made by Finance Act 2008 Sch 41. Failures in respect of businesses that started before 6 April 2009 were and remain subject instead to a £100 penalty if notification was not made within three months of commencement. The penalty would not have been charged if throughout the period of failure to notify Ken had been able to claim exception from Class 2 national insurance because his expected earnings were below the small earnings exception limit (£5,885 until 6 April 2016), although there was a new small profit threshold of £5,965 from that date against which he could measure his profits once they were known, rather than guessing them in advance.

A new facet to the interpretation of the term 'trade' emerged in 2012 in the decision of the First-tier Tribunal in *Eclipse Film Partners No 35 LLP* (TC01963), a decision later upheld by the Upper Tribunal (see [2013] UKUT 639), and the Court of Appeal (see [2015] EWCA Civ 95). A new limited liability partnership of 289 very high net worth members acquired a licence to certain film rights and sub-licensed those rights to a distributor. The contracts involved cash flows of up to £1 billion, so significant amounts of tax were at stake. Ordinarily, a film partnership venture would meet all the requirements to constitute a trading venture, but the Eclipse arrangements included complex financing arrangements involving loans to members of the partnership and a defeasance deposit by the distributor. In essence, HMRC argued, and the First-tier Tribunal decided, that this was an investment LLP, not a trading LLP. Carrying on a trade was a precondition (under s 362 Taxes Act 1988) for members to claim relief for a prepayment of interest for a 10-year period on their borrowings to join the LLP and invest in the films. The tribunal decided that the arrangements as a whole were designed to give a series of pre-determined cash flows with the object of giving members allowable interest payments with no taxable income for many years, and that the licensing of film rights with wholly pre-programmed cash flows from Disney was not a trading activity. The LLP was not carrying on a trade, but a non-trade business. The key point for the tribunal, and a new badge of trade, was that there was no element of the speculation or risk that is inherent in a genuine trade, since the LLP structure was designed to result in cash flows that were set at the outset, with the benefit to members being the tax deduction against other income for front-loaded interest.

It is difficult to see how having pre-determined cash flows balanced by financing costs differs conceptually to any material extent from a leasing business, which is generally treated as trading despite having pre-programmed cash flows and often a blue chip lessee with little or no risk of default. It is clear, however, that the film partnership was perceived as a tax avoidance scheme and that this fact influenced the decision and the creation of a new badge of trade concerning risk or speculation to add to the traditional six.

Mr Justice Sales in the Upper Tribunal discussed the importance of the fiscal motive in constructing the business model and how, where the primary motive was a fiscal advantage for the investors rather than making a profit out of the transactions, there might be a business but no trade. Where there is a non-trade business, tax will be chargeable under ITTOIA 2005, s 610 on the full amount of income arising in the year, less any expenses attributable to the generation of the income received, but the net income need not be calculated using UK GAAP principles because ITTOIA 2005, s 25 (trading profits and GAAP) does not apply. This consideration need not trouble Ken as he is clearly making (or losing) money on buying and selling antiques in an open market.

In April 2013, HMRC announced that it had reviewed its policy on sleeping and limited partners and stated that 'sleeping and inactive Limited Partners are—and have in the past been—liable to pay Class 2 National Insurance contributions (NICs) as self-employed earners and Class 4 NICs in respect of their taxable profits. "Inactive Limited Partners" are Limited Partners who take no active part in running the business. This view represents a change from that previously held by HMRC and the Department for Work and Pensions.'

Sleeping or inactive Limited Partners who had not paid Class 2 or Class 4 NICs for a past period would not, however, be required by HMRC to pay those contributions. The policy change is plainly incorrect in those cases where the partner is no more than an investor. It is not possible for Class 4 NICs to be due in respect of anything other than the profits immediately derived from the carrying on of a trade, profession or vocation taxed under Chapter 2 of Part 2 of ITTOIA 2005 (SSCBA 1992 s 15) and Class 2 liability depends on there being a business of some kind. In *Eclipse* above, HMRC argued successfully that the profits of the LLP investor members should be taxable under ITTOIA 2005, s 610, so there is no conceivable way that their profits could be liable to Class 4 NICs. In the case of *Rashid v Garcia* (SC 3095/02) a landlord of a small portfolio of investment properties, mixed residential and commercial in nature, failed to persuade the Special Commissioners that he was in fact carrying on a business because there was negligible activity on his part in managing the properties. He was therefore not entitled to pay Class 2 NICs. If activity that is more than insignificant is a pre-requisite for there to be a business for Class 2 purposes, then the LLP investor members in *Eclipse* could equally not be liable, as their active involvement in the trade was nil. HMRC appears to have missed this fundamental point in formulating its NICs policy change on sleeping and limited partners.

The point, however, ceased to be relevant from 6 April 2015 when the reform of Class 2 NICs under NICA 2015 was implemented, as Class 2 is now only chargeable on earners who have, or would if they made a profit have, profits in respect of which Class 4 NICs are due under SSCBA 1992, s 15 and which exceed the small profits threshold (SPT), formerly known as the small earnings exception limit. Ken's antiques trade will clearly fall within Class 4 and he will therefore be liable to pay Class 2 contributions if his profits are high enough. He will pay Class 2 contributions in his self-assessment payments every January (payments on account are not required). Even if Ken's profits are below the SPT, he will be able to pay Class 2 voluntarily (under SSCBA 1992, s 11(6)) to maintain his record for benefit purposes.

## (d)

January

Selling unwanted items that have been lying around in the attic is not sufficient to constitute a trade. The original purchases were presumably made for personal use. If items are being sold for more than their original cost, it is necessary to consider capital gains tax, but assuming they were individually worth less than £6,000 per item they would be exempt as chattels.

March

As stated under (c) **above**, the way a sale is carried out is a badge or indicator of trading. Setting up an online shop makes her activities appear more 'commercial'. However, no one factor can outweigh the others and provided the 'stock' being sold is still the same as before, Lily has not commenced trading. HMRC are known to monitor online retailers looking for unregistered businesses. It would therefore be prudent to retain proof, where reasonably practical, that the items being sold were her personal items.

July and August

Selling items on behalf of another person/buying stock for resale constitutes trading and Lily should register her business as soon as possible. Lily will also have to maintain records that allow her to separate the resale of her own personal items and 'business' transactions. She should also find out about the VAT margin schemes for second-hand goods and check when she might need to register. If she sells to buyers elsewhere in the EU, she needs to take great care (for as long as the UK remains a member) because other states will not necessarily have a VAT registration threshold (see http://europa.eu/youreurope/business/vat-customs/buy-sell/index_en.htm).

E-trading has grown phenomenally in recent years. EBay trading in particular often starts as a personal project to resell unwanted items and then develops into a business. This can generate problems for individuals who fail to register and fail to separate personal transactions from business ones. EBay provides guidance to users on their obligations to register with HMRC. It also makes various reports to HMRC. HMRC in turn use various tools to monitor online unregistered traders.

## (e)

When Julian designs websites for his own clients, he is likely to be self-employed, so any profits he makes will be subject to tax under ITTOIA 2005, Part 2, Chapter 2 and Class 4 NICs, and he will be liable to Class 2 NICs.

However, finding work through the agency of the Geekshop means that the agency rules in ITEPA 2003, s 44–47 for income tax and Social Security (Categorisation of Earners) Regs 1978 potentially come into play. Until 5 April

2014, the fact that Julian need not carry out any of the agency work personally would have meant that the agency rules did not apply, so the agency could have paid him gross without worrying about PAYE or Class 1 NICs.

From 6 April 2014, however, amendments to both the income tax and NICs provisions mean that, where Julian does carry out the work himself, under the usual contracts between (a) himself and the agency and (b) the agency and its client, Julian will, but for tax and NIC purposes only, be deemed to be an employee of the agency and his earnings will have to be payrolled, with The Geekshop liable to account for secondary Class 1 contributions as well as the deductions it makes from Julian's pay (see ITEPA 2003, s 44(3)).

The fact that Julian must follow the client's procedures in carrying out the work means that he and the agency cannot escape PAYE and Class 1 liability by using the exception in s 44(2)(a) for those workers who are not subject to a right of supervision, direction or control as to the manner in which they work. The existence of a right of supervision also means that, from 6 April 2016, under new rules introduced by FA 2016, s 18, Julian will no longer be able to claim a deduction from the earnings from his deemed employment for the costs of his commuting to the client's premises, as each assignment via the agency of The Geekshop will be treated as a separate employment. The client's premises therefore become a permanent workplace for his deemed employment.

If Julian has a mixture of employed and self-employed earnings in the year, he should take care not to overpay Class 2 and Class 4 NICs, settling the final liability for both types of contribution in his annual self-assessment tax return only once his Class 1 earnings for the year have been finalised. Extra care is needed this year as tax software generally and HMRC's ITSA system do not yet deal correctly with the annual maximum calculations for NICs, which only came into scope for ITSA with the transfer of Class 2 onto the same basis of Class 4 in April 2015, with the first returns due at the latest by 31 January 2017.

The agency might insist that Julian set up his own personal service company (PSC) to provide the web design services. This would absolve the agency from any PAYE or NIC obligations, as any remuneration or commuting expenses between home and the offices of Geekshop clients that Julian drew from his PSC would already be employment income (and any dividends would not be remuneration, so would be disregarded). The agency would be obliged to make quarterly online reports to HMRC of payments to Julian's PSC, identifying both Julian and the PSC and the amounts paid for the services in the quarter. If the client of The Geekshop is in the public sector, The rules are likely to change in April 2017, although the detail is not yet certain.

## Explanatory Notes

*Employment or self-employment*

(1) The distinction between employment and self-employment is often hard to draw. It is not set out in the legislation. Instead it is a question of fact based upon a series of tests developed from case law. A number of different elements have to be considered and a picture needs to be drawn from all the relevant factors. The question was well summarised by Mummery J in *Hall v Lorimer*, the summary being approved by Nolan LJ when the case went to the Court of Appeal (1993): 'In order to decide whether a person carries on business on his own account it is necessary to consider many different aspects of that person's work activity. This is not a mechanical exercise of running through a check list to see whether they are present in, or absent from, a given situation. The object of the exercise is to paint a picture from the accumulation of detail. The overall effect can only be appreciated by standing back from the detailed picture which has been painted, by viewing it from a distance and by making an informed, considered, qualitative appreciation of the whole.'

The difficulty is determining what weight to give to any individual item and what conclusion to draw from the whole. Very few tests or facts give a conclusive answer. The strongest single indicator of self-employment is the exercised ability to provide a substitute. A contract of service (employment) cannot exist unless it contains an obligation on the part of the employee to provide his/her services personally. In the case of *Express & Echo Publications Ltd v Tanton* (1999), it was made clear that if a worker did not have to perform the duties personally then he could not be an employee. However, the reverse, ie the requirement to undertake the duties personally, does not automatically make the worker an employee (*McManus v Griffiths* (1997)), but will be a strong pointer, and it has proven to be very helpful to HMRC in IR35 cases where it has been argued that, eg, an IT worker is in disguised employment. It is also now crucial in agency work, where actual personal service under an agency contract will often mean that the worker is deemed to be an employee of the agency for the duration of the contract.

The courts use the test of 'mutual obligations' between employer and employee extensively. If no obligations exist there can be neither a contract of service (ie, a contract of employment) nor a contract for services (ie, the provision of services by a self-employed person).

In the case of typical agency workers, there are two sets of mutual obligations (worker–agency and agency-client) and the minimum mutual obligations needed to form a contract of service are split across the two contracts, so there can be no contract of service. In the case of agency workers, the typical contract therefore amounts to a contract for service (ie, *not* employment), so the legislation has to deem such a contract to exist in order to levy PAYE and Class 1 NICs.

Equally, where a person may, but need not, be asked to perform a service and, if asked, is free to decline to provide the service asked for, there exists no mutuality of obligation and thus no overarching contract of service. Between engagements, the person would certainly not be an employee, but during the engagement a worker may be under a contract of service or a contract for services, depending on the exact terms of engagement for the period. Note, however, mutual obligations may be created by custom and habit, which in turn may give rise to an enforceable contract of service. Once the contract is made, however, the key to determining whether it is one 'of service' or 'for services' is the nature of the mutual obligations in that contract, which involves considering a number of factors.

The major factor to take into account is the 'economic reality'. How much freedom does the worker have and what risks does he run, since these are very different when comparing employed and self-employed workers. Is the worker really in business on his own account? Does he have the ability to subcontract work to others? Is he responsible for his own actions? In summary, can he gain or lose by his own actions? Is there any element of speculation or risk?

In any given case all of the factors will not be relevant. Each case must be determined on its own facts. The factors include:

- Mutual obligations – long-term, personal commitment, perhaps even spanning periods of absence on holiday or for sickness or even just weekends, or something more loose for the delivery of a project to a timetable
- Freedom to substitute, the ability to subcontract work, or hire one's own employees to help, or to take on more than one contract at the same time and decide how and when to work on each
- Financial risk
- Whether there is a written (or unwritten) contract of service
- Business management, own office, notepaper etc
- Number of providers of work
- Provision of business and public liability or professional indemnity insurance
- A proper accounting system
- Contract for fixed term or job
- Basis of remuneration
- Capital invested in business
- Equipment – who provides major items
- Control or, more importantly, the right of the work-giver to control the method and manner of performance of the duties

- Place of duties
- Provision of benefits, sick pay, holiday pay or pension scheme
- Organisation (integration with or separation from client's business).

(2) Over the years HMRC have taken a different view in relation to various activities, and has succeeded in some cases taken before the courts, eg *Sidey v Phillips* (1987), where a non-practising barrister who lectured part-time on legal subjects and had two other separate sources of earnings was held to be an employee, and *Walls v Sinnett* (1987), where a part-time lecturing appointment held by a professional singer was also held to be an employment. They had succeeded in the much earlier (1973) case of *Fall v Hitchen*, where a dancer on a six-month Equity contract was held to be an employee. They then, however, decided that self-employment would usually be more appropriate for most people in the performing arts (although they were often deemed to be employed for NI purposes unless they were paid a fee per performance rather an hourly rate). Employment treatment was restricted for income tax purposes to cases where someone received a regular salary to perform in a series of productions, with a period of notice required to end the contract, such as permanent members of orchestras, and of opera, ballet and theatre companies. More recently, however, HMRC challenged the self-employed status of a number of performers working for ITV and the tribunals determined that most were working under contracts of service (ie, employees), so HMRC have changed once more their policy on the determination of the status of artistes. The *ITV Services Ltd* decisions ([2010] TC00836 and [2012] UKUT 47) were subject to an appeal to the Court of Appeal but were held to be a sound basis for categorising entertainers. Where entertainers are indeed taxed as employees they may claim a deduction for agent's fees up to a maximum of 17½% of their earnings in the relevant tax year (ITEPA 2003 s 352). The deeming provisions for entertainers in the Categorisation of Earners Regulations 1978 were revoked from 6 April 2014, so some entertainers will have moved back from Class 1 to Class 2 and 4 when that change took effect.

HMRC have lost some other status cases, including the case of *McMenamin v Diggles* (1991), in which a barrister's senior clerk had changed his contractual arrangements to bring himself into the self-employed category, and *Hall v Lorimer* mentioned in 1 above (CA 1993), concerning a vision mixer who undertook short-term engagements for various production companies. The Revenue won the case of *Barnett v Brabyn* (1996), where they successfully argued that the taxpayer was self-employed despite only working for one client, but lost the case of *Andrews v King* (1991), where they argued that a gangmaster should be treated as self-employed. The court disagreed, holding that Andrews was selecting workers and hiring on behalf of his employers.

In *Parade Park Hotel & Paul May v HMRC* (2007) SpC, M, a builder and decorator worked for several years as the odd-job man at a small hotel. He was an alcoholic and his attendance was patchy. He had little other work and provided his own tools. M could refuse work and choose his own hours. The proprietor of the hotel would list work needing to be done in a book and M would do it as it suited him. The case involved a review of mutuality of obligation with the defence arguing the hotel was never obliged to provide work and M was never obliged to carry it out. The commissioners found there was no mutuality and insufficient control to constitute a contract of service.

The case highlights the current approach of the courts where there is no determinative or credible written contract of an irreducible minimum requirement for three components to be present for a contract of service:

- mutuality of obligation (ie, a commitment on both sides to offer and accept work on a regular basis and for the employer to pay for any work done);
- control (ie, a commitment by the employer to give direction and control and by the worker to accept the directions); and
- personal service (ie, a commitment by the worker to do the work himself, with no right to employ another to do it).

Where one or more of these components is missing, the contract cannot be one for service regardless of other factors indicating otherwise. This court approach is not always followed by HMRC's status officers. In the case of *Autoclenz v Belcher* [2011] UKSC 41, while an HMRC status inspector had accepted that a group of workers was self-employed, the Supreme Court held that their contracts were employment contracts. While the contracts included a substitution clause so that there was apparently no personal service obligation, the court held that the particular clause was not genuine and that there was no realistic intention that the men should be able to send a substitute.

(3) The same treatment should apply both to tax and national insurance, but someone (in any business) who has been retrospectively reclassified as self-employed has the option of not claiming a refund of Class 1 contributions, so that the contributions will remain on his record for the purpose of earnings-related pension. Employers will be able to reclaim their share of the Class 1 contributions wrongly paid for such self-employed workers, subject to SSA 1998 s 54, which provides for a time limit of one year after the end of the year in which the Class 1 contribution is wrongly paid. Earlier contributions are deemed to have been correctly paid irrespective of the employment status. This also applies to Class 1A and 1B contributions. Where contributions have been wrongly paid in the belief that someone was an employee, then after the end of the next following tax year (eg after 5 April 2016 for contributions paid in respect of 2014/15) the contributions will be treated as having been correctly paid for the relevant period, which means there will be no need for the HMRC National Insurance Contributions & Employer Office (NIC&EO) to amend the contribution record of the worker concerned or to make repayments. The rules on NIC for entertainers used to be different – see Tax Bulletin 65 June 2003.

(4) Contractors in the construction industry are required to certify on their monthly CIS returns that none of their subcontractors is an employee. Penalties are charged if this statement is false. Determining the status of construction workers is notoriously difficult because of the variation in contracts and practices. HMRC lost an argument that all the subcontractors at Castle Construction (Chesterfield) Ltd were employees (2008 – SpC 723) but succeeded in a similar argument with a contractor called PJ Wright (2008 – TC00032). Construction workers whose services as self-employed subcontractors are supplied by employment agencies are taxed as employees (see **Example D1** for full details).

(5) Since 6 April 2000, under the 'IR35' rules, the provision of personal services that amounts to disguised employment through a partnership or limited company has been 'looked through' and the individual is treated as an employee of the partnership or limited company supplying his services and a deemed employment payment, subject to PAYE and NIC, is imputed to him on 5 April at the end of the year (see **Example N2** for full details).

The application of these rules was temporarily thrown into some doubt following the employment case of *Cable and Wireless v Muscat CA* (2006). In that case an individual was held to have been an employee even though engaged through a personal service company. However, the facts were unusual, in that Mr Muscat was required by the employer to transfer from his existing employment into the personal service company, and the court found that he had never in fact ceased to be an employee of his original employer. HMRC wisely refused to take precedent from this employment law case and a subsequent employment law case has attempted to rein back the principle (see Taxation magazine dated 2.7.07 'Back to source').

(6) The main points of difference between employment and self-employment are dealt with in **part (a)** of the Example, and **part (b)** illustrates some of the consequences in terms of allowable expenditure. **Example B3** describes the rules on travel and subsistence expenses for employees. The rules for the self-employed may be summarised as follows.

All expenses incurred by the self-employed must wholly and necessarily incurred for the purposes of the trade if they are to be deductible in the computation of taxable profits.

Relevant cases concerning travelling expenses for the self-employed are *Horton v Young* (1971), where the expenses of travelling from home to the sites of the main contractor by a bricklaying subcontractor were allowed, and *Newsom v Robertson* (1953), where a barrister's expenses of travelling between his home, where he did some of his work, and his London chambers were disallowed.

In the High Court case of *Powell v Jackman* (2004) the Court found that a milkman's business base was not his home, where he kept his business records, nor his depot where he kept his milk float, but that he had a defined area of business being his milk round, so the cost of travel from home to that base area was not deductible.

More recently, in *TD Hanlin* (TC001078), a self-employed construction worker was denied a deduction for his travel and subsistence expenses between home and the customer site, because his work base was seen to have shifted from his home in Coventry to the customer site in Dungeness, Kent, where he had been working for seven or eight years, He travelled at weekends and stayed locally during the week, and tried unsuccessfully to claim a deduction for all of the travel and subsistence costs.

The most recent significant case on travel expenses for a self-employed person is *Samadian v Revenue & Customs Comrs* [2014] UKUT 0013, where it was decided that a doctor could not claim certain travel expenses. Dr Samadian was employed by the NHS in two hospitals and operated his own private practice in two others, but based his office at home. He argued that, since his home office was a place of business, and he was working as a doctor in the NHS hospitals, any travel between those locations and his two private clinics should be deductible. The Upper Tribunal disagreed, finding that the reason the costs of travelling to and from home were incurred was the taxpayer's decision to live there rather than close to one of his clinics. Equally, the cost of travelling between NHS and private hospitals was a result of the taxpayer's choosing to work as an employee in the NHS locations, not a result of practising as a self-employed consultant. It could therefore not be said that the expenses had been incurred wholly and exclusively in the course of his profession.

The travel and subsistence rules are currently under review, with a particular focus on preventing a claim for the expenses of travel between home and work by those who work through employment intermediaries such as umbrella companies. Where a self-employed person works via an agency and is subject to supervision, direction or control as to the manner of carrying out the task, there is usually a deemed employment (see ITEPA 2003, s 44), so any expenses incurred fall under the ITEPA 2003 rules described in **Example B3** rather than ITTOIA 2005.

*Clothing*

As far as clothing is concerned, it has been held in various cases concerning employees (*Woodcock v IRC* (1977), *Hillyer v Leeke* (1976)) that clothing is 'partly for cover and comfort' and thus does not come within the 'wholly and exclusively' rule. The same rules were applied in the case of *Mallalieu v Drummond* (1983), relating to a self-employed barrister. However, protective clothing and uniforms that are not suitable for private use (eg, bearing printed or sewn-in business logos) will still qualify for both employees and self-employed workers.

*Nature of a trade*

(7) **Parts (c)** and **(d)** of the Example indicate the main considerations in determining whether or not a trade exists. Where there are one or more isolated transactions it has to be decided whether they are 'in the nature of trade' or merely the conversion of capital in one form into capital in another. A purchase and sale is either a trading transaction or a capital transaction. There is no other interpretation, and a charge could not, for example, be raised under the 'miscellaneous profits or gains' provisions.

(8) The traditional badges of trade mentioned in **part (c)** of the Example were reviewed in the case of *Marson v Morton* 1986, in which it was held that the sale of land originally bought as an investment to be held for a year or two but in fact sold only a few months later was not 'an adventure in the nature of trade'. The following points were made, which re-state and in some respects add to the indicators listed by the Royal Commission:

(i) Although not conclusive, lack of repetition is a pointer that may indicate something other than a trade.

(ii) Is the transaction related to the taxpayer's existing trade or trades?

(iii) Was the subject matter a typical trading commodity which can only be turned to advantage by realisation?

(iv) Was the transaction carried out in a typical trading way for that type of commodity?

(v) If the item was bought with borrowed money, that points to an intention to short-term re-sale (the judge, strangely, did not make a distinction between long-term and short-term borrowings, which itself can often be a useful indicator).

(vi) Was the item re-sold in one lot or broken down into smaller lots?

(vii) What was the intention of the purchaser at the time of purchase?

(viii) Did the item yield either enjoyment or pride of ownership, or produce income, any of which would point to investment rather than trading?

The judge stated that 'in 1986 it is not any longer self-evident that unless land is producing income it cannot be an investment'.

HMRC's argument about whether a film partnership investor is trading is outlined above. The decision in *Eclipse Film Partners No 35 LLP* seems to mean, in HMRC's view, that any investor in a film partnership other than the main partner running the LLP will not be carrying on a trade. .

*Mutual trading*

(9) Where there is mutual trading, so that the people carrying on the trade and the customers are the same persons, as with members' clubs, any resulting surplus is not taxable as a trading profit, because it represents an excess of the members' contributions over the association's expenditure. This does not extend to trading with those who are not members, since the principle of mutuality does not then apply. Care must be taken to put into place a system to clearly identify the turnover attributable to members, so as to eliminate the non-taxable proportion. Many 'club licences' no longer restrict bar sales only to members. The club would also be taxable on any other profits, such as investment income and capital gains, and as an unincorporated association other than a partnership it would be liable to corporation tax rather than income tax and/or capital gains tax (see **Example I1 explanatory note 1**). Banks and building societies have for some time been able to pay interest to clubs without deducting tax, so the clubs will be due to account for corporation tax on the full amount of the interest at the appropriate rate. HMRC may be prepared to treat a club as dormant if it is mainly for recreational and other non-commercial purposes, even though there is strictly a small tax liability. Unless HMRC have given written notification of dormant status, however, clubs must complete returns and account for tax under the self-assessment system. Where dormant status has been granted, clubs must notify HMRC within twelve months after the end of the relevant accounting period if their circumstances change, or if chargeable assets are likely to be disposed of (see HMRC's Guide to corporation tax self-assessment CTSA/BK4). See also http://www.hmrc.gov.uk/ct/clubs-charities-agents/clubs.htm.

HMRC have stated they will not seek returns or tax from clubs or unincorporated associations, where the annual corporation tax liability is expected to be below £100. See also **Example N3 part b** and **explanatory notes 10–12** for the tax exemptions for registered community amateur sports clubs (CASCs), which can earn trading profits from sales to non-members of up to £50,000 and rent of up to £30,000 before a tax liability arises, provided the club spends money only on qualifying activities. Note that the CASC limits for corporation tax do not apply for VAT: if taxable turnover breaches the registration threshold, irrespective of profits, the CASC must register for VAT.

Mutual status can also bring with it complications with VAT partial exemption when supplies are made to non-members (see, for example, the ECJ decision in *Bridport and West Dorset Golf Club Ltd* and Revenue & Customs Brief 25/14).

*Illegal trading*

(10) It is established case law that profits of illegal trading are nonetheless taxable. The unlawful nature of the contracts cannot be used as a defence to avoid paying tax on the proceeds. Hence the profits from illegal gambling machines were assessable in *Mann v Nash* (1932), from illegal street betting in *Southern v AB* (1933) and from prostitution in *CIR v Aken* (1988). As to betting, it was held in *Partridge v Mallandaine* (1886) that a racecourse bookmaker's profits were assessable as the profits of a vocation even though he could not at law enforce the wagering contracts. In contrast someone whose means of livelihood was betting on horses from his private address at starting prices was held not to be carrying on a trade (*Graham v Green*, 1925). If any contract is for an illegal purpose, it cannot be a contract of service as it is void, either by statute or in common law. The worker under that contract will therefore be a self-employed earner for tax and NI purposes.

*Trading or investment*

(11) The general conclusion to be drawn from the legislation and case law is that in cases where an activity is not clearly established as a trade at the outset, there may nonetheless come a point where its character is such that it may be challenged as a trading activity. An example is buying and selling Krugerrands. Occasional purchases and sales of Krugerrands with fairly lengthy intervening periods of ownership would be treated as capital transactions subject to capital gains tax. If, however, the scale and frequency of the transactions became such as to indicate a trading motive they would be challenged by HMRC as assessable as trading income.

(12) Individuals pay tax on gains at 10% or 20% on most gains, and 18% or 28% on residential property that is not a principal private residence, rather than income tax rates, and companies pay tax at the same rates on both income and gains. There are, however, significant differences between the treatment of income and gains that need to be borne in mind, particularly the following.

Capital profits of companies are reduced by an indexation allowance. For individuals the indexation allowance (up to April 1998) and taper relief were available for periods up to April 2008 but the charge is now at the rate of 10% or 18% for basic rate taxpayers and 20% or 28% for higher or additional rate taxpayers, subject in certain cases where entrepreneurs' relief is available to a reduction to 10%. Capital profits may also be eligible for some relief or even exemption, including, for individuals, an annual exemption of (currently) £11,100. Income profits, on the other hand, may be reduced or eliminated by paying pension premiums, or acquiring tax-efficient investments. Trading losses may be set against total income and capital gains (subject to a limit of £50,000 or, if more, 25% of adjusted total income (ITA 2007 s 24A)), whereas capital losses may only be set against capital gains (except for losses on shares subscribed for in an unquoted trading company).

*Agency workers*

(13) A contract of employment is always between two parties: one does the work in exchange for the wage and accepts a measure of supervision, direction or control, while the other is obliged to offer work on a regular basis, direct the worker in his duties, and pay for the work done. The minimum mutual obligations required to create a contract of service were set out in *Ready Mixed Concrete (South East) Ltd v Minister of Pensions and National Insurance* [1968] 1 All ER 433.

Where a worker works through an agency, those mutual obligations become a tripartite arrangement: the agency pays a wage, but the client directs and controls the work. An agency worker cannot therefore be an employee under a contract of service, so he is automatically a self-employed earner, even though he may be working alongside the client's own employees doing the same job in the same way. To ensure that such workers are taxed and subjected to NICs in the same way as the employees with whom they work, ITEPA 2003, ss 44–47 and the Social Security (Categorisation of Earners) Regulations 1978 (SI 1978/1689) deem such agency workers to be employees of the agency if they do the work personally and are subject to a right of supervision, direction or control. Each engagement under an agency contract will have its own permanent workplace, so agency workers cannot claim tax-free expenses for travel between home and work.

Some 'agency workers' are actually employed by 'umbrella' companies, so called because they take on their workers under a permanent employment contract that covers all their work in a series of temporary workplaces. HMRC refers to this as an 'overarching contract'. Others work through their own personal service company (PSC). The deeming rules in ITEPA 2003 and the Categorisation Regs 1978 are not needed to make these umbrella and PSC workers employed: they already have an employment contract. The agency that supplies their services to a client will pay the umbrella employer or PSC gross, and the umbrella employer or PSC is obliged to operate PAYE and NICs on any wages it pays to the workers. The umbrella contract or PSC employment contract means that the worker, until the rules were changed at 6 April 2016 by FA 2016, generally had a series of temporary workplaces and the employer could pay tax- and NIC-free travel expenses for home-to-work travel, often reducing taxable pay by the same amount.

Similar considerations arose where workers operated through their own personal service company that fell within IR35.

The changes made by FA 2016 (and SI 2016/352 for NICs) deem each agency assignment to be a separate employment, so that most agency engagements undertaken by the umbrella or IR35 PSC worker will now result in the worker having a series of permanent workplaces, which means that home-to-work travel and subsistence expenses cannot now be paid tax- and NIC-free. This rule will not apply if the umbrella worker is free from any right of supervision, direction and control, but there is no such escape route for IR35 workers and their PSCs.

# Question

Huguenot Ltd, a UK company, has been taken over by a French group, Chasseur SA, which has group companies in various parts of the world. The parent company is considering sending some of its employees to the UK subsidiary to integrate its systems with those at head office in Nantes, gain work experience and improve their business English language skills.

They are also proposing to appoint Michel du Maurier, one of their French directors, to the board of the UK company. He will come to the UK for quarterly board meetings, which will last 1½ days each, but will not change his residence. He will be paid £10,000 pa by Huguenot.

Huguenot's top research scientist, Bruce, is an Australian. He is also to take a three-year secondment to the group's US R&D company, moving to California with his Scottish wife, Sheila, and their children, and letting his UK home while he is away. His contract will remain with Huguenot, but Bruce will be transferred onto the US payroll and it is agreed that the US company will pay all removal costs, all US medical and dental insurance, and a rent subsidy, and will ensure that any extra tax and social security costs that Bruce incurs will be met by that company. Bruce will remain a member of the UK pension scheme while on secondment. When Bruce was recruited, he was awarded some CSOP options that will mature while he is working in California. If Bruce's secondment is a success, he and his wife may extend their stay in the US, or even move to Australia, where Huguenot also has laboratories.

Chasseur is keen to use Huguenot's intellectual property to expand into the Far East, so it asks Huguenot's UK business development director, Clyde, an American who was recruited only two years ago from a US business, to spend six months based in Singapore to research opportunities for acquisitions in the region. You are told that Clyde has significant longstanding investments in US technology stocks that generate large US dividends each year.

Explain to the UK finance director the main points about the mobile workers' personal tax and social security position, and the company's UK PAYE and NIC obligations, in respect of:

(a) engineers who come to the UK for three month secondments;

(b) IT department staff who plan to spend around two years in the UK working on integration, but will go back regularly to France, one week in four, to work on the French end of the project (none of them have been UK resident before);

(c) Michel du Maurier, who intends to remain a UK director for at least the next five years;

(d) Bruce's remuneration and pension scheme membership;

(e) Clyde's tax and social security position.

Do not go into detail on the UK statutory residence test. Ignore non-tax and non-NIC considerations. You need not mention any detail of foreign taxes.

# Answer

## (a) Engineers

Short-term assignees such as the engineers should not become resident in the UK and should remain resident and taxable in France. Whether they have to pay income tax in the UK will depend on whether their costs are to be recharged to Huguenot.

If their costs are not recharged to the UK company (ie, the French company treats their work in the UK as a training experience and bears all the cost), they should fall within the exemption provided by the employment income article of the UK-France double tax treaty.

Article 15 of that treaty, 'Income from employment', provides the basic rule that the engineers' income from UK duties may be taxed in the UK, but it is to be taxed only in France if three conditions are fulfilled:

- the worker is present in the UK for a period or periods not exceeding 183 days in total within any period of 12 months,
- the remuneration is paid by, or on behalf of, an employer who is not resident of the UK, and
- the remuneration is not borne by a permanent establishment which the employer has in the UK.

HMRC regards the business that controls the workers and takes the risks and benefits of their work to be their 'economic employer'. In this case, even if Huguenot controls the workers and benefits from their work while they are in the UK, the fact that Chasseur does not recharge their costs should mean that the men qualify for exemption from UK tax under this article of the treaty.

This does not, however, mean that Huguenot has no obligations. Treaty relief is normally available only on the making of a claim by the taxpayer concerned. Huguenot is, in effect, the host employer of the workers and should be obliged to operate PAYE on their earnings unless specific permission is given by HMRC for nothing to be reported.

In practice, Huguenot should request a short-term business visitors agreement from HMRC as set out in the PAYE manual under the heading 'EP Appendix 4'. With such an agreement in place, HMRC will accept provisionally an advance claim under article 15 of the treaty. Huguenot will have to track the days spent in the UK and supply information to HMRC in respect of anybody who spends at least 60 days in the UK in a year.

Where the engineers in fact spend no more than 30 days in the UK, there are no requirements to fulfil, unless that period is part of a longer period of 60 days or more.

Where they spend no more than 59 days in the UK during the tax year, PAYE may be disregarded provided Huguenot confirms to HMRC that there is no formal contract of employment between it and the French engineers and the 59 days do not form part of a more substantial period.

For those engineers who spend up to 90 days in the UK, Huguenot can disregard PAYE provided it supplies to HMRC, by 31 May after the end of the tax year, certain details about the employees in question and their assignments, and confirms that the UK company does not ultimately bear the cost of the employee's remuneration or function as the employer during the UK assignment.

Where the engineers spend more than 90 days in the UK but no more than 150 days in the tax year, Huguenot can again disregard PAYE provided all of the information requested for visitors up to 90 days is provided and the engineers concerned provide a statement from the French tax authority confirming their residence in France for tax purposes throughout the period in the UK. This statement should be passed to HMRC by 31 May following the end of the relevant French tax year (ie, the calendar year).

In the circumstances, it would seem that Huguenot will not be responsible for operating PAYE provided it meets the conditions of the short-term business visitors agreement.

If any of the conditions for exemption under a short-term business visitors agreement are not met, Huguenot will be responsible for any arrears of PAYE. This will include reporting any benefits in kind which would otherwise not be taxable in the UK. The engineers' travel, subsistence and accommodation expenses should not be taxable because they will be regarded as the costs of being at a temporary workplace.

For social security purposes, the engineers should be subject to the French rules and should remain so throughout any short-term secondments to the UK. Chasseur should request A1 portable documents (ie, certificates of continuing liability) from the French social security authorities and supply a copy to Huguenot. Even in the absence of an A1, Huguenot should not be required to account for UK NICs in respect of the engineers' earnings where it is clear that they fall within article 12 of EC Regulation 883/2004, which keeps migrant workers insured under their home scheme where their employer posts them temporarily (ie, for no more than 24 months) to work in another EEA member state.

## (b) IT staff

Because the IT staff will be in the UK for two years, the earnings will not be exempted by article 15 of the UK-France double tax treaty. Their earnings from the UK duties will therefore be subject to PAYE, for which Huguenot will be responsible even if they continue to be paid into French bank accounts by Chasseur. Huguenot may take over responsibility for paying the IT workers on behalf of Chasseur or it may operate a dummy payroll using information provided by Chasseur and accounting for the PAYE due.

Like the engineers, the IT staff should qualify under regulation 883 /2004, article 12 to remain insured under the French Social Security system for the duration of their secondment and Chasseur should apply for A1 portable documents to certify this fact. If any of the engineers are likely to stay for more than two years, the certificate may be extended or an application may be made under article 13 because the workers will be working regularly in two EU member states. Because they are habitually resident in France and spending 25% of their working time there, France will be the competent state for social security purposes throughout the period of secondment, even if it extends beyond two years.

Huguenot should therefore simply disregard the IT staff for NIC purposes, leaving all NIC fields blank in the RTI record. Because the European regulations mean that the IT staff will not be insurable under UK rules, they will not be eligible for a National Insurance number and need not apply for one.

The staff should take up residence in the middle of the UK tax year and split year treatment will apply automatically. All income before arrival should not be taxable in the UK, while income earned from UK duties for the rest of the year (and the rest of the secondment) will be taxable under PAYE. The same principle in reverse should apply when the staff leave the UK after the end of their secondment.

Because they are non-domiciled and they have not been resident in the UK in the last three tax years, they will fall within ITEPA 2003, s26A, so their earnings from the one week in four that they spend back at their base in France after becoming UK resident should be subject to overseas workday relief and not be taxable in the UK, provided those foreign earnings are not remitted to the UK. Similarly, any investment income or gains that accrue to them during their period living in the UK should only be taxable if that income or those gains are remitted to the UK. Any income or gains from the period before they became UK resident may be remitted without a UK tax charge, so they should arrange for their earnings for the whole period of the UK secondment to be paid into a separate bank account, in order to be able to demonstrate that none of the earnings from the French duties are remitted.

Huguenot's primary duty is to operate PAYE on the whole of the earnings for the period of UK residence, but it may make an application under ITEPA 2003, s690 to HMRC for permission to apply PAYE deductions to only 75% of the earnings (i.e. the proportion not covered by overseas workday relief). Once that permission has been granted, Huguenot should need to operate PAYE only on the 75% of the earnings that relate to UK duties.

If the staff remained subject to home country payroll taxes while working on secondment in the UK, Huguenot could make an application for net of foreign tax credit relief to be applied through the payroll so that double tax relief was given provisionally at source. However, France does not have a PAYE payroll tax regime, and instead requires taxpayers to make payments in quarterly instalments based on the annual tax return, so this should be irrelevant in this case.

Huguenot should ask them for expat starter checklists (the successor to the P46(Expat) starter form), ticking box A to indicate that they will be working for the employer in the UK for more than six months. For any staff who joined the payroll before 6 October, a cumulative emergency PAYE code should be allocated provisionally, but in the second half of the year the emergency code should be used on a week 1/month 1 basis. HMRC should issue a correct code in due course. Any UK benefits provided should be reported on P11D, although travel and temporary accommodation expenses should be exempt, following the changes to ITEPA 2003 made by FA 2015 with effect from 6 April 2016.

## (c) Michel du Maurier

Michel will remain a French resident throughout and will therefore be taxable in the UK only on earnings derived from the UK duties. Article 16 of the UK-France double tax treaty permits the UK to tax Michel on his UK earnings as a director even if he is paid from France. The costs of his travel between two group companies should not attract a tax charge.

For PAYE purposes, Huguenot should ask Michel to complete the expat starter checklist and it should apply the relevant emergency code, taking account of the date of his arrival in the UK in the same way as for the IT staff. As an EU citizen, Michel is currently entitled to a full personal allowance (although the employer should review this once 'Brexit' happens), so none of his fees should in fact attract PAYE. He will also remain on a French employment contract, and will be taxable under French rules as a French resident. Overseas tax regimes typically provide some relief for foreign taxes, either by credit or exemption (eg, the US will exclude from US tax foreign income earned by expatriate US citizens up to $101,300 in calendar year 2016, even though US citizens in principle remain fully taxable in the US when non-resident), but however the French rules might apply, they are irrelevant to Michel's UK tax position because the UK has primary taxing rights as the jurisdiction where the duties are performed.

Michel's NIC's position is similar to that of the IT staff and the engineers: he will be making only brief visits to the UK and should, under the EU regulations, remain insured in respect of all of his earnings under the French system. Chasseur should apply for an A1 portable document to certify to the UK authorities that the earnings are not subject to UK National Insurance contributions. However, in practice, HMRC is unlikely to query the NIC position because Michel attends only four board meetings and spends only eight working days in the UK.

## (d) Bruce

Bruce will become non-UK resident as soon as he moves to California. He will require a visa and will transfer onto the US company's payroll, paying US wage taxes from the date of his arrival. He and his wife will also be required to file annual US tax returns for state and federal taxes.

Huguenot should have no immediate PAYE obligations as he is technically not leaving the UK company and does not need to be shown as such in any RTI submissions. His US earnings after leaving the UK will not be taxable in the UK because he will be able to split the UK tax year into resident and non-resident periods, so he will be entitled to a refund of UK taxes by taking into account unused personal allowance and basic rate band at the point of departure. In most countries, tax reliefs for foreign pension funds are irrelevant, but under the terms of the UK-US double tax treaty, Bruce's membership of the UK company pension scheme should create no tax complications as his personal contributions should continue to be deductible, and contributions by the UK employer to a UK registered pension scheme should not be treated as his taxable income in the US.

If Bruce was given a US contract of employment, he could be treated as a leaver and given a P45, allowing him to submit a P85 requesting a tax refund, or he could file a self-assessment tax return at the end of the year to the same end. Because he will be paid by the US company, his taxation position while living in the US is determined principally by US tax law.

However, the social security position complicates matters.

If Bruce's UK contract of employment continues while he is on secondment in California, he will fall within the terms of the UK-US reciprocal agreement on social security, article 4 of which allows for posted workers to remain insured under their home scheme, and not fall within the host country's scheme, during secondments of up to five years.

Huguenot should therefore submit a form CA9107 to HMRC in Newcastle requesting a certificate of coverage, US/UK1, which evidences to the US company and the US IRS Bruce's right to remain insured in the UK and not to pay US federal insurance contributions and federal unemployment taxes while working in California. In the circumstances, Huguenot will continue to operate a parallel UK payroll so as to account for UK national insurance contributions throughout the secondment. Bruce and Huguenot should apply to HMRC in advance of the commencement of the secondment for a 'NT' (no tax) PAYE code so that no UK tax must be accounted for in respect of the earnings during the period in the US.

While Bruce should be taxable only in the US in respect of his earnings during the secondment, UK NI contributions will be due on his earnings.

- If the UK company pays his removal costs, the excess over £8,000 will be subject to UK social security rules (although no NICs should in fact be due because excess relocation costs fall within Class 1A, for which liability only arises in respect of amounts taxable in the UK, and the excess relocation costs relate to the non-UK employment, the earnings from which are not taxable in the UK).
- It is likely that the US medical and dental insurance will be paid by the US host company, but since Bruce will have no P11D benefit in respect of the costs incurred while he is non-resident, there should be no Class 1A liability in the UK.
- The rent subsidy, however, is likely to be classed as earnings as it will not represent a specific and distinct expense incurred in carrying out the employment.
- If the company meets Bruce's extra tax costs (i.e., because the total tax payable by him to California and the US federal government exceeds the tax he would have paid in the UK on the same income), that payment will have to be grossed up for US tax and UK social security, and any payment will be subject to UK contribution liability.

If Bruce is treated as a leaver in the UK and becomes an employee solely of the US company for the three-year period, he will not be treated as a posted worker under the terms of the treaty and all tax and social security contributions will be payable in the US under US rules. The US host company will be responsible for all payroll matters, including employer social security contributions.

Bruce's CSOP option could give rise to tax charges in the US, where the tax advantages granted by UK law are irrelevant. US rules may grant tax advantages to certain kinds of incentive stock options but it is unlikely that the terms of the UK CSOP will meet the US requirements for special treatment. If Bruce exercises the option while in the US, any gain realised will be split on a pro rata basis between UK and US duties from the date of grant to the date of exercise. While the UK gain should be given capital treatment, just like any other UK CSOP option exercised in the UK, the US tax rules will treat the part of the gain attributable to his US working days as taxable income. The company may therefore have to meet that tax liability on a grossed-up basis unless CSOP gains are explicitly excluded from the tax protection guarantee given in his assignment letter or revised contract.

While Bruce is in the US, his UK home will be let, so he and his wife will be subject to UK income tax on any net rents received. They will also be subject to US income taxes, subject to double tax relief with the UK rules applying in priority to the US rules.

Because Bruce is not an EEA citizen or a government employee, he will not be entitled to UK personal allowances for years of non-residence, although his Scottish wife will be entitled to set her personal allowance against her share of any net rents.

In the UK the couple will be classed as non-resident landlords, which means that the letting agent should deduct basic rate tax from any rents passed to them and account for that tax to HMRC. However, if his UK tax affairs are up-to-date, Bruce may make an application on form NRL1i to receive UK rental income without deduction of UK tax. If Bruce's wife is a joint owner of the property, she will also have to complete her own application form. Any tax due on the rents will then be accounted for through the self-assessment tax return. It may be advantageous for the net rents to be split for tax purposes on other than a 50:50 basis (eg, because Sheila has the benefit of a personal allowance while Bruce does not), so they could submit a declaration of beneficial interests in joint property and income (Form 17) to adjust the allocation of the jointly-held property for UK tax purposes. It may also be possible to achieve the same in the US, but local advice will be necessary.

If Bruce and his wife sell their UK property while away in the US, any gain may be taxable in the US, subject to local exemptions (but the US has a $250,000 per person capital gains exemption for what the UK would term principal private residences that have been occupied as such for two years in the last five, with extensions for job-related relocations), but Bruce's absence from the UK home is likely to fall within the UK CGT disregard for periods spent working away. If the couple's plans change and they stay longer in the US, they may need to consider the CGT rules introduced in April 2015 making non-residents chargeable on the disposal of UK residential property.

If Bruce and his wife emigrate from the UK, they may be able to transfer their pension funds without a UK tax charge on exiting the UK scheme into a Qualifying Recognised Overseas Pension Scheme, provided the tax laws and the transferee fund in the jurisdiction in which they then live meet the conditions.

## (e) Clyde

Clyde has only been in the UK for two years and is non-domiciled. He will therefore have become UK resident for tax purposes and, given that he will return in six months' time, he should remain taxable in the UK on all his salary and benefits while working in the Far East, with the normal relief for pension contributions. His additional medical insurance during the assignment should be exempt in the UK. Note that, although Clyde is domiciled in a US state rather than the UK, he is not eligible for overseas workday relief (OWR) in respect of his Singapore earnings because his pay comes from a UK employer rather than a foreign source.

Huguenot should simply continue to tax his salary as normal through the PAYE system, but with no NIC deductions (see further below). His expenses incurred in travelling and performing the duties should be deductible or exempt, and the company may reimburse £10 per night in respect of personal incidental expenses unrelated to the job, such as laundry costs and personal telephone calls. Because he is going to be away for more than 60 days, the company could pay for Clyde's family to visit without incurring a UK tax charge. Clyde could only make a claim for OWR if he had earnings from a foreign source (eg, he was employed by the French holding company for the work in Singapore).

As Clyde is non-domiciled, his US dividend income is only taxable in the UK if it is remitted to the UK (see https://www.gov.uk/government/uploads/system/uploads/attachment_data/file/528018/RDR1-residence-domicile-remittance.pdf). If Clyde's dividends are paid into a US bank account and not remitted to the UK, he need not pay UK income tax on those dividends until they are remitted.

He is unlikely to become resident in Singapore if he spends less than 183 days there (it does not matter whether the period spans the end of a year so that the days fall into two tax years). If he spends more than 60 days in Singapore, his employment income for work in Singapore (but not elsewhere in the Far East) will be taxed as a non-resident at rates determined by local law, and the UK will grant double tax relief for any local taxes suffered. If he spends most of his time travelling around the Far East and spends less than 60 days in Singapore, his income is likely to be exempt from local tax. Huguenot should take local advice in Singapore about Clyde's tax position. However, since the income is taxable in the UK in any event, an absence of liability in Singapore means no more than that the administration involved in a double tax relief claim is avoided.

For social security purposes, Clyde should not be liable to UK or Singapore social security rules during his period in the Far East.

The UK does not have a social security reciprocal agreement with Singapore, so the normal domestic rules apply. Clyde is resident in the UK immediately before being sent abroad by his UK employer, but after living in the UK for only a year before going overseas again, he is unlikely to be classed as ordinarily resident, which is a condition set by regulation 146 of the Social Security (Contributions) Regulations 2001 for continuing UK liability during periods of absence from the UK working in non-EEA and non-treaty countries. Unless Clyde can show that he has settled in the UK for the long term, the obligation to account for National Insurance contributions should therefore cease when Clyde leaves the UK and recommence at the end of the secondment when he returns.

Singapore does not require or even permit short-term expatriates to join its domestic social security scheme, the Central Provident Fund.

Because Clyde is a US citizen, he will also remain liable to US tax rules wherever he happens to live and work, albeit with the benefit of exclusions for foreign earned income, so he will still have to file a US tax return each year.

## Explanatory Notes

*(i) Effects of residence on UK tax liability*

ITEPA 2003 Part 2 Chapters 2 to 5 (ss 3 to 41L) set out the rules for taxing the income of resident and non-resident employees.

The basic principles are that,

- unless a treaty makes alternative provision, earnings from carrying out UK duties (other than merely incidental visits on behalf of a foreign employer) are subject to UK income tax, whether a worker is resident or non-resident, and
- a UK resident is liable to UK tax on worldwide income on an arising basis, but
- a non-domiciled person with foreign duties who is either non-resident or only a short-term resident (subject to a three-year test set out in s 26A) should be eligible for overseas workday relief and therefore be taxable on income from the non-UK duties only if they are remitted to the UK.

Residence for tax purposes is now determined by a statutory residence test in FA 2013, Sch 45 which provides a series of objective criteria against which a taxpayer's circumstances can be measured (see Example F1 and HMRC guidance in RDR3 for details of residence rules, and RDR4 for details of overseas workday relief).

When a worker comes to or leaves the UK at the start or end of an assignment that results in a change of residence, the UK tax year may be split into resident and non-resident periods, with income arising in those periods taxed according to the relevant residence status. See Part 3 of Schedule 45.

Residence for social security purposes is not based on the FA 2013 test but on the long-standing case law tests that applied for tax purposes before 2013.

*(ii) PAYE*

A UK employer is obliged to operate PAYE when paying any of its workers unless HMRC has authorised the use of an 'NT' (no tax) code. When UK workers are sent overseas for extended periods, the NT code should be requested from HMRC before the start of the assignment. Where workers are recruited overseas to work solely overseas, albeit on a UK payroll, the issue of the NT code should be a mere formality.

Where a UK employer will pay a non-UK resident worker, or a worker who is UK resident but meets the requirements of s 26A, who will work both in the UK and outside the UK during the tax year, the employer may make an application under ITEPA 2003, s 690 for a direction that only a proportion of any payment of earnings (representing earnings from UK duties) made in the year should be treated as PAYE income and subjected to PAYE deductions through payroll.

Employees seconded from abroad rather than recruited in the UK still fall within PAYE but the rules for tax codes and information included in the payroll record differ. A secondee should complete an expatriate starter checklist (which used to be the P46(Expat)). The tax code for a seconded worker is determined in accordance with the following table:

| *Employee's present circumstances* | *Tax code to use for 2016/17* |
|---|---|
| Intends to live in the UK for 183 days or more | 1100L cumulative |
| Intends to live in the UK for less than 183 days | 1100L week 1/month 1 (unless employee is an EEA citizen) |
| Will be working for the UK employer both inside and outside the UK, but will be living abroad | 1100L week 1/month 1 (unless employee is an EEA citizen) |
| EEA citizen | 1100L cumulative, even if the employee has confirmed statements 2 or 3 in the New Starter questions |

| *Employee's present circumstances* | *Tax code to use for 2016/17* |
|---|---|
| The employee hasn't given enough information about present circumstances before the first payday | 0T week 1/month 1 |

*(iii) Double tax treaties and employees*

The state where the work is carried out has a right to tax workers in its jurisdiction, but so does the state in which the worker is resident. Some states treat all of their citizens as tax resident even when they are overseas (eg, the USA), others require presence for at least 183 days, others look to the ownership and occupation of an abode or home, so it is not uncommon for posted workers to be dual resident because different states have different rules. To determine which states have taxing rights, most countries enter into double tax treaties. Note: the EU and EEA have no competence in direct tax matters, but the EU treaty does include broad anti-discrimination provisions for EU citizens which can affect member states' rights to tax, and obligations to relieve posted workers from taxes.

The member states of the Organisation for Economic Cooperation & Development (OECD: see http://www.oecd.org/) have devised common interpretations that are generally applied globally, and proposed a model double tax convention that states may adopt as a template when negotiating or renegotiating bilateral agreements to prevent double taxation in cross-border situations. Note that social security matters are quite separate and not within the OECD's competence. Note also that even those countries with the most bilateral double tax treaties in place may not have a treaty with a particular state, and even if there is such a treaty, it might differ from the OECD model in various ways, so it is important to consider the exact terms of every treaty individually.

A typical double tax treaty based on the OECD model convention includes provision for avoiding double taxation on earnings from 'dependent personal services' or employment income. Article 15 of the model convention (http://www.oecd.org/tax/treaties/model-tax-convention-on-income-and-on-capital-2015-full-version-9789264239081-en.htm) provides that income from employment earned by a resident of a contracting state shall be taxable only in that state unless the employment is exercised in the other state. Where the employment is so exercised, such earnings as are derived from that employment in the other state may be taxed by that state. This principle has remained broadly unchanged over many years and many versions of the model convention, so appears in most treaties that encompass employment income. Note that some are restricted to just shipping and international transport, and some do not need to include employment income because the local tax code does not include foreign workers or does not include an income tax, and some are no more than tax information exchange agreements aimed at preventing tax evasion.

The model Article 15 goes on to provide for an exception in respect of short-term visitors so that the host state gives up its right to tax their income. The host state agrees not to tax the earnings of residents of the home state provided that:

- the visiting worker is present in the host state for a period or periods not exceeding 183 days in total in any 12-month period beginning or ending in the tax year;
- the earnings are paid by, or on behalf of, an employer who is not a resident of the host state; and
- the cost of those earnings is not borne by a permanent establishment which the employer has in the host state.

In some treaties, the 183-day maximum period of visit is measured within the tax year, while in others it is measured within the calendar year. Each relevant treaty must be examined to establish which rule applies.

The UK interprets the third condition as referring to a permanent establishment of the 'economic employer', ie, the business that benefits economically from the posted employee's work and bears the risk of the employee's mistakes. In other words, if the overseas home employer recharges the costs of the employee's remuneration to the UK host employer, the third condition is breached and no relief will be granted under the employment income article, even if the worker is in the UK for less than 183 days.

*(iv) Short-term business visitors*

Where employees of a foreign affiliate are sent to the UK for short periods and could make a claim for double tax relief or exemption from UK income tax under the dependent personal services or employment income article of the relevant tax treaty between the UK and their home base country, HMRC allows employers to avoid PAYE obligations by entering into a short-term business visitor arrangement. The details were set out originally in Appendix 4 to the Employment Procedures Manual (an 'EP Appendix 4' agreement) and are now found under the same name in the PAYE Manual at PAYE82000.

The agreement allows employers not to operate PAYE in respect of short-term secondees if certain conditions are met, the conditions varying according to the length of time the employee is likely to spend in the UK. Employees who will become resident in the UK by virtue of spending 183 days here are not eligible to be covered by the agreement.

The employer must put in place some form of internal reporting system to keep accurate records of employees visiting UK on business, with employees periodically reporting days spent in the UK to a central point controlling the arrangement. No PAYE is deducted in respect of employees covered by the agreement, but where liability is subsequently found to arise on payments of PAYE income made to an employee, the employer will be expected to pay the tax that ought to have been deducted from or otherwise paid in respect of each payment.

There are no reporting requirements in respect of employees who spend fewer than 30 days in the UK.

Where an employee spends no more than 59 days in the UK during the tax year, PAYE can be disregarded provided it is confirmed that there is no formal contract of employment with the UK employer and the 59 days do not form part of a more substantial period.

The employer will have to make reports of specified information by 31 May in respect of all visitors who spend between 60 and 90 days in the UK in the tax year, but PAYE may be disregarded. HMRC needs to know:

- the full name of the employee;
- the last known UK and overseas addresses of the employee;
- the nature of the duties undertaken;
- the date of the assignment commenced;
- the date it ceased; and
- the name of the country to which a tax return covering worldwide income is submitted.

The employer must also confirm that it does not ultimately bear the cost of the employee's remuneration or function as the employee's employer during the UK assignment.

Where an employee is in the UK for between 91 and 150 days in the tax year, PAYE can still be disregarded provided that all the information required for visitors up to 90 days is given and, in addition, other than for US citizens and green card holders, the employee provides a statement from the overseas tax authorities confirming residence in the other state throughout the period in the UK. Because US law automatically treats its citizens and green card holders as tax residents, they merely have to provide evidence of continuing residence in the US.

Individuals who spend more than 151 days but no more than 183 days in the UK require an individual application for authority to be included in the STBV arrangement. The application must include a statement by the employee giving reasons why he or she is treated resident in the treaty partner country by reference to the appropriate article in the double tax treaty. Instead of including the employee in the STBV agreement, HMRC may issue an NT code.

*(v) Net of foreign tax credit relief*

Employees who leave the UK on secondment without becoming non-resident and those who come to the UK on short-term assignments that do not meet the conditions for exemption under the double tax treaty may suffer payroll taxes in both the UK and the other state. Double tax relief may be available on the making of a claim under the treaty, but there is a short-term cash flow issue because both countries will be collecting payroll taxes and one of them will make a refund when the treaty claim is made.

For those employees on UK payrolls sent to work overseas, where the host country has priority in taxing the employment income, HMRC is prepared to grant provisional treaty relief through the PAYE system by allowing the UK employer to retain some of the tax otherwise payable in the UK and remit only the tax due net of foreign tax credit relief.

The CWG2 Employer's Further Guide to PAYE and NICs advises employers to contact HMRC if they have to deduct tax under two regimes. The employer technical team in HMRC NIC&EO in Sunderland deals with applications under 'EP Appendix 5', now found in the PAYE Manual at PAYE82001. Once authorised, the employer may give credit for foreign tax actually payable on and deducted from the employee's pay and paid to the overseas tax authority. Credit is given by reducing the amount of UK PAYE deducted from earnings by the amount of the foreign tax deducted from gross wages in the same UK tax year. Any net UK PAYE tax remaining due is returned under RTI.

*(vi) Overseas-based directors*

The tax rules for overseas-based directors are not significantly different from the rules for ordinary workers, although some double tax treaties apply slightly different rules from the normal Article 15 approach. In the UK-France treaty, for example, Article 16 provides that a director's fees and other similar payments derived by a resident of either state in his capacity as a member of the Board of Directors of a company which is a resident of the other state may be taxed in that other state. There are no 183-day time limits or thresholds.

Directors who are EEA citizens qualify for a UK personal allowance even if they are non-resident, and similar provision is made by a number of non-EEA double tax treaties. In Michel du Maurier's case, the UK has primary taxing rights, but the fees are covered by his UK personal allowance (for as long as the UK remains in the EU). French law exempts from French income tax directors' fees earned overseas from foreign companies provided they are subject to host country tax, so in this example Michel should have no UK or French tax to pay on his director's fees.

*(vii) Employment-related securities*

Gains realised from employee share awards and option exercises, unless under a tax-advantaged employee share scheme, are usually subject to UK income tax at award or exercise as 'securities income'. If the shares are readily convertible assets, PAYE may be due.

A simple award of shares will normally be classed as a payment of general earnings, and the resulting receipt will be taxed in the same way as cash earnings, which may be taxed on an arising basis, a remittance basis, or not at all, depending on the employee's circumstances.

Where a share award or option gain falls within Part 7 of ITEPA 2003, it will instead be treated as specific employment income. Before April 2015, specific residence rules were included in Part 7 (eg, ss 421E and 474) and most tax charges would have been based on the residence of the employee at the time of the award. However, from 6 April 2015, FA 2014 introduced changes so that only that element of share-based income that relates to UK duties is taxed in the UK, even where the share awards or option grants were made before the date of the change in the legislation.

The securities income of internationally mobile employees is now taxed under Chapter 5B of Part 2 of ITEPA 2003, which applies if the award or exercise counts as employment income. Tax is calculated by establishing the relevant period to which the securities income relates and time-apportioning it between UK and non-UK periods of working, using workdays as the basis of the apportionment.

If the employee meets mobility conditions in the 'relevant period', the amount of securities income other than 'foreign securities income' (FSI) is treated as taxable specific income for UK purposes. The 'relevant period' is measured from the date of grant to the date of vesting, except in the context of UK-US transfers, where the period from grant to exercise is taken into account instead.

FSI may be either chargeable or 'unchargeable'. Chargeable FSI is taxable in the UK if it is remitted. Unchargeable FSI relates to periods of non-UK duties to which the remittance basis would not apply if the earnings were paid in cash (ie, typically, work wholly outside the UK for a non-UK employer).

*(viii) Overseas workday relief*

Non-domiciled workers earning overseas income from a non-UK employer may, if they meet residence conditions (broadly, arrival in the UK within the last three years), claim the remittance basis and have the income from at least some overseas (non-UK) workdays excluded from UK liability until income is brought to the UK. This overseas workday relief (OWR) applies for up to a maximum of three tax years at a time, where the conditions are met, to earnings for any year in which the individual is resident, and to the UK part of a qualifying split year. The OWR rules are statutory and may be summarised as follows:

| | | |
|---|---|---|
| Is the person UK domiciled? | Yes → | OWR unavailable |
| No ↓ | | |
| Non-UK resident for all of last 3 years? | Yes → | OWR available for the tax year, provided the individual claims has foreign-source employment income and claims remittance basis |
| No ↓ | | |
| UK resident last year, but non-UK resident for the 3 years before that? | Yes → | |
| No ↓ | | |
| UK resident for the last 2 tax years, but non-UK resident for the 3 years before that? | Yes → | |
| No ↓ | | |
| Non-UK resident last year, UK resident the year before that, but non-UK resident for the 3 years before that? | Yes → | |
| No ↓ | | |
| OWR unavailable | | |

*(ix) Special mixed funds*

Special mixed fund rules apply to help simplify the identification of remittances to the UK from a bank account that receives foreign employment income. Because of the limitations of the special mixed fund rules, most individuals wishing to use them need to set up a new account into which UK assignment-related earnings are paid. The key points of the rules are outlined in summary form below.

Under these rules, all remittances from a qualifying bank account are deemed to have been made in a single year-end transfer of the relevant amount of income and gains in that account. This simplifies the analysis of funds remitted so that the taxpayer is able to manage affairs in a way that reduces any risk of bringing taxable income or gains to the UK by mistake.

The chosen bank account must be held in the taxpayer's sole name or in joint names for the individual's benefit. Two people cannot nominate the same account: if they do, this will disqualify the account. The balance in the account before the first deposit of employment income for the UK tax year must be no more than £10. The taxpayer must nominate the account to HMRC, usually in the ITSA return, by 31 January following the end of the tax year in which it became a qualifying account. The account must contain only employment income and any interest generated by the funds in the account.

All earnings paid into the chosen account are deemed to comprise UK and foreign earnings in proportion to the taxpayer's workdays in the UK and the overseas jurisdiction(s). At the end of the year, all transfers during the year (or period since arrival in the UK) to single transfers are deemed to take place: a transfer to the UK and a foreign transfer. Note that any amounts paid or delivered in the UK are automatically treated as remitted.

*(x) National Insurance contributions*

The NIC rules for internationally mobile workers are completely different from the tax rules, generally because cross-border social security coordination is as much about benefit entitlements as about contribution liabilities.

In the UK, domestic rules apply unless they are overridden by either the European rules in EC Regulations 883/2004 and 987/2009 or a social security reciprocal agreement that the UK has made with another state (eg, the USA). It is too early to say how these rules will be affected by the UK's decision to leave the EU.

Where an employee is sent by a UK employer to work overseas for a period, normal domestic rules in Social Security (Contributions) Regulations 2001, Reg 146 require the operation of Classes 1, 1A and 1B NIC to continue for the first 52 weeks of absence if three conditions are met:

- the employer has a place of business in the UK;
- the employee is ordinarily resident in the UK (now solely a term used in NIC legislation rather than the tax term, which was abolished by FA 2013); and
- immediately before the commencement of the employment overseas the earner is resident in the UK.

If any of the conditions are not met, UK NIC liability ceases as soon as the employee leaves the UK. An employee sent overseas on a permanent basis will cease to be ordinarily resident on departure and will therefore immediately escape UK NIC liability even if the employment by a UK-based business continues. The UK employer has no liability if the employee has none under this rule. An employee who leaves the UK to take up a contract overseas with a foreign employer will also fail the first condition and thereby cease to be liable in the UK.

Where the conditions are met, and liability continues for the first 52 weeks of the overseas assignment, it is irrelevant to the UK liability whether the host state is also charging social security contributions in respect of the earnings received for working there. There is no unilateral relief in UK law for double contribution liability.

Where an employee is sent by a non-EEA and non-treaty state foreign employer to work in the UK for a period, normal domestic rules in Social Security (Contributions) Regulations 2001, Reg 145(2) exclude the operation of Classes 1, 1A and 1B NIC for the first 52 weeks of presence if:

- the worker is ordinarily neither resident nor employed in the UK; and
- he comes to the UK in pursuance of employment which is mainly employment outside the UK by an employer whose place of business is outside the UK.

Other states with social security regimes tend to operate similar rules to exclude short-term visitors from their social security schemes, although Singapore explicitly excludes expatriates from membership of its Central Provident Fund.

Domestic rules are currently overridden by European regulations on social security coordination for migrant workers. These are contained in EC Regulations 883/2004 and 987/2009.

Where a worker is posted for up to 2 years to work in another EEA state on behalf of the home state employer, Article 12 of Regulation 883 provides that the worker automatically continues to be subject to the legislation of the home state if he has not been sent to replace another posted person.

Where a worker splits his time between two or more member states, Article 13 provides rules to determine which state is competent to collect contributions and take responsibility for state benefits. If the worker spends at least 25% of his time in each of two or more member states and one of those states is his state of habitual residence, he will be subject to the social security legislation of only that state, and will be treated as earning all of his income in that one state.

In either case, the home social security authorities will issue on request a certificate of continuing liability to the relevant member state's law known as an 'A1 portable document' or attestation. This is provided as evidence to the host state authorities that no contributions are due under its domestic law.

The UK also has bilateral treaties with a number of non-EEA states that govern the coordination of social security coverage. Typically, they make similar if less comprehensive provision to the EEA rules. Where for example a worker is posted by a UK employer to the USA and remains under contract solely to the UK employer, he will remain subject to UK social security law provided the period of posting is no more than five years. If, however, the employee is given a US contract, under the terms of the UK-US treaty he will fall under US social security rules in respect of the earnings from that US contract.

Note that the EU rules differ slightly in the case of non-EEA citizens. While most EEA member states apply the provisions outlined whatever the nationality of the posted worker, the UK (and Denmark) handle non-EEA citizens (known as 'third country nationals' or TCNs) under the old EEC Regulation 1408/71, which had slightly different posting provisions. The rules on dual-state workers can also differ markedly: if Bruce had been sent to work in Paris instead of Pasadena, as an Australian he would have fallen under Reg 1408/71. If he had taken up residence in Paris but worked four days per week back in London and one day per week in Paris, under the Reg 1408/71 he and his employer would have been subject to French rather than UK social security, even though most of the work was done in the UK. An EEA citizen with the same working pattern would have fallen under Reg 883/2004, which disregards any work that takes less than 25% of working time, and he would have been subject to UK social security instead.

*(xi) Domicile reform*

The government announced in 2015 that it would consult on possible reforms to the taxation of non-domiciled individuals. Final proposals were published in August 2016, for implementation on 6 April 2017.

In the context of the internationally mobile employee, the key changes in outline are:

- Those individuals born with a UK domicile of origin who emigrate and adopt a domicile of choice will no longer be able to claim to be treated as non-domiciled during any year where they return to the UK and resume residence for a period.

- Individuals resident in the UK for more than 15 out of the last 20 tax years will be deemed domiciled in the UK for the purposes of income tax and capital gains tax. This will, however, include any years spent in the UK as a minor, because the government did not want the 15 years to start to run only from age 18. A deemed domiciled individual will need to be non-UK resident for six consecutive tax years if he wishes to reset the deemed domicile clock for income tax and capital gains tax. For IHT purposes, as is currently the case, a taxpayer will lose deemed domicile status if he is non-UK resident for four complete tax years.

- Subject to certain conditions, individuals who become deemed domiciled on 6 April 2017 should be able to re-base their foreign assets so that they will only pay capital gains tax on any increase from 6 April 2017.

- For one tax year (2017–18) all non-domiciled individual will have the chance to re-arrange their mixed offshore bank accounts. This will be subject to their identifying the income and gains and removing the 'clean' capital from the mixed accounts. This concession will only be available to those who are able to identify the source of funds.

# Trading Income

# Question

Define capital expenditure and revenue expenditure and receipts and explain how they are treated differently for tax purposes.

# Answer

## Capital and revenue expenditure

The terms capital and revenue expenditure are not defined in the legislation. However, profits must be calculated in accordance with generally accepted accounting practice (GAAP) (ITTOIA 2005 s 25 for income tax and CTA 2009 s 46 for corporation tax). GAAP means UK GAAP or, where appropriate, International Financial Reporting Standards (IFRS). There are provisions to prevent groups of companies gaining a tax advantage by one company using IFRS and another UK GAAP. The normal accounting distinction between capital and revenue expenditure is that expenditure that is going to affect only the current accounting period is revenue expenditure, whereas expenditure that is going to give benefit to the business over more than one accounting period is capital expenditure.

There is an exception to the requirement to calculate profits in accordance with GAAP for individuals carrying on small businesses who may elect instead to use the cash basis to calculate their profits for tax purposes. (See **Example C2 explanatory note 20**). The distinction between revenue and capital is still of significance to such businesses, although they may deduct capital expenditure on plant or machinery (other than cars).

For other individuals and trustees, interest is a revenue item whatever the nature of the loan (ITTOIA 2005 s 29). Capital expenditure (s 33) and capital receipts (s 96) are excluded from profits unless specifically included by legislation. For example, the deduction of part of a short lease premium is spread over the term of the lease and revenue profits are reduced by capital allowances on certain capital assets. Capital expenditure that does not qualify for capital allowances forms part of the allowable cost for capital gains purposes, but on certain assets, such as leases, the expenditure is deemed to waste away over the tax life of the asset, so that no tax relief at all is given for the expenditure that is so treated. The same applies to any revenue expenditure that is specifically disallowed, such as entertaining expenses.

The tax treatment of capital and revenue expenditure has been varied for companies, with certain items being taken out of capital gains and brought into the computation of revenue profits. The main areas are the treatment of loan relationships (see **Example K2**) and the treatment of goodwill and intangible assets (see **Example K3**). In other instances, companies are entitled to deduct a greater amount in calculating profits than the expenditure incurred, in particular in relation to research and development expenditure (see **Example I5**) and qualifying expenditure in the creative sector (see **Example I7**). These differences need to be borne in mind when considering what follows.

The question of whether expenditure is revenue or capital is often something that has to be decided on a case by case basis, looking at the facts and circumstances giving rise to the expenditure. Guidance can be obtained from the many cases that have come before the courts, some of which give conflicting opinions. Lord Wilberforce, in the 1979 case of *Tucker v Granada Motorway Services Ltd* said that 'reported cases are the best tools that we have, even if they may sometimes be blunt instruments'. It is important to remember that the cases are only a guide, and each new situation must be considered on its own facts. In the case of *Vodafone Cellular Ltd v Shaw* (CA 1997 – see below) the judge in the High Court said that the decision involved 'a measure of gut reaction' in an area with 'an over-abundance of case law and the danger of over-citation'.

A case that considered the distinction between capital and revenue was *CIR v John Lewis Properties plc* (2003). In that case the Court of Appeal set out certain tests to determine whether an item is capital or revenue:

(1) If the item is long lasting it is more likely to be a capital item. On the other hand, if it is appropriate to classify the item as part of the fixed, rather than the circulating capital of the business, then it will be a capital item even though it has a brief life. The context is therefore important.

(2) The value of the asset is important, the higher the relative value the more likely the item is capital.

(3) The fact that a payment causes a diminution in value of the asset is important but this diminution need not be permanent. It should be judged at the time of the disposal, and the size of the reduction is material.

(4) A single lump sum payment is more likely to be capital and a series of recurring payments revenue.

(5) Where a disposal of an asset is accompanied by the transfer of risk this indicates a capital transaction.

In some of the older cases, two different tests emerged. The first was the distinction between fixed and circulating capital (essentially the difference between the fixed and current assets of a business) and the second was the 'enduring benefit' test stated in *Atherton v British Insulated and Helsby Cables Ltd* (1926): 'When an expenditure is made not only once and for all, but with a view to bringing into existence an asset or an advantage for the enduring benefit of a trade, I think that there is very good reason (in the absence of special circumstances leading to an opposite conclusion) for treating such an expenditure as properly attributable, not to revenue, but to capital'. This case was cited by HMRC in the Vodafone case mentioned above, HMRC contending that a cancellation payment by Vodafone to escape from a requirement to pay 10% of their profits by way of annual fees to an American company holding 15% of Vodafone's shares yielded an enduring benefit to Vodafone and was therefore a capital payment. This was rejected by the court, but the Commissioners and the High Court found against Vodafone on the grounds that the payment, although accepted as revenue expenditure, benefited not only the parent company but its subsidiaries as well, so that it failed the 'wholly and exclusively' test in what is now CTA 2009 s 54(1)(a). This decision was reversed by the Court of Appeal, which held that the *purpose* of the payment was to remove a liability from Vodafone and it did exclusively benefit that company, even though the *effect* was to benefit the other companies in the group as well.

In the *Tucker* case mentioned above, the House of Lords considered that the first step was to decide on what asset the expenditure had been incurred. (So if it was a current asset, such as a motor vehicle for resale by a car dealer, sums spent on putting it into saleable condition would be revenue expenditure.) If the asset was a capital asset, it was then necessary to consider the nature of the expenditure, so that expenditure linked to its acquisition or disposal (such as legal expenses on buying or selling a property) would be capital expenditure, whereas expenditure on maintaining and repairing it would be revenue. This general principle has been extended to the treatment of liabilities, particularly in the field of exchange losses, where it was held by the House of Lords in *Beauchamp v Woolworth* (1989) that capital borrowing was something that is to be borrowed once and for all and income borrowing is going to recur every year. The company's exchange losses on repaying substantial sums that it had borrowed for a five-year period were therefore capital losses and could not be deducted in calculating income profits. (The treatment of foreign exchanges losses and gains on loan relationships is now determined under the loan relationship rules – see CTA 2009 s 328.)

## Repairs or improvements

One of the key areas where the distinction is important is that of repairs. There are two aspects, first the treatment of repairs to newly acquired assets, and second the question of whether an item is a repair and thus allowable or an improvement or replacement and thus not allowable.

Where a newly acquired asset is repaired, the expenditure will not be allowed for tax purposes if the repairs must be done in order to bring the asset into use in the business (*Law Shipping v CIR* (1924)). If the asset is usable and commercially viable in its existing state, the subsequent repair expenditure will be allowable (*Odeon Associated Theatres Ltd v Jones* (1972)).

As far as improvements are concerned, the essential question is whether you are left with what you had originally or whether you have something extra. Money spent by a railway company in increasing the number of sleepers under each rail was capital expenditure, but expenditure on replacing worn rails and sleepers was revenue expenditure (*Rhodesia Railways Ltd v Income Tax Collector of Bechuanaland Protectorate* (1933)).

If the expenditure is on a renewal, the crucial test is what is the entirety of the asset in question. If you incur expenditure on renewing a subsidiary part of an asset, you have repaired the asset. If you replace the entire asset, you have incurred capital expenditure. Thus the cost of demolishing and rebuilding a colliery chimney was held to be capital expenditure, since the chimney was the entirety (*O'Grady v Bullcroft Main Collieries Ltd* (1932)), whereas in different circumstances the cost of removing and replacing a factory chimney was a repair to part of the factory building and was allowable (*Samuel Jones & Co (Devondale) Ltd v CIR* (1951)).

For certain assets integral to the fabric of a building or structure, known as 'integral features', CAA 2001 s 33B applies a simpler, statutory, test of capital vs revenue. Expenditure on replacement features is classified as capital expenditure (attracting the relevant capital allowances) if more than 50% of the current replacement cost of the asset is spent in any 12-month period (which may span two accounting periods).

## Provisions and impairment

The 1998 case of *Jenners Princes Street Edinburgh Ltd v CIR* raised the question of when a sum is expended for repairs. The departmental store had carried out a survey relating to external repairs and at the year-end was in the process of granting contracts to carry out the repair work. The actual work was done in the following two years. The Special Commissioners agreed with the company that a specific provision had been made, that it accorded with sound commercial accounting principles and therefore the amount had been 'expended' in the accounting sense even though not paid out.

In the 1999 case of *Herbert Smith v Honour* the High Court held that the expected future loss on a lease of vacated premises was an allowable deduction in the year of vacating the property, the provision being required under Financial Reporting Standard 12 (FRS 12) issued September 1998, which states that 'if an entity has a contract that is onerous, the present obligation under the contract should be recognised and measured as a provision'.

Under FRS 12, provisions must be made, and can only be made, when at the balance sheet date 'a business has a present obligation (legal or constructive) as a result of a past event, it is probable that expenditure will be required to settle the obligation, and a reliable estimate can be made of the obligation'.

In addition, post balance sheet events must be considered in arriving at the quantification of the provision. For example, a stock obsolescence provision cannot value stock at an amount below that subsequently achieved on an actual sale, ie its net realisable value. In the same way a provision cannot be made against a debt which has subsequently, but before the finalisation of the accounts, been paid in full. If settled at a reduced amount then the provision is restricted to the actual loss (FRS 21).

The wording of chapter 21 of FRS 102 is similar (to FRS 12 above) and 21.4 states that an entity shall recognise a provision only when:

(a) the entity has an obligation at the reporting date as a result of a past event;

(b) it is probable (ie more likely than not) that the entity will be required to transfer economic benefits in settlement; and

(c) the amount of the obligation can be estimated reliably.

Also the impairment should be subsequently measured:

> 21.10 An entity shall charge against a provision only those expenditures for which the provision was originally recognised.
>
> 21.11 An entity shall review provisions at each reporting date and adjust them to reflect the current best estimate of the amount that would be required to settle the obligation at that reporting date. Any adjustments to the amounts previously recognised shall be recognised in profit or loss unless the provision was originally recognised as part of the cost of an asset (see paragraph 21.5). When a provision is measured at the present value of the amount expected to be required to settle the obligation, the unwinding of the discount shall be recognised as a finance cost in profit or loss in the period it arises.

HMRC set out their views on the relationship between tax law and accountancy practice generally in the Business Income Manual, at BIM 31000 onwards, and on provisions in particular at BIM46515 onwards. A provision will be deductible provided it is a revenue amount that can be accurately quantified, the provision is required by GAAP and it does not conflict with statute.

## Income recognition

Where the business supplies services under a contract, the income for the period must include all services performed up to the balance sheet date, irrespective of any arrangements which prevent those services being billed for until later. The value of partially completed services is not treated as work in progress, but is recognised as income and the related profit included in the reporting period. This is in accordance with FRS 5 Application Note G and applies particularly to professional businesses.

## Goodwill and intangible assets

Another Accounting Standard that has a particular bearing on tax computations is FRS 10 – Goodwill and intangible assets. FRS 10 broadly requires *purchased* and intangible assets (but not internally created goodwill and intangibles) to be written off over the expected economic life of the asset. The commencement of FRS 102 has made some changes in this area, but the principles of the accounting treatment remain the same. In some cases the tax law prescribes a different treatment, for example, expenditure incurred by individuals on goodwill is wholly capital expenditure and a deduction against profits cannot be made. As indicated above, the tax treatment of goodwill and intangible assets for companies is largely as prescribed by accounting standards, but with some recent changes to the treatment of purchased goodwill and customer related intangibles **Example K3** has more details.

### Capital profit or trading income

Similar principles to those outlined above are used to distinguish receipts which are part of the trading income from capital profits. Receipts of the trade form part of income, whereas capital receipts are dealt with under the capital gains rules.

The disposal of trading stock clearly gives rise to trading income, whereas the amount received for disposal of a fixed asset is a capital receipt. Particular difficulty arises in relation to compensation payments. Lump sums are not necessarily capital receipts. It depends on whether the compensation is to make good damage to, or for the physical destruction of, a capital asset of the business.

Compensation relating to the cancellation of trading contracts, including agency contracts, is usually treated as a trading receipt, unless the contract is so dominant that its loss accounts for substantially the whole of the company's trade (*Barr Crombie and Co Ltd v CIR* (1945)), or the contract regulates the whole structure or framework of the trade as in the case of *Van den Berghs Ltd v Clark*, (HL 1935). The Van den Berghs decision was followed in the case of *Sabine v Lookers Ltd* (1958), where the Court of Appeal held that compensation for a material variation of a 'continuity clause' that had previously given a car distributor an ongoing option to renew its main distributorship was a capital receipt because the agreement 'governed Lookers' whole trade and was not merely one of several contracts or engagements'.

## Explanatory Notes

(1) In the absence of a specific statutory provision, the trading rules would not permit a deduction for expenses incurred prior to the commencement of trade. Such expenses are, however, specifically dealt with in ITTOIA 2005 s 57, which provides that pre-trading expenditure incurred by an individual within seven years prior to the commencement of a trade, which would have been allowable expenditure if it had been incurred after the commencement, is treated as incurred on the first day of trading and is thus allowable as an expense of the first accounting period. The same applies to companies, except for pre-trading interest, for which different rules apply (see **Example I1 explanatory note 6**).

(2) Legal charges on acquiring an asset such as a lease are part of the capital cost and are not allowed in computing taxable profits. HMRC will by concession allow the cost of *renewing* a short lease (ie one with 50 years or less to run) but not the cost of the original acquisition.

(3) For full details of the tax treatment of intangible assets for companies see **Example K3**.

(4) HMRC has published an online 'Capital v Revenue Expenditure Toolkit' at www.gov.uk/government/publications/hmrc-capital-vs-revenue-expenditure-toolkit. This is aimed at helping advisers avoid common errors in distinguishing between capital and revenue expenditure. It incorporates a checklist of common problem areas with a brief summary of the principles applicable to each area and links to the appropriate pages of the main guidance manuals.

# Question

Jason Lamb runs a catering business which has been in operation since 2002. He makes up his accounts to 31 March each year. The following is a summary of his Profit and Loss Account for the year to 31 March 2017:

| | | | £ |
|---|---|---|---|
| Sales | | | 897,251 |
| *Less*: Cost of sales | | | 482,359 |
| Gross profit after kitchen and delivery wages etc | | | 414,892 |
| Rent from temporary letting of kiosk | | | 10,000 |
| Bank interest | | | 40 |
| Profit on sale of equipment | | | 78 |
| Dividend on holding of shares Nature's Pantry plc | | | 314 |
| | | | 425,324 |
| *Less*: Salary – Mark Foyle (civil partner) | | 13,000 | |
| Other salaries | | 39,846 | |
| Rates and insurances | | 3,330 | |
| Light and heat | | 2,000 | |
| Broadband | | 1,520 | |
| Repairs | | 16,250 | |
| Motor car expenses: | | | |
| Lamb's own car | 3,000 | | |
| Head chef's car | 1,600 | 4,600 | |
| Bank interest | | 90 | |
| Loan interest | | 2,250 | |
| Bad and doubtful debts | | 138 | |
| Legal and professional expenses | | 1,206 | |
| General expenses | | 2,810 | |
| Depreciation | | 800 | |
| Business use of home | | 456 | |
| Own salary – J Lamb | | 15,000 | 103,296 |
| Net profit | | | 322,028 |

The following further information is available:

(1) Lamb's civil partner, Mark Foyle assists with specialist cake decorating and taking telephone orders. His salary was paid monthly at the rate of £950, a further £1,600 bonus for 2016/17 being paid at the end of April 2017 and included in creditors.

(2) Sophie Lewis, Lamb's niece is a student at the local university and lives on the premises and it is calculated that one-quarter of the insurance, light and heat relate to the living accommodation. She is not an employee of the business and does not act as caretaker.

(3) Rates and insurance comprise:

| | |
|---|---|
| Business rates | £2,100 |
| Insurances | £1,230 |
| | £3,330 |

(4) The broadband charge relates to the telephone and wi-fi for the business, but it includes two landlines, one of which is in the living accommodation although Sophie uses this very little. She does however regularly access the wi-fi. Lamb estimates that one-tenth of the expenditure relates to Sophie's use.

(5) Repairs comprise:

| | £ |
|---|---|
| Work on main ovens | 400 |
| Redecoration of the kitchen | 850 |
| Conversion of front office to glass-fronted shop and kiosk | 15,000 |
| | 16,250 |

When the premises were purchased in March 2016, the main ovens were quite old. They were still functioning but very inefficient.

Had the front office not been divided to accommodate the shopfront and kiosk, the front wall would have needed attention for damp at a cost of £4,000.

(6) The expenses for Lamb's car are the total running expenses for the year. Lamb's mileage in the year to 31 March 2017 was as follows:

| | | |
|---|---|---|
| Home to business | 4,000 | |
| Purely private journeys | 4,000 | |
| Purely business journeys | 10,000 | |
| Trip to the Birmingham area<br>Lamb spent a week there, three days manning a stall at the Food and Drink Show and<br>the remaining four days on holiday | 2,000 | |
| | 20,000 | miles |

The head chef's car was bought new in the year for £12,000. He uses the car 50% for private purposes. No private petrol is provided.

(7) The premises from which trade was carried on were purchased at the beginning of the year, having previously been rented. The loan interest relates to the purchase thereof. Having created the kiosk from part of the old front office he now sells cupcakes from it, but it was rented out to an ice-cream vendor for the summer while Lamb was recruiting staff for the cupcake side of the business.

(8) The bad debts account was:

| | | £ | | | £ |
|---|---|---|---|---|---|
| Trade debts written off | | 390 | Specific debt reserve } | B/F | 230 |
| | | | 2% of debtors reserve } | | 800 |
| Loan to customer written off | | 54 | | | |
| | | | Debts recovered | | |
| Specific debt reserve } | C/F | 250 | (previously charged and allowed | | |
| 2% of debtors reserve } | | 1,000 | in computing trading profits) | | 526 |
| | | | Profit and loss account | | 138 |
| | | 1,694 | | | 1,694 |

(9) Legal and professional expenses were:

| | | £ |
|---|---|---|
| Legal costs | – debt collection | 250 |
| | – negotiation of loan re premises | 316 |
| Accountancy | | 640 |
| | | 1,206 |

(10)

(a) General expenses comprise:

| | £ |
|---|---|
| Printing, stationery and web-hosting | 500 |
| Annual payment through gift aid to local hospital (gross) | 40 |
| Subscription – trade association | 70 |
| Gift to local charity | 30 |
| Entertaining expenses and gifts (see below) | 2,120 |
| Donation to the Caterers Charity Foundation to which all the employees belong | 50 |
| | 2,810 |

(b) Entertaining expenses and gifts were made up as follows:

| | £ |
|---|---|
| Entertaining customers | 550 |
| Christmas gifts to staff | 366 |
| Gift to employee on marriage | 50 |
| Gifts to customers (One pocket diary to each customer at Christmas – cost £3.40 each) | 850 |
| Expenses of staff dinner at Christmas | 304 |
| | 2,120 |

(11) Lamb maintains an office at his home. He has been charged business rates on the office amounting to £306, and the lighting and heating costs are estimated at £150.

(a) Mr Lamb has taken various goods for his own use or consumption, the selling price being £864 and the cost price £558. He has paid for these goods at cost price, £558 being included in his sales for the year.

(b) In June 2016, Lamb designed a weekly diet programme for his sister's health spa, a service for which he would normally charge a fee of £500 since this is one of the activities of his trade. He did not, however, make any charge.

(13) All amounts are adjusted appropriately for VAT.

Using the format of the full self-employment pages, SA103F, compute the trading profit for tax purposes (before deducting capital allowances).

## Answer

### Computation of Lamb's taxable profit for the year ended 31 March 2017

| | £ | £ | Explanatory Note |
|---|---|---|---|
| Turnover | | 897,251 | |
| Other business income | | 10,354 | 2 |
| | | *Disallowable* | |
| | £ | £ | |
| *Less:* | | | |
| Cost of goods bought for resale or goods used | 482,359 | | |
| Construction industry – payments to subcontractors | – | | |
| Wages, salaries and other staff costs | 52,846 | | |
| Car, van and travel expenses | 4,600 | 1,500 | 14 |
| Rent, rates, power and insurance costs (£3,330 + £2,000 + £456) | 5,786 | 808 | 3(a), 15 |
| Repairs & renewals of property and equipment | 16,250 | 15,000 | 3(b), 5 |
| Phone, fax, stationery and other office costs (£1,520 + (£2,810 – £2,120)) | 2,210 | 192 | 3(a), (d), 6, 8 |
| Advertising and business entertainment costs | 2,120 | 550 | 7 |
| Interest on bank and other loans | 2,250 | 562 | 9 |
| Bank, credit card and other financial charges | 90 | | |
| Irrecoverable debts written off | 138 | 254 | 3(c) |
| Accountancy, legal and other professional fees | 1,206 | 79 | 10 |
| Depreciation and loss/(profit) on sale of assets | 722 | 722 | 3(e) |
| Other business expenses | 15,000 | 15,000 | 4 |
| Total expenses/disallowable expenses | 585,577 | 34,667 | |
| Net profit | | 322,028 | |
| Goods and services for own use | 306 | | 13 |
| Total additions to net profit or deductions from net loss | | 34,973 | |
| Income, receipts and other profits included in business income or expenses but not taxable as business profits | 354 | | 2 |
| Total deductions from net profit or additions to net loss | | 354 | |
| Net business profit for tax purposes (before CAs) | | 356,647 | |

## Explanatory Notes

All references in these notes are to ITTOIA 2005 unless otherwise stated.

*Self-assessment – self-employment pages*

(1) For tax purposes, the profit shown in a trader's accounts has to be adjusted in accordance with the tax rules to arrive at the taxable profit (or allowable loss) for the accounting period. Section 25 requires profits for a trade to be calculated in accordance with generally accepted accounting practice, subject to any adjustment required or authorised by law. For information on the effect of Accounting Standards on tax computations relating to capital and revenue expenditure – see **Example C1**.

Under self-assessment, the accounts figures are shown in tax returns in a standardised format on the self-employment pages, except for certain very large partnerships – see **Example G2 explanatory note 2**. The headings under which information must be given are those shown in the Example. Taxpayers whose accounts include a balance sheet are also required to show the balance sheet details on the return. Those whose turnover is less than the VAT registration threshold (£83,000 for 2016/17) may instead complete the short self-employment pages, SA103S, which provides for a simpler summary of allowable expenses only, and no balance sheet. As an alternative, they may simply enter their expenses as a single figure in box 9 of SA103S (or box 30 of SA103F) and need provide no additional analysis.

The net business profit arrived at after the various tax adjustments is reduced by capital allowances to arrive at the taxable profit (see **Example C6**).

*Non-trading income*

(2) The 'other income' comprises rent of £10,000, bank interest of £40 and the dividend of £314. The profit on sale of equipment of £78 is not included because it is netted off against the depreciation figure (see **explanatory note 3**(e)). The interest and dividends are excluded from the taxable income because they are taxable under other provisions. The same should strictly apply to the rent from letting, but where a small part of business premises is let because it is temporarily surplus to requirements and is likely to be used by the business within three years, the rent may be treated as part of the trading income.

*Expenditure 'wholly and exclusively' for the trade*

(3) Unless it is covered by a specific statutory provision, expenditure is not allowable in computing profits unless it is wholly and exclusively for the purposes of the trade (s 34). A payment that satisfies the general rule is even so not allowable if it is a criminal payment, such as a bribe or protection money to terrorists, or a payment made in response to threats, menaces, blackmail and other forms of extortion. This restriction includes any payment made overseas which, if it were made in the UK, would constitute a criminal offence (s 55).

A distinction is drawn between expenditure incurred in the capacity of trader, and in the capacity of taxpayer, the latter being an appropriation of profit and not allowable. So the expenses of an appeal against business rates would be allowable, since they relate to the trade, whereas the expenses of an appeal against a tax assessment would not, because they are incurred in the capacity of taxpayer. In the case of accountancy expenses, some of the expense is clearly related to the agreement of the tax liability on the profits, but by HMRC practice the full amount is allowable. This does not extend to the expense of preparing self-assessment returns and calculating capital gains, but HMRC accepts that the additional costs are likely to be minimal for someone whose personal tax affairs are straightforward. The relief for accountancy expenses does not apply to additional accounting charges relating to an in-depth investigation of the trader's affairs by HMRC. Such expenses are only allowed if no adjustment to profit results from the investigation, or where there is an adjustment to the year of enquiry only and the additional profits do not arise out of careless or deliberate behaviour (HMRC Enquiry Manual – EM3981). Under self-assessment, HMRC is able to undertake random checks under the enquiry procedure, in addition to their powers to investigate cases of failure to take reasonable care or deliberate understatement (see **Example G2 explanatory notes 14** and **16**).

The wholly and exclusively provision in s 34 is interpreted in practice in the following way:

(a) Living expenses and private payments are not allowable as they are not for the purpose of the trade. Therefore the expenses of the living accommodation occupied by Sophie are not allowable. The accommodation expenses would be allowable if she were an employee or acting as caretaker and therefore treated as occupying the accommodation as an employee.

As the only person occupying the living accommodation is a student, there is no council tax payable on the living accommodation. If Sophie continues to live there once she graduates any council tax in respect of the living accommodation would have to either be paid by her or, if paid by Lamb, would have to be added back. The disallowed premises costs of £808 comprise ¼ of the insurance and light and heat (£308 and £500 respectively). 1/10th of the broadband costs, ie £152, is part of the disallowance of £192 on general administrative expenses (the other £40 relating to the charitable gift aid – see **explanatory note** 3(d)).

(b) Nothing can be allowed for repairs which might have been but have not been carried out. The £4,000 which would have been spent on addressing the damp problem in the office front wall is therefore not allowable and the whole cost converting the office into a shopfront and kiosk is capital expenditure (see **explanatory note** 5).

(c) Debts cannot be written off except for bad debts that were incurred wholly and exclusively for the purpose of the trade, doubtful debts to the extent that they are respectively estimated to be bad and debts released by the creditor in a voluntary arrangement under the 1986 Insolvency Act. (The debtor in a voluntary arrangement will not have to bring into his trading profit debts that have been released in this way, but debts released other than under such arrangements must be treated as a trading receipt – ITTOIA 2005 s 97.) A general bad debts provision is therefore disallowed when it is made. If it is subsequently increased the increase is disallowed, and if it is decreased, the decrease is excluded from the profit. For detailed notes on deductibility of provisions see **Example C1**.

Writing off a loan to a customer is not allowable (unless lending money is part of the taxpayer's trade), since it was not for trading purposes. The disallowance of £254 comprises the increase of £200 in the general reserve and the loan of £54 written off. Writing off a loan to an employee where the loan was made by reason of the employment would (in the absence of special circumstances) be an allowable expense to the employer – but the employee would usually be liable to tax on the amount so released. The employer would need to show that the loss was connected with or arose out of the trade. For the detailed provisions on employee loans see **Example J2**.

(d) Payments such as pension contributions for the sole trader or under the 'gift aid' scheme (personal donations – see **Example N4** for details) are not allowed as trading expense, so Lamb's payment of £40 to the local hospital is disallowed. If Lamb had paid any patent royalties, they would be deductible if they were wholly and exclusively for the purpose of the trade. Patent royalties that do not meet the wholly and exclusively test above would be deducted under ITA 2007 s 448 in calculating an individual's net income.

(e) Any capital items and expenses connected with the acquisition or disposal of capital items are not allowable (the depreciation of equipment of £800 is thus not allowable and the profit on sale of equipment of £78 is not included in the taxable profit, giving a net disallowance of £722). See **Example C1** for the tests that apply to determine capital expenditure.

*Family wages and drawings*

(4) Mark Foyle's salary and bonus are allowable provided they can be shown to be commercially justifiable (ie wholly and exclusively for the trade). Earnings that are paid after the end of the account to which they relate may only be taken into account in that period if paid within nine months after it ends and as long as a valid provision exists at the balance sheet date, in accordance with GAAP. Otherwise they are deducted in the period in which they are paid (s 36). These provisions do not affect Foyle's bonus since it is paid within one month. The bonus will form part of Foyle's income for 2017/18 (in which it is received).

The payment described as a management salary to Mr Lamb actually represents drawings of profit and is not allowed. The same applies to profit shares allocated to partners that are described as salaries, interest, etc.

*Repairs*

(5) The repair work on the main ovens and indeed the decorating of the kitchen is allowable since there was no question of these not being usable at the time of acquisition (*Odeon Associated Theatres Ltd v Jones* (1972)). If repairs are necessary before an asset can be used in a business, they are part of the capital cost. Expenditure on extensions, improvements and additions is capital expenditure and is not allowable, as in the case of the conversion of the office into a shop and kiosk in the Example.

*Entertaining, gifts, donations and subscriptions*

(6) The donation to the Caterers Charity Foundation is allowable since it is for the benefit of employees.

(7) Expenditure on entertaining and gifts is covered by s 45 which disallows expenditure on entertaining and gifts except for the following:

(a) Gifts carrying a conspicuous advertisement, not consisting of food, drink or tobacco and not exceeding £50 per person per annum (s 47(3)). This covers Lamb's expenditure on diaries.

(b) Gifts for employees (s 47(4)). The wedding gift will come under this heading. It will escape tax in the hands of the employee as a trivial, but not if it is regarded as paid as a reward for or in return for services performed as part of the employment.

Expenditure on staff entertaining (s 46(3)), although allowable to the employer as being for the benefit of staff, will result in a benefits charge on a director or P11D employee, unless covered by the £150 exemption (see **Example B2 explanatory note 31**). The VAT position on staff entertaining costs is that input tax can be recovered on the proportion relating to employees only and not that relating to other guests (since business entertaining expenses other than those relating to staff are disallowed – see **explanatory note 16**).

(c) Gifts to charities (s 47(5)) (other than gift aid payments – see **explanatory note 3(d)**), providing they are *wholly* and *exclusively* for the purposes of the trade. It will usually be difficult to show a trading motive for a gift to a charity. The trader may be able to show that being known as a subscriber to the charity benefits his trade. A modest gift to a charity with which the trader has a direct connection could usually be justified on 'wholly and exclusively' grounds. It has been assumed that this applies to Lamb's gift to the local charity. HMRC have stated that subscriptions to hospitals, churches, chapels etc are not normally regarded as admissible except in a small community where the trader is the dominant employer and the employees are the predominant users of the facilities. There are separate provisions to allow relief for gifts of trading stock to charities and educational establishments (s 108). For details see **Example I1 explanatory note 4(vi)** and **Example N4**.

Where a business makes sponsorship payments of a revenue nature, they are allowed providing they satisfy the 'wholly and exclusively' rule, ie the purpose must be to provide the payer with a commensurate benefit, usually in the form of advertising.

(8) Subscriptions to trade associations are normally allowable, the association bearing tax on any excess of its subscription income over its allowable expenses. Any other subscriptions need to be considered under the 'wholly and exclusively' rule.

*Finance costs*

(9) Whilst disallowing capital expenditure in computing profits, s 29 and s 34 permit the deduction of interest paid wholly and exclusively for the trade. The loan interest has therefore been allowed, except for the proportion relating to Sophia's living accommodation (assumed to be one-quarter).

(10) The incidental costs of raising loan finance (excluding stamp duty) are allowed providing that the interest on the loan qualifies as a deduction from profits (so the private proportion of ¼, ie £79, is disallowed) (s 58). HMRC have stated that if a life policy is taken out as a condition of obtaining loan finance, the premiums would not be 'incidental costs' of obtaining the finance, although any incidental costs of taking out the policy would be.

(11) Interest paid (or received) on delayed payment on contracts for the supply of goods or services will be a revenue expense (or trading receipt). The interest is not subject to deduction of tax at source (see **Example A5 part (a)**).

*Security expenditure*

(12) Expenditure to meet a special threat to the personal security of a sole trader or partner, such as from terrorists, is allowable subject to various restrictions (s 81). Revenue expenditure, such as on bodyguards, is allowed as a business expense. Capital expenditure, such as on alarm systems and bullet resistant windows, qualifies for capital allowances (see **Example C6**). Where expenditure is incurred in relation to employees, there are parallel provisions to exempt the employee from any benefit in kind charge on the security assets and security services provided.

*Goods and services for own use*

(13) Own goods should be accounted for at selling price by virtue of s 172B, a provision which gives statutory force to a principle established by case law in *Sharkey v Wernher* (1955). There is no equivalent rule requiring services to be accounted for at any greater figure than any charge made (*Mason v Innes* (1967)), although any costs incurred in providing those services would be disallowed under the 'wholly and exclusively' rule in s 34(1)(a). VAT is due on the price paid by the business.

*Motor expenses*

(14) Motor expenses are capable of division into a part which is wholly and exclusively for the purposes of the trade and a part which is not, the former part being allowable on an apportionment basis (s 34(2)). Private motoring includes home to business travelling even though there are some duties undertaken at the private residence for which an allowance is made in computing profits (*Newsom v Robertson* (1953)). Half of the expenses on Lamb's car have been disallowed on the basis of 10,000 private miles. Expenses that are *partly* for business are not allowed. The essential point is whether the trader had only a business purpose in mind when incurring the expenditure. If so the expenditure would be allowable, even if some incidental private benefit was obtained. But if there was more than one purpose, even if the trading purpose was the main one, the whole of the expenditure is strictly disallowed. For this reason the trip to the Birmingham area, having both a private and a business purpose, is disallowed. HMRC may be prepared to accept a claim for a proportion of travelling expenses for a mixed purpose journey on the basis of the time spent on business. This could not be done on a mileage basis for Lamb's trip, because he has clearly covered extra miles during his holiday. Under self-assessment, a trader's assessment of such a business element would only be questioned if HMRC enquired into his return or later made a discovery that it contained an inaccuracy which was careless or deliberate, or that insufficient disclosure of the area of doubt had been made. In addition to claiming the appropriate proportion of running expenses, Lamb will be able to claim the same proportion of capital allowances of the cost of the car (see **Example C8 part (b)**).

Under the provisions in ITTOIA 2005 Chapter 5A (introduced in Finance Act 2013) unincorporated traders may choose to compute allowable motoring expenses, whether by a car, goods vehicle or motor cycle, by reference to fixed mileage amount. For 2015/16 the rates of deduction available are 45p per mile for the first 10,000 business miles in a tax year and 25p per mile thereafter (the rate for motor cycles is 24p per mile).Capital allowances may not be claimed in addition. As Lamb has already claimed capital allowances on his own car, he cannot opt for the flat rate deduction The trader has to use the same basis for computing the motor expenses deduction, whether the fixed rate and actual costs, consistently for each vehicle. On changing the vehicle he can make a fresh decision in respect of the new vehicle. This option is only open to individuals or partnerships made up entirely of individuals and cannot be used if any part of the cost of the vehicle has been deducted in computing profits on the cash basis (see **explanatory note 20**). Before 2013/14, this option was only open to traders whose turnover was below the VAT threshold. Note that if more than one vehicle is charged using the fixed rate deduction, only one band of 10,000 miles at the higher rate is available to the business.

Private use by *employees* does not cause any restriction either in allowable running expenses or in capital allowances The private use will be the subject of a benefit in kind charge (see **Example B2 explanatory note 13**).

If a trader leases a car on or after 6 April 2010, and its official emissions rating exceeds 130 g/km $CO_2$, then the allowable hire charge is restricted to 85%. If the car was first leased before 6 April 2013 this restriction in the allowable hire charge applies to cars with emissions of more than 160g/km. (ITTOIA 2005 s 48 as amended by FA 2009 Sch 11) (see **Example C8 explanatory note 17**).

*Business use of home*

(15) Where a room at home is used for business purposes, a deduction may be claimed for the additional costs of the business use, such as light and heat. Where part of a property is used for business purposes, business rates are payable if the business use prevents the continued domestic use of that part of the property. This means strictly that there must always be mixed use to avoid a business rates charge, and where a room is exclusively set aside as an office business rates should be payable. Where business rates are not paid, the appropriate part of the council tax may be deducted as a business expense. The inclusion of £456 in the premises costs covers the home expenditure on rates, light and heat.

The HMRC guidance on the use of home by the self-employed is in its Business Income Manual at BIM47800 onwards. The guidance states that expenses can be apportioned using area, usage or time. The guidance includes examples and the higher the claim, the more likely the claim will be calculated by reference to more than one of these points eg, calculated on area and then time-apportioned. The guidance confirms that, in the right circumstances, it is possible to claim a portion of:

- Insurance – a portion of general household or where separate business insurance, that policy only in full.
- Council tax.
- Mortgage interest.
- Rent.
- Repairs and maintenance – examples include the full cost of decorating an area used solely for business purposes and the relevant portion of general redecoration of the exterior/roof.
- Cleaning.
- Heat, light and power.
- Telephone – including portion of line rental and all aspects of use including incoming calls where appropriate.
- Broadband – a flexible approach is suggested for all inclusive packages.
- Metered water – although the guidance incorporates the idea of apportioning some expenses that would be incurred regardless (eg, mortgage interest/council tax) there still seems to be a historic reluctance to accept claims for fixed water rates hence the title heading 'metered' water. That said, guidance to childminders (see BIM2751) allows them to claim up to 10% of their water regardless of whether metered or fixed. If the nature of the trade involves heavy water usage it may be advisable to arrange for that part of the property to be separately metered, in which case the resultant separate change would be deductible in full.

The guidance also states that where a claim is small and there is only minor business use of the home, for example the taxpayer writes up their business records at home, HMRC should accept a claim based on any reasonable basis.

Finance Act 2013 introduced a statutory method for an optional fixed rate method of computing deductions for business use of home. Under ITTOIA 2005 s 94H unincorporated traders may choose to deduct a fixed rate per month according to the number of hours per month spent by the trader, or any employee of the trade, working at the trader's home (if the trader has more than one home, the hours spent at each should be aggregated). The rate of deduction available for 2016/17 is:

| *Number of hours worked* | *Amount deductible per month* |
|---|---|
| 25–50 | £10.00 |
| 51–100 | £18.00 |
| 101 or more | £26.00 |

This option is only open to individuals or partnerships made up entirely of individuals. If the business chooses not to use the fixed rate deduction the cost of use of home will be arrived at by apportioning the relevant costs according to HMRC guidance in BIM47800. Estimated round sum deductions are no longer permitted – the business must use the amounts in the above Table if a flat rate deduction is desired. Finance Act 2016 section 24 correct the legislation to make it available to partners in a partnership, but requires that if more than one partner makes a claim for office use of home, they must all either claim the fixed rate deduction or must all claim on the strict apportionment basis.

From 2013/14, there is also a corresponding fixed rate adjustment that a trader can make in respect of any part of business premises occupied as his home (see ITTOIA 2005 s 94I). The adjustment is fixed by reference to the number of occupants using that part of the premises as a home and calculated on a monthly basis. The rate of the adjustment for 2016/17 is:

| *Number of occupants* | *Monthly amount* |
|---|---|
| 1 | £350 |
| 2 | £500 |
| 3 or more | £650 |

The amount as determined above is deducted from the expenses that would otherwise be claimed as a deduction from profits in respect of the business premises. Like the fixed rate deduction of use of home, this option is only open to individuals or partnerships made up entirely of individuals.

*Value added tax*

(16) As a VAT registered trader Lamb will account for VAT on his sales (including the sale of equipment), less a deduction for allowable input VAT he has suffered. He cannot claim a deduction for the VAT on business entertaining. It was, however, decided in the case of *Thorn EMI plc v C & E* (1994) that input tax should be apportioned where expenditure is partly for business entertaining and partly for other business purposes. He will have to pay a VAT scale charge for his private car fuel and this is similarly not deductible. If he had provided private fuel to employees, he would have to pay VAT scale charges for each employee, but the amounts charged would have been included as part of his deductible car expenses. As far as the car bought for the warehouse manager is concerned (and any other cars bought, but not commercial vehicles) Lamb will not be able to reclaim the input VAT, but he can claim capital allowances on the VAT-inclusive amount. The VAT-inclusive cost is presumably £12,000, since the example states that amounts have been adjusted appropriately for VAT and no adjustment is appropriate in this instance.

As far as cars that are leased rather than purchased are concerned, leasing companies are entitled to reclaim input VAT in full on cars acquired for leasing. (The same applies to other businesses that use cars wholly for business purposes, such as self-drive hire firms and driving schools.) Where the leasing company has recovered the input VAT, the lessee may recover only 50% of the input VAT on the leasing charges if there is any use of the car for private purposes. The disallowed input VAT forms part of the deductible leasing charges in computing profit (subject to any restriction for private use by a sole trader or partner).

Where a VAT registered trader makes a gift of business goods costing more than £50 in total in a year, VAT output tax will be due based upon input tax claimed on the goods. Gifts of lower value than £50 made to several individuals employed by the same company will be regarded as gifts to different recipients for this purpose. However, if the gift is to a charity for resale in a charity shop the supply will be zero-rated.

A non-VAT registered trader includes VAT as part of his allowable expenses or capital costs, subject to the disallowance of VAT on business entertaining and on any private use proportion. A partly exempt trader may recover any non-deductible input VAT in a similar way. Some approximation may be necessary in allocating the VAT to the various items of expenditure and this will be accepted by HMRC providing it is reasonable.

For the treatment of VAT where small business flat rate scheme is used see HMRC's Business Income Manual at BIM31585. Expenses should then be shown as VAT inclusive and the amount payable to HMRC can either be deducted from the VAT inclusive turnover or shown as an expense in 'other expenses' on the tax return. The maximum turnover to join the flat rate scheme is £150,000 so it is not available to Lamb. See **Example M2** for details of the flat rate scheme, and **Example M4** for more details on partial exemption.

*National insurance*

(17) As an employer, Lamb will have to pay employers' Class 1, Class 1A (and if appropriate Class 1B) national insurance contributions, which are deductible in arriving at his taxable profit, although he is entitled to claim an Employment Allowance of up to £3,000 to reduce the amount of employers' Class 1 NIC payable (see **Example H1** for details). He will also have to pay self-employed Class 2 and Class 4 contributions, but these are not tax deductible (see **Example H1**).

*Interest surcharges and penalties on income tax and VAT paid late*

(18) These are not deductible in arriving at the taxable figure of business profits, this includes interest on late paid CIS deductions, NI and student loan repayments (s 54).

*Miscellaneous*

(19) This example deals with the treatment of most common items of expenditure. For the treatment of expenditure incurred prior to the start of a trade, see **Example C1 explanatory note 1**. For the treatment of premiums paid on short leases, see **Example D3 part (h)**.

*Cash basis for small businesses*

(20) Although not applicable to Lamb's business, from 2013/14 there is a simpler basis for computing the profits of certain small businesses, available on election. Where an individual (or partnership of individuals) carries on a trade, profession or vocation which, taken together with any other such business carried on by that individual, has a turnover below the VAT threshold £83,000 from 1 April 2016), he can elect to calculate the profits of that trade, profession or vocation on a cash basis (ITTOIA 2005 s 25A). The effect of such an election is that rather than using GAAP to compute the profits of the business, the trader calculates his profits on the basis of receipts less expenses for the period in question.

Although that calculation is still subject to any adjustment required by law, many of the rules regarding the computation of profit are disapplied for users of the cash basis. A number of rules, such as those regarding relief for bad debts or employee remuneration accruals (in ITTOIA 2005 ss 35 to 37), are disapplied as there is no need for them in the absence of the concepts of accrual and provisions inherent in GAAP, Modified rules apply with regard to the capital/revenue divide in that the distinction is ignored where the receipt or expense is in connection with plant or machinery (other than a car) which would qualify for capital allowances (ITTOIA 2005 ss 33A and 96A). Expenditure on interest and the incidental costs of finance can be deducted as cash basis expenses up to a limit of £500 per month, provided they are incurred wholly and exclusively for the purposes of the trade (ITTOIA 2005 s 51A).

There is a broad-brush anti-avoidance provision, which allows for a just and reasonable adjustment to be made where the amount which would otherwise be brought into account on the cash basis is otherwise than would have been the case had the transaction in question been on an arm's length basis (ITTOIA 2005 Part 2 Ch 6A).

The key principle that still has to be applied to expenses deducted under the cash basis is that they must be wholly and exclusively incurred for the purposes of the trade. For more on the cash basis see **Example C3**.

*Changes of accounting policy*

(21) The use of GAAP as the starting point for calculating taxable profits (see **explanatory note 1**) means that if there is a change in GAAP this could have a knock-on effect on the amount of the taxable profits. The most recent significant change in UK GAAP has been the replacement of previous accounting standards with FRS 102 for accounting periods starting on or after 1 January 2015.

Where there is a change from one accounting policy to another, the provisions of ITTOIA 2005 ss 227 – 240 apply (the equivalent for corporates is CTA 2009 ss 180 – 187). Those provisions look at the periods immediately before and after the change in policy to ensure that no receipts or expenses fall out of account or are counted twice as a result of the transition. If there are any such amounts these are adjusted for in the first period under the new policy. A single adjustment is calculated bringing all such amounts together as an adjustment expense or as adjustment income.

# Question

(a) State and explain the eligibility criteria for using the cash basis of accounting for income tax.

(b) Describe what issues the adviser might consider in advising a client to adopt the cash basis of accounting.

(c) Which businesses can use the fixed rate deductions for some expenses, and what should a business or adviser consider in making a decision to use fixed rate deductions?

(d) Peter has been using the cash basis of accounting since it was introduced, but his turnover has now exceeded the exit limit, and so for the year ended 31 December 2016 he must prepare accruals accounts which comply with GAAP. He has prepared a cash based profit for the year of £27,600 but is unsure what to do next and has asked for help.

You ascertain the following information:

| | *31.12.15* | *31.12.16* |
|---|---|---|
| Trade debtors | 12,000 | 17,000 |
| Trade creditors | 1,400 | 800 |
| Stock | 4,200 | 2,200 |
| Accruals | 900 | 990 |
| Prepayments | 600 | 950 |

Compute Peter's profit for tax purposes for the year ended 31 December 2016, explain the tax implications of the change from the cash basis to the accruals basis.

# Answer

## (a) Eligibility for the cash basis

Only unincorporated businesses are permitted to use the cash basis. Beyond this, there are some eligibility criteria, covering the size and type of business. An eligible business will need to decide on a year by year basis whether to enter (or leave) the regime; when a partnership wishes to use the cash basis the election must be made by the partner responsible for the tax return.

The maximum turnover for entering the cash basis is the VAT threshold at the end of the relevant tax year – currently £83,000 (although universal credit claimants can start using the cash basis if their turnover is up to twice the VAT threshold – currently £166,000). However, the VAT threshold relevant to 2016/17 is the threshold on 5 April 2017. This would normally be announced in budget 2017, to take effect from 1 April 2017, so the turnover threshold poses some practical difficulty. However, there is no provision for the threshold to be reduced, so working with the threshold for the start of the year will be sufficient. Once using the cash basis, businesses will be required to leave when their turnover for the preceding year exceeds twice the VAT threshold – currently £166,000.

Where a person carries on more than one business, the turnover limits apply to the combined receipts of both businesses, and where a person has a self-employment and is also a partner in a partnership which they control, the turnover of the partnership is aggregated with that of his sole trade to test the turnover limit. If the total turnover is below the entry limit, then either or both of the sole trader and the partnership can elect for the cash basis. Once made, an election applies to all trades, professions and vocations undertaken by the person during the tax year.

The following businesses are specifically excluded from using the cash basis:

- partnerships in which any partner is not an individual;
- limited liability partnerships;
- Lloyd's underwriters;
- businesses with a current herd basis election;
- persons with a profit averaging election under ITTOIA 2005 s 221 (farmers and creative artists);
- persons who have received business premises renovation allowances under Capital Allowances Act 2001 Part 3A (CAA 2001), in the preceding seven years;
- persons carrying on a mineral extraction trade, as defined in CAA 2001 s 394(2);
- persons owning an asset on which research and development allowances have previously been claimed under CAA 2001 Part 6.

## (b) Practical considerations before adopting the cash basis

Taxpayers are likely to benefit from cash accounting for the following reasons:

(i) It is **easier** than GAAP accounting – as there is no need to value stock, include trade debtors, or creditors, or calculate accruals and prepayments;

(ii) There may be **cash flow advantages** as tax payable under cash accounting may be lower than under GAAP.

These benefits can be examined in more depth to establish what is the appropriate advice for the represented client (as opposed to the unrepresented business for whom the rules are really designed).

### *Business model considerations*

Where a business offers credit to customers, has little credit available to it, and / or is slow raising invoices for supplies of services, then cash accounting will inevitably reduce profits at the point of election, whether from the commencement of the business or at a later date.

However, any income deferred will come into charge eventually, whether at the point of moving to a full GAAP accounting basis, or at the end of the life of the business. By advising clients to adopt the cash basis, tax charges are deferred. The adviser might therefore consider whether the overall rates of tax on income are likely to rise or fall in the medium to longer term. He might also consider that for a particular client managing the variable cash flow demands of tax liabilities will be difficult in any event, without adding the potential for these to be further distorted by moving to a cash basis.

Where the business model offers the reverse scenario, clients could end up paying tax on more profit than they have earned initially, making it difficult to bear the tax liabilities. This is quite common in the building trade, where cash is often taken ahead of work being done to finance material purchases, which may be purchased through a credit account.

### *Fee considerations*

Clients might anticipate a reduction in fees if they move from the full GAAP basis to the cash basis, but any reduction is unlikely to be significant. For many small businesses, the work in balancing the bank and cash and verifying that expenses are tax deductible will not change; nor will the work required in completing the tax return. The only changes are to remove the requirement to account for debtors, creditors, stock and work in progress. For an experienced practitioner this is not normally a challenge and is likely to account for only a small part of the fee, unless a stocktake has to be undertaken.

In slightly larger businesses, a reconciliation of debtors and the check on gross profit provided by a stocktake (in for example, a pub) are essential business management tools, and therefore any saving by using a different basis for tax would be lost, and indeed we might argue that fees will increase.

### *Loss relief*

Probably the most contentious area in the legislation is the fact that there is no sideways loss relief or capital gains relief. If the business is likely to be loss making it is therefore unlikely to benefit from adopting cash accounting.

This is particularly problematic for business start-ups where an individual who has been made redundant, and has paid tax during their employment, starts in business and makes a loss in the first year. They will be unable to set that loss against their employment income if using the cash accounting basis. They will probably be forced into using GAAP accounting where loss relief is available, and indeed HMRC appears to accept that incurring losses is a legitimate reason to stop using the cash basis.

### *Low profits*

Where a business is making modest profits, it is common for the adviser to manage capital allowance claims so that best use is made of the personal allowances, where necessary delaying the capital allowances until a later period.

There is no option to do this under cash accounting, as when an allowable expense is paid, this becomes the amount deducted in the period, so clients with low income may end up not being able to use capital allowances in the most efficient way.

### *Interest restriction*

The restriction of interest and finance charges to £500 maximum under the simplified accounting basis will act as a deterrent to businesses with significant bank borrowings which are business related loans. The deduction of up to £500 allows mixed use interest charges to be deducted, which is frequently beneficial for clients, but where a specific bank borrowing incurs interest in excess of £500 in a year, this would not be relieved under the simplified accounting basis.

## (c) Fixed rate deductions eligibility and practical issues

Fixed rate deductions apply to almost all income tax trades and professions, with the exception only of partnerships in which one or more of the partners is not an individual. They do not apply to companies.

### *Expenditure on vehicles*

The fixed rate deduction for vehicles can be used where a deduction would be allowable in computing the profits of a trade for expenditure on a vehicle (or would be allowed if the expenditure were not capital in nature). The vehicles covered are cars, motorcycles and goods vehicles used for the purpose of the trade. Vehicles are excluded if capital allowances, or in the case of motorcycles and goods vehicles, a deduction under the cash basis, has been claimed in respect of them.

If a business elects to use the flat rate allowance, then the flat rate allowance must be used for that vehicle for the remaining period during which it is in use for the purpose of the business.

The relief is calculated at a rate of 45p for the first 10,000 business miles in a year and 25p a mile after that for cars and goods vehicles, and 24p a mile for motorcycles. Note that there is only a single annual band of 10,000 miles at the higher 45p rate, even where more than one vehicle is used in the business and an election is made in respect of them; where several vehicles are in use with total annual mileage in excess of 10,000 the business will very likely suffer tax relief on less than the actual motoring costs incurred, and this should be considered before deciding to use the fixed rate deduction. Also, where the vehicle running expenses are very high then the use of a fixed rate deduction would not be beneficial.

If a business operating the cash basis does not choose to use the fixed rate deduction in respect of a business car, then there will be a capital allowances claim available on the vehicle (business proportion only) as a car cannot qualify for deduction under the cash basis.

### *Use of home for business purposes*

The deduction may be claimed if the business uses the facilities in the proprietor's home for business use. The deduction is optional for all businesses, including those operating the cash basis, which would otherwise have to calculate a deduction on an apportioned basis according to the payments made. The alternative approach of apportioning use of home costs on a reasonably scientific basis is still available for those who choose to use it.

The calculation is performed on a monthly basis, and allows a deduction each month according to the number of hours spent per month wholly and exclusively on work done by the person or any employee of the person. Only one deduction is available, even if the business owner has more than one home used in the business.

**Deduction: per month or part month**

| *Number of hours worked* | *Applicable amount* |
|---|---|
| 25 or more | £10.00 |
| 51 or more | £18.00 |
| 101 or more | £26.00 |

Note that where only a few hours per month are spent doing office work, there is no deduction for use of home under the fixed rate deduction rules. Deciding to use the fixed rate deduction, does, however, carry associated accounting requirements – the client would need to make a record of hours worked each month in order to support a claim, although arguably such a record would also be needed to support a claim on the alternative strict basis.

### *Premises used as both home and business premises*

Where business premises are used mainly for the purpose of the trade, but also as the person's home, the person can elect for the flat rate of deduction to apply.

The calculation of the deduction is based on the total expenditure incurred, **less** a flat rate private use adjustment, based on the number of occupants using the premises as a home or staying there, otherwise than for the purpose of the trade. So this fixed rate amount is an **add back** rather than a deduction from profits. It may be useful to pubs, B&B's and similar. Once again, a strict apportionment of costs is also available as an alternative, but advisers should be ready to justify their calculations if they have not used the fixed rate amounts.

**Private use adjustment: per month or part month**

| *Number of relevant occupants* | *Applicable amount* |
|---|---|
| 1 | £350 |
| 2 | £500 |
| 3 or more | £650 |

## (d) Peter's adjusted profit

Peter's profit for the year ended 31 December 2016 should be adjusted as follows:

| | | £ | £ |
|---|---|---|---|
| Cash profit as calculated | | | 27,600 |
| Opening balance sheet adjustments | | | |
| Increasing profit | Creditors | 1,400 | |
| | Accruals | 900 | 2,300 |
| Reducing profit | Debtors | (12,000) | |
| | Stock | (4,200) | |
| | Prepayments | (600) | (16,800) |
| Closing balance sheet adjustments | | | |
| Reducing profit | Creditors | (800) | |
| | Accruals | (990) | (1,790) |
| Increasing profit | Debtors | 17,000 | |
| | Stock | 2,200 | |
| | Prepayments | 950 | 20,150 |
| Net profit for tax purposes | | | 31,460 |

We should also confirm that the cash based accounts do not include any purchases of fixed assets. These will not alter the taxable amount, as AIA is likely to cover any expenditure, but we would need to keep track of a Nil balance on the pool in the event of any disposals in future. Peter should also have disallowed any interest in excess of £500; we would need to check to ensure that the correct amount of interest has been charged against profit for the year.

The opening balance sheet adjustments have not been included in the previous year's profit which was taxed on a cash basis. The opposite effect therefore is effectively a profit which appears to escape tax. The net amount -

£16,800 – 2,300 = £14,500 crystallises as adjustment income and is taxed over the coming six years, or Peter may elect to be taxed quicker by bringing in additional adjustment income in any year he chooses. The adjustment income taxable in 2016/17 is £2,417 unless Peter elects to pay tax on a greater amount. Adjustment income is not liable to Class 4 NIC. See **explanatory notes 10 and 11.**

## Explanatory Notes

References in these notes are to ITTOIA 2005 unless otherwise stated.

*Simplified accounting measures*

(1) There are two distinct and separate elements of the legislation which was introduced by Finance Act 2013.

(a) **Eligible businesses** can elect to use cash basis accounting rather than GAAP. This is governed by Chapter 3A, and an election under s 25A. This is done by ticking a box on the tax return, and the default position is that GAAP must be followed, unless the appropriate election is made.

(b) **Most unincorporated businesses** can elect to use simplified, fixed rate deductions for expenses rather than actual expenses incurred on the basis of GAAP, apportioned where necessary between private and business use, for some expenses. This is governed by Chapter 5A. The areas covered are use of motor vehicles, use of home as office and private use of business premises.

Property businesses are not permitted to use cash accounting, but can use the simple "three line" method of displaying rent and expenses on the tax return.

*The cash basis of accounting*

(2) The legislation underpinning the cash basis of accounting sets up a separate process for computing profits, parallel to s 25 which requires profits to be computed accounding to UK GAAP. New s 31E applies to professions, vocations and trades and states that:

> 'To determine the profits of a trade for a tax year on the cash basis–
>
> *Step 1*
>
> Calculate the total amount of receipts of the trade received during the basis period for the tax year.
>
> *Step 2*
>
> Deduct from that amount the total amount of expenses of the trade paid during the basis period for the tax year.'

This is subject to, 'any adjustment required or authorised by law in calculating profits for income tax purposes'. This places the cash basis (Steps 1 and 2) on equivalent footing to the requirement in s 25 for accounts to be prepared according to GAAP, which is also followed by the qualifier above. The legislation does not define 'receipts' or 'payments' so it is unclear whether it is regarded as cleared funds or receipts and payments as recorded in the cash book.

The rules in ss 27 and 28 concerning receipts and expenses and s 30 concerning animals kept for trade purposes are disapplied.

There then follows a number of specific adjustments to tax provisions that do or do not apply under the cash basis.

(3) The following general principles in computing the profits of a business do not apply when the business elects to use the cash basis:

- section 33 – capital expenditure; replaced by new s 33A cash basis: capital expenditure;
- section 35 – bad and doubtful debts;

- sections 36 and 37 – unpaid remuneration;
- section 43 – employee benefit contributions, profits calculated before the end of the nine month period;
- sections 48 to 50B – car hire;
- sections 60 to 67 – tenants under taxed leases;
- section 68 – replacement and alteration of trade tools.

New ITA 2007 s 384B also excludes the right to claim relief for interest paid on loans in relation to a partnership if the partnership concerned has made an election for the cash basis. The loans affected are a loan to buy plant and machinery for partnership use (under ITA 2007 s388) and a loan to invest in a partnership (under ITA 2007 s 398) which has not been used to purchase a share in the partnership.

(4) Specific rules applying to specialist business sectors are disapplied in calculating the profits for tax purposes, if the business uses the cash basis:

- dealers in securities;
- relief for mineral royalties;
- lease premiums (reduction of receipts);
- ministers of religion;
- mineral exploration and access;
- pool betting duty;
- intermediaries treated as making employment payments;
- managed service companies;
- waste disposal;
- cemeteries and crematoria.

(5) There is also a list of exclusions of special rules in specific Chapters of ITTOIA 2005, so that none of these apply in calculating the profits of a trade on a cash basis:

- Chapter 8 – herd basis;
- Chapter 9 – sound recordings;
- Chapter 10 – telecommunications rights;
- Chapter 10A – long funding leases;
- Chapter 11A – trade profits: changes in trading stock;
- Chapter 13 – deductions from profits: unremittable amounts;
- Chapter 14 – disposal and acquisition of know-how;
- Chapter 16 – averaging profits of farmers and creative artists;
- Chapter 16ZA – compensation for compulsory slaughter of animals;
- Chapter 16A – oil activities.

(6) There are then some specific rules applying only to the cash basis.

- Section 33A – this permits expenditure on plant and machinery which would normally attract capital allowances to be deducted as incurred (with the exception of expenditure on cars).
- Section 51A – this prohibits the deduction of interest paid on a loan, but permits deductions under new s 57B. This rather unusually provides that interest and loan arrangement fees of up to £500 may be deducted in a year (on a paid basis) and there is no requirement that the loan is wholly and exclusively for the purposes of the business.
- Section 55A – this allows for expenditure on integral features to be deducted as incurred.
- Section 96A – capital receipts in respect of assets for which a deduction has been given under the cash basis (or would have been if an election had been made at the time they were acquired) are to be accounted for as a receipt under the cash basis. Where there is mixed use, the receipt is apportioned as appropriate.
- Section 97A – trading stock held at cessation when a cash basis election is in place is to be valued on a just and reasonable basis, and included as a receipt.
- Section 97B – work in progress at cessation of the trade when a cash basis election is in place is to be valued on a just and reasonable basis, and included as a receipt.
- TCGA 1992 s 47A provides an exemption from a chargeable gains on a wasting chattel used in the trade where a cash basis election is in force at the date of disposal.

There is also a requirement (ITTOIA 2005 s 106C) that all amounts taken into account are based on an arm's length amount, and adjustments will be required if a transaction is not at arm's length, subject to some minor exclusions.

(7) The following general principles in computing the profits of a business are amended to reflect the cash basis (all references are to ITTOIA 2005):

- section 38 – restriction of deductions in respect of employee benefit contributions;
- section 72 – payroll deduction schemes: contributions to agents' expenses;
- section 94A – costs of setting up SAYE option scheme or CSOP scheme;
- section 105 – industrial development grants;
- sections 246 and 254 – post-cessation receipts;
- section 786 – rent-a-room receipts;
- section 805 – qualifying care receipts;
- section 820 – periods of account not ending on 5 April.

*Losses*

(8) There is no relief for losses under the cash basis other than carry forward against future profits of the same trade. Sideways relief in the year and carry back (including opening year loss relief provisions) are not available to cash basis users, and this may well influence the choice of basis for some businesses who appoint an adviser. Similarly, relief against capital gains is also excluded for cash basis users.

*Special rules for barristers and advocates in the early years of practice*

(9) These rules have provided for a cash basis to apply in the first seven years of practice. These rules were abolished by the introduction of the cash basis, and barristers and advocates may elect to apply the new cash basis at any point in their business, provided the qualifying conditions are met. Where a barrister or advocate has been taxed under the special rules in 2012/13 and does not meet the qualifying conditions for

the cash basis, they may continue to apply the special basis until the expiry of the seven year period. The transitional rules which apply after the seventh year of practice are also retained for those who have been taxed under the special rules prior to 2013/14.

*Transitional rules*

(10) The provisions of ITTOIA 2005 Part 2 Chapter 17 in relation to adjustment income in relation to accruals accounts, apply equally to the cash basis by the introduction of new ITTOIA 2005 s 227A. This section applies ITTOIA 2005 Part 2 Chapter 17 to the cash basis if:

- an election has been made for the cash basis for the current tax year but not for the following one ie, a business leaving the cash scheme; or
- no such election was made for a tax year but one has effect for the following tax year ie, a business joining the scheme.

The provisions are designed to prevent abuse by moving from one basis to another to avoid income being taxed, or enable double relief for expenses. The general approach requires an amount by way of adjustment to be calculated in accordance with ITTOIA 2005 s 231. In particular it is worth noting that adjustment income (which will normally arise on the transition to a GAAP basis, as a result of recognising stock, work in progress and debtors) can be spread forwards over a period of up to six years.

(11) Most of the complications for a business entering the cash basis from GAAP, and moving from the cash basis to GAAP relate to capital allowances. The rules need to cover the following situations.

(a) Before entering the cash basis, an existing business will have been eligible to claim capital allowances.

(b) Capital allowances may not be claimed whilst applying the cash basis (with the exception of capital allowances on cars).

(c) After leaving the cash basis, capital allowances can be claimed.

New ITTOIA 2005 Part 2 Chapter 17A provides for adjustments for capital allowances. If Peter has previously claimed fixed rate deductions in respect of a car, he is not permitted to claim capital allowances on the car after leaving the cash basis. However, it is still open to him to claim fixed rate expenses, which is an election independent of the availability of the cash basis.

*Fixed rate deductions*

(12) Guidance on the computation of a charge for office use of home is in BIM starting at BIM47800, which is an alternative to using the fixed rate deduction, but is somewhat time consuming to do. Some small businesses have previously used a concession of £3 per week to account for business use of home. As the new fixed rates provide a statutory basis for the deduction, they should either choose the strict basis of apportionment following the guidance in the manual or the fixed rate deductions set out above.

(13) Where a business has more than one car, the fixed rate deduction is restricted to a total of 10,000 miles at the higher rate for all cars for which fixed rate deductions are claimed. This would effectively deny a deduction for the fixed costs of running a second car if the 10,000 limit was exceeded taking both cars together. In this case the owner may choose instead to elect for ordinary motor expenses and capital allowances to be claimed.

# Question

**Please note: This applies to unincorporated businesses and limited liability partnerships (LLPs) carrying on a trade.**

In (a) and (b) below, all calculations are to be taken to the nearest month.

(a) Show the assessments arising in the following four examples, assuming that the traders all started in business on 1 January 2016 and made profits (net of capital allowances) as shown:

| | | |
|---|---|---|
| (i) | Year to 31 December 2016 | £12,000 |
| | Year to 31 December 2017 | £18,000 |
| (ii) | Six months to 30 June 2016 | £3,000 |
| | Year to 30 June 2017 | £17,000 |
| (iii) | 15 months to 31 March 2017 | £3,750 |
| | Year to 31 March 2018 | £16,000 |
| (iv) | 16 months to 30 April 2017 | £4,400 |
| | Year to 30 April 2018 | £18,000 |

(b) Show the assessments for the final tax year for the businesses in (a) if they had all continued to make up accounts annually to the dates shown and had ceased on 31 August 2020, the profits for each of them in the final two years being at the rate of £5,000 a month and the final accounting periods being:

(i) 8 months from 1.1.2020 to 31.8.2020

(ii) 14 months from 1.7.2019 to 31.8.2020

(iii) 5 months from 1.4.2020 to 31.8.2020

(iv) 16 months from 1.5.2019 to 31.8.2020

(c)

(i) State how trading stock is valued on discontinuance of a business.

(ii) State how post cessation receipts and expenditure are treated.

## Answer

References in this Example are to the Income Tax (Trading and Other Income) Act 2005 (ITTOIA 2005) unless otherwise stated.

(a) Although s 203(3) states that apportionments should be made in days, all calculations in the Example have been taken to the nearest month in accordance with s 203(4) which permits apportionments either in days, or months, or months and fractions of months, providing the chosen method is used consistently. The 2015/16 profit in **part** (i) of the Example works out at £3,000 when apportioned in months, with the overlap profit being the same amount. It would be 96/366 of £12,000, ie £3,148 if apportioned in days, and the overlap profit would then be £3,148.

Where a business makes up accounts to 31 March, HMRC is prepared to treat an apportionment of profit for a period of 5 days or less as nil in accordance with s 209. On this basis, a business that started on 1 April 2016 and made up accounts to 31 March 2017 would have no assessable profit in 2015/16 and would pay tax in each succeeding year on the profit of the year to 31 March; overlap profits would not arise unless the accounting date was changed. HMRC is similarly prepared to treat a change of accounting date to 31 March as being equivalent to a change to 5 April (per s 220(5)), all existing overlap relief being deducted at the time of the change (see **part B(iii)** for an illustration).

| | | | | | £ |
|---|---|---|---|---|---|
| (i) | 2015/16 | 1.1.16 – 5.4.16 | 3/12 × | 12,000 = | 3,000 |
| | 2016/17 | Yr to 31.12.16 | | | 12,000 |
| | 2017/18 | Yr to 31.12.17 | | | 18,000 |
| | Overlap profit 1.1.16 – 5.4.16 (3 months) | | | £3,000 | |
| (ii) | 2015/16 | 1.1.16 – 5.4.16 | 3/6 × | 3,000 = | 1,500 |
| | 2016/17 | 1st 12 months: | | | |
| | | 6 mths to 30.6.16 | | 3,000 | |
| | | + 1.7.16 – 31.12.17 | + (6/12 × 17,000) | 8,500 | 11,500 |
| | 2017/18 | Yr to 30.6.17 | | | 17,000 |
| | Overlap profit | 1.1.16 – 5.4.16 | | £1,500 | |
| | (total 9 mths) | 1.7.16 – 31.12.17 | | 8,500 | |
| | | | | £10,000 | |
| (iii) | 2015/16 | 1.1.16 – 5.4.16 | 3/15 × | 3,750 = | 750 |
| | 2016/17 | 1.4.16 – 31.3.17 | 12/15 × | 3,750 = | 3,000 |
| | 2017/18 | Yr to 31.3.18 | | | 16,000 |
| | Overlap period 1.4.16 – 5.4.16 (ignore) | | | | |
| (iv) | 2015/16 | 1.1.16 – 5.4.16 | 3/16 × | 4,400 = | 825 |
| | 2016/17 | 6.4.16 – 5.4.16 | 12/16 × | 4,400 = | 3,300 |
| | 2017/18 | 1.5.16 – 30.4.17 | 12/16 × | 4,400 = | 3,300 |
| | 2018/19 | Yr to 30.4.18 | | | 18,000 |
| | Overlap profit 1.5.16– 5.4.17 (11 months) | | | £3,025 | |

Relief for the overlap profits is given either when the business ceases or on an earlier change of accounting date if more than twelve months' profits is being taxed in one year.

(b) If the businesses in (a) closed down on 31 August 2020, the tax year of cessation would be 2020/21. At £5,000 per month, the profits of the final accounting period would be:

| | | |
|---|---|---|
| In (a)(i) | 8 months to 31.8.20 | £40,000 |
| In (a)(ii) | 14 months to 31.8.20 | £70,000 |
| In (a)(iii) | 5 months to 31.8.20 | £25,000 |
| In (a)(iv) | 16 months to 31.8.20 | £80,000 |

The final assessments would be as follows:

| | | | |
|---|---|---|---|
| (i) | Profits 1.1.20 to 31.8.20 | 40,000 | |
| | Less overlap relief | (3,000) | £37,000 |
| (ii) | Profits 1.7.19 to 31.8.20 | 70,000 | |
| | Less overlap relief | (10,000) | £60,000 |
| (iii) | Profits 1.4.20 to 31.8.20 | | |
| | (No overlap relief) | | £25,000 |
| (iv) | Profits 1.5.19 to 31.8.20 | 80,000 | |
| | Less overlap relief | (3,025) | £76,975 |

(c)

(i) *Valuation of trading stock*

The valuation of stock and work in progress is dealt with in Chapter 12 of ITTOIA 2005.

Any unsold trading stock at the date of discontinuance of a business is treated as follows:

(1) Any stock sold to an unconnected UK trader who can deduct the cost of it in his computation of assessable trading profits is brought into the final accounts or computations at the amount for which it is sold (s 173). Where stock is transferred with other assets, the consideration is apportioned on a just and reasonable basis.

(2) Any stock sold to a UK trader who is connected with the vendor (eg through a family link, or as companies in the same group), is treated as sold for an arm's length price (s 177). If, however, that amount is greater than both the actual sale price and the cost of the stock, the two parties may make a claim to use the higher of cost and sale price instead of arm's length value. The claim must be made within two years after the end of the chargeable period (ie tax year or company accounting period) in which the trade ceased (s 178).

(3) Any other stock (eg stock given away or retained for private purposes) is adjusted in the final income tax computation to reflect the amount it would have realised if it had been sold in the open market at the discontinuation of the trade (s 175(4)).

(4) The provisions of notes 1 to 3 do not apply where a business ceases because of the death of the sole proprietor (s 173(4)), and the closing stock is valued at the lower of cost and market value. Its acquisition value for executors or beneficiaries is, however, its market value at the date of death, both for capital gains purposes and for income tax purposes if they carry on the business. Work in progress is valued at consideration received, or at market value if no consideration (s 184). In the case of a profession the taxpayer may elect for work in progress to be valued at cost. An excess amount subsequently received being treated as a post-cessation receipt (s 185). The election must be made within one year from 31 January following the tax year of cessation.

(ii) *Post-cessation receipts*

Where income is received after a business has ceased, and it has not been included in the final accounts, it is charged to tax under Chapter 18, at s 242. The taxable amount may be reduced by any expenses, capital allowances or losses that could have been set against it if it had been received before the business ceased (s 254). The taxable amount is treated as earned income of the tax year in which it is received. If, however, the income is received in a tax year beginning not later than six years after the cessation date, an election may be made to have it taxed as if it had been received on the date of cessation (s 257). The election must be made within one year from 31 January following the tax year in which the amount is received. Although the tax adjustment from backdating is calculated by reference to the earlier year, the claim is treated as relating to the tax year in which the amount is received and is given effect by increasing the tax payable for that later tax year. The additional tax is not, however, treated as part of the tax *assessed* for the later year and does not therefore affect payments on account for the next following year (see **Example G3**).

The treatment of post cessation receipts is particularly relevant to anyone preparing their accounts on the basis of cash received (either the cash basis for small business or the scheme for barristers in their early years of practice) rather than on an earnings basis.

*Post-cessation expenditure*

Where qualifying payments are made within seven years after cessation (or debts for which provision was not made in the final accounts become irrecoverable), then unless there are post-cessation receipts against which the amounts may be set, a claim may be made to set them against the total income and capital gains of the tax year in which the payment is made (or the debt proves to be irrecoverable) (ITA 2007 s 96). The claim must be made within twelve months after 31 January following the end of the relevant tax year.

Qualifying payments are those made wholly and exclusively for professional indemnity insurance, or to remedy defective work, goods or services, or paid by way of damages in respect of such defects, including related legal and other professional expenses, or in respect of debt recovery costs.

The relief for post cessation expenses does not apply for corporation tax purposes, nor is any relief given when computing income for tax credit purposes.

# Explanatory Notes

*Current year basis of assessment*

(1) Trading profits are charged to tax on the 'current year basis', which broadly means the profits of the accounting year ending in the current tax year. The detailed rules are given below. Businesses commencing on or after 6 April 1994 have used the current year basis from the outset. For businesses already in existence at that date the current year basis took effect from 1997/98, with 1996/97 being a transitional year – which may have given rise to transitional overlap relief.

*Current year basis rules and overlap relief*

(2) The current year basis rules are contained in Chapter 15 of Part 2 of ITTOIA 2005. The essence of the rules is that businesses will be taxed over their lifetime on the taxable profits made. Although overlaps occur on commencement and possibly on changes of accounting date, they are dealt with by calculating the amount of profit that has been double charged (overlap profit) and allowing that amount as a deduction either when the business ceases or on an earlier change of accounting date if and to the extent that more than twelve months' profit is being taxed in one year. It is possible, however, that tax will be charged overall on more than the profits earned, for example where there are insufficient profits and/or other income against which to set overlap profits (see **explanatory note 5**).

(3) A record needs to be kept not only of the amount of any overlap profits but also the length of the overlapping period. If an overlap period shows a loss, it must be recorded as an overlap of nil for the appropriate period. This is important because overlap relief is given at the time of a change of accounting date if and to the extent that more than twelve months' profit would otherwise be chargeable in one year (see **Example C5 part B(iii)**). Self-assessment returns provide for entries to be made for overlap profits brought forward and carried forward. The deduction of overlap relief is not affected by the cap on income tax reliefs introduced in April 2013.

*Opening years*

(4) The rules for the opening tax years are as follows (ITTOIA 2005 ss 199 to 201):

*Year 1* Profit from date of commencement to the end of the tax year.

*Year 2*
- (a) If there is an account of at least twelve months ending in year 2, profits of twelve months to the end of that account (as in **part (a)(i)** and **(iii)** in the Example).
- (b) Where the first account ends in year 2 but is for less than twelve months, profits of twelve months from commencement (as in **part (a)(ii)** in the Example).
- (c) Where no account ends in year 2, profits of the tax year itself (as in **part (a)(iv)** in the Example).

*Year 3 onwards* Normally profits of accounting year ending in the tax year, but with special rules for changes of accounting date, under which the basis period will never be less than twelve months but may be longer. (Changes of accounting date are dealt with in **Example C5**.)

If, however, the tax year is the first year in which there is an accounting date not less than twelve months after commencement (as in the third year 2017/18 in **part (a)(iv)** in the Example), the profits of twelve months to the accounting date are taken, even though the accounting period itself is longer.

Where there are losses, a loss that would otherwise be taken into account in two successive years is not included in the computation for the second year (see **Example E2** for an illustration).

(5) When a taxpayer acquires a new source of income, details must be shown in his return for the tax year in which income first arises. If the taxpayer does not receive a tax return for that tax year, he must notify HMRC within 6 months after the end of the year that he is chargeable to tax, otherwise interest and penalties may arise (TMA 1970 s 7 – see **Example G2 explanatory note 6**). This is particularly important for new businesses.. The penalty for failure to notify is behaviour based, with a penalty based on a percentage of the potential lost revenue, broadly similar to the structure for penalties for inaccuracies described in **Example G2 explanatory note 12**. The penalty rates are 100% for a deliberate and concealed failure to notify, 70% if the failure is deliberate but not concealed, and 30% in other cases. As for other penalties, reductions are given for disclosure. (FA 2008 Sch 41 para 6). A new business must notify HMRC for Class 2 NIC purposes 'immediately' after commencement of trading (SI 2001/1004 reg 87AA). Immediately is not defined within the legislation, although it is reasonable to assume that this means as soon as possible following commencement of trading. HMRC may allow further time to register, but it is not clear in which circumstances this will be offered (SI 2001/1004 reg 87AA(4)). All the businesses in **part (a)** of the Example have taxable profits for 2015/16, even though their first accounts would not have been available until 2016/17 or later. Even though accounts may not be available in time, the tax finally found to be due for any year attracts interest from the original due date. It is important, therefore, to make estimated payments in order to avoid the interest charge (see **Example C5**). The legislation does not stipulate the length of the first account (or of subsequent accounts) but clearly the interest provisions discourage taxpayers from preparing a very long account to delay their tax liabilities.

*Cessation of business*

(6) The basis period for the tax year in which a business ceases is from the end of the basis period for the previous tax year to the date of cessation, unless the business ceases in the second tax year, in which case the basis period for that tax year is from 6 April to the date of cessation (s 202). This means that there will often be two accounts that together form the final basis period, for example if in **part (b)** of the Example the trader in **part (a)(iv)**, instead of making up a 16 month account, had made up an account for the year to 30 April 2020 and a final 4 month account to 31 August 2020.

Any overlap profit for which relief has not already been given is deducted in full from the assessable profit of the last *tax year* (as distinct from the profit of the final period of account), and if that results in a loss, the normal loss reliefs will be available. See **Example E3**, in particular **explanatory note 6**.

**Part (b)** of the Example shows how overlap relief is dealt with on cessation. It should be noted that choosing an accounting year-end of 30 April still has the cash flow benefit of delaying the assessment of profits while the business continues, as shown in **parts (a)(iii)** and **(iv)** of the Example, in which profits are broadly being earned at the same rate in both cases but are being taxed a year later in **part (iv)**. However, on cessation this results in a final basis period that includes 11 months of the previous tax year.

This is illustrated in **part (b)(iv)** of the Example, where the basis period is 16 months, even though the business ceases only 5 months into the tax year. Although the available overlap relief covers 11 months' profits, the overlap profits were at a much lower rate than those being earned on cessation, hence the difference between the final assessment on the business with the 31 March year end (£25,000) and that on the business with the 30 April year end (£76,975). If there had been a loss in the first accounting period there may be no overlap relief at all.

On a practical note, as time passes the amount of the overlap profits, and therefore the relief due on cessation can be forgotten if an inadequate record is retained. HMRC does not have records going back far enough to provide this information, so taxpayers would be unable to claim relief if they cannot identify the amount of overlap profits. A careful record should therefore be retained, and when taking on a new client, every effort should be made to establish the amount of overlap profits at the outset.

*Capital allowances*

(7) Capital allowances are treated as a trading expense of the accounting period. If the accounting period is shorter or longer than twelve months, the annual writing down allowances are reduced or increased proportionately (see **Example C6 part (a)**).

*Transitional overlap relief*

(8) Under the previous year basis of assessment, which applied before 1996/97, profits were charged more than once when a business started, and sometimes on a change of accounting date, balanced by profits escaping tax for an equivalent length of *time* when the business ceased. Under the current year basis, profits may also be charged more than once at the start and on changes of accounting date, but the balancing adjustment when the business ceases is equal to the *amount* of profits that were double charged (see **explanatory note 2**).

On the replacement of the previous year basis by the current year basis, all profits up to 5 April 1997 were treated as having been taxed under the previous year basis rules, but the profit for the period from the end of the basis period for 1996/97 to 5 April 1997 was also included in the taxable profits for 1997/98 under the current year basis. This profit therefore represents a transitional overlap profit, for which relief will be given as in **explanatory note 2**, ie when the business ceases, or possibly earlier if the accounting date is changed. Unlike normal overlap profits, transitional overlap profits were calculated *before* capital allowances. Where, as a result of a change of accounting date, further overlap profits arise, these will be merged with transitional overlap profits to form a single figure.

The same comments apply as in **explanatory note 6** regarding records of transitional overlap relief due.

# Question

**Please note: This applies to unincorporated businesses and limited liability partnerships (LLPs) carrying on a trade.**

## A – Choice of accounting date

On 31 January 2015 David, a supervisor with a building supplies company, was made redundant. During the next twelve months he applied for many jobs, and attended a number of interviews but without success. On 1 February 2016, he set up his own business as a self-employed plumber providing services to local houseowners.

His turnover for the first three months was £2,000 per month, and David expects this monthly turnover to rise each quarter by £200 to a turnover of £2,800 per month in the quarter to April 2017. He estimates his turnover in future years to increase above the April 2017 level of £8,400 per quarter by approximately 10% per annum.

David estimates that his profits, adjusted for tax purposes, will be approximately 80% of his turnover.

He is considering preparing his first accounts either for the year to 31 January 2017 and annually thereafter, or for the 15 months to 30 April 2017 and annually thereafter.

(i) What are the tax consequences of David's accounts being prepared annually to 30 April, rather than 31 January?

(ii) State whether David is *required* to register his business for VAT purposes and irrespective of whether David is required to register or not, whether he is *able* to register if he so wishes, and the advantages or disadvantages of registration.

## B – Change of accounting date

(i)

Janet is a self-employed photographer who has been in business for a number of years making up her accounts to 31 August each year. Early in 2016 she successfully negotiates a number of major contracts at local events and decides to change her accounting date to 30 April. Her accounts before and after the change were as follows:

| | |
|---|---|
| 12 months to 31 August 2015 | £24,000 |
| 8 months to 30 April 2016 | £37,000 |

She has overlap profit from when she started trading of £925 (217 days)

Explain the rules for changing accounting date and show what Janet's taxable profits would be for 2016/17 and 2017/18.

(ii)

What would be the position if instead of making up accounts to 31 August each year, Janet's accounting date had been 31 December and her accounts before and after the change were as follows:

| | |
|---|---|
| 12 months to 31 December 2015 | £24,000 |
| 16 months to 30 April 2017 | £42,000 |

Overlap profit: £1,250 (3 months)

(iii)

Jade is in businesses as a fitness instructor and for a number of years has run a variety of classes and courses. Her accounting date is 30 April. During 2016 Jade decides to change her accounting date to 31 March. She makes up accounts as follows:

| | |
|---|---|
| Year to 30 April 2016 | £45,540 |
| 11 months to 31 March 2017 | £36,800 |

Overlap profit £17,600 (240 days).

Compute Jade's assessable profits for 2016/17 (assume there are no capital allowances).

# Answer

## A – Choice of accounting date

(i) David's anticipated turnover for the two alternative accounting dates is:

| | | | Turnover | Profits (80%) |
|---|---|---|---|---|
| | | | £ | £ |
| *Year to 31 January 2017* | | | | |
| 1st quarter | 6,000 | | | |
| 2nd quarter | 6,600 | | | |
| 3rd quarter | 7,200 | | | |
| 4th quarter | 7,800 | | | |
| | | | 27,600 | 22,080 |
| *Year to 31 January 2018* | | | | |
| 1st quarter (3 × £2,800) | 8,400 | | | |
| 2nd quarter (8,400 × 110%) | 9,240 | | | |
| 3rd quarter (8,400 × 110%) | 9,240 | | | |
| 4th quarter (8,400 × 110%) | 9,240 | | | |
| | | 36,120 | (say) 36,000 | 28,800 |
| *15 months to 30 April 2017* | | | | |
| 1st 12 months (as calculated above) | 27,600 | | | |
| 5th quarter (3 × £2,800) | 8,400 | | | |
| | | | 36,000 | 28,800 |
| *Year to 30 April 2018* | | | | |
| 4 quarters @ £8,400 × 110% | | 36,960 | (say) 37,000 | 29,600 |

On those figures, the taxable profits for 2015/16 to 2016/17, using the two alternative accounting dates would be:

| Using 31 January accounting date: | | | £ |
|---|---|---|---|
| 2015/16 | 1.2.16 – 5.4.16 | 2/12 × 22,080 | 3,680 |
| 2016/17 | 1.2.16 – 31.1.17 | | 22,080 |
| 2017/18 | 1.2.17 – 31.1.18 | | 28,800 |
| | | | 54,560 |
| Overlap profit: 1.2.16 – 5.4.16 | | £3,680 | |

| Using 30 April accounting date | | | |
|---|---|---|---|
| 2015/16 | 1.2.16 – 5.4.16 | 2/15 × 28,800 | 3,840 |
| 2016/17 | 6.4.16 – 5.4.17 | 12/15 × 28,800 | 23,040 |
| 2017/18 | 1.5.16 – 30.4.17 | 12/15 × 28,800 | 23,040 |
| | | | 49,920 |
| Overlap profit: 1.5.18 – 5.4.17 | | 11/15 × 28,800 = £21,120 | |

In each case the overlap profits represent the excess of profits charged to tax over the profits earned, ie (54,560 – 50,880 =) 3,680 with a 31 January year-end and (49,920 – 28,800 =) £21,120 with a 30 April year-end.

If David makes up accounts to 30 April, therefore, there is a reduction in the taxable profits of the first three years of (54,560 – 49,920) = £4,640. If profits continue to rise, there will be an ongoing benefit of paying tax each year on earlier, lower profits. With a year-end of 31 January the taxable profits are very little different from the profits of the tax year itself, whereas with a year-end of 30 April nearly all the taxable profit relates to the previous year.

Unless there are losses for which relief is unavailable, however, the profits eventually charged to tax under the current year basis are the same as the profits earned. Paying tax each year on lower profits than have actually been earned is therefore effectively building up an amount of deferred profits on which tax must be paid when the business ceases. Furthermore, there is no inflation proofing of the overlap relief.

Say David ceased business on 31 January 2019, not having changed his accounting date in the meantime. The position in the final year would be:

Accounts to 30 April annually

2018/19 Profits of 21 months from 1.5.17 to 31.1.19 less overlap relief of £21,120

Accounts to 31 January annually

2018/19 Profits of 12 months from 1.2.19 to 31.1.19 less overlap relief of £3,680

Clearly if the rate of profits in 2018/19 is much higher than when the business started, the length of the final basis period means that final assessment with the 30 April year-end will be very much higher than with the 31 January year-end.

As well as giving lower taxable profits when profits are rising, so long as the business continues, a 30 April year-end gives more time for preparation of accounts and tax computations. Under self-assessment, tax returns are due by 31 January following the tax year, eg by 31 January 2017 for 2015/16 if filed online, but 31 October after the end of the tax year if filed on paper, eg by 31 October 2016 for 2015/16. This normally allows 21 months' preparation time with a 30 April year-end, compared with twelve months with a 31 January year-end. The 30 April year-end, however, makes the calculation of tax bills more difficult at the start of the business.

A year end early in the tax year, such as 30 April, can allow scope for pre-tax year end planning. For example, personal pension contributions can be made before the end of the tax year to maximise higher rate tax relief as profits are likely to be known before the end of the tax year. A year end close to the end of the tax year, such as 31 March, does not allow for any degree of accuracy in such planning.

No matter which year-end is chosen, David has taxable profits for 2015/16, the tax on which is due for payment on 31 January 2017. Since the accounts will not be finalised by that date with either year-end, he will have to estimate the amount due, and will be charged interest from that date if his estimate falls short of the actual figure. (If he overestimates, he will receive a much lower rate of interest on the repayment than is charged on an underpayment.) He will know the exact amount of his profits sooner if he makes up accounts to 31 January. Furthermore, any tax due for 2015/16 will affect payments on account for 2016/17, unless it is covered by the de minimis limits, interest being payable from the half-yearly due dates of 31 January 2017 and 31 July 2017 based on the final figure of tax due for 2015/16. Estimated payments on account may therefore also be required, unless the 2015/16 tax on his business profits are less than the de minimis limits of £1,000 or 20% of his total tax liability for the year.

Where taxable profits are lower as a result of the choice of year-end there will also be a saving in Class 4 national insurance contributions provided the profits are above the Class 4 nil rate band. This would be the case for David in 2016/17, and probably in 2017/18 as well. However, the Class 4 NIC savings would be comparatively lower (2% as opposed to 9%) if the profits exceeded the upper profits limit (£43,000 in 2016/17).

(ii) As far as VAT registration is concerned, David is required to register at any time if his turnover in the next *thirty days* is expected to exceed the VAT threshold (currently £83,000). He is also required to register at the end of any *month* if his turnover in the year ended on the last day of that month exceeded the threshold, unless HMRC is satisfied that his turnover in the coming year will not exceed (from 1 April 2016) £81,000.

Clearly David's turnover is expected to be below these limits for at least the first few years. He may register voluntarily if he wishes. This will not be to his advantage, because he would have to charge VAT to the houseowners for whom he works, and they would not be able to recover it, and he would also have to comply with the administrative requirements for keeping records and accounting to HMRC for the VAT charged to his customers (less a set-off for VAT he has suffered) although this could be simplified by using the Flat Rate Scheme. For more details of the Flat Rate Scheme for VAT see **Example M2**.

It is also worth noting that as David's turnover is not expected to reach the level of the VAT threshold in the early years, he is likely to be eligible to use the simplified cash basis for small businesses. See **Example C3**.

If he remains non-registered, the VAT that he incurs forms part of the cost of the item concerned. If the item is an allowable deduction against his profit, such as his purchases of materials, he will save tax on the VAT suffered. If it is not, it may qualify for capital allowances, in which case the VAT forms part of the cost on which allowances are given. Where the asset is a chargeable asset for capital gains tax, any VAT not recovered forms part of the allowable expenditure taken into account when the asset is disposed of. Some VAT is not recoverable at all, such as on business entertaining.

## B – Changing accounting date

Under ITTOIA 2005 s 214, an accounting change, ie a change from one accounting date to another, is treated as made in the first tax year in which accounts are not made up to the old date, or are made up to the new date, or both. In order for the change to become effective at the time it is made, then unless the change takes place before the end of the third tax year, the following rules must be satisfied (s 217):

(1) The first account to the new date does not exceed 18 months.

(2) Notice of the change is given to HMRC by 31 January next following the tax year of change.

(3) Either:

  (a) No earlier change has been made in any of the 5 previous tax years

  or

  (b) The notice sets out the reasons for the change and HMRC either accept that the change is for bona fide commercial reasons or do not notify their dissatisfaction within 60 days of receiving the notice. (Obtaining a tax advantage is not a bona fide commercial reason.) If HMRC object to the change, the taxpayer has a right of appeal.

The fact that (apart from in the second and third tax year) HMRC does not recognise a change of accounting date unless the change is notified to them means that accounts may be made up to an intermediate date for commercial reasons, for example when a partner leaves, without the annual accounting date being altered (see **explanatory note** 7).

The provision that the new accounts period must not exceed 18 months does not prevent a longer account being made up. It merely prevents the account being recognised until the change of accounting date conditions can be satisfied. Thus, if the rules are not satisfied for the first relevant year, the change to the new date is treated as made in the next following year and so on until the rules are satisfied (s 219). (See **Example C4 explanatory note 4** re the effect of making up a long first account in a new business, such an account not, of course, being covered by the change of accounting date rules.)

Where the change of date occurs in the second or third tax year, or the provisions of s 217 apply, the basis period for the tax year in which the change occurs depends on the 'relevant period', ie the period from the end of the basis period for the previous tax year to the new accounting date in the current tax year. (Note that depending on the periods for which accounts are made up, there may not be an account made up to the new date in the current year – see **(ii)** below.) If the relevant period is less than 12 months the basis period for the tax year of change is 12 months to the new date. If the relevant period is more than 12 months, the basis period is that longer period.

What this means is that if the new date is *earlier* in the tax year than the old date, the basis period will be 12 months and profits will be double charged, for which overlap relief will be available in due course. If the new date is *later* in the tax year than the old date, more than 12 months' profit will be charged in the tax year of change, but the assessable profit will be reduced by the appropriate proportion of any available overlap profits according to the excess of the basis period over 12 months compared with the length of the period in which the overlap profits arose (see **(iii)** below).

Taxpayers need to maintain a running computation of overlap relief and the period to which it relates. The overlap period may be calculated in days, months, or months and fractions of months. For businesses in existence at 5 April 1994, transitional overlap relief on the changeover to the current year basis of assessment was maximised by calculating the overlap period in days. If that was done, then the overlap relief has to be worked out in days during the life of the business. Where a change of accounting date creates further overlap relief, the relevant period and amount are added to existing overlap relief to give a new single period and amount. Where a change of accounting date uses up some overlap relief, this reduces the period and amount of overlap relief carried forward. Where there is a loss in an overlap period it must be counted as a profit of nil for the appropriate period (see **Example E2** for illustrations).

## (i) *Changing date from 31 August to 30 April*

The change of accounting date takes place in 2016/17. The 'relevant period' is 1.9.15 to 30.4.16, which is less than 12 months, so the basis period for 2016/17 is the year to 30.4.16, giving assessable profits of:

| | |
|---|---|
| 1.5.15 – 31.8.15 (123/365 × £24,000) | 8,088 |
| 8 mths to 30.4.16 | 37,000 |
| | £45,088 |

The profits of £8,088 have also been taxed in 2015/16, so they are added to the existing overlap profit, the combined amount of (£925 +£8,088 =) £9,013 then relating to a period of (217 + 123 =) 340 days. The overlap profit will qualify for relief on a later change of accounting date to the extent that more than 12 months' profits is being charged, or otherwise on cessation.

The change of accounting date does not affect any other tax year and so Janet's 2017/18 assessable profits will be those for the year to 30 April 2017.

## (ii) *Changing date from 31 December to 30 April (long accounting period)*

The change of accounting date takes place in 2016/17, since accounts are not made up to the old date in that year (or in fact to the new date, since no account ends in 2016/17). Assessments for previous tax years are not affected.

The 'relevant period' for the change in accounting date is 1.1.16 to 30.4.16 (ie the date of the new year-end in 2016/17). Since that period is less than 12 months, the taxable profit is based on 12 months to the new date. This gives the following results for 2016/17 and 2017/18:

| | | | | |
|---|---|---|---|---|
| 2016/17 | Yr to 30.4.16 | | | |
| | 1.5.15 – 31.12.15 | 8/12 × 24,000 | 16,000 | |
| | 1.1.165 – 30.4.16 | 4/16 × 42,000 | 10,500 | £26,500 |
| 2017/18 | Yr to 30.4.17 | 12/16 × 42,000 | | £31,500 |

The profits of £16,000 for 8 months have also been taxed in 2015/16, so they will be added to the initial overlap profit of £1,250 (for 3 months), with the total amount of £17,250 covering an overlap period of 11 months qualifying for relief in a later year.

## (iii) *Changing date from 30 April to 31 March*

The change of accounting date takes place in 2016/17, since accounts are made up to the new accounting date in that year, and the 'relevant period' is 1.5.15 to 31.3.17. As that period exceeds 12 months, it is the basis period for 2016/17.

On the change of accounting date to 31 March, the transitional overlap relief is given in full against the 2016/17 assessment, since 31 March may be regarded as equivalent to the tax year (**Example C4 part** (**a**)).

This means that Jade's 2016/17 assessment is on:

| | | | |
|---|---|---|---|
| | | £ | £ |
| 2016/17 | Yr to 30.4.16 | 45,540 | |
| | 11 months to 31.3.17 | 36,800 | |
| | | 82,340 | |
| | *Less* Transitional overlap relief | 17,600 | 64,740 |

The change of accounting date does not affect any other tax year.

## Explanatory Notes

*Choice of accounting date*

(1) For the detailed provisions on opening and closing years' assessments, see **Example C4**. Self-assessment is dealt with in **Example G2**.

(2) Under the current year basis, the profits earned are normally taxed over the life of the business, any overlaps at the outset and on changes of accounting date being reflected in overlap relief when the business ceases. The effect of inflation, however, could mean that overlap relief is of limited value in real terms. A year-end of 30 April has an ongoing cash flow benefit where profits are rising and also a benefit in the time for preparing accounts and computations, as indicated in the Example.

If a year-end of 31 March is chosen, no overlap relief arises, since HMRC is prepared to treat the accounting year as equivalent to the tax year (see **Example C4 part** (**a**)), so there is no adverse effect from inflation. If a business with a different year-end faces falling profits, switching to a 31 March year-end would trigger any available overlap relief and would reduce the ongoing assessments (see **Part B** (**iii**) of this Example).).

*Notifying liability and sending in returns*

(3) Not all taxpayers regularly receive tax returns for completion. By TMA 1970 s 7, a taxpayer is required to notify HMRC if he is liable to tax for any tax year, the notification being required to be made not later than six months from the end of that tax year (TMA 1970 s 7 – see **Example G2 explanatory note 6**). In David's case, if he does not get a return, he needs to notify HMRC that he has taxable income for 2015/16 not later than 5 October 2016. As stated below, David will be required to register his new business with HMRC within three months by completing form SA1, which can be completed and submitted online. Normally this registration will result in HMRC issuing a tax return for the relevant year with no notification being required under s 7.

(4) Penalties arise both for failure to send in a return on time (Finance Act 2009 Sch 55) and for failure to notify liability to tax (Finance Act 2008 Sch 41). Penalties for 2015/16 returns apply if they are not submitted by 31 October 2016 for paper submissions, and 31 January 2017 for online. The penalty for late returns is a flat initial penalty of £100, with additional penalties increasing according to the length of the delay in submitting the return. The penalty for failure to notify is a tax geared penalty based on behaviour. For the interest provisions see **Example G2** and for the penalty provisions see **Example G6**.

*Class 2 and 4 national insurance contributions*

(5) A self-employed person is liable to pay Class 2 and Class 4 national insurance contributions. Class 2 contributions are due if earnings exceed the small profits threshold (SPT) (£5,965 for 2016/17). It is necessary to notify liability upon commencement of self-employment, although HMRC offer a single

registration process for those starting self-employment which incorporates notification of Class 2 liability. There is a penalty for late notification if not made by 31 January following the end of the year in which liability first arose (see **Example H1**(a)). Until 2015/16 Class 2 contributions were payable in January and July in the tax year unless the individual's earnings were expected to be below an exemption level (equivalent to the SPT) in which case the individual could apply for a certificate of exemption. As from 2015/16 onwards, Class 2 contributions are calculated and collected as part of the self-assessment process. There is a transitional arrangement in place for existing direct debit payers for whom the July 2015 payment is the last to be collected under direct debit. There are proposals to abolish Class 2 contributions and determine benefit entitlement by the payment of Class 4 contributions.

Class 4 national insurance contributions are calculated on profits net of capital allowances. Under self-assessment, they are calculated by HMRC if the taxpayer does not wish to calculate his own tax and submits his return either online or on paper by 31 October following the end of the tax year, and otherwise by the taxpayer. The Class 4 contributions are payable at the same time as income tax, so they are included in half-yearly payments on account. See **Example H1** for detailed notes on national insurance contributions.

*Changes of accounting date*

(6) As indicated in the Example, where accounts are made up to an earlier date in the tax year, this results in profits being charged more than once. The amount double charged represents an overlap profit. Relief is available either on a further change of accounting date if more than 12 months' profit would otherwise be taxed in one year or on cessation. Where on a change of date the new date is later in the tax year, more than twelve months' profit will be charged, as indicated in **part (ii)** the Example, and an appropriate proportion of earlier overlap profits will be deducted.

If profits of a business with overlap relief start to fall, the ongoing assessments may be reduced by switching to a 31 March year-end. The extended basis period that results from changing to the 31 March accounting date is offset by the fact that the profits are reduced by the whole of the overlap relief.

*Notification of changes*

(7) Changes of accounting date are not recognised unless they are notified to HMRC, except where they occur in the second or third tax year (ITTOIA 2005 ss 200 and 215).

Where a business ceases and accounts to the date of cessation are to a date other than the annual accounting date, the cessation provisions of s 202 override the change of accounting date provisions for the final tax year. Depending on the dates to which accounts are made up, the change of accounting date rules may apply for the penultimate year, but this may be overcome by not notifying HMRC of the change as indicated above.

Where, however, a business is of very short duration, and a long account is made up to the date of cessation, a change of accounting date might technically occur in the second or third tax year for which no notification is required. HMRC have, however, stated that they will not object if computations are submitted on the basis that the old date continues to apply. For example:

A business starts on 1 July 2014 and makes up accounts to 30 November 2015. The business ceases on 31 May 2017 and accounts are made up for the 18 months to that date. The basis periods are:

| | |
|---|---|
| 2014/15 | 1.7.14 – 5.4.15 (9/17 × 1st accounts) |
| 2015/16 | 1.12.14 – 30.11.15 |
| 2016/17 | Technically the change of accounting date rules should apply to give a basis period of the 12 months to 31.5.16, but HMRC will allow basis period to be left at: |
| | 1.12.15 – 30.11.16 (12/18 × 2nd accounts) |
| 2016/17 | 1.12.16 – 31.5.17 (6/18 × 2nd accounts) |

Overlap relief would be computed on profits of 4 months from 1.12.14 – 5.4.15 and relieved in 2017/18.

# Question

(a) Lindley, LJ in *Yarmouth v France* (1887) said 'Plant... includes whatever apparatus is used by a businessman for carrying on his business – not his stock in trade which he buys or makes for sale, but all goods and chattels, fixed or moveable, live or dead, which he keeps for permanent employment in his business'.

Discuss in the light of later cases and legislation how far this statement can be said to be true today.

(b) Where assets qualify for plant and machinery allowances, explain what expenditure may be taken into account, and state the date on which the expenditure is treated as incurred.

(c) Briefly explain when plant and machinery allowances may be available in respect of leased assets.

(d) Explain the various rates of capital allowances available, and give details of common allowances on expenditure other than plant and machinery.

(e) Explain the way in which capital allowances are given to traders and investors.

(f) Explain the meaning of the expression 'connected person' in relation to capital allowances, and outline the treatment of transactions between connected persons.

# Answer

References in this Example are to the Capital Allowances Act 2001 (CAA 2001) unless otherwise indicated.

## (a) Meaning of 'plant'

The meaning of the words 'plant' and 'machinery' has been considered by the courts on many occasions. 'Machinery' is given its ordinary meaning, but no definition of 'plant' that can be regarded as all embracing has been arrived at. Many of the cases described below have treated parts of buildings and structures as plant. CAA 2001 ss 21 to 23 attempt to clarify the boundary between plant and buildings, and to limit any further additions to the 'plant' category, while not disturbing the effect of existing case law. The legislation specifically states that an asset cannot be plant if its principal purpose is to insulate or enclose the interior of the building or provide an interior wall, floor or ceiling intended to remain permanently in place.

For many years, books in a professional library were held not to be plant following *Daphne v Shaw* (1926), but this was overruled in *Munby v Furlong* (1977), since when the professional libraries of solicitors etc have been accepted as plant.

The case of *Yarmouth v France* was heard in 1887 and it concerned not taxation but employer's liability. An employee who had been injured by his employer's horse claimed under the workers' compensation provisions that he had been injured by his employer's 'plant', and the courts found in his favour.

The statement made by the judge in that case still forms the basis of the accepted definition of plant, and it was expanded in the war damage compensation case of *J Lyons & Co Ltd v AG* (1944) to emphasise that the basic distinction is between apparatus *with* which the trade is carried on and the setting *in* which it is carried on. This was echoed in the case of *Jarrold v John Good & Sons Ltd* (1962), where expenditure by a firm of shipping agents on moveable office partitioning which was used in order to give them maximum continuing flexibility in relation to the subdivision of their floor space was held to be on plant. Similarly, expenditure by a ship repairing company on the concrete work used in the construction of a dry dock and on excavating the land for the dock was held to be expenditure on plant (*IRC v Barclay, Curle & Co Ltd* (1969)), as was expenditure on a swimming pool at a caravan site (*Cooke v Beach Station Caravans Ltd* (1974)).

On the other hand, the 'setting' argument was used to disallow pre-fabricated moveable buildings used as a laboratory and gymnasium in a school (*St John's School v Ward* (1975)), the canopy over a petrol station (*Dixon v Fitch's Garages Ltd* (1975)), a false ceiling in a restaurant (*Hampton v Fortes Autogrill Ltd* (1980)), a floating ship used as a restaurant (*Benson v Yard Arm Club Ltd* (1979)), a fan-inflated polythene tennis court cover in a tennis coaching business (*Thomas v Reynolds* (1987)), car wash halls and sites (*Attwood v Anduff Car Wash Ltd CA* (1997)) and the structure of an electrical substation (only the equipment within it qualifying as plant – *Bradley v London Electricity plc* (1996)).

Two cases heard during 2004 show how subtle the distinction can be between plant and setting. In *Shove v Lingfield Park*, the Court of Appeal, overturning the finding of the Special Commissioner, held that an artificial surface on a racetrack allowing racing throughout the year was part of the setting. On the other hand, the Scottish Court of Session held that the construction of a five-a-side pitch could qualify for allowances (*CIR v Anchor International Ltd*).

Several cases have gone partly for and partly against the taxpayer. In *Cole Bros v Phillips* (1980), the electrical switchboard and most of the electrical equipment in a department store were held to be plant, but not certain light fittings whose only function was to provide light in areas with few windows. The court held in that case that items had to be considered individually and not as a single installation. In the case of *Carr v Sayer* (1992), it was held that permanent quarantine kennels were not plant but temporary, moveable, quarantine kennels *were* plant. In two 1992 cases, heard together, concerning single storey warehouses (*Hunt v Henry Quick Ltd* and *King v Bridisco Ltd*), it was held that platforms erected to increase the floor space in the warehouses were plant, but lighting beneath the platforms was not. A glasshouse constructed as a 'planteria' to protect plants and create an appropriate growing environment, but without any mechanical controls, was not plant (*Gray v Seymours Garden Centre* (CA 1995)). HMRC accepts, however, that glasshouses that incorporate a sophisticated, probably computerised, system to control and monitor temperature, humidity etc will usually qualify as plant, and they confirmed in their Tax Bulletin of June 1998 that such glasshouses will not normally be 'long life assets' (as to which see **Example C8 explanatory note 21**).

Although the question of what is and what is not plant is broadly a functional test, some of the cases involving buildings used by the public have held that various items forming part of the setting created atmosphere and thus performed the function of making the premises more attractive to customers. This has been applied to decor, murals, light fittings etc in hotels (*IRC v Scottish and Newcastle Breweries Ltd* (1981)) and to decorative screens in the shop front windows of building societies (*Leeds Permanent Building Society v Proctor* (1982)). But in *Wimpy International Ltd v Warland* (1988), only expenditure on light fittings was held to be plant on this criterion. Expenditure on shopfronts, floor and wall tiles, suspended ceilings, and mezzanine and raised floors was all disallowed, with the exception of one ceiling made of metal strips with gaps for visual interest. The Court of Appeal emphasised in that case that the starting point was the decision of the Appeal Commissioners. They considered there were two tests, the premises test and the business use test, and the business use test was only considered if the premises test was satisfied. Under the premises test, something which becomes part of the premises, instead of merely embellishing them, is not plant, except in the rare cases where the premises are themselves plant, like the dry dock in Barclay Curle, and the computerised glasshouses mentioned above. Under the business use test, if the item is not part of the premises and is not stock in trade, it is plant if it is used in carrying on the trade. (Although initial expenditure on a shopfront is disallowed, HMRC allows the cost of a subsequent replacement as a trading expense, except to the extent that the replacement does more than merely replace the original, ie any improvement element is disallowed.)

These principles were reconsidered by the Special Commissioners in *J D Wetherspoon plc v HMRC* (2007) in the context of wood panelling in a pub. It was held by the Special Commissioners that the panelling had become so standardised in the chain of pubs that it no longer represented a feature in its own right and had become subsumed as part of the building.

The distinction between plant and premises has been further confused by statute. FA 2008 introduced s 33A which provides that expenditure on integral features (as defined) are to qualify as if on plant or machinery provided that the purpose of the feature is not to insulate the interior of a building or to provide an interior wall, floor or ceiling which is intended to remain permanently in place. The meaning of integral feature includes some assets that were previously treated as plant but also some that were previously excluded from the definition of plant. Integral features are defined as the following:

- an electrical system (including a lighting system);
- a cold water system;
- a space or water heating system, a powered system of ventilation, air cooling or air purification and any floor ceiling comprised in such a system;
- a lift, escalator or moving walkway;
- external solar shading.

It can be seen, therefore, that although the statement in *Yarmouth v France*, as expanded in *J Lyons & Co Ltd v AG*, still forms the essence of the currently accepted definition of plant, the extent of its application is frequently contested before the courts and often some very narrow distinctions are drawn.

## (b) Qualifying expenditure

On assets that qualify for capital allowances, the expenditure that may be taken into account is qualifying capital expenditure incurred in the *chargeable period* (s 6 – see **(e) below**). If expenditure is funded by borrowing, it is still treated as having been incurred, although interest on the borrowing is allowed as a business expense and not as part of the capital cost (*Ben-Odeco Ltd v Powlson* (1978)).

It is specifically provided by s 25 that expenditure on alterations to an existing building incidental to the installation of plant or machinery is treated as expenditure on plant or machinery. *In J D Wetherspoon plc v HMRC* [2012] it was held that this could apply to apportioned preliminary expenditure preparatory to alteration of a building incidental to the installation of plant, provided the cost of the alterations themselves was eligible expenditure. In the latter category fell partitions around toilets in a pub but the test excluded easy-wipe tiles in the pub's kitchen.

Where plant and machinery is moved from one site to another, the cost of removal and re-erection, if not allowed as an expense, may be treated as expenditure on plant and machinery for capital allowances. Where plant and machinery is demolished and replaced, the net cost of demolition is treated as expenditure on the replacement plant and machinery. If the plant and machinery is not replaced, the demolition cost is treated as qualifying expenditure for the period in which it is incurred (s 26).

Where someone brings into a trade plant and machinery that has been given to him, the plant and machinery is treated as having been bought at that time for its open market value (s 14). The same applies where plant and machinery that has previously been used other than for trading purposes is brought into a trade, except that if the cost is less than market value, the cost figure is substituted (or, for connected persons transactions, the cost to the connected person if less) (s 13).

Where a building is constructed and plant and machinery is installed therein, it will be necessary to apportion ancillary expenses such as professional fees of architects, surveyors and engineers and overhead costs between the building and the plant. Since such expenses often form a significant part of the cost, it is important to ensure that the allocation is appropriate and supported by the facts.

Certain expenditure that would not otherwise qualify as expenditure on plant is specifically treated as such, namely:

- Expenditure on adding thermal insulation to a building (s 28).
- Expenditure on safety at sports grounds (ss 30 to 32).
- Expenditure on security assets, such as alarm systems and bullet-proof windows, to improve the personal security of those under *special* threat, eg from terrorists (s 33).

In all these cases, the disposal value in respect of such expenditure is treated as nil (s 63).

Expenditure on integral features (as defined) qualifies as expenditure on plant and machinery (see above) (s 33A).

Conversely, expenditure on plant or machinery is not qualifying expenditure if incurred for leasing under a long-funding lease (s 34A).

If a trader other than a finance lessor acquires plant and machinery on hire purchase, the full capital cost is treated as incurred as soon as the asset is brought into use (s 67). The hire purchase charges are a revenue expense allowed over the term of the contract. Where plant and machinery is acquired under a lease, except for long-funding leases it is the lessor and not the lessee who is entitled to the allowances, whether the lease is an operating lease or a finance lease. Special anti-avoidance provisions apply to finance leases (see **Example C8 part A (a)**).

Where a third party (for example, the Government, or a local authority) makes a contribution or subsidy towards cost, that amount is excluded from the qualifying expenditure (subject to certain exceptions) (s 532). Where such contributions are paid by traders or investors, the payer can claim allowances even though he does not strictly have an interest in the asset (ss 537–541).

## Date expenditure treated as incurred

Section 5 provides that expenditure is deemed to be incurred on the date on which the obligation to pay becomes unconditional, but if any part of the payment is not due until more than four months after that date, that part of the expenditure is regarded as incurred on the due date of payment. The due date of payment is also substituted where the unconditional obligation to pay is earlier than normal commercial usage and the sole or main benefit is that expenditure would be treated as incurred in an earlier chargeable period. The date when the obligation to pay becomes unconditional depends on the terms of the contract. It will usually be either the invoice date or the delivery date. Where ownership is transferred in one chargeable period but the obligation becomes unconditional in the first month of the next, the obligation is regarded as having arisen in the earlier period. (This sometimes happens on a large construction contract, where the ownership of the asset is transferred, but the obligation to pay does not become unconditional until, for example, an architect's certificate is presented.)

Where plant and machinery is acquired under a hire purchase contract, the purchaser is treated as owning the asset throughout the period, rather than at the end when the 'option to purchase' is technically paid. The date that the expenditure is treated as incurred is the date that the plant and machinery is brought into use (CAA 2001 s 67(3)).

Note that with the recent changes to AIA , there may be more than one critical date for the acquisition of plant and machinery. The transitional rules mean that there can be two or even three critical dates in an accounting period for capital allowances purposes. (See **Example C9**).

Where expenditure on plant and machinery is incurred prior to the commencement of a trade, it is deemed to be incurred on the first day of the trade (s 12).

## (c) Leased assets

### Allowances on leased assets

Capital allowances on plant and machinery are not normally available unless the plant and machinery belongs to the taxpayer at some time in the relevant period (s 11). Allowances are, however, available for expenditure incurred by a tenant on lifts, heating and ventilating equipment, etc, even though in law such items become landlord's fixtures. Where such fixtures are not bought outright but are acquired on lease, either by a landlord or a tenant, there are provisions to enable the allowances to be given to the equipment lessor, instead of to the landlord or the tenant as the case may be. These provisions are dealt with in more detail in **Example C8**.

### Long funding leases

Since 1 April 2006 expenditure on assets acquired for the purpose of long-funding leasing have ceased to qualify for plant and machinery allowances (s 34A). Instead, the lessee is entitled to be treated as the owner of the expenditure (s 70A).

A long-funding lease is, broadly, a lease longer than seven years. Leases of between five and seven years are long-funding leases if:

(a) they are treated as finance leases under GAAP;

(b) the residual value of the plant or machinery is 5% or less of the market value at the commencement;

(c) the total rentals due in the first year (if less than those due in the second year) are between 90% and 100% of the second year's rentals; and

(d) the total rentals due in any year after the second (if greater than those due in the second year) are between 100% and 110% of the second year's rentals.

Certain leases of plant or machinery for a building or leased with land are excluded (ss 70G, 70R and 70U).

## (d) Rates of allowance on plant and machinery and other important capital allowances

### Rates of capital allowances on plant and machinery

For 2016/17 the rates of capital allowances on plant and machinery are as follows:

- An annual investment allowance (AIA) of up to £200,000, available on all plant and machinery including integral features, but with the exception of cars in relation to expenditure on or after 1 January 2016 (the previous limit was £500,000). The annual amount is available only once to a group of companies and other related parties. Accounting periods spanning 1 January 2016 are subject to transitional rules (see **Examples C8** and **C9**). – A writing down allowance of 18% on assets in the main pool. This can be given in addition to the annual investment allowance on additions which do not qualify for first-year allowances.

- A writing down allowance of 18% on assets in the main pool. This can be given in addition to the annual investment allowance on additions which do not qualify for first-year allowances.

- A writing down allowance of 8% on assets in the special rate pool. This is also available on additions in excess of the annual investment allowance.

– A first year allowance of 100% on new plant and machinery purchased by a business for use wholly in a designated development area within an enterprise zone. However, the plant must be for use in a new business activity not previously carried on before by the purchaser, or in the expansion of the activity. Plant for use in specific types of activity is excluded (s 45M(1)–(6)). The plant cannot be replacement plant, and the allowances are capped under the state aid rules at €125 million for each investment project. The expenditure must be incurred within eight years of the zone being designated.

### Businesses premises renovation allowances (Pt 3A)

Businesses which incur qualifying expenditure on converting or renovating a building (or structure) in a designated area may qualify for an allowance. The building has to have been unused throughout the year before the commencement of the conversion or renovation work (s 360C).

The business is entitled to a 100% 'initial' allowance in the chargeable period in which the expenditure was incurred (s 360G). To the extent that any expenditure is unrelieved, relief of up to 25% of the expenditure may be relieved as a writing-down allowance in subsequent chargeable periods (s 360J).

The allowance is available in respect of expenditure incurred on or after 11 April 2007 until April 2017.

## (e) Capital allowances given to traders and investors

Some capital allowances are given by way of a deduction when calculating the profits of a trade, profession, employment or property business following a claim in a tax return; others are given by a claim made other than in a return (s 3).

### Capital allowances given in taxing a trade etc or property business

Capital allowances given in taxing a trade, profession, employment or property business are treated as an expense of the relevant *chargeable period*, both for individuals and companies. The meaning of chargeable period is as follows (s 6):

Chargeable period – companies:

For a company the chargeable period is the company's accounting period. An accounting period for corporation tax cannot exceed twelve months (CTA 2009 s 10(1)), so a period of account that exceeds 12 months is split into a 12-month chargeable accounting period or periods and the remainder.

Chargeable period – individuals:

For sole traders and partners, the chargeable period is the period of account. A period of account is a period for which accounts are made up. The legislation prescribes rules for overlaps and gaps in periods of account, but in practice these will virtually never arise, because it would be very unusual for a business to produce more than one set of accounts for the same period, or to have a period for which accounts were not made up at all.

If a period of account is longer or shorter than 12 months, annual writing down allowances are proportionately increased or reduced. But if a period of account exceeds 18 months it is regarded for the purpose of computing allowances as being split into successive 12-month periods plus the balance (s 6(6)). The aggregate allowances for the separate periods are then treated as a business expense of the whole period. This prevents undue advantage being gained as a result of the long account, as follows:

For a company – account made up for 26 months to 31.3.2017

If s 6(6) had not been enacted:

| | £ |
|---|---|
| Plant and machinery expenditure brought forward | 100,000 |
| Additions November 2015 (in excess of annual investment allowance) | 20,000 |
| | 120,000 |
| Writing down allowance (18% × 26/12) | 46,800 |
| Written down value carried forward | 73,200 |

Applying s 6(6):

| | £ |
|---|---|
| Plant and machinery expenditure brought forward | 100,000 |
| Additions November 2014 (in excess of annual investment allowance) | 20,000 |
| | 120,000 |
| Writing down allowance 18% for first 12 months | 21,600 |
| | 98,400 |
| Writing down allowance 18% for next 12 months | 17,712 |
| | 80,688 |
| Writing down allowance 18% × 2/12 | 2,421 |
| Written down value carried forward | 78,267 |

The s 6(6) rule restricts the allowances for the period to (£21,600 + £17,712 + £2,421) = £41,733 instead of £46,800.

Where qualifying expenditure is incurred by an employee, or by an individual investor (including landlords of let property), the chargeable period for allowances is the tax year itself. The chargeable period for company investors is the accounting period, as for trading companies. As indicated above, capital allowances in connection with let property (including capital allowances on leased plant and machinery where the lettings are in the course of carrying on a property business) are treated as an expense of the property business (s 248).

## Capital allowances given by a claim made other than in a return

Allowances are given by a separate claim where plant and machinery is leased other than in the course of a 'qualifying activity', for example, a trade or property letting (see **Example C8 explanatory note 1**). Such leasing is referred to in the legislation as 'special leasing' (s 19). Leasing in such circumstances will be extremely rare. For income tax, relief for any such item of let plant and machinery is given against income from similar special leasing activities, unless the *lessee* does not use it for a trade etc throughout the relevant accounting period, in which case the set-off in that period is restricted to the time proportion of the accounting period that the plant and machinery has been leased (s 258). Excess allowances are carried forward to set against similar leasing income in later years. Similar rules apply for corporation tax, except that a claim may be made for excess allowances to be surrendered in a group relief claim (CTA 2010 s 101(1)), or carried back against previous accounting periods for an equivalent period of time to that in which the excess occurred, unless the plant and machinery had not been used by the *lessee* for a trade etc for the whole of the relevant accounting period, in which case the treatment of the allowance is the same as for income tax (ss 259, 260).

## Capital allowances claims

Claims for capital allowances by both traders and investors (other than claims relating to 'special leasing', as indicated above) are made in tax returns. For details see **Example G3**.

## Treatment of excess allowances

Excess allowances relating to a trade form part of a trading loss for which the usual loss reliefs are available.

Where an individual makes a claim for capital allowances on assets used in his employment, then in the unlikely event that the allowances exceed his employment income, the excess is available for a loss claim against other income under ITA 2007 s 64 (s 262 and annex to Explanatory Notes to the Act).

The treatment of excess allowances for which relief is available by a special claim is indicated above.

For individuals carrying on a 'property business', excess allowances form part of a UK property business loss. A claim may be made, for the tax year of loss or the following tax year, to set an amount equal to the capital allowances included in the loss against total income (ITA 2007 s 118). This set-off, however, is subject to the rules on capping income tax claims which will cap the loss claim at £50,000 or 25% of the claimant's gross income for the year. (See **Example E1** for more details). The time limit for the claim is one year from 31 January following the end of the tax year. Any loss not relieved in this way is carried forward against future rent income. Losses arising from claiming Business Premises Renovation Allowance are not subject to the cap.

A corporate investor's capital allowances are similarly incorporated within the company's UK property business loss but no separate claim relating to excess allowances may be made. Relief for a company's UK property loss is given against the total profits of the same accounting period. A claim may be made (within two years after the end of the accounting period) for any remaining loss to be surrendered to another company in the same group under the group relief provisions (see **Example K1**). Otherwise it is carried forward to set against the *total* profits of later accounting periods.

Companies (but not unincorporated traders) are entitled to tax credits in respect of trading losses that arise, to the extent that they relate to the obtaining of first-year allowances in respect of expenditure on energy-saving plant or machinery (s 45A) or environmentally-beneficial plant or machinery (s 45H). The rules apply only until 31 March 2018. The tax credits equal 19% of the surrenderable loss subject to a cap, being the higher of the company's PAYE and NICs payments for the chargeable period and £250,000 (CAA 2001 Sch A1).

## (f) Connected persons – definition

The basic definition of connected persons in ITA 2007 s 993 (for income tax) and CTA 2010 s 1122 (corporation tax) covers close family, trustees, partners, and companies one of which controls the other or under common control. Close family means spouse, relatives, and relatives' spouses and civil partners (relative being brother, sister, ancestor or lineal descendant). As far as business partners are concerned, however, s 993(4) (or s 1122) provides that partners are *not* connected with fellow partners and their spouses/civil partners and relatives in relation to acquisitions or disposals of partnership assets pursuant to genuine commercial arrangements. An expanded definition of connected persons is used in relation to *plant and machinery* in s 266, however, which brings partnership transfers within its scope.

### Effect on plant and machinery allowances

First-year allowances and the annual investment allowance (see **Example C8 explanatory note 2**) are not available on assets acquired from a connected person (s 217).

When plant and machinery is disposed of, the disposal value to be brought into account is normally the net sale proceeds, except that it cannot exceed the original cost (or, where plant has been transferred between connected persons, the highest price paid by any of the connected persons – ss 61 and 62). Where, however, the plant and machinery is sold for less than its open market value, open market value is substituted unless the buyer's expenditure will be taken into account for capital allowances or there will be a benefit taxable on an employee under the benefits code (ss 61, 63(1)). Normal intra-group transfers can therefore be made at the price paid on the transfer if the companies so wish, but there is no provision to use written down value.

Where a *trade* is transferred between connected persons (as defined in s 266 and ITA 2007 s 993 and CTA 2010 s 1122), the disposal value for plant and machinery is the open market value, but first-year allowances are not available (s 265(4)). An election may, however, be made within two years of the transfer for a deemed disposal value such as gives no balancing allowance or balancing charge. The transferor then gets no allowances in the period of transfer, and the transferee stands in the transferor's shoes as regards allowances and balancing charges (ss 266, 267). The main instances when this applies are on incorporation of a business, or on a transfer of trade between companies in the same group (but see below under *Reconstructions* where there is 75% common ownership). Partnership changes are not treated as a cessation of the business, so the capital allowances computation is not affected.

There are special rules affecting the availability of the Annual Investment Allowance for businesses which are 'associated', as defined by the AIA rules. See **Example C9**.

### Effect on other allowances

Where property other than plant and machinery is transferred between connected persons, or between bodies one of whom controls the other or controlled by the same persons, the property is treated as having been sold at open market value (ss 567, 568). An election may however, be made not later than two years after the transfer, for the transfer of industrial and enterprise zone buildings, hotels and research and development assets to be treated as made at written down value, so that balancing adjustments do not have to be made (s 569). This is relevant, for example, where a business is incorporated, or where assets are transferred from one group company to another.

### Reconstructions

The above provisions relating to plant and machinery and other property transferred between connected persons are not relevant where a trade is transferred from one company to another, and at some time within one year before and two years after the transfer, the same persons own three quarters or more of the trade. This is treated by CTA 2010 Part 22 Chapter 1 as a reconstruction of a company without a change of ownership. As far as the capital allowances computation for the period of transfer is concerned, first-year allowances on plant and machinery are claimed by whoever incurred the expenditure and balancing adjustments are made on the company carrying on the trade at the time of the disposal. Writing down allowances are split on a time basis. CTA 2010 s 944 also provides for trading losses to be carried forward into the successor company, subject to anti-avoidance provisions in CTA 2010 s 945 if the successor company does not take over the predecessor's unpaid liabilities.

### Tax avoidance schemes

Where a business enters into artificial transactions which depress the market value of an asset prior to its sale to a connected person then the balancing allowance on disposal is blocked. However, the acquirer can claim allowances only on the reduced price. This provision applies in relation to any balancing event where there is a tax avoidance motive to the transactions.

## Explanatory Notes

*Chargeable periods*

(1) For detailed notes on chargeable periods for capital allowances see **part (b)** of this Example and for the allowances for plant and machinery in detail, including the annual investment allowance, see **Examples C7, C8** and **C9**. For provisions on disclaiming capital allowances see **Examples** C7 and C8.

(2) Capital allowances for individuals relate to the period of account, and writing down allowances are proportionately reduced or increased if the period of account is less than or more than 12 months, subject to special rules for periods exceeding 18 months (see **part (b)**) and for finance lessors (see **Example C8 part (a)**).

# Question

All figures in the following examples are shown net of VAT.

(a) AB is a long established trader making up accounts annually to 30 September. Using the following information relating to the years to 30 September 2015 and 2016, show the capital allowances claimable on the plant and machinery main pool for 2015/16 and 2016/17.

| | £ |
|---|---|
| Pool written down value brought forward at 30.9.14 | 150,000 |

Disposal proceeds totalled £15,000 in the year to 30 September 2015 and £9,500 in the year to 30 September 2016.

| | *Additions* £ |
|---|---|
| Year to 30 September 2015 – | |
| General plant (November 2014) | 80,000 |
| Computer (June 2015) | 37,000 |
| Year to 30 September 2016 – | |
| General plant (October 2015) | 33,000 |
| Van (May 2016) | 28,000 |

(b) Margaret was made redundant by Hi Fi plc on 31 March 2014. On 1 May 2014 she registered for VAT and commenced a trade as a producer and distributor of musical records and tapes. Her first accounts covered the seventeen months to 30 September 2015 and accounts were made up annually to 30 September thereafter.

Capital expenditure on and disposals of business assets up to 30 September 2016 were as follows:

| | |
|---|---|
| 9 April 2014 | Jaguar 3.0L car costing £17,400 ($CO_2$ emissions 224g/km). Business use has been provisionally agreed at 70%. |
| 1 May 2014 | Office fixtures and fittings and mixing deck costing £28,000. |
| 2 November 2015 | Installation of computerised musical and recording equipment costing £30,000. |
| 23 March 2016 | Video equipment costing £35,000. |
| 28 March 2017 | Computer costing £7,000. |
| 1 April 2018 | Computer used as a music design system costing £25,000. |
| 4 June 2019 | New mixing deck costing £8,000. This amount was after deducting a part-exchange allowance of £2,000 for a mixing deck bought in May 2014 for £2,800. |

Prepare capital allowances computations for the first two accounting periods, assuming Margaret wishes to claim allowances as early as possible, and indicate how relief will be given. State any elections required and the time limit by which they should be made.

(c) Calculate the optimum capital allowances claims for the relevant income tax year or chargeable accounting period, in respect of the following businesses.

If any options or elections are available these should be indicated and explained.

(i) Falstaff is a single man entitled to a personal allowance of £11,000 in 2016/17. For the year ended 30 November 2015 his adjusted business profits before capital allowances were £11,910.

The written down value brought forward of assets on which capital allowances are claimed was £10,500.

On 7 March 2016 he purchased new plant costing £8,000.

He has no income other than from the business.

(ii) B Wise Ltd, a manufacturing company, has adjusted profits (before capital allowances) of £80,000 for its accounts year ended 31 December 2016.

The written down value of the capital allowances pool as at 1 January 2016 was £42,500.

In the year ended 31 December 2016:

| | |
|---|---|
| 1 January 2016 | Purchased new plant costing £142,500 |
| 1 March 2016 | Sold plant for £6,000 (it had cost £7,500) |

B Wise Ltd has a single subsidiary company and this company has incurred a trading loss in the corresponding accounting period which results in group relief being available of £42,800. The subsidiary is not able to carry back the loss and is not expected to trade profitably for some years to come. No AIA claim has been, or will be made, by the subsidiary company.

(d) C and D had been in business for many years, making up accounts annually to 31 January and sharing profits 3:1. The following information relates to their plant and machinery in the two years ended 31 January 2016 and 2017:

Written down values brought forward at 1.2.15:

| | | £ |
|---|---|---|
| Main pool | | 47,000 |
| Car used by C (Purchased June 2010, emissions 157 g/km) | | 5,600 |
| Car used by D purchased 2008 | | 21,000 |
| Disposal proceeds during period: | | |
| March 2015 Van (original cost £7,500) | | 3,500 |
| October 2015 Car used by works manager (purchased 2010, emissions 138 g/km) | | 4,000 |
| April 2016 C's car | | 6,500 |
| Additions during period: | | |
| March 2015 | Replacement van | 20,000 |
| October 2015 | Car to replace that used by works manager; $CO_2$ emissions 125 g/km | 14,500 |
| July 2015 | New fixtures (qualifying for main pool) | 55,000 |
| January 2016 | Plant (main pool) | 18,000 |
| March 2016 | Replacement car for C; $CO_2$ emissions 157 g/km | 23,000 |

The partners' cars were used privately to the extent of one third. The works manager's car was used one quarter privately.

An amount of £1,200 relating to an electric sign bought in May 2016 had been disallowed in computing trading profit.

(i) Compute the maximum capital allowances available for 2015/16 and 2016/17.

(ii) Without making computations, state what the position would be if the motor cars were owned personally by C and D.

Comment on the treatment of capital allowances for partnerships.

(e) B Green (London) Ltd, a trading company, has adjusted profits (before capital allowances) of £15,000 for its accounting year ended 31 March 2017. The company does not have any associated companies. The written down value of the capital allowances plant pool at 1 April 2016 was £6,400. On 1 May 2016 the company purchased a new car costing £14,000 with a carbon dioxide emissions figure of 72 g/km.

Show the optimum claim for capital allowances for the year to 31 March 2017.

# Answer

## (a) AB – Capital Allowances Computation 2015/16 and 2016/17

| | | *Main pool* | *Total allowances* |
|---|---|---|---|
| | | £ | £ |
| *2014/16 (1.10.14 to 30.9.15)* | | | |
| Written down value brought forward | | 150,000 | |
| Additions – Computer & plant | 117,000 | | |
| AIA* | (117,000) | | 117,000 |
| Disposals | | (15,000) | |
| | | 135,000 | |
| WDA at 18% | | (24,300) | 24,300 |
| | | 110,700 | 141,300 |
| *2016/17 (1.10.15 to 30.9.16)* | | | |
| Additions – (general plant and van) | 61,000 | | |
| AIA** | (61,000) | | 61,000 |
| Disposals | | (9,500) | |
| | | 101,200 | |
| WDA 18% | | (18,216) | 18,216 |
| Written down value carried forward | | 82,984 | 79,216 |

* The maximum AIA for the year ended 30 September 2015 is £500,000.

* The maximum AIA for the year ended 30 September 2016 is as follows:

92/366 × £500,000 + 274/366 × £200,000 = £275,410

Of this amount, a maximum of £149,727 applies to expenditure on or after 1 January 2016. The restriction does not affect the spend in this period as the allowance is so substantial.

## (b) Margaret – capital allowances computations

| | *Main pool* | *Jaguar (30% private)* | | *Total allowances* |
|---|---|---|---|---|
| | £ | £ | | £ |
| *Period to 30 September 2015* | | | | |
| Purchases 9.4.14, 1.5.14 | 28,000 | 17,400 | | |
| AIA* | (28,000) | | | 28,000 |
| WDA (8% x 17/12) | | (1,972) | × 70% = | 1,381 |
| WDV | Nil | 15,428 | | 29,381 |
| *Year to 30 September 2016* | | | | |

| | | *Main pool* | *Jaguar (30% private)* | | *Total allowances* |
|---|---|---|---|---|---|
| | | £ | £ | | £ |
| Qualifying for AIA | 107,000 | | | | |
| AIA** | (105,000) | 2,000 | | | 105,000 |
| Disposal 4.6.15 | | (2,000) | | | |
| WDA 8% | | | (1,234) | × 70% = | 864 |
| | | Nil | 14,194 | | 105,864 |

* The maximum AIA for the period ended 30 September 2015 is as follows:

518/365× £500,000 = £709,589

** the maximum AIA for the year ended 30 September 2016 is as follows:

Of this amount, a maximum of £149,727 applies to expenditure on or after 1 January 2016. This does not restrict the allowances available as it is so large in relation to the expenditure incurred.

There is no point in de-pooling the computer as a short life asset, as the full cost has been allowed through AIA.

The capital allowances will be deducted as trading expenses in arriving at the trading profit or loss of each accounting period. Assuming Margaret makes profits, the profits will be charged to tax as follows:

| | | |
|---|---|---|
| 2014/15 | Profit from 1.5.14 to 5.4.15 | = 11/17 × 1st profit |
| 2015/16 | Profit from 1.10.14 to 30.9.15 | = 12/17 × 1st profit |
| | Overlap profits 1.10.14 to 5.4.15 (6 months) | |
| 2016/17 | Profit for year to 30.9.16 | |

The effect of the overlapping income tax basis periods for 2014/15 and 2015/16 is that over the two years relief will be given for 23/17 of the capital allowances of £29,381 = £39,751. The extra relief of £10,370 is, however, reflected in a similar reduction in the overlap relief available in respect of the six months to 5 April 2015.

## (c)

(i) **Falstaff – 2016/17**

| | £ |
|---|---|
| Falstaff's taxable profits are | 11,910 |
| and he has a personal allowance of | (11,000) |
| which leaves him with income unabsorbed of | £910 |

He should therefore claim capital allowances for 2016/17 of £910 only, in order to reduce his income to the point where it is fully absorbed by his personal allowance (see **explanatory note 5**).

*Capital allowances computation for year to 30 November 2016*

| | *Pool* | *Total Allowances* |
|---|---|---|
| | £ | £ |
| WDV brought forward at 1 December 2015 | 10,500 | |
| Additions 7 March 2015 (AIA not claimed) | 8,000 | |
| | 18,500 | |
| Writing down allowance 18% × £18,500 = £3,330) restricted to | (910) | 910 |
| WDV carried forward to account commencing 1 December 2016 | 17,590 | |

Alternatively Falstaff could consider leaving some profits within the tax charge at 20% (plus 9% Class 4 national insurance). This would give a tax saving (at the cost of a cash-flow disadvantage) if he is likely to be paying tax in the near future at 40% plus Class 4 contributions of 2%. This Example ignores the impact of tax credits.

A variation would be to claim AIA of 100% restricted to £910 with no WDA. The tax savings would be the same.

**B Wise Ltd – Chargeable accounting period to 31 December 2016**

| | £ |
|---|---|
| B Wise Ltd has profits before capital allowances of | 80,000 |
| against which group relief is available of | 42,800 |
| which would leave unabsorbed profits of | 37,200 |

The capital allowances claim should therefore be restricted to this figure (see **explanatory notes 5 and 6**). The computation will be as follows:

| | | *Pool* | *Total Allowances* |
|---|---|---|---|
| | | £ | £ |
| WDV brought forward at 1 January 2016 | | 42,500 | |
| Additions | 142,500 | | |
| AIA (claim restricted to taxable profits) | 37,200 | | 37,200 |
| | | 105,300 | |
| | | 147,800 | |
| Sale proceeds | | (6,000) | |
| Writing down allowance not claimed | | 141,800 | |
| WDV carried forward at 31 December 2016 | | 141,800 | |

## (d) C and D

(i) **Capital Allowances Computations**

| | | *Main pool* | *C's first car (private use)* | | *C's second car (private use)* | | *D's car (private use)* | | *Total allowances* |
|---|---|---|---|---|---|---|---|---|---|
| | | £ | £ | | £ | | £ | | £ |
| B/f 1.2.15 | | 47,000 | 5,600 | | | | 21,000 | | |
| **2015/16** | | | | | | | | | |
| Additions qualifying for AIA | | | | | | | | | |
| Van Mar 2015 | 20,000 | | | | | | | | |
| Fixtures Jul 2015 | 55,000 | | | | | | | | |
| Plant Jan 16 | 18,000 | | | | | | | | |
| | 93,000 | | | | | | | | |
| AIA* | (91,986) | | | | | | | | 91,986 |
| | | 1,014 | | | | | | | |
| Additions not qualifying for AIA — cars | | 14,500 | | | | | | | |
| Disposals | | | | | | | | | |
| Van | | (3,500) | | | | | | | |
| Car | | (4,000) | | | | | | | |
| | | 55,014 | | | | | | | |
| WDA 18% | | (9,903) | | | | | | | 9,903 |
| | | | (1,008) | 2/3 | | | | | 672 |
| | | | | | | (Max) | (3,000) | 2/3 | 2,000 |
| | | | | | | | | | 104,561 |
| C/f to 2016/17 | | 45,111 | 4,592 | | | | 18,000 | | |
| 2016/17 | | | | | | | | | |
| Additions qualifying for AIA | 1,200 | | | | | | | | |
| AIA* | (1,200) | | | | | | | | 1,200 |
| Additions not qualifying for AIA | | | | | 23,000 | | | | |
| Disposal | | | (6,500) | | | | | | |
| Balancing charge | | | 1,908 | 2/3 | | | | BC | (1,272) |
| WDA 18% | | (8,120) | | | | | | | 8,120 |
| | | | | | | Max | (3,000) | 2/3 | 2,000 |
| WDA 8% | | | | | (1,840) | 2/3 | | | 1,227 |
| C/f to 2017/18 | | 36,991 | | | 21,160 | | 15,000 | | 11,275 |

* Although very substantial amounts of AIA apply in this period, the transitional rule as the limit reduced from £500,000 to £200,000 affects the partnership. While the overall limit for the year ended 31 January 2016 is substantial There is a restriction in relation to expenditure for the month of January 2016, where the maximum AIA on expenditure in that month would be 31/365 x £200,000 = £16,986, so the expenditure of £18,000 does not attract full AIA.

The capital allowances as computed will be deducted from the taxable profits, the balancing charge will be added to the profits, and the resulting amount will be divided three quarters to C and one quarter to D.

(ii) If instead of the motor cars being partnership assets they had been owned personally by C and D, then the allowances on them would have been computed separately but still claimed by the partnership. They would not have been taken into account in computing the partnership profit divisible between the partners in the profit sharing ratio but would instead have been deducted separately from each partner's profit share. The total capital allowances, including those on the partners' cars, would be shown on the partnership self-assessment tax return and the share of profits after capital allowances (both partnership and individual) on the partnership statement. The net figure is then transferred to the tax returns of C and D respectively. For example, in 2015/16 the adjusted profit of the year to 31 January 2016 would be reduced by AIA and the writing down allowances on the main pool totalling £101,889, the balance being split three quarters to C and one quarter to D. D's share would then be reduced by his capital allowances of £2,000 and C's share would be reduced by net allowances of £672.

(iii) Partnership capital allowances are treated as a trading expense of a period of account and are deducted in arriving at taxable profits. Partners are taxed separately on their shares of the profit as if it had arisen from a separate individual trade. Allowances on assets that are partnership assets reduce the overall profit and allowances relating to a partner's own property reduce his share of the profit as indicated in **(ii)** above, but in both cases the allowances must be claimed in the partnership return and cannot be claimed separately by an individual partner.

(e)

(i) **B Green (London) Ltd – Chargeable accounting period to 31 March 2017**

| *Capital allowances computation* | | *Main pool* | *Total Allowances* |
|---|---|---|---|
| WDV brought forward at 1 April 2016 | | 6,400 | |
| Additions | 14,000 | | |
| First year allowance 100% | (14,000) | | 14,000 |
| WDA at 18% — restricted to | | (1,000) | 1,000 |
| WDV carried forward at 31 March 2017 | | 5,400 | 15,000 |

## Explanatory Notes

*Basis period for capital allowances*

(1) Capital expenditure on plant and machinery is taken into account according to the chargeable period in which it is incurred (CAA 2001 ss 2 and 6). Capital expenditure incurred before a trade starts is treated as incurred on the first day of trading, as with Margaret's expenditure in April 2014 prior to commencing trading in May 2014 in **part (b)** of the Example (CAA 2001 s 12).

See **Example C6 part (b)** for detailed notes on the chargeable period rules. Where a period of account exceeds 12 months but does not exceed 18 months, writing down allowances are proportionately increased, as shown in **part (b)** of the Example.

(2) For a further detailed illustration of the application of the plant and machinery provisions and detailed notes on other aspects, including the provisions for allocating assets to pools, the treatment of short life and long life assets and the availability of 100% first-year allowance for low emission cars see **Example C8**.

*Rates of writing-down allowances*

(3) Writing-down allowances are given at an annual rate of 18% for assets in the 'main pool'. For cars with emissions of more than 130 g/km and long life assets and integral features the rate is 8%. For more detail on these types of asset see **Example C8**.

*Small pools*

(4) Pool balances of £1,000 or less are permitted to be written off immediately rather than reduced proportionately until the cessation of a business. The £1,000 limit is tested after accounting for additions and disposals for the period — that is, just at the point when the writing down allowance would be calculated. This applies only in respect of the main (18%) pool and the special rate (8%) pool.

The £1,000 limit is proportionately increased or reduced in cases of longer or shorter chargeable periods or where the qualifying activity has not been carried on for the whole of the chargeable period. CAA 2001 s 56A.

*Capital allowances claims and disclaims*

(5) Both individuals and companies must make a specific claim for capital allowances, claims being made in tax returns (CAA 2001 s 3). Where the individual or company does not wish to claim all the plant and machinery allowances they are entitled to, the claim may be restricted to the amount required (CAA 2001 ss 52(4) and 56(5)). Allowances may be left unclaimed to avoid wasting personal allowances or other reliefs, as shown in **part (c)** of the Example. The availability of first-year allowances on certain expenditure provides another reason for partial claims, as shown in **part (d)** of the Example. If there would otherwise be a balancing charge, all or the appropriate part of expenditure on which a first-year allowance is available may instead be included in the pool to cover a balancing charge (CAA 2001 s 58(5)).

(6) Under income tax self-assessment capital allowances are subject to the same time limits as other entries in a return, ie any amendment must normally be made within 12 months after the 31 January filing date for the return.

Companies are able to make, vary and withdraw capital allowances claims up to two years after the end of their accounting period.

For detailed notes on claims procedures see **Example G3**.

(7) If B Wise Ltd in **part (c)(ii)** of the Example had claimed the full available allowances of £149,070 (AIA of £142,500 plus WDA of £6,570) its profits would have been reduced to a loss of (£80,000 – £149,070 =) £(69,070) and group relief restricted accordingly. The subsidiary company would then have been left with unrelieved losses of £42,800 to carry forward, with no prospect of early relief in view of its anticipated unprofitable trading forecast. B Wise Ltd would also have unrelieved losses of £69,070 to carry forward.

*Private use*

(8) Note in **part (d)** of the Example that the private use restriction for the use of cars applies only to the cars used by the partners. Private use of assets by *employees* does not require any restriction of the capital allowances. The employees are charged on the benefit under the benefit in kind legislation in ITEPA 2003. This applies to the manager's car.

*Business use of partner's own assets*

(9) Where partners own assets personally and use them in the business, the same capital allowances are available as if the partnership owned them (CAA 2001 s 264), but the allowances are deducted in arriving at each partner's taxable profit, as indicated in **part (d)(ii)** of the Example.

*Cars*

(10) For cars purchased prior to 1 April 2009 (6 April 2009 for income tax), cars costing in excess of £12,000 are put into single asset pools. The purpose of this pool was to limit the writing-down allowance each year to £3,000.

Although the main rate of writing-down allowance has been reduced to 18%, the restriction of £3,000 is unchanged.

One unexpected advantage of single asset pooling for cars is that balancing allowances might be available on the disposal of a vehicle. This is not available for assets in the main pool until a cessation of the qualifying activity.

(11) The £12,000 cost limit does not apply to qualifying hire cars or cars which are entitled to 100% first-year allowances (s 74(2)).

(12) Cars purchased on or after 1 April 2009 (6 April 2009 for income tax) are subject to the capital allowance regime under which allowances are determined by $CO_2$ emissions.

- New cars with emissions of no more than 75g/km (95g/km before 1 April 2015 and 110g/km before 1 April 2013) are subject to 100% first-year allowance, the net WDV of nil being treated as added to the main pool unless the car has private use in an income tax business. This emissions limit is due to change to 50g/km in April 2018.

- Cars with emissions of no more than 130g/km (including second hand low emission cars) are added to the main pool where they attract 18% WDA. The emissions limit for the main pool was 160 g/km before 1 or 6 April 2013.

- Cars with emissions of more than 130g/km are added to the special rate pool where they attract 8% WDA.

- Cars with private use in income tax businesses will remain subject to the single asset pooling rules and will attract WDA based on their emissions.

The main consequence of this new regime is that balancing allowances are no longer available on cars added to the pools. The self-employed and partners with private use adjustments will find that they benefit from accelerated allowances under the new regime, but companies will suffer significant delays in obtaining the benefit of expenditure on cars.

*Annual investment allowance*

(13) Businesses incurring capital expenditure on plant or machinery are given an annual investment allowance (AIA). Subject to some exceptions (eg expenditure on cars), the first £200,000 of expenditure on plant and machinery in any year is immediately relievable. For expenditure incurred between 1 April 2014 and 31 December 2015 the limit was £500,000, and from 1 January 2016 the limit will be £200,000. Periods spanning the date of change are subject to transitional arrangements which are illustrated in the case of AB in **part (a)** of the Example and CD in **part (d)** of the Example. Groups of companies have only a single AIA allocated to the group as a whole which may be claimed as desired. The allowance is discussed further in **Examples C8** and **C9** where there is a detailed explanation of the transitional rules illustrated in this Example.

*Value added tax*

(14) Value added tax is not taken into account as part of the expenditure for capital allowances if it is recoverable through the VAT system (see **Example C2 explanatory note 16**). Similarly, output VAT on disposals is excluded from disposal proceeds. VAT on cars is not normally recoverable, and in that event it forms part of the cost for capital allowances, as shown in this Example. On the sale of a car VAT is not normally due but there are special rules for second-hand car dealers and in some other circumstances.

Special rules also apply for items of plant costing £2,000 or more (VAT inclusive) where the trader has elected to use the small business flat rate scheme. In those cases VAT input tax is recoverable and capital allowances are only due on the net cost. On the sale of these items output tax at 20% is payable but only the net sale proceeds are included in the capital allowances pool. For capital assets costing less than £2,000, under the flat rate scheme both output and input VAT-inclusive figures are used in the capital allowances computation. The only exception to this rule is where the asset was purchased before the trader joined the scheme in which case the VAT-exclusive price is deducted from the pool on sale. (Where the VAT-exclusive price is shown in the capital allowances pool, the sale is not included in the turnover for the purposes of the flat rate scheme and the output tax at 20% must be accounted for separately.) The Flat rate scheme for VAT is examined in detail in **Example M2**.

# Question

## A.

Alley plc, a company that qualifies as medium-sized, carries on a trade of multiple retailing. The company has traded for many years making up accounts to 31 December annually.

The company acquired some lorries under a finance lease for a two year period, 1 September 2016 to 31 August 2018. The lease rental payments are £485,000 per annum and the lorries have been capitalised in the accounts at £750,000, that amount being the cost of the lorries to the lessor company on 1 September 2016. Alley plc has charged depreciation on the lorries and the interest element of the rental payments in its accounts. The lessor company makes up accounts to 30 November annually.

The company made the following purchases and sales of plant and machinery in the two years ended 31 December 2016:

- 4 January 2016 purchased computer equipment costing £180,000.
- 12 January 2016 purchased three vans for £90,000.
- 21 March 2016 purchased a desk and office furniture for £76,000.
- 7 June 2016 purchased a motor car for use by the chairman for £16,000; the $CO_2$ emissions were 210 g/km.
- 19 June 2016 sold two motor cars for £3,000 each, which had previously cost £9,500 each in 2005.
- 31 March 206 purchased shop fittings for £45,000.
- 14 May 2017 disposed of the car purchased for use by the chairman for £7,000. It was replaced by the acquisition on lease of a new Jaguar with a retail value of £28,000 and $CO_2$ emissions of 174 g/km, on which lease payments of £6,500 were made in 2017. These were charged in arriving at the operating profit.

In October 2017 the company spent £570,000 on repairs to its electrical systems. It would have cost £750,000 to replace the systems.

The written down value at 1 January 2015 for the main pool was £104,100. There was no balance on the special rate pool.

(a) Show the treatment of the leased lorries and the leased Jaguar car for Alley plc and also indicate the capital allowances treatment of the lorries for the lessor company.

(b) Compute the capital allowances on plant and machinery for the two years ended 31 December 2017, assuming that the maximum reliefs are claimed as early as possible.

## B

EF Limited regularly purchases assets which are expected to have a relatively short life. During the year ended 31 December 2013 the company purchases two such assets for £20,000 each. One of the assets was not expected to be sold within its writing down period of 8 years, and so was added to the main pool. The second was to be sold within that time period, and therefore was de-pooled. In the event both of the assets were sold for scrap for £2,000 in April 2018. Assume that the assets attract writing down allowance at 18% throughout the period and that the company has a substantial balance on the main pool.

Show the capital allowances given on each from 2013 to 2018.

# Answer

## A. Alley plc

### (a) *Tax treatment of leased items*

**Lorries under finance lease**

The lorries acquired by Alley plc under the finance lease, although capitalised in the company's accounts, are not treated as purchased for tax purposes. Instead the rental payments of £485,000 per annum are treated as a trading expense. The payments must be allocated to periods of account under the accruals concept. Where the treatment under FRS 102 section 20 has been applied, Revenue Statement of Practice (SP3/91) permits the charge to comprise a mixture of the finance charge element and the accounting depreciation charge.

Assets acquired on long-funding leases are treated differently (CAA 2001 ss 70A–70YJ). Finance leases are also subject to detailed anti-avoidance provisions (see **explanatory note 22**). As far as the lessor company is concerned, the expenditure of £750,000 on the lorries qualifies for a restricted writing down allowance covering the three-month period from 1 September to 30 November 2016. The legislation puts this into effect by restricting the allowable expenditure in the first period, but the whole of the remaining expenditure goes into the pool at the end of that period, so it is more straightforward to apply the restriction to the writing down allowance. The position is therefore as follows:

**Lessor company's year to 30 November 2016 – relevant entries in plant and machinery pool**

| | £ |
|---|---|
| Cost of lorries 1 September 2016 | 750,000 |
| WDA 18% × 3/12 | 33,750 |
| Written down value carried forward | 716,250 |

**Jaguar car leased for use by chairman**

Alley plc is entitled to a deduction from its profits in respect of the Jaguar car lease payment in the year to 31 December 2017. Since the car emits more than 130g/km, Alley plc cannot deduct the full amount paid of £6,500. The restriction is 15% of the lease payments, so 85% is allowed for tax.

So £975 will be disallowed and £5,525 allowed.

### (b) *Alley plc – Capital allowances on plant and machinery for two years ended 31 December 2017*

| | *Main pool* | *Short life asset computer* | *Special rate (8%) pool* | *Total Allowances* |
|---|---|---|---|---|
| *Yr ended 31.12.2016* | £ | £ | £ | £ |
| WDV bf 1.1.16 | 104,100 | – | – | – |
| Additions qualifying for AIA: | | | | |
| Computer equipment (4.1.16) | | 180,000 | | |

| | | *Main pool* | *Short life asset computer* | *Special rate (8%) pool* | *Total Allowances* |
|---|---|---|---|---|---|
| Vans (12.1.16) | 90,000 | | | | |
| Furniture (21.3.16) | 76,000 | | | | |
| | 166,000 | | | | |
| AIA to 31.12.16 | (20,000) | | (180,000) | | 200,000 |
| Balance to main pool | | 146,000 | | | |
| Additions not qualifying for AIA: | | | | | |
| Car (7.6.16) | | | | 16,000 | |
| Sales proceeds (19.6.16) | | (6,000) | | | |
| | | 244,100 | | | |
| WDA 18% | | (43,938) | | | 43,938 |
| WDA 8% | | | | (1,280) | 1,280 |
| | | 200,162 | Nil | 14,720 | 245,218 |
| *Yr ended 31.12.2017* | | | | | |
| Additions — shop fittings 31.3.17 | | 45,000 | | | |
| Electrical system repairs (October 2016) | 570,000 | | | | |
| Annual investment allowance | (200,000) | | | | 200,000 |
| Balance to special rate pool | | | | 370,000 | |
| Sale proceeds (14.5.17) | | | | (7,000) | |
| | | 245,162 | | 377,720 | |
| WDA 18% | | (44,129) | | | 44,129 |
| WDA 8% | | | | (30,218) | 30,218 |
| WDV cf 31.12.16 | | 201,033 | | 347,502 | 274,347 |

## B. EF Limited – Capital allowances claims for five years to 31 December 2018

| | *Asset 1(de-pooled)* | *Asset 2 (in pool)4* |
|---|---|---|
| *Yr ended 31.12.2013* | £ | £ |
| Additions : April 2013 | 20,000 | 20,000 |
| WDA at 18% | (3,600) | (3,600) |
| | 16,400 | 16,400 |
| *Yr ended 31.12.2014* | | |
| WDA at 18% | (2,952) | (2,952) |
| | 13,448 | 13,448 |
| *Yr ended 31.12.2015* | | |
| WDA at 18% | (2,421) | (2,421) |
| | 11,027 | 11,027 |
| *Yr ended 31.12.2016* | | |
| WDA at 18% | (1,985) | (1,985) |
| | 9,042 | 9,042 |
| *Yr ended 31.12.2017* | | |
| WDA at 18% | (1,628) | (1,628) |

| | *Asset 1(de-pooled)* | *Asset 2 (in pool)4* |
|---|---|---|
| | 7,414 | 7,414 |
| *Yr ended 31.12.2018* | | |
| Disposal proceeds deducted from pool | (2,000) | (2,000) |
| Balancing allowance | 5,414 | |
| WDA at 18% (main pool) | | (975) |
| WDV c/f in main pool | | 4,439 |

# Explanatory Notes

All references in these notes are to CAA 2001 unless otherwise stated.

*Qualifying expenditure and qualifying activities*

(1) For a company, the entitlement to capital allowances depends on qualifying expenditure incurred in the chargeable accounting period. Expenditure on a building preparatory to the installation of plant and machinery counts as expenditure on plant and machinery (s 25). For detailed notes on the expenditure qualifying for relief and the timing of reliefs, including the chargeable period provisions relating to allowances for income tax purposes, see **Example C6.**

Plant and machinery allowances are available to those carrying on 'qualifying activities'. The main examples of qualifying activities are trades, professions, vocations and employments, property letting businesses, including furnished holiday lettings businesses, and special leasing businesses (as to which see **Example C6 part (b)** under *Capital allowances given by a claim made other than in a return*) (s 15). Allowances must be calculated separately for each qualifying activity (s 11).

FA 2006 brought some changes to the availability of capital allowances in respect of leased assets. They apply to leases longer than seven years (in some cases to leases longer than five years). See **explanatory note 22** below.

*Allowances available*

(2) The allowances available are writing down allowances and balancing allowances. In some instances a balancing charge is made to take away allowances previously given. Writing down allowances and balancing allowances and charges are dealt with under a 'pooling' system, as outlined later in these notes.

Although expenditure incurred before a trade starts is normally treated as incurred on the first day of trading (s 12), the actual date of the expenditure is the relevant date for FYAs. Where available, FYAs are given in full regardless of the length of the chargeable period (unless they are not or only partly claimed – see **explanatory note 9**).

From 1 April (6 April, income tax) 2009 the definition of a car was changed to exclude motor cycles and include hire cars (cars used as taxis, daily hire cars and cars leased to the disabled) (s 268A).

(3) From April 2008 the annual investment allowance (AIA) was introduced. More details of the Annual Investment Allowance are in **Examples C7** and **C9** and **explanatory note 7** below.

*Computers*

(4) Computer software is an intangible asset, but it is specifically provided that capital expenditure on licensed software (except where acquired with a view to sub-licensing) and electronically transmitted software qualifies for plant and machinery allowances (s 71). Software is usually either developed 'in house' or acquired on lifetime licence for a particular user or users rather than being purchased outright. If licensed

software is acquired on rental, the rentals are charged against profit over the life of the software. Where a lump sum is paid, HMRC normally takes the view that the cost of software with an expected life of less than two years may be treated as a revenue expense and deducted from profit (BIM35810). Otherwise it will usually be treated as capital expenditure for which plant and machinery allowances may be claimed (under the short life asset rules if appropriate). The treatment of in-house software is broadly similar, being either treated as capital or revenue depending on the expected period of use.

Separate rules apply for companies in relation to intangible assets. Computer software treated as part of the cost of the related hardware is not affected by these rules. Software that is not so treated is dealt with under the intangible assets provisions unless the company makes an election for capital allowances to apply. The election must be made within two years after the end of the accounting period in which the expenditure was incurred. Once made the election is irrevocable. (CTA 2009 s 815). For the detailed provisions on intangible assets see **Example K3**.

*Energy saving and environmentally beneficial plant and machinery*

(5) 100% FYAs are available on new plant and machinery that is energy-efficient (ss 45A–45C) or classified as environmentally beneficial. The FYA is available for qualifying expenditure on qualifying assets and technologies which are either energy or water efficient. Qualifying products are listed on the UK Energy Technology List, which is available on the Internet at https://www.gov.uk/guidance/energy-technology-list . Businesses purchasing relevant products may establish whether the 100% FYA is available by obtaining a certificate from the manufacturers, or alternatively via the website. The list is updated annually. Assets which attract subsidy through Feed in Tariff payments (FIT) are excluded from Enhanced Capital Allowances (ECA) and are treated as special rate assets, attracting 8% WDA.

The rules for fixtures in ss 172 to 204 (see **explanatory note 28**) have been adapted to enable energy service companies to claim the 100% first-year allowances on qualifying energy saving plant and machinery as outlined above where the plant and machinery is provided and becomes a fixture on a client business's premises, and the plant and machinery is operated by the energy service company under an energy services agreement.

Under s 45E, 100% first-year allowances may be claimed for expenditure incurred between 17 April 2002 and 31 March 2018 inclusive on new plant and machinery for gas refuelling stations.

The general exclusion from FYAs of plant for leasing (see **explanatory note 2**) does not apply to plant and machinery for leasing that is energy-saving plant and machinery (s 45A), gas refuelling equipment (s 45E) or environmentally beneficial plant (s 45H).

*Low emission cars*

(6) Expenditure on certain new cars purchased between 17 April 2002 and 31 March 2018 inclusive is eligible for 100% FYAs (s 45D). The eligible cars are those with a carbon dioxide emissions figure of 75g/km or less (95 g/km or less up to 31 March 2015 and 110g/km up to 31 March 2013), and electric cars. Where the car is a bi-fuel car, the rate of FYA is based on the lower of the published emissions figures. 'Car' for this purpose includes a taxi but does not include a motor cycle. The allowance was also available for leasing companies up to 31 March 2013.

Such cars are also excluded from the restrictions relating to cars costing more than £12,000 for those purchased before 1 April 2009 (see **explanatory note 15**).

*Annual investment allowance*

(7) The annual investment allowance (AIA) replaced the first-year allowance regime for small and medium sized enterprises. It is available to all businesses (whatever their size) but will proportionately be of more value to smaller enterprises.

The value of the allowance has changed several times since the regime was introduced in 2008, and each change is accompanied by transitional rules, under which time apportioned allowances are computed for each spanning period, but with further restrictions on those parts of an accounting period that fall either before or after the date of change. The impact of those transitional rules is illustrated in **Example C7**, and the transitional rules are explained in detail in **Example C9**.

The expenditure qualifying for AIA can be expenditure that would otherwise be allocated to either the main pool or to the special rate pool, but the allowance is not available in respect of expenditure on cars.

Given the fact that expenditure is generally written off more slowly in the special rate pool, it would be generally favourable for such the annual investment allowance to be allocated to such expenditure in preference to expenditure qualifying for the main (18%) pool.

See also **Example C9**, in particular where claims are to be made by related businesses.

*Partial claims for allowances*

(8) Individuals and companies *need not claim* the full allowances available on plant and may instead claim the amount which gives the most favourable tax position taking all other circumstances into account (ss 52(4) and 56(5)). The main reason for making partial claims for allowances or waiving claims to allowances is to enable the taxpayer to claim other reliefs or allowances that cannot be claimed in a later period, or where future profits are expected to be taxed at a higher marginal rate.

*Pooling*

(9) Expenditure on plant and machinery is pooled for the purposes of writing down allowances, balancing allowances and balancing charges (s 53). There are three kinds of pool, single asset pools, class pools and the main pool. Where someone carries on more than one qualifying activity, separate pools are required in relation to each activity.

Single asset pools (which contain only one asset) are required for:

(i) A car costing more than £12,000 (other than a low emission car) purchased before 1 April 2009 (6 April for income tax) (s 74) (see **explanatory note 15**).

(ii) A short life asset (s 86) (see **explanatory note 19**).

(iii) An asset used privately by the proprietor (s 206) (see **explanatory note 14**).

Class pools (which may contain more than one asset) are required for:

(i) Long life assets, high emission cars and integral features (see **explanatory note 20**).

(ii) Expenditure on assets leased outside the UK (s 109) (see **explanatory note 27**).

All other qualifying expenditure goes into the main pool.

*Writing down allowances and balancing adjustments*

(10) The calculation of the capital allowances position on the pool depends on whether the disposal proceeds are more than or less than the available qualifying expenditure (s 55), ie the disallowed expenditure brought forward, plus additional qualifying expenditure in the current period (other than expenditure on which FYA is claimed), less any disposal proceeds. (Businesses are not in fact *required* to bring expenditure into the pool in the earliest available period, so that if for example some of the expenditure was omitted in error it could be brought in when the error was discovered.) If the proceeds *exceed* the disallowed expenditure, a balancing charge is made to withdraw the excess allowances (but see **explanatory note 12** re the limit on the disposal proceeds). This may occur either while the business is continuing or on cessation.

Where the proceeds are less than the available expenditure, the available allowance is either a writing down allowance of 18% per annum on the reducing balance method (see **explanatory note 11** re accounting periods of more or less than 12 months), or a balancing allowance if the period is the 'final chargeable period'.

For a single asset pool, the final chargeable period is the period in which the asset is disposed of. For the main pool and class pools the final chargeable period is that in which the qualifying activity is permanently discontinued (s 65), although this is varied slightly for assets leased abroad (see **explanatory note 27**). A balancing allowance does not arise other than in the final chargeable period even if, say, the whole plant in the main pool were destroyed by fire and the compensation fell short of the balance on the pool. In those circumstances, the pool balance after deducting the compensation would continue to attract writing down allowances.

Where a claim for first-year allowance is made, the balance of expenditure (including a nil balance) is strictly not allocated to a pool until (at earliest) the commencement of the following period, unless the asset is also disposed of in the period in which it is acquired. In practice it is sensible to bring the balance of the expenditure into the relevant pool at the end of the period of expenditure, so that it forms part of the opening figure for the next period.

The practical working order in respect of a pool for periods other than the final chargeable period is as follows (although some steps are clearly not relevant for single asset pools):

| | | £ | £ |
|---|---|---|---|
| Written down value (WDV) brought forward | | ? | |
| *Add*: Expenditure qualifying for AIA | ? | | |
| AIA | (?) | | X |
| Balance of expenditure allocated to pool | | ? | |
| *Add:* Expenditure not qualifying for AIA or FYA or on which AIA/FYA not claimed | | ? | |
| *Less:* Disposal proceeds | | (?) | |
| | | X | |
| WDA on X (or balancing charge if X is a negative figure) | | (?) | X |
| Expenditure qualifying for FYA | ? | | |
| FYA | (?) | | X |
| Balance of expenditure allocated to pool | | ? | |
| WDV carried forward | | X | |
| Total allowances | | | X |

In the final chargeable period, if the qualifying activity is discontinued in that period, first-year allowance is not available (see **explanatory note 2**) and there would be a balancing allowance rather than a writing down allowance if X was positive. On a single asset pool, if an asset was disposed of in the period in which it was acquired for less than its cost, there would be a balancing allowance on the shortfall. If it was disposed of in that period for more than cost, it would not be brought into account for capital allowances at all and the capital profit would be dealt with under the capital gains legislation (see **Example L9**).

*Accounting periods of more than or less than 12 months (s 56)*

(11) If a company's chargeable accounting period is less than 12 months the writing down allowance is proportionately reduced.

Under the income tax rules, capital allowances are treated as a trading expense of a period of account, which may be more or less than 12 months. Writing down allowances are proportionately decreased where the accounting period is less than 12 months and increased where the accounting period exceeds 12 months (but there are special rules for accounting periods exceeding 18 months – see **Example C6 part** (e)).

For both companies and individuals, the writing down allowance is proportionately reduced if a qualifying activity has been carried on for only part of the accounting period (s 56).

*Limit on disposal proceeds*

(12) If plant is disposed of for more than its cost, the disposal proceeds brought into the computation are limited to the original value placed into the pool, except when the plant was acquired from a connected person, in which case the limit of disposal proceeds is the highest price paid by one of the connected persons (s 62). For the connected persons rules see **Example C6 part (f)**.

A capital profit is dealt with under the capital gains legislation (see **Example L10**).

*Hire purchase*

(13) Hire purchase does not prevent allowances being given as though there were an outright purchase at the time of the first use of the relevant asset, except for finance lessors (see **explanatory note 21**) (s 67). The cash price is therefore brought in at that time and the subsequent instalments of capital ignored, the interest element being charged in arriving at taxable profit.

*Private use*

(14) Where directors or employees are allowed to use company assets, such as cars, for private purposes, this does not affect the employer's allowances. The employee is charged on the benefit under the benefits code of ITEPA 2003.

It is only where business assets are used partly for private purposes by the *proprietor* of the business (ie by a sole trader or by partners) that the capital allowances are restricted. In these circumstances the asset is kept separate in a single asset pool (s 206). The asset is written down by allowances calculated on the full cost, but only the business fraction is allowed in calculating taxable profits. When the asset is sold there is a final adjustment by way of balancing charge or balancing allowance (again restricted to the business fraction). If more than one asset is used privately then a separate single asset pool is set up for each asset (s 54). For an illustration see **Example C7 part (a)**.

*£12,000+ cars purchased before 1 April / 6 April 2009*

(15) Where a car, other than a low emission car, costs more than £12,000 a single asset pool is set up for it (s 74). 'Car' for this purpose is defined as a mechanically propelled road vehicle (including a motor cycle) other than one primarily suited for carrying goods or a vehicle not commonly used as a private vehicle and unsuitable to be so used. Qualifying hire cars (ie cars normally hired to the same person for less than 30 consecutive days and less than 90 days in any twelve months and cars let to someone receiving the mobility component of disability living allowance or a mobility supplement) are not subject to the £12,000 restriction and they go into the main pool, unless there is private use.

The writing down allowance is restricted to £3,000 per annum and where there is private use (see **explanatory note 14**), to the business fraction of £3,000 (ss 75, 77). Once the written down value falls to £15,000 or less WDAs are calculated at 18% per annum in the usual way, but the car remains in the single asset pool until it is disposed of. There is no limit on a balancing allowance. Cars will remain in a single asset pool for five years after the new rules commence (see below) at which point the car will be moved to the appropriate pool.

*Cars purchased on or after 1 April / 6 April 2009*

(16) Cars are allocated to a pool according to their official $CO_2$ emissions, as follows:

- new cars with emissions of no more than 75g/km are subject to 100% first-year allowance, the net WDV of nil being treated as added to the main pool unless the car has private use in an income tax business; (this reduces on 1 April 2018 this limit reduces to 50g/km).

- cars with emissions of no more than 130g/km (including second hand low emission cars) are added to the main pool where they will attract 18% WDA;

- cars with emissions of more than 130g/km are added to the special rate pool where they will attract 8% WDA;

- cars with private use in income tax businesses will remain subject to the single asset pooling rules and will attract WDA based on their emissions.

No balancing allowances are therefore available on cars in future unless the car is subject to a private use adjustment.

*Leased cars*

(17) For leases entered into on or after 1 April 2009 (6 April for income tax) the lease restriction is simply 15% of the rentals where the emissions of the car exceed 1 g/km. There is no restriction on lease rentals for cars with emissions of up to 130 g/km. The allowable deduction may be further reduced where there is private use as set out in **explanatory note 14**.

Although a hire purchase agreement is an agreement for hire, with an option to purchase, it is expressly provided by ITTOIA 2005 s 49(2) that the hire charge restriction does not apply to a hire purchase agreement under which the option to purchase is exercisable on payment of an amount not exceeding 1% of the retail price of the car when new.

*Short life assets*

(18) Where a trader purchases machinery or plant for use wholly and exclusively for the purposes of the trade, an election may be made to treat the machinery or plant as a short life asset (s 85). The asset is then kept in a single asset pool. The scheme is intended to apply when a trader expects to dispose of an item of machinery or plant at less than its written down value within the 'relevant period' from the year of its acquisition, and it is particularly relevant for assets with a high rate of obsolescence, such as computers. (The normal 18% WDA system takes twelve years to write off approximately 90% of any expenditure.) The relevant period is eight years.

The election for short life asset treatment is to be made by companies within two years after the end of the chargeable period in which the capital expenditure was incurred (or, where the capital expenditure was incurred on different dates, as is the case with the building expenditure preparatory to the installation of the computerised control system in this Example, within two years after the end of the period in which the first expenditure was incurred). For individuals the time limit is one year from 31 January following the tax year in which the relevant accounting period ends. When a short life asset is sold within four years after the end of the period in which the capital expenditure was incurred (or the first capital expenditure if it was incurred on different dates), there is a final adjustment by way of a balancing charge or balancing allowance.

However, if the short life asset is not sold within that time its written down value is transferred to the main pool and thereafter dealt with as if it had never been in a single asset pool.

In part (b) of the Example the computer equipment is treated as a short life asset, in spite of the fact that AIA reduces the cost immediately by a substantial amount. It is very likely that at the end of its life the computer would have minimal value, so the decision to de-pool the asset is unlikely to have negative consequences, such as the crystallisation of a balancing charge on disposal. Nevertheless, careful thought may be needed in practice where AIA is available in full or in part.

For further illustrations of the short life assets provisions see **Example C7 part (b)**.

Short life asset treatment does not apply to machinery or plant otherwise dealt with outside the main pool, as detailed in **explanatory notes 9, 14** and **15** above.

*Long life assets – the special rate pool*

(19) Special rules apply to long life assets (ss 90 to 104). Expenditure on a second-hand asset is included if these rules applied to the vendor in respect of that asset.

Long life assets are those with an expected economic life of 25 years or more. The provisions do not apply to machinery or plant in dwelling houses, retail shops, showrooms, hotels or offices, nor to cars (nor to certain ships and railway assets bought before the end of 2011). There is also a de minimis limit of £100,000 a year (reduced pro rata for companies with associated companies). There are various provisions to prevent the de minimis limit being exploited.

Assets within the provisions are pooled in a separate class pool known as the special rate pool and writing down allowances are presently given at 8% per annum on the reducing balance method. A balancing adjustment does not arise on disposal unless the trade has also ceased.

The special rate pool also includes expenditure on integral features and on cars purchased on or after 1 April 2009 with $CO_2$ emissions of more than 130 g/km (160 g/km before 1 April 2013). Details on integral features are included at **explanatory note 28.**

*Finance leases*

(20) For accounting purposes assets acquired under operating leases are treated as owned by the lessor, whereas assets acquired under finance leases are treated as owned by the lessee. Complex anti-avoidance provisions relating mainly to finance leases are included in ss 213 to 233. These rules have been augmented by Finance Act 2004 with additional restrictions on certain sale/lease and leaseback schemes to prevent double benefits accruing. In addition, FA 2006 introduced rules that ensure that assets acquired on long funding leases qualify for capital allowances in the hands of the lessee rather than the lessor (CAA 2001 ss 70A–70YJ). See below.

The main targets of the legislation are finance leases involving lower rentals with compensating capital payments (the capital sums being taxed at lower rates or possibly not at all, either through indexation allowance or by using a separate leasing company in which the shares are sold rather than the asset), and finance leases with back loaded payments, ie with rents concentrated towards the end of the lease. The provisions align the tax treatment more closely with the recognised accounting treatment. The receipt of a 'major lump sum' is treated as a disposal for capital allowances purposes and the rental income for tax purposes is normally the higher of the actual rent and the earnings recognised in the lessor's commercial accounts.

The first writing down allowance for finance lessors is restricted on a time basis according to the period from the date the expenditure is incurred to the end of the accounting period, as illustrated in **part (a)** of the Example (s 220). Where a finance lessor obtains an asset on hire purchase, he will be entitled to capital allowances only as and when the capital expenditure is incurred, rather than being entitled to allowances on the full capital cost at the outset as indicated in **explanatory note 15** (s 229). There are rules to prevent unused past allowances being transferred to finance lessors through sale and leaseback arrangements (ss 221–228). Provisions also limit the amount of lease rentals that may be deducted by the lessee where there has been a sale or lease followed by a finance leaseback (ss 228A–228G). The term 'finance lease' is defined in s 219 as meaning arrangements which are, according to generally accepted accounting practice, treated as a finance lease or a loan in the books of one or more of the parties.

First-year allowances are not available on plant and machinery for leasing, as indicated in **explanatory note 2.**

FA 2006 introduced some anti-avoidance measures – particularly looking at the sale of lessor companies and the use of losses by leasing partnerships. CAA 2001 s 228K removed the restriction on the disposal value where the lessor is required to bring in a disposal value but remains entitled to some or all of the rentals payable after that time. Even where the limit would not have applied, the disposal value is the actual consideration plus the net present value of these amounts to which the lessor remains entitled.

FA 2008 has further eroded avoidance opportunities by introducing ICTA 1988 s 785A, which is designed to tax certain capital receipts (such as premiums) in connection with plant and machinery leases. FA 2008 led to the consequential repeal of certain aspects of CAA.

For HMRC's interpretation of various aspects of the anti-avoidance rules on finance leases, see the HMRC Capital Allowances manual starting at CA28000.

*Long funding leases*

(21) CAA 2001 ss 70A–70YJ provide an exception to the general tax rule that restricts capital allowances to the legal owner of an asset. The purpose of the rules is to bring closer alignment between the economic effect of a transaction and the tax consequences.

Where the rules apply in respect of an operating lease, the deemed capital expenditure is the market value of the plant or machinery at the beginning of the lease (or, if later, when the asset is first used) (CAA 2001 s 70B).

Where the rules apply in respect of a finance lease, the deemed capital expenditure is the present value of the minimum lease payments plus any unrelievable pre-commencement rentals (CAA 2001 s 70C).

(22) A long funding lease (CAA 2001 s 70G) is a lease which is:

- not a short lease (see below);
- not an excluded lease because of background plant or machinery (ie equipment that one would ordinarily expect to be installed in a building to add functionality to the building (CAA 2001, s 70R)); and
- not excluded because the plant is attached to land but:
  - is not background plant or machinery, and
  - either:
    - is worth no more than 10% of the value of any background plant or machinery, or
    - is worth no more than 5% of the land and buildings (s 70U).

(23) A short lease is:

- one of five years or less in duration, or
- a finance lease:
  - with a lease term of between five and seven years;
  - where the expected implied residual value at the end of the lease is 5% or less than the commencement value;
  - the first-year rentals in the first year are at least 90% of those in the second year; and
  - the rentals in any year after the second year are no more than 10% more than those in the second year (s 70I).

*Leasing plant and machinery together with land and buildings*

(24) Where plant and machinery is leased out as part of a letting of land and buildings, the property lettings are treated as a qualifying activity for plant and machinery allowances both for income tax and corporation tax (ss 15, 16). The effect is that a landlord's expenditure on plant and machinery is pooled, and relief is given when expenditure is incurred rather than when the particular letting commences (except for expenditure before the first property is let, which is treated as incurred when the first letting starts – s 12). . For the way in which relief is given for excess allowances see **Example C6 part** (e). See also **explanatory note 28** for the special rules relating to integral features.

(25) There are special provisions in s 19 relating to machinery and plant let other than in the course of a qualifying activity, but these circumstances will rarely arise (see **Example C6 part** (e)).

Where equipment leasing is a trade, the capital allowances are treated as a trading expense, and can therefore create or increase a trading loss. There is no restriction on the relief available for such a loss incurred by a company. If such a loss is incurred by an individual, however, the relief available is restricted to set-off against later rental income, rather than being set against other income under ITA 2007 ss 64 and 72 (see **Examples E1** and **E2**), unless the trade is carried on by the individual for a continuous period of at least six months in, or beginning or ending in, the tax year of loss, and the individual devotes substantially the whole of his time to that trade (ITA 2007 s 75). See also **explanatory note 20** re finance leases and **explanatory note 28** re fixtures. There are some anti-avoidance provisions relating to leasing in ITA 2007 ss 76–78 concerning partnerships with one or more company members.

(26) Plant and machinery leased to non-residents for use overseas usually attracts writing down allowances of only 8% on the reducing balance basis, with all such expenditure being kept in a separate class pool (s 109). The final chargeable period for the pool is the period at the end of which there can be no more disposal receipts in any later period (s 65).

*Fixtures*

(27) Sections 172 to 204 contain special rules relating to fixtures, ie plant and machinery that in law is treated as part of the building in which it is installed or otherwise fixed. The main intention of the provisions is to enable allowances to be claimed by whoever incurs capital expenditure on fixtures, whether or not that person has an interest in the land or buildings. The provisions are lengthy and complex, and what follows is only a brief summary.

As indicated in **explanatory note 24**, landlords may claim relief for expenditure on fixtures (other than in dwelling houses). Allowances on fixtures may also be claimed by a tenant if he incurs the expenditure (s 176). Where fixtures are provided by equipment lessors, a joint election may be made by the equipment lessor and the equipment lessee (who may be the owner or tenant of the property) for the equipment lessor to claim the allowances (s 177). Equipment lessors cannot claim allowances on fixtures in dwelling houses, nor can they claim allowances on fixtures leased to non-taxpayers, such as charities.

Allowances are not available on any amount in excess of the original cost of the fixtures when new plus any costs of installation (s 185). Vendors and purchasers may make a joint election (within two years of the date of the contract) fixing how much of the purchase price of a building relates to fixtures, the agreed amount being limited, however, to the vendor's original cost (s 198). Strictly elections should be made in respect of each fixture, but HMRC will accept a single election covering all the fixtures in a single property, split between those assets which are integral features and therefore liable to WDA at only 8%, and other plant and machinery. Where a claim in a tax return becomes incorrect, for example, because of such an election, the claimant must notify an amendment to the return within three months after becoming aware of that fact (s 203). In the absence of an election under s 198, s 562 requires a 'just apportionment' of the purchase price between building and fixtures. See **Example C6 part (a)** for comments on apportionment and **Example C9** for a detailed illustration of this in practice, together with details of the changes in Finance Act 2012 which took effect in 2012 and 2014.

There are anti-avoidance provisions to prevent double allowances and to prevent allowances on fixtures being artificially accelerated.

*Integral features*

(28) Expenditure on integral features after April 2008 ceases to qualify for the main pool and expenditure on such assets will be allocated to the 8% pool. Expenditure on integral features (as defined below) qualifies as if on plant or machinery provided that the purpose of the feature is not to insulate the interior of a building or to provide an interior wall, floor or ceiling which is intended to remain permanently in place. The meaning of integral features includes some assets that were previously treated as plant but also some that were previously excluded. Integral features are defined as the following:

- an electrical system (including a lighting system);
- a cold water system;
- a space or water heating system, a powered system of ventilation, air cooling or air purification and any floor or ceiling comprised in such a system;
- a lift, escalator or moving walkway;
- external solar shading.

Expenditure on repairs to integral features will be treated as capital expenditure, and disallowed in computing profits if more than 50% of the current replacement cost of the asset is spent during any twelve-month period, for an illustration of this, note the treatment of the expenditure on the repair of the electrical systems in **Part A(b)** of the Example. Capital allowances can be claimed on the expenditure as s 33A classifies it as expenditure on replacement features.

*VAT capital goods scheme*

(29) For value added tax, a capital goods scheme applies to items of computer equipment with a tax-exclusive value of £50,000 or more per item, and land and buildings with a tax-exclusive value of £250,000 or more. Under the scheme, adjustments may be made over a period of five years for computers and buildings on a ten-year or shorter lease and over ten years for other land and buildings where the VAT exempt/taxable use of the asset varies during the adjustment period, VAT being payable or repayable accordingly.

Any VAT adjustments are reflected in capital allowances computations, extra expenditure being treated as incurred when any additional VAT is paid and VAT refunds being taken into account when received. Where an additional VAT liability relates to expenditure that qualifies for first-year allowance, the FYA is also available on the additional VAT amount, depending on the availability of FYA's at the time the VAT is incurred.

The date the VAT is treated as paid or repaid for the purpose of deciding in which capital allowances period the adjustment has to be made will normally be six months after the end of the taxpayer's VAT year. The adjustment to the plant and machinery pool therefore occurs in the period in which that date falls. If the adjustment relates to a building qualifying for capital allowances, the VAT adjustment is added to or deducted from the residue of expenditure at that date and writing down allowances are recomputed over the remainder of the building's life. Very few buildings that qualify for capital allowances are affected by VAT capital goods scheme adjustments.

# Question

## A.

Describe the operation of the annual investment allowance. Explain how the annual investment allowance is allocated to different businesses in common or overlapping ownership.

## B.

Parsnip Limited purchased a commercial building on 15 June 2016. The total price paid was £475,000. Outline what Parsnip needs to do to enable a capital allowance claim in respect of the fixtures in the building in the year ended 31 December 2016.

## C.

Carrot Limited has purchased the following plant in the year ended 30 June 2016.

| | | |
|---|---|---|
| 15 November 2015 | Solar photovoltaic panels and control systems to be used to generate electricity. | £82,500 |
| 11 December 2015 | Rainwater harvesting system meeting the requirements of the environmentally beneficial plant scheme. | £38,000 |
| 24 April 2016 | Biomass heating system with controls. The whole system is certified under the ECA scheme. It will be used to heat the company's premises, and payments under the renewable heat incentive scheme will be made for 25 years to Carrot. | £47,500 |

Describe the capital allowances available on these purchases. There is no need to provide detailed calculations.

## D.

When may tax relief be claimed for the renovation of business premises in designated assisted areas? What other special allowances are available in respect of businesses in assisted areas?

## E.

Beetroot, a sole trader, prepares accounts to 30 June annually. On 31 July 2014 he acquired patents having ten years to run at a cost of £5,000. The patents were sold outright for £6,000 on 30 April 2017.
Show the tax position for all the years.

## F.

Turnip, a sole trader, has been in business for many years and makes up accounts to 30 September annually. In December 2015 he incurred capital expenditure of £100,000 on research and development. He also gave £20,000 to the South Riding University in June 2017 to be used for scientific research connected with his trade.
Show how these payments will be treated for tax purposes.

## G.

Swede makes up accounts annually to 30 April. In May 2014 he paid £8,400 for know-how for use in his trade. On 31 August 2016 he ceased trading. The business was not transferred to anyone else but he sold the know-how for £9,000.
Show the capital allowances available to him.

# Answer

Except where stated otherwise, all statutory references are to CAA 2001.

## A. Annual investment allowance

Finance Act 2008 included measures that were intended to simplify tax for smaller businesses by giving them, in many cases, an immediate write-off for capital expenditure.

The measures provide for an annual allowance (the annual investment allowance – AIA) of the following amounts:

- £50,000 in respect of expenditure between 1 April (6 April) 2008 and 31 March 2010 (5 April);
- £100,000 in respect of expenditure between 1 April (6 April) 2010 and 31 March (5 April) 2012;
- £25,000 in respect of expenditure between 1 April (6 April) 2012 and 31 December 2012 (this date applies to all businesses);
- £250,000 in respect of expenditure between 1 January 2013 and 31 March 2014;
- £500,000 in respect of expenditure between 1 April (6 April) 2014 and 31 December 2015;
- £200,000 in respect of expenditure on or after 1 January 2016.

(Where a different date appears in brackets above, that date applies for businesses subject to income tax).

Each time the limit has changed, there have been transitional rules applying to accounting periods spanning the date of change. These transitional rules have become increasingly complex, and can give rise to unexpected results. It is fair to say that advisers will have to be very cautious when advising clients who are contemplating large amounts of expenditure, as the timing of the expenditure can significantly affect the allowances available.

### Change on 1 January 2016

The allowance reduced to £200,000 on 1 January 2016. As before, the overall limit for an accounting period is calculated by time apportioning the limits across the date of change. This time there is a single change date for both income and corporation tax.

There is then a restriction on the AIA available for the part of the period falling after the date of change – that is the part of the accounting period which falls after 31 December 2015. In this case, the maximum allowance for that part of the accounting period is the time apportioned amount included in the full year computation.

Example — An income tax business with a year end of 31 March 2016 will benefit from AIA as follows in that accounting period.

Period 1 April 2015 to 31 December 2015 = 275 days

Period 1 January 2016 to 31 March 2016 = 91 days (leap year)

Total allowance for the year: (275/366 x £500,000) + (91/366 x £200,000) = £425,410

However, of this only £49,727 is available against expenditure between 1 January and 31 March 2016.

### Who qualifies for the annual investment allowance?

The AIA is available to individuals and companies. It is also available to partnerships if all the members are individuals (s 38A).

Therefore, trustees and partnerships with corporate partners will not be eligible for the annual investment allowance.

### When AIA is not available

The AIA is not available in the following cases (s 38B).

(1) In the chargeable period in which the qualifying activity is permanently discontinued.

(2) In respect of capital expenditure on a car.

(3) In respect of expenditure incurred wholly for the purposes of a ring-fence trade.

(4) Where there is a change in the nature or conduct of the qualifying activity and obtaining the AIA might objectively be seen as a main benefit of making the change.

(5) Where the plant or machinery was acquired for other purposes, for long-funding leasing or where it was acquired as a gift.

### Claiming AIA

AIA is equal to the financial limit for the period (or the amount of AIA qualifying expenditure if lower).

If the taxpayer's chargeable period is longer or shorter than a year, the value of the AIA is proportionately adjusted (s 51A(4)).

If the AIA is allocated to expenditure on plant or machinery that will not be used wholly for the purposes of the qualifying activity, then the AIA is subject to a just and reasonable reduction (s 205).

Unused AIA may not be carried forward. Conversely, the AIA is not compulsory. Consequently taxpayers who would rather defer the allowances until a later year are not required to claim the AIA in full or at all. However, even in such circumstances any unused element may not be carried forward.

## AIA and businesses under common control

### Individuals and partnerships

For individuals and partnerships, an AIA is generally available in respect of each qualifying activity carried on. Therefore, supposing an individual owned a confectioner's, ran a tuition service and was also a partner (with another individual) in a farming business, that individual would be entitled to two AIAs in addition to the AIA available to the partnership.

However, there are restrictions if there are two or more qualifying activities which are:

- carried on by a partnership or an individual;
- controlled by the same person; and
- related to each other.

Where this applies, there will be a single AIA available to the person(s) carrying on the qualifying activities.

Qualifying activities are related if either:

- they are carried on from the same premises; or
- they are similar activities within the same 'NACE classification' under European Law (s 51J). The NACE classification referred to are the 'letter' headings, and therefore encompass very broad categories of business.

## Companies

Companies are subject to four restrictions.

(1) First, companies are entitled to only one AIA, irrespective of how many qualifying activities they carry on (s 51B).

(2) Secondly, groups of companies are entitled to only one AIA (s 51C).

(3) Groups of companies under common control are entitled to only one AIA if they are related to each other (s 51D).

(4) Other companies under common control are entitled to only one AIA if they are related to each other (s 51E).

As with unincorporated taxpayers, companies are related if at the end of the chargeable period, they carry on qualifying activities from the same premises.

However, the other definition of related differs slightly from that applying with respect to unincorporated businesses. Companies are also related if more than 50% of each company's turnover is derived from qualifying activities within the same NACE classification (s 51G).

Note that there is no restriction that seeks to limit allowances when an individual carries on a trade and also controls a company.

## When restrictions apply

When the AIA is restricted, the taxpayers can choose how to allocate the allowance between the chargeable activities or companies.

## B.

As Parsnip has purchased the building after the changes imposed by FA 2012, there must be an agreement as to the value of the plant for capital allowance purposes if the company wishes to claim capital allowances in respect of the fixtures in the building (new s 187A CAA 2001 inserted by FA 2012 Sch 10). Parsnip will have to agree a split of the proceeds between building and plant with the vendor, which will be binding on both parties, and also on HMRC. If the parties cannot agree on a value, they will need to obtain a ruling from the Tribunal within two years of the date of purchase. If neither of these is done, then no capital allowances can be claimed by Parsnip. The maximum value the parties can agree is the vendor's original cost, but there is no minimum value. Obviously if Parsnip wishes to maximise the allowances available the company will be seeking as high a value as possible, but as this is the disposal proceeds for the vendor's pool, the vendor will be keen to keep the value as low as possible.

However, an important change that applies from 1 April 2014 is that unless the vendor has pooled the fixtures, Parsnip will not in any event be able to claim allowances on them. This excludes allowances on assets treated as integral features since 2008, but which were purchased by the vendor before that date, at a time when the relevant assets were treated as part of the building. This includes the basic electricity and cold water supplies within the building. So as part of the purchase agreement, Parsnip will need to obtain a warranty from the vendor that he has pooled the relevant assets at cost prior to the sale. This is now normally part of the pre-contract enquiries.

If Parsnip had been aware of the changes, it is likely that the negotiation of the value of fixtures acquired would have formed part of the overall negotiations preceding the sale of the building, as at this point the company had more leverage to influence the value.

## C.

Carrot's purchases will attract the following allowances:

The solar photovoltaic system attracts payments under the feed in tariff (FIT) scheme, but this does not affect the capital allowances claim. The timing of the purchase means that annual investment allowance is available against the purchase, which will cover the full cost unless Carrot has incurred other capital expenditure in the year.

The residual expenditure after the AIA has been deducted (if any) must be added to the special rate pool. Contracts for FIT assets normally run for 25 years, so this would be regarded as the useful life of the installation. In any event, after 1 April 2012 statute requires that these are added to the special rate pool.

The rainwater harvesting system qualifies for 100% first year allowances under the enhanced capital allowances (ECA) water scheme. Provided purchases meet the specification, the full allowance is available. If Carrot decides not to claim the full allowance, the system would be added to the general pool. Annual investment allowance is available against this item too, but given the ECA allowances, it is preferable to use the AIA on other purchases.

The biomass heating system is covered by the ECA scheme. However, after 1 April 2012 the company can choose either to receive ECA allowances, or to receive the payments under the RHI scheme. As the incentive payments are significant amounts, payable for an extended period, Carrot would be better to claim the RHI payments. If there is any AIA remaining after the claim against the solar system, the company can claim AIA on the heating system.

## D. Renovation of business premises in disadvantaged areas

Finance Act 2005 Sch 6 introduced a new business premises renovation allowance (BPRA) from 11 April 2007 for a period of five years; this period was extended to April 2017 in March 2012. The allowance provides tax relief on 100% of the cost of renovating or converting business property where the building has been unused for one year and is situated in either Northern Ireland or an area specified as a development area by the Assisted Areas Order 2014 (SI 2014/1508). There is a useful assisted areas map and postcode checker available through gov.uk and also at http://www.ukassistedareasmap.com. The new assisted areas came into force on 1 July 2014; before that the designation was in the Assisted Areas Order 2007 (SI 2007/107).

BPRA is available as a capital allowance to an individual or company being an initial allowance of up to 100% of the qualifying expenditure (CAA 2001 s 360G). If any part of the initial allowance is disclaimed a writing down allowance of up to 25% of the qualifying expenditure is available in subsequent years until costs are fully claimed (CAA 2001 s 360J). No balancing charge or allowance will occur providing there is no disposal event within seven years of the premises being brought back into use (s 360M). No allowance is available to the purchaser of the renovated building.

Qualifying expenditure means any capital expenditure, including fixtures, used on the repair, conversion or renovation of the building into a qualifying business premise (s 360B). Finance Act 2014 refined the definition of qualifying expenditure to include planning fees and similar, but to exclude a range of expenditure on fixtures and integral features as defined by new s 360B(3A) (as inserted by FA 2014, s 66). There is also an exclusion if there is a delay in carrying out the works.

The building must have been last used for the purpose of a trade or profession, or as an office. It must have been unused for at least one year before the expenditure is incurred and situated in either Northern Ireland or an area specified as a development area by the Assisted Areas Order 2014 (SI 2014/1508). It must not have been used wholly or partly as a dwelling (s 360C).

The renovated building must be a qualifying business premises, that is, premises used or available for use for the purpose of a trade, profession or vocation or as an office. It must not be used wholly or in part as a dwelling (s 360D).

The initial allowance is available in the chargeable period in which the qualifying expenditure is incurred (s 360G) but will be withdrawn if the building is sold before first letting or use (s 360H).

A balancing allowance or charge occurs if the building is disposed of within seven years of being available for use. Normally sale price (or market value) is compared with the unclaimed residue to arrive at the adjustment, any balancing charge to be restricted by restricting proceeds to cost. In the case of death proceeds are to equal the residue of unclaimed expenditure (s 360O).

There is also a 100% first year allowance available on plant and machinery purchased by a trading company for use in an assisted area which is also in an enterprise zone. The plant and machinery must be for use in a new activity or for expansion of an existing activity (FA 2012 s 44).

### E. Beetroot – Patents Allowances

| | | | |
|---|---|---|---|
| | | | £ |
| 2015/16 | Year ended 30 June 2015 | Cost | 5,000 |
| | | WDA 25% | 1,250 |
| | | | 3,750 |
| 2016/17 | Year ended 30 June 2016 | WDA 25% | 938 |
| | | | 2,812 |
| 2017/18 | Year ended 30 June 2017 | | |
| | Sale proceeds 30 April 2017 (limited to original cost) | | 5,000 |
| | Balancing charge | | 2,188 |

The capital profit of £1,000 is taxed (ITTOIA 2005 ss 587–599) over six years commencing with the year in which it is received, ie 2017/18 (unless Beetroot elects under s 590(3) to have all the tax charged in one sum in 2017/18).

### F. Turnip – Research and development

December 2015 capital expenditure qualifies for capital allowances of £100,000 in 2016/17 (chargeable period year to 30 September 2016). CAA 2001 s 439.

June 2017 gift of £20,000 to South Riding University is treated as a trading expense of the accounting year to 30 September 2017, reducing the taxable profit in 2017/18. ITTOIA 2005 s 88.

### G. Swede – Know-how

| | | | |
|---|---|---|---|
| | | | £ |
| 2015/16 | Year ended 30 April 2015 | Cost | 8,400 |
| | | WDA 25% | 2,100 |
| | | | 6,300 |
| 2016/17 | Year ended 30 April 2016 | WDA 25% | 1,575 |
| | | | 4,725 |
| 2017/18 | 1 May 2016 to 31 August 2017 | | |
| | Sale proceeds | | 9,000 |
| | Balancing charge (not restricted to allowances given) | | £4,275 |

## Explanatory Notes

(1) AIA is not available in respect of expenditure on a car. The meaning of car changed from 1 (6) April 2009 to exclude motorcycles and include hire cars (cars used as taxis, daily hire cars and cars leased to the disabled). Vans, are excluded from the definition. HMRC have confirmed that some double-cab pickups also fall outside the definition of car (see HMRC Manuals EIM23150), so these also qualify for AIA.

(2) AIA applies in respect of chargeable periods in which capital expenditure is incurred. See s 12 for the meaning of this.

(3) It will generally be advisable for the AIA to be allocated to expenditure qualifying for the special rate (8%) pool before expenditure which may be allocated to the 18% pool. This is because the former would otherwise be written off more slowly than the latter.

Care should be taken before allocating the AIA to expenditure destined for a single asset pool. In the case of assets used only partly for the purposes of a qualifying activity, the AIA will be similarly restricted. In respect of other assets, the AIA might lead to a balancing charge when the asset is disposed of.

However, different considerations may apply if a taxpayer's marginal rates are likely to differ in future years.

(4) The NACE classification can be found on the internet at the EC statistical service on http://ec.europa.eu/competition/merger/cases/index/nace_all.html and in CA23090.

(5) Although elections under CAA 2001 s 198 have been available for many years, it has been rare for elections to be made. This is principally because the joint election sets a maximum value of the vendor's cost, and purchasers have found that by choosing to split the proceeds under CAA 2001 s 562 they are able to obtain a better value for the plant element of the purchase.

This has been amplified by the number of specialist capital allowance consultancy businesses, who can conduct a physical survey of the building and identify all of the fixtures. Since the introduction of the integral features legislation in 2008, this has extended the scope for identifying qualifying expenditure under s 562, as the main electrical and water supply and services can form part of a capital allowances claim (albeit at the lower rate of writing down allowance).

From 1 April 2012 if the purchaser wishes to claim capital allowances on fixtures purchased in the building they must either agree a value with the vendor (subject to a maximum of the vendor's cost), fixing the value of the plant for both parties for tax purposes, or settle the value at Tribunal.

Where an election under s 198 is not available because the purchaser has never claimed capital allowances on the fixtures, there is a provision for a valuation to be agreed for tax purposes, so that the same process applies.

From 1 April 2014, no allowances are available to the purchaser unless the vendor has pooled the expenditure at cost to him before sale.

*Patents*

(6) Where a trader incurs expenditure on devising and patenting an invention etc or in connection with a rejected patent application, the expenditure is allowable in computing trading profits (ITTOIA 2005 s 89). Where a trader purchases patent rights, he is entitled to capital allowances of 25% per annum on a reducing balance basis for expenditure. This rate has not changed despite the changes to the rates available for plant and machinery allowances.

Balancing adjustments are made on sale. If the sales proceeds exceed original cost, the capital profit is *not* charged to capital gains tax. It is charged over six years commencing with the tax year of receipt, unless the trader elects to have the whole amount charged in the year of receipt (ITTOIA 2005 ss 587–599).

For companies, the treatment of patents changed from 1 April 2002. Capital allowances do not apply in respect of patent rights acquired on or after that date and the acquisition and disposal of the rights, and royalty payments on them, are dealt with under the intangible assets rules. For details see **Example K3**. Capital allowances continue to be available in respect of patents already owned by companies on 1 April 2002.

*Research and development*

(7) Where a trader incurs capital expenditure on research and development related to his trade he is entitled to a capital allowance equal to the full amount of that expenditure (CAA 2001 ss 437–451). The normal rules for chargeable periods apply. Expenditure on land is, however, excluded. Expenditure on dwellings is also excluded, except that where a building is used partly as a dwelling and partly for scientific research and not more than one quarter of the expenditure on the building relates to the dwelling, the whole of the expenditure is allowable.

Balancing adjustments are made upon the asset ceasing to belong to the trader. For this purpose, disposal value is taken into account rather than sale proceeds. Disposal value is defined as:

(a) the proceeds of sale, if the asset is sold at open market value or higher;

(b) the deemed proceeds of sale if the asset is deemed to be sold because of its destruction; it is treated as sold immediately before its destruction for any insurance proceeds, compensation, demolition proceeds etc (any demolition costs being added to the expenditure);

(c) open market value, in any other event (CAA 2001 ss 443–445).

See **Example I5** for the treatment of revenue expenditure on research and development, including enhanced deductions and tax credit payments available to companies in certain circumstances.

*Know-how*

(8) Know-how allowances are dealt with in CAA 2001 ss 452–463. Know-how means industrial information and techniques of assistance in manufacturing or processing goods or materials, working (or searching for) mineral deposits or carrying out agricultural, forestry or fishing operations. HMRC considers that the term does not include commercial know-how, such as information about marketing, packaging or distributing a product.

If know-how is sold as part of a business that is being disposed of, the payment is treated both as regards the seller and the buyer as a payment for *goodwill*, unless they jointly elect (within two years of the disposal) for it to be treated as a payment for know-how (ITTOIA 2005 s 194). If the election is made, or if know-how is disposed of other than as part of a business, capital allowances are available by way of annual writing down allowances of 25% on a reducing balance basis. Any additional expenditure is added to the written down value and any sale proceeds deducted before the writing down allowance is calculated. A balancing charge is made if know-how is sold for more than the written down value, and either a balancing charge or allowance is made when the trade ceases. Unlike balancing charges on other types of assets, a balancing charge is not restricted to the allowances that have been given in respect of the know-how, so if it is sold for more than cost, the excess is charged to tax within the balancing charge (CAA 2001 s 462).

For acquisitions by companies on or after 1 April 2002, know-how is dealt with under the rules for intangible assets. See **Example K3** for details.

# Question

(a) The partnership of Amy, Ben and Charlie commenced on 1 September 2015, accounts being made up annually to 31 August. They shared profits Amy one half, Ben one third, Charlie one sixth after a salary of £6,000 to Charlie. The profits for the first two years, net of capital allowances on partnership assets, were as follows:

| | £ |
|---|---|
| Year to 31 August 2016 | 42,000 |
| Year to 31 August 2017 | 48,000 |

In addition each partner uses their own car for the business, capital allowances being due as follows:

| | *Yr to 31.8.16* | *Yr to 31.8.17* |
|---|---|---|
| | £ | £ |
| Amy | 2,500 | 2,500 |
| Ben | 1,800 | 1,350 |
| Charlie | 2,000 | 1,833 |

Show the tax position of each partner arising out of the above, and state what the situation would be if Charlie left the partnership on 31 October 2017.

(b) Partners Danny and Ella have been in business for 25 years, sharing profits equally and making up accounts annually to 30 April. Fiona joined as an equal partner on 1 January 2017.

Taxable profits net of capital allowances around the time Fiona joined were as follows:

| | |
|---|---|
| Year to 30 April 2017 | £36,000 |
| Year to 30 April 2018 | £45,000 |

Show the taxable income arising to each partner in respect of these profits and indicate their position regarding overlap relief.

(c) Glen, Harry and Joe have been in partnership for many years, making up accounts annually to 30 June and sharing profits and losses equally. The partners were entitled to transitional overlap relief of £25,500 each. Glen retired on 30 September 2016. Harry and Joe continued as equal partners. Recent taxable profits after capital allowances were as follows:

| | | £ |
|---|---|---|
| Year to 30 June 2016 | | 84,000 |
| Year to 30 June 2017: | | |
| 1 July 2016 to 30 September 2016 | 25,650 | |
| 1 October 2016 to 30 June 2017 | 51,300 | |
| | | 76,950 |

Show the taxable income arising to each partner in respect of these profits and the treatment of overlap relief.

(d) Outline the treatment of partnership non-trading income.

# Answer

## (a) Partnership of Amy, Ben and Charlie

### Division of profits:

| | *Total* | *Amy* | *Ben* | *Charlie* |
|---|---|---|---|---|
| | £ | £ | £ | £ |
| *Year to 31.8.16* | | | | |
| Salary | 6,000 | | | 6,000 |
| Balance 3:2:1 | 36,000 | 18,000 | 12,000 | 6,000 |
| | 42,000 | 18,000 | 12,000 | 12,000 |
| *Less*: capital allowances on partners' cars | (6,300) | (2,500) | (1,800) | (2,000) |
| | 35,700 | 15,500 | 10,200 | 10,000 |
| *Year to 31.8.17* | | | | |
| Salary | 6,000 | | | 6,000 |
| Balance 3:2:1 | 42,000 | 21,000 | 14,000 | 7,000 |
| | 48,000 | 21,000 | 14,000 | 13,000 |
| *Less*: capital allowances on partners' cars | (5,683) | (2,500) | (1,350) | (1,833) |
| | 42,317 | 18,500 | 12,650 | 11,167 |

### Profits taxable on individual partners:

| | *Amy* | *Ben* | *Char-lie* |
|---|---|---|---|
| | £ | £ | £ |
| *2015/16* | | | |
| 1.9.15 – 5.4.16 | | | |
| 7/12 × profit share for yr to 31.8.16 | 9,042 | 5,950 | 5,833 |
| *2016/17* | | | |
| 1.9.15 – 31.8.16 | 15,500 | 10,200 | 10,000 |
| *2017/18* | | | |
| 1.9.16 – 31.8.17 | 18,500 | 12,650 | 11,167 |
| Overlap relief (1.9.15 – 5.4.16) | 9,042 | 5,950 | 5,833 |

As the partnership began on 1 September 2015 the partners are taxed on their profits under the opening year rules for basis periods in ITTOIA 2005 ss 198-201 (ITTOIA 2005 ss 852-853). In year 1 (2015/16), the profits from the date of commencement to the end of that tax year are taxable. In year 2 (2016/17) there is a 12-month accounting period ending in the tax year so the profits for the 12 months ending with the accounting date are taxable. However this means the profits from 1 September 2015 to 5 April 2016 have been taxed twice. This is known as overlap profits or overlap relief and is relieved when the partner retires or the accounting date is moved

(ITTOIA 2005 ss 204-205, 220). In year 3 (2017/18) current year basis applies which means the profits for the accounting period ending in the tax year (ie the year to 31 August 2017) are taxable. For a detailed discussion of the basis period rules, see **Example C4 explanatory notes 1–6.**

If Charlie leaves the partnership on 31 October 2017, the profit of the year to 31 August 2018 would be split as to the first two months (September and October 2017) between Amy, Ben and Charlie according to their profit sharing arrangements and the remaining 10 months between Amy and Ben according to whatever profit sharing arrangement they agree after Charlie's departure.

Charlie's 2017/18 income from the partnership would comprise his share of the profit of the year to 31 August 2017 and his two months' share of the profit of the year to 31 August 2018, reduced by his overlap relief of £5,833 (ITTOIA 2005 ss 202, 205). Amy and Ben would continue to be taxed each year on their shares of the profits, and would deduct their overlap relief when they retire from the partnership or on an earlier change of accounting date if, and to the extent that, more than 12 months' profit was charged to tax in one year.

## (b) Partnership of Danny, Ella and Fiona

### Division of profits:

| | *Total* £ | *Danny* £ | *Ella* £ | *Fiona* £ |
|---|---|---|---|---|
| *Year to 30.4.2017* | | | | |
| 1.5.16 – 31.12.16 (8 mths) | 24,000 | 12,000 | 12,000 | |
| 1.1.17 – 30.4.17 (4 mths) | 12,000 | 4,000 | 4,000 | 4,000 |
| | 36,000 | 16,000 | 16,000 | 4,000 |
| *Year to 30.4.18* | 45,000 | 15,000 | 15,000 | 15,000 |

Danny and Ella are taxed on their profit shares for the years ended 30.4.2017 and 30.4.2018, as shown above, in 2017/18 and 2018/19 respectively under the current year basis (see **answer (a)** above). Their position regarding overlap relief is unchanged in that they are still entitled to transitional overlap relief on their shares of the profits (before capital allowances) for the 11 months from 1 May 1996 to 5 April 1997 (the full 12 months to 30.4.97 being assessed in 1997/98) (ITTOIA 2005 Sch 2 para 52). See **Example C4 explanatory note 8.**

Fiona is taxed as follows:

| | | | £ |
|---|---|---|---|
| 2016/17 | 1.1.17 – 5.4.17 | 3/4 × 4,000 | 3,000 |
| 2017/18 | 1.1.17 – 31.12.17 | 4,000 + (8/12 × 15,000) | 14,000 |
| 2018/19 | Yr to 30.4.18 | | 15,000 |
| Overlap profit*: | 1.1.17 – 5.4.17 | | 3,000 |
| | 1.5.17 – 31.12.17 | (8/12 × 15,000) | 10,000 |
| | | | 13,000 |

As discussed in answer (a) above, as a new partner Fiona's profits are taxed according to the opening year basis period rules.

## (c) Partnership of Glen, Harry and Joe

### Division of profits:

The taxable profits of the years to 30 June 2016 and 30 June 2017 are divided between the partners as follows:

| | *Total* | *Glen* | *Harry* | *Joe* |
|---|---|---|---|---|
| | *£* | *£* | *£* | *£* |
| Yr to 30.6.16 | 84,000 | 28,000 | 28,000 | 28,000 |
| Yr to 30.6.17: | | | | |
| To 30.9.16 | 25,650 | 8,550 | 8,550 | 8,550 |
| To 30.6.17 | 51,300 | — | 25,650 | 25,650 |
| | 76,950 | 8,550 | 34,200 | 34,200 |

**Profits taxable on individual partners:**

| | Total | Glen | Harry | Joe |
|---|---|---|---|---|
| | £ | £ | £ | £ |
| *2016/17* (yr to 30.6.16) | 84,000 | 28,000 | 28,000 | 28,000 |
| On retirement of Glen | | | | |
| Period to 30.9.16 | | 8,550 | | |
| *Less* overlap relief | | (25,500) | — | — |
| | | 11,050 | 28,000 | 28,000 |
| *2017/18* (yr to 30.6.17) | 76,950 | | | |
| *Less* allocated to Glen | (8,550) | | | |
| | 68,400 | | 34,200 | 34,200 |
| Overlap relief | | | 25,500 | 25,500 |

As discussed in answer (a) above, as Glen has retired from the partnership, in the year of cessation he is taxed on all of his share of the profits which have not already been taxed, less his overlap relief (ITTOIA 2005 ss 202, 205, 852-853).

## (d) Partnership non-trading income

Non-trading partnership income, such as rents and interest, is taxed separately on each partner (ITTOIA 2005 s 851). The way in which each partner's taxable income is arrived at depends on whether the income has been taxed at source.

If the income is taxed at source, then although it is divided according to the sharing arrangements of the partnership accounting period, each partner must show the income relating to each tax year in his own self-assessment. Shares of taxed income, together with the tax thereon, are therefore shown in partnership tax returns for the tax year rather than for the accounting period (BIM82290).

Note that dividends are always treated as taxed income, even where no tax credit is attached (ITTOIA 2005 s 854(6)). Therefore even though the dividend tax credit was abolished for dividends paid on or after 6 April 2016, dividends received by a partnership continue to be taxed on a tax year basis (FA 2016 Sch 1 para 1(1)).

As far as untaxed income is concerned, it is treated as if it arose in a separate notional trade that started when the partner joined the firm (not when he started business on his own if he was a sole trader before becoming a partner) and ceased when he left (even if he continues as a sole trader, and even if the source of income actually ceased much earlier) (ITTOIA 2005 ss 854-855). Therefore this income is taxed under the normal basis period rules mentioned in answer (a) above.

A partner may therefore generate to overlap profits in respect of untaxed income in the same way as for trading profits when he joins the firm. The overlap relief will be given by reducing his share of the untaxed income when he leaves the firm (unless it has been given on an earlier change of accounting date), even if he then carries on business alone (ITTOIA 2005 s 856). This is different from overlap relief relating to the trade (see **explanatory note** 2).

If the partner's share of untaxed income in the relevant tax year is less than the overlap relief to be deducted, the balance is relieved against other income of that tax year (ITTOIA 2005 s 856(3)). Relief for any transitional overlap profits arising on the change to the current year basis of assessment is given in the same way as for normal overlap profits.

The deduction of tax at source on bank and building society interest ceased on 6 April 2016 (FA 2016 Sch 6). Therefore, as far as partnerships are concerned, a source of taxed income became a source of untaxed income on 6 April 2016, which is likely to be in the middle of an accounting period.

Therefore taxed interest received before 6 April 2016 is reported on a tax year basis as normal. In 2016/17 the interest received from 6 April 2016 to the end of the basis period is taxed in the 2016/17 tax year. In 2017/18 and subsequent years, the interest is untaxed income and so is taxed under the normal basis period rules.

# Explanatory Notes

*Taxation of trading profits*

(1) The trading profits of the accounting period are shared between the partners according to their sharing arrangements, and each partner's share is regarded as his profit from a separate business (ITTOIA 2005 ss 852-853). A new partner is therefore treated as commencing a new business when he joins (as illustrated in **answer (b)** above), unless he had previously carried on the business as a sole trader. A partner is treated as ceasing business when he retires from the partnership (as illustrated in **answers (a)** and **(c)** above), unless he continues the business as a sole trader.

Unless given on an earlier change of accounting date, overlap relief is given when the partner leaves the partnership, or if he continues the business as a sole trader, when the sole trade ceases (ITTOIA 2005 s 856). The partnership itself is not treated as discontinued on a change of partners except where none of the old partners continue.

Where the partnership is a mixed partnership, such that one or more partners is a limited company, targeted anti-avoidance rules apply to prevent manipulation of the profit allocation to avoid tax. See **Example C12.**

If there are large prior share salaries in the partnership's profit sharing agreement, it is entirely possible that even if the firm as a whole has a taxable profit (or loss), the allocation will result in some of the partners showing a large profit with others showing losses (or vice versa). For tax purposes, the allocation of a partnership's profits between the partners must result in a straight apportionment of the actual profits made by the partnership. If the allocation of the profits using the firm's profit sharing arrangements for all the partners produces both profits and losses, then the actual profit will need to be reallocated between the profit making (or loss making) partners alone in proportion to the profits initially allocated to them. The same applies for losses.

In summary, if the partnership as a whole makes a profit, then no individual partner can claim a loss (or vice versa) (ITTOIA 2005 ss 850-850B.

*Non-trading income*

(2) Non-trading partnership income is divided according to the sharing arrangements in the accounting period (ITTOIA 2005 ss 850, 851). As discussed in **answer (d)** above, If it is untaxed income, it is taxed as if it arose from a separate notional trade, which is treated as having started when the partner joined the firm and ceased when a partner leaves the firm (not when the source of income ceases) (ITTOIA 2005 ss 854-855). The rules for overlap relief apply equally to untaxed income (ITTOIA 2005 s 856).

In a tax year in which overlap relief on untaxed income is to be deducted (ie usually in the year when the partner leaves the firm, but possibly earlier if the accounting date is changed), then if it exceeds the partner's non-trading income it may be set against any other income of that year (ITTOIA 2005 s 856(3)). There is, however, no provision for carrying any excess back to an earlier year.

There are no overlap problems with taxed income and dividends (ITTOIA 2005 s 854(6)). Such income is allocated to the appropriate tax year.

*Calculation of overlap relief*

(3) The detailed rules on the calculation of overlap relief are in **Example C4**. Even though partners may share profits and losses equally, their overlap relief may have been calculated at different times, so that the amounts of profits on which each has paid tax more than once are different.

On a cessation of business, therefore, the profits assessable on each equal partner will reflect the differences in the overlap relief available. In **answer** (**c**) above, Glen, Harry and Joe were equal partners and each is entitled to the same amount of overlap relief.

In **answer** (**b**) above, although Danny, Ella and Fiona are equal partners, the overlap relief available to Danny and Ella is based on their profit shares for the 11 months to 5 April 1997, whereas that for Fiona is based on her profit shares for the 3 months to 5 April 2017 and the 8 months from 1 May 2017 to 31 December 2017.

*Partnership self-assessment*

(4) For the self-assessment provisions as they relate to partnerships see **Example G2**.

*Limited liability partnerships*

(5) A further type of commercial structure known as a 'limited liability partnership' (LLP) is available. An LLP has limited liability as though it were a limited company but its members are taxed as though it were a partnership as long as it is carrying on a trade. For details see **Example C13**.

*Inactive partners – NIC liability*

(6) Following a change of view announced on 4 April 2013, HMRC takes the view that sleeping and inactive partners in a partnership are gainfully employed as self-employed earners for the purposes of SSCBA 1992 s 2(1)(b). This means that HMRC expects all such partners to be registered for Class 2 NIC from 6 April 2013 and to account for Class 4 NIC for the tax year 2013/14 onwards. See **Example H1** for more about NIC.

# Question

The partnership of Pipe and Ross has traded as architects since 1991 and decided to merge with another partnership of architects founded in the early 1990s, Simpson, Eriksson and Capello, to form the new firm of Pipe Simpson with effect from 6 October 2016. Pipe and Ross made up their accounts to 5 July each year and Simpson, Eriksson and Capello made up accounts to 5 May each year. The recent tax adjusted profits and sharing arrangements are as follows:

| | Pipe & Ross | | Simpson, Eriksson & Capello |
|---|---|---|---|
| | £ | | £ |
| Year to 5 July 2016 | 58,400 | Year to 5 May 2016 | 85,600 |
| Period to 5 October 2016 | 23,750 | Period to 5 Oct 2016 | 33,250 |

| | Profit share | Overlap relief bf | | Profit share | Overlap relief bf |
|---|---|---|---|---|---|
| | % | £ | | % | £ |
| Pipe | 60 | 21,870 | Simpson | 40 | 28,600 |
| Ross | 40 | 14,580 | Eriksson | 30 | 21,450 |
| | | | Capello | 30 | 21,450 |

No formal notices of change of accounting date have been or are being given in respect of the accounts to 5 October 2016.

The merged partnership accounts are to be made up to 5 July and profits are to be shared as detailed below:

### 6 October 2016 to 5 July 2017

First slice of £10,000 per annum to each partner.

Balance split:

| | |
|---|---|
| Pipe | 22% |
| Ross | 16% |
| Simpson | 22% |
| Eriksson | 20% |
| Capello | 20% |

### From 6 July 2017

Profits shared equally.

The profit for the period 6 October 2016 to 5 July 2017 amounted to £121,000 and for the year to 5 July 2018 £200,000.

(a) Compute the taxable profits for the years 2016/17 to 2018/19, the division between the partners and the overlap relief to be carried forward at 5 April 2019;

(b) Explain the compliance obligations of the partnerships in 2016/17 and 2017/18.

# Answer

## (a) Profits taxable on individual partners

Partners are individually taxed on their shares of the partnership taxable profits for the accounting period ended in the tax year as follows:

| | *Pipe* | *Ross* | *Simpson* | *Eriksson* | *Capello* | *Total* |
|---|---|---|---|---|---|---|
| | £ | £ | £ | £ | £ | £ |
| **2016/17** (N1)–(N3) | | | | | | |
| (yr to 5.7.16) | 60% | 40% | | | | |
| | 35,040 | 23,360 | | | | 58,400 |
| (yr to 5.5.16) | | | 40% | 30% | 30% | |
| | | | 34,240 | 25,680 | 25,680 | 85,600 |
| **2017/18** (period to 5.7.17) (N2), N3) | | | | | | |
| Merger took place 6.10.16 | | | | | | |
| 6.7.16 to 5.10.16 | 14,250 | 9,500 | | | | 23,750 |
| 6.5.16 to 5.10.16 | | | 13,300 | 9,975 | 9,975 | 33,250 |
| 6.10.16 to 5.7.17: | | | | | | |
| First slice (9/12) | 7,500 | 7,500 | 7,500 | 7,500 | 7,500 | 37,500 |
| Balance | 18,370 | 13,360 | 18,370 | 16,700 | 16,700 | 83,500 |
| | 40,120 | 30,360 | 39,170 | 34,175 | 34,175 | 121,000 |
| *Less*: 2 months' overlap relief for Simpson, Eriksson and Capello (N4) | — | — | (5,200) | (3,900) | (3,900) | |
| Total 2017/18 | 40,120 | 30,360 | 33,970 | 30,275 | 30,275 | |
| **2018/19** | | | | | | |
| (yr to 5.7.18) | 40,000 | 40,000 | 40,000 | 40,000 | 40,000 | 200,000 |
| Overlap relief carried forward | 21,870 | 14,580 | 23,400 | 17,550 | 17,550 | |

## Notes

Notes

(1) Partners are taxed on their profit share from a partnership according to the basis period rules in ITTIOA 2005 ss 198-220 (ITTOIA 2005 ss 852-853). For long-standing partnerships who have had the same accounting date for years, this means the current year basis applies. The current year basis means that the partner is taxed on their profit share for the accounting period ending in the tax year.

(2) The merger of two partnerships to form one new partnership does not necessarily constitute a cessation of the old trade and commencement of a new trade for the purposes of the basis period rules for any partner who is a member of both the old and new partnership. However if the new business of the partnership is different in nature from either of the two businesses of the old partnerships this may be treated as a cessation. In that event it would be advisable to seek the view of HMRC as to whether the merger could be regarded as the continuation of an existing business or whether it has resulted in a new business

emerging, in which case all partners in the previous firms would be regarded as having ceased trading (with the full amount of any available overlap relief being given, see N3) and having commenced a new venture.

Based on the facts in the Example above, the merger of the two partnerships to form Pipe Simpson would not constitute a cessation for the purposes of the basis periods of the five partners.

(3) Strictly there is a later accounting date in the 2016/17 tax year for each of the old partnerships (5 October 2016). The temporary use of a new date need not, however, trigger the change of accounting date rules unless the taxpayers choose to notify the change under ITTOIA 2005 s 217. If no notification is made, the old date continues to apply.

(4) As the partnerships have made up accounts regularly to the same accounting date since the early 1990s, transitional overlap relief will have arisen (see **Example C4 explanatory note 8**). The transitional overlap period for Pipe and Ross is the period from 6 July 1996 to 5 April 1997, ie nine months, and for Simpson, Eriksson and Capello is the period from 6 May 1996 to 5 April 1997, ie eleven months.

Since the 2017/18 basis period for Simpson, Eriksson and Capello runs for the 14 months from 6 May 2016 to 5 July 2017, each partner is entitled to deduct a two month proportion of his available overlap relief, ie 2/11ths from his taxable profits for 2017/18.

## (b) Compliance obligations

As indicated in **answer (a)** above, the old partnerships need not notify HMRC of a formal change of accounting date to 5 October, but accounts have even been drawn up to 5 October 2016, which ends in the 2016/17 tax year. In view of the fact that 5 October has not been formally adopted as a new accounting date, the partners' profit shares for that period do not form part of their taxable profits for the 2016/17 tax year. Instead the profits to 5 October 2016 form part of their 2017/18 income.

However, the old partnerships should notify HMRC that they have ceased so that partnership returns are not issued in future years.

Simpson, Eriksson and Capello have changed their accounting date from 5 May to 5 July upon the merger, but the accounts to 5 July 2017 are made up by the new merged firm.

It is necessary for a partnership return to be completed by the new merged firm for 2016/17. The position regarding returns is as follows:

### *2016/17*

#### Pipe and Ross:

A partnership return is required to the date of cessation on 5 October 2016. The return should include accounting details for the year to 5 July 2016 and a second set of trading income pages for the period 6 July 2016 to 5 October 2016 (with a comment in the additional information box that the profit of this period will form part of the taxable profits to 5 July 2017).

There should be two partnership statements: one covering the year to 5 July 2016 and the other covering the period 6 July 2016 to 5 October 2016. The statements should also include taxed income etc for the period 6 April 2016 to 5 October 2016 (although see **Example C10 part (d)** in relation to the abolition of tax at source on bank interest with effect from 6 April 2016).

#### Simpson, Eriksson and Capello:

Again, a return with two sets of trading statements and partnership statements is required, covering the year ended 5 May 2016 and the period 6 May 2016 to 5 October 2016.

**Pipe Simpson:**

This partnership will have a separate unique tax reference (UTR) number and the 2016/17 partnership return will not include accounts, as no accounts ended in the year to 5 April 2017. The return will show a start date of 6 October 2016 and the partnership statement will include details of taxed interest etc for the period 6 October 2016 to 5 April 2017 (although see **Example C10 part (d)** in relation to the abolition of tax at source on bank interest with effect from 6 April 2016).

## *2017/18*

No partnership returns will be required from the old partnerships. If partnership returns are issued, the nominated partner should contact HMRC to ask for the returns to be withdrawn under TMA 1970 s 12AAA.

**Pipe Simpson:**

A partnership return is required, including the accounting details for the period 6 October 2016 to 5 July 2017. The partnership statement will cover the same period for trading and non-trading untaxed income. The taxed income will be for the year ended 5 April 2018. See **Example C10 part (d)**.

In the personal returns for 2017/18 the individual partners will complete separate partnership supplementary pages for each business, eg Pipe will complete a partnership page for the income from Pipe and Ross for the period 6 July 2015 to 5 October 2016 and a further partnership page for the income from Pipe Simpson for the period 6 October 2016 to 5 July 2017. However, no entry will be required for a commencement or a cessation, as each individual has continued to trade throughout the year. The overlap profits will be brought forward on the pages for Pipe and Ross and carried forward on the pages for Pipe Simpson.

For more on the compliance obligations associated with self-assessment, see **Example G2**.

# Question

(a) The Ben Williams Partnership carries on a retail trade and is UK resident. For the past 20 years its partners, all of whom are UK resident, have been Ben Williams Ltd, Henderson Traders Ltd and John Wilson. The first £100,000 profit is allocated to John Wilson and the remaining profits are shared:

| | |
|---|---|
| Ben Williams Ltd | 56% |
| Henderson Traders Ltd | 42% |
| John Wilson | 2% |

The partnership prepares its accounts to 31 December, as do the two corporate partners. John Wilson has transitional overlap relief brought forward of £46,700.

On 1 July 2016 Daniel Grant joined the partnership. He is entitled to a prior charge share of profits of £30,000 plus 1% of the remaining profits, Henderson Traders Ltd's share of profits reducing to 41% of the balance of profits from that date.

Assume that profits and capital allowances, both for income tax and corporation tax purposes, are as follows:

| *Year to* | *Profits (before capital allowances)* | *Capital allowances* |
|---|---|---|
| | £ | £ |
| 31.12.2015 | 5,200,000 | 70,000 |
| 31.12.2016 | 5,000,000 | 65,000 |
| 31.12.2017 | 5,500,000 | 76,000 |

Show the amounts declared by each partner as self-assessments in respect of the three years concerned, and state when tax will be payable.

(b) Smiley Faces is a children's entertainment firm which runs an activity centre as well as providing children's entertainers for parties and events. It is run as a partnership between Lucy Coles, Camilla Bright and Colebright Ltd. Lucy and Camilla each own 50% of the share capital in Colebright Ltd. The company owns and provides use of the activity centre premises as its contribution to the partnership (a commercial rate of rent would be £50,000 per year), but provides no other services.

Assume that profits and capital allowances, both for income tax and corporation tax purposes, are as follows:

| *Y/e* | *Profits* | *Capital allowances* |
|---|---|---|
| 30.9.16 | 192,000 | 9,000 |

The partnership is aiming to expand into a neighbouring town. The plan is for Colebright Ltd to acquire more premises and for the partnership to run another activity centre in those new premises. With this in mind, the partnership profit allocations have been fixed to ensure that the maximum amount is available to the company. The profit-sharing arrangements for both years are that Ms Coles and Ms Bright are each entitled to £20,000 each per year which they draw throughout the year, plus 10% of the remainder of the profits, with the company being entitled to the other 80%.

Show why and how the partnership's profit allocations for each year may be affected by the anti-avoidance rules for reallocation of mixed partnership profits.

# Answer

## (a) Ben Williams Partnership:

Where partnerships have both individual and corporate partners, separate computations have to be made for income tax and corporation tax, the computations being made *before* deducting shares of capital allowances according to the partnership agreement (see **explanatory note 2**). The total partnership profits for corporation tax purposes may therefore differ from those for income tax purposes. The Example assumes, however, that profits are the same in each case. The division of the capital allowances, and the profit shares taking the capital allowances into account, are therefore as follows:

| | Total | Ben Williams Ltd | Henderson Trad-ers Ltd | John Wilson | Daniel Grant |
|---|---|---|---|---|---|
| **Division of capital allowances** | £ | £ | £ | £ | £ |
| Year to 31.12.2015 | 70,000 | 39,200 | 29,400 | 1,400 | – |
| Year to 31.12.2016 | | | | | |
| Up to 30.6.2016 | 32,500 | 18,200 | 13,650 | 650 | – |
| 1.7 to 31.12.2016 | 32,500 | 18,200 | 13,325 | 650 | 325 |
| | 65,000 | 36,400 | 26,975 | 1,300 | 325 |
| Year to 31.12.2017 | 76,000 | 42,560 | 31,160 | 1,520 | 760 |
| **Division of profits** | | | | | |
| *Year to 31 December 2015* | | | | | |
| First allocation | 100,000 | – | – | 100,000 | – |
| Remainder (56:42:2) | 5,100,000 | 2,856,000 | 2,142,000 | 102,000 | – |
| | 5,200,000 | 2,856,000 | 2,142,000 | 202,000 | – |
| Less capital allowances | (70,000) | (39,200) | (29,400) | (1,400) | – |
| | 5,130,000 | 2,816,800 | 2,112,600 | 200,600 | – |
| *Year to 31 December 2016* | | | | | |
| *Up to 30.6.2016* | | | | | |
| First allocation | 50,000 | – | – | 50,000 | – |
| Remainder (56:42:2) | 2,450,000 | 1,372,000 | 1,029,000 | 49,000 | – |
| | 2,500,000 | 1,372,000 | 1,029,000 | 99,000 | – |
| *1.7 to 31.12.2015* | | | | | |
| First allocation | 65,000 | – | – | 50,000 | 15,000 |
| Remainder (56:41:2:1) | 2,435,000 | 1,363,600 | 998,350 | 48,700 | 24,350 |
| | 5,000,000 | 2,735,600 | 2,027,350 | 197,700 | 39,350 |
| Less capital allowances | (65,000) | (36,400) | (26,975) | (1,300) | (325) |
| | 4,935,000 | 2,699,200 | 2,000,375 | 196,400 | 39,025 |
| *Year to 31 December 2017* | | | | | |
| First allocation | 130,000 | – | – | 100,000 | 30,000 |
| Remainder (56:41:2:1) | 5,370,000 | 3,007,200 | 2,201,700 | 107,400 | 53,700 |
| | 5,500,000 | 3,007,200 | 2,201,700 | 207,400 | 83,700 |
| Less capital allowances | (76,000) | (42,560) | (31,160) | (1,520) | (760) |
| | 5,424,000 | 2,964,640 | 2,170,540 | 205,880 | 82,940 |

### *Amounts self-assessed by the partners*

The corporate partners will self-assess on their shares as shown above.

The profits of the individual partners are as follows:

*John Wilson*

John Wilson will self-assess on his shares as shown above in 2015/16, 2016/17 and 2017/18 the amounts being based on the accounting period ending in the tax year, under the current year basis (ITTOIA 2005 ss 852-853 as read with ITTOIA 2005 s 198).

*Daniel Grant*

| | | | | |
|---|---|---|---|---|
| | | | | £ |
| 2016/17 | 1.7.16 – 31.12.16 | | | 39,025 |
| | 1.1.17 – 5.4.17 | 3/12 × £82,940 | | 20,735 |
| | | | | 59,760 |
| 2017/18 | Yr to 31.12.17 | | | 82,940 |
| Overlap profits: | 1.1.17 – 5.4.17 | 3/12 × £82,940 | £20,735 | |

As a new partner, Daniel Grant's profits are taxed according to the opening year basis period rules (ITTOIA 2005 ss 852-853 as read with ITTOIA 2005 ss 198-201). In year 1 (2016/17), the profits from the date of commencement to the end of that tax year are taxable. In year 2 (2017/18) there is a 12-month accounting period ending in the tax year so the profits for the 12 months ending with the accounting date are taxable. However this means the profits from 1 January 2017 to 5 April 2017 have been taxed twice. This is known as overlap profits or overlap relief and is relieved when the partner retires or the accounting date is moved (ITTOIA 2005 ss 204-205, 220).

### *Due date of payment of tax liabilities*

Self-assessment applies both for income tax and corporation tax (see **explanatory note 8**). Ben Williams Ltd and Henderson Traders Ltd will be required to make quarterly payments on account of corporation tax if their profits are £1.5 million or above (SI 1998/3175).

John Wilson and Daniel Grant will include their profits in their self-assessment returns. Payments on account will be made on 31 January and 31 July each year, based on the partner's total net income tax liability for the previous year, with a balancing payment (or claim for a refund) on the next 31 January (TMA 1970 ss 59A, 59B).

The self-assessment returns will show overlap relief carried forward of £46,700 for John Wilson and £20,735 for Daniel Grant.

## (b) Smiley Faces

Where partnerships have both individual and corporate partners, separate computations have to be made for income tax and corporation tax, the computations being made *before* deducting shares of capital allowances according to the partnership agreement (see **explanatory note 2**). The total partnership profits for corporation tax purposes may therefore differ from those for income tax purposes. The Example assumes, however, that profits are the same in each case. The initial division of the capital allowances, and the profit shares taking the capital allowances into account, before consideration of the mixed partnership reallocation rules, are as follows:

| | *Total* | *Colebright Ltd* | *C Bright* | *L Coles* |
|---|---|---|---|---|
| **Division of capital allowances** | £ | £ | £ | £ |
| Y/e 30.9.2016 | 9,000 | 7,200 | 900 | 900 |

| | *Total* | *Colebright Ltd* | *C Bright* | *L Coles* |
|---|---|---|---|---|
| **Division of profits** | £ | £ | £ | £ |
| Y/e 30.9.2016 | | | | |
| First allocation | 40,000 | - | 20,000 | 20,000 |
| Remainder (80:10:10) | 152,000 | 121,600 | 15,200 | 15,200 |
| | 192,000 | 121,600 | 35,200 | 35,200 |
| Less capital allowances: | (9,000) | (7,200) | (900) | (900) |
| | 183,000 | 114,400 | 34,300 | 34,300 |

*Consideration of the mixed partnership reallocation rules:*

The mixed partnership reallocation rules (ITTOIA 2005 ss 850C-850E) only apply to periods of account starting on or after 6 April 2014.

In the case of the Smiley Faces partnership, for the year to 30 September 2016, Condition Y in ITTOIA 2005 s 850C(3) is met for the following reasons:

(1) The share of profits allocated to Colebright Ltd is more than an appropriate consideration for the services it provides to the partnership (use of the activity centre premises valued at £50,000). As the company has made no other contribution to the partnership, this represents its notional profit for the year – at £121,600 the company's share of partnership profits for the year exceeds this amount (ITTOIA 2005 s 850C(3)(a));

(2) As Ms Bright and Ms Coles each own 50% of the share capital of the company they are connected with it (ITTOIA 2005 s 850C(18)(a)) and they both have the power to enjoy the company's profit share as that profit share increases the value of their shareholding in it (ITTOIA 2005 s 850C(20)(b));

(3) It is reasonable to suppose that as Ms Coles and Ms Bright own the company between them, the profit allocation is attributable to their power to enjoy the company's share and it is apparent that the combined tax bill of all three parties is lower than would have been the case had the individuals not had the power to enjoy the company's profit share, in which case the individual partners would have been taxable on some of their shares at 40% rather than 20% (ITTOIA 2005 s 850C(3)(c)).

As a result, the profit shares for the year ended 30 September 2016 have to be reallocated so that the company share does not exceed its notional profit of £50,000 for the year.

Revised division of profits:

| | *Total* | *Colebright Ltd* | *C Bright* | *L Coles* |
|---|---|---|---|---|
| | £ | £ | £ | £ |
| **Division of profits** | | | | |
| Original allocation as above | 192,000 | 121,600 | 35,200 | 35,200 |
| Year ended | | | | |
| Reallocation under ITTOIA 2005 s 850C(4) | | (71,600) | 35,800 | 35,800 |
| | 192,000 | 50,000 | 71,000 | 71,000 |
| Less capital allowances: | (9,000) | (7,200) | (900) | (900) |
| | 183,000 | 42,800 | 70,100 | 70,100 |

If no other reliefs are available to Ms Coles and Ms Bright, this reallocation pushes them over the threshold for higher rate tax at 40%.

# Explanatory Notes

*Treatment of partnerships with company members*

(1) Where a partnership has companies as members, the normal income tax rules of ITTOIA 2005 Part 9 apply to partners who are individuals (see **Example C10**), but special rules CTA 2009 Part 17 apply to corporate partners.

*Computation of profits*

(2) Two computations are made, one for income tax using income tax principles and one for corporation tax using corporation tax principles. The corporation tax computation treats the partnership as a notional company. The reason for having two separate computations is that there are various points of difference in the computations, in particular:

(a) Interest paid by a company is dealt with under the loan relationships rules, whether or not tax is deducted at source, and if it relates to the trade it is taken into account (usually on an accruals basis) in arriving at the trading profit. See **Example K2** for full details of loan relationships rules;

(b) Different rules apply in relation to transactions in financial instruments (see **Example K2**) and the treatment of intangible assets (see **Example K3**);

(c) The rules for calculating rental income of individuals and companies are broadly the same, but there are some differences that affect the computation.

*Mixed partnership reallocation rules*

(3) The mixed partnership reallocation rules (ITTOIA 2005 ss 850C–850E) apply to accounting periods starting on or after 6 April 2014. Where the accounting period straddles that date and the conditions for the reallocation rules to apply are met (see below), the accounting period should be split into two notional accounting periods (one ending on 5 April 2014 and one starting on 6 April 2014) and the reallocation rules applied to the notional period of account starting on 6 April 2014.

The reallocation rules apply where a mixed partnership or a mixed limited liability partnership (LLP) (ie one which is made up of both individuals and non-individuals) makes a profit for tax purposes, a profit share is allocated to a non-individual partner (B) and either Condition X or Condition Y is met:

- Condition X is that the profits represent deferred profit of an individual member (A) (ITTOIA 2005 s 850C(2));
- Condition Y is that B's profit share exceeds the appropriate notional profit and that individual partner (A) has the 'power to enjoy' all or any part of B's profit share (ITTOIA 2005 s 850C(3)).

In both cases, it must be reasonable to assume that A's profit share is less than it would be apart from the profit deferral arrangements, or the circumstances that lead to the power to enjoy condition being met, and that, overall, less tax is paid because of the allocation of profits to the non-individual.

In the case of Condition Y, it must also be reasonable to assume that all or part of B's profit share relates to A's power to enjoy.

If these conditions are met then instead of being taxed on their profit shares according to the ratio agreed between the partners, the partners' profit shares are adjusted for tax purposes so that:

- The individual is taxed on the profits that would have been allocated to him had the deferral arrangements not been entered into or that reflect his power to enjoy, as determined on a just and reasonable basis;
- The increase in the profit shares allocated to the individual partner(s) is deducted from the share allocated to the non-individual partner(s).

Where Condition Y applies, the maximum additional profit that the individual can be taxed on is the difference between the appropriate notional profit for the non-individual and the profit allocated to that non-individual (the non-individual's 'excess profit'). In the Example, the allocation to Colebright Ltd is reduced to the appropriate rent on the premises, ie £50,000.

If a reallocation of profit shares has taken place for tax purposes under this legislation, the non-individual partner may make a payment to another person out of the excess profit share and that payment is not treated as income of the recipient, taken into account in calculating the profits or losses of the non-individual or otherwise allowed as a deduction against the non-individual's income and it is not treated as a distribution (ITTOIA 2005 s 850E).

*Mixed partnership losses*

(4) Where a partnership includes both individuals and non-individuals and a loss arises to a partner who is an individual, that partner will be denied loss relief if the loss arises due to arrangements intended to secure that the losses of the trade are allocated to that partner rather than the non-individual partner(s) (ITA 2007 s 116A). This has effect for losses incurred in 2014/15 and later tax years.

*Treatment of the company's share of profits*

(5) The share allocated to each corporate partner is reduced by the capital allowances and charges allocated to that company. The company's share of interest paid will be taken into account on an accruals basis either as a trading expense or in arriving at a loan relationship credit surplus or deficit (see **Example K2**). The company's share of patent royalties paid will also be taken into account on an accruals basis under the intangible assets rules (see **Example K3**). The profit is charged to corporation tax as if it arose from a separate trade carried on by the company. Each corporate partner must include its share of the profits in its own corporation tax return. If the accounting periods of the company and partnership are different, the partnership share is time apportioned to the accounting periods of the company. If a loss arises the normal loss reliefs are available, subject to some anti-avoidance provisions.

*Treatment of individual partners' profit shares*

(6) The share of the capital allowances relating to the individual partners is treated as a trading expense and deducted from the profit, each individual partner's share then being dealt with according to the normal rules. Each individual will include his share of the profits in the partnership pages of his own self-assessment return (see **explanatory note 8**).

*Changes of partner*

(7) As far as changes of partner are concerned, the firm is not treated as ceasing when an individual partner joins or leaves. Similarly, changes in the corporate partners do not have any effect on the continuance of the partnership business, unless a change occurs in which none of the company partners continues but one or more new company partners joins the partnership. In that event the trade is treated as having been transferred to a different 'notional' company.

*Self-assessment*

(8) Under self-assessment, partnerships are required to send in partnership returns (TMA 1970 s 12AA). This applies even if there are no individual partners in the partnership. Where all the partners are companies, accounts and computations must be submitted with the partnership return (see **Example G2 part 2**).

If all the partners are individuals, the due date for sending in the partnership return is 31 January following the end of the tax year. If all partners are companies, the return is due 12 months after the end of the accounting period. In both cases where notice to submit a return is received late, the due date becomes 3 months from the date the notice is received.

For mixed partnerships (partnerships with both company and individual members), the due date for the partnership return is the later of the company date and the date for individuals.

The due date of filing for income tax returns is 31 October for paper returns, and 31 January for electronic returns.

For the year to 31 December 2016 the due filing date is therefore the later of 31 December 2017 and 31 January 2018 for electronic returns (ie 31 January 2018), or the later of 31 December 2017 and 31 October 2017 for paper returns (ie 31 December 2017).

The individuals and companies also have to file their separate returns, the due dates for those separate returns being the same as stated above for partnerships of all individuals or all companies.

*Limited partnerships*

(9) Under the provisions of the Limited Partnership Act 1907, it is possible for one or more partners to restrict liability for partnership debts to the amount of the limited partner's agreed capital contribution, providing there is at least one general partner with unlimited liability. The limited partner cannot take part in the management of the partnership, and his share of partnership profits would normally rank as unearned income.

A company could act as either a limited partner or a general partner in such a partnership, and if a limited company is the general partner this effectively limits the liability of that general partner.

(10) Certain reliefs available to a limited partner cannot exceed the amount of the partner's agreed capital contribution plus undrawn profits (ITA 2007 ss 104, 105). The main items concerned are reliefs for trading losses (including capital allowances) against the partner's income (or company profits) other than trading income, group relief for companies and interest paid in connection with the trade by an individual. ITA 2007 s 103C limits trade loss relief against other income or capital gains ('sideways' relief) to £25,000 per fiscal year per limited partner or 'non-active' partner. Relief is denied under this anti-avoidance legislation where the main purpose of making a contribution to a partnership is to obtain tax relief. See **Example E4**. A limited partner is also not entitled to relief for interest on a loan to buy an interest in a partnership, or lend money to it. See **Example A1 explanatory note 14 (iii)**.

(11) The national insurance treatment of limited partners who are individuals depends on the circumstances. Class 2 national insurance contributions are payable by someone who is 'gainfully employed' otherwise than as an employee (SSCBA 1992 s 2(1)(b)). Class 4 contributions are payable where profits are 'immediately derived' from carrying on a trade, profession or vocation (SSCBA 1992 s 15(1)). Although a limited partner cannot take part in managing the business, he may participate in a lesser capacity, and if he does, contributions will be payable.

# Question

(a) Daniel Brown and his wife Sharon who both previously worked for other firms, propose to commence trading on 1 January 2017 as a partnership of chartered surveyors. They have heard that other firms of chartered surveyors often operate through LLPs and want to know what the difference is in tax treatment between an ordinary general partnership and an LLP. Write brief notes for a meeting with them setting out the legal and taxation aspects of both a general partnership and an LLP, highlighting any key differences.

(b) DHP Davies LLP runs several dairy farms in South Wales, and has done so since 2003. The members of the LLP are DHP Holdings Ltd and brothers Julian and Ivor Davies who both work on various aspects of running the farms. The capital contributions made to the LLP by Julian and Ivor are £250,000 and £150,000 respectively. There is no other connection between the brothers and the company. One of the farms operated by the LLP was originally rented from Julian's ex-wife but was inherited by Julian's daughter Lily on her mother's death in 2010. The LLP now rents the farm from Lily Davies for £30,000 per year (this figure was negotiated based on the average prevailing rental rate on similar holdings in the area).

The partnership makes up its accounts to 30 April each year and its results have not varied by more than 10% in any year. The results for years ended 30 April 2017 are as follows:

| | *Profits* | *Capital allowances* |
|---|---|---|
| Y/e 30.4.2017 | £1,020,000 | £52,000 |

Assume that the profits for income tax and corporation tax purposes are the same.

The profit-sharing arrangements are that the brothers are entitled to £72,000 each per year which they draw throughout the year, with the remainder of the profits being shared 60% to the company, 25% to Julian Davies and 15% to Ivor Davies. These profit-sharing arrangements have been in place since 2010.

On 1 November 2016, Julian's daughter Lily becomes a member of the partnership, initially taking on responsibility for transporting the animals from farm to farm and to and from market. She introduces just £2,000 in capital. At that point the profit sharing arrangements are adjusted so that the brothers are still entitled to £72,000 and Lily is entitled £24,000 a year to be drawn evenly each month during the year. Lily is also entitled to 1% of any profits of the LLP over £5 million. The remainder of the profits are split: 61% to the company, 24% to Julian Davies and 15% to Ivor Davies.

Show the amounts that each member of the partnership should include in their self-assessments in respect of each of the years concerned, and discuss whether and how the salaried member rules might apply to Julian, Ivor or Lily Davies (for the purposes of this example you can accept that the salaried members rules have been tested and found not to apply to any previous period).

# Answer

(a) **General partnerships**

In order for a partnership to exist there must be an agreement, which should preferably although not necessarily be in writing, and there must be evidence that the agreement has been acted on.

There is therefore little formality attached to the formation of the partnership, although there are requirements on each partner and the partnership as a whole to notify HMRC of the commencement of the trade and the existence of the partnership. Both Mr and Mrs Brown would each have to register with HMRC for Class 2 NIC purposes 'immediately' after commencement of trading (SI 2001/1004 reg 87AA). Immediately is not defined within the legislation, although it is reasonable to assume that this means as soon as possible following commencement of trading. HMRC may allow further time to register, but it is not clear in which circumstances this will be offered (SI 2001/1004 reg 87AA(4)). Registration for Class 2 is normally made at the same time as registering the partnership and partners for self-assessment ( although if Mr and Mrs Brown are currently within the self-assessment regime the latter will not be necessary). This can be done via the GOV.UK website [www.gov.uk/log-in-file-self-assessment-tax-return/register-if-youre-a-partner-or-partnership]. In doing so, the couple would also have to decide who will be the nominated partner, acting as the contact point for HMRC. Once HMRC has issued a unique taxpayer reference to the nominated partner, the other partner will also have to register with HMRC as a member of the partnership, using that reference number. Each year the nominated partner must make a partnership self-assessment return to HMRC in addition to each partner submitting their own self-assessment return.

Partners are free to divide profits or losses between individual members in whatever way they wish according to the provisions of the partnership agreement. This division is accepted as valid for tax purposes (although profits may be reallocated where the partnership includes both individual and corporate partners – see **Example C12** part (**b**)).

Historically, HMRC has looked critically at partnership arrangements between husband and wife where a spouse joining a partnership takes a profit share out of all proportion to the contribution made, either in relation to the capital they have introduced or to the level of work done to produce the partnership profits. HMRC sought to remove the tax benefit of such arrangements using the settlements legislation but given a high profile defeat in the Courts in 2007, such a challenge is less likely (see **explanatory note 1**).

**Limited liability partnerships**

A Limited Liability Partnership (LLP) has to be registered with Companies House. Most LLPs are formed through formation agents as is the case for private limited companies. The name chosen must end with 'LLP' or 'Limited Liability Partnership', and names are subject to the same restrictions as company names. LLPs may not choose a name closely similar to an existing company's name, and vice versa. See the GOV.UK website for more information [www.gov.uk/set-up-and-run-limited-liability-partnership].

If the partners do not wish to use a formation agent or other third party they can download Form LL IN01 from the GOV.UK website [www.gov.uk/government/publications/register-a-limited-liability-partnership-ll-in01] and file it with Companies House with the appropriate signatures and fee. At the time of writing, the fee is £40 although Welsh partnerships using the Welsh language and registering an office in Wales only pay £20. A 'same day service' is offered for a higher fee [www.gov.uk/set-up-and-run-limited-liability-partnership/register-your-llp].

The LLP has similarities to a company in that it is a separate legal entity contracting in its own right, it provides limitation on individuals' liability, and has accounting and administrative burdens similar to those of companies, including an obligation for annual reporting to Companies House.

A key advantage of an LLP as opposed to a general partnership from a member's point of view is the limited liability of individual members. Normally an LLP member's liability will be restricted to capital provided plus undrawn profits. If this is below a specified amount, a member may be required to contribute on winding up. As for a limited company, an individual can, however, still remain personally liable under the law of tort where a duty of care to another exists. This particularly applies to professional firms. Furthermore, members can be sued for wrongful or fraudulent trading and can be disqualified from being a member of an LLP.

**Taxation aspects of LLPs**

Members of an LLP carrying on a trade are broadly taxed as if they were members of a partnership (ITTOIA 2005 s 863 and TCGA 1992 s 59A). All activities of the LLP are treated as carried on by the members and property is held by the members. All references to a partnership in the tax legislation include an LLP. This means that the registration and self-assessment requirements are exactly the same as those described above for a general partnership.

Unless treated as salaried members (see **explanatory note 6**), the members are taxed under the same income tax rules as partners. This means that the basis periods are as for partnerships (see **Example C10**) and that the benefits in kind rules do not apply to partnership assets used by the members, such as cars.

On liquidation, however, the LLP becomes subject to corporation tax.

Tax should not be the major consideration in deciding between a traditional partnership and an LLP, as the tax treatment of both formats is intended by legislation to be as nearly identical as possible (leaving aside anti-avoidance provisions).

The choice for Mr and Mrs Brown is therefore likely to rest on non-tax factors, such as the benefit of limited liability status and their plans for the future of the business. If they choose to set up as a general partnership to begin with, they can always transfer the business to an LLP at a later date. That transfer would be tax-neutral (see **explanatory note 5**).

(b) DHP Davies LLP

Where partnerships have both individual and corporate partners, separate computations have to be made for income tax and corporation tax, the computations being made *before* deducting shares of capital allowances according to the partnership agreement (see **Example C12 explanatory note 2**). The total partnership profits for corporation tax purposes may therefore differ from those for income tax purposes. The Example assumes, however, that profits are the same in each case.

The division of the capital allowances, and the profit shares taking the capital allowances into account, are therefore initially as follows (before consideration of the salaried partner rules):

| | *Total* £ | *DHP Holdings Ltd* £ | *Julian* £ | *Ivor* £ | *Lily* £ |
|---|---|---|---|---|---|
| **Division of capital allowances** | | | | | |
| Y/e 30.4.2017 | | | | | |
| Up to 31.10.2016 | 26,000 | 15,600 | 6,500 | 3,900 | - |
| 1.11.2016 to 30.4.2017 | 26,000 | 15,860 | 6,240 | 3,900 | - |
| | 52,000 | 31,460 | 12,740 | 7,800 | - |

**Initial division of profits:**

| | *Total* £ | *DHP Holdings Ltd* £ | *Julian* £ | *Ivor* £ | *Lily* £ |
|---|---|---|---|---|---|
| **Division of profits** | | | | | |
| Y/e 30.4.2017 | | | | | |
| Up to 31.10.2016 | | | | | - |
| First allocation | 72,000 | - | 36,000 | 36,000 | - |

| | Total £ | DHP Holdings Ltd £ | Julian £ | Ivor £ | Lily £ |
|---|---|---|---|---|---|
| Remainder (60:25:15) | 438,000 | 262,800 | 109,500 | 65,700 | - |
| | 510,000 | 262,800 | 145,500 | 101,700 | - |
| 1.11.2016 to 30.4.2017 | | | | | |
| First allocation | 84,000 | - | 36,000 | 36,000 | 12,000 |
| Remainder (61:24:15:0) | 426,000 | 259,860 | 102,240 | 63,900 | - |
| | 1,020,000 | 522,660 | 283,740 | 201,600 | 12,000 |
| Less capital allowances: | (52,000) | (31,460) | (12,740) | (7,800) | - |
| | 968,000 | 491,200 | 271,000 | 193,800 | 12,000 |

**Consideration of the salaried partner rules**

The salaried partner rules in ITTOIA 2005 ss 863A-863G apply from 6 April 2014 onwards. The salaried member rules apply if all of three conditions (A, B and C) are met. The legislation sets down at which point each of the conditions has to be tested.

The first point at which the conditions had to be considered was 6 April 2014 when Julian and Ivor were the only individuals who were members of the LLP. Subsequently Conditions B and C have to be tested on 6 April every year (in practice only if Condition A is met) and all three tests have to be applied in respect of any new member joining the LLP as at the date of joining. See **explanatory note 6** for other events that mean one or more of the conditions has to be re-tested. The Example assumes that Conditions A, B and C have been tested for Julian and Ivor and that the salaried member rules were found not to apply to them for any period up to and including the year ended 30 April 2016.

This means that the first point during the year ended 30 April 2016 that the salaried members rules have to be considered is 1 November 2016 when Lily Davies joins the LLP. The conditions then have to be tested afresh in respect of each of the individuals who are members of the partnership.

The position has not changed for Julian and Ivor Davies, but Lily Davies does trigger the salaried members rules:

*Condition A* (ITTOIA 2005 s 863B): is it reasonable to expect that at least 80% of the amounts payable to Lily from the LLP represent disguised salary? The fixed entitlement to £24,000 a year counts as disguised salary as it is a payment in respect of the services she performs and it is not in practice affected by the overall amount of profits or losses of the LLP (on the basis that it is reasonable to assume that the LLP is unlikely to incur losses or make a profit of more than £5 million). It is also more than 80% of the total amount payable to Lily by the LLP so Condition A is met. For the purposes of this test, the £30,000 per annum rent received by Lily Davies is disregarded as it is rental income in her hands and not payable to her in respect of performance of her services.

*Condition B* (ITTOIA 2005 s 863C): does Lily have significant influence over the affairs of the partnership. Given that Lily's role is to transport the animals and there is no indication that she has responsibility in the business, she does not have significant influence so Condition B is met.

*Condition C* (ITTOIA 2005 s 863D): is the amount of Lily's capital contribution to the LLP amount to less than 25% the amount payable to her as disguised salary for the tax year 2016/17? Lily only invested £2,000. As this was made part of the way through the tax year it is time apportioned under ITTOIA 2005 s 263D(8) to £833 (5/12 x £2,000). This is less than 25% of the £10,000 (£12,000 x 5/6) disguised salary she is due to receive in 2016/17. Condition C is met.

This means that Lily is treated as a salaried member – ie an employee. Lily is treated for income tax and NIC purposes as receiving £2,000 per month in employment income. For the year ended 30 April 2017 the LLP is entitled to a deduction of £12,000 plus 13.8% in secondary Class 1 NIC on the monthly excess over the secondary threshold, totalling £13,096, giving a revised profit for the year of £1,006,904 (£1,020,000 - £13,096), allocated as follows:

| | Total £ | DHP Holdings Ltd £ | Julian £ | Ivor £ |
|---|---|---|---|---|
| **Division of profits** | | | | |
| Y/e 30.4.2017 | | | | |
| Up to 31.10.2016 | | | | |
| First allocation | 72,000 | - | 36,000 | 36,000 |
| Remainder (60:25:15) | 431,452 | 258,871 | 107,863 | 64,718 |
| | 503,452 | 258,871 | 143,863 | 100,718 |
| 1.11.2016 to 30.4.2017 | | | | |
| First allocation | 72,000 | - | 36,000 | 36,000 |
| Remainder (61:24:15) | 431,452 | 263,186 | 103,548 | 64,718 |
| | 1,006,904 | 521,057 | 283,411 | 201,436 |
| Less capital allowances: | (52,000) | (31,460) | (12,740) | (7,800) |
| | 954,904 | 490,597 | 270,671 | 193,636 |

The LLP should check whether Lily (or any other individual member) is caught by the salaried member rules as at 6 April each year, so that it can correctly operate PAYE in respect of payments to her.

A further check also needs to be made is a new member joins the LLP or if any of the factors relevant to each of Conditions A, B or C changes.

## Explanatory Notes

*General partnerships between spouses*

(1) It is common to see general partnerships made up of husband and wife. Although partners are free to divide profits in whatever way they wish according to the provisions of the partnership agreement, the division being accepted as valid for tax purposes, the settlements provisions of ITTOIA 2005 ss 619-648 are wide enough to catch artificial partnership arrangements between husband and wife where a spouse joining a partnership takes a profit share out of all proportion to the contribution made. However, the success of Mr and Mrs Jones in *Jones v Garnett* [2007] STC 1536, otherwise known as Arctic Systems, means that such a challenge by HMRC is currently unlikely.

(2) One factor that couples may not wish to think about but can be important in the event of a marriage breakdown, is that a deserted spouse may be left to meet the firm's liabilities. This is different to the position with an LLP where individual partners are not jointly and severally liable for all business debts as in a general partnership.

*Limited Liability Partnership – wider points*

(3) LLP administration

The disclosure requirements for LLPs are similar to those for companies, although the LLP does not have a Memorandum of Association. The Members' Agreement is a private document.

The LLP must have at least two members, and members' names must be notified to Companies House in the prescribed form, as for officers in the case of limited companies. A minimum of two members must be designated as 'designated members', who are in particular responsible for the filing and compliance obligations. The LLP must complete an annual return, and notify changes of members' details, of accounting periods, and place details of mortgages or charges on record.

The LLP has very similar arrangements for setting an Accounting Reference Date, appointing auditors, for filing accounts, and similar penalties for non-compliance, as a limited company. Abbreviated accounts are available to small and medium-sized LLPs as for private limited companies.

(4) Limited liability

As the LLP is a separate legal entity which contracts and holds property in its own right, in the case of a prudently run LLP, its liabilities should be limited to its assets. The individual partners are therefore not jointly and severally liable for all business debts as in a traditional partnership. This is the case as long as the agreement does not automatically allocate losses. As for companies, in the case of an individual acting negligently or in contravention of professional guidelines, a legal challenge may seek to look through the corporate veil and hold an individual personally responsible. A liquidator may seek to recover any funds (eg loans, profit, expenses) or property withdrawn from the LLP within two years of commencement of winding-up if the member knew or had reasonable grounds for believing that the firm would be made insolvent by the withdrawal.

The members should therefore consider the solvency of the LLP before withdrawing funds. The LLP offers significant limitation of liability in comparison with traditional partnerships.

(5) Taxation

The transfer of a partnership to an LLP is tax neutral, eg no balancing adjustments for capital allowances, the existing overlap relief of a partner continues, no capital gains charges or SDLT. Class 2 and 4 NICs are payable as before. A single partnership tax return can be made for the tax year of change. It is not possible to re-register a limited company as an LLP or to convert an LLP to a limited company.

LLPs are not eligible to elect for the simplified cash basis for small businesses under ITTOIA 2005 s 25A, as they come within the definition of excluded persons by virtue of ITTOIA 2005 s 31C. Anti-avoidance legislation applies to LLPs that are property investment or investment LLPs (defined in CTA 2010 s 1135 and ITA 2007 ss 399(6), 1004(1)) to prevent abuse. No interest relief is available on loans used to buy an interest in, or lend money to, such partnerships (ITA 2007 s 399). Other provisions affect pension funds, insurance companies and friendly societies.

Although an LLP is free to allocate profits among its members, if the LLP includes both individual and non-individual members (ie it is a mixed partnership) the rules in ITTOIA 2005 ss 850C- 850E may apply to reallocate the partnership profits. For these rules apply either it must be reasonable to suppose that some or all of the individual's profit share has been 'deferred' by including it in the profit allocated to the non-individual partner resulting in a lower combined tax bill or there must be a connection between the individual and the non-individual partner such that the individual may derive benefit from the non-individual's share of the profit (either at once or in the future). If either of these conditions are met then the profits have to be reallocated on a just and reasonable basis to reflect the respective contributions of the partners. For further discussion of these rules, see **Example C12**.

Where a close company makes a loan to an LLP or other partnership in which there is an individual partner who is a participator in the close company (or an associate of an individual who is a participator), a tax charge arises of 32.5% of the amount of the loan under ITTOIA 2005 s 455 (25% for loans made before 6 April 2016). This tax is payable by the close company as if it were corporation tax payable for the accounting period in which the loan is made. The same rules apply regarding the due date for payment and repayment of the tax charged in the event that the loan is repaid as apply to other loans to participators. See **Example J2 Part (d)** for more information on the tax charge under CTA 2010 s 455. If a loan made to a partnership which was subject to a charge under CTA 2010 s 455 is subsequently written off or released, an amount is brought into the charge to tax equal to the amount of the loan written off or released (ITTOIA 2005 s 416) . The person liable for that tax charge is any partner in the partnership who is an individual (where there is more than one such partner the charge is apportioned between them in a just and reasonable manner) (ITTOIA 2005 s 417).

An LLP is treated as an entity for VAT, and registration is made using form VAT1 [www.gov.uk/government/publications/vat-application-for-registration-vat1]. The LLP can become part of a VAT group.

(6) Salaried members rules

ITTOIA 2005 ss 863A- 863G, effective from 6 April 2014, treats amounts received by certain members of LLPs as if those amounts were employment income and so subject to income tax and Class 1 NIC under PAYE. These rules bite in respect of a member of an LLP who is an individual is if three conditions are met:

- Condition A - it must be reasonable to expect that 80% of the member's share of the profits of the LLP is 'disguised salary';
- Condition B - the individual must not have significant influence over the affairs of the LLP; and
- Condition C - the individual's capital contribution to the LLP must be less than 25% of the disguised salary.

If all three conditions are met, then the individual is deemed to be a salaried member of the LLP, ie an employee, for income tax and NIC purposes and any monies or benefits that the member receives by reason of that deemed employment are subject to tax and Class 1 NIC, and subject to PAYE.

Conditions A, B and C have to be tested in respect of any new member of the LLP as at the time of joining. Condition A should also be retested if arrangements that affect the amounts the member may receive for services performed are put in place, modified or ended. Conditions B and C should be retested on 6 April each year. Additionally Condition B should be retested if the member's level of influence in the LLP changes and Condition C should retested if the member's capital contribution changes or there is another change that could affect the outcome of Condition C.

In considering methods of preventing members of LLPs falling foul of the salaried members rules, it is worth examining ITTOIA 2005 s 863G which contains specific anti-avoidance provisions as well as bearing in mind the possible application of the general anti-abuse rule (see **Example N6**).

(7) Tax treatment of trading and professional losses of LLPs

Where professional partnerships operate through an LLP, loss relief will be due as for an unlimited partnership, except that relief for losses will be restricted to a member's subscribed capital. Undrawn profits will normally be regarded as a debt of the LLP rather than part of a member's capital unless the members' agreement provides otherwise. Where the restriction causes losses to be unrelieved, the unrelieved amount will be carried forward and treated as a loss available for relief against other income under ITA 2007 s 64 and s 72 in later years, subject to the 'subscribed capital' restriction in those years (ITA 2007 ss 107-114).

There is also a restriction on losses where a partnership is made up of both individuals and non-individuals that applies for losses incurred in 2014/15 onwards. If a loss arises to a partner who is an individual due to arrangements intended to secure that the losses of the trade are allocated to that partner rather than the non-individual partner(s), then the individual partner is denied loss relief (ITA 2007 s 116A).

Partnership losses are discussed in more detail in **Example E4**.

(8) Winding-up of an LLP

When a liquidator is appointed (or, if earlier, when a winding-up order is made), the tax treatment changes. Any income will thereafter belong to the LLP and will be taxed as that of a corporate body. Any chargeable gains will be computed by reference to the date the asset was acquired by the LLP and taxed on the LLP. Members will then be taxed (or obtain relief) on the gain/loss arising on their capital interest, the base cost being determined by the historical capital contribution made by the member to the LLP as if it had been a limited company. This treatment does not apply on an informal winding-up without the appointment of a liquidator.

Where, in respect of the acquisition of a share in an LLP asset, a member had claimed business assets roll-over relief under TCGA 1992 ss 152, 153, or gains on depreciating assets had been held over under TCGA 1992 s 154, or the acquisition cost had been reduced by gifts holdover relief under TCGA 1992 ss 165 or 260, then on appointment of a liquidator the postponed gain will become chargeable (TCGA 1992 ss 156A, 169A).

# Question

## A.

Rodney Rogers has been farming in England since 1985.

His recent results (after capital allowances) have been:

| *Year ended* | *Profit (loss)* £ |
|---|---|
| 30 April 2012 | 50,000 |
| 30 April 2013 | 20,000 |
| 30 April 2014 | 25,000 |
| 30 April 2015 | (9,000) |
| 30 April 2016 | 23,000 |

(a) State the original taxable profits for all relevant tax years, assuming that a general income s 64 loss relief claim was made for the first available year, and

(b) State the amended profits for all years assuming that Rodney makes claims for 'averaging relief' wherever possible and assuming that a loss relief claim under ITA 2007, s 64 is made for the most advantageous year.

(c) Comment on the effect of the averaging adjustments.

## B.

Harold Pendragon had farmed Tintrim Farm for many years.

In 2014 Harold moved from Tintrim Farm to Bishops Farm, but the move was unsuccessful, so he moved in April 2015 to Green Leasowes Farm.

His recent farming results (after capital allowances) were as follows, accounts always having been prepared to 30 April:

| | | | £ | £ |
|---|---|---|---|---|
| 9 months ended 31 January 2014 | Tintrim Farm | Profit | 64,200 | |
| 3 months ended 30 April 2014 | Bishops Farm | Loss | (12,000) | 52,200 |
| 11 months ended 31 March 2015 | Bishops Farm | Loss | (11,000) | |
| 1 month ended 30 April 2015 | Green Leasowes | Profit | 2,450 | (8,550) |
| Year ended 30 April 2016 | Green Leasowes | Profit | | 44,000 |

Harold has savings income taxed at source of £5,000 gross per annum (2016/17 paid gross).

(i) Calculate Harold's income for all years affected by the above trading results, making averaging and loss claims to the best advantage, and show the effect on Class 4 national insurance contributions.

(ii) Show the effect of the averaging claims on payments on account, assuming claims are made to reduce such payments based upon the most favourable averaging/loss choice.

C.

Kay Connor is an author who has written many books.

Her income as an author fluctuates and for recent years her results have been:

| | | |
|---|---|---|
| Year ended 30 April 2013<br>(Fully relieved against 2012/13 taxable profits under ITA 2007 s 64) | Loss | (£3,650) |
| Year ended 30 April 2014 | Loss | (£11,760) |
| Year ended 30 April 2015 | Profit | £90,400 |
| Year ended 30 April 2016 | Profit | £32,550 |

Kay has no other income. Her income from appearances and talks is included in her literary accounts.

Show the tax and Class 4 national insurance contributions payable by Kay for each year, assuming all available reliefs are claimed.

Relevant allowances and tax bands in addition to those in the front of this book are as follows:

| | *Starting rate band** | *Basic rate threshold* | *Personal allowance* | *Starting point for higher rate tax* |
|---|---|---|---|---|
| | £ | £ | £ | £ |
| 2012/13 | 2,710 | 34,370 | 8,105 | 42,475 |
| 2013/14 | 2,790 | 32,010 | 9,440 | 41,450 |
| 2014/15 | 2,880 | 31,865 | 10,000 | 41,865 |
| 2015/16 | 5,880 | 31,765 | 10,600 | 42,385 |

* The starting rate was 10% for years 2012/13 to 2014/15 inclusive, reducing to 0% for 2015/16 onwards, and applies only to savings income. If taxable non-savings income is above this limit the starting rate is not applicable.

Class 4 national insurance contributions are payable at the rates indicated on profits between the following limits:

| | | |
|---|---|---|
| 2012/13 | @ 9% on | £7,605 to £42,475 and 2% thereafter |
| 2013/14 | @ 9% on | £7,755 to £41,450 and 2% thereafter |
| 2014/15 | @ 9% on | £7,956 to £41,865 and 2% thereafter |
| 2015/16 | @ 9% on | £8,060 to £42,385 and 2% thereafter |

# Answer

## A. Rodney Rogers

### (a) *Original self assessments for 2012/13 to 2016/17 assuming s 64 claim made for first available year*

| | | £ | £ |
|---|---|---|---|
| 2012/13 | Year ended 30.4.12 | | 50,000 |
| 2013/14 | Year ended 30.4.13 | | 20,000 |
| 2014/15 | Year ended 30.4.14 | 25,000 | |
| | Less s 64 claim re loss of yr to 30.4.15 | (9,000) | 16,000 |
| 2015/16 | Year ended 30.4.15) loss, therefore | | – |
| 2016/17 | Year ended 30.4.16 | | 23,000 |

### (b) *Amended self assessments for 2012/13 to 2016/17 assuming averaging relief claimed wherever possible and assuming s 64 claim made for most advantageous year*

Self assessments before loss claims are:

| | | £ | | £ |
|---|---|---|---|---|
| 2012/13 | (7/10ths = £35,000) | 50,000 | revised after full averaging: | 35,000 |
| 2013/14 | | 20,000 | revised after full averaging: | 35,000 |
| | | 70,000 | | 70,000 |
| 2013/14 | (7/10ths = £24,500, 3/4 = £26,250) | 35,000 | revised (partial averaging): | 31,250 |
| 2014/15 | | 25,000 | revised (partial averaging): | 28,750 |
| | | 60,000 | | 60,000 |
| | Partial averaging calculation: | | | |
| | Difference in profits: | 10,000 | | |
| | × 3 = | 30,000 | | |
| | Less (3/4 × 35,000) | 26,250 | | |
| | Adjustment to deduct from higher, add to lower profit = | 3,750 | | |
| 2014/15 | (7/10ths = £20,125) | 28,750 | revised after full averaging: | 14,375 |
| 2015/16 | | – | revised after full averaging: | 14,375 |
| | | 28,750 | | 28,750 |
| Consider 5 year averaging for 2016/17 | Original profit | 23,000 | | |
| Average of previous 4 years | (£35,000+£31,250+£14,375+£14,375)/4= | £23,750 | 75% = £17,813 | |
| 5 year averaging not available | | | | |

| | | | | |
|---|---|---|---|---|
| 2015/16 | | 14,375 | revised after full averaging: | 18,688 |
| 2016/17 | (7/10ths = £16,100) | 23,000 | revised after full averaging: | 18,687 |
| | | 37,375 | | 37,375 |

It will be better to claim loss relief in 2015/16 rather than 2014/15 (see **part** (c) for more detailed consideration). Taxable profits after loss claims will therefore be as follows:

| | | £ | £ |
|---|---|---|---|
| 2012/13 | | | 35,000 |
| 2013/14 | | | 31,250 |
| 2014/15 | | | 14,375 |
| 2015/16 | | 18,688 | |
| | Less s 64 claim re loss of yr to 30.4.15 | (9,000) | 9,688 |
| 2016/17 | (subject to any averaging claim re 2017/18) | | 18,687 |

## (c) *Effect of averaging adjustments*

Where an averaging adjustment decreases the income of an earlier year, this does not result in any change to the self-assessment of that year, because although the *tax saving* is calculated according to the tax position of the earlier year, the claim is *given effect* for the later year (see **explanatory note 9**).

Averaging 2012/13 and 2013/14 is worthwhile because it eliminates the higher rate tax in 2012/13. However, this saving is partially offset by additional NIC liability, brought about because the original profits exceeded the Class 4 national insurance contributions upper profits limit threshold of £42,475 for 2012/13. The profits over the threshold without averaging are charged at 2% whereas averaging reduces the profits each year to below the upper profits limit and they are all therefore charged to NIC at 9%.

Averaging 2013/14 and 2014/15 does not, in fact, achieve any immediate tax saving because no higher rate tax was payable in either year.

Without an averaging claim for 2014/15 and 2015/16, there would be no trading income in 2015/16 because of the loss. Averaging brings income into 2015/16 to cover the balance of the personal allowance. Claiming relief for the 2015/16 loss in 2014/15, however, would reduce the trading income of that year to only £5,375, thus wasting some of the nil-rate Class 4 band. It would be better to make the loss claim for 2015/16, at the same time making an averaging claim for 2015/16 and 2016/17 to increase the 2015/16 trading income to £18,688. The time limit for the loss claim is 31 January 2018. After setting off the loss of £9,000, there is then sufficient income remaining (trading income £9,688) to cover almost all of the personal allowance and all of the nil-rate Class 4 national insurance contributions band. If 2015/16 and 2016/17 were not averaged, the trading income of £14,375 would be reduced to £5,375 after the loss claim, so that part of the Class 4 nil-rate band would again be wasted, and more of the personal allowance would be unused. Five year averaging in 2016/17 is not possible as the volatility tests are not met (see **explanatory note 8**).

The effect of averaging on Class 4 contributions payable by Rodney is as follows:

**Class 4 national insurance contributions payable:**

| | *No averaging* | | *Averaging* | |
|---|---|---|---|---|
| | *Profit* | *Class 4* | *Profit* | *Class 4* |
| | £ | £ | £ | £ |
| 2012/13 | 50,000 | 3,289 | 35,000 | 2,466 |
| 2013/14 | 20,000 | 1,102 | 31,250 | 2,115 |
| 2014/15 | 16,000 | 724 | 14,375 | 578 |
| 2015/16 | – | – | 9,688 | 147 |
| 2016/17 | 21,000 | 1,165 | 18,687 | 956 |
| | | 6,280 | | 6,262 |

From 2012/13 to 2016/17 there is a net reduction of only £18 but it is still worthwhile making the averaging claims because of the tax savings achieved.

## B. Harold Pendragon

### (i) *Total income and Class 4 national insurance contributions*

### (a) Self assessments of trading income, subject to averaging (see explanatory note 9)

| | | £ |
|---|---|---|
| 2014/15 | Year ended 30.4.14 | 52,200 |
| 2015/16 | Year ended 30.4.15 (Loss of £8,550) | – |
| 2016/17 | Year ended 30.4.16 | 44,000 |

Relief for the loss of £8,550 for 2015/16 may be claimed under s 64 in 2015/16 or 2014/15, or the loss may be carried forward to 2016/17.

### (b) Possible averaging adjustments

| | | £ | | £ |
|---|---|---|---|---|
| Profits if all three years are averaged | 2014/15 | 52,200 | becomes | 26,100 |
| | 2015/16 | – | becomes | 26,100 |
| | | 52,200 | | 52,200 |
| | 2015/16 | 26,100 | becomes | 35,050 |
| | 2016/17 | 44,000 | becomes | 35,050 |
| | | 70,100 | | 70,100 |
| Profits if only 2014/15 and 2015/16 are averaged | 2014/15 | | | 26,100 |
| | 2015/16 | | | 26,100 |
| | 2016/17 | | | 44,000 |

It is possible that 2016/17 could be subject to a five year averaging claim, but we do not have sufficient data to establish whether this would be possible and whether it would be beneficial.

## (c) Total income, taking into account averaging and loss claims

Averaging all three years will eliminate the higher rate tax for 2014/15 and 2016/17 (bearing in mind the other income of £5,000 per annum) and ensure that personal allowances are fully utilised for 2015/16. Relief for the loss could then be claimed in 2015/16, thus reducing the tax of that year and reducing the payments on account required for 2016/17. If losses are carried back, the tax saving from the loss claim does not reduce payments on account for *any* year (see **explanatory note 9**). One further alternative is to make no claim for loss relief and carry the loss forward to 2016/17. The tax saving is the same, but the cashflow benefits of obtaining earlier relief make it more advisable for the loss claim to be made under s 64 in 2015/16.

Higher rate tax could be substantially eliminated and 2015/16 personal allowances fully utilised by averaging only 2014/15 and 2015/16, and carrying the loss forward to reduce the profits of 2016/17. This would, however, result in tax being paid at an earlier stage because it significantly increases the payments on account required for 2017/18. The best overall position is achieved by averaging all three years and claiming relief for the 2015/16 loss against the income of that year. This gives the following results:

| | *2014/15* | *2015/16* | *2016/17* |
|---|---|---|---|
| | £ | £ | £ |
| Farm profits (a) | 52,200 | – | 44,000 |
| Averaging adjustments (b) | (26,100) | 35,050 | (8,950) |
| Averaged trading profits | 26,100 | 35,050 | 35,050 |
| Savings income | 5,000 | 5,000 | 5,000 |
| | 31,100 | 40,050 | 40,050 |
| Less: Loss relief under s 64 | | (8,550) | |
| Total income | 31,100 | 31,500 | 40,050 |

## (d) Effect on Class 4 national insurance contributions

| | | | | *2014/15* | *2015/16* | *2016/17* |
|---|---|---|---|---|---|---|
| | | | | £ | £ | £ |
| Profits before averaging, with 2015/16 loss set against 2014/15 profits (i) | | | | 43,650 | | 44,000 |
| Profits after averaging and with loss set against 2015/16 profits (ii) | | | | 26,100 | 26,500 | 35,050 |
| Contributions payable | | | | | | |
| (i) | 43,650 – 41,865 | @ 2% | 36 | | | |
| | 41,865 – 7,956 | @ 9% | 3,052 | | | |
| | | | | 3,088 | | |
| (ii) | 26,100 – 7,956 | @ 9% | | 1,633 | | |
| (i) | – | | | | – | |
| (ii) | 26,500 – 8,060 | @ 9% | | | 1,660 | |
| (i) | 44,000 – 43,000 | @ 2% | 20 | | | |
| | 43,000 – 8,060 | @ 9% | 3,145 | | | |
| | | | | | | 3,165 |
| (ii) | 35,050 – 8,060 | @ 9% | | | | 2,429 |
| Increase/(decrease) | | | | (1,455) | 1,660 | (736) |

There is thus a net decrease in national insurance contributions of £531.

## (ii) *Effect of averaging claims on payments on account*

### (a) Before averaging claims

| | | | | | £ | £ | *Payable* £ |
|---|---|---|---|---|---|---|---|
| 2014/15 | Trading income | | | | | 52,200 | |
| | Savings income | | | | | 5,000 | (1,000) |
| | | | | | | 57,200 | |
| | Personal allowance | | | | | 10,000 | |
| | | | | | | 47,200 | |
| | Tax thereon: | 31,865 | | @ 20% | | 6,373 | |
| | | 15,335 | | @ 40% | | 6,134 | |
| | | 47,200 | | | | 12,507 | |
| | Class 4 NIC | | (52,200 – 41,865) | @ 2% | 207 | | |
| | | | (41,865 – 7,956) | @ 9% | 3,052 | | |
| | | | | | | 3,259 | |
| | | | | | | | 15,766 |
| | Tax due by payments on account 31.1.15 and 31.7.15 with balancing payment 31.1.16 | | | | | | 14,766 |

**Note**

It is not possible to reduce this amount because of the loss/averaging claim to be made for 2015/16. The amount will be repayable in part when the 2015/16 return is filed.

| | | |
|---|---|---|
| 2015/16 | Payments on account due on each of 31.1.16 and 31.7.16 – half of £14,766 | £7,383 |

### (b) Following averaging claims re 2014/15 and 2015/16 and s 64 loss claim

| | | | | £ | *Payable* £ |
|---|---|---|---|---|---|
| 2014/15 | Trading income | | | 26,100 | |
| | Savings income | | | 5,000 | (1,000) |
| | | | | 31,100 | |
| | Personal allowance | | | 10,000 | |
| | | | | 21,100 | |
| | Tax thereon: | 21,100 | @ 20% | 4,220 | |
| | Class 4 NIC | (26,100 – 7,956) | @ 9% | 1,633 | 5,853 |
| | | | | | 4,853 |
| Paid for year (as in (a)) | | | | | 14,766 |
| Repayment given effect for 2014/15 on filing 2015/16 return | | | | | (9,913) |
| 2015/16 | Trading income | | | 26,100 | |
| | Savings income | | | 5,000 | (1,000) |

| | | | | £ | Payable £ |
|---|---|---|---|---|---|
| | | | | 31,100 | |
| | *Less*: s 64 claim re loss of year | | | (8,550) | |
| | | | | 22,550 | |
| | Personal allowance | | | 10,600 | |
| | | | | 11,950 | |
| | Tax thereon: | 11,950 | @ 20% | 2,390 | |
| | Class 4 NIC | (26,100 – 8,550 – 8,060) | @ 9% | 854 | 3,244 |
| | | | | | 2,244 |
| Payments on account due 31.1.16 and 31.7.16 as in (a) | | | | 14,766 | |
| Reduced to actual following claim on Form SA303 | | | | (12,522) | 2,244 |
| 2016/17 | Payments on account due on each of 31.1.17 and 31.7.17 – half of £2,244 | | | | 1,122 |

## (c) Following averaging claim re 2015/16 and 2016/17

| | | | | | | |
|---|---|---|---|---|---|---|
| 2015/16 | Trading income | | | | 35,050 | |
| | Savings income | | | | 5,000 | (1,000) |
| | | | | | 40,050 | |
| | *Less* s 64 claim re loss of year | | | | (8,550) | |
| | | | | | 31,500 | |
| | Personal allowance | | | | 10,600 | |
| | | | | | 20,900 | |
| | Tax thereon: | | | | | |
| | | 20,900 | @20% | 4,180 | | |
| | Class 4 NIC | (35,050 – 8,550 – 8,060) | @ 9% | 1,660 | | 5,840 |
| | | | | | | 4,840 |
| Paid for year (as in **(b) above**) | | | | | | (2,244) |
| Due with 2016/17 liability | | | | | | 2,596 |

| | | | | | £ | Payable £ |
|---|---|---|---|---|---|---|
| 2016/17 | Trading income | | | | 35,050 | |
| | Savings income | | | | 5,000 | |
| | | | | | 40,050 | |
| | Personal allowance | | | | 11,000 | |
| | | | | | 29,050 | |
| | Tax thereon: | Non savings: | 24,050 | @ 20% | 4,810 | |
| | | Savings income: | 1,000 | @ 0% | – | |
| | | | 4,000 | @ 20% | 800 | |
| | Class 4 NIC: | (35,050 – 8,060) | | @ 9% | 2,429 | 8,039 |
| Payments on account per (b) | | | | | | (2,244) |

| | £ | Payable £ |
|---|---|---|
| | | 5,795 |
| Due for 2015/16 re averaging claim as above | | 2,596 |
| Payable re 2016/17 on 31.1.18 | | 8,391 |
| Plus | | |
| First payment on account due on of 31.1.18 for 2017/18 (half of £8,039) | | 4,019.50 |
| Total payable 31.1.18 | | 12,410.50 |

**Summary of payments due**

| | | £ | £ |
|---|---|---|---|
| 2014/15 | Total due by 31.1.16 (a) | | 14,766 |
| 2015/16 | Due 31.1.15 (1st payment on account) | 7,383 | |
| | Reduced by claim | (6,261) | |
| | Revised amount due 31.1.16 (b) | | 1,122 |
| | 2nd payment on account due 31.7.16 (b) | | 1,122 |
| 2016/17 | Due 31.1.17 (c) | | 1,122 |
| | Due 31.7.17 (c) | | 1,122 |
| | Balance due 31.1.18 (c) | 8,391.00 | |
| 2017/18 | 1st payment on account due 31.1.18 | 4,019.50 | 12,410.50 |
| Repayable re 2014/15 by claim with 2015/16 tax return | | | (9,913) |

## C. Kay Connor

### *Tax and Class 4 national insurance contributions payable*

**Assessable profits**

| | | £ | £ | £ |
|---|---|---|---|---|
| 2013/14 | | | | |
| | Year ended 30.4.13 | | | Nil |
| | (Loss carried back to 2012/13) | | | |
| 2014/15 | | | | |
| | Year ended 30.4.14 – Loss | (11,760) | | |
| 2015/16 | | | | |
| | Year ended 30.4.15 – Profit | 90,400 | | |
| Claim for averaging with 2014/15 made by 31.1.16: | | | | |
| | Year ended 30.4.14 | | – | |
| | Year ended 30.4.15 | | 90,400 | |
| | Average | | 45,200 | |
| **Revised trading results:** | | | | |
| 2014/15 | | | | |
| | Average profits | | 45,200 | |
| | *Less*: s 64 loss claim re: year to 30.4.14 | | (11,760) | 33,440 |
| 2015/16 | | | | |

| | | | | £ | £ | £ |
|---|---|---|---|---|---|---|
| | Average profits | | | 45,200 | | |
| 2016/17 | | | | | | |
| | Year ended 30.4.16 | | | 32,550 | | |
| | Difference | | | 12,650 | | |
| | Averaging by claim made by 31.1.19: | | | | | |
| | 75% of higher profit = | | £33,900 | | | |
| | 70% of higher profit = | | £31,640 | | | |
| | Averaging adjustment is: | | | | | |
| | 3 × 12,650 | | | | 37,950 | |
| | Less 75% × 45,200 | | | | 33,900 | |
| | Deduct from higher and add to lower | | | | 4,050 | |
| **Revised trading results:** | | | | | | |
| 2015/16 | | (45,200 – 4,050) | | | | 41,150 |
| 2016/17 | | (32,550 + 4,050) | | | | 36,600 |
| | (subject to any claim to average with 2017/18) | | | | | |

## *Tax payable*

| | | | | £ | £ |
|---|---|---|---|---|---|
| 2013/14 | | | | | Nil |
| 2014/15 | Income from profession | | | 33,440 | |
| | Personal allowance | | | (10,000) | |
| | Taxable income | | | 23,440 | |
| | Tax thereon: | 23,440 | @ 20% | 4,688 | |
| | Class 4 NIC | (33,440 – 7,956) | @ 9% | 2,294 | |
| | | | | | 6,982 |
| 2015/16 | | | | | |
| | Income from profession | | | 41,150 | |
| | Personal allowance | | | (10,600) | |
| | Taxable income | | | 30,550 | |
| | Tax thereon: | 30,550 | @ 20% | 6,110 | |
| | Class 4 NIC | (41,150 – 8,060) | @ 9% | 2,978 | 9,088 |
| 2016/17 | | | | | |
| | Income from profession | | | 36,600 | |
| | Personal allowance | | | (11,000) | |
| | Taxable income | | | 25,600 | |
| | Tax thereon: | 25,600 | @ 20% | 5,120 | |
| | Class 4 NIC | (36,600 – 8,060) | @ 9% | 2,569 | 7,689 |

## Explanatory Notes

*Averaging claims*

(1) ITTOIA 2005 s 221 gives averaging relief for individuals and partnerships who are farmers or creative artists who make a claim in their tax return or an amended return. It need not be claimed unless required. Profits to be averaged are taken into account *after* capital allowances. The amount of capital allowances *claimed* may be varied using the disclaimer provisions (see **Example C7**). The profits taken into account for averaging are before deducting losses.

(2) No averaging claims may be made by individuals or partnerships using the cash basis for small businesses under ITTOIA 2005 s 25A, by virtue of s 221A. For more on the cash basis for small businesses, see **Example C3**.

*Creative artists*

(3) A 'creative artist' is someone whose profits are:

(a) derived wholly or mainly from literary, dramatic, musical or artistic works, or from designs, created by the taxpayer personally or by someone in partnership with the taxpayer, and

(b) chargeable to income tax as trading income.

'Artistic works' would include paintings and sculpture. The inclusion in profits of appearance fees and speaking fees would not prevent a claim for averaging.

*Time limits for claims*

(4) The time limit for making averaging claims is 12 months from the 31 January following the end of the second tax year (eg by 31 January 2017 for an averaging claim for 2013/14 and 2014/15).

*The averaging adjustment*

(5) The averaging rules provide that if, in respect of consecutive years of assessment, profits in either year do not exceed 7/10ths of the other year or are nil, a claim may be made for the profits of each year to be adjusted so that one-half of the profits for the two years taken together, or for the year for which there are profits, is assessed in each year.

Where profits are nil because there is a loss, any independent claim for loss relief is not affected and in calculating available losses the original results and not the averaged results are used. A nil value is included in the averaging calculation for the loss making year.

(6) Marginal relief is available where profits for either year exceed 7/10ths but are less than three-quarters of the profit for the other year. Profits for each year may then be adjusted by adding to those that are lower and deducting from those that are higher three times the difference between them less three-quarters of the higher profits. This is illustrated in **part A(b)** of the Example in relation to the 2013/14 and 2014/15 assessments.

Once an averaging calculation has been done, the average itself is the figure to use if the next year's profits are to be averaged. Averaging claims must be performed in sequence, and therefore if an averaging claim is made for a recent year, it precludes averaging claims for earlier years.

No claim can be made for the first and last years of the business.

(7) A claim is nullified if profits for either year are adjusted for any other reason (for example because of a change of accounting date, or cessation of trade), but any further claim in respect of the profits as adjusted is not out of time if made before one year from 31 January following the tax year in which the adjustment is made.

*Five-year averaging*

(8) Finance Act 2016, s 25 introduces a new five-year averaging rule for farmers but not creative artists (new s 222A ITTOIA 29915). The first year for which a five-year averaging claim may be made is 2016/17. A claim may be made in any year from 2016/17 onwards to average a year with the four preceding tax years. There are no changes to the mechanics of averaging or to any of the provisions regarding tax payment or repayment.

There are two alternative volatility tests to be met in order for a five year average claim to be made. These are that either:

- Any one of years 1 to 5 are zero, or
- The average profits of years one to four when compared to year five have a less than 75% relationship

Where there has been a zero result in any year, it is very likely that in practice this will already have been subject to an averaging claim – as for 2015/16 in Part A of the Example. So normally the first volatility test will be met in any year from 2016/17 onwards when there is a zero result (i.e. a loss). Part A of the Example illustrates the check on the second volatility test, but the profit of 2016/17 is very close to the average of years 1 to 4 so five-year averaging is not available. In fact, the option for five-year averaging is likely to be preferable only where there is a very substantial profit in year 5, allowing the higher rate liabilities to be eliminated by spreading the additional profit over four years rather than one.

*Carry-back claims under self-assessment*

(9) The treatment under self-assessment of claims that affect an earlier year is that although the effect of the adjustment is *calculated* by reference to the tax position in the earlier year, the adjustment is *given effect* in the later year (TMA 1970 Sch 1B). The adjustment does not, however, affect the tax *assessed* for the later year. For taxpayers who are calculating their own tax, the amount of any tax underpaid for the earlier year is shown in box 14 on the Tax Calculation Summary accompanying the tax return and any overpayment is shown in box 15.

Carried back amounts do not affect payments on account for the first of the two years that are averaged, because the tax of the earlier year is not adjusted. The payments on account for the second of the averaged years will initially be based on the unaveraged profits of the first year. Once the liability for the second year can be accurately ascertained, based on the averaged profits, a claim can be made to reduce payments on account if appropriate. The change to the assessable profit of the second year affects the payments on account for the next following year, which are based on the tax *assessed* for the second year.

The treatment of averaging claims under self-assessment means that even if an averaging adjustment which reduces the profits of the current year does not save any tax overall, because it is balanced by an increase of the same amount in the tax payable for the previous year, a cash flow advantage will still arise. This is because the reduction in the current year's tax reduces the payments on account for the next following year. Furthermore, if the reduction of the current year's liability reduces the amount payable below the payments on account made for that year, repayment supplement will be payable on the overpaid amounts as at 31 January in the tax year and 31 July following, even though the overpayment will be balanced by an underpayment for the previous year, that underpayment being payable by 31 January following the current year.

Thus in **part B(ii)** of the Example, the repayment based on 2013/14 does not alter the payments for that year, or payments on account for 2015/16, but is repayable after any outstanding tax (and tax due within 35 days) is settled. Once the revised liability for 2015/16 is known, a claim may be made to reduce payments on account for that year to the revised liability, repayment supplement being paid where appropriate. Following the next claim to average 2015/16 with 2016/17, this increases the liability for 2015/16, the increase being added to the tax due for 2016/17 (ie on 31 January 2018) but the adjustment does not affect the payments on account for any year, nor does it affect the tax *due under self-assessment* for 2016/17, so that the payments on account for 2017/18 are based on the 2016/17 tax due of £8,039. Note that the issue of additional tax payable for a previous year is important when a five-year averaging claim is made. The additional tax due for any earlier years is only due when the averaging claim is made, so there is no question of interest on those additional liabilities.

Interest on overdue or overpaid tax is charged from 31 January following the second year. There is therefore no interest benefit from an adjustment that reduces the tax of the earlier year as in 2014/15 in **B(ii) above**. On the other hand there is no interest disadvantage from an averaging adjustment that increases the tax of the earlier year as in 2015/16 in **B(ii) above**. And where the tax of the second year is reduced as a result of the adjustment, then interest will be paid on overpaid payments on account for the second year as indicated above. For detailed notes on carry-back claims see **Example G3**.

*Partnerships*

(10) Under the current year basis, averaging claims are made by individual partners in respect of their shares of the profit and not in respect of the partnership as a whole.

*Farming treated as one trade*

(11) In **part B** of the Example, Harold's trade is treated as continuing notwithstanding his change of farms, since all farming carried on by any particular person is treated as one trade (ITTOIA 2005 s 9). Where the trade is carried on by a firm then that trade is separate from any farming trade carried on by an individual who is a partner of the firm (s 859).

*Restrictions on relief for farming losses*

(12) The farmers in both parts of this Example have made intermittent profits and losses. There are special rules where farmers sustain losses over a long period. Relief for a loss against general income (ITA 2007 s 64) in a trade of farming and market gardening is not available if a loss (calculated without reference to capital allowances) has been made in each of the five tax years preceding the loss-making year in question. Certain exceptions are made to this rule (ITA 2007 s 67). One such exception applies where the trade is carried on with 'a reasonable expectation of profit'. Note that when considering the rule in s 67 the practice is to compute losses and profits on a strict fiscal year basis, apportioning the accounting periods between them. This can produce unexpected results, with profits in an accounting period subsumed within losses either side.

Similar rules apply to a loss in a company accounting period following a five-year run of losses (CTA 2010 s 48).

Losses prevented from being relieved against general income (ITA 2007 s 64) under the above provisions can be carried forward (under ITA 2007 s 83) against later profits from the same trade.

Although under the current year basis rules, capital allowances are treated as trading expenses, and are thus part of a trading loss, losses are still calculated before capital allowances for the purpose of ITA 2007 s 67.

*National insurance contributions*

(13) For detailed notes on national insurance contributions see **Example H1**.

# Property Business

# Question

## A.

Joe, who has worked for many years as an employee, has recently set up his own construction company, Specialists All Aspects Ltd. He has two employees, and the plant and equipment needed for general building work, but uses subcontractors at busy times, and for electrical, plumbing and decorating work.

He has asked for a meeting to go over the construction industry scheme (CIS), which he heard about as an employee.

Compile bullet points of the main features of the CIS scheme, to prepare for the meeting.

## B.

(a) George, a part-time employee with Barchester town council, has just received a legacy, and plans to buy two flats which he will renovate at a cost of £35,000, using local tradesmen. He plans to let one flat, but to sell the other at a profit, and buy further properties for renovation/let with the proceeds. He hopes eventually to make this his full-time occupation.

(b) Master Builder plc commenced trading on 1 January 2013, establishing a nationwide chain of DIY outlets. It has a 31 December year end, and has incurred or expects to incur the following amounts on construction expenditure (excluding land):

| | |
|---|---|
| Y/e 31 December 2013 | |
| Master Builder retail outlets | 1.7 million |
| Y/e 31 December 2014 | |
| Master Builder retail outlets | 0.9 million |
| Master Builder corporate HQ | 0.5 million |
| Y/e 31 December 2015 | |
| Master Builder retail outlets | 0.7 million |
| Master Builder sales office | 0.5 million |
| Y/e 31 December 2016 | |
| Master Builder retail outlets | 0.4 million |
| Refurbishment of disused building for commercial letting | 0.5 million |

(c) Patrick is a builder with electrical and plumbing skills. He builds conservatories, extensions and outhouses for householders, and occasionally carries out minor property maintenance or building on the premises of small non-construction businesses, taking about £25,000 per year plus materials.

State the obligations of each of the above as regards the construction industry scheme.

## C.

Specialists All Aspects Ltd has won a contract with Luxury Leisure Lodges Ltd, a company owned by a firm of architects, for the clearance of land and construction of holiday lodges, over a period of 18 months. Specialist All Aspects Ltd has not previously had to operate the CIS scheme.

At the end of the first month of July 2016 SAA Ltd's director reports that he has failed to grasp what is required by CIS regulations, and has taken no action towards compliance. He requests assistance in compliance, and in preparation of the first month's return. He advises that the following transactions have taken place:

**Payments/invoices for costs**

| | |
|---|---|
| (1) £1,750 + VAT | Paid to Rayne Forestry Enterprises, a forestry contractor providing its own timber harvester, loader and labour for clearing scrub and trees. Its previous activity has been limited exclusively to harvesting timber. Fuel for the timber harvester and the loader amounted to £85. |
| (2) £2,000 | Paid to Heavyweight Plant Hire for the hire and transport of a roller to prepare the site, to be operated by one of Specialists All Aspects Ltd's employees. |
| (3) £25,000 | Invoiced by Latvian Larch Lodges Inc (a Latvian-based company operating abroad for the first time) for provision and erection of one large Larch lodge, no customs duty or VAT has been charged. The lodge cost £20,000 and the erection £5,000. Payment was made during the month, but was subject to a 10% retention. |
| (4) £1,500 | Paid to John Smith, a local joinery contractor for joinery work. This payment was for a single job, but it has been agreed that in future Mr Smith will be paid £1,500 each month during the course of the project, for working Mondays, Tuesdays and Wednesdays each week. This will include the months of July and December, when he will be on holiday for two weeks. He will provide his own hand tools and van, although it is unlikely the van will be used for project purposes. |
| (5) £2,500 | Paid to Mega Tile plc, a major UK-wide decorative tile supplier, for supplying and installing decorative tiles in the bathroom. The payment is made up of £750 for tiles, £1,250 for labour and £500 for travel and subsistence. |
| (6) £2,500 | Paid to Darren, who recently became self-employed, for ground works. The payment is made up of £1,900 for labour, £350 for plant hire at cost, £75 fuel for machinery at cost and £175 travel expenses. |

**Company income**

Specialists All Aspects Ltd invoiced Luxury Leisure Lodges Ltd for £38,000, plus VAT, subject to 2.5% retention, and received payment on 27 July. The quantity surveyor certified materials and plant hire costs to be £23,260.

PAYE for the month to 5 August 2016 amounted to £1,237.

(a) State what action needs to be taken, and what reports must be produced, with due dates.

(b) Calculate deductions, on the basis that Darren and John Smith registered for net payment, Mega Tile plc for gross payment, and the others are not registered.

**D.**

Henry, director of Gross Builders Ltd, was discussing tax saving schemes with his friend Keran, a sole trader, in the pub. Both have remarkably similar construction industry businesses with a turnover of £85,000 per year, including rechargeable materials costs of about £30,000, and annual profit of around £20,000 (Henry has a low salary and pays dividends). PAYE amounts to around £1,250 per quarter, and CIS deductions withheld from subcontractors to around £600.

Both businesses have a 31 March year-end, but Keran's business is registered for gross payment whereas Gross Builders Ltd is still registered for net payment. Keran says that he has taken his wife into partnership from 1 July 2016 – she does substantial work for the business – to use both rate bands. Henry asks you why we have not provided him with similar proactive advice.

Respond, forecasting CIS payments/receipts for the next year on a quarterly basis, and state when final repayment is due.

# Answer

## A. Points for preparation for meeting with Joe

The construction industry scheme, applies where:

- a subcontractor receives payment from;
- another subcontractor, a contractor or deemed contractor;
- under a 'construction contract'.

'Contractors' include any businesses carrying out defined construction operations. They are required to:

- Review subcontractors' status for employment/self-employment;
- Verify their payment status with HMRC's database. There are three types of payment status, gross (gross payment status often being referred to as 'GPS'), 20% withholding, or 30% withholding;
- Calculate deductions correctly, excluding defined materials expenses;
- File monthly (but not annual) CIS returns and pay over deductions monthly;
- Issue monthly payslips to subcontractors subject to deduction.

Construction operations are defined in FA 2004 s 74, and listed in HMRC's guide, CIS340, covering most construction work in the UK and within the 12-mile limit offshore.

The deductions from payment do not reduce the amount of income liable to tax, but are on account of year-end tax and, for non-corporate subcontractors, NIC. A company may offset CIS deductions it has suffered against its own payroll deductions and CIS amounts that it has deducted itself, but only has a right of set-off against those within the same tax year. A sole trader or partnership does not have a right of set-off against PAYE or CIS deductions paid.

Payments for construction operations will be subject to CIS deductions, unless the subcontractor can prove compliance with strict criteria that assure HMRC that all tax and NIC will be paid on time.

## B.

(a) George is engaging in the repair of buildings, which is within the definition of construction operations. The activity is clearly not carried out in the capacity of a private householder, as he does not occupy the flats. The pattern and scale of expenditure will almost certainly cause the activity to be considered as a property developing business, altering buildings to make a profit.

The fact that some flats will be let, creating a separate letting business, does not affect CIS obligations, and it is common for the CIS scheme to apply to only parts of a business.

George should register as a contractor from the start of renovation of the first flat, and verify the tradesmen's payment status with HMRC, using the CIS online service, to operate CIS deductions accordingly. Exceptionally, George may verify a subcontractor's status by telephone, but must still use the online service shortly thereafter to check that the correct status has been recorded in his list of verified subcontractors on HMRC's system.

(b) As a retailer, Master Builder plc is not automatically within the construction industry, and the supply of building materials is not within the scope of construction operations.

However, as a non-construction business with an average spend on construction of over £1 million per year, Master Builder plc is a 'deemed contractor', under the construction industry scheme.

Payments made for construction operations for fixed assets used for the group's business are not within the scheme, so no deductions need to be made in respect of these.

As a result, Master Builder plc does not need to report the payment in respect of the sales office and retail sales outlets. Although because of its turnover it remains a deemed contractor, the company will submit nil returns, or report a period of inactivity until it expects to make contract payments. The payments in respect of the investment property are caught by the scheme, so these will be reported on a monthly return as they arise.

In the year ending 31 December 2016 it expects to incur less than £1 million on construction expenditure, but as the annual average at £1.16 million still exceeds the threshold, it remains a contractor.

(c) Patrick's business is undoubtedly a construction business, and potentially within the construction industry scheme. However, he appears not to work for contractors within the scheme. Householders are never contractors for payments on their own properties, and small non-construction businesses are unlikely to spend an average of £1 million per year over three years. The persons paying him are not within the scheme, so no deductions will be made. Patrick is free not to register as a subcontractor, but it would be advisable to register for 20% deduction, in case he was offered subcontract work by a construction company or other registered contractor. If he took on a CIS contract without being CIS-registered with HMRC, the contractor would have to withhold 30% of the payment for labour.

If he wanted to take on subcontractors, he would be obliged to register immediately as a contractor (even if he was still only working for householders and non-contractor businesses), and make the appropriate deductions from contract payments to them. This would also require him to make monthly returns, and there are penalties for late filing of monthly returns. HMRC is likely to issue a penalty automatically, even for the failure to submit a nil return when no payments have been made in a month, but such penalties for missing nil returns (which are no longer required by the regulations) will be cancelled on request. The penalty for failure to submit returns is £100 per return, then £200 once two months have passed from the penalty date, then after six months the penalty will be the greater of £300 or 5% of the payments that should have been shown on the return. If the delay lasts more than a year, deductions have not been made or reported and HMRC considers that the withholding of the information has prevented them from assessing liability, the penalty is higher still. Penalties generally are under review, but no announcements have been made about new policies on CIS penalties yet.

## C.

(a) Specialists All Aspects Ltd (SAAL) must contact HMRC immediately to register as a contractor, as it should have registered as soon as it took on subcontractors. HMRC will no longer issue a paper monthly return, which used to be filed by 19th of the following month. Instead, all returns must be made online, by the same deadline.

SAAL must then review the terms under which subcontractors work, and identify those who should be categorised as employed. These are excluded from the CIS scheme, as PAYE and NI are operated instead.

When registered, SAAL will be able to verify the status of the subcontractors, online, using the CIS online service (if the number of subcontractors is small) or commercial CIS software, to determine whether they should be paid gross, or subject to 20% or 30% deduction. The regulations now require online verification, but the CIS helpline can be used exceptionally to carry out a verification, although SAAL will still have to check online subsequently that the correct details have been recorded. It is then necessary to calculate the deductions, and pay them over by 19th of the following month (22nd if paid electronically).

(b) Calculation of deductions

(1) Forestry operations are not within the CIS scheme, so for the bulk of its activity, Rayne Forestry Enterprises, has no need to register. However, clearing scrub on a construction site falls within the definition of construction operations, and brings the business within the scheme. As it is not registered, tax will be deducted at 30% from the payment, net of VAT, and less the *cost* of fuel of £85; (1,750–85) × 30% = £500. The company must give Rayne Forestry Enterprises written confirmation of the CIS deduction.

The verification reference given by HMRC in respect of any unregistered subcontractor such as Rayne must be stated on the monthly pay advice.

(2) Hire and transport of equipment *without* an operator is excluded from the definition of construction operations, so this cost will not be reported on the return.

(3) The CIS scheme applies only within the UK, but applies to foreign businesses operating in the UK. Latvian Larch Lodges should contact HMRC to register, and arrange for repayment of tax in line with double tax treaty arrangements, using the written confirmation of deduction as evidence. As the company is not registered, the higher rate of deduction of 30% applies. The deduction is made to the amount paid excluding materials costs, not the amount invoiced, so will be (5,000 – 500) × 30% = £1,350.

The verification reference given by HMRC must be given on the monthly pay advice.

(4) As John Smith is clearly carrying out construction operations as a contractor, he will be CIS-registered, and will be paid subject to deduction at 20% (1,500 × 20%) = £300.

Contractors must review the self-employed status of workers regularly. As John Smith's future work seems likely to meet employment criteria, he will be subject to PAYE in future. The fact that he is part-time will have no effect, but the fixed times suggest a degree of control. Paid holidays are not necessarily an indicator of employee status: under the Working Time Regulations 1998, genuinely self-employed workers who contract to provide their own personal service are entitled to paid holiday. Many labour-only subcontractors who cannot send a substitute to do the work will qualify. HMRC disregards the provision of hand tools in determining status, and the van is not used for contract work.

(5) As Mega Tile plc is registered for gross payment, no deduction need be made, nor is there any requirement to analyse the payment.

Work on artistic works such as statues is outside the definition of construction operations, but anything with a construction function, such as tiles, is included.

(6) Ground works are clearly within construction operations, so withholding will have to be applied to the payment net of specified expenses. Hire of plant, and fuel for machinery, are deductible expenses, but travel expenses, and fuel for travel are not. The deduction will therefore be (2,500 – 350 – 75) × 20% = £415.

As this subcontractor is paid net, the monthly return must show the gross payment, the expenses deducted, and the amount withheld. A payslip must be issued to him within 14 days of the end of the month.

The amounts withheld therefore amount to 500 + 1,350 + 300 + 415 = £2,565.

The professional services of the firm of architects that owns Luxury Leisure Lodges Ltd are not within the CIS scheme. However, when they act as property developers, as in this case, they are required to operate the scheme like any other contractor in the construction business, and can exclude materials and plant hire costs that are passed on to them. The amounts withheld from SAAL are ((38,000 – 2.5%) – 23,260) × 20% = £2,758. Deductions are always operated on amounts paid, not on the basis of the invoice.

As this is a company, the amount suffered can be offset against amounts due within the same tax year, against payroll liabilities first. Any excess of CIS deductions suffered over PAYE, NIC and corporation tax due should be refunded once the final RTI return of the tax year has been submitted and processed.

| | |
|---|---:|
| PAYE due for month to 5 August 2016 | 1,237 |
| CIS deductions withheld by SAA | 2,565 |
| *Less*: CIS deductions suffered | (2,758) |

| | |
|---|---|
| Payable for the month | 1,044 |

Payment is due by 19th August 2016, or 22nd if paid electronically. The set off is made by filing an EPS return under RTI, which is presently filed after the end of the relevant tax month but before the following 19th of the month. The EPS shows the cumulative CIS set off so far in the tax year.

**D.**

The cost of materials is excluded from turnover for CIS purposes, so annual turnover is £55,000, or £13,750 per quarter, subject to a quarterly CIS deduction of £2,750 if applicable.

PAYE and CIS subcontractor deductions withheld amount to (1,250 + 600) = £1,850 per quarter or £7,400 per annum.

## *Gross Builders Ltd*

As a limited company, Gross Builders Ltd can offset CIS deductions suffered against CIS and PAYE paid, with the result that cash flow from turnover will be as follows:

| *Quarter Ending* | *Turnover* | *CIS deductions suffered* | *PAYE/CIS payable* | *Net flow* | *Cumulative cash flow* |
|---|---|---|---|---|---|
| 30/06/16 | 13,750 | (2,750) | Nil (offset) | 11,000 | 11,000 |
| 30/09/16 | 13,750 | (2,750) | Nil (offset) | 11,000 | 22,000 |
| 31/12/16 | 13,750 | (2,750) | Nil (offset) | 11,000 | 33,000 |
| 31/03/17 | 13,750 | (2,750) | Nil (offset) | 11,000 | 44,000 |
| | | 11,000 | | | |
| Less offset | | (7,400) | | | |
| 30/06/17 | Repayment or offset against other liabilities | 3,600 | | 3,600 | 47,600 |
| | 55,000 | Nil | 7,400 | 47,600 | |

Gross Builders Limited can submit a claim for the balance of the deductions suffered to be repaid after the end of the 2016/17 tax year. HMRC's service commitment is for repayments to be made within 25 working days of online claims or receipt by HMRC of a written claim form, assuming there are no queries with the claim, so the company should receive repayment in the quarter ended 30 June 2017. Alternatively, it can offset the refund against its next quarterly VAT liabilities or its corporation tax liability of £4,000 for the year, normally due by 31 December.

## *Keran*

By taking his wife into partnership at 1 July 2016, Keran has formed a new business which needs to be separately registered for the construction industry scheme. The partnership will not be able to register immediately as it has no trading record to demonstrate the required turnover level to qualify for gross payment. A partnership must have a minimum of £30,000 turnover from construction operations per partner, or £100,000 for the whole partnership, before it can qualify for gross payment status. Keran's cash flow is therefore as follows:

| *Quarter Ending* | *Turnover* | *CIS deductions suffered* | | *PAYE/ CIS payable* | *Net flow* | *Cumulative Cash flow* |
|---|---|---|---|---|---|---|
| 30/06/16 | 13,750 | | | (1,850) | 11,900 | 11,900 |
| 30/09/16 | 13,750 | (2,750) | | (1,850) | 9,150 | 21,050 |
| 31/12/16 | 13,750 | (2,750) | | (1,850) | 9,150 | 30,200 |
| 31/03/17 | 13,750 | (2,750) | | (1,850) | 9,150 | 39,350 |
| | IT offset | 8,250 | 8,250 | | 8,250 | 47,600 |
| | | Nil | | (7,400) | | |

Keran has suffered a cash flow disadvantage of (£44,000 – £39,350) £4,650 by the fourth quarter. In an unincorporated business with a high PAYE or CIS liability, loss of gross payment status can be severely damaging. Great care must be taken to avoid breaching the conditions of the compliance test for gross payment status, which requires that all returns be filed on time and all taxes be paid by the due date. Retention of gross payment status will repay the care and commitment needed to achieve it.

If Keran's turnover (excluding VAT and materials) had been at least £60,000, HMRC would probably have registered the new partnership for gross payment without a problem. Under changes introduced in April 2015, the new partnership can rely on the fact that Keran already has gross payment status and at least a 50% interest in the partnership assets and income when making its application.

It is possible that HMRC would argue that a partnership share in a construction business with its attendant book-keeping, scheduling and administrative requirements involves income shifting and could potentially be challenged under the settlement provisions in ITTOIA 2005 s 624. However, challenges of this nature are rare, and the fact that Keran's wife becomes liable for the debts of the business by becoming a partner is normally an effective response to any challenge. There remains the issue with loss of gross payment status, and it might have been better for Keran's wife to be paid for her work through payroll, perhaps at a rate that attracted little or no PAYE or NIC contributions (eg, employer contributions might have been covered by the employment allowance), so as to avoid losing gross payment status. Furthermore, as a partner, any failure in respect of her personal tax filing obligations would put the firm's gross payment status at risk.

## Explanatory Notes

*The construction industry scheme*

(1) The first construction industry scheme (CIS) was introduced in 1972 as a measure to cut evasion and police tax compliance in an industry which offered short-term work and often paid itinerant workers in cash. The current construction industry scheme, which came into effect on 6 April 2007, is the third of its kind. It retains many of the principles of the previous schemes, but instead of issuing certificates and cards it features control of compliance and verification by means of a centralised computerised database, without the need for cards. Stringent criteria for compliance are set and HMRC is given wide powers to cancel registration for gross payment, in which case a 20% deduction rate applies, and also to cancel registration for the 20% rate, in which case a 30% rate applies. It places a huge compliance burden upon contractors, as gross payment status can inadvertently be lost by late payment of any taxes, or delay in filing tax returns (in the past, further aspects of statutory compliance were taken into account, such as filing accounts at Companies House, and filing directors' personal tax returns on time, but these tests no longer apply).

The current scheme was introduced by FA 2004 Chapter 3 and Sch 12, with detailed regulations provided by SI 2005/2045 Income Tax (Construction Industry Scheme) Regulations 2005, and guidance provided by HMRC's publication CIS 340 on the construction industry scheme. As for previous schemes, its main purpose is to deduct tax at source, unless HMRC is satisfied that the tax will be properly accounted for by the recipient. This is achieved by requiring both payers and payees to register as contractors or subcontractors with HMRC, and for contractors to make monthly returns of payments made to subcontractors.

*Online facility*

(2) At present it is almost always required to:

- register for payment under deduction online (but a supplementary identity check is needed for identification if a sole trader has no NI number or HMRC cannot trace the NI number used);
- verify contractors online;
- make monthly returns online.

Those with strong religious objections to the use of computers may be excused the online filing obligations, as may those for whom it is not reasonably practicable to do so, eg, those who live and work in areas with no broadband connections.

Guidance is given at https://www.gov.uk/topic/business-tax/construction-industry-scheme. Contractors may register by calling 0300 200 3211 (ie, the helpline for new employers), and subcontractors on 0300 200 3210.

If returns are made online, the subcontractors to be paid can be selected from the HMRC database, hopefully increasing accuracy in establishing deduction status. Where, exceptionally, a subcontractor's status is verified by telephone, the contractor must still check online subsequently that his records have been linked with the correct subcontractor. It is no longer possible for contractors who verify a subcontractor by telephone to input the subcontractor's details to his own list, as this facility was withdrawn because it was prone to error.

The free HMRC facility is intended for small contractors with 50 or fewer subcontractors. If the maximum number is exceeded, the submission times out and fails. Contractors are then required to delete some of the subcontractors in their list if they wish to continue using the HMRC software, but HMRC advises the use of commercial software instead. A number of proprietary software suppliers have been approved by HMRC, and are listed on their website. As well as being able to supply up-to-date information, the system will be able to collect instances of non-compliance routinely. Given the stringent compliance conditions, it may be necessary to use reliable software if compliance is to be achieved.

Where CIS suffered is set off by a company against PAYE and NIC due, this must be indicated by filing EPS returns under RTI within the fourteen days after the end of the tax month for which the set-off is due.

*Application of the scheme*

(3) The scheme applies where:

- a subcontractor receives a contract payment from,
- another subcontractor, a contractor or deemed contractor,
- under a 'construction contract'.

*Subcontractors*

(4) A subcontractor is a person, partnership or company under a duty to carry out operations or provide labour, or responsible for operations carried out by others (FA 2004 s 58).

*Contractors*

(5) Private persons not acting in a business capacity cannot be contractors, with the result that the scheme does not apply to them, and they can never be required to withhold CIS deductions.

Contractors include:

- any person carrying out a business which includes construction operations (usually known as mainstream contractors even if they are not recognised as building or construction businesses);

- local authorities, NHS trusts, housing associations and a number of specified public bodies, subject to spending an average of at least £1,000,000 annually on construction operations over the last three years;

- persons not carrying on a construction business, but whose business spends on average at least £1,000,000 annually on construction operations over the last three years. There are some exceptions to this, detailed below.

*Deemed contractors*

(6) Deemed contractors are persons or bodies who do not operate as construction businesses, but who are deemed contractors because they have spent £1,000,000 on construction operations annually over the last three years. If they have been in existence for less than three years, this limit is scaled down proportionately; in the event of a reconstruction, the previous history is aggregated with the new structure.

The requirement for deemed contractors to operate the CIS scheme ceases only after expenditure on construction operations has been less than £1,000,000 in each of three successive years following a year in which the average of £1,000,000 was reached. For public bodies, 'year' means the year ended 31 March, while for businesses 'year' means the period of account.

*Small payments exemption*

There is a small payments exemption which applies to small amounts up to a maximum of £1,000 paid by deemed contractors only, not those paid by mainstream subcontractors. The contractor must be specially approved by HMRC for the purpose. The £1,000 must cover the whole cost of the contract, not stage payments on a larger contract, excluding materials.

*Construction contracts*

(7) Construction contracts are contracts relating to construction operations. Certain operations are defined as being within construction operations, while other operations are defined as being excluded. The CIS scheme operates only in the UK up to the 12-mile offshore limit, but it applies to non-UK businesses operating in the UK.

A summary of operations considered to be construction operations as defined in FA 2004 s 74(2) is as follows:

(a) construction, alteration, repair, extension, demolition or dismantling of buildings or structures (whether permanent or not), including offshore installations (ie, inside the 12-mile limit);

(b) construction, alteration, repair etc of any works forming, or to form, part of the land. This particularly includes walls, roadworks, power-lines, electric communications apparatus, aircraft runways, docks and harbours, railways, inland waterways, pipe-lines, reservoirs, water-mains, wells, sewers, industrial plant and installations for the purposes of land drainage, coast protection or defence;

(c) installation of heating, lighting, air-conditioning, ventilation, power supply, drainage, sanitation, water supply or fire protection into buildings;

(d) painting or decorating the internal or external services of any building or structure;

(e) preparatory operations such as site clearance, and earthmoving, excavation, tunnelling, laying foundations, site restoration, landscaping and the provision of roadways and other access works.

A summary of operations which are excluded from the definition of construction operations as per FA 2004 s 74(3) is as follows:

(a) drilling for, or extraction of, oil and gas;

(b) extraction of minerals (whether by surface or underground working) and tunnelling, boring or construction works for this purpose;

(c) manufacture or building of engineering components, equipment, materials, plant or machinery, or delivery to the site;

(d) manufacture of components or systems of heating, lighting, air-conditioning, ventilation, power supply etc or delivery to site;

(e) professional work of architects or surveyors, consultants in building, engineering, interior/ exterior decoration or landscaping;

(f) the making, installation and repair of artistic works, being sculptures murals or other works which are wholly artistic in nature;

(g) signwriting, or erecting, installing or preparing signboards and advertisements;

(h) installation of seating, blinds and shutters;

(i) installation of security systems including burglar alarms, closed-circuit television and public address systems (but closed-circuit television systems for non-security purposes, such as traffic monitoring, would be construction operations).

*Employment status*

(8) There is, however, one major exclusion from CIS subcontractor status which is crucial to compliance with CIS and PAYE regulations. A contract of employment is not within the CIS scheme: PAYE and NIC deductions must be made instead. From 6 April 2013 RTI applies to PAYE see **Example B1**, and from 6 April 2014 the employer may usually claim employment allowance to reduce or eliminate the employer NIC liability, see **Example H1**.

In particular, the fact that a non-corporate subcontractor was or is registered under the CIS scheme is no indication of self-employed status. Contractors must work out the employment status of subcontractors at the time they are taken on, and this must be reviewed regularly, certainly at any change in contract terms or working practice.

HMRC emphasises that employed or self-employed status is not a matter of labelling, but a fact derived from the terms of engagement. If a worker who had been treated as self-employed is recategorised by HMRC as an employee, the employer is liable for PAYE, NICs and penalties and interest. See **Example B6** 'Employment or self-employment'.

By the primary legislation of FA 2004 s 70, contractors must declare on each monthly return that 'The employment status of each individual included on this return, and any continuation sheets, has been considered and payments have not been made under contracts of employment.' This is a monthly reminder of the importance of implementing procedures to ensure that workers are correctly classified.

If workers are reclassified as employees, the resulting additional PAYE and NIC due but unpaid may cause the contractor to fail the compliance test, and lose gross payment status.

*Mixed contracts*

(9) Some contracts may include construction operations and non-construction operations. In the case of such mixed contracts, the CIS regulations apply to all operations under the whole contract.

*Registration*

(10) Registration is central to the centralised database system. It provides notification to contractors of whether the subcontractor is to be paid gross, after deduction of 20% from the labour element, or whether a 30% deduction may need to be applied. It provides no information on whether the individual should be classified as employed or self-employed, a matter to be considered separately at the beginning of each new project, and reviewed throughout its duration.

Both contractors and subcontractors need to register under separate schemes. Therefore, a business operating both as a contractor and subcontractor will require two registrations, one for each activity. The contractor registration is the same as that for an employer. An existing employer will use his existing employer PAYE reference when registering as a contractor. A new contractor who has no employees nevertheless has to register as an employer, but inform HMRC that he will not be filing PAYE or P11D returns.

*Contractors' obligations*

(11) FA 2004 empowers HMRC to make regulations detailing the obligations of contractors, which are found in SI 2005/2045 and the HMRC publication CIS 340 'Guide for contractors and subcontractors'.

*Contractor registration*

Contractors are required to register when they take on their first subcontractors, irrespective of whether the subcontractor is likely to be paid gross or subject to deduction of tax. Contractors may have multiple registrations (for instance different registrations for different construction sites), but the increased number of returns required will increase the risk of penalties and non-compliance.

As a result of registration, contractors will gain access to the centralised database to enable them to 'verify' the payment status of subcontractors, and they will also be required to make monthly returns of contract payments. Annual returns are not required. Nil returns were required by the regulations until 5 April 2015 for any month without contract payments, but that obligation was removed as a simplification measure (by SI 2015/429, Reg 2(2)).

*Verification*

(12) The contractor must contact HMRC's systems online to verify the registration status of newly-hired subcontractors, or those re-hired after a break of more than two years, before making any payment. The contractor must provide the name and UTR, together with the NI number for individuals and partnerships, or the company registration number for companies.

The HMRC system will advise the contractor of a verification number. This must be retained in all cases, and is required on the monthly return for subcontractors paid at the higher rate of deduction.

(13) Verification is not required if the payee has been included on a monthly return of contract payments within the last two years, and the HMRC system lists those payees for the contractor (older records for those inactive and unpaid for two years are now automatically deleted by HMRC and must be re-verified). A company within a group may rely on a verification carried out within the last two years by another group company. However, HMRC are required to notify contractors of any change in the registration status of subcontractors who have appeared on the contractors' monthly returns within the last two years. The contractor must implement these changes in payment status, so it is very important that the contractor is able to manage these notifications.

The contractor may not verify the status of any subcontractor before work has been offered. The contractor may verify the subcontractor status only when a contract has been entered into, or where a tender has been formally accepted.

*Contractors' monthly return CIS 300*

(14) Returns are now made online, for the tax month, from the 6th of the month to the following 5th, and must be returned within 14 days, that is by the 19th of the month.

The return must include all payments and deductions made, including payments made gross and costs of materials, giving the contractor's name, the UTR and accounts office reference, the NI number or company registration number if known, and the verification number for contractors subject to the higher rate of deduction. These requirements are set out in SI 2005/2045 reg 4.

The monthly return also requires the following declarations to be made.

- The employment status of each individual included on this return, and any continuation sheets, has been considered and payments have not been made under contracts of employment.

- Every subcontractor included on this return has either been verified with HMRC or been included in previous CIS returns in this, or the previous two tax years.
- That the return contains all the information, particulars and supporting information, and that it is complete and accurate to the best of the contractor's knowledge and belief.

The return must now be be filed electronically by all except (a) those with religious objections to computer use and (b) those for whom it is not reasonably practicable to use a computer to file and who do not use an agent, and to whom a direction has been issued by HMRC. Payment of the deductions must be made within 14 days, or within 17 days if made electronically. E-payment is mandatory for businesses which are large payers for PAYE purposes. If average monthly payments of PAYE, NIC, CIS and student loan deductions are less than £1,500, the contractor may opt to pay quarterly. Nil returns are not technically required from registered contractors if no payments are made in a period (but HMRC's computer will still issue an invalid penalty notice if none is filed, so in practical terms it is usually better to file a nil return), but contractors who know that no payments are likely to be made for some time can tick a box and stop making returns for six months, or until the next payment is in fact made if that occurs sooner.

*Payment and deduction of tax*

(15) The contractor is required to deduct tax at the appropriate rate and remit it on a monthly basis together with the monthly return. Those small traders with monthly deductions averaging less than £1,500 may pay quarterly, but they must still file returns monthly.

For details of the calculation of deductions, see **explanatory note 21** below.

*Subcontractor registration*

If the subcontractor is newly starting up on a self-employed basis, he will of course need to register online, notifying the start of self-employment, to avoid a penalty. FA 2008 s 118 and Sch 41 provide for this penalty to be a behaviour- and tax-based penalty.

The subcontractors may apply to register for payment under deduction or, if they can meet the conditions described below, for gross payment.

Subcontractors should register before they are due to receive contract payments, failing which tax will be deducted at the higher rate of 30%. The primary route to registration is by logging in to HMRC's website with a Government Gateway ID, and providing name, the trading name if any, address, telephone number, UTR, NI number and VAT registration number if already registered for VAT. Sole traders can also register by telephone (0300 200 3210).

Provided that the applicant supplies all details, particularly relating to identity, HMRC will register the subcontractor for payment under deduction at 20%. The legislation provides that HMRC may refuse registration under deduction if they are not satisfied with the documents and identity. In this case the individual could still work in the construction industry, but would suffer deduction at 30%.

*Registration for gross payment*

(16) Details of the criteria for registration of the gross payment are set out in FA 2004 ss 63 and 64, which are summarised below. All businesses must meet the following three tests for the qualifying period of the 12 months prior to registration:

- the business test;
- the turnover test;
- the compliance test.

The compliance test is waived where the applicant is either:

- a partnership where one or more of the partners is already registered for gross payment, alone or as a partner in another firm, and has (or together have) an interest in at least 50% of the assets and income of the firm (FA 2004, Sch 11 para 8A), or
- a company where one of the members is already registered for gross payment and that member has at least a 50% interest in the share capital or voting rights or in the proceeds of a winding up, and the same rule applies where two members of the company are registered for gross payment and they together have 50% of the share capital or 50% of the voting rights (FA 2004, Sch 11 para 12A).

*The business test*

(17) Applicants must provide evidence that they are carrying on business in the UK involving construction operations, substantially using a business bank account. HMRC will require evidence of business address, invoices and contracts for construction work, details of payments for construction work, the books and accounts of the business and details of the business bank account including bank statements.

*The turnover test*

(18) The turnover threshold for an individual is £30,000 from construction operations for provision of labour, and excluding materials, to be earned in the 12 months following application.

The turnover threshold for partnerships is now the lesser of £100,000 (£200,000 before 6 April 2016), or the individual threshold of £30,000 multiplied by the number of partners.

The turnover threshold for companies is the lesser of £100,000 (£200,000 before 6 April 2016), or the individual threshold of £30,000 multiplied by the number of directors, or in the case of a close company multiplied by the number of directors, plus beneficial shareholders who are not also directors.

Evidence of future turnover is likely to be derived from historic turnover or a large contract already entered into.

*The compliance test*

(19) Applicant subcontractors (except those noted at (16) above) must have met all their specified compliance obligations during the previous 12 months. This means (FA 2004, Sch 11, Paras 4, 8 and 12):

- paying the amount liable to be deducted and submitting returns under the CIS scheme
- paying any tax liable to be deducted under the PAYE regulations (Paras 4, 8 and 12 make no mention of amounts due under the NIC regulations) and
- submitting a self-assessment return.

The former requirement for CIS-registered individuals, partners and directors in contractor companies to keep all their personal self-assessment payments up to date was removed by SI 2016/404, Reg 2 from 6 April 2016. The return-filing test applies to the applicant for gross payment status, ie, to the company or partnership, not to all the people who are partners or directors.

The compliance conditions are set out in detail in FA 2004 Sch 11 and SI 2005/2045 paras 32 to 37. HMRC may, at 90 days' notice, cancel gross payment status if it 'appears' that:

- an application for registration for gross payment, if made at this time, would be refused; or
- that an incorrect return or incorrect information under any provision of the CIS regulations has been made; or
- there has been a failure to comply with any provisions under the regulations.

A number of breaches of conditions are considered as acceptable under para 32 (as amended by SI 2016/348 from 6 April 2016), but the breaches include failures by the firm/company and any individual subcontractor. These breaches are any or all of:

- not more than two late submissions of the monthly CIS return in the last 12 months – submission up to 28 days late will be disregarded;
- not more than two late payments of CIS/PAYE deductions in the last 12 months – payment up to 14 days late will be disregarded, as will any underpaid liability of under £100; and
- any self-assessment return made late – submissions up to 28 days late will be disregarded.

The government announced in December 2014 that directors' individual filing obligations were to be removed from the compliance test as a simplification measure. This was legislated with effect from 6 April 2016 as indicated.

HMRC have limited power of mitigation on these compliance conditions and the conditions are sufficiently stringent to be breached accidentally. The contractors' records are reviewed annually and automatically on a rolling basis (known as the 'scheduled review'). The withdrawal of gross payment status is notified first to the affected subcontractor, who has a right of appeal and can advance any reasonable excuse: some appeals have succeeded before the First-tier Tribunal (eg, *Cormac Construction Ltd* TC00315) while others have failed (eg, *Westview Rail Ltd* TC00215). Contractors should be notified of the change of status of a subcontractor only after the appeal deadline has expired, although HMRC postal and computer processing delays sometimes prevent this order of events. The introduction of the scheduled review and a rigid computer-driven system for issuing GPS withdrawal notices initially led to many notices and successful appeals, HMRC has stopped the issue of automatic notices and is taking a more reasonable view of whether GPS should be withdrawn, although a number of cases are still reaching the tribunals (eg, *Shaw Cleaning Service* TC01233, reported in July 2011).

Monthly returns are pre-populated by HMRC and are available for completion online each month. The returns must be submitted online by the 19th of the following month (even if they are nil returns made without statutory obligation that cannot lead to penalties). Failure to make a return other than a nil return incurs the following penalties: an initial penalty of £100; a further £200 when the return is three months late; if the return is six months late the penalty is a further 5% of deductions due for the return period (minimum £300), and another 5% if twelve months late. Once more than twelve months late, the return could attract a penalty of 70% of the deductions due if the contractor's delay was deliberate but not concealed, or 100% if deliberate and concealed.

*Subcontractor registration*

*Registration for gross payment*

(20) A subcontractor registered for gross payment is paid without any deductions. The amount paid, excluding VAT, must be reported monthly giving UTR plus NIC number or company registration number. There is no requirement to analyse the CIS gross payment (ie, net of VAT) between materials and labour. No payslip need be issued.

*Registration for net payment*

(21) Where a subcontractor is registered for net payment, tax at 20% must be withheld from the CIS gross (net of VAT and CITB levy) payment, as reduced for specific defined costs which are:

- materials;
- consumables;
- fuel (but not fuel for travelling);
- plant hire;
- cost of manufacture of prefabricated materials.

The amount deductible is the cost to the subcontractor, plus irrecoverable VAT, if appropriate. The contractor may estimate the cost to the subcontractor in the absence of evidence. The contractor must ensure that any profit element on any of the above items is excluded, whether evidence is presented or not.

Expenses of travel, in particular, are not deductible from the gross payment.

For the monthly return, the costs of materials must be split from the labour element. The contractor must make a monthly report of the total of amounts paid to the subcontractor, showing name, UTR, NIC or company registration number, 'gross' payment, materials element and tax deducted.

Where the subcontractor is unregistered and the contractor performing a verification is informed that the higher rate must be used, and a 30% deduction is made, the verification number must also be shown.

Contractors must issue a payment analysis to subcontractors paid under deduction of tax (but not to those paid gross) within 14 days of payment.

*Recovery/offset of deductions*

(22) Subcontractors liable to income tax are able to offset CIS deductions against their year-end income tax liability, and then Class 4 national insurance contributions liability. Payment slips issued by the contractor will be required, and in the case of subcontractors subject to deduction of higher rate, it is essential that the verification numbers are provided.

Regulation 17 of SI 2005/2045 provides for in-year repayments for subcontractors other than companies, subject to proof that deductions are excessive in relation to subcontractors' profits, contractors' profits and other income for the year to date at the time of application, after deducting proportional allowances. The applicant(s) must sign a declaration that this information is given to the best of their knowledge and belief.

Companies, but not partnerships or those who are self-employed, have separate rules in Reg 56 of SI 2005/2045. They may offset CIS deductions withheld from their income, firstly against NICs the company is due to pay to HMRC, then PAYE liabilities, then student loan repayments withheld, then advances against statutory payments obligations, and finally against CIS deductions withheld from other subcontractors and due to HMRC. HMRC may set any overpaid CIS withholdings suffered by the company contractor against corporation tax due for an accounting period ending before those relevant CIS deductions were withheld by the contractor. . Where CIS deductions suffered are offset against payroll taxes or deductions withheld, they may be offset only within the same tax year. Any excess of deductions suffered over amounts available for set-off cannot be repaid to the subcontractor until after the end of the tax year, except where the corporate subcontractor in question is subject to a winding-up order under Part 4 of Insolvency Act 1986 and the subcontractor has ceased trading, and/or permanently ceased making CIS contract payments as a contractor.

For example, Faith and Hope Foundations Ltd has a 30 September 2016 year-end.

For the quarter ended 31 March 2016, the company suffers £4,000 surplus deductions. For the two quarters to 30 June and 30 September 2016, it has payroll, student loan and CIS liabilities of £1,200 and £1,800 respectively (net of employment allowance). In the quarter to 31 December 2016, it suffers deductions at source of £1,500 in excess of PAYE and CIS liabilities.

Its corporation tax liability for the year ended 30 September 2016 was £7,500.

Offset would be as follows:

The £4,000 surplus deductions to 31 March cannot be offset against the liabilities of June and September 2016, as these fall into a different tax year. These liabilities must be paid on time to achieve the compliance conditions for gross payment.

The £1,500 excess deductions of the quarter 31 December 2016 cannot be set against the corporation tax liability for the period ended 30 September 2016, because they arose after the end of that period. They could be offset against subsequent PAYE and CIS liabilities arising later in the 2016/17 year.

Corporation tax for the period ended 30 September 2016 will therefore be offset by the surplus at 31 March 2016 only, giving £3,500 (£7,500 – £4,000).

Offset against corporation tax could represent a delay of 19 months for deductions suffered at the beginning of the period of account, and a claim for repayment would normally be preferable – particularly now that repayments are made much quicker.

For self-employed/partnerships, self-assessment returns may be filed online, shortly after 6 April, to speed repayment.

*Collection of unpaid deductions*

(23) Where contractors fail to make payments of deductions, or where it appears to an HMRC officer that the payment is insufficient, HMRC may prepare a certificate to the best of the officer's judgement for the combined amount of CIS, PAYE, NIC and student loan deductions. The amount specified on such a notice is payable in seven days, under SI 2005/2045 reg 11.

# Question

**(A)** Fred Stone owns the following properties in the UK which he lets.

| | |
|---|---|
| *Shop 1* | A butcher's shop, the annual rental of which is £13,200 under a seven-year lease expiring on 28 September 2016 and the lease was renewed at £18,800 per annum for seven years. |
| *Shop 2* | A shop selling textiles, the annual rental of which is £12,000 under a seven-year lease expiring on 25 March 2018. The quarter's rent due on 25 March 2017 was not paid until 30 April 2017. |
| *Shop 3* | A shop selling light fittings. This was let to a relative of Mr Stone at an annual rental of £2,400 when a commercial rent would have been £10,000. Mr Stone's relative is responsible for all outgoings, with the exception of insurance amounting to £2,500. |
| *Shop 4* | This shop had been let at an annual rental of £14,000 until 23 June 2016 when the tenant, who had been selling clothing, informed Mr Stone that he could not afford to pay the rent and vacated the premises forthwith. Mr Stone agreed through his agent to re-let the premises from 25 March 2017 to a new tenant who would be selling pottery imported from Scandinavia. The new rental was £16,000 per annum for 10 years and Mr Stone also received a premium of £6,000 from the incoming tenant on 25 March 2017. |

Mr Stone borrowed money to buy Shops 1, 2 and 4 and the interest payable for 2016/17 was £8,200.

| | |
|---|---|
| *House 1* | A furnished house let on weekly tenancies. The house was purchased in November 2004 with the aid of a bank loan of £62,500. Interest of £5,000 was paid for 2016/17. The property was let throughout 2016/17. The all-inclusive weekly rental was £160. |
| *House 2* | A furnished house also let on weekly tenancies. During 2016/17 the property was let for 43 weeks. The all-inclusive weekly rental was £120. |

The houses are not holiday accommodation and are regularly let to one tenant for lengthy periods. House 2 had been empty and available for letting during the weeks when it was not let. Council tax had been paid by the tenants, apart from the period when House 2 was not let, when the tax was paid by Mr Stone.

On 31 December 2016, Mr Stone received a property income distribution of £8,000 from Super Alpha REIT plc.

With the exception of the houses, the rents are due in advance on the normal English quarter days: 25 March, 24 June, 29 September and 25 December.

Mr Stone draws up his rental accounts to 5 April annually. Details of expenditure for the year ended 5 April 2017, as adjusted for amounts in arrears and advance, were as follows:

| | £ |
|---|---:|
| Insurance | |
| Buildings | 3,122 |
| Contents | 216 |
| Ground rent | 610 |
| Repairs and decorating (see notes) | 7,145 |
| Accountancy | 370 |
| Newspaper advertising | 134 |
| Gardeners' wages | 380 |
| Water supply charges (house 1 £230, house 2 £310) | 540 |
| Council tax | 60 |
| | 12,577 |

Mr Stone employs an agent to manage the properties, except that of Shop 3. He pays them 10% of the amount receivable (not applicable to the premium). The agent is not registered for VAT.

## Notes on repairs

(1) £3,854 was spent on putting Shop 4 into proper condition after the previous tenant had vacated it.

(2) £1,050 was spent on dry-rot remedial treatment to House 1. The dry-rot was present in the house when Mr Stone purchased it in November 2004.

(3) £1,428 was spent on repairing cracked roof tiles and re-flashing the chimneys of the roof of House 2.

(4) All the expenditure on the houses in respect of repairs and decorating relates to the property and not the furniture.

In 2013/14 Mr Stone gave £20,000 to his son Donald as part payment for the son's flat, Donald borrowing a further £80,000. The net interest in 2016/17 was £3,200. To help with expenses, Donald let a furnished room in the flat to a friend and received rent of £60 a week throughout the year. He did not provide any other services. Donald paid for the buildings and contents insurance on the flat amounting to £150, and spent £250 on repairs during 2016/17. He also paid a service charge of £300, water supply charges of £110 and council tax of £400 (his friend making a contribution of £100 to the council tax).

(a) Calculate Fred Stone's net rental income for tax purposes for 2016/17.

(b) Explain:

(i) Donald's position in 2016/17 in relation to his rents and expenses;

(ii) the position if Donald took up a job where he was required to live on the premises, and he let the whole flat for an annual rent of £5,500 from 6 April 2017.

**(B)** Mrs Morley is a married woman aged 47, whose husband is the director and owner of a prosperous engineering company with profits averaging £300,000 per year.

She has a pensionable salary of £30,000 per annum. Her only other source of income is rent from two houses that she purchased on 1 January 1997. One is in London and has been let furnished at a commercial rent continuously since purchase. The other is a furnished holiday home in Suffolk used partly by the family and partly for holiday letting on commercial terms. The house in Suffolk cost £100,000 and there has been no major improvement since that date.

Both properties were purchased with the assistance of bank loans, the interest paid in the year ended 5 April 2017 being £3,739 on the loan for the London house and £5,586 on the loan for the Suffolk house.

The Morleys are considering buying a house in Ruritania, which will principally be let as holiday accommodation, but used by the family in the skiing season. The Ruritanian lawyer has advised that this should be purchased through a company formed for the purpose, and they ask your advice as they are concerned about possible benefit in kind charges. Assume that Ruritania is in the EEA.

The Suffolk house has been occupied as follows:

| | | *Year ended 5 April 2016* | *Year ended 5 April 2017* |
|---|---|---|---|
| Number of weeks – | let | 10 | 20 |
| | occupied by family | 20 | 20 |
| | empty, available for letting | 22 | 12 |
| | | 52 | 52 |

The Suffolk house was only let on a short-term basis, with all the tenants staying for less than a month.

The income and expenditure for each property for the year ended 5 April 2017, adjusted for accruals and prepayments, was as follows:

| | | *London* | *Suffolk* |
|---|---|---|---|
| | | £ | £ |
| Income – | rent receivable | 16,735 | 7,000 |
| Expenditure – | business rates | | 1,300 |
| | water supply charges | 730 | 520 |
| | insurance | 485 | 364 |
| | cleaning on change of occupants | – | 996 |
| | replacement of furniture | 390 | 777 |
| | repairs and decorations | 940 | 1,810 |
| | advertising for lettings | – | 263 |

(a) Calculate Mrs Morley's property income for 2016/17.

(b) State the position relating to pension contributions on the income from the Suffolk house.

(c) Suggest any tax planning issues that may be relevant in relation to the Suffolk house.

(d) Prepare notes for a response to the request for advice on the foreign letting property.

(C) Mr and Mrs Turner own fifteen residential properties in Yorkshire, having built the business up over the last twenty years. The properties, which are currently worth £3m, bring in £180,000 in rents each year and their mortgage interest costs are £70,000 per year (at an interest rate of 3.5%pa). Other costs, including repairs are normally around £30,000.

The Turners own the properties jointly, sharing the profits and losses equally, and report the income and expenses on the UK property supplementary pages of their tax returns. They actively manage the portfolio, with Mrs Turner doing most of the administration work and Mr Turner doing any general repairs which do not require specialist skills. They do not use an agent to manage the properties, but do pay an agent to find them new tenants when necessary and deal with the legalities around the properties. The mortgages for the properties are in the names of Mr and Mrs Turner.

Both Mr and Mrs Turner are also employed, with Mr Turner working full time for an engineering firm and Mrs Turner working four days a week in the NHS. Their employment income is sufficient for both of them to be higher rate taxpayers.

The Turners have heard about the changes to tax relief on mortgage interest and are concerned about how this will affect them. Their neighbour has told them that they may be able to avoid the tax liability by incorporating their property business. Consider their tax position with regard to the property business and of the tax implications of incorporation.

# Answer

(A)

## (a) *Fred Stone*

All UK rental income is treated as single UK property business (whether commercial or residential property) with the exception of accommodation which qualifies as furnished holiday lettings (ITTOIA 2005 s 264).

Mr Stone's property income for the 2016/17 tax year is as follows:

| | £ | £ |
|---|---|---|
| UK property business income (W1) | 52,456 | |
| Less: allowable expenses (W2) | (30,365) | |
| | | 22,091 |
| REIT income (£8,000 x 100/80) (N1) | | 10,000 |
| | | 32,091 |

| (W1) | UK property business income | | £ | £ |
|---|---|---|---|---|
| Shop 1 (N2) | | | | |
| | 6.4.16 – 28.9.16 (176 days/365 days) | @ £13,200 pa | 6,365 | |
| | 29.9.16 – 5.4.17 (189 days/365 days) | @ £18,800 pa | 9,735 | |
| | | | | 16,100 |
| Shop 2 (N2) | | | | 12,000 |
| Shop 3 | | | | 2,400 |
| Shop 4 (N2) | | | | |
| | 6.4.16 – 23.6.16 (79 days/365 days) | @ £14,000 pa | 3,030 | |
| | 25.3.17 – 5.4.17 (12 days/365 days) | @ £16,000 pa | 526 | |
| | | | | 3,556 |
| Premium (W3) | | | | 4,920 |
| House 1 (£160 × 52 weeks) | | | | 8,320 |
| House 2 (£120 × 43 weeks) | | | | 5,160 |
| | | | | 52,456 |

| (W2) Allowable expenses | £ | £ |
|---|---|---|
| Interest re Shops 1, 2, 4 and House 1 (£8,200 + £5,000) (N5) | | 13,200 |
| Other expenditure as listed (N4) | 12,577 | |
| *Less*: Shop 3 excess of insurance paid over rent received (N3) | (100) | |
| | | 12,477 |
| Agent's commission – 10% of rent collected except for Shop 3 and the premium (£52,456 (W1) - £2,400 - £4,920 (W3)) | | 4,688 |
| | | 30,365 |

| (W3) | The part of the premium to be taken as additional rent is: | £ |
|---|---|---|
| | Premium | 6,000 |

| | | |
|---|---|---|
| Less 2% × (10 – 1) = 18% | | (1,080) |
| | | 4,920 |

| (W4) Agent's commission | £ | |
|---|---|---|
| Shop 1 (£13,200 / 4) + ((£18,800 / 4) x 3) | 17,400 | |
| Shop 2 | 12,000 | |
| Shop 4 (£16,000 / 4) | 4,000 | |
| House 1 (£160 × 52 weeks) | 8,320 | |
| House 2 (£120 × 43 weeks) | 5,160 | |
| | 46,880 | (N7) |
| Commission £46,880 x 10% | | £4,688 |

## Notes

1. The property income distribution from the real estate investment trust (REIT) is received net of basic rate tax which has been withheld by the company. Therefore the amount received must be grossed up. See **explanatory note 21**.
2. Property income must be calculated in accordance with generally accepted accounting practice (GAAP) and therefore the income and expenses for the tax year must be determined using the accruals basis (ITTOIA 2005 s 25 as read with ITTOIA 2005 s 272). HMRC accepts calculations on the cash basis, but only where the gross rental income does not exceed £15,000. Fred's income exceeds this amount so the accruals basis must be used. See **explanatory note 4**.
3. As Shop 3 is let at an uncommercial rent, the expenses are limited to the amount of income received. The excess cannot be set against the profits of other properties or carried forward to future years; the excess is lost. As the Shop 3 income is £2,400 and the expenses are £2,500 the excess needs to be disallowed. See **explanatory note 3**.
4. The expenditure on repairs is all allowable for tax purposes. As discussed in **explanatory note 5**, the expenditure is wholly and exclusively for the purposes of the business and is not capital in nature. The dry rot treatment is allowable despite the dry rot being present when the property was purchased because the property was in a useable state at that time (evidenced by the fact it has been let).
5. Until 2017/18, loan interest on residential properties is a revenue expense and can be deducted from the rents received. This includes mortgage interest, interest on loans used to fund repairs/extensions and any incidental costs of obtaining loan finance (ITTOIA 2005 s 272 as read with ITTOIA 2005 ss 29, 58; PIM2105).

   However from 2017/18, relief for finance costs relating to residential property (in the UK or overseas) is to be restricted to the basic rate of income tax. From 2017/18 to 2020/21, the revenue deduction is phased out and instead relief is given by a tax reduction of 20% in Step 6 of the income tax calculation in ITA 2007 s 23 (ITTOIA 2005 ss 272A, 274A):

   | Tax year | Percentage of expense given as revenue deduction | Percentage of expense given as a tax reduction at 20% |
   |---|---|---|
   | 2016/17 | 100% | 0% |
   | 2017/18 | 75% | 25% |
   | 2018/19 | 50% | 50% |
   | 2019/20 | 25% | 75% |
   | 2020/21 | 0% | 100% |

   Therefore, in 2017/18, assuming the same fact pattern, Mr Stone would have a revenue deduction of £11,950 (£8,200 + (£5,000 x 75%)) and a tax reduction of £250 ((£5,000 x 25%) x 20%).

   This restriction affects residential property finance costs only. The rules on the allowability of finance costs for commercial property are unchanged, meaning Mr Stone will still be able to deduct the whole amount of the mortgage interest in relation to the shops from his property income in 2017/18. See **explanatory note 16**.

6. Wear and tear allowance was repealed with effect from 6 April 2016 by Finance Act 2016. See **explanatory note 7.**
7. Property agents provide a service of collecting rents due from tenants on behalf of landlords. Under agency law, rental income should be paid into a client money bank account. The agent then deducts (transfers) its fee and passes the balance onto the landlord. The agent should issue an invoice for each deduction from rent. The question states that the agent charges based upon rent receivable. This is usual as this is the time when the agent performs its service (checks rent paid and chases arrears). On this basis, the agent would issue invoices dated when each rent payment is due. Such fees are potentially liable to VAT, although in this case the question states the agent is not registered. If the agent were VAT registered the VAT charged would represent an additional cost to Mr Stone.
   Under normal accountancy principals as the recipient of a service, Mr Stone enters the agent's invoices into his book keeping based upon the invoice dates. As stated above, these are the same as the date the rent is due. Therefore for Shop 1 £3,300 (13,200/4) rent is payable 24 June 2016 followed by three instalments of £4,700 (£18,800/4) on 29 September 2016, 25 December 2016 and 25 March 2017. No adjustment is made for Shop 2 when the rent is paid a month late as the agent's fee for collecting this rent will still be dated 25 March 2017.

## (b) *Donald Stone*

### (i) Donald's position in 2016/17

Donald receives rent of 52 weeks × £60 + £100 towards council tax = £3,220 and has incurred expenses of £4,410 (£150 + £250 + £300 + £110 + £400 = £1,210 plus £3,200 interest), part of which relates to his own occupation.

Under the 'rent-a-room' relief provisions, he is exempt from tax on the rents, since they do not exceed £7,500 (ITTOIA 2005 ss 789, 791, 793). It is unlikely that once the private use element of the expenses is removed he would be in a loss position so it would not be a good idea for him to elect for the alternative treatment under ITTOIA 2005 s 799).

For a discussion of rent-a-room relief, see **explanatory note 15**. For more on private use adjustments, see **explanatory note 13.**

### (ii)

If Donald let the whole property, then he would be taxed on the rental income of £5,500 less allowable expenses, including interest. Although see N5 in relation to Fred Stone above for the phased restriction to relief for finance costs in relation to residential properties from 2017/18 (ITTOIA 2005 ss 272A, 274A).

Rent-a-room relief cannot be claimed unless the property is the claimant's main residence at some time in the letting period, so the relief would not be available from 6 April 2016 (ITTOIA 2005 s 784(1)). See **explanatory note 15.**

## (B) Mrs Morley

## (a) *Computation of Mrs Morley's UK property income for 2016/17*

| | *London house* | | | *Suffolk house* (N1) | |
|---|---|---|---|---|---|
| | £ | £ | | £ | £ |
| Rent receivable | | 16,735 | | | 7,000 |
| *Less:* Business rates | – | | (32/52) | 800 | |
| Water supply charges | 730 | | (32/52) | 320 | |
| Insurance | 485 | | (32/52) | 224 | |
| Cleaning on change of occupants | – | | | 996 | |

| | *London house* | | | *Suffolk house* (N1) | |
|---|---|---|---|---|---|
| | £ | £ | | £ | £ |
| Repairs and decorations | 940 | | (32/52) | 1,114 | |
| Advertising for lettings | – | | | 263 | |
| Replacement of furniture (N2) | 390 | | | – | |
| Interest paid (N3) | 3,739 | | (32/52) | 3,438 | |
| | | (6,284) | | | (7,155) |
| Profit / (loss) | | 10,451 | | | (155) |

The taxable property income for the 2016/17 tax year is £10,451.

The Suffolk house qualifies as a furnished holiday let. This is because (ITTOIA 2005 s 325):

- it was available for letting for 224 days (ie 52 weeks - 20 weeks);
- it was actually let for 140 days (ie 20 weeks);
- it is not let for longer-term accommodation.

Any losses on furnished holiday lets can only be set against future profits. They cannot be set against UK property business income or overseas property business income (ITA 2007 s 127). See **explanatory notes 22-23**.

## Notes

1. As Mrs Morley and her family used the Suffolk house for 20 weeks in the 2016/17 tax year, the expenditure must be pro-rated to remove the private use element. This is done by multiplying the total expenses by ((52 weeks - 20 weeks)/52 weeks)). See **explanatory note 13**. There is no need to pro-rate the cleaning and advertising costs as there is no personal element to these expenses.
2. Wear and tear allowance was repealed with effect from 6 April 2016 by Finance Act 2016. It is replaced with a new statutory renewals basis called 'replacement of domestic items relief'. It is available to people letting residential property, whether in the UK or abroad, and allows a deduction against income for the capital costs of replacing a domestic item, such as free-standing white goods, furniture, carpets or curtains (ITTOIA 2005 s 311A). Furnished holiday lets are excluded, as is any expenditure on items which are not exclusively used by the tenant (ie there is an element of private use of the item). See **explanatory note 7**. Therefore Mrs Morley can deduct the cost of the replacement furniture for the London house but not the Suffolk house. Instead, Mrs Morley is able to claim capital allowances in respect of the Suffolk house (see **part (c)** and **explanatory notes 22, 25**) however there is insufficient information in the question to calculate the allowances available.
3. As noted above in relation to Fred Stone, from 2017/18, relief for finance costs relating to residential property (in the UK or overseas) is to be restricted to the basic rate of income tax. From 2017/18 to 2020/21, the revenue deduction is phased out and instead relief is given by a tax reduction of 20% in Step 6 of the income tax calculation in ITA 2007 s 23 (ITTOIA 2005 ss 272A, 274A):

| Tax year | Percentage of expense given as revenue deduction | Percentage of expense given as a tax reduction at 20% |
|---|---|---|
| 2016/17 | 100% | 0% |
| 2017/18 | 75% | 25% |
| 2018/19 | 50% | 50% |
| 2019/20 | 25% | 75% |
| 2020/21 | 0% | 100% |

Therefore, in 2017/18, assuming the same fact pattern, Mrs Morley would have a revenue deduction of £2,804 (£3,739 x 75%)) and a tax reduction of £186.95 ((£3,739 x 25%) x 20%) in respect of the London house. See **explanatory note 16**.
The rules do not apply to furnished holiday lets (ITTOIA 2005, s 272B(4)).

## (b) *Personal pension contributions*

Income from furnished holiday lettings in the UK is considered 'relevant UK earnings' for purposes of calculating the amount of pension contributions on which tax relief is available (ITTOIA 2005 s 328; FA 2004 s 189(2)). Although in Mrs Morley's case there is no FHL income in the year as it ran at a loss.

## (c) *Advice regarding tax planning in relation to the Suffolk home*

Mrs Morley has incurred a loss on the furnished holiday letting (FHL) activity (the Suffolk house). With effect from 2011/12, this loss can no longer be set against her other income, nor is it available to set against other property income (arising on the London house). The loss is carried forwards and set against the profits of her UK holiday letting activity in the future (ITA 2007 s 127).

Mrs Morley should review the position regarding the Suffolk property, and decide whether she wishes to reorganise the costs etc so as to provide a profit on an ongoing basis, otherwise it would seem that she may create marooned losses.

However, no data is provided about capital allowance claims. It is possible that Mrs Morley is not aware that extensive claims to capital allowances may be possible in relation to the Suffolk home. Even if not claimed at the date of purchase, there is still time to make claims to capital allowances on many of the fixtures in the property; the availability of allowances can be ascertained by a study of List C in CAA 2001 s 23. It is possible that claims for allowances on integral features may also be available. From 6 April 2012, the value of fixtures must be established within two years of transfer. Therefore, anyone buying or selling a commercial property (including a FHL) after this date should consider whether they wish to make a CAA 2001 s 198 election with the other party to fix the price of fixtures. For Mrs Morley the availability of capital allowances should be explored – but the usefulness of such a claim will of course depend on the improved profitability of the FHL business.

She should also be aware that the periods during which the house must be available for letting and actually let increased significantly from 6 April 2012. The Suffolk house currently meets the new criteria but Mrs Morley would be well advised to be aware of the limits. The details are:

- it must be available for letting for at least 210 days (30 weeks) in a tax year (ITTOIA 2005 s 325(2)). In 2016/17 the property was available for letting but not let for 12 weeks, and actually let for 20 weeks, bringing the total to 224 days (32 weeks) so there is capacity in hand on the availability test. She should review whether occupation by the family is likely to increase in the future as if the property does not meet the availability test, it will not be an FHL property. There is no period of grace; once the property is not available for sufficient days in the year, it immediately ceases to be FHL. While exiting the FHL regime will allow losses on the Suffolk property to be set against profits on the London house, there are other disadvantages to this outcome – not least of these the loss of entrepreneurs' relief on eventual sale (see **Example L5**) and restriction of finance costs from 2017/18 onwards (see explanatory note 16). There would also be a disposal at market value of any assets on which capital allowances had been claimed, and in view of the availability of the annual investment allowance, this could produce a significant balancing charge. See **explanatory note 25**;

- The property must also be actually let for 105 days (15 weeks) in the tax year (ITTOIA 2005 s 325(3)). In 2016/17 Mrs Morley has achieved 140 days (20 weeks) letting so again the conditions have been met. If it is not possible to meet the actual letting condition in one year, Mrs Morley can make an election that the condition is deemed to have been met for the next two tax years, so by meeting the criteria for 2016/17 she would be able to elect to be treated as meeting the letting criteria for both 2017/18 and 2018/19. An election is required in the first year of failing the letting test, for it to be available in the subsequent year (ITTOIA 2005 s 326A). This election (or period of grace) is not available in relation to the availability condition.

For more details of the qualifying conditions, see **explanatory note 23**.

Mrs Morley does seem to be in a relatively safe position regarding the availability and letting conditions, so her main thoughts should be regarding the losses. Obviously, if she can increase lettings the additional income is likely to produce a profit for her, against which the 2016/17 loss can be set.

If she is concerned about the losses, or has doubts about meeting the letting and availability periods in the future, she also has the opportunity to cease her FHL activity and sell the property. If she sells within three years of cessation of the activity, the gain in relation to the FHL activity will attract entrepreneurs' relief provided the business qualified for the 12 months up to the date of cessation. See **explanatory note 27**.

No details are provided in relation to whether a main residence election has been made by Mr and Mrs Morley under TCGA 1992 s 222(5). It is possible that the Suffolk property could be considered a 'residence' for the purposes of only or main residence rules in TCGA 1992 s 222. However, if no nomination has been made within the two years from the time the couple had two residences the decision as to which is the main residence would be based on fact and this would probably mean that the family home would be the main residence.

However, there are ways in which the nomination period could be reopened (such as by renting a third property and using it as a residence) and this might be worth looking into if the gain on the Suffolk property is substantial. This is discussed further in **Example D4**.

Note that if the Suffolk property was the couple's main residence for TCGA 1992 s 222 at any time during the ownership period, the gain which relates to the FHL let period may qualify for letting relief (TCGA 1992 s 223(4)). Although HMRC took the view that letting relief was only available if the lettings had some degree of permanence (so a series of short lets would not qualify), it lost a case on the point (*Owen v Elliott* [1990] STC 469, see **Example L8 explanatory note 8**).

## (d) *Notes for response on Ruritanian holiday property*

- We are unable to advise on foreign tax matters. It is essential that these are dealt with by a competent professional trained in the tax law of the jurisdiction concerned. We can obtain a specialist opinion at additional cost if requested.
- The tax treatment of the property will be determined by the double tax treaty (if any). However, it is likely that the income will be taxable in both countries, with the result that tax will be paid at the higher of the two rates. If Ruritanian tax is higher than UK tax, then no refund will be available in the UK; if Ruritanian tax is lower than UK tax, then there will be additional UK tax to pay. See **Example F3**.
- If Ruritania is in the European Economic Area (EEA), the purchase of the property as a furnished holiday letting activity in private hands (as opposed to through a limited company) would attract favourable tax treatment. The property would have to be let on a commercial basis and meet the availability and actual letting conditions set out above and would be treated as a separate FHL business to the Suffolk house, as UK and non UK FHLs are treated as separate businesses. The offset of losses between the two would not be possible, but all of the favourable rules for FHL are available on an EEA FHL if it meets the relevant conditions (see above).
- Individuals owning a property through a company are exempt from benefits in kind chargesi f the following conditions are met (ITEPA 2003, s 100A):
  - the property is owned by a company owned by individuals;
  - the company's only activities are incidental to its ownership of the property;

– the property is the company's only or main asset;

– the property must not be funded, directly or indirectly, by a connected company.

The property must therefore not be funded by Mr Morley's company. The matter of what activities are planned for the holiday property, and to what extent they are merely incidental to ownership, must be resolved. It is however probable that it will be possible to escape the benefit in kind charge.

## (C) Mr and Mrs Turner

Mr and Mrs Turner's situation is not straightforward. Based on the facts, there may be significant tax charges on incorporating their property business, but this might still be the best option for them if they intend to continue running the business in the long-term.

As higher rate taxpayers, they pay income tax at 40% on the profits of the business. If the business were run via a company the profits would be taxed at 20% corporation tax (19% from 1 April 2017), although they would have to consider the tax costs associated with extracting profits from the company.

The restriction to relief for finance costs of dwelling houses is phased in from 2017/18 onwards and applies to unincorporated residential property businesses, not companies (see **explanatory note 16**). Companies receive relief for interst costs under the loan relationships rules, see **Example K2.**

Based on the facts in the question, and assuming the interest rate on their mortgage remains 3.5%, the tax payable by **each person** if they carry on their property business jointly will be:

| | 2016/17 | 2017/18 | 2018/19 | 2019/20 | 2020/21 |
|---|---|---|---|---|---|
| | £ | £ | £ | £ | £ |
| Rents | 90,000 | 90,000 | 90,000 | 90,000 | 90,000 |
| Less: mortgage interest | (35,000) | (26,250) | (17,500) | (8,750) | — |
| Less: other expenses | (15,000) | (15,000) | (15,000) | (15,000) | (15,000) |
| Property income | 40,000 | 48,750 | 57,500 | 66,250 | 75,000 |
| Tax on property income | | | | | |
| @ 40% | 16,000 | 19,500 | 23,000 | 26,500 | 30,000 |
| Less: tax reduction for mortgage interest | — | (1,750) | (3,500) | (5,250) | (7,000) |
| Tax payable on property income | 16,000 | 17,750 | 19,500 | 21,250 | 23,000 |

The difference would be even more pronounced if mortgage interest rates were to rise.

The levels of Mr and Mrs Turner's employment incomes are not given in the question, but once the changes to the relief for mortgage interest take their adjusted net incomes over £100,000 the personal allowance(s) will be abated. During the abatement (which is between £100,000 and £100,000 plus twice the personal allowance) the marginal rate of tax is, in fact, 60% so the figures for tax payable above would be slightly higher. Since they are both higher rate taxpayers, this is likely to be the case from 2018/19, if not before. See **Example A3, explanatory note 1.**

The immediate tax issues which need to be considered when incorporating a residential property business are:

- stamp duty land tax (land and buildings transaction tax for disposals in Scotland);
- capital gains tax.

There are also non-tax issues to consider here, including:

- the need to move the mortgages into the name of the new company (which may mean redemption penalties and administration fees depending on the mortgage terms);
- the legal costs in drawing up new tenancy agreements in the name of the company;
- the increased administration requirements which apply to companies, including filing public accounts with Companies House.

## *Stamp duty land tax*

Stamp duty land tax (SDLT) is charged on transactions of land in England, Wales and Northern Ireland. For these purposes, 'land' includes buildings. Land and buildings transaction tax (LBTT) applies to transactions of land in Scotland and the rules are similar, but they will not be considered further as the Turners' properties are in Yorkshire.

Normally SDLT is levied on the 'chargeable consideration' paid, or deemed to be paid in the case of assumption of debt, to acquire a 'chargeable interest' in land. Land transactions are chargeable to SDLT unless they are specifically exempted or there is no chargeable consideration. SDLT is payable by the purchaser, in this case the company.

Whilst normally a gift of land would not be liable to SDLT, or only be liable to SDLT on the amount of the debt assumed by the transferee (FA 2003 Sch 3 para 1; FA 2003 Sch 4 para 8), this is not the case where the property is 'gifted' to a connected company. As the Turners would be connected with the new company, this means that the disposals of the properties to the company would be deemed to take place at market value (FA 2003 s 53; CTA 2010 s 1122).

The question then becomes, are the transfers treated as one transfer with deemed consideration of £3m, or is each property treated as a separate transfer? The latter will produce a lower SDLT liability, not least because where the purchaser is a non-natural person and the consideration exceeds £500,000, SDLT of 15% is charged on the entire consideration (FA 2013 Sch 4A).

Firstly, as the fifteen properties are transferred from the same seller to the same buyer, these are linked transactions under FA 2003 s 108 which is designed to prevent transactions being split up to avoid SDLT. However, since July 2011, multiple dwellings relief (MDR) applies to limit the SDLT to the average price per dwelling multiplied by the number of dwellings (FA 2003 s 58D Sch 6B). As the properties are to be transferred after 1 April 2016 the additional 3% SDLT rate applies (FA 2003 Sch 4ZA para 7).

The average price per dwelling is £200,000 (£3m/15 properties). Therefore the SDLT charge, applying MDR will be:

| | £ |
|---|---|
| £125,000 @ 3% | 3,750 |
| £75,000 @ 5% | 3,750 |
| Average SDLT charge per property | 7,500 |
| | |
| Total SDLT charge (£7,500 x 15) | 112,500 |

This SDLT liability has to be paid and the return filed within 30 days of the transfer (FA 2003 ss 76-78). This is a significant amount of cash to find for a new company, and indeed it exceeds the annual profits of the business. The company may need to borrow from the bank or Mr and Mrs Turner may need to loan this money to the company.

However, had the Turners run their property business as a bona fide **partnership**, with a partnership agreement and partnership tax returns it would have been possible to transfer the properties to a new company without an SDLT charge using FA 2003 Sch 15 paras 18-20. In summary, these rules provide full or partial relief from the SDLT charge where one or more of the partners will remain a relevant owner of the property after the transfer to the company. If the same individual shareholders own the properties, in the same proportions, as they did when they operated the business as a partnership, there will be no SDLT charge. Although the anti-avoidance rule on transfers to connected companies in FA 2003 s 53 also applies, HMRC confirms in SDLTM34160 that the partnership rules take precedence.

It is unlikely, on the facts, that HMRC would accept an argument that the Turners had actually been carrying on a parthership (rather than jointly owning a property business). However it is worth considering HMRC's guidance on the existence of a partnership in PM10100, PM102000 and PM10400.

If the Turners were to convert their joint property business into a partnership with a view to then incorporating the partnership in future and saving SDLT, this is likely to fall into the targeted anti-avoidance rules in FA 2003 s 75A. This attacks arrangements which are introduced to avoid SDLT and was specifically introduced to prevent this type of avoidance via partnerships (PM60330).

SDLT is discussed in detail in **Example D6.**

## *Capital gains tax*

Transfers of chargeable assets otherwise than a bargain at arm's length are deemed to take place at market value (TCGA 1992 s 17). The question is whether the resulting gain can be deferred under:

- incorporation relief (TCGA 1992 s 162); or
- business asset gift relief, also known as hold-over relief (TCGA 1992 s 165)

Incorporation relief applies where a business is incorporated as a going concern, all the assets (except cash) are transferred to the company and the consideration paid by the company is wholly or partly in shares. The amount of the relief will be proportionally restricted if any of the consideration is not paid in shares (eg part of the consideration is left outstanding on loan account). Strictly, the assumption of the mortgage debts by the company could be deemed to be a form of non-share consideration (as it is in SDLT) but HMRC does not treat assumption of debt as consideration for the purposes of TCGA 1992 s 162 (ESC D32).

Business asset gift relief is often used as an alternative to incorporation relief. This relief is considered in relation to the gift of each chargeable asset, rather than on the transaction as a whole. It can be useful if the individual does not want to transfer all the assets to the company.

In the Turners' case, the key point is whether a residential property business qualifies as a 'business' for the purposes of incorporation relief and business asset gift relief.

For incorporation relief purposes, the key case is *Ramsay v HMRC* [2013] STC 1764, in which the Upper Tribunal held that the taxpayer was carrying on a business. However, for this to be the case the business had to represent a "serious undertaking earnestly pursued" and be conducted using "sound and recognised business principles". As far as the Turners are concerned this would be a question of fact and more information would be needed to understand the detail of the runnings of the property business so as to be able to give a view on whether incorporation relief would apply.

However, business asset gift relief would not be available because the assets must be used in the individual's "trade, profession or vocation". Property businesses of the type pursued by the Turners might be considered to be a business but they do not normally amount to a trade (which is decided based on the badges of trade, see **Example B6, Part (C)**.

Therefore it is possible that Mr and Mrs Turner could defer all or part of the capital gains on incorporation using incorporation relief (with the relief depending on the amount left on loan account).

For a further discussion of incorporation, see **Example N3**. For more on business asset gift relief, see **Example L9.**

## *ATED*

The annual tax on enveloped dwellings (ATED) is payable by companies which hold high value residential dwellings. This tax charge was introduced April 2013, and for accounting periods which begin on or after 1 April

2016 this applies to any property worth £500,000 or more (FA 2013 ss 94, 99). Properties which are let to a third party on a commercial basis or those which are not currently let but are available for letting can claim an exemption from the charge (FA 2013 s 133).

It is unclear from the facts whether any of the Turners' properties are valued at over £500,000. This should be established and, if any are worth over £500,000 an ATED return should be made within 30 days of incorporation, claiming the property rental business exemption (FA 2013 ss 159, 159A). Penalties apply if the return is submitted late, even where no tax is at stake (FA 2009 Sch 55). Therefore should the Turners transfer the properties to a company, the company would not suffer ATED charges.

For a full discussion of ATED, see **Example D5**.

### *Extraction of profit from the company*

It is important to consider how the Turners could extract profits from the business, as amounts extracted by way of dividends will increase the effective tax rate (assuming the dividends exceed the dividend nil rate band of £5,000).

For a discussion of strategies to extract profit from the business and the tax implications of these, see **Examples N3** and **J3**.

### *Conclusion*

On the assumption that the capital gain can be deferred via incorporation relief, the main cost of incorporation is the SDLT charge of £112,500. Although this is a significant one-off hit, it may be that this is still the best option for the Turners if they intend to continue to run the business in the long term, given the availability of full relief for the mortgage interest, the potential for interest rate rises and lower rates of corporation tax.

However the Turners would be vulnerable to future changes in the law, such as changes to the rental exemption for ATED (coupled with rises in property values or reduction in the ATED threshold) or restriction of finance costs on dwelling houses for companies. The restriction of relief for mortgage interest is predictably leading unincorporated businesses to incorporate and the Government may decide that this 'avoidance' of these rules is unacceptable.

## Explanatory Notes

*Taxation of rental income*

(1) The same rules broadly apply to the calculation of rental income for individuals and companies, although there are some differences.

The rules that apply to both individuals and companies are dealt with in **explanatory notes 2–12** below. Rules that apply only for income tax are dealt with in **explanatory notes 13-16** and rules that apply only for companies in **explanatory notes 17-18**.

*UK property business rules for rental income*

(2) All UK rental income is treated as relating to a single 'UK property business'. This applies whether the income is from sizeable businesses or from letting a single property, commercial or residential and no matter whether the property is let furnished or unfurnished (ITTOIA 2005 s 264; CTA 2009 s 205).

The income from UK furnished holiday lettings is, however, calculated separately as the rules on the utilisation of losses are different. See **part B** of this Example and **explanatory notes 22-28**.

Special rules also apply under the 'rent-a-room' scheme for individuals letting rooms in their own homes (see **explanatory note 15**).

Those who run hotels or guest houses, or individuals who provide meals to lodgers or tenants in their own homes, are usually regarded as trading (although the 'rent-a-room' scheme may apply). HMRC considers that where let property is not the taxpayer's home, the income will rarely constitute trading income, even if managing the properties takes up virtually all of the owner's time, although where additional services are provided over and above those normally provided for let property the income from those additional services may be treated as trading income (PIM4300).

*Calculation of rental profits*

(3) Under ITTOIA 2005 s 272, the profits of an unincorporated UK property business are computed broadly in the same way as business profits.

Similarly, CTA 2009 s 210 imports trading income rules to calculate the profits of an incorporated UK property business.

The overriding rules in relation to allowable expenses is that they must be 'wholly and exclusively' for the purposes of the business and not be capital in nature (ITTOIA 2005 ss 33-34 as read with ITTOIA 2005 s 272; CTA 2009 ss 53-54 as read with CTA 2009 s 210). Adjustments may need to be made to expenses of unincorporated businesses to disallow any proportion relating to private use (see **explanatory note 13**). No private use adjustments are needed for companies, although there may be a benefit in kind charge if an employee or director uses the property for personal purposes.

Typical allowable property expenses include:

- agent fees or commission;
- mortgage interest (but not any capital element, as this is prevented by the general rule above) for unincorporated property businesses (PIM2105). For incorporated property businesses, mortgage interest is not allowed as a deduction from property income and is instead dealt with under the loan relationship rules (see **explanatory note 16**);
- legal and professional costs in relation to the renewal of a short lease (ie with a term of 50 years or less). The costs in relation to the initial lease are not allowable unless the term is for less than a year (PIM2205);
- bad and doubtful debts for unincorporated property businesses (ITTOIA 2005 s 35 as read with ITTOIA 2005 s 272; PIM2054). For incorporated property businesses, bad debts are likely to be money debts falling under the loan relationships rules (see **explanatory note 17**);
- the cost of repairs (which are not capital improvements, as this is prevented by the general rule above) (see **explanatory note 5**);
- insurance costs (PIM2040).

For a more extensive list of expenses, see PIM2050.

This may include the expenses of travelling to and from the let properties, unless in the case of an individual the trip is partly for private purposes (PIM2210).

As mentioned above, capital expenditure is disallowed in calculating the profit on a property business. However, relief may be available under specific tax provisions:

- capital allowances may be claimed in relation to let commercial property or qualifying furnished holiday lets (see **explanatory note 6**);
- replacement of domestic items relief may be available in respect of let residential property (see **explanatory note 7**).

Allowable expenditure incurred in the seven years before the business started is treated as incurred on the first day of the business (ITTOIA 2005 s 57 as read with ITTOIA 2005 s 272; CTA 2009 s 61 as read with

CTA 2009 s 210). Any interest paid by a company prior to the start of the property business is dealt with under the loan relationships rules (see **explanatory note 17**).

If property is let for less than a commercial rent for personal reasons (for example, to a relative or friend), expenses relating to the property are restricted by the 'wholly and exclusively' rule, and are not allowed to the extent that they exceed the rent received, nor can the excess expenses be carried forward to a later year (PIM2220). In part A of this Example, therefore, Fred cannot deduct the excess insurance premium on Shop 3 from his other rental income and the excess is not carried forward.

(4) Rental income and expenses should be calculated in accordance with generally accepted accounting practice (GAAP), subject only to adjustments required by tax legislation (ITTOIA 2005 s 25 as read with ITTOIA 2005 s 272; CTA 2009 s 46 as read with CTA 2009 s 210). In accordance with GAAP, property income and expenditure should be determined using the 'accruals basis', ie with adjustments for amounts in arrears and in advance.

For income tax purposes, HMRC will, however, accept figures based on receipts and payments for 'small' cases, ie where the gross rental income does not exceed £15,000, providing the cash basis is used consistently and does not produce a result substantially different from the earnings basis (PIM1101). Property businesses do not qualify to use the simplified cash basis for unincorporated businesses introduced from 2013/14 onwards, because these rules are not imported by ITTOIA 2005 s 272 into the calculation of income from a property business.

The basis period is the tax year for individuals and the accounting period for companies. If individuals do not draw up their UK property business accounts for the tax year, the results must be apportioned on a time basis (ITTOIA 2005 s 275; PIM1010). For example, if accounts are drawn up to 30 June, the 2016/17 income would be 86/366ths of the result to 30 June 2016 and 279/365ths of the result to 30 June 2017. In practice HMRC accepts accounts drawn up to 31 March as being the same as the tax year, providing this is done consistently and does not give materially different results from the strict tax year basis.

*Repair expenditure*

(5) As mentioned in **explanatory note 3**, for repair expenditure to be allowable, it must not be capital in nature (ITTOIA 2005 s 33 as read with ITTOIA 2005 s 272; CTA 2009 s 53 as read with CTA 2009 s 210). Expenditure on improvements, additions and extensions is capital and so is not allowable (PIM2020).

Where maintenance and repairs of property are made unnecessary because of improvements, additions and alterations, no allowance will normally be given (ie there is no deduction for the notional cost of a repair, see BIM46930).

However if assets are replaced with broadly the same asset a full deduction can be claimed for the replacement and only additional amounts will be capital, eg a replacement kitchen with extra storage (only the extra storage will be disallowed). When deciding whether the replacement of an asset is a 'repair' it is necessary to look at the identity of the asset and decide whether the entire asset is being replaced. If the entire asset (rather than a distinct part of the asset) is replaced the expenditure is capital and so is disallowed. See BIM46910 for a discussion of the 'entirety' principle. Also see **explanatory note 7**.

If the asset (whether the entirety or a distinct part) is substantially upgraded then the cost is disallowed (BIM46915). HMRC accepts that certain improvements are not capital (for example the cost of replacing single glazed windows with double glazed equivalents is allowable). The key point is whether after the repair the asset performs exactly the same function as before (BIM46920).

Under GAAP, expenditure to rectify dilapidations that occurred in a previous ownership is allowable so long as the property was in a usable state when acquired. This follows the principle in *Odeon Associated Theatres Ltd v Jones* 48 TC 257 (see BIM31095, BIM35450). Hence the cost of rectifying the dry-rot was allowable in **part A** of this Example.

*Capital allowances and replacement of domestic items relief*

(6) Capital allowances are available on plant and machinery used for the maintenance, repair or management of let commercial premises. Residential lets do not qualify for capital allowances, with the exception of qualifying furnished holiday lets (FHLs) (CAA 2001 ss 15(1)(c), (da), 35).

The rules on qualifying expenditure and calculation of capital allowances are the same as for trades (see **Examples C6-C9** for in-depth discussion of the capital allowances rules).

In relation to **part A** of this Example, it is possible that capital allowances claims may be available in respect of the fittings in the shops, although no details are given of the costs or written down value in the question. Specialist help might be appropriate in identifying the value of equipment for the purposes of capital allowances claims, particularly as some plant may be treated as integral features.

Where property is let as furnished holiday accommodation, a significant amount of capital allowances may be available, including bathroom fittings etc. On the initial purchase you will need to establish the value available for capital allowances. However, the downside is that if the FHL conditions are not met, there is a disposal at market value for capital allowances purposes, which adds complexity. See **explanatory note 25**.

Capital allowances are deducted as a business expense and are thus taken into account in arriving at the UK property business profit or loss.

(7) Landlords who let furnished residential property which does not qualify for capital allowances can obtain some tax relief for their capital outlay. Revenue deductions can be claimed for:

- replacement of domestic items (ITTOIA 2005 s 311A; CTA 2009 s 250A). These rules apply for expenditure incurred on or after 6 April 2016 for unincorporated property businesses and on or after 1 April 2016 for companies. This relief replaces wear and tear allowance and the statutory renewals basis; and
- the replacement of fixtures (under case law)

Replacement of domestic items relief is available to those letting residential property, whether in the UK or abroad, and allows a deduction against income for the capital costs of replacing a domestic item, such as free-standing white goods, carpets or curtains. It is only the cost of the replacement that it allowed, not the initial outlay. The domestic item must be provided soley for the use of the tenant; if the property owner is an individual there must be no element of private use.

Furnished holiday lets and those letting a room in their own property are exempt and cannot claim a deduction under these rules (ITTOIA 2005 s 311A(7), (8); CTA 2009 s 250A(7)).

The amount of the revenue deduction is the cost of the new domestic item, including any incidental charges (such as delivery or VAT). Any amount received for the old item in money or money's worth must be deducted from the allowable cost. If the new item is an improvement on the old item then the amount treated as the improvement (ie the cost of the new item less the cost of a like-for-like replacement) must also be taken off the allowable cost (ITTOIA 2005 s 311(9)-(13); CTA 2009 s 250A(8)-(12)).

In addition to replacement of domestic items relief, a deduction may be claimed for the cost of replacing fixtures that are an integral part of buildings, such as baths, toilets, central heating (but excluding any 'improvement element' where the replacements are significantly better than the original items). Until 6 April 2013 (for unincorporated businesses) or 1 April 2013 (for companies) this treatment was given by ESC B47 (now withdrawn). There has been confusion as to the treatment of fixtures under the statutory rules, however HMRC clarified the position in a letter to ICAEW and CIOT in April 2014 (www.lexisnexis.com/tolley/guidance/personaltax/signOn.faces). The key point to consider is whether or not the expenditure is considered to be a repair. HMRC confirmed in the letter that the replacement of fitted kitchen appliances is a repair but the replacement of free-standing white goods is not. See **explanatory note 5**.

Wear and tear allowance was repealed with effect from 6 April 2016 for unincorporated businesses and 1 April 2016 for companies. Prior to this date it was available where the residential accommodation was let furnished. HMRC interpreted 'furnished' to mean that the property was let with sufficient furniture, furnishings and equipment for normal residential use (PIM3205). The deduction available was of 10% of the gross rent for the year less any payments made by the landlord that would normally be borne by a tenant (eg water rates or council tax). This stopped the landlord increasing the rent, paying these charges and benefiting from an increased wear and tear allowance. Council tax is usually paid directly by the tenants, but where a property is multi-occupied, the landlord may pay it instead (see **explanatory note 10**).

An election was required for the wear and tear allowance to apply. For unincorporated businesses the time limit was the first anniversary of 31 January following the end of the tax year (ITTOIA 2005 s 308A(2)). For companies the time limit was two years from the end of the accounting period to which the allowance related (CTA 2009 s 248A(2)).

Up to April 2016, instead of electing for wear and tear allowance the landlord could claim a deduction for expenses under the statutory renewals basis (ITTOIA 2005 68 as read with ITTOIA 2005 s 272; CTA 2009 s 68 as read with CTA 2009 s 210).

HMRC's view was that a deduction under the statutory renewals basis was only available for the replacement of small items used routinely in the business (BIM46960). For a property business this might have included lightbulbs, smoke detectors, carbon monoxide detectors etc.

The landlord needed to decide each tax year whether to make an election for wear and tear allowance or claim the statutory renewals basis. It was not possible to benefit from both provisions (ITTOIA 2005 s 308C(2); CTA 2009 s 248C(2)).

*Deductions for expenditure on energy-saving items*

(8) Up to April 2015, landlords carrying on a property business involving a dwelling-house could deduct expenditure on certain energy-saving items which was otherwise disallowed as capital expenditure (ITTOIA 2005 ss 312–314; CTA 2009 ss 251-253).

To qualify, the expenditure on cavity wall insulation, loft insulation, floor insulation, hot water system insulation or draft proofing had to be incurred before 6 April 2015 (or 1 April 2015 for companies) (ITTOIA 2005 s 312; SI 2008/1520). A limit of £1,500 per dwelling was imposed, with each flat in a block of flats counting as a separate dwelling (SI 2007/3278, reg 3; SI 2008/1520, reg 3).

No deduction was allowed if the energy-saving item was installed in a dwelling-house in the course of construction, neither in respect of rent-a-room receipts, nor in respect of commercial letting of furnished holiday accommodation (ITTOIA 2005 s 313; CTA 2009 s 252).

*Premiums on leases*

(9) The premium arising on the grant of a short lease (ie for 50 years or less) by a landlord, as distinct from the assignment of such a lease from one tenant to another, is partly assessable as income, whilst the remainder forms part of a capital gains computation (ITTOIA 2005 s 277; CTA 2009 s 217).

The proportion taxed as income is treated as additional rent and is therefore available to cover expenses (as in Shop 4 in **part A** of this Example).

The formula given in the legislation is devised so that the longer the term of the lease, the more of the premium falls into the capital gains computation and the less is regarded as additional rent.

The premium is reduced by 2% for each complete twelve-month period of the lease except the first, in ascertaining that part to be left in as rent.

Thus:

| *Lease for* | 5 yrs | 10 yrs | 25 yrs | 40 yrs | 50 yrs |
|---|---|---|---|---|---|
| Premium £ or % | 100 | 100 | 100 | 100 | 100 |
| Reduce by 2% for each year except the first(and take this part into a capital gains computation as a part disposal) | (8) | (18) | (48) | (78) | (98) |
| Include as additional rent | 92 | 82 | 52 | 22 | 2 |

The formula for including the discounted part in a capital gains computation is dealt with in **Example D3**, which also deals with other aspects of the tax treatment of premiums.

*Council tax and business rates*

(10) Council tax on let domestic property is usually paid by the tenants, but the landlord may pay when property is in multiple occupation. The landlord must pay the council tax for periods when, as in this Example, the property is empty between lettings, although various periods are exempt, such as the first six months for unfurnished property which is empty following the death of the owner. There is no exemption for empty furnished property.

For property that is not domestic property, such as business premises, business rates are payable, and the payments are deductible as an expense in the normal way, subject to the rules for void periods for company landlords.

For more on the rules for council tax and business rates for empty properties, see the GOV.UK website (https://www.gov.uk/council-tax/second-homes-and-empty-properties and https://www.gov.uk/apply-for-business-rate-relief/exempted-buildings-and-empty-buildings-relief).

*UK property let by a non-resident*

(11) Where property is let by a non-resident, the rental income is computed in the same way as for a resident *individual* (ITA 2007 ss 971–972; SI 1995/2902). This applies whether the non-resident landlord is an individual, or trustees, or a company, except that it does not apply to the rental income of a UK branch of a non-resident company.

'Non-residents' for the purpose of ITA 2007 s 971 are those whose 'usual place of abode' is outside the UK, rather than the definition used for other purposes (as to which see **Example F1**). HMRC regards an individual as having a usual place of abode outside the UK if he is away for more than six months (PIM4800). Companies will not be so treated if they are UK resident for tax purposes. References to non-residents in the remainder of this note should be read accordingly.

The non-resident landlord scheme operates to ensure that basic rate tax is withheld from property income either by a UK agent handling the let property, or by the tenant where there is no agent (SI 1995/2902 reg 8). The tax is paid over to HMRC 30 days after the end of each calendar quarter (SI 1995/2902 reg 10). The landlord must review the position and file a self-assessment tax return if further tax is payable or a repayment is due. Where the tenant pays VAT on the rent, tax need only be deducted from the net of VAT amount. A tenant paying rent of £100 a week or less does not have to deduct tax unless told to do so by HMRC.

The tax withheld is 20% of the gross rents less any expenses paid by the agent/tenant in the calendar quarter which the agent/tenant is reasonably satisfied will be allowable expenses (SI 1995/2902 reg 9). This might include management fees, repairs and gas/electricity safety checks. No allowable expenses paid by the landlord can be taken into account (eg mortgage interest).

Neither tenants nor agents have to deduct tax at source if the non-resident applies to HMRC to receive the rent gross. The application is made using:

- Form NRL1i for individuals https://www.gov.uk/government/publications/non-resident-landlord-application-to-receive-uk-rental-income-without-deduction-of-uk-tax-individuals-nrl1i;
- Form NRL2i for companies https://www.gov.uk/government/publications/non-resident-landord-application-to-receive-uk-rental-income-without-deduction-of-uk-tax-companies-nrl2i;
- Form NRL3i for non-resident trustees https://www.gov.uk/government/publications/trusts-and-estates-application-to-receive-uk-rental-income-without-deduction-of-uk-tax-non-resident-trustees-nrl3i.

The landlord agrees to complete any self-assessment tax returns he receives and pay any tax due on the property income (ITA 2007 s 972). If the non-resident landlord makes significant profits, payments on account may be required (see **Example G2**).

The HMRC Centre for Non-Residents does not normally issue self-assessment returns to non-resident individual landlords who have no net tax liability, although returns may still be sent occasionally to ensure that the tax position remains the same. If no self-assessment tax return is issued, the landlord must monitor the UK tax position as a notification of chargeability may be necessary by 5 October after the end of the tax year if there is UK tax to pay (FA 2008 Sch 41, see **Example G2**).

For the capital gains tax implications of disposals of UK residential properties by non-residents (as determined under the statutory residence test), see **Example F2.**

*Overseas property lettings*

(12) Income from property let abroad is calculated broadly in the same way as for a UK property business (except that the rules for FHLs do not apply outside the European Economic Area (EEA)).

Note that the income tax rules in ITTOIA 2005 ss 92–94 relating to board and lodging and travelling expenses in connection with foreign trades do not apply to overseas property businesses (as these rules are *not* imported into the property income rules by ITTOIA 2005 s 272).

In order to calculate the amount of double tax relief available where the foreign tax has been paid on overseas property income, profits and losses are calculated separately for each property and then aggregated and taxed as the profits of an 'overseas property business' (ITTOIA 2005 s 265; CTA 2009 s 206). Again, the profits of any overseas FHLs in the EEA are calculated separately from profits from non-FHL property as losses are ring-fenced.

For more on overseas property lettings, see **Example D4**.

*Provisions applicable to individuals*

**Private use adjustment**

(13) If an expense incurred by an unincorporated property business is incurred for a 'dual purpose' (both a business and a private element to the expense), HMRC may permit a tax deduction for the business proportion only (PIM2005).

This can be common with second homes which are used by the owner at times during the tax year and rented out at other times. The private element of the expenses such as mortgage interest and insurance costs must be disallowed.

**Relief for losses**

(14) If losses arise, they are carried forward to set against future property income of the same type (eg UK property losses are set against future UK property profits and overseas property losses are set against future overseas property profits) (ITA 2007 ss 118-119).

See **Example C6 part E** for details of the relief available to individuals for excess capital allowances included in a UK property business loss.

**Rent-a-room relief**

(15) Under the 'rent-a-room' relief provisions of ITTOIA 2005 ss 784-802, an owner or tenant who lets furnished rooms in his home is exempt from tax on gross rent of up to £7,500 a year from 2016/17 (£4,250 a year prior to this). This applies whether the rent would have been charged as UK property income or trading income where the services provided are such that the income would be treated as being from a trade.

The rent taken into account for the relief is the payment for the accommodation plus payments for related goods and services, such as meals, cleaning, laundry etc.

The property must have been the claimant's only or main residence at some time during the letting period in each relevant tax year. The relief cannot be claimed if part of the property is let unfurnished in the same year.

If during the basis period someone else receives rent for letting a room in the property while it is the claimant's only or main residence the available exemption is halved to £3,750. This would apply, for example, to a couple who were jointly receiving rent from tenants, or to other joint owners.

The automatic tax treatment depends on whether the rent received is within the available exemption or exceeds it:

- if the rent is within the available exemption (ie not more than £7,500 or £3,750 as appropriate) — rent-a-room relief is automatic although the individual can elect for the profit or loss to be calculated under normal business income principles (eg if he would realise a loss);
- if the rent is more than the available exemption (ie more than £7,500 or £3,750 as appropriate) — the profit or loss is automatically calculated under normal business income principles although the individual can elect for only the excess over the available exemption to be taxable (eg if the allowable expenses are less than the available exemption).

Elections for alternative treatment must be made by the first anniversary of 31 January following the end of the tax year.

For HMRC guidance on rent-a-room relief, see PIM4000.

For the effect of letting part of the home on the capital gains tax exemption see **Example L8.**

**Relief for finance costs**

(16) Until 2017/18, loan interest is a revenue expense and can be deducted from the rents received. This includes mortgage interest, interest on loans used to fund repairs/extensions and any incidental costs of obtaining loan finance (ITTOIA 2005 s 272 as read with ITTOIA 2005 ss 29, 58; PIM2105).

However from 2017/18, relief for finance costs relating to residential property (in the UK or overseas) is restricted to the basic rate of income tax. From 2017/18 to 2020/21, the revenue deduction is phased out and instead relief is given by a tax reduction of 20% in Step 6 of the income tax calculation in ITA 2007 s 23 (ITTOIA 2005 ss 272A, 274A, 274AA):

| Tax year | Percentage of expense given as revenue deduction | Percentage of expense given as a tax reduction at 20% |
|---|---|---|
| 2016/17 | 100% | 0% |
| 2017/18 | 75% | 25% |
| 2018/19 | 50% | 50% |
| 2019/20 | 25% | 75% |
| 2020/21 | 0% | 100% |

These rules do not apply to commercial properties or to furnished holiday lets (ITTOIA 2005 s 272B(4)).

If the tax reduction is limited by the amount of the property income (after property losses brought forward) or if the property income is covered by the personal allowance, the excess finance costs may be carried forward (ITTOIA 2005 s 274AA). Note that finance costs are not within the cap on income tax reliefs.

*Provisions applicable to companies*

**Treatment of interest paid and losses**

(17) Interest paid by a company in relation to rented property is dealt with under the 'loan relationships' rules (see **Example K2**). If the interest relates to a furnished holiday letting it is deducted from the letting income. See **Example I1 explanatory note 6** for the treatment of interest incurred before the commencement of a trade.

(18) If a loss arises, it may be set against the total profits of the same accounting period, or surrendered by way of group relief (see **Example K2 Part A**), with any unrelieved balance carried forward to set against future *total* profits.

*UK real estate investment trusts (REITs)*

**Overview**

(19) The REIT regime provides that profits from a company's or group's ring-fenced property rental business are exempt from corporation tax, provided that at least 90% of those profits are passed through to shareholders as property income distributions (PIDs) within 12 months of the company's year end (CTA 2010 s 530; GREIT02050).

These profits are liable to income tax or corporation tax in the hands of the recipients as income from a separate property business.

**UK REIT company – key points**

(20) The UK REIT legislation is found in CTA 2010 ss 518–609, and a number of regulations. The exemption is obtained by making an application to HMRC, stating that a number of properties have been moved into the exempt property business ring fence, and that a number of conditions have been fulfilled.

Prior to 17 July 2012 there was an entry charge of 2% of the market value divided by the company's tax rate for properties entering the ring fence (CTA 2010 s 538). However this was deemed to discourage the use of REITs and was abolished.

Provided that conditions are met, the tax exemptions available to the REIT company are:

- exemption from corporation tax on the rental income;
- exemption from capital gains tax on disposal of ring fence properties.

The main conditions to be met by the company are (CTA 2010 ss 527-529, 531):

- it must be admitted to trade on a recognised stock exchange (ie the REIT can be listed on AIM). Prior to 17 July 2012 the REIT needed to be a quoted company;
- it must not be a close company (although where the company applies to be a REIT on or after 17 July 2012 there is a three year grace period where this condition does not have to be met);
- it must be UK resident and not dual resident;
- it must have one class only of ordinary shares, but may have fixed interest preference shares;
- there is an interest cover restriction, charging excessive interest to tax;
- interest paid on loans must be fixed interest, and not participate in profit;
- there must be a minimum of three properties (individual units count as separate properties) (GREIT02025);
- no property may represent more than 40% of the portfolio (IFRS valuation/fair value) (GREIT02035);
- no property may be owner occupied;
- 75% of total profits must arise from the tax-exempt property rental business (GREIT02070);
- 75% of the company's assets at the beginning of the period must relate to the tax-exempt property rental business (GREIT02075);

- the maximum individual shareholding in the company is limited to less than 10% (CTA 2010 ss 551-553; GREIT02100-GREIT02150).

Note that, at the time of writing, the HMRC manual has not been fully updated to reflect the rewrite of the provisions into CTA 2010, however as an insight into HMRC's view it is still useful.

Failure to meet these conditions may cause a tax charge to arise, or for the company to cease qualifying for REIT exemptions.

**Distributions**

(21) Distributions of property income from REITs (known as property income distributions (PIDs)) are not dividends, but are treated as profits of a separate UK property business. There is no tax credit on these distributions; instead tax must be withheld by the REIT at the basic rate (20%).

The distributions are treated as profits of a *separate* property business, and as such, losses from other property businesses cannot be offset against them. The non-residents landlord regime does not apply to these distributions.

There are no tax exemptions for recipients of distributions, the purpose of the scheme being to facilitate holdings in property portfolios. However, because profits have not been subject to corporation tax, the distributions should be higher than they otherwise would have been.

If the shareholder sells shares in the REIT this is subject to tax in the usual way (ie capital gains tax for individuals, trustees and personal representatives and corporation tax for companies).

Shares in REITs may be held in tax efficient wrappers such as ISAs and self-invested personal pensions (SIPPs), where tax relief may be available.

*Furnished holiday lettings*

(22) The commercial letting of furnished holiday accommodation in the UK is treated differently for tax purposes to the letting of other residential or commercial property. It is assessable to tax as property income but deemed to be a trade for the purposes of various aspects of the legislation meaning that reliefs are available.

To qualify for the special FHL treatment:

- there must be qualifying holiday accommodation;
- the accommodation must be furnished;
- the accommodation must be let out commercially.

See **explanatory note 23**.

The original UK tax legislation restricted the benefits of the furnished holiday let (FHL) regime to properties in the UK. This was contrary to EU law and the legislation was changed in FA 2011 such that the FHL regime applies to any property within the European Economic Area (EEA) that meets the qualifying conditions. However these changes had a negative impact on UK FHLs. From 2011/12 the ability to offset FHL losses against other income was removed, and from 2012/13 the 'qualifying holiday accommodation' definition was tightened up.

From 6 April 2011 FHL losses can only be set against profits from the FHL business (and not profits from a normal property business). Since the letting of UK properties and the letting of non-UK EEA properties are deemed to be separate businesses, losses on UK FHLs cannot be offset against profits on non-UK EEA FHLs and vice versa (ITA 2007 ss 127-127ZA).

Income from FHLs held by individuals is considered 'relevant UK earnings' for pension purposes (ITTOIA 2005 s 328; FA 2004 s 189(2)).

See **explanatory notes 27-28** for the capital gains position. See **explanatory note 25** for the capital allowances position.

*Qualifying conditions*

(23) To meet the 'qualifying holiday accommodation' definition from April 2012 onwards the following three conditions must be met in the tax year/accounting period (ITTOIA 2005 s 325; CTA 2009 s 267):

- the availability condition – the property must be available for commercial letting as holiday accommodation for at least 210 days (formerly 140);
- the letting condition – the property must be commercially let as holiday accommodation for at least 105 days (formerly 70).
- the pattern of occupation condition – not more than 155 days of longer-term occupation. Long-term occupation being defined as a continuous period of more than 31 days during which the property is let to the same person or persons (any days of occupation which are due to abnormal circumstances being disregarded for the letting condition).

If the property was not let as furnished holiday lettings in the previous tax year/accounting period then the above tests apply for the period of 12 months from the date of first letting as qualifying furnished holiday accommodation (ITTOIA 2005 s 324; CTA 2009 s 266).

Meeting the above conditions can be difficult. There are two elective provisions which might assist.

The first is the averaging election (ITTOIA 2005 s 326; CTA 2009 s 268), which can apply where:

- there is more than one property;
- some properties meet all three conditions and some only fail the letting condition.

The averaging election can be made to average out the let days with respect to properties specified in the election. If the average is over 105 then all the properties are deemed to meet the FHL conditions. The election applies separately to properties in the UK and properties in EEA states other than the UK.

The second provision is referred to as the 'period of grace' election (ITTOIA 2005 s 326A; CTA 2009 s 268A). Broadly, where the conditions are met in one tax year they will also be deemed to be met during: (i) the next tax year; or (ii) the next two tax years provided that:

- the election is made (the election can only be made for the second of the two following tax years if it has been made for the first tax year);
- only the failure to meet the letting condition prevented the property from meeting the 'qualifying holiday accommodation' definition for the tax year (or both tax years); and
- there was a genuine intention to meet the condition in the tax year (or both tax years).

HMRC guidance on FHLs is available in Helpsheet HS253 (https://www.gov.uk/government/publications/furnished-holiday-lettings-hs253-self-assessment-helpsheet).

In the light of the less favourable regime advisers should consider whether the FHL business activities are such that they amount to a trade. The status of the business will depend on the particular facts of the case. For the business to be seen as a trade it would be necessary for services to be provided (for example a proprietor providing meals). The case of *Elisabeth Moyne Ramsay v HMRC* [2013] STC 1764 looked at whether a taxpayer was carrying on a business for the purposes of TCGA 1992 s 162 rollover relief on incorporation in exchange for shares.

As far as inheritance tax is concerned, business property relief may not be available, because the lettings would probably be regarded as investments (IHTA 1984 s 105(3)). This view is supported by the decision in *HMRC v Personal Representatives of Pawson (dec'd)* [2013] STC 976.

*Rent-a-room relief*

(24) The 'rent-a-room' relief provisions outlined in **explanatory note 15** above could be claimed if appropriate in respect of furnished holiday accommodation instead of the above rules if the accommodation consisted of furnished rooms in the taxpayer's only or main residence, but not where, as in this Example, the holiday home is not the main home. For HMRC's view, see PIM4004.

*Capital allowances*

(25) Capital allowances may be claimed in respect of FHLs where appropriate (ITTOIA 2005 ss 327, 328A; CTA 2010 ss 269-269A).

Where FHL property ceases to qualify as such and later once again meets the conditions, the capital allowance assets are disposed of at market value, and subsequently reacquired when the property qualifies once again. This requires some detail in the record keeping to allow the owner to identify which assets have been the subject of a capital allowances claim.

Once the property no longer qualifies, replacement of domestic items relief could be claimed (see **explanatory note 7**), but given the substantial amount of expenditure which can qualify for capital allowances it is likely that the owner will wish to return to capital allowances claims once the property qualifies for FHL treatment. Where the taxpayer has a single FHL property, the sale will produce a balancing charge or allowance on the relevant pools (which will have a private use adjustment in these circumstances) as the qualifying activity has ceased.

*Council tax and business rates*

(26) Council tax is payable on domestic property. Self-contained holiday accommodation is, however, liable to business rates if it is available for letting for 140 days or more a year (no matter for how long it is actually let), hence the rates payable on the Suffolk house.

As far as the London house is concerned, if it is let long-term the tenant will pay the council tax. If it is no-one's only or main residence Mrs Morley will pay the council tax, which would be an allowable expense of the letting.

*Capital gains tax*

(27) The property and other chargeable assets used in the FHL business are eligible for capital gains roll-over relief if they are replaced (see **Example L9**) (TCGA 1992 s 241).

Where a sole trader either sells his business as a going concern, or ceases trading and sells the assets used in the business, entrepreneurs' relief is available on the sale – known as a material disposal (TCGA 1992 ss 169H-169S). The business must have been carried on for at least 12 months. It is therefore necessary that the furnished holiday letting conditions are met for the tax year 2016/17 and the period leading up to the date of sale to ensure that the relief is available. See **Example L5** for further discussion of entrepreneurs' relief.

(28) As far as Mrs Morley is concerned, roll-over relief could be claimed in respect of the lettings proportion of the gain providing the full business proportion of the proceeds of sale was reinvested in the business proportion of the new property (TCGA 1992 ss 152-157). Gains can continue to be rolled over on a succession of such sales.

# Question

Calculate the taxable income and chargeable gains that would arise in the following circumstances (assuming that a general 31 March 1982 rebasing election has not been made in any of these Examples).

The retail prices index for July 2001 is 173.3. Assume the index to be 260.0 for December 2016.

(a) An individual acquired a freehold for £188,000 on 16 May 1994. On 24 June 2016 he grants a lease of the whole premises for 21 years for a premium of £120,000 and a rent of £20,000 per annum, payable quarterly in advance on usual quarter days. The value of the reversion was £256,000.

(b) A lease is granted for 60 years for a premium of £230,000, the value of the reversion being £80,000. The other circumstances are as in (a).

(c) An individual was granted a 40 year lease on 25 December 2009 at a market rental of £20,000 per annum payable quarterly in advance on the usual quarter days and paying a market premium of £50,000. The property is used as a second home. On 25 December 2016 he assigns the unexpired portion of the lease for a premium of £70,000.

(d) The individual in (c) above, instead of assigning the lease, grants a sub-lease at the same rent for 20 years from 25 December 2016 for a market premium of £49,000.

(e) On 1 July 2011 Eric Forbes granted a lease to Jeremy Poulton on payment of a premium of £7,500. The lease was for a period of 17 years and it is considered, having regard to the terms of the lease, that a premium of £120,000 could have been demanded. On 15 January 2016 Jeremy sold the lease to Peter Long for £100,000 and Peter in turn sold the lease on 18 June 2016 to John Field for £150,000.

Compute the amount, if any, chargeable to income tax for 2015/16 and 2016/17 on the assumption that none of the persons involved is a dealer in land.

(f) Newco Ltd prepares accounts to 31 March. It has a wholly owned subsidiary from which on 2 December 2016 it acquired freehold property at the then market value of £500,000. The cost to the subsidiary in July 2002 was £360,000.

On 31 December 2016 Newco Ltd granted a 21-year lease over three quarters of the property to Antiques Ltd. Newco Ltd received a premium of £220,000, and the rent was £1,000 per month payable in advance on the 1st of each month.

There are three-yearly rent reviews at which point the tenant has an option to terminate the lease, the rent to be determined in the absence of agreement by arbitration. The residual value of the whole property at 31 December 2016 following the grant of the lease was £352,000.

(g) Newport, a trader who has been in business for many years, making up accounts annually to 31 December, was granted a 21 year lease of business premises on 1 July 2016 at a premium of £90,000 and a rent of £20,000 per annum payable quarterly in advance. Show the deductions to be made in respect of the lease in Newport's accounts to 31 December 2016 and indicate the tax treatment if Newport were to assign the lease in five years' time.

# Answer

## (a) Grant of short lease out of freehold

| | £ |
|---|---|
| Premium – 24 June 2016 | 120,000 |
| *Less*: Discount (21 – 1) = 20 × 2% = 40% | 48,000 |
| Additional rent | 72,000 |
| Normal rent: 24 June 2016 to 5 April 2017 (286 days) (£20,000 × 286/365 ) | 15,671 |
| 2016/17 UK property income subject to expenses | 87,671 |
| | |
| Capital proceeds (total premium 120,000 – 72,000 taxed as additional rent) | 48,000 |
| *Less*: Cost May 1994 | 24,000 |
| 2016/17 Capital gain | 24,000 |

## (b) Grant of long lease at a premium

No UK property income liability on the premium since this is a long lease, but a liability on rent as (a):

| | |
|---|---|
| 2016/17 UK property income – rent (286 days) | £15,671 |

| | | £ |
|---|---|---|
| Capital gain – premium 24 June 2016 | | 230,000 |
| Less: Cost May 1994 | $£188,000 \times \frac{230{,}000 \text{ (cash received)}}{310{,}000 \text{ (cash and reversion)}}$ | 139,484 |
| 2016/17 Capital gain | | 90,516 |

## (c) Assignment of short lease

Since the lease was acquired at full market value there will be no income tax liability on the premium when the assignment takes place (see **explanatory note 3**).

| | | £ |
|---|---|---|
| The capital gain is: | | |
| Premium 25 December 2016 | | 70,000 |
| *Less*: Cost December 2009 | $£50{,}000 \times \frac{\text{33 years unexpired on disposal}}{\text{40 years unexpired on acquisition}}$ | |
| Substituting relevant percentages: | $£50{,}000 \times \frac{\text{(33 years = ) 90.280}}{\text{(40 years = ) 95.457}}$ | 47,288 |
| 2016/17 Capital gain | | 22,712 |

## (d) Grant of sub-lease out of short lease

| | | £ | £ |
|---|---|---|---|
| Premium received 25 December 2016 | | | 49,000 |
| *Less:* Discount (20 – 1) = 19 × 2% = 38% | | | 18,620 |
| | | | 30,380 |
| *Less:* Fraction applicable to sub-lease of premium paid on acquisition – | | | |
| Premium paid | | 50,000 | |
| *Less:* (40 – 1) = 39 × 2% = 78% | | 39,000 | |
| Additional rent | | 11,000 | |
| 20 (years of sub-lease) /40 (years of head lease) × 11,000 | | | 5,500 |
| Additional rent | | | 24,880 |
| Normal rent: 25 December 2016 | | 5,000 | |
| 25 March 2017 | 5,000 | | |
| Less in advance (79 days out of 91) | 4,341 | 659 | 5,659 |
| 2016/17 UK property income subject to expenses | | | |
| | | | 30,539 |

*Capital gain*

| | |
|---|---|
| Proceeds (full premium) | 49,000 |
| *Less:* Cost December 2009 | |

*Less*:

$$£50{,}000 \times \frac{\text{33 years unexpired when sub-lease granted less 13 years unexpired when sub-lease ends}}{\text{40 years unexpired when lease acquired}}$$

Substituting relevant percentages:

$$£50{,}000 \times \frac{(33\text{ years}) = 90.280 - (13\text{ years}) = 56.167}{(40\text{ years}) = 95.457}$$

$$= £50{,}000 \times \frac{34.113}{95.457}$$ 17,868

| | |
|---|---|
| | 31,132 |
| *Less:* Part of premium assessable as UK property income | 24,880 |
| 2016/17 Capital gain | 6,252 |

Note that where there is a capital gain the rent deduction cannot convert it to a loss; it can only reduce the gain to nil, so that if the gain had been say £24,000, the result would have been no gain no loss. If the capital gains calculation had resulted in a loss, then that would be the allowable loss for capital gains purposes and the taxable UK property income could not be used to increase the allowable loss.

## (e) Grant of lease at an undervalue

Amount forgone by Eric Forbes on the grant of the lease to Jeremy Poulton on 1 July 2011 was (120,000 – 7,500 =) £112,500.

**Assignment by Jeremy Poulton to Peter Long 15.1.16**

| | |
|---|---|
| Excess of premium received over premium paid (100,000 – 7,500) | 92,500 |
| *Less*: (17 – 1) x 2% = 32% | 29,600 |
| Chargeable on Jeremy as UK property income for 2015/16 | £62,900 |

Leaving (112,500 – 92,500 =) £20,000 to be dealt with on subsequent assignments.

**Assignment by Peter Long to John Field 18.6.16**

| | |
|---|---|
| Excess of premium received over premium paid (150,000 – 100,000 =) £50,000 but restricted to balance of amount forgone | 20,000 |
| *Less*: 32% as above | 6,400 |
| Chargeable on Peter as UK property income 2016/17 | £13,600 |

Unlike other amounts charged to income tax, the amounts charged under these provisions are not excluded from the proceeds in the capital gains computation (TCGA 1992 Sch 8 para 6(2)), so Jeremy will have a capital gains liability by reference to proceeds of £100,000 and Peter by reference to proceeds of £150,000 (see **explanatory note** 3).

## (f) Newco Ltd – intra-group transfer and subsequent lease

Property income liability on grant of lease:

| | £ | £ |
|---|---|---|
| Amount received 31 December 2016 | | 220,000 |
| *Less:* Discount (21 – 1) × 2% = 40% | | 88,000 |
| Portion taxable as additional rent is | | 132,000 |
| Rent: 1.1.17 to 31.3.17 3 months @ £1,000 | | 3,000 |
| Property income (subject to expenses) yr ended 31.3.17 | | 135,000 |
| Chargeable gain portion | | 88,000 |
| *Less:* Allowable expenditure | | |
| Cost to subsidiary July 2002 | 360,000 | |
| Indexation allowance $\frac{260 - 173.3}{173.3} = 50.0\%$ | 180,000 | |
| Deemed acquisition cost to Newco Ltd December 2016 | 540,000 | |
| Cost of part disposed of December 2016 (no further indexation allowance since disposed of in same month as acquired) $0.75 \times 540,000 = 405,000 \times \frac{88,000}{220,000 + 352,000}$ | | 62,308 |
| | | £ |
| Chargeable gain year ended 31 March 2017 | | 25,692 |

* Assumed figures

### (g) Newport – premium paid on short lease of business premises

| | | £ | £ |
|---|---|---|---|
| Premium payable 1 July 2016 | | 90,000 | |
| *Less:* | Discount (21 – 1) × 2% = 40% | 36,000 | |
| Assessable on landlord as additional rent | | 54,000 | |

Therefore allowable to Newport $\frac{54,000}{21}$ = £2,572 per annum

| | £ |
|---|---|
| In year to 31 December 2016: | |
| Deduction re lease premium (6 months) ½ × 2,572 | 1,286 |
| Rent payable (2 quarters) | 10,000 |
| | 11,286 |

If Newport assigned the lease in five years' time, the assignee, providing he was a business tenant, would take over the right to make the annual deductions of £2,572 in respect of the premium (ITTOIA 2005 s 61). Newport would be treated as having made a disposal for capital gains tax, the allowable cost being the premium paid of £90,000, less the total annual deductions allowed to him, less depreciation under TCGA 1992 Sch 8 (see **explanatory note 11**).

## Explanatory Notes

*Difference between grant and assignment of lease*

(1) **Example D2** deals with the income tax/corporation tax treatment of let property. This Example deals with some additional income aspects and also the capital gains treatment of lease premiums.

(2) A *grant* of a new lease by a landlord to a tenant and an *assignment* of an existing lease from one tenant to another must be carefully distinguished for tax purposes. A grant of a new lease for a capital sum is a part disposal of the property for capital gains purposes, but part of the capital sum is charged as income if the lease is for 50 years or less, as detailed below (ITTOIA 2005 s 279). An assignment of an existing lease on the other hand is a disposal of the whole of the assignor's interest in the property and is normally subject only to a capital gains charge.

(3) If, however, the premium obtained on the *grant* of a lease for 50 years or less is less than could have been obtained, successive assignors of the lease may be liable to an income tax (or corporation tax) charge on part of the proceeds instead of the proceeds on assignment being wholly a capital gains matter. This situation will prevail until the whole of the premium originally forgone has been charged on subsequent assignments (ITTOIA 2005 s 283). The charge is calculated in the same way as additional rent would have been calculated for the grantor of the lease, using the original lease term, as illustrated in **part (e)** of the Example. Despite the income tax or corporation tax charge, there is no deduction from the proceeds in a capital gains computation on the premium (TCGA 1992 Sch 8 para 6(2)). The charge under ITTOIA 2005 s 283 is treated as part of the profits of a UK property business.

*Income tax treatment on grant of short lease followed by sub-lease*

(4) A premium received on the *grant* of a lease not exceeding 50 years is partly taxable as additional rent. That part so taxable is the premium less 2% for each complete year of the lease except the first (ITTOIA 2005 s 279).

(5) If the lessee then sublets at a premium, he may deduct from the amount of his additional rent calculated as in note 4 above the appropriate proportion of the base premium that is taxable, being the proportion that

the sub-lease bears to the head lease (ITTOIA 2005 s 288). If he sublets at a rent rather than at a premium, he may deduct the appropriate proportion of the premium he paid from the rent on a day to day basis (ITTOIA 2005 s 292).

(6) In **part (d)** of the Example, half of the £11,000 'additional rent' on which the head landlord was taxed relates to the 20 year sub-lease, ie £5,500, and this would have been deducted at £275 per annum from the rent payable by the sub-tenant if he had not paid a premium.

(7) Similar provisions apply where a premium is paid by a business tenant – see **explanatory note 11.**

(8) For both individuals and companies, rental income and expenses are normally calculated according to commercial accounting principles, with adjustments for amounts in arrear and in advance. Full details are in **Example D2.**

*Grant of short lease out of freehold/long lease*

(9) Where a short lease (ie not exceeding 50 years) is granted out of a freehold or long lease, that part of the premium not taxed as additional rent is a part disposal for capital gains purposes.

The value of the reversion (ie the right to receive the rent and possession of the premises at the end of the lease) must be taken into account in calculating the gain arising.

The denominator in that calculation includes the full premium received, not just the deemed capital portion (TCGA 1992 Sch 8 para 5).

(10) The normal rules for part disposals apply to the capital gains computation (TCGA 1992 s 42). Note that for companies the indexation allowance is calculated on the cost of the part disposed of (or on the same proportion of the 31.3.82 value if appropriate), not on the total cost.

*Grant of sub-lease out of short lease*

(11) Where a short lease is granted out of another short lease, then for capital gains purposes the gain or loss is calculated on the *full premium* according to the wasting asset rules, taking as the cost figure that part of the original expenditure that will waste away during the sub-lease. The part that has wasted away is worked out on a curved line basis, the percentages appropriate to the years concerned being in TCGA 1992 Sch 8 (see **page (xvi)**). For companies, the available indexation allowance is calculated on the depreciated amount. Where the original short lease was acquired before 31 March 1982, then unless a general rebasing election has been made, the gain or loss is calculated using pre-March 1982 and post-March 1982 rules, with the allowable expenditure being the depreciated 31.3.82 value or depreciated cost, and indexation allowance being on the higher of the depreciated 31 March 1982 value and depreciated cost as the case may be. When the gain has been calculated, the part of the premium chargeable as UK property income is then deducted from the capital gain, but not so as to create a loss, nor can it be added to a loss (TCGA 1992 Sch 8 paras 4 and 5).

*Assignment of short lease*

(12) In calculating the capital gain arising on an *assignment* of a short lease, the cost has to be depreciated on the same curved line basis as in note 8 above, and, for companies, the same provisions apply in relation to the indexation allowance and assets acquired before 31 March 1982.

*Intra-group transfer; term of lease*

(13) The cost to be used on the acquisition by Newco (**part (f)**) from its subsidiary is the cost to the subsidiary plus indexation allowance (TCGA 1992 s 171). See **Example L10 explanatory note 1 and 2** for the special rules which apply where the asset was originally acquired before 31 March 1982 and for the effect of the provisions preventing the use of indexation allowance to create or increase a loss.

The term of the lease for the purpose of calculating the exclusion from property income and inclusion as a chargeable gain is considered to be 21 years, even though the tenant has an option to terminate the lease at each three-yearly rent review.

If the term had been artificially extended in the lease, whilst encouraging the tenant to terminate it earlier because of harsh rent review provisions, the term for calculating the exclusion from property income and inclusion as a chargeable gain would have been taken as the period for which the lease was likely to run (CTA 2009 s 244).

*Income tax treatment of lease premium paid by business tenant*

(14) Where a business tenant pays a premium on the grant of a short lease, that part of the premium that is assessable on the landlord as additional rent is allowable to the payer as rent payable, but spread over the period of the lease rather than as a single deduction. The appropriate fraction may accordingly be deducted in arriving at trading profits as shown in **part (h)** of the Example (ITTOIA 2005 s 61).

Relief is no longer available on a lease that is only deemed to be short (less than 50 years) by virtue of rule 1 in CTA 2009 s 243 (or ITTOIA 2005 s 303) (with effect from 1 or 6 April 2013).

If the business tenant then assigns the lease, the part of the premium that has been allowed as an expense against income must be excluded from the allowable cost in the capital gains computation, as shown in **Example L10**. A new business tenant would then take over the right to make the annual deductions for the balance of the premium.

*Surrenders and variations*

(15) Where a tenant surrenders a lease in exchange for a new longer lease on broadly the same terms but at a different rent, the surrender is not normally treated as a disposal and acquisition for capital gains purposes (Extra Statutory Concession D39).

(16) Where a leaseholder acquires a superior interest in the land, such as a freehold reversion, HMRC, by Extra Statutory Concession D42, allow indexation allowance on the original cost of the lease, reduced as appropriate under Sch 8, by reference to the date of the original acquisition, even though strictly indexation should run from the date the superior interest is acquired. Indexation on the consideration for the superior interest runs from the date of its acquisition.

*Reverse premiums*

(17) Where an inducement is provided by a landlord to a tenant to encourage the taking of a lease of land or buildings it is known as a reverse premium. CTA 2009 Sch 2 para 24 (corporation tax) and ITTOIA 2005 ss 101 and 311 (income tax) provide that the receipt of a reverse premium is taxable in the hands of the recipient. If the taxpayer receives the amount in the course of a trade or profession then the amount is taxed in that trade. Under Accounting Standards, the amount will normally be spread over the period of the lease (or to the date of the first rent review if shorter) and taxed over that period. There are anti-avoidance rules to prevent exploitation of this principle by granting a lease on uncommercial terms between connected persons. In such cases the reverse premium is taxable in full in the period in which the lease is granted. Where the tenant is not in business, the premium received is taxed as UK property income, again spread over the lease. No charge arises if the property is the tenant's only or main residence or if the same amount is a deduction as a contribution towards expenditure for capital allowances.

# Question

(a) Peter and Lucy Hobday, who are UK resident and domiciled, jointly own a villa in southern France, which they spend some weeks at during the summer as well as going out for the Easter holidays and at other times during the year when their diary makes this possible. They purchased the villa on 1 June 2015.

In 2016/17 the 'season' lasted for 18 weeks. The couple used the property personally for seven weeks during the season so it was only available for commercial letting for 11 weeks. They tried to let the property for all 11 weeks but some of the lettings fell through so they only managed to let the property out for a total of eight weeks. The total rent they received was £12,000.

The interest on the loan to purchase the property amounts to £8,000 for the year, and the couple pay a service charge for the upkeep of the property of £2,400 per annum. On 20 July 2016 they replaced the broken washing machine with a new machine costing £300 including installation and removal of the old machine.

Each visit to the property costs £400 in travelling expenses, and the couple visit the property twice a year to 'open' and 'close' it at each end of the season, attending to cleaning and other tasks while there for two days on each occasion. These visits do not coincide with their own holidays there and in total they spent 53 days in France in 2016/17.

Explain the treatment of the income on the property for UK tax purposes. Advise the couple of any other tax implications that they should consider with regard to their holiday home.

(b) Kate and Richard Simpson are UK resident, but Kate is not UK domiciled. Both will pay UK income tax in 2016/17 at the additional rate. They own a substantial villa in Utopia, which Kate inherited from her grandparents 10 years ago and transferred a half share to Richard. The couple use the villa whenever they visit Utopia and have no plans to let it out.

It is the couple's intention to retire to Utopia in around six years (when family commitments permit). In the first few years after leaving they are unlikely to return to the UK, as their only child (a daughter) is likely to be working abroad. Even when she returns to the UK their visits will not be such that they would fall back into being UK resident.

The couple spend increasing amounts of time in Utopia – around 14 weeks per annum now, and this is likely to increase steadily towards retirement. They have not decided whether they will use their current villa in Utopia as their retirement home or whether they will sell it and acquire a different property in the country.

Kate and Richard's home in the UK (which they own jointly) will probably be let for several years after they leave the UK for retirement in Utopia. Letting of the UK property will continue until their daughter (currently expected to be working in Australia for the next eight to 10 years) returns to the UK. When this happens the couple will transfer ownership of the UK property to her.

Advise the couple of the tax issues associated with their foreign property. Note that Kate has been UK resident since 2001/02 and, apart from the Utopian property, her only foreign asset is a Utopian bank account on which she receives minimal interest (in sterling terms less than £5 per tax year). She has no foreign employments or other sources of foreign income apart from the small amount of bank interest.

The rate of capital gains tax (CGT) in Utopia is a fixed 20% on gains (with no relief for incidental selling expenses). To date the Utopian villa has increased in value such that in sterling terms it is worth £575,000 more than its probate value. If the property is sold assume: (i) incidental selling expenses of £10,000; (ii) if they are UK resident at the time of the sale, the entire CGT annual exemption (£11,100 for 2016/17) is available (as there are no other gains in the tax year); and (iii) there are no exchange rate fluctuations.

(c) Janek has been working in the UK for four years, running a building company. His UK income in 2016/17 is £85,000 (so he will pay income tax at the higher rate but not lose any of his personal allowance). Janek does not own property in the UK.

He purchased a house in Nettopia in the first year he was working in the UK. This is presently rented to his cousin at a rent of £200 per month (which is less than the market rent). The cousin transfers £600 quarterly in advance to Janek's Nettopian bank account in settlement of the rental amount agreed. In addition Janek's cousin bears all of the expenses related to the house, and carries out any minor repairs that are needed. The rent is banked in Nettopia in Janek's name. The interest rate is low so he receives less than the sterling equivalent of £5 per annum.

Janek is now considering moving back to Nettopia, as the economy there is booming. However, he is seeking advice regarding his house there. It has increased substantially in value and he is considering selling it and trading up. He would most likely do this before returning to Nettopia, so that the new property would be ready for him on his return. He estimates that the increase in value of the property is equivalent to around £80,000 over the period he has owned it.

It is June 2016, advise him of the UK tax issues. Assume that the rental income is the only source of foreign income he has and that he has no other chargeable foreign assets.

The rate of tax on income in Nettopia is 19%, as is the rate of tax on capital gains. Gains on property owned for more than five years are, however, exempt from Nettopian tax. Assume that Janek has no allowances available to set against his Nettopian tax liabilities.

# Answer

## (a) Peter and Lucy Hobday

For the purposes of the UK taxation of their French property income (N3), the taxable profits are:

| | £ | £ |
|---|---|---|
| Rent received | | 12,000 |
| *Less:* allowable expenses (N1, N2) | | |
| Loan interest 11/52 × £8,000 | 1,692 | |
| Service charges 11/52 × £2,400 | 508 | |
| | | (2,200) |
| Overseas property income (N4, N5, N8) | | 9,800 |

### Notes

(1) In terms of expenses only 11weeks/52 weeks of the annual expenses are allowable as in 2016/17 the property was only available for letting commercially for 11 weeks in the tax year. This means that the rest of the expenses must be disallowed as they are not wholly and exclusively for the purposes of the business (ITTOIA 2005 s 34 as read with ITTOIA 2005 s 272).

(2) Peter and Lucy's travel to their villa in France at the beginning and end of the season is not allowable. It has a dual purpose, as although the trip does not relate to their own holidays specifically, the season to which the travel relates comprises both let periods and owner occupation. The travel expenses are not, therefore, allowable because:

- the 'wholly and exclusively' rule is breached (ITTOIA 2005 s 34 as read with ITTOIA 2005 s 272); and
- the relaxation in ITTOIA 2005 ss 92–94 which allows for travel to the place where a foreign trade is carried out does not apply for the purposes of computing the profit of an overseas property letting business (see **explanatory note 5**).

(3) The double tax treaty with France allows both France (as the Source State) and the UK (as the Residence State) to tax income derived from immovable property situated in France. As such the couple will be taxed on the rental profit in both France and the UK. As the Residence State, the UK gives credit for the French tax paid. The French tax charge will normally be levied on a different income figure as the basis of assessment and allowable expenses is likely to vary from that in the UK.

For UK tax purposes since the property is jointly owned, the profit of £9,800 should be split equally between the couple and disclosed on their respective tax return (as discussed in N4). Relief will be given in the UK tax computations for the French tax suffered by each individual. This will be the lower of (i) the French tax suffered; and (ii) the UK tax due. See **Example F3**.

(4) The couple should each enter their share of the income and expenses on the foreign supplementary pages of the self-assessment tax return (SA106), on page F4, which requires a summary of the rent and allowable expenses for all foreign properties, and a further analysis by country to claim double tax relief.

(5) Wear and tear allowance was repealed with effect from 6 April 2016 by Finance Act 2016. It is replaced with a new statutory renewals basis called 'replacement of domestic items relief'. It is available to people letting residential property, whether in the UK or abroad, and allows a deduction against income for the capital costs of replacing a domestic item, such as free-standing white goods, carpets or curtains. However Peter and Lucy cannot deduct the cost of the replacement washing machine because it is not exclusively for

use by the tenants; they have private use of the appliance when they visit the property (ITTOIA 2005 s 311A(1)–(5)). See **Example D2, explanatory note** 7.

This means that they have lost the benefit of the wear and tear allowance (which was a flat deduction of 10% of the rents), but cannot benefit from the new relief.

(6) It is not clear what the UK CGT position is with regard to the French villa. The level of use by the family indicates that it would be correct to refer to the villa as a 'residence' rather than just a property they own. It is assumed that the couple only own two properties (their UK home and this French villa) and that the French villa was acquired and used as a residence after the UK property.

Up until 6 April 2015 it would have been possible for the couple to make a main residence election under the rules in TCGA 1992 s 222(5). However the rules changed with effect for disposals made after that date which means that for the election to be valid the individual or his spouse/civil partner either had to be tax resident in that country or present in the property for 90 days or more (TCGA 1992 ss 222B-222C). As Peter and Lucy are not resident in France and were present in the villa for only 53 days in 2016/17, this condition is not met for that year. However if circumstances were to change it may be possible for them to make the election at a later date.

If a main residence was made in favour of the French villa before 6 April 2015 (which would not be valid after that date for the reasons discussed above) any only or main residence relief accumulated up to that point is 'banked' under TCGA 1992 s 222B(2). Also, as it had qualified as a main residence at some point in the ownership, the last 18 months of ownership would be treated as deemed occupation for the purposes of the relief (TCGA 1992 s 223(1)). See **explanatory note 9**.

(7) The couple should also seek advice about the impact of French VAT (TVA) on their letting income, which amounts to charges for holiday accommodation, as this is frequently subject to standard rate VAT. There is a risk that they could exceed the VAT limit in France if their letting income in any year was substantial – and given the length of the season this is possible. VAT registration limits in the rest of the EU are significantly lower than in the UK. They should seek specialist advice on this point as a matter of urgency.

(8) The extension of favourable furnished holiday letting (FHL) treatment to properties in the EEA is not available to Peter and Lucy as they do not let the property for sufficiently long enough to meet the ITTOIA 2005 s 325 conditions. The period of grace election at ITTOIA 2005 s 326A (see **explanatory note 3**) cannot assist as there has never been a tax year during which the FHL conditions have been met.

(9) Until 2017/18, loan interest is a revenue expense and can be deducted from the rents received. This includes mortgage interest, interest on loans used to fund repairs/extensions and any incidental costs of obtaining loan finance (ITTOIA 2005 s 272 as read with ITTOIA 2005 ss 29, 58; PIM2105). In Peter and Lucy's case the interest that can be deducted from their rental income is limited to the amount which relates to the let period (see N1).

However from 2017/18, relief for finance costs relating to residential property (in the UK or overseas) is to be restricted to the basic rate of income tax. From 2017/18 to 2020/21, the revenue deduction is phased out and instead relief is given by a tax reduction of 20% in Step 6 of the income tax calculation in ITA 2007 s 23 (ITTOIA 2005, ss 272A, 274A):

| Tax year | Percentage of expense given as revenue deduction | Percentage of expense given as a tax reduction at 20% |
|---|---|---|
| 2016/17 | 100% | 0% |
| 2017/18 | 75% | 25% |
| 2018/19 | 50% | 50% |
| 2019/20 | 25% | 75% |
| 2020/21 | 0% | 100% |

Therefore, in 2017/18, assuming the same fact pattern, Peter and Lucy would have a revenue deduction of £1,269 (£1,692 x 75%) and a tax reduction of £84.60 ((£1,692 x 25%) x 20%). See **Example D2, explanatory note 16.**

## (b) Kate and Richard Simpson

Disregarding inheritance tax (covered in **Taxwise II 2016/17**), since Kate and Richard do not plan to let their villa in Utopia, their tax issues are limited to CGT. However, the situation is complex. This is particularly the case as Kate and Richard are undecided about whether on retirement they will live in their current Utopian property or to sell it and acquire a different property in Utopia to live in during their retirement.

It is assumed that Kate and Richard just have the two properties (their UK home and the Utopian villa) and that a main residence nomination has not been made within the two year deadline (TCGA 1992 s 222(5)).

Kate and Richard should seek more specific advice about the incidence of CGT in Utopia on the possible sale of the property.

### *Selling the current Utopian property whilst UK resident*

A husband and wife (or civil partners) who are not separated can only have one main residence between them (TCGA 1992 s 222(6)(a)).

Kate and Richard have not made any election under TCGA 1992 s 222(5) to nominate which of their residences is to be regarded as their main residence for the purposes of only or main residence relief (TCGA 1992 s 222). For a full discussion of this relief, see **Example L8**. Whilst we do not have all the facts, it appears that the quality of the time that Kate and Richard have spent at the Utopian villa would be such that from quite close to the date that Kate inherited the property it was factually a residence of the couple. We are told that Kate inherited the property 10 years ago and, therefore, the couple have missed the chance to nominate one of their two residences as the main residence (as two years have elapsed since the combination of residences was acquired). They could reopen the nomination period by:

- acquiring a third residence (which could be by taking a short-term tenancy on another property anywhere in the world); or
- relinquishing a residence by granting a shorthold lease (eg 12 months) meaning the property would no longer be a residence for Kate and Richard. At the end of the lease the couple could resume their pattern of occupation and this would be a 'new' residence for the purposes of the nomination period.

As neither Kate nor Richard is tax resident in Utopia, they are only able to consider reopening the nomination period because they spend at least 90 days in the property each year (TCGA 1992 ss 222B-222C).

The absence of a nomination means that on disposal of one or both of the properties it will be necessary to decide on the facts which property should be regarded as their main residence, qualifying for exemption (CG64545). Under self-assessment, on the first disposal Kate and Richard must make the decision when preparing their tax returns (providing appropriate disclosure in the white space and a calculation of the gain). Within a specified time period HMRC has the power to enquire into the tax return and question the decision made should it so wish to (see **Example G2 explanatory note 14**). Where the tax return is submitted on time, provided adequate disclosure is made on the tax return, the HMRC enquiry window will close one year after the submission of the tax return (TMA 1970 s 9A).

It would be wise to assemble the exact facts regarding their use of the two properties during the period since the property in Utopia was acquired, to ensure that sufficient detail can be provided to HMRC to establish which of the properties should be treated as their main residence for CGT relief when a disposal occurs. CG64545 lists a number of factors which HMRC will wish to consider.

At present, whilst the couple do spend increasing amounts of time in Utopia, they still spend the majority of the year in the UK. Given what is known of the circumstances to date, this makes it likely that on the facts the main residence of Kate and Richard would be determined to be the home in the UK.

Assuming that the UK home is currently regarded as their main residence, for so long as it remains a residence for them, its status as the main residence for the purposes of the CGT principal private residence relief legislation cannot alter until either:

- the nomination period is reopened (see above); or

- the couple's occupation of their home in the UK diminishes, and their occupation of the Utopian villa increases, such that the UK property is no longer their factual main residence.

From what we have been told, rather than a gradual decrease in the use of the UK residence, it is likely that the UK property will cease to be the couple's main residence at the same time as it ceases to be used by them as an actual residence. The couple's plan when they move to Utopia does not involve returning to the UK and using the UK property (since they intend first to let it out commercially and then transfer it to their daughter) so on their departure from the UK the UK property ceases to be a residence or any sort for them.

From what we know, if they sell the Utopian villa when they are UK resident it is likely that there will be no main residence relief available. The couple can, however, claim relief for the Utopian tax suffered (the fixed 20% on the capital gain). As additional rate taxpayers selling residential property they will be taxed on the gain at the 28% rate, so using the current £575,000 increase in value and the assumptions provided in the question, if they sold the property whilst UK resident, Kate and Richard would each have a CGT liability of £18,492 (£75,992 – £57,500):

- UK tax liability without the foreign tax credit relief (((£575,000/2) – (£10,000/2) – £11,100) × 28%) = £75,992;
- foreign tax suffered ((£575,000/2) × 20%) = £57,500.

Richard has no choice but to be taxed on his half of the gain on the arising basis as he is UK resident and UK domiciled. Kate, however, is foreign domiciled and could be taxed on the remittance basis meaning that she could shelter any gains on her share of the Utopian property by not remitting them to the UK (ITA 2007 s 809L). However, given Kate's situation there are problems with this approach.

As explained in **Example F4 explanatory notes 6-8**, adults who have been UK resident for in excess of six of the preceding nine tax years can only automatically access the remittance basis for a given year if they have unremitted income or gains of less than £2,000 for the tax year (ITA 2007 s 809D). Where this is not the case access to the remittance basis comes at the price of (ITA 2007 ss 809B, 809G):

- forfeiting the personal allowance (though since Kate is an additional rate taxpayer she would have forfeited this anyway under ITA 2007 s 35(2));
- forfeiting the CGT annual exemption;
- paying the remittance basis charge. For foreign domiciliaries who, like Kate, have been UK residence in at least 12 of the preceding 14 tax years, the remittance basis charge is £60,000.

Even if the entire Utopian property were in Kate's sole name a remittance basis claim would not be beneficial with an increase in value of £575,000 and a foreign tax credit of 20%. This is because the tax liability if Kate was assessed on the entire gain on the arising basis would only be £40,092 (£155,092 – £115,000):

- UK tax liability without the foreign tax credit relief ((£575,000 – £10,000 – £11,100) × 28%) = £155,092;
- foreign tax suffered (£575,000 × 20%) = £115,000.

The remittance basis claim would be more expensive than the tax due under the default arising basis and the only other foreign income and gains that she could shelter as a result of making the remittance basis claim would be gross foreign interest (which as set down in the question is less than £5).

Note that if something were to change it might be worth considering Richard transferring back his half of the property to Kate. Possible reasons for this could be:

- the gain increasing materially;
- the Utopian tax credit reducing significantly;
- the gain became exempt from Utopian taxes.

It should, however, be remembered that although he could gift his share back to Kate, this may trigger an inheritance tax problem if he dies within seven years. This is because, unless Kate makes the IHTA 1984, s 267ZA

election (that is the election to be treated as domiciled in the UK) he is limited to an inter-spouse exemption of £325,000 as Kate is not UK domiciled (and has not yet been UK resident for sufficient time to become deemed domiciled). Before considering seriously the UK tax issues that would result from a transfer of Richard's half share to Kate it would be necessary to establish whether similar beneficial CGT rules for interspouse gifts apply in Utopia to our UK no gain/no loss provisions.

## Selling the Utopian property after they have become non-UK resident

### *Leaving the UK for good*

Once the couple leave the UK for good on retirement, they are likely to become non-UK resident under the statutory split year provisions. From what we have been told they are likely to qualify for split year treatment by meeting the FA 2013 Sch 45, para 46 Case 3 (ceasing to have a home in the UK) conditions since:

- they will have been resident in the UK in the previous tax year;
- at the start of the tax year they had a home in the UK but during the tax year this ceases to be the case and from then on in the tax year they have no UK home;
- they will not return to the UK at all in the tax year (so, from the date of departure, will spend fewer than 16 days in the UK to the end of that tax year);
- they will not be resident in the UK in the next tax year (by spending fewer than 16 days in the UK and so meeting the first automatic overseas test in FA 2013 Sch 45 para 12); and
- they will immediately establish a sufficient link with Utopia by virtue of having their only home there.

The UK is no longer a home once it is rented out and not available to them.

For more details on the statutory residence test and the split year rules, see **Example F1**.

As non-residents with UK residential property, they would be liable to UK CGT on the disposal of their UK home (which includes a gift to their daughter) (under the non-resident CGT (NRCGT) rules in TCGA 1992 ss 14B-14F). However, the period during which the property was their main residence would be exempt from UK CGT and the last 18 months would be treated as deemed occupation for the purposes of the only or main residence rules (TCGA 1992 s 223(1)). Lettings relief should also be considered. There are various methods of calculating the gain (TCGA 1992 Sch 4ZZB):

- the rebasing method - the property is valued at 5 April 2015 and this is substituted for the original cost of the property and the gain is then reduced by the post-5 April 2015 period qualifying for main residence relief and lettings relief;
- the time apportionment method - the gain is assumed to accrue evenly over the entire period and only the amount arising after 5 April 2015 is chargeable (although this is then reduced by the post-5 April 2015 period qualifying for main residence relief and lettings relief);
- the retrospective method - it is assumed that the non-resident CGT rules have always applied and the entire gain from the original date of acquisition is taxable, however this also allows the entire period of main residence relief and lettings relief to be applied and can lead to a lower gain in certain circumstances.

It is important to run all the computations to decide which gives rise to the most tax efficient result. If the time apportionment method or the retrospective method is used, the individual must make an election on the NRCGT return or the self-assessment tax return (TCGA 1992 Sch 4ZZB para 2). The NRCGT return must be filed within 30 days of conveyance of the property (TMA 1970 s 12ZB). On the assumption that Kate and Richard will be filing UK self-assessment tax returns to declare their UK rental income on the property, the gain on disposal of the property can be declared on that return and the CGT due can be paid by the normal due date of 31 January following the end of the tax year (TCGA 1992 ss 12ZE, 12ZG, 12ZH). See **Example F2 explanatory notes 9–17**.

Note that there may also be Utopian tax to pay on disposal of the UK property whilst Kate and Richard are resident in Utopia.

The non-resident CGT rules take precedence over the temporary non-residence anti-avoidance provisions at TCGA 1992 ss 10A-10AA. If a gain on UK residential property has been taxed under the non-resident CGT rules it cannot be taxed again under the temporary non-resident rules if the individual returns to the UK within five years.

### *Summary*

Kate and Richard will be subject to UK CGT on any transfer of the UK house that takes place in the period of non-UK residence. However it is likely that most of the gain will be covered by main residence relief and lettings relief.

The most appropriate advice regarding the UK home is for the couple to review their ownership of it regularly once they leave the UK.

Note that if the UK property is let out by Kate and Richard when they are non-UK resident they will need to register under the non-resident landlords' scheme to receive the rental income gross or the tenants/agent will need to deduct basic rate tax (at 20%) and pay this across to HMRC (ITA 2007 ss 971–972; SI 1995/2902). For more on on-resident landlords, see **Example D2 explanatory note 11.**

UK rental income is not classified as disregarded income (see ITA 2007 s 825) for the purposes of the limit on the income tax liability of non-residents in ITA 2007 s 811. This means that non-UK residents are subject to tax in full on UK property income so it will be necessary for Richard and Kate to submit self-assessment tax returns to disclose the UK rental income received. For details of the rules which limit the income tax liability of non-residents, see **Example F2 explanatory note 4**.

## (c) Janek's Nettopian home

The situation can be complex as Janek is eligible for the remittance basis and has both foreign income and the potential to realise a foreign chargeable gain. The amounts are not that significant so the most tax efficient choice is not as obvious as in cases where the amounts are greater.

Janek should seek more specific advice about the incidence of CGT in Nettopia on the sale of the property.

### *Selling the Nettopian property prior to leaving the UK*

Janek has never occupied the house in Nettopia so no UK CGT relief under TCGA 1992 s 222 (only or main residence relief) will be available to him. This means that if he is taxed on the arising basis he will be taxed at a rate of 28% (assuming he continues to be a higher rate taxpayer) on any gain. The gains will be reduced by the CGT annual exemption (assuming it is not utilised on other gains) and he can claim credit against his UK tax liability for the Nettopian tax paid. See **Example F3.**

The additional UK CGT that would be due if the gain were taxed on the arising basis would be £4,092 (((£80,000 – £11,100) × 28%) – (£80,000 × 19%)), if for the purposes of the estimated computation we use:

- the £80,000 estimated increase in value as the chargeable gain;
- the 2016/17 CGT annual exemption of £11,100;
- a 28% UK CGT rate (on the basis he is a higher rate taxpayer and the asset is residential property); and
- a 19% foreign tax credit on the £80,000 gain.

As a foreign domiciliary Janek could be taxed on the remittance basis meaning that he could shelter any gains on his share of the Nettopian property by not remitting them to the UK (ITA 2007 s 809L). If he is taxed on the remittance basis then provided he does not remit the funds he will also shelter the property rental income received in the period up until the disposal. See **Example F4** for a full discussion on the meaning of remittance.

Janek has a level of UK income that is too high for him to qualify for the automatic remittance basis under ITA 2007 s 809E. This means that he can only qualify automatically under ITA 2007 s 809D for 2016/17 if for the tax year he either (i) received less than £2,000 of aggregate foreign income and gains or (ii) remitted sufficient foreign income and gains so that he had less than £2,000 of aggregate unremitted foreign income and gains at the end of the year. The expenses in relation to the property would seem very small. It is, therefore, likely that his foreign rental profit for the UK tax year exceeds £2,000.

A remittance basis claim would *not* be worthwhile for a tax year assuming:

- there is no disposal in the year of the Nettopian property;
- the Nettopian property is rented out for the full year; and
- the £2,400 (£200 per month for twelve months) of foreign rental income is the only foreign income and gains.

Whilst he has not been in the UK long enough to have to pay the remittance basis charge under ITA 2007 s 809B, and he would have no need of the CGT annual exemption as he has no gains, losing the personal allowance would cost him more than being taxed on the arising basis and claiming relief for foreign tax paid (ITA 2007 s 809G).

Losing the personal allowance, which for 2016/17 is £11,000 would, since he is a higher rate taxpayer (whose adjusted income is less than £100,000 so he can benefit from the entire £11,000), increase his tax bill by £4,400 (£11,000 x 40%). Being taxed on the arising basis, on the foreign income, will only result in a maximum of £504 of additional tax. This is because he has a 19% foreign tax credit to set against the 40% tax liability he would have to pay on the profits from his overseas property business (which we know will not be higher than £2,400).

Janek should assemble the details of the expenses he bears in relation to the Nettopian property, and be prepared to account for UK tax on the rental income. In terms of planning, it might be most efficient if Janek could remit sufficient of the income to bring him within ITA 2007 s 809D (that is he remits sufficient income in the tax year that less than £2,000 is unremitted as at the end of the tax year, see **Example F7 explanatory note 17**). This would mean that Janek would automatically be entitled to the remittance basis such that the unremitted income would not be subject to UK income tax but the personal allowance and the CGT annual exemption would still be available. Following this strategy might not, however, be practical for him.

If, in addition to profits from his overseas property business, Janek disposes of the Nettopian property and realises a gain in the tax year the decision as to whether or not to make the remittance basis claim would need to be evaluated. Whilst Janek remains UK resident for less than seven of the preceding nine tax years the cost of making the claim is relatively low as the £30,000 remittance basis charge is not in point. He would, however, not be able to benefit from the personal allowance or the CGT annual exemption.

Assuming that (i) the only chargeable gain that Janek will realise is on the foreign property; and (ii) he does not need to remit the proceeds from the sale of the property, he would have no need of the CGT annual exemption should he be taxed on the remittance basis. The only benefit to him of being taxed on the arising basis as opposed to the remittance basis would, therefore, be the retention of the personal allowance (which for 2016/17 saves him £4,400 – see above).

We know from the calculation in the second paragraph of this answer that if Janek is taxed on the estimated £80,000 gain on the arising basis he will pay UK tax of £4,092. When one considers the CGT saving and the income tax on the foreign property income (assuming a sale mid-year such that there will be a few months of rental profit), it is touch-and-go whether the arising basis or the remittance basis is the cheapest option (assuming no remittances are anticipated). On the basis that the property is rented out up until the sale the remittance basis option will become more favourable the later in the tax year that the sale takes place (since the profits from the overseas property business that can be sheltered will be greater).

For a discussion of the remittance basis and the remittance basis charge, see **Example F4** and **Example F5**.

## *Selling the Nettopian property after leaving the UK*

Janek will leave the UK after 5 April 2013, meaning that the statutory residence test and statutory split year rules within FA 2013 Sch 45 will apply.

If Janek waits until his return to Nettopia to sell the Nettopian property and then acquires a new home, provided: (i) his circumstances are such that he falls within at least one of the five cases for split year treatment available on leaving the UK specified in FA 2013 Sch 45 Part 3; or (ii) the sale takes place after the UK tax year during which he left the UK, he will not be liable to UK tax.

Delaying the sale until such time as he has owned the Nettopian property for five years would also mean that the gain realised would not be subject to Nettopian tax, although as an investment decision, advice on the timing of the sale is regulated. Janek should, however, be warned that as a UK resident for at least four years of the preceding seven tax years, the temporary non-resident rules (TCGA 1992 s 10A) could apply to him. This would mean that if he returned to the UK, before five years of non-residence have elapsed, the gain on the Nettopian property could come into charge on his return. If there was no Nettopian tax charge on the sale there would be no foreign tax credit and the gain could be subject to UK CGT at 18%/28%. To avoid this, assuming he remained foreign domiciled, Janek would be able to make a remittance basis claim for the tax year that he returned to the UK.

For more on the temporary non-residence rules, see **Example F1 explanatory notes 24-25**.

## Explanatory Notes

*Foreign let property*

(1) For UK resident individuals income from foreign lettings is taxed as property income (ITTOIA 2005 ss 263, 265, 269(2)). The basis of computation of the profit or loss follows the same rules as UK property income (see **Example D2**). In particular, expenses incurred wholly and exclusively for the purpose of the overseas letting trade are allowed against the income. Any costs, which relate to private use of the property or periods when it is not available for letting, are split so as to only provide a deduction for the costs incurred in relation to the period when the property is actually let or available for letting.

(2) All overseas property (with the exception of furnished holiday lets (FHLs) in EEA states, see **explanatory note 3**) is treated as one business (ITTOIA 2005 s 265). This means the income and expenses are aggregated to give the overall profits of the business. Double tax relief for the rental income is provided on a jurisdiction-by-jurisdiction basis. Where the property is situated in a State that the UK has a double tax agreement, the double tax relief available will be determined by the treaty. Where there is no double tax agreement, relief is provided on a unilateral basis and will be through a tax credit for the lower of: (i) the tax suffered in the foreign jurisdiction; and (ii) the UK tax payable on the income. See **Example F3**.

(3) The commercial letting of furnished holiday accommodation in the UK is treated differently for tax purposes to the letting of other residential or commercial property. It is assessable as property income but deemed to be a trade for the purposes of various aspects of the income tax and CGT legislation meaning that various reliefs are available.

To qualify for the special FHL treatment:

- there must be qualifying holiday accommodation;
- the accommodation must be furnished;
- the accommodation must be let out commercially.

The original UK tax legislation restricted the benefits of the furnished holiday let (FHL) regime to properties in the UK. This was contrary to EU law and the legislation was changed in FA 2011 such that the FHL regime applies to any property within the European Economic Area (EEA) that meets the qualifying conditions. However these changes had a negative impact on UK FHLs. From 2011/12 the ability to offset FHL losses against other income was removed and from 2012/13 the 'qualifying holiday accommodation' definition was tightened up.

To meet the 'qualifying holiday accommodation' definition for a tax year from 2012/13 onwards the following three conditions must be met in relation to (i) the availability for letting; (ii) the actual let period; and (iii) the pattern of occupation (ITTOIA 2005 s 325). These conditions are discussed in **Example D2 explanatory note 23**.

In the light of the new less favourable regime advisers should consider whether the FHL business activities are such that they amount to a trade. The status of the business will depend on the particular facts of the case. For the business to be seen as a trade it would be necessary for services to be provided (for example a proprietor providing meals). The case of *Elisabeth Moyne Ramsay v HMRC* [2013] STC 1764 looked at whether a taxpayer was carrying on a business for the purposes of TCGA 1992 s 162 rollover relief on incorporation in exchange for shares.

(4) Accounts for foreign property letting may be drawn up to a date that is required for foreign tax purposes. For UK tax purposes this is unimportant as, in contrast to trading income, the date to which accounts are drawn up is not relevant for UK tax purposes. UK tax is charged on the full amount of profits arising in the UK tax year (ITTOIA 2005 s 275).

The rules which determine the profit for foreign tax purposes are irrelevant to the UK tax computation. Profits must be calculated as if the letting were a normal UK letting. The general rule set down in ITTOIA 2005 s 272(1) is that the 'profits of a property business are calculated in the same way as the profits of a trade'. There are, however, exceptions and not all the trading provisions apply when calculating the profits of a property business. ITTOIA 2005 s 272(2) lists the specific trading provisions which apply to a property business (see **explanatory note 5**).

(5) As stated in **explanatory note 4,** ITTOIA 2005 s 272(2) lists the trading income provisions that apply to property income. There are minor differences in allowable expenditure in relation to a foreign trade and an overseas property letting business.

Primarily, ITTOIA 2005 ss 92–94 (expenses connected with foreign trades – with ITTOIA 2005 s 92 providing relief for travel and accommodation, plus family expenses) do not apply for the purposes of computing overseas property business profits. For foreign trades these sections permit travel to the place where the trade is carried on to be tax deductible even where the 'wholly and exclusively' rule would not apply. Note that where the expenses would qualify as 'wholly and exclusively' for the purposes of the overseas property letting business, ITTOIA 2005 s 92 is not necessary, and such travelling expenses are deductible overseas property expenses under standard rules.

(6) As regards completing the foreign pages of the self-assessment tax return to declare income from foreign let property, taxpayers are required to prepare multiple copies of boxes 14 to 24 on pages 4 and 5 to report the income of more than one let property overseas in the year if the properties are in different countries and foreign tax has been suffered. There is no longer any necessity to provide the address of each let property abroad.

(7) Where the owner of the property is UK resident but not UK domiciled and is a remittance basis user the letting income arising is taxed only to the extent it is remitted to the UK (ITA 2007 s 809L). Accessing the remittance basis and the working of the remittance basis regime are discussed in **Example F4**. Where the remittance basis claim is made (or the remittance basis applies automatically) the net rental profit comes within the definition of relevant foreign income (ITTOIA 2005 s 830(2)(c)).

(8) The treatment of losses on foreign property lettings is given by ITA 2007 s 118. Losses on an overseas property business are treated in the same way as losses on a UK property business, and carried forward against future profits of the same business. It is important to note that for this purpose, a foreign property business (comprising all overseas lettings wherever situated) are separate from a UK property business, and thus any losses on overseas lettings cannot be offset against profits on a UK property business and vice versa. Also, as discussed in **explanatory note 3**, these losses must also be kept separate from the profits or losses of FHLs.

*CGT on foreign property*

(9) In general, the CGT rules apply to foreign property in exactly the same way as to UK property. However, as far as the only or main residence relief rules are concerned, from 6 April 2015 a property cannot be considered a residence unless either (TCGA 1992 ss 222B):

- the individual or his spouse/civil partner were tax resident in the country in which that residence is situated (assessed either via the rules in the local jurisdiction or by deeming the UK statutory residence test to apply in that jurisdiction); or
- the individual or his spouse/civil partner spent 90 days or more in that residence (or in any other residence in that jurisdiction, as these days of presence can be added together).

A day is counted as being spent in the residence if either (i) the individual is present in the house at midnight, or (ii) the individual is present in the house at some point during the day (but not at midnight) and stays overnight the following night (TCGA 1992 s 222C). The 90 day period is pro-rated if the house is bought or sold during that tax year.

Main residence relief up to 5 April 2015 has been 'banked' and will apply if the foreign residence is later sold (TCGA 1992 s 222B(2)). Equally pre-6 April 2015 main residence relief means that the final 18 months will also be treated as deemed occupation (TCGA 1992 s 223(1)).

Whilst main residence relief can relieve a foreign property from UK tax it does not affect the treatment of the disposal of that property for foreign tax purposes. As the incidence of foreign CGT can be higher than the UK rates on residential property gains of 18%/28%, where an individual has residences in the UK and overseas, there may be no (or little) benefit in electing for a foreign home to be the main residence, even if this is possible under the post-5 April 2015 rules, as double tax relief could prevent (in whole or in part) UK tax from being due on disposal.

It used to be HMRC practice to restrict the foreign tax credit allowed against UK tax where either (i) different periods of ownership were in point or (ii) due to the availability of a UK CGT relief (such as main residence relief) the gain assessable in the UK was lower than the foreign gains assessed. However, Revenue & Customs Brief 17/10 [http://webarchive.nationalarchives.gov.uk/20140109143644/http://www.hmrc.gov.uk/briefs/cgt/brief1710.htm] states that: 'We have reconsidered our view and are revising our practice so that the whole of the foreign tax is allowable as foreign tax credit relief (FTCR) up to the amount of the UK tax on the gain'.

For a detailed study of capital gains in relation to the main residence see **Example L8**, and in particular **explanatory notes 1 to 4**.

(10) The UK CGT elections available should be reviewed carefully in light of any potential foreign tax charges, for which specific professional advice should be sought.

(11) Where the foreign property is owned by a UK resident but non-domiciled individual, unless an election is made for the remittance basis (or the individual qualifies automatically), any gains on the property will be taxed on the arising basis. In the case of both Kate (**part B**) and Janek (**part C**) in this Example, the foreign gains are unlikely to be remitted to the UK given the facts. On the facts it is also unlikely that the remittance basis will be automatic for the relevant tax year if the individuals are still UK resident at the date of disposal of the foreign property. In real life scenarios, consideration will have to be given to the tax saving the remittance basis will result in (bearing in mind any foreign tax relief claim, which would reduce the tax payable on the arising basis) and the cost of making the remittance basis claim. See **Example F4** for a discussion on accessing the remittance basis.

(12) Each situation should be reviewed in the light of the specific facts and the future plans of the client so that appropriate advice can be given about the interplay between the foreign tax likely to arise on the overseas property, the incidence of UK CGT on the disposal and whether any decisions will have an impact on the tax liabilities that could arise on other assets (as may be the case where main residence elections are made). In addition, CGT should not be considered in isolation but rather all the tax consequences need to be covered off to ensure that everything relevant has been taken into account.

# Question

(a) You are due to meet a potential new client, Mr Brown. He has contacted you because he is concerned about a 'mansion tax'. You have established that he has recently inherited shares in a UK company that owns a large residential property in the country together with a large acreage of land.

Make some notes in preparation for your meeting and in particular, specify the key questions to ask in order that the potential tax issues can be identified.

# Answer

(a) Mr Brown is presumably concerned about the annual tax on enveloped dwellings (ATED). This applies if the company owns a dwelling and the value of that dwelling on 1 April 2012 (or on the date of purchase by the company, if later) was more than £500,000 (see **explanatory note 1**). However, there is a lot of detail to the tax and it requires expert consideration. If ATED does apply, then a return must be made even if a relief applies (see **explanatory notes 14-16**).

The starting point is to establish the valuation of the property and the use to which it is applied. As Mr Brown has only recently acquired his shares then there may have been a recent valuation in any case – probably for inheritance purposes but otherwise for capital gains tax on a gift. However, the valuation for those purposes may require further consideration to establish what land should be included with the dwelling for the purposes of ATED. This is likely to require further discussion with the valuers concerned.

A detailed understanding of the usage to which the property is put is required. Is it an historic house? Is it a farmhouse? Is the property in multiple occupation such that it amounts to several dwellings? See **explanatory notes 9-13**.

It is important to establish a detailed understanding of the property so that liability to ATED can be assessed. It is also important for Mr Brown to appreciate that ATED applies to both UK and overseas owners as opposed to the media comment at the time the tax was first proposed which implied that it would only be assessed on foreign owners.

Who occupies the property? Does Mr Brown live there, or intend to live there? Mr Brown does not need to occupy the property all of the time for ATED to apply.

If ATED applies and if the annual tax will be burdensome on the company then action could be considered to liquidate the company – especially if the shares have a market value base cost following a recent death. However, a capital gains tax charge would apply on the disposal of the property on any gain accruing from 1 April 2013 (or date of purchase if later), so if this route is chosen, action will be needed promptly (see **explanatory note 17**). You might also check whether the advisers to the company have already filed ATED returns, as if the property value exceeds £2 million, returns were first due in October 2013, and substantial late filing penalties may also have been accrued. For property worth in excess of £1 million, returns were first due in October 2015, and for property valued at between £500,000 and £1 million the first returns were due by 30 April 2016.

# Explanatory Notes

*How is the tax calculated?*

(1) ATED is a tax payable on high value residential property (a dwelling). It came into effect from 1 April 2013 and is payable each year. It applies to dwellings, situated in the UK, valued at more than the specified limit on 1 April 2012, or acquisition if later, where owned, completely or partly, by a company, a partnership where one of the partners is a company, or a 'collective investment vehicle' – for example, a unit trust or an open ended investment company (FA 2013 s 94).

| *Chargeable periods beginning* | *Value on 1 April 2012 or date of purchase* |
|---|---|
| 1 April 2013 | £2 million |
| 1 April 2015 | £1 million |

| *Chargeable periods beginning* | *Value on 1 April 2012 or date of purchase* |
|---|---|
| 1 April 2016 | £500,000 |

There are reliefs that can reduce, or eliminate, the tax (see **explanatory note 16**).

(2) No distinction is drawn between UK and offshore companies.

(3) The term 'enveloped' refers to assets owned or partly owned by one of the above vehicles and are said to be 'enveloped' because they sit within a corporate 'wrapper' or 'envelope' (FA 2013 s 94(2)(b), (4)-(6)).

(4) Individuals or trusts (including trusts with a corporate member) who own 'dwellings' with a value in excess of the current limit are not affected by the ATED rules.

(5) The amount of ATED is worked out using a banding system based on the value of the property. The rates for 2015-16 showing a very significant increase on the previous rates:

**Rate bands**

| *Property Value* | *Annual tax 2015–16* | *Annual tax 2016–17* |
|---|---|---|
| £500,000 to £1,000,000 | £3,500 | N /A |
| £1,000,000 to £2,000,000 | £7,000 | £7,000 |
| £2,000,001 to £5,000,000 | £23,350 | £23,350 |
| £5,000,001 to £10,000,000 | £54,450 | £54,450 |
| £10,000,001 to £20,000,000 | £109,050 | £109,050 |
| £20,000,001 and over | £218,200 | £218,200 |

(6) If the dwelling is only owned for part of a year, or the usage changes so that it moves into or out of ATED, then ATED applies on a proportionate basis (that is, the ATED will be calculated by reference to the number of days in the year the property falls within ATED) (FA 2013 s 105). The charging period for ATED is the year commencing on 1 April, with returns filed and payment made at the beginning of the year; this means that provisional claims to relief may be necessary based on the expected use of the property during the coming year (FA 2013, s 100).

(7) The value at 1 April 2012 is used for the ATED return periods beginning 1 April 2013. The property needs to be re-valued at 1 April 2017 (FA 2013 s 102). The valuation on 1 April 2017 will be used as the basis for returns due on 30 April 2018 (in respect of the year 1 April 2018 to 31 March 2019), giving time for valuations to be made before they are needed to file returns. Note that any property which is enveloped but not currently affected by ATED will need to be revalued on 1 April 2017 to establish whether it comes within the regime at that point.

(8) Should the properties valuation be within 10% either side of a rate band then you can ask HMRC for pre-return banding check (PRBC) to confirm which banding they accept the property falls into.

*Meaning of dwelling*

(9) ATED applies to UK residential properties (dwellings). A dwelling may be all or part of a residential or mixed use property (FA 2013 s 112). Where it is part of a mixed use property only the dwelling will be subject to ATED and will need to be valued separately. Gardens and grounds and any building in them are included (FA 2013 s 112(2)). Where a property consists of self-contained flats, each flat will need to be valued separately and considered separately against the limits. (FA 2013 s 108).

(10) Where connected persons (eg shareholders, relatives, beneficiaries, etc) also have an interest in the dwelling, the interests will be added together for ATED purposes (FA 2013 s 110). Where there is more than one

dwelling in a property and they are owned by a company or connected person, and there is internal access between them, they will be classed as a single dwelling for ATED, as will two dwellings in adjoining buildings with internal access between them (FA 2013 ss 116-117).

(11) Hotels, guest houses, boarding school accommodation, hospitals, student halls of residence, military accommodation, care homes and prisons are not classed as dwellings and are therefore outside the scope of ATED.

(12) If a company owns an historic house that is open to the public or provides access to the dwelling as part of its services (for example, as a wedding venue) with the intention of being open for at least 28 days per year it may be able to claim a relief that will reduce its ATED charge to nil. The company's activities in the historic house must be commercial and with a profit-seeking motive, even if that profit doesn't cover the full costs of the house. Also, access must be to a significant part (relative to the size, nature and function of the areas opened to the public) of the property (FA 2013 s 137).

(13) If a farming company owns a farmhouse it may be able to claim a relief that will reduce its ATED charge to nil as long as a 'farm worker' occupies the property. The relief is available where a person connected to the owner occupies the farmhouse, so long as they are a 'farm worker' and the relevant conditions are met (FA 2013 s 148).

*Returns and payment*

(14) For the ATED period beginning 1 April 2014 and for all future years, the return and the payment are due by 30 April (FA 2013 ss 159, 163). For example, for the ATED period 1 April 2014 to 31 March 2015, both the return and payment are due by 30 April 2014. However, for properties first coming within the regime on 1 April 2015 (that is, those valued at in excess of £1 million on 1 April 2012) the return must be submitted by 1 October 2015 and the tax paid (if any) by 31 October 2015 (FA 2014 s 109(5)-(7)). Properties first coming within the regime on 1 April 2016 had no period of grace, and returns for the year ended 31 March 2017 were all due on 30 April 2016.

(15) The obligation is on the owner to self-assess (FA 2013 s 161). If a dwelling that falls within ATED is jointly owned, all the owners are jointly responsible for completing and sending the returns and payments (FA 2013 s 97). A return must be completed per dwelling. Failure to submit a return and/or payment may be subject to penalties and/or interest charges (FA 2009 Schs 55, 56). It is now becoming clear that many companies affected by ATED were unaware of its existence, and are now facing very significant late filing penalties.

*Reliefs*

(16) Reliefs exist which can prevent ATED being payable on a dwelling (FA 2013 ss 132-150). These are claimed through the return. These include where a dwelling is:

- let to a third party on a commercial basis and is not occupied, or available for occupation, by any connected person;
- held for charitable purposes;
- open to the public for at least 28 days a year; or
- a farmhouse.

For chargeable periods beginning 1 April 2015 a new "relief return" was introduced to allow an owner to claim relief in respect of more than one property on a single return. A separate return is needed for each type of relief claimed, but this replaces the necessity to make a separate return for each property (FA 2013 s 159A). This remains necessary, however, when a property is in charge to ATED rather than subject to relief.

*Capital gains tax*

(17) Where ATED applies then on disposal of the dwelling by the company, a charge to capital gains tax at 28% applies rather than a charge to corporation tax on the capital gain arising. This applies to gains accruing

from 1 April 2013, calculated on a time apportioned basis (TCGA 1992 ss 2B-2F). This charge is extended to properties valued at between £1 and £2 million on 1 April 2012 with effect from 1 April 2015, and further to properties valued in excess of £500,000 from 1 April 2016.

# Question

## A.

Briefly describe when a liability will arise to stamp duty land tax (SDLT)

## B

Briefly outline the significance of the effective date for stamp duty land tax purposes.

| | |
|---|---|
| 8 May 2016 | He purchased a holiday home in the Lake District for £500,000. He retains ownership of his main residence in London. |
| 7 August 2016 | He sold non-residential land and standing timber, with a value of £450,000, to a timber merchant. |
| 10 January 2017 | A gift of £350,000 cash was made to his eldest son to help with a property purchase. |

Provide Mr Capaldi with a memorandum that sets out the stamp taxes liabilities of each transaction.

## C

Mr Capaldi has been involved in the following transactions during the year ended 5 April 2017:

# Answer

## A. Stamp Duty Land Tax (FA 2003 ss 42–124 and Schs 3–19)

Stamp duty land tax (SDLT) applies to transactions involving land and buildings anywhere in the UK other than Scotland. It applies regardless of where the contract is executed and is not dependent on UK residency. The charge arises when the transaction is 'substantially performed' (ie when consideration paid or the purchaser, or someone connected with the purchaser, takes possession) or on completion. SDLT does not apply to transactions in land in Scotland with an effective date on or after 1 April 2015. Such transactions are instead subject to land and buildings transaction tax.

SDLT is charged on land transactions entered into in return for 'chargeable consideration'. A land transaction is defined as the 'acquisition of a chargeable interest'.

The definition of 'acquisition' is widely drawn, and encompasses the creation, surrender and in some cases, variation, of a chargeable interest. In every instance, liability to pay the tax rests with the purchaser.

In a straightforward sale of land, it is clear who fits the description of 'purchaser'. The legislation sets out rules for identifying the purchaser in all the different scenarios.

Where a chargeable interest has been *created*, the 'purchaser' is the person who becomes entitled to the interest created, for example, the buyer of a freehold property.

Where there is a *surrender* of a chargeable interest (for example, where a tenant surrenders a lease to the landlord), the 'purchaser' is the person whose benefit or interest is enlarged thereby, in this case, the landlord.

The *variation* of a chargeable interest *other than a lease* is also a land transaction, and in this case, the purchaser is the party benefiting from the variation. On the other hand, the *variation of a lease* qualifies as a land transaction for SDLT purposes in two circumstances. The first is if the variation takes effect, or is treated for SDLT purposes, as the grant of a new lease (see **explanatory note** 8 below; SDLT provisions on rent). The second is if the variation is such as to reduce the rent or term of the lease.

Except where explicitly provided in the legislation, a charge to SDLT arises regardless of the means by which the transaction is effected. In other words, it is generally irrelevant whether the 'acquisition' is by agreement of the parties, court order, legislative provision, or operation of law.

'Chargeable interests' are estates, interests, rights or powers in or over land in England and Wales or Northern Ireland. The definition also includes the benefit of any obligation, restriction or condition affecting the value of such estates, interests, rights or powers. These all qualify as chargeable interests only insofar as they are not specifically declared by the legislation to be 'exempt'.

Examples of exempt interests are security interests, tenancies at will, and licences. The position for tenancies at will is somewhat unclear. FA 2003 Sch 17A para 4 makes provision for leases for an indefinite term. Broadly, these are treated in the first instance as leases for one year, and if the lease continues beyond one year, as a lease for two years, and so on. As a result of such a continuation, SDLT may eventually become payable under the lease. The problem with tenancies at will is that para 4 includes them under the ambit of leases for an indefinite term. It is therefore a possibility, on the reading of that paragraph, that a charge to SDLT could arise in relation to a tenancy at will.

SDLT applies to consideration in money or money's worth. If there is a contingency it is charged on the assumption that the full amount is payable. The tax is then adjusted when the contingency occurs or it is clear that it will not occur. VAT is included unless the vendor/landlord has not opted to tax the land/building at the time of sale/granting of the lease (see **explanatory note 2**).

Where the consideration is uncertain (for example, where it is based on future turnover), or unascertained (for example, based on a set of accounts which have not been finalised), then a reasonable estimate is made. The purchaser may apply to defer payment in respect of contingent and uncertain consideration. There is no such provision for unascertained consideration.

Special rules apply where the land is acquired by a connected company (see **explanatory note 4**) so that SDLT is payable even when the land is gifted to the connected company.

The acquisition of land by a partnership from a partner or an incoming partner, or, the acquisition of land by a partner or former partner from a partnership or from another partner is liable to SDLT. The SDLT provisions in respect of partnerships are extremely complex. Different rules apply to trading partnerships as opposed to investment partnerships.

Land transactions on marriage breakdown, variations following death, assents and appropriations by personal representatives and certain leases granted by registered social landlords or social housing providers are exempt from SDLT.

The rates of SDLT are based upon chargeable consideration and are:

***Residential property*** *(rates apply to the consideration in each slice)*
*Effective date after 31.3.16*

| Main rate* | Higher rate* | £ |
|---|---|---|
| 0% | 3% | Up to 125,000 |
| 2% | 5% | 125,001–250,000 |
| 5% | 8% | 250,001–925,000 |
| 10% | 13% | 925,001–1,500,000 |
| 12% | 15% | Over 1,500,000 |

***Non-residential or mixed property*** *(rates apply to the consideration in each slice)*
*Effective date after 16.3.16*

| Rate* | Non-Residential or Mixed £ |
|---|---|
| 0% | 150,000 |
| 2% | 150,001–250,000 |
| 5% | Over 250,000 |

* A rate of 15% may apply, where the purchaser is a non-natural person. The rate applies to transactions in residential property where the chargeable consideration exceeds £500,000. The 15% rate applies to the whole of the consideration. There are a number of reliefs and exemptions from this charge, which reflect the reliefs and exemptions in the Annual Tax on Enveloped Dwellings (ATED). ATED is dealt with in **Example D5**.

The higher rate of SDLT applies to certain transactions in residential property with an effective date on or after 1 April 2016, except, broadly, where the contract was entered into and substantially performed before 26 November 2015. The rate applies to purchases of additional residential property by individuals and to purchases of residential property by companies and certain trusts. It does not apply to transactions under £40,000. There is provision for relief where an individual's main residence is replaced and there is a gap in ownership of such a residence, or an overlap in ownership, not exceeding 36 months.

Where interests in more than one dwelling are transferred in a single transaction or under a scheme, arrangement or series of linked transactions the rate of tax charged on the consideration attributable to the dwellings is determined by taking the mean consideration (ie the aggregate consideration attributable to the dwellings divided by the number of dwellings), subject to a minimum rate of 1%.

Where a lease is granted, there are two potential elements which are chargeable to SDLT.

The first is the premium payable on the grant. This is subject to SDLT in the same way as on a sale.

The second element is the rental payable during the term of the lease. This is subject to SDLT at the following rates:

*Effective date after 16.03.16*

| *Rate (%)* | *Net present value of rent* | |
|---|---|---|
| | **Residential** | **Non-residential or Mixed** |
| 0% | First £125,000 | First £150,000 |
| 1% | Excess over £125,000 | £150,001–£5,000,000 |
| 2% | N/A | Excess over £5,000,000 |

Note that the rates apply to the amount of the net present value in each slice.

The 'net present value of rent' is defined in FA 2003 Sch 5 para 3 and is effectively the aggregate of the rent payable over the term of the lease, discounted by the 'temporal discount rate' which is currently 3.5% per year.

A land transaction is a chargeable transaction for SDLT, unless it falls within an exemption. The most important exemptions are:

(a) transactions where there is no chargeable consideration for the disposal (ie gifts);

(b) transactions in connection with divorce;

(c) variations of wills etc after death.

No land transaction return is required if one of the exemptions applies.

SDLT on property with a mortgage based on unconventional principles (eg Islamic rules) will be the same as that payable on a property with a conventional mortgage.

If two pieces of land are exchanged, there will be two separate SDLT transactions. The chargeable consideration for each transaction is the higher of the market value of the land acquired by each purchaser and what the chargeable consideration would be for each purchaser under the normal rules. There are special reliefs for certain exchanges of residential property. These include the situation where a house-building company acquires a dwelling in part exchange for the disposal of a newly constructed dwelling. The old dwelling must have been the only or main residence of the individual disposing of it and he must intend to occupy the new dwelling as his only or main residence. The effect of the relief will usually be that no SDLT is payable on the old dwelling.

A return and payment of SDLT must be made by the purchaser within 30 days of the effective date. The tax is self-assessed. A return is required for every 'notifiable transaction' even if no tax is chargeable. A return is also required within 30 days of any event altering the SDLT liability eg confirmation of consideration or contingency, withdrawal of any relief such as SDLT group relief.

In order to register a notifiable land transaction the purchaser must produce a certificate, issued by HMRC, showing compliance with SDLT.

## B. Memorandum for Mr Capaldi

8 May 2016
The purchase of an additional residential property attracts SDLT at the higher rate. Mr Capaldi is liable for SDLT of £125,000 × 3% + £100,000 × 5% + £275,000 × 8% = £30,750.

7 August 2016
The sale of land and standing timber is a transfer of property valued in excess of £150,000. It therefore attracts SDLT of £100,000 × 2% + £200,000 × 5% = £12,000, unless Mr Capaldi had elected to waive his exemption for VAT. If the sale was subject to VAT, the VAT would amount to 20% of £450,000 = £90,000, making total consideration of £540,000. SDLT payable is therefore £100,000 × 2% + £290,000 × 5% = £16,500. The purchaser is liable for the tax (FA 2003 s 85).

10 January 2017
SDLT is a tax on land and buildings. As cash does not fall into this category no duty is payable.

The 'effective date' of a transaction is significant for many reasons. It identifies the date of the transaction for the purposes of determining, among other things, the following:

## C. The effective date

The 'effective date' of a transaction is significant for many reasons. It identifies the date of the transaction for the purposes of determining, among other things, the following:

- when the land transaction return should be filed;
- when the tax should be paid;
- the date from which interest begins to run, and from which penalties may be charged; and
- the market value of the consideration, eg where non-monetary consideration is given for a land transaction, FA 2003 Sch 4 para 8 provides that its value is taken to be its market value at the effective date of the transaction.

Generally speaking, the effective date of a transaction is the date of completion. However, there are certain circumstances in which a different date applies.

In the case of a contract to transfer land where the transaction will be completed by a conveyance, the effective date is the date of completion. However, if the contract is 'substantially performed' without being completed, the effective date is the date when the contract is substantially performed. The effect of this provision is to catch attempts to avoid tax by 'resting on contract'. Without the 'substantial performance' provision, SDLT could be avoided by the purchaser, for example, taking possession of the property without the contract ever being completed.

A contract may be made between two parties, providing for a chargeable interest to be conveyed by one party (A), at the request or direction of the other party (B), to a third party. If the contract is substantially performed, B is treated as having acquired a chargeable interest at the date that the contract is substantially performed.

Where an agreement for lease is made, and is substantially performed without being completed, the agreement is treated as the grant of a lease under the terms of the agreement, with the effective date being the date of substantial performance.

Where an agreement for lease has been made, and the lessee under the agreement assigns his interest under the agreement after it has been substantially performed, the assignment is taken as a separate land transaction, the effective date being the date of assignment.

A contract is taken to be 'substantially performed' if the purchaser, or a connected person, takes possession of the whole, or substantially the whole, of the subject matter. 'Taking possession' includes the receipt of rents or the right to receive them. Also, it is immaterial whether possession is taken under the contract or under a licence or lease of temporary character.

A contract is also taken to be substantially performed if a substantial amount of the consideration is paid or provided. In a case where none of the consideration is rent, such as the outright sale of land, this condition is taken to have been met if the whole, or substantially the whole, of the consideration is paid or provided. Where the consideration includes rent and some other consideration, such as a premium, the condition is met if either the whole, or substantially the whole of that other consideration (eg the premium) is paid or provided, or when the first payment of rent is made. Where the consideration consists of rent only, the condition is met when the first payment of rent is made.

The acquisition of an option or right of pre-emption is a land transaction in its own right, distinct from any land transaction arising from its exercise. In the case of the acquisition of the option or right, the effective date is the date it was acquired.

## Explanatory Notes

*SDLT legislation*

(1) SDLT applies to transactions in land and buildings in England and Wales or Northern Ireland and stamp duty applies to documents relating to stocks and marketable securities and the issue of bearer instruments. SDLT also applies to the acquisition of a partnership which holds land in England and Wales or Northern Ireland. SDLT has been replaced in Scotland by the land and buildings transaction tax from April 2015.

SDLT is dealt with by HMRC (Stamp Taxes).

*Value added tax*

(2) Where property that is conveyed or leased is property on which the option may be taken to charge VAT (broadly all land and buildings except domestic, relevant residential or non-business charity buildings) then SDLT is payable on the value *plus VAT* if the option is exercised. The availability of a claim to recover input tax will not alter the charge to SDLT.

Chargeable consideration does not include any VAT that may become payable as a result of an election to waive exemption after the effective date. This means that, for example, if a landlord 'opts to tax' *after* granting a lease, the VAT payable will not form part of the chargeable consideration.

The notice to waive exemption from VAT (option to tax) is not liable to SDLT, and SDLT itself is never liable to VAT.

On the sale of the land and standing timber in **part B** on 7 August 2016 the option to charge VAT may have been available. If Mr Argenton did not exercise the option before sale, SDLT is not payable on the VAT that might have become due. If, on the other hand, the option was exercised at any time before completion, then SDLT would be payable on the VAT inclusive value.

If the transaction is part of a sale of a business, then VAT is not chargeable under the transfer of a going concern provisions. If this is expected to be the case, it may well be that the provisions relating to contingent consideration will apply.

*Mortgaged property*

(3) Care must be taken with transfers of mortgaged property, as the value for SDLT is the sum of the price paid plus the outstanding loan (see *CIR v City of Glasgow Bank* (1881), a case decided under stamp duty). This also applies where there is no actual consideration; duty is payable on the value of the debt taken over (see Revenue Statement of Practice SP6/90).

This is particularly relevant where the transaction is between connected persons, eg a mortgaged property held in the name of one spouse is transferred into joint names, or into the name of the other spouse, or from joint names to a single name.

Where the transferor covenants to pay the debt and the transferee does not assume any liability for it, no consideration has been given. The transfer is then not liable to SDLT as no chargeable consideration is provided by the purchaser (FA 2003 Sch 3 para 1 and Sch 4 para 1).

If, however, the transferee agrees to pay the debt or to indemnify the transferor against his personal liability to the lender that will constitute valuable consideration liable to SDLT. A covenant or agreement may be in writing or implied.

The above rules do not affect any statutory exemption from SDLT, eg transfers to a charity or a charitable trust (FA 2003 Sch 8) and certain transfers from one party to the other in connection with a divorce or separation (FA 2003 Sch 3 para 3).

*Transfer to connected company*

(4) Special rules apply where the purchaser is a company and either:

(a) the vendor is connected with the company; or

(b) some or all of the consideration for the transaction is the issue or transfer of shares in a company with which the vendor is connected.

An example would be where land is transferred from a sole trader or partnership to a company on incorporation. In this case, the chargeable consideration is the market value of the land at the date of the transaction. This rule applies even if the land is gifted to the company, as the exemption in FA 2003 Sch 3 para 1 is disapplied (FA 2003 s 53).

*Transfers between associated companies and company reconstructions*

(5) Transfers of property between associated companies and on company reconstructions are exempt from SDLT (FA 2003 Sch 7). Group relief applies where one company is the parent of the other company, or both are subsidiaries of a common parent, and the parent company owns in each case not less than 75% of the ordinary share capital of the subsidiary, and is entitled to 75% or more of the profits, and on a winding up 75% or more of the assets (Sch 7 para 1). Exemption also applies to the grant of a lease by one group company to another group company or an agreement for a lease between group companies. There are anti-avoidance provisions in Sch 7 para 3 to prevent these provisions being used to avoid SDLT when property, or an economic interest in it, passes out of the group.

Group relief may be withdrawn if the vendor and purchaser companies cease to be members of the same group within three years, in certain circumstances. The tax that would originally have been paid becomes chargeable. It becomes payable 30 days after the event which causes the withdrawal of the group relief. Group relief is not withdrawn where the companies cease to be members of the same group because the vendor leaves the group.

SDLT group relief must be claimed in a land transaction return and a further return made if the relief is withdrawn.

A reduced rate of SDLT of ½% applies to land transactions entered into for the purposes of or in connection with the acquisition by a company of the whole or part of an undertaking of another company in exchange for shares (Sch 7 para 8). This is subject to anti-avoidance provisions where the undertaking includes UK land (Sch 7 para 9).

*Transfer to a limited liability partnership*

(6) There is an exemption from SDLT where land is transferred to a limited liability partnership (LLP) in connection with its incorporation.

Three conditions must be satisfied:

(a) the effective date of the transaction is not more than one year after the incorporation of the LLP;

(b) the partners in the old partnership and the new LLP are the same and the transferor is one of those partners;

(c) the interests of the partners in the old and new partnerships are the same or any change in the interests is not part of a tax avoidance scheme (FA 2003 s 65).

*Variable or contingent consideration*

(7) Where all or part of the consideration payable on a land transaction is not in money or money's worth then market value at the effective date of the transaction is used. However, this rule only applies in the absence of any contrary provision. 'Market value' is determined using the capital gains tax rules in TCGA 1992 (FA 2003 s 118 and Sch 4 para 7). There is no discount for postponed consideration (Sch 4 para 3). Where, however, the consideration is ascertainable but not fixed, SDLT is paid on the basis that any contingent

amount will be payable. Where consideration is uncertain SDLT is paid on the amount that could reasonably be certain to be received (FA 2003 s 51). Where the value is based upon an annuity payable for more than 12 years the value is restricted to the twelve highest annual payments (FA 2003 s 52).

Special rules apply to leases in the case of variable or uncertain rent (see FA 2003 Sch 17A para 7). See **explanatory note** 8 below.

*SDLT provisions on rent*

(8) Different provisions apply where the rent payable under a lease is contingent, uncertain or unascertained. If the rent payable relates to any period before the end of the fifth year of the lease, the normal rules for contingent, uncertain and unascertained consideration apply. If it relates to a period after the end of the fifth year, the 'annual amount' is taken to be the highest amount of rent payable in any consecutive 12-month period within the first five years of the lease. Finance Act 2003 Sch 17A para 7 gives details on how to determine this figure.

For contingent, uncertain or unascertained rent payable within the first five years of the lease, an adjustment must be made, either at the end of year five, or if the rent payable ceases to be uncertain at an earlier time at that time. If, at the end of year five, the rent is still uncertain, it is calculated using the rules in the preceding paragraph. If, as a result of the rent ceasing to be uncertain, a transaction becomes notifiable, or tax (or additional tax) becomes payable, the purchaser must make a return (together with self-assessment) to HMRC within 30 days, and pay the tax due not later than the filing date for the return. The tax is calculated using the rates in force at the effective date of the transaction. This is beneficial for the taxpayer if rates have risen since then. If it turns out that the purchaser had initially paid more tax than turned out to be in fact due, a refund is given.

Where a lease is varied so as to increase the rent payable within the first five years of the term, this is treated as a grant of a new lease, in consideration for the additional rent payable. However, this rule does not apply where the increase in rent is made in pursuance of a provision within the lease itself. It also does not apply to leases under certain legislation relating to agricultural holdings and tenancies.

*SDLT administration*

(9) Where there has been a 'notifiable transaction', the purchaser must, within 30 days of the effective date of the transaction, submit to HMRC a land transaction return. The following are notifiable transactions:

(a) the acquisition of a 'major interest' in land, other than one falling within one or more of the exceptions listed below:

A 'major interest' means, in relation to land in England and Wales, an estate in fee simple absolute, or a term of years absolute. In relation to land in Northern Ireland it means any freehold or leasehold estate.

(b) an acquisition of a chargeable interest which is not a 'major interest' if there is chargeable consideration in respect of which SDLT would be chargeable at a rate of 1 per cent or higher, or would be so chargeable, but for a relief;

(c) the substantial performance of a contract in circumstances envisaged by FA 2003 s 44A(3) dealing with a contract under which a chargeable interest is to be conveyed to a third party (see notes to **Question C** above); and

(d) a notional land transaction under the anti-avoidance provisions of FA 2003 s 75A.

The exceptions to (a) above are:

(i) an acquisition which is exempt under FA 2003 Sch 3;

(ii) an acquisition (other than the grant, assignment or surrender of a lease) where the chargeable consideration is less than £40,000;

(iii) the grant of a lease for a term of at least seven years where any chargeable consideration other than rent is less than £40,000 and the annual rent is less than £1,000;

(iv) the assignment or surrender of a lease originally granted for a term of at least seven years where the chargeable consideration for the assignment or surrender is less than £40,000;

(v) the grant of a lease for less than seven years where the chargeable consideration does not exceed the zero rate threshold; and

(vi) the assignment or surrender of a lease originally granted for a term of less than seven years where the chargeable consideration for the assignment or surrender does not exceed the zero rate threshold.

Payment of SDLT must be made on or before the filing date for the return.

The disclosure of tax avoidance schemes regime in FA 2004 Pt 7 and the high-risk promoter regime in FA 2014 Pt 5 apply to SDLT.

*Interest and penalties*

(10) SDLT is subject to a regime similar to income tax self-assessment with penalties for failure to deliver a return, for a careless or deliberate error in a return, failure to keep or preserve records, failure to comply with notices to provide documents or information and criminal sanctions for fraudulently evading SDLT. Interest is paid on overpaid tax and charged on overdue SDLT.

From a date to be appointed, SDLT will fall within the cross-tax penalties for failure to make returns (under FA 2009 Sch 55) and payments on time (under FA 2009 Sch 56) and the cross-tax interest regime (FA 2009 s 103).

# Losses

# Question

(a) William Smith has been trading for some years preparing accounts to 31 December each year. He made a trading profit of £10,000 for the year to 31 December 2015 and a trading loss of £16,000 for the year to 31 December 2016. He has reorganised the business and expects to show a profit of around £11,000 in 2017, increasing in later years. Capital allowances have been taken into account in these figures. The business is undertaken on a commercial basis.

His unearned income for 2015/16 and 2016/17 was as follows:

| | *2015/16* | *2016/17* |
|---|---|---|
| | £ | £ |
| Rental income | 4,720 | 11,000 |

His only savings income is derived from are ISAs and can therefore be disregarded in calculating his annual tax liabilities, In 2015/16 Smith had sold some shares he had inherited many years ago and made a chargeable gain of £11,500. He had no capital losses brought forward and he had no capital transactions in 2016/17.

Indicate what claims are available to Smith in respect of the 2016 loss and state the time limits involved.

(b) Georgia Brown, who is 53, has run a successful confectionary business for many years in addition to having a significant portfolio of rental properties. After a spate of ill-health combined with an increase in competition, she incurs significant losses in the confectionary business in her accounting year ended 31 December 2016. Her results from both her self-employment and her property business for 2015/16 and 2016/17 are as follows (after taking capital allowances into account):

| | 2015/16 | 2016/17 |
|---|---|---|
| | £ | £ |
| Confectionary business profit/(loss) | 26,000 | (95,050) |
| Rental income | 123,030 | 65,220 |

In July 2016 to help ease her cashflow she sold one of her rental properties, giving rise to a capital gain of £13,500, but has no other capital transactions in either 2015/16 or 2016/17. She has bank interest of £3,500 gross each year.

She has not made any contributions to a registered pension scheme or gift aid donations in either year.

Indicate what claims are available to Ms Brown in respect of the 2016 loss and what restrictions may apply to those claims.

For the relevant rates and allowances, see the front of this book.

(c) John Riddell started a new sportswear business on 1 December 2015 and had the following results:

| | | |
|---|---|---|
| 6 months from 1 December 2015 to 31 May 2016 | Profit | £9,000 |
| Year to 31 May 2017 | Loss | £20,400 |
| Year to 31 May 2018 | Profit | £16,200 |

Show the alternative ways in which Mr Riddell could obtain relief for his loss, assuming that he has enough other income to obtain full relief for any loss claimed under ITA 2007 ss 64 or 72.

(d) Lionel Drake, who had been in business as a bookseller for many years, drawing up accounts to 30 April, has had the following results (after capital allowances) in recent years:

| | | |
|---|---|---|
| Year to 30 April 2014 | Profit | £30,000 |
| Year to 30 April 2015 | Profit | £24,000 |
| Year to 30 April 2016 | Loss | £18,000 |

He has transitional overlap profit of £34,000, the overlap period being 340 days. He has no other sources of income.

(i) show his tax position for the relevant years;

(ii) show what the position would have been if he had changed his accounting date to 31 March, and had made a loss of £16,500 in the 11 months to 31 March 2016.

For the relevant rates and allowances, see the front of this book.

# Answer

## (a) Loss claims available to William Smith in respect of 2016 loss

The loss of £16,000 in the year to 31 December 2016 is treated as the loss of the tax year 2016/17 (see **explanatory note 1(b)**). The loss claims available to Mr Smith are as follows:

(i) he may carry forward the loss to set against his first available later profits from the same trade (carry forward trading loss relief ITA 2007 s 83);

(ii) he may claim to set the loss against his total income of 2016/17 or 2015/16, or, if he wishes, of both years (trade loss relief against general income ITA 2007 s 64);

(iii) he may claim to set the balance of the loss after a general income (ITA 2007 s 64) claim (and after any other claims, such as under ITA 2007 s 64 for the previous year) against his capital gains for the tax year(s) of the ITA 2007 s 64 claim (ITA 2007 s 71).

The time limit for the carry forward of trading loss relief claim is four years from the end of the tax year of the loss (TMA 1970 s 43). Once the loss claim has been established, relief is given automatically against the first available later trading profits.

The time limit for claims under ITA 2007 s 64 and against capital gains is one year from 31 January after the tax year of loss (ITA 2007 s 64(5)), ie by 31 January 2019 for a 2016/17 loss.

The effect of the different claims would be as follows:

### *(i) Carry forward trading loss relief*

The loss would be set against the trading profit of the year to 31 December 2017. If this is £11,000 as expected, there would still be an unrelieved loss of £5,000 to carry forward to a later year. Smith's other income currently covers his personal allowance, although this might not be the case in 2017/18. The claim would reduce or eliminate the tax and Class 4 national insurance contributions for 2017/18, which is payable by way of payments on account on 31 January 2018 and 31 July 2018, with a balancing payment (or repayment) on 31 January 2019. Tax would remain payable for 2015/16 and 2016/17.

### *(ii) and (iii) Claim against general income of 2016/17 and/or 2015/16, and possibly against 2015/16capital gains*

Smith's income tax position for the relevant years before loss claims is as follows:

**2016/17**

| | £ |
|---|---|
| Trading income (loss in yr to 31.12.16) | – |
| UK property income | 11,000 |
| | 11,000 |
| Personal allowance | (11,000) |
| Taxable income | NIL |

**2015/16**

| | | | | |
|---|---|---|---|---|
| | | | | £ |
| Trading income (year ended 31.12.15) | | | | 10,000 |
| UK property income | | | | 4,720 |
| | | | | 14,720 |
| Personal allowance | | | | (10,600) |
| Taxable income | | | | 4,720 |
| Tax thereon: | | | | |
| | 4,120 | @ | 20% | 824 |
| Class 4 NIC | | | | |
| (£10,000 – £8,060 =) | 1,940 | @ | 9% | 175 |
| | | | | 999 |
| His capital gains tax liability in 2015/16 is (£11,500 – annual exemption £11,100) | | | | |
| | £400 | @ | 18% = | £72 |

Clearly a claim in 2016/17 would not be appropriate, since his personal allowance would be wasted and very little tax would be saved.

His income of 2015/16 does not fully cover the loss, so if he makes a claim for that year he cannot avoid wasting his personal allowance. The claim would save tax and Class 4 national insurance of £999 and leave an unrelieved loss of (16,000 – 14,720 =) £1,280, which could be carried forward under trading loss relief provisions against future profits of the same trade. Relief would be obtained at the basic rate in 2017/18 if his anticipated profit is realised and there remains some rental income. The loss carried forward for Class 4 national insurance purposes would be £6,000, being loss of £16,000 relieved against trading income only of £10,000 (see **explanatory note 7**).

Alternatively, Smith could set the balance of the loss of £1,280 against his 2015/16 capital gains of £11,500. The loss of £1,280 would reduce the gains to £10,220 which would be below the annual exemption of £11,100. There would therefore be no capital gains tax payable, saving an additional £72; however Smith would obtain no benefit from £880 of the loss, being the loss of £1,280 less the chargeable gain before relief is claimed of £400. It is not possible to restrict the claim to leave £11,100 in charge (equal to the annual exempt amount).

## Optimum loss claim(s)

Claiming the maximum relief against general income (ITA 2007 s 64), including relief against capital gains, means that the 2015/16 personal allowance is wasted and the remainder of the loss saves tax at 20%.

Furthermore, under self-assessment, carried back losses do not affect the calculation of payments on account either for the loss year or the next following year (see **explanatory note 8**), and interest on tax and Class 4 national insurance contributions refunded as a result of the loss claim is payable only from 31 January following the loss year. Assuming Smith made a ITA 2007 s 64 claim for 2015/16 (possibly extended to capital gains), his tax position would be as follows:

| | |
|---|---|
| *2015/16* | Income tax and Class 4 national insurance totalling £999 refunded; a further capital gains tax refund of £72 made if loss set against gains. No interest on refund unless made after 31 January 2018 (balancing payment date for 2016/17). |
| *2016/17* | Payments on account would be have been due on the basis of tax/national insurance of £999 payable for 2015/16. |
| *2017/18* | Payments on account would not be required, because the 2016/17 tax is below the de minimis level of £1,000. |

If the loss is carried forward under ITA 2007 s 83, tax might be saved at the basic rate, depending on the level of his 2017/18 income, and there could be further relief in a later year if his 2017/18 trading profits do not fully cover the loss.

Smith may be able to delay the decision on what loss claim(s) to make until he is reasonably certain of the level of his 2017/18 income. On the other hand, he may prefer to make the general income (ITA 2007 s 64) claim in order to obtain immediate cash repayments.

## (b) Loss claims available to Georgia Brown in respect of 2016 loss

The loss of £95,050 in the year to 31 December 2016 is treated as the loss of the tax year 2016/17 (see **explanatory note 1(b)**). The loss claims available to Ms Brown are as follows:

(i) she may carry forward the loss to set against her first available later profits from the same trade (carry forward trading loss relief ITA 2007 s 83);

(ii) she may claim to set the loss against his total income of 2016/17 or 2015/16, or, if she wishes, of both years (trade loss relief against general income ITA 2007 s 64);

(iii) she may claim to set the balance of the loss after a general income (ITA 2007 s 64) claim (and after any other claims, such as under ITA 2007 s 64 for the previous year) against her capital gains for the tax year(s) of the ITA 2007 s 64 claim (ITA 2007 s 71).

The time limit for claims under ITA 2007 s 64 and against capital gains is one year from 31 January after the tax year of loss (ITA 2007 s 64(5)), ie by 31 January 2019 for a 2016/17 loss.

The cap on income tax reliefs in ITA 2007 s 24A is likely to limit Ms Brown's claims under (ii) above to the greater of £50,000 or 25% of her income for the year in which she wishes to utilise the loss (see **explanatory note 10**).

The effect of the different claims would be as follows:

### (i) *Carry forward trading loss relief*

The loss would be set against the trading profit of the year to 31 December 2017. If this is a profit but less than £95,050, the balance would be carried forward to a later year. If Ms Brown again makes a loss in 2017/18, the 2016/17 loss can only be added to the amount of that later loss for the purpose of carry-forward to set against profits of later years. For all other types of claim the losses of each year have to be considered separately.

### (ii) and (iii) *Claim against general income of 2016/17 and/or 2015/16, and possibly against 2016/17capital gains*

Ms Brown's income tax position for the relevant years before loss claims is as follows:

**2016/17**

| | | |
|---|---|---|
| | | £ |
| Trading income (loss in year to 31.12.16) | | – |
| UK property income | | 65,220 |
| Savings income | | 3,500 |
| | | 68,720 |
| Personal allowance | | (11,000) |
| Taxable income | | 57,720 |
| Tax: | | |
| On non savings income: | | |
| £32,000 @ 20% | 6,400 | |
| £22,220 @ 40% | 8,888 | |
| On savings income | | |
| £500 @ 0% | — | |
| £3,000 @ 40% | 1,200 | |
| | | 16,488 |
| Capital gain (£13,500 – £11,100 = £2,400 @ 28%)* | | 672 |
| | | 17,160 |

| | | £ |
|---|---|---|
| * - the gain is on residential property | | |

**2015/16**

| | | £ |
|---|---|---|
| Trading income (year to 31.12.15) | | 26,000 |
| UK property income | | 123,030 |
| Savings income | | 3,500 |
| | | 152,530 |
| Personal allowance (nil as income exceeds £121,200 – see below) | | – |
| Taxable income | | 152,530 |
| Tax: | | |
| £31,785 @ 20% | 6,357 | |
| £150,000 – £31,785 @ 40% | 47,286 | |
| £152,530 – £150,000 @ 45% | 1,138 | |
| | | 54,781 |
| Class 4 NIC: | | |
| £26,000 – £8,060 @ 9% | | 1,615 |
| Total | | 56,396 |

## Optimum loss claim(s)

The amount of Ms Brown's trading loss available to set against other income in 2016/17 is limited to £50,000 (this being more than 25% of her adjusted total income for that year). Reducing her taxable income by £50,000 would reduce her income tax liability to £1,344 (a saving of £15,144).

The amount of losses available for set-off against 2015/16 general income is also affected by the cap on income tax relief, but £26,000 of those losses may be used against the previous profits of the confectionary business before the £50,000 cap is applied, giving an overall amount of loss relief available of £76,000. An ITA 2007 s 64 claim made for both years, taking 2015/16 first would be advantageous, not only because a greater amount of relief is available for this year than in 2016/17, but also because using this relief in 2015/16 would remove Ms Brown's liability to tax at the additional rate as well as restoring her entitlement to the personal allowance. Personal allowances are withdrawn at a rate of £1 for every £2 of income above £100,000 (ITA 2007 s 35(2)).

The cap on income tax reliefs does not restrict the amount of loss that can be set against trading profit for Class 4 NIC purposes.

The remainder of the loss should then be used against 2016/17 general income.

As Ms Brown can use the whole of the 2016/17 trading loss against her income tax liabilities for 2015/16 and 2016/17 there is no surplus available for her to claim against her 2016/17 capital gains tax liability.

Revised computations of tax/NICs payable are as follows:

**2015/16**

| | £ |
|---|---|
| Trading income (loss in year to 31.12.15) | 26,000 |

| | | £ |
|---|---|---|
| UK property income | | 123,030 |
| Savings income | | 3,500 |
| Loss claim under s 64 | | (76,000) |
| | | 76,530 |
| Personal allowance | | (10,600) |
| Taxable income | | 65,930 |
| Tax: | | |
| £31,785 @ 20% | 6,357 | |
| £65,930 – £31,785 @ 40% | 13,658 | |
| | | 20,015 |
| Class 4 NIC: | | |
| £26,000 – £26,000 = nil profit for Class 4 purposes | | – |
| Total | | 20,015 |

## 2016/17

| | | £ |
|---|---|---|
| Trading income (loss in year to 31.12.16) | | – |
| UK property income | | 65,220 |
| Savings income | | 3,500 |
| Loss claim under s 64 (95,050 – 76,000 used 15/16) | | (19,050) |
| | | 49,670 |
| Personal allowance | | (11,000) |
| Taxable income | | 38,670 |
| Tax: | | |
| On non savings income | | |
| £32,000 @ 20% | 6,400 | |
| £3,170 @ 40% | 1,268 | |
| On savings income | | |
| £500 @ 0% | | |
| £3,000 @ 40% | 1,200 | |
| | | 8,868 |

For Class 4 NIC purposes, £69,050 (£95,050 - £26,000) remains available to carry forward against future profits of the same trade.

## (c) John Riddell – interaction of losses and overlap relief

| | | | |
|---|---|---|---|
| 2015/16 | 1.12.15 – 5.4.16<br>4/6ths × £9,000 profit | | £6,000 |
| 2016/17 | Since no 12 month account ends in the second year, the basis period is 1.12.15 to 30.11.16: | £ | |
| | Profit to 31.5.16 | 9,000 | |
| | Loss 1.6.16 – 30.11.16 (6/12 × £20,400) | (10,200) | |
| | Loss available for relief | (1,200) | |

| | | |
|---|---|---|
| | Profit | Nil |

Profit of £9,000 is offset by an equivalent amount of loss in arriving at a nil result. £6,000 of the profit of £9,000, ie for the four months from 1.12.15 to 5.4.16, is an overlap profit for which overlap relief will be available (see **explanatory note**).

2017/18 — Basis period is 1.6.16 to 31.5.17 but cannot include the loss to 30.11.16 that was already taken into account in 2016/17. Since there is still a loss in the remainder of the period, the result is nil and the loss available for relief is 6/12 × £20,400 = £10,200.

There is a further overlap period of 6 months from 1.6.16 to 30.11.16 with an overlap profit of nil (since there is a loss in the period). This is aggregated with the previous 4 month overlap period to give a total overlap period of 10 months with an overlap profit of (£6,000 + nil =) £6,000.

2018/19 — Basis period is year to 31.5.18. Taxable profit is £16,200.

£9,000 of the loss was offset against profit in arriving at the nil result for 2016/17. If relief for the 2016/17 loss of £1,200 and the 2017/18 loss of £10,200 has been claimed against other income (ITA 2007 s 64), the loss will therefore have been fully relieved. If no claims have been made against other income, there will be losses of £11,400 brought forward to set against the 2018/19 trading profit(ITA 2007 s 83).

For a discussion of relief for trading losses in the first four years of the trade under ITA 2007 s 72, see **Example E2.**

## (d) Lionel Drake's tax position – loss with change of accounting date

### (i) *Tax position for relevant years*

| | £ |
|---|---|
| 2014/15 (yr to 30.4.14) | 30,000 |
| 2015/16 (yr to 30.4.15) | 24,000 |
| 2016/17 (yr to 30.4.16) | nil |
| Loss available for relief | £18,000 |

Relief for the loss could be claimed in 2016/17 or in 2015/16 under ITA 2007 s 64. Assuming no other income, the carry back to 2015/16 would be preferable unless Drake is likely to be a higher rate taxpayer in 2017/18 (yr to 30.4.17).

| *Tax position* | *2014/15* | *2015/16 before loss* | *2015/16 after loss* | *2016/17* |
|---|---|---|---|---|
| | £ | £ | £ | £ |
| Trading income | 30,000 | 24,000 | 24,000 | Nil |
| *Less*: ITA 2007 s 64 loss claim | | | (18,000) | |
| | | | 6,000 | |
| *Less*: Personal allowance | (10,000) | (10,600) | (10,600) | |
| | 20,000 | 13,400 | Nil | Nil |
| | £ | £ | £ | £ |
| Tax @ 20% | 4,000 | 2,680 | | |
| Class 4 NIC | | | | |
| 9% × (£30,000 – £7,956) | 1,984 | | | |
| 9% × (£24,000 – £8,060) | | 1,435 | | |
| 9% × (£6,000 – £8,060) | | | Nil | |
| | 5,984 | 4,115 | Nil | Nil |

| *Tax position* | *2014/15* | *2015/16 before loss* | *2015/16 after loss* | *2016/17* |
|---|---|---|---|---|
| Tax and NIC repayable (for 2015/16) | | | £4,115 | |

## (ii) *With change of accounting date to 31 March 2016*

| | | | |
|---|---|---|---|
| *Self assessments* | | £ | £ |
| 2014/15 – as above | | | 30,000 |
| 2015/16 (1.5.14 to 31.3.16) | | | |
| yr to 30.4.15 | Profit | 24,000 | |
| period ended 31.3.16 | Loss | (16,500) | |
| | | 7,500 | |
| *Less*: overlap relief | | (34,000) | |
| Loss available for relief | | (26,500) | |

The loss may be relieved in 2015/16 or 2014/15 under ITA 2007, s 64. Assuming no other income, the carry back to 2014/15 would be preferable unless Drake is likely to be a higher rate taxpayer in 2016/17 (ie accounts year ended 31 March 2017).

| *Tax position* | *2014/15 before loss* | | *2014/15 after loss* | *2015/16* |
|---|---|---|---|---|
| | £ | | £ | £ |
| Trading income | 30,000 | | 30,000 | Nil |
| *Less*: ITA 2007 s 64 loss claim | | | (26,500) | |
| | | | 3,500 | |
| *Less*: Personal allowance | (10,000) | | (10,000) | |
| | 20,000 | | Nil | |
| Tax and NIC (as above) | £5,984 | | Nil | Nil |
| Tax and NIC repayable | | £5,984 | (and no liability in 2015/16) | |

By changing his accounting date to a date nearer to 5 April, Drake has increased his available loss by means of overlap relief. In this Example he has fully used the available overlap relief, as the change is to 31 March, and as a result has wasted part of his personal allowances. A change to 28 February would give an estimated repayment of:

| | | |
|---|---|---|
| *2015/16 (1.5.14 to 28.2.16)* | | £ |
| | yr to 30.4.13 | – |
| | period ended 28.2.16 (say) | 24,000 |
| | | (15,000) |
| | | 9,000 |
| Less: overlap relief 309/340 × £34,000 | | (30,900) |
| Loss available for relief | | (21,900) |

| | | | *2014/15 after loss* |
|---|---|---|---|
| | | | £ |
| Trading income | | | 30,000 |
| *Less*: ITA 2007 s 64 loss claim | | | (21,900) |
| | | | 8,100 |
| *Less*: Personal allowance | | | (10,000) |
| | | | Nil |
| | | | £ |
| Tax: | | | Nil |
| Class 4 NIC | (£8,100 – £7,956) | @ 9% | 13 |
| | | | 13 |

With a February year-end, the loss of £1,500 in March (and £1,500 in April) would reduce the taxable profits of 2016/17 (yr ended 28.2.17) and overlap relief of £34,000 – £30,900 = £3,100 would be carried forward at the cost of £13 payable for 2014/15. This is not as favourable as the position with the 31 March year-end.

## Explanatory Notes

*Loss reliefs available – income tax*

(1) The reliefs available for a trading loss are as follows:

(a) The loss may be carried forward to set against the first available later profits from the *same trade* (ITA 2007 s 83). Where part of a loss remains unrelieved after other loss claims, the balance is carried forward under this section. The amount will include any allowable interest, relieved outside the accounts, incurred for trading purposes and not utilised in the year (ITA 2007 s 88).

(b) The loss of a tax year may be set against the net total income of that tax year, or of the previous tax year, or, if the loss is large enough and the claimant so wishes, of both tax years (ITA 2007 s 64). Unrestricted relief for trading losses against general income is not available unless:

(i) the trade is commercial (ITA 2007 s 66); and

(ii) the individual spends an average of more than 10 hours a week personally engaged in activities of the trade (ITA 2007 ss 74A and 74C).

The first condition is met if the trade is carried on throughout the period on a commercial basis and with a view to the realisation of profits.

Where an individual incurs a loss from carrying on a trade in a non-active capacity, ie spending an average of less than ten hours a week personally engaged in activities of the trade, there is an annual limit of £25,000 on the total amount of sideways loss relief that the individual can claim. That £25,000 limit applies to the total of any losses arising in the year from all trades carried on by the individual in a non-active capacity (ITA 2007 s 74A).

Where a person carries on alone or in partnership a trade profession or vocation, and makes a loss from that activity in the year, and the loss arises directly or indirectly in consequence of or in connection with relevant tax avoidance arrangements, no sideways loss relief or capital gains relief is available in respect of the loss (ITA 2007 s 74ZA).

Where claims are to be made for both the current and the previous tax years, relief may be given in the order specified by the claimant. The trade does not have to have been carried on in the previous year. If relief is claimed in a tax year both for a loss of that year and a loss carried back from the following year, the current year's loss is relieved first (ITA 2007 s 65).

Losses are calculated using the *same basis periods* as are used for calculating profits, for claims under general income (ITA 2007 s 64) and early trade-loss relief (ITA 2007 s 72) (ITA 2007 ss 61, 62). Where a loss would otherwise enter into the calculations for two tax years, for example in the first year of business or on a change of accounting date, it is taken into account only in the first year.

(c) For new businesses, relief may be claimed under early trade-loss relief (ITA 2007 s 72) where losses are incurred in the first four tax years. For details see **Example E2**.

(d) A general income (ITA 2007 s 64) claim may be extended to include set-off against capital gains, in either or both of the tax year of loss and the previous year (ITA 2007 s 71). The claim against income of the claim year must be made first (personal allowances therefore being wasted) and the loss available to set against capital gains is also reduced by any other loss relief claimed, for example under general income claim (ITA 2007 s 64) in the previous year or by carry back under early trade-loss relief (ITA 2007 s 72) in a new business. The amount of capital gains *available* to relieve the trading loss is the amount of the capital gains of the relevant year after deducting current and brought forward capital losses, ignoring any later claim that affects the chargeable gains for the year (TGCA 1992 s 261C). Having identified the amount *available* for relief in this way, that amount is then treated as an allowable capital loss of the relevant year and is therefore relieved *in priority* to brought forward capital losses (TCGA 1992 s 261B). Where there are no losses brought forward, the claim may mean wasting all or part of the annual capital gains exemption. Where there are capital losses brought forward this will sometimes avoid wasting annual exemption, but in some cases there would be no immediate tax saving and it would be a question of whether the taxpayer wanted to have unrelieved trading losses carried forward or unrelieved capital losses carried forward.

In most instances it would probably be preferable to have unrelieved trading losses carried forward rather than capital losses, but if the business had closed down, the reverse would apply. If a later claim, such as a claim to business assets roll-over relief, reduces the amount of the gains against which ITA 2007 s 71 relief has been claimed, the ITA 2007 s 71 losses which thereby become unrelieved are carried forward for relief against later gains, but they cannot be relieved in any tax year after the tax year in which the trade ceases (TGCA 1992 s 261B(7)(b)). Such losses must therefore be separately identified in the amount of unrelieved capital losses carried forward (see **Example L4**).

(e) The capital gain tax rate for basic rate taxpayers is 10%. Those liable to income tax at higher and additional rate pay capital gains tax at 20% although gains on residential property are charged at 18% and 28%.. Basic rate taxpayers can use the balance of their income tax basic rate band to secure capital gains tax rate of 10%, thereafter paying 20% on the balance of gains. Losses and the annual exemption can be set off in the most beneficial way.

(f) Where a business has ceased, terminal trade-loss relief may be claimed under ITA 2007 s 89 in respect of the loss of the last twelve months of trading (see **Example E3**).

*Time limits for claims etc*

(2) A valid loss claim must state the source of the loss, the year of loss, and either the year of claim or the statutory reference under which the relief is claimed. The time limit for loss claims under general income (ITA 2007 s 64) and early trade (ITA 2007 s 72) is one year from 31 January following the tax year of loss. The time limit for claims under carry-forward (ITA 2007 s 83) and terminal relief ITA 2007 s 89 is four years from 31 January following the tax year of loss/cessation. Late claims cannot be accepted, but in very limited circumstances HMRC may grant relief as if a claim had been made within the time limit (see SACM10035).

HMRC have stated that where claims are made under general income (ITA 2007 s 64) both against the current year's and the previous year's income, the loss will be dealt with according to the order in which the claims are made. If the claim relating to the previous year were made first, the loss would be set against the previous year's income first. If both claims were made together the loss would be set off according to the order specified by the claimant. Where, however, relief is claimed in one tax year in respect of a loss both of the current year and of the following year, the current year's loss is relieved first (ITA 2007 s 65).

*Capital allowances*

(3) Capital allowances are automatically included in loss claims, since they are deducted as trading expenses in arriving at the trading result. There is some flexibility, in that some capital allowances may be wholly or partly disclaimed. See **Examples C7** and **C8** for further details on capital allowances.

*Class 4 national insurance contributions and trading losses*

(4) Class 4 national insurance contributions are payable on profits above the lower threshold, as indicated in the Example, and they are included in the calculation of payments of account and balancing payments (or repayments) under self-assessment. Although a trading loss may be set against non-trading income following a claim under general income ITA 2007 s 64, Class 4 national insurance contributions are based solely on trading profits and losses can only reduce trading profits for Class 4 purposes to nil. Any part of the loss set against non-trading income for tax purposes under ITA 2007 s 64 may be carried forward to reduce future profits for Class 4 NIC purposes. The self-assessment return provides a working sheet to calculate the appropriate adjustment to be made in the return. For detailed notes on national insurance contributions see **Example H1**.

*Effect of carry back claims on payments on account and repayment supplement*

(5) Carrying back a loss for relief in an earlier year has an unwelcome effect on payments on account. The tax saving from the carry back claim is *calculated* by reference to the tax rates of the earlier year, but relief is given *in relation to* the later year (TMA 1970 Sch 1B). Since the tax of the earlier year is not altered, the claim does not affect payments on account for the loss year (although the refund flowing from the loss claim may enable those payments to be discharged or repaid). Nor does it affect the payments on account for the next following year, which are based on the tax *assessed* for the loss year.

Similarly, repayment supplement on any repayment arising out of a carry back claim does not relate to the payment dates for the carry back year. Supplement is not payable unless the claim is given effect after 31 January following the loss year, and in that event it runs from that 31 January (see **Example G2** for an illustration).

*Losses and registered pension scheme contributions*

(6) See **Example A6 explanatory note 13** for the effect of loss claims on earnings for registered pension scheme contributions.

*Effect of restriction on income tax reliefs*

(7) Under ITA 2007 s 24A (as introduced by FA 2013), relief for trade losses against general income under ITA 2007 s 64 is among the list of reliefs which are subject to an annual aggregate limit of £50,000 or, if greater, 25% of the individual's adjusted total income for the tax year. The amount of any ITA 2007 s 64 claim that is utilised against profits of the same trade are ignored in applying the cap on reliefs, and may be allowed in addition to the capped loss (see part (b) of this Example).

A taxpayer's adjusted income is the total income for the tax year plus the amount of any deductions given for payroll giving less the gross amount of any pension contributions qualifying for relief under FA 2004 s 192(1) and the amount of any deductions for relief under FA 2004 ss 193(4) or 194(1).

The cap on income tax reliefs operates independently of the rules for set-off of losses for Class 4 NIC purposes, which continue to look simply at the amount of the trading loss and set this against the profits of the same trade.

Relief for trade losses against capital gains tax is not included in cap on income tax reliefs, so any trade loss not set against general income under ITA 2007 s 64 because of the operation of the cap on income tax reliefs, may still be used against capital gains tax liability under ITA 2007 s 71.

*Overlap profits and overlap period*

(8) Under the current year basis, care needs to be taken in the calculation of overlap profits and the overlap period.

ITTOIA 2005, s 204 defines an overlap profit as profits which arise in a period which falls within two basis periods (overlap periods may be calculated in days, months, or months and fractions of months providing the chosen method is used consistently). HMRC's guidance states that any overlap period must be identified as such, even if it shows a loss, and the period must be aggregated with any subsequent overlap period as in part (c) of this Example. This affects the amount of overlap relief that may be claimed where more than 12 months' profit is being taxed in one year because of a change of accounting date,

(9) Transitional overlap profits qualifying for relief on the change to the current year basis (see **Example C4 explanatory note 8**) are treated as overlap profits (ITTOIA 2005, Sch 2, para 52).

(10) As indicated in **explanatory note 1(b)**, ITA 2007 s 64 losses under the current year basis are calculated for the same periods as profits (ITA 2007 ss 61–62). Where, therefore, there is an accounting period of more than 12 months showing a loss, the loss is the loss of the tax year in which that accounting period ends. The loss in such an extended basis period is increased by the appropriate amount of overlap relief.

In **part (d)** of this Example, the long accounting period does not in itself show a loss, but the profit is turned into a loss by the overlap relief deduction. The change of accounting date to a date nearer to 5 April enhances the available loss relief, and also has the effect of turning a profit into a loss.

# Question

You have been consulted by Rod Bridges who commenced business as an engineering consultant on 1 August 2015. He had previously been employed, his taxable salary being:

| | |
|---|---|
| 2012/13 | £45,000 |
| 2013/14 | £35,000 |
| 2015/16 | £35,000 |

He was unemployed from 6 April 2015 to 1 August 2015, receiving taxable state benefits of £2,785.

He has a part-time bookkeeper who has prepared a draft profit and loss account to 31 March 2017 covering the first 20 months' trading which showed:

| | | £ |
|---|---|---|
| Fees receivable | | 27,384 |
| *Less*: Office rent, rates and insurance | 9,344 | |
| Office salaries | 7,527 | |
| Travelling expenses | 1,210 | |
| Motor expenses | 4,740 | |
| Stationery, postages and telephone | 2,079 | |
| Professional indemnity insurance | 2,400 | |
| General expenses | 385 | |
| | | (27,685) |
| Loss for the period | | (301) |

You ascertain:

(i) On 1 August 2015 Bridges bought a motor car for £15,400 which he used both for business and private purposes as to three-quarters and one-quarter respectively. The car's emissions are 125g/km.

(ii) At the same time he bought a computer and printer for £2,600 and subsequently purchased a scanner in August 2016 for £600. The scanner has been included in stationery in the accounts.

(iii) Although expenses accrued evenly over the entire period, of the total fees receivable only £5,617 related to the first eight months.

(iv) Bridges also has savings income as follows:

| | *Building society interest (gross amounts)* | *Dividends (including dividend tax credits where applicable)* |
|---|---|---|
| | £ | £ |
| 2012/13 | 2,100 | 1,300 |
| 2013/14 | 1,400 | 600 |
| 2014/15 | 1,000 | 920 |
| 2015/16 | 2,500 | 1,100 |
| 2016/17 | 1,400 | 300* |

* No tax credit available in 2016/17

Assume the savings income and dividend income remains the same for 2017/18 to 2019/20 ie interest of £1,400 and dividends £300.

(v) Bridges is registered for VAT and all amounts are shown net of recoverable input tax.

(vi) Bridges informed HMRC of his self-employment in October 2015. He received a 2015/16 tax return in April 2016, but has not yet completed it.

(vii) You have agreed with Bridges to advise on the optimum tax claims, and will prepare accounts either to 31 March 2016 (and 2017) or for 20 months to 31 March 2017.

Tax data (in addition to that in the front of this book):

| | *2012/13* | *2013/14* | *2014/15* | *2015/16* |
|---|---|---|---|---|
| | £ | £ | £ | £ |
| Personal allowance | 8,105 | 9,440 | 10,000 | 10,600 |
| Tax rates: | | | | |
| Savings rate limit | 2,710 | 2,790 | 2,880 | 5,000 |
| Basic rate limit | 34,370 | 32,010 | 31,865 | 31,785 |
| Savings starting rate* | 20% | 20% | 20% | 0% |
| Dividend rate on income up to basic rate limit | 10% | 10% | 10% | 10% |

40% higher rate tax or dividend upper rate of 32.5% apply between the basic rate limit and £150,000. 45% additional rate or dividend additional rate of 37.5% (50% and 42.5% respectively in 2011/12 and 2012/13).

*If taxable non-savings income is above the savings rate limit, the starting rate is not applicable.

Advise Bridges on how to finalise his draft accounts for submission to HMRC, and on his optimum loss claim(s), and compute the tax payable or repayable for 2015/16 and 2016/17.

# Answer

The alternatives suggested are to complete accounts for two separate periods of eight and twelve months, or to complete accounts for 20 months to 31 March 2017.

The profits or losses and tax payable under each alternative are:

## (1) Two Accounts

| | | *8 months to 31.3.16* | *12 months to 31.3.17* |
|---|---|---|---|
| | £ | £ | £ |
| Fee income | | 5,617 | 21,767 |
| Expenses | 27,685 | | |
| *Less*: Scanner | (600) | | |
| One-quarter car expenses | (1,185) | | |
| Divisible 8: 12 | 25,900 | (10,360) | (15,540) |
| Capital allowances (see below) | | (3,986) | (2,429) |
| | | Loss (8,729) | Profit 3,798 |

### Capital allowances

| | *Car* | *Business use* | *Pool* | *Total allowances* |
|---|---|---|---|---|
| | £ | | £ | £ |
| Period 1.8.15 to 31.3.16: | | | | |
| Purchases | 15,400 | | 2,600 | |
| Qualifying AIA | | | (2,600) | 2,600 |
| WDA at 18% × 8/12 | (1,848) | × 75% | | 1,386 |
| | 13,552 | | Nil | 3,986 |
| Period 1.4.16 to 31.3.17: | | | | |
| WDA @ 18% | (2,439) | × 75% | | 1,829 |
| Addition Aug 2016 | | | 600 | |
| Qualifying AIA | | | (600) | 600 |
| WDV c/fwd | 11,113 | | Nil | |
| | | | | 2,429 |

### Taxable profits

| | | £ |
|---|---|---|
| 2015/16 (1.8.15 to 31.3.16) | | – |
| Loss in basis period | 8,729 | |
| ITA 2007 s 72 loss claim 2012/13 | (8,729) | |
| 2016/17 (yr to 31.3.17) | | 3,798 |

## Tax repayable

Taxable income:

| | 2012/13 | 2015/16 | 2016/17 |
|---|---|---|---|
| | £ | £ | £ |
| Employment income/Unemployment benefit | 45,000 | 2,785 | – |
| Trading income | | – | 3,798 |
| Building society interest | 2,100 | 2,500 | 1,400 |
| Dividends (including tax credits where appropriate) | 1,300 | 1,100 | 300 |
| | 48,400 | 6,385 | 5,498 |
| *Less*: Loss relief under ITA 2007 s 72 | (8,729) | | |
| | 39,671 | | |
| *Less*: personal allowance | (8,105) | (10,600) | (11,000) |
| | 31,566 | Nil | Nil |

Tax repayable following loss claim:

| | | | | 2012/13 Without loss claim | 2012/13 With loss claim | 2014/15 | 2016/17 |
|---|---|---|---|---|---|---|---|
| | | | | £ | £ | £ | £ |
| Taxable income (£48,400 – £8,105) | | | | 40,295 | 31,556 | | |
| *Before loss* | *With loss* | | Tax rate | | | | |
| £34,370 | £28,156 | @ | 20% | 6,874 | 5,631 | | |
| | £2,100 | @ | 20% | | 420 | | |
| | £1,300 | @ | 10% | | 130 | | |
| £2,525 | | @ | 40% | 1,010 | | | |
| £2,100 | | @ | 40% | 840 | | | |
| £1,300 | | @ | 32.5% | 422 | | | |
| £40,295 | £31,556 | | | | | | |
| Tax due | | | | 9,146 | 6,181 | Nil | Nil |
| Tax repayable on loss claim | | | | | (2,965) | | |
| Tax deducted at source from interest | | | | | | (500) | — |
| Total tax repayable (£2,965 + £500) = £3,465 | | | | | | | |

**Notes:**

Although Bridges has earnings below the Class 2 national insurance contributions exemption limits (2015/16 £5,965), repayment for 2015/16 had to be claimed by 31 January 2017 (SI 2001/1004, reg 47). From 2015/16 Class 2 contributions are collected via the self assessment tax return. Bridges' earnings are below the small profits threshold so no Class 2 contributions would be due for 2016/17. However, it is possible that Bridges would prefer to maintain a full national insurance record for maximum benefits.

No Class 4 contributions are due, but as the loss has been fully relieved against non-trading income, an equivalent loss can be carried forward for Class 4 purposes from 2015/16 to 2016/17. After deducting £3,798 in that year (on which no contributions would in fact have been payable), £4,931 of the loss remains to be carried forward to 2017/18. Relief must be taken against the first available trading profits from any trade.

## (2) One Set of Accounts

| | *20 months to 31.3.16* |
|---|---|
| | £ |
| Loss per draft accounts | (301) |
| Add: Scanner | 600 |
| One-quarter car expenses | 1,185 |
| | 1,484 |
| Less Capital allowances (see below) | (6,415) |
| Revised loss | (4,931) |

### Capital allowances

| | *Car* | | *Pool* | *Total allowances* |
|---|---|---|---|---|
| | £ | | £ | £ |
| Period 1.8.15 to 31.7.16: | | | | |
| Purchases | 15,400 | | 2,600 | |
| Qualifying for AIA | | | (2,600) | 2,600 |
| WDA 18% | (2,772) | × 75% | | 2,079 |
| | | | | 4,679 |
| WDV c/fwd | 12,628 | | Nil | |
| Period 1.8.16 to 31.3.17: | | | | |
| WDA ($^8/_{12}$ × 18%) | (1,515) | × 75% | | 1,136 |
| Addition | | | 600 | |
| AIA | | | (600) | 600 |
| WDV c/fwd | 11,113 | | Nil | |
| | | | | 6,415 |

**Taxable profits**

| | £ | £ |
|---|---|---|
| 2015/16 (1.8.15 to 5.4.16) | | |
| Loss in basis period 8/20 × £4,931 | 1,972 | |
| ITA 2007 s 72 loss claim 2012/13 | (1,972) | |
| | | Nil |
| 2016/17 (yr to 31.3.17) | | |
| Loss in basis period 12/20 × £4,931 | 2,959 | |
| ITA 2007 s 72 loss claim 2013/14 | (2,959) | |
| | | Nil |

**Tax repayable**

| | *2013/14* | *2014/15* | *2015/16* | *2016/17* |
|---|---|---|---|---|
| | £ | £ | £ | £ |
| Employment income/ Unemployment benefit | 45,000 | 35,000 | 2,785 | – |
| Trading income | | | – | – |
| Building Society Interest | 2,100 | 1,400 | 2,500 | 1,400 |
| Dividends (including tax credits where applicable) | 1,300 | 600 | 1,100 | 300 |
| | 48,400 | 37,000 | 6,385 | 1,700 |
| *Less*: Loss relief under 72 | (1,972) | (2,959) | | |
| | 46,428 | 34,041 | | |
| *Less*: Personal allowance | (8,105) | (10,000) | (10,600) | (11,000) |
| | 38,323 | 24,041 | Nil | Nil |
| Tax repayable: | | | | |
| £1,972 @ 40% | (788) | | | |
| £2,959 @ 20% | | (592) | | |
| *Tax deducted at source repayable to Bridges* | | | | |
| Building society interest @ 20% | | | (500) | — |
| *Total repayable*: (£788 + £592 + £500) | £1,880 | | | |

**Note:**

Similar comments apply re Class 2 national insurance contributions as for separate accounts. For Class 4, again the loss has not been relieved against trading income, the loss carried forward being £4,931.

## Overall conclusion on accounts submission

As the income tax repayment is £2.965 – £1,880 = £1,085 lower with one account compared with two accounts, it is advisable to submit separate accounts to HMRC.

## Explanatory Notes

*Notifying new sources of income and sending in tax returns*

(1) The rules for opening years' assessments do not prevent a taxpayer deciding the period covered by the first accounts. If a tax return is not received, however, HMRC must be notified not later than 5 October following the tax year that a new source of income has been acquired, ie by 5 October 2016 in the case of Bridges. For further details see **Example C4 explanatory note 5**. Failure to notify before 31 January following the end of the tax year of commencement results in a penalty geared to the contributions lost and the behaviour leading to the failure: careless, deliberate but not concealed or deliberate and concealed (SI 2001/1004, regs 87A-87F).

Although Bridges notified HMRC in good time, he has to send in his 2015/16 tax return by 31 January 2017. Failure to send in the return currently attracts a fixed penalty of £100, rising after six months (see **Example G2 explanatory note 12**), followed by automatic daily penalties once the return is three months late (see **Example G2 explanatory note 12**).

*Effect of basis periods: overlap relief, cessation*

(2) For the basis periods in the opening years see **Example C4 explanatory note 4**.

Where accounts are drawn up to 31 March annually, the problem of overlap profits does not arise. If accounts are drawn up other than to 31 March (or 5 April), and the accounts for the opening period show a loss, then it is probable that the overlap relief available will be nil. For example, if Bridges had drawn up accounts for the 21 months to 30 April 2017 showing a loss of £4,931, his taxable profits would be:

| | | | |
|---|---|---|---|
| 2015/16 | 1.8.15 to 5.4.16 | | Nil |
| | ITA 2007 s 72 loss available 8/21 (carry back to 2012/13) | £1,878 | |
| 2015/16 | 6.4.16 to 5.4.17 | | Nil |
| | ITA 2007 s 72 loss available 12/21 (carry back to 2013/14) | £2,818 | |
| 2016/17 | yr to 30.4.17 | | Nil |
| | ITA 2007 s 72 loss available 1/21 (carry back to 2014/15) | £235 | |

(Overlap period 1.5.16 to 5.4.17 = 11 mths shows a loss, therefore overlap relief is nil. There is no doubling up of losses and the loss for the period 1.5.16 to 5.4.17 is treated as arising in 2016/17 only.)

As a consequence of the above, Bridges would waste most of his personal allowance in 2017/18.

If, for example, Bridges had ceased business on 31 March 2020, having made profits as follows, assuming the same profits for years/periods to 31 March or 30 April for simplicity:

| | |
|---|---|
| Year to 31 March or 30 April 2018 | £30,000 |
| Year to 31 March or 30 April 2019 | £46,000 |
| Year or 11 months to 31 March 2020 | £27,500 |

With a 31 March year-end, he would have been taxed on those profits in 2017/18, 2018/19 and 2019/20, amounting to £103,500, with possibly a small higher rate tax liability in 2018/19.

With 30 April year-end, he would have taxable profits as follows:

| | | £ | £ |
|---|---|---|---|
| 2017/18 | | | – |
| 2017/18 | | | 30,000 |
| 2017/18 | Yr to 30.4.2019 | 46,000 | |
| | 11 mths to 31.3.2020 | 27,500 | |
| | | 73,500 | |
| | *Less*: overlap relief | – | |
| | | | 73,500 |
| | | | 103,500 |

Although the total assessable profits are the same with either year-end, it is clear that a significant amount of higher rate tax would be payable for 2019/20 with the 30 April year-end. This would need to be set against the benefit of paying no tax in 2017/18 and paying less tax in 2018/19. The effect on Class 4 national insurance contributions also needs to be considered (see **explanatory note 7** below).

*Early trade losses relief*

(3) Where a loss is incurred in any of the first four tax years of a new business, relief may be claimed under ITA 2007 s 72 against the *total income* of the previous three tax years, *earliest* first (ITA 2007 s 73). ITA 2007 ss 61-62 provide that losses made in a tax year means losses made in the basis period for the tax year. This is subject to ITA 2007 s 63, which prohibits double counting.

(4) As with a general income claim (ITA 2007 s 64), relief cannot be claimed under ITA 2007 s 72 unless the trade is conducted on a commercial basis (ITA 2007 s 74). It is also necessary to show that a profit could reasonably have been expected in the loss period or within a reasonable time thereafter.

Under ITA 2007 s 24A (as introduced by FA 2013), early trade losses relief under ITA 2007 s 72 is among the list of reliefs which are subject to an annual aggregate limit of £50,000 or, if greater, 25% of the individual's adjusted total income for the tax year. The amount of any ITA 2007 s 72 claim that is utilised against profits of the same trade are ignored in applying the cap on reliefs, and may be allowed in addition to the capped loss. See **Example E1 explanatory note 10** for more information.

*Capital allowances*

(5) Capital allowances are treated as trading expenses of the accounting period and writing down allowances are proportionately reduced or increased if the period is less than or more than 12 months. If, however, the period exceeds 18 months, it is split into a 12-month period plus the remainder, as illustrated in the Example in relation to the 20-month account (see **Example C6 part** (e)).

*Repayment supplement*

(6) For losses, repayment supplement on repayments arising from carry back claims is payable from 31 January following the loss year (TMA 1970 Sch 1B). It runs to the date the repayment order is issued (see **Example G2**).

*National insurance*

(7) The amounts payable (using 2016/17 rates for later years) with a 31 March year-end would be:

| | *2015/16* | *2016/17* | *2017/18* | *2018/19* | *2019/20* |
|---|---|---|---|---|---|
| | £ | £ | £ | £ | £ |
| Class 2 (assuming not abolished) | 98* | 146 | 146 | 146 | 146 |
| Class 4 | – | – | | | |
| (£30,000 – £4,931 – £8,060) @ 9% | | | 1,531 | | |

| | | 2015/16 | 2016/17 | 2017/18 | 2018/19 | 2019/20 |
|---|---|---|---|---|---|---|
| | | £ | £ | £ | £ | £ |
| (£43,000 – £8,060) | @ 9% | | | | 3,145 | |
| (£46,000 – £43,000) | @ 2% | | | | 60 | |
| (£27,500 – £8,060) | @ 9% | | | | | 1,750 |
| | | 98 | 146 | 1,677 | 3,351 | 1,896 |
| Total | £7,168 | | | | | |

* Subject to a claim for repayment for small earnings exemption if made. Note that as Bridges only commenced his self-employment on 1 August 2015, he is only liable for 35 weeks at £2.80 per week in 2015/16. For 2016/17 Bridges is within the small profits threshold for Class 2 and no refund is due because the contributions are not collected until after the end of the tax year, when the profits for the year are known.

Whereas with a 30 April year end, the liability would be:

| | | | 2015/16 | 2016/17 | 2017/18 | 2018/19 | 2019/20 |
|---|---|---|---|---|---|---|---|
| | | | £ | £ | £ | £ | £ |
| Class 2 | | | 98* | 146 | 146 | 146 | 146 |
| Class 4 | | | – | – | | | |
| (£30,000 – £4,931 – £8,060) | @ 9% | | | | | 1,531 | |
| (£43,000 – £8,060) | @ 9% | | | | | | 3,145 |
| (£73,500 – £43,000) | @ 2% | | | | | | 610 |
| | | | 98 | 146 | 146 | 1,677 | 3,755 |
| Total | | £5,822 | | | | | |

* Subject to a claim for repayment for small earnings exemption if made. Note that as Bridges only commenced his self-employment on 1 August 2015, he is only liable for 35 weeks at £2.80 per week in 2015/16. For 2016/17 Bridges is within the small profits threshold for Class 2 and no refund is due because the contributions are not collected until after the end of the tax year, when the profits for the year are known.

This gives a saving of £1,346 (£7,168 – £5,822).

*Effect of accounting date on loss claims*

(8) There are points for and against drawing up accounts to a date early in the tax year (see **explanatory notes 2** and **7** above and **Example C5**). Where losses are concerned, drawing up accounts to 30 April restricts the losses that may be taken into account in ITA 2007 s 72 claims where successive losses are made in the early years of a new business. For example, if such a business started on 1 May 2014, the first accounts being either for the 11 months to 31 March 2015 or for the 12 months to 30 April 2015, the position regarding ITA 2007 s 72 claims would be:

| | *Accounts to 31 March* | *Accounts to 30 April* |
|---|---|---|
| 2014/15 | Loss of 11 months to 31.3.15 | 11/12 × loss to 30.4.15 |
| 2015/16 | Loss of yr to 31.3.16 | 1/12 × loss to 30.4.15 |
| 2016/17 | Loss of yr to 31.3.17 | Loss of yr to 30.4.16 |
| 2017/18 | Loss of yr to 31.3.18 | Loss of yr to 30.4.17 |

The ITA 2007 s 72 loss claims would cover 47 months with the 31 March year-end and only 36 months with the 30 April year-end.

Overall, if there is a loss in the opening period which will cause personal allowances and lower rate bands to be wasted, and it is expected that significant amounts of higher rate tax will be payable in the near future, it is advisable to use a 31 March (or 5 April) year-end.

*Anti-avoidance provisions*

(9) ITA 2007 s 74 contains anti-avoidance provisions to prevent husband and wife transferring a trade from one to the other after the first four years of assessment and effectively starting again.

ITA 2007 s 110 onwards restrict the relief for trading losses in the first four years of assessment to capital contributions made by the partner where the claimant is a partner who does not spend a significant amount of time personally engaged in the trade. See **Example E4 part** (e).

ITA 2007 s 74A contains anti-avoidance provisions to prevent the offset of losses against other income by sole traders. The restrictions apply where the sole trade is not carried on by the individual spending a significant amount of time personally engaged in the trade, which is carried on on a commercial basis with a view to the realisation of profits as a result of the trading activities. This parallels the similar provision for partners. The limit on relief is £25,000 in total in any tax year, but there is no relief at all if the loss arises in connection with tax avoidance.

*Miscellaneous*

(10) Bridges needs to show his accounting results in his self-assessment tax returns in standard format. For an illustration see **Example C2**. For capital allowances on plant see **Example C6**, for the disclaimer rules see **Example C7**.

# Question

(a) Bob Sewell has been trading as a sole trader for many years, drawing up accounts to 30 September each year. As a result of serious decline in trade he decided to cease trading at 31 January 2017.

His results after capital allowances for the last few periods of trading have been:

| *Profit (loss)* | £ |
|---|---|
| Year ended 30 September 2013 | 21,000 |
| Year ended 30 September 2014 | 15,000 |
| Year ended 30 September 2015 | 6,000 |
| Year ended 30 September 2016 | 5,000 |
| Four months to 31 January 2017 | (20,000) |

Overlap relief available was £11,579.

(i) Compute the amount of losses arising and show how these losses may be relieved.

(ii) State what alternative form of relief is available to Sewell if the trade were to be transferred to a limited company solely in exchange for shares in the company.

(b) From the following details of the income of Karen Waters, a sole trader who has been carrying on the business of light engineering since 1980, show details of all taxable profits covered by the figures given and how relief for the loss on cessation may be obtained.

Tax adjusted profits or losses (after capital allowances):

| | *Profit* £ | *Loss* £ |
|---|---|---|
| Year to 30 June 2013 | 94,100 | |
| Year to 30 June 2014 | 60,500 | |
| Year to 30 June 2015 | 13,200 | |
| Year to 30 June 2016 | 8,000 | |
| Nine months to 31 March 2017(when business ceased) | | 100,600 |

Overlap relief available was £9,900.

Ms Waters has no income other than from the business.

(c) Ken Tranter ceased business on 30 June 2016. His results in the period leading up to the cessation were as follows:

| | *Profit* £ | *Loss* £ |
|---|---|---|
| Year to 31 December 2013 | 10,000 | |
| Year to 31 December 2014 | 15,000 | |
| Year to 31 December 2015 | 6,000 | |
| Six months to 30 June 2016 | | 21,200 |
| Overlap relief available was | | 5,800 |

Tranter had previously had no other sources of income, but he took up employment after ceasing trading and earned £15,000 in 2016/17.

Show the alternative loss claims available to Tranter and calculate his tax position for the relevant years. For tax allowances and rates and Class 4 national insurance rates for years before 2016/17 see **Example E2.**

# Answer

## (a)

### (i) *Bob Sewell – terminal loss relief*

The position before loss relief is as follows:

| | | | £ |
|---|---|---|---|
| 2013/14 | yr to 30.9.13 | | 21,000 |
| 2014/15 | yr to 30.9.14 | | 15,000 |
| 2015/16 | yr to 30.9.15 | | 6,000 |
| 2016/17 | 1.10.15 to 31.1.17 | | |
| | To 30.9.16 | 5,000 | |
| | To 31.1.17 | (20,000) | |
| | Loss | (15,000) | |

The whole of any available overlap relief is included in the terminal loss of the final tax year (see **explanatory note 6**).

The losses available for relief are calculated as follows (see **explanatory notes 1** to **6**):

#### General income

The loss of 2016/17 comprises the loss of £15,000 in the 16 months to 31 January 2017, augmented by the overlap relief of £11,579, giving a loss of £26,579. This loss can be set against general income in 2016/17 or 2015/16 under ITA 2007 s 64 (see **Example E1**).

#### Terminal trade loss relief

£5,000 of the loss has already been relieved against the profit of the year to 30 September 2016 in arriving at the 2016/17 nil self assessment and cannot be included in the terminal loss. The terminal loss is therefore as follows (ITA 2007 s 90):

| | | £ |
|---|---|---|
| Loss | 1.2.16 – 5.4.16: | |
| | Profit therefore | – |
| Loss | 6.4.16 – 31.1.17: | |
| | To 30.9.16 6/12 × £5,000 profit | (2,500) |
| | To 31.1.17 (£20,000 – £2,500 loss already relieved against balance of profit) | 17,500 |
| | Overlap relief | 11,579 |
| | | £26,579 |

The same amount is thus available for relief both under ITA 2007 s 64 and ITA 2007 s 89.

If Sewell has no other income the terminal loss would be relieved against trading profits under ITA 2007 ss 89, 91 as follows:

| | | £ |
|---|---|---|
| 2016/17 | | – |
| 2015/16 | | 6,000 |
| 2014/15 | | 15,000 |
| 2013/14 | (reducing taxable profit to £15,421) | 5,579 |
| | | 26,579 |

Had any loss remained unrelieved after setting against the 2013/14 profit, no further relief would be available.

Personal allowances of 2014/15 and 2015/16 would be wasted.

If Sewell has other income, the ITA 2007 s 64 claim would be against the *total* income of 2016/17 and/or 2015/16. Unless the other income is very substantial, however, the terminal loss claim would still be preferable, because it would leave the other income to cover personal allowances.

### (ii) *Alternative relief available to Sewell*

If the trade were transferred to a limited company solely in exchange for shares, then so long as the shares continued to be held, the loss could be carried forward and relieved against income received by Sewell from the company, both earned income (eg director's fees) and unearned income (eg dividends) (ITA 2007 86). See **explanatory note 7**.

## (b) Karen Waters – Taxable profits and relief for losses

The tax position before relief for the loss on cessation is as follows:

| | | £ |
|---|---|---|
| 2013/14 | Yr to 30.6.13 | 94,100 |
| 2014/15 | Yr to 30.6.14 | 60,500 |
| 2015/16 | Yr to 30.6.15 | 13,200 |
| 2016/17 | 21 months to 31.3.17 | Nil |

Claims under ITA 2007 s 64 are not relevant, since Ms Waters has no income other than from the business. However, she can claim terminal loss relief under ITA 2007 s 89. The position is therefore as follows:

### Terminal trade loss relief

| | | | £ |
|---|---|---|---|
| Loss 1.4.16 – 5.4.16: | (this period shows a small profit) | | Nil |
| Loss 6.4.16 – 31.3.17 | | | |
| 6.4.16 – 30.6.16 | Profit 86/365 × £8,000 | (1,885) | |
| 1.7.16 – 31.3.17 | Loss | 100,600 | |
| | | 98,715 | |
| | Overlap relief | 9,900 | |
| Terminal loss available for relief | | | 108,615 |
| Set against: | | | |

| | |
|---|---|
| 2015/16 profits | (13,200) |
| 2014/15 profits | (60,500) |
| 2013/14 profits (balance) | (34,915) |
| | Nil |

Leaving profits taxable in 2013/14 of (£94,100 – £34,915) = £59,185

## (c) Ken Tranter – loss relief available on cessation of business

Before loss relief claims Tranter's taxable profits are as follows:

| | | | £ |
|---|---|---|---|
| 2013/14 | Yr to 31.12.13 | Profit | 10,000 |
| 2014/15 | Yr to 31.12.14 | Profit | 15,000 |
| 2015/16 | Yr to 31.12.15 | Profit | 6,000 |
| 2016/17 | Six mths to 30.6.16 | Loss | – |

### *If terminal trade loss relief is claimed followed by a claim for relief against general income*

*Terminal trade loss relief*

| | | £ |
|---|---|---|
| Loss 1.7.15 – 5.4.16: | | |
| Profit 1.7.15 – 31.12.15 6/12 × £6,000 | (3,000) | |
| Loss 1.1.16 – 5.4.16 3/6 × £21,200 | 10,600 | |
| | | 7,600 |
| Loss 6.4.16 – 30.6.16 3/6 × £21,200 | 10,600 | |
| Add overlap relief (see **explanatory note 5**) | 5,800 | |
| | | 16,400 |
| Terminal trade loss available for relief | | 24,000 |

Since there are no trading profits in 2016/17, the terminal loss will be relieved as follows (ITA 2007 ss 89, 91):

| | £ |
|---|---|
| 2015/16 | 6,000 |
| 2014/15 | 15,000 |
| 2013/14 (balance) | 3,000 |
| | 24,000 |

Leaving taxable profits in 2013/14 of (£10,000 – £3,000 =) £7,000.

*Relief against general income*

| | £ |
|---|---|
| Loss of 2016/17 (£21,200 + overlap relief £5,800) | 27,000 |
| *Less*: already relieved under s 89 | (24,000) |
| Loss available for relief | 3,000 |

Tranter's 2016/17 income of £15,000 (from new employment) will be reduced to £12,000 via a claim under ITA 2007 s 64.

## *If loss relief is claimed against general income, followed a terminal loss relief claim*

*Relief against general income*

| | £ |
|---|---|
| Loss of 2016/17 (£21,200 + overlap relief £5,800) | 27,000 |
| Set against 2016/17 employment income | (15,000) |
| Loss remaining unrelieved | 12,000 |

There would be no point in making a ITA 2007 s 64 claim for 2015/16 since there is no non-trading income and the terminal loss claim is available against the trading profits.

### Terminal trade loss relief

The part of the terminal loss relieved under ITA 2007 s 64 is regarded as being (£15,000 – £3,000) = £12,000, since £3,000 of the ITA 2007 s 64 loss is not included in the terminal loss (see **explanatory notes 2** and **5(b)**). The terminal loss is therefore as follows (ITA 2007 s 90):

| | £ | £ |
|---|---|---|
| Loss 1.7.15 – 5.4.16: | | |
| Profit 1.7.15 – 31.12.15 | (3,000) | |
| Loss 1.1.16 – 5.4.16 3/6 × £21,200 | 10,600 | |
| | 7,600 | |
| *Less*: already relieved under ITA 2007 s 64 | (7,600) | |
| | | – |
| Loss 6.4.16 – 30.6.16 as above | 16,400 | |
| *Less*: already relieved under ITA 2007 s 64 (£12,000 – £7,600) | (4,400) | |
| | | 12,000 |
| Terminal loss available for relief | | 12,000 |

This will be set against the 2015/16 profits of £6,000 and £6,000 of the 2014/15 profits of £15,000, leaving £9,000 taxable for that year.

## *Tax position with alternative loss claims*

*Taxable income after loss claims*

| | *Terminal loss relief first* | *Relief against general income first* |
|---|---|---|
| | £ | £ |
| 2013/14 | 7,000 | 10,000 |
| 2014/15 | – | 9,000 |
| 2015/16 | – | – |
| 2016/17 | 12,000 | – |
| | 19,000 | 19,000 |

*Tax and Class 4 national insurance contributions payable*

| | | | | | *Terminal loss first* £ | *Relief against general income first* £ |
|---|---|---|---|---|---|---|
| **Terminal loss relief first** | | | | | | |
| 2013/14 | (£7,000 – £9,440) | = 0 | tax | @ 20% | – | |
| | (£7,000 – £7,755) | = 0 | NI (Class 4) | @ 9% | – | |
| 2014/15 | Nil | = 0 | | | – | |
| 2015/16 | Nil | = 0 | | | – | |
| 2016/17 | (£12,000 – £11,000) | = £1,000 | tax | @ 20% | 200 | |
| | (£15,000 – £8,060) | = £6,940 | NI (Class1) | @ 12% | 833 | |
| **Section 64 claim first** | | | | | | |
| 2013/14 | (£10,000 – £9,440) | = £560 | tax | @ 20% | | 112 |
| | (£10,000 – £7,755) | = £2,245 | NI (Class 4) | @ 9% | | 202 |
| 2014/15 | (£9,000 – £10,000) | = 0 | tax | @ 20% | | – |
| | (£9,000 – £7,956) | = £1,044 | NI (Class 4) | @ 9% | | 94 |
| 2015/16 | Nil | = 0 | | | | – |
| | (£15,000 - £8,060) | = £6,940 | NI (Class 1) | @12% | | 833 |
| | | | | | 1,033 | 1,241 |

There is therefore a reduction of £208 (£1,241 - £1,033) in the tax and Class 4 national insurance contributions payable if the terminal loss claim is made first. Under self-assessment there is no longer any repayment supplement advantage from carry-back claims, and there is a disadvantage in terms of payments on account (see **Example E1 explanatory note 8**).

# Explanatory Notes

*Calculation of losses available for relief*

(1) Under the current year basis rules, losses under ITA 2007 s 64 and ITA 2007 s 72 are calculated not only in the same way as profits but also for the *same periods* (subject to excluding any loss already included in a previous tax year where basis periods overlap) (ITA 2007 ss 61–62). Any apportionment of losses or profits to basis periods may be computed by reference to days or any other length of period, provided the method chosen is used consistently (ITTOIA 2005, s 203(3), (4)). Apportionment by reference to months is illustrated in parts (a) and (c) of the Example, whereas part (b)shows apportionment by reference to days.

It is worth noting that the terminal loss rules have not been properly adapted to fit in with the accounting period treatment, and terminal losses still have to be calculated separately for the parts of the last 12 months falling up to and after the end of the tax year (ITA 2007 s 90). This may restrict the terminal loss available for relief where there is a profit in part of the last 12 months. This is illustrated in **part (c)** of the Example, where £3,000 of the loss of £21,200 in the last six months does not form part of the terminal loss, although Tranter does in fact get relief for it under ITA 2007 s 64 because he has other income in 2016/17. See **explanatory notes 2** and **5(a)**.

(2) Where more than one loss claim is available in respect of a loss, the strict position is that losses that reduce trading profits (such as terminal losses) take priority over losses that reduce total income (such as ITA 2007 s 64 losses). If, however, relief under ITA 2007 s 64 has become final before relief is given under ITA 2007 s 89, the ITA 2007 s 64 relief will not be altered. The HMRC Manuals state that in practice a taxpayer may choose which claim he wishes to become final first (BIM85080).

The effect of making alternative claims is shown in **part (c)** of the Example. The calculation of the terminal loss where the ITA 2007 s 64 claim is made first is not clear. The view has been taken that the amount of relief given under ITA 2007 s 64 may be regarded as covering first that part of the loss that is excluded from the terminal loss because of the way in which the terminal loss is calculated. This enables relief to be given overall for the full amount of the loss in that Example. It is considered that this approach would be acceptable to HMRC.

(3) In the calculation of NIC savings (as in the **part (c)** of the example), it has to be remembered that loss relief for the purposes of Class 4 NIC cannot be set against income from other sources in the same was a loss relief can be set against general income for tax purposes under ITA 2007 s 64. Thus Tranter remains liable to the same amount of Class 1 NIC on his employment income regardless of what claims are made in respect of his trading losses.

*Calculation of terminal trade loss and relief available*

(4) The terminal loss is calculated under ITA 2007 s 90 as follows:

(a) the loss (if any) made in the trade in the period beginning with the start of the final tax year and ending with the cessation; and

(b) the loss (if any) made in the trade in the period consisting of so much of the previous tax year as falls in the 12 months prior to the cessation.

(5) The following points should be noted:

(a) if 4 (a) or (b) is a profit it is treated as nil in the computation – it is *not* deducted from the terminal loss, as shown in **part (a)** of the Example. If, however, there is a profit for *part* of the period concerned, it is taken into account in *arriving at* the loss for (a) or (b), as shown in **parts (a)** and **(b)** of the Example;

(b) the terminal loss cannot include any loss for which relief has already been obtained (eg under ITA 2007 s 64 or ITA 2007 s 83). See **explanatory note 2** regarding the interpretation of this provision.

If a terminal loss claim is made, the loss is set first against the trading profits of the final tax year and then against the trading profits of the three previous tax years, latest first (ITA 2007 s 91). ITA 2007 s 92 provides relief for the terminal loss against interest and dividends from the trade where trade profits are insufficient to fully utilise the loss.

Note that because terminal loss relief is not a relief against general income, it is not affected by the cap on income tax reliefs in ITA 2007 s 24A and neither are these losses taken in account when deciding whether the cap is exceeded.

*Overlap relief*

(6) ITTOIA 2005, s 205 provides for overlap relief to be taken into account in computing the result of the *tax year of cessation*. This means that it does not need to be apportioned over the last 12 months in the terminal loss calculation. This is confirmed in HMRC's Helpsheet HS222, www.gov.uk/government/publications/how-to-calculate-your-taxable-profits-hs222-self-assessment-helpsheet in the section on 'Overlap Relief used this year'. For the calculation of transitional overlap relief, see **Example C4 explanatory note 8**.

*Transfer of a business to a company*

(7) Where a business is transferred to a company by a sole trader or partners in exchange solely or mainly for shares in the company, then it is provided by ITA 2007 s 86 that any income from the company, such as director's fees and dividends, can be regarded as trading income for the purposes of a carry-forward trade loss (ITA 2007 s 83) claim. This is the case provided that the business has been carried on and the shares held throughout the tax year for which the claim is made (or in the tax year in which the transfer takes place, for the whole of the remainder of that year). In practice HMRC give the relief providing at least 80% of the shares are retained (BIM85060).

# Question

(a) Sonny, Tyler and Don have been trading in partnership for many years sharing profits and losses after charging interest on capital and salaries in the proportions of one-half, one-fifth and three-tenths respectively, drawing up accounts to 30 April annually. Interest on capital amounts to £3,200, £2,260 and £940 respectively. Don is entitled to a salary of £16,000 and Sonny to a salary of £8,000.

The partnership results for the years to 30 April 2016 and 2017 are as follows:

| | | *Profit (loss)* £ |
|---|---|---|
| Year to 30 April | 2016 | 18,600 |
| | 2017 | (9,600) |

Show the tax allocation of trading profits and losses for the two years, and show what ITA 2007 s 64 claims may be made assuming that the partners have substantial other income.

(b) John, Paul and George have been partners in a firm of turf accountants for many years, drawing up accounts annually to 31 July and sharing profits and losses in the ratio 40:35:25. Profits and losses have been shared in these proportions since commencement. The accounts for recent periods, as adjusted for tax purposes, have shown the following profits and losses:

| | £ |
|---|---|
| Year to 31 July 2015 | 53,200 |
| Year to 31 July 2016 | 11,800 |
| Period to 31 January 2017 | (43,920) |
| Total of overlap profits of the firm for eight months from 1 August 1996 to 5 April 1997 | 19,867 |

On 31 January 2017 John retired due to ill health.

Calculate the taxable profits for 2015/16 and 2016/17 and show the allocation of these profits among the partners. Show also how the loss to 31 January 2017 is treated and indicate the loss claims available to each partner.

Ignore capital allowances.

(c) Graeme is a limited partner in a partnership and under the partnership agreement his share of the profits or losses of the business is 25%. His capital introduced was £10,000.

During the year to 31 March 2017 the partnership suffered a loss of £60,000.

Calculate Greame's share of the loss for income tax purposes.

(d) Victoria became a member of Becks LLP, a trading limited liability partnership, on 6 April 2011, introducing capital of £10,000 into the LLP. The LLP draws up accounts annually to 5 April. During the year ended 5 April 2017 Victoria made a further capital contribution of £27,000 for the purposes of the partnership's trade. Victoria has sufficient other income to claim full loss relief under ITA 2007 s 64 in all years. Victoria is not active in Becks LLP and spends very little of her time on this business.

The profit/losses allocated to Victoria are as follows:

| | Profit (loss) |
|---|---|
| | £ |
| Year to 5 April 2015 | (6,000) |
| Year to 5 April 2016 | (6,000) |
| Year to 5 April 2017 | (30,000) |
| Year to 5 April 2018 | 34,000 |

Set out the amounts of sideways loss relief available for each year.

(e) Richard and Judy commence trading as property developers on 6 April 2016. The partnership is funded by capital introduced of:

| | |
|---|---|
| Richard | £500,000 |
| Judy | £10,000 |

It is agreed that Richard be entitled to a salary of £50,000 and profits and losses be divided equally. Richard works full time in the business but Judy only works five hours per week, on average, for the partnership.

The results for the first three years are:

| | Profit (loss) |
|---|---|
| | £ |
| Year to 5 April 2017 | (100,000) |
| Year to 5 April 2018 | (30,000) |
| Year to 5 April 2019 | 80,000 |

On 31 March 2019 Judy contributes further capital of £20,000 for the purpose of the partnership's trade. Both Richard and Judy have sufficient other income to utilise their share of losses for all relevant years. They have made no capital withdrawals from the partnership.

Set out the amount of ITA 2007 ss 64 or 72 loss relief available for Richard and Judy for each year and the amount of loss relief carried forward after making maximum claims against other income.

# Answer

## (a) Sonny, Tyler and Don

### Profit of year to 30 April 2016

| | *Total* £ | *Sonny* £ | *Tyler* £ | *Don* £ |
|---|---|---|---|---|
| Interest on capital | 6,400 | 3,200 | 2,260 | 940 |
| Salaries | 24,000 | 8,000 | – | 16,000 |
| Balance 50:20:30 | (11,800) | (5,900) | (2,360) | (3,540) |
| | 18,600 | 5,300 | (100) | 13,400 |
| Eliminate Tyler's 'loss' £5,300 : £13,400 | | (28) | 100 | (72) |
| Division of taxable profit | | 5,272 | Nil | 13,328 |

The partners self assess individually on their profit shares in 2016/17 as above. See **explanatory note 4** for more on the elimination of Tyler's 'loss'.

### Loss of year to 30 April 2017 available for relief against general income

| | *Total* £ | *Sonny* £ | *Tyler* £ | *Don* £ |
|---|---|---|---|---|
| Interest on capital | 6,400 | 3,200 | 2,260 | 940 |
| Salaries | 24,000 | 8,000 | – | 16,000 |
| Balance 50:20:30 | (40,000) | (20,000) | (8,000) | (12,000) |
| | (9,600) | (8,800) | (5,740) | 4,940 |
| Eliminate Don's 'profit' £8,800 : £5,740 | | 2,990 | 1,950 | (4,940) |
| Final division of loss | | (5,810) | (3,790) | Nil |

See **explanatory note 4** for more on the elimination of Don's 'profit'.

Each partner's share of the loss is a loss of 2017/18 for ITA 2007 s 64 claims, relief for which may be claimed against total income of 2017/18 and/or 2016/17 (see **explanatory note 2**). Since they have substantial other income, they will be able to obtain full relief in either year. If relief is claimed against 2016/17 income, Sonny's loss of £5,810 would eliminate his 2016/17 profit of £5,272 and the balance of £538 would be set against his other income. Since Tyler's 2016/17 profit share was nil, his share of the loss of £3,790, would all be set against his other income. (The losses set against non-trading income would still be available to reduce the partners' later profit shares for calculating Class 4 national insurance contributions.)

Carrying back losses does not, however, reduce the tax of the earlier year (see **Examples G2** and **G3** for details). Relief is *calculated* by reference to the earlier year but is *given effect* in relation to the loss year. Furthermore, the tax saving through the carryback claim does not affect the calculation of payments on account for any year (although the refund flowing from the loss claim may enable payments on account to be discharged or repaid). Sonny and Tyler may prefer to claim relief against their 2017/18 income, providing the rate of tax saved was the same. This would then reduce the tax *self assessed* for that year, enabling 2017/18 payments on account to be repaid and affecting the calculation of payments on account for 2018/19.

## (b) John, Paul and George 2015/16 and 2016/17self assessments

Each partner is treated as if he carried on a separate notional trade, which ceases when he leaves the partnership, unless he continues the business on his own, in which case the actual date of cessation is taken. When John retires on 31 January 2017, therefore, his business is treated as having ceased and he can claim terminal loss relief if appropriate.

The accounting date has been changed by making up accounts to 31 January. Unless the partnership chooses to notify the change to HMRC, the accounts to 31 January 2017 could be regarded as interim (see **Example C5**). The next accounts could be made up for the six months to 31 July 2017 and the two sets of results amalgamated as far as Paul and George are concerned. On the assumption that the accounting date is in fact changed permanently, the position would be as follows:

### Individual self assessments 2015/16

The 2015/16 self assessments are based on the profit of the firm for the year to 31 July 2015, which is divided as follows:

| Total | John (40%) | Paul (35%) | George (25%) |
|---|---|---|---|
| £ | £ | £ | £ |
| 53,200 | 21,280 | 18,620 | 13,300 |

### Position for 2016/17

There will be nil self assessments in 2016/17, since the basis period runs from 1.8.15 to 31.1.17 and the combined result of the accounts of that period shows losses for each partner as follows:

| | Total | John (40%) | Paul (35%) | George (25%) |
|---|---|---|---|---|
| | £ | £ | £ | £ |
| Yr to 31.7.16 | 11,800 | 4,720 | 4,130 | 2,950 |
| Six mths to 31.1.17 | (43,920) | (17,568) | (15,372) | (10,980) |
| Loss in basis period | | (12,848) | (11,242) | (8,030) |

### Division of overlap profits

| Total | John (40%) | Paul (35%) | George (25%) |
|---|---|---|---|
| £ | £ | £ | £ |
| 19,867 | 7,947 | 6,953 | 4,967 |

As indicated in the Example, the overlap relief covers the eight months from 1 August 1996 to 5 April 1997. John's share of the overlap relief would be taken into account in full on the cessation of his business. Since the 2016/17 basis period spans 18 months, Paul and George would include in their allowable losses for 2016/17 a six months' proportion of their overlap relief, ie 6/8ths = £5,215 and £3,725 respectively, leaving overlap profits carried forward of £1,738 and £1,242 respectively.

### Share of 2016/17 losses for relief against general income

Losses are calculated for the same periods as profits for ITA 2007 s 64 claims (ITA 2007 s 62. Available losses are therefore as follows.

| | *John (40%)* | *Paul (35%)* | *George (25%)* |
|---|---|---|---|
| | £ | £ | £ |
| Loss as above | 12,848 | 11,242 | 8,030 |
| Overlap relief | 7,947 | 5,215 | 3,725 |
| Loss for ITA 2007 s 64 purposes | 20,795 | 16,457 | 11,755 |

Relief is available against the *total* income of 2016/17 and/or 2015/16. Although the partners' other income is not known, each has sufficient *trading* income in 2015/16 to obtain full relief for his loss share, although unless there is other income most of their personal allowance would be wasted.

In addition to the tax saving, the loss claim would eliminate the 2015/16 Class 4 national insurance contributions. If loss relief was claimed against other income in 2016/17, John would lose the benefit of reducing Class 4 contributions, as he has no future trading profits against which to set relief, but Paul and George would be able to set the losses against later *trading* income for Class 4 purposes.

If Paul and George did not wish to claim relief under ITA 2007 s 64 their shares would be carried forward under ITA 2007 s 83 to set against later trading profits.

### John's loss for terminal loss relief

John's terminal loss is the loss from 1.2.16 to 31.1.17, excluding any loss for which relief has already been obtained, and including the *whole* of any available overlap relief (ITA 2007 s 90; ITTOIA 2005 s 205).

John had a loss of £12,848 in the 18 months' basis period for 2016/17, and the whole of his share of the profit of the year to 31 July 2016, ie £4,720, was taken into account in arriving at that amount. His loss of £17,568 has therefore been relieved to that extent, so that only £12,848 can be included in the terminal loss claim. This is then augmented by the overlap relief of £7,947 to give a terminal loss of £20,795, which is the same as under ITA 2007 s 64. Since John has no trading income in 2016/17, this could be fully relieved against his 2015/16 trading profit. Had the loss been larger it could have been carried back against his 2014/15 profits and then his 2013/14 profits (ITA 2007 ss 89, 91).

### Effect of carry-back claims

As indicated in **part (a)**, carry-back claims are *calculated* by reference to the tax position of the earlier year but are *given effect* for the later year (see **Examples G2** and **G3** for details).

## (c) Grame

Graeme's share of the loss of £60,000 for the year to 31 March 2017 is £15,000. Since his capital contribution is only £10,000, however, and he is a limited partner, he may not claim loss relief against income other than from the business on any amount in excess of £10,000, plus the amount of his undrawn profits, less any part thereof that has been offset by earlier losses. See **explanatory note 5**.

## (d) Victoria, partner in Becks LLP

As a member of Becks LLP, Victoria is entitled to ITA 2007 s 64 relief for losses allocated to her, subject to maximum loss claims not exceeding her subscribed capital. This restriction would not apply if the LLP carried on a profession.

Her ITA 2007 s 64 loss claims are as follows:

| | | |
|---|---|---|
| 2014/15 | £6,000 | (capital remaining £4,000) |
| 2015/16 | £4,000 | (capital remaining nil, loss carried forward £2,000) |
| 2016/17 | £25,000 | (capital contributed £27,000 of which £25,000 used, leaving £2,000 carried forward) |

In 2016/17 her actual loss of £30,000 can be increased by the unrelieved loss of £2,000 brought forward, making £32,000 available for relief against future profits of the partnership trade, or partially at relievable against other income subject to restrictions of ITA 2007 ss 102-116A. Since Victoria contributed £27,000 for the purposes of the trade, her sideways loss relief for 2016/17 is limited to the lower of £32,000 available losses, £27,000 capital contribution and £25,000 annual cap ie £25,000, leaving £7,000 available to carry forward.

## (e) Richard and Judy

### Loss of year to 5 April 2017

| | *Total* | *Richard* | *Judy* |
|---|---|---|---|
| | £ | £ | £ |
| Salary | 50,000 | 50,000 | |
| Balance equally | (150,000) | (75,000) | (75,000) |
| | (100,000) | (25,000) | (75,000) |

The 2016/17 self assessments will be *nil* for both partners. Relief will be available under ITA 2007 s 64 in 2016/17 or 2015/16 or under ITA 2007 s 72 in 2014/15 or 2011/12 against other income as follows:

| | *Richard* | *Judy* |
|---|---|---|
| | £ | £ |
| Loss as above | 25,000 | 75,000 |
| ITA 2007 ss 64, 72 | | |
| Restricted to contribution to trade | (25,000) | (10,000) |
| Restricted loss carried forward | Nil | 65,000 |

### Loss of year to 5 April 2016

| | *Total* | *Richard* | *Judy* |
|---|---|---|---|
| | £ | £ | £ |
| Salary | 50,000 | 50,000 | – |
| Balance equally | (80,000) | (40,000) | (40,000) |
| | (30,000) | 10,000 | (40,000) |
| Eliminate Richard's 'profit' | | (10,000) | 10,000 |
| | | Nil | (30,000) |

The 2017/18 self assessments will be *nil* for both partners. Richard does not have a share of loss to use in an ITA 2007 ss 64 or 72 claim. See **explanatory note 4.**

Judy has fully used her 'contribution to trade' and therefore can only add the loss of £30,000 to the amount of restricted loss brought forward of £65,000 to carry forward £95,000 to 2018/19. See **explanatory note 5.**

**Profit of the year to 5 April 2019**

| | *Total* | *Richard* | *Judy* |
|---|---|---|---|
| | £ | £ | £ |
| Salary | 50,000 | 50,000 | – |
| Balance equally | 30,000 | 15,000 | 15,000 |
| | 80,000 | 65,000 | 15,000 |

Richard will self assess profits of £65,000 in 2018/19.

For 2018/19 Judy has:

| | |
|---|---|
| | £ |
| Profits | 15,000 |
| Restricted loss brought forward | (95,000) |
| Available restricted loss | 80,000 |
| ITA 2007 ss 64, 72 loss claim (being contribution to trade) | (20,000) |
| Restricted losses carried forward | 60,000 |

Her self assessment will be nil with relief for £20,000 given under ITA 2007 s 64 in either 2018/19 or 2017/18, or under ITA 2007 s 72 in 2016/17 or 2015/16.

Had the £20,000 been contributed for purposes of obtaining loss relief, not for purposes of the trade, no further sideways loss relief would be due (ITA 2007 s 113A). See **explanatory note 5**.

## Explanatory Notes

*Commencement and cessation*

(1) Each partner is treated as starting a new business when he joins a partnership (unless he previously carried on the business as a sole trader) and as ceasing business when he leaves, unless he continues the business on his own, in which case he will not be treated as ceasing until that business is permanently discontinued (ITTOIA 2005 s 852).

As and when a partner is treated as ceasing business, he may claim terminal loss relief if appropriate (ITA 2007 s 89) (see **part (b)** of the Example, and also **Example E2**).

Losses are personal to the partners, so if anyone retires or dies with unrelieved losses, the losses cannot be transferred to the other partners.

*Losses for relief against general income*

(2) Under the current year basis rules, loss relief under ITA 2007 s 64 is given against the income of the current and/or previous tax years. See **Example E1**.

*Losses carried forward*

(3) In calculating a loss available to carry forward under ITA 2007 s 83, any loss that has been relieved in some other way must be excluded. This includes not only relief by way of another loss claim but also relief by aggregating the loss with a profit in arriving at the assessable result for a year. Hence the restriction on the losses available to be carried forward by Paul and George in **part (b)** of the Example.

See **Example E1**.

*Unusual profit/loss allocations*

(4) It is not possible for one partner to show a loss for tax purposes whilst there is an overall profit, and vice versa. (ITTOIA 2005 ss 850A, 850B).

Hence the elimination of Tyler's 'loss' in the year to 30 April 2016 and Don's 'profit' in the year to 30 April 2017 in **part (a)** of the Example. The amount that has to be eliminated is split between the other partners in the ratio of their shares of the original allocation.

If, exceptionally, the partnership agreement provides that losses are to be shared in a different proportion to profits and the accounting results show a profit whereas the taxable amount is a loss then the partnership agreement applies to the accounting results even if the effect is to divide the loss for taxation in a different proportion to that provided for by the partnership agreement.

In both of the above cases it would be possible to provide in the partnership agreement for a tax indemnity for any tax costs arising to a partner due to the taxable division being different to that provided for by the profit share in the partnership agreement.

*Non-active partners'/limited partners' loss relief restriction*

(5) Loss relief is restricted for limited or non-active partners in traditional partnerships (ITA 2007 ss 103–105) and LLPs (ITA 2007 ss 107–114). Loss relief is limited to a maximum of capital contributed (provided it is not contributed for the purposes of obtaining a tax advantage) and capped to a maximum of £25,000 per tax year. There are exclusions and alternative restrictions for film relief.

These restrictions apply to ITA 2007 s 64 'sideways relief' for losses against general income, ITA 2007 s 72 losses in the early years of the trade, and set off against capital gains (TCGA 1992 s 261B). These restrictions were introduced to counter tax avoidance schemes using partnership losses to reduce income tax liabilities. These restrictions do not apply to general partners, and losses continue to be available for offset against profits arising from the partnership trade.

The definition of 'limited partner' is widely drawn and covers any person in partnership who acts in substance as a limited partner, who is not entitled to take part in the management of the trade, and whose liability for debts incurred for the purposes of the trade is limited (ITA 2007 s 103A). A 'non-active partner' is an individual who does not devote a significant amount of time to the trade specified as an average of at least ten hours per week personally engaged in activities of the trade (ITA 2007 s 103B). Those activities must be carried out on a commercial basis with a view to the realisation of profits as a result of those activities. This applies both to LLPs and traditional partnerships.

ITA 2007 s 74ZA provides that where a person carries on alone or in partnership a trade profession or vocation, and makes a loss from that activity in the year, and the loss arises directly or indirectly in consequence of or in connection with relevant tax avoidance arrangements, no sideways loss relief or capital gains relief is available in respect of the loss.

Capital contributions specifically include any share of profit added to capital, as well as funds contributed. However, ITA 2007 s 113A disallows amounts contributed for the purposes of obtaining tax relief. Capital contributions are reduced by amounts paid back at any time (five years for an LLP) while the individual is in partnership, unless the withdrawal gives rise to an income tax charge as profits of the trade.

*Film partnership*

(6) The provisions of ITA 2007 ss 115–116 restrict loss relief in film making partnerships. They are targeted at individuals using such partnerships for the purposes of obtaining loss relief, and apply particularly to individuals who do not devote a significant amount of time to the trade.

*Limited liability partnerships*

(7) For detailed notes on LLPs see **Example C13**. A specific point as far as losses are concerned is that in order for a partner to benefit from limited liability, losses are not shared amongst partners in the way that they are for an unincorporated partnership. A loss will therefore only arise to a member of an LLP if

allocated by the firm to them. This is to be contrasted with profits which are allocated in accordance with a profit sharing ratio.

*Mixed partnerships*

(8) Where a partnership includes both individuals and non-individuals and a loss arises to a partner who is an individual, that partner will be denied loss relief if the loss arises due to arrangements intended to secure that the losses of the trade are allocated to that partner rather than the non-individual partner(s). This restriction, in ITA 2007 s 116A, was introduced by FA 2014 Sch 17 para 8, and has effect for losses incurred in 2014/15 and later tax years. See **Example C12** for more detail.

*National insurance contributions*

(9) For detailed notes on national insurance contributions see **Example H1**.

# International aspects

# Question

## A.

Determine the residence status in 2016/17 of (i) Jamie; (ii) Chloe; and (iii) Katie:

(i) Jamie decided to go travelling on 17 March 2016, returning to the UK on 3 April 2017. As such, he only spent three days in the UK in 2016/17. Throughout the tax year his only home was in the UK. He had a UK employment but had taken an extended period of unpaid leave.

(ii) Chloe is a Brazilian citizen. In 2009/10 she spent one year at university in the UK to improve her English. This is the only time that she has been UK resident. During that time she acquired a flat in London. She keeps various belongings there and generally spends 60 to 70 days a year there (using it as a base when she visits Europe). Since ceasing to be UK resident in 2010/11 she has never spent more than 75 days in the UK in a tax year.

Whilst Chloe thinks of the London flat as a home she has always had a more substantial home in Sao Paulo where she spends most of her time. However, Chloe sold her home in Sao Paulo in November 2016 (having received an unexpectedly high offer for the property). She decided to acquire a new property but it was not going to be ready until May 2017 so she went travelling in the Southern hemisphere for four months. She decided to visit Europe to meet up with friends in mid-March 2017 and landed in London on 15 March 2017. She spent most of the next six weeks in her London flat using the Eurostar to travel to Paris, Brussels etc to meet up with friends. She left the UK on 30 April 2017.

In total Chloe spent 69 days in the UK in 2016/17. She spent 170 days in Brazil of which 165 were in the property in Sao Paulo that she sold in November 2016.

Chloe had sold her overseas business in 2015/16 at a significant profit and did not work in 2016/17. Throughout 2016/17 she was single and had no children.

(iii) Katie and her family left the UK to live permanently in Austria in 2014/15. In 2014/15 (the year of departure) she spent in excess of 90 days in the UK. In 2015/16 her UK days dropped to 40.

In 2016/17 Katie's main home (where she spends 270 days) is in Vienna, where she lives with her husband and their two young children. Katie has various other residences across the world, including a property in London. The London property is rented out throughout 2016/17.

Katie and her husband both work full time. Her husband qualifies as being non-UK resident by virtue of the third automatic overseas test as he meets the sufficient hours test and restricts his UK work days to 12 in the 2016/17 tax year (one board meeting a month) and overall UK days to 20. Katie meets the sufficient hours test but her UK workdays for the year are 41, with her overall UK day count being 50 for the tax year. Her overseas workdays are 289. As such, she works less than 75% of her workdays in the tax year in the UK.

Katie's two children spend less than 16 days in the UK in 2016/17.

When they are in the UK Katie, her husband and the children use hotel accommodation. Katie does not stay in the same hotel more than once in any 15-day period.

## B.

Mr Carey, a single man, is a British subject who is resident and domiciled in the United Kingdom. He is taking up full time employment (working 40 hours a week) in France on 1 August 2016. His contract of employment with the French company is for three years.

He was employed in the UK prior to departure and his employer deducted income tax and primary Class 1 national insurance contributions from his gross salary under PAYE as usual. Mr Carey also receives interest on the funds in his UK bank account.

The following additional information is available:

- Mr Carey spent 127 days in the UK in 2016/17;
- Mr Carey has full time employment in the UK up until 26 July 2016. He, therefore, worked in excess of 31 days in the UK in 2016/17;
- until 31 July 2016 he only had one home, which was in the UK;
- he returned to the UK for 10 days after leaving on 31 July 2016;
- his first day of work overseas was 1 August 2016 and he worked for 8.5 hours on that day. The only breaks from work in the period to 5 April 2017 were with respect to reasonable holidays;
- he takes 15 days of holiday (three actual weeks) between 1 August 2016 and 5 April 2017 and works for 45 hours on average per week during the rest of the period. None of his work from 1 August 2016 is carried out in the UK;
- he retained the UK bank account and the interest credited on 31 December 2016 was £100;
- he rented out his house furnished, with the rental income collected by an agent. In accordance with the non-resident landlords' scheme the agent deducted tax at the basic rate from the net rents and paid it over to HMRC. Mr Carey has no mortgage on the property.

*Questions*

(i) Assuming that he is not be UK resident in 2017/18 as a result of meeting the third automatic overseas test, will Mr Carey be eligible to split the tax year 2016/17 such that he is taxed as a non-UK resident from 1 August 2016?

(ii) State what action Mr Carey should take in relation to his UK tax position before he leaves.

(iii) Show how Mr Carey's tax position would alter if his circumstances changed such that he was UK resident in 2017/18. Assume that he submitted his self-assessment tax return for 2016/17 on 27 January 2018 and claimed split year status as at that date he thought he would qualify as being non-UK resident for 2017/18 as a result of satisfying the third automatic overseas test.

# Answer

## A.

An individual's residence status in 2016/17 must be determined under the statutory residence test (FA 2013 Sch 45). This means working through the tests in the order below:

(1) if any of the automatic overseas tests are met, the individual is non-resident in the UK for the tax year;

(2) if none of the automatic overseas tests are met, one must move on to the automatic UK tests. If any of the automatic UK tests are met, the individual is resident in the UK for the tax year;

(3) if none of the automatic overseas tests and none of the automatic UK tests are met then the sufficient ties test must be considered. If the sufficient ties test is met then the individual is UK resident for the tax year. If the sufficient ties test is not met then the individual is not resident in the UK for the tax year.

### Jamie

Jamie spent less than 16 days in the UK in 2016/17. As such he is automatically not UK resident as a result of meeting the first automatic overseas test (FA 2013 Sch 45 para 12).

See **explanatory note 6**.

### Chloe

Chloe's UK days are greater than 46 so are too high for her to be automatically not UK resident as a result of her UK day count (FA 2013 Sch 45 para 13). She does not have any employment and does not die in the tax year. As such she did not meet any of the automatic overseas tests (see **explanatory note 5**).

Moving onto the automatic UK tests, since she sells her overseas home in November 2016 and does not acquire another one until May 2017 there is a period of in excess of 91 days during which she has no overseas home. She retained her London home through this period and in excess of 30 days of the period falls within 2016/17. As such, for 2016/17 both conditions A and B of the second automatic UK test are met and Chloe is seen as being automatically UK resident for the tax year (FA 2013 Sch 45 para 8).

See **explanatory note 16**.

### Katie

Katie's aggregate UK days (50 for the 2016/17 tax year) are too high for her to be automatically not UK resident as a result of her UK day count (FA 2013 Sch 45 para 12). Katie works full-time abroad but cannot meet the third automatic overseas test because her UK workdays exceed 30 (FA 2013 Sch 45 para 14(1)(c)). She does not die in the tax year (FA 2013 Sch 45 para 15). As such, she does not meet any of the automatic overseas tests.

Her UK days are too low for her to be automatically UK resident (FA 2013 Sch 45 para 7). She retains her home in Vienna throughout the tax year so does not meet the second automatic UK test (only home in the UK) (FA 2013 Sch 45 para 8). Her UK workdays did not exceed 75% of the total workdays so she does not meet the third automatic UK test (FA 2013 Sch 45 para 9(1)(d)) and since she did not die in the tax year she does not meet the fourth automatic UK test (FA 2013 Sch 45 para 10). As such, she does not meet any of the automatic UK tests.

Therefore, the sufficient ties test needs to be considered (see **explanatory note 22**). The sufficient ties test compares the days spent in the UK in the tax year with the number of UK ties to decide if an individual is UK resident in that tax year. As Katie was UK resident in at least one of the previous three tax years, she must use the table in FA 2013 Sch 45 para 18.

Her ties with the UK for the purposes of the sufficient ties test are:

| UK tie | |
|---|---|
| Family tie | **No** – her husband and children are all not UK resident (FA 2013 Sch 45 para 32). |
| Accommodation tie | **No** – Katie has a London property but it is rented out throughout the tax year. When she came to the UK she used hotels and never the same hotel within a 15-day period. There was, therefore, no UK accommodation that was used by her for a continuous period of at least 90 days (FA 2013 Sch 45 para 34). |
| Work tie | **Yes** – Katie's workdays in the year exceed 39 so she has a UK work tie (FA 2013 Sch 45 para 35). |
| 90 day tie | **Yes** – Katie did not spend in excess of 90 days in the UK in 2015/16 but she did in 2014/15 (FA 2013 Sch 45 para 37). |
| Country tie | **No** – Katie spent far more time in Austria than in the UK (FA 2013 Sch 45 para 38). |

Overall Katie has two UK ties for the 2016/17 tax year. Based on the table in FA 2013 Sch 45 para 18, she is not UK resident in 2016/17 as her UK days are less than 91.

## B.

### (i) *Will Mr Carey qualify for split year treatment from 1 August 2016?*

Before considering whether Mr Carey qualifies for split year treatment under any of the cases which apply to people leaving the UK, we have to consider the statutory residence test. The split year cases only need to be reviewed if Mr Carey is UK resident for the tax year. If an individual is non-resident in the UK under the statutory residence test in FA 2013 Sch 45 there is no need to split the tax year into periods of residence and non-residence.

As mentioned in answer (A) above, for the statutory residence test the various tests should be considered in a specific order.

Mr Carey's aggregate UK days (127 for the tax year) are too high for him to be automatically not UK resident as a result of his UK day count (FA 2013 Sch 45 para 12). He cannot meet the third automatic overseas test because his UK workdays exceed 30 (FA 2013 Sch 45 para 14). He did not die in the tax year (FA 2013 Sch 45 para 15). As such, he does not meet any of the automatic overseas tests.

His UK days are too low for him to be automatically UK resident (FA 2013 Sch 45 para 7). However, he is automatically UK resident for the tax year as a result of only having a home in the UK for the period from 6 April 2016 to 31 July 2016 (in excess of 90 days) and, therefore, meeting the second automatic UK test (FA 2013 Sch 45 para 8).

As Mr Carey is UK resident in 2016/17, the split year rules can be considered.

As explained in **explanatory note 23**, FA 2013 Sch 45 Part 3 introduces statutory split year treatment. There are three cases where the tax year can be split when an individual is leaving the UK. These are:

- Case 1 – starting full time work overseas (FA 2013 Sch 45 para 44);
- Case 2 – accompanying a partner who qualifies under Case 1 (FA 2013 Sch 45 para 45);
- Case 3 – ceasing to have a home in the UK (FA 2013 Sch 45 para 46).

It is possible that an individual could meet the conditions for more than one Case, which could lead to a conflict as to which date the period of non-residence begins (as each Case has a different measurement as to when non-residence begins). Therefore, the legislation gives an order of priority. Case 1 has priority over Cases 2 and 3. Case 2 has priority over Case 3 (FA 2013 Sch 45 para 54). As such, if Mr Carey meets the conditions for Case 1, there is no need to consider the only other relevant Case in his circumstances, Case 3.

Mr Carey was resident in the UK in 2015/16 and is UK resident in 2016/17, so he meets the initial qualifying conditions for Case 1. The question assumes he will be not UK resident in 2017/18 as a result of meeting the third automatic overseas test. Therefore, he will qualify for split-year treatment for 2016/17 under Case 1 because:

- he satisfies the sufficient hours overseas test as set down in FA 2013 Sch 45 para 44(7) for the period from 1 August 2016 to 5 April 2017 (only taking reasonable holiday and averaging 45 hours of work overseas in the working weeks);
- there are no significant breaks from overseas work in the period from 1 August 2016 to 5 April 2017;
- he has no UK workdays after 31 July 2016, so his UK workdays clearly do not exceed the permitted limit (FA 2013 Sch 45 para 44(8)); *
- his UK days after he left are within the permitted limit. *

* His period of non UK residence begins with the first work day in the overseas country, ie 1 August 2016 (FA 2013 Sch 45 para 53(2)(a) as read with FA 2013 Sch 45 para 44(3)). On this basis, the permitted limit for UK workdays is 20 days and the permitted limit for UK days is 60 days (see Table E in the HMRC booklet RDR3 https://www.gov.uk/government/publications/rdr3-statutory-residence-test-srt).

As stated above, because Mr Carey meets the conditions for Case 1 to apply there is no need to consider the other Cases. Having said this, it is likely that Mr Carey would also qualify for split year treatment under Case 3 since his UK home is let commercially. It is assumed he would have a 'sufficient link' with France within the necessary six month period for the purposes of FA 2013 Sch 45 para 46(7). For Case 3, the period of non-residence begins with the date on which the individual ceases to have a home in the UK. It appears from the question that this is also 1 August 2016, but it could easily be later where there are delays in letting the property.

## (ii) *Action to be taken by Mr Carey before leaving the UK*

Before Mr Carey leaves the UK he should arrange for agent to receive rental monies and pay tax quarterly to HMRC on the net rental income.

If Mr Carey wishes to receive his rental income gross he must register with HMRC and ask for permission to receive payment gross by way of completing form NRL1i https://www.gov.uk/government/publications/non-resident-landlord-application-to-receive-uk-rental-income-without-deduction-of-uk-tax-individuals-nrl1i.

To be able to receive rental payments gross Mr Carey must have complied with all his UK tax obligations to date by submitting tax returns and paying any tax liabilities by the due dates (ITA 2007 s 971; SI 1995/2902).

In signing a NRL1i, Mr Carey undertakes to:

(i) tell HMRC if his usual place of abode ceases to be outside the UK;

(ii) comply fully with UK tax obligations (that is submitting self-assessment tax return forms, paying tax due on time and answering questions relevant to his UK tax affairs); and

(iii) where an application is made in advance of a tenant being found tell HMRC when he expects to become liable to UK tax.

If HMRC allows the application and discover at any time that Mr Carey is not meeting his undertakings it will revoke the permission granted to him to receive gross rental income payments.

Note that there is no longer a general requirement for taxpayers who are required to complete self-assessment tax returns to submit form P85 to HMRC to provide notification that they are leaving the UK. Such taxpayers may, however, wish to submit the form to provide advanced notification to HMRC. In addition taxpayers with employment income, who have not submitted self-assessment returns, may submit form P85 to claim a tax refund where excess PAYE has been deducted at source.

Form P85 (https://www.gov.uk/government/publications/income-tax-leaving-the-uk-getting-your-tax-right-p85) should be used by both self-assessment and non self-assessment taxpayers to request an NT tax code where the individual leaves the UK to work full-time for a UK-based employer overseas. The P85 should be sent to HMRC no earlier than eight weeks before the date the overseas work is due to commence and be accompanied by a letter requesting a NT tax code. In such cases the completed form should be sent to:

HM Revenue & Customs, Pay As You Earn, BX9 1AS

Since 6 April 2016 there is no need for a leaver to complete form R105 (application to receive interest without tax taken off) as the rules regarding deduction of tax on interest at source were repealed by FA 2016.

### (iii) *If Mr Carey was UK resident in 2017/18*

If Mr Carey is UK resident in 2017/18 he cannot qualify for split year treatment for the 2016/17 tax year as he would not meet the condition in FA 2013 Sch 45 para 44(4). This means that he will be regarded as having been resident in the UK for tax purposes for the whole of 2016/17.

In this situation, he is liable to UK tax on his earnings in France, subject to double tax relief for tax suffered in France (the exact terms of the UK/French double tax treaty would need to be consulted). Since his UK income has been fully charged to tax anyway, there is no other change to his tax position (unless other foreign income had arisen to him while he was in France).

Mr Carey claimed split-year treatment for 2016/17 as he expected to meet all the Case 1 conditions. He would therefore have excluded his French earnings from the return, and it is likely a repayment would have been due to him. A repayment would be expected because his full year's personal allowance is set against four months' salary rather than against the full year's salary (as expected when the employer deducted income tax via PAYE).

He should file an amendment to the return to bring the French earnings into charge and the tax position will need to be recalculated. Depending on the tax deducted by the French authorities he may still have overpaid tax for 2016/17. If there is a liability he will be charged interest on any underpayment from 31 January 2018. The first 5% late payment penalty will arise if the tax is not paid by 2 March 2018 (FA 2009 Sch 56 paras 1, 3(2)).

If Mr Carey is resident in France from the date of his departure from the UK, he should consider the residence tie-breaker (Article 4) of the UK/French double tax treaty which will decide his treaty residence status. If he is treaty resident in France from 1 August 2016, he should complete an amended 2016/17 return to include the Helpsheet HS302 claim form (https://www.gov.uk/government/publications/dual-residents-hs302-self-assessment-helpsheet) and obtain certification from the French tax authorities confirming his French residence status. As a dual resident who is treaty resident in France, his French employment income will not be liable to tax in the UK.

The tax position for non-residents is considered in detail in **Example F2**.

## Explanatory Notes

These notes are divided into two parts. **Part A (explanatory notes 1–28)** provides an overview of the statutory residence test (SRT) introduced by FA 2013 Sch 45 and effective for tax years from 2013/14 onwards. **Part B (explanatory notes 29–36)** provides an overview of the pre-6 April 2013 tax rules on UK residence and ordinary residence (the concept of ordinary residence having been abolished from 6 April 2013 by FA 2013 Sch 46).

## PART A – THE STATUTORY RESIDENCE TEST (SRT)

*Introduction*

(1) The SRT is effective for tax years from 2013/14 for the purposes of income tax, capital gains tax (CGT), inheritance tax (IHT) and, in so far as it is relevant, corporation tax. For these purposes it generally supersedes all existing legislation, case law and guidance. The only exception is with respect to the Constitutional Reform and Governance Act 2010, which has priority, so MPs and active members of the House of Lord will continue to be deemed UK resident.

An individual's residence status for previous tax years will still have to be determined according to the former, uncertain, principles (as discussed in **explanatory notes 29–36**). The SRT has transitional provisions (see **explanatory note 26**) but these are relevant only when assessing past residence status for the application of the SRT in 2013/14 onwards. The SRT cannot be applied retrospectively so as to determine an individual's residence status for earlier tax years.

The SRT is not currently applied for other purposes where residence is a determining factor. In particular the SRT does not apply for the purposes of national insurance contributions or tax credits.

HMRC has published various information and guidance about the SRT on its website.

- guidance on residence, domicile and the remittance basis (RDR1 https://www.gov.uk/government/publications/residence-domicile-and-remittance-basis-rules-uk-tax-liability);
- detailed guidance on the SRT (RDR3 https://www.gov.uk/government/publications/rdr3-statutory-residence-test-srt);
- guidance on overseas workday relief (RDR4 https://www.gov.uk/government/publications/rdr4-overseas-workday-relief-owr);
- an on-line residence indicator tool (tools.hmrc.gov.uk/rift/). A second indicator allows an individual to obtain a 'decision' on whether split year treatment applies on leaving the UK.

The Joint Forum on expatriate tax and national insurance contributions involves representatives of HMRC, employers, the professional bodies and payroll advisers. At the meetings various issues are discussed with respect to the operation of the tax and national insurance system for international secondees. Issues with respect to residence, domicile and the remittance basis are often covered and important insights into HMRC's thinking can be obtained from reading the minutes (all of which are posted on the HMRC website and can be accessed at:

https://www.gov.uk/government/groups/joint-forum-on-expatriate-tax-and-national-insurance-contributions

*The main provisions*

(2) The SRT is based on the principles that:

- residence should have an adhesive character. It should be more difficult for those who are resident and seek to leave the UK to lose their UK resident status, than for those who visit the UK, without having been UK resident in any of the three preceding tax years, to acquire UK residence;
- alongside physical presence, certain factors linking an individual to the UK may need to be considered in determining residence. The SRT, therefore, takes into account both time spent in the UK (UK days) and a limited number of specified UK ties.

The SRT legislation (FA 2013 Sch 45) is divided into five parts as follows:

- Part 1 – the SRT rules;
- Part 2 – definitions of key concepts;
- Part 3 – split-year treatment;
- Part 4 – anti-avoidance provisions applicable to temporary non-UK residents;
- Part 5 – miscellaneous (interpretation, consequential amendments, commencement and transitional provisions).

FA 2013 Sch 46 abolished the concept of ordinary residence, for the purposes of income tax, CGT, IHT and (where relevant) corporation tax, with effect from 6 April 2013. There were transitional provisions up to and including 2015/16, so as not to disadvantage individuals who were not ordinary resident as at 5 April 2013 (see **explanatory note 27**).

Relief for overseas workdays is retained for internationally mobile employees (see **Example F4 explanatory note 3**). The scope has been restricted in that it is now only available to foreign domiciliaries. The relief itself, however, has been widened in that it is now available for the first three tax years of residence for all qualifying individuals arriving in the UK, regardless of how long they intend to stay in the UK.

*How does the SRT work?*

(3) It is simplest to think of the SRT as being divided into three parts:

- the automatic overseas tests;
- the automatic residence tests; and
- the sufficient ties test.

These are ranked in order of priority, so if somebody qualifies under one of the automatic overseas tests as not resident, there is no need to move on to the automatic residence or sufficient ties tests.

Each test takes account of days when an individual is present in the UK. These are referred to as 'UK days'. Days on which work is carried out in the UK are separately defined as 'UK workdays'.

*Definition of 'UK days' and 'UK workdays'*

(4) FA 2013 Sch 45 para 22 defines UK day for the purposes of the SRT as follows:

- the standard SRT definition of a 'UK day' (presence in the UK at midnight) is the same as the pre-6 April 2013 definition, subject to the anti-avoidance provision explained below;
- the let-out for transit passengers is retained (broadly, where just one midnight is spent in the UK and the only substantive activities are with respect to travelling through the UK, ie no work activities or seeing family or friends);
- in addition, a day may be disregarded if there are exceptional reasons for someone's presence. However, this disregard for 'exceptional days' is subject to a maximum of 60 such days per tax year. HMRC's interpretation of the concept of exceptional circumstances is discussed in Annex B of RDR3 (https://www.gov.uk/government/publications/rdr3-statutory-residence-test-srt).

The anti-avoidance provision is to prevent manipulation of the 'midnight rule'. It is aimed at individuals who:

- have been UK resident in at least one of the preceding three tax years;
- have three or more ties to the UK in the tax year under the sufficient ties test (see **explanatory note 22**); and
- are present in the UK but leave before midnight on more than 30 occasions during the year.

Where these conditions are met the midnight rule will generally be overridden, so that from (and inclusive of) the 31st occasion on which the individual is present in the UK but leaves before midnight, all days on which he or she is present for any length of time will count as UK days (FA 2013 Sch 45 para 23).

It is important to remember that the term 'UK workday' is defined differently from a 'UK day'. A UK workday is one on which more than three hours of work is carried out in the UK (FA 2013 Sch 45 paras 9, 14). 'Work' is defined at FA 2013 Sch 45 para 26 and includes incidental and non-incidental duties and most business travel and training. The location of work concept is covered at FA 2013 Sch 45 para 27.

*The automatic overseas tests*

(5) Regardless of any other factor (save for being a member of one of the Houses of Parliament), an individual will not be UK resident if one (or more) of the following five tests is met:

- first automatic overseas test – UK resident in one or more of the previous three tax years and present for fewer than 16 UK days in the current tax year (FA 2013 Sch 45 para 12);

- second automatic overseas test – non-UK resident in the previous three tax years and present in the UK for fewer than 46 UK days in the current tax year (FA 2013 Sch 45 para 13);
- third automatic overseas test – the 'sufficient hours' working overseas test (FA 2013 Sch 45 para 14);
- fourth automatic overseas test – died in the year and was non-UK resident in the previous two years and present for fewer than 46 UK days in the current tax year (FA 2013 Sch 45 para 15);
- fifth automatic overseas test – died in the tax year and would have been treated as meeting the third automatic overseas test if the conditions had been amended to take account of the death (FA 2013 Sch 45 para 16).

*First automatic overseas test – fewer than 16 UK days test*

(6) An individual (regardless of the previous pattern of UK residence) is non-UK resident if he is present in the UK for fewer than 16 days in the tax year (FA 2013 Sch 45 paras 12, 13).

This test does not apply to someone who dies in the tax year. Such a person will have to meet one of the other four tests to be automatically non-UK resident in the year of death (FA 2013 Sch 45 para 12(c)).

*Second automatic overseas test – fewer than 46 UK days test*

(7) An individual is non-UK resident if he (FA 2013 Sch 45 para 13):

- is present in the UK for fewer than 46 days in the tax year; and
- was not UK resident in *any* of the preceding three tax years.

## Third automatic overseas test – sufficient hours working overseas test

*Overview*

(8) As can be seen from Part B of these explanatory notes, the way in which the non-statutory rules on UK residence were operated up to 6 April 2013 was more favourable to those who left the UK to work full time abroad than to other categories of individuals. This 'lighter touch' was seen as encouraging UK business, and it was felt desirable to reproduce this as closely as possible in the new SRT. This is what the third automatic overseas test seeks to do.

An individual is non-UK resident for a given tax year if all four of the following conditions are satisfied (FA 2013 Sch 45 para 14):

- he works 'sufficient hours' overseas. This is to establish whether, after adjusting the 365 day averaging period (366 days if a leap year) by subtracting certain days (broadly UK workdays, reasonable holiday leave, reasonable sick leave and parenting leave), over 35 hours a week on average have been worked overseas (see **explanatory note 9**);
- there are no 'significant breaks' (see **explanatory note 10**) from overseas work;
- the number of UK workdays in the tax year is fewer than 31. This means that an individual could spend up to 30 working days in the UK carrying out substantive duties and still qualify;
- he is present in the UK for fewer than 91 days in the tax year (not including days deemed to be spent in the UK under the day-counting anti-avoidance provision discussed in **explanatory note 4**).

Day-counting and UK workdays are discussed in **explanatory note 4** above. A day can count as a UK workday and *not* be a day of UK presence and vice versa. Careful record keeping is necessary.

Note that because of the way the calculation works to achieve the 35 hour target it will generally be necessary to work in excess of 35 hours on average during working weeks. Broadly, 37 to 40 hours should be sufficient depending on the adjustments made to the averaging period as a result of holiday leave etc.

Within the specified limits the test allows an individual to carry out substantive duties in the UK without jeopardising his non-UK residence status. Remuneration related to the performance of non-incidental duties in the UK remains, however, fully liable to UK income tax unless exempted under a double tax treaty. For more on double tax relief, see **Example F3**.

**This test does NOT apply to someone who (FA 2013 Sch 45 para 14(4)):**

- has a relevant job on board a vehicle, aircraft or ship (as defined under FA 2013 Sch 45 para 30) at any time in the tax year; and
- makes at least six job related trips involving cross border travel (ie ones that begin or end in the UK).

Such workers must consider the other tests when determining their residence status.

*'Sufficient hours' working overseas*

(9) FA 2013 Sch 45 para 14(3) sets down a prescriptive methodology for the third automatic overseas test that has to be followed to establish if sufficient hours have been worked overseas. If the individual has more than one employment, or carries on more than one trade during the tax year (whether consecutively or concurrently), the hours worked should be aggregated for this. Broadly, the test seeks to establish that, on average, at least 35 hours a week are worked abroad during the period of absence. The process is follows:

(i) the number of 'disregarded days' in the tax year has to be ascertained. A 'disregarded day' is any UK workday (that is a day on which the individual does more than three hours of work in the UK);

(ii) the total 'net overseas hours' must be obtained by adding up the total number of hours worked overseas in the tax year but excluding any hours spent working overseas on 'disregarded days' (as in step (i));

(iii) the 'reference period' must be determined. To do this one subtracts from 365 (or 366 for a leap year) the total number of 'disregarded days' and also the following days (FA 2013 Sch 45 para 28):

- reasonable amounts of annual leave and parenting leave (which depends on the country and sector in which the individual works);
- sick leave where the individual cannot reasonably be expected to work;
- non-working days (for example weekends or bank holidays if the individual is not expected to work on these days) embedded within a block of leave falling into either of the above two categories. See FA 2013 Sch 45 para 28(5)–(6) for the definition of embedded non-working days;
- gaps of up to 15 days between employments being allowed for one change of employment and a maximum of 30 days where there is more than one change of employment.

(iv) divide the reference period arrived at in step (iii) by 7 (rounding down to the nearest whole number but with a minimum result of one);

(v) divide the 'net overseas hours' figure arrived at in step (ii) by the figure arrived at in step (iv).

If, at the end of this procedure, the answer is 35 or more, sufficient overseas hours have been worked in the tax year for the individual to comply with the third automatic overseas test. If the answer is less than 35 then the test is not met.

*'Significant break' from overseas work*

(10) There is a 'significant break' from overseas work if there is a continuous period of 31 days or more during which time (FA 2013 Sch 45 para 29(2)):

- the individual does not work overseas for more than three hours per day on any day throughout the period; and
- the reason for this is not because he or she is absent from work due to annual leave, parental leave or illness (and the individual would have worked for in excess of three hours overseas if it had not been for this reason).

*Other definitions*

(11) The concept of work is discussed at FA 2013 Sch 45 para 26 and location of work at FA 2013 Sch 45 para 27 (see **explanatory note 4**).

*Fourth automatic overseas test – first test specific to those who die in the tax year*

(12) Someone who dies is not UK resident in the tax year of death if he has spent fewer than 46 days in the UK in that year and either (FA 2013 Sch 45 para 15):

- had not been resident in the UK for either of the preceding two tax years; or
- was not resident in the UK in the preceding tax year and had qualified for split year treatment (see **explanatory note 23**) for part of the tax year before that as a result of:
  - Case 1 – starting full time work overseas (FA 2013 Sch 45 para 44);
  - Case 2 – accompanying a partner who qualifies under Case 1 (FA 2013 Sch 45 para 45).
  - Case 3 – ceasing to have a home in the UK (FA 2013 Sch 45 para 46).

*Fifth automatic overseas test – second test specific to those who die in the tax year*

(13) Someone who dies is not UK resident in the tax year of death if (FA 2013 Sch 45 para 16):

- he would have met the sufficient hours working overseas test for that year, looking just at the period up to death (the conditions are modified to take into account the shorter period); and
- the individual qualified as not resident under the sufficient hours working overseas test(s) either:
  - in the two preceding tax years; or
  - in the preceding tax year and qualified for split year treatment in the tax year before that under Case 1 (starting full time work overseas – FA 2013 Sch 45 para 44).

*The automatic UK tests*

(14) Provided none of the automatic overseas tests (discussed above) are met, an individual will be UK resident if one (or more) of the following four automatic UK tests are met:

- first automatic UK test – present in the UK for 183 days or more (FA 2013 Sch 45 para 7);
- second automatic UK test – the only substantive home in the UK test (FA 2013 Sch 45 para 8);
- third automatic UK test – 'sufficient hours' working in the UK test (FA 2013 Sch 45 para 9);
- fourth automatic UK test – died in the tax year, had a home in the UK and was UK resident for the previous three tax years (and the immediately preceding year was not a split year) (FA 2013 Sch 45 para 10).

*First automatic UK test – 183 UK days test*

(15) An individual is UK resident if he is present in the UK for 183 days or more in the tax year (FA 2013 Sch 45 para 7).

*Second automatic UK test – only substantive home in the UK test*

(16) In the course of discussions over the terms of the SRT, it became clear that having an 'only home' in the UK during the tax year, even for only a short time, is considered by the Government to be such a significant tie that, unless one of the automatic overseas tests applies, it should cause a person to be UK resident. Accordingly the SRT provides that someone is UK resident for a tax year if (FA 2013 Sch 45 para 8):

- during the tax year, the individual has at least one 'home' in the UK where he is present for a total of at least 30 days during the tax year (such days do not need to be consecutive and presence in the home includes any time spent there in a day, no matter how short a length of time);
- there is at least one period of 91 consecutive days (at least 30 days of which must fall within the tax year) during which the individual:
  - has a home in the UK; and
  - either (i) has no home overseas in that 91 day period, or (ii) does not have a substantive home overseas.

A substantive home overseas is not a statutory term. However it is a useful shorthand for the situation where the individual has been present in the home for a total of at least 30 days during the tax year. As above, days need not be consecutive, and for these purposes presence at any point during the day will count. Where an individual has more than one home overseas, he or she must be present in at least one of the homes for at least 30 days (FA 2013 Sch 45 para 8(8)). As such, presence in two foreign homes for only 25 days each would not qualify and it is possible that the individual could meet the second automatic UK test and be considered UK resident.

Therefore, to avoid being UK resident because of this test, an individual either has to ensure that he:

- does not spend 30 days in a UK home; or
- retains a 'substantive home overseas' throughout the tax year concerned.

There is a trap if someone with a UK home disposes of their only qualifying foreign home without acquiring another within three months (91 days), as is the situation in the example of Chloe above. There will be cases where the split year rules will not provide adequate relief (though if such a person is dual resident, treaty relief may be available).

## Third automatic UK test – 'sufficient hours' work in the UK test

*Overview*

(17) Full time work in the UK is seen by the Government as another fundamental connection to the UK which should cause a person to be automatically UK resident. An individual meets the third automatic UK test if all of the following four conditions are met (FA 2013 Sch 45 para 9):

- he works 'sufficient hours' in the UK as assessed over a period of 365 days (of which only part needs to fall within the relevant tax year). This is a test which approximately corresponds to that applying to overseas work and seeks to establish whether, after adjusting the 365 day averaging period by subtracting days falling within certain designated categories (broadly overseas workdays, reasonable holiday leave, reasonable sick leave and parenting leave), over 35 hours a week on average have been worked in the UK (see **explanatory note 18**);

- on at least one day, falling within both the period above and the relevant tax year, the taxpayer works more than three hours in the UK;
- during the period there are no 'significant breaks' from UK (see **explanatory note 19**); and
- More than 75% of the total number of workdays within the 365-day period are UK workdays (ie works more than three hours).

Since the test looks at a 365-day period (only one day of which, in theory, needs to be in the relevant tax year), an individual could be resident as a result of meeting this test when he comes to the UK late in the tax year – but only if none of the automatic overseas tests apply. In such cases it is likely that split year treatment will apply as a result of meeting the Case 5: starting full time work in the UK (see **explanatory note 23**).

**This test does NOT apply to someone who (FA 2013 Sch 45 para 9(3):**

- has a relevant job on board a vehicle, aircraft or ship ship (as defined under FA 2013 Sch 45 para 30) at any time in the tax year; and
- makes at least six working trips that are cross border (ie which either begin or end in the UK).

**Such workers must consider the other tests when determining their residence status.**

*'Sufficient hours' working in the UK*

(18) As with the 'sufficient hours' work overseas test (see **explanatory note 9**), the legislation sets down a prescriptive methodology to determine if sufficient hours have been worked in the UK.

If an individual has more than one employment, or carries on more than one trade during the period (whether consecutively or concurrently), the hours worked should be aggregated when determining whether the test has been met. Broadly, the test seeks to establish that, on average, at least 35 hours a week are worked in the UK. The process is follows (FA 2013 Sch 45 para 9):

(i) the number of 'disregarded days' in the period has to be ascertained. A 'disregarded day' is any day during which more than three hours of work is carried on overseas (even if work is also carried out in the UK on that day);

(ii) the 'net UK hours' figure must be obtained by adding up the total number of hours that an individual has worked in the UK in the period but excluding any hours worked in the UK on 'disregarded days' (see step (i)).

(iii) the 'reference period' must be determined. This is done by subtracting from 365 the total number of 'disregarded days' (see step (i)), and the following (FA 2013 Sch 45 para 28):

- reasonable amounts of annual leave and parenting leave;
- sick leave where the individual cannot reasonably be expected to work;
- non-working days (for example weekends or bank holidays if the individual is not expected to work on these days) embedded within a block of leave falling into either of the above two categories. See FA 2013 Sch 45 para 28(5)–(6) for the definition of embedded non-working days;
- gaps during employment (provided no work is carried out in the gap period) with up to 15 days being allowed for one change of employment and a maximum of 30 days where there is more than one change of employment.

(iv) divide the reference period arrived at in step (iii) by 7 (rounding down to the nearest whole number but with a minimum result of 1);

(v) divide the 'net UK hours' figure arrived at in step (ii) by the figure arrived at in step (iv).

If at the end of this procedure the final answer is 35 or more sufficient UK hours will have been worked in the tax year for the individual to comply with the third automatic UK test. If the final answer is fewer than 35 then this part of the test is not met.

*'Significant breaks' from UK work*

(19) There will be a 'significant break' from UK work if there is a continuous period of 31 days or more during which time (FA 2013 Sch 45 para 29(1)):

- the individual does not work in the UK for more than three hours per day on any day throughout the period; and
- the reason for this is not because he or she is absent from work due to annual leave, parental leave or illness (and the individual would have worked for in excess of three hours in the UK if it had not been for this reason).

*Other Definitions*

(20) The concept of work is discussed at FA 2013 Sch 45 para 26 and location or work at FA 2013 Sch 45 para 27 (see **explanatory note 4**).

*Fourth automatic UK test – test specific to those who die in the tax year*

(21) Someone who dies meets the fourth automatic UK test in the tax year of death if the following conditions are all met (FA 2013 Sch 45 para 10):

- in all the three tax years preceding the year of death, he was UK resident by virtue of meeting one of the automatic UK tests. Where the transitional election (see FA 2013 Sch 45 para 154) is not made and his residence status for tax years prior to 2013/14 needs to be established (that is tax years before the SRT is effective) this will have to be determined in accordance with the principles previously applying;
- the preceding tax year did not qualify as a split year, even assuming non-UK residence for the tax year of death;
- when the individual died either: (i) his only home (or homes) was in the UK; or (ii) he had a home in the UK and a home overseas but insufficient time was spent in the overseas home in the year of death.

Where there is a home overseas in the year of death, sufficient time will have been spent there where (FA 2013 Sch 45 para 10(2)):

(i) there were at least 30 days in aggregate when the individual was present in the home; or

(ii) the individual was present there on each day of the tax year up to and including the day on which he died.

For these purposes, the individual is 'present' in the home if he was in the property at any point during the day.

*The sufficient ties test*

(22) An individual only needs to consider this third part of the SRT test where none of the automatic overseas tests and none of the automatic UK tests are met. Where this is the case, residence is determined by considering the number of UK days in relation to the number of defined UK ties (FA 2013 Sch 45 paras 17–20).

The rules are stricter for those who were UK resident in one or more of the three preceding tax years than for those who were non-resident in the UK in those years (FA 2013 Sch 45 paras 18-19).

| *Days* | *Non-UK resident in any of the three preceding tax years ('arrivers')* | *UK resident in one or more of the three preceding tax years ('leavers')* |
|---|---|---|
| Fewer than 16 | Always non-UK resident | Always non-UK resident |
| 16 to 45 | Always non-UK resident | 4 or more UK ties = UK residence |
| 46 to 90 | 4 UK ties = UK residence | 3 or more UK ties = UK residence |
| 91 to 120 | 3 or more UK ties = UK residence | 2 or more UK ties = UK residence |
| 121 to 182 days | 2 or more UK ties = UK residence | 1 or more UK ties = UK residence |
| 183 days or more | Always UK resident | Always UK resident |

The UK ties are set down at FA 2013 Sch 45 para 31:

- family tie – there are important qualifications but, broadly, a UK resident partner and/or UK resident minor child or children (see the answer to Mrs Harding in **Example F2** for further discussion of this tie) (FA 2013 Sch 45 paras 32-33);
- accommodation tie – again there are important qualifications but, broadly, in the tax year having a place to live in the UK for at least 91 days and using that place for at least one night. Staying with a close relative is ignored for the purposes of this tie so long as the number of days spent there is fewer than 16 (FA 2013 Sch 45 para 34);
- work tie – at least 40 UK work days in the tax year (see **explanatory note 4** for the definition of a work day) (FA 2013 Sch 45 paras 35-36);
- 90-day tie – more than 90 days of UK presence in either or both of the two preceding tax years) (FA 2013 Sch 45 para 37); and
- country tie (only applicable for those who have been UK resident in one or more of preceding three tax years) – broadly, spending more days in the UK than in any other country (FA 2013 Sch 45 para 38).

*Statutory split year treatment*

(23) Before tax year 2013/14 there were no statutory provisions allowing a tax year to be split, the general principle being that residence in any part of a tax year equated to residence for the entire year. Split-year treatment was, in practice, available either (see **explanatory note 35**):

- where a relevant double tax treaty applied to determine residence in another state; or
- through claiming relief under extra statutory concessions that allowed a tax year to be split (where specified qualifying conditions were met and there was no tax avoidance motive).

For 2013/14 onwards, these extra statutory concessions have been withdrawn and incorporated as far as possible into the SRT.

To be eligible for split year treatment, the individual must first be UK resident in the year under the SRT. Where this is the case, there are eight situations (referred to as Cases) in which it will be possible to split a tax year into periods of UK residence and non-UK residence.

The first three cases relate to individuals leaving the UK and are:

- Case 1 – starting full time work overseas (FA 2013 Sch 45 para 44);
- Case 2 – accompanying a partner who qualifies under Case 1 (FA 2013 Sch 45 para 45);
- Case 3 – ceasing to have a home in the UK (FA 2013 Sch 45 para 46).

Cases 4 to 8 relate to individuals coming to the UK and are:

- Case 4 – starting to have an 'only' home in the UK (FA 2013 Sch 45 para 47);
- Case 5 – starting to work full time in the UK (FA 2013 Sch 45 para 48);
- Case 6 – ceasing full-time work overseas (FA 2013 Sch 45 para 49);
- Case 7 – accompanying a partner who qualifies under Case 6 (FA 2013 Sch 45 para 50);
- Case 8 – starting to have a home in the UK which continues throughout the following tax year (FA 2013 Sch 45 para 51).

Technically, where someone qualifies for split year treatment, he will be UK resident throughout the tax year, but taxed as a non-resident for the appropriate part. Broadly, UK tax will not be due on foreign income or gains arising or accruing, unless the anti-avoidance provisions affecting a temporary non-resident apply (see **explanatory note 24**).

There are a number of differences between the statutory split year treatment introduced from 6 April 2013 and the concessionary treatment which was in place for tax years prior to that date. However, one of the most fundamental changes is that it is no longer the date of departure or arrival in the UK which determines the date on which the year is split (FA 2013 Sch 45 para 53). It is often the date that the overseas work starts or finishes or the date the individual starts to have a home in the UK or ceases to have a home in the UK, which may be some time after the individual arrived or left the UK.

For more guidance on split year treatment under the SRT, see Chapter 5 of RDR3 (https://www.gov.uk/government/publications/rdr3-statutory-residence-test-srt).

Split year treatment applies to an individual's personal tax situation only. It does not apply if the individual also acts as a personal representative and there are special provisions where the individual acts as a trustee. An individual trustee is not regarded as UK resident, for the purposes of determining the residence status of the trust, where:

- split year treatment applies; and
- the entire period during which the individual is a trustee falls within the overseas part of the split year.

## Temporary non-residence

*Overview*

(24) Leaving the UK and becoming non-UK resident allows for UK tax to be avoided (see the explanatory notes to **Example F2**). There are specific anti-avoidance provisions, which apply where the individual is only temporarily non-resident in the UK. Broadly, the aim of the provisions is to tax in the year of return income and/or gains which have been accumulated prior to leaving the UK and which are received or realised in the period of temporary non-residence (and were not taxable in the UK during that period).

In summary, to be caught by these provisions (FA 2013 Sch 45 para 110):

- the individual must have been UK resident in at least four of the seven tax years (whether these were split years or not) immediately preceding the 'year of departure' (see **explanatory note 25**); and
- the period of non-UK residence is fewer than five years.

Prior to 6 April 2013, these anti-avoidance provisions only applied (so as to tax the income or gains in the year of return) to:

- capital gains;
- offshore income gains;
- income withdrawals under certain foreign pension schemes;
- income withdrawals under registered pension schemes; and
- remittances of relevant foreign income.

The SRT enables individuals to manage their affairs so as to leave the UK and be certain of being non-UK resident for a tax year, even when absence from the UK is for fewer than five years. To prevent tax being avoided by individuals arranging matters so as to receive substantial income (relating to years when they were UK resident) during a temporary period of non-UK residence FA 2013 Sch 45 Part 4 widens the anti-avoidance provisions applying to such individuals.

The target is income where the time of receipt can be determined by the person leaving the UK. As such, from 6 April 2013 as well as the areas which were already caught under the old temporary non-residence rules, these further areas are also within the provisions:

- distributions from close companies (and companies that would be close if they were UK resident);
- chargeable event gains from life assurance contacts; and
- various pension benefits.

The opportunity was also taken to re-write the pre-existing legislation (as listed above), which was introduced piecemeal and, in some cases, had been modified more than once. Therefore the new definition of temporary non-residence applies to all the areas caught. To tie in with the new statutory split year provisions, an individual now has only to be non-UK resident for more than five years to avoid the anti-avoidance provisions, rather than for five tax years.

Note that although not included in FA 2013 Sch 45 Part 4, the new temporary non-residence rules also apply to offshore income gains (OIG). This is because although the gain is subject to income tax, the regulations import rules from capital gains tax, including temporary non-residence. The new rules apply to OIG arising from 2013/14 onwards (SI 2009/3001 regs 23-23A).

For more guidance on temporary non-residence under the SRT, see Chapter 6 of RDR3 (https://www.gov.uk/government/publications/rdr3-statutory-residence-test-srt).

*Effective date*

(25) The new legislation is effective where the 'year of departure' from the UK is 2013/14 or thereafter (FA 2013 Sch 45 para 153(3)). This means that only the old rules can apply to individuals with a 'year of departure' from the UK prior to 6 April 2013. However, care must be taken when applying the rules as there may be situations where the individual physically left the UK on or after 6 April 2013 but the 'year of departure' is deemed to be the 2012/13 tax year (meaning the old rules would apply). This is discussed in the article 'Temporary structure' in Taxation magazine dated 13 March 2013.

*Transitional provisions – years prior to 2013/14*

(26) As discussed above, the SRT came into force from 6 April 2013 and does not apply to determine residence in any prior tax year. However, when applying the SRT or deciding upon eligibility for split year treatment, it may be necessary to determine someone's residence status for a tax year prior to 2013/14. Where this is the case, an irrevocable written election may be made for tax years 2013/14 to 2017/18 to determine 'residence' with respect to 2010/11 to 2012/13 as if the SRT had applied. The deadline for the election is one year after the end of the relevant tax year. The election can be made either on the individual's tax return or in a standalone letter to the individual's HMRC office (FA 2013 Sch 45 para 154).

This election is effective only in relation to determining the individual's residence status for 2013/14 onwards, and will have no impact on his or her actual taxable status for those earlier years (which still have to be determined according to the former, uncertain, principles).

*Ordinary residence – abolition and transitional provisions*

(27) For income tax, CGT, IHT and (where relevant) corporation tax, the Government has abolished the concept of ordinary residence from 2013/14 onwards. However the concept remains for the purposes of national insurance and when considering tax credits. Overseas workday relief has been retained (see **explanatory note 28**).

Except where transitional provisions apply (see below), this means that now:

- only foreign domiciliaries are able to claim the remittance basis; and
- the attribution of income arising in foreign entities to UK residents (known as the 'transfers of assets abroad code') applies to all UK residents.

Those who were resident but not ordinarily resident in the UK at the end of 2012/13 benefited from transitional provisions such that they were no worse off as a result of the change.

The areas subject to the transitional provisions were (FA 2013 Sch 46 paras 26, 73):

- overseas workday relief (for those who already qualified before 2013/14);
- the remittance basis of taxation;
- foreign service relief for termination payments;
- transfer of assets abroad;
- seafarers earnings deduction.

As long as the conditions for the relevant provision were met and the individual continued to be considered not ordinarily resident in the UK (as if the concept of ordinary residence still existed), he continued to receive the beneficial tax treatment for (FA 2013 Sch 46 paras 26(3), 73(5):

- 2013/14 if he was UK resident in the 2010/11 and 2011/12 tax years;
- 2013/14 and 2014/15 if he was not UK resident in the 2010/11 tax year but was UK resident in the 2011/12 tax year; and
- 2013/14 to 2015/16 if he was not UK resident in the 2011/12 tax year.

The concept of ordinary residence is discussed in **explanatory note 36.**

*Overseas workday relief*

(28) The general rule is that the remittance basis applies to employment income only where the foreign employment is with an overseas employer and the employment duties are wholly performed abroad (with the exception of incidental UK duties). It can be very difficult for employment income to come within the remittance basis because of this and a specific rule has always applied to mitigate the severity of the general rule for short-term UK residents. 'Overseas workday relief' is the term used when referring to this relief.

Prior to 6 April 2013, a remittance basis user could claim overseas workday relief for the tax years during which the individual remained not ordinarily UK resident. Provided the income was paid into an offshore account, it meant that the remittance basis could be claimed in connection with foreign employment duties where a single contract covered both UK and overseas duties.

The earnings from the employment were apportioned between UK and overseas duties on a days basis and there was only a UK remittance if the total of the below exceeded the total UK portion of the earnings (SP 1/09):

- the total amount of earnings received in the UK; plus
- the amount remitted from the offshore account set up to receive the overseas portion of the earnings.

This relief was very valuable to internationally mobile employees (and their employers). As such, the relief has been retained but only for foreign domiciliaries.

From 6 April 2013 overseas workday relief can be claimed for a tax year if the individual (ITEPA 2003 ss 15, 26-26A):

- is domiciled outside the UK;
- accesses the remittance basis;
- has employment where the duties are performed in the UK and overseas; and
- he is resident for no more than two years immediately before the tax year in question (having been non-resident in the UK for at least three years prior to the first year of that period of UK residence).

Therefore the claim for overseas workday relief relates to one of the first three tax years of UK residence (counting the year of arrival as the first year even though it is unlikely to be a full year).

For HMRC guidance on overseas workday relief, see RDR4 (https://www.gov.uk/government/publications/rdr4-overseas-workday-relief-owr).

Allowing relief for the first three tax years of residence, regardless of the future intentions of the employee, is a particularly welcome change as it provides certainty and is helpful in attracting highly skilled internationally mobile workers to the UK. As a further relief for such individuals FA 2013 Sch 6 paras 4-6 enacted special rules (based on SP 01/09 that applied for tax years from 2008/09 to 2012/13) to enable a simplified version of the mixed fund rules for the remittance basis to apply, if certain conditions are met, to the offshore account that individuals eligible for overseas workday relief use for their earnings. For more details of how this works and the conditions which must be met, see the HMRC FAQs (now archived - http://webarchive.nationalarchives.gov.uk/+/hmrc.gov.uk/international/faqs-special-mixed-fund-rules.htm).

# PART B – THE LAW ON RESIDENCE PRIOR TO 2013/14

*The law prior to 2013/14 – overview*

(29) The following paragraphs state the law as it was prior to 6 April 2013. There is not space within these notes for a detailed discussion of the law in this area and the following paragraphs only provide a brief overview of some key considerations. HMRC guidance on the rules which applied prior to 6 April 2013 can be found in HMRC6 (https://www.gov.uk/government/publications/tax-on-foreign-income-rules-for-the-tax-year-ending-5-april-2013). The situation facing an individual leaving the UK to work full time abroad under a contract of employment spanning at least one complete tax year is discussed in more detail within **explanatory notes 31–32**.

Although it was such a fundamental concept for tax purposes, prior to 2013/14 there was no comprehensive statutory provision defining when an individual was and was not resident in the UK for tax purposes. Instead, when considering UK residence prior to 2013/14 the matter is left to case law much of which relates to the 19th and early 20th centuries and the issue is treated as one of fact based on each individual's circumstances.

The one absolute test pre-2013/14, set down in statute, is that an individual was for UK tax purposes taxed as if they were UK resident if he or she was present in the UK for 183 days or more in a tax year.

For tax years prior to 2013/14, the so called '91 days averaging' test was not a statutory test but was extracted by HMRC from historic case law and first set down within IR20 (the guidance which preceded HMRC6) as a test to determine whether an individual who made repeated visits to the UK over a number of tax years was UK resident. In addition to the test not being statutory it was clear from the approach taken by HMRC in a series of cases (the most well known being *Gaines-Cooper v HMRC* [2011] STC 2249) that HMRC for tax years prior to 2013/14 will challenge an individual's claim to be non-UK resident where he or she has been UK resident and cannot evidence that any return to the UK was merely for a temporary purpose. As such, the 91-day test could be seen more as a potential trap than as being of assistance to the taxpayer. Basically, in order to engage the 91-day test the individual first had to be non-resident. It only applied to check whether a non-resident would become UK resident rather than a test to break UK residence. Therefore, if an individual had been successful in establishing non-UK residence, breaching the 91-day averaging test could lead to an HMRC challenge on the basis that UK residence had resumed.

The need to be able to show that any return to the UK was merely temporary led to an emphasis on the individual who was seeking to become non-UK resident needing to evidence that he or she had made a 'distinct break' from the UK.

The phrase 'distinct break' was originally used by Lord Sands and comes from the case of *CIR v Combe* 17 TC 405 in 1932. The Respondent left the UK on 24 April 1926, having been UK resident and ordinarily resident, to enter into a three year apprenticeship with a financial firm in New York (he was to learn the business with a view to becoming the European representative).

Whilst he returned to the UK, living in hotel rooms as he had no available UK accommodation, for significant periods (52 days in 1926/27; 175 days in 1927/28; and 181 days in 1928/29) it was held that for the three years he had a permanent base in New York and so should be seen as neither UK resident nor ordinarily UK resident.

Prior to the FA 2013 changes, the legislation stated that in determining whether an individual is UK resident one should ignore any living accommodation available in the UK if he worked full time abroad in one or both of a foreign trade (trade included profession and vacation) or a foreign employment (employment included an office). The legislation specified that:

- a trade could only be foreign if no part of it was carried on in the UK; and
- an employment could only be foreign if either:
  - all of its duties were performed outside of the UK; or
  - the only duties of the employment performed outside of the UK were duties which were merely incidental to the duties of the employment performed outside of the UK in the year.

*The law prior to 2013/14 – the 'distinct break' test*

(30) The 'distinct break' test used prior to tax year 2013/14 was one of fact and so each individual's circumstances had to be reviewed as a whole. In the Court of Appeal decision in *HMRC v Grace* [2009] STC 2707 Lloyd LJ, in rejecting the argument that the appellant's presence in the UK for employment purposes was a factor which necessarily showed residence, referred to the need to take into account, weigh up and balance all relevant factors.

When considering whether there had been a distinct break, case law indicated that some factors (such as the presence of a UK employment or where the individual's immediate family was based) might be given more weight than others. However, only presence in the UK in excess of 182 days was so significant that, regardless of other factors, the only possible conclusion was that the individual should be treated as being UK resident for income tax and capital gains tax purposes.

Since the decision turned on making specific judgments based on the specific facts of a case, there was significant inherent uncertainty as to how profound a change an individual needed to make to sever UK ties sufficiently to be said to have made a distinct break.

When considering UK residence prior to 2013/14 where other factors were present, such that it could be said that a distinct break from the UK had been made, case law shows that not setting foot in the UK for a whole tax year could result in a finding of non-UK residence and non-UK ordinary residence. In *Reed v Clark* [1985] STC 323, the period of absence from the UK was 13 months (spanning an entire tax year).

The decision that the individual was neither UK resident nor ordinarily resident in the UK was predicated on the specific facts. These were that the individual:

- left the UK before the start of a tax year with a settled intention not to return to the UK for at least one whole tax year;
- took steps to ensure he did not have a residence available in the UK;
- had a settled intention (which he subsequently fulfilled) to take up residence in a specific territory (providing a base for himself in this new territory) and an established purpose for doing so; and
- did not return to the UK for a whole tax year (that is, he made no return visits to the UK whatsoever during the whole of the tax year outside the UK).

The lack of an available UK residence during the period away, the settled intention and the purpose for residence in another territory, the fact that a fixed base was established in that other territory and that Mr Clark did not visit the UK at all led Nicholls J to conclude that:

'*In this case there was a distinct break in the pattern of the taxpayer's life which lasted (as from the outset he intended) for just over a year.*'

When considering tax years prior to 2013/14, leaving the UK before the start of a tax year, to work full time abroad under a contract of foreign employment (or to become self-employed abroad) was sufficient, in the eyes of HMRC, to establish a distinct break provided days of physical presence in the UK were kept within the limits specified in HMRC6 (discussed below). HMRC accepted that where an individual qualified for the 'working abroad route' an accompanying spouse was also be deemed to be non-UK resident if the day count tests were not breached.

Prior to 2013/14, where an individual could not arrange his affairs so as to be able to follow exactly the ground rules set down in *Reed v Clark* and was not leaving the UK for full time employment abroad, it was necessary to demonstrate a distinct break by a severing of ties with the UK. The aim when advising in advance was to establish a position such that the non-resident status was unchallengeable.

For tax years prior to 2013/14, when considering whether there was a 'distinct break', as well as the UK employment issues already mentioned, the courts may give significant weight to the availability of UK accommodation.

Registration with UK doctors and dentists could also be an issue. A claim of non-residence when coupled with repeated visits to the UK for NHS medical and dental treatment could be expected to attract a challenge from HMRC. Indeed any use of UK services by the individual or dependants or claims to social security benefits whilst non-UK residence was claimed can be expected to lead to HMRC scrutiny and a potential challenge to the claim to be non-UK resident.

There would be no issue with an individual who chose to spend his retirement abroad and received the UK state pension to which he was entitled. As a practical point, where an individual is to establish residence in an EU member state they should not have applied for a European Health Insurance Card (EHIC) from the UK as these are only available to UK residents making temporary visits abroad.

In terms of severing other ties with the UK, the following actions would have been helpful to demonstrate a severing of UK ties (note the list is not exhaustive and would need to be tailored to the specific individual):

- removing all personal possessions from the UK;
- cancelling UK mobile telephone and internet service provider contracts;
- removing oneself from the UK electoral roll;
- closing UK bank accounts, opening accounts abroad and changing direct debits and standing orders;
- cancelling UK credit cards and store cards;

- changing car licence plates and taking steps to acquire a driving licence abroad; and
- cancelling UK club memberships or, where membership is particularly important to the individual, switching to overseas membership.

## The law prior to 2013/14 – full time work abroad

*The law prior to 2013/14 – overview*

(31) Leaving the UK to work full time abroad under a contract of foreign employment (or to become self-employed abroad) which spanned a complete UK tax year was sufficient, in the eyes of HMRC, to establish a distinct break provided days of physical presence in the UK were kept within the limits specified. HMRC's settled view on this was set down within section 8.5 of HMRC6 (https://www.gov.uk/government/publications/tax-on-foreign-income-rules-for-the-tax-year-ending-5-april-2013).

In summary HMRC accepted that, for tax years prior to 2013/14, individuals would become non-UK resident and not ordinarily resident from the day after the day of their departure from the UK, as long as:

- they were leaving to work full time abroad under a contract of employment (or to become self-employed abroad) for at least a whole tax year;
- they actually physically left the UK to begin their employment/self-employment abroad and not, for example, to have a holiday until they began their employment/self-employment;
- they would be absent from the UK for at least a whole tax year; and
- visits to the UK after individuals had left to begin their overseas employment/self-employment would:
  - total less than 183 days in any tax year; and
  - average less than 91 days a tax year. (This average was taken over the period of absence up to a maximum of four years.) Any days spent in the UK because of exceptional circumstances beyond the individual's control were not normally counted for this purpose.

To place any reliance on section 8.5 of HMRC6, the taxpayer must have met all of the conditions in full. Where an individual left the UK to work full time abroad an HMRC challenge to his residence status prior to 2013/14 normally took the form of an argument that one or more of these conditions has not been met:

- the case of *Farquhar v HMRC* [2010] UKFTT 231 (TC) concerned the averaging method used with respect to the non-statutory '91-day averaging test'. The averaging method used on behalf of the taxpayer, although allowed by one HMRC tax office (as evidenced to and accepted by the tribunal in the course of the hearing), was not the method specified in HMRC6.
- in the case of *Hankinson v HMRC* [2009] UKFTT 384 (TC) (discussed in **explanatory note 32**) HMRC successfully challenged the individual's non-UK residence claim on the grounds that the foreign employment was not full time.

For tax years prior to 2013/14, ESC A78 extended split year treatment to a spouse/civil partner who accompanied the individual or later follows him abroad provided the accompanying partner:

- would be absent from the UK for at least a whole tax year; and
- kept visits to the UK after departure down to:
  - less than 183 days in any tax year; and
  - averages less than 91 days a tax year.

*The law prior to 2013/14 – the concept of full time work abroad*

(32) An employment/self employment was foreign where either:

- all duties were performed outside the UK; or
- the duties of the employment/self-employment were in substance performed outside the UK and the only duties performed in the UK in the year were duties which were merely incidental to the duties performed outside the UK.

Incidental was not defined in the legislation. The case of *Robson v Dixon* 48 TC 527 gave us the following definition:

'*The words "merely incidental to" are upon their ordinary use apt to denote an activity (here the performance of duties) which does not serve any independent purpose but is carried out in order to further some other purpose.*'

It was also clear from the case that for UK duties to have been incidental they needed to be distinguishable from foreign duties to the extent that it was possible to give a satisfactory answer to the question: 'What exactly were the duties outside the UK to which the performance of the duties were incidental?' In the case, Pennycuick VC accepted as clearly right the contention that an emergency landing would be seen as incidental and also that one might have a de minimis position (a single landing).

HMRC6 (particularly at section 10.6 in the sub-sections on 'Other workers' - https://www.gov.uk/government/publications/tax-on-foreign-income-rules-for-the-tax-year-ending-5-april-2013) suggested that HMRC would argue for the term 'incidental duties' to be construed strictly. HMRC considered this issue in 2011 and its view was that, as a general rule, if the UK work was for less than 10 days per year HMRC would, for the purposes of determining if there was a foreign employment when considering an individual's UK residence status, accept UK duties were incidental without further investigation. See The ten day test' in Taxation magazine 27 April 2011. If there were more than 10 UK days this does not mean that HMRC would automatically argue that there was no full-time contract of employment abroad. It would depend on the facts.

Full-time employment was also not defined in the old legislation. It is understood that HMRC regarded a normal working week as being at least 35 hours. Although, it may have been possible to argue that an individual was working full time where their hours were below this figure. This would only be where the hours the individual worked were in line with what counted as full-time employment in the sector and territory where they were living. Several part-time foreign employments and/or self-employments could be aggregated so as to count as full-time employment.

In order to meet the conditions the reason for leaving the UK needed to be to take up the foreign contract of employment or to work abroad for oneself in a trade, profession or vocation. This meant that there needed to be a demonstrable commercial rationale for the overseas contract of employment or the self-employed business venture rather than it being used purely as a route to non-residence. In addition, the actual work carried out must have been genuinely and demonstrably full-time.

In *Hankinson v HMRC* [2009] UKFTT 384 (TC), the First-tier Tribunal judges found that as a question of fact the work undertaken for the UK company was of such an extent in comparison to the duties for the foreign company that the individual could not have been employed full-time abroad.

The *Hankinson* case shows that the courts tested whether a contract of employment was full-time by looking at what work the individual could actually be said to have carried out for the foreign company.

*The law prior to 2013/14 – day count*

(33) For tax years from 2008/09 onwards, there was a statutory definition of a day of UK presence. From 2008/09 to 2012/13 inclusive, a day counted as one of UK presence where the individual was in the UK at the end of that day (meaning the individual was present in the UK at midnight). However, a day was not be counted where the transit exemption applied.

Prior to 2013/14, by extra-statutory concession, provided the statutory 183-day test was not breached, a day could be disregarded where a visit had to be extended as a result of exceptional circumstances beyond the individual's control (such as an illness so serious that it prevented the individual from leaving the UK). It was strongly recommended that individuals did not rely on this concession and if at all possible ensured that their aggregate number of days (including days in the UK as a result of exceptional circumstances) of UK presence was comfortably less than 91.

When considering tax years prior to 6 April 2008 there was no statutory definition and the generally accepted rule is that days of arrival and departure were discounted (though this could be challenged by HMRC if an individual made repeated visits to the UK in a tax year).

Strictly, the statutory definition of a day of UK presence that applied between 2008/09 and 2012/13 only had effect with respect to the statutory 183-day provision that an individual was taxed as if he were UK resident if he had spent over 182 days in the UK in the tax year in question. However, HMRC stated that it would normally use the statutory definition of a day of presence in the UK when it applied its non-statutory '91-day averaging' test. HMRC6 (https://www.gov.uk/government/publications/tax-on-foreign-income-rules-for-the-tax-year-ending-5-april-2013) made it clear that HMRC viewed things differently if an individual made a significant number of one-day trips to the UK (in such cases it appeared that HMRC reserved the right to argue that all days of UK presence should be counted when considering the non-statutory 91 day test).

When applying the averaging test to individuals who came to the UK prior to 6 April 2008 it was necessary to determine the number of days of UK presence in the relevant period by using the statutory day count definition for tax years 2008/09 to 2012/13 and the non-statutory practice for relevant tax years before then.

*The law prior to 2013/14 – Temporary absences*

(34) If the absence abroad was not permanent and did not span a complete tax year, a person was regarded as remaining resident and ordinarily resident in the UK throughout. Prior to tax year 2013/14 and the introduction of the SRT, case law showed us that even not setting foot in the UK for a whole tax year would not result in non-UK resident status where:

- the absence was only of a temporary nature; and
- the individual had not established his residence in any place other than the UK and could have been said to retain links to the UK.

The specific case law authority for the assertion that an individual could be UK resident in a tax year during which he spent no time here came from the 1879 case of *Rogers v Inland Revenue* 1 TC 225. The facts in this case can be contrasted with those in *Reed v Clark* (see **explanatory note 30**). As explained in **explanatory note 6** above, this changes from 2013/14 as an individual who spends fewer than 16 days in the UK will be automatically non-UK resident under the SRT.

As discussed in **explanatory note 30**, HMRC accepted that the pre-6 April 2013 'distinct break' test was met, such that the absence was not just of a temporary nature, where an individual left the UK to work full time abroad under a contract of foreign employment (or to become self-employed abroad) which spaned a complete tax year. There would be an issue if something went wrong and the individual returned to the UK prematurely such that the absence did not span a tax year.

Anti-avoidance provisions (known as temporary non-residence) applied if:

- prior to the tax year of departure the individual had been UK resident for at least four or the preceding seven tax years;
- an individual returned to the UK prior to having spent five complete tax years outside the UK.

The legislation did not impact the residence status of the taxpayer but it meant that gains or income which had not been taxable in the UK due to the individual's residence status fell to be taxed in the UK in the year of return. The temporary non-residence rules applied to:

- capital gains;

- offshore income gains;
- income withdrawals under certain foreign pension schemes;
- income withdrawals under registered pension schemes; and
- remittances of relevant foreign income.

For guidance on the temporary non-residence rules prior to 6 April 2013, see HMRC6, para 5.11 (https://www.gov.uk/government/publications/tax-on-foreign-income-rules-for-the-tax-year-ending-5-april-2013), CG26100 and RDRM32510. The rules which apply from 6 April 2013 are discussed in **explanatory note 24.**

*The law prior to 2013/14 – split-year treatment*

(35) Prior to 2013/14, the UK tax legislation made no provision for splitting a tax year in relation to residence. This meant that an individual who was resident in the UK for any tax year was chargeable strictly on the basis that he was resident for the whole year.

There were two exceptions to the strict rule that the tax year could not be split:

(i) the provisions of a relevant double tax treaty (the exact relief depends on the exact wording of the specific treaty);

(ii) where relief could be claimed under ESC A11 for income tax and ESC D2 for CGT. A taxpayer was not by right entitled to a concession. There has always been a general caveat that a taxpayer should not use HMRC guidance for tax avoidance purposes. This rule applies to HMRC guidance, statements of practice or any other such pronouncements made by HMRC.

Provided tax avoidance was not in point, ESC A11 (the income tax split year concession) should have been granted for tax years prior to 2013/14 where:

- in the year of arrival where an individual came to the UK to take up permanent residence or to stay for at least two years;
- in the year of departure where an individual ceased to reside in the UK if he left for permanent residence abroad; or
- in the years of departure and return where an individual went abroad for full-time service under a contract of employment and the following conditions were met:
  - the individual's absence from the UK and the employment itself both extended over a period covering a complete UK tax year; and
  - any interim visits to the UK during the period did not amount to:
    - 183 days or more in any tax year; or
    - an average of 91 days or more in a tax year (the average was taken over the period of absence up to a maximum of four years).

A further concession (ESC A78) extended the same treatment to a non-working spouse or civil partner who accompanied or later joined his or her spouse or civil partner who was working full-time abroad.

Where the tax year was split under ESC A11, the limit on income chargeable on non-residents outlined in **Example F2 explanatory note 4** did not apply for that tax year. Even though income for each part of the year was calculated according to whether the individual was, or was not, resident, full personal allowances were available for that tax year.

As mentioned, ESC D2 was relevant for the split-year rules in relation to capital gains tax. Where this treatment applied, gains in the non-resident part were not charged, and losses in the non-resident part were not allowed. However, for the pre-2013/14 temporary non-residence rules to be avoided the individual would have to be non-resident for five complete tax years (see **explanatory note 34**).

*The position prior to 2013/14 – ordinary residence*

(36) Prior to 6 April 2013, in the UK tax system there were three concepts that determined the liability of an individual to direct taxation: residence, ordinary residence and domicile. Of these, residence and domicile were the more important, but being not ordinarily resident in the UK could reduce an individual's liability to tax. For example, where an individual was resident but not ordinary resident in the UK:

- the rules were more favourable when applying the remittance basis to foreign employment income (overseas workday relief, see **explanatory note 28**);
- the anti-avoidance code relating to the transfer of assets abroad could not apply; and
- a UK domiciled individual was able to claim the remittance basis with respect to foreign income (but not capital gains).

Liability to CGT was determined by whether a taxpayer was UK resident or ordinarily resident in the UK. It was, therefore, envisaged that an individual might be liable to UK tax solely because he was ordinarily UK resident.

For HMRC guidance on the meaning of ordinary residence, see HMRC6, Chapters 7 and 8 (https://www.gov.uk/government/publications/tax-on-foreign-income-rules-for-the-tax-year-ending-5-april-2013).

# Question

Mr Harding, a married man born in 1957, is a British subject who is not resident in the UK.

His income for 2016/17 is:

| | £ |
|---|---|
| UK rental income (net amount after basic rate tax deducted under the provisions of the non-resident landlords' scheme) | 67,200 |
| Interest from 3½% War Loan | 1,500 |
| UK dividends | 10,000 |
| Earnings from employment abroad | 110,000 |
| Interest from Canada (gross) | 150 |

Mr Harding sold a rental property in London on 1 April 2017 for £1,250,000. He originally purchased it on 27 May 1995 for £350,000, with costs of acquisition of £6,000. He has never lived in the property. He has no mortgage on the property and it has always been held in his sole name. It is valued at £1,125,000 on 5 April 2015. The costs of sale were £20,000. He used the proceeds to buy a rental property in Geneva, which completed on 2 April 2017.

Mr Harding was non-UK resident in 2013/14, 2014/15 and 2015/16. His employment is with a Swiss company whom he has worked for since he left the UK and none of the duties of his employment are performed in the UK. He lives in Geneva.

He qualifies as automatically non-UK resident by virtue of meeting the third automatic overseas test (working sufficient hours overseas – with no significant breaks – in the tax year and keeping his UK days within the permitted limits).

Compute the amount of UK income tax and capital gains tax payable by Mr Harding for the year 2016/17 assuming that any available relief is claimed. Ignore double taxation agreements.

Mrs Harding (Mr Harding's wife) accompanied him to Geneva. Like her husband she was non-UK resident to 2014/15 inclusive. However, in 2015/16 her mother died and the additional time she spent in the UK meant that her UK days exceeded 183 so she was UK resident for tax purposes (under the first automatic UK test).

Throughout 2016/17 the couple had a home in Geneva and a home in the UK. They occupied the UK home when staying in the UK. Mrs Harding:

- had no employment anywhere in the 2016/17 tax year;
- spent 80 days in the UK (seeing her minor children, who attended UK boarding schools, on 76 of these days), 250 days in Switzerland and 35 days elsewhere;
- her children are both minors who are automatically UK resident in 2016/17 by virtue of spending in excess of 183 days in the UK but for 2016/17, outside of term time both children only spent 10 days in the UK.

Mrs Harding has UK building society interest of £8,130 for 2016/17, an annuity from a family trust of £10,000 gross per annum (from which basic rate tax is deducted), and interest of £250 on a foreign bank account.

Determine whether Mrs Harding is UK resident or not for 2016/17 and compute the amount of UK income tax payable by or repayable to Mrs Harding for the year 2016/17 assuming that any available relief is claimed. Ignore double taxation agreements.

# Answer

## Mr Harding

### UK income tax position 2016/17

| | UK income |
|---|---|
| *Mr Harding* | £ |
| UK rental income (N1) | 84,000 |
| UK dividend income (N3) | 10,000 |
| | 94,000 |
| Personal allowance (N4) | (11,000) |
| Taxable income | 83,000 |
| Tax thereon: | £ |
| £32,000 @ 20% | 6,400 |
| £41,000 @ 40% | 16,400 |
| £5,000 @ 0% (N3) | — |
| £5,000 @ 32.5% | 1,625 |
| | 24,425 |
| Less: income tax treated as paid on dividends (N3) | (750) |
| Less: tax withheld from rent | (16,800) |
| Tax due | 6,875 |

*Notes*

(1) Under the non-resident landlords' scheme the letting agent (or the tenant if there is no agent) must withhold income tax at the basic rate on the gross rent and pay this over to HMRC (ITA 2007 s 971; SI 1995/2902). The tax withheld is £16,800 (£67,200 x 20/80), meaning the gross rent is £84,000 £67,200 + £16,800). For further details of the non-resident landlord scheme, see **Example D2 explanatory note 11.**

(2) As a non-resident, Mr Harding is only taxable on UK source income. However, UK gilt interest received by non-residents is not taxable in the UK because of a specific exemption from tax (ITTOIA 2005 ss 713-714). These investments are referred to in practice as FOTRA securities (free of tax to residents abroad). Therefore the interest on the 3½% War Loan bonds are not taxable in the hands of Mr Harding.

(3) Dividends no longer attract a tax credit from 2016/17 onwards. However, under ITTOIA 2005, s 399 (as amended by Finance Act 2016), non-residents in receipt of UK dividends are entitled to treat income tax equivalent to the dividend ordinary rate of 7.5% as paid (see **explanatory note 7**). This can be deducted from the UK tax liability for the year but it cannot generate or increase a repayment. Non-residents also qualify for the £5,000 dividend nil rate band (ITA 2007, s 13A). The balance is taxable at the marginal rate, which is the dividend upper rate of 32.5%.

(4) Mr Harding is entitled to a personal allowance as a British national (ITA 2007 s 35 as read with ITA 2007 s 56). Although his income from the UK and overseas exceeds £100,000, for the purposes of abating the personal allowance it is only the income which is taxable in the UK which is taken into account, so no reduction is necessary (ITA 2007 s 35(2) as read with ITA 2007 s 58 and ITA 2007 s 23).

*UK capital gains tax position 2016/17*

Mr Harding sold a UK sited residential property in 2016/17 which he had owned prior to becoming non-resident in the UK. This means two sets of rules need to be considered:

- temporary non-residence rules in TCGA 1992 s 10A, which apply to assets disposed of during a period of temporary non-residence (fewer than five years) which were owned prior to departure from the UK. Where these rules apply, the gain is charged in the tax year of return to the UK;
- non-resident capital gains tax (NRCGT) rules in TCGA 1992, s 14B, which apply to disposals of UK residential property by UK non-residents from 6 April 2015. The gain is charged to UK tax in the year in which it arises.

The NRCGT rules take precedence over the temporary non-residence rules, such that the gain is chargeable to UK tax in the year in which it arises under NRCGT and if the taxpayer becomes UK resident again within the five year window there is no second tax charge on the same gain (TCGA 1992 s 10A(5)).

Under the NRCGT rules, three different methods can be used to calculate the chargeable gain, with the taxpayer able to elect for whichever one is produces the lowest gain. The methods are (TCGA 1992, Sch 4ZZB):

- the rebasing method, where the property is valued at 5 April 2015 and only the gain from this date is taxable. This is the default method and will apply unless an election is made for one of the other options;
- the straight-line apportionment method, where only the gain arising from 6 April 2015 is taxable but the gain is assumed to have accrued evenly over the entire ownership of the property. The apportionment is made on a days basis;
- the retrospective method, where the taxpayer can deem the NRCGT rules to have always applied. Although this might seem only to be appropriate where a loss arises, this method is also worth considering in cases where there is a gain and principal private residence (PPR) relief applies.

Based on the facts in this question, these three methods give the gains:

| | *Rebasing method* | *Straight-line method* | *Retrospective method* |
|---|---|---|---|
| | £ | £ | £ |
| Proceeds | 1,250,000 | 1,250,000 | 1,250,000 |
| Less: costs of sale | (20,000) | (20,000) | (20,000) |
| | 1,230,000 | 1,230,000 | 1,230,000 |
| Less MV 5 April 2016 | (1,125,000) | — | — |
| Less: acquisition costs | — | (356,000) | (356,000) |
| Less: pre-6 April 2015 gain | | | |
| (£874,000 x 7,253 days/7,980 days) | — | (794,376) | — |
| Chargeable gain | 105,000 | 79,624 | 874,000 |

Therefore, Mr Harding should elect for the straight-line apportionment method. As he is entitled to the annual exempt amount, the tax due is £19,187 ((£79,624 – £11,100) x 28%). Tax is charged at 28% (rather than 20%) as this is a disposal of a residential property interest. The election should be made on the NRCGT return, which must be filed within 30 days of the date of completion, and should declare details of the gain. However, as Mr Harding already submits a UK self-assessment tax return he has until 31 January 2018 to pay the CGT of £19,187, in addition to his UK income tax liability calculated above.

See **explanatory notes 10–16**.

## Mrs Harding

Mrs Harding's residence status in 2016/17 must be determined under the statutory residence test (FA 2013 Sch 45). This means working through the tests in the order below:

(1) if any of the automatic overseas tests are met, she is non-resident in the UK for the tax year;

(2) if none of the automatic overseas tests are met, one must move on to the automatic UK tests. If any of the automatic UK tests are met, she is resident in the UK for the tax year;

(3) if none of the automatic overseas tests and none of the automatic UK tests are met then the sufficient ties test must be considered. If the sufficent ties test is met then she is UK resident for the tax year. If the sufficent ties test is not met then she is not resident in the UK for the tax year.

Based on Mrs Harding's day count, lack of any employment/self employment and homes in both the UK and overseas she does not meet any of the automatic overseas tests(see **Example F1 explanatory note 5**) or automatic UK resident tests (see **Example F1 explanatory note 14**). The only one of these tests which requires careful thought is the second automatic UK test (home in the UK test) (FA 2013 Sch 45 para 8). This is not met because although she has a home in the UK which was available for at least 91 consecutive days (of which at least 30 fall in the 2016/17 tax year), she also has an overseas home and is present at that home for 30 days or more in 2016/17.

Therefore, the sufficient ties test needs to be considered (see **Example F1 explanatory note 22**). The sufficient ties test compares the days spent in the UK in the tax year with the number of UK ties to decide if an individual is UK resident in that tax year. As Mrs Harding was UK resident in 2015/16, she must use the table in FA 2013 Sch 45 para 18.

Her ties with the UK for the purposes of the sufficient ties test are:

| **UK tie** | |
|---|---|
| Family tie | **No** because:<br>• her husband is not UK resident.<br>• whilst her minor children are UK resident for the purposes of this tie that is disregarded as a result of special provisions at FA 2013 Sch 45 para 33(3)–33(6). This is because the minor children are only UK resident as a result of being in full time education in the UK and they spend less than 21 days in the UK outside of term times. |
| Accommodation tie | **Yes** – Mrs Harding has a place to live in the UK which was available for a continuous period of 91 days or more and she spent more than one night there in the tax year (FA 2013 Sch 45 para 34) |
| Work tie | **No** – Mrs Harding does not have any employment or self-employment (FA 2013 Sch 45 paras 35–36) |
| 90 day tie | **Yes** – Mrs Harding spent more than 90 days in the UK in either of the last two preceding tax years (FA 2013 Sch 45 para 37) |
| Country tie | **No** – Mrs Harding spent more time in Switzerland than in the UK in 2016/17 (FA 2013 Sch 45 para 38) |

Overall Mrs Harding has two UK ties for the 2016/17 tax year. Based on the table in FA 2013 Sch 45 para 18, she is not UK resident in 2016/17 as her UK days are less than 91. As such, she is subject to tax as a non-UK resident meaning her UK tax computation for 2016/17 is as follows:

| | UK source income | UK tax deducted |
|---|---|---|
| | £ | £ |
| UK annuity | 10,000 | 2,000 |
| UK building society interest | 8,130 | – |
| | 18,130 | 2,000 |
| Less: personal allowance (N1) | (11,000) | |
| Taxable income | 7,130 | |
| Tax thereon: | £ | £ |
| £5,000 @ 0% (N2) | — | |
| £1,000 @ 0% (N3) | — | |
| £1,130 @ 20% | 226 | |
| | | 226 |
| Less: tax withheld from annuity | | (2,000) |
| Tax repayable | | (1,774) |

*Notes*

(1) Mrs Harding is entitled to a personal allowance as a British national (ITA 2007 s 35 as read with ITA 2007 s 56).

(2) Since Mrs Harding's taxable income is all savings income (the annuity being set off against her personal allowance), she is entitled to the 0% starting rate for savings income (ITA 2007 s 12).

(3) As Mrs Harding is a basic rate taxpayer, she is entitled to savings nil rate on her first £1,000 of taxable savings income (which applies after the starting rate for savings) (ITA 2007 s 12A). The balance after the starting rate for savings and the savings nil rate (£7,130 – £5,000 – £1,000) is taxable at 20%.

(4) As a non-resident, Mrs Harding is not subject to UK tax on the £250 of foreign source interest.

## THE TAXATION OF NON-UK RESIDENTS

*Personal allowances for non-residents*

(1) Non-residents are not entitled to UK personal allowances unless they qualify under the provisions of ITA 2007 s 56, or under the terms of a double taxation agreement. The main categories of qualifying non-resident are EEA nationals (the EEA covers the European Union plus Iceland, Liechtenstein and Norway) and residents of the Isle of Man or the Channel Islands. Non-residents will not normally be able to register as blind and will not therefore be entitled to blind person's allowance. The personal allowance may be set against any of the person's income that is liable to tax in the UK (ITA 2007 s 34(2)), whereas married couple's allowance is a tax reducer set against the person's tax liability (ITA 2007 s 42(4)). No allowances are available to those who qualify only on grounds of being citizens of former Commonwealth, but many affected individuals will qualify in any event under double taxation agreements.

To qualify for UK child tax credit or working tax credit, claimants have to be 'in the UK' (physically present here) and ordinarily resident within the meaning of the Tax Credits legislation (see TCTM02026 as to how HMRC interpret ordinary residence for this purpose although, at the time of writing it has not been updated to reflect the change to the tax rules in **Example F1 explanatory note 27**). In this Example, it is unlikely that either Mr Harding or Mrs Harding would qualify as ordinarily resident under the tax credits tests so no entitlement to CTC will arise. If Mrs Harding was able to establish ordinary residence for the future she would make a claim for tax credits as a single person based on the number of days she was 'in the UK' (ignoring certain periods of temporary absence – see SI 2003/654 reg 4). Only her income would count in the tax credits claim. ***Note that for the purposes of the tax credits legislation the concept of ordinary residence is retained.***

*Government 'FOTRA' securities*

(2) ITTOIA 2005 s 713 states that Government securities are not liable to UK income tax whilst in the beneficial ownership (that is either held directly or through a trust provided a qualifying individual is entitled to the interest) of persons not resident in the UK. Prior to 6 April 2013 the person beneficially entitled had to be not ordinarily resident in the UK.

Such securities are referred to as FOTRA securities (free of tax to residents abroad). The exemption does not, however, apply where the interest is received as part of a trade carried on in the UK.

*Taxation of non-residents and provision of information*

(3) Since 6 April 2016 UK deposit-takers, such as banks and building societies are no longer required to deduct basic rate income tax at source from interest. This was introduced in tandem with the savings nil rate (mentioned in the answer to Mrs Harding above). This removes the need for non-UK residents to complete form R105 in order to receive interest gross without deduction of tax.

Since 6 April 2001 banks, building societies etc have been required to provide information to HMRC on interest paid to depositors in the UK. Paying and collecting agents who handle interest and dividends from abroad are included in the provisions.

In addition, FA 2006 replaced the existing arrangements for exchange of information with overseas jurisdictions with more extensive arrangements that cover not only the exchange of information with overseas tax authorities in both directions, but will also allow for enforcement of foreign taxes in the UK, and of UK taxes abroad. Additional measures were brought in by FA 2011 Sch 25 which gives effect to the EU Council Directive 2010/24/EU which is concerned with mutual assistance for the recovery of claims relating to taxes, duties and other measures. This directive was adopted by the EU to expand the situations in which a Member State (the Applicant State) may obtain assistance from another member state (the Requested State) in recovering taxes owing to the Applicant State. The directive covers all taxes and essentially enhances the ability of EU Member States to enforce tax recovery crossborder.

See also **Example F3 explanatory note 2.**

*Income tax liability of non-residents*

(4) Non-residents are not liable to UK tax on foreign income.

With respect to UK source income, in addition to being exempt from tax on interest on Government stocks (see **explanatory note 2**), and possibly on other sources of income under a double tax agreement, non-UK resident individuals and trustees are subject to special rules on certain categories of UK income (referred to as disregarded income and listed out at ITA 2007 s 813).

Employment income, trading income and income from renting UK land does not come within the definition of disregarded income and is taxable in full. This means that a non-UK resident receiving such UK source income is always liable to tax at basic, higher and additional rates as appropriate.

Most UK savings and investment income (defined in ITA 2007 s 825) falls within the disregarded income category as do annual payments (ITA 2007 s 826), most pension income, including UK state pensions (ITA 2007 s 813(3)), social security income and disregarded transaction income (ITA 2007 s 814).

The special rules for the taxation of disregarded income are set down at ITA 2007 s 811. Broadly, the UK tax liability of non-UK resident individuals and trustees on disregarded income can be limited to the amount of tax deducted at source from that income (even if, in the case of interest, no tax was deducted at source because it was paid gross). This means that neither the higher nor the additional rate of income tax has to be paid. An individual has a choice between: (i) benefiting from this limitation; and (ii) being taxed on all UK income and where applicable, benefiting from personal allowances, age-related allowances, blind person's allowance, married couples' allowance, or any tax reliefs that would otherwise be due under ITA 2007 ss 457–459. For example, a non-UK resident individual whose only source of UK income in the tax year is a dividend of £100,000 from a UK company would have no UK tax to pay. As explained, this is because dividend income is 'disregarded savings and investment income' by ITA 2007 s 825(1)(a) and ITA 2007 s 811 provides that the UK tax liability is limited to the income tax treated as paid at source on that dividend (see **explanatory note 7**). In contrast, if personal allowances were claimed instead (assuming they are available under a double tax agreement or otherwise) the dividend income would not be taxed under the disregarded income rules so the UK tax liability would be higher as shown below:

| | | | £ | £ |
|---|---|---|---|---|
| Dividend income (gross) | | | | 100,000 |
| Less: personal allowance | | | | (11,000) |
| Taxable income | | | | 89,000 |
| | | | £ | £ |
| Tax thereon | £5,000 | @0% | — | |
| | £27,000 | @7.5% | 2,025 | |
| | £57,000 | @32.5% | 18,525 | |
| | | | | 20,550 |
| Less: tax treated as paid on the dividend | | | | (7,500) |
| | | | | 13,050 |

The effect of the rules in ITA 2007 s 811 is unchanged by the changes introduced in 2016/17.

The ITA 2007 s 35(2)–(4) reduction provisions mean that individuals with adjusted net income between £100,000 and £122,000 (for 2016/17) can only access a reduced personal allowance (a £1 deduction for every £2 of income received in excess of £100,000). For 2016/17 no personal allowance is due where income exceeds £122,000. This needs to be taken into account when carrying out computations to determine whether claiming the personal allowance or benefiting from the disregarded income rules will be more beneficial to an individual.

A non-resident individual who receives a dividend of £1 million from a UK company would have no higher rate or additional rate liability to UK tax. As explained above, with income at this level the personal allowance would not be available.

In this Example, Mr Harding has UK income which would be taxable in the UK of £94,000. Apart from the £84,000 of UK property income, Mr Harding's only other UK source of taxable income is £10,000 of dividends (the interest on government stocks is exempt). As such, it is beneficial for him to claim the personal allowance.

Looking at the position of Mrs Harding, she has UK income of £18,130 (£8,130 of building society interest which qualifies as disregarded income and £10,000 of annuity income). Building society interest, in contrast to interest from government stocks, is not exempt in the hands of a non-UK resident. It has to be taken into account in any repayment claim as she is claiming the personal allowance. As the answer shows, this means she can reclaim only £1,774 of the £2,000 deducted from her annuity. In this situation, even though claiming the personal allowance means that the building society interest cannot be disregarded, it is still more favourable to make the personal allowance claim. In contrast, if Mrs Harding's UK building society interest had amounted to £25,000, it would have been beneficial for her to forgo personal allowances and be taxed in accordance with the 'disregarded income' provisions, which would exclude the interest from her tax computation, such that she would be taxed as follows:

| | UK income | UK tax paid |
|---|---|---|
| | £ | £ |
| UK annuity | 10,000 | 2,000 |
| Tax thereon: @ 20% | | 2,000 |
| Further tax payable | | Nil |

Had personal allowances been claimed the computation would have been:

| | | UK income | UK tax paid |
|---|---|---|---|
| | | £ | £ |
| UK annuity | | 10,000 | 2,000 |
| UK building society interest | | 25,000 | |
| | | 35,000 | |
| Less: personal allowance | | (11,000) | |
| | | 24,000 | |
| Tax thereon: | £5,000 @ 0% | — | |
| | £1,000 @ 0% | — | |
| | £18,000 @ 20% | 3,600 | |
| | | | 3,600 |
| Less: tax deducted at source | | | (2,000) |
| Tax repayable | | | 1,600 |

(5) A non-resident who carries on a trade in the UK (on his own or in partnership) is taxed on his profits that relate to the UK trade, measured on an arm's length basis.

(6) This Example sets out the basic principles of the taxation of non-residents. Reference must always be made to any relevant double tax agreements, the provisions of which may restrict the taxing rights which a participant state has under domestic tax law and specify how double tax relief should be given.

*Non-residents with UK dividends*

(7) As covered in **explanatory note 4** above, where the non-UK resident claims allowances he is taxed on all UK source income. Even though dividend tax credits have been abolished, ITTOIA 2005, s 399, as amended by Finance Act 2016, means non-residents are entitled to treat UK dividends as having income tax treated as paid equivalent to the dividend ordinary rate of 7.5%. This does not mean that the dividend is paid net and a gross up is required. Instead the income tax treated as paid is calculated on the amount received, such that if the dividend is £10,000 the tax treated as paid is £750. The income tax treated as paid can be deducted from the UK tax liability, but it cannot generate or increase a loss.

Prior to 2016/17, non-residents were not automatically entitled to a UK tax credit on UK dividends (ITTOIA 2005 s 397). A person who claimed UK personal allowances under ITA 2007 Part 3 (in accordance with ITA 2007 s 56) was, however, entitled to a tax credit (ITTOIA 2005 s 397(4)). Sometimes a double tax agreement may provide for income that is not exempt from UK tax to be charged at a reduced rate, for example interest may be taxed only at 10%. Tax credits for non-residents are provided in most double taxation agreements (TIOPA 2010 s 2) and the agreement may provide that the UK tax is not to exceed 15% of the tax credit inclusive amount. However, as the UK tax credit rate was only 10% such a restriction was not relevant. Although UK dividend tax credits were not repayable to UK residents, non-residents were still entitled to repayment under double tax agreements if the credit exceeded the rate under the agreement, but the reduction of the UK tax credit to 10% meant that repayments rarely arose. Where a dividend was received by a non-resident who was neither within the categories entitled to UK allowances as in **explanatory note 1**, nor entitled to relief under a double tax agreement, he was liable to tax only on the tax credit exclusive amount and then only to the extent, if any, of higher/additional rate tax over ordinary rate tax (ITTOIA 2005 ss 399, 400).

*Income from property letting*

(8) Where rent is paid to someone who usually lives abroad, tax must be deducted at the basic rate, as shown in the Example, unless the landlord has applied to HMRC for permission to receive the rental payments gross and the tenant/agent has received directions from HMRC that he or she can make gross rental income payments. For further details see **Example D4 explanatory note 11**.

*Capital gains tax liability of non-residents*

(9) In general, a non-UK resident individual is not subject to tax on capital gains (with the exception of UK residential property, see **explanatory notes 10–16**), unless these arise from assets used in a UK trade (TCGA 1992 s 10). However, gains realised or remitted by or attributed to individuals during a period of temporary non-residence may be charged to tax on return under anti-avoidance provisions (see **Example F1 explanatory note 24**).

(10) Where a UK non-resident disposes of UK residential property on or after 6 April 2015, he is liable to UK capital gains tax (TCGA 1992, s 14B). As well as individuals, these rules also apply to trusts, personal representatives, companies and funds. These provisions are referred to as the non-resident capital gains tax (NRCGT) rules.

(11) The following buildings are not treated as residential property for these rules (TCGA 1992 Sch B1 para 4(3)–(9):

(a) residential accommodation used by school pupils or members of the armed forces;

(b) home or institution providing residential accommodation to children, old age pensioners, disabled people, people with mental illness or those dependent on alcohol or drugs;

(c) hospital, hospice or prison;

(d) hotel or inn;

(e) residential accommodation with at least 15 bedrooms which is purpose built/converted for occupation by students and is occupied by them for at least 165 days in the tax year; and

(f) residential accommodation used as an institution that is the main residence of its residents (and not covered by one of the exclusions listed above)

(12) Under the NRCGT rules, three different methods can be used to calculate the chargeable gain, with the taxpayer able to elect for whichever one produces the lowest gain. The methods are (TCGA 1992, Sch 4ZZB):

- the rebasing method, where the property is valued at 5 April 2015 and only the gain from this date is taxable. This is the default method and will apply unless an election is made for one of the other options;
- the straight-line apportionment method, where only the gain arising from 6 April 2015 is taxable but the gain is assumed to have accrued evenly over the entire ownership of the property. The apportionment is made on a days basis;
- the retrospective method, where the person can deem the NRCGT rules always to apply. Although this might seem only to be appropriate where a loss arises, this method is also worth considering in cases where there is a gain and principal private residence (PPR) relief applies.

The election is made on the NRCGT return. When calculating the gain, any NRCGT losses which have not yet been relieved can be set against the gain.

(13) A NRCGT return must be submitted to HMRC within 30 days of the date of conveyance (not the date of exchange, which is the date of disposal for tax purposes) (TMA 1970 s 12B). The NRCGT return must include a calculation of the gain or loss and the amount of UK CGT due, unless the person has already been issued with a notice to file a self-assessment tax return (or one has been issued for the previous year) or filed an annual tax on enveloped dwelling (ATED) return for the previous period (TCGA 1992 ss 12ZE, 12ZG).

(14) As the NRCGT return is likely to be filed before the end of the year, individuals may not have enough information to correctly determine (a) their UK residence status, or (b) their UK taxable income (which is necessary to determine the rate of UK capital gains tax due (TMA 1970 ss 12ZF, 12ZJ). In this situation it is possible to submit a provisional return and revise it later. The person has until the first anniversary of 31 January after the end of the tax year in which the disposal occurs to amend the NRCGT return (TMA 1970 s 12ZK).

(15) The UK CGT due must also be paid over to HMRC within 30 days of the date of conveyance. However there is an exception where the person has been issued with a notice to file a self-assessment tax return, in which case the normal due date for payment applies. For individuals, personal representatives and trustees this will be 31 January after the end of the tax year in which the disposal occurs (TMA 1970 s 59AA).

(16) As the asset involved is residential property, the rates of NRCGT are 18% or 28%, depending on the non-resident's UK taxable income. The rate of CGT for carried interest and disposals of interests residential property were uncoupled from the main rates of CGT from 2016/17 onwards. The main rates of CGT which apply from that date are 10% and 20%. See **Example L3**.

(17) Penalties are charged under FA 2009 Sch 55 for late submission of the NRCGT return (see **Example G2 explanatory note 13**). Penalties are charged under FA 2007 Sch 24 for submission of an incorrect NRCGT return (see **Example G2 explanatory note 12**), athough HMRC will take into account that full information may not be available at the time of filing (TMA 1970 s 12ZF(6)).

*Self-assessment*

(18) HMRC sometimes makes a provisional repayment to someone who leaves the UK if the individual has no continuing sources of UK income.

(19) The residence, remittance basis etc supplementary pages (SA109) to the self-assessment return contain various sections which must be completed if an individual was not UK resident or eligible for overseas workday relief or split year treatment in the tax year (see **Example F1 explanatory notes 23** and **28**).

*HMRC offices*

(20) There are separate offices within HMRC which deal with operational and technical work (including compliance) relating to non-resident individuals, non-resident trusts and certain non-resident companies. The work of these offices includes dealing with non-resident landlords and double tax relief claims. Specialist residence and domicile queries are also generally dealt with by these units, although where the individual is within the High Net Worth Unit their affairs are likely to be dealt with by experts within that unit.

*Payment of tax or national insurance in Euros*

(21) Self-assessment liabilities can be paid in Euros or other foreign currencies. The payment is converted at the current rate of exchange. Any overpayment is repaid in sterling.

# Question

(a) During 2016/17 Johnson, a single man who is resident and domiciled in the UK, has the following income:

| | £ |
|---|---|
| Salary from employment | 41,185 |
| UK bank interest | 715 |
| Dividends received | |
| From UK companies | 4,000 |
| From Ruritanian company | 1,700 |
| From Utopian company | 1,250 |
| The following foreign tax was deducted from the overseas dividends before receipt: | |
| Ruritanian company | 300 |
| Utopian company | 1,250 |
| and additionally the following underlying (indirect) tax had been suffered: | |
| Utopian company | 500 |

No double taxation agreements exist between either: (i) Ruritania and the United Kingdom; or (ii) Utopia and the UK. Relief for the foreign tax suffered is, therefore, given unilaterally. There is no tax charge on company profits in Ruritania.

Showing the workings of overseas credits, compute the amount of United Kingdom income tax remaining to be paid by Johnson for the year 2016/17 presuming that his salary had been subject to deduction of tax under PAYE of £6,037.

(b) In 2016/17 Boswell, a married man, born on 17 February 1935, who is resident and domiciled in the UK, had UK income comprising state pension of £12,000, UK building society interest of £7,051, gross foreign interest from Ruritania of £2,000 on which the foreign tax was £300 and gross foreign interest from Narnia of £1,000 on which the foreign tax was £100.

Show his liability to UK tax if he claims double tax relief where appropriate. His wife is aged 71 at the start of the tax year.

# Answer

## (a) Income tax payable by Johnson for 2016/17

| | | | | £ |
|---|---|---|---|---|
| Salary | | | | 41,185 |
| Bank interest | | | | 715 |
| Dividends – | United Kingdom | | | 4,000 |
| | Ruritania (£1,700 + £300) | | | 2,000 |
| | Utopia (£1,250 + £1,250) (N1) | | | 2,500 |
| | | | | 50,400 |
| Less: personal allowance | | | | (11,000) |
| | | | | 39,400 |
| Tax thereon: | | | £ | |
| Non-savings income | | (£30,185 @ 20%) | 6,037 | |
| Savings income (N2) | | (£500 @ 0%) | — | |
| | | (£215 @ 20%) | 43 | |
| Dividend income (N2) | | (£5,000 @ 0%) | — | |
| | | (£3,500 @ 32.5%) | 1,137 | |
| | | | 7,217 | |
| *Less: foreign tax relief (N3)* | | | | |
| *Utopian company* | | | | |
| Foreign tax credit: lower of: | | | | |
| | Foreign tax | £1,250 | | |
| | UK tax (£2,500 @ 32.5%) | £812 | | |
| | | | (812) | |
| *Ruritanian company* | | | | |
| Foreign tax credit: lower of: | | | | |
| | Foreign tax | £300 | | |
| | UK tax (£1,000 @ 32.5%) + (£1,000 @ 0%) | £325 | | |
| | | | (300) | |
| | | | 6,105 | |
| Less: | PAYE deducted at source | | (6,037) | |
| | Tax due | | 68 | |

*Notes*

1. As an individual Johnson cannot claim relief unilaterally for the underlying tax of £500 suffered by the Utoptian company (see **explanatory note 3**).
2. As Johnson is a higher rate taxpayer, he is entitled to the savings nil rate of 0% on his first £500 of savings income (ITA 2007 ss 12A-12B). He is also entitled to the dividend nil rate of 0% on the first £5,000 of dividend income (ITA 2007 s 13A). The first £1,100 of the dividend income uses up this remaining basic rate band, saving tax of £82 (£1,100 x 7.5%). The balance of the dividend income taxed at the nil rate, £3,900, saves tax of £1,267 (£3,900 x 32.5%). The dividend tax credit was abolished and the rates of tax on dividend income changed with effect from 6 April 2016 (FA 2016, s 5).

3. Foreign tax relief is deducted from the UK tax liability in priority to taking off tax paid at source (a step 6 tax reduction in the ITA 2007 s 23 income tax calculation, see ITA 2007 ss 26-27). The amount of relief available is the lower of (i) the amount of foreign tax paid, and (ii) the UK tax due on that foreign income.
   Strictly, the calculation of the UK tax due on the foreign income is done by comparing the actual UK tax liability with the UK tax liability after the foreign income has been removed from the calculation. The workings shown in the proforma above are just a shortcut to the same result.
   As explained in HMRC Helpsheet HS263, where multiple sources of foreign income are concerned, the relief is calculated separately but account has to be taken of sources upon which relief has already been claimed.
   In the calculation above this means that for the Utopian dividends the claim for foreign tax relief is the lower of:

- foreign tax paid on the Utopian income £1,250;
- UK tax on the foreign income (ie the difference between (i) the actual UK tax liability of £7,217 and (ii) the UK tax liability if the Utopian income was excluded) of £812.

The lower of the two figures is £812.
Then, when it comes to calculating the foreign tax relief for the Ruritanian dividends, the calculation of the UK tax due on the interest must take into account that relief has already been claimed on the Utopian dividends. Therefore, the foreign tax relief is the lower of:

- foreign tax paid on the Ruritanian income £300;
- UK tax on foreign income (ie the difference between (i) the UK tax liability after exclusion of the Utopian income and (ii) the UK tax liability if the Ruritanian income is also excluded). In this situation, the Ruritanian income is taxed partly at the dividend nil rate of 0% and partly at the dividend upper rate of 32.5% meaning the UK tax liability in (ii) is £325.

The lower of the two figures is £300.
See also **explanatory note 4**.

## (b) Boswell's income tax liability for 2016/17

**The income tax calculation if Boswell claims double tax relief on interest from Ruritania and Narnia.**

| | | | £ |
|---|---|---|---|
| State pension | | | 12,000 |
| UK interest | | | 7,051 |
| Foreign interest | – Ruritania | | 2,000 |
| | – Narnia | | 1,000 |
| | | | 22,051 |
| Less: personal allowance (N1) | | | (11,000) |
| Taxable income | | | 11,051 |

| | | | £ |
|---|---|---|---|
| Tax thereon: | £1,000 @ 20% | | 200 |
| | £4,000 @ 0% (N2) | | — |
| | £1,000 @ 0% (N3) | | — |
| | £5,051 @ 20% | | 1,010 |
| | | | 1,210 |
| Less: age-related married couple's allowance £8,355 @ 10% (N4) | | | (835) |
| | | | 375 |
| Less: double tax relief: | | | |
| On interest – Ruritania | | | |
| Lower of foreign tax | | £300 | |

| | | |
|---|---|---|
| and UK tax £2,000 @ 20% = £400 but restricted by allowances to £375 (N5) | £375 | |
| | | (300) |
| On interest – Narnia | | |
| Lower of foreign tax | £100 | |
| and UK tax (N5) | Nil | |
| | | — |
| UK tax liability | | 75 |

*Notes*

1. Although Boswell was born before 6 April 1938, he is not entitled to an age-related personal allowance as these have been abolished with effect from 6 April 2016 since the normal personal allowance exceeds age-related allowances.
2. The 0% rate applies to the first £5,000 as, once the personal allowance has been deducted from non-savings income, the starting rate for savings band has not been fully utilised by non-savings income (ITA 2007 s 12). In the calculation above, £1,000 of the starting rate for savings band is unavailable because Boswell's taxable non-savings income after taking into account the personal allowance is £1,000. This leaves £4,000 of the band remaining to set against savings income. See **explanatory note 1**.
3. As Boswell is a basic rate taxpayer, he is entitled to the savings nil rate of 0% on £1,000 of savings income (ITA 2007 ss 12A-12B). The savings nil rate applies after the starting rate for savings (if the starting rate for savings is applicable, as it is in Boswell's case).
4. Boswell is entitled to the married couple's allowance as he is married and one of the couple was born before 6 April 1935 (ITA 2007 s 45). As his income is below the threshold of £27,700, the full amount of the allowance is available as a 10% tax reducer (deducted at step 6 of the ITA 2007 s 23 income tax calculation). Although foreign tax relief is also a step 6 tax reducer, married couple's allowance must be deducted in priority (ITA 2007 s 27).
5. See the discussion in N3 for part (a) above. In order to calculate the foreign tax relief for the Narnian interest, the calculation of the UK tax due on the interest must take into account that relief has already been claimed on the Ruritanian interest. Therefore, the foreign tax relief is the lower of:
   - foreign tax paid on the Narnian income £100;
   - UK tax on foreign income (ie the difference between (i) the UK tax liability after exclusion of the Ruritanian income and (ii) the UK tax liability if the Narnian income is also excluded). When the Ruritanian income is excluded the UK tax liability is nil. Excluding the Narnian income as well would restrict the married couple's allowance and so would also give a tax liability of nil. Therefore the UK tax on the Narnian income is nil.

   The lower of the two figures is nil. The foreign tax paid on the Narnian income is lost as it cannot be relieved and it cannot be carried forward.

In this situation, Boswell could not claim foreign tax relief and instead benefit from credit by deduction (TIOPA 2010 s 112). The difference this makes to the income tax calculation is shown below.

| | | £ |
|---|---|---|
| State pension | | 12,000 |
| UK interest | | 7,051 |
| Foreign interest – Ruritania | | 2,000 |
| Foreign interest net of foreign tax – Narnia (N1) | | 900 |
| | | 21,951 |
| Less: personal allowance | | (11,000) |
| Taxable income | | 10,951 |
| | | £ |
| Tax thereon: | £1,000 @ 20% | 200 |
| | £4,000 @ 0% | — |
| | £1,000 @ 0% | — |
| | £4,951 @ 20% | 990 |

| | |
|---|---:|
| | 1,190 |
| *Less*: age-related married couple's allowance £8,355 @ 10% | (835) |
| | 355 |
| *Less*: foreign tax relief on interest – Ruritania: | |
| Lower foreign tax paid £300 | |
| and UK tax £2,000 @ 20% = £400 but restricted by allowances to £355 | (300) |
| UK tax liability | 55 |

*Notes*

1. As Boswell was unable to obtain any relief from the Narnian tax paid he would be better advised to use the credit by deduction method (TIOPA 2010 s 112). Under this method, instead of subjecting the gross Narnian interest of £1,000 to UK tax, the tax paid is deducted from the income so that only £900 (£1,000 gross income less £100 tax paid) is taxable. This reduces Boswell's tax liability by £20. See **explanatory note 6**.

## Explanatory Notes

*Tax on savings and dividend income*

(1) Potentially UK taxpayers have a 0% starting rate band for savings income that for 2016/17 covers the first £5,000 of savings income (ITA 2007 s 12). However, this starting rate band only applies where the band is not exhausted by non-savings income (taxable at the basic rate).

If the starting rate for savings is unavailable because it has been exhausted by non-savings income, the tax rate on both UK and foreign savings income, excluding dividends, is:

- 0% on the first £1,000 (for basic rate taxpayers) or £500 (for higher rate taxpayers) of savings income, called the savings nil rate. Additional rate taxpayers cannot benefit;
- 20% on any excess over the saving nil rate band limit if the savings income, taxed after non-savings income but before dividend income, does not exceed the basic rate limit;
- 40% on any excess over the basic rate limit to the extent that this does not exceed the higher rate limit; and
- 45% on any excess above the higher rate limit.

The tax rate on both UK and foreign dividend income is (ITA 2007 s 13):

- 0% on the first £5,000 of dividend income, called the dividend nil rate. The dividend nil rate applies to the first £5,000 of dividend income irrespective of the marginal rate of the taxpayer;
- 7.5% on the excess over the dividend rate band limit if the dividend income, taxed after non-savings and savings income, does not exceed the basic rate limit;
- 32.5% on any excess to the extent that this does not exceed the higher rate limit; and
- 38.1% on any excess above the higher rate limit.

The savings rates and the dividend rates do not apply to foreign dividend income that is charged on the remittance basis (broadly where it is received by someone who is not domiciled in the UK and is a remittance basis user either: (i) as a result of making a claim (ITA 2007 s 809B); or (ii) being automatically entitled to the remittance basis as a result of meeting the conditions in ITA 2007 s 809D or s 809E, see **Example F4 explanatory notes 5–10**). In these situations the foreign dividends are treated as 'relevant foreign income', and taxed at non-savings rates of 20%, 40% and 45%.

*Double tax relief*

(2) For the in-force double tax treaties, see https://www.gov.uk/government/collections/tax-treaties-signed-and-in-force.

Where the same income and capital gains are liable to tax in more than one country, relief for the double tax is given either under the provisions of a double tax treaty or unilaterally (TIOPA 2010 s 2 onwards).

Where there is a double tax treaty, it may provide for certain income and gains to be wholly exempt, or for tax to be deducted at a reduced rate. Income that is not exempt is charged to UK tax, but a credit is given for the lower of the overseas tax and the UK tax.

Where there is no double tax treaty, unilateral relief may be claimed against the UK tax at the lower of the overseas tax and the UK tax (as explained in the answers to parts (a) and (b) above).

To counter tax evasion both nationally and internationally, HMRC has the power to obtain relevant tax information from taxpayers and third parties and for such information to be exchanged with, or obtained for, other EU states and countries with whom the UK has made either a double taxation agreement or a tax information exchange agreement (TIOPA 2010 s 129). See also **Example F2 explanatory note 3.**.

FA 2006 gave HMRC powers to cancel existing arrangements, and replace them with more comprehensive information exchange arrangements, and also powers to recover tax in overseas courts.

Note that in recent years there has been a huge jump in the number of countries with which the UK either:

- has a treaty with a specific exchange of information article; or
- has entered into a standalone tax information exchange agreement.

A good summary of the history is given in the introduction to the 'Implementing Agreements under the Global Standard on Automatic Exchange of Information to Improve International Tax Compliance' consultation in 2014 https://www.gov.uk/government/consultations/implementing-agreements-under-the-global-standard-on-automatic-exchange-of-information:

"In September 2012 the UK became the first jurisdiction to sign an enhanced automatic tax information exchange agreement with the United States of America (US) to implement the reporting required under US FATCA legislation (automatic exchange of financial account information on US citizens and entities). In 2013 the UK signed automatic tax information agreements with its Crown Dependencies (Isle of Man, Jersey and Guernsey) and Overseas Territories (Anguilla, Bermuda, the British Virgin Islands, the Cayman Islands, Gibraltar, Montserrat and the Turks and Caicos Islands). The US agreement and the agreements with the Crown Dependencies and Gibraltar impose obligations on UK financial institutions to report financial account information to HMRC for onward transmission to these territories, the agreements with the remaining Overseas Territories are non-reciprocal so while the UK will receive information there is no obligation to provide information to them.

In April 2013 the UK along with France, Germany, Italy and Spain (the G5) set up a pilot to explore the possibility of developing a common approach to automatic exchange of financial account information. This was adopted by the G20 leading to work being commissioned with the OECD to develop a new global standard. In February 2014 the OECD delivered the Model Competent Authority Agreements for a Common Reporting Standard (the CRS) which was approved by the G20 as the Global Standard for Automatic Exchange of Financial Account Information. The CRS is designed to provide maximum consistency with US FATCA. This is in order to minimise the additional costs and burdens to business from the increased reporting requirements. There are areas where the CRS does not exactly mirror the US model due to differences in context, for example the taxation systems of the participating jurisdictions.

As at 14 July 2014, 45 jurisdictions, including the UK, have agreed to early adoption of the CRS. Under the proposed regulations that are the subject of this discussion financial institutions will be required to capture information in relation to accounts in existence as at 31 December 2015 and new accounts opened on or after 1 January 2016 with first reporting in 2017."

The regulations implementing the CRS came into force on 15 April 2015 (SI 2015/878). Guidance on the CRS was published on 17 September 2015 [https://www.gov.uk/government/publications/informal-consultation-guidance-notes-for-the-automatic-exchange-of-financial-account-information]. For a list of the jurisdictions which will begin reporting un the CRS in 2017 and those which will follow on in 2018, see [https://www.gov.uk/guidance/automatic-exchange-of-information-introduction].

(3) Double tax relief is available only for direct foreign taxes on the income. Where the income is dividend income, no credit is available for the underlying tax on the profits out of which the dividend is paid (TIOPA 2010 s 18). Where the overseas country operates a system under which dividends have tax credits attached and withholding tax is not deducted, the tax credits represent underlying tax and are not eligible for double tax relief unless specifically provided for by the double tax agreement. Where the treaty does not so provide, the net dividend paid is the amount charged to UK tax.

(4) When computing the amount of double taxation relief, available sources of overseas income may be taken in the order most advantageous to the taxpayer (TIOPA 2010 s 36). The answer to **part (a)** illustrates this principle.

If the Ruritanian dividend had been regarded as the top slice of income in **part (a)** of the Example, the credits would have been less advantageous, as follows:

**Relief taken in the opposite order to the answer in part (a)**

| | | | | | | |
|---|---|---|---|---|---|---|
| *Ruritanian company* | | | | | | |
| Lower of: | foreign tax | | | £300 | | |
| | UK tax£2,000 @ 32.5% | | | £650 | | |
| | | | | | £300 | (the same as in the answer to **part (a)**) |
| *Utopian company* | | | | | | |
| Lower of: foreign tax | | | | £1,250 | | |
| UK tax | | £1,500 @ 32.5% | £487 | | | |
| | | £1,000 @ 0% | — | | | |
| | | | | £487 | | |
| | | | | | £487 | (comparing unfavourably with the higher figure of £812 in the answer to **part (a)**) |

(5) If, following a double tax relief claim, the amount of foreign tax payable is later adjusted, the amount of double tax relief claimed must be similarly adjusted. If an adjustment to foreign tax results in an excessive amount of relief having been claimed, HMRC must be notified within one year of the adjustment being made (TIOPA 2010 s 19).

*Not claiming double tax relief*

(6) If double tax relief is not claimed, the income or gain is charged to UK tax net of the overseas tax suffered (TIOPA 2010 s 112). This will rarely be more beneficial. Potential examples of cases where it could be beneficial are where the net overseas income is covered by allowances, or tax arising is reduced by other deductions, such as age-related married couple's allowance. This is illustrated in **part (b)** of the Example above.

*Basis of assessment of foreign income*

(7) Where foreign income is subject to tax on the arising basis, it is converted into sterling at the exchange rate on the date it arises. Where over the course of the tax year there are frequent income receipts, an average exchange rate for the year may be used providing it is used consistently and does not materially affect the taxable amounts. HMRC publish average rates (based on data published by the Financial Times) at [https://www.gov.uk/government/collections/exchange-rates-for-customs-and-vat].

See **Example F7 explanatory notes 15 to 17** for further details and a discussion of the issues with respect to remittance basis users.

*UK tax credits in respect of foreign dividend income (repealed with effect from 6 April 2016)*

(8) Prior to 6 April 2016, a UK resident who received dividend income from a foreign company which was brought into charge to UK tax was, as a result of the provisions at ITTOIA 2005 ss 397A–397C, entitled to a deemed one-ninth UK tax credit on the value of the grossed up distribution. This was the case as long as at least one of the following three conditions was met (referred to in ITTOIA 2005 s 397AA as conditions A to C):

(A) the distribution was made by a company with issued share capital and at the time the person receives the distribution the person was a minority shareholder (broadly, a person whose holding in the issued share capital of the company was less than 10% but see ITTOIA 2005 s 397C for the full definition) in the company;

(B) the company that makes the distribution was an offshore fund and ITTOIA 2005 s 378A (offshore funds distributions), which would result in the distribution being taxed as if it were interest income, did NOT apply;

(C) The following conditions were met:

(i) the distribution was made by a company which was a resident of (and only a resident of) a qualifying territory at a time when the distribution was made. A qualifying territory was a territory with which the UK has a double tax treaty that contains a non-discrimination provision;

HMRC included a list of qualifying territories, and companies within those territories that were excluded from benefiting from the tax treaty, in Revenue & Customs Brief 76/09 (issued on 12 January 2010 and available to view at http://webarchive.nationalarchives.gov.uk/20140109143644/http://www.hmrc.gov.uk/briefs/income-tax/brief7609.htm);

(ii) if the distribution was one of a series of distributions made as part of a scheme: (i) each company that made a distribution in the series was a resident of (and only of) a qualifying territory at the time that the scheme distribution was received; or (ii) the scheme was not a tax advantage scheme.

(9) The ITTOIA 2005 s 397A deemed tax credit was in addition to any foreign tax credit and increased the gross income treated as received. For example, if the net foreign dividend received was £200 and foreign tax withheld was £50, the taxable income for the purposes of his UK income tax computation would have been £277 (£250 × (100/90)), with an attached UK tax credit of £27.

Where the foreign tax relief covers the tax liability on the dividend, no additional ITTOIA 2005 s 397A deemed tax credit is available.

(10) As with normal UK dividend tax credits, the ITTOIA 2005 s 397A deemed tax credit could reduce the UK tax due but could not generate or increase a loss. Furthermore, the credit was reduced by any deductions which decreased the amount brought into charge (ITTOIA 2007 s 397A(3)).

(11) HMRC initially sought to deny the ITTOIA 2005 s 397A deemed tax credit to trustees of interest in possession trusts but upon review this decision was reversed.

# Question

## A.

At the end of 2016/17 Henry Non-Dom is a 29-year-old UK resident foreign domiciliary. He arrived in the UK at the age of 21 (arriving in the UK on 17 March 2009) remained here and was UK resident until 17 March 2010 (when he left for a two-year secondment in New York) and returned on 30 April 2012.

Taking each scenario below in turn, explain whether ITA 2007 ss 809D, 809E or 828C applies for 2016/17.

SCENARIO A

For 2016/17 Henry had gross foreign interest income of £1,800, no foreign chargeable gains and made no remittances. He also had UK self-employment income of £35,000 and £10 of UK gross bank interest that was taxed at source. He had no other UK income and made no disposals of UK situs chargeable assets in 2016/17.

SCENARIO B

For 2016/17 Henry had gross foreign interest income of £23,000, aggregate foreign chargeable gains of £250,000 and makes no remittances. He also had £85 of UK bank interest. He had no other UK income and made no disposals of UK situs chargeable assets in 2016/17.

SCENARIO C

For 2016/17 Henry had foreign income of £501,175:

- £1,175 of gross bank interest; and
- an offshore income gain of £500,000 (total proceeds £1.5 million) that was realised on 17 March 2017.

He has just the one offshore account. He remits £500,000 on 20 December 2016. At that time the account contained £1,116,080 of foreign income:

| | *Gross* |
|---|---|
| | £ |
| 2016/17 receipts to date | 875 |
| 2015/16 receipts | 365,795 |
| 2014/15 receipts | 485,750 |
| 2013/14 receipts | 263,660 |

No foreign chargeable gains accrued to him in 2016/17.

SCENARIO D

Henry has foreign income and foreign chargeable gains in 2016/17 of £365,000. This breaks down as £150,000 of gross interest (received on 31 December 2016) and a foreign chargeable gain of £215,000 (the disposal taking place on 24 June 2016 with proceeds of £650,000 being received and no foreign tax credit). Clean capital (an inheritance received in 2011/12) was originally used to acquire the asset. Henry has just the one offshore account. He remits £363,300 on 17 January 2017. At that time the account contained £1,680,555 that breaks down as follows:

| | Gross £ |
|---|---|
| 2016/17 receipts to date | 800,000 |
| 2015/16 receipts | 295,555 |
| 2014/15 receipts | 350,000 |
| 2013/14 receipts | 235,000 |

He has UK self-employment income of £315,000 and £2,750 of UK gross bank interest that is taxed at source and paid into his UK current account. He has no other UK income and made no disposals of UK situs chargeable assets in the tax year.

SCENARIO E

In the year to 5 April 2017 Henry did not make any disposals of chargeable assets and received the following income:

- £25,000 of gross UK employment income;
- £10 of UK grossed up dividend income;
- £8,500 of gross taxed foreign employment income (taxed at 15%);
- £75 of gross foreign taxed bank interest (taxed at 15%).

Henry's has no further UK tax liability with respect to his UK income. His PAYE code correctly deducted the necessary income tax from his UK employment income and as a basic rate taxpayer the 10% notional tax credit on his UK dividend income covers that liability. He did not remit any remittance basis foreign income or gains relating to prior tax years and will not be making a remittance basis claim (ITA 2007 s 809B) for 2016/17. Accordingly, if it were not for the foreign income that arose in the tax year he would not have to file a UK self-assessment tax return.

## B.

Nicolas Non-Dom is 26 years old. He first came to the UK in 1996/97. His residency pattern between then and 2015/16 is as follows:

| *Tax year* | *UK resident at any time in the tax year* |
|---|---|
| 1996/97 – 2012/13 | Yes |
| 2013/14 | No |
| 2014/15 | No |
| 2015/16 | No |

He returned to the UK on 15 October 2016 and starts to have a home in the UK from that date. For the purposes of the statutory residence test, he is resident in the UK from that date.

He has significant UK income so cannot qualify for the automatic remittance basis under ITA 2007 s 809E. In addition, Nicolas's aggregate foreign income and gains and the level of his remittances do not qualify him for automatic access to the remittance basis in 2016/17 under ITA 2007 s 809D. As such, if he wishes to access the remittance basis he must make a claim (ITA 2007 s 809B). Would a claim to access the remittance basis mean that he has to pay the remittance basis charge (RBC) for the year?

## C.

Lauren and Ellie Non-Dom are UK resident foreign domiciliaries. They are twins who have been UK resident since 29 August 2007 when they started their UK private schooling. Lauren is the elder and was born at 11:51 pm on 5 April 1999. Ellie was born at 00:05 on 6 April 1999.

Both Lauren and Ellie have significant offshore wealth as the result of interest in possession trusts established by their paternal grandparents. They will take an absolute interest at the age of 21 and during their minority are entitled to the income (which is around £300,000 per annum). The trust, whilst an offshore settlement, provides the twins with the same beneficial entitlement to the income as a trust established under the law of England and Wales. The trustees ensure that no trust property is UK situs so all the trust income is foreign situs. The income arising from the trusts has been invested in personal portfolios (held for them, whilst they are minors, on bare trust by their mother) with instructions that investment in UK situs assets is prohibited.

The twins' parents (both of whom are not UK resident) settle all the twins' UK expenses and provide them with a generous monthly allowance.

For 2016/17 the twins' foreign income and foreign chargeable gains are identical and as follows:

| | | *Gross* | *Foreign tax credit* |
|---|---|---|---|
| | | £ | £ |
| Trust | Interest income | 160,000 | Nil |
| Trust | Property income | 150,000 | 37,500 |
| Personal | Interest income | 55,000 | Nil |
| Personal | Dividend income | 45,000 | 6,750 |
| Personal | Offshore income gains | 95,000 | Nil |
| Personal | Capital gains | 50,000 | 5,000 |

Neither Lauren nor Ellie will make any taxable remittances to the UK in 2016/17. Both have a UK non-interest bearing current account with BZS Bank plc. They have no UK source income.

The twins did not dispose of any UK situs chargeable assets in 2016/17.

Explain whether either twin can automatically access the remittance basis of taxation and, if not, whether making the remittance basis claim will mean the RBC is due and whether, based on the foreign income and gains arising in 2016/17, the remittance or arising basis will be the cheaper alternative.

## D.

Lauren and Ellie Non-Dom's cousin Chloe Non-Dom was born on 3 April 1997. She came to the UK on 27 February 2003 and lived here with her parents until 17 August 2012 when the family moved to Geneva. She returned to study in the UK on 25 September 2015 and has been UK resident ever since.

Like her cousins, she has an interest in possession in a substantial offshore trust. Her income entitlement for 2016/17 is around £600,000, all of which is foreign income. She only remits £100,000 in the tax year all of which matches to the 2016/17 income from the trust.

If she wants to claim the remittance basis will she have to pay the RBC and if so how much will she have to pay?

## E.

In 2016/17 Jake Non-Dom is a 36 year old UK resident foreign domiciliary. Jake's taxable UK income in 2016/17 equates to £165,345. His foreign income and foreign chargeable gains are such that he does not qualify for the automatic remittance basis in 2016/17 and so makes the remittance basis claim and pays the £30,000 RBC (he has not been UK resident for long enough to have to pay either the £60,000 or £90,000 RBC). A nomination of foreign income or gains needs to be made. Jake has the following BCDE Jersey Plc bank accounts:

- Account A – an account containing the proceeds from the sale of various foreign chargeable assets disposed of prior to 6 April 2016. Interest arising on this account is paid into account C;
- Account B – an account containing £75,000 of interest income that derives originally from successful source ceasing exercises (the interest relating to tax years prior to 2008/09). The £75,000 is part of a larger sum that was remitted to the UK on 17 March 2012. Jake had kept some of the funds in the UK and transferred the surplus offshore on 25 August 2012. Interest arising on this account is paid into account C;

- Account C – an income account receiving gross interest income earned with respect to a number of the other accounts. A total of £950 of interest was paid into this account in 2016/17. The figure of £950 breaks down as £85 of interest earned on the funds within account C and £865 with respect to interest earned on other accounts with the bank;
- Account D – an account into which £1,000 of clean capital was transferred in January 2017. Interest is paid each December so the account balance at 6 April 2017 was still £1,000. Interest of £4 was received in December 2017;
- Account E – an account receiving gross Swiss bond interest of £270,000 in 2016/17. Interest arising on this account is paid into account C;
- Account F – an account into which his Swiss director's fees for April 2016 to February 2017 are paid. The account received £82,500 of net income with tax of £27,500 having being deducted at source. Interest arising on this account is paid into account C;
- Account G – an account opened in February 2017 into which his March 2017 net Swiss director's fees of £7,500 was paid (with tax of £2,500 having been deducted at source). No interest income arose in 2016/17 and no further funds have been paid into the account;
- Account H – an account that in March 2017 was established with a £1,000 transfer from account E. The intention both when the transfer was made and at the end of 2016/17 was that the funds remain in the account indefinitely. Immediately before the transfer to this new account the transferor account (Account E) contained £1,052,000 of which £160,000 related to 2012/13, £220,000 to 2013/14, £177,000 to 2014/15, £225,000 in 2015/16 and £270,000 to 2016/17. No interest income arose on this account in 2016/17 and no further funds were paid into account H.

Explain, taking each account in turn, whether funds within the account could be nominated for the purposes of a long-term UK resident foreign domiciliary making a valid remittance basis claim.

# Answer

## A. Henry Non-Dom

ITA 2007 ss 809D, 809E are provisions under which the individual can automatically qualify for the remittance basis without having to make a claim. An individual who qualifies automatically is able to preserve his personal allowances for income tax and annual exempt amount for capital gains tax, whereas these are lost if a claim is made for the remittance basis to apply. The conditions which must be met for ITA 2007 ss 809D or 809E to apply are discussed below and also in **explanatory notes 6-8**.

ITA 2007 s 828C allows certain non-domiciled individuals to exempt their foreign income from UK tax. As you might expect with such a valuable exemption, the conditions are narrowly drawn in ITA 2007 s 828B. These conditions are considered below and also in **explanatory note 4**.

**SCENARIO A:** In this scenario Henry automatically qualifies for the remittance basis under ITA 2007 s 809D.

In 2016/17 Henry meets all the necessary conditions set down in ITA 2007 s 809D(1):

- he is UK resident in the tax year;
- he is not domiciled in the UK in the tax year;
- his unremitted foreign income and gains are less than £2,000; and
- he does not meet the ITA 2007 s 828B conditions (see **explanatory note 4**).

Without going through all the ITA 2007 s 828B conditions, Henry cannot qualify for the ITA 2007 s 828C exemption as for 2016/17 he has no UK employment income.

Should Henry not wish to be taxed on the remittance basis he can opt out (ITA 2007 s 809D(1B)) by giving notice on his 2016/17 self-assessment tax return that he does not wish ITA 2007 s 809D to apply to him for 2016/17.

See **explanatory note 7**.

**SCENARIO B:** In this scenario Henry does not automatically qualify for the remittance basis or the ITA 2007 s 828C exemption.

He cannot qualify under ITA 2007 s 809D as his unremitted income and gains are not less than £2,000.

He cannot qualify under ITA 2007 s 809E due to the knock-on effect of the abolition of tax at source on bank interest. As from 2016/17 this is no longer within the definition of 'taxed investment income' for ITA 2007 s 809E(1)(c), (2A), this prevents him for meeting the conditions for the automatic remittance basis.

However had the same scenario occurred in 2015/16 or earlier years, Henry would have qualified for the automatic remittance basis under ITA 2007 s 809E. See **explanatory note 8**.

Therefore, if Henry wants to access the remittance basis he will have to make a claim under ITA 2007 s 809B. Note that if he does not make the claim and is taxed on the default arising basis he will be taxed on the entire 23,000 of foreign income and £250,000 of foreign gains arising in the tax year. By making a claim under ITA 2007 s 809B he will forfeit his personal allowance and annual exemption (ITA 2007 s 809G).

Henry arrived in the UK in 2008/09 (on 17 March 2009), was UK resident until 17 March 2010 (when he left for a two-year secondment in New York) and returned on 30 April 2012 (so he was not UK resident in 2010/11 and 2011/12). When considering the position for 2016/17 the nine-year look back period is from 2007/08 to 2015/16 inclusive:

| *Tax year* | *UK resident at any time in the tax year* |
|---|---|
| 2007/08 | No |
| 2008/09 | Yes |
| 2009/10 | Yes |
| 2010/11 | No |
| 2011/12 | No |
| 2012/13 | Yes |
| 2013/14 | Yes |
| 2014/15 | Yes |
| 2015/16 | Yes |

He was UK resident for six out of the nine tax years preceding the 2016/17 tax year and so does not need to pay the RBC if he makes a claim under ITA 2007 s 809B.

The £60,000 and £90,000 remittance basis charges do not need to be considered as Henry only arrived in the UK in 2007/08.

Without going through all the ITA 2007 s 828B conditions, Henry cannot qualify for the ITA 2007 s 828C exemption as for 2016/17 he has foreign chargeable gains (see **explanatory note 4**).

**SCENARIO C**: In this scenario Henry does not qualify for the automatic remittance basis or the ITA 2007 s 828C exemption.

He cannot qualify under ITA 2007 s 809E as he remitted £500,000 in the tax year.

In order to see whether the conditions for ITA 2007 s 809D are met, the unremitted income and gains for 2016/17 must be calculated. The £500,000 is remitted on 20 December 2016 (that is before the disposal of the units in the non-reporting fund). At the time of the remittance only £875 of foreign income and gains has arisen in 2016/17 and so the £500,000 remittance is matched as follows:

(1) £875 of current year foreign income;

(2) £365,795 of foreign income arising in 2015/16;

(3) £133,330 of foreign income arising in 2014/15.

Henry does not qualify under ITA 2007, s 809D as the £500,000 remittance is matched to just £875 of foreign income arising in 2016/17 (the remaining £499,125 being matched to prior years' income) (ITA 2007 s 809U). That is remittances made by Henry in 2016/17 are matched to just £875 out of a total of £501,175 of foreign income and gains for the tax year. This means that the amount of Henry's unremitted foreign income and gains for 2016/17 is not less than £2,000, so ITA 2007 s 809D(1)(c) is breached. For details of how to quantify unremitted income and gains in sterling, see **Example F7 explanatory note 17**.

If Henry wants to access the remittance basis he will have to make a claim under ITA 2007 s 809B. Note that if he does not make the claim and is taxed on the default arising basis he will be taxed on the entire £501,175 of foreign income arising in the tax year and the element of the £500,000 remittance that was matched to tax years prior to 2016/17 (that is he will also be taxed on a remittance of £499,125 of foreign income).

Without going through all the ITA 2007 s 828B conditions, Henry cannot qualify for the ITA 2007 s 828C exemption as he has no UK employment in 2016/17 and his foreign interest is greater than £100 (see **explanatory note 4**).

**SCENARIO D**: In this scenario Henry automatically qualifies for the remittance basis under ITA 2007 s 809D.

In 2016/17 Henry meets all the necessary conditions set down in ITA 2007 s 809D(1):

- he is UK resident in the tax year;

- he is not domiciled in the UK in the tax year;
- his unremitted foreign income and gains are less than £2,000 (see below); and
- he does not meet the ITA 2007 s 828B conditions (see **explanatory note 4**).

Without going through all the ITA 2007 s 828B conditions, Henry cannot qualify for the ITA 2007 s 828C exemption as for 2016/17 he has no UK employment income.

Should Henry not wish to be taxed on the remittance basis he can opt out (ITA 2007 s 809D(1B)) by giving notice on his 2016/17 self-assessment tax return that he does not wish ITA 2007 s 809D to apply to him for 2016/17.

In order to see whether the conditions for ITA 2007 s 809D are met, the unremitted income and gains for 2016/17 must be calculated. The £363,300 is remitted on 17 January 2017 from an account that immediately before the remittance contains £800,000 of 2016/17 receipts (ie foreign interest of £150,000 and foreign proceeds of £650,000 which represent £215,000 of gain and £435,000 of clean capital).

The account from which the money was remitted is a mixed fund for the purposes of the remittance basis. This means it includes multiple different sources of income or gains and/or income or gains from more than one tax year (RDRM35220). Matching the £363,300 remittance in line with ITA 2007 s 809Q one deems the remittance to represent:

(1) £150,000 of 2016/17 relevant foreign income; and

(2) £213,300 of 2016/17 foreign chargeable gains.

See **Example F6** for more on the mixed fund rules.

Accordingly, in 2016/17 Henry remitted £363,300 out of a total of £365,000 of foreign income and gains for that year so his unremitted foreign income and gains for 2016/17 is less than £2,000. This means that he meets all the necessary ITA 2007 s 809D qualifying conditions in the tax year. For details of how to quantify unremitted income and gains in sterling, see **Example F7 explanatory note 17.**

See **explanatory note** 7.

**SCENARIO E**: On the basis that Henry will not make a remittance basis claim for 2016/17, in this scenario Henry meets the conditions at ITA 2007 ss 828A-828B such that the ITA 2007 s 828C exemption is available.

| *Condition* | |
|---|---|
| UK resident and foreign domiciled | Met |
| No ITA 2007 s 809B remittance basis claim in the tax year | Met |
| In receipt of UK employment income | Met |
| No foreign chargeable gains | Met |
| All foreign income subject to foreign taxes | Met |
| The only foreign income that can arise in the tax year is: | Met, only foreign income is £8,500 gross of employment income and £75 of gross bank interest |
| (1) foreign employment income and interest income (as defined in ITTOIA 2005 ss 369-380A); and | |
| (2) the income arising must not exceed specified limits being (1) £10,000 or less of foreign employment income and (2) no more than £100 of interest | |
| When considering the total worldwide income, if it were all subject to UK tax, the individual would not pay tax on any of this income at a rate in excess of the basic rate of tax | Met, worldwide income of £33,585. Accordingly no income would be taxed at a rate higher than the 20% basic rate |
| The individual does not submit a self-assessment tax return for the tax year, and other than the foreign income, has no reason to have to submit a return | Met |

For 2016/17 Henry's UK tax paid was correct and he meets all the other ITA 2007 ss 828A-828B conditions meaning he falls within the exemption and does not have to pay UK income tax on his foreign income.

As ITA 2007 s 828C is a complete exemption from tax on foreign income arising in the year it is more favourable than the remittance basis. An individual, whose financial affairs in every other respect meet the qualifying conditions, should be warned not to put himself outside the ITA 2007 s 828C exemption. The individual could do this by, for example, making a remittance basis claim under ITA 2007 s 809B for the year.

An individual could not qualify for both ITA 2007 s 809E and ITA 2007 s 828C. To fall within ITA 2007 s 809E there can be no UK employment income whilst, in contrast, the ITA 2007 s 828B qualifying conditions cannot be met unless the individual receives UK employment income for the relevant tax year.

It is possible (though in Henry's case it has not happened as he has not remitted any of his £8,575 of foreign income) to come within the qualifying conditions for both ITA 2007 s 828C and ITA 2007 s 809D. As ITA 2007 s 828C is more favourable than the automatic remittance basis, this provision has priority (ITA 2007 s 809D(1A)).

Note that if an individual who potentially met the ITA 2007 ss 828A–828B conditions and qualified under ITA 2007 s 809D were to submit a UK self-assessment tax return for the year, that would breach the ITA 2007, s 828B conditions such that the ITA 2007 s 828C exemption would be lost for the year. This would mean that for the tax year the individual would be an automatic remittance basis user unless he made a claim for ITA 2007 s 809D not to apply. As the ITA 2007 s 828C exemption is more favourable, the individual should be advised not submit a UK self-assessment tax return.

See **explanatory note 4**.

## B. Nicolas Non-Dom

When considering whether the RBC is in point for 2016/17, the 20-year look back period runs from 1996/97 to 2015/16, the 14-year look back period runs from 2002/03 to 2015/16 and the nine-year look back period runs from to 2007/08 to 2015/16. From the information provided in the case of Nicolas Non-Dom, the facts are as follows:

| *Tax year* | *UK resident at any time in the tax year* |
|---|---|
| 1996/97 – 2012/13 | Yes |
| 2013/14 | No |
| 2014/15 | No |
| 2015/16 | No |

For the purposes of the RBC tests in ITA 2007 s 809C the 17 of 20 preceding tax years test is met. In 2016/17 Nicholas has been UK resident in 17 of the immediately preceding 20 tax years (1996/97 to 2015/16) and would, therefore, have to pay the £90,000 RBC in order to access the remittance basis in 2016/17.

It is interesting to note that neither the 12 out of 14 years test nor the seven out of nine years test is met. If it had not been for the new RBC added from 2015/16 by FA 2015 s 24, Nicholas would not have had to pay any RBC in the 2016/17 tax year.

See **explanatory note 9**.

## C. The Twins

In the case of Lauren and Ellie Non-Dom the 14-minute interval between their birth times means that in 2016/17 their tax affairs are different:

- Lauren, being born on 5 April 1999, is 18 on 5 April 2017 (the end of the 2016/17 tax year);

- Ellie, being born on 6 April 1999, is under 18 throughout the tax year to 5 April 2017.

Ellie automatically qualifies for the remittance basis under ITA 2007 s 809E. This is because in 2016/17 Ellie meets all the necessary conditions set down in ITA 2007 s 809E(1):

- she is UK resident in 2016/17;
- she is not domiciled in the UK in 2016/17;
- she has no UK income and gains in 2016/17 other than taxed investment income not exceeding £100;
- no foreign income or gains are remitted to the UK in 2016/17; and
- as she is under 18 throughout the tax year the fact that Ellie has been UK resident for more than six of the nine tax years immediately preceding 2016/17 does not disqualify her from meeting the ITA 2007 s 809E conditions.

See **explanatory note 8**.

Ellie can automatically access the remittance basis and does not have to pay the RBC. Since she made no remittances in 2016/17 she has no UK tax to pay on her foreign income and gains. Being taxed on the remittance basis will clearly result in a far better tax position for 2016/17 for Ellie than opting out and being taxed on the arising basis.

Lauren does not qualify under ITA 2007, s 809E as she is over 18 at the end of the tax year and has been UK resident for more than six of the nine tax years immediately preceding 2016/17.

As she has made no remittances and has foreign income well in excess of £2,000 she does not qualify for automatic access to the remittance basis in 2016/17 under ITA 2007 s 809D. She has no UK employment income so cannot qualify for the ITA 2007 s 828C exemption (see **explanatory note 4**).

Accordingly, to access the remittance basis Lauren needs to make a claim under ITA 2007 809B and it is necessary to establish whether the arising basis or the remittance basis is more cost effective for her in 2016/17.

When considering whether the RBC is in point for 2016/17, the 20-year look back period runs from 1996/97 to 2015/16, the 14-year look back period runs from 2002/03 to 2015/16 and the nine-year look back period runs from to 2007/08 to 2015/16. From the information provided in the case of Lauren Non-Dom the facts are as follows:

| *Tax year* | *UK resident at any time in the tax year* |
|---|---|
| 1999/00 – 2006/07 | No |
| 2007/08 | Yes |
| 2008/09 | Yes |
| 2009/10 | Yes |
| 2010/11 | Yes |
| 2011/12 | Yes |
| 2012/13 | Yes |
| 2013/14 | Yes |
| 2014/15 | Yes |
| 2015/16 | Yes |

Note that the 20-year look back does not apply to Lauren as she is only 18 years old in 2016/17.

Lauren is an adult at the end of the tax year and has been UK resident for nine of the preceding 14 tax years, meaning that she has to pay the basic £30,000 RBC if she wishes to access the remittance basis (ITA 2007 s 809C). In addition, since she has to make a claim for the remittance basis, she will not be entitled to her personal allowance or capital gains tax (CGT) annual exemption (ITA 2007 s 809G).

See **explanatory note 10.**

However, if she were taxed on the arising basis her personal allowance would be lost anyway given her adjusted net income level would be significantly in excess of £122.000 (£100,000 + (2 × £11,000)) (ITA 2007 s 35(2)). As such, she only forfeits her CGT annual exemption as a result of the remittance basis claim and since she has no UK capital gains this does not result in additional tax being payable.

We know that Lauren made no remittances in 2016/17 so this means that if she claims the remittance basis her additional UK tax liability with respect to her foreign income and gains will be limited to the £30,000 RBC. Aggregating her trust and personal foreign income and chargeable gains she has:

| | *Gross* | *Foreign tax credit* |
|---|---|---|
| | £ | £ |
| Interest income | 215,000 | Nil |
| Property income | 150,000 | 37,500 |
| Dividend income | 45,000 | 6,750 |
| Offshore income gains | 95,000 | Nil |
| Capital gains | 50,000 | 5,000 |

If she were taxed on the arising basis it is clear that even taking into account foreign tax credits her tax liability with respect to her foreign income and gains will be well in excess of £30,000.

Accordingly, based on the foreign income and gains arising in 2016/17, the remittance basis will be the cheaper alternative even though Lauren has to pay the £30,000.

## D. Chloe Non-Dom

Chloe does not qualify under ITA 2007 s 809E as she is over 18 at the end of the tax year and has been UK resident for more than six of the nine tax years immediately preceding 2016/17 (see below).

Her foreign income for 2016/17 is well in excess of £2,000 and, whilst she has made remittances, she has around £500,000 of unremitted foreign income for the 2016/17 tax year. She does not, therefore, qualify for automatic access to the remittance basis under ITA 2007 s 809D. She has no UK employment income so cannot qualify for the ITA 2007 s 828C exemption (see **explanatory note 4**).

Therefore in order to access the remittance basis for 2016/17, Chloe must make a claim under ITA 2007 s 809B.

When considering whether the RBC is in point for 2016/17, the 20-year look back period runs from 1996/97 to 2015/16, the 14-year look back period runs from 2002/03 to 2015/16 and the nine-year look back period runs from to 2007/08 to 2015/16. From the information provided in the case of Chloe Non-Dom the facts are as follows:

| *Tax year* | *UK resident at any time in the tax year* |
|---|---|
| 1996/97 – 2002/03 | No |
| 2003/04 | Yes |
| 2004/05 | Yes |
| 2005/06 | Yes |
| 2006/07 | Yes |
| 2007/08 | Yes |
| 2008/09 | Yes |
| 2009/10 | Yes |
| 2010/11 | Yes |
| 2011/12 | Yes |

| *Tax year* | *UK resident at any time in the tax year* |
|---|---|
| 2012/13 | Yes |
| 2013/14 | No |
| 2014/15 | No |
| 2015/16 | Yes |

To access the remittance basis she will have to pay the RBC. Since she has been UK resident for 12 of the preceding 14 tax years she will have to pay a RBC of £60,000 (ITA 2007 s 809C).

See **explanatory note 10.**

## E. Jake Non-Dom

See **explanatory notes 11** to **19.**

In order to pay the RBC, the individual must attach it to foreign income or gains by nominating the foreign income and/or gains to which it relates. However, if any of the nominated income or gains are later remitted to the UK, draconian rules are triggered in relation to the order of funds remitted. For this reason it is usually best not to remit nominated income or gains. See **explanatory note 16.**

For nominations relating to tax year 2012/13 onwards, a nomination of £10 or less will mean that regardless of what is done with the nominated funds the penal provisions in ITA 2007 ss 809I, 809J cannot be triggered. Provided £10 or less of funds are nominated there is no need for ring-fencing as the funds can be remitted to the UK without the taxpayer suffering any detriment.

The shortfall in the required tax increase, which results from a token £10 or less nomination, will be made up by the deeming provisions at ITA 2007 s 809H(4). See **explanatory note 12.**

In order for the nomination to be valid:

- it must relate to foreign income or gains which arose in the relevant tax year (ie 2016/17) (ITA 2007 s 809C(2), (3) as read with ITA 2007 s 809Z7);
- the UK tax liability on the income or gains must be such that it does not exceed the RBC of £30,000, £60,000 or £90,000 as appropriate (ie the nomination must not be excessive) (ITA 2007 s 809C(4)). See **explanatory note 13.**

ACCOUNT A

This account was the source of foreign interest income arising in 2016/17 (the bank having instructions to pay the *interest* for this account into account C). For 2016/17 a nomination can, therefore, be made with respect to the whole or part of the interest arising from this source in 2016/17.

Account A does not contain any funds representing or derived from foreign income or gains for 2016/17. Accordingly, a valid nomination for 2016/17 cannot be with respect to any foreign income or chargeable gains that are actually within the account.

ACCOUNT B

Again this account was the source of foreign interest income arising in 2016/17 (the bank having instructions to pay the interest for this account into account C). For 2016/17 a nomination can, therefore, be made with respect to the whole or part of the *interest* arising from this source in 2016/17.

Account B does not contain any funds representing or derived from foreign income or gains for 2016/17. Accordingly, Jake cannot make a valid nomination for 2016/17 with respect to any foreign income or chargeable gains that are actually within this account.

ACCOUNT C

This account received £950 of interest income in the 2016/17 tax year. Of this figure the account was the source of £85 of interest and the recipient account for £865 derived from other sources (accounts A, B, E and F).

All or part of this £950 of foreign income could be nominated and, provided the relevant details are provided, that would be a valid nomination for 2016/17. However, generally to avoid the need for ring-fencing, a token nomination of £10 or less should be made. See **explanatory note 17**. The shortfall in the tax increase will be made up by the deeming provisions at ITA 2007 s 809H(4). See **explanatory note 12**.

## ACCOUNT D

The deposit made in 2016/17 relates to clean capital. This account has not received any foreign income or gains for 2016/17 with the first income receipt being in 2017/18. Accordingly:

- the account is not the source of any income in 2016/17; and
- there is no foreign income and gains for 2016/17 within the account so Jake cannot make a valid nomination for 2016/17 with respect to any foreign income or chargeable gains within this account.

## ACCOUNT E

This bank account, as with accounts A and B above, was the source of foreign income arising in 2016/17 (its interest income having been paid into account C). As such a nomination can be made with respect to the whole or part of the interest arising from this source in 2016/17.

The account received £270,000 of gross bond interest income in the tax year (no foreign tax credits). He cannot nominate the entire £270,000 as it would give rise to a tax increase in excess of £30,000 and, thereby, break the provision at ITA 2007 s 809C(4) meaning the nomination would not be valid. See **explanatory note 13**.

Disregarding any foreign income that he receives, the quantum of Jake's UK income is such that he pays tax at the additional income tax rate (his UK income for the tax year being £165,345). This means that to make a valid nomination the maximum amount of bond interest that he can nominate is £66,666 (£66,666 × 45% = £30,000) with the minimum being £1.

Whilst the bond interest is within account E, that account is not the source of the income. When providing details of the source of income on Jake's self-assessment tax return, details of the Swiss bond interest will need to be provided. See **explanatory note 10**. If Jake did decide to nominate the bond interest then, provided he restricts the nomination to £10 or less, there is no need for him to specify what account the funds are in or be concerned about ring-fencing the funds.

If Jake wishes to make a full nomination (unlikely but see **explanatory note 19**) then he would need to nominate £66,666 and ring-fencing would be necessary.

## ACCOUNT F

This bank account, as with accounts A, B and E above, was the source of foreign income arising in 2016/17 (its interest income having been paid into account C). As such a nomination can be made with respect to the whole or part of the *interest* arising from this source in 2016/17.

This account received £110,000 of gross income in the tax year (£82,500 plus £27,500 foreign tax paid). All or part of this £110,000 could be nominated and that would be a valid nomination for 2016/17. This is because the £27,500 foreign tax paid means that the relevant tax increase if the entire £110,000 is nominated will only be £22,000 ((£110,000 × 45%) – £27,500) so there is no possibility of the nomination resulting in a relevant tax increase in excess of £30,000. There will be an insufficient nomination and the deemed nomination provisions at ITA 2007 s 809H(4) come in to make up the tax increase shortfall. See **explanatory note 12**.

Whilst the Swiss director's fees are within account F, that account is not the source of the income. When providing details of the source of income on Jake's self-assessment tax return details of the Swiss director's fees will need to be provided including information with respect to the foreign tax paid. See **explanatory note 10**.

If Jake did decide to nominate the Swiss director's fees then he would probably prefer to restrict the nomination to £10 or less, as this will mean that regardless of what is done with the nominated funds the penal provisions in

ITA 2007 ss 809I, 809J cannot be triggered. Provided the nomination does not exceed £10 there is no need for him to specify what account the funds are in or be concerned about ring-fencing the funds.

ACCOUNT G

The account is not the source of any income in 2016/17. In prior years diverting a month's foreign salary to a specially set up account may have been appropriate so as to ring-fence a small amount to avoid inadvertent remittances of nominated funds. The new rules mean that this is not necessary as, for tax year 2012/13 onwards, there is no need to ring-fence funds where a token nomination of £10 or less is made.

Where this income is nominated, even for a token nomination, when providing details of the source of income on Jake's self-assessment tax return details of the Swiss director's fees will need to be provided including information with respect to the tax credit. See **explanatory note 10**.

ACCOUNT H

The account is not the source of any income in 2016/17.

This account was established though an offshore transfer from account E. No remittances were made from account H in 2016/17 and at the end of 2016/17 there is no intention for remittances to be made from the account. Accordingly, the offshore transfer provisions at ITA 2007 s 809R(4) apply. This means that the funds transferred are deemed to be "the appropriate proportion of each kind of income and gain in the fund immediately before the transfer". The appropriate proportion is logically defined as, the proportion the funds that are transferred equate to when assessed against the value in the mixed fund immediately before the transfer.

The composition of the accounts is as follows:

| | *In Account E prior to the transfer* | *Transferred to Account H* | *Retained in Account E* |
|---|---|---|---|
| | £ | £ | £ |
| 2016/17 foreign interest | 270,000 | 257 | 269,743 |
| 2015/16 foreign interest | 225,000 | 214 | 224,786 |
| 2014/15 foreign interest | 177,000 | 168 | 176,832 |
| 2013/14 foreign interest | 220,000 | 209 | 219,791 |
| 2012/13 foreign interest | 160,000 | 152 | 159,848 |
| | 1,052,000 | 1,000 | 1,051,000 |

For a discussion of the mixed fund rules and offshore transfer provisions, see **Example F6**.

Accordingly, account H is deemed to contain £257 of Swiss bond interest relating to 2016/17. All or part of this £257 could be nominated and that would be a valid nomination for 2016/17. When providing details of the source of income on Jake's self-assessment tax return, details of the Swiss bond interest will need to be provided. See **explanatory note 10**.

However, with the new rules for tax years from 2012/13 onwards it is not necessary to ring-fence nominated funds provided the nomination made is for £10 or less of current year income or gains. This means that where a token nomination of £10 or less is made it does not matter where the funds are retained so ring-fencing and transferring funds to a special account are no longer necessary.

## Explanatory Notes

*What is the remittance basis?*

(1) The default basis of taxation for income tax and capital gains tax (CGT) for individuals is known as the 'arising basis'. Where this basis of taxation applies for a tax year, individuals are taxed on a worldwide basis on the taxable income deemed to arise and the chargeable gains deemed to accrue to them in the tax year.

All UK tax residents, whatever their domicile status, are subject to 'arising basis' tax on their UK source income and chargeable gains realised on the disposal (or deemed disposal) of UK situs assets. The 'remittance basis' is an alternative basis of UK taxation which can only be accessed by foreign domiciliaries (see **explanatory note 2**). It can apply to foreign income and foreign chargeable gains of such individuals. Where it does apply, such funds are only taxable when remitted (brought) to the UK.

There are specific rules that govern the remittance basis of taxation. There are also some specific items of foreign income and/or gains to which the remittance basis cannot apply. In particular gains on the surrender of all rights under a policy of life assurance, life annuity or on a capital redemption policy are always taxable on the arising basis. The rules in relation to partial surrenders are more complicated and depend on the source of the funds used to pay the original premiums (see RDRM33540).

Fundamental changes to the remittance basis were made in FA 2008 (with some modifications enacted in FA 2009). The 2008 changes extended the meaning of 'remittance', introduced financial penalties for accessing the remittance basis and generally complicated the remittance basis rules.

FA 2012 made the following changes to the remittance basis all of which were effective from 6 April 2012:

- a higher RBC for adult longer-term UK residents (individuals who have been resident in the UK for at least 12 of the preceding 14 tax years). Originally set at £50,000 per year, this increased to £60,000 per year from 2015/16 onwards (ITA 2007 s 809C);
- a new exemption for commercial investment in UK qualifying businesses (referred to in the legislation as 'business investment relief') (ITA 2007 ss 809VA-809VO)
- a new exemption to tie in with the cultural gifts scheme to incentivise foreign domiciliaries to make gifts to the nation of pre-eminent works of art (ITA 2007 s 809YE);
- The simplification of the existing remittance basis rules in respect of:
  - nominated income (ITA 2007 s 809I(5));
  - foreign currency bank accounts (TCGA 1992 s 252);
  - the taxation of assets remitted to and sold in the UK (ITA 2007 s 809YA).

FA 2013 made a number of helpful modifications to the exempt asset rules and to the exemption for 'Money paid to the Commissioners' (specifically targeting the practical problems encountered where payments on account are required) (ITA 2007 s 809UA). In addition, after a lengthy consultation exercise, FA 2013 introduced legislation into the statutory mixed fund provisions to replace SP 1/09 (employees resident but not ordinarily resident in the UK). Provided certain conditions are met, these new provisions simplify the mechanics of the mixed fund rules for individuals entitled to overseas workday relief (ITA 2007 ss 809RA-809RD).

FA 2015 introduced a third level of the RBC, with an annual charge of £90,000 in respect of adult longer-term UK residents who have been resident in the UK for at least 17 out of the preceding 20 tax years (ITA 2007 s 809C). See **explanatory note 9**. It is expected that this will be abolished from 6 April 2017, as part of the introduction of deemed domicile rules for income tax and CGT in Finance Bill 2017.

The remittance basis is a highly complex area of UK taxation. These explanatory notes address the issues of eligibility for and access to the remittance basis. Other aspects of the remittance basis are covered in the Examples that follow:

- the meaning of remittance is discussed in **Example F5** and its explanatory notes;
- the mixed fund rules and some investment issues are explained in greater detail in **Example F6** and its explanatory notes;
- the particular issues with respect to capital gains tax are discussed in **Example F7** and its explanatory notes.

*Who is potentially eligible to access the remittance basis?*

(2) From 2013/14 onwards the concept of ordinary residence has been abolished for direct tax purposes and so, apart from when the transitional rules apply, the remittance basis is only available to foreign domiciliaries (note that for income tax and capital gains tax purposes the concept of deemed UK domicile does not apply). The transitional rules are discussed in **Example F1 explanatory note 27**.

Prior to 6 April 2013, individuals who were UK resident and domiciled but not ordinarily resident in the UK could potentially access the remittance basis with respect to their foreign income (though never on foreign chargeable gains).

*Foreign employment income – overseas workday relief*

(3) The general rule is that the remittance basis can apply to employment income only where the foreign employment is with an overseas employer and the employment duties are wholly performed abroad (with the exception of incidental UK duties). It can be very difficult for employment income to come within the remittance basis because of this and a specific relief has always been available to mitigate the severity of the general rule for short term UK residents. 'Overseas workday relief' is the term used when referring to this relief.

Prior to 6 April 2013, overseas workday relief could be claimed by a remittance basis user for the tax years during which the individual remained not ordinarily UK resident. Provided the income was paid into an offshore account, it meant that the remittance basis could be claimed in connection with foreign employment duties where a single contract covered both UK and overseas duties.

The earnings from the employment were apportioned between UK and overseas duties on a days basis and there was only a UK remittance if the total of the below exceeded the total UK portion of the earnings (SP 1/09):

- the total amount of earnings received in the UK; plus
- the amount remitted from the offshore account set up to receive the overseas portion of the earnings.

This relief was very valuable to internationally mobile employees (and their employers). As such, the relief has been retained but only for foreign domiciliaries.

The rules are discussed in **Example F1 explanatory note 28**.

*Non-domiciliaries – exemption for small earnings*

(4) The general rule is that a claim has to be made to benefit from provisions within double tax agreements. This rule when coupled with the changes with respect to accessing the remittance basis (see **explanatory note 5**) would mean that a significant number of tax returns would have to be submitted where there was little or no tax due. This would place a significant administrative burden on both taxpayers and HMRC.

An exemption at ITA 2007 s 828C addresses the problem partially. Where the qualifying conditions in ITA 2007 ss 828A-828B are met, the legislation exempts the individual's foreign income from UK tax. Those meeting the conditions would not have had to submit a self-assessment tax return if it were not for the foreign income, so the exemption from paying UK tax on this income removes the need for qualifying individuals to have to file UK tax returns.

To qualify for the exemption, in the relevant tax year the individual must (ITA 2007 ss 828A–828B):

- be UK resident;
- not be domiciled in the UK;
- not have made a claim for the remittance basis under ITA 2007 s 809B;
- have income from an employment, the duties of which are performed wholly or partly in the UK;

- have no foreign income other than (1) £10,000 or less of foreign employment income subject to a foreign tax; and/or (2) £100 or less of foreign interest income subject to a foreign tax;
- have no foreign chargeable gains;
- not pay UK tax on any of this foreign income at a rate higher than the basic rate of tax (assuming all the individual's worldwide income were subject to UK tax); and
- not make a self-assessment tax return under TMA 1970 s 8.

Where the conditions are met, this exemption gives a more favourable result than applying the remittance basis to the foreign income for the tax year. This is because the exemption means that no UK tax will arise on the foreign income regardless of whether it remains offshore or is remitted to the UK.

*Accessing the remittance basis*

(5) One of the fundamental principles underpinning the remittance basis regime is that, with limited exceptions, those who access the remittance basis should suffer a financial penalty.

Individuals who are eligible to access the remittance basis are, by default, taxed on the arising basis and are only able to access the remittance basis if they make a formal claim (the standard means for doing this being to complete the relevant boxes on the 'Residence, remittance basis etc' supplementary pages of their UK self-assessment tax return). Note that a 'claim' must be made on the tax return even if the individual is able to access the remittance basis automatically under ITA 2007 ss 809D or 809E (see **explanatory notes 6–8**) (Residence, remittance basis etc notes, https://www.gov.uk/government/publications/self-assessment-residence-remittance-basis-etc-sa109, page RRN10).

Where a claim must be made for the remittance basis under ITA 2007 s 809B (as opposed to the automatic remittance basis), the deadline for making the remittance basis claim is the standard claims deadline. This means that for the claim to be valid it must be made before the fourth anniversary of the tax year for which the remittance basis claim is being made (TMA 1970 s 43). The following table provides the claims deadlines for tax years from 2008/09 to 2016/17:

| *Tax year* | *Remittance basis claim deadline* |
|---|---|
| 2008/09 | 5 April 2013 |
| 2009/10 | 5 April 2014 |
| 2010/11 | 5 April 2015 |
| 2011/12 | 5 April 2016 |
| 2012/13 | 5 April 2017 |
| 2013/14 | 5 April 2018 |
| 2014/15 | 5 April 2019 |
| 2015/16 | 5 April 2020 |
| 2016/17 | 5 April 2021 |

Making a remittance basis claim comes with a cost attached. The basic cost is set down at ITA 2007 s 809G and entails the loss of:

- the income tax personal allowance (and where applicable the age allowance);
- the blind person's allowance (if applicable);
- the capital gains annual exempt amount; and
- the married couples'/civil partners' allowance (only claimable where one of the individuals was born on or before 5 April 1935).

It should be noted that given the provisions with respect to the personal allowance, which withdraw the tax free amount (in whole or part) from taxpayers with adjusted net income in excess of £100,000, a foreign domiciliary may forfeit his personal allowance simply as a result of the level of his taxable income regardless of whether the remittance basis claim is made (ITA 2007 s 35(2)).

There is one exception to the general rule that a remittance basis claim results in the loss of allowances in the relevant tax year. The exception arises because certain double tax agreements (DTAs) the UK has entered into have specific provisions which, if the individual meets the conditions, establish that the individual has a right to the same allowances and reliefs as British subjects not resident in the UK.

The precise treaty provision needs to be consulted, but very broadly for the treaty provision to apply in this situation, the individual must be dual resident with the treaty tiebreaker provisions awarding residence to the other territory. At the time of writing the countries with whom the text of the DTA with the UK is such that this can happen are: Austria, Barbados Belgium, Fiji, Ireland, Kenya, Luxembourg, Mauritius, Namibia, Netherlands, Portugal, Swaziland, Sweden, Switzerland and Zambia (Residence, remittance basis etc notes, https://www.gov.uk/government/publications/self-assessment-residence-remittance-basis-etc-sa109, page RRN5). When FA 2008 came into force France and Germany also had the requisite provisions in their treaties with the UK but:

- for France the provisions of the treaty signed on 19 June 2008 (which has effect from 6 April 2010 for income tax and capital gains tax) do not preserve the individual's entitlement to the personal allowance; and
- for Germany the provisions of the treaty signed on 30 March 2010 (which has effect from 6 April 2011 for income tax and capital gains tax) do not preserve the individual's entitlement to the personal allowance.

There are lists showing treaties in force and treaties signed but not in force on the HMRC website with the home page for tax treaty news being https://www.gov.uk/government/collections/tax-treaties-signed-and-in-force.

Claiming the remittance basis (as opposed to being an automatic remittance basis user) also has an impact on the individual's capital loss relief entitlement (TCGA 1992 s 16ZA) as explained in **Example F7 explanatory notes 5–7**.

In addition to the basic cost of accessing the remittance basis, the RBC is due where the individual is aged 18 or over in the tax year and meets the definition of a long-term UK resident (ITA 2007 s 809C). An individual will be a long-term resident if he or she meets the 'seven out of nine preceding tax year', the '12 out of 14 preceding tax year' or the '17 out of 20 preceding tax year' residence tests.

The 'seven out of nine preceding tax year' residence test is met where an individual has been UK resident for at least seven of the preceding nine tax years but does not meet the '12 out of 14 preceding tax year' or '17 out of 20 preceding tax year' residence tests. Where just the 'seven out of nine preceding tax year' residence test is met the basic £30,000 RBC is payable.

The '12 out of 14 preceding tax year' residence test was introduced for tax years from 2012/13 onwards and is met where an individual has been UK resident for at least 12 of the preceding 14 tax years but does not meet the '17 out of 20 preceding tax year' residence test. Where the 12-year residence test is met a higher £60,000 RBC is payable (for the tax years 2012/13 to 2014/15 inclusive the RBC was £50,000).

The '17 out of 20 preceding tax year' residence test was introduced for tax years from 2016/17 onwards and is met where the individual has been UK resident for at least 17 of the preceding 20 tax years. Where the test is met, the RBC is £90,000. It is expected that this will be abolished from 6 April 2017, as part of the introduction of deemed domicile rules for income tax and CGT in Finance Bill 2017.

For 2016/17 one therefore has to look at an individual's pattern of UK residence from 1996/07 onwards to establish whether the RBC is payable and at what rate. See **explanatory note 9**. There are two statutory exceptions (ITA 2007 ss 809D and 809E – see **explanatory notes 6–8**) to the rule that the remittance basis must be claimed. The determination as to whether the individual qualifies for the remittance basis without having to make a claim is made on a year-by-year basis. An individual might meet the conditions such that the remittance basis can be accessed without the need to make a claim in one tax year and not in another.

For individuals who meet either the ITA 2007 ss 809D or 809E qualifying conditions the position is reversed in that the remittance basis is the default basis of taxation. Individuals qualifying automatically for the remittance basis will only be able to access the arising basis if they give notice on their tax return for the relevant year that they wish to opt out of being taxed on the remittance basis for that year.

Whether the arising or remittance basis of taxation applies by default to a UK resident foreign domiciliary's UK tax affairs for a tax year, he has a free choice as to whether to take action so that the other basis will apply. Decisions made in previous years in no way fetter an individual's choice in later years. Furthermore, the choices made have no impact on the individual's actual domicile status.

*Automatic entitlement to the remittance basis*

(6) Where an individual automatically qualifies for the remittance basis under ITA 2007 ss 809D or 809E, his entitlement to personal allowances and the CGT annual exemption are unaffected. A self-assessment tax return does not need to be submitted in order to make HMRC aware of the automatic entitlement, however if a self-assessment tax return has to be submitted for other reasons, the necessary questions on the 'Residence, remittance basis etc' supplementary pages must be completed (Residence, remittance basis etc notes https://www.gov.uk/government/publications/self-assessment-residence-remittance-basis-etc-sa109, page RRN10).

*Unremitted foreign income and foreign chargeable gains under £2,000*

(7) ITA 2007 s 809D provides that the remittance basis is automatic for a tax year during which an individual:

- is UK resident;
- is not domiciled in the UK;
- has aggregate unremitted foreign income and foreign chargeable gains equating to less than £2,000; and
- does not benefit from the ITA 2007 s 828C exemption (which takes priority, see **explanatory note 4**).

The 'less than £2,000' test is with respect to the quantum of total foreign income and foreign chargeable gains that arise in the tax year and are not remitted to the UK in the same tax year. Accordingly, it is not necessary for the individual's total foreign income and gains for the tax year to be less than £2,000. For example, the total foreign income and gains figure could be £500,000 for the tax year and the individual would qualify if £498,001 of those foreign income and gains were remitted to the UK in that year.

Note than there is no split year treatment with respect to the £2,000. This means that, if an individual arrives mid-way through the tax year, foreign income and gains that arose or accrued in the part of the tax year before UK residence began are taken into account for the purposes of the test (RDRM32120).

Individuals who qualify for the automatic remittance basis as they have aggregate unremitted foreign income and foreign chargeable gains for the tax year of less than £2,000 do not have to pay the RBC regardless of how long they have been resident in the UK.

For details of how to quantify unremitted income and gains in sterling for the purposes of ITA 2007 s 809D, see **Example F6 explanatory note 17.**

*Child or short-term UK resident making no remittances and with minimal UK income arising in the tax year*

(8) ITA 2007 s 809E provides that the remittance basis is automatic for a tax year during which an individual:

- is UK resident;
- is not domiciled in the UK;
- meets at least one of the following two qualifying conditions:
  - under 18 throughout the tax year;

  - has been UK resident in not more than six of the nine tax years immediately preceding the year in question;

- either has no UK income or chargeable gains whatsoever or only has £100 or less of investment income that has had actual tax (as opposed to a deemed tax credit) deducted at source, for example bank interest paid net; and

- does not remit any property representing or derived from remittance basis foreign income or foreign chargeable gains.

The definition of UK investment income for this purpose is given in ITA 2007 s 946 (ITA 2007 s 809E(2A)). From 6 April 2017 this no longer covers interest paid by UK banks, building societies and deposit takers. Instead the definition is limited to interest/annual payments/patent royalties paid by UK companies.

This change is a result of the abolition of tax at source on interest by these institutions and it means those who previously met the conditions and had small amounts of UK bank interest are no longer able to qualify:

- In the case of those over 18, this would mean making a claim for the remittance basis under ITA 2007, s 809B or being taxed on the arising basis. Making a claim would result in the forfeit of the personal allowance and CGT annual exemption. See the answer to Henry Non-Dom scenario B above;

- for those under 18 the consequences could be more significant if they have been in the UK for more than six out of the last nine years, as the loss of automatic remittance basis may mean they must pay the RBC to benefit from the remittance basis. Consider the answer to Ellie Non-Dom above if she had received £85 of UK bank interest; she would have had to pay the RBC like her sister.

*Long-term UK residents: the RBC*

(9) The tax liability for an individual who claims the remittance basis if he is aged 18 or over in the tax year and is a long-term UK resident, is increased by the RBC. As explained above, for tax years from 2016/17 onwards there are three categories of long-term UK resident with a basic £30,000 RBC, an intermediate £60,000 RBC and a higher £90,000 RBC (ITA 2007 s 809C).

The £90,000 is payable by individuals who claim the remittance basis and have been UK resident for at least 17 out of the preceding 20 tax years. The £60,000 RBC is payable by individuals who claim the remittance basis and have been UK resident for at least 12 of the preceding 14 tax years and do not meet the '17 out of 20 preceding tax year' residence test. For tax years between 2012/13 and 2014/15 inclusive, the intermediate RBC was set at £50,000. The £30,000 RBC payable by individuals who do not meet the '12 out of 14 preceding tax year' or the '17 out of 20 preceding tax year' residence tests but have been UK resident in at least seven of the nine tax years immediately preceding the year in which the remittance claim is made.

The following table sets down the RBC look back periods for tax years from 2008/09 to 2016/17:

| | *'Seven out of nine' test RBC look back period* | *'12 out of 14' test RBC look back period* | *'17 out of 20' test RBC look back period* |
|---|---|---|---|
| 2008/09 | 1999/00 to 2007/08 | Not applicable | Not applicable |
| 2009/10 | 2000/01 to 2008/09 | Not applicable | Not applicable |
| 2010/11 | 2001/02 to 2009/10 | Not applicable | Not applicable |
| 2011/12 | 2002/03 to 2010/11 | Not applicable | Not applicable |
| 2012/13 | 2003/04 to 2011/12 | 1998/99 to 2011/12 | Not applicable |
| 2013/14 | 2004/05 to 2012/13 | 1999/00 to 2012/13 | Not applicable |
| 2014/15 | 2005/06 to 2013/14 | 2000/01 to 2013/14 | Not applicable |
| 2015/16 | 2006/07 to 2014/15 | 2001/02 to 2014/15 | 1995/96 to 2014/15 |
| 2016/17 | 2007/08 to 2015/16 | 2002/03 to 2015/16 | 1996/97 to 2015/16 |

When determining whether the individual has been resident in the tax year for the purposes of the RBC, split years count as a year of residence as do years of dual residence even where, under a tie breaker clause, the individual is resident in the other territory (RDRM32220). A child under the age of 18 throughout the tax year does not have to pay the RBC (ITA 2007 ss 809C(1)(a), 809H(1)(b)). However, as illustrated in **part C** and **part D** of this Example, one should bear in mind that years of UK residence during the individual's minority are counted when determining if an individual who is over 18 in the tax year has met either residence test (RDRM32230). Where a child is a long-term UK resident (possibly having been born in the UK) this means that free access to the remittance basis will end in the tax year that the child reaches 18. As **part D** shows, this may mean that the individual has to pay the RBC from the tax year that he reaches 18. Consideration should be given to what tax efficient transactions and re-arrangements of the child's affairs could be carried out in the tax year preceding the tax year during which the child has his 18$^{th}$ birthday.

The RBC is collected through the self-assessment system and where the RBC is derived from an actual or a deemed income nomination (see **explanatory note 12**) the resulting income tax feeds into the payments on account calculation.

When considering payments on account and whether a reduction can be made it is important to consider whether the taxpayer will pay the RBC for the following tax year and whether the residence position will mean that the RBC payable for the next tax year will increase, either from £30,000 to £60,000 or from £60,000 to £90,000.

The legislation contains a specific exemption (see **Example F5 explanatory note 19** for details) where funds representing or derived from remittance basis income and/or gains are used to pay the RBC (whether this is the basic £30,000, the intermediate £60,000 or the higher £90,000) (ITA 2007 s 809V). Being able to pay the RBC from remittance basis income and/or gains without incurring a tax liability means that the individual can preserve his or her clean capital. This exemption should be kept in mind when comparing the tax consequences under the arising basis (where any payment of the UK tax due that comes from prior years' unremitted income or gains will result in a tax liability) and the remittance basis.

The exemption will only cover £90,000 if the individual meets the '17 out of the preceding 20' residence test in the tax year such that the £90,000 RBC is payable. Similarly, where the £60,000 or £30,000 RBC is due the exemption will only cover £30,000 or £60,000 as appropriate.

*Long-term UK residents: making the remittance basis claim*

(10) In addition to making the basic remittance basis claim, an adult long-term UK resident foreign domiciliary must:

- make an actual nomination of at least £1 of foreign income or foreign chargeable gains that have arisen in the relevant tax year (ITA 2007 s 809C(2)); and
- avoid making an excessive actual nomination such that the nominated foreign income or chargeable gains gives rise to a relevant tax increase exceeding £30,000/£60,000/£90,000 (whichever amount is due as a result of the numbers of preceding tax years where there was UK residence) (ITA 2007 s 809C(4)).

The choice the individual makes with respect to the foreign income or gains to nominate has no impact on his or her nomination choice in future years.

The nomination is made on the tax return on the 'Residence, remittance basis etc.' supplementary pages (SA109).

The 2016/17 self-assessment tax return, supplementary pages and associated notes are not available. For 2015/16 the nomination of foreign income or chargeable gains arising in the tax year is made using box 34 (for foreign income) and/or 35 (for foreign gains). Where foreign gains are nominated it is necessary to complete box 36 (the amount of RBC coming from capital gains) so that the RBC amount coming from capital gains does not feed through to the payments on account calculation for the next year.

Additional information about the nominated income and/or gains needs to be provided in box 40 'any other information'. Strictly if box 40 is not completed the nomination will not be complete. Merely putting a number into box 34 and/or 35 of the supplementary pages for 'Residence, remittance basis etc.' is insufficient to satisfy the statutory requirements that a nomination of income or gains be made.

*Long-term UK residents: the nomination process*

(11) The nomination process has been put in place to try to establish that the RBC is either income tax or CGT, and so should be given credit in the same way as any other income tax or CGT paid, rather than it being seen as a stand-alone tax charge.

As discussed in **explanatory note 10**, it is a statutory requirement that in order to make a valid remittance basis claim a long-term resident makes a nomination of at least £1 of actual foreign income or gains arising or accruing in the tax year for which the claim is being made.

The provisions state that nominated foreign income and gains are treated as being taxed on the arising basis (ITA 2007 s 809H(2)) and the tax increase due as a result of the nomination is calculated. Credit is given, in the standard manner, for any foreign tax suffered. As the nominated foreign income and gains are treated as being taxed on the arising basis, one calculates tax on foreign dividend income using the dividend tax rates.

A valid nomination will always result in a relevant tax increase of £30,000, £60,000 or £90,000 (as appropriate) and, therefore, a RBC of £30,000, £60,000 or £90,000. The legislation achieves this result by artificially increasing an insufficient actual nomination (see **explanatory note 12**) and rejecting an excessive nomination (see **explanatory note 13**).

*The additional top-up deemed nomination provisions*

(12) Where a long-term UK resident foreign domiciliary wants to make a remittance basis claim and makes an actual nomination that results in a tax increase of less than the applicable RBC (£30,000, £60,000 or £90,000 depending on the individual's record of UK residence in the preceding 20 tax years), specific deeming provisions are triggered.

For the purposes of carrying out the RBC calculation these provisions deem an additional top-up 'notional' nomination of foreign income, sufficient to result in the necessary tax increase, to have been made (ITA 2007 s 809H(4)(a)). Note that it is irrelevant whether the individual does or does not have foreign income that could have been so nominated (ITA 2007 s 809H(4)(b)).

The foreign income deeming provisions feed through to the self-assessment tax computation. This means that the income tax calculated on the deemed foreign income impacts on the payments on account. However, the deeming provisions are specifically disapplied when considering whether nominated foreign income or gains have been remitted (ITA 2007 s 809H(6)). Accordingly for the purposes of the ITA 2007 ss 809I-809J legislation (see **explanatory note 16**) one only considers actual nominated income or chargeable gains and, for tax years from 2012/13 onwards, only when an actual nomination of in excess of £10 is made.

*Excessive nominations*

(13) The legislation specifies that the nomination must be such that the resulting tax increase does not exceed the RBC due (that is £30,000, £60,000 or £90,000 depending on the individual's record of UK residence in the preceding 20 tax years) (ITA 2007 s 809C(4)). This means that a remittance basis claim made will not be valid if there is an excessive nomination.

If an invalid claim is not repaired within the claims deadline (four years from the end of the relevant tax year, TMA 1970 s 43) then the taxpayer will not have been entitled to the remittance basis for that tax year. Accordingly, great care should be taken to avoid making an excessive nomination. Generally the preferred tactic will be to make a token nomination of £10 or less (see **explanatory note 16**).

*Little chance of credit in the UK for the RBC*

(14) The individual is unlikely to ever receive credit for the RBC against UK tax as to do so it is necessary for him to make a full nomination (that is an actual nomination which increases the tax by the necessary £30,000/£60,000/£90,000) and have first remitted *all* foreign income and gains subject to tax on the remittance basis since 6 April 2008 (ITA 2007 s 809I). This is unlikely to be achievable because even the deduction of £1 in bank fees from funds representing post-5 April 2008 remittance basis foreign income and/or gains would mean that the individual would not be able to remit *all* such foreign income and gains.

*Is credit for the RBC given in other territories?*

(15) It was thought that where an individual's tax affairs were such that they would wish to claim credit for the RBC against foreign tax, they would not want to make an insufficient nomination. Making an actual nomination such that the increase in the tax liability can be traced to actual foreign income or gains was felt to be advisable as it would give the individual the best possible chance of being successful in making a claim for credit for the RBC in a foreign territory.

**Giving credit for the RBC – the US position**

The main jurisdiction where the creditability of the RBC for foreign taxes is important is the US. The Internal Revenue Service (IRS) opined in Revenue Ruling 2011–19 (issued on 6 September 2011) on the creditability of the RBC against American income. The full ruling is accessible at www.irs.gov/irb/2011-36_IRB/ar06.html. The ruling takes a pragmatic stance concluding that the entire RBC is creditable against US tax whether an insufficient or full nomination is made.

The reason for this is stated as being that the RBC, when viewed in conjunction with other UK income and CGT paid in accordance with the remittance basis provisions, should be seen as conforming with the requirements of section 901 of the Internal Revenue Code such that it is creditable whether the remittance nomination made is a full nomination or an insufficient nomination. The IRS ruling specifies that credit can be claimed even where only a token actual nomination is made.

This should mean that US citizens can benefit from the £10 exemption easement with respect to nominated income/gains for 2012/13 onwards such that full credit for the RBC can be obtained in the UK whilst avoiding difficulties with ITA 2007 ss 809I, 809J.

Whilst Revenue Ruling 2011–19 is good news, it is important to note the qualifications set down at the end of the Ruling. The credit from the RBC will only be available where the other legal requirements for obtaining a foreign tax credit are met. It is also important to remember that for some US taxpayers the question may be academic as:

- the individual may be better off being taxed on the arising basis; or
- where the remittance basis claim is made, the level of UK tax paid may be higher than in the US, meaning that individual will have excess foreign tax credits.

The ruling was based on the legislation in force as at 6 September 2011 so considered just the £30,000 RBC. The changes to the legislation to introduce the intermediate charge (which is £60,000 for tax years 2015/16 onwards) and the higher charge of £90,000, are so closely aligned to the old rules for just the £30,000 RBC that it is assumed that now the £30,000, £60,000 and £90,000 RBC will be creditable for US tax purposes.

Given the potential complexities, where credit in the US is required specific advice should be sought from the individual's US tax adviser to ensure that what is done with respect to the nomination is optimal.

*Remitting nominated income or gains*

(16) The legislation has deeming provisions (ITA 2007 s 809I) which mean that, apart from a crucial £10 de minimis introduced for tax year 2012/13 onwards, if the individual does remit actual nominated income or gains before having remitted *all* foreign income and gains subject to tax on the remittance basis since 6 April 2008, special matching provisions (ITA 2007 s 809J) are triggered which for tax purposes change reality.

The provisions are potentially penal so, for tax years from 2012/13 onwards, it will generally be important to ensure that the nomination made does not exceed £10 so as to qualify under the de minimis and avoid these rules.

**Where the provisions are triggered**

As discussed in **explanatory note 14**, in practical terms it is very unlikely that an individual will be able to remit *all* of their foreign income and gains subject to tax on the remittance basis since 6 April 2008. This means that unless the remittance is for tax years from 2012/13 onwards and comes within the £10 de minimis discussed below, it is likely that if nominated income or gains are remitted these penal rules will be triggered.

The provisions are highly complex. It is necessary to quantify the actual foreign income and gains remitted in the tax year and then determine the actual foreign income and gains received in that tax year and the previous tax years for the periods back to 2008/09. The individual is taxed on the same amount of relevant foreign income and gains that have been remitted but this amount is matched to foreign income and gains in the order set down in the legislation (ITA 2007 s 809J(2)).

Generally the legislative matching order will mean that, where the individual has more than one category of foreign income or gains, the taxpayer will pay more UK tax on the income or gains remitted than would otherwise have been the case.

**Example**

Lucy is a long-term UK resident foreign domiciliary who pays tax at the additional income tax rate. She made the remittance basis claim and paid the RBC for all tax years from 2008/09 onwards. Lucy has two Jersey bank accounts:

- a Jersey income account containing foreign bank interest of £100,000 relating to 2011/12 (with no tax credit); and
- a Jersey capital proceeds account containing the proceeds (£300,000) from the sale in 2008/09 of a foreign chargeable asset which on sale realised a gain of £100,000 (the £200,000 to acquire the asset having come from clean capital).

On 17 May 2011 Lucy remitted £50,000 from the Jersey capital proceeds account. Under normal circumstances this remittance would have been taxable at 28%. However, if with respect to a prior transaction Lucy remitted nominated income or gains and so triggered the ITA 2007 ss 809I, 809J provisions, what actually happened is ignored. Should these provisions have applied, Lucy would have been taxed as if £50,000 of the foreign bank interest were remitted (so the tax rate is 45% rather than the CGT rate of 28%).

It should be noted that these provisions have no bearing where clean capital is remitted since in such cases the quantum of the remittance is zero. The rules only work to re-characterise remittances of foreign income and gains.

**The £10 de minimis**

As the example above shows, the rules that apply if ITA 2007 s 809J is triggered are particularly onerous. Prior to 2012/13 these rules led to the creation of specific accounts to ring-fence the funds nominated and much professional time was spent explaining and supervising this process.

Recognising that the lengths to which the legislation was making taxpayers go were excessive and unnecessary, the rules were amended in FA 2013. For tax years from 2012/13 onwards, the penal matching provisions are not triggered on remittance of up to £10 of nominated income or gains for a relevant tax year (ITA 2007 s 809I(1)(c), (5)).

In simple terms, provided that for each tax year from 2012/13 onwards, the nominated amount is less than or equal to £10, the penal matching rules can never apply and even if the nominated funds are in whole or part remitted there will be no tax charge. The £10 de minimis amount is so small that the tax impact is insignificant. The important point is that for 2012/13 onwards the ring-fencing requirements can fall away provided the nomination for the tax year is less than or equal to £10.

*Considerations when making the nomination*

(17) Care needs to be taken when making the nomination to ensure that a valid nomination is made. As discussed in **explanatory note 10**, to make a valid nomination it is necessary to ensure that:

- at least £1 of foreign income and/or gains arising in the relevant tax year is nominated; and
- that the actual nomination made does not result in an additional tax liability in excess of the RBC.

In addition, when making the nomination one will want to avoid triggering the penal matching provisions at ITA 2007 ss 809I, 809J (see **explanatory note 16**). As discussed above, with the relaxation in the nominated income/gains rules from 2012/13 onwards the normal approach will be to nominate foreign income or gains of £10 or less. That way there will be a valid nomination and no possibility of triggering the ITA 2007 ss 809I, 809J provisions.

*Nominating foreign income as opposed to foreign gains*

(18) Where foreign income is nominated, or deemed to have been nominated, there is an impact on the payments on account situation going forward (and with respect to the current tax year if a reduction claim was made).

In contrast, if foreign gains are nominated the payments on account are unaffected, with the £30,000, £60,000 or £90,000 being part of the balancing payment due by 31 January following the tax year. Accordingly, from a cash flow perspective, it would be advantageous to nominate foreign chargeable gains where an individual:

- is certain he can ring-fence proceeds from gains sufficient to increase his tax liability by £30,000/£60,000/£90,000 (as appropriate) and will never remit these proceeds;
- is happy to provide details with respect to the capital disposal to HMRC; and
- is confident that their tax liabilities will not be increased overall through not being able to remit the proceeds as there will be no need to remit from funds which would give rise to a liability in excess of 28%.

It would seem unlikely that the cash flow advantage of making a full nomination of foreign gains will be significant enough to mean that it is worth making a full nomination (with the dangers of coming within ITA 2007 ss 809I, 809J that would come with this decision) rather than making a token nomination of £10 or less (such that for tax years from 2012/13 onwards ITA 2007 ss 809I, 809J cannot apply). However, with the remittance basis regime there is no 'one size fits all' answer and individual circumstances need to be considered carefully.

# Question

## A.

Claude Non-Dom first came to the UK in 2007/08 and has been UK resident every year since then. He made remittance basis claims for tax years 2008/09 to 2015/16. He had also made the necessary claims for his relevant foreign income to be taxed on the remittance basis in prior years (any foreign employment income and foreign chargeable gains automatically being subject to the remittance basis in 2007/08). He will make a remittance basis claim for 2016/17.

Claude will pay income tax at the additional rate in 2016/17. Taking each in turn state whether the following 2016/17 transactions will result in a taxable remittance:

(a) to pay for various home improvements Claude remitted £60,000 from his Jersey account containing foreign employment income (on which no foreign tax had been paid);

(b) Claude sold offshore at a loss an antique table acquired prior to 12 March 2008 from £12,000 of relevant foreign income. The auctioneer wired the net proceeds received (£11,000) direct to his UK account;

(c) Claude used £7,500, from an ABC Jersey account containing post-5 April 2008 foreign employment income, to buy his wife jewellery for her 30th birthday present. The gift occurred offshore but his wife brought the jewellery back to the UK and uses it personally;

(d) Claude had an offshore portfolio, which is managed by XYZA UK Investment Managers (a London based fund management team). The fund manager had strict instructions to never acquire UK situs assets. Fixed £2,500 per quarter investment management fees were settled from Claude's Jersey income account with XYZA UK Investment Managers by the means of electronic transfers to the fund manager's Jersey account;

(e) a standing order of £3,000 per month from his Jersey account containing post-5 April 2008 foreign employment income was made to his adult daughter's Jersey account. His daughter then remitted the funds to the UK to help with her household expenditure. The monthly gifts were absolute and unconditional and neither Claude nor any other relevant person in connection with Claude benefited from the gifts;

(f) Claude gifted £15,000 to his wife offshore, from a Jersey account containing pre-6 April 2008 foreign employment income, which she remitted and used to finance her PhD studies;

(g) in January 2017 Claude arranges for an electronic transfer from his post-5 April 2008 foreign employment income account to HMRC to settle his £67,100 tax liability. The transfer is straight from Claude's Swiss account to HMRC. This breaks down as a £45,000 balancing payment for 2015/16 and a first payment on account for 2016/17 of £22,100. Claude had settled the payments on account for 2015/16 from UK funds.

## B.

Claudine Non-Dom is a long-term UK resident foreign domiciliary. She made remittance basis claims for tax years 2008/09 to 2015/16. She had also made the necessary claims for her relevant foreign income to be taxed on the remittance basis in prior years (any foreign employment income and foreign chargeable gains automatically being subject to the remittance basis in 2007/08). She will make a remittance basis claim for 2016/17.

In 2016/17 she makes the following sales through a UK auction house. The chattels are brought to the UK specifically for the sale and the sales proceeds (less selling costs) are paid directly to her Geneva account:

(a) an antique table funded from Claudine's foreign employment income;

(b) a painting inherited from Claudine's grandmother;

(c) a diamond necklace funded partly from a birthday present from her father and Claudine's relevant foreign income.

Taking each of these in turn, state whether bringing these assets into the UK constitutes a remittance and, if not, whether the sale of the assets in the UK is a remittance.

## C.

Katya Non-Dom wants to take advantage of business investment relief. She has £500,000 of relevant foreign income and various potential investment opportunities. Assuming that she would make the necessary claim by the due date, taking each in turn explain whether the following would be qualifying investments:

(a) loaning £500,000 to a UK trading partnership;

(b) loaning £500,000 to an unquoted foreign company that carries on a UK trade;

(c) using £500,000 to provide additional working capital for her sole tradership;

(d) using £500,000 to subscribe for quoted shares in a UK trading company;

(e) using £500,000 to subscribe for shares in an unquoted UK trading company;

(f) using £500,000 to acquire shares in an unquoted UK trading company from the existing owners.

## D.

Jake Non-Dom wants to take advantage of business investment relief. Explain whether the following would be a qualifying company for the purposes of the relief:

(a) an unquoted foreign company whose only asset (apart from an incidental bank account) is a UK residential property used by the only shareholder without the payment of any rent;

(b) an unquoted foreign company whose activities consist solely of carrying on a hotel business in the UK;

(c) a quoted UK trading company;

(d) an unquoted UK company that is the parent company of an eligible trading group;

(e) an unquoted UK company that exists wholly for the purpose of making investments in eligible trading companies and holds several such investments.

## E.

Heidi Non-Dom makes a qualifying £10 million investment under the business investment relief scheme. Which of the following breaches the extraction of value rule in ITA 2007 s 809VH(1)(c):

(a) Heidi enters into a contract of employment with the company as the finance director and receives market value remuneration all of which is subject to UK tax;

(b) the company is successful and Heidi receives dividend income on the same basis as all the other shareholders and pays tax on the dividends received;

(c) Heidi does not work for the company. A foreign company connected to the company that Heidi invested in acquires a chalet in Verbier and Heidi uses the chalet as if it were her own. No tax is paid in connection with this free use of the property.

# Answers

## A. Claude Non-Dom

For more on the remittance basis and when it is available, see **Example F4**.

Individuals who are taxed on the remittance basis are only taxed on their foreign income and gains if these are remitted (brought) to the UK. The meaning of remittance changed on 6 April 2008 and the rules must be considered carefully with the facts of the situation to decide whether a remittance has occurred, see below. See **explanatory note 1**.

For more on matching remittances to foreign income and gains in mixed funds, see **Example F6**.

(a) The £60,000 cash remittance is taxable (ITA 2007 s 809L(2), (3)). Claude pays tax at the additional income tax rate and there is no foreign tax credit so there will be a UK liability of £27,000 (£60,000 × 45%).

(b) The £11,000 is not a taxable remittance. The table was sold at a loss so no chargeable gain is remitted. The funds to acquire the table represent relevant foreign income. Normally there would be a UK tax liability in this scenario. However, the transitional provisions in FA 2008 Sch 7 para 86(3) switch off the normal ITA 2007 s 809L remittance definition where before 12 March 2008 property (other than money) was acquired from an individual's relevant foreign income and an event occurs that would otherwise result in a remittance of this relevant foreign income. Accordingly, as Claude acquired the table prior to 12 March 2008 from relevant foreign income, there is no remittance in this scenario (see **explanatory note 8**).

For a discussion of foreign capital losses of UK resident non-domiciliaries, see **Example F7 explanatory notes 5–7**.

(c) The £7,500 is not a remittance. Claude's wife is a relevant person in relation to Claude (ITA 2007 s 809M) and she remits the property representing Claude's post-5 April 2008 foreign income. However, since the property is jewellery and it is used personally by a relevant person, the personal use exemption applies (ITA 2007 s 809X(4) as read with ITA 2007 s 809Z2, see **explanatory note 22**). There will be a remittance of the £7,500 of income used to acquire the jewellery should the jewellery be in the UK at a time when:

- Claude's wife does not use it personally;
- no other relevant person uses it personally;
- no other relevant rules applies (that is the public access rule, the repair rule or the temporary importation rule, see **explanatory notes 24–26**); and
- within 45 days of no relevant rule applying there has been no qualifying investment of the property for the purposes of business investment relief (see **explanatory note 11**).

(d) The £2,500 quarterly fee payments are not remittances even though the investment manager is based in the UK. This is because the service exemption conditions at ITA 2007 s 809W are met as payment for the fees is made offshore to an account held by the service provider and the services are wholly in connection with foreign property. See **explanatory note 20** for further details with respect to the services exemption.

(e) The monthly standing order of £3,000 is not a remittance because:

- the gift occurs offshore;
- Claude's daughter is an adult and, therefore, not a relevant person in connection with Claude (ITA 2009 s 809M);
- neither Claude nor any other relevant person in connection with Claude receives any UK benefit whatsoever from the gifted property;

- there is no arrangement which would result in Claude, or any other relevant person in connection with Claude, receiving a UK benefit from other property as a result of the gift he made to his daughter.

Therefore none of the conditions in ITA 2007 s 809L is met. See **explanatory note 5**.

(f) The gift to Claude's wife of £15,000 is not a remittance because:

- the gift occurs offshore;
- Claude's wife is a relevant person in connection with Claude (ITA 2007 s 809M). However, when determining whether a taxable remittance has taken place, FA 2008 Sch 7 para 86(4) provides that relevant persons other than the taxpayer can only be taken into account with respect to foreign income and chargeable gains for tax years from 2008/09 onwards. That is a successful alienation of pre-6 April 2008 remittance basis income and gains can still be effected through a gift offshore to a spouse;
- Claude's wife remits the funds to the UK but Claude does not benefit in any way. If Claude did benefit the alienation would not be successful (see **explanatory note 9**).

(g) The remittance of £67,100 is partially taxable and partially exempt. This is because part of the sum remitted falls within the conditions at ITA 2007 s 809V. Provided the payment is made from offshore directly to HMRC (as is the case with the entire £67,100), this exemption allows tax free remittances to be transferred from funds representing or derived from foreign income and/or foreign gains, to settle all or part of the remittance basis charge (RBC) tax liability for a tax year for which the RBC is payable.

In Claude's case the RBC payable for 2015/16 is only £30,000 (as he has been UK resident long enough to qualify for the basic £30,000 RBC but not the intermediate £60,000 RBC or higher £90,000 higher RBC, see **Example F4 explanatory note 5**). This means that there is a cap such that where the RBC is due for a tax year only £30,000 of that year's tax liability can be paid by way of a remittances (or remittances) of foreign income and gains and be within the exemption (for further details see **explanatory note 19**).

We are told that Claude has paid his two payments on account for 2015/16 from UK funds and that he had a £45,000 balancing payment to make for 2015/16 and we know that the RBC was payable for 2015/16. Accordingly, £30,000 of the £67,100 payment can be taken as a tax free remittance with respect to the 2015/16 RBC.

We also know that £22,100 of the £67,100 payment relates to the first payment on account for 2016/17 and that Claude will make the remittance basis claim and pay the RBC for 2016/17 (when again the basic £30,000 RBC will be due). This means that the £22,100 paid for 2016/17 comes within ITA 2007 s 809V.

With respect to his 2016/17 tax liabilities Claude can only remit a further £7,900 (this being £30,000 less £22,100) from foreign income and gains and come within the exemption. Any additional payments from foreign income or gains to settle his 2016/17 tax liability will result in taxable remittances.

On the basis that the 2015/16 remittance basis claim is not withdrawn and the 2016/17 remittance basis claim is made (and not withdrawn) out of the total of £67,100 remitted in January 2017 £52,100 is covered by the ITA 2007, section 809V exemption (RDRM34020).

As a safeguard against a reversal of the decision to make the remittance basis claim, one should advise clients that where tax liabilities are to be paid from remittance basis income and/or gains in the hope of coming within ITA 2007 s 809V the payment should come from the foreign income or gains of the relevant year for which the claim is to be made. By doing this:

- if the remittance basis claim is made use will have been made of the exemption; and
- if the remittance claim is not made for the tax year there is no additional tax with respect to the remittance as the foreign income or gains used will be subject to tax on the arising basis anyway.

To get the most advantage from the exemption the RBC should be paid from the foreign income or gains that would give rise to the highest tax liability if remitted.

## B. Claudine Non-Dom

See **explanatory note 27**.

(a) It is assumed from the question that the table is in the UK for less the 275 days so the remittance itself will qualify as exempt property under the temporary importation rule (ITA 2007 s 809X(5)(b) as read with ITA 2007 s 809Z4). As the table is exempt property, the subsequent sale also qualifies for exemption because the proceeds are taken out of the UK within 45 days (ITA 2007 s 809YA).

Therefore the sale of the table in the UK does not constitute a remittance of the underlying funds used to buy the table. The full conditions for the exemption for sales of exempt property are discussed in **explanatory note 27**. The rules also treat any capital gain on the disposal as being a foreign gain, despite the sale occurring in the UK (ITA 2007 s 809YD).

If the sale of the table had not been exempt it would have triggered a remittance of the foreign employment income which had been used to acquire the table. Also the gain would have chargeable to UK capital gains tax.

(b) The painting inherited from Claudine's mother is acquired from clean capital. As such, the remittance into the UK does not need to be covered by an exemption. HMRC, therefore, does *not* accept that the painting is exempt property (RDRM34070) and so the exemption in ITA 2007 s 809YA cannot apply. As ITA 2007 s 809YA does not apply, neither does the favourable capital gains tax treatment discussed in (a) above. Therefore the gain on sale of the painting is chargeable in the UK.

(c) The necklace is a mixed fund (acquired through a mixture of clean capital and relevant foreign income). It is assumed from the question that the necklace is in the UK for less the 275 days so again the remittance itself will qualify under the temporary importation rule exemption such the foreign income is not taxable at that point ITA 2007 s 809X(5)(b) as read with ITA 2007 s 809Z4).

Since the necklace is exempt property, HMRC accepts that the exemption for sales in ITA 2007 s 809YA applies so long as the proceeds are taken out of the UK within 45 days. The full conditions for the exemption for sales of exempt property are discussed in **explanatory note 27**. Again, as ITA 2007 s 809YA applies, the gain is treated as a foreign gain under ITA 2007 s 809YD.

## C. Katya Non-Dom

Business investment relief was introduced on 6 April 2012. Provided conditions are met in relation to the investment, a UK resident non-domiciliary can bring what would otherwise be taxable foreign income and/or gains into the UK for business investment and the remittance will be exempt. See **explanatory notes 11–18**.

(a) The investment in a UK trading partnership does not qualify as business investment relief is only available where there is investment in an unquoted company (ITA 2007 ss 809VC–809VD).

(b) The investment in an unquoted foreign company that carries on a UK trade qualifies for business investment relief (ITA 2007 ss 809VC–809VD). The fact that the company is foreign is not a bar to meeting the conditions. Either new loan finance or share subscriptions will qualify (ITA 2007 s 809VC(1)).

(c) The investment in working capital for Katya's self-employed trade does not qualify as business investment relief is only available where there is investment in an unquoted company (ITA 2007 ss 809VC–809VD).

(d) The investment in quoted shares in a UK trading company does not qualify for business investment relief as the company must be unquoted (ITA 2007 s 809VD(2)(a)).

(e) The investment in shares in an unquoted UK trading company qualifies for business investment relief as the business is in an unquoted company that is carrying out a commercial trade (ITA 2007 ss 809VC–809VD). Either new loan finance or share subscriptions will qualify (ITA 2007 s 809VC(1)).

(f) The investment used to acquire shares in an unquoted UK trading company from existing owners does not qualify as the shares must be acquired via subscription (the legislation stipulates the shares must be 'issued', see ITA 2007 s 809VC(1)(a)). For the meaning of subscription, see **Example N7 explanatory note 8**.

## D. Jake Non-Dom

See **explanatory notes 11-18.**

(a) The unquoted foreign company whose main asset is UK residential property does not qualify for business investment relief. This is because the residential property is used by the sole shareholder rent-free rather than there being a business carried on for the purposes of generating income from land (ITA 2007 s 809VE as read with CTA 2009 s 207).

(b) The foreign company carrying on a UK hotel business qualifies for business investment relief as it is unquoted and carries on a commercial trade in the UK (ITA 2007 ss 809VD–809VE). It is an eligible trading company for the purposes of the relief.

(c) The quoted UK trading company does not qualify for business investment relief as relief is only available where there is a qualifying investment in an unquoted company (ITA 2007 s 809VD).

(d) The UK holding company qualifies for business investment relief as it is unquoted and is the parent company of a trading group (ITA 2007 s 809VD). It is an eligible holding company for the purposes of the relief.

(e) The UK company investing in trading companies qualifies for business investment relief as it is unquoted, exists just to make investments in eligible trading companies and has several such investments (ITA 2007 s 809VD). It is an eligible stakeholder company for the purposes of the relief.

## E. Heidi Non-Dom

See **explanatory note 14.**

(a) Heidi is employed on arm's length terms and her employment income is subject to tax so the extraction of value rule is not breached (ITA 2007 s 809VH(3); RDRM34420).

(b) The dividends received by Heidi represent an arm's length return for the investment and are subject to tax so the extraction of value rule is not breached (ITA 2007 s 809VH(3); RDRM34420).

(c) The extraction of value rule is breached when the connected foreign company allows Heidi to use company assets rent-free (RDRM34420). This is because the foreign company is:

- an 'involved company' in connection with the company that Heidi invested in (since they are connected) (ITA 2007 s 809VH(2)(b)(i));
- the free use of the Verbier chalet is value in money's worth received otherwise than from a disposal of the holding (ITA 2007 s 809VH(2)(a), (c)); and
- the use of the asset does not represent arm's length remuneration or an arm's length return on the investment and the value received is not subject to tax (ITA 2007 s 809VH(3)).

# Explanatory Notes

*The meaning of 'remitted to the UK'*

(1) From 6 April 2008 there is one set of rules governing remittances to the UK. These rules are found at ITA 2007 s 809L which specifies that there can be a remittance if:

- conditions A and B are met;
- condition C is met; or

- condition D is met.

The standard core definition of remittance is given in ITA 2007 s 809L as conditions A and B. This very wide definition covers cash remittances, goods, services and the payment of UK-related debts (RDRM33160, RDRM33170) traced directly or indirectly to previously unremitted foreign income or foreign chargeable gains.

In summary the conditions are met where:

- money or other property representing or derived from foreign income or foreign chargeable gains is brought to, received or used in the UK by or for the benefit of a relevant person (defined in **explanatory note 4**); or
- a service is provided in the UK to, or for, the benefit of a relevant person (this is the case regardless of whether the service is paid for offshore or the payment is made in the UK).

ITA 2007 s 809L condition C (gift recipient provision) and condition D (third party connected operation provision) are both anti-avoidance provisions. These provisions cover gifts to other individuals and transactions with third parties where the property transferred represents or is derived from foreign income or foreign chargeable gains. There *is* a taxable remittance where such transactions result directly or indirectly in any relevant person receiving a benefit in the UK.

The extended meaning of remittance means there is a risk of inadvertent remittances under these rules. It is important to appreciate how wide this definition is and that it encompasses far more than just cash remittances. Potentially it covers:

- any form of property brought to, received or used in the UK for the benefit of a relevant person;
- payment (whether to the service provider's UK or offshore account) for any services provided in the UK to or for the benefit of a relevant person;
- any use of property representing or derived from foreign income or foreign chargeable gains in connection with a loan or debt which provides, whether directly or indirectly, any UK person with a UK benefit (either in connection with property enjoyed or a service provided to them or for their benefit).

*The extent of the definition of remittance*

(2) The definition of 'remitted to the UK' in ITA 2007 s 809L is potentially wide enough to catch payments made offshore to acquire UK situs property even where funds do not enter the UK.

In addition where previously unremitted foreign income or gains are first remitted to the UK after 5 April 2008 there is a tax charge on taxable remittances made in the tax year regardless of whether, in the tax year of remittance, the individual is subject to tax on the arising or remittance basis.

There are important transitional provisions relating to:

- pre-6 April 2008 foreign income and gains (FA 2008 Sch 7 para 86, see **explanatory notes 6-9**); and
- the payment from relevant foreign income of the interest on qualifying pre-12 March 2008 residential mortgages (FA 2008 Sch 7 para 90, see **explanatory note 6**).

There are also ongoing exemptions with respect to the remittance of property (not money) which, when in point, mean that there is no tax liability even though an ITA 2007 s 809L remittance of foreign income and/or foreign chargeable gains has been made (see **explanatory note 10**).

*Tracing*

(3) Where there is a remittance, one has to trace to the source of the original funds and where at any point one finds unremitted foreign income and/or gains there will be a tax charge (unless one of the transitional provisions or ongoing exemptions apply, see **explanatory notes 6, 10**).

This is best explained by an example. On 11 November 2016 Toby remits £70,000 from his Jersey bank account. This represents the proceeds of sale of a painting. A £20,000 foreign chargeable gain arose on the sale. The £50,000 used to acquire the painting was derived from the sale of foreign securities where a gain of £10,000 was realised. The original funds (£40,000) to acquire the securities came from Toby's Jersey interest income account (the account being opened on 19 September 2008 so all the income is post 5 April 2008 meaning the FA 2008 Sch 7 para 86 transitional provisions cannot apply). In total, therefore, Toby will be taxed on foreign chargeable gains of £30,000 and foreign bank interest of £40,000.

*The 'relevant person' concept*

(4) There is a deemed remittance where the property represents or derives from foreign income and foreign chargeable gains arising or accruing after 5 April 2008, by the individual to whom the foreign income or gains originally arose where any relevant person in connection with the individual (ITA 2007 s 809L):

- remits property representing or derived from foreign income or foreign chargeable gains; or
- receives a UK benefit derived from foreign income or foreign chargeable gains.

The meaning of a 'relevant person' is widely drawn and great care must be taken to avoid inadvertent remittances.

'Relevant person' is defined in ITA 2007 s 809M as:

(a) the individual;

(b) the individual's spouse or civil partner (or those living together as if they were spouses or civil partners);

(c) a child under 18 or grandchild under 18 of someone within category (a) or (b);

(d) a close company in which a person falling within any other category is a participator (see **Example J1 explanatory notes 1–7** for the meaning of these terms);

(e) with effect from 22 April 2009, a company which is a 51% subsidiary of a company meeting the category (d) conditions;

(f) a foreign company, that would be a close company if UK resident, in which a person falling within any other category is a participator;

(g) with effect from 6 April 2010 a company which is a 51% subsidiary of a company meeting the category (f) conditions;

(h) the trustees of a settlement where a person falling within any other category is a beneficiary; or

(i) a body connected with such a settlement if the body falls within one of the following categories (ITA 2007 s 809M(3)(g) as read with ITA 2007 s 993(3)(c)–(f)):

   (i) any close company whose participators include the trustees of the settlement;

   (ii) any non-resident company which, if it were UK resident, would be a close company whose participators include the trustees of the settlement;

   (iii) any body corporate controlled by a company within (i) or (ii); or

   (iv) if the settlement is the principal settlement in relation to one or more sub-funds settlements, a person in the capacity as trustee of such a sub-fund settlement.

The individual is taxed on the remittance in exactly the same way whether the action is effected or the benefit enjoyed, by the individual himself or any other relevant person connected with him.

*Anti-alienation provisions*

(5) As explained in **explanatory note 1**, specific provisions cover gifts to other individuals (condition C at ITA 2007 s 809L(4) and ITA 2007 s 809N) and transactions with third parties (condition D at ITA 2007 s 809L(5) and ITA 2007 s 809O) where the property transferred represents or is derived from foreign income or foreign chargeable gains. There is a taxable remittance where such transactions result directly or indirectly in any relevant person (see **explanatory note 4**) receiving a UK benefit.

The provisions are wide ranging. However, there are *no* provisions restricting offshore gifts from foreign income and gains to non-relevant persons provided a relevant person does not receive any benefit. This is illustrated in **part A**(e) of this Example, where Claude uses his foreign income to make regular monthly gifts to his adult daughter.

It should be noted that whilst adult children are not relevant persons in connection with their parents, their minor children will be (being minor grandchildren), and particular care needs to be taken to avoid a benefit to a relevant person where a gift is made to an adult child who has minor children.

Important transitional provisions (FA 2008 Sch 7 para 86(4)) narrow the definition of relevant person when considering pre-6 April 2008 foreign income and/or foreign chargeable gains (see **explanatory note 9**).

*Transitional provisions*

(6) For individuals there are four main transitional provisions:

- two specific provisions override the remittance definition in ITA 2007 s 809L with respect to property brought to, received or used in the UK: (1) relating to property (including money) consisting of or derived from relevant foreign income brought to the UK prior to 6 April 2008 (see **explanatory note 7**); and (2) relating to property (excluding money) consisting of or derived from relevant foreign income acquired prior to 12 March 2008 (see **explanatory note 8**);
- the relevant person definition - which narrows the definition of relevant person to only consider the individual to whom the income or gains arose where the foreign income or gains relates to a tax year prior to 2008/09 (see **explanatory note 9**);
- interest paid on a pre-12 March 2008 qualifying loan relating to UK residential property (FA 2008 Sch 7 para 90). Where the conditions are met the provision overrides the ITA 2007 s 809L remittance definition where the interest is paid from relevant foreign income. The conditions are strict and there is a sunset clause, so that even if all other conditions are still met the provision will not apply to interest payments made after 5 April 2028 (RDRM31500).

*Transitional provisions – property (including money) brought to, received or used in the UK prior to 6 April 2008*

(7) FA 2008 Sch 7 para 86(2) is a comprehensive exclusion provision which provides that a remittance, on or after 6 April 2008, will be disregarded where the property (including money) remitted:

- consists of, or derives from, an individual's relevant foreign income; and
- before 6 April 2008 was brought to, received or used in the UK by or for the benefit of a relevant person (in this context the definition of relevant person is the wider definition even though the relevant foreign income relates to before 6 April 2008).

Provided the conditions are met the property can be exported, re-imported or sold in the UK without triggering a remittance charge on the relevant foreign income (RDRM31460).

The inclusion of money means that there will be no taxable remittance with respect to funds derived from successful source ceasing exercises, which have been brought to the UK prior to 6 April 2008. This is the case regardless of whether the funds remain within the UK.

*Transitional provisions – property (excluding money) acquired by a relevant person before 12 March 2008*

(8) FA 2008 Sch 7 para 86(3) is another comprehensive exclusion provision. If the conditions are met the ITA 2007, s 809L remittance rules with respect to the relevant foreign income is permanently disapplied (RDRM31470).

The legislation states that, where relevant foreign income would otherwise be deemed to have been remitted, no remittance of relevant foreign income should be treated as having taken place where:

- before 12 March 2008 property (other than money) was acquired by a relevant person (in this context the definition of relevant person is the wider definition of ITA 2007 s 809M, even though the relevant foreign income it relates to arose before 6 April 2008); and
- the acquisition was financed from relevant foreign income or funds derived from relevant foreign income.

Where a taxpayer has been in the habit of investing income returns this could be a very generous provision.

Note that money (which cannot benefit from this transitional provision) has a wide definition in ITA 2007 s 809Y(5), which includes travellers' cheques, promissory notes, bills of exchange or any other (i) instruments that are evidence of a debt; or (ii) vouchers, stamps or similar tokens or documents which are capable of being exchanged for money, goods or services.

*Transitional provisions – pre-6 April 2008 foreign income and gains*

(9) Where the remittance represents or derives from pre-6 April 2008 foreign income and/or gains, the relevant person definition (ITA 2007 s 809M) does not apply when considering if a remittance has been made.

For pre-6 April 2008 foreign income and/or gains, it is only the individual to whom the foreign income or gains arose that needs to be considered (FA 2008 Sch 7 para 86(4); RDRM31480).

This means that funds representing or derived from pre-6 April 2008 foreign income or foreign chargeable gains can be gifted to any person and remitted by that person to the UK without there being a taxable remittance provided the individual to whom the remittance basis foreign income or gains arose or accrued does not receive any benefit. This is illustrated in **part A(f)** of this Example, where Claude uses his pre-6 April 2008 remittance basis income to make a lump sum gift to his wife which she used to finance her PhD studies.

*Ongoing exemptions*

(10) The legislation contains the following ongoing exemptions from the remittance definition. These are:

- business investment relief – ITA 2007 ss 809VA–809VO, 809Z8–809Z10; (see **explanatory notes 11–18**);
- money paid to HMRC – ITA 2007 ss 809UA–809V (see **explanatory note 19**);
- consideration for certain UK services (known as the 'services exemption') – ITA 2007 s 809W (see **explanatory note 20**);
- property which is considered 'exempt property' under ITA 2007 s 809X because it falls into one of the categories below:
  - the public access rule – ITA 2007 ss 809X(3), 809Z (see **explanatory note 26**);
  - the personal use rule (applicable only to clothing, footwear and jewellery) – ITA 2007 ss 809X(4), 809Z2 (see **explanatory note 22**);
  - the repair rule – ITA 2007 ss 809X(5)(a), 809Z3 (see **explanatory note 25**);

- the temporary importation rule (across all tax years the property should not have been in the UK for more than 275 countable days) – ITA 2007 ss 809X(5)(b), 809Z4 (see **explanatory note 24**); and

- the de minimis provision where the notional remitted amount is less than £1,000 – ITA 2007 ss 809X(5)(c), 809Z5 (see **explanatory note 23**).

- exemption for sales of exempt property – ITA 2007 ss 809YA–809YD (**explanatory note 27**);

- exemption for assets transferred under the gifts to the nation scheme (also known as the cultural gift scheme) – ITA 2007, s 809YE (see **explanatory note 28**).

Each ongoing exemption has its own qualifying conditions. Great care must be taken when advising as it can be easy to confuse the conditions.

The exemptions with respect to money paid to HMRC and consideration for UK services will generally involve the payment of money. This will also generally be the case for business investment relief (though it would be possible to make a qualifying investment in specie).

The 'exempt property' reliefs apply to property brought to, received in or used in the UK (property being defined as not including money, which has an extended meaning for remittance basis purposes (ITA 2007 s 809Y(5), see **explanatory note 8**).

*Business investment relief*

**Overview**

(11) An exemption is available to encourage UK resident foreign domiciliaries to invest in UK businesses. The exemption, referred to as business investment relief, can be claimed where the qualifying investment occurs on or after 6 April 2012. The exemption:

- disapplies the remittance rules in ITA 2007 s 809L with respect to remittances of foreign income or gains used to invest in a qualifying business (which must be carried out through an unquoted company);

- is available in respect of any unremitted foreign income or gains, regardless of whether the remittance basis is claimed for the tax year in which the qualifying investment is made. In other words, electing for the arising basis in a particular tax year will not preclude relief being claimed if the individual makes a qualifying investment using prior years' unremitted foreign income and/or gains;

- is relevant to non-domiciled individuals returning to the UK, and caught by the temporary non-residence rules (discussed in **Example F1 explanatory note 24**). These individuals can use business investment relief in the same way as any other taxpayer accessing the remittance basis;

- applies not only to direct investment by the taxpayer, but also to investment by any other relevant person (such as an offshore trust or company which is a relevant person in connection with the taxpayer) or a nominee (see RDRM34330).

While the concept behind business investment relief is simple, the actual provisions are relatively complex and care needs to be taken when advising in this area. **Explanatory notes 12-18** provide a summary of the relief.

It should be noted that business investment relief applies only where the actual investment in the company is from relevant foreign income and/or gains. Business investment relief does not apply where the investment is made from UK source income and/or gains on UK situs property. Such income and/or gains will be taxed as normal in the UK (although it possible that the investment may qualify for tax relief under the enterprise investment scheme (EIS) or seed enterprise investment scheme (SEIS), see **Example N7**).

Similarly, there are no IHT provisions specifically associated with business investment relief; the normal business property relief rules must be considered on a case by case basis (IHTA 1984 s 105).

The legislation contains an anti-avoidance provision, which disapplies the exemption where the investment is made as part of or as a result of a scheme or arrangement the main purpose or one of the main purposes of which is to avoid tax (ITA 2007 s 809VA(7)). The context in which it is thought this provision will be applied is unclear.

As well as the guidance available in the Residence, Domicile and Remittance Basis Manual there is also HMRC guidance which was released in May 2012 and covers all the changes to the remittance basis contained within FA 2012. Chapter 2 covers business investment relief. This can be found at https://www.gov.uk/government/publications/guidance-note-changes-to-the-remittance-basis.

**Qualifying conditions**

(12) For business investment relief to be due (ITA 2007 s 809VC(4)):

- there must be a 'qualifying investment' into a 'target company' (see below) (ITA 2007 s 809VD(1));
- no relevant person may (directly or indirectly) receive a benefit (ITA 2007 s 809VF):
  - as the result of either making the investment or the commitment to do so (it does not matter whether the benefit is received before or after the investment is made); or
  - where it is reasonable to assume that the benefit is only provided as a result of the investment.

A relevant person (as defined in ITA 2007 s 809M, see **explanatory note 4**) will be viewed as having received a benefit where, as the result of an arrangement entered into, he is provided (whether temporarily or permanently) with anything (thus embracing money or money's worth, including property, capital, goods or services of any kind) that would not be provided to him in the ordinary course of business, at least on the same terms.

The legislation states that there can be three types of 'target company' (ITA 2007 ss 809VD–809VE):

- an 'eligible trading company'. Broadly, this is an unquoted company that carries on one or more commercial trades (or is preparing to do so within two years) and carrying on commercial trades is wholly or substantially what it does (or what it will do) (RDRM34345);
- an 'eligible holding company'. An eligible holding company must be an unquoted company that is a member of an eligible trading group (or a group that within two years is reasonably expected to become an eligible trading group). Eligible trading group being defined as a parent company and 51% subsidiaries, all private limited companies, where taken as a whole carrying on commercial activities is substantially all of what the group does. In addition to be an eligible holding company the company must have at least one 51% subsidiary that is an eligible trading company (either holding the ordinary share capital in that company directly or through intermediary companies such that each intermediary is a member of the group) (RDRM34355);
- an 'eligible stakeholder company'. Broadly, this is an unquoted company that exists wholly or mainly to invest in eligible trading companies and has invested in such companies or will within two years of the qualifying investment (RDRM34350).

The target company does not have to be UK resident. For the purposes of this relief trade has a special extended meaning, it includes (ITA 2007 s 809VE):

- anything that is treated as a trade for corporation tax purposes;
- a business carried on for generating income from land as defined in CTA 2009 s 207 (this would include, but is not limited to, a residential letting business); and
- research and development from which it is intended that a commercial trade will be derived, or will benefit (note that merely preparing to carry out such activities is not sufficient).

For an investment to be a qualifying investment it must represent an injection of new funds (whether in cash or in specie) into the target company. It can either be by way of new loan finance or a share subscription

(ITA 2007 s 809VC(1); RDRM34330). Provided the conditions are met, there are no upper or lower limits on the amount of previously unremitted foreign income and gains that can be invested.

The qualifying investment can either be made directly into the target company or the funds can be brought into the UK so that the qualifying investment can be made. Where the funds are brought to the UK the individual has 45 days in which to make the investment (ITA 2007 s 809VA(5)). If, however, the investment in whole or part does not go ahead there will be no remittance provided within the 45 day period the funds are taken offshore (ITA 2007 s 809VB(1)–(2); RDRM34370). Where only a portion of the relevant funds are taken offshore, the part of the relevant foreign income or gains that are treated as remitted is to be determined on a just and reasonable basis (ITA 2007 s 809VB(3)). It is assumed that this will mean apportionment.

Initially there was concern that a narrow reading of the legislation could result in remittance issues in the following circumstances:

- where a UK resident foreign domiciliary made an investment in the UK in a close company (or a foreign company that would be close if it were UK resident) and that company (being a relevant person in connection with the individual) uses the funds in the UK;
- where an individual made an investment offshore in a foreign company which would be close if UK resident and that company (being a relevant person in connection with the individual) brings to/uses the funds in the UK; and
- where an individual made an investment in a company by taking out a loan and relevant foreign income or gains are used to service the loan and/or make repayments of capital.

It is understood that in the first two situations HMRC's settled view is that once a qualifying investment has been made, the foreign income and gains will only be taxed under the remittance basis if there is a potentially chargeable event and the appropriate mitigation steps are not taken within the grace period, see **explanatory note 13** (HMRC guidance https://www.gov.uk/government/publications/guidance-note-changes-to-the-remittance-basis, para 2.28). In essence, ITA 2007 s 809VA trumps ITA 2007 s 809L so that the use by a relevant person of the income and gains in the UK would not be a remittance. However, there is no statutory underpinning of this treatment, so taxpayers will be vulnerable if HMRC decides to change its practice at a later date.

In the third case, it is understood that HMRC takes a wide view of the meaning of ITA 2007 s 809VA(1)(b) and specifically the words 'by virtue of the event' such that there would not be a remittance issue provided a qualifying investment has been made. Note that where the initial investment is made from loaned funds the claim for the exemption has to be made in relation to the repayment of the loan from remittance basis income and gains. If this happens in different tax year it will impact on the claims deadline.

**Potentially chargeable events and mitigation steps**

(13) Where a potentially chargeable event occurs, and appropriate mitigating action is not taken within the grace period, the relevant foreign income or gains exempted as a result of the qualifying investment (or the appropriate portion where the chargeable event does not relate to the entire investment) are treated as having been remitted to the UK immediately after the end of the grace period.

The following are potentially chargeable events (ITA 2007 s 809VH):

(a) the investor disposes of all or part of the qualifying investment;

(b) the target company does not meet any of the qualifying company definitions;

(c) the extraction of value rule is breached (discussed below);

(d) the two-year start-up rule is breached (discussed below).

Liquidation resulting from insolvency will not itself be a chargeable event but any value received will potentially give rise to a tax charge unless mitigating action is taken.

The appropriate mitigating action is (ITA 2007 ss 809VI, 809Z9; RDRM34440, RDRM34460):

- to take the proceeds offshore within the grace period;
- to re-invest the proceeds in a further qualifying investment for business investment relief within the grace period. A qualifying re-investment can be in the same or a different company. A new claim for business investment relief must be made within the time limit. If no new claim is made by the deadline the mitigating action will not be treated as having been made; or
- a combination of these two actions.

The amount of the proceeds which must be taken offshore or re-invested is defined in ITA 2007 s 809VI(4) (RDRM34450). Where there is an insolvency or a winding up this is modified, see ITA 2007 s 809VI(8).

There are potentially two separate grace periods (ITA 2007 s 809VJ; RDRM34480):

- where a disposal is required (ie the potentially chargeable event falls into (b)–(d) above) 90 days is allowed for the necessary disposal to be made and then the individual has 45 days from receipt of the proceeds to take the appropriate mitigating action;
- if the potentially chargeable event falls into (a) above, the individual has 45 days from receipt of the disposal proceeds to take the appropriate mitigating action.

An Officer of HMRC may agree to extend the grace period allowed for an appropriate mitigation step in exceptional circumstances (see RDRM34490). The extension can be for an indefinite period provided it is capable of becoming definite by means identified in the agreement (such as the satisfaction of conditions). Where the target company ceases to be a qualifying company as a result of becoming quoted, SI 2012/1898 specifically enables an Officer of HMRC to extend the period of grace during which the disposal can take place if there are lock up agreements or statutory or legal bars to a sale.

The disposal of all or part of the investment is a potentially chargeable event for the purposes of business investment relief. There are no exceptions to this rule for gifts/sales at undervalue or even for transfers to a spouse/civil partner. However, in such cases, since there are no proceeds to take offshore or re-invest, an amount equal to the market value of the investment at the time of the disposal must either be taken offshore or reinvested (ITA 2007 809Z8(4)). Where the disposal consideration is received in instalments, each instalment is treated as a separate potentially chargeable event (with its own period of grace starting from the date the instalment proceeds are received (ITA 2007 s 809VH(8))).

On disposal there are special matching rules for the purposes of business investment relief (ITA 2007 s 809VN) where:

- there are multiple investments in the same target company;
- there are multiple investments made in companies within the same eligible trading group;
- there are investments made in an eligible trading company and in an eligible stakeholder company that holds investments in that trading company.

If this is the case, all the qualifying investments in the same company are treated as a single holding (RDRM34530).

There are also special rules for certain part disposals (see **explanatory note 16**).

**Extraction of value**

(14) The extraction of value rule is breached if (ITA 2007 s 809VH(2); RDRM34420):

- value (in money or money's worth) is received by or for the benefit of the investor or any other relevant person (as defined in ITA 2007 s 809M, see **explanatory note 4**, although see also **explanatory note 12**);

- the benefit is received from:
  - an 'involved company'; or
  - anyone else where the circumstances are directly or indirectly attributable to the investment, or to any other investment made by a relevant person in an involved company; and
- the value is received other than by a disposal of the qualifying holding (since this is a potentially chargeable event in its own right).

The extraction of value rule is not breached merely because a relevant person receives value that (ITA 2007 s 809VH(3)):

- is treated for income tax or corporation tax purposes as the receipt of income, or would be so treated if that person were liable to such tax; and
- is paid or provided to the person in the ordinary course of business and on arm's length terms.

This rule will not, therefore, prevent a relevant person from receiving commercial remuneration, dividends, interest or other income in respect of their rights as a shareholder or lender, provided that, where appropriate, tax is paid on such payments (see **part E** of this **Example**).

'Involved company' means (ITA 2007 s 809VH(4)):

- the company which received the original investment (ie the target company);
- where the target company is an eligible stakeholder company, all eligible trading companies in which it has or intends to make an investment;
- where the target company is an eligible holding company, any eligible trading company that is a 51% subsidiary of it; and
- any companies connected with a company falling within one of the above bullet points.

The 'involved company' provision is a potential problem where:

- the investor (on his or her own or together with persons connected to him) controls the target company; or
- the investor is one of a consortium acting together in relation to the target company to secure or exercise control over it.

The problem here is that in addition to the target company and any company it controls (or in the case of a stakeholder company any eligible trading company it invests in) the involved company definition can include potentially any other company controlled by: (i) those companies; (ii) the investor or (iii) persons connected with the investor. In this context connected has the standard definition as set down at ITA 2007 s 993 so a company comes within the 'involved company' definition if, for example, it is controlled by the investor's parents, siblings or a trust of which the investor is a settlor.

This is a real practical problem:

- in a family situation – where the investor has control over the target company the 'involved company' definition will catch companies, controlled by close family members (such as parents), which the investor may have no control over. In such situations it may not be possible for the investor to ensure that a relevant person does not receive a benefit from such a company;
- in an international situation – with complex groups this could cover so many companies that ensuring that a relevant person does not receive a benefit that would breach the extraction of value rule could be challenging.

**Two-year start-up rule**

(15) This rule will be breached where (ITA 2007 s 809VH(5); RDRM34430):

- the target company is non-operational within two years of the investment having been made; or
- at any time after the end of that period the target company becomes non-operational.

The definition of non-operational depends on the target company's classification (that is which of the three target company definitions it meets in **explanatory note 12**) (ITA 2007 s 809VH(6)). An eligible trading company is non-operational if it is not trading. An eligible stakeholder company is non-operational if:

- it holds no investments in eligible trading companies; or
- none of the eligible trading companies in which it has invested are trading.

An eligible holding company is non-operational if:

- the group of which it is a member is not an eligible trading group; or
- none of its 51% subsidiaries in the eligible trading group of which it is a member is an eligible trading company which is trading.

**Part disposals**

(16) Where only part of the qualifying investment is subject to disposal, taking the required mitigation action may be difficult where the disposal proceeds (defined below) received are insufficient to enable the individual to (ITA 2007 s 809VK):

- take offshore or re-invest proceeds equal to the relevant foreign income or gains used to fund the original investment; and
- pay the highest potential capital gains tax liability — this being computed by multiplying the gain by the highest rate of tax applicable in the tax year (ie 28% for individuals).

The shortfall between the above and the proceeds actually received can be retained in the UK to pay the capital gains tax liability without triggering a tax liability, provided (i) the funds are used, within the grace period, to acquire a certificate of tax deposit (CTD); and (ii) the CTD conditions are not breached (RDRM34500).

The CTD conditions are as follows (ITA 2007 s 809VM; RDRM34520):

- the tax deposit must only be used to pay the UK capital gains tax due on the part disposal of the qualifying investment;
- if any of the tax deposit is withdrawn, the funds withdrawn must within 45 days either be taken offshore or used to make another qualifying investment;
- any part of the tax deposit not used to pay the tax due on the part disposal of the qualifying investment must be taken offshore or reinvested within 45 days of the due date for the capital gains tax payment (31 January following the tax year of the chargeable disposal).

It is necessary to inform HMRC at the start (this means when details of the deposit are confirmed with HMRC) that the 'business investment relief retention of funds to meet CGT liabilities' legislation is intended to apply to the deposit (ITA 2007 s 809VK(8); RDRM34510).

**Claiming the exemption**

(17) The exemption has to be specifically claimed by the taxpayer. The deadline for making a claim is the first anniversary of 31 January following the tax year in which the investment is made (ITA 2007 s 809VA(8)). Where the qualifying investment is made in 2016/17 the claim deadline is 31 January 2019.

Making the claim by the due date where the investment has been made by the taxpayer should not be difficult. There are, however, potential practical difficulties where a relevant person makes the investment (in particular a foreign company or trust). Maintaining lines of communication are crucial.

The claim should be made on the individual's UK self-assessment tax return (specifically by completing the relevant boxes on the 'Residence, remittance basis etc supplementary pages' SA109) or by way of an amendment to a return already filed. Someone who would not otherwise file a return will have to do so if they wish to claim this relief. Individuals claiming the exemption are required to state in box 38 of the supplementary pages:

- how much has been invested in total (but without a requirement to show the constituent elements of the funds invested); and
- the company registration numbers for the companies in which they have invested.

**Clearance procedure**

(18) The Government wants business investment relief to be successful in attracting investment into UK businesses. Recognising that certainty is important to taxpayers, it gave a commitment that there would be a non-statutory pre-transaction clearance procedure in order to provide investors with certainty that an investment will qualify for relief. Details of the procedure are available at https://www.gov.uk/non-statutory-clearance-service-guidance.

There is a special checklist (referred to as Annex B – Business Investment Relief Advance Assurance checklist) to use for business investment relief queries (accessible at https://www.gov.uk/government/publications/non-statutory-clearance-service-guidance-annexes) and the request goes to a special unit (the address being shown on the checklist).

Where a relevant person (other than the taxpayer him or herself) makes the investment, to obtain the advance clearance full details about both the taxpayer and the relevant person have to be provided.

*Money paid to the Commissioners exemption*

(19) This ongoing exemption overrides the ITA 2007 s 809L conditions such that it allows for a total equivalent to the individual's RBC amount for the tax year to be transferred to HMRC from funds representing or derived from relevant foreign income and/or gains, without there being a tax charge.

For the exemption to apply the following conditions must all be met (ITA 2007 s 809V):

- the transfer(s) must be from offshore direct to HMRC;
- the transfer(s) must be made in relation to a tax year for which the RBC is due; and
- the cumulative amount(s) of all transfers made for a given tax year must not exceed the RBC amount due for that tax year (£30,000 or £60,000 or £90,000 depending on the individual's residence history, see **Example F4 explanatory note 9**).

Where these conditions are met the exemption applies regardless of the tax year that the foreign funds arose or accrued in.

The provisions with respect to claiming the remittance basis and the RBC are complicated and outside the scope of this chapter (see **Example F4 explanatory note 5** for an overview). For some clients there may be considerable uncertainty over whether or not the remittance basis will result in a lesser tax liability than the default arising basis. Since the exemption is only available if a remittance basis claim is made for the tax year for which the tax payment is made this means that great care must be taken when advising clients in this area. Where possible payments should be made out of foreign income or gains arising/accruing in the tax year to which the tax payment relates.

In a payments on account situation, where the RBC was paid in the preceding year, taking full advantage of the exemption has been especially difficult. In some cases the decision for a particular tax year will only be taken in the following January (that is just before the electronic filing deadline).

With respect of payments on account for the tax year 2012/13 onwards, dealing with this situation has been made much easier. Provided the RBC was due for the preceding tax year, the taxpayer can pay, in direct settlement of his or her tax liabilities for the year, an amount equal to or less than the RBC that was due in the preceding year (that is the maximum amount of RBC that could have fed into the payments on account computation without an automatic adverse tax result if the remittance basis claim is not made). The amount paid to HMRC in accordance with these conditions is referred to as the 'relevant amount' (ITA 2007 s 809UA).

If the remittance basis claim is not made for the tax year the individual can take mitigating action to prevent a taxable remittance in connection with the 'relevant amount' from crystallising. This is done by the individual taking money equal to the 'relevant amount' offshore by (ITA 2007 s 809UA):

- the 15 March following the end of the relevant tax year; or
- such later date as HMRC may allow on a claim made by the individual (such a claim must be made within a year of the end of the relevant tax year and can only be made where the individual files a self-assessment tax return for the relevant year and reasonably expects to receive a repayment of tax paid in respect of that year).

*The service exemption*

(20) Where the qualifying conditions are met, the 'services exemption' overrides the ITA 2007 s 809L remittance provision, such that there is no taxable remittance. The 'service exemption' applies regardless of the source of relevant foreign income and/or gains used to make the payment.

For the exemption to apply (ITA 2007 s 809W):

- there must otherwise be a remittance under the standard remittance basis charging provisions (that is conditions A and B of ITA 2007 s 809L). The exemption does not apply where there is a deemed remittance as a result of the ITA 2007 s 809L gift recipient (condition C) or associated operations (condition D) remittance charging provisions; and
- both the service condition and the payments condition must be met.

The exemption is specifically disapplied (ITA 2007 s 809W(5); RDRM34050) where the relevant service relates to any extent to the provision in the UK of a benefit under the income tax transfer of assets abroad anti-avoidance provisions (ITA 2007 s 735) or the offshore trust capital gains tax anti-avoidance provisions applicable to foreign domiciliaries (TCGA 1992 s 87B).

For the services exemption to be in point, the UK service must be wholly or mainly (over 50%) in connection with foreign property. HMRC accepts that the condition can be met with respect to qualifying services where one invoice for services is issued covering qualifying and non-qualifying services (RDRM34040). However, it will generally be simplest for clients to be issued with separate invoices for qualifying services (not least to avoid confusion with respect to the funds to use to settle the invoices).

In addition to meeting the service condition, the payment condition must be met meaning that the qualifying invoice must be settled outside the UK by one or more payments to an offshore bank account held by or on behalf of the service provider (ITA 2007 s 809W(4)).

Where the conditions are met, the provisions with respect to the services exemption mean there will never be a tax liability with respect to foreign income and/or gains used in this way.

*The exempt property exemptions*

(21) There are five ongoing exemptions where goods are brought to, received in or used in the UK (ITA 2007 s 809X). For so long as one or more of these rules apply, the property is 'exempt property' such that the ITA 2007 s 809L rules with respect to remittances to the UK are disapplied.

Should the exempt property be in the UK at a time when none of the ongoing exemptions apply and the individual is UK resident, the remittance amount that would have been taxable when the property was first brought into the UK will come into charge unless within 45 days the property is used to make a qualifying investment under the terms of the business investment relief exemption (see above).

FA 2013 made some favourable changes to these provisions. The changes improve the 'exempt property' rules by:

- providing that there is not a taxable remittance where exempt property is lost, stolen or destroyed whilst it is in the UK;
- widening the definition of qualifying property for the purposes of the public access rule; and
- widening the conditions under which a day, on which property is present in the UK, may be disregarded for the purposes of the temporary importation rule.

From 6 April 2013, provided compensation is not received, property will not cease to be exempt property (meaning that a tax charge will not be crystallised) where it is lost stolen or destroyed whilst in the UK (ITA 2007 s 809Y(4A)).

There is a potential taxable remittance where a compensation payment is released in respect of the exempt property that has been lost, stolen or destroyed (ITA 2007 s 809Y(4B)). The tax charge can, however, be avoided provided conditions A and B within ITA 2007 s 809YF are met. Broadly these are:

- within a period of 45 days, beginning with the day on which the compensation payment is released (that is the day on which the compensation payment first becomes available for use in the UK by or for the benefit of any relevant person), the whole of the compensation payment is taken offshore or used by a relevant person to make an investment qualifying for business investment relief (see **explanatory notes 11–18** above);
- where the above condition is satisfied, wholly or in part by using a compensation payment to make an investment qualifying for business investment relief, the taxpayer makes a claim for relief on or before the first anniversary of the 31 January following the tax year in which the compensation payment is released.

*The personal use rule*

(22) For the personal use rule to apply the property must be clothing, footwear, jewellery or watches and two conditions must be met (ITA 2007 s 809Z2; RDRM34170):

- the property must be property of a relevant person (as defined by ITA 2007 s 809M, see **explanatory note 4**) in connection with the taxpayer to whom the foreign income and/or foreign chargeable gains are derived; and
- the property must be for the personal use of a relevant individual (ie spouse/civil partner, minor child or minor grandchild) in connection with the taxpayer to whom the foreign income and/or foreign chargeable gains are derived.

The asset does not have to be owned and used by the same individual, but use by a relevant individual is not sufficient to qualify if the owner is not a relevant person. It is important to remember that an asset will cease to meet the personal use rule if it is in the UK at the time that a relevant individual ceases to use the property personally and/or a relevant person disposes of the property. This is the case regardless of whether the individual, with respect to whom the foreign income and/or foreign chargeable gains from which the property derives, receives any value in the UK with respect to the asset.

Gifts to individuals who are not relevant persons, which are derived from foreign income and/or foreign chargeable gains, will not come within this exemption even though the gift recipient may use the asset personally. Accordingly, to avoid a tax liability such gifts should occur offshore and while the gifted property (or property derived from the original gift) is in the UK a relevant individual should not benefit from it whether directly or indirectly.

*The less than £1,000 de minimis provision*

(23) The exemption applies with respect to the importation of property of any description provided the notional remitted amount is less than £1,000 (ITA 2007 s 809Z(5)(c)).

The notional remitted amount is the amount that would be treated as remitted if the exemption did not apply, which means it is the amount of foreign income and/or gains used to acquire the property (ITA 2007 s 809Z5). If the property was acquired with a mixture of clean capital and foreign income/gains then the property may be worth in excess if £1,000 and the exemption still apply (RDRM34180).

Special valuation provisions apply with respect to sets where only part of the set is imported to the UK. The notional remitted amount is such portion of the total value of foreign income or gains used to acquire the set as is just and reasonable having regard to what has been remitted to the UK and what has been left offshore (ITA 2007 s 809P(13)).

Where the £1,000 de minimis rule applies, the conditions can only be broken should the asset be converted to money while in the UK. Should this occur it will be the amount of foreign income and/or gains used to acquire the asset that comes into charge (that is the original taxable amount avoided by the exemption being in point). If there is a gain and if this is not covered by the chattels exemption there will be tax with respect to both: (i) the original remittance basis income and/or chargeable gains used; and (ii) the gain on the disposal of the asset.

*The temporary importation rule*

(24) Property is covered by this rule where the aggregate countable number of UK days that the property is deemed to be present in the UK does not exceed 275 (ITA 2007 s 809Z4). Effective with respect to property imported after 5 April 2008, the 275-day limit is across all tax years from the date that the property first came into the UK.

The remittance is disregarded for as long as the countable days remain below 276 (intention does not come into the test).

From 6 April 2013, days on which the property is in the UK are *not* a countable day if during any part of the day (ITA 2007 s 809Z4(3)):

- the property meets the public access rule (see **explanatory note 26**);
- the property meets the personal use rule (see **explanatory note 22**);
- the property meets the repair rule (see **explanatory note 25**);
- the notional remitted amount is less than £1,000 (see **explanatory note 23**);
- the property cannot be enjoyed as it has been lost, stolen or destroyed and, as yet, no compensation payment has been received;
- any part of the foreign income or gains used to purchase the property is treated as not remitted to the UK under either:
  - (i) the business investment relief provisions (see **explanatory notes 11–18**);
  - (ii) the sales of exempt property rules apply (see **explanatory note 27**); or
  - (iii) a compensation payment has been received and has been taken offshore within 45 days or re-invested under the business investment relief provisions (see **explanatory note 21**).

If the property which is lost, stolen or destroyed is recovered, and prior to the property being lost or stolen there were 231 or more countable days, then the individual will have a fixed 45 countable days period during which the property can remain in the UK prior to the temporary importation exemption being breached (ITA 2007 s 809Z4(3B)). This applies from 6 April 2013.

For property last brought to the UK prior to 6 April 2013 the 'countable day' disregard where the property met the public access rule was more limited. The disregard for the purposes of the countable days test only applies to a day when the public access rule is met if *one* of the following three specified conditions is also met:

- the property meets the public access rule during the *whole* of the period of importation;
- the period of importation begins with a period of no public access and ends with a period of public access which immediately follows the initial period of no public access; or
- the property meets either the public access rule or the repair rule *throughout* the period of importation.

*The repair rule*

(25) The repair conditions are met, such that there is no taxable remittance, where (ITA 2007 s 809Z3; RDRM34190):

- the property is under repair or restoration;
- in advance or following repair or restoration the property is in transit:
  (i) from a place outside the UK to repair rule premises (defined below);
  (ii) in transit between repair rules premises; or
  (iii) from repair rule premises to a place outside the UK;
- in advance of, or following, repair or restoration the property is in storage at repair rule premises.

  The legislation is strict in that it states that the repair rule will only apply where either (ITA 2007 s 809Z3(6)):

  - the property meets the repair rule throughout its time in the UK from the importation to the exportation; or
  - where throughout the time in the UK, from the importation to the exportation, the property meets either the repair rule or the public access rule.

Repair rule premises are (ITA 2007 s 809Z3(4); RDRM34200):

- premises in the UK that are to be used, or have been used, for the repair or restoration of property; or
- other commercial premises in the UK used by the restorer (the person who is to carry out or has carried out, the repair or restoration work) for the storage of property in advance of, or following, repair or restoration of property by the restorer.

*The public access rule*

(26) Where property is brought to the UK on or after 6 April 2013 the exemption will apply providing (ITA 2007 s 809Z):

- there is 'qualifying public access' to the exempt property; and
- that from the time of importation to the time when it ceases to be in the UK the exempt property meets the 'qualifying public access' condition for a period of no more than two years (or such longer period as HMRC may specify).

For there to be qualifying public access the exempt property must be (ITA 2007 s 809Z(3)):

- available for public access at an approved establishment; or

- available for public access and in connection with this availability is:
  - (i) in transit to/from public access rule premises; or
  - (ii) in storage at public access rule premises.

Broadly an approved establishment is a designated museum, gallery or other institution or any other premises or institution designated by HMRC (ITA 2007 s 809Z(5)).

Public access rule premises are (ITA 2007 s 809Z(6)):

- premises in the UK at which the property is to be, or has been, available for public access; or
- other commercial premises in the UK used by the approved establishment for the storage of property either:
  - – in advance of the property being available for public access at the approved establishment; or
  - – after the property has been available for public access at the approved establishment.

For property last brought to the UK prior to 6 April 2013, for the exemption to apply the exempt property had to meet the strictly worded qualifying property definition which only allows property qualifying under the meaning of Council Directive 2006/112/EC (that is a qualifying work of art, collectors' item or antique of educational, scientific or cultural value) to qualify. This meant that some modern art (for example sound art) did not qualify.

*Sales of exempt property*

(27) Prior to 6 April 2012, if an exempt asset was sold in the UK:

- the foreign income or gains used to acquire the asset were treated as remitted and fell to be taxed in the UK; and
- any gain on the disposal was subject to capital gains tax on the arising basis (unless the proceeds were less than £6,000 such that the chattels exemption applied).

This made the UK unattractive as a place for the sale of assets owned by UK resident foreign domiciliaries. An exemption was introduced with effect from 6 April 2012 to enable UK resident foreign domiciliaries to sell 'exempt property' in the UK:

- without crystallising an UK income tax or capital gains tax charge on the underlying foreign income and/or gains used to acquire the asset; and
- without crystallising a UK capital gains tax charge on any chargeable gain on disposal of the exempt property (where the sale takes place during a tax year for which the seller is a remittance basis user).

In this context property meets the 'exempt property' definition if it meets the public access rule, the personal use rule, the repair rule, the temporary importation rule or if the notional remitted amount is less than £1,000 (that is the remittance of the property falls within one of the ITA 2007 s 809X exemption categories).

Broadly, to qualify the following conditions must be met (ITA 2007 s 809YA):

- the sale is on arm's length terms to someone other than a relevant person (as defined in ITA 2007 s 809M, see **explanatory note 4**);
- a relevant person cannot benefit in any way from the property after the sale;
- the proceeds are all be paid over by the first anniversary of 5 January following the end of the tax year that the property ceased to be exempt property (referred to as the 'final deadline'). So for a sale in 2016/17 the proceeds would have to be paid over by 5 January 2019;

- the proceeds are either taken offshore or used to fund a qualifying investment under the business investment relief provisions (see **explanatory notes 11–18**) within 45 days of receipt or (if earlier) by the final deadline.

Where the proceeds are used to make a qualifying investment for business investment relief purposes a claim under that legislation must be made by the first anniversary of 31 January following the tax year that the property is sold in order for the reliefs to apply (ITA 2007 s 809YA(9)).

Where the proceeds are received in instalments there are separate 45 days periods for each instalment. What happens to the actual asset itself after the sale is irrelevant to the operation of the exemption (assuming that a genuine third party sale has taken place). Where a specific request is made HMRC Officers have discretion to extend any 45 day period (ITA 2007 s 809YB). This will, however, only be done in exceptional circumstances.

Any subsequent remittance of the proceeds from the sale or any property derived from these proceeds will be taxable (unless one of the exemptions applies). The legislation provides that where the asset was acquired from a mixed fund, the offshore transfer rules will apply to both the sale of the property and the re-exported funds. For more on mixed funds, see **Example F6**.

The capital gains tax treatment (which deems any gain to be a foreign chargeable gain despite the sale occurring in the UK) only applies for the purposes of chargeable gains. This means that losses will remain UK allowable losses. Whilst the gains treatment is automatic, an election can be made (in writing by the first anniversary of 31 January following the end of the tax year during which the disposal occurs) such that provision is switched off so the gain remains a UK capital gain taxable on the arising basis (ITA 2007 s 809YD).

The reliefs can apply where property is imported to the UK for sale at a UK auction house, as the initial remittance will be deferred by the temporary importation rule (see **explanatory note 24**). HMRC's settled view is that the capital gains tax exemption will only apply where the underlying funds used to acquire the asset were unremitted foreign income or gains, such that a disposal would otherwise constitute a remittance if not for these rules.

HMRC does not accept that the capital gains tax exemption applies where the property was acquired from clean capital and/or UK taxed income, even if all the other conditions are met (RDRM34070).

The legislation contains a similar anti-avoidance provision to that within the business investment relief provisions. In this case the provision disapplies the exemption where the sale of the exempt property occurs as part of, or as a result of, a scheme or arrangement the main purpose or one of the main purposes of which is to avoid tax (ITA 2007 s 809YA(11)). Again the context in which the Government thinks this provision will be applied is unclear.

*The cultural gift scheme exemption*

(28) Foreign domiciliaries can benefit from the cultural gift scheme provisions (also known as the gifts to the nation scheme).

The cultural gift scheme is, broadly, a scheme which seeks to encourage the gifting of objects (or collections of objects), which are either considered to be preeminent or associated with an historic building in public ownership, to the nation through the incentive of income tax reductions (30% of the value of the object for individuals with the possibility of spreading this over five tax years) (FA 2012 Sch 14).

Total funding of £30 million is available annually to cover the cost to the Exchequer of both the tax relief under this scheme and IHT taken as offset in the acceptance in lieu scheme.

To secure the tax relief the individual has to make a formal offer to donate the object to the nation and a Panel will assess whether the object is suitably pre-eminent (assessments being carried out on a first come, first served basis). In addition to the tax reduction available under the cultural gift scheme provisions, there is an exemption from any UK income tax or capital gains tax charge that would otherwise crystallise as a result of the object deriving from foreign income or gains (ITA 2007 s 809YE). This works as follows:

- where tax has been deferred as a result of one of the existing exemptions the gift will not trigger the deferred charge, meaning that the tax is avoided permanently;
- where the object is brought into the UK specifically to be gifted to the nation there will be no taxable remittance.

*Statutory matching rules with respect to remittances from mixed funds*

(29) Statutory rules apply to mixed funds containing either different types foreign income and foreign gains arising or accruing after 5 April 2008 or the same type of foreign income and gains but arising over different tax years. There are different rules for matching with respect to remittances to the UK (ITA 2007 s 809Q) and offshore transfers (ITA 2007 s 809R(4)). There is also a targeted anti-avoidance rule (ITA 2007 s 809S).

Where a fund contains pre- and post-5 April 2008 funds, two sets of matching rules apply (the post-5 April 2008 statutory rules having priority until these funds are deemed to have been remitted). The issues are explained in greater detail in **Example F6**.

*Irish source income*

(30) For the purposes of these explanatory notes Irish source income refers to income arising from sources in the Republic of Ireland. Income from sources in Northern Ireland is UK source income.

From 6 April 2008 Irish source income is treated in the same way as income from any other territory outside the UK. This means a remittance basis user is only be taxable on Irish source income if it is remitted to the UK. To prevent double taxation there is a specific provision exempting Irish income arising before 6 April 2008, which had previously been subject to UK tax on the arising basis, from being taxed a second time if it is remitted to the UK after 5 April 2008 (FA 2008 Sch 7, paras 82, 83(3); RDRM31420, RDRM31530). If they have not already done so individuals and offshore trustees (of a trust with UK resident and foreign domiciled beneficiaries) can amend investment mandates so that investment managers can freely invest in Irish investments.

*The remittance basis and foreign dividend income*

(31) With effect from 6 April 2008, remittance basis users cannot access the dividend tax rates with respect to remitted foreign dividend income. This is because this is 'relevant foreign income' and is excluded from the definition of dividend income in ITA 2007 s 19. Therefore remittance basis users are subject to tax at 20%, 40% or 45% on remittances of foreign dividend income depending on their marginal tax rate.

*Extension of the accrued income scheme*

(32) With effect from 6 April 2008, the scope of the accrued income scheme was extended to apply to remittance basis users acquiring and disposing of foreign securities.

The accrued income scheme rules operate to break down the proceeds of sale figure into a capital element and an accrued income element (with this being relevant foreign income). This means that one has a mixed fund.

Where there would otherwise be no gain or a minimal gain and the security has been acquired from clean capital, the practical impact is that the clean capital has been tainted as one has a fund containing both accrued income and clean capital. In such a case the statutory matching rules mean that any remittances will first be matched to the accrued income element.

HMRC has considered the issues in this area and the matter is covered in RDRM33550:

> " . . . For consistency of treatment between the [accrued income scheme] AIS and the remittance basis regime, HMRC will follow the tax treatment delivered by the AIS and accept that an 'income amount' can be transferred to a separate 'income account' immediately upon transfer, that is, the proceeds are 'split' into two separate accounts immediately upon receipt into the individual's account. This 'income' could then be identified and taxed as such, without creating a mixed fund refer to RDRM35200.
>
> To the extent that the remainder of the proceeds consist of capital or UK or non-taxable income (as opposed to, say, untaxed foreign income or gains) originally used in the purchase of the security (refer to RDRM35030) the remainder of the proceeds could therefore be separately identified and remitted as such."

In practical terms this would seem to mean that provided the accrued income element is immediately and demonstrably transferred out of the individual's account HMRC will accept that there no mixed fund is created. Where there is reliance on this HMRC statement it is recommended that a copy of the HMRC guidance as at the time the advice is given is provided to the client, that a record is made of this on the file and that there is disclosure on the tax return.

# Question

## A.

Ethan Non-Dom is a UK resident foreign domiciliary. He first became resident in the UK on 7 April 2005 and made ITA 2007 s 809B remittance basis claims for the tax years from 2008/09 to 2016/17. He also made the necessary claims for his relevant foreign income to be taxed on the remittance basis in prior years (any foreign employment income and foreign chargeable gains automatically being subject to the remittance basis in 2007/08 and prior years).

Ethan has various offshore assets. State whether the following are mixed funds:

(a) a non-interest bearing Swiss bank account into which Ethan's Swiss dividend income (subject to foreign tax) is paid (the account is opened in 2016/17 so for that tax year it can only contain 2016/17 income);

(b) shares in XYZ Jersey Ltd bought for £800,000 with a mixture of 2009/10 clean capital (£630,000) and 2009/10 relevant foreign income (£170,000);

(c) a Swiss account opened on 17 June 2016 to receive a £5.6 million inheritance from his grandmother. The account pays interest once a year on 31 December and instructions have been given that the interest should be paid into a separate specially opened account.

## B.

Clarisse Non-Dom is a UK resident foreign domiciliary. She made ITA 2007 s 809B remittance basis claims for the tax years from 2008/09 to 2016/17. She also made the necessary claims for her relevant foreign income to be taxed on the remittance basis in prior years (any foreign employment income and foreign chargeable gains automatically being subject to the remittance basis in 2007/08 and prior years).

She has a number of offshore bank accounts and made various transfers in 2016/17. State the rules which govern how one matches the following transfers to the various categories of income and capital:

(a) she has a number of Jersey bank accounts. One contains a mixture of income and gains with respect to tax years 2008/09 onwards. She transfers £125,000 from this account to her UK current account;

(b) her Geneva bank account also contains a mixture of income and gains with respect to tax years 2008/09 onwards. She uses £1.4 million to acquire a property in Florida which at the end of the tax year she has no intention of ever selling;

(c) another Jersey bank account contains a mixture of income and capital but all with respect to tax years prior to 2008/09. She remits £500,000 to the UK;

(d) her final Jersey bank account contains a mixture of income and capital with respect to tax years from 2001/02 to 2011/12. She remits £1 million to the UK.

## C.

Ethan Non-Dom (in **part A**) sold his shares in XYZ Jersey Ltd on 18 May 2016 for £950,000 (there is no foreign capital gains tax payable). He bought the shares on 17 March 2010 for £800,000 with a mixture of 2009/10 clean capital (£630,000) and 2009/10 relevant foreign income (£170,000 of gross bank interest).

Ethan pays the proceeds from the disposal of the XYZ Jersey Ltd shares into a newly opened bank account in Jersey (with this being the first receipt into the account). On 17 June 2016 he remits £250,000 to the UK.

What categories of income and capital will the £250,000 remittance be matched with? On the basis that he is an additional rate taxpayer what will his additional UK tax liability be as a result of the remittance?

## D.

Megan is a UK resident foreign domiciliary. She has made ITA 2007 s 809B remittance basis claims for the tax years from 2008/09 to 2016/17. She also made the necessary claims for her relevant foreign income to be taxed on the remittance basis in prior years (any foreign employment income and foreign chargeable gains automatically being subject to the remittance basis in 2007/08 and prior years).

As at 6 April 2016 Megan has an offshore account containing £700,000 of 2015/16 relevant foreign earning (not subject to foreign tax). The following receipts are paid into the account in April 2016:

(i) 10 April 2016 – £50,000 of gross foreign bank interest; and

(ii) 27 April 2016 – £750,000 inheritance from the estate of Megan's godmother.

There are no further transactions until a withdrawal of £750,000 on 3 May 2016. What categories of income and gains would be matched to the withdrawal if:

(a) she remits the funds to the UK?

(b) she spends the funds on a foreign property that, at the end of the tax year, she does not intend to sell?

## E.

Clara is a UK resident foreign domiciliary. She has made ITA 2007 s 809B remittance basis claims for the tax years from 2008/09 to 2016/17. She also made the necessary claims for her relevant foreign income to be taxed on the remittance basis in prior years (any foreign employment income and foreign chargeable gains automatically being subject to the remittance basis in 2007/08 and prior years).

On 17 May 2016 Clara sells her Guernsey house for £1 million realising a gain of £200,000. She acquired the property in February 2007 and financed it from a mixture of relevant foreign income and clean capital as follows:

| | |
|---|---|
| Gross foreign interest income – no tax credit | £200,000 |
| Net foreign interest income – 15% foreign tax paid | £500,000 |
| Clean capital | £100,000 |

She pays the proceeds into a newly opened Jersey bank account (such that the proceeds are the funds within the account). After this initial £1 million deposit the following transactions occur, with respect to this account, in tax year 2016/17:

- on 18 May 2016 £600,000 is transferred to a Swiss lawyer's client account to finance the acquisition by Clara of a chalet in Verbier;
- on 25 June 2016 Clara deposits £1 million into the account which represents a legacy from her great aunt's will;
- on 31 December 2016 gross foreign bank interest income of £75,000 is credited to the account;
- on 19 March 2017 Clara uses funds within the account to make a £1 million transfer to her UK deposit account for the acquisition of a UK residential property.

What categories of income and capital will the £1 million remittance be matched with? On the basis that Clara is an additional rate taxpayer what will her additional UK tax liability be as a result of the remittance?

## F.

Nico is a UK resident foreign domiciliary. He has made ITA 2007 s 809B remittance basis claims for the tax years from 2008/09 to 2016/17. He also made the necessary claims for his relevant foreign income to be taxed on the remittance basis in prior years (any foreign employment income and foreign chargeable gains automatically being subject to the remittance basis in 2007/08 and prior years).

## F6.3 THE REMITTANCE BASIS – MIXED FUNDS

As at 6 April 2016 Nico's Guernsey bank account contained £1.1 million of clean capital relating to tax year 2005/06. Interest is paid into a separate account.

On 14 July 2016 he sold his Guernsey summer house (acquired with £535,000 of 2009/10 relevant income on which no foreign tax was due) for £470,000. By mistake he paid the proceeds into the Guernsey bank account such that the balance was then £1,570,000. He transferred £600,000 to his UK current account on 27 July 2016.

What categories of income and capital will the £600,000 remittance be matched with? On the basis that Nico is an additional rate taxpayer what will his additional UK tax liability be as a result of the remittance?

# Answer

## A. Ethan Non-Dom

When deciding whether foreign income and gains have been remitted, special rules apply if the remittance is from a mixed fund. Therefore it is important to examine the facts of the situation carefully. See **explanatory note 3** for the mixed fund definition.

(a) The Swiss account only contains one of the kind of income listed at ITA 2007 s 809Q(4) and that income relates to just one tax year (2016/17). As such this is not a mixed fund. It will be a mixed fund in 2017/18 if the Swiss dividend income continues to be paid into the account.

(b) The shares derive from funds that match to more than one kind of income and capital listed at ITA 2007 s 809Q(4), meaning that they come within the 'mixed fund' definition.

(c) The Swiss account only contains one of the kind of income and capital listed at ITA 2007 s 809Q(4) and the funds within the account relate to just one tax year (2016/17). A separate account has been opened to receive the interest income so the clean capital within the account will not be tainted with relevant foreign income. The account is not a mixed fund.

## B. Clarisse Non-Dom

For a discussion of the meaning of remittance in ITA 2007 s 809L, see **Example F5**.

See **explanatory note 3** for the meaning of mixed fund. See **explanatory notes 7–22** for details of how transfers out of mixed funds are matched.

(a) Clarisse has brought money into the UK from an offshore account containing income and capital relating to tax years from 2008/09 onwards (ie a mixed fund). As such condition A of ITA 2007 s 809L is met and the statutory mixed fund matching rules at ITA 2007 ss 809Q-809S are relevant (see **explanatory note 7**). These rules operate to match the transfers with the appropriate income or gains to decide whether condition B of ITA 2007 s 809L is met (RDRM35210) such that there is a taxable remittance and to decide what has been remitted (determined by ITA 2007 s 809Q(3), see **explanatory note 8**).

(b) Clarisse has used money from an offshore account containing income and capital relating to tax years from 2008/09 onwards (ie a mixed fund) to acquire an offshore asset which at the end of the tax year she has not sold and does not intend to sell. As such the ITA 2007 ss 809Q–809S provisions are effective (see **explanatory note 7**) and there has been an offshore transfer (see **explanatory note 11**). ITA 2007 s 809R(4), therefore, deems that the transfer comprises the appropriate proportion of each kind of income and capital in the fund immediately before the transfer. For example, if the transfer represents 21% of the funds in the account immediately prior to the transfer, the Florida property is deemed to derive from 21% of each kind of income and capital in the fund immediately before the transfer with the post transfer offshore account being deemed to contain 79% of each kind of income and capital in the fund immediately before the transfer. The Florida property itself is also a mixed fund for the purposes of this rule.

(c) Clarisse has brought money into the UK from a Jersey bank account and has, therefore, met condition A of ITA 2007 s 809L. The Jersey bank account contains pre-6 April 2008 income and capital. As such the common law matching rules apply for remittances from an account which contains a mixture of income and gains (see **explanatory notes 14-20**) rather than the statutory matching rules (FA 2008 Sch 7 para 89).

(d) Clarisse has brought money into the UK from an offshore account and has, therefore, met condition A of ITA 2007 s 809L (ie taxable funds have been remitted). The Jersey account contains pre-6 April 2008 income and capital and post-5 April 2008 income and capital. This means that both the common law matching rules and the statutory matching rules apply. In such cases the statutory rules have priority unless and until all the post-5 April 2008 funds have been removed (RDRM35330). Where the remittance is such that it does remove all the post-5 April 2008 income and capital, the common law rules will apply from the moment one matches to pre-6 April 2008 income and capital (see **explanatory note 21**).

## C. Ethan Non-Dom (continued)

For a discussion of the meaning of remittance in ITA 2007 s 809L, see **Example F5**.

See **explanatory notes 7–9** for details of how transfers out of mixed funds are matched.

The £950,000 of proceeds from the sale of the XYZ Jersey Ltd shares breaks down as follows:

| | | £ |
|---|---|---|
| 2016/17 | Foreign chargeable gains – not subject to foreign tax | 150,000 |
| 2009/10 | Relevant foreign income (interest) – not subject to foreign tax | 170,000 |
| 2009/10 | Clean capital | 630,000 |
| | | 950,000 |

A remittance by Ethan of £250,000 to the UK meets condition A of ITA 2007 s 809L and, because the cash is from a mixed fund, the ITA 2007 ss 809Q-809S provisions are effective as the income and gains relate to tax years from 2008/09 onwards.

In order to see whether condition B of ITA 2007 s 809L (ie the amount brought to the UK relates to taxable foreign income or gains) is met, the mixed fund rules apply to match the £250,000 remitted to the UK as follows:

- £150,000 is matched to the 2016/17 funds (foreign chargeable gains – no foreign tax credit attached);
- £100,000 is matched to the 2009/10 relevant foreign income (no foreign tax credit attached).

Ethan is an additional rate taxpayer so suffers tax on his capital gains at the highest rates. This means that:

- the £150,000 matched to foreign chargeable gains is taxed at 20%, the highest rate which applies to gains arising from disposals of shares (tax of £30,000 being due); and
- the £100,000 of relevant foreign income is subject to tax at 45% (tax of £45,000 being due).

In total, therefore, UK tax of £75,000 will be due as a result of the remittance.

## D. Megan Non-Dom

For a discussion of the meaning of remittance in ITA 2007 s 809L, see **Example F5**.

See **explanatory notes 7–8 and 11** for details of how transfers out of mixed funds are matched.

(a) If Megan remits the funds to the UK she will meet condition A of ITA 2007 s 809L and, because the cash is from a mixed fund, the ITA 2007 ss 809Q-809S provisions are effective as the income and gains relate to tax years from 2008/09 onwards.

In order to see whether condition B of ITA 2007 s 809L (ie the amount brought to the UK relates to taxable foreign income or gains) is met, the mixed fund rules apply to match the £750,000 remitted to the UK as follows:

- £50,000 is matched to the gross foreign bank interest arising in 2016/17;
- £700,000 to the inheritance (clean capital) received in 2016/17.

Therefore the remittance of £750,000 would result in £50,000 of taxable income being brought to the UK.

After the transfer the account balance would be £750,000, which would be broken down as follows:

- £50,000 relating to the 2016/17 inheritance; and
- £700,000 relating to the 2015/16 relevant foreign earnings.

(b) If Megan spends the funds on a foreign property that at the end of the tax year she does not intend to sell, since the funds relate to post-5 April 2008 income and capital the ITA 2007 ss 809Q-809S provisions are effective.

The transfer meets the conditions such that it qualifies as an offshore transfer and the rules at ITA 2007 s 809R(4) apply. Since the transfer equates to 50% of the funds within the account immediately prior to the transfer this means that each of (i) the property acquired and (ii) the transferor account are deemed to contain 50% of each kind of income and capital held immediately prior to the transfer. So each comprises £25,000 of 2016/17 relevant foreign income (not subject to foreign tax), £375,000 of 2016/17 clean capital and £350,000 of 2015/16 relevant foreign earnings (not subject to foreign tax).

## E. Clara Non-Dom

For a discussion of the meaning of remittance in ITA 2007 s 809L, see **Example F5**.

See **explanatory notes 7–8** and **11** for details of how transfers out of mixed funds are matched.

It is clear from the question that Jersey bank account is a mixed fund. Where there are multiple transactions from a mixed fund one takes a step by step approach.

The first step is to determine the composition of the Jersey bank account immediately after the receipt of the proceeds from the sale of the Guernsey property:

| *Tax year* | *Category* | £ |
|---|---|---|
| 2016/17 | Foreign capital gain – no foreign tax paid | 200,000 |
| Pre-6 April 2008 | Gross foreign interest income – no foreign tax paid | 200,000 |
| Pre-6 April 2008 | Net foreign interest income – 15% foreign tax paid | 500,000 |
| Pre-6 April 2008 | Clean capital | 100,000 |
| Total within the bank account after proceeds deposited | | 1,000,000 |

The next transaction through the Jersey account is the withdrawal of funds in order to acquire the Verbier chalet. An amount of £600,000 (that is 60% of the £1 million mixed fund) is taken from this account by Clara to finance the acquisition of the chalet. The acquisition of the chalet is an offshore transfer (the £600,000 has not been remitted to the UK and as at the end of 2016/17 Clara has no expectation there will be any such remittance). This means that the rule at ITA 2007, s 809R(4) applies and the transfer is deemed to remove 60% of every category of income and gain within the account immediately before the transfer (with 40% remaining within the Jersey account). After having done this, the composition of the Jersey account and the chalet is, therefore, said to be as follows:

| *Tax year* | *Category* | *Left in Jersey account (40%)* | *In Verbier chalet (60%)* |
|---|---|---|---|
| 2016/17 | Foreign capital gain – no foreign tax paid | £80,000 | £120,000 |
| Pre-6 April 2008 | Gross foreign interest income – no foreign tax paid | £80,000 | £120,000 |
| Pre-6 April 2008 | Net foreign interest income – 15% foreign tax paid | £200,000 | £300,000 |
| Pre-6 April 2008 | Clean capital | £40,000 | £60,000 |

On 25 June 2016 Clara deposits £1 million into the Jersey account, which represents a legacy from her great aunt's will. On 31 December 2016 gross foreign bank interest income of £75,000 is paid into her Jersey account. On 19 March 2017 she remits £1 million to the UK.

The remittance to the UK is in accordance with ITA 2007 s 809L condition A and, therefore, to the extent that the £1 million remittance can be matched to post-5 April 2008 foreign income and capital (in this scenario it can be matched to such income and capital in its entirety) the statutory matching rules in ITA 2007 ss 809Q-809S apply.

To determine what kind of income and capital the £1 million remittance is matched with (for the purposes of ITA 2007, s 809L condition B), one must determine the composition of the Jersey account immediately prior to the remittance:

| *Tax year* | *Category* | *In Jersey account before remittance to the UK* |
|---|---|---|
| 2016/17 | Gross foreign interest income – no foreign tax paid | £75,000 |
| 2016/17 | Foreign capital gain – no foreign tax paid | £80,000 |
| 2016/17 | Clean capital (inheritance) | £1,000,000 |
| Pre-6 April 2008 | Gross foreign interest income – no foreign tax paid | £80,000 |
| Pre-6 April 2008 | Net foreign interest income – 15% foreign tax paid | £200,000 |
| Pre-6 April 2008 | Clean capital | £40,000 |

The £1 million remittance to the UK will be matched as follows:

| *Tax year* | *Category* | *Remittance* | *Tax rate* | *Tax liability* |
|---|---|---|---|---|
| 2016/17 | Gross foreign interest income – no tax credit | £75,000 | 45% | £33,750 |
| 2016/17 | Foreign capital gain – no tax credit | £80,000 | 28% | £22,400 |
| 2016/17 | Clean capital (balancing figure) | £845,000 | Nil | Nil |
| | | | | £56,150 |

As an additional rate taxpayer selling a residential property, Clara is subject to the higher 28% capital gains tax rate.

Note that appropriate segregation of clean capital, proceeds from the disposal of chargeable assets and income would have resulted in Clara being able to remit £1 million from clean capital and, therefore, suffer no UK tax liability. She should have set up two new accounts one to receive the £1 million legacy from her great aunt's will and one to receive the bank interest with respect to the legacy. She could then have remitted solely from the account containing the legacy.

## F. Nico Non-Dom

For a discussion of the meaning of remittance in ITA 2007, s 809L, see **Example F5**.

See **explanatory notes 7-9** for details of how transfers out of mixed funds are matched.

A remittance by Nico of £600,000 to the UK meets condition A of ITA 2007 s 809L and, because the cash is from a mixed fund relating to the 2008/09 tax year onwards, the ITA 2007 ss 809Q-809S provisions are effective in order to see whether ITA 2007 s 809L condition B is met.

To determine what kinds of income and capital the £600,000 remittance is matched to one must determine the kinds of income and capital within the mixed fund immediately prior to the remittance:

| *Tax year* | *Category* | *£* |
|---|---|---|
| 2009/10 | Relevant foreign income – no foreign tax paid | 535,000 |
| Pre-6 April 2008 | Clean capital | 1,100,000 |
| | | 1,635,000 |

Note that the total of the categories of income and capital within the mixed fund (£1,635,000) is greater than the actual money in the bank account (£1,570,000) as a result of the property derived from the relevant foreign income having been sold at a loss of £65,000. The loss may or may not be available for relief depending on whether Nico has made a TCGA 1992 s 16ZA election (see **Example F7**).

Since there are no income or gains within the account relating to tax years later than 2009/10, one matches first to the income and gains relating to 2009/10. For 2009/10 there is only £535,000 of relevant foreign income. The remittance of £600,000 is, therefore, matched first to the £535,000 of 2009/10 relevant foreign income. Applying the 45% tax rate gives a UK tax liability of £240,750.

There is now no post-5 April 2008 income and/or gains to match to and £65,000 of the remittance is not matched. The only pre-6 April 2008 funds are clean capital. The remaining £65,000 is, therefore, matched to £65,000 of pre-6 April 2008 clean capital which carries no tax liability.

Note that if the proceeds from the sale of the Guernsey summer house had not been paid into this account by mistake the entire £600,000 could have been transferred from this account and remitted to the UK free of tax, as it would have been matched entirely to clean capital. Since the mistake was made by Nico, rather than the bank (see **explanatory note 23** for comment about when there are bank errors or mistakes), the mistake cannot be corrected such that the contamination of the clean capital can be undone.

## Explanatory Notes

*Introduction*

(1) A remittance basis user will suffer a UK tax charge on relevant foreign income and foreign chargeable gains where there is a remittance to the UK of funds representing or derived from actual or deemed/attributed foreign income and/or chargeable gains. This charge would be in addition to any remittance basis charge (RBC) paid that may have to be paid to access the remittance basis (see **Example F4: explanatory note 5**).

This means that the following are crucial issues:

- the definition of 'remitted to the UK' (see **Example F5**); and
- if there has been a remittance to the UK, whether it is derived from actual or deemed/attributed foreign income and/or chargeable gains.

Where funds are remitted to the UK that represent or derive from 'clean capital' there is no tax charge. Funds deriving from capital gains will be taxed at 10%, 18%, 20% or 28% rate as applicable. Funds deriving from income will be taxed at the individual's marginal rate. Some foreign income and foreign chargeable gains will have suffered tax in other territories such that relief for foreign tax can be claimed (see **Example F3**).

Accordingly determining from which source the funds derive is crucial to ascertaining (a) whether there is a tax liability and (b) the quantum of any tax liability.

*Remitting nominated foreign income or gains*

(2) These explanatory notes do not consider the rules (ITA 2007 ss 809I–809J) that apply where a remittance basis user remits nominated income or gains in excess of the £10 de minimis (introduced for tax year 2012/13 onwards), before the remittance of *all* foreign income and gains subject to tax on the remittance basis since 6 April 2008.

Where the ITA 2007 ss 809I–809J provisions are triggered, specific matching rules come into operation. Broadly, the aggregate amount remitted in the year is matched to foreign income or gains received in a specified order regardless of the foreign income or gains that have actually been remitted. Generally this order will be unfavourable to the taxpayer and overturn any planning based on remitting from the foreign income or capital account containing funds which will give rise to the lowest tax liability. As such, it is very important that the individual is aware of the rules and has a strategy in place to avoid triggering them (from 2012/13 this will generally be by ensuring that the ITA 2007 s 809C nomination of foreign income and/or gains does not exceed £10).

For a discussion of these rules, see **Example F4 explanatory note 16**).

*Definition of a mixed fund*

(3) A mixed fund exists where, immediately before the transfer, the money or other property contains or derives from more than one of the following kinds of income and capital (ITA 2007 s 809Q(6)):

(a) employment income (other than income within (b), (c) or (f));

(b) relevant foreign earnings (other than income within (f));

(c) foreign specific employment income (other than income within (f));

(d) relevant foreign income (other than income within (g));

(e) foreign chargeable gains (other than chargeable gains within (h));

(f) employment income subject to a foreign tax;

(g) relevant foreign income subject to a foreign tax;

(h) foreign chargeable gains subject to a foreign tax; and

(i) income or capital not within another category above.

Any account that receives the proceeds of sale of an asset sold at a gain will automatically become a mixed account under this definition.

Prior to 6 April 2012, a foreign currency bank account was a chargeable asset (unless the foreign currency gains were exempt from capital gains tax because the currency was acquired for personal expenditure of the individual and his family/dependants). This meant that merely having a non-sterling account could result in potentially highly complex mixed fund issues.

The capital gains tax rules on this changed with effect from 6 April 2012 such that foreign currency within a bank account is no longer a chargeable asset (TCGA 1992 s 252). Gains realised in prior years but not remitted will, however still remain within the mixed fund pool.

The bank account is also deemed to be a mixed fund where, immediately before the transfer, the money or other property contains or derives from income or capital of more than one tax year (see above). For example, an income account that only contains gross foreign interest becomes a mixed account as soon as income is received for a second tax year. An account that contains clean capital relating to two separate tax years will also be a mixed account, although if these are the only two credits to the account it is very unlikely that this provision will have any practical effect.

It is important to remember that a mixed fund is not just a bank or building society account. The legislation refers to 'money or other property'. For example a painting would be a mixed fund if it had been acquired from more than one of the types of income or capital stated above, or from the same kind of income or capital but for more than one tax year.

*Bank account issues*

(4) Having more than one account with the same branch of a specific bank is not an issue as funds are only deemed to be mixed if they are in the same bank account. This common law assertion is backed up by case law (*Hart v Sangster* (1957) 37 TC 231 and *Kneen v Martin* 19 TC 33) and HMRC accepts that this is the position where the mixed funds legislation enacted by FA 2008 applies (RDRM33560).

*Avoiding a mixed fund*

(5) Up to a point a mixed fund can be avoided through segregation. Where funds are invested in appreciating capital assets it is, however, impossible to avoid having a mixed fund after the sale. It is not possible to avoid the creation of a mixed fund by paying the gain element (whether this be with respect to a capital gain, an

offshore income gain or the profit element subject to income tax under the deep discounted securities rules) into a separate account.

The extent to which one takes segregation of income and capital will depend on the sums at stake (see **explanatory note 25**).

*Why we need rules with respect to mixed funds*

(6) Where money or other property represents or derives from more than one kind of income or gains (ie a mixed fund) and that money or other property is only partly remitted, there is a need for special rules to determine what has been remitted to the UK. This is so that it is possible to determine whether a remittance is taxable as representing or being derived from foreign income and/or gains (ie whether condition B of ITA 2007 s 809L is met) (ITA 2007 s 809Q(2)).

The mixed fund rules are complex. There are three very different sets of rules that can apply:

- statutory rules (ITA 2007 ss 809Q–809S) where the income or gains arose after 5 April 2008 and the remittance to the UK falls within the standard remittance condition (that is condition A of ITA 2007 s 809L is met, see **Example F5** for more on the meaning of remittance). See **explanatory notes 7-13** below;
- for tax years from 2013/14 onwards, within these statutory mixed fund rules there are special rules at ITA 2007 ss 809RA–809RD (based on SP 1/09, which was effective up to 5 April 2013 with grandfathering provisions for those who were not ordinarily resident at that date). These rules enable a simplified version of the mixed fund rules to apply to the offshore account that individuals eligible for overseas workday relief use for their earnings, provided specified conditions are met. These explanatory notes do not consider these special simplified rules. An overview is provided in **Example F4 explanatory note 3** and **Example F1 explanatory note 28** and readers should consult the HMRC FAQs (now archived) (http://webarchive.nationalarchives.gov.uk/+/hmrc.gov.uk/international/faqs-special-mixed-fund-rules.htm) for details;
- in all other cases one applies common law rules based on case law and accepted practice. See **explanatory notes 14-20** below.

Where the mixed fund contains a mix of post-5 April 2008 foreign income and gains and also pre-6 April 2008 foreign income and gains, see **explanatory note 21.**

***The statutory matching rules***

*When do these rules apply?*

(7) The statutory matching rules do *not* apply for the purposes of either (FA 2008 Sch 7 para 89):

(i) determining whether income or chargeable gains for the tax year 2007/08 or any earlier tax years are remitted to the UK; or

(ii) establishing the quantum of such a remittance.

As such, where categories of capital and/or income relate to 2007/08 or earlier years one has to apply the common law matching rules (see **explanatory note 14**).

Furthermore, the statutory matching rules can *only* apply where condition A in ITA 2007 s 809L applies (ITA 2007 s 809Q(1)). That is where:

- money or other property is brought to, received or used in the UK by or for the benefit of a relevant person; or
- a service is provided in the UK to or for the benefit or a relevant person (this will be the case regardless of whether the service is paid for offshore or the payment is made in the UK).

As such where there is a condition C (gift recipient provision) or condition D (third party connected operation provision) ITA 2007 s 809L remittance, the statutory matching rules do not apply meaning that the common law rules must again be used. For more on these types of remittances, see **Example F5 explanatory note 1**.

*Overview of the rules*

(8) The basic remittance basis statutory matching rules are found within ITA 2007 s 809Q which establishes the rules where there is a remittance to the UK as a result of condition A of ITA 2007 s 809L being met.

In contrast to the common law practice (see **explanatory note 14**), a fundamental principle which underpins the statutory mixed fund rules is that of matching within tax years.

One matches in the order specified in the legislation to receipts in each tax year looking firstly at the period from 6 April to the point of remittance and *not* at the tax year as a whole. If the remittance is in excess of the funds added since the start of the current tax year one firstly exhausts current year funds and then matches to funds added in the preceding tax year, again in the specified order set down in the legislation, and so on until the entire amount remitted has been matched. This means that in effect one matches on a year-by-year basis with tax years being taken on a last-in, first-out, basis until the remittance has been exhausted.

The statutory rules can be favourable to the taxpayer where a mistake is made such as clean capital being paid into an account containing past years' accumulated income as a transfer to the UK will be matched to the clean capital receipt of that year before the income from earlier tax years.

Where there is a qualifying remittance to the UK, a specific sequence of five steps (set down at ITA 2007 s 809Q(3)) has to be followed to determine if the remittance to the UK is out of the individual's foreign income or chargeable gains (ie whether condition B of ITA 2007 s 809L is met).

Broadly speaking, for tax year 2016/17 the steps can be explained as follows:

(A) break down the mixed fund into its component parts in accordance with the categories at ITA 2007 s 809Q(4) for the period from 6 April 2016 until immediately before the remittance. The ITA 2007 s 809Q(4) categories of income and capital being:

(a) employment income (other than income within (b), (c) or (f));

(b) relevant foreign earnings (other than income within (f));

(c) foreign specific employment income (other than income within (f));

(d) relevant foreign income (other than income within (g));

(e) foreign chargeable gains (other than chargeable gains within (h));

(f) employment income subject to a foreign tax;

(g) relevant foreign income subject to a foreign tax;

(h) foreign chargeable gains subject to a foreign tax; and

(i) income or capital not within another category above.

Two rules (discussed below) set down in ITA 2007 s 809R feed into this step to determine the categories of income and gains remaining within the fund immediately before the remittance to the UK. These are the rule with respect to debt (ITA 2007 s 809R(3)) and the rule with respect to offshore transfers (ITA 2007 s 809R(4)–(6)). See **explanatory note 10** for a discussion of the debt rule and **explanatory note 11** for a discussion of the offshore transfer rule.

(B) match as much of the remittance amount as possible to the highest category (in the above list) of income and gains available;

(C) where the remittance amount has not been fully matched, treat the amount as reduced by the amount matched in step B;

(D) continue with the matching process in the order of priority specified in the above list until either all the remittance amount has been matched or all income and gains in the current tax year (up to the date of the remittance) has been matched;

(E) if the remittance amount is still not exhausted then repeat the process for the tax year immediately before the current tax year and so on taking tax years in a last-in, first-out, order until the remittance amount has been matched in full.

Only UK employment income has priority over the other kinds of income and capital. This is different to (and less favourable than) the common law rules.

*The statutory matching rules: more can go into the categories than enters the bank account*

(9) The normal rules apply to quantify the remittance amount as follows (ITA 2007 s 809P(3)):

- where the remittance is of foreign income or chargeable gains the amount remitted is equal to the income or chargeable gains; and
- where the remittance derives from foreign income or chargeable gains the amount subject to tax will not be the market value of the asset on the date that the remittance is effected but rather the amount of foreign income or foreign chargeable gains directly or indirectly used to acquire the asset or to acquire any asset(s) from which the asset is derived.

These rules mean that it is possible to remit a greater sum than the market value of the money or other property brought to the UK. In the same way, when depositing funds within a mixed fund account it is possible for an aggregation of the amounts added to the matching categories (being the different kinds of income and capital within the mixed fund) as a result of the deposit to be higher than the actual amount deposited into the bank account (see **part F** of this Example).

Where there are remittances from a mixed fund account, the mixed fund rules place a cap on the taxable amount. This means that only the amount *transferred* can be matched and, therefore, limiting the amount which can be a taxable remittance (ITA 2007 s 809Q(7)).

*'Just and reasonable' provision with respect to satisfying a debt*

(10) There is a specific provision which impacts the composition of mixed fund property where a debt relating (wholly or in part, and directly or indirectly) to that property has been satisfied (wholly or in part) by foreign income or foreign chargeable gains or anything deriving (directly or indirectly) from such funds (ITA 2007 s 809R(3)).

ITA 2007 s 809R applies for the purposes of determining the constituent element of a mixed fund immediately prior to a remittance to which ITA 2007 s 809Q applies (that is it feeds into step 1 of the ITA 2007 s 809Q(3) composition of mixed funds matching rules explained above). ITA 2007 s 809R(2), (3) are tracing provisions, which (on a just and reasonable basis) attempt to ensure that where income or gains are applied in satisfaction of a debt, or where property derives from income or chargeable gains, the relevant property is treated as consisting of the income or gains so used, or from which the property derives.

Whether or not a debt relates to property is a question of fact. The legislation does not provide a special definition of 'relates to' and it, therefore, bears its normal everyday meaning. One obvious example of where this rule would apply is where a loan is taken out to acquire offshore property, and the loan is paid off using funds from an offshore bank account that is a mixed fund. In such a case the property acquired would, to the extent that it is just and reasonable, be treated as comprising the income or capital used to repay the loan.

*The offshore transfer rule*

(11) **Explanatory note 8** explained that, where the statutory matching rules are in point and certain specified transfers from the offshore account (referred to as 'offshore transfers') occur, the 'offshore transfer rule'

needs to be applied to determine what is left within the bank account immediately prior to a remittance to the UK.

An 'offshore transfer' is a transfer that meets the following two conditions (ITA 2007 s 809R(6)):

- the transfer does not result in a remittance to the UK (as a result of ITA 2007 s 809L condition A being met) prior to the end of the tax year in which the transfer took place; and
- it is not thought, at the end of the tax year in which the transfer takes place, that the transfer will result in a remittance to the UK as a result of ITA 2007 s 809L condition A being met.

As such, the offshore transfer rule potentially applies where there has been either (1) a transfer between offshore accounts or (2) where part of a mixed fund is used to finance foreign expenditure (including the acquisition of foreign investments).

The second condition (which looks to the 'intention at the end of the tax year') can lead to significant uncertainty since, at the end of the tax year, the individual might be undecided. It is suggested that where there is genuine uncertainty the transfer is treated as an offshore transfer such that the ITA 2007 s 809R(4) provisions explained below apply.

Some transfers will be partly a remittance and partly an offshore transfer (for example the repayment of an offshore loan used to acquire both UK and non-UK property). ITA 2007 s 809R(8) specifies that in such cases the transfer is deemed to be split into two with the matching to occur in the following order of priority:

- the remittance – with the remittance matching rules at ITA 2007 s 809Q applying;
- the offshore transfer with the ITA 2007 s 809R(4) matching rule applying.

ITA 2007 s 809R(4) provides that where an offshore transfer occurs, the funds transferred out are deemed to be 'the appropriate proportion of each kind of income and gain in the fund immediately before the transfer'. The appropriate proportion is defined as the proportion of the funds that are transferred. For example, the appropriate proportion would be 17% where £1,700 was transferred from a mixed fund bank account containing £10,000 immediately before the transfer.

Genuine offshore expenditure where the asset or service required will not result in a UK benefit being conferred on a relevant person will always qualify as an offshore transfer, this means that every withdrawal/transfer from the offshore account to settle offshore expenditure will have to be matched with 'the appropriate proportion of each kind of income and gain in the fund immediately before the transfer'. Where there are numerous small transfers to settle offshore expenditure in the year the matching procedure will be laborious. Where a mixed account has to be operated, an individual should try to ensure that the funds are either used exclusively for offshore expenditure or exclusively for remittances to the UK.

Where a transfer offshore does not fall within the offshore transfer conditions (for example there has been a remittance from the transferee account prior to the end of the tax year in which the transfer takes place) it appears that one has to use the matching rules at ITA 2007 s 809Q (subject to any potential application of the ITA 2007 s 809S(2) just and reasonable test).

*Mixed fund matching rules – anti-avoidance provision*

(12) ITA 2007 s 809S is an anti-avoidance provision aimed at preventing taxpayers manipulating the statutory matching rules to reduce their tax liability. The provision applies only in circumstances where all of the following conditions are met:

- the taxpayer enters into an arrangement. Arrangement meaning any scheme, understanding, transaction or series of transactions (whether or not enforceable);
- the main purpose (or one of the main purposes) of the transaction entered into is to secure an income tax advantage or capital gains tax advantage (both terms being defined within ITA 2007 s 809S).
- by reason of the arrangement, the mixed fund contains:

- one or more of the kinds of income or capital subject to a foreign tax (that is income or gains falling within one of the ITA 2007 s 809Q(4)(f)–(h) categories);

- income or capital that is classified as falling within the ITA 2007 s 809Q(4)(i) residual category. This means funds where there would be no tax liability on remittance as, for example, the funds represent or derive from: (1) clean capital, (2) income or capital not subject to UK tax or (3) income – other than UK source employment income – or capital that has already suffered UK tax or is subject to UK tax on the arising basis.

Where the anti-avoidance provision applies, the statutory matching rules are disregarded and the relevant mixed fund is treated as containing so much of the income or capital as is 'just and reasonable' (ITA 2007 s 809S(2)). It is not clear what would constitute just and reasonable in these circumstances.

HMRC states the following at RDRM35480:

*"The practical effect of this provision is that any such arrangement is ignored so that a 'mixed fund' is regarded as containing the same amounts of foreign income and chargeable gains that would have been present if the arrangements had not been made. This is subject to a 'just and reasonable' test in s809S(2)."*

The following is an example of a situation where HMRC said in 2008 that the ITA 2007 s 809S would apply:

*"A non-domiciled individual could obtain a loan at the beginning of the tax year, put the loan capital into a mixed fund and then remit sums up to the amount of the loan before repaying it. Under the ordering rules, the remittance would be capital for the year, and the anti-avoidance rule would prevent that manipulation of the mixed fund."*

At the time of writing the RDRM provides very little detail on how HMRC will seek to apply ITA 2007 s 809S. At RDRM35480 it merely states that:

*"A full report should be made to Specialist Personal Tax, PTI Advisory, Foreign Income and Remittance Basis Team for any cases where ITA07/s809S may be applicable, or where representations are made by a taxpayer that refer to the 'just and reasonable' provisions in s809S(2)."*

*Problems with the anti-avoidance rule*

(13) It is assumed that ITA 2007 s 809S is intended to apply in circumstances where there is an arrangement which increases, as a proportion, the amounts of income or capital within the specified sub-paragraphs of ITA 2007 s 809Q(4) contained in a particular mixed fund. As explained above, these paragraphs cover all of the remittance basis income and gains that have been subject to foreign tax, together with any income or capital which would not be taxable if remitted.

The anti-avoidance rule is not well drafted. On a literal reading it could be interpreted as only being able to apply to re-classify remittances from the transferee account. This is because any arrangement entered into could only result in the transferee account containing one or more of the specified kinds of income or capital (the transferor account might be cleansed by the transaction but it will not contain income or capital as a result of it). If this is the case, given that the rules with respect to offshore transfers contain an anti-avoidance element (as the pro-rata basis will not apply if that is a remittance in the tax year or a remittance is envisaged) it is hard to see how much impact the ITA 2007 s 809S provisions can have.

As this is explicitly an anti-avoidance provision, a Court is likely to go to some lengths to give it a useful meaning. However, whatever its precise meaning, it is clear that it can only apply to a mixed fund which, either potentially or actually, contains income or capital within paragraphs (f) to (i) of ITA 2007 s 809Q(4).

*The common law matching rules*

*When do these rules apply?*

(14) The common law matching rules apply whenever the statutory matching rules do not (see **explanatory note 7** for when the statutory matching rules apply). In brief, the common law matching rules apply in the following situations:

- whenever the categories of income and gains relate to tax year prior to 2008/09; or
- in situations where there is an ITA 2007 s 809L remittance as a result of condition C or condition D (see **Example F5: explanatory note 1**).

*Overview of the common law matching rules*

(15) The common law matching rules rest on a mixture of principles drawn from case law and generally accepted practice.

*Common law rules – taxed income has priority*

(16) Where immediately before a transfer an account contain funds which have been subject to UK tax, these funds should be deemed to be remitted in priority to anything else within the account. This assertion is supported by comments in *Duke of Roxburghe's Executors v IRC* (1936) 20 TC 711 (and accepted in *Walsh v Randall* (1940) 23 TC 55). This is supported by RDRM35320, which refers to the case of *Sterling Trust v CIR* 12 TC 868 on this point.

*Common law rules – general rule that income has priority over capital*

(17) The decision in the *Scottish Provident Institution v Allan* (1901) 4 TC 409 established the principle that where there is an account containing a mixture of income and capital and there are remittances, the remittances are deemed to be income in priority to capital (regardless of the year in which the income or capital arose). The judgment was, however, more nuanced than this general rule, with it being made clear that one looks to the substance of the transaction. On the facts, an argument that the remittance should be seen as one of capital might, in certain circumstances, be correct. This more nuanced judgment is acknowledged by HMRC at RDRM35320 and RDRM35330 where it states that although the initial supposition should be that the remittance is of income, this supposition might be overturned by a consideration of the particular facts of the case. This guidance is worth considering if you need to apply the common law matching rules in this situation.

*Common law rules – capital gains*

(18) Where a remittance is made from an account containing the proceeds of the sale of an asset at a gain, it is generally accepted that the correct treatment under the common law rules is to pro-rate the remittance between the gain and the base cost (RDRM35320). It was also generally accepted that where an amount, which was capital in nature, was deemed to be income (for example in the case of the profits on sale or redemption of a deeply discounted security) then the same principles as for capital gains should apply to the deemed income element.

*Common law rules – capital gains and pure capital*

(19) There are no cases concerned with remittances where immediately before the transfer the fund contained capital gains and pure capital. Under the common law rules, accepted practice is to treat remittances as capital gains in the proportion that total chargeable gains in the account from which remittance was effected bore to the full amount in the account (RDRM35320).

*Common law rules – offshore transfers*

(20) The *Scottish Provident* case looked specifically at remittances back to the UK. There are no cases which have looked specifically at the issues of foreign expenditure and transfers between foreign bank accounts.

One could say that, where the substance of the transaction does not suggest otherwise, a logical extension of the reasoning of their Lordships in *Scottish Provident Institution v Allan* (1901) 4 TC 409 would be to argue that where an account contains income and capital immediately before the offshore withdrawal (to fund foreign expenditure or the transfer to another foreign bank account) the expenditure should be taken to draw off the income first. However, there is an alternative school of thought which argues that one should pro-rate the contents of the originating account across the amount of the transfer.

The position is uncertain and where this is relevant to a UK filing position full disclosure should be provided on the self-assessment tax return.

*Where a fund contains pre- and post-5 April 2008 funds*

(21) Whilst the legislation is not explicit, it is accepted that where a mixed fund account contained pre-6 April and post-6 April 2008 funds and condition A in ITA 2007 809L is met, the statutory rules have priority unless and until all the post-5 April 2008 funds have been removed. The common law rules will apply from the moment there is matching to pre-6 April 2008 income and capital.

*What happens where there is a mixed funds account and a taxpayer is taxed on the arising basis in some years and the remittance basis in other tax years?*

(22) The planning opportunities will generally be greater with pre-6 April 2008 funds as a result of the FA 2008 Sch 7 para 86 transitional provisions. As such, where a fund contains both pre-6 April 2008 and post-5 April 2008 income it will often be desirable to clear out the post-5 April 2008 income. It is clear that this can be achieved by remitting an amount equal to the post-5 April 2008 funds. Where the individual has been taxed on the arising basis since 2008/09 this can be done without triggering an additional tax liability (the income and gains being subject to tax anyway). There will, unless an on-going exemption (see **Example F5 explanatory note 10**) is in point, be an additional tax charge if the individual has been a remittance basis user for one or more of the tax years that the post-5 April 2008 income in the fund arose.

Where there is an offshore transfer the tax analysis is more problematic as an offshore transfer only removes a pro-rata portion of income, gains and capital. There are two schools of thought:

- the mixed fund is the money or other property 'as a whole' meaning that an offshore transfer equal to the post-5 April 2008 funds will only carry out a portion of such income and gains;
- where a mixed fund contains pre-6 April 2008 and post-5 April 2008 funds there are two mixed funds. The statutory matching rules including the pro-rate offshore transfer rule at ITA 2007 s 809R(4) can only apply to the post-5 April 2008 funds meaning that an offshore transfer, equal to the post-5 April 2008 funds, will carry out all such funds leaving behind the pre-6 April 2008 funds.

***Practical points***

*Bank errors and mistakes*

(23) The classic case with respect to bank error is that of *Duke of Roxburghe's Executors v IRC* (1936) 20 TC 711 (the case actually concerned the Duchess of Roxburghe but was heard under the name of the Duke as independent taxation did not apply at that time). In this case the bank made the transfer to the UK from the wrong account (funds that had already been subject to UK tax should have been remitted rather than untaxed foreign income). It was held that:

- it was the legal right of the Duchess to determine from where the funds should come from; and
- the bank had acted contrary to her instructions and she should not be penalised because of its poor administration/record keeping.

In this case a confusion over the name of the account was not found to be an issue in allowing the remedy as taking the instructions as a whole (the actual source of the funds to be remitted was specified and it was also stated that the funds were those with respect to which no further tax would be due on remittance to the UK) it was felt that the meaning was sufficiently clear.

HMRC accepts that the conclusions with respect to bank errors and mistakes in the Roxburghe case are relevant where the statutory matching rules apply. In addition, provided express instructions have been given to the bank or investment manager, it appears that HMRC accepts that the principle can apply where income is incorrectly segregated but not yet remitted (see RDRM33560).

HMRC may accept that the remedy can apply in connection with investments other than bank accounts. There would have to be a failure to segregate which is contrary to express instructions (for example where there is a distributor fund with income segregation). In addition HMRC may allow a similar remedy where:

- there is an error trade; and

- the trade is taken onto the institutions own books such that the individual is in the position he or she would have been in if the error had not taken place.

Where there is an error by the bank or an investment manager the key points are that (i) an error has been made contrary to clear instructions and (ii) that the error is rectified as soon as possible, and before the taxpayer has received any benefit in consequence of the erroneous transfer. If the taxpayer has received a benefit, or if the transaction is not reversible by simple bookkeeping entries, it is likely to be much harder to convince HMRC to accept that the principle should apply.

*Interest credits to a capital account*

(24) Even though clear instructions have been given to the offshore bank to pay interest income into a special segregated 'income account' it is possible that the bank's systems may not be able to do this. It may be that the system has to credit the interest to the source account in the first instance and can only transfer the interest out to the special 'income account' as a second step.

HMRC accepts that no mixed fund has been created provided the transfer to the segregated account is clearly identifiable and happens immediately after the initial deposit (RDRM33560).

*How far to take segregation*

(25) Segregation of funds avoids tax inefficiencies and opens the door for significant planning opportunities.

The extent to which one takes segregation of income and capital will depend on the sums at stake, but where it is practical one should advise clients against having accounts with different kinds of income and capital. This might be thought less pressing where one is certain that the funds within the account will never need to be remitted. However, circumstances change and maximum flexibility to make tax efficient remittances should be retained whenever possible.

Depending on the amounts involved and how the funds will be used it might also be sensible to segregate on a tax year basis and avoid the mixed fund rules altogether.

Where it is expected that a client will be a remittance basis user in some years and an arising basis user in others, segregating not just between different kinds of income and capital but also on a tax year basis will make sense as this will ring-fence arising basis income and gains which can be remitted without any additional UK tax liability.

Where practical the following should be avoided:

- creating or adding to a mixed fund account;
- remittances to the UK from mixed fund accounts; and
- joint accounts (in particular where funding from the account derives from both individuals).

Where a remittance needs to be made from a mixed fund account one should try to avoid using the same account for foreign expenditure as this leads to a more complicated calculation when trying to determine the type of funds remitted.

# Question

## A.

Anne-Marie Non-Dom is a UK resident foreign domiciliary. She makes a remittance basis claim for 2016/17 and pays tax at the additional rate on her UK income. She is the owner of a significant residential property portfolio in Switzerland.

In the period from 17 January to 11 March 2017 she disposes of three residential properties as follows:

| *Property* | *Sterling equivalent proceeds* | *Sterling chargeable gain/(loss)* |
|---|---|---|
| | £ | £ |
| Verbier chalet | 1,500,000 | 100,000 |
| Geneva property | 2,500,000 | 500,000 |
| Zurich property | 3,000,000 | 750,000 |
| | 7,000,000 | 1,350,000 |

The properties were all acquired before she came to the UK in 2006/07, meaning that clean capital was used to purchase them.

She remits £1,500,000 to the UK on 29 March 2017. Explain:

(a) the amount of foreign chargeable gains taxed in the UK if she paid the proceeds from the sale of all three properties into one specially established bank account;

(b) if there is anything she could have done to improve her tax position.

## B.

Yelena Non-Dom is a foreign domiciliary who came to the UK on 6 April 2016 on a five year contract of employment.

Taking the following scenarios in turn explain what basis of taxation Yelena is likely to choose:

(a) for 2016/17 Yelena had £90,000 of UK employment income and relevant foreign income of £3,200 (all unremitted). She has a share portfolio and realised gains of £23,000 with respect to UK securities and losses of £28,000 on foreign securities;

(b) for 2016/17 Yelena had £1.5 million of foreign income (no foreign tax suffered) and £275,000 of UK income. She did not dispose of any chargeable assets and made no remittances in the tax year;

(c) for 2016/17 Yelena had foreign income of £750,000 and realised foreign losses of £50,000. She has no UK income arising in 2016/17. During the tax year she lived off of her clean capital and made no remittances of foreign income or gains;

(d) for 2016/17 Yelena had foreign income of £7,000 of which £5,500 was remitted to the UK. She did not realise any foreign gains during the year but disposed of foreign chargeable assets realising losses of £100,000. She had UK chargeable gains of £75,000.

When answering consider whether Yelena does not qualify for standard capital loss relief in the year and, therefore, has a choice between the default position of doing nothing (thereby forfeiting entitlement to foreign capital loss relief) and making the TCGA 1992 s 16ZA(2) election (thereby opting into the alternative loss relief regime as per TCGA 1992 ss 16ZB–16ZD).

C.

Lucille Non-Dom is a UK resident foreign domiciliary. She has significant UK income and pays tax in 2016/17 at the additional income tax rate. She came to the UK in 2013/14 and made remittance basis claims for the tax years from 2013/14 to 2015/16. She made a TCGA 1992 s 16ZA capital losses election.

(a) In 2013/14 Lucille disposed of foreign securities realising gains of £300,000; she has not remitted these disposal proceeds. In 2014/15 she disposed of foreign securities incurring losses on all disposals, with her aggregate losses for the year totalling £55,000. She made no chargeable gains in 2015/16 so the £55,000 capital loss is carried forward to 2016/17.

In 2016/17 Lucille disposed of various securities with the following results:

- UK chargeable gains of £75,000 and losses of £10,000; and
- foreign chargeable gains of £150,000 and losses of £25,000.

For 2016/17 she is taxed on the arising basis on foreign income and gains and does not remit prior year remittance basis chargeable gains. What is her UK capital gains tax position?

(b) In 2013/14 Lucille disposed of foreign securities realising gains of £300,000. She made no remittances until tax year 2016/17 (see below). In 2014/15 she disposed of foreign securities incurring losses on all disposals with her aggregate losses for the year totalling £195,000. She made no chargeable gains in 2015/16 so the £195,000 loss is carried forward to 2016/17.

In 2016/17 Lucille disposed of various securities with the following results:

- UK chargeable gains of £75,000 and losses of £10,000; and
- foreign chargeable gains of £150,000 and losses of £25,000.

For 2016/17 she is taxed on the arising basis on foreign income and gains and she remits £100,000 of prior year (2013/14) remittance basis chargeable gains on 27 February 2017. What is her UK capital gains tax position?

(c) In 2013/14 Lucille disposed of foreign securities realising gains of £300,000 that she has yet to remit. In 2014/15 she disposed of foreign securities incurring losses on all disposals with aggregate losses for the year totalling £55,000. She made no chargeable gains in 2015/16 so the £55,000 loss is carried forward to 2016/17.

In 2016/17 Lucille disposed of various securities with the following results:

- UK chargeable gains of £75,000 and losses of £10,000; and
- foreign chargeable gains of £150,000 and losses of £25,000.

For 2016/17 she is taxed on the remittance basis and remits £10,000 of 2016/17 gains on 27 February 2017 but no prior year gains. What is her UK capital gains tax position?

(d) In 2013/14 Lucille disposed of foreign securities realising gains of £300,000. No remittances were made until 2016/17 (see below). In 2014/15 she disposed of foreign securities incurring losses on all disposals with her aggregate losses for the year totalling £55,000. She made no chargeable gains in 2015/16 so the £55,000 loss is carried forward to 2016/17.

In 2016/17 Lucille disposed of various securities with the following results:

- UK chargeable gains of £75,000 and losses of £10,000; and
- foreign chargeable gains of £150,000 and losses of £25,000.

For 2016/17 she is taxed on the remittance basis and remits £100,000 of the 2013/14 gains on 27 February 2017. What is her UK capital gains tax position?

## F7.3 UK RESIDENT FOREIGN DOMICILIARIES, CAPITAL GAINS TAX ISSUES AND FOREIGN EXCHANGE

### D.

Lulu is a UK resident foreign domiciliary who for 2016/17 is a remittance basis user paying the remittance basis charge. She is also an additional rate taxpayer by virtue of her UK income. She was also a remittance basis user in prior tax years and made the TCGA 1992 s 16ZA election on 27 January 2010 in respect of the 2008/09 tax year. In 2016/17 she realised the following gains and made the following remittances:

- £105,000 foreign chargeable gain from residential property unremitted relating to 2016/17;
- £150,000 foreign chargeable gain from shares remitted relating to 2016/17;
- £85,000 foreign chargeable gains on a painting remitted relating to 2015/16 (when she was also a remittance basis user);
- £97,000 UK gains realised on share disposals in 2016/17;
- £550,000 UK gain realised in 2016/17 with respect to which Lulu makes a valid entrepreneurs' relief claim;
- £400,000 of capital losses relating to 2016/17 disposals.

She has made no remittances from prior year remittance basis gains other than those described above. How will her £400,000 of capital losses be set off and how much UK capital gains tax will be payable?

### E.

Jasper Non-Dom is a UK resident foreign domiciliary in 2016/17 who has UK income totalling £285,000. He makes a remittance basis claim for 2016/17. He came to the UK in 2006/07. Prior to coming to the UK for the first time he had acquired a holding in Wow Ltd, a Utopian company. He paid 150,000 Utopian dollars for the holding at a time when 1 Utopian dollar was equivalent to 1.5 pounds sterling.

Jasper sold his entire holding in Wow Ltd on 21 April 2016 for 750,000 Utopian dollars. At this time 1 Utopian dollar was worth 1.4 pounds sterling. The Utopian dollar proceeds were paid into a specially opened bank account with interest being paid into a separate account.

Jasper remitted the entire 750,000 Utopian dollars to his UK account on 21 June 2016. On this date one Utopian dollar was equivalent to 1.43 pounds sterling. What are the tax consequences of the remittance?

# Answer

## A. Anne-Marie Non-Dom

For details of who can access the remittance basis, see **Example F4**. For a discussion of the meaning of remittance, see **Example F5**.

(a) The £7,000,000 within the account represents chargeable gains of £1,350,000 (relating to tax year 2016/17) and clean capital of £5,650,000 (pre 2008/09). The account is therefore a mixed fund and the matching rules in ITA 2007 s 809Q apply (see **Example F6**).

The £1,500,000 remittance is, therefore, matched first to the £1,350,000 of chargeable gains and then to £150,000 of clean capital. As Anne-Marie is an additional rate taxpayer and the gains relate to residential property, the foreign gains are subject to 28% UK capital gains tax (CGT). As she makes a claim for the remittance basis under ITA 2007 s 809B, she is not entitled to a CGT annual exemption for the tax year (ITA 2007 s 809G).

(b) Ideally she would have segregated the proceeds from each gain such that each was kept in its own specially established bank account. At a minimum, she should have segregated the proceeds from the sale of the Verbier chalet. This would have enabled her to remit the £1,500,000 from the sale of the Verbier chalet and only have chargeable gains of £100,000 accruing.

## B. Yelena Non-Dom

For a discussion of the statutory residence test, see **Example F1**.

See **explanatory note 5** for the treatment of foreign capital losses in the hands of UK resident non-domiciliaries.

Yelena's first tax year of UK residence is 2016/17, so there are no issues with respect to prior years and she will not have to pay the remittance basis charge if she makes a remittance basis claim under ITA 2007 s 809B.

(a) Yelena does not qualify for the automatic remittance basis as:

- her UK employment income means she does not qualify under ITA 2007 s 809E, as for that section to apply the individual needs to have little to no UK income (see **Example F4**); and
- her level of unremitted foreign income for the year is not less than £2,000 so she does not qualify under ITA 2007 s 809D (see **Example F4 explanatory note 7** and also **explanatory note 17** to this Example).

If Yelena wishes to be taxed on the remittance basis for 2016/17 she will have to make a claim under ITA 2007 s 809B and will forfeit her personal allowance (£11,000) and annual exemption (£11,100) (ITA 2007 s 809G). She has no foreign gains and her amount of foreign income is less than the personal allowance so making the remittance basis claim would result in her paying more tax than if she accepts being taxed on the arising basis.

Provided she accepts being taxed on the arising basis she will be entitled to standard capital loss relief meaning that the £28,000 of foreign losses can be set off against her £23,000 of UK gains. As such she will have £5,000 of foreign losses to carry forward to 2017/18.

(b) Yelena does not qualify for the automatic remittance basis as:

- her taxable level of UK income means she does not qualify under ITA 2007 s 809E; and
- her level of unremitted foreign income for the year is not less than £2,000 so she does not qualify under ITA 2007 s 809D.

If Yelena wishes to be taxed on the remittance basis she will have to make a claim under ITA 2007 s 809B and will forfeit her personal allowance and annual exemption (ITA 2007 s 809G). Her level of foreign income is such that it is clearly beneficial for her to be taxed on the remittance basis. This is even more apparent as, with her level of income, the tapering away of the personal allowance from individuals with adjusted net income in excess of £100,000 means that if taxed on the arising basis, Yelena would not be entitled to a personal allowance anyway (ITA 2007 s 35(2)). This means that the remittance basis claim only results in her losing entitlement to the CGT annual exemption (and since she did not realise any chargeable gains in the tax year this will not result in her suffering financial detriment).

If Yelena makes a remittance basis claim for 2016/17 she will satisfy the conditions in TCGA 1992 s 16ZA(1) as she is a foreign domiciliary and will have made an ITA 2007 s 809B remittance basis claim. This means that 2016/17 triggers her ability to make an election under TCGA 1992 s 16ZA. The fact that she made no chargeable disposals in the 2016/17 tax year is irrelevant.

This is an election that allows her to benefit from foreign capital losses, which as a non-domiciled remittance basis user she is unable to do without the election. However the one-off election is irrevocable and comes with strict rules as to the matching of both foreign and UK capital losses which may not be beneficial (see **explanatory note 7**).

She will have until 5 April 2021 (see **explanatory note 8**) to decide whether to make the election.

(c) Yelena qualifies for the automatic remittance basis for 2016/17 as she meets the ITA 2007 s 809E(1) requirements:

- she is UK resident and non-domiciled;
- she is not a long-term resident;
- she makes no remittance in the tax year; and
- she has no UK income.

As such she is entitled to standard capital loss relief, meaning relief for her foreign losses is on the same basis as if she had UK losses (see **explanatory notes 5–6**). No chargeable gains have accrued to her in 2016/17 so her capital losses of £50,000 will be carried forward to 2017/18.

(d) Yelena qualifies for the automatic remittance basis for 2016/17 as she meets the ITA 2007 s 809D requirements (her unremitted foreign income and gains amount is less than £2,000, see **explanatory note 17**). As such she is entitled to standard capital loss relief (see **explanatory notes 5–6**). This means that her £75,000 of UK chargeable gains are reduced to nil by her foreign losses. She has £25,000 of capital losses to carry forward to 2017/18.

## C. Lucille Non-Dom

For details of who can access the remittance basis, see **Example F4**. For a discussion of the meaning of remittance, see **Example F5**.

Lucille made the TCGA 1992 s 16ZA election (see **explanatory notes 5–7**) in respect of the first tax year in which she claimed the remittance basis under ITA 2007 s 809B, ie 2013/14.

(a) Lucille is taxed on the arising basis for 2016/17 so she is subject to UK tax on her worldwide gains and the provisions at TCGA 1992 s 16ZC do not apply. In 2016/17 she does not make any remittances which represent or derive from remittance basis foreign chargeable gains so TCGA 1992 s 16ZB does not apply.

Her CGT position is therefore as follows:

| | £ |
|---|---|
| UK chargeable gains | 75,000 |
| Foreign gains – arising basis | 150,000 |
| Total chargeable gains | 225,000 |
| Current year capital losses (£10,000 + £25,000) | (35,000) |
| Net gains of the year | 190,000 |
| B/f foreign capital losses (2014/15) | (55,000) |
| Net gains | 135,000 |
| Annual exemption | (11,100) |
| Taxable amount | 123,900 |
| | |
| UK CGT at 20% | £24,780 |

The gains are taxed at 20% as Lucille is an additional rate taxpayer who has disposed of securities.

(b) Lucille is taxed on the arising basis for 2016/17 so she is subject to UK tax on worldwide gains and the provisions at TCGA 1992 s 16ZC do not apply.

She has made the TCGA 1992 s 16ZA election so, since she remits £100,000 of remittance basis foreign chargeable gains from 2013/14, the provisions at TCGA 1992 s 16ZB apply.

As such, one has to consider her CGT position in two distinct stages:

The gains remitted from 2013/14:

- the £100,000 of foreign gains remitted must be treated in isolation without the benefit of capital losses or the annual exemption, so Lucille has UK capital gains tax to pay of £20,000 (£100,000 × 20%).

The position with respect to gains arising in 2016/17:

- in total she has £225,000 of capital gains for 2016/17, aggregate capital losses of £230,000 (current year capital losses of £35,000 and brought forward capital losses of £195,000). Her current year gains are, therefore, reduced to nil with capital losses to carry forward of £5,000.

Overall her total UK CGT liability for the year is £20,000 (relating to the gains remitted from 2013/14).

(c) Lucille is taxed on the remittance basis for 2016/17 so she is subject to UK tax on foreign gains for the year only when remittances are made and the provisions in TCGA 1992 s 16ZC apply. She makes no remittances of foreign gains arising in previous tax years, so TCGA 1992 s 16ZB does not apply.

For 2016/17 she has:

- UK chargeable gains of £75,000;
- foreign chargeable gains of £150,000 of which £10,000 is remitted and £140,000 unremitted;
- aggregate capital losses (UK and foreign) of £90,000 (£55,000 relating to 2014/15 and £35,000 being current year losses).

Her capital losses are set off in the order specified in TCGA 1992 s 16ZC(3):

| | | £ |
|---|---|---|
| (1) | Current year remitted foreign gains | 10,000 |
| | Relief for current year capital loss | (10,000) |
| | Taxable in 2016/17 | Nil |

| | | £ |
|---|---|---|
| (2) | Current year unremitted foreign gains | 140,000 |
| | Remaining current year loss (£35,000 – £10,000) | (25,000) |
| | B/f foreign capital losses (2014/15) | (55,000) |
| | Remaining 2016/17 unremitted foreign gains | 60,000 |

The foreign gains are sufficiently high to utilise all the capital losses. As the capital losses were insufficient to reduce the unremitted foreign gains down to zero, for the purposes of potential future remittances the losses are deemed to be set against foreign gains realised in the tax year in reverse chronological order (ie last-in first-out) (TCGA 1992 s 16ZC(2) Step 1(a)–(b)). Should there be insufficient losses to offset the total quantum of gains realised on the same day then losses are deducted from all the gains realised on that day proportionately (TCGA 1992 s 16ZC(2) Step 1(c)).

Since all the losses have been offset against foreign gains, Lucille will be subject to tax on the £75,000 of UK chargeable gains at 20% (as she is an additional rate taxpayer disposing of securities). The tax payable is £15,000.

(d) Lucille is taxed on the remittance basis for 2016/17 so she is subject to UK tax on foreign gains for the year only when remittances are made and the provisions in TCGA 1992 s 16ZC apply. She has remitted £100,000 of remittance basis gains relating to 2013/14 so TCGA 1992 s 16ZB also applies.

As both TCGA 1992 ss 16ZB and 16ZC both apply her CGT position has to be considered in two distinct stages:

The gains remitted from 2013/14:

- neither the current year nor the brought forward capital losses can be set against that remittance as the gain was made in an earlier tax year. Lucille, therefore, has UK capital gains tax to pay of £20.000 (£100,000 × 20%).

The position with respect to gains arising in 2016/17:

- Lucille did not remit any current year foreign chargeable gains. She has unremitted foreign chargeable gains of £150,000 and UK gains of £75,000.

  Her capital losses are set off in the order specified in TCGA 1992 s 16ZC(3):

| | £ |
|---|---|
| Current year unremitted foreign gains | 150,000 |
| Current year capital losses (UK and foreign) | (35,000) |
| B/f foreign capital losses (2013/14) | (55,000) |
| Remaining 2016/17 unremitted foreign gains | 60,000 |

  The foreign gains are sufficiently high to utilise all the capital losses. As the capital losses were insufficient to reduce the unremitted foreign gains down to zero for the purposes of potential future remittances they are deemed to be set against gains realised in the tax year in reverse chronological order (ie last-in first-out) (TCGA 1992 s 16ZC(2) Step 1(a)–(b)). Should there be insufficient losses to offset the total quantum of gains realised on the same day then losses are deducted from all the gains realised on that day proportionately (TCGA 1992 s 16ZC(2) Step 1(c)).

  Since all the losses have been offset against foreign gains Lucille will have to pay UK CGT of £15,000 (£75,000 × 20%) on the £75,000 of UK chargeable gains realised in the tax year.

In total, therefore, Lucille has a UK CGT liability for 2016/17 of £35,000 which breaks down as £20,000 on the remittance of £100,000 of prior year remittance basis capital gains and £15,000 of tax payable on the UK chargeable gains realised in the tax year.

## D. Lulu Non-Dom

For details of who can access the remittance basis, see **Example F4**. For a discussion of the meaning of remittance, see **Example F5**.

Lulu is a remittance basis user who has made the TCGA 1992 s 16ZA election (see **explanatory note 7**).

For 2016/17 she has:

- UK chargeable gains of £550,000 subject to the 10% rate where a valid entrepreneurs' relief claim has been made;
- UK chargeable gains on the disposal of shares of £97,000;
- foreign chargeable gains of £255,000 (£105,000 from residential property and £150,000 from shares) of which the share gains of £150,000 have been remitted and residential property gain of £105,000 is unremitted;
- aggregate capital losses (UK and foreign) of £400,000 all relating to current year losses

In the tax year she also remitted £85,000 of foreign chargeable gains on a painting relating to 2015/16 (when she was also a remittance basis user).

The current year capital gains and losses must be dealt with separately to the remitted gains from the prior tax year. This is because different rules apply under the legislation.

The current year capital losses cannot be set against the £85,000 of prior year remittance basis gains remitted in 2016/17 (TCGA 1992 s 16ZB). The UK CGT due on these gains is £17,000 (£85,000 × 20%).

The £400,000 of current losses is set off against current year gains as follows (TCGA 1992 s 16ZC):

| | | | *Loss* |
|---|---|---|---|
| | | £ | £ |
| (1) | Current year remitted foreign gains | 150,000 | 400,000 |
| | Relief for capital losses | (150,000) | (150,000) |
| | Taxable in 2016/17 | Nil | 250,000 |
| | | £ | |
| (2) | Current year unremitted foreign gains | 105,000 | |
| | Relief for capital losses | (105,000) | (105,000) |
| | Remaining 2016/17 unremitted foreign gains | Nil | 145,000 |
| | | £ | |
| (3) | UK share portfolio gains | 97,000 | |
| | Relief for capital losses | (97,000) | (97,000) |
| | Chargeable gains for 2016/17 | Nil | 48,000 |
| | | £ | |
| (4) | UK gain qualifying for entrepreneurs' relief | 550,000 | |
| | Relief for remaining capital losses | (48,000) | (48,000) |
| | Chargeable gains for 2016/17 | 502,000 | Nil |

The ordering rules at TCGA 1992 s 16ZC are first applied such that losses are offset against foreign gains (remitted and unremitted) in priority to UK gains. Since there are no provisions in TCGA 1992 s 16ZC specifying which UK gains the loss should go against, in line with TCGA 1992 s 4B, Lulu can choose to set the remaining losses off against the non-entrepreneurs' relief gains (taxable at 28% and 20%) in priority to the qualifying entrepreneurs' relief gain (taxable at 10%).

The total UK CGT payable for 2016/17 is £67,200, which breaks down as £23,800 (£85,000 × 20%, see above) plus £50,200 (£502,000 × 10%) due as a result of UK gains qualifying for entrepreneurs' relief. For more on entrepreneurs' relief, see **Example 15**.

## E. Jasper Non-Dom

See **explanatory note 12**.

The 750,000 of Utopian dollars that Jasper remitted on 21 June 2016 represents 2016/17 foreign chargeable gains (the gain on the shares) and pre-6 April 2008 clean capital.

The foreign chargeable gain on the disposal of the Wow Ltd shares is:

| | *Utopian $* | *Exchange rate: Ut$ to £* | *£* |
|---|---|---|---|
| Proceeds | 750,000 | 1:1.4 | 1,050,000 |
| Base cost | (150,000) | 1:1.5 | (225,000) |
| Chargeable gain | 600,000 | | 825,000 |

The amount remitted on 21 June 2016 equated to £1,072,500 (the exchange rate being Ut$1: £1.43). Jasper was, therefore, fortunate that in the period between the funds being paid into his Utopian account and being remitted to the UK the sterling value of the currency increased.

Also, luckily for Jasper, from 6 April 2012 foreign currency within bank accounts is not a chargeable asset for individuals, trustees and personal representatives so Jasper is not taxed on the gain. Equally if there has been a foreign currency loss he would not be entitled to any relief and would still have to pay tax on the entire £825,000 gain.

The transfer to Jasper's UK bank account results in foreign chargeable gains of £825,000 being remitted (the balance of £247,500 brought to the UK being clean capital or exempt foreign currency gain). The foreign gain is taxed in the UK at 20% since Jasper is an additional rate taxpayer and the asset subject to disposal is foreign shares.

# Explanatory Notes

*Foreign chargeable gains: remittance rules*

(1) In contrast to the situation where capital is invested and a straight-forward income return is received, it is not possible on the sale of an asset to split the capital appreciation element from the original cost for tax purposes. This means that (unless a loss is made) the proceeds received on the sale of an investment are automatically a mixed fund regardless of where the funds to acquire the asset derived from. The mixed fund rules are explained in **Example F6**.

Under the ITA 2007 s 809Q statutory matching rules, where an investment acquired from clean capital is subject to disposal such that a gain is realised and then the proceeds are remitted to the UK, the foreign chargeable gain is deemed to be remitted *before* the clean capital. The rules make it all the more important to segregate out different capital proceeds where the sums are significant and it is possible to isolate significant proceeds where the acquisition was entirely or mostly funded from clean capital and the gain element is low. This issue is illustrated in **part A** of this example.

*UK CGT reporting requirements*

(2) Normally an individual does not need to report chargeable disposals on his self-assessment tax return where (i) the aggregate gains are less than the CGT annual exempt amount; and (ii) the aggregate proceeds are less than four times the CGT annual exempt amount (TCGA 1992 s 3A). However, these statutory reporting requirement relaxations do not apply where (TCGA 1992 s 3A(5A)):

- in the relevant tax year the individual has made a claim to be taxed on the remittance basis (as opposed to meeting the conditions such that they are automatically entitled to be a remittance basis user, see **Example F4 explanatory notes 5–8**); or
- the individual is not a remittance basis user in the relevant tax year but the following conditions are met:
  - the one-off irrevocable foreign losses election has been made under TCGA 1992 s 16ZA (see **explanatory note 7**);
  - in the period starting from the relevant tax year with respect to which the need for the loss election was triggered and ending in the preceding tax year the individual has realised foreign chargeable gains which have been sheltered by the remittance basis; and
  - the individual is deemed to have remitted prior year remittance basis foreign chargeable gains in the tax year.

Where either of the above applies *all* UK chargeable disposals and all remitted foreign gains must be disclosed on the tax return.

Where a remittance basis claim is made and no foreign chargeable gains have been remitted there may still be additional compliance issues as a result of the reporting relaxation not applying. This is because it will be necessary to disclose details of all UK chargeable disposals (if there are any).

*CGT rates*

(3) For 2016/17 the following UK CGT rates apply:

- trustees and personal representatives are subject to tax at a fixed rates of 28% or 20% depending on the nature of the asset subject to disposal;
- individuals are subject to 28% or 20% rates of CGT on gains, with potential 10% or 18% rates applying to all or part of the gains where the individual does not pay tax on any income at the higher rate or dividend upper rate (that is the 10% or 18% rates are only available to the extent that an individual has unutilised basic rate band);
- 10% on gains qualifying for entrepreneurs' relief (which applies to trustees and individuals) or investors' relief (which applies to individuals only)

The rates of 28% or 20% and 18% or 10% depend on the nature of the underlying asset. Gains resulting from the disposal of residential property (both by UK residents on worldwide residential properties and non-UK residents on UK residential property) and carried interest are taxed at 28% (or 18% in the case of individuals to the extent the gains fit within the unutilised basic rate band). Gains on all other assets are taxed at 20% (or 10% if the taxpayer is an individual and to the extent that the gain fits within the unutilised nil rate band).

Where gains are subject to CGT at different rates the allowable capital losses may be deducted from those gains in the most beneficial manner for the taxpayer (TCGA 1992 s 4B). This provision is subject to any other provisions in the CGT legislation which restrict the use of losses such as the losses order of set off for a remittance basis user who has made the TCGA 1992 s 16ZA capital loss election (see **explanatory note 7**).

*Foreign chargeable gains accruing on a disposal made other than for full consideration*

(4) Prior to 6 April 2008 when an individual taxed on the remittance basis gifted foreign situs assets to another person and did not receive any disposal proceeds he might still have been deemed to have realised a gain (ie the difference between the market value at the date of the transfer and the cost of the asset) on the disposal (TCGA 1992 s 17).

However, as that gain was not represented by any money or money's worth in the hands of the individual making the gift, it was not possible for the individual to remit the gain. This meant that the gain arising on making the gift could never become assessable (RDRM36260).

The law changed with effect from 6 April 2008. Where such disposals occur on of after that date, the gain arising on foreign situs assets by a remittance basis user will become taxable should the asset, proceeds from the sale of the asset or funds derived from proceeds from the sale of the asset, be remitted to the UK for the benefit of the individual who made the gift, or any other relevant person in connection with the individual (ITA 2007 s 809T). Relevant person is defined at ITA 2007 s 809M and discussed in **Example F4 explanatory note 4**.

*UK resident foreign domiciliaries: treatment of capital losses*

(5) Prior to 6 April 2008 the remittance basis of taxation for foreign capital gains was automatic. This meant that a gain on a foreign situs asset was only taxable on a UK resident foreign domiciliary if the proceeds were remitted to the UK. The legislation contained a blanket provision disallowing capital losses accruing to foreign domiciliaries on the disposal of foreign situs assets (RDRM31340).

Although the rules on foreign capital losses of remittance basis users changed from 6 April 2008 (see below), the above rules still apply in relation to disposals which occurred prior to 6 April 2008. This means that there is still no question of being able to claim relief for foreign losses where the disposal occurred prior to 6 April 2008. This blanket disallowance of foreign losses with respect to pre-6 April 2008 disposals applies regardless of when the remittance of the proceeds occurs or what basis of taxation applies during the year that such a remittance takes place.

The post-5 April 2008 regime is complex. It is possible for a remittance basis user to obtain relief for foreign capital losses by making a one-off irrevocable election but the rules are very strict and the effect may not always be beneficial to the individual (see **explanatory note** 7).

The determinative factor is whether or not for tax years from 2008/09 onwards the individual has made a remittance basis claim (TCGA 1992 s 16ZA(1)). The ability to make the foreign loss election is triggered by the *first time* a claim is made under ITA 2007 s 809B and, if the loss election is to be made, it must be made in relation to that tax year. The choices available to the individual are:

- do nothing, which includes failing to make the election by the deadline, see **explanatory note** 8 (in which case the default rules apply, see **explanatory note 6**); or
- to make the 'one off' irrevocable election into an alternative capital loss relief regime (TCGA 1992 s 16ZA, see **explanatory note** 7).

It is important to remember that the issue is not whether the individual is a remittance basis user in the tax years considered but *whether he made a claim* to access the remittance basis. This is an important distinction as it means that where an individual meets the conditions in ITA 2007 ss 809D or 809E, such that he is automatically entitled to the remittance basis, it is not necessary for him to opt to be taxed on the arising basis in order to preserve his entitlement to standard capital loss relief on UK and foreign capital losses (RDRM31170).

Note that it is the mere making of the remittance basis claim under ITA 2007 s 809B which is the trigger event for the decision on the foreign loss election regardless of whether or not the individual has made capital disposals in the tax year (TCGA 1992 s 16ZA(1)).

Making the irrevocable election may mean that, during the course of an HMRC enquiry, significant disclosure (which otherwise would not have been required) has to be made with respect to unremitted chargeable gains.

*No election – the default rules*

(6) If, for 2008/09 or a subsequent tax year, a remittance basis claim is made and the one off election is not made, the default rules apply. These rules are the same as those which applied to UK resident foreign domiciliaries prior to 6 April 2008. In summary for as long as the individual remains foreign domiciled:

- standard relief is available for UK capital losses; and
- all foreign capital losses are disallowed.

The disallowance of foreign losses is a blanket provision applying to all foreign losses; the basis of taxation applying in the tax year being considered is irrelevant. So the individual will not be entitled to relief on foreign capital losses whilst he or she remains foreign domiciled even if the individual is taxed on the arising basis in a later year (TCGA 1992 s 16ZA(3); CG25330A).

Should the individual acquire a UK domicile (meaning he can no longer access the remittance basis with respect to foreign income or foreign chargeable gains), his capital loss relief treatment will change. With effect from the tax year during which the change in domicile status takes place, an individual who did not make the election will be entitled to the standard form of capital loss relief with respect to both UK and foreign situs assets for that and subsequent tax years. However, there would be no relief with respect to capital losses relating to prior remittance basis years where the disposal proceeds are remitted after the change in domicile status. This means that:

- remittance basis gains remitted when the individual has become UK domiciled will be taxable; but
- there will be no relief for foreign capital losses realised in the period from the start of the trigger year to the end of the last tax year in which the individual was foreign domiciled.

*What happens if the election is made?*

(7) Where the individual wishes to receive relief for foreign capital losses a one-off irrevocable election must be made under TCGA 1992 s 16ZA(2). By making the election the individual irrevocably opts for the TCGA 1992 s 16ZA(1) trigger year (that is the first tax year from 2008/09 onwards for which a remittance basis claim is made) and all subsequent tax years to receive a modified form of capital loss relief in respect of both UK and foreign capital losses.

As stated in **explanatory note 5**, in effect this means that an alternative capital loss regime applies to individuals who make the election. Making the election impacts on the benefit the individual receives from both UK and foreign capital losses.

The alternative regime applies to *all* capital losses realised in the trigger year and subsequent years. Any losses brought forward at the start of the TCGA 1992 s 16ZA(1) trigger year are unaffected and relievable in accordance with the standard provisions (see **Example L4**).

Where the election is made, the capital loss relief available for losses in the trigger year and subsequent years is complex. The rules are different depending on whether the individual is taxed on the arising or remittance basis in the year.

In brief where the individual who has made an election is subject to tax on the *arising basis* in the tax year (TCGA 1992 s 16ZB):

- the CGT annual exemption is set against current year gains (UK and foreign) accruing in the tax year and any remittance basis gains accruing which relate to tax years prior to the TCGA 1992 s 16ZA(1) trigger year;
- all losses (current year and brought forward) can be set against current year gains (UK and foreign) accruing in the tax year and any remittance basis gains accruing which relate to tax years prior to the TCGA 1992 s 16ZA(1) trigger year;
- remittance basis foreign gains accruing in or after the trigger year *cannot* be reduced by either the CGT annual exemption or losses. This means that the entire remitted amount is subject to CGT at the tax rate applicable to the individual;
- unutilised losses are carried forward to be used in future tax years to offset *current year* capital gains accruing.

See **parts C(a)–(b)** and **D** of this Example.

Broadly, where the individual who has made an election is subject to tax on the *remittance basis* for the tax year (TCGA 1992 s 16ZC):

- the CGT annual exemption is not available if a remittance basis claim is made (ITA 2007 s 809G). If the individual is automatically entitled to the remittance basis such that the CGT annual exemption is available this *cannot* be set off against foreign chargeable gains accruing in the TCGA 1992 s 16ZA(1) trigger year or subsequent years prior to the current tax year.

- all losses (current year and brought forward) are set against *current year* gains in the following order:

  - remitted foreign chargeable gains;

  - unremitted foreign chargeable gains;

  - UK gains.

See **parts C(a)–(b)** and **D** of this Example.

Where losses are deducted from unremitted foreign chargeable gains but the quantum of the losses is insufficient to exhaust the gains, the losses are set off against the gains accruing in the tax year in reverse chronological order (that is starting from the last foreign chargeable gains to accrue and working backwards). Where the quantum of losses is insufficient to exhaust gains accruing on the same day the available losses are set against all the gains on the same day proportionately (TCGA 1992 s 16ZC(2)).

Segregation of proceeds from the various sales in the tax year may mean that proceeds from later sales can be remitted in a subsequent year free from tax as the gains are covered by the losses. Losses *can never* be offset against remittance basis foreign gains where the disposal took place in an earlier tax year (ie earlier years' gains remitted in the year of a loss cannot benefit from that current year loss). This is because losses cannot be carried back (which is effectively what would happen if relief was allowed against earlier years' unremitted gains) (CG25330B).

Unutilised losses are carried forward to be used in future years against *current year* capital gains accruing.

*The deadline for making the election*

(8) The deadline for making the claim is the standard deadline set down in TMA 1970 s 43. This is four years from the end of the tax year in which the first remittance basis claim (for a tax year from 2008/09 onwards) is made. Therefore the following deadlines apply:

| *Tax year of first remittance basis claim (trigger year)* | *Deadline for making the election and claiming relief for the foreign losses for the trigger tax year* |
|---|---|
| 2008/09 | 5 April 2013 (deadline passed) |
| 2009/10 | 5 April 2014 (deadline passed) |
| 2010/11 | 5 April 2015 (deadline passed) |
| 2011/12 | 5 April 2016 (deadline passed) |
| 2012/13 | **5 April 2017 (next deadline date)** |
| 2013/14 | 5 April 2018 |
| 2014/15 | 5 April 2019 |
| 2015/16 | 5 April 2020 |
| 2016/17 | 5 April 2021 |

*How the election is made*

(9) There is no standard form to make the election. An election can be made by an appropriate white space note on the self-assessment tax return for the year in which the first remittance basis claim (for tax years from 2008/09 onwards) is made. Where the taxpayer has to complete capital gains tax supplementary pages, the capital loss election should be included in the white space supplementary information box on these pages.

Where capital gains tax supplementary pages are not required, the capital loss election should be made in the white space additional information box on the main return.

It may be that the decision to make the election is not made until after the tax return for the trigger year has been submitted and possibly even until after the amendment window has closed. In such cases a stand-alone election can be made before the deadline expires. Where it is decided to delay until closer to the deadline, any tax returns submitted in the meantime would need to be on the basis of the default rules, these being that UK capital loss relief is available as normal and all foreign capital losses are disallowed.

Where the self-assessment amendment window is closed you will need to submit a revised capital gains tax calculation for that year if:

- a valid election were made after the submission of the tax returns; and
- the alternative loss regime would result in the losses claimed on the tax returns submitted having to be set off in a different manner to the default regime rules used when preparing the returns.

Since the tax return cannot be amended this would have to be done by way of a letter to the taxpayer's tax office and if additional tax is due as a result it will be necessary for HMRC to raise an assessment.

*Should the election be made?*

(10) Advice as to whether a client should make the election has to be based on a detailed understanding of the client's circumstances past (as far back as 2008/09), present and future. For some clients (such as those who do not and never will own UK assets directly), making the election will be the appropriate choice, while for others (such as those with material UK chargeable assets held directly), it could be highly disadvantageous.

Given the magnitude of the decision, it may in some cases make sense to hold off until closer to the deadline so as to better assess actual information and changes in the asset portfolio and intentions of the individual.

As **explanatory note 8** makes clear, where 2012/13 was the trigger year the deadline for making the election (if it has not already been made) is 5 April 2017. It is important that an informed decision is made rather than by default doing nothing. Using the 2015/16 tax return preparation cycle as a chance to raise the issue with relevant clients is advisable.

*Foreign currency issues*

(11) It is a basic rule that in order to calculate the tax payable in the country of assessment, taxable income and gains must be expressed in the currency of the country. This means that for UK purposes gains must be in sterling and income received in foreign currency must be converted into sterling. The CGT details are covered in **explanatory notes 12–13** and **16**. The income tax issues are outlined in **explanatory notes 14–16**.

*Capital gains must be converted in sterling*

(12) Capital gains must be computed in sterling. As such, where foreign assets are involved the sales proceeds, costs of acquisition, enhancement costs and any incidental expenses must be translated into sterling at the exchange rate prevailing on the appropriate date. Under *Bentley v Pike* [1981] STC 360 the appropriate date for conversion into sterling is the date the expenditure was incurred or the proceeds received (RDRM31190).

This rule will also apply where there is a disposal of units in a non-reporting fund and an offshore income gain is calculated and, in HMRC's view, when calculating the profit on the disposal of a deeply discounted security.

The GOV.UK website (accessible at https://www.gov.uk/government/collections/exchange-rates-for-customs-and-vat) gives average exchange rates for tax years and spot rates on 31 December and 31 March of each year for certain foreign currencies (this information is based on figures published in the Financial Times). As such, using the appropriate Financial Times exchange rates would seem certain to be acceptable. The Bank of England also publishes daily exchange rates on its website. It is, however, thought that HMRC will accept tax return figures in all cases where the source used is reputable and it is reasonable to use that exchange rate for the particular transaction (RDRM31190). There should be consistency in the rates applied and disclosure is recommended.

*Foreign currency within a bank account*

(13) From 6 April 2012, foreign (non-sterling) currency within bank accounts (including joint accounts) is not a chargeable asset for capital gains tax for individuals, trustees and personal representatives (TCGA 1992 s 252). This is the case regardless of the domicile status of the bank account holders. The corollary to gains not being chargeable is that there is no relief for losses.

It should be stressed that the exemption applies only to foreign currency bank accounts, and does not:

- cover investment in structured cash products such as money market funds;
- prevent foreign exchange gains from being indirectly subject to tax where an asset is sold. For example, a property bought for €250,000 (when that was worth £125,000) and sold for €250,000 (when that is worth £150,000) will still result in a taxable gain of £25,000.

The exemption only applies for disposals effected on or after 6 April 2012. Disposals prior to that date are not re-characterised. Therefore if pre-6 April 2012 foreign currency chargeable gains were sheltered by the remittance basis there will still be a CGT liability if these gains are remitted after 5 April 2012.

When considering transactions in tax years prior to 2012/13, the version of this question in **Taxwise I 2011/12** should be consulted for a detailed discussion of the position prior to 6 April 2012 when for individuals, trustees and personal representatives foreign currency within bank accounts was chargeable (apart from a narrow personal use exemption).

*Foreign income received in a foreign currency*

(14) For income tax purposes, foreign domiciliaries who are taxed on the arising basis will be subject to tax on foreign income arising in the tax year in the same way as any other UK taxpayer. The foreign exchange rate used will be that applying on the date the income arises or the average rate for the year where the income arises frequently throughout the year (eg dividend and interest income). HMRC has confirmed that although the narrative and text in the RDRM31190 only refers to the foreign exchange rate on the date that the income arises, this should not be construed to mean HMRC will no longer accept the use of the average rate where appropriate.

For a number of foreign currencies HMRC publishes average exchange rates for tax years at https://www.gov.uk/government/collections/exchange-rates-for-customs-and-vat and it is suggested that where an average rate is required the HMRC average rate for the year is used.

*Exchange rates and the remittance basis*

(15) HMRC's settled view is that where foreign income is remitted which was received originally in a currency other than sterling, the sterling amount is determined by using the exchange rate on the date of remittance for the currency in which the income was originally received (RDRM31190).

The alternative view is that the conversion methodology is the same for arising and remittance basis taxpayers. For a remittance basis user, this means that where foreign income is received in a currency other than sterling the exchange rate to use to determine the sterling amount is the rate on the date the income arises (or, where reasonable, the average for the tax year in which the income arises).

As there is no consensus between the profession and HMRC on this point, practitioners will have to take a view and ensure that they have made full disclosure.

*Exchange rate to use for the conversion to sterling of a foreign tax credit*

(16) HMRC's view is that, for the purposes of calculating foreign tax relief, foreign tax paid is converted into sterling at the date the foreign tax is payable (INTM162620). This is in line with the principle from *Greig v Ashton* (1956) 36 TC 581.

*Exchange rate and the threshold for automatic remittance basis*

(17) To qualify for the automatic remittance basis under ITA 2007 s 809D, aggregate unremitted foreign income and gains must be less than £2,000 (see **Example F4 explanatory note 7**). Where foreign income is received in a currency other than sterling there must be a method by which one calculates the unremitted foreign income.

HMRC's normal position on the foreign income of remittance basis users is that the exchange rate at the date of remittance must be used, but this is obviously unsuitable for deciding the sterling amount of unremitted income. Instead the balance of unremitted foreign income is converted to sterling at the exchange rate on the final day of the tax year (RDRM31190). For unremitted gains the normal rules discussed in **explanatory note 12** apply (ie the exchange rates on the dates the expenditure was incurred and proceeds received are used). RDRM31190 goes on to provide an example calculation.

If the unremitted foreign income is later remitted to the UK, this is converted to sterling at the rate of exchange at the date of remittance (RDRM31190). The calculation for the purposes of ITA 2007 s 809D does not fix the sterling amount of that income.

It will be appreciated that supporters of the alternative view with respect to the conversion of remittance basis foreign income received in a currency other than sterling will not agree with the approach explained at RDRM31190. If you believe that the better view is that, where foreign income is received in a currency other than sterling, the exchange rate to use is that on the date the income arises (or, where reasonable, the average for the tax year in which the income arises) it naturally follows that for a ITA 2007 s 809D computation you would use the same methodology. Given there is no agreement on this issue, where it makes a difference, practitioners should take a view and make full disclosure on the self-assessment return.

# Tax administration

# Question

Mr and Mrs Norton, who are resident and domiciled in the United Kingdom, have previously dealt with their own tax affairs. In May 2016 they instructed you to prepare their income tax returns, and compute all tax liabilities, for the year ended 5 April 2016.

You have not received any documents from them other than notice to make a return for 2015/16 but at your initial meeting you were informed that their personal circumstances were as follows:

(1) They are married and Mrs Norton has one child, James, from a previous marriage. Mr Norton was born on 11 May 1972 and Mrs Norton on 5 October 1975. James was born on 7 June 2005.

(2) Mr Norton is the overseas purchasing manager of Rumwell plc, a London department store, and receives gross remuneration of approximately £45,000 per annum. A car is provided by his employer.

(3) He has a bank deposit account.

(4) He pays an annual subscription to his professional association and gift aid payments to his local church.

(5) The couple have a mortgage of £80,000 on their private house in London, which is currently valued at £875,000.

(6) Mrs Norton is a director (working part time only) of Priddy Ltd, undertakers. She receives gross remuneration of between £2,500 and £10,000 per annum, depending upon results, and receives mileage allowance for use of her own car. As this is her family company, she also receives a dividend on her shareholding based upon the tax planning requirements of the company.

(7) She has stock exchange investments and building society deposits.

(8) She paid a premium under a personal pension plan in the year ended 5 April 2016.

(i) Prepare schedules to be sent to Mr and Mrs Norton listing documents and information that you will require for completion of their tax returns and computation of tax liabilities for the year ended 5 April 2016.

(ii) It is your office policy to undertake a review of the file of each personal taxation client before the end of each tax year. Explain why this is advisable and outline the matters which you would include in your review in February 2017. Is there any matter (other than the tax return) which needs to be dealt with before February?

# Answer

## (i) Schedules to be sent to Mr and Mrs Norton listing documents and information required to complete tax returns and to compute liabilities for year to 5 April 2016

*Schedule to be sent to Mr Norton*

### 1. Earnings

(a) The following are required from Mr Norton in respect of his job at Rumwell plc for 2015/16:

- P60 year-end certificate of pay and tax deducted;
- Coding notices issued for 2015/16 (and also coding notice for 2016/17) (Form P2), together with details of any underpayments brought forward from 2013/14 or 2014/15 to 2015/16, or amounts carried forward to 2016/17 in respect of 2015/16. These amounts may be shown on forms P800 if issued for the relevant years;
- Form P11D (details of benefits and expenses received), together with any additional schedules provided by the employer;
- Details of expenses incurred in performance of duties of the employment which were either not reimbursed by the employer or not covered by a dispensation and so included on his P11D;
- Details of share options and incentives, with particulars of any options exercised during 2015/16;
- Details of any amounts received, other than from Rumwell plc in respect of the employment;
- Confirmation of whether Mr Norton is a member of Rumwell's pension scheme, whether the scheme is an occupational scheme or a group personal pension scheme, together with details of his contributions for the year.

(b) Confirmation that there are no earnings from other sources. If there are any such earnings, details required of amount, source and date of payment. If employment changed in the year, Form P45 (part 1A) is required.

(c) National insurance number (should be shown on P60).

### 2. Bank deposit account

Details of the interest credited during the year to 5 April 2016, including name of deposit taker and account number. Confirmation that the account is a UK based account and that interest for the year was paid after deduction of basic rate tax. Tax vouchers for amount of tax deducted on such interest.

Details of any compensation payments for mis-selling.

### 3. Professional subscription

Amount and date paid and name of professional association.

## 4. Details of gift aid payments

Amounts paid to church in the tax year with confirmation that he has signed a gift aid declaration.

Details of any other charitable gifts made under gift aid during the year ended 5 April 2016 (name of charity, date and amount). Could include entry to museums or other attractions where gift aid may apply.

Details of any gift aid payments made since 5 April 2016, so that consideration may be given to a claim to carry such payments back to 2015/16.

## 5. Information for tax credits

Confirmation whether a claim was made for child tax credits in 2015/16.

Mr and Mrs Norton probably not entitled to child tax credits for 2015/16 and 2016/17 due to level of income. Check to ensure no other factors (income disregard, large gift aid/pension premiums, etc) enabled a claim to be made for 2015/16. Consider if James's father could make any child's tax credit claim in respect of James.

## 6. Information about child benefit

If Mr Norton's income exceeded £50,000, information on child benefit received by Mrs Norton is needed (see below).

Confirm Mr and Mrs Norton were not separated during the tax year (if they were, no charge may apply to Mr Norton).

## 7. Other income and outgoings, and capital transactions

Details of any other income and outgoings, or changes therein, and capital assets acquired or subject to disposal. Details of capital assets acquired are not required for the tax return, but are essential for the adviser's file. Details of any capital gains tax losses brought forward reported on earlier years' tax returns.

Confirm that no investments in James's name were provided by Mr Norton, otherwise full details needed to determine if treated as Mr Norton's taxable income.

## 8. 2014/15 tax calculation working sheet

Copies of the 2014/15 self-assessment tax return and calculation of the tax liability for the year (ie the working sheet for 2014/15 or HMRC's calculation of liability).

## 9. Statements of account

Copies of statements of account since April 2014, and details of any claim to reduce payments on account (form SA303).

## 10. Form 64-8

Signed form 64-8 giving authority to HMRC to issue copies of formal notices to you (as his agent) and to discuss all taxation, national insurance and tax credit issues. Online registration as agent for the clients is an alternative, but best practice indicates that a signed 64-8 should be retained on file.

## 11. Electronic filing

If not covered in engagement letter, confirmation that electronic filing of the return is acceptable.

*Schedule to be sent to Mrs Norton*

## 1. Earnings

The following are required from Mrs Norton in respect of her job at Priddy Ltd for 2015/16:

- P60 from Priddy Ltd for 2015/16, together with coding notices issued for 2015/16 and 2016/17 (Form P2) and details of any benefits and expenses received (Form P11D, together with any additional schedules provided by the employer;
- Expenses incurred in performance of duties of employment either not reimbursed or not covered by a dispensation and so included on her P11D;
- Details of business mileage undertaken in her own car and the amount paid by her employer;
- Confirmation that there are no earnings from other sources. If there are any such earnings, amount, source and date of payment required;
- National insurance number (should be shown on P60).

## 2. Investments

Dividend vouchers for dividends paid by Priddy Ltd during 2015/16.

Dividend and interest vouchers on stock exchange investments and contract notes covering any purchases and sales of securities.

Details of original acquisitions of investments and details of any capital gains tax losses brought forward reported on previous tax returns. Copies of any capital gains tax elections in force (eg gains held-over)

Details of building society accounts including account numbers and interest credited in the year. Confirmation that these are UK-based accounts and interest for the 2015/16 tax year was paid net of basic rate tax. Tax vouchers for such interest.

## 3. Personal pension policy

Name of insurance company to which personal pension premium paid and amount contributed. Form PPCC or other evidence of payment, and confirmation that the premium was paid net of basic rate tax. Details of amount paid in the three preceding tax years to calculate any annual allowance carried forward.

Confirmation that Priddy Ltd has not included her in a company pension scheme (Priddy Ltd may be required to do so under auto-enrolment). If so, details of any contributions needed.

## 4. Gift aid payments

Confirmation of any donations to charity under gift aid made during year to 5 April 2016 or since 5 April 2016.

## 5. Provision for James

Details of any investments in her name for the benefit of James.

## 6. Information about child benefit

Details of any child benefit received in respect of James in 2015/16 or confirmation of election not to receive child benefit.

### 7. Self-assessment details for 2014/15 and statements of account

Copies of 2014/15 self-assessment tax return and tax calculation for the year (ie working sheet for 2014/15 or HMRC calculation of liability).

Copies of her statements of account since April 2014 and details of any claims to reduce payments on account (form SA303).

### 8. Other income and outgoings, and capital transactions

Details of any other income and outgoings or changes therein, and capital assets acquired or subject to disposal.

### 9. Form 64-8

Signed form 64-8 giving authority to HMRC to issue copies of formal notices to you (as her agent) and to discuss all taxation, national insurance and tax credit issues. See above regarding online authorisation.

### 10. Electronic filing

If not covered in engagement letter, confirmation that electronic filing of the return is acceptable.

## (ii) Year end review to be undertaken in February 2017

### *Need for annual review*

An annual review is essential in order that opportunities for tax mitigation are considered and any necessary action may be taken before the end of the tax year.

A record of the review should be kept in the file of each personal taxation client, and also those for whom one prepares accounts and agrees business taxation liabilities in so far as the personal taxation aspect of their affairs is concerned.

The main areas to be covered in the review are:

### Areas relevant to Mr and Mrs Norton

### 1. Pension provision

The schedule received from Mr Norton re 2015/16 will confirm whether Rumwell plc operates a pension scheme of which he is a member. Assuming that this is the case, consider whether any additional pension contributions are appropriate, after establishing whether it is possible to make further contributions in the unlikely event that Mr Norton has elected for protection from lifetime allowance tax charges.

Mrs Norton's pension provision should similarly be reviewed, including the possibility of paying £3,600 per year into her pension even if that is more than her earnings.

The impact of auto-enrolment on Mr and Mrs Norton should also be established. Presumably, Rumwell Plc has already reached its staging date and hence has enrolled Mr Norton in a pension scheme (although he may have opted out following enrolment). Mrs Norton may be required to be auto enrolled by Priddy Ltd very shortly, depending on the company's staging date and her earnings at that time. Both clients may need advice or information about opting out, or in Mrs Norton's case, opting in if her earnings are not sufficient to require her to be auto-enrolled. The impact of this on any clients might have elected for lifetime allowance protection will need to be explained.

**2. Is income sufficiently large to utilise personal allowances, loss etc claims, and the basic rate bands of each spouse and child?**

Mr Norton clearly uses his available allowances.

The position for Mrs Norton and her child should be checked. If possible, Mrs Norton should receive income to utilise for 2016/17 her:

- personal allowance, £11,000;
- the savings nil rate band of £1,000 (as she is presumably a non-taxpayer or basic rate taxpayer);
- the dividend nil rate band of £5,000;
- the starting rate for savings band of £5,000 (this band is not available if taxable non-savings income exceeds £16,000) and it applies before the savings nil rate band.

Although, in practice, if allowances etc are not being used there may be nothing that can be done.

**3. Gifts to charities**

It is important to ensure that a gift aid declaration has been made in respect of all charitable donations and that all such donations are noted contemporaneously. Records to support the payments should be retained.

It is worth checking that charitable gifts are being made by the spouse with the highest marginal rate of tax, ie Mr Norton unless Mrs Norton's investment income is substantial. If the gifts were made by Mrs Norton, and she was a non-taxpayer, she will have to account for basic rate tax (see **Example N4**).

**4. Potential capital gains tax position**

It is important to check if Mrs Norton has made sufficient gains to utilise the annual exemption (£11,100 for 2016/17). If gains above that level have already been realised, are there assets standing at a loss which should be sold before 6 April 2017 in order to reduce the chargeable gains? Remember that the contract date is the date of disposal for capital gains tax. However you should not give investment advice to Mrs Norton unless you are authorised to do so.

If Mr or Mrs Norton have assets standing with a potential capital gain, the seed enterprise investment scheme (SEIS) offers a capital gains tax exemption on half of any gains made that are reinvested in an SEIS investment plus 50% income tax relief regardless of tax rate. Also, if a loss arises on the investment it may be possible to turn this into an income tax loss giving relief at marginal rate. Again this is regulated advice, although you can discuss the existence of this relief and the tax benefits without this being investment advice. See **Example N7** for further details of SEIS.

**5. Transfers between spouses and inheritance tax planning**

It appears that Mr Norton has no investments. You should consider whether it would be appropriate for Mrs Norton to transfer some investments to him to utilise his annual exemption for capital gains tax, or into joint ownership (see **explanatory note 4**). Such transfers must be absolute gifts to be effective.

However, Mr Norton is probably liable to tax at 40%, therefore he will be liable for capital gains tax at 20% (assuming the investments are not residential property) once his annual exemption has been utilised compared to Mrs Norton who may (depending on her level of investment income) be liable to capital gains tax at only 10%.

Provided Mr Norton does not become an additional rate taxpayer (income of £150,000) he should be entitled to the savings nil rate band of £500 per annum which may cover any interest income on such investments up to the limit.

When reviewing the investment position, a review of current wills could be made, incorporating a calculation of the potential inheritance tax liability. Consideration should be given to the FA 2015 and 2016 changes relating to the residence nil rate band and the transfer of this plus the transfer of the normal nil-rate band between spouses. Any necessary advice about new wills and mitigation of potential inheritance tax liabilities by insurance, use of trusts, or other means could then be given.

If appropriate, Mr and Mrs Norton should be made aware of the inheritance tax provisions for small gifts, gifts out of income and annual exemptions, and the facility to make potentially exempt transfers.

## Areas for consideration generally

### 6. Maximising allowances, basic rate band and reliefs

Consider whether justifiable payments for one spouse assisting in the other's business can be made before 6 April where appropriate. This is relevant not only for trades, professions and vocations but also in relation to a UK property business and for occupations such as clergymen and examiners. PAYE regulations must be followed, and the administrative impact of RTI filing should not be underestimated. The national insurance implications should also be considered. In 2016/17 a spouse could be paid £155 a week without attracting national insurance contributions, but the first £3,000 of employer contributions may be covered by employment allowance (provided the company is not a one man company or has not already used the allowance). Pay at or above £112 makes the year a qualifying year for benefits purposes (including state pension). On the other hand, if a spouse's pay was at a much higher level (in order to use the basic rate band) the national insurance cost would be substantial.

In the case of discretionary trusts or deceased's estates, should a distribution be made before 6 April?

Where there is a family company, should a dividend be paid by the company before 6 April rather than after 5 April? Conversely would the tax position of the recipient be improved by delaying a dividend or indeed other income until a later tax year if that is possible?

All taxpayers are entitled to the dividend nil rate band of £5,000. Although it may be referred to as a dividend allowance, it actually uses part of a taxpayer's basic or higher rate band (hence potentially causing other income to be taxed at a higher rate). However, it is normally preferable for a family company to pay each individual shareholder £5,000 per annum as opposed to £10,000 one year and no dividend the following year.

In the past, general advice was to avoid paying dividends where they would be covered by the personal allowance. Due to the changes in the taxation of dividends this is no longer automatically the case. If a taxpayer had a choice of receiving a dividend this year, which would be covered by their personal allowance and dividend nil rate band versus a dividend next year, which would be taxable at the dividend ordinary rate of 7.5%, it is preferable to advance the dividend.

Various other HMRC approved planning ideas (EIS, SEIS, EMI, VCT, ISA, junior ISA etc) have annual limits. February 2017 is a good time to review whether those limits have been utilised or could be utilised before the end of the tax year. See **Example N5** for general tax planning ideas.

### 7. Child benefit

A couple living together where one is entitled to child benefit payments, and where the net income of either exceeds £50,000, are liable to a tax charge to claw back the child benefit payments in full or in part. It is possible that Mr Norton's income exceeds £50,000, so he may be liable to a tax charge in 2015/16 to partially recoup child benefit paid to Mrs Norton. Where the higher income in the household exceeds £60,000, all of the child benefit paid will be clawed back. It is likely that if affected Mr and Mrs Norton will face only a partial withdrawal of child benefit. The calculated amount should be reflected in the 2015/16 self-assessment tax return for the partner with the higher income. See also **explanatory note 9**.

### 8. Other points

There is a cap on income tax reliefs of the higher of 25% of income or £50,000. This should be considered if any reliefs are claimed in respect of the Nortons.

## Explanatory Notes

*Notifying HMRC of agent's appointment*

(1) Upon receiving instructions the agent should file form 64-8 with National Insurance Contributions and Employer Office, HM Revenue and Customs, BX9 1AN or use the online agent authorisation process (see below). It should be noted that form 64-8 is not sent to this address where:

- it accompanies other correspondence, in which case it should be sent to that HMRC office;
- it is for a high net worth individual, in which case it should be sent to the HMRC High Net Worth Unit;
- it is for an expatriate, in which case it should be sent to the Manchester Expat Team
- it is solely for corporation tax affairs;
- it accompanies a VAT registration application, in which case it should be sent to the relevant VAT Registration Unit;
- it has been specifically requested by an HMRC office, in which case it should be submitted to that office.

If the agent files electronically, or uses a computer produced tax return, then the client will no longer receive a tax return for completion, but a formal notice requiring the submission of a completed return by the relevant date.

If the clients both have unique taxpayer reference numbers (UTRs) and are within self-assessment then it is possible to obtain authorisation to act as an agent through the SA Online system, using a tool known as Online Agent Authorisation Service. The agent initiates the process, using the taxpayer's UTR and postcode, after which HMRC sends an activation code through the post to the taxpayer, who can then pass this to his agent. Provided the agent logs on and enters the code within 30 days of issue by HMRC, no further authorisation will be needed. HMRC would like to see the agent authorisation process go fully online in the future. See Example G4.

Where the client does not have a UTR you should submit form SA1 with form 64-8. The UTR will be notified to you when allocated. SA1 can also be completed online, and the UTR will be notified to the taxpayer at which point the agent can be advised.

*Pension provision*

(2) Mrs Norton pays personal pension premiums net of basic rate tax. Her employment income is low, but if her investment income is high enough to take her income above the basic rate limit, further relief will be due on the premiums.

As an alternative, it may be possible to get Mrs Norton's employer (Priddy Ltd) to make the payments to the personal pension. Employer contributions are paid gross. The pension contribution is deductible for trading income purposes to the extent that it is incurred wholly and exclusively for the purpose of the trade. However, it is the remuneration package in total that must be wholly and exclusively for the purposes of the trade. HMRC has stated that the proportion that the pension contribution bears to salary will not affect the deduction, but the total amount must be justified by the work done.

The pension contribution is paid from funds that have not been reduced by national insurance contributions. It is, therefore, possible to effect a salary sacrifice of an amount that would have been liable to national insurance contributions, and enhance the contribution (and, therefore, total remuneration) by the amount of the national insurance saved. This can increase the value of the amount invested into the pension by up to 32% (20% + 12%) for a basic rate taxpayer.

(3) All files should be reviewed each year in time for appropriate action to be taken in relation to pension contributions before 6 April 2017. If Mr Norton is not a member of an occupational scheme, a personal pension plan would be appropriate.

*Transferring assets between spouses*

(4) Rather than transferring assets outright, spouses may prefer to put them into joint ownership. In that event the income will be divided 50:50 for tax purposes regardless of the actual ownership proportions (ITA 2007 s 836). This provision does not apply to close company shares. In that case the division of income always follows the actual ownership.

If the taxpayers prefer, a declaration may be made of the true beneficial ownership of the investment. Provided HMRC is notified (on form 17) within 60 days of the date of the declaration, the true division of income will apply from the date the declaration was made (ITA 2007 s 837). HMRC's view is that joint bank and building society accounts are held equally and cannot be the subject of a s 837 election unless the parties have changed the legal basis on which the account is held, for example, by way of deed.

(5) Where action is being contemplated to reduce the income of the main earner from a family company full regard must be given to the anti-avoidance legislation relating to settlements in ITTOIA 2005 ss 619-648. If an element of bounty is provided, then the income remains taxable on the main earner. The decision in *Pearce v Young* [1995] STC (SCD) 196 should be noted. In this case, preference shares without voting rights were issued to wives, entitling them to dividends of 30%. It was held that the preference dividends remained assessable on the husbands (under what is now ITTOIA 2005 s 626) since the property given was wholly or substantially a right to income. HMRC gave its view as to when the settlement provisions apply in Tax Bulletin 64 published in April 2003 [http://webarchive.nationalarchives.gov.uk/20140109143644/http://www.hmrc.gov.uk/bulletins/tb64.htm].

HMRC will review cases where it appears that:

- the main earner draws a low salary leading to enhanced dividends paid to other family members or friends;
- dividends represent disproportionally large returns on capital investments;
- there are different classes of shares enabling dividends to be directed to shareholders only paying the lower rate of tax;
- there are dividend waivers in favour of shareholders who only pay at the lower rate of tax;
- there is income transferred from the earner to other members of the family or friends who pay tax at a lower rate.

Commonly, the settlements legislation will be considered to apply where:

- shares are subscribed for that carry only restricted rights;
- shares are gifted that carry only restricted rights;
- shares are subscribed for at par in a company where the income is derived mainly from the earnings of a single employee;
- a share in a partnership is transferred at below market value;
- there are dividend waivers;
- dividends are only paid on certain classes of share;
- dividends are paid to a settlor's minor children.

In the case of *Jones v Garnett* [2007] STC 1536 (also known as the Arctic Systems case), the main earner was paid a salary well below the going rate, which provided funds that could be distributed equally between husband and wife by a way of a dividend. A decision in 2005 confirmed that taking a salary below the market rate provided bounty, and therefore the dividend declared to the wife was taxable on the husband. This decision was reversed by the House of Lords; see **Example A2 (b) part (iii)** for more detailed comments on income shifting between spouses, and **Example N5** for comments on the general anti-abuse rule (GAAR).

*National insurance*

(6) Employees have entitlement to benefits if their earnings exceed the lower limit (£112 per week in 2016/17). Their contributions are 12% of earnings over £155 per week to a maximum of the upper earnings limit of £827 per week and 2% thereafter. Employers' contributions of 13.8% commence at earnings above £156 per week. Accordingly an employee could have earnings of £8,060 per annum without attracting any national insurance contributions. A PAYE scheme would be needed to establish the employee's entitlement to benefits.

*Inheritance tax and taxation of trusts and estates*

(7) For detailed provisions see companion book **Tolley's Taxwise II 2016/17.**

*Tax credits*

(8) All taxpayers with a qualifying child, or who work 30+ hours per week and are aged 25 or over should consider making a protective claim for tax credits by 6 May in a tax year. Any later claim can only be backdated by one month. As an award is eventually based upon income for the actual year it will not be known, by 6 May, whether or not an amount will be payable. If the claimant waits until the award can be quantified it will often be too late to make any claim. See **Example A7** for full details. As stated above, they may wish to make a protective claim although, based upon current levels of income the Nortons are unlikely to qualify for tax credits.

*High income child benefit charge*

(9) The high income child benefit charge applies to anyone who either has an entitlement to child benefit for a week in a tax year, or is a partner (as defined in ITEPA 2003 s 681G) of someone who has an entitlement to child benefit for a week in the tax year. The definition of partner includes married couples, civil partners and couples living together as husband and wife or civil partners.

The charge arises when income of the individual exceeds £50,000, and applies to the person with the higher income in the household. Any taxpayer who is affected by these rules will be brought into self-assessment from 2012/13, even where they elected to pay the tax through the PAYE system. At income of £60,000 the entire amount of income is clawed back, and a proportion is clawed back at income of more than £50,000, so that 1% of the child benefit payments are lost for each £100 of income over £50,000.

There is more detail on the charge and the means by which it is collected in **Example A2.**

# Question

Outline the self-assessment provisions that apply to individuals and partnerships.

# Answer

## Outline of self-assessment provisions for individuals and partnerships

### 1. *General*

#### (a) Requirement to send in partnership returns

Taxpayers within self-assessment and partnerships are required to submit a self-assessment return in response to a notice to make a return issued by HMRC. Notice may be given by simply issuing a paper return, but more commonly the notice is a separate notification usually issued during the April following the end of the tax year.

Partnerships must complete partnership returns (TMA 1970 s 12AA), and then each partner brings his profits into his own personal self-assessment. The responsibility for completing the partnership return is usually that of a representative partner to whom it (or the notice) is sent, but it may be issued in the name of the partnership, in which case the partners may nominate a partner to complete it. If the partner originally responsible for filing returns is no longer available, provision is made for a successor to be nominated by the partners, or if they do not do so, by HMRC.

The filing deadline varies depending on whether the return is to be filed electronically or not. (TMA 1970 ss 8(1D), 12AA(4D)). On receipt of a notice from HMRC requiring a return to be made, taxpayers and partnerships must send in their return, together with supporting schedules by:

- 31 October following the end of the tax year if the return is non electronic, (ie, by 31 October 2017 for 2016/17); or
- 31 January following the end of the tax year for an electronic return (ie by 31 January 2018 for 2016/17).

If a notice is given after 31 July following the tax year the return must be filed by:

(1) three months from the date of notice (for a non-electronic return); or

(2) 31 January, if later (for an electronic return).

If a notice is given after 31 October following the tax year, the return must be filed within three months of the date of the notice, whether by electronic or non-electronic means. HMRC encourages taxpayers to file online if possible. There are facilities for most individual returns to be filed via the Personal Tax Account provided by HMRC, but some individuals (particularly non-residents) and partnerships and trusts must purchase commercial software to file their returns electronically.

Computer generated substitute returns (that is, paper output from computer software) are no longer accepted by HMRC. However, there are a small number of self-assessment taxpayers who cannot file online because of their particular circumstances. HMRC allow this small minority to file on paper up to 31 January. See https://www.gov.uk/government/publications/self-assessment-reasonable-excuse-for-not-filing-return-online for the claim form to accompany the paper return to avoid a penalty being issued. The solution is only intended for the small minority but HMRC have confirmed they will accept 'other' paper returns filed up to 31 October provided they are identical to HMRC printed forms.

If precise figures are not available when the return is submitted, best estimates should be used. Where provisional figures are used, box 20 on page TR8 should be ticked and a note should be made in the white space on page TR7 detailing the figures which are provisional, an explanation for the delay and an estimated date by which the final figure will be provided. If the figures are not available within the time limit for taxpayer amendments or HMRC enquiries (see **Parts 7 and 14 of this Answer**), HMRC may accept a recovery of overpaid tax claim under TMA 1970 Sch 1AB (see **Example G3**) to reduce the tax payable, or will issue a discovery assessment under TMA 1970 s 29 (see **Part 17 of this Answer**) to recover any additional tax payable.

If HMRC receives an unsatisfactory return it will be rejected. This includes:

- non-standard return form;
- unsigned return;
- relevant supplementary pages (or accompanying calculation in the case of capital gains) not enclosed with the return.

If HMRC sends back an unsatisfactory return between 18 January and 31 January following the end of the tax year, then in cases of genuine oversight 14 days are allowed for the return to be resubmitted without incurring a penalty.

Where a taxpayer starts a business or joins a partnership, it may not be possible to submit accurate information relating to the business if the first year-end is after the relevant 5 April. The procedure for provisional figures set out above should be used.

## (b) Calculation of tax payable

Taxpayers do not have to work out their own tax and HMRC will make the calculations if the return is sent in by 31 October (eg by 31 October 2017 for 2016/17). A tax calculation is provided automatically as part of filing online. Calculations of amounts on which the tax is based must, however, be done by the taxpayer, for example capital allowances and capital gains. Taxpayers may ask HMRC to check valuations used in calculating their capital gains before they send in their returns using form CG34 [www.gov.uk/government/publications/sav-post-transaction-valuation-checks-for-capital-gains-cg34]. Partnership returns do not include tax payable, as the amounts are entered on the partners' personal returns.

HMRC will still calculate the tax for returns received after 31 October if required, but will not guarantee to advise the amounts due in time for the taxpayer to avoid interest (and possibly a late payment penalty). As far as employees are concerned, even if they are working out their own tax they must meet the 31 October (or 30 December if filed online) deadline if there is a tax underpayment of up to £3,000 that they wish to have collected through the PAYE scheme rather than being required to pay it on 31 January following the end of the tax year (SI 2003/2682, reg 186). If the 31 October deadline is missed but HMRC receives the paper return by the end of November, it will still try to collect the underpayment through PAYE but cannot guarantee to do so, although submission of a paper return at this point could attract a late filing penalty.

Where a taxpayer with employment income settled an underpayment in excess of £500 by payment in the previous year then the HMRC system will not code out underpayments in excess of £500 in the current year. Care should be taken to warn clients of this problem if they fail to file their return by 31 October and therefore have to pay the balance of tax due on 31 January following. For some taxpayers, coding out can also be refused due to HMRC working practices. If the tax coded out take the tax collected under PAYE to over 50% of the taxpayer's income, HMRC will not code out the liability, even where it meets the necessary constraints (SI 2003/2682, regs 23(5), 28(5), 144(4) as read with SI 2003/2682, regs 2, 4).

Taxpayers need not include pence on the return, and income and gains may be rounded *down* and tax paid rounded *up*. If an entry in a particular box covers several different items, it is the total figure that should be rounded. Tax must be calculated to the penny.

## (c) Trust and estate returns

To minimise delays in winding up estates and trusts and distributing estate or trust property, HMRC will, on request, issue tax returns before the end of the tax year of death, or of winding up an estate or trust, and will give early confirmation if they do not intend to enquire into the return. Those wishing to file returns online for trusts or estates will need to purchase third party software, as HMRC's facility to file online only covers individuals.

The death of the taxpayer does not automatically cancel the payments on account due for that year based upon the previous year's liabilities. It is necessary to compute the likely liabilities to the date of death, then make a claim on form SA303 [www.gov.uk/government/publications/self-assessment-claim-to-reduce-payments-on-account-sa303] to reduce the payments on account to the expected liability.

HMRC has a dedicated bereavement services team [www.gov.uk/government/organisations/hm-revenue-customs/contact/bereavement-and-deceased-estate] and a section on the GOV.UK website for dealing with a tax return for someone who has died [www.gov.uk/after-a-death/overview]. HMRC's Bereavement helpline can be reached on 0300 200 3300.

### (d) Partnership statement

The partnership return must be accompanied by a statement showing the names, addresses and tax references of everyone who was a partner at some time in the year, the dates of joining or leaving where relevant, each partner's share of profits, losses and charges on income, and tax deducted or credited (TMA 1970 s 12AB). The amounts on the partnership statement will normally be transferred to the partner's individual return on the partnership pages. This may vary when someone joins a partnership part way through a tax year.

There is a short version of the partnership statement for partnerships with only trading or professional profits and taxed interest and a full version for partnerships with other types of income and/or capital gains. In the latter case, the statement shows each partner's share of the proceeds for chargeable assets, each partner calculating his gain or loss according to his own circumstances.

### (e) Partners' personal returns

Each partner is required to complete supplementary partnership pages in his personal return. As with the partnership return, the personal return contains a short version of the partnership pages if the partnership has only trading profits and taxed interest. The income shown in the personal return should agree with that shown in the partnership statement. In some circumstances, however, the partner will not receive the relevant information in time to give the correct figures in his personal return.

For example, if an established partnership makes up accounts to 31 December and a new partner joins on 1 January 2017, the new partner will be taxed in 2016/17 on his profit to 5 April 2017, but his profit share will form part of the profit shown on the 2017/18 partnership statement. In these circumstances, he should include a provisional figure in his 2016/17 return, and notify the exact figure as soon as possible.

Say that following the admission of the new partner, an existing partner left the partnership on 31 March 2017. He would have a basis period for 2016/17 covering the 15 months from 1 January 2016 to 31 March 2017, and he would similarly have to include a provisional figure for the three months' profits to 31 March 2017 in his 2016/17 return. He would be entitled to deduct any available overlap relief from the profits of the 15 months' period to the date he left the firm.

It is possible for the partnership to prepare intermediate accounts without permanently changing its accounting date, because a change of accounting date does not take effect unless notice is given to HMRC (see **Example C5**). It might then be possible for the partnership to let the incoming/retiring partner know the provisional profit share for the relevant period. If this were done, the intermediate accounts would not be shown in the partnership statement for the full year, but would be combined with those for the rest of the accounting period and shown as a single set of figures for the full year in the partnership statement.

In normal circumstances a partner's personal return includes the amount that the partnership statement states is their share of the partnership profit or loss. However in exceptional circumstances where an individual partner does not agree with the profits allocated to them they can enter what they consider to be the correct amount. They must advise HMRC that they have done so by making an entry in the white space of the return to show:

- the profits allocated in the partnership statement;
- the disputed amount; and
- an explanation about why they think the profit allocated to them in the partnership statement is wrong.

Partners should normally seek to resolve any disputes between themselves and hence genuine disputes should be rare. See EM7025. The principle that an individual partner's return should show the 'correct' figure and not the amount shown in the partnership statement was supported in *King and others v HMRC* [2016] UKFTT 409 (TC).

Class 4 national insurance contributions are included in partners' personal returns. The personal tax return makes provision for a partner to indicate that he is excepted from contributions or that contributions have been deferred. See **Example H1** for detailed notes on national insurance contributions.

Partners are individually responsible for paying their own tax. If a partnership pays the bill on behalf of the partners, the partners' names, tax reference numbers and amounts applicable to each partner must be provided.

### (f) Limited liability partnerships (LLPs)

An LLP is taxed as a partnership and will receive a partnership tax return as if the members were partners carrying on a business in partnership. Accordingly all of the rules set out above apply to an LLP which carries on a trade. Where an existing partnership incorporates as an LLP during an accounting period, then a single partnership return can be made for the tax year. This will apply even if there is a change of accounting date.

### (g) No tax liability for year

If a taxpayer receives a return, and he has no tax liability, HMRC used to take the view that the return had to be completed. Upon request by the taxpayer, HMRC can withdraw the notice to file and cancel any related penalty for late filing if a return was not necessary (TMA 1970 ss 8B, 12AAA). FA 2016 s 169 removes the requirement that this process has to be initiated by the taxpayer, allowing the cancellation of the notice to file to be undertaken autonomously by HMRC. Although this is necessary to facilitate the introduction of simple assessments (see **Part 16 to this Answer**), this change has in fact been backdated to 2014/15 (TMA 1970 s 8B). Note that this change applies only to personal tax returns and not to partnership tax returns, where the process still has to be initiated by the taxpayer.

### (h) Part-year residents

Where an individual leaves the UK and becomes non-resident part-way through the tax year, HMRC will accept a return made after the departure date but before the end of the tax year if it is accompanied by form P45.

## 2. *Self-employment and business profits of partnerships*

When completing the self-employment pages of the tax return or the business profits of the partnership return, the profit or loss is required to be shown in standard layout. Smaller businesses with turnover of below the VAT limit (£83,000 for 2016/17) (see **Example C2** for an illustration) can complete the short self-employment pages, or the three line entry on the partnership return. In this case, only turnover, tax deductible total expenses and profit are shown. For taxpayers completing the full self-employment pages or partnerships the balance sheet details must also be provided if there is a business balance sheet prepared.

Where more than one accounting period relates to the basis period for the year (for example where the accounting date has changed), a separate set of trading pages must be completed for each account.

The simplified cash basis allows certain small business to account for business profits on a cash basis (FA 2013 Sch 4). Primarily a trade, vocation or profession can only be considered for the simplified cash basis if it falls below the VAT registration threshold at the end of the tax year (£83,000 at the start of the 2016/17 tax year, and potentially more than this at the end of the year). See Example C3.

Accounts need not be sent in with returns except for partnerships with profits greater than £15 million or when all members of the partnership are companies. Taxpayers may send whatever supporting information with their returns they consider is necessary in order to make a full disclosure, but unless the relevance of any additional material is pointed out, this will not stop HMRC later trying to make a discovery assessment. The return forms include various blank spaces for additional information (known as 'white space'), and it would be sensible to use the white space to refer to any additional information that is being sent with the return.

Any expenses paid personally by partners and capital allowances on partners' own cars *must* be included in the *partnership* return and cannot be separately claimed in the partners' own personal returns. Such items must be included before apportioning the profit between the partners, with the share of the relevant partner then being adjusted appropriately. If expenses incurred individually are not shown in the partnership accounts, it will be necessary to reconcile the accounts figures with those shown in the partnership return. To avoid the possibility of discrepancies leading to an HMRC enquiry, it would be appropriate to file both the accounts and the details of the adjustments with the partnership return.

## 3. *Retaining records*

Even though accounts need not be submitted with returns, taxpayers must retain their records for a statutory period. Traders, partnerships and those with letting income must keep the records until the fifth anniversary of the 31 January next following the relevant tax year. Other taxpayers must retain records until the first anniversary of that 31 January date. So for 2016/17 the time limit for traders and landlords is 31 January 2023 and for other taxpayers 31 January 2019. If HMRC enquires into the return (see **Part 14 of this Answer**), the records must be retained until the enquiry is completed if later than the normal retention date (TMA 1970 s 12B).

Where a claim is made other than in a return (see **Example G3**), records relating to the claim must similarly be retained until any HMRC enquiry into the claim is completed, or until HMRC is no longer able to start such an enquiry (TMA 1970 Sch 1A para 2A).

A penalty of up to £3,000 per tax year may be charged for non-compliance. (TMA 1970 s 12B(5))

HMRC is able to expand the definition of statutory records contained within TMA 1970 s 12B by way of regulations and also by notice. Statutory records have a specific identity under the inspection powers discussed in **Part 14 to this Answer.**

## 4. *Information from employers*

Employers must provide employees with appropriate information relating to their earnings to enable the employees to complete their tax returns. Form P60 (pay and tax details) must be supplied by 31 May, and Forms P11D (details of expenses payments and benefits, including calculations of cash equivalents) by 6 July.

Employers sometimes make PAYE 'tax equalisation' arrangements for foreign national employees. There is a special Help Sheet HS212 to assist such employees and their advisers in the completion of their tax returns [www.gov.uk/government/publications/tax-equalisation-hs212-self-assessment-helpsheet].

## 5. *Non-trading income of partnerships*

The partnership return includes details of income other than from the trade or profession and of disposals of partnership chargeable assets. The details provided normally relate to the accounting year ended in the tax year. Details of taxed income and of disposals of chargeable assets are, however, shown for the tax year itself rather than for the accounting year ended in the tax year, in order that the partners have the information they need to complete their own returns.

The return states that the taxed income of the relevant accounting periods should be apportioned to arrive at the figure for the tax year. A straight time apportionment would, however, give anomalous results if tax rates changed. It is acceptable, and probably more appropriate, to enter the taxed income actually received in the tax year itself. Similarly, where profit shares change, the partners' actual shares of the taxed income may be shown rather than time apportioning the total for the tax year.

## 6. *Notification of liability if no return received*

Anyone who is liable to income tax or capital gains tax (including a liability to the high income child benefit charge from 2012/13) and does not receive a notice under TMA 1970 s 8 must notify HMRC that he is so chargeable within six months from the end of the tax year, ie by 5 October 2017 for 2016/17 (TMA 1970 s 7).

Penalties for failure to notify liability are calculated on a behaviour-based tax-geared penalty of increasing amount depending on whether the failure was deliberate or not (FA 2008 Sch 41). The rules are very similar to penalties for incorrect returns (see **Part 12 of this Answer**). They also apply to failures to notify liability to VAT and corporation tax and a similar penalty applies for failing to register as self-employed and paying Class 2 NIC (see **Example C5 explanatory note 5**). However, historically HMRC has offered a number of 'disclosure opportunities' (also known as 'campaigns') aimed at various business sectors, types of investment income and compliance failures and more favourable penalties may be available if a relevant campaign is still open. For details of the open campaigns, see the GOV.UK website [www.gov.uk/government/publications/2010-to-2015-government-policy-tax-evasion-and-avoidance]. If the taxpayer could have disclosed his income or gains under a relevant campaign and did not do so, HMRC will levy higher penalties.

The penalty is determined (as a percentage) of the potential lost revenue (PLR). This is the tax unpaid at a specified date or to which the person is liable for the relevant period. For failure to notify liability to income tax or capital gains tax this is the amount unpaid on 31 January next following the tax year (FA 2008 Sch 41 para 7(2)).

Example: Daniel doesn't normally file tax returns but he makes a capital gain on 28 February 2017 that generates a tax liability of £10,000. He notifies liability on 15 January 2018 and at the same time makes a payment on account of the tax liability of £6,000. He failed to notify liability by 5 October 2017 and therefore he is liable to a penalty. His PLR is £4,000 (£10,000 less £6,000). This penalty could therefore have been avoided if Daniel had paid the tax in full prior to 31 January 2018.

Taxpayers can appeal against the imposition and amount of a penalty. They can also request a review of the decision to apply a penalty. Other similarities to penalties for incorrect returns (see **Part 12 of this Answer** for full details) are:

- behaviour – the rate of penalty increases when the omission is deliberate or deliberate and concealed;
- disclosure – the penalty can be reduced according to the 'quality' of the disclosure;
- whether a disclosure is unprompted or prompted.

The amount of the penalty is increased where the inaccuracy involves an offshore matter (from 2011/12 onwards). See **Part 12 of this Answer** for further details including the percentage increases. The way in which the penalty for late notification involving domestic matters works is best demonstrated by a diagram, as follows:

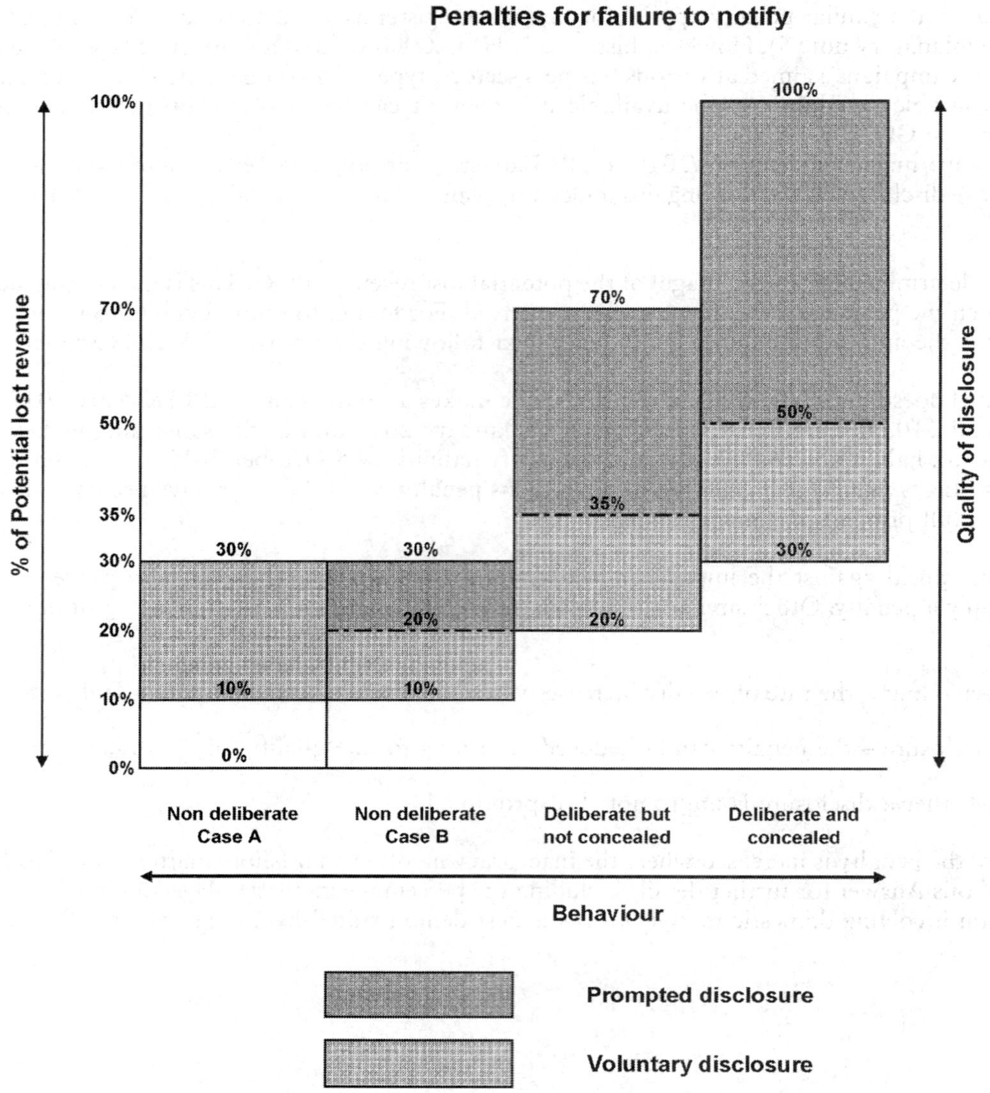


To encourage disclosure, if the failure is non deliberate and notified within 12 months of the tax becoming unpaid, the penalties are those shown above for case A. Otherwise, case B applies.

For further information see HMRC manual CH72500.

For failures to notify before 1 April 2010 there was a penalty of up to the amount of tax payable as at 31 January following for non-notification.

There is no liability to notify if the individual has no capital gains or liability to higher rate tax, and tax on all income has been accounted for under PAYE, or by deduction at source. Employees will not usually have received their coding notices by 5 October, but if they have a copy of Form P11D they may assume HMRC is aware of its contents unless they have reason to believe otherwise.

## 7. *HMRC corrections and taxpayer amendments*

HMRC has nine months from the date a return is received to correct obvious errors in the return, or (since April 2009) anything else in the return that the officer has reason to believe is incorrect in the light of information available to him (TMA 1970 s 9ZB). Taxpayers may make amendments within a year from the filing deadline

(TMA 1970 s 9ZA), but if the return is selected for further enquiry – see **Part 14 of this Answer** – amendments made between the time HMRC gives notice that they intend to enquire into the return and the time the enquiries are completed only take effect on the completion of the enquiry (TMA 1970 s 9B). HMRC will accept an amendment from a taxpayer's agent unless they believe the taxpayer may not have authorised it. HMRC's right to correct a return extends to making consequential corrections within nine months after a taxpayer amendment.

The taxpayer has an explicit right under TMA 1970 s 9ZB to reject an HMRC correction to a return, providing notice of rejection is given within 30 days, similar rights being given in relation to partnership returns by TMA 1970 s 12ABB. In practice any rejection outside that period will be accepted if it is as a result of an HMRC error.

If an amendment results in extra tax payable, the due date of payment for the extra tax is 30 days after the amendment or, where relevant, the date of completion of an HMRC enquiry (TMA 1970 Sch 3ZA), although interest on overdue tax runs from the original due date for the return.

Under TMA 1970 s 30B, HMRC may amend a partnership statement outside the twelve-month enquiry period if it discovers that profits have been understated and the understatement was 'brought about carelessly or deliberately' by a partner, or because of inadequate information.

## 8. *Payments on account*

Under TMA 1970 s 59A, provisional payments on account are due half-yearly on 31 January in the tax year and 31 July following. The payments on account are equal to half of the *net* income tax and Class 4 national insurance liability of the previous tax year (ie after deducting tax paid at source (such as under PAYE and tax deducted from subcontractors' payments) and excluding student loan repayments. Class 2 national insurance, although collected via the tax return from 2015/16 onwards, is not included in the payments on account calculation (SSCBA 1992 s 11A(2)). Payments on account are not required where more than 80% of the previous year's tax liability was covered by tax deducted at source and dividend tax credits, or where the previous year's net tax and Class 4 national insurance was less than £1,000 (TMA 1970, s 59A(1); SI 1996/1654).

At any time before the 31 January filing date for the return, a taxpayer (or his agent) who believes he would otherwise overpay tax may make a claim (on form SA303 or using the online facility) for the payments on account not to be paid, or to be reduced. Care needs to be taken in working out appropriate payments on account for a taxpayer whose PAYE coding includes a previous year's underpayment or, a recovery of overpaid tax credits. The tax return provides for claims to reduce payments on account to be made in the return itself. Reduction in payments on account can also be conveniently actioned online through the Personal Tax Account.

Following a claim, if either or both of the payments on account have already been made, the appropriate amount will be repaid, with repayment supplement from the payment date. If, however, the final tax figures for the year show that all or part of the reduction in the payments on account should not have been made, interest will be charged on the shortfall from the original due dates. In addition to being charged interest, a taxpayer who fraudulently or negligently reduces his payments on account is liable to a penalty not exceeding the shortfall in payment (TMA 1970 s 59A(6)). HMRC will calculate payments on account for taxpayers who do not calculate their own tax.

Taxpayer's account information is available online to agents (and taxpayers). Digital developments are being rolled out rapidly and new services are becoming available. See **Example G4**.

## 9. *Balancing payments/repayments*

Under TMA 1970 s 59B, the total income tax, Class 4 national insurance and capital gains tax due for the tax year is compared with the amount already paid and the balance is payable or repayable on or before the following 31 January. For 2015/16 until abolished, Class 2 national insurance contributions due are added to the balancing payment. If, however, a taxpayer had given notice of liability by 5 October following the tax year as indicated in **Part 6 of this Answer**, and did not receive a notice to complete a return until after 31 October, the balancing payment is due three months from the date of the notice (TMA 1970 s 59B(3)). In either case, the first payment on account for the next tax year is due at the same time.

Where a return shows an overpayment, it will be refunded if the appropriate box is ticked in the return, but overpaid payments on account are not refunded automatically. The refund should be requested online or a letter sent.

## 10. *Interest on overdue tax/Class 4 national insurance and repayment supplement*

*Interest on overdue tax*

Under TMA 1970 s 86, interest is normally charged on Self Assessment tax liabilities and (by SSCBA 1992 Sch 2 para 6) on Class 4 national insurance paid late, from the date the payment was due to the date the tax is paid, ie from 31 January in the tax year and 31 July following for payments on account, and from 31 January following the tax year for the balancing payment.

Interest also runs from 31 January following the tax year to which the assessment relates for assessments issued by HMRC (unless otherwise provided) regardless of when the assessment was issued (see **Part 17 of this Answer** for a discussion of HMRC assessments). For amendments to self-assessments, interest runs from 31 January following the relevant tax year.

In addition to being charged on unpaid tax, interest is payable on late paid penalties.

Any interest charged under these provisions is not an allowable deduction for tax purposes (ITTOIA 2005 s 54).

Discovery assessments, in addition to carrying interest, also affect payments on account. TMA 1970 s 59A(4B) provides that the payments on account that should have been made for the following year are increased accordingly, subject to a claim under TMA 1970 s 59A(3), (4) to eliminate or reduce them because they exceeded the tax payable for that following year.

*Repayment supplement*

Interest paid by HMRC on tax and national insurance or penalties overpaid by the taxpayer is known as repayment supplement. The interest is tax-fee in the hands of the taxpayer (ITTOIA 2005 s 749). Repayment supplement accrues from the date the amount was paid until the date the repayment order is issued. If, however, a taxpayer pays more than the amount that is legally due at the payment date, the overpayment does not attract supplement.

Where there is a refund of tax deducted at source, supplement runs from 31 January following the relevant tax year (FA 2009 s 102(3), (4) as read with FA 2009 Sch 54 paras 1–5). Tax deducted at source includes PAYE tax, except that amounts deducted in respect of previous years are excluded.

*Claims involving more than one year*

Special provisions apply to claims involving more than one year (see **Example G3**). Where such claims result in an *increase* in tax for the earlier year (for example through farmers' averaging), any additional tax payable is regarded as relating to the later year and is due for payment on 31 January following that later year. Where a claim *reduces* the tax for the earlier year (for example through farmers' averaging, or where trading losses or gift aid donations are carried back), *effect is given* to the claim in relation to the later year, by repayment or set-off, or by an increase in the amount to be deducted in arriving at the balancing payment for the year under TMA 1970 s 59B, or 'otherwise' (TMA 1970 Sch 1B).

Interest due on the tax for earlier years will cease from the date of the claim. Thus an early claim can stop interest accruing against a taxpayer even if no supplement would be due if the same amount was repaid. Supplement will only be relevant if the claim is given effect after the 31 January following the later year, supplement then running from that 31 January date.

*Date when payments regarded as made*

Payments of income tax and national insurance have historically been treated as made as follows for the purpose of calculating interest or repayment supplement:

- the payment date for postal payments is the day they are received by HMRC, except those received following a day when the HMRC office was closed, which are treated as received on the first day the office was closed (see below re cheques);
- online payments by debit/credit card or electronic funds transfer (Faster Payments/CHAPS) are usually treated as received by HMRC on the date of payment;
- funds transfer by BACS may take up to three bank working days to be received by HMRC;

- payments by bank Giro or Girobank are received on the date payment is made at the bank or post office.

HMRC recommend that tax is paid electronically and for some taxes (eg corporation tax) it is compulsory. There are facilities to make payment directly through the new Tax Account online system, which are pre-populated with reference numbers, and requires only the insertion of the taxpayer's card details to make payment

## 11. *Penalties for late payment of tax*

The penalty regime for late payment of taxes was brought into line across a range of taxes (income tax, corporation tax, PAYE, national insurance, construction industry scheme, stamp duty land tax, stamp duty reserve tax, inheritance tax, pension and petroleum tax) by FA 2009 Sch 56. Tax credits are not included in the reform. Taxpayers have a right of appeal against all penalties and no penalty can be charged if they have a reasonable excuse (see **Part 13 of this Answer**). Not all of the regimes affected have moved to the new system of penalty as of 2016/17.

For income tax and capital gains tax the new late payment penalties commenced on 6 April 2011 in respect of tax due for 2010/11 onwards. The following late payment penalties can arise (FA 2009 Sch 56 para 3):

(1) penalties of 5% of the amount of tax unpaid 30 days after the payment due date;

(2) further penalties of 5% of any amount of tax still unpaid at five and eleven months after the payment date at (1) above.

For example, John Connor's 2015/16 tax return showed a balancing payment due by 31 January 2017 of £10,000. If the tax is not paid, penalties will accrue as follows:

| *Trigger date* | *Penalty* |
|---|---|
| 3 March 2017 | £500 (5%) |
| 1 August 2017 | £500 (5%) |
| 1 February 2018 | £500 (5%) |

HMRC also has the power to reduce, stay or agree a compromise if it thinks it is right because of special circumstances (FA 2009 Sch 56 para 9). Ability to pay and the fact that the potential loss of revenue from one taxpayer is balanced by a potential overpayment by another are not special circumstances for this purpose. See CH170000.

When a late payment penalty is incurred HMRC will issue a penalty notice which is copied to the agent. The penalty is payable within 30 days, and the amount due is treated as tax for enforcement purposes. The taxpayer can appeal against the penalty notice (within 30 days) provided he has reasonable excuse for the late payment, which cannot be lack of funds (FA 2009 Sch 56 para 13). However, the taxpayer does not have to pay the penalty until the appeal is determined. Penalty notices are issued automatically by HMRC's computer system. Late payment penalties will not normally apply where the taxpayer has agreed a time to pay arrangement before the penalty date (subject to meeting the terms of the arrangement). A couple of other exceptions apply to prevent the automatic issue of penalty notices including where the taxpayer is subject to bankruptcy or IVA.

Late payment penalties are applied to balancing payments, determinations, amendments and revenue assessments but not to interest, late filing penalties or payments on account (although if still outstanding is included in any balancing payment penalty).

HMRC guidance is at CH150000.

## 12. *Penalties for incorrect returns and errors in documents*

FA 2007 Sch 24 sets out the framework for charging and assessing penalties on incorrect tax returns and inaccuracies in documents. These cover income and corporation tax, PAYE, national insurance and VAT. FA 2008 extended this framework to all other taxes and duties (inheritance tax, environmental taxes, stamp duties etc) except tax credits.

With effect for 2011/12 and subsequent years, the amount of the penalty may be increased where the inaccuracy involves an offshore matter. See below for further details, including the increased percentages.

The relevant percentages are slightly different to those for failure to notify, and those applying to domestic matters are set out in the diagram below:

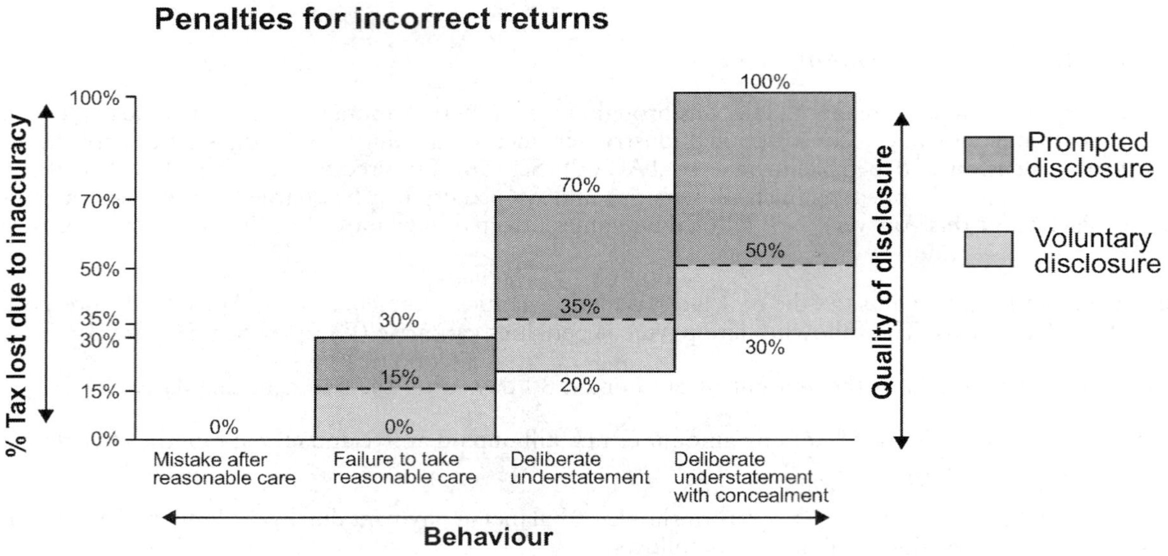


## Potential lost revenue

For a penalty to be charged two conditions must be satisfied:

(1) The document given to HMRC must contain an inaccuracy that leads to:

- an understatement of tax liability;
- an excessive tax loss; or
- an excessive tax repayment claim; and

(2) The inaccuracy was careless or deliberate.

The list of documents covered is wide. These penalties do not only apply to documents which are normally thought of as tax returns. For example, they can also apply:

- to a statement or declaration in connection with a claim for an allowance, deduction or relief;
- accounts in connection with ascertaining liability to tax;
- any other document likely to be relied on by HMRC to determine the taxpayers liability to tax.

Plus, for these purposes, giving HMRC a document includes giving HMRC information in any form and by any method.

In order to arrive at the penalty it is necessary to know the amount of potential lost revenue (PLR). The basic rule is the PLR is the additional amount due as a result of correcting the inaccuracy (FA 2007 Sch 24 para 5). For the purpose of calculating PLR 'tax', national insurance is included. In addition, group relief and relief given on repayment of a loan by a close company (CTA 2010 s 458) are ignored.

Special rules apply to losses, groups, multiple errors and delayed tax, so that the legislation prescribes an amount to be potential lost revenue in some cases, for example, where no relief for an overstated loss has yet been given (FA 2007 Sch 24 paras 7, 8).

## Behaviour

The penalty regime focuses on behaviour. There are no penalty for errors/omissions where the taxpayer took reasonable care but there are substantially higher penalties in all other cases. Behaviour is divided into four separate groups. An inaccuracy made by a person in a document or return may be:

- made despite taking reasonable care (**no penalty**);
- careless;
- deliberate but not concealed; or
- deliberate and concealed.

HMRC has published considerable material, including in CH80000 onwards, e-learning packages and various leaflets. These contain examples of the various behaviours.

## Error despite taking reasonable care – no penalty

What is 'reasonable care' will be different for every taxpayer and depends on their ability and circumstances. HMRC has confirmed it does not expect the same level of knowledge from a self-employed unrepresented individual, as from a publicly listed company.

An example of an error despite taking reasonable care is an arithmetical or transposition inaccuracy that is not so large (either in absolute terms or relative to overall liability) as to produce an obviously odd result or be picked up by a quality check (see CH81130). An example might be transposing a figure incorrectly when filing a tax return – car benefit shown as £5,190 instead of £5,910 (from CH81131).

It is important, when completing documents (tax returns etc) to fully disclose any contentious positions as this shows reasonable care and may protect the taxpayer from a penalty if the tax treatment is subsequently changed.

If an inaccuracy was made despite taking reasonable care at the time the document was submitted (normally no penalty), it can be treated as careless (ie, potential penalty) if the person discovered the error at some later time and did not take reasonable steps to inform HMRC of the inaccuracy.

Penalties can be raised where an adviser makes an error, however, no penalty can be charged if the taxpayer took reasonable care to ensure the document was correct.

It was announced in Budget 2016 that the government is considering legislating the definition of reasonable care in tax avoidance cases. It is expected to make it clear that avoiders cannot rely on generic, third party legal advice received via the promoter or other enabler of the scheme to establish reasonable care.

## Failure to take reasonable care 'careless' – penalty 0% to 30%

Careless is likened to the previous long-standing concept of 'negligence' which was the basis for a penalty under the old system for direct taxes. This includes omitting to do something a reasonable person would do or doing something a reasonable person would not do. For example, a plumber failing to keep accurate records to prepare his return.

HMRC expects taxpayers to take their tax affairs seriously and seek advice on unfamiliar transactions. If failing to seek such advice leads to an error it would be considered 'careless'. For example, Jack the trade electrician changes from using a van to a car to facilitate personal use (at weekends) but continues to claim all input tax on fuel without seeking advice from HMRC or his accountant. If advice is sought but subsequently found to be wrong (after disclosing all facts and from a reliable source) the taxpayer would have shown reasonable care and no penalty applies.

To encourage taxpayers to improve their systems and procedures, the careless penalty can be suspended for a maximum of two years provided the taxpayer complies with various conditions (FA 2007 Sch 24 para 14). The conditions relate to compliance with a view to preventing further problems. Provided such conditions are met, the penalty will be cancelled at the end of the suspension period.

Failure to notify an under-assessment within 30 days is a separate offence but subject to the same maximum penalty of 30%.

### Deliberate but not concealed – penalty 20% to 70%

The key word here is 'deliberate' which implies the person knew what they were doing (see CH81150). An inaccuracy can arise by deliberately not doing something or deliberately getting something wrong. For example, knowingly failing to record all sales such as taking £50 'pocket money' or entering an inflated input figure on the VAT return and hoping the return would not be checked.

### Deliberate and concealed – penalty 30% to 100%

The distinction between this category and the previous one can be a fine line, as almost any deliberate inaccuracy is likely to have some element of concealment. HMRC guidance states the person has taken active steps to cover their tracks by making arrangements (see CH81160). For example, taking 'pocket money' of £50 or entering the wrong input tax figure on the VAT return and creating false paperwork to support the transaction, representing it is a business expense.

### Disclosure

A disclosure is unprompted if it is made at a time when the person making it has no reason to believe that HMRC has discovered, or is about to discover, the error (FA 2004 Sch 24 para 9; CH82400).

A disclosure can be treated as unprompted even if:

- the full extent of the disclosure is not known, as long as full details are provided within a reasonable time;
- made following a national campaign highlighting an area of the trading community;
- exceptionally during a visit/compliance check *if* the disclosure is about something the officer has not discovered or is about to discover. For example, during a compliance check on a capital gain, the taxpayer discloses a car benefit or during a PAYE audit they disclose transfer pricing errors.

For VAT purposes, correcting errors on a subsequent VAT return (as under de minimis limit) does not count as a voluntary disclosure of the inaccuracy. Therefore all mistakes other than those made after reasonable care (and under the de minimis limit) should be disclosed in full. Where, however, an error corrects itself on the next return, the potential lost revenue is calculated under the delayed tax rule, and is therefore only 5% of the error.

### Quality of disclosure

All of the penalties can be substantially reduced depending on the 'quality' of the disclosure. Quality is defined to include the timing, nature and extent of three elements. These elements are (CH82430):

> **Telling:** admitting, disclosing and explaining in full.
> **Helping:** helping to quantify inaccuracies by volunteering information; actively engaging and providing positive assistance.
> **Giving access:** responding positively to requests for information; allowing access to relevant documents.

For example, Mel has been systematically diverting taxable receipts into an undisclosed bank account and covering the traces. He is willing to make a full disclosure and is sure HMRC have no knowledge of his wrong doings. The maximum penalty for this type of behaviour is 100%. This can be reduced to 30% if the quality of Mel's disclosure warrants such a reduction.

The disclosure is to be seen as a continuous process involving much more than the initial contact. This means that in order to secure the maximum possible reduction (ie, reduce the penalty to 30%), Mel needs to make a reasonably full initial disclosure at the earliest possible stage and to cooperate fully with HMRC's subsequent enquires as required.

## Offshore matters

Where an inaccuracy on a return relates to an offshore matter, and the tax concerned is income tax or capital gains tax, the penalty regime set out above is scaled up depending on the territory involved. The territories are grouped into different categories depending on the jurisdiction's cooperation with HMRC. Currently there are three categories, with Category 1 attracting the same penalties as shown in the diagram above. The tax-geared penalty percentages are increased for Category 2 and Category 3 territories. Where the inaccuracy relates to a Category 2 territory the maximum penalties above are increased by 50% in all cases. Where the inaccuracy relates to a Category 3 country then the penalties described above are increased by 100%. The offshore penalty regime applies from 6 April 2011, and therefore affects 2011/12 returns onwards. The categorisation of countries is listed on HMRC's website, where Category 1 and Category 3 countries are listed, all other countries being Category 2 [www.gov.uk/government/publications/territory-categorisation-for-offshore-penalties].

The same extension of penalties to offshore matters also applies to late notification and tax-geared penalties for late returns. From April 2016 the offshore matters penalty regime is (FA 2015, Sch 20; SI 2016/456):

- extended to encompass offshore transfers (from the 2016/17 tax year onwards). An offshore transfer is one where UK source income/proceeds are received in the UK and moved offshore or are received offshore. It also includes a situation where an inheritance tax chargeable transfer is made and the asset is transferred out before the return is filed;
- amended to include inheritance tax (for transfers made on or after 1 April 2016).

A further change to the offshore penalty regime was made by FA 2015 Sch 20, which is not yet in force. From a date to be appointed by regulations, a further category of penalty (Category 0 is to be introduced and those in the new Category 1 territories will attract a 25% increase on the above percentages. The territory classification system is to be updated to reflect the jurisdictions that adopt the new global common reporting standard and the new system of four levels of penalty will be effective following this review. Meanwhile, factsheet CC/FS17 provides details of the current regime [www.gov.uk/government/publications/compliance-checks-penalties-for-income-tax-and-capital-gains-tax-for-offshore-matters-ccfs17].

There is also an additional penalty of 50% of the original penalty when a taxpayer changes residence or moves an asset (including sterling) from a specified territory to a non-specified territory on or after 26 March 2015 (FA 2015 Sch 21). These are known as penalties for offshore asset moves (and is not the same as an offshore transfer). To fall within the rules, the taxpayer must have incurred an original penalty for a deliberate inaccuracy or a deliberate failure to notify chargeability or to make a return. Specified territories are listed in SI 2015/866. If the territory is not on that list it is a non-specified territory.

From a date to be appointed, FA 2016 Sch 21 retains the scale ups above when calculating the maximum penalty but increases the minimum penalties. The penalty provisions in FA 2007 Sch 24 new paragraph 10A for inaccuracies involving an offshore matter or offshore transfer are as follows:

Category 1

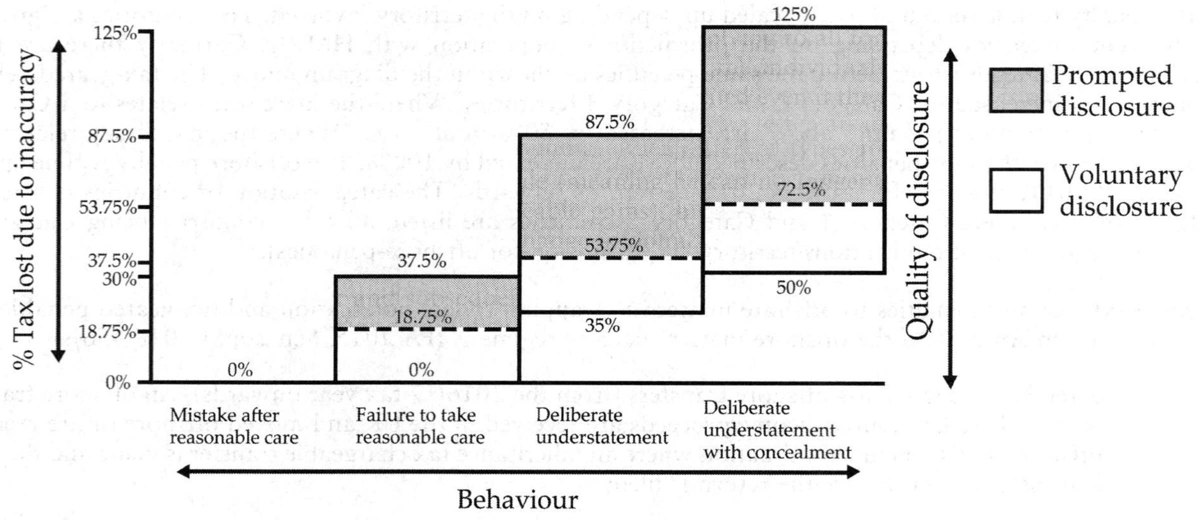


Category 2

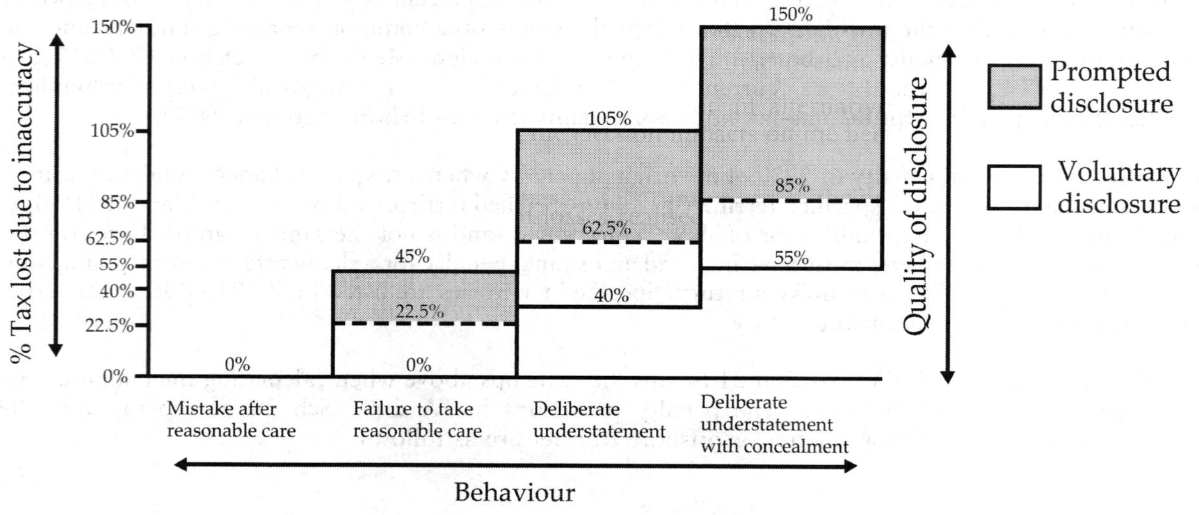

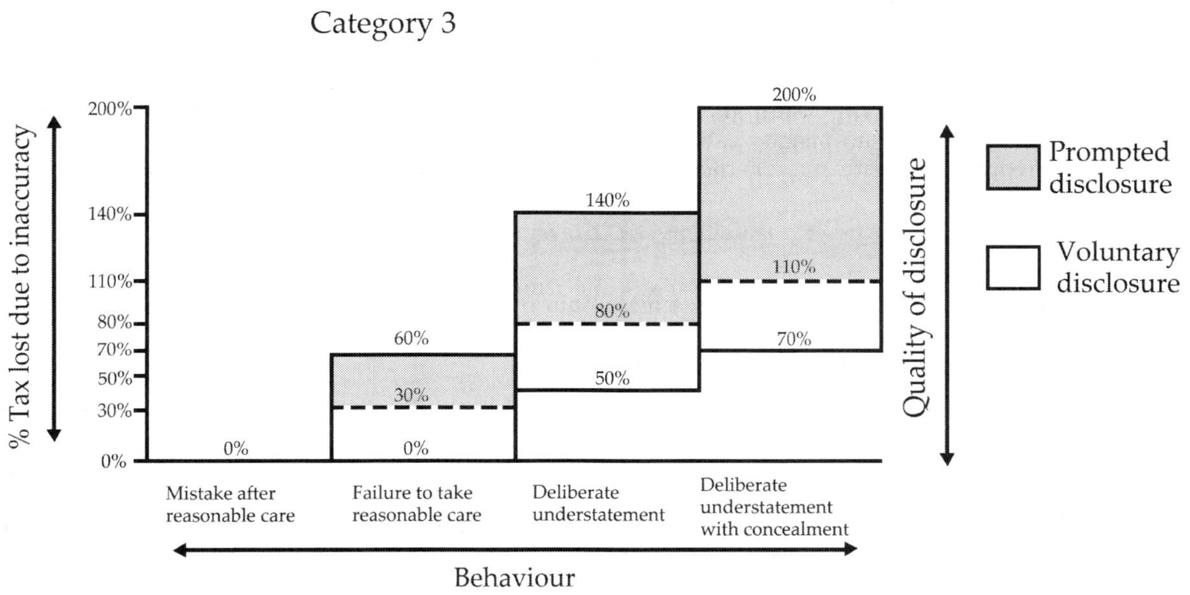


* The dotted line marks the minimum percentage for a prompted disclosure. The maximum percentage for a voluntary disclosure (unprompted) is the top of each category. For example, for an unprompted disclosure of a careless inaccuracy the penalty will be 30% (max), or 0% (min) or any amount in between.

The late notification rules (FA 2008 Sch 41) and tax geared penalties for late returns (FA 2009 Sch 55) are also amended by FA 2016 on the same basis and the new tables of rates can be found at FA 2008 Sch 41 para 13A and FA 2009 Sch 55 para 15A. FA 2016, also provides that deliberate offshore related failures require the taxpayer to provide 'additional information' to obtain the maximum penalty reduction under these two sets of rules. The meaning of 'additional information' is to be set by regulations following a consultation.

Again from a date to be appointed, FA 2016 Sch 22 introduces a new asset-based penalty for deliberate offshore inaccuracies and failures where the PLR exceeds £25,000. The taxpayer must be liable for one or more of the 'standard' offshore tax penalties above (namely failure to notify chargeability, failure to file a return or inaccuracies in a return or document). The penalty is the lower of:

- 10% of the value of the asset; and
- 10% of the PLR associated with that asset.

This amount can be reduced for disclosure, co-operation and in special circumstances.

Again from a date to be appointed, FA 2016 introduces new criminal offences where the income tax or capital gains tax relates to offshore income, assets or activities of:

- failing to give notice of being chargeable to tax (TMA 1970 s 106B);
- failing to deliver a return (TMA 1970 s 106C);
- making an inaccurate return (TMA 1970 s 106D).

To be convicted the tax at stake must exceed a threshold to be set by regulations (and is not to be less than £25,000). The minimum sentence is up to 51 weeks in prison in England and Wales (six months in Scotland and Northern Ireland). The taxpayer may also be fined. There is no need to prove any intent; it is a strict liability offence. There are exclusions for trustees of settlements, executors or administrators of deceased persons and those with a reasonable excuse.

## 13. *Penalties for late returns*

The penalty regime for late filing of returns is set out in FA 2009 Sch 55 and applies across the range of taxes (income tax, corporation tax, PAYE, national insurance, construction industry scheme, stamp duty land tax, stamp duty reserve tax, inheritance tax, pension and petroleum tax) excluding tax credits. Taxpayers have a right of appeal against all penalties and no penalty can be charged if they have a reasonable excuse. For income tax and capital gains tax involving domestic matters the following late filing penalties apply to 2016/17 income tax returns filed late (FA 2009 Sch 55):

- a £100 penalty;
- daily penalties of £10 per day up to a maximum of 90 days once the return is three months late;
- tax geared penalties for prolonged failures:

  at six months, the greater of £300 or 5% of tax due (tax payable for period not tax outstanding);

  at twelve months, the basic penalty is again the greater of £300 or 5%. However, much higher penalties apply if by failing to make the return the taxpayer is deliberately withholding information. These start at 70% and increase to 140% depending upon the category of the information deliberately withheld. If the withholding is also concealed the range changes to 100% to 200%.

It is important to note that the penalties for late filing always apply, unless HMRC cancels the return (see **Part 1(g) of this Answer**). Therefore where a taxpayer has no liability or is owed a small repayment it is worth contacting HMRC to see if the return can be cancelled. Similar penalties apply to partnership returns, except there is no tax due on the partnership return so a fixed penalty will apply at each occasion of charge.

The taxpayer may appeal against a penalty, and the First-tier Tribunal may set it aside if the taxpayer has a reasonable excuse (FA 2009 Sch 55 paras 20-23). Interest is charged on late paid penalties as it is on late paid tax (TMA 1970 s 103A). See **Part 10 of this Answer.**

In a reasonable excuse case the onus is on the taxpayer to show that the excuse should be considered reasonable and that excuse must exist throughout the period of default (CH61580). The HMRC guidance indicates that a reasonable excuse for late filing of a tax return is when some unforeseeable and exceptional event beyond the taxpayer's control prevented the return being filed on time and could include:

- fire or flood at the Post Office that handled the return, or prolonged industrial action within the Post Office (if a paper return is filed);
- loss of records through fire, flood or theft;
- very serious illness such as coma, stroke, major heart attack or serious mental or life threatening illness;
- death of a close relative or domestic partner;
- a failure in HMRC's computer system;
- the taxpayer's computer breaks down just before or during the preparation of the online return.

See the HMRC guidance at www.gov.uk/tax-appeals/reasonable-excuses.

HMRC will not accept an excuse where the taxpayer has not made a reasonable effort to meet the deadline and the following reasons are not a reasonable excuse (FA 2009 Sch 55 para 23(2); CH61600; EM5173; EM75175):

- pressure of work;
- shortage of funds to pay the tax;
- lack of information;
- considering the tax form/online system too difficult;
- ignorance of the law;

- HMRC did not remind the taxpayer of the deadline;
- taxpayer did not have the relevant software on their computer to enable online filing;
- did not try to re-submit the tax return once a problem was rectified.

However, on appeal to the First-tier Tribunal, the taxpayer may find that they are granted more latitude. Interesting quotes from the Tribunal include:

- "An excuse is likely to be reasonable where the taxpayer acts in the same way as someone who seriously intends to honour their tax liabilities and obligations would act." *B&J Shopfitting Services v HMRC* [2010] UKFTT 78 (TC) at [14];
- "HMRC argues that a 'reasonable excuse' must be some exceptional circumstance which prevented timeous filing. That, as a matter of law, is wrong. Parliament has provided the penalty will not be due if the appellant can show it has 'reasonable excuse'. If Parliament had intended to say that the penalty would not be due only in exceptional circumstances, it would have said so in those terms. The phrase 'reasonable excuse' uses ordinary English words in everyday usage which must be given their plain and ordinary meaning." *NA Dudley Electrical Contractors Ltd v HMRC* [2011] UKFTT 260 (TC) at [4].

HMRC accepts that the inclusion of provisional or estimated figures does not enable it to impose a late filing penalty (unless reasonable care was not taken with the figures, or final figures could have been obtained before the return was sent in), although it will be a factor to take into account in deciding whether to open an enquiry.

The amount of the penalty is increased where the inaccuracy involves an offshore matter (from 2011/12 onwards). See **Part 12 of this Answer** for further details.

## 14. *HMRC enquiries and compliance checks*

HMRC have wide powers to enforce tax compliance. The main powers relate to enquiries into self assessment tax returns. However they operate in tandem with other powers to obtain evidence both directly from the taxpayer and from third parties. This includes obtaining specialist and bulk data.

The enquiry period is linked to the date a return is filed. For returns made on time, HMRC have a year after the day on which a return is delivered to open an enquiry, eg to 31 May 2018 for a 2016/17 return filed on 31 May 2017 (TMA 1970 s 9A(2)(a)). If the return or an amendment to it is made after the due date, then the time limit is a year from the time the return or amendment is delivered plus the period to the next quarter day, ie the next 31 January, 30 April, 31 July or 31 October) (TMA 1970 s 9A(2)). Otherwise the tax as calculated will normally stand unless there has been inadequate disclosure or failure to take reasonable care or deliberate understatement.

Following completion of the enquiry, HMRC will issue a closure notice informing the taxpayer of their conclusions and any amendments they have made to the return (TMA 1970 s 28A). The taxpayer has 30 days to appeal against the conclusions stated and amendments made by HMRC, and the appeal and postponement procedures dealt with in **Example G6** apply (TMA 1970 s 31).

If HMRC enquires into a partnership return, this automatically means that the enquiry extends to partners' personal returns, since the personal returns must reflect any changes to the partnership return (TMA 1970 s 12AC). An enquiry into a personal return relating to non-partnership matters does not affect the other partners. HMRC will notify each partner when they open and close an enquiry, but the partner responsible for the return must keep the other partners aware of how the enquiry is progressing.

HMRC has similar powers to enquire into claims made separately from the return (TMA 1970 Sch 1A para 5) (for claims procedures see **Example G3**). The time limit for opening an enquiry into such a claim is the same as for an enquiry into an amendment to a return, and the same procedures apply for the taxpayer to appeal against HMRC amendments when the enquiry is completed. There is, however, no provision for tax to be postponed.

HMRC may select cases for enquiry at random, and are not required to state whether the enquiry is a random one or whether it suspects something is wrong. There is no statutory relief for accountancy fees incurred in dealing with an enquiry, although HMRC has confirmed that if an enquiry results in no addition to trading profits, or only in an adjustment to the year of enquiry that does not arise because of careless or deliberate inaccuracies, accountancy expenses relating to the enquiry will be allowed (SP 16/91). If it is considered that an enquiry has been unnecessarily prolonged, taxpayers may ask the First-tier Tribunal to direct that it should be closed (TMA 1970 s 28A(4)), and they may also complain to the Adjudicator or Ombudsman, each of whom has the power to recommend compensation.

FA 2008 Sch 36 sets out the powers available to HMRC to check that businesses and individuals have paid the correct amount of income tax, capital gains tax, corporation tax, VAT and PAYE. The powers include the right to request information from the taxpayer, from third parties, and to visit business premises to carry out a check. Since 2008, these powers have regularly been added to, with new powers from 1 April 2012 allowing HMRC to demand information from a wide variety of third parties on a 'bulk' basis – that is, not in respect of a named taxpayer, but in relation to any and all (also known as data-gathering powers under FA 2011 Sch 23). For example, HMRC can ask rental letting agents for detailed information about rent they have collected on behalf of landlords, together with the names and addresses of the landlords for whom the agent acts, and amounts due to each. Since 17 July 2013 HMRC can also ask merchant acquirers (card payment handling businesses) for information about the payments they handle, which is intended to allow HMRC to identify businesses which are not registered for tax, or which understate their sales figures. FA 2016 extended HMRC powers to enable them to collect data from third party providers of electronic stored-value payment services – so called "digital wallets" (eg companies like Paypal, Airbnb etc) and business intermediaries. See **Example G6 explanatory note 3**.

The information powers in FA 2008 Sch 36 Part 1 can be exercised without opening a formal enquiry. HMRC can issue information notices to any person requiring the production of information and or documents provided it is reasonably required to check a person's tax position (FA 2008 Sch 36 para 1 taxpayer notices and para 2 third party notices). The notice may be appealed against unless it relates to the production of statutory records which the taxpayer is obliged to keep, or the First-tier Tribunal has approved the issue of the notice (FA 2008 Sch 36 paras 29, 30).

FA 2006 Sch 36 para 10 provides the power to inspect a person's business premises including vehicles and parts of homes used for business purposes and inspect documents on those premises provided reasonably required for the purposes of checking that person's tax position. This is not a right to *search* premises and a person has a right to refuse entry (CH25650). Therefore even when an officer has been given access to the premises he can be asked to leave at any time and HMRC's instructions make it clear that the officer must leave straight away. Where there is no reasonable excuse for the obstruction, HMRC can seek a penalty of £300 where the inspection was preapproved by the First-tier Tribunal (FA 2008 Sch 36 para 39).

The power of inspection does not extend to a person's home used *solely* as a dwelling, unless invited (although see CH25240 where the home is used as business premises).

Business records become statutory records when they are created. As stated in **Part 3 of this Answer** the normal time limit for a trader to retain their statutory records is over five years (TMA 1970 s 12B). For example, on 1 July 2016 a sole trader, with a 31 March year end, who has filed all tax returns on time and has not been subject to an enquiry in the last six years will hold statutory records for the period 1 April 2010 to 1 July 2016.

Non-business records which must be kept for tax purposes only become statutory records after the end of the chargeable period to which they relate. For example, Joanne gifts a precious ring to her sister on 1 July 2016 and on that date has an independent valuation carried out to calculate the gain arising. The valuation does not become a statutory record until after 5 April 2017 and assuming she files her return on time and no enquiry is opened must be retained until 31 January 2019 (TMA 1970 s 12B).

An information notice or inspection may only be issued where it is 'reasonably required to check a person's tax position'. However, when a return has been made for the period, the notice must be issued within the enquiry window, unless a discovery has been made. Notices may, however be issued in respect of periods for which no return has yet been made, and the enquiry window principle does not apply to PAYE and VAT compliance checks.

HMRC has issued a Charter for taxpayers titled 'Your Charter' [www.gov.uk/government/publications/your-charter]. It sets out seven rights and seven obligations of individuals, businesses and other groups who deal with HMRC. HMRC's commitments include those to respect, treat as honest and accept that someone else can act for a taxpayer. In return, they expect taxpayers to be honest, respect their staff and take care to get things right.

## 15. *HMRC determinations of tax due*

HMRC has the power to determine the amount of tax due if a return is not submitted. The determination is treated as a self-assessment until superseded by an actual self-assessment (TMA 1970 s 28C). A determination under TMA 1970 s 28C cannot be made more than three years after the filing date for the return, and a superseding self-assessment can only be made within twelve months after the determination.

## 16. *Simple assessments*

For 2016/17 onwards, HMRC can issue an assessment (known as a 'simple assessment') of an individual's or trustee's income or capital gains tax liability without the taxpayer submitting a self-assessment tax return (TMA 1970 ss 28H, 28I). This is intended to be used where HMRC believes it already has all the information needed to calculate a taxpayer's liability.

An individual who receives a simple assessment is removed from the need to notify HMRC of that income under TMA 1970 s 7, however he or she remains liable to notify any other income or gain excluded from the simple assessment. The taxpayer the right to query the simple assessment within 60 days of issue (TMA 1970 s 31AA). If no objections are raised the simple assessment becomes final.

HMRC can issue more than one simple assessment for the same tax year (even if the earlier assessment has not been withdrawn). Where a notice to file a self-assessment tax return has already been issued, this notice must be withdrawn before or at the same time as a simple assessment is issued (see **Part 1(g) to this Answer**). HMRC has four years from the end of the tax year to issue a simple assessment (TMA 1970 s 34).

The due date for payment of the tax remains the same as it would be under self-assessment, unless the simple assessment is issued after 31 October following the tax year, in which case it is extended to three months from the date of issue (TMA 1970 s 59BA). The late payment rules in FA 2009 Sch 56 are extended to include simple assessments.

## 17. *HMRC assessments*

The main assessments issued under self-assessment are for 'discovery' (since simple assessments are outside of the self-assessment regime). Discovery assessments under TMA 1970 s 29 are issued to prevent a loss of tax in cases of failure to take reasonable care and deliberate understatement or where there has been inadequate disclosure (see **Example G6 explanatory note 23**).

There are some other limited occasions when assessments will be raised outside the self-assessment system (excluding simple assessments), for example:

- Under ITA 2007 s 424 to recover tax deemed deducted from a gift aid payment to charity where the payer has insufficient income tax or capital gains tax chargeable to cover the tax – see **Example N4**;
- Under ITA 2007 s 234 to withdraw relief under the enterprise investment scheme – see **Example N7**;
- Under TCGA 1992 s 153A to withdraw capital gains rollover relief provisionally given in respect of business assets – see **Example L9**;
- Under FA 2004 s 192(9) to recover basic rate or other tax relief on excessive pension contributions.

Tax under HMRC assessment is due for payment thirty days after the issue of the assessment (TMA 1970 s 59B(6)). Interest is, however, payable from 31 January following the tax year to which the assessment relates, regardless of when the assessment is issued (TMA 1970 s 86).

## 18. *Online filing*

Accountants and tax agents may submit tax returns in respect of individuals, partnerships and trustees electronically (TMA 1970 Sch 3A), where the taxpayer or agent has registered with HMRC online services.

HMRC is very keen to increase the number of returns filed digitally, but in response to appeal decisions are also developing an 'assisted digital' programme to support taxpayers who are unable to move online. See Example G4.

For agents initial registration is via the GOV.UK website using the agent's code [www.gov.uk/guidance/client-authorisation-an-overview]. For new agents, requests for a code must be made in writing including name, business name, address and telephone number to Central Agent Authorisation Team in Longbenton. The agent must then register via the Government gateway at www.gateway.gov.uk. The agent is required to keep a copy of the filed tax return and accompanying schedules which must have been approved by the client before submission. The approval must authorise the electronic submission of the return.

Users of SA Online have the facility to view the client's self-assessment statement of account and perform basic housekeeping tasks online. The online account facility enables agents to see liabilities and allocation of payments, and to expand details relating to the current and earlier years. Agents can also check when repayments are issued, request repayments, apply to reduce payments on account, view the previous year's tax account and check the filing status (ie which returns have been filed for self-assessment and when) online. It is also possible to print the forms needed to support some mortgage applications – form SA302 (the HMRC calculation of the tax liability for the year). Agents who file using commercial software can do this though their software.

## 19. *Non-statutory clearances*

HMRC provides clearance across all business taxes where there is a material uncertainty. For direct tax changes older than the last four Finance Acts there is an additional requirement that the uncertainty relates to a commercially significant issue. HMRC aims to respond to applications within 28 days although reserves the right for longer in complex cases.

## 20. *Certificates of tax deposit*

Individuals, partnerships, personal representatives, trustees or companies may purchase certificates of tax deposit, subject to an initial deposit of £500, with minimum additions of £250. The certificates may be used to pay any tax except PAYE, VAT, annual tax on enveloped dwellings-related capital gains tax, tax deducted from payments to subcontractors and corporation tax. The only purpose for which companies may use tax deposit certificates is to pay income tax due under the quarterly accounting system. A certificate purchased in the name of a partnership can only be used against partnership liabilities. See www.gov.uk/guidance/certificate-of-tax-deposit-scheme.

Interest at a variable rate accrues daily for a maximum of six years (for certificates under £100,000 the current rate is 0%). A lower rate of interest applies if the deposit is withdrawn for cash rather than used to cover tax liabilities. The interest accrued at the time the deposit is used or cashed is charged to tax as savings income.

The certificates are a way of ensuring that funds are available to meet tax payments when due. They also prevent interest charges on tax in dispute, because interest on overdue tax is not charged when the certificates are used to pay tax, except to the extent if any that the deposit was made after the due date of payment for the tax.

## 21. *Short tax return*

A short tax return can be issued by HMRC to taxpayers whose affairs are straightforward. These include employees and pensioners with limited investment income and those self-employed with turnover below £83,000 (VAT threshold for 2016/17 return). The return does not include the facility to self-calculate so needs to be completed by 31 October for HMRC to perform the calculations before the following 31 January. There is an option to file the short return over the telephone using voice recognition software, but cannot be filed online through the self assessment system. A short tax return cannot be used by a company director, those receiving trust income or those who require supplementary pages. A short return will not be issued on demand or to taxpayers who failed to file on time in the previous tax year. A taxpayer whose affairs have changed such that they are not eligible for a short return must request a full return.

## 22. *Disclosure of use of tax avoidance schemes*

Taxpayers who use tax avoidance schemes are required to include on their tax return the registration number of the scheme. If the scheme has been implemented offshore or developed in-house then taxpayers will be required to provide details of the scheme directly to HMRC. See **Example N5** for more details of this issue.

## 23. *Student loans*

Where an individual is self-employed, their student loan repayment is made together with their tax payment, ie, by 31 January after the end of the year of assessment (SI 2009/470). Student loan repayments for a Plan 1 loan are calculated as 9% of the income over the starting limit of £17,495 for 2016/17 (£17,335 for 2015/16). Plan 2 student loans relate to English and Welsh students who started on their course on or after 1 September 2012. They are repaid at 9% of earnings over £21,000. Student loan repayments are not included in the payments on account for the following year.

For example, Jo's 2016/17 profits amounted to £30,000 and her tax calculation is:

| | | | | | | |
|---|---|---|---|---|---|---|
| Income | | | | | | 30,000 |
| Less personal allowance | | | | | | (11,000) |
| | | | | | | 19,000 |
| Tax thereon | 19,000 | | | @ 20% | 3,800 | |
| Class 4 NIC | 30,000 | – | 8,060 | @ 9% | 1,975 | |
| Student loan | 30,000 | – | 17,495 | @ 9% | 1,125 | |
| Total | | | | | | 6,900 |
| Less payments on account for 2016/17 say | | | | | | (6,000) |
| Balancing tax payment due 31 January 2018 | | | | | | 900 |
| First payment on account for 2017/18 due 31.1.18 | | | | | | 2,888 |
| Second payment on account for 2017/18 due 31.7.18 | | | | | | 2,888 |

The payments on account are half the total excluding the student loan, ie, £6,900 – £1,125 = £5,775/2 = £2,888.

Where an individual is an employee, student loan deductions are made by the employer each pay day, ie, normally monthly or weekly. Each pay day is treated separately and therefore varies based on earnings. If earnings are below the starting limit for that period (ie, £17,495/12 or 52) the employer should not make a deduction.

Student loan borrowers have historically been known to overpay their loan due to the time delay between employers making deductions from salary each month and submitting their annual return with details of repayments. To avoid this the Student Loans Company introduced an initiative under which a borrower can opt out of PAYE and make payments by direct debit. Where this happens HMRC issue a SL2 Stop Notice to the employer. Guidance can be found at www.gov.uk/repaying-your-student-loan/overview.

Student loan repayments can also be affected by large savings income (over £2,000 pa), when a liability will arise in respect of this income. Repayments can be made voluntarily direct to the Student Loans Company, but voluntary repayments do not reduce the amount payable in respect of income, so this should be borne in mind when planning them.

## 24. *Internal review*

All tax appeals are heard by either the First-tier Tribunal or the Upper-tier Tribunal. For direct taxes, taxpayers have an additional route to resolving disputes with HMRC of requesting an internal review. The HMRC case reviewer reviews the decision made by the case worker; objectively checking whether the disputed decisions are in line with HMRC's legal and technical guidance, policy and current practice (ARTG4060, ARTG4080).

The review may conclude that the decision should be (TMA 1970 ss 49E, 49G):

- upheld – the taxpayer can appeal within 30 days and proceed to a tribunal;
- varied – the original decision is changed in some way. The taxpayer has the right to appeal within 30 days;
- cancelled – HMRC backs down and accepts the taxpayer's argument.

The internal review is not part of the appeal procedure. It is not intended as a substitute for tribunal hearings, but rather to avoid unnecessary and costly hearings. A review can be offered by HMRC or requested by the taxpayer, but will always be offered if the taxpayer has asked for an appeal (TMA 1970 ss 49B, 49C). The taxpayer may refuse this offer and proceed direct to appeal if he wishes. Where requested by a taxpayer, HMRC will provide its view of the matter. HMRC must then carry out a review within 45 days (unless a different period is agreed) (ARTG4850).

HMRC also uses mediation to resolve disputes with business customers. The alternative dispute resolution (ADR) process is available if the disagreement is making no progress. It allows a facilitator (from HMRC) to mediate between the two parties. See www.gov.uk/guidance/tax-disputes-alternative-dispute-resolution-adr.

## 25. *Business Payment Support Service (BPSS)*

The BPSS exists to help viable businesses having difficulty in paying their tax liabilities due to the economic climate. Upon making contact with the service it is usual to agree a time to pay arrangement. These typically allow a business to repay accrued tax debts over a period which meets the taxpayer's individual needs (often six to twelve months). Interest is normally charged on the late payment of liabilities but penalties and surcharges can be avoided where a taxpayer complies with the agreement. The business support telephone number is 0300 200 3835.

A business which is incurring losses in the current period of trade can ask for relief for the loss to be taken into account in negotiating the time to pay arrangement. Strictly, relief for losses cannot be given until the accounting period producing the loss has come to an end. This arrangement allows a time to pay arrangement to bridge the period from when a tax liability falls due to when relief for the loss can formally be claimed. If the BPSS does take current period losses into account it will ask the business to undertake to submit the return for the current year on time.

HMRC uses debt collection agencies to provide additional capacity to pursue and collect tax debts. HMRC charges fixed costs on cases in county courts (chasing debts) where judgement is awarded in HMRC's favour (although see **Part 27 to this Answer** below).

## 26. *Collection of small debts through PAYE*

Debts can be collected through the PAYE system. Balancing payments due under self-assessment of less than £3,000 can be collected via an adjustment to the individual's PAYE code (often referred to as coding out). This is possible providing the self-assessment tax return is submitted by 30 December after the end of the tax year (SI 2003/2682 reg 186).

Older self-assessment debts, overpaid tax credits and late paid Class 2 national insurance contributions are subject to a different collection limit. The amount that can be collected is determined by the taxpayer's PAYE income for the year (SI 2003/2682 reg 14D):

| *Estimated PAYE income for the tax year* | *Coding out limit* |
|---|---|
| Up to £29,999 | £3,000 |
| £30,000 to £39,999 | £5,000 |
| £40,000 to £49,999 | £7,000 |
| £50,000 to £59,999 | £9,000 |
| £60,000 to £69,999 | £11,000 |
| £70,000 to £79,999 | £13,000 |
| £80,000 to £89,999 | £15,000 |
| £90,000 and above | £17,000 |

Collection via the coding out of debts cannot take the total amount deducted from the PAYE income to over 50% (SI 2003/2682, regs 23(5), 28(5), 144(4) as read with SI 2003/2682, regs 2, 4).

The taxpayer can object to his code being amended to collect the debt(s), but if he or she does so then HMRC will start immediate collection proceedings (SI 2003/2682, reg 14C(1)).

## 27. *Direct recovery of debts*

HMRC has the right to recover tax debts from the bank accounts of individuals and companies who have sufficient funds to pay, but have not paid their tax liability (F(No 2)A 2015 Sch 8). There is a long and prescriptive process, which involves HMRC contacting banks for details of the accounts held by debtors, and then issuing a hold order over the funds, provided that at least £5,000 remains available to the debtor. The debtor then has a right of appeal to the courts, after which the funds will be paid over to HMRC. The power will only be used in respect of debts in excess of £1,000, and there must be a face-to-face meeting with the debtor before the power can be used. Vulnerable taxpayers, such as those in poor physical or mental health, will not have their debts collected via direct recovery; they will be referred to a specialist debt team within HMRC and may also be referred to tax charities, such as Tax Aid or Tax Help For Older People, for support.

# Question

Outline the procedure for making claims and elections, both for individuals and companies.

# Answer

## Claims procedure for income tax and capital gains tax

The procedure for making claims and elections and for giving notices was formalised with the introduction of self-assessment. TMA 1970 s 42 provides that where notice to submit a return has been given, claims must normally be made in the return or an amendment to the return, which means that the time limit for making the claim is normally twelve months from the filing date for the return. TMA 1970 s 42(1A) requires claims to be quantified when made.

Where it is not possible to include a claim in a return, a separate claims procedure is laid down in TMA 1970 Sch 1A, under which similar provisions apply as for entries in returns, ie HMRC has nine months from the date of the claim to correct obvious errors and the taxpayer has twelve months to amend it (TMA 1970 Sch 1A para 3). HMRC may enquire into a claim made outside a return, or amendment to such a claim, within the period ending 12 months after 31 January following the tax year to which the claim relates, or if later, the quarter day (31 January, 30 April, etc) next following 12 months after the date of the claim (TMA 1970 Sch 1A para 5). Unless another time limit is stipulated in the legislation, the time limit for claims made outside the return is four years from the end of the tax year (TMA 1970 s 43). The claims procedures discussed above do not apply to capital allowances claims by traders, as these claims are required to be made in a return or amendment to a return (CAA 2001 s 3(3)(a)).

Where HMRC enquires into a return or claim, and as a result it makes amendments to the return or claim, the taxpayer may appeal against the amendments within 30 days of being notified of them (TMA 1970 ss 31, 31A, Sch 1A para 9).

*Claims for relief involving two or more years*

TMA 1970 Sch 1B deals with claims and elections that involve two or more years. It does not apply to claims to treat payments made under gift aid to be deemed paid in the preceding tax year under ITA 2007 s 426 (see **Example N4**).

Where relief is claimed for a loss incurred or payment made in one tax year to be set against the income of an earlier year, then although the tax adjustment resulting from the claim is calculated by reference to the tax position of the earlier year, the claim is treated as relating to the later year and is given effect in relation to that later year. Normally this is achieved by showing the tax repayment or the extra tax due for the earlier year on the self-assessment tax return for the later year.

These provisions also apply to carrying back post-cessation receipts (see **Example C4 part (c)(ii)**) and claims for averaging farming profits and creative artists (see **Example C14**).

For claims to carry back losses, the recalculated tax will be lower than that originally payable. Farmers' and creative artists' averaging claims may result in the earlier year's tax being reduced or increased. Claims to carry back post-cessation receipts result in the tax of the earlier years being increased. Since the claim is *given effect* in relation to the later year, however, it is the view of HMRC that interest on underpaid tax or supplement on overpaid tax runs from the balancing payment date for the later year, ie 31 January following that later year.

When recalculating the tax position of the earlier year following a carry back claim, any relevant claims for allowances, reliefs etc, may be made or revised, for example transferring surplus married couple's allowance.

## Claims for coding adjustments under PAYE

Taxpayers may make claims for coding adjustments (for example claim for higher rate relief for personal pension contributions) either in their tax returns or separately from the return. A claim made in-year may subsequently be reflected in a tax return. Where no such return is issued the claim will normally become final 22 months after the end of the tax year (for example by 31 January 2019 for a 2016/17 claim) and cannot be reopened by HMRC unless there has been deliberate understatement or incomplete disclosure. HMRC has confirmed it will apply the same time limits where coding claims are carried forward automatically, or are implemented on the basis of preliminary information from the taxpayer, even though HMRC may strictly enquire into such claims at any time up to four/six years after the end of the tax year.

The assessment time limits for IT, CGT, CT, VAT and PAYE are normally (TMA 1970 s 36; FA 1998, Sch 18 para 46):

- four years for mistake (despite reasonable care);
- six years (except VAT which is four) for failure to take reasonable care; and
- 20 years for deliberate understatement.

## Claims procedure for companies

Under corporation tax self-assessment, the provisions for claims and elections are similar to those for income tax self-assessment. The general provisions are in FA 1998 Sch 18 Part VII. Unless there is a specific provision giving a longer or shorter period, the time limit for making claims is four years from the end of the accounting period. Where a discovery assessment is made, other than one arising from the taxpayer's deliberate understatement, provision is made for claims, elections, notices etc to be made, revoked or varied within one year after the end of the company accounting period in which the assessment is made.

Where possible claims must be included in the corporation tax return (CT600) or in an amended return and the claims will be given effect in the company's self-assessment. This means that claims must normally be made within two years from the end of the accounting period.

The enquiry period for companies that are not members of large groups is linked to the date a return is filed (FA 1998 Sch 18 para 24). For returns made on time, HMRC has a year after the day on which a return is delivered to open an enquiry, eg to 30 August 2017 for a 31 May 2016 year end return filed on 31 August 2016. For large groups, the enquiry period (for returns filed on time) is one year after the filing due date, eg 30 January 2018 for a 31 January 2016 year end return filed on 31 August 2016, on the basis the different returns from such groups need to be looked at together. There is, however, a concession to allow groups to fix their enquiry window by reference to the filing date for the last company in the group.

If HMRC enquire into the return the time limit is extended to thirty days after the time when the profits or losses of the period are finally determined. The provisions of TMA 1970 Sch 1A mentioned under the income tax self-assessment provisions above also apply to companies in respect of claims that cannot be included in a return. The time limit for an HMRC enquiry into a claim made outside a return is the quarter day (31 January, 30 April, etc) next following 12 months after the date of the claim.

Also see **Examples G6, I1** and **I2** regarding HMRC's compliance checks.

The group relief claims provisions are in FA 1998 Sch 18 Part VIII. The provisions enable group relief claims to be made without being accompanied by copy notices of consent to surrender, and enable one company to act on behalf of the group in making claims and surrenders and amending returns where the group is dealt with mainly within one tax district.

The four-year time limit for claims does not apply. Group relief claims must be made by the latest of (FA 1998 Sch 18 para 74):

(1) one year after the filing date for the return;

(2) 30 days after the completion of an HMRC enquiry into the return;

(3) thirty days after notice of HMRC amendments to the return following an enquiry; and

(4) 30 days after the final determination of an appeal against such an amendment.

The order in which claims are treated as made for the purpose of determining amounts previously surrendered or claimed in respect of group or consortium relief for overlapping periods is dealt with in CTA 2010 s 141(1). See also CTM80220.

Capital allowances claims are dealt with in FA 1998 Sch 18 Part IX and CAA 2001 s 3(3)(b). The four-year time limit does not apply and claims are subject to the same time limits as stated above for group relief (FA 1998 Sch 18 para 82). If the effect of a claim following an enquiry is to reduce the allowances available for a later period for which a return has been submitted, the company has 30 days from the settlement of the enquiry to make any necessary amendments to that return, failing which amendments will be made by HMRC (FA 1998 Sch 18 paras 61-64).

*Late claims*

HMRC has discretion to admit late claims by companies. It has stated that this will only be done in exceptional circumstances, for example where the delay was due to circumstances beyond the company's control, or where an HMRC error was a major reason for the delay; not where claims are late because the company has changed its mind or because a different combination of claims would be more advantageous.

For late claims involving losses, group relief and or capital allowances see SP 5/01.

## Overpaid tax

Relief is available for overpaid tax under TMA 1970 Sch 1AB and FA 1998 Sch 18 paras 51-51G. The rules tighten up the old error or mistake rules, restricting the claims for overpaid tax which can be made (TMA 1970 Sch 1AB, para 2; FA 1998 Sch 18 para 51A). Claims for a refund of overpaid tax are subject to the normal rules on HMRC rights of enquiry into claims made outside of the return. The time limit for claims is four years (TMA 1970 Sch 1AB para 3; FA 1998 Sch 18 para 51B).

FA 2016 reverses HMRC defeat in the Upper Tribunal in *R (oao Higgs) v HMRC* [2015] STC 1600 and ensures the four year time limit applies to self-assessment tax returns in the future (TMA 1970, s 34A). In the *Higgs* case the Upper Tribunal held that a self-assessment tax return submitted by a taxpayer more than four years after the tax year to which it related should be accepted by HMRC and that the four year time limit in TMA 1970 s 34(1) had no application to a self-assessment return. The return in question resulted in a repayment of tax being due to the taxpayer. There is a very small window (up to 5 April 2017) to submit 'late' returns in the right circumstances (TMA 1970 s 34A(4)) – see www.gov.uk/government/publications/income-tax-time-limits-for-self-assessment/income-tax-time-limits-for-self-assessment.

HMRC accepts that any interest, penalties or surcharge for the claim year should be mitigated, in line with the relief granted under the claim.

## Equitable liability/special relief

Once the time limits for appealing against assessments, or for substituting a taxpayer's own self-assessment for an HMRC determination under self-assessment, have expired, the tax assessed or determined becomes legally due.

HMRC has, however, stated that where income tax (including PAYE tax) or capital gains tax is higher than it would have been if all the relevant information had been submitted at the proper time, it may be prepared to accept an amount equal to what the correct liability would have been, providing the taxpayer's affairs are brought fully up to date. Having said this, such discretion should rarely be necessary under the self-assessment system. This practice used to be known as 'equitable liability'. HMRC proposed abolition of the practice, regarding it as unnecessary, but the response to the consultation indicated that there was a clear need for this. As a result it was legislated with effect from 1 April 2011 under the new name of 'special relief', see SACM12215 onwards (TMA 1970 Sch 1AB para 3A; FA 1998 Sch 18 para 51BA).

# Explanatory Notes

*Time limits and late claims*

(1) There are many exceptions to the normal time limits for claims and it is essential that the time limit for the relevant claim is complied with. Although HMRC usually has discretion to admit late claims, it will only

exercise that discretion in exceptional circumstances. See SP 5/01 for HMRC's approach to late company claims for loss relief, capital allowances and group relief (CTM97060).

*Requirements for valid claims*

(2) The requirements for making a valid claim have often not been clear-cut, and it was only as a result of losing a case on what a group relief claim needed to contain that HMRC specified the minimum information required. Group relief claims are now made in accordance with specific statutory provisions (FA 1998 Sch 18 para 68).

As far as income tax loss claims are concerned, a loss claim may be made by indicating the source of the loss, the year of loss and either the year of claim or the statutory reference under which the relief is claimed. Providing that claim is made within the relevant time limit, the supporting accounts may follow later.

(3) Many claims are required by the provisions of the legislation to be made in writing. However HMRC has the power to direct that specified income tax claims may be made by the use of a telecommunications system (TMA 1970 s 43E). This applies to claims by individuals or their agents (but not to claims by partners, trustees or personal representatives). Claims can be made electronically in so far as they are included within a tax return filed online.

# Question

Write a letter to your client Peter explaining the implications for him of HMRC's proposals for making tax digital. He is a longstanding self-employed client with annual turnover of around £40,000, per annum, showing an annual profit of around £25,000, although this does fluctuate, according to his workload. His wife keeps his business records in an exercise book, and makes out invoices in a duplicate book. He does not use software and is not convinced that the internet is secure enough to use internet banking, preferring to visit the bank on a weekly basis to make bankings and draw cash needed for expenses. He also has some bank interest on a savings account. His wife is paid a modest salary of £50 per week for her help in the business, and she has no other income.

# Answer

Dear Peter

The purpose of this letter is to advise you of developments that may affect the way you keep records for your business in the future. Although these proposals are in their early stages, it is very likely that they will be implemented in some form over the next two years, so I wanted to give you some time to reflect on them before we discuss what is the right way forward for you and your business.

HMRC is planning a major modernisation of their computer system, and as part of this will be moving in 2018 to a much more digital tax administration system. There are hopes that the changes will benefit everyone – HMRC, their staff and taxpayers, by providing a more responsive service which is easy for taxpayers to understand.

As part of these changes, HMRC will be implementing a new requirement for most businesses to keep their records digitally, using software and "apps" on portable digital equipment such as smart phones and tablets, although ordinary computers will also be able to access this software. There are plans for the smallest businesses to be excluded from the new requirement, but at present it is very likely that your business is too large to be excluded.

What this means to you and your wife is that (with our help) your business records must be moved onto a computer based system of record keeping. Your records will need to be kept up to date at least quarterly, and the summary information submitted to HMRC within one month of the end of each quarter. You will be able to choose which quarter ends you would prefer, so with an accounting date of 31 May, I would suggest that you think in terms of quarters ending 31 August, 30 November, 28 (or 29) February and 31 May. You would then be supplying HMRC with an update by the end of September, December, March and June each year.

There is quite a wide range of suitable software available now, but it is likely that more will become available over the coming year, so we will sit down with you both in 2017 and help you decide what you and your wife would be able to do, and how we can help you with this. It may be that you would prefer us to take over your bookkeeping for you but we would also be very happy to give you both the support you need to do this for yourselves. The first quarter for which digital records will be mandatory is likely to be the period starting on 1 June 2018, so we would be planning to start you with software from 1 June 2017, to give you a year to find your feet before the new system starts. Most businesses find it easier to make changes to their accounting system at the start of a new accounting period, which is why we are recommending starting in June 2017. HMRC will not be imposing penalties for late returns for 12 months after the start of the new system, so penalties will not be a problem for you is you struggle at first.

On a personal level, both you and your wife will have access to your personal digital tax account (which is already available), which will show your tax position once the new system is introduced. The tax account for you will show the tax you are likely to have to pay at the end of the year as you provide the quarterly updates, on which the tax computation will be based. It is likely that this will give you confidence that you have put enough money away to meet your tax bill – and you will be able to make voluntary payments against your tax liability if you wish to. You will also find your state pension prediction on your digital tax account, which many people find very useful. If you have not yet accessed your digital account and would like some help to do this, we have a member of staff trained to help our clients with this – please just ask.

As the new system beds in more information will be collected by HMRC and shown on your digital tax account – for instance, from April 2018 any interest you receive is likely to be reported directly to HMRC. Instead of completing this information on a tax return you will be able to log on to your account and check the figure directly. Of course, we shall be very pleased to do this for you if you prefer. HMRC predicts that by 2020 there will be no more tax returns.

We are quite excited by these new developments, but do not underestimate the change for both us and our clients. We are developing new ways of working with businesses to support them through the changes, and will be looking forward to meeting with you early in 2017 to discuss the specific help you are likely to need. This will be followed by a new letter of engagement, as the services we provide to you are likely to change quite significantly. In the meantime, if you are worried about any aspect of this, do ring the office and we'll do our best to put your mind at rest.

With very best wishes,

## Explanatory Notes

(1) HMRC unveiled six consultation documents on 15 August 2016:

- bringing business tax into the digital age
- simplifying tax for unincorporated businesses
- simplified cash basis for unincorporated property businesses
- voluntary pay as you go
- tax administration
- transforming the tax system through better use of third party information

The consultation on the detail of Making Tax Digital (MTD), as the project is known ended on 7 November, and the next detail on this development is likely to be in December 2016, with the release of draft legislation for the Finance Bill 2017.

Much of the detail in the consultation documents is beyond the understanding of the average small business, so the letter includes none of the detail about the simplification measures proposed; a represented client is not likely to be interested in technical changes to accounting methods.

*Digital record keeping*

(2) The proposals depend on the mandation of digital record keeping by businesses. This is the first time any tax authority in the world has sought to dictate the way in which tax records are kept. Further, at present, digital does not include the use of spreadsheets but instead depends on record keeping 'apps' which could be used on any digital device including a smartphone.

Apps will, using technology known as application programme interfaces (APIs) shared by HMRC with developers, identify potential miscoding of transactions and spot unusual transactions or patterns in data, offering advice to the taxpayer through 'prompts' and 'nudges'. This new way of checking records at a transactional level support HMRC's ambition to close the tax gap through reducing errors and careless mistakes, which in turn will help finance the whole project.

At least once every three months (or more often if the taxpayer chooses) he will review the data and upload a summary to HMRC for which a time limit of one month is suggested. The uploaded data will be displayed on his digital tax account, together with an estimate of his tax liability for the year to date, offering the chance for taxpayers to save for their tax in real time.

(3) Some help is provided for the smallest businesses in the following terms:

- businesses with a turnover of below £10,000 and / or landlords with gross rents of less than £10,000 will be exempt from the requirement to keep digital records and update HMRC quarterly. However, if a small business owner also has rental income the threshold is applied to the total. This is in addition to an exemption announced in Budget 2016 for taxpayers with a secondary source of self-employment or rental income of no more than £10,000 gross
- the next rank of businesses (i.e. those with turnover of more than the threshold but up to an unspecified limit) will have an extra year to join digital record keeping and quarterly updating.
- businesses which cannot use digital technology (a definition carried across from the current VAT rules where online returns have been mandatory for a while), often referred to as the 'digitally

excluded', will be exempt from the requirements. However, they may still have to update HMRC quarterly by other means

- charities and community amateur sports clubs will be exempt from the requirement

Note that the threshold mentioned above is subject to the consultation outcomes but the Government confirms it will not be lower than £10,000.

In general, the design approach is to allow as much choice as possible, within minimum parameters to allow businesses to continue to use the format and approach of accounting systems that they have already. Adjusting for accruals and prepayments, stock etc. and the tax adjustments such as disallowances and capital allowances can be made either periodically or in a separate year end update (called an end of year declaration), for which nine months will be allowed. In any event, the year end declaration finalises the information for the year, in a similar way to the submission of a complete tax return. Penalties for inaccuracies will not apply to quarterly updates, but only to the year end declaration.

Partnerships will submit periodic updates for the whole firm, with the relevant partner profit or loss shares being fed through onto each partner's digital tax account.

The actual commencement date is also the subject of the consultation, with the most likely option being businesses joining the digital record keeping requirements from the first day of their accounting period starting on or after 6 April 2018. So, Peter who has a 31 May year end will join MTD from 1 June 2018.

*Simplifying tax for unincorporated businesses*

(4) Part of the consultation process has been to examine approaches to simplifying tax for businesses, to ease the introduction of MTD. Four main areas of simplification have been proposed:

- increasing the entry threshold for the simplified cash basis which is currently linked to the VAT registration threshold
- reforming the basis period rules for the self-employed
- changing the calculation of taxable profits for those not using the simplified cash basis by removing some accounting requirements, including accruals and prepayments, stock adjustments, revenue recognition of long-term contracts and bad debt provisions, and
- further reforming the capital / revenue divide under the simplified cash basis

Some of these ideas will provide real simplification, but they are of minimal interest to the client, and are therefore not discussed in the letter.

(5) There is also a proposal to introduce an optional simplified cash basis for landlords, potentially without a limit on gross rents. It is suggested that this could apply to residential properties, commercial properties and furnished holiday lets (FHL) owned by unincorporated businesses. It may also be available to unincorporated non-resident landlords.

There would be some changes to the cash basis as used by trading businesses, but once again, this represents a marked simplification.

*Voluntary pay as you go*

(6) There was a separate consultation setting out the options for taxpayers to make payments towards their eventual tax liability, aided by information on their digital tax account. Some businesses may find this a useful aspect of MTD, but the reliability of the tax figures will depend on the accuracy of the data submitted in the quarterly updates. If this data needs substantial corrections at the end of year stage, the usefulness of the tax projections will be severely undermined.

Government has confirmed that the actual due dates for payment of income tax liabilities under self-assessment will not change before 2020.

*Tax administration*

(7) There will need to be significant changes to tax administration legislation to meet the new rules. At the same time, HMRC has taken the opportunity to move away from the fixed penalty regime for late returns which has been so unpopular since the last change in 2011. Changes will very likely be included in Finance Bill 2017.

In principle powers (and safeguards) such as enquiry and other compliance powers, determinations, discovery assessments and corrections to 'returns' will be carried across into the new regime with only the necessary changes to articulate with the effective abolition of the tax return. Compliance powers will not be directed at quarterly updates, as the Government recognises that taxpayers may need to make corrections in the end of year declaration.

(8) For late submission and late payment sanctions some new proposals are advanced, based on a discussion paper on penalties issued in early 2015.

Non-deliberate late submission penalties could move to a more flexible points based system, imposing a penalty when a certain level of points have been reached through multiple failures across all tax obligations. Two potential models are included in the consultation for comment. Deliberate late submission penalties may be tax-geared (as opposed to the initial flat £100 penalty which applies currently).

Late payment sanctions could move to a 'penalty interest' model (in addition to the normal interest charge) which would escalate as the default lengthens. An alternative is to align all late payment penalties across both the direct and indirect tax regimes.

*Transforming the tax system through better use of third party information*

(9) The benefits of these proposals are clear – no taxpayer would ever be required to tell HMRC about information already in the tax authority's possession. So as early as April 2017 details of pay, pensions and benefits reported by employers and pension providers would be shown on the individual tax account.

From April 2018, this would be supplemented by interest from banks and building societies. The interest from each account will be displayed separately.

Beyond that, HMRC is considering additional powers to require information from third parties – the most obvious of which is dividends. Also mentioned is rent paid to landlords (presumably by letting agents).

# Question

Your firm has recently been appointed as advisers to Sparks Manufacturing Ltd. Following your appointment the accountant of the company has informed you that HMRC is shortly to carry out a PAYE compliance visit and he has asked that your firm review the procedures in operation prior to the HMRC visit. The following information is relevant:

(1) The company has 36 full-time and ten part-time workers. These include three full-time office staff, one sales representative, two apprentices recruited straight from school, and the directors, who are Mr and Mrs Sparks. Mr and Mrs Sparks own all the shares in the company.

(2) The manufacturing workers are paid weekly in cash, and earnings are variable depending on hours worked. Any production bonuses are paid on a month-by-month basis.

(3) The office staff are paid monthly by cheque. The sales representative is paid gross on a commission basis and is treated as self-employed. His commission is in excess of £44,000 per annum.

(4) Mr and Mrs Sparks receive monthly standing order payments of £500 each. Any additional amounts for expenses are drawn by cheque on a monthly basis.

(5) The accountant applies PAYE and national insurance to the wages and bonus payments made to the full-time employees with the exception of Mr and Mrs Sparks and the salesman. He pays over the deductions monthly, taking care to post the cheque to the HMRC Accounts Office on the 19th of each month.

(6) Part-time employees are all production workers, who each receive £150 per week gross. The production bonus for part-time workers in April 2015 amounted to £110 each and was paid gross.

(7) The company does not hold signed Forms P46 or starter declarations for the following part-time workers:

   (a) Mrs Acorn (aged 35) – a married lady with no other employment.

   (b) Mrs Beech (aged 65) – in receipt of a state pension based upon her husband's contributions and with no other employment.

   (c) Mr Chestnut (aged 19) – a student who only works during vacations.

   (d) Mr Dallow (aged 40) – also working as a milkman.

   It is understood that all part-time workers were first employed on 6 April 2013 when the evening shift commenced.

(8) The company pays £18 per week to each of its full-time employees and £10 per week to each of its part-time employees as subsistence payments. These amounts do not appear on the payroll records and the full-time employees have received them since 6 April 2011 and the part-time workers since they joined the company.

(9) The company provides an old car first registered in 2005 (1,298 cc, Euro-IV diesel, $CO_2$ rating 109g/km) with fuel to the foreman, who travels 10,000 business miles per year. The list price of the car when new was £23,200, although it is now worth only about £3,000. The foreman's wage in 2015/16 was £18,000.

(10) Miss Fallow, part-time secretary to the managing director, also has a Euro-IV diesel car provided for her own use with all fuel paid for by the company. The current car is three years old (1,298 cc) and had a list price of £10,200 when new and a $CO_2$ emissions figure of 109g/km. In 2015/16 she travelled approximately 1,000 business miles. Her salary in that year was £8,400.

(11) Mr Sparks, whose salary is shown in the company accounts as £45,000 per annum, is provided with a 2,500 cc car which had a list price of £26,000 and a $CO_2$ emissions figure of 232g/km when new in 2014. He travels 25,000 business miles each year. Mrs Sparks only attends directors' meetings and is paid £4,700

per annum. She is provided with a three-year-old car (1,988 cc, $CO_2$ figure 219g/km) which had a list price of £19,500 when new. Business mileage is minimal. Fuel is provided for both cars.

Because being contactable is crucial for his business, Mr Sparks has two mobile telephones on different networks in case the signal is poor on one of the networks while he is travelling. The telephone bills on his main number in 2015/16 amounted to £1,200 plus VAT. From the bills it would appear that 40% of the calls are non-business. His second number is also on a company contract. With a full data plan so that he can receive and send emails and access cloud storage using the phone as a hotspot with his laptop while away from the office, the subscription costs £720 plus VAT per year.

(12) Mr Jones, the accountant, uses his own petrol car (1,998 cc) for business purposes and is paid 75p per mile.

(13) Miss Fallow prefers to buy her own fuel, which is reimbursed to her through petty cash.

The other car users and the sales representative have obtained petrol on company credit cards, the amounts for 2015/16 being as follows (amounts excluding VAT):

| | £ |
|---|---|
| Foreman | 1,480 |
| Sales representative | 2,040 |
| Mr Sparks | 3,880 |
| Mrs Sparks | 300 |

As car parking is limited at the factory, five season tickets for the car park in the next street are purchased by the company for £2,000 per annum plus VAT each for use by the above.

All VAT on the above items has been recovered in full without any adjustments for private usage.

The apprentices are allowed to claim their bus fares for travel to their FE College when they are on day release.

(14) The following expenses have been drawn in the year 2015/16 (amounts shown net of VAT where appropriate):

| | *Subsistence* | *Entertaining* | *Round Sum* | *Motoring* | *Home telephone* |
|---|---|---|---|---|---|
| | £ | £ | £ | £ | £ |
| Sales representative | 2,460 | 428 | – | – | 940 |
| Foreman | 820 | – | – | – | 280 |
| Mr Sparks | – | – | 10,500 | – | 770 |
| Mrs Sparks | – | – | 4,300 | – | – |
| Mr Jones | – | 1,842 | – | 1,452 | 320 |
| Miss Fallow | – | – | – | 460 | – |

(15) Forms P11D have been completed only for Mr Sparks and Mr Jones showing the figures above and Mr Sparks's car.

(16) Sparks Manufacturing Ltd arranged a golf weekend for its customers in 2015/16 and invited ten managing directors to join Mr Sparks and the sales representative for the event. The total cost was £12,000.

The firm also gives its suppliers Christmas hampers, the size of which reflects the value of transactions undertaken in the year. At Christmas 2015 the cost of the hampers varied from £50 to £500.

(17) The apprentices are entitled to a £100 bonus every time they pass a set of formal exams at the FE College, and this has typically been paid out of petty cash without being recorded in the payroll. When a previous apprentice came top in his year at FE College, the company gave him a new bike costing £800 as a special reward.

Set out the implications of the above in respect of PAYE, national insurance, VAT and corporation tax as regards Sparks Manufacturing Ltd, and the effect on the individual's taxable earnings under the following headings:

(a) Part-time employees

(b) Directors' remuneration

(c) Cars and fuel

(d) Other benefits

(e) Sales representative

(f) Apprentices

Without calculating precise figures, indicate the possible basis on which a settlement with HMRC might be negotiated for the period to 5 May 2016, and any steps which could be taken to minimise the liability.

# Answer

## (a) Part-time employees

Part-time employees are subject to PAYE and national insurance in the same way as other staff. For those employees for whom Form P46 or a newer starter declaration is held showing that this is the main or only employment, no PAYE or national insurance liability arises unless their weekly pay equals or exceeds the following limits. The LEL is relevant because earnings between the LEL and the employee threshold should have been reported separately in the FPS submissions:

| | *Thresholds* | | | *Lower earnings limit* |
|---|---|---|---|---|
| | *PAYE* | *NI Ee* | *NI Er* | *LEL* |
| | £ | £ | £ | £ |
| 2012/13 | 156 | 146 | 144 | 107 |
| 2013/14 | 182 | 149 | 148 | 109 |
| 2014/15 | 192 | 153 | 153 | 111 |
| 2015/16 | 204 | 155 | 156 | 112 |
| 2016/17 | 212 | 155 | 156 | 112 |

Before the advent of RTI, there would have been no reporting requirement if earnings did not pass the LEL. Under the RTI regime, every payment of earnings, however small, must be reported online on or before the date of payment. Since the company is small, a concession was available until 5 April 2014 permitting reporting by the end of the tax month, which was limited to those with 9 or fewer employees at 6 April 2014, but that has now been withdrawn from 6 April 2016, so Sparks must now operate RTI correctly, although it is unlikely to be penalised by HMRC for late submission provided everything is reported within three days of the statutory deadline.

Their current weekly pay inclusive of round sum subsistence payments is £160 a week, and they receive a variable monthly bonus. The cumulative pay inclusive of bonuses needs to be checked to ensure that the PAYE limit has not been exceeded. The same check needs to be made for national insurance, but on a non-cumulative basis. As far as national insurance is concerned, there is clearly a small liability each week, and a much larger one in the weeks when bonus payments are made. Under RTI, there is a reporting requirement throughout. For those employees who have not signed a Form P46 or starter declaration, or where it is not possible to obtain a signed starter declaration certifying that this is the main or only employment, income tax at the basic rate of tax should be deducted from all remuneration (see below re Mrs Beech). Failure to do so could result in HMRC assessing the tax not deducted on the company by way of a determination under regulation 80 of the PAYE regulations.

It would appear that the company has been in breach of its obligations under the PAYE/NI scheme since April 2013. It will be necessary to agree a settlement with HMRC for that period. The potential penalty for failing to submit Form P46 for pre-RTI periods was up to £3,000, on a sliding scale depending on the number of failures in a tax quarter. Given the small number of employees in Sparks Limited, the maximum penalty is likely to have been £100. For returns due for submission after 31 March 2009, the penalties for incorrect returns set out in FA 2007 Sch 24 apply where there has been failure to take reasonable care or deliberate understatement. With regard to any PAYE and national insurance underpaid, HMRC may issue a determination of the amount of PAYE tax due under SI 2003/2682 reg 80 and a notice of decision under SSCTFA 1999 s 8 and SI 1999/1027 for NICs underpaid. For pre-RTI underpayments, interest is charged on unpaid tax and national insurance from 14 days after the end of the tax year (except to the extent that HMRC has required an amount to be paid by an employee) without the need for a formal determination. From April 2014, interest is chargeable from the 19$^{th}$ or 22$^{nd}$ of each month when the deductions should have been paid to HMRC.

Since 19 May 2013, the company appears to have been liable to a penalty for paying over the monthly PAYE and NIC deductions late, as the cheque should have been sent to arrive at HMRC by the 19$^{th}$ of the month. On establishing that an underpayment has occurred twelve times in 2013/14 and 2014/15, HMRC is likely to issue a penalty of 4% of all PAYE and NIC deductions due during the two years, since all were paid over after the deadline.

The company should compute the actual liability for the 37-month period. It is possible that for a number of weeks the actual remuneration (inclusive of subsistence) would be under the earnings threshold for national insurance and therefore no liability to employer's or employees' contributions would arise. The company should also obtain signed Forms P46 (for pre-RTI periods) or starter declarations wherever possible. In the case of Mr Chestnut, a student, there are no longer any special rules and the Form P38(S) was withdrawn in April 2013. Again, it is unlikely that any income tax liability would arise. However, from 6 April 2015, there should be no secondary NICs payable because he is under the age of 21, but the nil rate of NICs did not apply for the earlier years that may be reviewed by HMRC. Since Mrs Beech receives a pension, the company should obtain a retrospective starter declaration from her now as it will have to be shown to the HMRC officers. Tax at the basic rate should be deducted from her pay. Mrs Beech is over state pension age, so no employee's national insurance would be payable on her wages, although employer's contributions would still be due. Provided the company is certain of her age (eg, it has a copy of her passport or birth certificate), it cannot be liable for employee contributions, whether or not an age exception certificate has been issued, although employer contributions will be due. It seems almost certain that basic rate tax and appropriate national insurance contributions will be applicable to Mr Dallow, unless his activity as a milkman is on a self-employed basis so that he has only one contract of employment.

If this matter is disclosed to HMRC and correct procedures are put in place, then it is possible that a settlement could be negotiated based upon the correct liability plus interest and penalties. For returns due for submission since 31 March 2009, the penalties for incorrect returns set out in FA 2007 Sch 24 apply. In relation to the type of errors here, under the FA 2007 system, disclosing the inaccuracies in full at the commencement of the visit would not count as an unprompted disclosure, but if the company could show that the failure was through a lack of reasonable care rather than deliberate, with the full discount for disclosure the penalty should be only 15%. It may also be possible to have the penalty suspended for up to two years, as these failures might be regarded as systemic. This would give the company the opportunity to restructure payroll and reporting procedures with the aim of future compliance.

## (b) Directors' remuneration

It is not clear whether the monthly standing order is intended to be remuneration or withdrawals from directors' current accounts, or whether any such current accounts are running in credit.

PAYE and national insurance are not relevant unless the amounts are on account of remuneration (see **Example J2 explanatory note 12**).

In the case of Mr Sparks it would appear that the remuneration of £45,000 per annum, when credited to his director's current account net of PAYE/NI, would be sufficient to provide funds for his withdrawals. If, however, the round sum drawings by Mr Sparks have not been charged to his director's current account, they would give rise to a liability. In that event, because he is a director (but see below), the amount drawn should be grossed up and PAYE applied to that gross figure. As Mr Sparks will already have paid the maximum higher rate employee's national insurance contributions, only employer's liability will apply to that grossed up figure, plus 2% employee's contributions.

Similar comments apply to Mrs Sparks. However, it is almost certain that Mrs Sparks will not have a credit balance on her director's current account and therefore if the round sum drawings are not in anticipation of earnings and they have been charged to her director's current account, the beneficial loans rules and the provisions of CTA 2010 s 455 will apply (see below). If the round sums have not been charged to the account, PAYE and national insurance must apply on each and every withdrawal. Unless there is evidence that the payment to Mrs Sparks is made by Mr Sparks as part of their personal relationships, it is not likely that HMRC would treat the withdrawal by Mrs Sparks as coming from the remuneration of Mr Sparks.

Directors' national insurance contributions are computed on a yearly pay period basis and liability strictly only arises when the cumulative drawings for the tax year exceed the earnings threshold. National insurance liability will of course arise on the total amount when the annual earnings threshold is reached, thus giving a material liability in that month for employer and director.

Should the company pay the PAYE liability due in respect of Mr and Mrs Sparks in any settlement, then that amount will be treated as a further benefit in kind taxable on the director unless it is charged to the director's loan account (ITEPA 2003 s 223), but only if the payment is not grossed up, with full PAYE accounted for. Any settlement by the company of a national insurance liability in respect of employee contributions applicable to the director will again be treated as a benefit in kind giving rise to further tax liabilities, again unless charged to the director's loan account.

If a director's account becomes overdrawn, then there will be a potential benefit in kind liability in respect of the interest due on that loan under ITEPA 2003 Part 3 Chapter 7. In addition, the company will have a charge to tax on the loan under CTA 2010 s 455, at 25% for drawings made before 6 April 2016, and 32½% thereafter. If drawings are made in anticipation of their being cleared later by voting a bonus, and those drawings make the account further overdrawn, the drawings must be treated as payments of earnings for NI purposes and Class 1 contributions accounted for, without any corresponding PAYE deduction. Later voting of the bonus to clear the account would then be subject to PAYE but not NI, because the NI has already been paid.

To avoid the problems with s 455 and the beneficial loans rules, it is suggested that regular monthly salaries should be drawn which are subject to PAYE and national insurance contributions. All round sum allowances should be stopped. Mr and Mrs Sparks should draw actual expenses against vouchers.

The VAT position of round sum allowances should be checked. If any input tax has been recovered because of purported VAT-inclusive expenditure in the round sum allowances this must be declared to HMRC and repaid to the extent that there is no evidence of input tax having been incurred on business expenses.

If the above was put into force then it is possible that Mrs Sparks would receive remuneration under the national insurance limit and contributions would not be payable. In addition, it should be suggested to her that fuel should not be provided for her car as the benefit in kind cost appears to be greater than the value of fuel provided (a similar comment will apply for VAT and Class 1A national insurance contributions – see (c)).

A Form P11D should have been completed for Mrs Sparks as she is a director. The penalty for failure to provide that information is as stated in **part (a)**. If the company had sent in Form P11D(b), which confirms that Forms P11D have been submitted for all relevant employees, this will probably be regarded as fraudulent or negligent conduct triggering the penalty of up to £3,000 in addition to the penalty for not sending in the Form P11D. For returns due for submission after 31 March 2009, the penalties for incorrect returns set out in FA 2007 Sch 24 apply.

HMRC may contend that the car provided to Mrs Sparks is in fact provided by reason of Mr Sparks's employment. Such a contention might be disputed on the grounds that ITEPA 2003 s 169 applies, ie, that the car was provided to Mrs Sparks by reason of her directorship and that it is normal commercial practice for a director to be provided with a motor vehicle, although it might be difficult to produce appropriate evidence of that contention (see S Barnard Limited (2010) TC00491). Although the charge is the same amount as would be charged on Mr Sparks, it is likely that Mrs Sparks's tax rate will be lower than her husband's.

It is possible that HMRC could argue that the remuneration paid to Mrs Sparks is excessive for her duties as a director. The remuneration for 2015/16 could be considered to have been:

| | | |
|---|---|---|
| Salary | | £4,700 |
| Round sum allowance | | £4,300 |
| Benefit in kind – | Car 37% × 19,500 | £7,215 |
| | Fuel 37% × 22,100 | £8,177 |
| | | £24,392 |

unless any of it is charged to Mrs Sparks's director's account.

It is therefore possible that a disallowance will occur in the taxable trading profit computation of the company.

The company should have paid Class 1A national insurance contributions in respect of the directors' cars (**see (c)**). The penalty for paying Class 1A contributions more than twelve months late is automatically 15% of the amount due (ie, 5% for payment more than 30 days late, plus 5% for payment more than six months late, and a final 5% for payment more than a year late). Interest runs from the normal payment date (19 or 22 July).

## (c) Cars and fuel

Clearly, both the foreman and Miss Fallow are employees who were not excluded from the benefits code before 6 April 2016 (they were not in lower-paid employment by virtue of ITEPA 2003 s 217) when the benefits charges for cars were added to their respective salaries. Both cars have the same size engine and $CO_2$ emissions and both meet the Euro-IV standard, although that standard no longer makes any difference to the scale charge. Should HMRC argue for liabilities to arise in 2010/11, the foreman's car will not have been subject for 2010/11 to the 3% diesel surcharge because it was registered before 1 January 2006, although it will have applied from 6 April 2011 and in later years.

Again Forms P11D should have been provided to HMRC in respect of the foreman, Miss Fallow and probably the sales representative (**see (e)**), so penalties may arise.

The company should have paid Class 1A national insurance contributions each year in respect of the cars and fuel provided to employees, including the directors' cars. Records should be available in respect of the business mileage travelled to 5 April 2016 to show that the correct contributions have been paid.

It would appear that no VAT adjustments have been made for private fuel. The company should apply the scale charges in respect of private fuel at the relevant rate. The VAT scale charges are based on $CO_2$ emissions, using the benefit in kind tables to set the emission bands. In addition, there will be a scale charge in respect of the sales representative if he is an employee. If he is not, VAT will be due on the full value of the supply to him.

For VAT returns, due for submission since 31 March 2009, the penalties for incorrect returns set out in FA 2007 Sch 24 apply. Interest will be chargeable where appropriate.

The company should consider the financial viability of providing cars. The combined tax, VAT and national insurance charges on employer and employee may well be greater than the benefits actually obtained, particularly for Miss Fallow.

Similar comments apply to the provision of fuel to all employees and directors. For Mr and Mrs Sparks the fuel charge for 2015/16 was 37% of £22,100 = £8,177 each and is now 37% of £22,200 = £8,214 each. If free fuel is to be withdrawn, the charge for a tax year will be reduced according to the period for which fuel is provided (unless free fuel is provided again later in the same tax year).

Mr Jones is paid a mileage allowance. If that amount exceeds the mileage allowance payment in ITEPA 2003 s 230 then it should be treated as remuneration. The figure of 75p per mile exceeds 45p per mile and therefore NI should have been applied to the excess of 30p per mile (ie, in total 1,936 miles @ 30p = £581, but accounted for monthly as mileage allowances were paid) and the excess of £581 should have been reported on Mr Jones's P11D for income tax purposes (but without Class 1A NIC). The authorised mileage allowance rate for tax for Mr Jones's car has, since April 2011, been 45p per mile up to 10,000 miles and 25p thereafter, the 45p rate applying to all miles for NI. If Mr Jones's mileage allowance was restricted to the authorised rate, it would no longer have to be taken into account for income tax and NI. The old 40p per mile rate should be taken into consideration for any periods before 6 April 2011.

## (d) Other benefits

### *Telephones*

The provision of a single mobile phone to Mr Sparks and private use thereof is not subject to an income tax charge, but Mr Sparks has two, so the cost of the second is a taxable benefit (£864 (i.e., £720 + VAT) in this case because he can nominate the phone that produces the lower tax charge). VAT is payable on the non-business use of the mobile. Assuming the second phone is used privately to the same extent as the car phone, this would appear to be 40% × ([1,200+£720] × 20%) = £153.60 in a normal year. This amount must be declared to HMRC and repaid assuming full input tax deduction had occurred.

The home telephone expenses for Mr Sparks and Mr Jones have already been shown on Forms P11D.

They should also be shown for the foreman and the sales representative (if he is an employee). It is then up to the individual employee to make an ITEPA 2003 s 336 claim for actual business calls. The balance will be liable to tax – if the company pays the bills directly to the telephone provider, the bills are reported on P11D, but if the company gives cash to the employees for them to pay their personal bills, the identified private element (rental and private calls) should be paid through payroll. For national insurance purposes, it does not matter whether the employer pays the bill or gives the employee the cash to do so: the same private element should be subject to Class 1 national insurance through the payroll. Identified business calls (but no part of the rental) may be excluded from the amount on which contributions are payable, or alternatively if there is an agreement with HMRC as to the business proportion for tax purposes, it is acceptable for NI purposes. The required adjustment for the telephones will be applied for all relevant years. Although the income tax liabilities are technically those of the individual employees it is possible that the company will wish to settle them, as it has been in breach of its obligations under ITEPA and the PAYE and NI regulations in not submitting Forms P11D. The penalties and interest within any such settlement would not be an allowable deduction for the company, but the tax and national insurance would be allowed in the year of payment if the amounts paid by the company in respect of the telephone bills had been grossed up to calculate that tax and national insurance. If the employer agrees to gross up the tax on benefits in kind (which is in law the liability of the employee), HMRC will generally accept that no penalty should be charged.

### *Entertaining*

The amounts to be shown on Forms P11D should be inclusive of VAT. If any input tax has been recovered on such sums then it must be repaid to HMRC. Interest will be charged and, for returns due to be submitted after 31 March 2009, the penalties for incorrect returns set out in FA 2007 Sch 24 apply. No deduction is allowed in calculating the business trading profits.

### *Car parking*

The cost of the car parking near the factory attracts no PAYE or national insurance liabilities.

### *Subsistence*

Subsistence will be an important part of the settlement. Subsistence payments in cash to employees who are not at a temporary workplace are pay, and PAYE and NI are due at the appropriate rates. Similar payments are due for earlier years back to 2010, because HMRC can look back six years where there has been a careless understatement of liabilities. If HMRC believed that the error was deliberate, it could seek arrears for up to 20 years having made a discovery. For example, 36 employees × £18 per week × 48 weeks = £31,104 per annum which at 20% + NI of 25.8% = £14,245 for 2011/12 onwards, with a slightly lower value for earlier years when the combined NIC rate was 23.8% (and lower still if the number of employees in the period was lower). As this error is likely to be classed as carelessness, the normal four-year time limit for mistakes is unlikely to apply. The tax, NI, interest and penalties will fall on the company, which could in theory recover the PAYE, and some of the NI from the most recent year, from workers who are still employed, but this is unlikely in practice because of the damage to employee relations. If it was the company's intention that the amounts should be gross, the tax and NI liabilities should be calculated on normal PAYE lines, with no grossing up (COG913010). The company could, however, agree that the amounts were net payments and therefore should be grossed up. In either case, it would normally be agreed that the whole of the PAYE and NI would be deductible in calculating trade profits of the accounting period when it was paid, as the payment is an employer payment wholly and exclusively in respect of employing staff. The fact that it is not necessary for the company to agree to bear the employees' tax and NI liabilities is irrelevant.

It should be noted that if the company, instead of paying a subsistence allowance, had an in-house canteen with subsidised or free meals or arrangements had been made with a local caterer to provide similar meals then no liability would arise. No dispensation would have been needed before 6 April 2016 (when dispensations were abolished) from HMRC as the benefit would not have been taxable. Although VAT would be due on amounts paid by employees, any costs involved would give rise to deductible input tax. A reasonable subsistence allowance may be paid tax- and NI-free to workers who work away from their normal permanent workplace on any particular day. This could in the past have been covered by a dispensation, but now needs to fall within the statutory rates set by HMRC, or a bespoke rate agreed specifically with HMRC. Since April 2009 HMRC has provided benchmark scale rates which employers may adopt, but a dispensation was still needed until they were abolished and replaced by statutory rates. For more details see the Employment Income Manual at EIM 05200 If the company wants to pay more than the new statutory rates, it will have to apply to HMRC to agree its own rates for the future if they are to be treated as exempt under the new rules.

To minimise the costs in this case, calculations should be made to ensure that the actual liabilities are applied rather than global calculations, eg, go back and exclude days for which allowances were not paid to employees because of illness, holidays etc. Also confirm any days for which subsistence allowance was genuinely due, eg, days out of the factory. Check if any employee was lower paid or on lower national insurance rates, thus avoiding liability or having a lower liability. Check when employees were recruited and use accurate headcounts.

The treatment of the subsistence paid to the sales representative depends on whether he is classified as employed or self-employed. If he is an employee the position is as described above, although he will probably be classed as a travelling appointment and be entitled to claim a tax-free amount. In the unlikely event that HMRC agrees that he is self-employed (**see** (e)), the subsistence payments to him will represent part of his fees. Unless he is VAT-registered and has submitted a VAT invoice, no VAT input tax should have been recovered on the subsistence, and if any has been, it should be repaid to HMRC. Any subsistence provided and paid for directly by a business for self-employed agents, etc, is disallowed as entertaining expenditure (*C & E v Shaklee International* (1981)).

## *Third party benefits*

Where an employer has *arranged* for a third party to provide benefits to employees the employer is required to include the benefits on Forms P11D. If third party benefits are provided other than by arrangement with the employer, the third party is required to provide written details of the cash equivalent of the benefits to the employees concerned by 6 July following the relevant tax year, ie, by 6 July 2016 for 2015/16 (SI 2003/2682 reg 95). The third party is treated as the employer in respect of the benefits and is required to provide details to HMRC for Class 1A national insurance purposes, and to pay the NI liability (SI 2001/1004 regs 70–80). The Incentive Award Unit in Chapel Wharf, Salford (albeit reached via the Glasgow postal address for Employer Compliance) will issue the third party Class 1A return on request, but no return is required for income tax purposes unless HMRC calls for a return under TMA 1970 s 15.

The third party benefits provisions do not apply to corporate hospitality, ie, entertainment or hospitality provided by someone who is not the employer or a person connected with the employer, where the employer or connected person has not arranged or procured the provision of the benefit, and it is not provided in return for particular services performed or anticipated to be performed by the employee in the course of his employment (ITEPA 2003 s 265).

Nor do they apply to benefits covered by ITEPA 2003 s 324. This excludes gifts from third parties that do not exceed a VAT-inclusive value of £250 to any individual in a tax year.

The golf weekend will be covered by the corporate hospitality provisions unless HMRC argues that the benefit was provided as a result of specific services performed or to be performed by the managing directors in their companies, eg, to give special favour to contracts with Sparks Manufacturing.

The provision of Christmas hampers up to a value of £250 would normally be covered by ITEPA 2003 s 324. Suppliers receiving hampers would only be chargeable if they received them as employees (ie, they are employees of the supplier). In this case hampers in excess of that value would need to be notified, and the company should consider entering into a taxed award scheme for the future. The same penalties apply for not notifying third party benefits as for not reporting the annual Class 1A liability on Form P11D(b).

If Sparks Manufacturing do not wish the recipients to pay tax on the benefit, they may arrange with the Incentive Award Unit of HMRC to pay tax on the grossed-up value of the award under the Taxed Award Scheme. In that event the recipients would receive information under the Taxed Award Scheme rules rather than the third party benefits reporting requirements and the company would pay tax and NI on the benefits.

Sparks Manufacturing will not be able to claim a deduction for VAT or in calculating trade profits for the golf weekend or the hampers.

Any amounts paid or reimbursed to Mr Sparks (and the sales representative if an employee) in respect of the golf weekend should be included on Forms P11D. A s 336 claim can then be made in respect of the whole amount, since it represents a specific payment for entertaining carried out in the performance of the director's duties (which has been disallowed in calculating trade profits).

## *National insurance on benefits in kind*

Employer's Class 1A national insurance contributions are payable on most taxable benefits (except those subject to Class 1 contributions, and certain childcare provision). The rate of Class 1A contributions is 13.8% (12.8%

before 5 April 2011). Benefits are shown separately from expenses on Form P11D. No liability arose before 6 April 2016 (from which date all employees fell into the scope of the benefits code) for non-directors who were lower paid, for whom P9D was used. The Class 1A liability is computed for all relevant directors/employees with a P11D and summarised on Form P11D(b). The P11D(b) is still used even if the employer elects to payroll the benefits for tax purposes. A separate payslip or online payment reference is then used to pay the Class 1A liability by 19 July (22 July for e-payers) following the tax year. Interest is charged on late payments and a penalty may be levied: £100 per 50 employees (or part thereof) for each month (or part thereof) the return is late. In addition, in respect of years after 5 April 2010, the penalties in FA 2009 Sch 56 for late payment extend to Class 1A NI, so as already noted late payment discovered at a PAYE inspection is likely to attract an automatic penalty of 5%, 10% or 15% of the underpayment, depending on how late the eventual payment is.

The employer is liable to Class 1A national insurance on any benefits received by an employee from a third party if the benefit has been arranged by the employer (eg, if any of the customers had arranged for their staff to be invited to the golf day by Sparks). However, HMRC will not impose that charge on the employer provided the third party has paid the Class 1A liability. As noted above, the third party is liable if the employer did not arrange the award of the benefit. Meeting the Class 1A liability can be done as part of the provision of a Taxed Incentive Award.

Sparks Manufacturing Ltd should carefully check the completion of Forms P11D to ensure that benefits are shown separately from expenses, and that Class 1 national insurance has been paid on round sum payments and the settlement of employees' pecuniary liabilities. No Class 1A liability arises on any amount liable to Class 1, or exempt from tax (eg, one mobile telephone per employee). Liability is as follows:

| | |
|---|---|
| Subsistence | Class 1 on profit element before 6 April 2016, on whole amount if paid in excess of statutory or bespoke rates agreed with HMRC from that date |
| Company cars and fuel | Class 1A on scale charges |
| Mileage payments | Class 1 on excess over 45ppm |
| Mobile telephones | No charge (one per employee), Class 1A on cost of second contract. |
| Reimbursed petrol | Class 1 (on profit element if business usage identified) |
| Car parking | No charge |
| Entertaining | No charge |
| Round sums | Class 1 on full amount |
| Home telephone | Class 1 (on rent and private calls provided business calls identified) |

Sparks Manufacturing Ltd will be liable to pay the employers' Class 1A national insurance due on the golf weekend if HMRC succeeds in treating the amount as a taxable third party benefit for the guests.

From 6 April 2016, tax and Class 1 liability arises on expenses reimbursed under a salary sacrifice arrangement, or in excess of approved round sum rates, and NICs are due on payments in respect of anticipated expenses that have not yet been incurred (even if those expenses are subsequently incurred).

## (e) Sales representative

The status of this worker should be clarified. The information provided suggests at point 1 that he is an employee, but at point 3 that he is treated as self-employed. The facts suggest that he is under the supervision, control or direction of the company. He would appear to be an integral part of the business and does not appear to be taking commercial risks. He draws all expenses from the company and is provided with benefits such as subsistence allowance, car parking space, etc. He would appear to work only for the company. It is therefore most likely that he will be treated as an employee throughout (see **Example B6** for a full discussion of employment status).

Reclassification can strictly take place from the date of the commencement of the employment, but if the position has been clearly disclosed to HMRC in earlier years, reclassification from a later date may be negotiated, particularly if the sales representative has prepared and submitted accounts and agreed and paid all of his tax and NI liabilities to date. In computing the liability HMRC should take into account the personal allowances of the employee and any potential s 336 expenses claims. The Class 2 national insurance contributions paid by the sales representative should be credited against his Class 1 employee's national insurance liability. Any Class 4 national insurance contributions and trading income tax paid may be repaid to the employee. As the sales representative still works in the business, negotiations should take place with him for part or all of the tax to be repaid to the company, or indeed set off in the settlement by agreement between the sales representative and the company. Strictly the company has no legal right to recover from the sales representative national insurance contributions for previous years and may not recover employer contributions in any event. Following the *Demibourne* case, new PAYE Regulation 72F was introduced from 6 April 2008 which potentially applies where an employer is required to account for PAYE but fails to do so and the employee has paid tax under self-assessment as though self-employed. These allow a direction to be made to transfer the PAYE liability from an employer to an employee. HMRC have published some FAQs on this legislation at www.hmrc.gov.uk/employers/faq-transfer-paye.htm.

If he were to be classified as an employee, the sales representative would be assessed on benefits in kind in the normal way.

The provision of personal services through a limited company or partnership, which amounted to disguised employment, became liable to PAYE/NI on a deemed salary payment from 6 April 2000. If the sales representative attempts to retain his self-employed status by use of a partnership (or limited company) it is likely to lead to his partnership or service company being liable to account for PAYE and NI on a notional payment of most of his profit deemed to happen on 5 April each year, so such an arrangement would probably be ineffective. However, in those circumstances Sparks Manufacturing Ltd would have no liability for any PAYE/NI arising on a reclassification. The case of *Cable & Wireless plc v Muscat* found there to be a continuing contract of employment between the company and an individual working via both his own limited company and an employment agency after he was forced to transfer into that structure after having been an employee for some time. It is unlikely that the sales representative's self-employed status can be maintained.

### (f) Apprentices

The status of the apprentices is clear: they are deemed to be employed by the company with which they have entered into an apprenticeship agreement.

The reimbursement of the bus fares to attend day release training is exempt from tax and NIC.

However, as they have recently left school, they will be under the age of 25, which means that the company will, from 6 April 2016, also have no secondary Class 1 liability in respect of their earnings (ie, their wage plus the £18 round sum subsistence payment and the exam rewards), unless they receive an exceptionally large production bonus and exam reward that takes their earnings in a week above the upper earnings limit for that week, in which case the excess will be liable. If they were taken on before 6 April 2016, their earnings in 2015–16 will also have benefited from a nil secondary NIC rate under the rule for under-21s.

The exam rewards are contractual pay so they should have been paid through payroll, with PAYE and primary NICs deducted. The gift of the bike constitutes a taxable benefit that should have been reported in a P11D at the VAT-inclusive value, with Class 1A NICs paid.

### *Generally*

The company clearly has material liabilities to HMRC in respect of failure to operate PAYE and national insurance in earlier years. These amounts should be quantified as soon as possible and declared to HMRC before the commencement of the visit. The company should regularise its position as follows:

(i) account for PAYE in respect of payments to the sales representative unless it can be specifically established with HMRC that he is self-employed;

(ii) cease paying subsistence and replace with canteen facilities (or add subsistence in the normal workplace to pay for payroll purposes, paying an allowance to those who incur costs while at a temporary workplace);

(iii) apply PAYE and NI to part-time staff and to the exam rewards paid to the apprentices;

(iv) regularise the position of Mr and Mrs Sparks and their monthly drawings;

(v) prepare and submit outstanding Forms P11D for all relevant employees, also providing the directors and employees with copy P11Ds for 2015/16;

(vi) give third parties written details of benefits provided in 2015/16;

(vii) obtain signed starter declarations for all workers joining after 5 April 2013;

(viii) use the Authorised Mileage Allowance Payment rate for the accountant's business mileage.

In addition, the VAT implications of all transactions mentioned above should be reviewed. A voluntary disclosure should be made to HMRC as soon as possible. If the net disclosure is under the greater of £10,000 or 1% of turnover in box 6 of the return on which the error is to be corrected, subject to an upper limit of £50,000, the adjustment can be made in the next VAT return. If the figure is in excess of these limits a written declaration must be made to HMRC showing the liability divided between VAT accounting periods so that interest may be calculated for the last four years.

The company should cease paying round sum allowances and should only reimburse expenses against actual vouchers, or it should adopt the statutory subsistence rates and pay them only on days when the workers in question are away from the factory on business for the requisite period. VAT input tax can then be recovered with the exception of that on entertaining. In the case of motoring, VAT will only be recoverable on the petrol element of the allowance paid to Mr Jones, using the VAT fraction applied to the current advisory mileage rate. It should be confirmed that VAT has only been recovered on the business proportion of telephone bills, not the total bill. Note that the European courts have ruled that the recovery of input VAT by an employer on company expenses where the expense was incurred by the employee is against EU rules. In Notice 700/64 HMRC states that input tax may be recovered in respect of business use if supported by a VAT invoice. Output tax must be accounted for in respect of private use.

It is probable that there will be significant settlements to be agreed with HMRC in respect of past breaches. Full co-operation and correction of past errors will be strong mitigating factors when negotiating the level of liability and penalties thereon.

## Explanatory Notes

*PAYE compliance visits*

(1) HMRC have power to visit employers' premises to undertake PAYE tax and national insurance inspections. Income Tax (PAYE) Regulations 2003 (SI 2003/2682 reg 97) and Social Security (Contributions) Regulations 2001 (SI 2001/1004 Sch 4) applied until April 2009. FA 2008 Sch 36 replaced both of these powers and extended HMRC powers to visit in other circumstances – see **Example G2 explanatory note 13.**

Employers are required to produce to HMRC investigators all records relating to the calculation of PAYE income, and the deduction of tax and national insurance therefrom. It is common for an inspection to reveal areas of non-compliance with the regulations by the employers, and in that event HMRC will typically require settlement for the current and previous six years, with the addition of interest and penalties depending on the nature of the irregularities. Where there has been no lack of care, the assessing time limit for PAYE (but not NIC) is reduced by FA 2008 Sch 39 to four years, although the six-year limit is otherwise unchanged for careless errors, but where understatements are found to have been deliberate the limit becomes 20 years. These new time limits apply in full from April 2010. The NIC limit is six years for all purposes.

HMRC may agree to accept the amount due by instalments. The example illustrates many of the typical points to be considered in a PAYE/NI investigation.

(2) Where HMRC consider that the employer has been guilty of fraudulent or negligent conduct, a penalty of up to 100% of the underpayment could be charged, but this will be subject to mitigation along the lines indicated in **Examples G6** and **G7**. HMRC factsheets EC/FS3 and EC/FS4 used to indicate their approach to negotiating PAYE settlements. For returns due for submission after 31 March 2009, the new penalties for incorrect returns set out in FA 2007 Sch 24 apply. Penalties for understatements over the last six years will be calculated separately according to the penalty regime that applied to the return which contained an inaccuracy. See **Example G2** for more details on the penalty regime from April 2009.

*Year-end returns*

(3) As far as employers' returns are concerned, year-end Forms P35 and P14 for 2012/13 were due to be submitted by 19 May 2013 (ie, within 44 days), although the tax was due for payment by 19 April 2013 (22 April for e-payers). Although Sparks will have been reporting under RTI since April 2013, the same penalty regime still applied to the final FPS or EPS return, with a 'final submission' tick box replacing the declaration. In-year penalties for late filing of FPSs began to apply from 6 October 2014 for large companies and from 6 March 2015 for the remainder of the employer population, although few penalties have been issued in practice.

TMA 1970 s 98A imposes penalties in respect of late submission at the year-end, which does not apply for years after the new RTI regime was implemented, but is still relevant for 2013/14 and earlier years. It is possible for HMRC to proceed instead under TMA 1970 s 98, in which case the penalties are the same as for Forms P11D etc as outlined in **part (A)** of the Example.

Under s 98A, there are automatic penalties for late year-end Forms P35 and P14 (and RTI final submissions for 2013/14) as follows:

(a) A non-mitigable amount of £100 a month or part month for every 50 employees (and an additional £100 where the number of employees is not a multiple of 50), for up to 12 months, plus

(b) If the returns are outstanding for more than 12 months, an amount not exceeding the amount unpaid at the original due date (ie, 19 April following the year to which the returns relate).

These penalties are imposed by a determination made by an officer under TMA 1970 s 100 and no proceedings before the First-tier Tribunal are necessary.

Similar penalties apply for late year-end Forms P11D(b) (SI 2001/1004 Sch 4 para 22). These have not changed with the introduction of RTI.

Where the statutory penalty exceeds the total tax and national insurance due, it will normally be reduced to that amount or to £100 whichever is greater.

The s 98A penalties based on number of employees cover both tax and national insurance. Where the returns are outstanding for more than twelve months, a penalty may be imposed up to the amount of national contributions unpaid at the original due date, in addition to the penalty on the unpaid tax (Social Security Contributions and Benefits Act 1992 Sch 1 para 7).

The company will have been obliged to report under RTI from 6 April 2013. As noted, for the first year, there were no penalties for late submission of FPS and EPS returns, although incorrect returns that lead to underpayments might have led to penalties for late payment on a sliding scale of between 1% and 4%, depending on the number of defaults in the tax year, with an extra 5% if any payment is made more than six months late and another 5% if twelve months late. In-year late monthly reporting penalties began from 6 October 2014, charged quarterly with the first charges levied in late Spring 2015. Late payment penalties apply for 2014/15 and 2015/16 as already described, on an annual basis and HMRC will take a 'risk-based approach', ie, only those employers caught will be charged. From 6 April 2015, in-year monthly late payment penalties were planned, but processing problems led to their introduction being deferred until April 2017 at the earliest.

(4) The time limit for sending in Forms P11D, P11D(b) and P9D is 6 July after the end of the tax year. The penalties outlined above will normally be imposed if the forms are not filed with HMRC by 19 July. Employers must provide employees with copies of Forms P11D and P9D by 6 July following the tax year (see **Example B2**), and the penalties that apply for failing to provide such copies are outlined in **part (A)** of the Example. HMRC will not normally impose penalties for failure to provide copy Forms P11D unless the amount involved is significant or the employer persists in failing to comply. As indicated in **part (D)** of the Example, similar penalties apply for not notifying third party benefits. The P9D was abolished for 2016/17 onwards and all employees now fall under the benefits code.

Penalties for late submission of these returns are also potentially subject to the legislation in Finance Act 2009 Sch 55, but implementation is to be delayed while HMRC systems are prepared. The late P11D(b) penalty remains for now based on the automatic £100 per month (or part-month) per 50 P11Ds showing taxable benefits, with employee numbers rounded up to the next 50.

*Determinations of tax due*

(5) Under SI 2003/2682 reg 75A HMRC have power to estimate the monthly payments due if no payment is made or they are not satisfied with the tax paid. The specified charge is added to the employer's account and must be paid within seven days of the issue of the notice unless the employer can satisfy HMRC that a lower amount is due. The specified charge can only be displaced by the filing of an FPS with the correct cumulative figures for tax and NICs due or the filing of a nil-payment EPS for the relevant month.

(6) Where an officer considers that tax and national insurance due under PAYE have not been paid, he may issue a formal determination of the amount due (SI 2003/2682 reg 80). Under the pre-Finance Act 2009 rules, where a regulation 80 determination was made, interest automatically ran on late paid tax and national insurance from 19 April after the end of the tax year (income tax SI 2003/2682 reg 82, national insurance SI 2001/1004 Sch 4 para 17). FA 2009 s 101 introduced provision for interest to run from the actual due date of the original payment until actual payment to HMRC, but HMRC announced in 2009 Budget Note 91 that it would apply these rules on a limited basis only, and this happened only from April 2014.

*Employees' national insurance position on PAYE settlements*

(7) Where an employer negotiates a settlement with HMRC and pays a sum representing tax that should have been deducted from the employees' earnings it is sometimes contended by HMRC that the employer is thereby meeting a pecuniary liability of the employee and that contributions are due on the payment as if a PAYE settlement agreement had been reached. There is no PSA (see **explanatory note 8**), and the cases of *CIR v Woollen* (1992) and *CIR v Nuttall* (1990) suggest that this approach is not correct, since the employer is statutorily liable to make the payment, the employee is not party to such an agreement and HMRC's right to recover the amounts from the employee has been subsumed within the overall amount payable by the employer.

*PAYE Settlement Agreements (PSAs)*

(8) Some employers negotiate annual voluntary settlements with HMRC in respect of the tax liability on certain expenses payments and benefits to employees, which are referred to as PAYE settlement agreements (ITEPA 2003 Part 11 Chapter 5). Class 1B national insurance applies to PSA's, under which contributions are payable on the benefits, etc, taxed under a PSA plus the tax thereon, to the extent that there would have been a national insurance liability under Class 1 or Class 1A. For details see **Example B2 explanatory note 9.**

*Recovery of underpaid tax and national insurance from employee*

(9) Where an employer has to account for tax and national insurance contributions that he has failed to deduct, his rights of recovery from the employee are limited. However, the case of *Kleinwort Benson Ltd v Lincoln City Council* (1998 4 AER 513) now allows recovery where money was wrongly paid under a mistake of law, such as incorrectly treating an employee as self-employed. For other recoveries from an employee the case of *Bernard and Shaw Ltd v Shaw* (1951) held that recovery of PAYE was restricted to later payments of remuneration, but *McCarthy v McCarthy & Stone plc* (2008) suggests that employers may nevertheless make claims in restitution if they meet the conditions for such a claim. As far as national insurance is concerned, the regulations provide that recovery of an underpayment that arose from an error made in good faith can be made only by deducting it from pay in the same year or the next following year, and then not exceeding an extra amount in each pay period equal to the normal deduction for that period (SI 2001/1004 Sch 4 paras 6 and 7), although the *McCarthy & Stone* principle should be equally applicable to NI. In any event, most employers would find it difficult to recover amounts from their employees, and may well suffer all or most of the payment themselves.

(10) Following the *Demibourne* case, new PAYE Regulation 72F was introduced from 6 April 2008 which potentially applies where an employer is required to account for PAYE but fails to do so and the employee has paid tax under self-assessment as though self-employed. These allow a direction to be made to transfer the PAYE liability from an employer to an employee. HMRC have published some FAQ on this legislation at www.hmrc.gov.uk/employers/faq-transfer-paye.htm (now archived but available via web search).

(See **Example B12** for a full discussion and recent court cases on employment status.)

*Childcare vouchers*

(11) See **Example B2 explanatory note 24** for details of the income tax and national insurance treatment of childcare vouchers provided by an employer.

*Personal service companies*

(12) This legislation is covered in detail in **Example N2**.

*Employment allowance*

(13) It is important for small employers to establish that any available employment allowance has been claimed against any arrears for periods after 6 April 2014. The allowance was increased for 2016/17 from £2,000 to £3,000.

# Question

*A*

Grenville is an antique dealer, and he has accounts professionally prepared to 31 October each year. The accounts for the year ended 31 October 2015, forming the basis of his self-assessment return for the tax year 2015/16, which was submitted to HMRC on 30 September 2016.

Grenville is married, his wife assisting minimally in the business, for which she has consistently received a wage just below the personal allowance. She has no other income.

On 28 February 2017 Grenville received a formal notice from HMRC under TMA 1970 s 9A(1) stating that they had decided to enquire into his 2015/16 self-assessment, and requesting the following documents and information:

(1) The business records for the accounting year to 31 October 2015;

(2) Grenville's private bank statements and building society account books covering the tax year ended 5 April 2016;

(3) An explanation of the source of £20,000 described as capital introduced;

(4) An analysis of the deduction in arriving at the self-employment profits for wages, casual labour and porterage.

Grenville is concerned at the apparent extent of HMRC's powers in pursuing its enquiry and in particular the implied ability of the officer to examine his private financial records.

He says that he can explain and prove the capital introduced, since it was from his wife's current account, but confides in you that when the officer sees his own private bank and building society accounts he is bound to be curious about large deposits and withdrawals, which Grenville acknowledges are for business transactions which have not been recorded in the business books and hence not reflected in the profits.

Advise Grenville:

(a) of the consequences of failing to comply with the officer's request for information and documents, and what protection he has if he finds that request unreasonable;

(b) given that the information and documents are provided, how the officer's enquiry is likely to proceed;

(c) to what extent the officer may extend his enquiry to cover the self-assessment for 2014/15 (which was filed on 31 December 2015, tax having been paid appropriately) and earlier years; and

(d) state what action you, as a tax adviser, must take to comply with your legal and professional obligations.

*B.*

Petersen's original net tax payable for 2013/14 was £25,000, so that 2014/15 payments on account of £12,500 each were payable on 31 January 2015 and 31 July 2015. A discovery assessment relating to 2013/14 was issued on 1 December 2017 for additional tax of £15,000.

State the consequences of the issue of the discovery assessment on tax payable for 2013/14 and 2014/15, and the position relating to interest on overdue tax, on the assumption that on 31 January 2016 a balancing payment had been made for 2014/15 amounting to:

(a) £20,000; or

(b) £5,000

# Answer

## (A) Grenville

## (a) HMRC's request for information and documents

If Grenville fails to comply with the request for information and documents, HMRC is able formally to demand these under FA 2008 Sch 36 para 1 by the issue of a taxpayer notice, the initial request to Grenville with the formal notice of enquiry being an opportunity for him to provide what HMRC requires without use of the formal powers.

Grenville cannot object to the officer enquiring into the return, but if he finds the request for information and documents unreasonable, he has the right to appeal to the First-tier Tribunal within 30 days from the date of the taxpayer notice (FA 2008 Sch 36 paras 21, 29, 32). If the Tribunal confirms the notice, the taxpayer has a further period allowed to produce the information and documents required, normally specified by the Tribunal, but alternatively such period as is reasonably specified by the officer in writing. There is no right of appeal against a request to produce documents which form part of the taxpayer's statutory records. If during the progress of the enquiry the taxpayer feels that HMRC has no reasonable grounds for continuing it and that it should therefore be concluded, he can ask the Tribunal to direct HMRC to issue a closure notice (TMA 1970 s 28A(4)).

## (b) Enquiry procedure

Upon seeing Grenville's bank and building society accounts, HMRC will undoubtedly come to the conclusion which Grenville predicts, and he would be advised at the time of submitting them to point out to HMRC the irregularities in his business records and accounts.

Despite Grenville's ability to explain the £20,000 capital introduced and provide proof as to the source of the funds, HMRC can also be expected to question how his wife, given her low level of income, could have accumulated that amount of money in her current account.

Due to the nature of independent taxation, HMRC cannot directly ask Grenville about this without first receiving permission to do so from his wife. Equally Grenville would need his wife's permission to disclose such information about her affairs to HMRC. However, HMRC can serve Mrs Grenville with a formal information notice (a third party notice) under FA 2008 Sch 36 para 2, which allows it to ask for documents in the possession or power of one person which might affect the taxation liability of another. Normally HMRC do this with the agreement of the taxpayer concerned, but the officer can seek prior approval of the Tribunal where appropriate (FA 2008 Sch 36 para 3). The taxpayer has a right to make written representations to the Tribunal in most cases.

The implication is that the wife's current account, like Grenville's own personal bank and building society accounts, have been used for business transactions and Grenville and his wife should be advised to agree a way forward with HMRC under which the omitted profits can be ascertained. This needs to consider not just direct tax liabilities but also whether VAT has been understated and the impact on any claims for tax credits.

Although the business records have been discredited ('broken' in HMRC terms), they may still be useful in piecing together what has happened, for example by seeking to match the recorded expenditure on purchases, restoration costs, hotels, credit card payments showing where petrol and meals have been purchased, with sales and stock records.

An overall reconsideration of personal and business finances over an agreed period, embracing the amended accounts after the specific matching exercise referred to in the previous paragraph, and the transactions through Mrs Grenville's account, will provide a basis for the computation of the taxable profits for the periods concerned.

In the course of the enquiry, HMRC will be concerned to prove the veracity of the recorded business expenditure, particularly in the areas highlighted by its request for information, there being a danger that amounts paid for casual labour and porterage should have been dealt with under PAYE or otherwise reported to HMRC under the procedures for providing information about monies paid to the employees of others.

When the enquiry is completed Grenville may be invited to make an offer to HMRC in consideration of its not taking criminal proceedings against him, the amount of the offer comprising the tax and interest plus a penalty.

Where income or gains have been understated, the penalty regime in FA 2007 Sch 24 will be applied to any potential loss of tax arising from the inaccuracy on the return. The size of the penalty is determined by the taxpayer's behaviour giving rise to the inaccuracy, and by the degree and type (whether prompted or unprompted) of disclosure. In this case assuming there are no offshore elements to the inaccuracies, it is likely that HMRC would argue that the understatement is deliberate, and therefore a penalty of up to 70% would apply, unless steps had been taken to conceal the inaccuracy, which would command a penalty of 100% of the potential lost revenue (PLR). The PLR is the amount of tax and Class 4 national insurance due as a result of correcting the errors in the return.

Where disclosure has been made during the course of the enquiry the penalty could be reduced to 35% for deliberate understatement or 50% if the understatement was also concealed. The exact details of how the reductions are calculated is discussed in CH82400. If HMRC accepts the taxpayer's offer, a binding contract is concluded, breach of which through non-payment by the taxpayer enables HMRC to take action for recovery of the amount outstanding.

## (c) Extending enquiry to earlier years

Except where a return is filed late, HMRC can only open an enquiry under TMA 1970 s 9A into the amount of a taxpayer's self-assessment within the period ending 12 months after the return is delivered. When the time for opening an enquiry has expired, however, HMRC have the power to issue a discovery assessment in cases of failure to take reasonable care or deliberate understatement, or where there has been inadequate disclosure by the taxpayer (TMA 1970 s 29). The time limit for such assessments in cases of inadequate disclosure is four years for mistake despite reasonable care, six years for failure to take reasonable care and 20 years for deliberate understatement (TMA 1970 ss 34, 36).

If, therefore, the enquiry into the 2015/16 self-assessment indicate that the profits declared on the self-assessment return were deliberately understated, HMRC can raise discovery assessments for all years back to 1996/97 to the best of the officer's judgment under TMA 1970 s 29. If HMRC accepts that the understatements arise from a failure to take reasonable care, only the last six years can be subject to discovery assessments.

Grenville and his advisers should agree with HMRC a suitable way of attempting to calculate the profits for a mutually acceptable number of years working back from 2015/16.

## (d) Other legal and professional implications

Tax practitioners, whether qualified or not, are bound by the money laundering regulations. These regulations require them to make reports not only of money laundering transactions, but also of the existence of any proceeds of crime. By under-declaring income, Grenville has obtained a monetary advantage in retaining funds that he otherwise would not have, and these are the proceeds. The proceeds of crime include the proceeds of tax evasion, bribery or any costs saved by failure to comply with regulatory requirements where failure to comply is a criminal offence – in this case the failure appears to be deliberate, and could be the subject of prosecution if HMRC so chose.

The fact that the tax authorities are aware of the matter does not obviate the need to make a report as soon as possible. The tax practitioner must report the matter to the firm's Money Laundering Reporting Officer (MLRO). The MLRO must then consider whether to report, and whether to make a full suspicious activity report (SAR) or a limited information value report (LIVR).

There is no indication that these omissions were unintentional, or particularly small (there is no de minimis limit for reporting), so clearly a report must be made. As there is good evidence for the identity of the person holding the proceeds of crime, and the whereabouts of the proceeds of crime themselves, a full SAR must be made.

The SAR must, therefore, be made to the National Crime Agency as soon as reasonably possible.

## (B) Petersen

Before the discovery assessment was made, the position was:

| | | |
|---|---|---|
| 2013/14 | Net tax payable | £25,000 |
| 2014/15 | 31 January 2015 payment on account | £12,500 |
| | 31 July 2015 payment on account | £12,500 |
| (a) | 31 January 2016 balancing payment (giving total 2014/15 tax of £45,000) | £20,000 |
| (b) | 31 January 2016 balancing payment (giving total 2014/15 tax of £30,000) | £5,000 |

The tax of £15,000 under the 2013/14 discovery assessment is due for payment on 31 December 2017, but interest would run from 31 January 2014 to the date the tax was paid. The revised tax for 2013/14 is £40,000 (£25,000 + £15,000).

In the case of (a) (ie 2014/15 balancing payment of £20,000), the amounts that should have been paid by way of payments on account for 2014/15 would be increased by £7,500 to £20,000 each, and interest thereon would run from the half yearly due dates of 31 January 2015 and 31 July 2015 to 31 January 2016 (the underpayments of £7,500 each being effectively paid as part of the balancing payment of £20,000).

In the case of (b) (ie 2014/15 balancing payment of £5,000), the effect of increasing the payments on account to £20,000 each would be to give an overpayment of £10,000 for the year, so that a claim could be made to reduce the additional amounts payable to £2,500 each. Repayment supplement thereon would run from the half yearly due dates of 31 January 2015 and 31 July 2015 to 31 January 2016.

# Explanatory Notes

*Conduct of an enquiry*

(1) This Example deals with the method of computing overall income or income omitted from tax returns, and the way in which a settlement will usually be concluded with HMRC. In making that calculation, allowance must be made for VAT on additional sales for which a liability exists.

*HMRC's sources of information*

(2) HMRC might already be in possession of information about Grenville and his affairs, and some of the documents or information called for may be to test that he is being completely open in providing them following the officer's challenge.

(3) HMRC uses the following powers to require persons to disclose income or transactions of others:

- third party information notices under FA 2008 Sch 36 para 2 (see **explanatory note 4** below);
- data-gathering notices under FA 2011 Sch 23 to request bulk data from 'relevant data holders', such as banks and building societies.

The data-gathering legislation allows HMRC to issue a notice to 'relevant data holders', who are specified in Part 2 ofFA 2011 Sch 23 (see CH28400). Each category of data has a list of data holders prescribed for that purpose. For example, in relation to rents and other payments arising from land, the following data holders are identified: a lessee; an occupier of land; a person having use of land, and a person who as agent, manages land or is receipt of rent or other payments arising from land (FA 2011 Sch 23 para 18). Clearly this enables HMRC to seek bulk data from letting management companies, concerning the landlords for whom they act and the amounts of rent collected for each. The list of types of data is very extensive, and even includes auctioneers as relevant data holders in respect of 'dealing in other property'. Data holders only have to provide data for the period of a maximum of four years ending on the date of the notice (FA 2011 Sch 23 para 3), and there are penalties for failure to comply (FA 2011 Sch 23 paras 30, 31, 38; CH29500). Data holders have a right to appeal on the grounds that compliance is unduly onerous, but not where the data requested forms part of the data holder's statutory records (accounting records) (FA 2011 Sch 23 para 28; CH29400).

Since originally enacted, the data-gathering powers have been extended to:

- merchant acquirers - those processing debit and credit card transactions for merchants and retailers (FA 2011 Sch 23 para 13A enacted on 17 July 2013 but applies retrospectively)
- business intermediaries - booking and reservation companies such as those taking payment for holiday accommodation, restaurants supplying takeaway food and outlets reselling tickets for entertainment events (FA 2011 Sch 23 para 13C enacted on 15 September 2016 and applies retrospectively)
- electronic payment service providers - those providing digital wallets which allow payment by smartphone (FA 2011 Sch 23 para 13B enacted on 15 September 2016 and applies retrospectively)
- Information is also obtained from other government departments such as HMRC Capital Taxes, Department for Work and Pensions, Companies House, DVLA, the Land Registry and in respect of holdings of government stocks.

(4) In addition to the persons that are required to provide information mentioned in **explanatory note 3**, HMRC has the power under FA 2008 Sch 36 paras 2, 3 to obtain information from third parties, with either the approval of the taxpayer, or the consent of the First-tier Tribunal. Under this provision an accountant may be required to make available his working papers relating to a client's tax affairs, except for audit papers and tax advice (FA 2008 Sch 36 paras 24, 25).

HMRC also has the power to visit business premises, but not people's homes, and review records in 'real time' (FA 2008 Sch 36 Part 2). FA 2008 s 114 allows an officer access to any computer used in relation to any relevant document – essentially part of anybody's statutory tax records.

For further details, see **Example G2 Part 14**.

(5) A considerable amount of information available to the public generally is also used by HMRC to check the accuracy of returns, such as share registers, planning applications, press and media coverage, entries in telephone and trade directories, and details of new company formations, not only in so far as the new company is concerned, but the other business activities of the personnel involved, which may be apparent from the documents submitted to Companies House. HMRC is also known to use various technologies such as Xenon, a data-mining tool which explores the internet looking for unregistered (with HMRC) businesses or trading websites. Another data-mining tool that has been developed by HMRC is Connect.

HMRC has a vast amount of information at its disposal from the files of other taxpayers. This might include information on loans, capital acquisitions and disposals. Also the HMRC officers glean considerably more in meetings with taxpayers and in examining business records, which will contain details of other businesses with which trade is conducted.

In Grenville's case, HMRC might well have been alerted to the apparent irregularities in his affairs through investigating the affairs of another trader with whom he has done business, or indeed by analysing his particular trade in his geographical area. For example, they might have seen the VAT records of an auction house and, by a combination of those and other means, have formed the view that declared profits were inadequate.

Finally, HMRC, like other authorities, receives information from informants. Someone suspecting Grenville's under-declarations might well have provided HMRC with information.

*Completion of enquiry*

(6) In addition to examining bank and building society accounts during an enquiry, HMRC will require a certified statement of assets and liabilities before agreeing the taxpayer's liabilities. This is to ensure that all of these have been included in considering the calculation of profits.

The taxpayer will also be asked to sign a certificate of full disclosure and of bank and building society accounts operated.

(7) From a combination of the certified statements at **explanatory note 6** above, the independent information which it holds (see **explanatory note 5**) and the detailed workings, HMRC will be as satisfied as in the circumstances it is possible to be that all income and gains have been taken into account.

(8) The enquiry will usually be settled by HMRC accepting an offer from the taxpayer (contract settlement), or for some self-assessment enquiries, by HMRC issuing a closure notice under TMA 1970 s 28A setting out HMRC's conclusions and the amendments to the self-assessment. For details of the settlement procedure see **explanatory notes 15–17**.

*Criminal proceedings*

(9) Whilst the usual practice of HMRC is to seek a pecuniary settlement with the taxpayer, it should always be borne in mind that it could take criminal proceedings in the case of provable fraud, being quite distinct from the civil proceedings for the recovery of unpaid tax, interest and penalties.

The offence of fraudulent evasion of income tax applies in to anyone knowingly concerned in the fraudulent evasion of income tax. This could be evasion on their own behalf or that of another (TMA 1970 s 106A).

Although tax penalties are considered to be 'criminal charges' under European law (see *Jussila v Finland* [2009] STC 29), and so the burden of proof sits with HMRC, it is the civil standard of proof which applies, not the criminal standard (see *HMRC v Khawaja* [2008] STC 2880), Therefore, HMRC must prove 'on the balance of probabilities that the penalty is due.

Usually in criminal cases HMRC needs to prove its case beyond all reasonable doubt (instead of on the basis of the balance of probability) (although see **explanatory note 10** below). The taxpayer is not required to incriminate himself. The onus of proof is on HMRC and only admissible evidence may be used to prove the case. As the burden of proof is so heavy, HMRC often prefers in cases of suspected serious fraud to investigate a taxpayer under its civil investigation of fraud procedures (known as the contractual disclosure facility), although in recent years it has been under pressure to try more criminal cases and is targeted to prosecute over 1,000 taxpayers per year. Under the contractual disclosure facility (see **explanatory note 28**), the taxpayer receives a letter stating that HMRC believes he has made deliberate error (without stating what the nature of the error) and offers him the choice of disclosing the error or not to cooperate. The taxpayer has 60 days to respond. If he accepts the offer, there will be no criminal prosecution provided he discloses his error in full, desists from the activity and agrees to pay the relevant tax, interest and penalties. If he refuses the offer to make a full disclosure, or fails to reply by the deadline, HMRC will continue the investigation, which may result in a criminal prosecution. In practice taxpayers will almost always prefer to negotiate a settlement rather than risk the possibility that HMRC may take a criminal prosecution.

In the matter of a deceased taxpayer, the Human Rights Act confirms that criminal liability ceases at the date of death. This prevents HMRC imposing tax-geared penalties on the personal representatives for actions of the taxpayer prior to death. However, the Upper Tribunal confirmed in *Personal representatives of Wood (Deceased) v HMRC* [2016] UKUT 346 (TCC) that discovery assessments do not amount to a criminal charge.

(10) FA 2016 introduces the first strict liability offences for tax which will apply from a date appointed by regulations. A strict liability offence is a criminal offence where it is not necessary for the taxpayer to have criminal intent to be convicted. It applies income tax or capital gains tax is due in relation to offshore income, assets or activities and the amount of tax due exceeds a certain threshold to be set by regulations (but will not be less than £25,000).

In relation to an enquiry, this offence could apply where the taxpayer has failed to correct an inaccurate return within the amendment window (usually the first anniversary of 31 January following the end of the tax year) (TMA 1970 s 106D). The taxpayer can be fined and be sentenced to a maximum 51-week prison sentence in England and Wales or a maximum six-month prison sentence in Scotland or Northern Ireland (TMA 1970 s 106H).

(11) Any adviser whose client is convicted of the criminal offences discussed in **explanatory notes 9 and 10** (or of the civil offences discussed in **Example G2 part 12 'Offshore matters'**) could be subject to a civil penalty from HMRC. The amount charged will be the higher of (a) 100% of the tax at stake in the client's case or (b) £3,000 (FA 2016 Sch 20). Again these rules are to apply from a date appointed by regulations. These penalties apply to 'enablers' but the definition is wide enough to catch a normal adviser/client relationship (FA 2016 Sch 20 para 1(2)(b)).

*Level of penalties and interest*

(12) In all cases HMRC has power to determine penalties at less than the maximum levels, by applying a 'special reduction' (FA 2007 Sch 24 para 11; CH82490, CH170000). However this must be applied in special circumstances, which does not include an inability to pay the tax concerned (FA 2007 Sch 24 para 11(2)(a)).

(13) HMRC will normally indicate to a taxpayer in Grenville's position (**Part A** of the answer) that his full disclosure in establishing the amount of unpaid tax will be to his advantage in determining the amount eventually required from him. In the circumstances he should be advised to make a complete disclosure to HMRC and to co-operate fully in ascertaining the tax underpaid for earlier years. The penalty discount will be determined by the degree of 'telling', 'helping' and 'allowing access' in the disclosure. That is (FA 2007 Sch 24 para 9(1)):

- telling HMRC that there is an inaccuracy on a return, and how the inaccuracy arose (CH82440);
- helping HMRC to quantify the amount of the understatement of tax (CH82450); and
- allowing HMRC full access to the records (if requested) to enable the officer to establish that the understatement has been correctly rectified (CH82460).

Where HMRC does not request access to the records, the full discount for the 'allowing' aspect is given.

Depending upon the level of profits there might also be liability for Class 4 national insurance contributions, and if so, this will have to be included in the amount due to HMRC and will be treated like tax due for the purposes of calculating interest and penalties.

(14) Interest will run at the prescribed rate on the unpaid tax (and Class 4 national insurance contributions) for the years concerned, and in order to restrict it, the taxpayer should be advised to make a meaningful payment on account to HMRC.

*Contract procedure for settlement of enquiry*

(15) When the unpaid tax and Class 4 national insurance contributions have been ascertained, the taxpayer will be invited to make an offer to HMRC in consideration of it not issuing formal assessments or additional assessments for its recovery and not formally determining the interest and penalties. Upon the taxpayer doing so and HMRC accepting that offer, there is a legally binding contract upon which HMRC can rely if the taxpayer does not make payment.

The amount of the offer will usually have to be for at least the unpaid tax and national insurance contributions plus interest and an appropriate uplift to cover the penalty element.

(16) The amount of penalty added to the agreement will be determined by applying the penalty rules in FA 2007 Sch 24 to any liabilities arising from April 2008 onwards, and the old rules to earlier liabilities. There is very little room for the officer to vary the penalty by subjective judgement as the discounts for disclosure are all included in primary legislation. CH82510 shows how penalties are calculated. The penalty rules under FA 2007 Sch 24 are covered in detail in **Example G2 Part 12**.

*Self-assessment enquiry closure notice*

(17) The legislation provides that at the end of an enquiry HMRC will issue a closure notice stating its conclusions and showing the revisions to the taxpayer's self-assessment and the additional tax and Class 4 national insurance due, if appropriate (TMA 1970 s 28A). The taxpayer then has 30 days in which to appeal in writing against conclusions stated or amendments made by the closure notice, giving the grounds of appeal (TMA 1970 ss 31, 31A).

*Taxpayer amendments notified in the course of an enquiry*

(18) A taxpayer may give HMRC notice of an amendment to the self-assessment return (within the permitted 12 months after the filing date for the return) whilst an enquiry is in progress. The amendment will not restrict the scope of the enquiry but may be taken into account by HMRC. If it affects the tax payable, it will not take effect unless and until it is incorporated into the TMA 1970 s 28A closure notice issued to the taxpayer (see **explanatory note 17** above) (TMA 1970 s 9B).

*Referral of questions to the Tribunal during enquiry*

(19) At any time during an enquiry, any question in connection with the subject matter of the enquiry may be referred to the Tribunal for determination. To do so, the referral must be made in writing jointly by the taxpayer and HMRC. Either party may withdraw from the referral process providing they give notice before the first hearing of the matter by the Tribunal. The determination is binding on both parties as if it were a decision on a preliminary issue under appeal (TMA 1970 ss 28ZA–28ZE).

*Class 4 national insurance contributions*

(20) Additional Class 4 national insurance contributions arising following the conclusion of an enquiry are treated as a tax debt as far as interest and penalties are concerned. Criminal proceedings may be taken for deliberate evasion of national insurance contributions (SSAA 1992 s 114).

*Litigation and settlement strategy*

(21) All enquiries and contract settlements must be compliant with the HMRC Litigation and Settlements Strategy (LSS) [www.gov.uk/government/publications/litigation-and-settlement-strategy-lss]. The LSS aims to ensure disputes are resolved consistently within the law, whilst meeting HMRC's objectives of maximising revenue flows, reducing costs and improving the experience for taxpayers. As a result HMRC will no longer do 'deals' or make compromises to close cases as every aspect of the case should comply with the legislation.

- This means that where HMRC believes it is likely to succeed in litigation on an 'all or nothing' point, and the customer does not concede in full, it will generally take the case to Court if it is cost effective to do so. It will also litigate cases where clarification of the law is necessary or the amount of tax at stake is such that the issue cannot be conceded by HMRC unless it loses in court.

- In cases which are not 'all or nothing', perhaps because the facts of the legal interpretation is uncertain, HMRC is required by the LSS to resolve the dispute in a way that secures the right tax due most efficiently. This may be by means of litigation and in making the decision to take the case to court, HMRC must consider the likely finding of the tribunal as well as the impact on other open cases.

*Acceptance of offer by an officer*

(22) The officer dealing with the enquiry has power to accept an offer by a culpable taxpayer (which is compliant with the LSS, see **explanatory note 21**) up to certain limits of size and gravity, but above those limits the offer has to be referred to a policy department who will consider it, endeavouring to preserve national consistency.

*Discovery assessments*

(23) Following the introduction of self-assessment, HMRC can make a 'discovery' where there has not been full disclosure and either (TMA 1970 s 29(4), (5)):

(a) the loss of tax is the result of a failure to take reasonable care or deliberate understatement by the taxpayer or his agent, or

(b) the officer could not reasonably be expected to have been able to identify the circumstances giving rise to the loss of tax either before the end of the normal enquiry period, or by using the information made available to him.

Information is treated as made available if (TMA 1970 s 29(6)):

(a) it is contained in the tax return or supporting accounts, statements or documents supplied; or

(b) it is contained in any claim made; or

(c) it is contained in any document, accounts or particulars supplied in relation to an enquiry into a return or claim; or

(d) it is information which could reasonably be expected to be inferred from the above; or

(e) it is information notified in writing by the taxpayer.

References to a return mean the return under review and either of the two previous returns. Information supplied by an agent is deemed to be supplied by the taxpayer (TMA 1970 s 29 (7)).

The case of *Langham v Veltema* [2004] STC 544 had a significant impact on the understanding of what it means to make information available to HMRC. In this case the taxpayer was advised by a professional valuer that the value of a house transferred to him in 1998 by his employer was £100,000. He used this figure in his self-assessment tax return which was received and acknowledged by HMRC as needing no correction on 9 September after the tax year. This figure was also used on the company's corporation tax return. Following an enquiry into the company's tax affairs the market value figure was revised to £145,000, however by the time this had been decided the enquiry window for the taxpayer's return had closed. HMRC issued a discovery assessment to the taxpayer and he appealed. The courts upheld HMRC's appeal, deciding there would not be sufficient disclosure of the uncertainty unless it is highlighted in the tax return as an actual, rather than a potential, insufficiency. On the basis of the initial information made available in the taxpayer's return, HMRC could not be expected to have been aware that the valuation was inadequate.

Following the case, HMRC issued SP 1/06 in which it recommends that taxpayers who rely on a valuation in determining their tax liability should state the following in the white space of the tax return:

– that a valuation has been used, and

– who carried out the valuation giving the name and qualification and stating that they are an independent suitably qualified valuer.

If a taxpayer has adopted a different view of the law from that published by HMRC the white space of the tax return should state that HMRC guidance has not been followed (SP 1/06 paras 18, 19).

If the return includes exceptional items the entry in the white space should give full details of the exceptional entries (SP 1/06 para 17).

If this guidance is followed then the return should become final at the end of the enquiry window if HMRC does not open an enquiry (or open and close an enquiry). A 'discovery' would not then arise unless the information provided was incorrect because of deliberate understatement by the taxpayer.

Recent tax cases on discovery include:

- *HMRC v Lansdowne Partners Ltd* [2012] STC 544 - the Court of Appeal found against HMRC as the partnership had submitted the relevant information by letter prior to the closure of the enquiry window and the officer could have been reasonably expected to be aware that the partnership profits were insufficient at that time, meaning there was no discovery;

- *HMRC v Charlton* [2013] STC 866 - HMRC failed to act on information (including SRN of tax avoidance scheme registered under DOTAS) within the normal enquiry window, meaning that it had inadvertently failed to open an enquiry into the return of one of the scheme members and subsequently tried to raise a discovery assessment. The Upper Tribunal decided that the officer could have been reasonably expected to be aware of the insufficiency, especially since the tax avoidance scheme had been defeated in court before the enquiry window for the taxpayer's return had closed. HMRC's appeal was dismissed;

- *Pattullo v HMRC* [2016] UKUT 270 (TCC) - the Upper Tribunal found that a 'discovery' can be a series of discoveries, rather than a single moment of discovery. However HMRC must act when the discovery is 'fresh', and issue the discovery assessment without undue delay or it would become 'stale'. It is not sufficient for HMRC merely to act within the statutory time limit for raising the assessment. The discovery assessment in this case was found to be valid;

- *Mieseages v HMRC* [2016] UKFTT 375 (TC) - the disclosure included in the trust tax return was not sufficient to prevent a discovery assessment for the life tenant. The trust return contained a large white space disclosure but the personal self-assessment for the life tenant had minimal disclosure. The First-tier Tribunal found that the information in the trust return had not been 'made available' for discovery assessment purposes.

*Appeals and postponement applications*

(24) Under TMA 1970 ss 31, 31A, a taxpayer has 30 days to appeal in writing against any HMRC conclusions stated or amendments made at the end of an enquiry, jeopardy amendments made during the course of an enquiry (see **Example G7 explanatory note 6**), 'discovery' amendments to partnership statements (see **Example G2**) and any assessments which are not self-assessments (ARTG2160). Appeals may also be made within 30 days under TMA 1970 Sch 1A para 9 against HMRC amendments to claims made outside the return (see Example G3).

The HMRC officer may accept a late appeal made without unreasonable delay after the 30 days if he is satisfied that there was a reasonable excuse for not bringing the appeal within the time limit. If the officer is not prepared to do so, the taxpayer can ask for his late appeal to be admitted by the First-tier Tribunal (TMA 1970 s 49; ARTG2220).

An appeal against a national insurance issue may be made, within 30 days of the decision, to the First-tier Tribunal or, if the tribunal rules so determine, the Upper Tribunal (SSC(TF)A 1999, ss 12, 13).

There is no prescribed form of appeal, although a tax assessment is usually accompanied by a form on which an appeal and, if appropriate, postponement application may be made (ARTG2140).

(25) An appeal does not alter the due date of payment of tax unless an application is made for postponement (TMA 1970 s 55; ARTG2510). Under self-assessment the postponement provisions apply only to amendments to self-assessments made by HMRC as a result of an enquiry into the return and to HMRC assessments.

The time limit for making a postponement application is also within 30 days after the date of the assessment/amendment as the case may be. Late applications for postponement may be made if changed circumstances since the original postponement application or lack of it result in the taxpayer having grounds for believing that he has been overcharged (ARTG2520). It is not sufficient in a postponement application to say that the tax may be excessive. The application must state by how much the taxpayer believes he has been overcharged and the specific reasons for that belief (TMA s 55(3)).

Where application is made for tax to be postponed, the due date for any tax not postponed becomes 30 days after the Tribunal's decision on the postponement and against which no appeal is pending. If the HMRC officer agrees the postponement without recourse to the Tribunal, the due date for the tax not postponed becomes 30 days after the officer's agreement to the postponement provided that no appeal is made against the postponement decision (TMA 1970 s 55(6)).

It is not possible to make a postponement application where the tax is subject to an accelerated payment notice or partner payment notice (TMA 1970 s 55(8B)-(8D)).

(26) When the appeal is settled, any tax and, if relevant, Class 4 national insurance contributions found to be due but previously postponed and any additional amounts become payable 30 days after the officer issues to the appellant notice of the total amount payable (TMA 1970 s 55(9); ARTG2550).

(27) If an assessment or HMRC amendment to a self-assessment is not appealed within the time limit (or within any further time allowed by HMRC), the assessment will stand. Where an appeal is made, it is most likely to be heard by the First-tier Tribunal, although the Tribunals Service may allocate the case under its own rules to the Upper Tribunal, whose decisions on questions of fact are normally binding on both parties, but with a right of further appeal on a point of law. Appeals from the First-tier Tribunal are made to the Upper Tribunal, and from there to the Court of Appeal (Court of Session in Scotland) and, where leave is granted, the Supreme Court (formerly the House of Lords). Once an appeal has been determined, it is final and conclusive (ARTG2750). TMA 1970 s 54 provides that an appeal can be settled by agreement between the taxpayer and HMRC before going to the Tribunal, in which case the agreement is treated as if the appeal had been determined by the Tribunal.

Most appeals are normally to the First-tier Tribunal, but an independent review by HMRC is offered to anyone notifying an appeal before the Tribunal is involved (TMA 1970 s 49C). Whilst the taxpayer can refuse the offer and proceed to the Tribunal, it is usual for the taxpayer to accept the offer of review as it gives the taxpayer a chance to resolve the dispute in his favour without having to go to the Tribunal (which will be stressful and expensive). The review officer will reconsider the decision in light of the LSS, see **explanatory note 21**. The review process is discussed in **Example G2 Part 24** and in ARTG4001-ARTG4860. If the taxpayer has accepted the offer of a review, it is not possible to appeal to the Tribunal until the review has concluded (TMA 1970 s 49G). If, following the outcome of the review the taxpayer disputes the decision, he has 30 days to appeal to the Tribunal (TMA 1970 s 49G).

Appeals are not managed by HMRC, and the appellant deals directly with the Tribunal once notice of appeal has been sent to HMRC.

In 2015 the Government ran a consultation on whether to introduce fees for tax appeals. The fee structure depends on the classification of the case by the Tribunal and there will be a registration fee and a hearing fee. Where the appeal relates to a penalty of £100 or less, the fees will be reduced. There will also be a fee to appeal a First-tier Tribunal decision and a hearing fee. The new fee structure is expected to apply from January 2017.

*Civil Investigation of Fraud*

(28) The civil procedure for dealing with cases of suspected serious fraud is set out in HMRC's Code of Practice 9 (COP9), the latest version of which applies from 30 June 2014 [www.gov.uk/government/publications/code-of-practice-9-where-hm-revenue-and-customs-suspect-fraud-cop-9-2012].

Under this procedure, known as the contractual disclosure facility, HMRC writes to a taxpayer to say it believes he has made deliberate error (without stating the nature of the error) and offers him the choice of fully disclosing the error or not to cooperate at all. Note that all mentions of 'fraud' were removed from the letters and contracts from 30 June 2014. The taxpayer has 60 days to decide whether to cooperate, which entails him signing and dating a contract acceptance letter, completing an outline disclosure form (ie a summary of the errors) and agree to cease making the deliberate errors immediately (FCIM201030). This is the only way in which a person can admit to a tax fraud without undergoing criminal investigation. A full formal disclosure of all deliberate errors and the tax due should follow at a later date (FCIM206040).

Obviously, some taxpayers will decide not to cooperate with HMRC, but they should be aware that the contractual disclosure facility is only offered when HMRC has a reasonable suspicion that fraud has been committed.

The Board of HMRC reserves complete discretion to pursue criminal investigations, and will refer cases to the Crown Prosecution Service if they deem the evasion to be unsuitable for the COP9 'Civil Investigation of Fraud' procedure. The COP9 procedure will not lead to prosecution for the original offence, but other related offences might be reported to the National Crime Agency and lead to prosecution, and on conviction, confiscation proceedings. The procedure gives the taxpayer the opportunity to make a complete disclosure of all irregularities in direct and indirect taxes. If the disclosures are found to be materially incorrect, then prosecution can follow.

*Amending claims on completion of enquiries*

(29) Where HMRC issues an assessment and the underpayment has arisen despite the taxpayer taking reasonable care, he can make, revise or withdraw claims which would otherwise be out of time (TMA 1970 s 43A). The time limit is one year from the end of the year of assessment in which the assessment is made. That right is extended to situations where a return is amended at the end of an enquiry (TMA 1970 s 43C). Claims affecting another person's liability will require the written consent of that other person (TMA 1970 s 43B). The ability to amend claims does not extend to the transferable tax allowance, the surrender of married couple's allowance or children's tax credit, and is restricted to claims which affect the amount of additional tax payable by the assessment or amendment.

*Tax Credits*

(30) Any adjustment to income may have a corresponding effect upon the income for tax credits. The fact that tax credits are based on joint income complicates the enquiry procedures in the event of a joint claim. TCA 2002 ss 19, 20 give HMRC appropriate enquiry and discovery powers. Where a taxpayer under enquiry has made a tax credits claim, both enquiries will be undertaken at the same time by the same officer. Separate opening and closing letters and 'offer' letters will be required. The time limit for a tax credit discovery assessment is five years after the end of the relevant tax year.

The tax credits settlement would not attract interest (unless the claim was fraudulent) and any penalties (if due) are flat amounts (TCA 2002 s 37). The maximum civil penalty is £3,000 for providing incorrect information fraudulently or negligently, or £300 for failure to provide information (TCA 2002 ss 31, 32; TCTM10410). In both instances the level of the penalty depends on the seriousness of the issue, amounts involved, co-operation and disclosure. Tax credit fraud can also be subject to criminal sanction, particularly where it is organised, when HMRC's policy is that it will never follow the civil route (TCA 2002 s 35; TCTM10910).

For more on tax credits, see **Example A7.**

*The Money Laundering Regulations and legal privilege*

(31) See **Example I2 explanatory notes 20 and 21.**

# Question

Feckless, a married man with three children all born between 2003 and 2012, has been in business on his own account as a UK market trader at shows, carnivals and race meetings since May 2010. HMRC had sent him self-assessment forms for the years 2010/11 onwards, but he had not submitted them, and in their absence HMRC determined the tax for each tax year up to 2014/15 in amounts which increased each year, Feckless having paid the tax and the fixed penalties for failing to make returns.

As a result of reading in the press in April 2017 that some £50,000 had been stolen from Feckless's house, HMRC wrote to him pointing out that although the determinations for earlier years had been made in amounts which were HMRC's then best estimates of what he should have paid, they were entitled to increase such estimates if they were discovered to be inadequate, the reported theft of such a large cash hoard suggesting that they were. The officer invited Feckless to provide HMRC with a statement showing his overall financial position, seeking thereby to ascertain his trading profit since he commenced in business, and enabling assessments in correct amounts for all years to replace the determinations.

A friend who had limited experience in this area produced for Feckless the following statement which purported to calculate the profits figures covering the period to 30 April 2015 and resulting tax position for the tax years 2010/11 to 2016/17:

| *Assets at 30 April* | *2010* | *2011* | *2012* | *2013* | *2014* | *2015* | *2016* |
|---|---|---|---|---|---|---|---|
| | £ | £ | £ | £ | £ | £ | £ |
| Cash hoard | 50,000 | 50,000 | 50,000 | 50,000 | 50,000 | 50,000 | – |
| Cash at bank – current account | 100 | 3,900 | 7,600 | 11,300 | 13,900 | 19,900 | 47,100 |
| Stock (minimal since everything sold at the end of a day) | – | 10 | 10 | 15 | 15 | 20 | 20 |
| Wife's jewellery (received from deceased relative) at original value | 6,000 | 6,000 | 5,000 | 3,000 | – | – | – |
| Freehold house at cost net of £150,000 mortgage | – | – | – | – | 20,000 | 20,000 | 20,000 |
| | 56,100 | 59,910 | 62,610 | 64,315 | 83,915 | 89,920 | 67,120 |
| At previous 30 April | | 56,100 | 59,910 | 62,610 | 64,315 | 83,915 | 89,920 |
| Increase/(Decrease) | | 3,810 | 2,700 | 1,705 | 19,600 | 6,005 | (22,800) |
| Expenses | | | | | | | |
| Rent (before buying house) | | 4,338 | 4,338 | 4,338 | 4,169 | – | – |
| Mortgage interest | | – | – | – | 720 | 10,440 | 10,440 |
| Housekeeping | | 5,156 | 5,156 | 5,156 | 5,156 | 5,156 | 5,156 |
| Miscellaneous | | 1,200 | 1,200 | 1,200 | 1,200 | 1,200 | 1,200 |
| | | 10,694 | 10,694 | 10,694 | 11,245 | 16,796 | 16,796 |
| Total of wealth increase + expenses | | 14,504 | 13,394 | 12,399 | 30,845 | 22,801 | (6,004) |
| Income | | | | | | | |
| Sale of jewellery | | – | (1,000) | (2,000) | (3,000) | – | – |
| Betting winnings | | (650) | (800) | (1,000) | (1,200) | (1,500) | (2,000) |
| Net increase/(decrease) | | 13,854 | 11,594 | 9,399 | 26,645 | 21,301 | (8,004) |

Total increases over the five trading years to 30 April 2015 are £82,793, giving an average income over that period of £16,558 per annum.

Loss of £8,004 for the year to 30 April 2016 establishes a nil profit for the tax year 2016/17 and the loss may be deducted from the 2015/16 profit of £16,558, reducing it to £8,554.

Feckless submitted this statement to HMRC accompanied by completed self-assessments for 2010/11 to 2015/16 in which estimated figures of turnover, purchases and business expenses were included to net off to the averaged profit figures.

HMRC responded saying that there are many anomalies and areas which the statement does not properly or sufficiently address, setting out their areas of concern and listing the information and documents that they require in order to resolve them.

(1) Without preparing an amended statement, set out what you believe HMRC's reaction to the content of the statement will have been and say what further information and evidence you think has been requested.

(2) Apart from an amended statement, amended self-assessments for those years in-date and eventually the self-assessment for 2016/17, what other certificates etc will HMRC require at the conclusion of its enquiry?

(3) Since Feckless had not put in false returns, as distinct from accepting HMRC determinations, is HMRC correct in suggesting in the summer of 2017 that it can amend the tax payable for those years for which the time limit for replacing a determination for that year has expired? What is the status of the self-assessment returns submitted for the earlier years?

# Answer

## (1) Officer's reaction to statement, and information etc required to take matter forward

### Cash hoard

(a) Whilst the theft might be evidence of the cash stolen, what evidence is there that it was consistent over the years?

(b) How did a hoard of £50,000 arise in 2010 before business commenced? It is far more likely to have arisen over the trading period.

(c) What evidence is there that the stolen cash hoard represented all the cash? A certificate is required of the present cash count. Was it kept in one place and in what sort of container? What is the result of insurance company investigations if a claim for loss was made?

(d) The amount stolen should be included in the statement for 2016. Its omission accounts for the apparent decrease in wealth for that year and before considering any other points, turns the loss of £8,004 into a profit of £41,996, which makes a nonsense of the figures Feckless has used for turnover, purchases and expenses in the calculation of the result for the year to 30 April 2016.

### Bank accounts etc

(a) A bank certificate is required, not only to confirm the current account balances but also as a check on other transactions and matters included by banks in the standard certificate required by HMRC, eg accounts at other branches (including abroad), securities held etc.

(b) Bank statements are required for examination. Particular deposits, withdrawals, indications of transfers to/from other accounts, and the pattern of transactions may lead to other relevant points. It is possible that bank statements are not received as a matter of routine as all banking is online. In which case bank statements should be requested from the bank.

(c) Has Feckless been trading on e-marketplaces (eBay or similar)? It may be possible to obtain a record of such sales.

### Trading stock

(a) Stock is very low despite the nature of the trade. More information is required on how the trade is operated.

(b) Are purchase invoices and dates of shows etc available? If so this will give some idea if stocks are, albeit exceptionally, carried.

(c) Such invoices will also give some idea of the potential profit achievement if, for example, a trading pattern, attempted profit margin, wastage etc, can be established.

### Jewellery

(a) What evidence is there that jewellery was inherited or received by way of gift, as distinct from being purchased, for which funds would be required?

(b) If purchased, then as with the cash, how could it have been accumulated before trading started? HMRC is likely to suggest that it did not exist, or if it did, that it was acquired after trading started. Also, what evidence of sales?

(c) Contents insurance policy required to confirm/contradict the point.

(d) It has, in any event, been included twice – once as a movement in assets and once more as income.

(e) Alternatively the income figure may represent the profit on sale. Determine the actual cost and sale proceeds, profits and likely gain, or exceptionally does this constitute a further trading source?

### House mortgage etc

(a) Consistent mortgage interest implies that house purchase was financed on an interest only mortgage on a fixed rate. Confirm this by reference to statements or adjust for capital repayments.

(b) There is no record of a deposit for the house being paid. Feckless would not have been able to raise a 100% mortgage, so cash must have been used to pay the deposit.

(c) A copy of the mortgage application form is required since this may indicate the level of income reported to the lender. How was that income calculated?

(d) The costs of buying the house and of furnishing it to be incorporated.

(e) The fixed mortgage suggests that it is possible that capital repayments may be being dealt with by other means. Does Feckless have a long-term fixed-rate mortgage? Is there a savings vehicle which is accumulating capital to repay the principal?

(f) Has there been any house improvement expenditure and, if so, how is it financed? Was the property previously occupied as a 'sitting tenant'?

### Living expenses

(a) Housekeeping is low for a family of this size.

(b) Further, it will have risen over the years with the cost of living and will not have been consistent.

(c) Sample costs are required at the present time, which will then be worked backwards using an appropriate index and taking into account known changes in circumstances.

(d) It would be surprising if there were no credit cards. This needs confirming and credit card statements should be obtained.

### Miscellaneous expenses

(a) What is covered under miscellaneous expenses?

(b) What should be covered, given the habits of the family; such as smoking, drinking, gambling, entertaining and holidays?

### Betting winnings

(a) Proof is required of the betting winnings.

(b) In the absence of proof, the inclusion of the winnings has admitted the activity and since it usually costs money, an additional expense instead of an item of income probably arises.

(c) The Officer will in all probability contend that proved winnings have, in any event, been cancelled by undisclosed losses, thus cancelling the winnings and involving further cash payments.

# Answer

## (1) Officer's reaction to statement, and information etc required to take matter forward

### Cash hoard

(a) Whilst the theft might be evidence of the cash stolen, what evidence is there that it was consistent over the years?

(b) How did a hoard of £50,000 arise in 2010 before business commenced? It is far more likely to have arisen over the trading period.

(c) What evidence is there that the stolen cash hoard represented all the cash? A certificate is required of the present cash count. Was it kept in one place and in what sort of container? What is the result of insurance company investigations if a claim for loss was made?

(d) The amount stolen should be included in the statement for 2016. Its omission accounts for the apparent decrease in wealth for that year and before considering any other points, turns the loss of £8,004 into a profit of £41,996, which makes a nonsense of the figures Feckless has used for turnover, purchases and expenses in the calculation of the result for the year to 30 April 2016.

### Bank accounts etc

(a) A bank certificate is required, not only to confirm the current account balances but also as a check on other transactions and matters included by banks in the standard certificate required by HMRC, eg accounts at other branches (including abroad), securities held etc.

(b) Bank statements are required for examination. Particular deposits, withdrawals, indications of transfers to/from other accounts, and the pattern of transactions may lead to other relevant points. It is possible that bank statements are not received as a matter of routine as all banking is online. In which case bank statements should be requested from the bank.

(c) Has Feckless been trading on e-marketplaces (eBay or similar)? It may be possible to obtain a record of such sales.

### Trading stock

(a) Stock is very low despite the nature of the trade. More information is required on how the trade is operated.

(b) Are purchase invoices and dates of shows etc available? If so this will give some idea if stocks are, albeit exceptionally, carried.

(c) Such invoices will also give some idea of the potential profit achievement if, for example, a trading pattern, attempted profit margin, wastage etc, can be established.

### Jewellery

(a) What evidence is there that jewellery was inherited or received by way of gift, as distinct from being purchased, for which funds would be required?

(b) If purchased, then as with the cash, how could it have been accumulated before trading started? HMRC is likely to suggest that it did not exist, or if it did, that it was acquired after trading started. Also, what evidence of sales?

(c) Contents insurance policy required to confirm/contradict the point.

(d) It has, in any event, been included twice – once as a movement in assets and once more as income.

(e) Alternatively the income figure may represent the profit on sale. Determine the actual cost and sale proceeds, profits and likely gain, or exceptionally does this constitute a further trading source?

**House mortgage etc**

(a) Consistent mortgage interest implies that house purchase was financed on an interest only mortgage on a fixed rate. Confirm this by reference to statements or adjust for capital repayments.

(b) There is no record of a deposit for the house being paid. Feckless would not have been able to raise a 100% mortgage, so cash must have been used to pay the deposit.

(c) A copy of the mortgage application form is required since this may indicate the level of income reported to the lender. How was that income calculated?

(d) The costs of buying the house and of furnishing it to be incorporated.

(e) The fixed mortgage suggests that it is possible that capital repayments may be being dealt with by other means. Does Feckless have a long-term fixed-rate mortgage? Is there a savings vehicle which is accumulating capital to repay the principal?

(f) Has there been any house improvement expenditure and, if so, how is it financed? Was the property previously occupied as a 'sitting tenant'?

**Living expenses**

(a) Housekeeping is low for a family of this size.

(b) Further, it will have risen over the years with the cost of living and will not have been consistent.

(c) Sample costs are required at the present time, which will then be worked backwards using an appropriate index and taking into account known changes in circumstances.

(d) It would be surprising if there were no credit cards. This needs confirming and credit card statements should be obtained.

**Miscellaneous expenses**

(a) What is covered under miscellaneous expenses?

(b) What should be covered, given the habits of the family; such as smoking, drinking, gambling, entertaining and holidays?

**Betting winnings**

(a) Proof is required of the betting winnings.

(b) In the absence of proof, the inclusion of the winnings has admitted the activity and since it usually costs money, an additional expense instead of an item of income probably arises.

(c) The Officer will in all probability contend that proved winnings have, in any event, been cancelled by undisclosed losses, thus cancelling the winnings and involving further cash payments.

### Wife and children

(a) Child benefit will have been received in respect of the children, mitigating the position.

(b) The statement includes certain items relating to his wife, eg jewellery. It does not include wife's income or expenses (eg personal expenditure, hairdresser, clothes, motoring costs of her vehicle if any). Although the officer has not opened an enquiry into the wife's affairs, clearly they interlink with those of Feckless. In practice the officer may ask for voluntary disclosure of the assets, liabilities, income and expenses of Mrs Feckless, only resorting to issuing a tax return to her (so that a formal enquiry notice may be issued) if she will not cooperate.

### National insurance and tax payments

(a) Self employed Class 2 national insurance contributions have not been included as an outgoing.

(b) The tax and Class 4 national insurance paid on the determinations have not been included as outgoings.

### Arriving at increases/decreases

(a) The increases/decreases cannot be averaged. Each year must stand on its own.

(b) The only decrease in this case has already been eliminated, but should one arise it may suggest further expenditure on assets, extraordinary items or living expenses, in the latter case with persuasive influence on other years.

(c) An increase may be used as an indication that other years should show a similar increase, or be persuasive as to profitability.

The 2014 increase arises directly as a result of the house purchase. It is undoubtedly not applicable solely to that year. Where were the funds previously held and did any of them arise before the business started?

### Fixed assets of the business

(a) The statement does not include anything for fixtures, fittings or vehicles. Presumably there will be some. When acquired and for how much?

(b) Specifically check the purchase and sale details for cars and vans.

## (2) Other certificates etc required

Apart from a new statement and (subject to (3) **below**) amended profit calculations, reflecting the above points, HMRC will require from Feckless a certificate of complete disclosure, a certified statement of assets and liabilities at a date approximating to that on which the officer concluded his enquiry and a certified list of bank and building society accounts operated throughout the period covered by the enquiry.

## (3) HMRC's position re time limits

In order to replace the determinations for 2010/11 to 2012/13 which are outside the normal statutory time limit of three years after the submission date for the tax return, HMRC must prove that Feckless deliberately understated his income (for 2012/13) or failed to take reasonable care. See **explanatory note 1**. It would undoubtedly succeed in their contention that the acceptance of determinations lower than would be compatible with living standards and accumulation of wealth amounts to dishonesty. This would be based on the understanding that a reasonable man would have known that his business was more successful than the profits which produced the income tax and Class 4 national insurance contributions payable under the determinations. As a result, HMRC can raise discovery assessments under TMA 1970 s 29 to recover the loss of tax.

The status of the self-assessment returns that Feckless submitted means that they are largely irrelevant. The time limit for replacing a determination with a self-assessment return is twelve months after the date the determination was issued, so most of the years have become final. See **explanatory note 1**. In any event, as indicated above, HMRC will seek to raise additional assessments based on the information collected during the enquiry. See **explanatory note 3**.

In consideration of not taking criminal proceedings against him, Feckless may be invited by HMRC to make an offer to them embracing tax, national insurance contributions, interest and penalties for the tax years 2010/11 to 2015/16. A binding contract ensues upon acceptance by HMRC, hence the expression a 'contract settlement'. See **explanatory note 5**.

The self-assessment for 2016/17 should be based on accurate figures and filed by 31 January 2018 (31 October 2017 if filed on paper).

## Explanatory Notes

*Determinations in the absence of a return*

(1) Where a return has not been filed by the due date, HMRC can issue a determination of the tax due which is then treated as if it were a self-assessment (TMA 1970 s 28C). The time limit for issuing a determination is three years from the filing date for the return for the relevant year, the filing date being 31 January after the tax year (TMA 1970 s 28C(5)(a), (6)). The determination can be superseded by filing a self-assessment return for that year, but the determination cannot be displaced after 12 months from the date of issue, so at that point the determination is final (TMA 1970 s 28C(3), (5)(b)).

In reality, the facts indicate that the determinations raised were insufficient, so HMRC is able to raise discovery assessments for the relevant years – see **part (3)** of the Answer above.

*VAT*

(2) As far as VAT is concerned, any amount due to HMRC is available to reduce the calculated trading profits so long as the VAT liability is agreed before the settlement of the direct tax with HMRC. In this Example, since all sales may have been zero-rated, Feckless may have registered for VAT as all returns would give rise to refunds. In that event, copies of VAT returns submitted may assist in allocating income and expenditure to accounting periods.

If incorrect VAT returns have been submitted, a further settlement will be necessary, with turnover and expenditure figures estimated using similar techniques to those for calculating trading profits.

*Deliberate under assessments*

(3) Under the self-assessment provisions, a taxpayer's self-assessment is final unless HMRC enquire into the return (see **explanatory note 4** below), except where there is a failure by the taxpayer to take reasonable care or deliberate understatement or inadequate disclosure, in which case HMRC may issue discovery assessments under TMA 1970 s 29.

HMRC can raise discovery assessments going back (TMA 1970 ss 29, 34, 36):

- four years for mistake despite reasonable care;
- six years for failure to take reasonable care; and
- 20 years for deliberate understatement or failure to notify liability.

Prior to April 2010, the time limit for HMRC assessments was five years from 31 January following the tax year, extended to 20 years in cases of fraudulent or negligent conduct.

(4) Under self-assessment, HMRC may serve a formal notice on the taxpayer that it has opened an enquiry into the accuracy of the tax return within 12 months after the date the return is filed (eg by 30 May 2018 for

a 2016/17 return filed on 31 May 2017) (TMA 1970 s 9A). The time limit is extended where, as in this example, the self-assessment is filed late (TMA 1970 s 9A(2)). See **Example G2 Part 14**.

*Penalties*

(5) The penalties included in the contract settlement are calculated under FA 2007 Sch 24 ('Penalties for errors'). A penalty is charged under FA 2007 Sch 24 where either the taxpayer has submitted an incorrect document, a return contains an inaccuracy which leads to an underpayment of tax or where the taxpayer has received an assessment from HMRC which shows an understatement and does not take adequate steps to notify HMRC.

In this Example, Feckless has not submitted returns for 2010/11 to 2015/16 so he cannot be liable to the higher penalties for making a dishonest return – which could be either 70% or 100% if the dishonesty is compounded by his concealing it. Instead, he is liable to the lower penalty of 30% for failure to notify an incorrect assessment (FA 2007 Sch 24 para 2; CH81170, CH82120). This amount may be subject to a reduction for disclosure, but as HMRC had to approach Feckless the disclosure would be prompted, and the minimum penalty would be 15% of the understated tax (FA 2007 Sch 24 paras 9, 10). To achieve a full discount, Feckless would need to have told HMRC that there is an understatement, given help in quantifying the understatement and provided full access to HMRC, allowing the authorities to check the position (CH82400). From the facts, and assuming there are no overseas elements to the settlement, it is likely that the penalty would be somewhere between 15% and 30%.

*Jeopardy amendments*

(6) HMRC has the power to issue 'jeopardy amendments' to a self-assessment to create an additional tax charge during the course of an enquiry if it thinks there is likely to be a loss of tax if no immediate amendment is made (TMA 1970 s 9C). This power should only be used when HMRC suspects that the taxpayer intends to dispose of assets, become non-resident or bankrupt, or is about to go to prison (EM1953).

A well-advised taxpayer will normally make a substantial payment on account at an early stage in the enquiry, thus negating the need for HMRC to consider a jeopardy amendment to the self-assessment.

*Tax credits*

(7) If the taxpayer made a claim for tax credits for the years under enquiry and the conclusion is that the income reported is insufficient, then the Tax Credits Office should be notified that the declared income is incorrect and amended details provided (TCA 2002 s 20; TCTM10330). An overpayment of tax credits may arise and possibly penalties for incorrect statements (TCA 2002 s 31). For more on tax credits, see **Example G6 explanatory note 30**.

# National insurance contributions

# Question

(a) There are various classes of contributions for national insurance purposes. Indicate the circumstances in which a liability arises under each class.

(b) State how earnings are defined for national insurance purposes, the payments that may be excluded and the way in which benefits in kind are treated.

(c) J Bond is a Member of Parliament and his salary is £66,000. He also carries on business as a management consultant and for the year ended 30 June 2016 his taxable profits were £22,000. His wife is employed by him as a research assistant for his Parliamentary duties and receives a salary of £7,500 per year. She is also employed by him in his management consultancy business for which she receives a salary of £7,500 per year.

Advise him and his wife of their national insurance position and calculate their national insurance liabilities for 2016/17.

(d) Mrs Williams and her son are the directors of Tation Ltd, which trades as a restaurant employing four waitresses and an apprentice who joined straight from school last summer and is working under a formal apprenticeship agreement with day release sessions at the local FE college. She has asked you to explain how contributions are charged on their directors' earnings and also to state whether the following items must be included in gross pay for the purposes of Class 1 contributions of the waitresses:

(i) Tips and gratuities.

(ii) Benefits in kind.

(iii) Payment of taxi fares home after late shifts and laundry costs.

(iv) Payments to a local florist for a £50 bouquet delivered to one of the staff when she was married during the year.

Draft a memorandum to answer the points raised by Mrs Williams.

(e) Outline the main provisions of the employment allowance rules, noting any limits and exclusions that apply.

(f) Set out how national insurance contributions are collected.

# Answer

## (a) Classes of national insurance contributions

National insurance contributions are payable under seven categories as follows:

### *Class 1 contributions (SSCBA 1992 ss 5–9)*

These relate to employed persons and are subdivided into primary contributions (payable by employees) and secondary contributions (payable by employers). Class 1 NICs are not an annual contribution: a liability arises on earnings that exceed the relevant threshold in any earnings period (SSCBA 1992 s 5). For 2016/17 the relevant threshold for employees is known as the primary threshold (PT), fixed at £155 per week. The secondary threshold (ST) for employers is £156 per week. There is also a lower earnings limit (LEL) of £112 per week, with a 'nil contributions' band for earnings between that limit and the two earnings thresholds. Even though no contributions are payable on that band of earnings, employers are required to report earnings at or above the LEL in order that the employee may earn entitlement to social security benefits.

There is an upper earnings limit (UEL) of £827 per week for employees' contributions that are charged at the main rate of 12%, but no upper limit for employers' contributions, which are paid at 13.8% on all earnings over the ST, except in respect of earnings paid to employees under the age of 21, and apprentices under the age of 25 following a government-approved apprenticeship framework, who attract a 0% rate on earnings up to the UEL and 13.8% on the excess. This does not affect their employee contributions.

On earnings above the UEL employees pay 2% contributions.

The employees' contributions are deducted by the employer from earnings and paid together with the employer's contributions and the PAYE tax to the HMRC Accounts Office. Payment must be received by HMRC by the 19th of the following month, unless the employer is classed as 'small' and payment is made quarterly.

Payment may be deferred until the 22nd of the month (or the last working day before that date if the 22nd is a non-working day) if payment is made electronically so that HMRC has cleared funds by that date.

The current (2016/17) earnings limits are:

| | Weekly | Monthly | Annual |
|---|---|---|---|
| Lower earnings limit (LEL) | £112 | £486 | £5,824 |
| Earnings thresholds (ET) | | | |
| • Employer | £156 | £676 | £8,112 |
| • Employee | £155 | £672 | £8,060 |
| Upper earnings limit for employees (UEL) | £827 | £3,583 | £43,000 |

An earnings period is the interval at which earnings are normally paid. Thus if pay is paid weekly the first limits apply; if fortnightly, twice the first limits apply, and so on. If pay is paid at intervals of less than one week then the weekly limit applies. If the employee is a director then the annual limit applies (except in the year of appointment, where a pro rata limit applies, based on the weeks from the week of appointment to the end of the tax year). Contributions for directors may, however, be payable provisionally according to the normal pay period, just like an employee's contributions, with an annual adjustment if necessary (SI 2001/1004 reg 8(6) – see **part (D)**).

Contributions are payable by employees on earnings paid on or after their 16th birthday until they are of state pension age. This is normally 65 years for a man and between 60 and 65 for a woman. A woman's state pension age now depends on her date of birth: women born before 6 April 1950 will obtain their state pension at age 60, but for every month after that date until 5 April 1953, pension age increases in stages, so that women will eventually all obtain state pension age at the same age as men, 65, from 6 December 2018, and the state pension age for both men and women will then move in stages to 66 by 6 October 2020. An employer has no liability to pay contributions for an employee under 16 but full secondary contributions are payable for persons over state pension age. In some circumstances, employees' contributions are credited rather than paid, such credits counting towards satisfying the contribution conditions for certain benefits, in particular the basic state pension (see under Class 3).

Married women who elected on or before 11 May 1977 – and have continued to qualify ever since – pay reduced rate (Table B) contributions in exchange for limited benefits. The employer still pays full secondary contributions. If a reduced rate election lapses or is revoked it cannot be revived (see **explanatory note 11**).

The liability is calculated on the earnings of a given pay period from a given employer (subject to anti-avoidance rules relating to uneven payments and pay from another business which is 'in association' with the employer – see **explanatory note 10**). There is now no maximum Class 1 national insurance liability for employed earners. Those earning over £43,000 in one or more employments generally have to pay 2% on that excess. For those with more than one employment (or with employment and self-employment) there are complex rules to ensure that they do not pay excessive contributions (see below under Maximum contributions payable). There is no maximum for employers' secondary contributions. 'Earnings' broadly means amounts paid in cash/cheques or paid on the direction of the employee, but it also includes some non-cash payments, such as credits to a director's loan account that are a reward for services, loans via third parties arranged by the employer, employee shares in quoted companies and payment in the form of vouchers (eg shopping vouchers and the excess of any childcare vouchers over the relevant tax-free limit). Payments in kind do not count as pay for Class 1 contributions unless the asset concerned is specifically included (see **part (B)**). The assets included are mainly assets that can be readily converted into cash. Employers' Class 1A contributions are payable on virtually all taxable benefits that are not within the Class 1 charge (see below).

The rates of contribution for 2016/17 are:

## Employer's contributions

| | |
|---|---|
| Earnings of over-20s up to secondary threshold (ST) | Nil |
| Earnings of under-21s and apprentices under 25 up to UST or Apprentice UST | Nil |
| Excess above ST/UST/Apprentice UST | 13.8% |

Most employers can set a £3,000 pa employment allowance off against their secondary NICs liability, except small companies where the sole paid earner is the director, when no allowance is available.

## Employee's contributions

The employee's contributions (full rate) are:

| | |
|---|---|
| Earnings up to primary threshold (PT) | Nil |
| Earnings between PT and upper earnings limit (UEL) | 12.0% |
| Earnings above UEL | 2.0% |

## Married women's reduced rate contributions are:

No liability if earnings do not exceed earnings thresholds.

| | | |
|---|---|---|
| Employee: | Earnings between PT and UEL | 5.85% |
| | Earnings above UEL | 2.0% |
| Employer: | Earnings above ST | 13.8% |
| | (No under-21 or apprentice rate can apply) | |

## *Class 1A contributions (SSCBA 1992 s 10)*

Class 1A national insurance contributions are payable by employers (not by employees) in respect of the provision of any taxable benefits except those specifically exempted (eg certain childcare provision), or already charged under Class 1 to a P11D employee or director, or included in a PAYE settlement agreement and thereby subject to Class 1B liability.

Where the employer chooses to tax employee benefits in kind through the payroll, only PAYE is charged: Class 1A NICs are still due after the end of the tax year. No Class 1 liability arises unless the benefits consist of the employer meeting the employee's personal pecuniary liability to a third party (eg, paying a home telephone bill), in which case no Class 1A liability arises.

The amounts on which the Class 1A contributions are payable are the cash equivalents of the benefits as measured for income tax purposes, reduced by any employee contribution. For 2016/17 the contributions are at the rate of 13.8% of the cash equivalents and are payable annually in arrears by 19 July (22 July if paid electronically), after the taxable benefits have been calculated by the employer for P11D purposes. The 13.8% rate still applies to benefits provided to under-21s and apprentices, despite the 0% secondary Class 1 rate applied to their earnings.

If the business ceases, then the liability for Class 1A contributions arises 14 days after the tax month of succession or cessation, eg, if an employer ceases in October 2016 then Class 1A contributions for the period 6 April 2016 to the date of cessation will be payable with the October national insurance payment on 19 November 2016. If the date of cessation is any day up to 5 July then the liability includes the Class 1A amount due for the preceding tax year. The same provisions apply to a predecessor employer if a business changes hands, but only in respect of employees not continuing with the successor. The successor takes over the liability for employees who continue in the business and includes them in the normal end-of-year return.

No Class 1A liability arises on any amount already charged to Class 1 or 1B, or not liable to income tax as general earnings, or benefits provided exclusively for business use. However Class 1A contributions are due on the full amount of benefit where there is mixed business and private use, and the benefit is not liable under Class 1 (ie, reimbursed personal bills with both business and private elements are shown on the P11D and lead to a Class 1 charge (through payroll) on the private element, but no Class 1A charge). Insignificant private use is ignored for this purpose.

The main benefits chargeable to Class 1A contributions are:

- Cars and fuel
- Vans
- Beneficial loans
- Living accommodation
- Private medical insurance
- Gifted assets
- Taxable gifts from third parties (chargeable on the provider)
- Goods and services provided for private use
- Taxable relocation benefits provided by the employer
- The value of employer-contracted childcare (other than an in-house nursery or crèche) above the relevant tax-free limit.

Non-taxable benefits are not subject to Class 1A liability. This applies to, eg, £55 per week of childcare vouchers, the provision of a single mobile telephone, subsidised qualifying travel, and qualifying trivial benefits.

## *Class 1B contributions (SSCBA 1992 s 10A)*

Employers are able to settle the tax and national insurance liability on minor and irregular benefits by making a lump sum payment under a PAYE Settlement Agreement (PSA) (see **Example B1 explanatory note 9**). Class 1B contributions are payable on all items in the PSA that would otherwise be liable to Class 1 or Class 1A contributions and on the tax payable under the agreement. The rate of contributions is the employers' secondary rate of 13.8%. Benefits provided to under-21s and apprentices are not separately identified and do not attract a 0% employer rate. The Class 1B contributions are payable with the tax on the agreement on 19 October (22 October for e-payment) following the relevant tax year, eg 19 October 2017 for 2016/17.

Class 1B contributions are not credited to an individual's national insurance contribution records even when paid in lieu of Class 1 contributions. However, an employee who has cash earnings just below the LEL may require earnings in the PSA to be taken into account for the purpose of qualifying for SSP, SMP, SAP, SPP (both ordinary and additional SPP) or Statutory Shared Parental Pay (ShPP).

## *Class 2 contributions (SSCBA 1992 ss 11, 11A, 12)*

Class 2 contributions are payable by 'self-employed earners', which means those who are gainfully employed other than as employed earners (SSCBA 1992 s 2). The scope of Class 2 is wider than for Class 4, because it relates to 'businesses', whereas Class 4 is restricted to trades, professions and vocations. Since 6 April 2015, a self-employed earner who carries on a trade, profession or vocation has been subject to a compulsory liability (subject to profits reaching a small profits threshold), while someone in a business that is not within Class 4 (eg, a property letting business with only rental income) has been allowed to opt to pay Class 2 voluntarily in order to create or protect state benefit entitlements. Trading and professional earnings are now based on the definition used for Class 4 (see below). Sleeping or limited partners in a trading partnership or trading LLP are liable to Class 2 as they are self-employed earners with income from the trade.

Class 2 contributions are due at the flat rate of £2.80 per week for 2016/17. Class 2 contributions used to be collected following the issue of six-monthly bills, with self-assessment tax payments on 31 January and 31 July, unless contributors elected to use a monthly direct debit. However, for 2015/16 onwards, they are reported on the income tax self-assessment return and are collected annually in arrears with the balancing tax payment under ITSA, so the Class 2 liabilities for 2016/17 will fall due by 31 January 2018. There is no need to make payments on account as happens with Class 4.

A liability arises whenever a person is self-employed in any week if he is over 16 and under pension age (ie, the contribution is payable annually but is calculated on the basis of weeks of ordinary self-employment during the year in question. A person who is also employed is liable to pay both Class 1 and Class 2 (and possibly also Class 4) contributions, subject to an annual maximum.

Liability to Class 2 must be notified no later than 31 January after the end of the tax year in which liability arises due to the commencement of trading. A penalty applies for failure to notify. The penalty may be 100% of the lost contributions if the failure is deliberate and concealed, 70% if deliberate but not concealed, or otherwise 30%. This will not be imposed if the contributor has a reasonable excuse or a successful claim for exemption is made (see below).

For 2015/16 onwards, no compulsory Class 2 contributions are due unless earnings exceed the small profits threshold (SPT: £5,965 for 2016/17), but earners may choose to pay voluntarily if profits are below the SPT.

Profits included in the accounts that arise from something other than trading (eg, rents, subpostmaster salaries) should be excluded in assessing whether the SPT has been reached.

Earners may choose to pay Class 2 even if their profits do not reach the SPT. If no Class 2 contributions are paid for a year then state retirement pension may be reduced in due course and entitlement to short-term benefit when unable to work through sickness (employment and support allowance) will be lost for two years. A voluntary Class 3 contribution could be paid to safeguard the basic state pension benefits, but state pension and sickness benefits can be safeguarded at a Class 2 cost of only £2.80 per week. As with Class 1 contributions, in some circumstances contributions are credited rather than paid, such credits counting towards satisfying the contribution conditions for certain benefits, in particular the state pension (see under Class 3). Neither Class 2 nor Class 3 contributions give rise to an entitlement to jobseeker's allowance.

A woman with a valid reduced rate contribution certificate (see Class 1 above) need not pay Class 2 national insurance contributions and cannot pay them voluntarily (without revoking the reduced rate election permanently) but will receive no contributory state benefits except the new state pension that begins to accrue from April 2016.

The government plans to abolish Class 2 in April 2018 and to make Class 4 (below) the basis of benefit entitlements for the self-employed.

### *Class 3 contributions (SSCBA 1992 ss 13, 14)*

Class 3 contributions are voluntary so there is no obligation to pay them. The contributions give an entitlement to basic retirement pension and bereavement benefits. Payment could be made by those not liable for other contributions, eg, non-employed, self-employed with small earnings, persons taking early retirement or moving abroad etc, to maintain a full national insurance record. Anyone who is registered as unemployed or is receiving jobseeker's allowance is credited with Class 1 contributions at the lower earnings limit and does not have to pay Class 3 contributions to maintain a full contributions record. An unemployed man aged 60 to 64 is credited with Class 1 contributions whether or not he is registered as unemployed, although this is being phased out as women's state pension age rises to the same level as men's. Class 1 credits used to be given to those aged 16 to 18 who would otherwise not have paid enough contributions, and also for certain periods of full-time training lasting up to 12 months, but not for longer courses such as university degree courses. The under-18 credits have now been withdrawn but should be applied for those who were at the relevant age before April 2010. Credits are also given to those claiming employment and support allowance, SSP, SMP, SAP, SPP, ShPP, maternity allowance, invalid care allowance, disability working allowance, working tax credits, or universal credit.

The Class 3 rate for 2016/17 is £14.10 per week. This should be compared to £2.80 per week for Class 2 contributions which can also be paid voluntarily by some people to protect benefits and protect short-term as well as long-term benefit entitlement. Payment is by six-monthly bill or monthly direct debit, although most Class 3 contributions are paid after the end of a tax year when the need to make up a deficiency in order to protect benefits can be ascertained.

### *Class 3A contributions (SSCBA 1992, ss 14A–14C)*

Class 3A contributions are also voluntary. They were created by the Pensions Act 2014, Sch 15 to allow those who were already state pensioners by 6 April 2016 (ie, men born before 6 April 1951 and women born before 6 April 1953) to enhance their state pension by up to £25 per week. From 12 October 2015 to 5 April 2017, eligible pensioners are able to buy extra state pension in units of £1 per week for the rest of their life by making a one-off lump sum Class 3A payment. The aim is to allow them to increase their state pension with an extra SERPS addition (even if they were never in SERPS while it existed) to somewhere near the new single-tier state pension basic amount of £155.65 per week.

The cost of the Class 3A contribution will vary with the age of the contributor on the date of payment, so the oldest pensioners with the shortest life expectancy will pay the least. Those who have only recently reached state pension age may pay both Class 3 and Class 3A contributions for relevant periods (with the former being much cheaper).

The official publicity material refers to the new Class 3A regime as 'state pension top-up' (SPTU). Eligibility is personal to each contributor, so either spouse or civil partner or both spouses or partners may choose to contribute and buy an amount of SPTU. This eligibility is not restricted by reference to the class of contribution paid during the working life.

Contributions will be refundable for 90 days if the contributor changes his or her mind and applies for a refund, or dies within that period. SPTU entitlements will be inherited wholly or partially by a spouse or civil partner in accordance with the SERPS rules.

Those who reach state pension age on or after 6 April 2016 are ineligible to pay Class 3A contributions as their pensions will be calculated in accordance with the new single-tier state pension rules.

### *Class 4 contributions (SSCBA 1992 ss 15–18)*

These contributions do not provide any benefits. The liability is calculated on trading profits, as agreed for income tax (ITTOIA 1995, Part 2, Chapter 2), after adjusting for capital allowances, balancing charges, trading losses and trade charges but before deducting registered pension scheme premiums. Where trading losses have been relieved against non-trading income for income tax purposes, they still reduce the first available current or later trading profits for Class 4 contributions (SSCBA 1992 Sch 2 para 3(4)). Note that the use of the Class 4 definition of earnings for Class 2 purposes (see above) does not extend the loss relief rules to Class 2.

Class 4 contributions are paid as part of payments on account and balancing payments under self-assessment. The rates for 2016/17 are:

| | | | |
|---|---|---|---|
| Profits up to | £8,060 | @ | Nil |
| Profits between | £8,060 and £43,000 | @ | 9% |
| Profits in excess of | £43,000 | @ | 2% |

The Class 4 contributions relate to a tax year, so the limits remain the same where more than one account is made up to a date within the tax year, or where the trader is involved in more than one business. Husband and wife are charged separately. A liability does not arise in any tax year in which the taxpayer is aged under 16 (and holds a certificate of exception) or over state pension age at the start of the year, or in which he is not resident in the UK for income tax.

If income taxed as trading income is also liable to Class 1 national insurance contributions (eg, sub-postmasters, certain actors, self-employed supply teachers working through an agency) then the amount liable to Class 4 contributions is reduced by the amount on which Class 1 contributions have been paid.

## Maximum contributions payable

### Maximum Class 1 and 2

Where a person has more than one 'employment' (and in this context that includes self-employment) the annual maximum of Class 1 and Class 2 contributions depends on the number of jobs, and how much is earned in each of those jobs. Each earner will therefore have his, or her, own individual maximum. This applies only to the employee's personal contribution liability: employer contributions are not subject to a maximum.

The computations are complex, involving eight steps, but basically each earner will be required to pay a maximum amount based on 12% charged on 53 times the difference between the primary earnings threshold and the upper earnings limit (£672 (£827 – £155) × 53 = £35,616 @ 12% = £4,273.92), plus 2% of the *aggregate* of all other 'employed earner's' earnings in secondary employments above the primary threshold in each job, plus 2% of all Class 4 profits above the lower annual limit. (The fact that the regulations take 53 times the difference between the upper earnings limit and the primary threshold means that the normal annual upper limit (£43,000) is effectively irrelevant for this one purpose.

Employees who think that they may have overpaid should write to HMRC Payment Reconciliation, NIC&EO, Benton Park View, Newcastle-upon-Tyne, NE98 1ZZ. A Class 1 refund is requested by letter, Class 2 on form CA8480 and Class 4 on form CA5610. For 2015/16 onwards, it is expected that Class 2 overpayments should be rare, because the liability will be self-assessed in arrears with the benefit of all figures being known before the return is prepared, although manual adjustments may be needed where software does not automatically take the NIC annual maximum into account.

The provisions determining the annual maxima are in SI 2001/1004 and work as follows:

An individual has three 'employments', A, B and C, receiving salaries of £52,000, £22,000 and £7,000. Steps 1 and 2 of Reg 21 of SI 2001/1004 require the calculation of the £4,273.92 as above (Step 1 calculates the £35,616, Step 2 takes 12%). Step 3 aggregates the earnings of each employed earner's employment which fall between the primary threshold and the upper earnings limit, in this case, in 2016/17:

| | | |
|---|---|---|
| A | 34,940 | (43,000 – 8,060) |
| B | 13,940 | (22,000 – 8,060) |
| C | – | (all below 8,060) |
| | 48,880 | |

Step 4 deducts from this figure 53 times the difference between the upper limit and the earnings threshold (that is the £35,616 of Step 1) leaving £13,264 (£48,880 – £35,616). Step 5 takes 2% of this figure, giving £265.28.

Step 6 takes the earnings of each employed earner's employment in so far as it exceeds the upper earnings limit, in this case just employment A, £52,000 less £43,000 = £9,000 and Step 7 takes 2% of that figure £180.00. The annual maximum for Class 1 for this individual becomes £4,719.20, the sum of Steps 2, 5 and 7 (£4,273.92 + £265.28 + £180.00).

Where an individual has Class 2 liability, and therefore more than one 'employment' the same procedure applies but the maximum calculated will be compared with the sum of his Class 1 and 2 payments, see the main example below and Example X in the Table below. Note that, in most years, 52 Class 2 contributions will be paid, but the annual maximum calculation is based on 53 weeks' contributions.

## Maximum Class 1, 2 and 4

Where a person has employment and is also self-employed and paying Class 4, there is also a maximum amount of contributions to be paid at the main Class 1 and Class 4 rates (12% and 9%).

Contributors should apply for a refund if they pay more in 2016/17 than:

- £3,293.00 at the Class 1 (12%) rate, Class 2 and Class 4 (9%) rate, or
- £4,273.92 at the Class 1 (12%) rate and Class 2.

The computation of the Class 4 refund is even more complex than the calculation for Class 1. It is a nine step process with three different 'Case' scenarios applying after the fourth step (see Reg 100 of 2001/1004). The method is best demonstrated by working through the steps in one main example and then giving summary figures for three further examples (X, Y and Z) in a Table below.

Take the situation of someone employed on a salary of £45,000, with self-employed profits of £48,000. His national insurance liability before applying any annual maxima will be:

| | | | |
|---|---|---|---|
| | | | £ |
| Class 1, assumed paid monthly, | (3,583 – 672) | @ 12% × 12 | 4,191.84 |
| | (3,750 – 3,583) | @ 2% × 12 | 40.08 |
| | | | 4,231.92 |
| Class 2 | £2.80 × 53 | | 148.40 |
| | | | 4,380.32 |
| Class 4 | (43,000 – 8,060) | @ 9% | 3,144.60 |
| | (48,000 – 43,000) | @ 2% | 100.00 |
| | | | 7,624.92 |

Steps 1, 2 and 3 involve computing the £3,293.00 maximum of Class 2 and 4 (53 × £2.80 = £148.40 plus (43,000 – 8,060) 34,940 × 9% = £3,144.60). Step 4 then requires the deduction of the Class 1 contributions at the main rate plus the total Class 2 contributions actually paid, in this case a total of £4,340.24 (£4,191.84 + £148.40).

| | |
|---|---|
| | £ |
| Steps 1, 2 and 3 | 3,293.00 |
| Step 4 | (4,340.24) |
| | (1,047.24) |

If a negative figure is achieved, the result of this step is nil, the maximum amount of Class 4 payable at the main rate is nil and four more steps have to be applied to compute the 2% liability. This is a Case 3 scenario. (See below for Case 1 and 2 scenarios.)

Step 5 involves taking the figure at Step 4 and multiplying it by 100/9. In this case the answer is still nil. Step 6 involves deducting the lower profits limit from the smaller of the actual profits and the upper profits limit. In this case, the latter applies:

| | £ |
|---|---|
| Step 6 | 43,000 |
| Lower profit limit | (8,060) |
| | 34,940 |

Step 7 requires Step 5 to be deducted from Step 6, in this case leaving £34,940 and Step 8 takes 2% of that figure ie £698.80.

Step 9 calculates the extra Class 4 that is due on profits over £43,000 (48,000 – 43,000 @ 2%), in this case £100.00 and the maximum Class 4 payable by this taxpayer is the sum of Steps 4, 8 and 9 ie £798.80 (Nil + £698.60 + £100.00). This is, of course, 2% of all the profits over the lower profits limit ((48,000 – 8,060) @ 2% = £798.80). This taxpayer should apply for a refund of Class 4 of £2,445.80 (£3,244.60 less £798.80).

This individual would also be entitled to a refund of some of the Class 2 as the following application of the eight step process shows:

| | | £ |
|---|---|---|
| Steps 1 and 2 | | 4,273.92 |
| Step 3, Employment income (43,000 – 8,060) | 34,940 | |
| Step 4 (827 – 155) × 53 | (35,616) | |
| Step 5, 2% of | – | Nil |
| Step 6, Employment income (45,000 – 43,000) | 2,000 | |
| Step 7, 2% of £2,000 | | 40.00 |
| Step 8 | | 4,313.92 |
| Class 1 and 2 paid (latter for 53 weeks) | | (4,380.32) |
| Refund due of Class 2 | | 66.40 |
| Refund of Class 4 as above | | 2,445.80 |
| Total refund | | 2,512.20 |

The Table below shows three further examples:

- Another case 3 scenario but where the Class 4 is only paid at the main rate (Example X);
- A Case 1 scenario – that is where the result at Step 4 is positive and exceeds the aggregate of Class 1 (12%) rate plus Class 2 plus Class 4 (9%) rate. For Case 1 the Steps 5 to 9 are unnecessary (Example Y); and
- A Case 2 scenario where the surplus at Step 4 does not exceed the NI paid at main rates, and Steps 5 to 9 become necessary to determine the total Class 4 maximum.

The Table assumes all salaries paid monthly.

| | X (Case 3) £ | | Y (Case 1) £ | | Z (Case 2) £ |
|---|---|---|---|---|---|
| Class 1 Salary £42,600 | 4,144.80 | Class 1 Salary £11,952 | 467.04 | Class 1 Salary £27,452 | 2,327.04 |
| Class 2 paid (× 52) | 145.60 | | 145.60 | | 145.60 |
| Class 4, profits £10,304 | 201.96 | Class 4, profits £18,060 | 900.00 | Class 4, profits £29,410 | 1,921.50 |
| Total NIC paid | 4,492.36 | | 1,512.64 | | 4,394.14 |
| Steps 1, 2 | 3,293.00 | | 3,293.00 | | 3,293.00 |

| | | | | |
|---|---|---|---|---|
| and 3 | | | | |
| Main rate | 4,290.40 | 612.64 | | 2,472.64 |
| Class 1 + Class 2 | | | | |
| Step 4 | Nil | 2,680.36 | | 820.36 |
| | | This figure exceeds all the NI paid at the main rates (£1,512.64), so the computation ends and the maximum Class 4 NI is £2,680.36 | | |
| Step 5 | Nil | | 820.36 × 100/9 | 9,115.11 |
| Step 6, deduct lower profit | 10,304.00 | | | 29,410.00 |
| limit | 8,060.00 | | | 8,060.00 |
| | 2,244.00 | | | 21,350.00 |
| Step 7, deduct Step 5 | – | | | 9,115.11 |
| | 2,244.00 | | | 12,234.89 |
| Step 8, take 2% of Step 7 | 44.88 | | | 244.70 |
| Step 9 not applicable | – | | | – |
| Max Class 4 sum of Steps 4, 8 and 9 | 44.88 | 2,680.36 | | 1,065.06 |
| Class 4 refund due | 157.08 | Nil | | 856.44 |

Example X would also give rise to an overpayment of Class 2 as the following application of the eight step process shows:

| | | £ |
|---|---|---|
| Steps 1 and 2 (12% × 53 weeks of UEL–PT) | | 4,273.92 |
| Step 3, Employment income (42,600 – 8,060) | 34,540 | |
| Step 4 | (35,616) | |
| Step 5, 2% of | Nil | Nil |
| Step 6, Employment income (42,600 – 43,000) | Nil | |
| Step 7, 2% of | Nil | Nil |
| Step 8 | | 4,273.92 |
| Class 1 and 2 paid | | 4,290.40 |
| Overpayment | | 16.48 |

An overpayment will normally be notified to the taxpayer by HMRC where the amount due exceeds £56.00, although the minimum amount that a taxpayer can request is £5.38 for a 2016/17 overpayment. They will invite an application for a refund. A claim for a Class 1 or 2 refund is made to HMRC, Payment Reconciliation (or Self-Employment Services for Class 2), NIC&EO, Benton Park View, Newcastle upon Tyne, NE98 1ZZ. A Class 4 refund request (minimum 50p) is made online, or by post on form CA5610 to Deferment Services at the same NIC&EO address.

Where contributions have been paid at the contracted-out rate (for years up to 5 April 2016) or married woman's reduced rate then they are recomputed at the standard rate in order to compare with the above limits.

For 2015/16 onwards, Class 2 liabilities are computed and paid in arrears, so overpayments should be unlikely to arise, other than where they are paid voluntarily in advance to protect entitlement to maternity allowance but Class 1 earnings in the year are unexpectedly high.

Where there are multiple sources of earned income, it used to be possible to apply for deferment of Class 1, 2 and 4 contributions so that foreseeable overpayments were mostly avoided. Deferment is now restricted to Class 1 payable in multiple employments.

If an individual has more than one employment and expects to pay primary Class 1 contributions on earnings of at least £827 per week (£3,583 per month) throughout the whole tax year in any one employment, or earnings of at least £9982 per week (£4,255 per month) in two jobs, then he can apply for deferment. If Class 1 deferment is granted then NI of 2% of all earnings above the earnings threshold will be payable in each employment to which the deferment applies. Note that each independent job attracts a separate earnings threshold: the calculation of maximum NICs due does not simply involve adding together all earnings and deducting one earnings threshold.

The position is complex and reference should be made to HMRC's leaflet CA72A (in respect of deferral of Class 1 contributions).

A person who is both employed and self-employed may no longer apply to defer payment of Class 4 contributions. Class 4 will be paid with income tax through the self-assessment form on all self-employed income above £8,060 for 2016/17, so the correct amount should always be self-assessed, together with the Class 2 liability.

Leaflet CA72A contains the necessary deferral form which can also be downloaded from HMRC's website, but HMRC promotes online applications using the contributor's Government gateway ID over paper applications.

The address for Deferment Services is HMRC NIC&EO Deferment Services, Benton Park View, Newcastle upon Tyne, NE98 1ZZ. Telephone: 03000 560 631.

### Interest on late paid contributions

Until 5 April 2014, late-paid Class 1 contributions attracted interest from 19 April after the end of the tax year in which the contributions were due for payment (22 April for e-payers). From 6 April 2014, with the full introduction of RTI filing, interest now runs from the 19$^{th}$ of each month and is automatically added to the employer's account by HMRC when remittances are received late. Late paid Class 1A contributions attract interest from 19 July after the end of the tax year (22 July for e-payers). Late paid Class 1B contributions attract interest from the due date of payment, ie 19 October (22 October for e-payers) following the tax year in respect of which the contributions were due. (SI 2001/1004 Sch 4 para 17.)

There is now provision for charging interest on late-paid Class 2 contributions because NICA 2015 applied to Class 2 the same rules as Class 4.

### Penalties

Failure to notify liability to Class 1A by 19 July on Form P11D(b) gives rise to a penalty of £100 per month (or part thereof) per 50 employees (or part thereof) for whom a P11D must be submitted, restricted to the Class 1A liability.

With effect from 1 April 2010 a unified penalty regime has applied to most taxes including NI. The former fixed £100 penalty for failure to notify liability to Class 2 within three months was dropped and replaced by a penalty based upon all NI not paid as a result of the notification failure.

If the failure is due to an innocent error, no penalty will be charged provided the contributor makes an unprompted disclosure of the facts to HMRC within twelve months of 31 January after the end of the tax year in which liability to register arose. If the disclosure is made later, the penalty will be between 10% and 30%.

If the error is due to carelessness, a penalty of up to 30% of the unpaid revenue will be due. That amount will not be charged if the taxpayer had a reasonable excuse for the failure (eg he had reasonable grounds for believing that no liability arose). If the late notification was unprompted and within twelve months of the end of the tax year in which the first day fell on which a liability became payable, then the penalty can be mitigated to nil. If notification was prompted, the maximum mitigation is to a 10% penalty. If prompted notification is over twelve months late, as above, the reduction is to not less than 20%.

For an unconcealed deliberate failure to notify, the penalty is 70% of the tax unpaid with mitigation for an unprompted disclosure to not less than a 20% penalty (35% if prompted).

For a concealed deliberate failure to notify, the penalty is 100% with discount for unprompted disclosure to not less than 30% (50% if prompted) (Finance Act 2008 Sch 41 and SI 2001/1004 regs 87B–87G).

Various breaches of the national insurance legislation may lead to criminal proceedings, although these are usually reserved for cases of fraud or 'cheating the public revenue'.

New penalties, harmonised with the new PAYE penalties (FA 2009 Sch 56), were introduced from 6 April 2010 for failure to pay contributions on time in respect of earnings from that point onwards (SI 2010/721).

For Class 1 underpayments, an escalating scale of surcharges applies. For the first late payment in a tax year there is no penalty. For up to three more failures to pay on time, there will be a surcharge of 1% of all amounts paid late except the first, which is disregarded. If there are up to three further defaults, the surcharge becomes 2% of amounts paid late in the months after the fourth, when those further late payments occurred, then 3% for up to three further defaults, again applied to late payments each month after the seventh default, and 4% if there are 11 or 12 defaults in a year, but only on late payments after the tenth. Penalty notices will be issued after the end of the relevant quarter in respect of late payments during that quarter. Any amount that is paid more than six months late attracts a 5% penalty, even if it is the only default in the year and otherwise avoids the escalating surcharge regime. If it remains outstanding for twelve months, another 5% penalty is added. This penalty regime changed from April 2014 from a similar but harsher type of escalating surcharge that was levied annually at the maximum rate triggered for the year.

The introduction of RTI included the announcement of new automatic in-year penalties, but penalties for late filing of FPS returns were deferred until 6 October 2014, while automatic in-year penalties for late payment were originally deferred until April 2015. The first penalty notices to employers, which should have identified the alleged defaults so that they could be checked and challenged, were scheduled to be issued in July 2015, then quarterly thereafter. That is not now likely to happen before July 2017. HMRC announced on 17 February 2015 that late payment penalties would continue to be reviewed on a risk-assessed basis, without putting a revised date on the introduction of automated penalties. Occasional filings of a FPS late by up to three days will be disregarded until at least 6 April 2017.

For Classes 1A and 1B, the system is much simpler: payment more than 30 days late attracts a 5% surcharge, more than six months late a further 5% and more than 12 months late a further 5%.

Classes 2 and 4 NIC for 2015–16 onwards fall within the normal regime for late-paid ITSA tax. Class 2 for earlier years may be payable at a higher rate if paid more than a full tax year in arrears.

## (b) Earnings for Class 1 national insurance contributions

### Meaning of earnings

Earnings for Class 1 national insurance contributions are defined in s 3 of the Social Security Contributions and Benefits Act 1992 as including 'any remuneration or profit derived from an employment'. The amount of a person's earnings for any period is computed in accordance with Part 2 of the Social Security (Contributions) Regulations SI 2001/1004. That statutory instrument provides that a liability arises on earnings paid, or treated as paid, in an earnings period (reg 2). The amount paid is the gross earnings from the employment.

### Payments that do not count as earnings

SI 2001/1004 Sch 3 lists certain payments that do not count as earnings, with a large number of exclusions from the provisions, and with the Schedule running to ten separate parts. This represents a minefield for employers struggling to know what does and what does not constitute earnings, and there are even longer lists in the Employer's Further Guide to PAYE and NICs (CWG2). Most of the exclusions, however, relate to items that are exempt from income tax. Some particular exclusions are as follows:

Payments in kind, unless specifically included – see below. (Virtually all taxable benefits that escape Class 1 liability are liable to employers' Class 1A contributions where they are provided to P11D employees and directors – see **part (A)** – even if the benefits are taxed by the employer voluntarily through payroll.)

Tips or gratuities not paid directly or indirectly by the employer or where the payment is not directly or indirectly allocated by the employer to the earner, providing the payments are not from a trust where the beneficiaries are employees or, if from a connected person, of an amount in excess of the amount that a non-connected person might give (SI 2004/173).

Any payments by way of a pension, other than certain lump sums.

An employer's contribution to an employee's personal or occupational pension.

A payment by shares or options over shares which form part of the ordinary share capital of the employer company or its holding company, where the shares or options are either obtained under an approved scheme or are not readily convertible assets.

Any value added tax chargeable on earnings (eg, where a worker is actually self-employed but is deemed to be an employee for NIC purposes).

Redundancy payments (although HM Treasury is consulting on aligning the tax and NIC rules in 2018).

Any specific and distinct payment of, or contribution towards, expenses actually incurred by an employed earner in carrying out his employment, other than expenses paid under salary sacrifice arrangements, round sum allowances above the statutory flat-rate limits that are not agreed in advance with HMRC, advances in respect of anticipated expenses yet to be incurred, and home-to-work travel expenses of most intermediary workers.

## Payments in kind treated as earnings

The following are exceptions to the 'payments in kind' exclusion and are treated as earnings (SI 2001/1004 reg 25 and Sch 3 Parts II, III and IV):

Stocks and shares, and warrants and options in respect of stocks and shares, that are readily convertible assets (other than as indicated above) (see **Example B1 explanatory note 12** and **Example N1**)

Unit trusts and units in collective investment schemes (eg enterprise zone trusts, interests in investment LLPs)

Commodity futures and other futures and hedging contracts

Options to acquire or dispose of:

- an asset falling under any other heading
- currency
- gold, silver, palladium or platinum

Assets capable of being sold on a recognised investment exchange (ie an investment exchange recognised under the Financial Services and Markets Act 2000) or on the London Bullion Market

The value of certain payments from tax avoidance planning transactions (after 2 December 2004) which involve employment-related securities

Money debts

Gemstones and certain fine wines

Assets (including vouchers) which are readily convertible assets (see **Example B1 explanatory note 12**)

Any voucher capable of being exchanged for any of the assets listed above and any other non-cash vouchers other than those falling within SI 2001/1004 Sch 3 Part V (see below)

Certain life insurance policies including:

- Life and annuity policies;
- Linked long-term policies;
- Capital redemption policies;

– Other policies with any of the foregoing elements.

Benefits received by an employee who makes a restrictive covenant with his employer (SSCBA 1992 s 4 – see **Example B5 part (A)**).

The exceptions from the voucher charging rules mainly mirror income tax provisions. They used to include transport vouchers for non-P11D employees working for passenger transport undertakings, but the P9D was abolished for 2016–17 onwards. They still include vouchers exchangeable for sports or recreational facilities, and vouchers exchangeable for meals on the employer's premises. For members of employers' childcare schemes before 5 April 2011, childcare vouchers up to £55 per week for children up to age 16 are free of NIC liability, but for employees who join such a scheme from 6 April 2011 onwards, the £55 limit applies only to those employees whose basic earnings are assessed as falling within the basic rate band. For employees whose basic earnings place them in the higher rate tax band, the NIC-free value is £28 per week, and for additional rate taxpayers it is only £25 per week.

Non-cash vouchers are valued as for tax purposes, but unlike the tax position, they must be dealt with on a weekly or monthly basis (the latter with a limit of £243, £124 or £110, depending on the basic earnings assessment) rather than at the year-end.

Under anti-avoidance provisions, amounts that count as employment income under Part 7 of ITEPA (employment-related securities) and Part 7A (disguised remuneration) are deemed to be earnings for NIC purposes (see Regs 22–22B, SI 2001/1004). The GAAR may also be used to counter NIC avoidance schemes in appropriate circumstances and subject to safeguards.

In addition to Class 1 contributions, employers (but not employees) have to pay Class 1A national insurance contributions at 13.8% on taxable benefits provided to employees and directors that are not within the Class 1 or Class 1B charge. Until 5 April 2016, Class 1A only applied to P11D employees, but from 6 April 2106 the P9D was abolished and all employees became subject to the benefits code, and their employers to Class 1A liability.

## (c) Mr and Mrs Bond – national insurance position

J Bond has employment liable to Class 1 contributions and self-employment liable to Class 2 and 4 contributions. As the total payments exceed the likely maxima, the overall liability on Mr Bond's 2016–17 record will be capped. The small technical liability that will arise because the maximum is based on 53 weeks' contributions in the past might not have been collected, but Class 2 is now self-assessed when completing the tax return, so should still be payable (see computation below).

Deferment might have been relevant in the past, but there is no longer any need to defer Class2 or Class 4 as they are self-assessed after the end of the relevant tax year as follows:

| | | | £ |
|---|---|---|---|
| Class 1, salary paid monthly, | (3,583 – 672) | @ 12% × 12 | 4,191.84 |
| | (5,500 – 3,583) | @ 2% × 12 | 460.08 |
| | | | 4,651.92 |
| Class 2 × 52 potential liability | | | 145.60 |
| Class 4, profits (22,000 – 8,060) | | @ 9% | 1,254.60 |
| Total NIC potentially payable | | | 6,052.12 |

### Class 4 refund computation

| | |
|---|---|
| Steps 1, 2 and 3 | 3,293.00 |
| Main rate Class 1 + Class 2 potentially | 4,337.44 |
| Step 4 | Nil |
| Step 5 | Nil |
| Step 6 | 22,000.00 |

| | |
|---|---|
| Deduct lower profit limit | 8,060.00 |
| | 13,940.00 |
| Step 7, deduct Step 5 | – |
| | 13,940.00 |
| Step 8, take 2% of Step 7 | 278.80 |
| Step 9 not applicable | – |
| Max Class 4, sum of Steps 4, 8 and 9 | 278.80 |
| Class 4 potentially payable | 1,254.60 |
| Class 4 reduction | 975.80 |
| Class 4 to be paid under self-assessment | 278.80 |

Mr Bond also needs only to pay a reduced Class 2 contribution as the following application of the eight step process shows:

| | | £ |
|---|---|---|
| Steps 1 and 2 ((827 – 155) × 53 × 12%) | | 4,273.92 |
| Step 3, Employment income (43,000 – 8,060) | 34,940 | |
| Step 4 | (35,616) | |
| Step 5, 2% of | Nil | Nil |
| Step 6, Employment income (66,000 – 43,000) | 23,000 | |
| Step 7, 2% of | 23,000 | 460.00 |
| Step 8 | | 4,733.92 |
| Class 1 paid and 2 potentially payable | | 4,797.52 |
| Excess Class 2 not payable | | 63.60 |
| Total Class 2 and Class 4 not due (63.60 + 975.80) | | 1,039.40 |
| Class 2 in SA, payable by 31 January 2018 (145.60 – 63.60) | | 82.00 |
| Class 4 in SA, payable with income tax | | 278.80 |

Mrs Bond has two employments, but both are with J Bond. The earnings must therefore be aggregated (unless it would be impracticable to do so, because for example earnings were worked out at different pay points, which is unlikely), giving a liability for primary (employee's) Class 1 contributions (assuming paid equally throughout the year) of:

| | £ |
|---|---|
| 8,060 @ nil | – |
| 6,940 @ 12% | 832.80 |
| 15,000 | |

J Bond will have a liability as employer to pay secondary contributions of £15,000 – £8,112 = £6,888 @ 13.8% = £950.54, which would be allowed in computing his earnings/profits in the year of payment. If Mr Bond has no other employees, and Mrs Bond is not a domestic employee, it should be covered by the employment allowance due to Mr Bond.

## (d) Memorandum for Mrs Williams re national insurance liabilities

### *Treatment of directors' earnings*

Contributions are charged on directors' earnings whenever they are drawn but on a cumulative, annualised basis. An employer may, however, use the normal pay period rules to compute the weekly or monthly contributions provided that the liability is recomputed at the end of the year (or when a director leaves) by reference to the annual limits.

This special treatment prevents irregular payments of bonuses, commissions, etc, being used to give reduced contributions because of the monthly upper limit. Where a regular salary is paid, the overall amount will be the same.

For example, if an employee is paid £43,215 at £3,601.25 a month, his monthly contributions using monthly limits and thresholds will be (349.32 + 0.37 =) £349.69, making £4,196.28 in the year and the employer will pay contributions on the excess of the monthly pay of £3,601.25 over the secondary earnings threshold of £676, ie £2,925.50 @ 13.8% = £403.72, giving £4,844.64 for the year. If a director is paid the same amount and the annual basis is used, the *total* amount payable is the same (allowing for monthly roundings), but the position will be as follows:

| | *Pay to date* | *Employee's contribution* | | | *Employer's contribution* | | |
|---|---|---|---|---|---|---|---|
| Mth | £ | £ | | £ | £ | | £ |
| 1 | 3,601.25 | 3,601.25 | @ nil | – | 3,601.25 | @ nil | – |
| 2 | 7,202.50 | 7,202.50 | @ nil | – | 7,202.50 | @ nil | – |
| 3 | 10,803.75 | 8,060 | @ nil | – | 8,112 | @ nil | – |
| | | 2,743.75 | @ 12% | 329.25 | 2,691.75 | @ 13.8% | 371.46 |
| 4 to 11 | 39,613.75 | 28,810.00 | @ 12% | 3,457.20 | 28,810.00 | @ 13.8% | 3,975.78 |
| 12 | 43,215.00 | 3,386.25* | @ 12% | 406.35 | 3,601.25 | @ 13.8% | 496.97 |
| | | 215 | @ 2% | 4.30 | | | |
| Total contributions payable | | | | 4,197.10 | | | 4,844.21 |

* 2% contributions on (43,215 – 43,000) = £215, therefore 12% contributions due on (3,601.25 – 215) = £3,386.25.

The pennies of difference between the monthly and annual calculations are due to roundings each month.

## *Treatment of payments/benefits for waitresses*

### (i) Tips and gratuities

If Tation Ltd collects the tips and divides them between the employees or controls the way in which they are divided, then they are earnings liable to Class 1 national insurance (providing the total earnings exceed the lower limit in an earnings period). If Tation Ltd does not control the division of the tips but leaves that to the employees, the amounts are not liable to national insurance, even if collected in the main till or via credit cards with other takings. Any amount paid directly from the customer to staff does not attract national insurance provided the employer does not influence the division of the tips. This also applies if the donor is connected to the employer provided that the tip does not exceed an amount an unconnected person might have given.

Any amounts collected by the employer and paid to staff under a legal obligation are liable to NI. Gratuities cannot now be used by employers to make up earnings to the level of the national minimum wage, but gratuities paid as part of earnings above the NMW can still be gratuities not liable to national insurance provided they are paid by the employer through its own payroll, albeit at the direction of the troncmaster or staff committee. Payment through the employer's payroll no longer qualifies tips, gratuities, etc to be treated as part of pay for NMW purposes.

For further details and examples on tips etc see HMRC booklet E24 (2015). To determine the tax, national insurance and VAT treatment it is necessary to divide tips into the following categories

- mandatory service charges,
- discretionary service charges,
- gratuity paid to the employer (eg by debit/credit card),

- gratuity put into a staff box, or
- cash gratuity handed directly to a member of staff.

A tip, freely given, is outside the scope of VAT and cannot count towards the national minimum wage. If a customer is required to pay a mandatory service charge, that amount is standard-rated as part of the price of the food and service and the employer can pay it to the employee as wages that count for NMW and are subject to NIC.

For PAYE the employer must deduct tax from all amounts paid to the employee. If a member of staff distributes the tips, this is known as a tronc and the troncmaster is responsible for deducting PAYE.

The individual member of staff is responsible for declaring tips received, and paying tax on amounts received. This may be done by way of a code number adjustment or direct payment of tax due.

For mandatory service charges (on which VAT is due), and where an employer has control over tips distributed by an employee, PAYE and NIC must be deducted by the employer.

### (ii) Benefits in kind

The basic rule for national insurance is that Class 1 contributions are not payable on benefits in kind. Instead they are chargeable to Class 1A contributions of 13.8% payable by the employer. However, where a benefit can be converted to cash merely by surrendering the asset (see **explanatory note 6**), or represents the settlement of a debt of the employee (**see (iii)**), or is a round sum payment or expense with a profit element, then Class 1 contributions are due. The provision of free meals to waitresses, provided all members of staff are entitled, in a staff dining room or a designated staff area of the restaurant, would be free of tax and NI. If Mrs Williams occasionally books and pays for a taxi home for a waitress who exceptionally has to work after 9pm, that should also be tax- and NI-free. The bouquet of flowers should qualify as a trivial benefit which, if exempt from income tax, will also be free of Class 1A and Class 1 NICs. The earnings of the apprentice will not attract Class 1 secondary contributions, as she is working under an apprenticeship agreement with an approved trainer and is under the age of 25 having just left school. However, Class 1A contributions will still be due on any taxable benefits she receives, as the 0% rate of secondary contributions for under-21s and apprentices under 25 does not extend beyond Class 1.

### (iii) Payment of bills

If an employer pays bills relating to the employee, the treatment depends on who made the contract. If the employer made the contract it is a payment in kind; if the employee made the contract the employer's payment is the settlement of a pecuniary liability of the employee (equivalent to handing over cash for the payment of the bill) and is therefore earnings for Class 1 national insurance.

For example, if Tation Ltd paid an employee's telephone bill the payment would be earnings (because the contract was between the employee and the telephone company) whereas if Tation Ltd was the subscriber for the telephone installed at the employee's home, Class 1 contributions would not be payable. However, because there is both private and business use of the line Class 1A contributions would be due on the total bill if the employee is a P11D employee or director.

If the company reimbursed an employee for the cost of parking near the restaurant, Class 1 contributions would not be payable, whether or not the company contracted directly with the car parking company. In that event there would also be no Class 1A charge, as the benefit is not taxable. If the company contracted with a supplier for the supply of meat and then gave the meat to its employees the gift would not be earnings for Class 1 but would be a taxable benefit liable to Class 1A contributions, on the basis of the cost, however much the employee earned. In contrast, if the employee went to the same supplier and ordered meat, giving the bill to the company for settlement, it would be earnings for Class 1 and payment would have to be included in an FPS when made.

Reimbursements of expenses incurred in the course of the employment or in travelling to and from a temporary workplace are not earnings or benefits provided the expenses are identified and quantified. Round sum allowances are earnings and are fully liable to Class 1 national insurance unless they represent mileage allowances for business travel, or meal allowances paid at or below the statutory rate, or the employer has a written agreement with HMRC to enable them to make such payments at a higher rate free of tax and national insurance and there is no salary sacrifice arrangement in place for the expenses. An advance paid against anticipated expenses that have yet to be incurred (whether or not such expenses are actually incurred after the payment is made) must be treated as earnings rather than expenses following a change made by SI 2016/352, reg 5(2) from 6 April 2016.

HMRC may no longer grant a dispensation to enable certain payments to be regarded as covering expenses incurred by the employee in carrying out his duties. Such a dispensation has for some years also been accepted for national insurance purposes. However, dispensations were abolished for 2016–17 onwards, and any round sum allowances, if they are to be tax- and NIC-free, must be within the statutory limits set by ITEPA 2003, s 289A or at a bespoke rate agreed with HMRC under s 289B. Where an employee is away from home overnight on business, contributions are not chargeable on payments or reimbursements of personal expenses up to £5 a night (£10 if outside the UK). HMRC will expect the employer to retain evidence of the personal expenses having been incurred, even where a round sum allowance has been paid.

## (e) Employment allowance

Most employers are entitled to claim the employment allowance from 6 April 2014 onwards, as a reduction in their Class 1 secondary NIC liability (not against Class 1A or 1B). It is worth a maximum of £3,000 per year (increased from £2,000 from April 2016), but is limited to the amount payable by the claimant in secondary NICs in the year.

Where employers are connected to other employers (eg, companies in a group, charities under common control, or two separate payrolls using different HMRC references in one business), they must choose and nominate which employer or PAYE scheme will claim the allowance. The allowance cannot be shared among connected employers, so the chosen scheme (which should be the scheme with the largest liability) must set the appropriate flag in its RTI submission and reduce its secondary NIC payments each month in the EPS until the allowance has been used up.

The rules determining whether businesses are connected look for common control and treat LLPs as companies. If one individual controls two separate companies, they are connected. However, if he or she controls a company and also has a sole trade with employees, the two payrolls are not connected, because the rules look only at companies, LLPs and charities, so two allowances will still be due. If a husband and wife share control of two separate companies, the companies are connected for employment allowance purposes. However, if each controls his or her own company and the businesses are otherwise unconnected and not interdependent, they are not connected for employment allowance purposes and each can claim up to £3,000.

Employers who are public authorities are not entitled to claim the allowance, and those who provide a service that is the statutory duty of a public authority (eg, GP practices that provide NHS medical services, or refuse collection businesses working for a local authority) are also disqualified. Businesses that provide services to public authorities (eg, cleaning or guarding public buildings, or IT services), rather than providing them on behalf of the authorities, are not disqualified. The disqualification does not apply to employers who are charities: an academy school or a FE college is providing public education but is usually a statutory charity and is therefore nevertheless eligible.

No employment allowance is available to a householder in respect of domestic employees (such as housekeepers, chauffeurs or nannies), except from 6 April 2015 where the employee works as a care & support worker looking after a qualifying infirm or disabled person in that person's own home. If a trader employs someone to work partly in the home and partly in the business, no allowance is due, with the exception of care & support workers whose sole duties in the home relate to qualifying care.

Personal service companies within IR35 can claim the allowance only against secondary NICs due on actual payments of earnings. The NICs due in respect of the 5 April deemed payment are not covered by the allowance. If the company has only one paid employee who is the director, no allowance is due for 2016–17 onwards. If a one-man company takes on and pays another director, or even just a casual employee for an occasional shift, the disqualification is lifted, and the allowance is available against the liability to secondary contributions on the earnings of the shareholder-director. HMRC believes the second employee must earn enough to trigger a secondary NIC liability, but the legislation merely requires a payment of earnings, not a payment of contributions.

## (f) Contracting out

Employees paying NICs currently accrue an entitlement to a state pension if their earnings in a year reach the lower earnings limit (LEL), even if they have no primary Class 1 liability because the earnings do not reach the primary threshold. Before 6 April 2016, they could also earn an entitlement to an additional earnings-related element, the

Second State Pension (S2P), if their earnings exceeded the LEL. An employee could be contracted out of the S2P element through membership of a registered occupational salary-related pension scheme that replaced the additional earnings-related component of the state pension. Contracting out was abolished by Pensions Act 2014 and associated regulations with effect from 6 April 2016, so there are no longer any rebated rates of NIC, and everyone accrues entitlement to the new flat rate state pension in the same way.

National insurance contributions are normally collected as follows (subject to what is said in part (a) about deferment of contributions):

| | |
|---|---|
| *Class 1* | Employees' (primary) contributions are deducted from earnings when paid, and together with the employers' (secondary) contributions, they are paid over to HMRC by the employer with the PAYE deductions either monthly or, if total payments average less than £1,500 a month and the employer so wishes, quarterly. Payment by cheque must reach HMRC by the 19th of the following month, and electronic payment must give HMRC cleared funds by the 22nd of the following month. |
| *Class 1A* | Employers' contributions on taxable benefits are paid to HMRC annually in arrears by 19 July (22 July for e-payment) following the tax year. |
| *Class 1B* | Employers' contributions payable under a PAYE Settlement Agreement (PSA) on benefits liable to NI plus the tax thereon are paid to HMRC together with the tax on the PSA annually in arrears on 19 October (22 October for e-payment). |
| *Class 2* | For 2015/16 onwards, Class 2 contributions for most contributors are paid annually with the self-assessment balancing payment by 31 January after the end of the tax year (half-yearly payments with the Class 4 payments on account are not required). Those who pay voluntarily or who are outside the ITSA regime (eg, those working in the EU who have no UK trading profits but remain insured in the UK) may pay by direct debit. |
| *Class 3* | Class 3 contributions may be paid annually once it is known how much is needed to make a year qualify, or may be paid monthly by direct debit. |
| *Class 4* | Provisional half yearly payments are made to HMRC on 31 January and 31 July in respect of all income tax and Class 4 national insurance due, with any remaining balance on the following 31 January. |

## Explanatory Notes

*Liability to pay national insurance contributions*

(1) HMRC frequently assess arrears of contributions for several years where, for example, someone has been reclassified as employed rather than self-employed. Although they have the right to assess arrears for as many years as they wish, their rights to *enforce payment* for more than six years may be restricted by the Limitation Act 1980, providing liability has not been admitted in writing or part payment made within the six-year limitation period (NB: the law in Scotland is different). NI has not been affected by the change to a four-year default period for income tax arrears.

See **Example B6 explanatory note 2** for the employment status of entertainers and **explanatory note 3** for the treatment of contributions paid in the mistaken belief that a worker was an employee.

(2) Where there is a dispute about national insurance contributions, there is a right of appeal to the First-Tier Tribunal on a question of fact or law relating to a decision of HMRC, with further rights of appeal on points of law to the Upper Tribunal, Court of Appeal and, in rare cases of wide importance, the Supreme Court.

*Structural changes to state pension scheme*

(3) The State Second Pension (S2P) replaced the State Earnings Related Pension Scheme (SERPS) from 6 April 2002. The scheme gave enhanced benefits to lower earners (below £15,300 per annum), carers and long-term disabled workers. As a consequence the rebate payable on contracting out by way of a money purchase pension plan was, until April 2012, biased to give lower earners a disproportionately higher rebate

than higher earners. These rebates were abolished for money-purchase pensions (occupational and personal schemes) from April 2012. Final-salary schemes were unaffected by the changes, except for a reduction in the rebate rate to the current 4.8% from that date. S2P was abolished from April 2016, although accrued rights up to that date are protected as a 'foundation amount' under the new single-tier state pension regime if they give the contributor a better flat-rate state pension than would be payable if the new rules alone were applicable. The excess of the old-style pension over the new-style pension is added to the new-style pension earned by contributions made in 2016–17 onwards. Only those who reached state pension age before 6 April 2016 will receive a pension based wholly on the old rules.

*Alignment of tax and national insurance legislation*

(4) There are already many areas where the national insurance legislation has been aligned with the income tax legislation, and this process is continuing. There are still some differences in treatment, however, for example where an employee receives a mileage allowance for business use of his own car, national insurance contributions are not payable on allowances that do not exceed the Authorised Mileage Allowance Payment rates for up to 10,000 miles (45p), whatever the mileage (for details see **Example B2 explanatory note 20**).

For details of permissible round sum allowances and the treatment of incidental personal expenses see **Example B2 explanatory notes 11** and **12**. For the national insurance position on relocation allowances see **Example B2 explanatory note 7**.

(5) The Department for Work and Pensions retains responsibility for benefit entitlement including pension credits, but not for tax credits, statutory sick pay, statutory maternity pay or old contracted-out pension schemes (which are now closed to new contracted-out contributions but will continue to collect normal contributions and to pay pensions to members), which are policed by HMRC. Appeals on those matters are, however, to a different chamber of the Tribunal from appeals about NI contributions.

(6) In Budget 2011 the Chancellor announced a review of tax and NIC with a view to aligning the operation of the two as a simplification measure. This was a result of early work by the Office of Tax Simplification. Work continued during 2012 and 2013, but the only signs of progress were in a new simplification report from the OTS, which considered only the treatment of benefits and expenses payments. This report was updated in early 2014 and further proposals were advanced in early 2016. The OTS has been tasked with considering divorcing employer and employee contributions by turning the former into a new payroll tax with its own rules (allegedly as a simplification measure). Once that has been done, it may be followed by moving Class 1 contributions onto an annualised, cumulative and aggregated basis, so that the primary threshold is shared across different employments, just like an income tax personal allowance, and NIC is collected like PAYE, with a separate NIC code and annual reconciliation process like the P800 used for income tax for those outside self-assessment.

*Benefits that can be surrendered for cash*

(7) The employer's further guide to PAYE and NICs (CWG2), Chapter 5 gives detailed notes on what is included in pay both for tax and national insurance.

It is the view of HMRC that even where a benefit is transferred from the employer to the employee it does not come within the definition of a benefit in kind if it can be converted into cash by mere surrender, rather than requiring to be sold, and they give as an example premium bonds (CWG2 page 80). Class 1 national insurance contributions would therefore be payable on such benefits.

*Cars – benefits or cash*

(8) Where an employee has a choice between the use of a company car and additional salary, the employee's tax and national insurance position is based on what he actually gets – either salary or the use of the car (ITEPA 2003 s 119), but so as not to reduce the taxable value below the relevant $CO_2$-based scale charge. The Class 1A NIC charge is based on the taxable value. If the employee is paid a mileage allowance for the use of his own car for business, any amount up to 45p per mile is free of NICs liability.

*Directors and other special classes of employees*

(9) Special rules apply for certain classes of employees – for example see booklets (or substituted web guidance):

| | |
|---|---|
| Directors | CA 44 |
| Foreign-going mariners and deep sea fishermen | CA 42 |
| Social Security abroad | NI 38 |

See **part (D)** of the example for the special annual earnings period rules for directors.

(10) Where payment by a company of a director's personal bills is charged to the director's loan or current account, the payment does not count as earnings for national insurance unless the payment represents drawings in anticipation of earnings and the credit balance in the account is insufficient to meet the cost or the account is overdrawn. This will occur where the overdrawn loan account is settled by way of a bonus. The liability then arises at the time the loan account becomes overdrawn. This is particularly important to employers who are required to file their pay and deductions data under the Real-Time Information rules, which has affected nearly all employers since April 2013. Very few businesses will keep real-time information about the balance on a director's loan account, and it is yet to be seen how HMRC intends to apply the RTI penalty rules where an amount debited to an overdrawn loan account gives rise to a NIC liability that is not included in an FPS at the time. The problem does not arise for PAYE, as the overdrawing of a loan account is not deemed to be a payment of earnings: instead, CTA 2010 s 455 and ITEPA 2003 ss 173-191 may be relevant.

*Associated employers etc*

(11) Class 1 national insurance contributions are payable on earnings from one employment in one earnings period without regard to any other payment of earnings (Social Security Contributions and Benefits Act 1992 s 6(4)). However where two or more employers 'carry on business in association' or where more than one job is held with the same employer, earnings are aggregated to compute the liability for that earnings period unless it is not reasonably practical to do so (Social Security Contributions and Benefits Act 1992 Sch 1 para 1). See the Inland Revenue's Tax Bulletin of August 2000 for their views on the meaning of 'not reasonably practicable'. It has been assumed that the two employments of Mrs Bond in **part (C)** of the Example would be aggregated as both jobs are with J. Bond. If however the research post was with her husband's political party then her liability in respect of each employment would be:

| | £ |
|---|---|
| 7,500 @ nil × 2 | Nil |

giving a reduction of £832.80, and the employer's liability in each case would also be reduced to nil, because each employer pays earnings below the secondary threshold of £8,112, compared with a total liability of £950.54 if the earnings have to be aggregated.

*Married women's reduced rate contributions*

(12) Married women who pay reduced rate contributions cannot claim contributory benefits, but they can claim retirement pension (at a reduced level) and widow's benefit, both based on their husband's contributions. This position has been protected with the introduction of the new single-tier state pension, despite the fact that the new rules otherwise treat each contributor independently and there is no married couple's pension for those who reach state pension age on or after 6 April 2016. A woman widowed after 5 October 2010 who reached state pension age before 6 April 2016 will, however, inherit only half of her late husband's SERPS/S2P entitlement. Those widowed between 6 October 2002 and 5 October 2010 will have inherited between 60% and 90% of the spouse's SERPS/S2P entitlement. Women lose the right to pay reduced contributions on divorce (effective immediately after the decree absolute) or widowhood (effective from the end of the tax year, or if the husband died between 1 October and 5 April, from the end of the next tax year). The right is also lost if a married woman neither pays Class 1 contributions nor has self-employed earnings for two consecutive tax years. A woman with a valid reduced rate election is not permitted to pay voluntary contributions without first permanently revoking the election. The reduced rate continues in April 2016, although only a few thousand women still have valid elections in place.

*Contracted-out contributions*

(13) When contributions were paid at contracted-out rates before 6 April 2016, the actual contributions were revalued to their full rate equivalent in order to test whether the maximum contribution levels had been exceeded. The order of repayment of excess contributions was:

| | |
|---|---|
| Class 4 | |
| Class 2 | |
| Class 1 | (full rate) |
| Class 1 | (contracted-out rate, contributions in respect of salary-related schemes being refunded before contributions in relation to money purchase schemes in years before 6 April 2012) |

therefore contracted-out contributions will not normally have been repaid unless there was more than one such employment. In that case the appropriate actual excess will have been refunded (not the full-rate calculated contribution). The same order of repayment still applies after the abolition of contracting out, with the exception that all contributions for 2016–17 onwards will be at the full rate (or, in a tiny number of cases, at the married women's reduced rate).

*Liability for outstanding national insurance contributions of employees*

(14) A culpable company director or other culpable officer (including any shareholder who exercises management powers) may be personally liable under SSAA 1992 s 121C for the arrears of a company in respect of national insurance contributions if a notice is issued under this section. The arrears must arise through the officer's fraud or neglect and the amount payable will include interest. The officer may appeal against the notice to the First-Tier Tribunal, with the burden of proof on HMRC.

This power extends to the NI debts of a managed service company (MSC) under ITEPA 2003 s 688A. For this section recovery is against a director, other office holder or an associate of the MSC, or a provider or person who directly or indirectly encouraged, facilitated or was actively involved in the provision by the MSC of the services of the individual.

Since 6 April 2014, when the categorisation rules were changed for self-employed agency workers, the s 121C personal liability notice regime has been available for use against the directors of any agency liable for paying contributions and, where an end client or any other person who has a contractual relationship with the agency has issued a fraudulent document with a view to painting a false picture of the absence of supervision, direction or control over the agency worker, against the culpable officers of any such organisation. The transfer of liability to individuals has also been extended to PAYE liabilities for the first time. Similar rules now apply where an intermediary is involved in paying, incorrectly, home-to-work travel expenses tax- and NIC-free to its workers. Any underpayments may be transferred to the directors if not paid by the company.

*Employer's liability to Class 1 contributions re unapproved share option schemes*

(15) When an employee exercises an unapproved share option in a company where the shares are marketable (ie, a readily convertible asset), then a PAYE/NI liability arises on the taxable value realised by exercise of the option. This gives the employer a liability on an amount that cannot be determined in advance by the employer and the timing of the liability depends on the actions of the employee. To prevent unexpected national insurance costs affecting the employer, in respect of unapproved options granted on or after 6 April 1999 that have not yet been exercised, the employer and employee may jointly elect that the secondary NIC liability will be that of the employee. Furthermore, in computing the income tax payable by the employee the national insurance Class 1 secondary contributions paid by the employee on behalf of the employer will be deductible from the taxable amount (ITEPA 2003 s 478). For example: Gain on exercise of option liable to income tax £10,000. Employer's NIC paid by employee £1,380. Income tax due (10,000 – 1,380) = £8,620 @ say 40% = £3,448, giving the employee an effective marginal rate of income tax of 48.28% (ie, 1,380 + 3,448 = £4,828 paid out of £10,000, plus typically a further 2% employee NI liability).

*Helpline*

(16) For general enquiries regarding NI and Individuals there is a helpline at 0300 200 3500.

# Corporation tax – Basic corporation tax computations

# Question

Holsworthy Ltd, which has no associated companies, commenced trading as a manufacturer of adhesives in 1990. It has always drawn up its accounts to 31 December and prepares its accounts under UK GAAP. It is not a close company.

For the year to 31 December 2016 the net profit before taxation was £5,467,185. The following information has been provided (VAT having been adjusted appropriately in the figures given):

(1) The following items of investment income have been included in the profit:

*Interest receivable*

| | £ |
|---|---|
| Lundy Building Society | 85,000 |
| Interest on 10% loan note (issued by Worth plc) | 68,000 |
| | 153,000 |

The amounts actually received in the year to 31 December 2016 were building society interest of £87,000 in March 2016 and interest on Worth plc loan note of £65,000 on 31 May 1016.

UK dividends of £18,000 were received in November 2016, and are reported in the accounts in accordance with s.23 FRS 102.

*Rent*

Rent received is shown as £24,800. £12,800 of this amount was rent received from a house behind the factory which is let furnished. The company paid £1,200 insurance premium for the house on 1 January 2015 and this has been included in the general charge for insurance. The tenant pays the council tax and water rates.

The remaining £12,000 was received in respect of a block of garages let on tenant's repairing leases. In the accounts a deduction has been made for £2,000 of rent arrears on the garages. The company has not yet taken any steps to recover the overdue rent.

(2) In January 2016 the company had sold its 6% stake in an unquoted trading company which it had acquired in October 2000, resulting in a chargeable gain (after indexation allowance) of £5,330. A share in a freehold investment property which cost £117,762 (including legal costs of purchase) in March 1997 was sold for £289,370 in March 2016. Assume indexation allowance for the period March 1997 to March 2016 was 68%. The profit figure of £5,467,185 is before taking these transactions into account.

(3) On 30 May 2016 Holsworthy Ltd acquired leasehold factory premises at Milford Parva to be used in its trade. The term of the lease is 30 years. No premium was payable. In June 2016, the company vacated its former leasehold factory premises at Milford Parva. The lease still had four years to run from the end of June 2016 and the company was likely to find it difficult to assign the lease in the foreseeable future. The annual rent was £100,000. In addition to the annual rent, a provision of £200,000 was made at 31 December 2016 and charged against profits (in accordance with s.21 FRS 102) for the company's future rental obligations under the lease (less its estimated income from sub-letting).

(4) An analysis of the salaries and wages account shows that the following payments were made during the year:

| | £ |
|---|---|
| Removal expenses of new employee | 8,700 |
| Expenses of employee seconded to Housing Charity | 15,400 |
| Misappropriation of funds by former employee | 12,000 |
| Ex gratia payment to former director to settle claims made by him on the company | 20,000 |
| Statutory redundancy payments | 70,000 |

(5) An analysis of legal charges shows that the following amounts have been expended:

| | £ |
|---|---|
| Debt recovery | 3,200 |
| Sale of investment property March | 10,360 |
| Lease of new factory at Milford Parva | 15,780 |
| Fine for breach of Health and Safety at Work Regulations | 3,700 |
| Penalty for infringement of a patent | 12,800 |
| Legal costs of (successful) defence of action for breach of contract | 3,890 |
| Preparation of service agreement for sales manager | 1,600 |

(6) The entries in the bad debts account may be summarised as follows:

| | £ |
|---|---|
| Debts written off | 35,000 |
| Debts recovered | (15,000) |
| Decrease in debt impairment | (8,000) |
| Increase in general bad debt provision | 9,000 |
| Charge to profit and loss account | 21,000 |

(7) Sundry expenses include the following items:

| | £ |
|---|---|
| Fees for apprentice training course at technical college | 2,500 |
| Contribution to Milford Parva Enterprise Agency | 3,000 |
| Donation to Political Party | 4,000 |
| Bribe | 1,000 |
| Gift Aid donations of £2,500 to Oxfam paid on 1 July 2016 and 1 Jan 2017 | 5,000 |
| Gift Aid payment to local charity (gross amount – paid January 2016) | 2,000 |
| Trade association subscription | 400 |
| Debit interest on quarterly instalments of corporation tax for 2015 | 4,360 |

(8) Entertaining and gifts were made up as follows:

| | £ |
|---|---|
| Entertaining and gifts – UK customers | 138,940 |
| – Foreign customers | 24,480 |
| Staff dinner | 42,460 |
| Pocket diaries for UK customers (company's name embossed thereon) costing £3.75 each | 13,125 |
| | 219,005 |

(9) Depreciation charged for the year on the factory and plant and machinery amounted to £521,000. In addition, amortisation of goodwill of £300,000 was written off to profit and loss account. This related to goodwill costing £1,500,000 that was acquired on the purchase of the Sven Glue Co Ltd business and assets in January 2013. The company is amortising the goodwill equally over five years. Capital allowances of £456,400 are available on assets used in the factory.

(10) Loan interest payable charged against the profit was £200,000. The loan was £2,000,000 borrowed from the trustees of the company's self-administered pension fund to provide additional finance for the trade on 1 October 2013, on which interest at 10% per annum was payable half yearly on 31 March and 30 September.

(11) Patent royalties of £42,000 per annum (gross) were charged against the profit. These were paid to Barmouth plc half yearly in June and December.

(12) A final dividend of £800,000 for the year ended 31 December 2015 was paid in June 2016 and an interim dividend of £500,000 for the year to 31 December 2016 was paid in January 2017.

(A) Compute the corporation tax liability for the year to 31 December 2016.

(B) Show how the company would account for the taxation liabilities arising out of the information given. (Note: The company was liable to pay its tax under the quarterly payment regime in 2015.)

## Answer

### (a) Computation of Corporation Tax liability for year to 31 December 2016

| | | £ | £ |
|---|---|---|---|
| Net profit per accounts | | | 5,467,185 |
| *Less*: | Interest receivable | 153,000 | |
| | UK dividends | 18,000 | |
| | Rent (24,800 income less 1,200 expenses) | 23,600 | |
| | Capital allowances on plant and machinery | 456,400 | 651,000 |
| | | | 4,816,185 |
| *Add*: | Legal expenses re sale of property | | 10,360 |
| | Legal expenses re new lease of factory | | 15,780 |
| | Fine for breach of Health and Safety at Work Regulations | | 3,700 |
| | Penalty for infringement of patent | | 12,800 |
| | Increase in general bad debt provision | | 9,000 |
| | Donation to Political Party | | 4,000 |
| | Bribe | | 1,000 |
| | Gift Aid donations to Oxfam | | 5,000 |
| | Gift Aid payment to local charity | | 2,000 |
| | Entertaining and gifts (other than staff dinner and diaries) (219,005 – 42,460 – 13,125) | | 163,420 |
| | Depreciation (**footnote 1**) | | 521,000 |
| | Trading income | | 5,564,245 |
| | Property business income (**footnote 2**) | | 23,282 |
| | Non-trading loan relationship credits | | |
| | Worth plc 10% loan note interest | | 68,000 |
| | Building society interest | | 85,000 |
| | Chargeable gains (**footnote 3**) | | 86,500 |
| | Total profits | | 5,827,027 |
| | *Less qualifying charitable donations relief (gross amounts paid):* | | |
| | Gift aid donations (paid gross) (2,500 + 2,000) (**footnote 4**) | (4,500) | |
| | Taxable total profits | | 5,822,527 |
| Total corporation tax @20% | | | 1,178,161 |

**Footnotes**

1. Goodwill purchased from a third party after 8 July 2015 is not deductible however amortisation of some of the component intangible assets may qualify if they are identifiable assets in their own right and are separated out and accounted for as distinct assets.
2. Property business income – rental income (12,800 + 14,000) — 26,800

| | | | |
|---|---|---|---|
| *Less:* | insurance (house) | 1,200 | |
| | wear and tear allowance (house – 10% of 12,800 * 91/366 (allowance withdrawn 1 April 2016) | 318 | |
| | provision for rent arrears (garages) | 2,000 | 3,518 |
| | | | £23,282 |

3. The chargeable gains are (see **explanatory note 10**):

| | | | |
|---|---|---|---|
| On sale of unquoted trading company shares January 2016 | | | 5,330 |
| On sale of freehold investment property March 2016: | | | |
| | Sale proceeds | 289,370 | |
| | *Less:* Costs of sale | (10,360) | |
| | | 279,010 | |
| | Cost of property – March 1997 | (117,762) | |
| | Gain before indexation allowance | 161,248 | |
| | *Less*: Indexation allowance £117,762 × 68% | (80,078) | |
| | | | 81,170 |
| | | | 86,500 |

4. The donations to Oxfam are charitable donations and as such allowable on a paid basis, not an accruals basis.

### (b) Accounting for taxation liabilities arising out of information given

As the company paid its 2015 tax liability under the quarterly instalment payment ('QIP') regime and its taxable total profits for the year ended 31 December 2016 exceed £1,500,000, the corporation tax payable of £1,165,405 per part (a) will be accounted for under the QIP regime. Thus 25% of the estimated liability is payable on each of 14 July 2016, 14 October 2016, 14 January 2017 and 14 April 2017 (see **explanatory note 15**).

During 2016, the company paid tax on account of its 2015 corporation tax liability. The last two 25% instalments of the 2015 liability were paid on 14 January 2016 and 14 April 2016. The debit interest of £4,360 on the QIPs arises due to insufficient tax being paid on the QIP basis compared with the relevant proportion of the final liability which should have been paid. Such interest is a non-trade loan relationship debit.

## Explanatory Notes

*Scope of corporation tax*

(1) Corporation tax is charged on the *profits* of *companies* (CTA 2009 s 2(1)). Profits means both income and chargeable gains (see **explanatory note 10** below). Most dividends, whether received from a UK company or foreign company are exempt from corporation tax. However the rules are written such that distributions are subject to corporation tax unless they fall within one of the exemptions. Capital distributions are excluded and are taxed under capital gains rules. See **explanatory note 4(x)** for share dealers (CTA 2009 s 1285).

The definition of company for corporation tax purposes is 'any body corporate or unincorporated association' (CTA 2010 s 1121). This would include a members' club, which is liable to corporation tax on its income from non-members, such as investment income and guests' fees. (Income from members, e.g. subscriptions, is not taxed under the 'mutuality' principle.) Registered community amateur sports clubs, broadly amateur sports clubs open to the whole community which require their surpluses to be reinvested in the club, enjoy a number of special tax exemptions (see **Example N4 explanatory note 9** for the detailed provisions).

The definition specifically excludes a partnership, a local authority or a local authority association. Most unit trusts fall within the definition (CTA 2010 ss 617 and 1119). LLPs carrying on a trade are treated as partnerships unless and until they go into formal liquidation, from which time they are taxed as companies. See **Example C12 part (b)** for details.

UK resident companies are charged on their worldwide profits (although see **Example K8** for an optional exemption for overseas permanent establishments). Non-resident companies carrying on a trade in the UK through a permanent establishment are charged on income arising from the permanent establishment and on capital gains on the disposal of assets in the UK used for the purposes of the trade or attributable to the permanent establishment.

From 1 April 2013 an annual tax on enveloped dwellings (ATED) is imposed on certain non-natural persons (NNP) which hold UK residential dwellings valued at greater than originally £2M ( £500,000 for 2016/17). NNP's include:

(a) Companies;

(b) Partnerships with at least one corporate member; and

(c) Collective investment schemes.

| Property value | Annual tax charge for 2016–17 |
|---|---|
| Less than £500k | Nil |
| £500k to £1M | £3,500 |
| £1M to £2M | £7,000 |
| £2M to £5M | £23,350 |
| £5M to £10M | £54,450 |
| £10M to £20M | £109,050 |
| Over £20M | £218,200 |

For 2016/17 a return and payment of the tax due are required by 30 April 2016. For properties purchased after 1 April 2016, the return and tax are due 30 days after purchase. Properties valued at between £500,000 and 1 million only came within the regime from 1 April 2016, and the first return for these properties is due on 1 October 2016, with tax due on 31 October 2016. If the taxpayer is not chargeable (e.g. a disposal) for the full year a later repayment claim can be made. However, a charge to capital gains tax arises on any gain since 6 April 2013 on a time apportioned basis, charged at 28%.

The property value above relates to the market value on the last valuation date. The first valuation date is 1 April 2012 and then reassessed every five years. A number of exemptions and reliefs exist including the property being used for various commercial purposes such as third party rental and development, for charities and for public/national bodies. **Example D5** covers ATED in more detail.

Certain companies, called close companies, are subject to special restrictions. A close company is broadly one under the control of five or fewer shareholders or of its directors. See **Example J1** for details.

*Chargeable accounting periods*

(2) The basis of the charge to tax is the profits of a 'chargeable accounting period'. This normally means the period for which a company makes up accounts, as in the case of Holsworthy's year to 31 December 2016. However, see **Example I3 explanatory note 1** for detailed notes on chargeable accounting periods.

*Calculation of profits*

(3) In computing a corporation tax liability, the Corporation Tax Acts (CTA) 2009, 2010 and TIOPA 2010 set out the basis on which profits are calculated.

Profits are computed separately for each source within the charge to corporation tax (see scope above). Debits and credits are calculated according to the relevant source legislation, although trading loan relationships and trading intangible assets are included as part of trading income rather than shown separately. Total profits are the aggregate of these sources including chargeable gains (after allowable losses but excluding gains chargeable under section TCGA 1992 2B(ATED)) with the resulting total being known as the total taxable profits (TTP) (previously profits chargeable to corporation tax (PCTCT)) for the period. The main sources of income and reliefs are:

| Source | Type |
|---|---|
| Trading income | Profits from a trade |
| Property income | Profits from letting UK and overseas property |
| Loan relationships | Debits and credits arising from money debts |
| Miscellaneous income | Sundry income |

| | |
|---|---|
| Chargeable gains | Capital gains and losses on disposals |
| Management expenses | Expenses of companies with investment business |
| Intangible assets | Receipts/expenditure on intangible assets |
| R & D relief | Relief for research and development |
| Qualifying charitable donations relief | Mainly gift aid donations |
| Loss relief | Relief for losses |

CTA 2009 s 46 requires that the profits of a trade are calculated in accordance with generally accepted accounting practice (GAAP), subject to any adjustment required or authorised by law. Losses must be calculated on the same basis as profits (CTA 2009 s 47). CTA 2009 s 51 contains provisions governing the relationship between rules prohibiting and allowing deductions. Also see **Example N5** for the general anti-abuse rule. GAAP is defined in CTA 2010 s 1127 to include either UK or International Financial Reporting Standards (IFRS).

See **Example I2 explanatory note 27** for International Financial Reporting Standards.

(4) Although accounts are required to be prepared in accordance with GAAP, tax law takes precedence over accounting practice and can require adjustments for certain types of expenditure. Two of the most fundamental rules in the calculation of taxable trade profits are whether items will be disallowed for tax purposes under the capital expenditure rule (CTA 2009 s 53) or the wholly and exclusively rule (CTA 2009 s 54). Applying the rules to this Example:

(i) *Crime related payments*

Expenses must not involve committing a criminal offence, such as paying a bribe or protection money (including payments overseas that would be illegal if paid in the UK), nor be paid in response to threats, menaces, blackmail and other forms of extortion (CTA 2009 s 1304). Any VAT input tax on legal expenses in court proceedings relating to illegal acts may, however, be recovered providing the criminal payment relates directly to the business (*C & E v Rosner* (1993)).

The Bribery Act 2010 sets out four categories of offence:

(1) A general offence of offering, promising or giving a bribe to another person;

(2) A further general offence of requesting, agreeing to receive or accepting a bribe from another person;

(3) A specific offence of bribing a foreign public official; and

(4) A corporate offence of failing to prevent bribery.

The Act covers both UK companies operating at home and abroad as well as overseas companies with a presence in the UK. Point four places wide obligations on 'commercial organisations' with potential prosecutions even if senior management were totally unaware that the bribery had taken place. The defence to this offence is to have 'adequate procedures' designed to prevent bribery. The onus is thus on the organisation to show 'adequate steps' have been taken.

Offenders convicted under the Act face up to ten years imprisonment and/or an unlimited fine. Directors convicted of bribery offences are likely to be disqualified.

Government guidance can be found at:

http://www.justice.gov.uk/downloads/legislation/bribery-act-2010-guidance.pdf

(ii) *Rents and provision for lease rental obligations*

Rent is normally expenditure incurred for trade purposes, even after a company has vacated its premises. *CIR v Falkirk Iron Co Ltd* (1933) held that rent payable on premises which had ceased to be occupied was an allowable deduction as the rent obligation arises from the lease which is taken out for trading purposes. Furthermore, it was decided that provision for future rental obligations on vacated premises was acceptable under GAAP in *Herbert Smith (a Firm) v Honour* (1999).

Following the High Court's decision in that case, HMRC conceded that there was no longer a (judge-made) rule which prevented provision being made for future expenditure in accordance with GAAP, and this has now been made statutory. In particular, accounting provisions required under s.21 FRS102 are accepted for tax purposes. Broadly, FRS 12 requires provision to be made where the business has a current (legal or constructive) obligation as a result of a past event; it is probable that expenditure will be required to satisfy it; and the provision can be reliably estimated. s.21 FRS102 would require provision to be made for future net rental obligations where the company is unable to assign the lease or can only sub-let it at a lower rent. By entering into the lease, the company has incurred the legal obligation to pay the rents – the lease becomes an onerous contract since the unavoidable costs of meeting the obligations exceed the benefits to be received under it. This applies to Holsworthy's rent provision in this Example.

It should be noted that provisions for other obligations that may arise under a lease, such as provisions to remove capital alterations and restore the building to its original state, may be capital in nature and not deductible on an accounts basis.

(iii) *Salaries and wages and redundancy payments*

The basic requirement is that the payments must be wholly and exclusively for the purposes of the trade. The removal expenses for the new employee satisfy this rule and are allowable. For the tax treatment of the employee see **Example B2 explanatory note 7**.

The expenses of an employee seconded to a charity would not usually satisfy the 'wholly and exclusively for the trade' rule, but they are specifically allowable by CTA 2009 s 70.

The ex gratia payment will be allowed as a deduction by the company providing it is wholly and exclusively for the trade, and will be charged on the director under the 'golden handshakes' provisions (see **Example B5**).

Misappropriations of funds by staff are an allowable expense provided they are the sort which one might expect to be an ordinary risk of the trade. Such losses are distinguished from those arising as a result of misappropriations by persons in controlling positions such as directors, which have been held in various cases to be not allowable – e.g. *Curtis v Oldfield Ltd* (1925), *Bamford v ATA Advertising Ltd* (1972).

In the case of an ongoing business, redundancy and other termination payments would normally be incurred as part of a rationalisation programme and would be allowed under general principles as expenditure incurred wholly and exclusively for the purposes of the trade (CTA 2009 s 54). Statutory redundancy payments are specifically deductible as a trading expense (CTA 2009 s 77). HMRC also allow *contractual* redundancy payments made on cessation of trade, following the Privy Council's decision in *Hong Kong CIR v Cosmotron Manufacturing Co Ltd* (1997). The rationale is that such payments are made under a pre-existing obligation to employees taken on for the purposes of the trade (CTA 2009 s 76).

The Cosmotron decision does not cover ex-gratia or non-contractual redundancy payments made on cessation. Under CTA 2009 s 79, however, an amount of up to three times the statutory redundancy payment is specifically allowed provided it would otherwise have satisfied the 'wholly and exclusively' rule.

See **Example N5 answer** (f) regarding deductibility of pension contributions.

(iv) *Legal charges*

Capital items, e.g. the charges on the sale of the property and the acquisition of the lease, are not allowable (CTA 2009 s 53). Fines and penalties for breaches of the law and costs connected therewith, are not allowable and fines and penalties by non-governmental regulatory bodies are also not allowable in certain cases (*McLaren Racing Limited v HMRC* [2012] TC02278). The costs of defending a civil action for breach of contract are wholly and exclusively for the purposes of the trade and are allowable, whether the action is successful or not.

In the case of *McKnight v Sheppard* (1999), the House of Lords held that legal expenses incurred by a stockbroker in an (unsuccessful) defence against Stock Exchange disciplinary proceedings for gross misconduct were to avoid the destruction of his business and satisfied the 'wholly and exclusively' rule, although the fines imposed by the Stock Exchange were not allowable, since they represented a loss which did not arise out of the trade.

(v) *Bad debts*

In relation to ordinary trading transactions with customers and suppliers, bad debts written off and specifically provided impairment losses for are allowable (CTA 2009 s 55). A general bad debts provision, or increase therein, is not. (Bad debt impairments are not covered by s.21 FRS102 (see **note (i)** above) as they reduce the value of an asset (the debtors) instead s.11 FRS102 applies.) Bad debts which do not relate to ordinary trading transactions are dealt with under the rules for 'loan relationships' (see **Example K2**).

(vi) *Sundry expenses*

Where expenses of training courses are met by the employer, they are allowable as part of the benefits provided to staff, and they are not assessable on the employees providing certain conditions are met (see **Example B2 explanatory note 33**). Employers may also deduct the cost of retraining employees who are about to leave or have just left their present jobs (CTA 2009 s 74).

For training involving employees who have a proprietary stake in the employer see BIM47080 in HMRC's Business Income Manual.

Contributions to approved local enterprise agencies, training and enterprise councils, Scottish local enterprise companies and 'business link' organisations are specifically allowable (CTA 2009 s 82).

Charitable and political donations are not allowable as trading expenses, unless exceptionally they satisfy the 'wholly and exclusively' rule. Charitable donations can be claimed, under the qualifying charitable donations relief as deductions from *total* profits (see **explanatory note 11**).

As far as trade association subscriptions are concerned, most trade associations have agreed with HMRC to pay tax on the excess of their receipts over their allowable expenditure and the subscriptions are accordingly allowed to the payer. Any other subscriptions would be considered under the 'wholly and exclusively' rule.

Interest on overdue and overpaid tax is brought into account as a trading loan relationship debit / credit and hence relief is given in calculating taxable profits (see **Example I2 explanatory note 6**).

(vii) *Entertaining and gifts*

With regard to entertaining and gifts, all expenditure in relation to customers, both home and overseas, is disallowed, except for gifts that are not food, drink, tobacco or gift vouchers, that carry a conspicuous advertisement and that cost not more than £50 per person in each accounting period, which applies to the pocket diaries in this Example (CTA 2009 s 1300) (see **Example C2**). The disallowance does *not* apply to anything provided for staff, unless it is incidental to entertaining customers. The cost of staff entertaining is allowed in calculating taxable profits providing it is wholly and exclusively for the trade. Staff entertaining may, however, result in a tax and national insurance charge on employees and directors under the benefits provisions (see **Example B2 explanatory note 31**), unless the conditions for staff entertaining are fulfilled and the expenditure in a tax year does not amount to more than £150 per head.

The disallowance also doesn't apply where the entertainment or gift is of a kind which it is the company's business to provide and it is so provided in the ordinary course of business in order to advertise to the public generally (CTA 2009 ss 1299 (2) and 1300 (2)).

Relief may be claimed for gifts of machinery, plant and trading stock to schools and other educational establishments (CTA 2009 s 105). Similarly, relief is available under CTA 2009 s 1300(5) for gifts in kind to a charity or heritage body (within CTA 2010 s 468)).

Under these provisions, nothing has to be brought into account either as a trading receipt if the item is from trading stock or as disposal proceeds for capital allowances if it has been used in the donor's trade. Relief is also given for trading stock consisting of medical supplies donated for humanitarian purposes to developing countries (together with transportation and delivery costs) (CTA 2009 s 107). These provisions are accompanied by an anti-avoidance provision which excludes the donor from receiving any benefit in return for the gift. (CTA 2009 s 108.)

VAT-registered traders donating used or obsolete items have to account for VAT only on the current value of such items, not on their original cost.

See **explanatory note 11** regarding charitable donations relief for gifts of stocks and shares and land.

(viii) *Depreciation of factory and plant etc and amortisation of goodwill*

Depreciation of owned assets is a capital item and is disallowed. (Most but not all assets qualify instead for capital allowances.) See BIM 61120 regarding the taxation of finance leases in the returns of lessees.

(ix) *Intangible assets*

Amortisation of goodwill purchased after 1 April 2002 and before 8 July 2015 is deductible as a trading expense under the intangible fixed assets regime (CTA 2009 Part 8 starting at s 711). Thus no adjustment should be required for the £300,000 goodwill amortisation charge. With effect from 8 July 2015, F(No2)A 2015 s 32 disallows corporation tax deductions for amortisation and impairment debits in respect of goodwill and other intangible assets linked to customers and customer relationships. See **Example K3** for details of the intangible fixed assets rules.

Patent royalties were brought within the intangible fixed assets rules by FA 2002, and are therefore also dealt with by CTA 2009 Part 8. The broad effect of these rules is to provide tax relief for all expenses, losses, profits etc relating to such assets, normally based on the amounts reflected in the accounts as part of the profits of the trade. This means that patent royalties are deductible as a trading expense. (Previously they were allowed as a charge on income.) Thus, in this Example, full relief can be taken for the patent royalties of £43,000 already charged against Holsworthy's profits, with no further tax adjustment being required.

(x) *Non-trading income*

Non-trading income is excluded from the trading profits computation. It is then brought in appropriately elsewhere, except qualifying dividends (see **explanatory note 1**), which are not chargeable to corporation tax.

For share dealers, dividend income and manufactured payments that are treated as dividends are trading income rather than investment income and are included in trading profits (exclusive of tax credits).

Interest from banks and building societies is received by companies in full without deduction of tax (CTA 2009 s 498). The same applies to interest on UK government stocks, unless application is made for net payment (ITA 2007 s 892). Companies receive most interest in full but in the rare cases where investment income is received net of income tax, the gross amount is nonetheless included in the taxable total profits. The income tax suffered is taken into account in the Schedule 16 quarterly income tax accounting (see **Example I3 explanatory note 9**) or set off against the corporation tax payable. The corporation tax treatment of interest is dealt with in **Example K2**.

(xi) *Property income*

UK property business income of companies is computed as a single figure under the 'UK property business rules' with separate computation for an overseas property business. Allowable deductions are broadly those that apply to business profits, hence a provision may be made for unpaid rents as indicated in the Example. The Example also includes a deduction for 10% wear and tear. This allowance wasabolished from 1 April 2016 via the 2016 Finance Act. Rent from sub-letting *part* of business premises (not land) that is *temporarily* surplus to requirements may for convenience be included in the trading income providing it is comparatively small and part of a building used in the trade. For detailed notes on the treatment of rents see **Example L10**.

*Loan relationships*

(5) For detailed notes on the loan relationships provisions see **Example K2**.

*Pre-trading expenditure*

(6) Pre-trading expenditure, other than interest (and elected research and development (R&D) expenditure – see below), incurred by a company within seven years before the start of the trade that would have been allowable if incurred after commencement is treated as paid on the first day of trading (CTA 2009 s 61).

Where interest is paid before the trade starts, it is deducted on an accruals basis in calculating the non-trading profit or loss. This does not apply if the company makes a claim, within two years after the end of the period in which the deduction was given, to bring the interest in as a trading expense of the first trading period. In order to be deductible in that period the trade must start within seven years after the end of the accounting period in which the interest would otherwise have been deducted as non-trading debits (CTA 2009 s 330).

Where a small/medium-sized company incurs qualifying R&D expenditure before it begins to carry on the relevant trade, it may elect to treat 230% (225% up to 31 March 2015) of the expenditure as if it were a trading loss, see **Example I5**. Where an R&D election is made, the amount cannot also be treated as a pre-trading expense.

*Capital allowances*

(7) When the trading profit has been ascertained using the above principles, capital allowances are then deducted as a trading expense and balancing charges included as a trading receipt (CAA 2001 s 2).

*Value added tax*

(8) For a company making wholly taxable supplies, VAT does not normally enter into the profits and expenditure for corporation tax, except as follows:

(a) Any non-recoverable VAT. Examples of non recoverable VAT are:

- on cars (hire or purchase),
- entertaining (other than staff, see **Example C2 explanatory note** 7 and from 1.5.11 reasonable business entertainment of overseas customers),
- repairs, refurbishments and other expenses relating to domestic accommodation provided for directors and deemed non business expenditure.
- split business/private expenditure; input tax reclaim may be restricted to business percentage, for example, mobile phone bills.

The non-allowable element forms part of the cost of the expenditure. E.g., the non-recoverable VAT on the hire of a car will form part of the allowable cost of hiring a car whilst the non-recoverable VAT on entertaining will form part of the disallowed cost of entertaining.

(b) Scale VAT charges for private fuel provided to employees are included in motoring expenses.

A partially or wholly exempt or unregistered company includes the VAT as part of its allowable expenses or capital costs, subject to the disallowance of VAT on business entertaining. Some approximation may be necessary for partly exempt companies in allocating the VAT to the various items of expenditure, and this will be accepted by HMRC providing it is reasonable. See **Example M2** for the use of the flat rate VAT scheme for small businesses.

*National insurance contributions*

(9) Companies are required to pay Class 1 secondary national insurance contributions at 13.8% in respect of their employees' earnings in excess of £156 a week from 6 April 2016. (Employees' Class 1 primary contributions are payable on earnings in excess of £155 a week. For 2016/17 the main charge runs out at the upper earnings limit of £827 a week, £43,000 a year, and a charge of 2% applies to earnings above this limit.) Earnings for Class 1 contributions comprise cash pay and certain benefits in kind that can be readily converted into cash. Employers (but not employees) also pay Class 1A contributions at 13.8% on most taxable benefits in kind that do not attract Class 1 contributions, and also Class 1B contributions at 13.8% regarding PAYE settlement agreements (see **Example B1** for details). The contributions are an allowable expense against the profits.

See **Example H1** for the detailed provisions on national insurance.

*Chargeable gains*

(10) Company chargeable gains are calculated using capital gains tax principles, but are then charged to corporation tax rather than to capital gains tax (CTA 2009 s 2(2), TCGA 1992 ss 1 and 8). References in the capital gains legislation to years of assessment are treated as references to accounting periods. If losses exceed gains, the excess is carried forward to set against later gains (see **Example L10 explanatory note 11**).

For companies, indexation relief continues to apply in the calculation of chargeable gains. However, companies have seen an increasing amount of capital assets being removed from the capital gains regime (where they are only broadly taxed on a 'realisation' basis) and taxed instead in accordance with profits and losses recognised in the accounts.

*Qualifying charitable donations relief*

(11) Qualifying donations to charities and certain gifts of shares and securities to charities are eligible for charitable donations relief (CTA 2010 Part 6 s 189 onwards) to the extent they are not:

(a) dividends or other distributions and

(b) are not already deductible in computing income.

Qualifying charitable donations relief is deducted from the company's total profits for the period after any other relief but before group relief (CTA 2010 s 189). The general rule is that where the amount of the donation exceeds the company's total taxable profits for a period the excess cannot be carried back or forward. Instead the excess will be lost unless a claim for group relief can be made. However, special provision is made for companies which are wholly owned by one or more charities under CTA 2010 s 199 (see **Example N4 explanatory note 7** for details).

A company will make a qualifying payment for the purposes of *CTA 2010, s 191* if:

(a) the payment is a payment of a sum of money;

(b) the payment is not subject to a condition as to repayment;

(c) the company making the payment is not a charity, and

(d) the payment is not disqualified under:

(i) s 193 – an associated acquisition is made by the charity,

(ii) s 194 – the payment is regarded as a distribution, or

(iii) s 195 – benefits are associated with the payment (see **Example D1.5**).

Prior to CTA 2010 relief for charitable donations was given as a charge on income.

The charity must be a UK registered charity, or an EU charity that would qualify as a UK charity if registered in the UK.

*Gross and net payments and quarterly income tax returns*

(12) See **Example I3 explanatory note 10** for details of when payments of interest, royalties etc are made gross or net of income tax and how such tax is accounted for to HMRC on quarterly income tax returns (form CT61).

*Corporation tax rates*

(13) The rate of corporation tax is fixed for years ended 31 March which are called 'financial years'. Financial years are identified by the calendar year in which they start. Thus the year ending 31 March 2017 is called the financial year 2016. The rate for the financial year 2016 is 20%.

The main rate is expected to be cut again in FY 2017 to 19% and 17% in FY 2019.

Where company accounting periods do not coincide with financial years, the total taxable profit is apportioned over the years concerned to determine the rates at which tax is payable (CTA 2009 s 8), unless the rate is the same for both years. This apportionment is done in days rather than months.

*Corporation tax self-assessment (CTSA)*

(14) See **Example I2 explanatory note 6** for full details.

*Payment of corporation tax*

(15) Although the corporation tax self-assessment return CT600 must be filed within twelve months of the year end, corporation tax must be paid within nine months and one day of the end of the accounting period (except for companies with large taxable profits that must pay by instalments). Interest on corporation tax unpaid after nine months is 2.75% since 23/08/16. The rate is responsive to bank base rate changes. Previous rates are:

| From | % |
|---|---|
| 29/09/09 | 3% |
| 24/03/09 | 2.5% |
| 27/01/09 | 3.5% |
| 6/01/09 | 4.5% |

*Quarterly instalments*

In Holsworthy's case the company qualifies as large and the tax must be paid in four equal instalments as follows:

| ***Instalment*** | ***Due*** | ***Date*** | ***Percentage*** |
|---|---|---|---|
| Instalment 1 | 6 months + 13 days after start of AP | 14/07/16 | 25% |
| Instalment 2 | 3 months after instalment 1 | 14/10/16 | 25% |
| Instalment 3 | 3 months after instalment 2 | 14/01/17 | 25% |
| Instalment 4 | 3 months plus 14 days after end of AP | 14/04/17 | 25% |

The number of instalments will be reduced if the accounting period is less than nine months in length. The taxable profits of acompany qualify as large if its profits (including non-group franked (for dividends received before 1 April 2016) investment income) exceed £1.5 million, as scaled-down for shorter accounting periods and for the number of related 51% group companies (previously associate companies see **explanatory note 22**).

A company is not large if:

(a) its tax liability does not exceed £10,000 (as scaled-down for shorter accounting periods); or

(b) its profits for the accounting period do not exceed £10 million (as adjusted for shorter accounting periods), *and* it was not large (disregarding the £10 million exclusion) in the previous accounting period.

Holsworthy's profits were below £10 million, but it was large in the previous year, and its profit is above £1.5 million so quarterly payments are required. A company will not be large in the previous period if it did not exist or have an accounting period in any part of the previous 12 months, or if it was not a large company for an accounting period that fell within or ended in the previous 12 months.

*Estimating quarterly instalment payments (QIPs)*

It is the company's responsibility to state on the self-assessment return CT600 that it is liable to make QIPs. It is also its responsibility to estimate the amount of the QIP, which involves estimating the profit for the year before the year has ended. Because the instalments are estimated the amount paid will rarely match the final liability, and interest is charged or paid on underpaid or overpaid instalments. Interest runs from the date of the first instalment, and is currently charged at 1.25% (from 15/08/16 previously 1.5%) on underpayments, and credited at 0.5% on overpayments. The rates would be expected to change quite frequently but are based on bank base rates that have been stable.

Interest on unpaid instalments is deductible, and interest on overpaid instalments is assessable in calculating profits for tax. See **Example I2 explanatory note 14** for further details.

Payments can be made at any time, and a system exists for reclaiming overpayments made during the year. Group payment arrangements can be made by groups of companies, with the effect that over and underpayments by a group member can be offset.

In July 2015 it was announced that the government propose to introduce new payment dates for companies with annual taxable profits of £20 million or more (again the limit is split between group companies). Affected companies will be required to pay their corporation tax wholly within the accounting year rather than half during and half afterwards. For an annual accounting period, a company would pay in the third, sixth, ninth and twelfth months. The measure was due to apply to accounting periods starting on or after 1 April 2017 but was deferred in the 2016 corporate tax road map to accounting periods starting on or after 1 Aril 2019.

*Related 51% group companies*

(16) As part of the abolition of the small profits rate (subject to certain exceptions) the associated companies rules (below) have been simplified by replacing them with a "related 51% group companies test" in CTA 2010 s 279F. This states that two companies are associated with one another if:

(a) One is a 51% subsidiary of the other,

(b) Each is a 51% subsidiary of a third company,

(c) One is owned by a consortium of which the other is a member,

(d) One has control of the other, or

(e) Both are under the control of the same person.

For the FY 2015 onwards the 51% group companies rules are applicable to:

(a) small ring fence profits,

(b) the long life assets legislation (CAA 2001 s 99),

(c) Patent Box (CTA 2010 s 357CL and 357CM) and

(d) the quarterly instalment payment rules (see Explanatory Note 15 above).

# Question

Your firm has acted for Captain H. Blower for many years, preparing rental income computations and personal tax returns. After a distinguished career in the forces, he started trading in executive cars in April 2015, as EEC (Extremely Expensive Cars). Accounts prepared by the bookkeeper, showing a profit of £40,000, have proved remarkably accurate, and give rise to a tax and NIC bill of £13,400 in respect of the car dealing business, after taking into account £20,000 of other income.

The following note of 12 December 2016 addressed to the senior partner who is on holiday, has just been found amongst the accounting records, and passed to you on 15 December 2016 to deal with.

> 'Jim, what a great round of golf last weekend – I'll get even with you next time!
>
> I had a fantastic first year, not just because of good profits, but I just love driving those wonderful cars. The hard bit is parting with them when I get to the customer. I have a good customer base now, although some of them make my jaw drop. One customer bought an old Audi from me for £14,995 in cash, which was a pretty steep price, and then I saw it advertised for sale at £7,500 a week later. And then he gave me an unbelievable price on my Aston Martin! Well, it takes all types to make a world. Anyway, I feel the time has come to transfer the business to a limited company. It does not have much in the way of assets, other than the Aston Martin, but I hope to buy a transporter next summer. Apparently, I can save tax by transferring the goodwill of EEC to the company, and closing it after a couple of years, and paying tax at only 10%. The rental income business is paying the bills, so I could put as much money as you advise from the car business into a pension. I set up the company myself on 3 February 2015, and immediately put £5,000 into a company deposit account, so it receives trivial amounts of interest every month. I put a couple of cars deals through it on 3 November 2016 to start it trading. On 10 November 2016 I issued a second share to my wife, and made her a Director. I have just put in Form 225 to extend the year end to get extra time for filing the accounts and I am changing the name to European Executive Cars Ltd. You probably do not know the answer to this, or would not know how to do it, but should my company adopt the new International Accounting Standards if it is allowed to? I would like to do so if it saved any tax. So, this will wait until you have recovered from your holiday. Have a good trip.
>
> Rodney'

Research on Companies House website shows that the directors are indeed as stated, and that the company was formed on 3 February 2015.

(a) Draft notes for a meeting with the captain, explaining the compliance and tax issues that the note raises for the limited company.

(b) State what action you, as a tax adviser, need to take to comply with money laundering requirements.

Disregard VAT & Excise Duty.

# Answer

## (a) Notes for a meeting with Captain H. Blower

### Money laundering

The captain has been a client for many years and has met the firm's procedures for existing clients. However, there is a need for ongoing monitoring of the business relationship, and risk assessment (SI 2007/2157). Examples of instances where ongoing due diligence methods may be applied are a change in business strategy or profile, as here. The firm must ensure that it holds evidence of the identity of the client and the ultimate owners and that it has knowledge of the purpose of the business relationship. As the level of due diligence is based on risk, the firm should perform a risk assessment.

### Company filing dates

As the captain's private company was formed on 3 February 2015, its accounting reference date (ARD) will initially be 28 February. For a newly formed company, the accounts must be filed within 21 months of the date of incorporation (not nine months from the ARD), that is by midnight on 3 November 2016. The accounts are therefore already overdue.

Extending the company's year end will not extend the date of filing of the accounts. Furthermore, the application must be made within the timescale for filing the accounts. As the application to extend the year end will be received after the due date for filing the accounts, it will be rejected. The company's ARD will remain 28 February.

### Company name

Companies House controls the use of 'sensitive words and expressions'. Examples are words such as 'British', 'International' or 'European' which may imply greater size and scope than the company actually possesses, so it is likely that the change of name application will be rejected, unless the company can show significant trading across Europe to justify it. A list of controlled and banned words and expressions can be found in the guidance section on company names in the Companies House website.

### Charge to corporation tax

The company must give notice to HMRC within 3 months of the start of the accounting period, in this case 3 February 2015of coming into charge to corporation tax, in this case of the company acquiring the deposit account which earns interest. If this has not already been done, notification should be made as soon as possible. Penalties may apply to late notification.

As the company receives interest, it is within the charge to corporation tax, and not dormant. The normal tax payment and tax filing deadlines apply to it. As a period of account for corporation tax cannot exceed one year, there are two periods of account: 3 February 2015 to 2 February 2016; and 3 February 2016 to 28 February 2016. Any tax on these accounting periods should have been paid by 3 November 2016 and 30 November 2016 respectively, after which interest would run, but after costs and fees it is unlikely that any actual corporation tax would fall due. Although the payment deadline is nine months, the filing deadline for the company tax return CT600 (of which two are required, one for each accounting period) is twelve months from the end of the period of account. A tax return is required for each period, failing which an initial penalty of £100 each will apply. The filing deadline is 28 February 2017 for both returns (see **explanatory note 7**), so these penalties should be easily avoided.

Consideration may be given to shortening the current accounting period (year ending 28 February 2017). The due date for filing the accounts for this year will be 28 November 2017 (not 30 November 2017), so an application to shorten the accounting period may be made at any time up to that date. An accounting period may not be less than six months in length, so it would be possible to shorten the accounting period to 31 October 2016, giving an eight-month period.

The amount of tax for this period will be minimal, as trading does not commence until November 2016. The effect of shortening the non-trading accounting period to 31 October 2016 will be to place all of the trading activity and profits into a year ending 31 October 2017. The due date for filing accounts will be 31 July 2018, and deferring the due date of corporation tax to 1 August 2018.

## Employment related securities (previously form 42)

The issue of shares to the founder before commencement of trade does not require a report. However a report still needs to be made on issue to directors after commencement of trade. A report must therefore be made by 6 July 2017 of the issue shares to Mrs Blower on 10 November 2016. If no more shares are to be issued before 6 April 2017, you may wish to prepare and file the report immediately with HMRC, to avoid having to diary this date, as the report may be made annually or on issue by issue basis. For 2014/15 and subsequent years the paper form 42 has been replaced by a spreadsheet that must be completed and uploaded to HMRC online. To access it the employer must register for the employment related securities service via PAYE online.

## Transfer of goodwill

Before 3 December 2014, it was common to value goodwill on the incorporation of a business as high as possible. FA 2015 removed two tax advantages in connection with goodwill. For disposals on or after 3 December 2014:

(a) CGT entrepreneurs relief no longer applies to disposals of goodwill (and certain other related intangible assets) by a sole trader or partnership to a related company, (the gains on other business assets are not affected) FA 2015 s 42 and

(b) When a company acquires goodwill (or similar assets) from a related individual/partnership the company cannot obtain tax relief on the cost of amortising the goodwill over its useful life / impairment. Any corporation tax relief is calculated on disposal. (There was an exception where the individual had originally purchased the goodwill from an unrelated third party) FA 2015 s 26.

The s 26 provisions above have been superseded by rules relevant to all acquisitions (not just incorporations) on or after 8 July 2015 by F(No2)A 2015 s 32. This disallows corporation tax deductions, such as amortisation and impairment debits, for goodwill (and certain other intangible assets linked to customers). On disposal any loss will be classified as a non-trading debit.

Mr Blower will therefore be unable to access the reliefs above. However, goodwill remains a capital asset and shouldn't be ignored as he may crystallise a capital gain if it has any market value.

The recognition of goodwill in the accounts at fair market value is a proper transaction for both tax and accounting purposes. Achieving an acceptable valuation is a matter of extreme uncertainty.

Because the goodwill introduced generates a liability as a credit to the director's loan account it has no effect on the value of the company, nor are there any tax implications in extracting the fair value.

Goodwill can be classified into three kinds (see HMRC Manual):

(i) Personal goodwill – the trader's name and reputation.

(ii) Inherent goodwill – the location of the business.

(iii) Free goodwill – the brand name, customers, business reputation and super-profits.

Personal goodwill cannot be transferred as it is specific to the individual. Inherent goodwill goes with the property, and can only be transferred if an interest in the property is transferred. HMRC accept that free goodwill of a sole trader business may be transferred to the owner's new limited company. If EEC cars has a website, contracts, premises, salesmen and therefore a business separate from the Captain himself, then there may be free and inherent goodwill to transfer to the Company and hence a market value. If the whole process of buying, selling and delivery is done by the Captain himself, this may be regarded as evidence that goodwill is not separable from him as an individual. The fact that a couple of deals can easily be put through another legal entity implies it is personal goodwill, unless there is some special reason for singling out these particular transactions.

It seems likely on the face of it that the goodwill has quite a low value. If it is placed on the company at over-value, HMRC may seek to treat the excess as a dividend, or even to tax it under PAYE as an inducement to take up employment.

It is possible to agree the value of goodwill with HMRC, via a post-transaction valuation check, but by definition this happens only after the transaction has been completed. The request for a post-valuation check should be made well before the deadlines for filing the personal or corporation tax returns, to allow them to reflect the agreed figure.

The value for goodwill that is agreed will be the disposal value for capital gains tax. That amount will be credited to the director's current account and can be withdrawn with no further tax liability.

## Tax avoidance

The client believes that he could save tax by transferring goodwill in the company, taking very low remuneration, and then liquidating the company to take advantage of the lower rate of tax applicable to capital gains. It will be necessary to consider the general anti-abuse rule in FA 2013 s 203 plus other anti-avoidance rules such as CTA 2010 Part 15 s 731 onwards (transactions in securities) may allow HMRC to cancel such an advantage where certain specific conditions are fulfilled. There is also the danger that surplus assets in the company would cause it to lose its qualifying status for entrepreneur's relief, in which case any gain would be taxed at 20% (assuming he is a higher rate taxpayer).

FA 2009 Sch 25 also introduced rules to prevent the transfer of income into gains, transfers of income streams that would need to be considered.

If the issue of one share to the Captain's wife is to divert income to her by means of dividends, then care must be taken that the arrangements do not fall within the settlements legislation (as described in **Example J3**). The settlements legislation involves a bounteous transfer, and in this context a high value placed on goodwill as a result of future earnings would be unhelpful. If the transfer of the business to the limited company goes ahead, the shareholdings and a dividend policy will have to be examined with great care.

In addition the work performed by the Captain's wife would need to be monitored. Whilst the 'Arctic Systems' (*Jones v Garnett* [2007 4 All ER 857]) was decided in favour of the tax payer, HMRC's guidance and subsequently published documents and statements indicated that they will scrutinise whether the reward received by an individual is proportionate to the risks and work actually performed.

## Pension payments

Qualifying pension payments are deductible against company profits in the same way as salary. If **employee** contributions are made by the company to an individual's personal registered pension scheme they will be treated as the settlement of a pecuniary liability and will be liable to tax and NIC. The premiums received by the personal pension are limited to 100% of remuneration and are paid net of basic rate tax. Consideration should also be had to the annual allowance (£40,000 gross 2014/15 onwards; although the annual allowance is tapered for those with total income (including employer pension contributions) of £150,000 to £210,000 if their total income excluding employer pension contributions is over £110,000 from 2016/17 onwards down to a minimum of £10,000) and any unused relief brought forward. Payments in excess of the annual allowance available attract an annual allowance charge at the taxpayer's marginal rate. See **Example A6**. Higher rate tax relief will be available to the individual. Effectively there is tax leakage in such circumstances caused by the NIC liabilities, although these are mitigated by the corporation tax deduction available for the company.

If the company sets up a registered pension scheme, then its contributions are not limited to 100% of earnings and are paid gross (ITEPA 2003 s 308). The amount that can be paid should still consider the individual's annual allowance available (as mentioned above). The company will obtain tax relief on the amount that is expended wholly and exclusively for the purposes of the trade (CTA 2009 s 54). This is measured in the same way as other deductions, which are also deductible only insofar as they are expended wholly and exclusively for the purposes of the trade. One informal guideline is that an amount that would have been taxed as profit on a sole trader will generally be allowable as remuneration for a controlling director. HMRC guidance on the deductibility of pension payments states that the proportion of pension to salary in the overall remuneration package will be disregarded (see Business Income Manual 46030). On this basis, it would appear subject to the cap imposed by the annual allowance that the captain's remuneration could be paid entirely as pension for him, and the company would still obtain a tax deduction for the remuneration.

The guidance also states that large or exceptional pension contributions are likely to attract attention, particularly if they were made on behalf of a controlling director. It is likely that such a high proportion of pension would attract scrutiny.

See **Example A6 explanatory note 31** for obligations and procedures under pension's auto enrolment.

## Other matters

As a sole trader in his car-dealing business, the captain has to make tax payments on account on 31 January 2017 and 31 July 2017. The payment on 31 January 2017 will therefore be £20,100, being £13,400 for 2015/16 plus the first payment on account of 2016/17 of 50% of the 2015/16 liability. The payment on account system accentuates the fluctuations in tax liabilities for sole traders with uneven profits. The transfer of a trade to a limited company may reduce the tax liability for 2016/17. Care should be taken to make payments on account of an amount sufficient to cover the tax liability on the income retained in the captain's own name. Any reduction should be claimed using the online 'reduce payments on account' option.

The Aston Martin should not be brought into the limited company since the scale charges, which are based on its list price when new and not the advantageous price paid for it, are likely to be prohibitive. A claim of 45p per mile (25p after 10,000 miles per annum) should be made for actual business miles travelled by the captain for the company, for which the captain should keep a mileage log to evidence the business journeys. As a sole trader, the captain receives a tax deduction on the proportion of motor expenses related to business use, and bears the actual cost of private mileage out of taxed profit.

## High value dealer

As EEC does not have a clear policy that it should not accept cash for sales of €15,000 or over, it is classed as a high value dealer, and should have registered with HMRC which monitors compliance with money laundering regulations for money service businesses (MSBs) and high value dealers. There are requirements to observe policies on identification and record keeping, to check Bank of England 'financial targets' for MSBs, and to make reports to the National Crime Agency (NCA – formerly SOCA) on suspicious transactions.

EEC should have registered as soon as practicable after commencing trade, and both it and the company must now register as soon as possible. Penalties for non-compliance with these regulations are up to £5,000 for each failure to comply and there are clearly major failures.

## Accounting Standards

UK GAAP is converging with international accounting standards, and the different standards are treated as equal as a basis for preparing accounts for UK tax. For a company without intangibles, financial assets or derivatives, the differences are likely to be small. All companies are entitled to adopt IFRS for accounting periods beginning after 1 January 2005. We can prepare IFRS accounts if requested. Adoption of the full standards would involve additional work and hence higher level of fees.

(a) FRS 105 – the standard applies to micro entities for periods commencing on or after 1 January 2016, early adoption available,

(b) FRSSE 2015 (accounts to 28 February 2016 only),

(c) Section 1A of FRS 102 – new standard for small entities applying to accounting periods commencing on or after 1 January 2016. Early adoption available for periods commencing on or after 1 January 2015 onwards,

(d) FRS 102, or

(e) EU-adopted IFRS.

EEC Ltd has a number of choices when preparing its accounts for the year ended 28 February 2016 and subsequent years.

See **Explanatory note 26** below.

### (b) Money laundering

Money laundering regulations apply to accountancy services Accountants should hold identification details on file for each client and have in place procedures:

- for identifying clients;
- an ongoing monitoring of the business relationship;
- to vary due diligence in higher risk situations;
- for training staff to detect signs of money laundering;
- for reporting to the Money Laundering Reporting Officer (MLRO); and
- for the MLRO to report to NCA.

These procedures are required by the Money Laundering Regulations 2007, SI 2007/2571.

Even though the captain's identity is on file, this change in business relationship requires a further risk assessment, possibly followed by additional due diligence. We must, therefore, ensure we have details of the identity of the business and its beneficial owners, and ensure that we know the purpose of the business relationship. We are also required to obtain identification details of the ownership of the limited company and of its directors. There is an obligation to retain the records of identification for five years after the business relationship ceases.

The training the firm has received in money laundering enables us to detect the likelihood of serious incidences of money laundering. It would appear that the captain's customers have bought cars for cash, both in the case of the Audi and the Aston Martin, and then resold them (accepting a loss) in exchange for bankable funds from a reputable source, a classic form of money laundering. These suspicions must be reported immediately to the MLRO, who will probably wish to make a report to NCA as a matter of urgency.

It is an offence under the money laundering regulations to 'tip off' a suspect, subject to a maximum term of imprisonment of five years, or a fine, or both. The captain is not the suspect, but under no circumstances must any member of our staff let him, or anyone else, know that a report may be/has been made to ensure compliance with this regulation. Indeed the MRLO should not inform anyone that he has made a report to NCA. We may continue to act for him as normal, indeed there is an obligation on us to do nothing to tip him off that our suspicions have been aroused.

The captain's failure to register as a high value dealer is a compliance failure that could potentially lead to prosecution. As such, it should be reported to the MLRO, who will probably decide to make a report – particularly since, had he registered, the HMRC guidelines supplied with the registration pack would have alerted the captain to what was going on. This makes it all the more important that he notifies HMRC voluntarily as soon as possible, before an enquiry is opened in response to information received from NCA.

## Explanatory Notes

*Company formation*

(1) A company is formed by registration with Companies House, whose website https://www.gov.uk/government/organisations/companies-house from whom full details and statutory forms may be downloaded from there.

A new company must file a:

- Memorandum of Association, signed by all subscribers and stating that they wish to form a company and agree to become members of the company;
- Application for registration. CA06 s 9 sets out information and includes:

- proposed name of company;
- whether limited liability;
- whether private or public company;
- statement of capital and initial shareholdings (number of shares, aggregate nominal value and amount paid up);
- statement of proposed officers (directors and company secretary if applicable);
- articles if applicable (otherwise model articles apply);
- a statement of compliance;
- details of registered office;
- statement of guarantee if applicable.

- Payment of the registration fee – currently £15.

Details of limited companies, and their accounts, are placed in the public domain by filing with Companies House, and can be obtained on payment of a fee. There are procedures and forms for changing these details, and an annual return confirming that details remain unchanged must be filed each year. Many of the company's statutory forms, documents and returns can be filed online.

A new company comes into existence when the Registrar of Companies issues a certificate of incorporation, which may be achieved within 24 hours for a private company. There are a number of restrictions on the company names the Registrar will allow.

The types of private company available are:

- limited by shares;
- limited by guarantee; or
- unlimited.

These companies may have only one member. A company is no longer required to appoint a company secretary, and may have a sole director as the single company officer. A sole director must be a natural person, not a legal entity.

A public limited company (plc) has a higher level of regulation and cost commensurate with access to financial markets. It must have at least two members, two directors, and a qualified company secretary. The minimum issued share capital is £50,000.

A Societas Europeae (SE) is a European company. These have been available since 2004. They have regulations similar to those of the plc, and a special tax regime to facilitate trading within Europe. They may be formed by merger, as a holding company or as a subsidiary, and can also be formed by a plc transforming into an SE. There are requirements for worker participation. Details can be found at https://www.gov.uk/government/publications/european-companies-in-the-uk-registration-and-administration.

*Accounting reference date*

(2) The company must specify its accounting reference date, which cannot exceed 18 months, nor less than six months after formation. As the accounting period for corporation tax may not exceed one year, longer periods of account will have to be split.

An accounting reference date may not be extended more than once in every five years unless specific circumstances apply.

*Companies House filing deadlines*

(3) Under company law, public companies must normally file accounts with the Registrar of Companies not later than six months after the end of the accounting period, the time limit for private limited companies being nine months. There are automatic penalties for late filing, the penalties for public companies ranging from £750 if accounts are up to three months late, to £7,500 if accounts are more than twelve months late, and for private companies from £150 to £1,500. The Companies Registry interpretation of six or nine months is that the accounts are due by the same day of the month as that in which the company's account ends, e.g. accounts to 28 February 2016 should be filed by 28 August/28 November 2016.

*Notification of chargeability*

(4) A company is chargeable to corporation tax for any accounting period which has not received notice requiring a return must notify HMRC that it is so chargeable within one year of the end of that period (FA 1998 Sch 18 para 2).

Penalties for failures to notify chargeability to corporation tax are based on behaviour and depend upon whether the failure was careless, deliberate but not concealed or deliberate and concealed. The same penalty provisions apply to failure to notify liability to income tax and VAT (see **Example G1 explanatory note 6**).

The penalty is determined (as a percentage) of the potential lost revenue (PLR). This is the tax unpaid at a specified date or to which the person is liable for the relevant period. For failure to notify liability to corporation tax this is the amount unpaid 12 months following the end of the accounting period. This includes any liability under CTA 2010 s 455 (loans to participators) excluding any relief under CTA 2010 s 458 (4), (5) (repayment and release). For example, MJD Ltd, an existing dormant company with a 31 January year end commences trading on 1 February 2015. It fails to notify HMRC until 4 March 2017 when it files a return for the year to 31 January 2016 showing a liability of £30,760 and at the same time makes an online payment. The company failed to notify liability by 31 January 2017 (within 12 months of the end of the accounting period) and is therefore potentially liable to a penalty. The company's PLR is £30,760 as no tax had been paid by 31 January 2017.

The rules for penalties for late notification are similar to those for incorrect returns (see **Example G1 note 12**) although the relevant percentages are slightly different. The percentages are summarised below (they are also shown in a diagram chart at **Example G1 explanatory note 6**):

| | *Minimum Voluntary Disclosure % PLR* | *Minimum Prompted Disclosure % PLR* | *Maximum Prompted Disclosure % PLR* |
|---|---|---|---|
| ***Behaviour*** | | | |
| Careless | 10% | 20% | 30% |
| Deliberate but not concealed | 20% | 35% | 70% |
| Deliberate and concealed | 30% | 50% | 100% |

To encourage disclosure, if the failure is notified within 12 months of the tax becoming unpaid, the penalty for a careless failure to notify may be reduced for:

- a prompted disclosure from 20% to 10%
- an unprompted disclosure from 10% to 0%

Thus in the Example above, MJD Ltd made an unprompted disclosure and assuming the failure was non-deliberate and they cooperated fully the penalty could potentially be reduced to 0%.

A taxpayer can appeal against the imposition and amount of a penalty. They can also request a review of the decision to apply a penalty. HMRC also have the power to apply a 'special reduction'. The amount of the penalty may also be reduced by the amount of any other penalty determined by reference to the same tax liability. No reduction is made for a tax related penalty in connection with failure to comply with

HMRC's investigatory powers under FA 2008 Sch 36. For advice on whether a disclosure is unprompted or prompted and the 'quality' of the disclosure see penalties for incorrect returns (**Example G1 note 12**).

In practise, HMRC are informed of the incorporation of a new company by Companies House. They then issue a UTR to the company's registered office. The company must then go online and register for corporation tax, https://online.hmrc.gov.uk/registration/newbusiness/introduction. The company will need its UTR, company registration number, the start date of its first accounting period (the date that it first obtains a source of taxable income or begins to carry on a business) and its accounting reference date.

*Corporation tax self-assessment and online filing*

(5) Corporation Tax legislation is generally found in CTA 2009, CTA 2010 and TIOPA 2010. However, the provisions relating to corporation tax payment dates and interest are found in TMA 1970 ss 59D, 59DA, 59E, 87 and 87A, and ICTA 1988 ss 826 and 826A and FA 2009 s 100.

The self-assessment provisions are contained in FA 1998 s 117 and Sch 18, with minor and consequential amendments in Sch 19 and also in FA 1999 Sch 11 and FA 2001 Sch 29. FA 1998 Sch 18 is amended by ICT (Electronic communications) regulations 2009 (SI 2009/3218) and HMRC directions SI 2003/282.

Companies have to file their company tax returns online and pay their corporation tax electronically. The vast majority of companies need to file their corporation tax return, accounts and tax computations in iXBRL. XBRL is machine readable which means HMRC's computer systems can automatically interrogate it. Inline XBRL, or iXBRL effectively enables the presentation in normal, human-readable format.

To comply with the iXBRL format companies and agents can:

- Purchase commercial compliant software to produce the tax return, accounts and computations. Such software looks 'normal' with the hard work (tags) being inserted behind the screens.
- Purchase commercial compliant conversion software to enable applications such as Word or Excel to be converted to iXBRL.
- Use HMRC free software for accounts and tax computations templates in iXBRL. This is only suitable for 'less complex tax affairs'. The current product which is based on a downloadable Adobe form is to be withdrawn for accounting periods ended on or after 1 January 2016. It will be replaced by a Companies House / HMRC joint filing facility called CATO. This latter facility will only be available to unrepresented companies, and not to agents. The old software will be retained until at least 31 December 2016, allowing accounts for periods up to 31 December 2016 to be filed within the permitted deadline.
- Manually tag, see 'XBRL – when to tag, how to tag, what to tag' https://www.gov.uk/government/publications/xbrl-tagging-when-what-and-how-to-tag.

Exceptions to full iXBRL online filing:

– Where directors (and any company secretary) are all practising members of a religious society or order whose beliefs are incompatible with the use of electronic methods of communications. In such cases it is necessary to write to HMRC providing full details to confirm exemption from online filing.

– In certain cases where a company is subject to a winding up order, in administrative receivership or managed by an administrator.

– Unincorporated bodies such as clubs and associations and some charities that do not have to prepare statutory accounts under CA 2006 must file online tax returns and computations but can submit accounts as a PDF or iXBRL.

A company only satisfies its filing obligation when it delivers online the completed corporation tax return CT600 (and relevant supplementary additions) together with a copy of its full financial statements and tax computations in the prescribed format.

The most important supplementary additions are:

| | |
|---|---|
| CT600A | For loans made to participators of close companies. |
| CT600B | For tax liabilities of controlled foreign companies. |
| CT600C | For claims to and surrenders of group and consortium relief. |
| CT600E | Charities and Community Amateur Sports Clubs. |
| CT600J | Disclosure of tax avoidance schemes. |

The company tax return CT600 contains a self-assessment of the amount of tax payable, including the tax on loans or advances by close companies' participators and tax relating to controlled foreign companies. This self-assessment creates the charge to tax.

HMRC have published an updated version (version 3; version 2 was published in 2008) of the company tax return CT600. The new version must be used for accounting periods starting on or after 1 April 2015. Version 2 must continue to be used for accounting period that start before 1 April 2015, including those that span 1 April 2015. There is no longer a "short" version of the form and the new form is eleven pages compared to the previous eight.

*Filing dates*

(6) HMRC issue a notice to deliver a corporation tax return (CT603) between three and seven weeks after the end of the return period. Tax agents receive a monthly listing (CT603A list) detailing their client companies to whom a CT603 has been sent. With the switch to compulsory online filing HMRC have ceased to issue paper forms CT600 with the CT603. The CT603 notice should be for the period that HMRC believes to be an accounting period of the company.

Dormant companies do not usually receive a notice to complete a corporation tax return, but if they do, then technically a nil return is required. The company should write to inform the officer that the company is dormant and ask whether the return is required. It is important not to ignore the notice, otherwise penalties may arise. Dormant companies may occasionally receive a form CT204 to review whether a return is required. This form asks if the company is trading, has any income/gains, is in liquidation/administration and the director's future intentions.

A notice to deliver a corporation tax return might specify a period that does not coincide with the company's accounting period. If so, the company has to make a return for any accounting period(s) ending in the specified period. If a period of account started but none ended within the specified period, a nil return has to be made for the period up to the date the period of account started. If the specified period is less than twelve months and falls wholly within an accounting period of the company, a return does not have to be made but the officer should be notified. If the company is outside the scope of corporation tax throughout the specified period (e.g. because it is non-resident and not trading in the UK, or because it is dormant), a nil return should be filed.

The return must usually be filed within one year of the end of the period of account for corporation tax, failing which penalties will be incurred.

If a *period of account* exceeds twelve months but does not exceed 18 months, the due date for filing the returns for the accounting periods within that period of account is twelve months from the end of the period of account, if later than the normal due date. If a period of account exceeds 18 months, the due date is 30 months after the beginning of the account, or the normal due date if later. For example, if accounts are made up for the 18 months from 1 October 2014 to 31 March 2016, the returns for the accounting periods to 30 September 2015 and 31 March 2016 are both due by 31 March 2017. If the accounts were made up instead for the 21 months from 1 October 2014 to 30 June 2016, the return for the accounting period to 30 September 2015 would still be due by 31 March 2017 (30 months after the start of the account). The return for the nine months to 30 June 2016 would be due by 30 June 2017 (twelve months after the end of the account).

A flat rate penalty of £100 is charged if the return is no more than three months late, and £200 if more than three months, but these rise to £500 and £1,000 if the returns are late for more than three accounting periods in a row.

In addition, if the company does not file a return within 18 months of the end of the accounting period and has not paid the right amount of tax, a tax related penalty of 10% is imposed. This rises to 20% if the return is late by 24 months or more.

FA 2009 s 106 and Sch 55 introduced new late filing penalties across the range of taxes (IT, CT, PAYE, NIC, CIS, SDLT, SDRT, IHT, pension and petroleum tax) excluding tax credits. Taxpayers have a right of appeal against all penalties and no penalty can be charged if they have a reasonable excuse. Penalties can be suspended where the taxpayer agrees a time to pay arrangement (subject to meeting the terms of the arrangement). Implementation of the new penalties requires changes to HMRC's computer systems and so the new penalties are being introduced in stages. The new late filing penalties have been introduced for income tax, bank payroll tax, pension scheme returns, PAYE and the construction industry scheme. The date of the introduction of the new rules for corporation tax has not yet been announced.

When introduced, the following late filing penalties will apply to corporation tax returns filed late:

- £100 penalty;
- daily penalties of £10 per day up to a max of 90 days;
- penalties of the greater of £300 or 5% of tax due (tax payable for period) for prolonged failures (over six and at twelve months);
- higher penalties of 70% of the tax due where a person fails to submit a return for over twelve months and has deliberately withheld information necessary to assess the tax due (100% penalty if deliberate with concealment).

*Payment of tax*

(7) See **Example I1 explanatory note 15**.

*Claims and elections*

(8) General provisions on claims are in FA 1998 Sch 18 paras 9 and 10 and Part VII. All claims must be for a specified amount and must be made where possible in a return or amendment to a return, although there is an overall time limit for most claims of four years from the end of the accounting period. Claims for group relief (Part VIII) and capital allowances (Part IX) can only be made in a return or amendment to a return. Where it is not possible to make claims on a return the provisions of TMA 1970 Sch 1A apply (see **Example G2**).

Unless HMRC otherwise allows, the time limit for capital allowances claims is the latest of twelve months after the filing date for the return, 30 days after the completion of a HMRC enquiry, 30 days after the issue of a HMRC amendment following an enquiry, and 30 days after the date when any appeal against such an amendment is finally determined. See **Example J5** regarding group relief claims.

*Keeping records*

(9) Companies are required to keep sufficient records to make a correct and complete return. These records must be kept until the sixth anniversary of the end of the period for which the company may be required to deliver a tax return, and there is a penalty of up to £3,000 per accounting period for failing to comply. The records, or the information in them, may be preserved in any form or by any means.

*HMRC corrections and taxpayer amendments*

(10) HMRC have nine months from the date a return is received to correct obvious errors in the return, and companies can make amendments within a year from the filing date. If the return is selected for further enquiry, amendments within the permitted twelve-month period will not restrict the scope of the enquiry but may be taken into account in the enquiry. If an amendment affects the tax payable for the current or another period, or by another company, it will not take effect unless and until it is incorporated in the closure notice issued to the company at the end of the enquiry (see **explanatory note 11**).

Taxpayers have a statutory right to repayment where tax has been overpaid (from 1 April 2010 under FA 2009 s 100). Repayment claims are subject to a self-assessment style regime with HMRC rights of enquiry. The time limit for claims is four years. This section replaces the previous 'error or mistake' rules.

*HMRC enquiries*

(11) Under FA 1998 Sch 18 para 24, unless a CT600 return is filed late, HMRC must initiate an enquiry into the return by the first anniversary of the date the return was filed for a single company or a company that is a member of a small group. Thus for a small company with an accounting period ended 31 December 2016, with the CTSA return filed 31 March 2017 the enquiry window closes on 31 March 2018. For larger groups HMRC retains the old time limit of two years after the end of the accounting period, although in practice, agreement can be reached to limit the enquiry window to 12 months after the date of the last filed return for any group company.

See **Example G6 explanatory note 24** regarding referring questions to the Tribunal during an enquiry, and see **Example G3** regarding HMRC enquiries into claims made separately from the return.

An enquiry may either be an aspect enquiry raising one or more specific queries in relation to the return, or it may be a full enquiry including a comprehensive review of the accounts and underlying records. HMRC have wide powers to request further information, documents etc. for the purpose of their enquiry.

HMRC CTSA guidance provides useful information about their approach to enquiries under CTSA. For example, it states that where relevant records are required for examination by HMRC they should be provided within a reasonable time. A request may be made to examine them at the company's premises, as this may be more convenient. Similarly, HMRC may request a meeting with relevant officers or employees of the company and their professional adviser. The company may be asked to comment on HMRC's notes of the meeting (noting any disagreement) and sign them. However, HMRC officers have powers to enter any business premises to inspect the premises and/or the records, if this is reasonably required for the purpose of checking the tax return. They are required to give at least 24 hours' notice, or to obtain authorisation from a senior officer.

A company may be invited to make a payment on account during the enquiry process to mitigate its potential interest exposure, although it is not legally obliged to pay any additional tax until HMRC invites it to amend its self-assessment.

A closure notice will be issued by HMRC when they conclude their enquiry, together with their findings. HMRC undertake to agree their findings with the company before inviting an amended return in accordance with their proposed adjustments. If the company disagrees and does not amend the return within the relevant 30-day window, HMRC make their own amendments, which can then be subject to the appeals process. (If the return or an amendment to it is made after the due date, the enquiry window runs from a year from the time the return or amendment is delivered plus the period to the next quarter day, ie the next 31 January, 30 April, 31 July or 31 October.) If an enquiry is not opened within the time limit, the tax as calculated will normally stand unless there is a HMRC 'discovery assessment' (see **explanatory note 13** below).

*Compliance checks*

(12) FA 2008 introduced new powers to enable HMRC to check that businesses and individuals have paid the correct amount of tax (IT, CGT, CT, VAT and PAYE). These powers are extensive and have been applied from 1 April 2009. The powers include the right to request information from the taxpayer, from third parties, and to visit business premises to carry out a check. Since 2008, these powers have regularly been added to, with new powers allowing HMRC to demand information from a wide variety of third parties on a 'bulk' basis – that is, not in respect of a named taxpayer, but in relation to any and all; for example, HMRC annually ask rental letting agents for detailed information about rent they have collected on behalf of landlords, together with the names and addresses of the landlords for whom the agent acts, and amounts due to each.

FA 2008 Sch 36 Part 1 can be exercised without opening a formal enquiry. HMRC can issue information notices to any person requiring the production of information and or documents provided it is reasonably required to check a company's tax position (Sch 36 Part 1 para 1 taxpayer notices and para 2 third party notices). The notice may be appealed against unless it relates to the production of statutory records which the taxpayer is obliged to keep or the First-tier Tribunal approved the issue of the notice. F(No 3)A 2011 s 86 extended the third party data gathering powers to include bulk data collected for risk assessment and provides a penalty if a person is aware of an inaccuracy when providing such information or documents.

Schedule 36 Part 2 (para 10) provides the power to inspect business premises including vehicles and parts of homes used for business purposes and inspect documents on those premises (provided reasonably required) for the purposes of checking that company's tax position. They cannot search premises and as stated in HMRC Compliance Handbook manual at CH25650 'the person . . . has the right to refuse you entry'. Therefore even when an officer has been given access to the premises he can be asked to leave at any time. HMRC's instructions make it clear that the officer must leave straight away. Where there is no reasonable excuse for the obstruction, HMRC may apply a penalty of £300 where the inspection was preapproved by a tribunal.

Business records become statutory records when they are created. The normal time limit for a company to retain their statutory records is six years. For example, on 1 July 2016 a company with a year end of 31 December who has filed all tax returns on time and has not been subject to an enquiry in the last six years will hold statutory records for the period 1 January 2009 to 1 July 2016.

An information notice or inspection may only be issued where it is 'reasonably required to check a person's tax position'. However, when a return has been made for the period, the notice must be issued within the enquiry window, unless a discovery has been made. Notices may, however, be issued in respect of periods for which no return has yet been made. Also the enquiry window principle does not apply to PAYE and VAT compliance checks.

HMRC has significantly changed its approach to compliance over the last few years. One target was to reduce the administrative burden around audits and inspections for businesses considered to be tax compliant. This works with large businesses where a business risk review is carried out and a low/high risk rating is given. Obtaining a low risk rating has considerable benefits.

In 2013, HMRC completed a trial/consultation on the Single Compliance Process (SCP). This is a framework for SME compliance checks, also known as 'standard working SME'. The main features/differences are:

- More focus on risks and behaviours with a proportional response, e.g. a different response where the risk is £10 in tax compared to £10,000.
- Early dialogue with customers. Where a meeting is deemed appropriate it will be requested much earlier than present as considered a quicker way to resolve. Also more requests for telephone contact.
- Where appropriate, sharing concerns about the risks that led to the intervention. For example, HMRC reviewing a new pub and concerned about a large capital allowances claim. The initial opening letter may say 'I will be looking at the capital allowances to understand what assets are involved and so that I can verify the amount claimed'.
- On site reviews to use sampling techniques to examine perceived risk areas as opposed to a full review of all records.
- More use of covert activities and unannounced visits, in appropriate cases.
- Meeting notes no longer issued as standard.

*Senior accounting officers (SAO)*

(13) Although not relevant in this Example, senior accounting officers of large companies are annually required to personally certify that their company's accounting systems are adequate for the purposes of accurate tax reporting (FA 2009 s 93). Large companies need to notify the name and contact details of the SAO to their Customer Relationship Manager at HMRC within 6 (PLC) or 9 (Ltd co) months after the end of the accounting period. The certificate of compliance must be submitted by the filing deadline for the accounts (or such later time as allowed by HMRC). Failure to comply makes the officer personally liable to a penalty of £5,000.

It is important to identify if the company is close to becoming a 'large' company and ensuring procedures are implemented to ensure that the SAO can certify that the company's systems are robust and adequate to provide an accurate self-assessment of corporation tax.

HMRC guidance can be found in a separate manual http://www.hmrc.gov.uk/manuals/saogmanual/index.htm.

*Interest and penalties on overdue and overpaid tax*

(14) Interest on overdue and overpaid corporation tax (including tax on close company loans to participators) is deductible/taxable as non-trading interest under the 'loan relationships' provisions (see **Example K2**). If interest on overpaid tax is received or receivable by a company in liquidation in its final accounting period, however, the interest is not included in taxable profits if it does not exceed £2,000. The rates of interest are adjusted to reflect the fact that the interest is taken into account in computing taxable profits, but the rate on underpaid tax is still much higher than that on overpaid tax.

Regardless of when leap years occur HMRC uses a denominator of 366 in all calculations of interest on overdue tax and a denominator of 365 for interest on overpaid tax, which in each case gives a slight benefit to the taxpayer company.

Interest regimes for the different taxes (including CT) were harmonised by FA 2009 (SI 2009/2032).

The penalty regime for late payment of tax is being reformed. FA 2009 s 107 introduces new late payment penalties across the range of taxes (IT, CT, PAYE, NIC, CIS, SDLT, SDRT, IHT, pension and petroleum tax) excluding tax credits. Taxpayers have a right of appeal against all penalties and no penalty can be charged if they have a reasonable excuse. Penalties can be suspended where the taxpayer agrees a time to pay arrangement (subject to meeting the terms of the arrangement). Implementation of the new penalties requires changes to HMRC's computer systems and so will be introduced in stages. The implementation date for corporation tax has not yet been announced.

Once in force for corporation tax the following late payment penalties will arise:

- penalties of 5% of the amount of tax unpaid one month after the payment due date;
- further penalties of 5% of any amount of tax still unpaid at six and twelve months after the payment due date.

*HMRC determinations and assessments*

(15) As with income tax self-assessment, HMRC are able to determine the tax payable in the absence of a return, and this will count as a self-assessment until superseded by an actual self-assessment. HMRC may still make discovery assessments under the self-assessment regime (FA 1998 Sch 18 para 41). Note that losses and other negative amounts are subject to self-assessment and are thus incorporated within the figure of tax payable under HMRC determination. They may also make 'discovery determinations' where a return incorrectly states an amount that affects another period or another company, see **Example G2 explanatory note 15.**

*Penalties for incorrect tax returns*

(16) Penalties for inaccurate documents (including returns) are based on a scale of percentages depending on the taxpayer's behaviour, and are applied to tax lost or delayed.

| *Behaviour* | *Maximum penalty % Potential Lost Revenue* | *Minimum penalty % Potential Lost Revenue* |
|---|---|---|
| Mistake after reasonable care | 0% | 0% |
| Careless | 30% | 0% |
| Deliberate not concealed | 70% | 20% |
| Deliberate and concealed | 100% | 30% |

HMRC are required to mitigate penalties for co-operation, broken down into prompted/unprompted disclosure, providing HMRC with reasonable help and with access to records.

The penalty provisions are covered in more detail in **Example G2**.

*Employment-related securities – reportable events*

(17) A report is required to be made to HMRC of securities issued in connection with employment. For 2014/15 onwards these details must to be returned online (the paper form 42 has been withdrawn) (FA 2003 Sch 22).

Reportable events must be notified to HMRC, online, by 6 July following the year in which the securities were issued, failing which penalties commencing at £300 per reportable event per employee may be charged.

Reportable events include acquisitions, transfers and disposals of securities, rights issues or alteration in the values and rights of securities. Securities include shares, debentures, loan stock, bonds, certificates of deposit, warrants, futures, units in collective investment schemes and rights under contracts for differences, all issued in connection with employment.

A report of the issue of such securities is required unless one of the exemptions applies. It is emphasised that these rules are concerned with the transfer of shares in connection with employment. Transfers of shares in the normal course of domestic, family or personal relationships do not have to be reported. However, it is up to the transferor to determine whether the transfer is being made for purely personal reasons, and to be able to demonstrate this. HMRC specifically states that it will accept that shares passing to children involved in the business will be considered as being made in the normal course of family relationships. However, if any element of remuneration rather than gift, is shown to be present, a report would be required (and the transfer would be liable to income tax and national insurance).

The transfer of founder shares to the owners of the new company need not be reported (see HMRC guidance issued April 2006) provided:

- all the initial shares are obtained at nominal value; and
- the shares are the only form of security that is obtained; and
- their shares are not acquired by reason of another employment; and
- the shares are acquired by a person who is to be a director of the company, or by somebody with a family relationship with the director (provided the transfer is in the normal course of family relationships, rather than by reason of employment).

Similarly, if prospective directors or other family members acquire additional shares before trading commences, a return will not be required. However, if additional shares are issued after the company commences trading, then a return is required but only for the shares issued after commencement of trade.

A report is only required if a reportable event occurs in the tax year, unless HMRC have issued a return, in which case it must be filed whether there was a reportable event or not. A report is not required for HMRC approved share schemes and options, as these have their own specific reporting requirements. For Enterprise Management Incentives (EMI), the grant of options up to the EMI limit of £250,000 will be reported on a special scheme form, while the excess over £250,000 must be reported on an employment related securities return.

The requirement affects not just current employees but directors and office holders, prospective employees, and former employees where the event was within seven years of the ex-employee leaving.

For unrestricted shares, the information required is the name of the employee, the employer's name, the description of the shares, date of transfer, number of shares, market value, price and whether PAYE was applied.

It is important to consider these reporting requirements whenever a security is transferred.

*Goodwill on incorporation after 3 December 2014*

(18) Where a sole trader or partner disposes of goodwill to a company that they control, the transfer is one between connected persons, so takes place at market value for tax purposes. A capital gain arises in this case for the individual (for disposals on or after 3 December 2014 entrepreneur's relief is no longer available on the sale of business goodwill)), while an asset and director's loan account will be established in the company's records.

Following the changes to the taxation of goodwill, the tax reliefs available on the disposal of goodwill and related intangible assets on incorporations on or after 3 December 2014 are:

(a) Incorporation hold-over relief. Under TCGA 1992 s 162 the gain on the disposal of the whole business is rolled over against the cost of the shares acquired.

(b) Gift relief. Under TCGA 1992 s 165 all or part of the gain on the disposal of one or more business assets are held over on a gift.

See **Examples L5** and **N2**.

The key difficulty is establishing the value of goodwill and to what it is attributable.

Where, as in the case of the skills of an individual tradesman, the goodwill is inseparable from the individual (termed personal goodwill), it is not capable of being transferred to the company. It is essential to demonstrate that goodwill attaches to the business rather than the owner or location of business premises. The goodwill associated with a particular location can be transferred to a Limited Company, if the Limited Company also obtains an interest in the property. Any goodwill which is able to be separated from the location of the business and the proprietor is known as free goodwill. It is the true worth of a business over and above its net assets. It is not fixed with any particular attribute of the business although there can be a slight overlap with the owner and or location. It could include the organisation separate from the owner, brand names, general reputation, contracts and or transferable customer lists.

The disposal of goodwill must be reported in the capital gains tax section of the individual's self-assessment return.

A tax deduction is available on goodwill acquired from a connected person if the goodwill was created wholly after 31 March 2002 and the transfer was before 3 December 2014. Where the goodwill has arisen through trading (internally generated goodwill) the date the goodwill is regarded as created for these purposes is the date that trade commenced (CTA 2009 s 882). Any pre-1 April 2002 assets (including goodwill) acquired from a related party are outside the intangible fixed asset rules. HMRC's view was supported in the case of *Greenbank Holidays Ltd v CRC* 6 April 2011. In this case, two connected companies, the trade of one was sold to other in 2003. The taxpayer tried to argue goodwill was only created on sale in 2003. The court upheld the HMRC view that although not recognised in the accounts goodwill existed before this date.

In circumstances where a connected party asset was created after 1 April 2002 and transferred before 3 December 2014 relief will normally be available. HMRC may seek to deny relief where the transaction was mainly motivated by tax avoidance (CTA 2009 s 864).

Where qualifying the company can claim a tax deduction for the purchased goodwill based on the amount amortised in their accounts in accordance with FRS 102. This applies from January 2015 and requires such intangibles to be written off over their economic life. Economic life is restricted to five years unless the company can determine otherwise (and can only exceed 20 years in exceptional circumstances).

The company may pay for the goodwill, but often will credit its value to a director's loan account. The director's loan may provide a means of extracting funds from the company without incurring a tax liability.

*Sale of goodwill at overvalue*

(19) HMRC offers a free post-transaction value check service, but as its name implies it can only be requested after the event has occurred.

If it proves that goodwill was transferred at overvalue, under exceptional circumstances it is possible to unwind the transaction, and have the individual repay the company or reduce the directors' loan account. Alternatively if the incorporation of the business involved a formal sale agreement between the company and the former proprietor, then a 'tax adjuster' clause may have be included and become active. This will substitute the correct market values for the assets acquired into the sale agreement.

This is only possible where the business goodwill was formally valued by a named qualified valuer, who was given adequate information to determine the value. However, if the reduction in the loan account causes it to become overdrawn, income tax will be due on the benefit, and tax may become payable under CTA 2010 s 455. In most cases it is likely to give rise to a tax charge, either as income of employment, or as a distribution.

If excess goodwill is shown to be an inducement for the individual to join the company, or to represent payment for future services, it will be treated as income of employment under ITEPA 2003 s 62. The company is required to account for income tax and national insurance contributions under RTI PAYE regulations, failing which penalties and interest will apply. It may, under certain circumstances, represent a benefit reportable on form PllD.

Where there is no evidence that the excess goodwill represents earnings from employment, particularly when transferred before the company commences trade: the excess will be treated as a distribution. If the distribution does not cause the individual to exceed the higher rate band, no further tax will arise on the individual.

*The money laundering regulations – tax practitioners*

(20) The Money Laundering Regulations 2007 apply the Proceeds of Crime Act 2003 and the Terrorism Act 2000 to regulating affected businesses.

The purpose of the regulations is to require relevant businesses to make reports to NCA of any knowledge or suspicions of money laundering activity. However, this is limited to knowledge or suspicions acquired in the course of business or employment, not knowledge acquired through personal social connections.

Firms affected must appoint an individual as the money laundering reporting officer (MLRO) to receive money laundering reports from staff, and to make reports to NCA. All staff must be trained in the recognition and reporting of potential money laundering transactions, and how to verify the identity of new clients.

The Money Laundering Regulations 2007 (SI 2007/2157) set out number of specific requirements, including 'due diligence', and record keeping.

**Due diligence:**

'Customer due diligence measures' (approximately equivalent to 'know your customer' procedures) involve identifying the customer and verifying the customer's identity on the basis of documents, data or information obtained from a reliable and independent source, and identifying the beneficial owner, if this is not the customer, and taking measures to establish their identity, and obtaining information on the purpose or intended nature of the business relationship.

**Ongoing monitoring**

There is a requirement for ongoing monitoring of the business relationship, which is defined as meaning:

- scrutiny of transactions undertaken throughout the course of the relationship, including the source of funds, to ensure that the transactions are consistent with the firm's knowledge of the customer, the business and the risk profile;
- retention of documentation obtained for the purpose of customer due diligence;
- enhanced customer due diligence must be applied on risk-sensitive basis, for instance where the customer is not physically present for identification.

**Record-keeping:**

The records, which must be kept for at least five years, are:

- a copy of the customers identity documentation;
- supporting records in respect of the business relationship which is the subject of customer due diligence and ongoing monitoring.

Businesses may rely on others for due diligence purposes, but they must have the agreement of the person being relied upon, and they are responsible for ensuring that the person can provide the necessary documentation plus it is correct. There is a slight relaxation from 2012 on whose due diligence can be relied upon: it is now anyone who is a member of a professional body listed in Schedule 3 of the MLR.

HMRC have issued revised Money Laundering Regulations 2007 (MLR 2007) which are intended for businesses registered with HMRC, and which are considered to form guidance for POCA 2004 and the Terrorism Act 2000.

These regulations summarise money laundering obligations as follows:

'**MLR 2007 Regulation 20** sets out the requirement for relevant businesses to establish and maintain appropriate and risk-sensitive policies and procedures relating to:

- customer due diligence;
- reporting;
- record keeping;
- internal control;
- risk assessment and management;
- the monitoring and management of compliance; and
- the internal communication of such policies and procedures, in order to prevent activities related to money laundering and terrorist financing.

These policies and procedures must include arrangements that:

- Identify and scrutinise
  - complex or unusually large transactions;
  - unusual patterns of transactions which have no apparent economic or visible lawful purpose;
  - any other activity which could be considered to be related to money laundering or terrorist financing;
- specify the additional measures that will be taken to prevent the use of products and transactions that favour anonymity for money laundering or terrorist financing;
- determine whether a customer is a politically exposed person (person holding a prominent public function outside the UK, or their associates);
- nominate an individual in the organisation to receive disclosures under Part 7 of POCA and Part 3 of TA;
- ensure employees report suspicious activity to the Nominated Officer; and

- ensure the Nominated Officer considers such internal reports in the light of available information and determines whether they give rise to knowledge or suspicion or reasonable grounds for knowledge or suspicion of money laundering or terrorist financing.'

The CCAB (treasury approved) guidance on money laundering, issued in December 2007, applies to accountancy and tax businesses, including those that are supervised by HMRC. (www.gov.uk/government/uploads/system/uploads/attachment_data/file/200701/aml_hmt_approved_guidance.pdf). This guidance is essentially similar to Money Laundering Regulations (MLR) 2007, being based on the same SI, but is applied to the circumstances of accountancy businesses.

The form of identification to be obtained is not specified by the Act, but is determined by the firm's own policies via a risk-based approach, and specific details and circumstances relating to acceptable identity are set out in MLR 2007. Furthermore, a firm's customer due diligence procedures need not be standard for all clients, but may vary on a risk-based approach. The guidance given them by the Joint Money Laundering Steering Group (originally intended FSA supervised businesses), is often followed, and this guidance was used in the preparation of MLR 2007. The offences to be reported include any criminal activity giving rise to proceeds, and in particular are not limited to terrorism or drug dealing. The proceeds of crime, termed criminal property, include the proceeds of tax evasion, bribery, or costs saved by failure to comply with regulatory requirements (where the failure to comply is a criminal offence). There is no de minimis limit for the value of the proceeds of crime to be reported, so even the smallest transactions may require a report. Requests for a de minimis for small businesses were considered and rejected in 2012 on the basis risk is not related to the size of a business and small payments or receipts can relate to serious crimes (an example given was the purchase of child pornography where sales were for trivial amounts in business terms but the crime was very serious).

Reports must be made as soon as is reasonably possible to NCA on a suspicious activity reports (SAR), and can be made online at http://www.nationalcrimeagency.gov.uk/. The details to be reported are specified on this site. The client should never be made aware of the adviser's suspicions because tipping off is a criminal offence.

Accountants and tax advisers in practice are expected to make reports on clients in circumstances where failure to comply with tax regulations has led to underpayment of tax or late payment.

The fourth European Money Laundering Directive, which is the source of the UK's MLR, was formally adopted in the UK in June 2015. The UK has two years to transpose the directive into national legislation. At this stage, the impact on tax professionals is expected to be minor. The biggest impact is expected to be in relation to increasing the transparency of beneficial owners. From January 2016, the Small Business, Enterprise and Employment Act 2015 will require UK companies to create and maintain a register of people who have "significant control" over the company.

*Legal privilege*

(21) In a relatively narrow range of circumstances, such as litigation or giving legal advice where making a report to NCA would compromise the client's rights to legal privilege, qualified accountants have the same legal privilege as the legal profession allowing them to claim protection from reporting suspicious transactions. This applies only to money laundering, not offences under the Terrorism Act 2000.

In 2010 following consultation regarding the reform of legal services, the Institute of Chartered Accountants of England & Wales argued to obtain wider legal professional privilege (LPP) for additional areas of the work undertaken by accountants and tax advisers. LPP has continued to be the subject of much debate, especially following the judgment in the *Prudential* case. The court held that LPP is available only in relation to advice from lawyers.

*Money laundering – HMRC responsibilities*

(22) HMRC has the responsibility for administering the money laundering regulations in respect of:

- money service businesses (MSB);
- high value dealers (HVD);

- trust and company service providers (TCSP);
- accountancy service providers (ASP).

Members regulated by specified recognised legal, accountancy or bookkeeping professional bodies are supervised by those bodies. All other businesses within the scope of the regulations are required to register with HMRC.

*Accountancy service providers (ASPs)*

Members of designated professional tax, accountancy and bookkeeping bodies continue to be regulated by those bodies, not by HMRC.

Unlike other businesses supervised by HMRC for money laundering regulations, ASPs:

- MLR 2007 requires ASPs to follow CCAB guidance rather than the MLR 2007 guidance;
- ASPs are not required to complete the 'fit and proper' test.

Registration is based on business premises and the fee is currently £110 per premises. Those with no business premises i.e. working from home have to list and pay a fee for their home address or contact address.

Accountancy service providers are businesses providing external accountancy, bookkeeping, payroll, and tax services. Internal providers are specifically excluded.

HMRC registration guide for accountancy service providers https://www.gov.uk/government/publications/notice-mlr9d-registration-guide-for-accountancy-service-providers.

*Trust or company service providers*

Services such as company formation, trustee, nominee, or representation services are not covered by the ASP designation, but by the trust or company service provider (TCSP) designation. HMRC have, however, stated that firms providing such services that are members of specified recognised legal, accountancy or bookkeeping professional bodies do not need to register with HMRC, but continue to be governed by those bodies.

TCSPs that are not governed by a specified professional body are required to register and complete a 'fit and proper' test.

HMRC registration guide for TCSP https://www.gov.uk/government/publications/notice-mlr9c-registration-guide-for-trust-or-company-service-providers.

HMRC general guidance https://www.gov.uk/money-laundering-regulations-introduction.

*MSBs and HVDs*

Failure to register or to comply with money laundering regulations may lead to prosecution by HMRC, or civil penalties. Businesses must register as soon as possible on commencing the above activities, which need not be their sole or main activities.

A money service business (MSB) is a business that carries out the activities of:

- bureau de change; or
- transferring a customer's money (money transmission); or
- third party cheque cashing.

Banks and businesses regulated by the FSA do not need to be registered under the MSB scheme.

The registration number issued to the MSB forms part of its identity, which it will use in its dealings with banks and other MSBs. A register is kept of all businesses not covered by the FSA register covering bureaux de change, money transmitters and third party cheque cashers.

A high value dealer (HVD) is any business that does not have a clear policy of not accepting payments over €15,000 per transaction in cash.

MSBs and HVDs are required to complete 'fit and proper' tests as well as registering. Specific additional requirements apply to them and to money transmission businesses, but basic requirements are essentially the same.

HMRC registration guide for MSB https://www.gov.uk/government/publications/notice-mlr9a-registration-guide-for-money-service-businesses.

HMRC general guidance for MSB https://www.gov.uk/money-laundering-regulations-money-service-business-registration.

HMRC registration guide for HVD https://www.gov.uk/government/publications/notice-mlr9b-money-laundering-regulations-registration-guide-for-high-value-dealers.

HMRC general guidance for HVD https://www.gov.uk/money-laundering-regulations-high-value-dealer-registration.

*Penalties*

**Civil Penalties**

HMRC have the power to impose civil penalties on businesses that fail to comply with the requirements of the Money Laundering Regulations in respect of:

- notification and registration requirements;
- customer due diligence measures;
- ongoing monitoring of a business relationship;
- enhanced customer due diligence and ongoing monitoring;
- record-keeping;
- policies and procedures to prevent money laundering and terrorist financing;
- appointing a Nominated Officer and internal reporting procedures;
- training of employees.

Penalties will be for an amount that is considered appropriate for the purposes of being effective, proportionate and dissuasive, with no upper limit.

Penalty and registration decisions can also be appealed to the VAT and Duties Tribunal.

*Criminal offences*

The Money Laundering Regulations 2007 provide for criminal sanctions for failure to comply with the detailed requirements of the regulations, by fine or prison sentence of up to two years. This includes failures relating to registration, customer due diligence, ongoing monitoring, verification, ceasing transactions, enhanced due diligence, record keeping and training. These are in additions to offences under POCA 2002 or the Terrorism Act 2000.

HMRC guidance on appeals and penalties under MLR https://www.gov.uk/money-laundering-regulations-appeals-and-penalties#3.

*Countering tax avoidance*

(23) See **Example N5** for details of HMRC's general anti-abuse rule (GAAR).

*International information and gathering powers*

(24) FA 2006 ss 173–177 provide for the cancellation of existing agreements to exchange information with overseas tax authorities, and replace them with arrangements giving increased powers to collect and disclose information. In addition, it provides for the possibility of recovery of foreign tax debts through UK courts, and therefore the recovery of UK tax debts in foreign courts.

These powers may have a greater effect on tax fraud rather than tax avoidance. Furthermore, HMRC obtained disclosure orders against banks, requiring them to disclose details of all offshore accounts held by customers with UK addresses and details of holders of credit cards linked to offshore accounts. This move does not change existing law, but has the effect of policing it more stringently.

F(No 3)A 2011 s 87 and Sch 25 introduced legislation to enable the UK to implement the Mutual Assistance Recovery Directive (MARD) agreed by the EU in 2010. The Directive applies from 1 January 2012. Under this Directive EU member states can provide each other with assistance in the recovery of tax debts and duties, which includes service of documents and exchanging information in connection with the recovery of claims. The legislation replaces and repeals the existing MARD set out in FA 2002 s 134 and Sch 39.

From 2013 the UK entered into enhanced automatic tax information exchange agreements with a number of individual countries, e.g. an agreement with the US to implement the reporting required under US FATCA legislation. They also participated in a pilot to develop a common approach to automatically exchanging financial information on a wider scale. This was supported by the G20 and OECD and led to the development of the Common Reporting Standard (CRS). The CRS came into force as European law on 1 January 2015 via the revised Directive on Administrative Cooperation (Council Directive 2014/107/EU). This is effected into UK law via the International Tax Compliance Regulations 2015 (SI2015/878). These regulations, require financial institutions to identify (includes due diligence procedures), collect and report specified information in a specified manner to HMRC.

Under CRS more than 90 countries will automatically exchange taxpayer information. The UK will begin to receive information on offshore accounts and financial assets under CRS from 2017 and at the same time will begin to share information with other tax authorities on accounts held in the UK. (Until that date information will continue to be shared under existing agreements with individual countries.)

F(No2)A 2015 s 46 introduces a power under which financial intermediaries and tax advisers will be required to notify their customers about the existence of the CRS, the penalties for tax evasion and the opportunities to disclose offshore evasion to HMRC.

*Accounting Standards and tax law*

(25) The relationship between accounting practice and law is stated in CTA 2009 s 46: 'the profits of a trade, must be calculated in accordance with generally accepted accounting practice subject to any adjustment required or authorised by law . . . '.

Generally Accepted Accounting Practice (GAAP) is defined in CTA 2010 s 1127 as follows: 'UK generally accepted accounting practice means generally accepted accounting practice in relation to accounts of UK companies (other than IAS accounts) that are intended to give a true and fair view . . . '. The same section specifies that this definition applies to individuals, non-UK companies and entities other than companies.

As GAAP is increasingly codified and becoming more uniform, there is a trend to align profits for tax with accounting profits. Furthermore, it is the intention of the FRC (Financial Reporting Council replaced the Accounting Standard's Board) to align UK GAAP with IFRS (International Financial Reporting Standards). See explanatory note below. It is the intention of the legislation that companies drawing up their accounts under either set of standards should receive broadly equivalent tax treatment.

While it is government policy to align tax and accounting profits, there will continue to be departures from the accounting rules, whether from IFRS-based accounts or from UK GAAP. There are a great many departures, arising from public policy, in the areas of anti-avoidance, the distinctions between capital and revenue, fiscal incentives or valuation rules. Also changes in accounting standards can create unintentional tax issues. For example F(No 3)A 2011 s 53 introduced rules to counter changes in accounting for leases. The section seeks to continue the existing tax treatment. Examples of differences between accounting and tax rules are given in context throughout the publication, and particularly in **Example I1**.

*International Financial Reporting Standards (IFRS)*

(26) Historically, most countries have had their own accounting standards. The primary objective of the IASB (International Accounting Standards Board) is to produce a set of accounting standards which are intended to be adopted on a worldwide level. To that end, International Financial Reporting Standards (IFRS) were introduced in 2005 by the European Union.

For accounting periods commencing after 1 January 2005, publicly-traded companies have been required to prepare consolidated accounts in accordance with IFRS. However, the individual company accounts may still be prepared in accordance with UK GAAP. All companies (not charities) may adopt IFRS, but must then apply it consistently. CTA 2010 s 1127 defines generally accepted accounting practice to include international accounting standards.

UK GAAP and IFRS are likely to give broadly similar results for trading, but there can be significant differences in some areas, for example on goodwill and financial instruments. The trend has been to align UK GAAP with IFRS. However the road to IFRS convergence has not been without its critics.

In 2012 and 2013 the UK's FRC (Financial Reporting Council replaced the Accounting Standard's Board) issued three new Financial Reporting Standards that fundamentally reform financial reporting:

(i) FRS 100 Application of Financial Reporting Requirements

(ii) FRS 101 Reduced Disclosure Framework

(iii) FRS 102 The Financial Reporting Standard applicable in the UK and ROI.

The new IFRS-based framework for UK GAAP is effective for accounting periods beginning on or after 1 January 2015.

The adoption of IFRS caused special problems for securitisation companies, where a mismatch in methods for valuation of financial assets and matching financial liabilities might have produced tax liabilities out of all proportion to profits or cash flow generated. In this case, a special regime for securitisation companies was provided for by FA 2006 s 101, which for tax purposes matches assets against liabilities, as had been done by UK GAAP.

In 2015 the FRC published a number of changes to accounting standards that dovetail with changes to company law. The changes:

(a) Introduce a new regime for micro-entities (FRS 105). This is effectively a replacement for the FRSSE and can be adopted straight away. It is the least complex standard and requires limited disclosures and constrains the accounting policies that can be applied.

(b) Introduce a new regime for small entities (FRS 102 section 1A). It applies to accounting periods commencing on or after 1 January 2016 but can be adopted early for periods commencing on or after 1 January 2015. It contains a number of financial reporting simplifications from full FRS 102 disclosures. Although, a number of additional disclosures are "encouraged" by the FRC. Directors of companies will need to assess the level of disclosure required to present a true and fair view. However their view may be affected by the removal of the option to file true abbreviated accounts and hence the information being available to anyone via Companies House. The new section also contains transitional exemptions around recognition and measurement requirements of FRS 102.

(c) Remove the Financial Reporting Standard for Smaller Entities (FRSSE) (effective January 2015). The FRSSE (effective January 2015) replaced the FRSSE (effective April 2008) and is effective for accounting periods beginning on or after 1 January 2015 although early adoption is permitted. It is effective for one year only and then for accounting periods commencing on or after 1 January 2016 it is necessary to move onto the micro or small (or normal FRS 102 if no longer qualify) entities rules above.

To qualify as micro or small it is necessary to not exceed two or more of the following criteria:

| | *Micro* | *Small* |
|---|---|---|
| Turnover | £632,000 | £10.2M |
| Balance sheet total | £312,000 | £5.1M |
| Number of employees | 10 | 50 |

Certain entities are also ineligible entities such as financial institutions and PLCs.

An entity may (in suitable circumstances) have the choice or reporting under IFRS or GAAP. GAAP is currently made up of six separate regimes see the table below:

**Choices of Financial Reporting Frameworks**

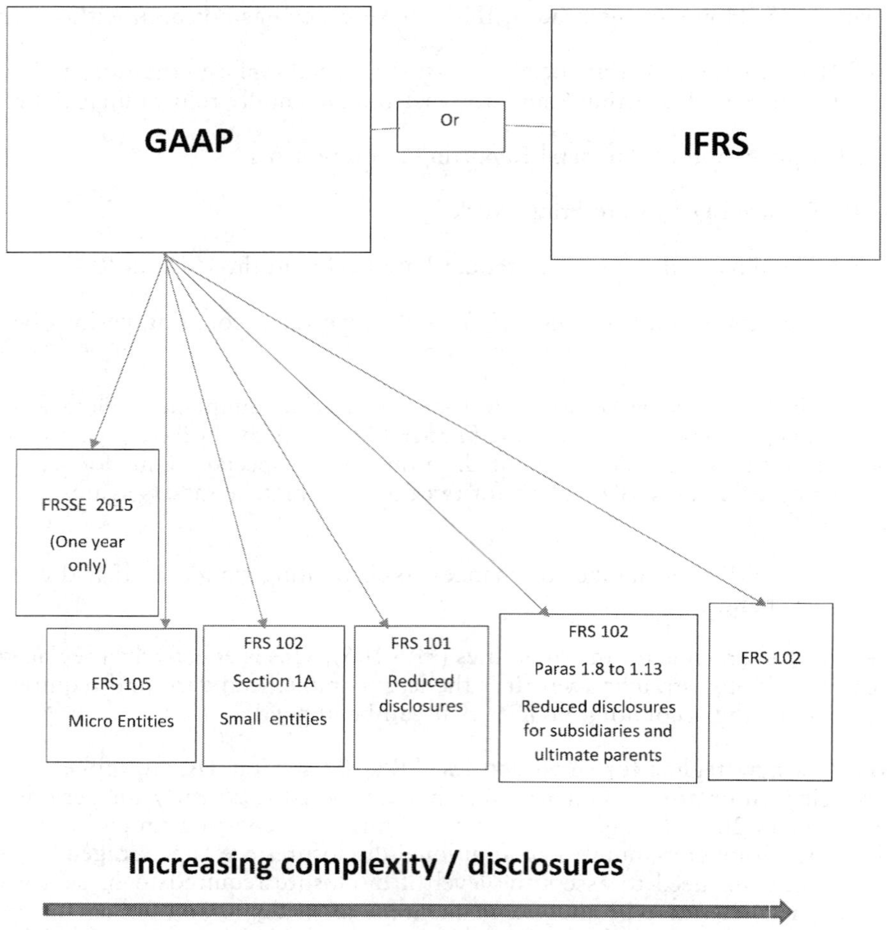


Where an entity qualifies to use more than one regime it will need to choose the most appropriate reporting framework particular to its circumstances.

*Updating the Corporate Tax Road Map*

(27) The Corporate Tax Road Map was first published in 2010. It set out the then Coalition Government's plans and signposted key changes planned to the corporate tax system. It was widely welcomed by UK business and most of the specific proposals were introduced. Understandably, there has been some unpredicted / rapid changes to international taxation such as the OECD's base erosion and profit shifting (BEPS) project and the introduction of the diverted profits tax from April 2015. However, the decision to update the roadmap at the start of the new parliament has again been welcomed. The new road map was published in April 2016 and set out the government's proposed timetable for reforms, key announcements included the proposed reform of corporate loss relief, restrictions on interest deductions for large companies, continued drive to support the BEPS project and clamp down on contrived avoidance.

# Question

Tweeters Ltd has traded as a manufacturer of specialist hi-fi speakers since 2000 and has no related companies. Accounts have previously always been prepared for years ended 31 March. The following information relates to the period of account for eighteen months ended 30 September 2016.

(a) Trading profits as adjusted for tax purposes but *before* making any adjustment for capital allowances are summarised as follows:

| | £ |
|---|---|
| Trading profits after finance costs | 2,389,770 |
| *Add*: Depreciation | 160,000 |
| Disallowable legal costs | 5,780 |
| Charitable donations to CAFOD (see (e) below) | 36,000 |
| Entertaining | 15,250 |
| | 2,606,800 |
| *Less*: Investment income | (75,600) |
| Adjusted trading profits before capital allowances | 2,531,200 |

(b) The written down value of the plant and machinery allowances pool at 31 March 2015 was £300,000. On 21 February 2016 a specialist manufacturing machine which had cost £100,000 in March 1994 was sold for £196,800 and a machine costing £80,000 was acquired on 10 September 2016.

(c) Investment income was:

| | | £ | £ |
|---|---|---|---|
| (i) | Bank deposit interest received | | |
| | 30 June 2015 | 3,000 | |
| | 31 December 2015 | 2,500 | |
| | 30 June 2016 | 5,500 | 11,000 |
| (ii) | Building society interest received 1 January 2016 | | 2,000 |
| (iii) | Gross debenture interest receivable from Dovedale plc | | |
| | (£100,000 at 8.4% per annum) | | |
| | (received half yearly on 1 March and 1 September) | | 12,600 |
| (iv) | Dividends from UK companies | | |
| | May 2015 (27,000 + tax cr 3,000) | 30,000 | |
| | May 2016 (18,000) | 18,000 | 48,000 |

The opening and closing accruals in respect of (i) to (iii) were as follows:

| | *At 01.04.15* | *At 30.09.16* |
|---|---|---|
| | £ | £ |
| Bank interest | 1,100 | 3,000 |
| Building society interest | 1,400 | 1,500 |
| Debenture interest | 700 | 700 |

(d) Interest at 10% per annum is paid on 1 July each year on a loan of £200,000 from Mr Woofer. Mr Woofer is a controlling shareholder of Tweeters Ltd and lent the money to provide additional working capital for trading purposes.

(e) Gift Aid donations of £25,000 were paid to CAFOD (a UK charity) on 30 April each year (gross amounts).

(f) A dividend of £800,000 was paid on 1 March 2016.

(g) Assume indexation allowance for the period March 1994 to February 2016 was 82.6%.

(h) Calculate the company's corporation tax liability for eighteen months ended 30 September 2016.

(i) Calculate the corporation tax payments due for that period (based on the final liability), stating the relevant due dates of payment. (In recent years Tweeters Ltd has always paid tax at the main rate.)

(j) Show any amount required to be reported on Form CT 61 (quarterly return of income tax) for the eighteen months to 30 September 2016.

# Answer

## (1) Corporation Tax Liability

| | | *12 months to 31.03.16* | *6 months to 30.09.16* |
|---|---|---|---|
| | £ | £ | £ |
| Trading profits (see **note 3**) (366:183 days) | | 1,687,467 | 843,733 |
| *Less*: Capital allowances: plant and machinery | | | |
| Year to 31 March 2016 | | | |
| WDV at 31 March 2017 | 300,000 | | |
| Sale proceeds 21 February 2016 | | | |
| (elimination from pool is limited to cost) | (100,000) | | |
| | 200,000 | | |
| WDA 18% | (36,000) | (36,000) | |
| | 164,000 | | |
| 6 months to 30 September 2016 | | | |
| Addition 10 September 2016 | 80,000 | | |
| AIA @£500,000 × (6/12) = max £250,000 | (80,000) | | (80,000) |
| WDA 18% × $^{6}/_{12}$ | | | |
| | (14,760) | | (14,760) |
| WDV cf | 149,240 | | |
| | | 1,651,467 | 748,953 |
| *Loan relationships* (see **explanatory note 7**) | | | |
| Bank deposit interest | | 8,592 | 4,308 |
| Building society interest | | 1,398 | 702 |
| Debenture interest | | 8,392 | 4,208 |
| *Chargeable gain:* | | | |
| Plant sale proceeds (February 2016) | 196,800 | | |
| *Less*: Cost | 100,000 | | |
| Unindexed gain | 96,800 | | |
| *Less*: Indexation allowance | | | |
| 100,000 @ 82.6% | (82,600) | | |
| Gain after indexation allowance | | 14,200 | |
| *Less*: *charitable donations relief:* | | | |
| Gift Aid donations paid | | (25,000) | (25,000) |
| Taxable total profits | | 1,659,049 | 733,191 |
| Corporation tax thereon at 20%: | | 331,910 | 146,638 |

## (2) Corporation tax payments

| | *Year to 31.03.16* | *6 months to 30.09.16* |
|---|---|---|
| | £ | £ |
| Corporation tax payable as in (1) | 331,910 | 146,638 |
| Due dates of payment: | | |
| 14 October 2015 | 82,978 | |
| 14 January 2016 | 82,978 | |
| 14 April 2016 | 82,977 | |
| 14 July 2016 | 82,977 | |
| 14 October 2016 | – | 73,319 |
| 14 January 2017 | – | 73,319 |

In practice, Tweeters Ltd would make instalment payments based on its *estimated* tax liability for the relevant periods, making appropriate adjustments to the payments when it had finalised its self-assessed liability. HMRC would compare the estimated payments with the payments which should have been made based on the final liability and calculate the appropriate (underpaid) debit interest or (overpaid) credit interest up to the normal nine month due date when the normal interest rates apply. The interest will be reflected on the company's statement.

Although not relevant to this question, see **Example I1 explanatory note 15** for proposals to change the dates of corporation tax payments for large companies.

## (3) Accounting for income tax (ITA 2007 Part 15)

| *Period* | *Date due* | | *Tax deducted from interest etc paid Tax rate* | | *Payable to HMRC* |
|---|---|---|---|---|---|
| | | £ | | £ | £ |
| *Year ended 31.03.2016* | | | | | |
| Qr to 30.6.2015 no return required | | | | | |
| Interest paid 01.07.2015 | [1] | 20,000 | | | |
| Qr to 30.09.2015 | 14.10.2015 | 20,000 | 20% | 4,000 | 4,000 |
| Qr to 31.12.2015 no return required | | | | | |
| Qr to 31.03.2016 no return required | | | | | |
| | | | | | 4,000 |
| *6 months ended 30.09.2016* | | | | | |
| Qr to 30.06.2016 no return required | | | | | |
| Interest paid 01.07.2016 | [1] | 20,000 | | | |
| Qr to 30.09.2016 | 14.10.2016 | 20,000 | 20% | 4,000 | 4,000 |

[1] Interest payable on loan of £200,000 from Mr Woofer

# Explanatory Notes

*Chargeable accounting periods*

(1) Full notes on the computation of profits for corporation tax are in **Example H1**.

(2)

(a) Corporation tax rates are fixed for financial years (defined as the year beginning 1 April), but corporation tax returns, including self-assessments are made by reference to chargeable accounting periods, and the profits arising in an accounting period are apportioned on a time basis between the financial years in which the accounting period falls in order to determine the rate of corporation tax applicable (CTA 2009 s 8(5)).

(b) An accounting period of a company begins whenever:

(i) the company, not then being within the charge to corporation tax, comes within it, whether by the company becoming resident in the UK or acquiring a source of income, or otherwise, or

(ii) an accounting period of the company ends without the company then ceasing to be within the charge to corporation tax (CTA 2009 s 9(1)).

(c) An accounting period of a company ends on the first occurrence of any of the following (CTA 2009 ss 10(1) and 12):

(i) twelve months after the beginning of the accounting period;

(ii) an accounting date of the company or, if there is a period for which the company does not make up accounts, the day before the date from which accounts are made up;

(iii) the company beginning or ceasing to trade or to be, in respect of the trade or (if more than one) of all the trades carried on by it, within the charge to corporation tax;

(iv) the company beginning or ceasing to be resident in the UK;

(v) the company ceasing to be within the charge to corporation tax;

(vi) the appointment of a liquidator on commencement of winding-up of the company (following which accounting periods end at twelve monthly intervals until the completion of the winding-up).

Since the period for which Tweeters Ltd has made up accounts exceeds twelve months, the eighteen month period ended 30 September 2016 must be divided into two chargeable periods, the year to 31 March 2016 and the six months to 30 September 2016.

*Allocating profits and losses to accounting periods*

(3) CTA 2009 s 52(2) provides that where it is *necessary* in order to arrive at profits or losses of an accounting period to apportion profits/losses to specific periods, the apportionment is made according to the days in the respective periods (CTA 2009 s 52(3)). In exceptional circumstances, a more accurate measure of profits may be obtained other than by time-apportionment, in which case time-apportionment is not *necessary* (*Marshall Hus & Ptnrs Ltd v Bolton* [1981] STC 18, 55 TC 539).

(4) Except for interest, in respect of which there are special rules (see **explanatory note** 7) and income from intangible fixed assets, such as patent royalties (see **Example K3**), a company's other sources of income are dealt with in the chargeable period in which they arise, using income tax principles. Capital gains and losses are dealt with in the chargeable period in which the disposal is made (TCGA 1992 s 8). Where gains and losses on disposal relate to a company's 'loan relationships' they are included in calculating income rather

than capital gains (see **Example K2**). The same applies to gains and losses on intangible fixed assets, although a special rollover relief applies where intangible fixed assets are replaced.

(5) For capital allowances purposes, additions and disposals are dealt with in the chargeable accounting period in which they occur.

(6) Charitable donations relief (formerly known as charges on income)(and the charitable Gift Aid donations in this Example) are deducted in the chargeable period in which they are paid, not as they accrue (CTA 2010 s 189(1)).

*Treatment of interest paid and received*

(7) Interest paid and received is normally taken into account on an accruals basis (see **Example K2** for details). If the interest relates to the trade (which, except for financial businesses, will usually apply only to interest *payable*), it is incorporated within the trading profit of the period of account, which is time apportioned over the chargeable accounting periods if the period of account exceeds twelve months. As far as non-trading interest is concerned, the same treatment would normally be used to arrive at the amounts included in the loan relationship's profit or deficit, unless the amounts involved were material and time-apportionment would not give a fair result.

In this Example, the loan interest paid will already be deducted in arriving at the trading profits. The non-trading interest received over the period to 30 September 2016 is arrived at as follows and has been time-apportioned as shown:

| | | *To 31.03.16* | *To 30.09.16* |
|---|---|---|---|
| | £ | £ | £ |
| Bank interest (11,000 – 1,100 + 3,000) | 12,900 | 8,592 | 4,308 |
| Building society interest (2,000 – 1,400 + 1,500) | 2,100 | 1,398 | 702 |
| Debenture interest (12,600 – 700 + 700) | 12,600 | 8,392 | 4,208 |

*Gross and net payments*

(8) Companies and local authorities pay patent royalties and annual interest on a gross basis (without deducting tax) where they believe the recipient to be a UK-resident company, local authority or a UK permanent establishment of a non-resident company (ITA 2007 ss 930–938). Interest is also paid gross on quoted Eurobonds. Quoted Eurobonds are interest-bearing securities issued by a company which is listed on a recognised stock exchange (ITA 2007 s 987). Companies can also continue to pay discount in relation to Original Issue Discount ('OID') notes without withholding tax.

In other cases, such as where the recipient is an individual, a non-exempt trust or a non-resident company, the amounts continue to be subject to deduction of tax at the relevant rate. (If the payment is made overseas with the benefit of a double tax treaty, a 'nil' or reduced rate of withholding may apply.)

Companies may still receive patent royalties net of tax where the payer is an individual.

*Quarterly accounting for income tax*

(9) A company has to make a return under ITA 2007 Chapter 15 from s 945 onwards to account for any income tax it has deducted in the return period from patent royalties, interest and any other annual payments (such payments being referred to as 'relevant payments'), subject to a set-off for any income tax suffered on taxed income. The return must be made within fourteen days after the end of the return period on form CT 61.

The return periods are the calendar quarters to 31 March, 30 June, 30 September and 31 December. If a company's accounting period does not end on one of those dates, however, the company must make up returns to each of those dates and also a return ending on the last day of the accounting period.

HMRC's corporation tax records have an automatic feed from Companies House into HMRC corporation tax system (COTAX). In practise this means forms CT61 can only be issued to a company's registered office.

Taxed receipts and payments are brought into the quarterly accounting system according to when they are received and paid. Where, looking at the cumulative position during a chargeable accounting period, too much income tax has been accounted for owing to later receipts of taxed income, the excess payments to HMRC are repayable upon completion of the appropriate CT 61 return form. HMRC will not, however, repay sums in excess of those already paid to them in the accounting period. Such excesses can be used to cover the company's liability on later payments in the same accounting period, any balance being treated as indicated in note 10. The rate of tax deducted from interest is 20%. The rate of tax deducted from other taxed amounts such as patent royalties is the basic rate, presently also 20%.

Note 8 above sets out details of when payments must be made net of income tax. Thus in the Example Tweeters Ltd receives its debenture interest from Dovedale plc gross, but must withhold 20% tax from its loan interest payments to Mr Woofer, since tax must be deducted from interest payments to individuals (other than on quoted Eurobonds). Companies are required to deduct tax on payments of annual interest, patent royalties and any annual payments where they are made to individuals, trustees (other than trustees of exempt bodies), or non-residents (such as overseas group or associate companies), and will suffer tax if they receive payments such as patent royalties from individuals.

In 2010 HMRC raised the proposal of an online return of income tax deducted (rather than a CT61), and the possibility of an annual (rather than quarterly) return for small cases. F(No 2)A 2010 introduced a new section 963A ITA 2007 which enables HMRC to amend the time and manner in which individuals and other non-corporate persons account to HMRC. It is understood this section has been introduced to enable a new online form CT61 at some time in the future.

*Excess income tax suffered*

(10) If at the end of an accounting period more income tax has been suffered on taxed income than the company is liable to account for in respect of its taxed payments, the excess income tax is set off against the corporation tax bill for the relevant accounting period. If it should *exceed* the corporation tax bill, then the balance will be *repaid to the company*. Since the majority of UK source investment income is now paid on a 'gross' basis, such situations are likely to be rare. However, in such cases, companies claim repayment of excess income tax suffered when they submit corporation tax returns (ITA 2007 ss 899(4), 977(1)).

(11) Companies are not *required* to set off income tax suffered against income tax payable under the quarterly return procedure, and may if they wish set the whole amount against the corporation tax payable for the relevant accounting period (ITA 2007 ss 18, 19, 953). In most cases, it will only be *excess* income tax suffered that is set against corporation tax payable. The relevant accounting period in which excess income tax suffered is set off is that in which the related income is taken into account (ITA 2007 ss 18, 19).

*Payment of corporation tax*

(12) See **Example I1 explanatory note 15.**

*Capital gains rollover relief*

(13) If the plant sold in this Example is fixed plant, the company may claim rollover relief in respect of the chargeable gain if the proceeds are reinvested in other business assets acquired within one year before and three years after the date of disposal (TCGA 1992 s 152(3)) (see **Example L9** for details).

If, on the other hand, the plant sold (or the replacement plant) is not fixed plant but moveable plant, then rollover relief is not available.

# Question

## A.

Streetfield Ltd, which has no associated companies, had made up its accounts to 30 September since its incorporation in 2000, but decided after the accounting year to 30 September 2014 to make up a six-month account to 31 March 2015.

The results of recent periods were:

| | *Year ended 30.9.14* | *6 mths ended 31.3.15* | *Year ended 31.3.16* |
|---|---|---|---|
| | £ | £ | £ |
| Adjusted trading profit (loss) | 15,000 | 84,500 | (210,000) |
| Loan relationship non trading profit – interest on debenture stock of Lane plc | 2,000 | 1,000 | 2,000 |
| Capital gains | – | – | 20,500 |

Having reorganised the business following its difficult trading period, the company has recently secured a major new contract and a (taxable) trading profit of some £320,000 is anticipated for the year to 31 March 2017. The company will continue to receive the debenture interest.

Corporation tax rates during the period have been as follows:

### Year ended 31 March

| | *2013* | *2014* | *2015* | *2016* | *2017* |
|---|---|---|---|---|---|
| Full rate on profits over £1,500,000 | 24% | 23% | 21% | 20% | 20% |
| Small profits rate on profits up to £300,000 | 20% | 20% | 20% | | |
| Effective marginal rate on profits between £300,000 and £1,500,000 | 25% | 23.75% | 21.25% | | |
| Marginal rate fraction | 1/100 | 3/400 | 1/400 | | |

(i) Illustrate the alternative ways in which relief may be obtained for the trading loss of the year to 31 March 2016, stating the time limits within which any claims must be made.

(ii) Indicate what the position would be if the company had made a Gift Aid donation to a charity of £1,000 gross on 31 March each year.

## B.

Calamity Ltd, a family-owned close company that had operated in an enterprise zone, ceased trading on 30 June 2016.

It was incorporated many years ago and the company has had no income other than from the trade. The company has paid a charitable Gift Aid donation of £1,000 per annum. The last payment under Gift Aid was made in December 2014. A summary of recent adjusted trading results is as follows:

| | | £ |
|---|---|---|
| *Year ended* | | |
| 31.12.12 | Profit | 150,000 |
| 31.12.13 | Profit | 143,000 |
| 31.12.14 | Profit | 35,000 |
| 31.12.15 | Loss | 65,000 |
| 6 months to 30.6.16 | Loss | 50,000 |

On 31 August 2016 the company's factory (on which enterprise zone allowances had been claimed) was sold, a balancing charge of £48,000 and a chargeable gain of £15,000 arising. The final accounting period is to 31 December 2016.

Assuming that the company claims relief for losses in the most effective way:

(i) Show the tax position in relation to the balancing charge and chargeable gain.

(ii) Show the final taxable total profits for each of the chargeable periods shown, after loss relief claims, together with the amounts of unrelieved losses and unrelieved charitable donations, if any.

(iii) Give the latest dates by which the loss claims could be made by Calamity Ltd.

# Answer

## A.
## Streetfield

(i) **The loss claims available in respect of the loss of the year to 31 March 2016 are as follows:**

(1) The adjusted trading loss of £210,000 can be carried forward under CTA 2010 s 45 to set against future profits of the *same trade* (not any other income nor chargeable gains). If the anticipated trading profit of £320,000 is made in the year to 31 March 2017, relief for the loss will be obtained in that year, reducing the corporation tax payable on 1 January 2016.

If this alternative is adopted, Streetfield Ltd will have taxable total profits for the year ended 31 March 2016 of £22,500 taxable at the rate of 20%.

(2) Alternatively a claim may be made under CTA 2010 s 37 to set the loss against the *total profits* of the same accounting period, viz.

| | |
|---|---|
| Trading loss for year ended 31 March 2016 | 210,000 |
| Set against total profits before charitable donations relief of same accounting period | 22,500 |
| Leaving a balance unrelieved of | £187,500 |

which may be carried forward under s 45.

The tax saving from this claim amounts to £4,500 (22,500 @ 20%). The claim against any current profits is a prerequisite if the company wishes to claim under the provisions of note 3 below.

(3) After a claim has been made under 2 above, then alternatively to carrying the unrelieved trading loss of £187,500 forward it may be carried back to set against the *total* profits of accounting periods ending wholly or partly within the previous twelve months, latest first. Results are apportioned where, as in this Example, an accounting period falls only partly within the twelve-month period. Any unrelieved balance is then carried forward.

The carryback claim is as follows:

| | £ | £ |
|---|---|---|
| Unrelieved loss of year to 31 March 2016 as above | | 187,500 |
| Set against total profits of six months to 31 March 2015: | | |
| Trading profits | 84,500 | |
| Loan interest | 1,000 | |
| | | (85,500) |
| Set against one half of total profits of year to 30 September 2014: | | |
| Trading profits | 15,000 | |
| Debenture interest | 2,000 | |
| | 17,000 | |
| Loss set off | (8,500) | (8,500) |
| Leaving taxable profits of | 8,500 | |
| Loss carried forward under s 45 | | 93,500 |

(4) Losses that are carried forward under s 45 are set off automatically against later trading profits without the need for a claim. The time limit for making current and carryback claims under s 37 is two years after the end of the loss period, i.e. by 31 March 2018 or within such further period as HMRC may allow.

The anticipated results for the year to 31 March 2017 are:

| | |
|---|---|
| Trading profits | 320,000 |
| Profit on non-trading loan relationship (say) | 2,000 |
| | £322,000 |

As can be seen in the table below, since the harmonisation of the main rate and small profits rates and therefore the abolition of the marginal rate there is no advantage from 2016 onwards in how losses are allocated in absolute cash terms, although cashflow and (re)payment interest advantages can occur. As corporate tax rates are reducing there will often bean advantage in carrying back to a previous period.

If the loss is carried back under s 37, usage will be as follows:

| | *Profit/(Loss)* | *Loss Relief* | *Tax Saving* |
|---|---|---|---|
| Year to 30.09.14 | 17,000 | 8,500 @ 20% | 1,700 |
| Six months to 31.03.15 | 85,500 | 85,500 @ 20% | 17,100 |
| Year to 31.03.16 | (210,000) | | |
| | 22,500 | 22,500 @ 20% | 4,500 |
| Year to 31.03.17 | 322,000 | 93,500 @ 20% | 18,700 |
| | | 210,000 | 42,000 |

(a) If the loss is carried forward under s 37:

| | *Profit/(Loss)* | *Loss Relief* | *Tax Saving* |
|---|---|---|---|
| Year to 31.3.16 | (210,000) | 0 | |
| | 22,500 | 0 | |
| Year to 31.3.17 | 322,000 | 210,000 @ 20% | 42,000 |
| | | 210,000 | 42,000 |

As can be seen in the table above, since the harmonisation of the main rate and small profits rates and therefore the abolition of the marginal rate there is no advantage from 2016 onwards in how losses are allocated. There would still be an advantage in carrying back to a previous period if the company was subject to the previous main companies or paid tax at the marginal rate.

Although there is no additional tax saved it is usually beneficial to carry the loss back from a cashflow perspective unless a very large profit is expected in the next period which could cause the company to be due to pay its liability by quarterly instalments. Generally speaking, with falling rates of corporation tax as have been experienced since 2011, the first option would be to carry back to seek deduction at higher rates (unless the company is only subject to the small profits rate). The opposite could be true if:

(b) The other factors to be considered in relation to the loss claims are the time when the tax saving will occur and whether any repayments will be boosted by tax-free interest.

Given that the carryback claim avoids payment of the 2016 liability of £4,500, and brings a cash advantage forward by about a year, the Streetfield directors are likely to give the carryback option serious consideration. There is an obvious cash flow advantage in a carryback claim, and it may be possible to bring forward the date of repayment by prompt filing of the tax return and the claim.

(c) To the extent that the loss is carried forward, the relief will reduce the corporation tax payable on 1 January 2018. Relief against current or earlier profits will either result in tax not yet paid being discharged, or in tax being repaid.

(d) Any repayment for the earlier years would attract interest, if any, from 1 January 2017, except for the six months to 31 March 2015, for which interest would run from 1 January 2016 (see **explanatory note 6**).

(ii) **If Streetfield Ltd had paid £1,000 gross annually on 31 March to a charity under Gift Aid**

A Gift Aid donation to charity is relieved under qualifying charitable donations relief (formerly known as charges on income) and can only be deducted where there are profits available to cover it. (Excess donations may, however, be surrendered under the group relief provisions – see **Example K1**.) Where losses are carried back, qualifying charitable donations relief such as donations are not protected and relief can be lost.

Streetfield Ltd would obtain full relief for the Gift Aid donations if it made the carry forward claim, sufficient profits being available in both the loss year to 31 March 2016 and the following year to cover the qualifying charitable donations relief. If the loss was set against the current and previous profits as indicated above, there would be £1,000 unrelieved in the loss year to 31 March 2016 and in the six months to 31 March 2015. In the year to 30 September 2014, the donation would be covered by the profits remaining after the loss claim.

## B.
## Calamity

(i) *Tax position on balancing charge and chargeable gain*

The balancing charge of £48,000, together with the chargeable gain of £15,000, totalling £63,000, will be taxed at 20% (see **explanatory note 12**), giving tax payable of £12,600. The balancing charge is, however, treated in the same way as a post-cessation receipt under CTA 2009 ss 196 and 285 (CAA 2001 s 354), so that it can be deemed to occur on the last day of trade and offset against the trade losses at that date reducing the loss in the period. It should be noted that on the cessation of trade all trading losses are eliminated and are therefore not available to offset against post-cessation receipts except by means of a s 198 election.

(ii) **Final taxable total profits, after loss claims:**

Taking into account (a) above, the position is as follows:

| *Accounting period to* | *Trade profits* | *Chargeable gains* | *Trading losses** | *Charitable donations relief*** | *Taxable total profits* |
|---|---|---|---|---|---|
| | £ | £ | £ | £ | £ |
| 31.12.16 | – | 15,000 | – | – | 15,000 |
| 30.6.16 | 48,000[2] | | 48,000[1] | – | – |
| 31.12.15 | – | | – | ** | – |
| 31.12.14 | 35,000 | | (35,000)[1] | ** | – |
| 31.12.13 | 143,000 | | (32,000)[1] | (1,000) | 110,000 |
| 31.12.12 | 150,000 | | | (1,000) | 149,000 |

[1]Losses are relieved as follows:

| | | Terminal loss |
|---|---|---|
| | *01.01.2015 – 30.6.2015* | *01.07.2015 – 31.12.2015* |
| *Year to 31.12.2015* (see **explanatory notes 10** and **11**) | £ | £ |
| Trading loss (£65,000) | 32,500 | 32,500 |
| Set against profits of previous year/three years (s 37): | | |
| Year to 31.12.2014 (£35,000) | (32,500) | (2,500) |
| Year to 31.12.2013 (balance) | | (30,000) |
| *6 months to 30.06.2016* | | |
| Trading loss | | 50,000 |
| Less balancing charge arising in period to 31.12.16 deemed under s 198 CTA 2009 to arise on 30.06.2016 | | (48,000) |
| Set against profits of previous three years (s 37): Year to 31.12.2013 | | (2,000) |
| Leaving unrelieved loss of | | Nil |

[2]The balancing charge is a post-cessation receipt under s.196 and s.285 CTA 2010 (s.354 CAA2001) so an election is made under s.198 CTA 2010 for the charge to be deemed to arise on the last day of trade (30 June 2016) reducing the loss of the final trading period.

Charitable donations relief is deducted after trade losses and, if there are no profits to cover them, no relief is available. The payments under Gift Aid for the years to 31 December 2014 and 31 December 2015 are therefore unrelieved.

(iii) The latest date for making the s 37 claim to carry back the loss of the year ended 31 December 2015 is 31 December 2017 (or such further period as HMRC may allow) (CTA 2010 s 37(7)).

## Explanatory Notes

*Loss relief against current and previous profits under CTA 2010 s 37*

(1) This Example outlines the reliefs available to a single company in a continuing business in respect of trading losses and excess qualifying charitable donations. Under CTA 2009 s 47 losses are calculated on the same basis as profits therefore all 'negative amounts', including trading losses, included in the CT 600 return become final in the same way as a self-assessment, subject to HMRC's ability to enquire into a return or make a discovery, although FA 2008 s 114 provides that an officer of HMRC may amend a tax return that appears to be incorrect.

(2) Relief for trading losses may be claimed under CTA 2010 s 37 against profits of whatever description in the current and carryback period, normally 12 months. Where there is a change of accounting date during the carryback period, as shown in this Example, s 37 provides that the reduction to be made in the profits of a period falling only partly within the carryback period shall not exceed the appropriate proportion of those profits. Current and carryback claims must be made within two years after the end of the loss period, or within such further period as HMRC may allow (CTA 2010 s 37(7)). See Statement of Practice 5/01 for the circumstances in which HMRC may accept late claims.

*Carrying trading losses forward under CTA 2010 s 45*

(3) Where relief is not claimed or part of a loss remains unrelieved, the loss is carried forward automatically under s 45 without the need for a claim. Losses can only be offset against profits of the same trade s 45(4)a.

HMRC have issued a consultation document regarding proposed changes to loss relief, the change proposed is to permit losses carried forward that arise after 1 April 2017 to be offset against any profits. A restriction will apply to companies with substantial losses which will reduce the available offset in any period where the profits exceed £5m to 50% of the profits over £5m, a similar restriction already applies to banking company profits.

*Qualifying charitable donations*

(4) The general rule is that charitable donations relief can only be claimed in respect of the period during which the payment or donations is made. Where losses are carried back relief for donations will be lost unless a claim for group relief can be made.

*Other loss claims*

(5) Losses may be the subject of a group relief claim for a company that is a member of a 75% group – for details see **Example K6**. That Example also deals with the treatment of excess management expenses of an investment company.

*Interest on repayments*

(6) Where tax is repaid following a loss claim, interest on the repayment normally runs from nine months and one day after the loss period (except for a repayment relating to an account falling wholly within the 12 months before the loss period, for which interest runs from nine months and one day after that earlier period).

Hence in this Example, interest on repayments would run from 1 January 2017, except for any repayment for the six months to 31 March 2015, on which interest would run from 1 January 2016, as indicated in Example A **part (i) note d**.

A 'large' company which is subject to the quarterly instalment payment rules may also generate repayments following the carryback of losses. However, even in such cases, interest will accrue only from the relevant nine months and one day due dates (ICTA 1988 s 826(7D) and (7E)).

Interest on underpaid and overpaid tax is taken into account in calculating taxable total profits.

*Relief for non-trading losses*

(7) Companies may generate non-trading losses on other activities. The relief available for such losses depends on the nature of the loss, as summarised below for the most important categories:

(a) Capital losses – offset against capital gains of the same accounting period, with any unrelieved loss being carried forward to reduce capital gains in future periods (see **Example L1 explanatory note 1**).

(b) Non-trading foreign exchange/loan relationships deficit – a claim can be made to relieve such deficits in various ways (see **Example K2 part A**).

(c) Property business losses on leased UK property – CTA 2010 s 62 (formerly ICTA 1988 s 392A) provides that losses on a UK property leasing business can be offset against the company's total profits of the same period and/or included in a group relief claim under CTA 2010 s 99. Any surplus property business loss is carried forward against future total profits (provided the property business continues). A company with investment business can carry forward an unrelieved property business loss (*after* the property business has ceased) as a management expense under CTA 2009 ss 1219 (1) and 1223(3). See **Example D2**.

(d) Overseas property letting business losses must be carried forward for future offset against profits of the same overseas property business (CTA 2010 s 66) (see **Example D2**).

(e) Miscellaneous losses (formerly known as Schedule D Case VI) can only be relieved under CTA 2010 s 91 against current or future miscellaneous income. Miscellaneous income is defined at CTA 2010 s 1173 other than offshore income gains. Most Schedule D case VI losses carried forward to accounting periods ending on or after 1 April 2009 are treated as a loss from a miscellaneous transaction with relief available under s 91.

*HMRC toolkit*

(8) HMRC publish a toolkit to assist with 'company losses' which may be a useful and maybe vital tool for small practitioners who wish to show they have taken 'reasonable care' (see **Example G2** penalties). The toolkit focuses on errors HMRC officers find commonly occur. It takes the form of a checklist followed by explanation and further sources of guidance.

Using the toolkit does not supplant the taxpayer's obligation to ensure that their Corporation Tax returns are complete and accord with the Taxes Acts. Indeed HMRC comment that their 'application to specific cases will depend on the law at the relevant time and on the precise facts', and 'it is not a comprehensive statement of all risks that may arise in any particular return'.

*Terminal loss relief*

(9) Relief for trading losses may be claimed under CTA 2010 s 37 against profits of whatever description in the current and carry-back period, which is normally 12 months. The normal one year carry back period is extended to three years by s 39 for terminal losses. The terminal loss is the loss of the last twelve months of trading.

First, losses in that twelve months may be carried back for a full three years. Where an accounting period falls partly within the last twelve months, the three year carryback applies to the appropriate proportion.

(10) In Calamity Ltd's case, the loss of the twelve months ended 31 December 2016 must be apportioned between:

– 6 months to 30 June 2016, which is available for carryback against the previous year only.

– 6 months to 31 December 2016, which falls within twelve months of the cessation date, and can therefore be carried back against the previous three years' profits.

The loss for the final 6 months to 30 June 2016 can also be carried back for up to three years (as part of the loss of the last twelve months), but is reduced by the s.198 claim which deems the post-cessation receipt to arise on the last day of trade and accordingly reduces the loss for the period.

(11) The general rule is that charitable donations relief (CTA 2010 s 191) can only be claimed in respect of the period during which the payment or donation is made. Where losses are carried back relief for the donation will be lost unless a claim for group relief can be made. (See **Example I1 explanatory note 11.**)

*Capital gains and balancing charges after cessation of trade*

(12) The capital gain after the cessation of trading illustrates the possible danger of disposing of capital assets after the cessation of a trade.

Trading losses of the *same accounting period only* are available for set-off against capital gains. Since the cessation of trade marks the end of an accounting period (CTA 2009 s 10(1)), any losses of the final trading period are automatically prevented from being allowed against gains arising on the subsequent disposal of the company's assets, resulting in practical difficulties since invariably the assets have to be retained until after the cessation of trading. Balancing adjustments on pooled items arise at the end of the final trading period, so are automatically offset against profits or losses. Adjustments on single pool assets, or enterprise zone buildings arise on sale of the asset, and therefore may fall outside the final trading period. Under CAA 2001 s 354 unrelieved trading losses may be set against such a balancing charge, as shown in the Example. But there can be no set-off against capital gains.

If, however, the *contract* for sale of the assets was made prior to the cessation of trading, with *completion* taking place after the cessation, the date of disposal would be the contract date (TCGA 1992 s 28), so that the chargeable gains would then arise in the final trading period and be available to offset any trading losses of that period.

*Company reconstructions without a change of ownership*

(13) Under CTA 2010 Part 22 Chapter 1 s 938 onwards (formerly ICTA 1988 s 343), where a trade is transferred from one company to another, and at some time within one year before the transfer and two years after the transfer the same persons have a 75% ownership, the trade is treated as being transferred to the successor company rather than being discontinued for the purposes of carrying forward capital allowances. This prevents the predecessor carrying trading losses back three years, and enables the successor to take over the unrelieved losses of the predecessor. Where, however, the successor does not take over all the predecessor's assets and liabilities, and the liabilities of the predecessor immediately after the transfer exceed the market value of its assets (including any consideration received or receivable for the transfer of the trade), the trading loss transferred to the successor is reduced by the excess.

The successor also takes over the predecessor's capital allowances computations. Any first-year allowances available on plant and machinery are claimed by whoever incurred the expenditure and balancing adjustments are made on the company carrying on the trade at the time of the disposal. Writing down allowances are split on a time basis.

# Question

## A

MJD Ltd, a trading company with no associated companies prepares accounts to 30 September 2016 making trading profits of £1,000,000. During the year the company spent £120,000 on research and development expenditure (all eligible under CTA 2009 Part 13 Ch 2). The company qualifies as an SME for R&D purposes and had no other sources of income.

(a) Calculate the taxable total profits, assuming that the £120,000 research and development costs were incurred evenly throughout the accounting period.

(b) State the main conditions required for an R&D tax relief claim under CTA 2009 Part 13 Chapter 2 (SME scheme).

(c) MJD Ltd is considering seeking a patent for its latest invention. Prepare a short outline of the patent box regime.

## B

Petunia Engineering Limited is a small company with 4 staff. The company has carried on research and development for many years, and has two products which are subject to a UK patent. The company makes up its accounts to 30 June each year.

*B1. Year ended 30 June 2016*

The detailed accounts and notes thereto for the year ended 30 June 2016 are as follows:

The following further information is available:

| | | £ |
|---|---|---|
| Sales | | 1,491,250 |
| *Less*: Cost of sales | | (282,359) |
| Gross profit | | 1,208,891 |
| Other income | | 14,406 |
| Salaries related to R & D work | 148,935 | |
| Other salaries | 54,911 | |
| Depreciation of equipment | 34,903 | |
| Office and laboratory rent | 74,044 | |
| Other R & D costs (all allowable) | 23,754 | |
| Sub-contract work (non R&D) | 39,846 | |
| Rates and insurance | 8,330 | |
| Light and heat | 3,502 | |
| Internet services | 4,520 | |
| Repairs | 4,250 | |
| Motor expenses | 8,647 | |
| Professional fees | 11,341 | |
| Staff training | 1,600 | |
| Subscriptions | 980 | |
| Bank interest and charges | 2,250 | |
| Travel and hotels | 4,544 | |
| Office general expenses | 3,776 | |

| | | |
|---|---|---|
| Miscellaneous expenses | 1,080 | |
| Staff welfare | 891 | |
| Donation to charity | 450 | |
| Amortisation of patents | 1,498 | |
| Entertaining | 847 | |
| | | 434,899 |
| Net profit | | 788,398 |

(1) Legal and professional fees includes £3,499 paid to patent lawyers who protect the company's patent rights.

(2) All amounts shown as salary include the related National Insurance contributions.

(3) The total sales relating to the two patented items are £844,508.

(4) Other income comprises exchange difference on sales abroad of £8,402, interest received of £3,000 and hire charges for patented items of £3,004.

(5) The capital allowances for the year have been calculated as £101,834.

(6) R & D charged to the profit and loss account in the preceding four years was:

| Year ended 30 June | £ |
|---|---|
| 2015 | 155,148 |
| 2014 | 201,664 |
| 2013 | 195,777 |
| 2012 | 149,021 |

The directors have decided to make a claim under the patent box regime for the year ended 30 June 2016, having not claimed previously. Calculate the corporation tax liability for the year ended 30 June 2016.

*B2. Year Ended 30 June 2017*

| *Petunia Engineering Ltd* | *Non-trade* | *Patent A* | *Patent B* | *Patent C* | *Total* |
|---|---|---|---|---|---|
| Sales | 450 | 500 | 500 | 500 | 1,950 |
| Less: Cost of sales | (200) | (0) | (0) | (0) | (200) |
| Gross profit | 250 | 500 | 500 | 500 | 1,750 |
| Bank interest | 50 | (0) | (0) | (0) | 50 |
| R&D costs within Heads 1-6 | (0) | (50) | (50) | (50) | (150) |
| In-house R&D | (0) | (150) | (200) | (10) | (360) |
| Sub-contracted R&D | (0) | (50) | (0) | (190) | (240) |
| Royalties | (0) | (20) | (5) | (0) | (25) |
| Net profit | 300 | 230 | 245 | 250 | 1,025 |

Notional royalties for patents per transfer pricing specialist:

| | | | | | |
|---|---|---|---|---|---|
| Notional royalties | (0) | (15) | (45) | (1) | (61) |

All sub-contracted R&d is with Petunia's branch in Notaxland, a country with which the UK has no double tax treaty. Petunia has elected not to treat the branch as taxable in the UK under s 357 CTA 2009. No expenditure was incurred on the acquisition of IP rights.

Petunia was granted each patent on the first day of trade. In the previous 6 years the patent pending IP profits were £300k.

Calculate the corporation tax liability for the year ended 30 June 2017.

# Answer

## A

*(a) Taxable total profits*

| | |
|---|---|
| MJD Ltd year ended 30 September 2016 | £ |
| Trading profits | 1,000,000 |
| Less additional % on research & development expenditure | |
| £120,000 @ 130% | (156,000) |
| Taxable total profits | 844,000 |

The enhancement rate since 1 April 2015 has been a130% uplift (230% total tax relief).

*(b) Main conditions for a research and development tax relief claim under CTA 2009 Part 13 Chapter 2*

Companies qualifying as an SME are able to claim research and development (R&D) tax relief equal to 225% or 230% of the qualifying expenditure, (capped at €7.5 million per project) giving an additional trading deduction of 125% and 130% from 1 April 2015.

For expenditure incurred before 1 April 2012 the rate was 200% (100% uplift). For these purposes, R&D is as defined in accordance with generally accepted accounting practice (GAAP) (and in particular, FRS 102 (or SSAP 13 for accounting periods starting before 1 January 2015) as qualified by the Department of Business Innovation and Skills (formerly the Department for Business, Enterprise and Regulatory Reform (BERR)) guidelines on the topic entitled 'Guidelines on the meaning of Research and Development for Tax Purposes', adopted by SI 2004/712.

Companies may surrender their unused losses generated by an R&D claim to obtain a cash tax credit equal to 14.5% (for expenditure incurred before 1 April 2014, 11%) of the loss (see **explanatory note 2**).

HMRC's Corporate Intangibles Research & Development manual at CIRD80000 onwards provides some helpful commentary.

The main conditions for a R&D relief claim under CTA 2009 Part 13 Chapter 2 are as follows:

- The claimant company is a small or medium-sized enterprise. For R&D purposes this means that the company (together with any 'linked enterprises' and 'partner enterprises') has:
  - fewer than 500 employees, *and*
  - annual turnover not exceeding €100 million (approx £75 million), *or*
  - gross balance sheet totals not exceeding € 86 million (approx £64.5 million).

  A company ceases to qualify as a small or medium-sized enterprise if it fails the above definition for two consecutive periods.
- The R&D expenditure is of a revenue nature, i.e. not capital expenditure, although 100% R&D capital allowances may be available on capital expenditure, but relief is not denied by virtue of the cost being capitalised for accounting purposes.
- The expenditure relates to the company's trade, an extension of that trade, or a trade that will be derived from the R&D
- The expenditure relates only to staffing costs (as defined in CTA 2009 s 1123), and to software or consumable items (as defined by CTA 2009 s 1125) or to R&D contracted out to someone else.

- The R&D does not relate to activities that have been contracted out to the company by any person.
- The R&D spending is not subsidised by the state or any other party (the R&D tax relief being ignored for this purpose).

The definition of R&D expenditure is complex. Essentially R&D requires that the company undertook a project to resolve a scientific of technological uncertainty where the answer is not readily deducible or available to a competent professional working in the field. Claimants need to be sure that their expenditure falls within it before making a claim. The claim should be supported by a written statement explaining this scientific or technological advance. When preparing the claim consideration must be had to the guidelines referred to above.

Claims must be made, amended or withdrawn on the company's corporation tax return, within one year of the anniversary of the filing date.

*(c) A short outline of the patent box regime*

*Introduction*

Part 8A (ss 357A–357GE) of CTA 2010 sets out a tax regime which deals with 'Profits arising from the exploitation of patents etc . . . ', colloquially known as the 'Patent Box' (though it applies to more than patents), which applies for accounting periods ending on or after 1 April 2013.

Whilst there is a large amount of detailed legislation, the new provisions broadly provide for a reduced rate of corporation tax of (eventually) just 10% for profits attributable to income from qualifying IP rights. The rate is being phased in over a four year period. From April 2013 60% of the benefit is available, giving an effective rate on patents of about 14%, rising by 10% each year, thus providing a reducing effective rate of tax until the full benefit is available in April 2017.

The patent box has been revised to account for concerns arising from the BEPS (Base Erosion and Profit Shifting) project by the OECD (Organisation for Economic Cooperation and Development) and the existing scheme will be closed to new entrants on 30 June 2016 and withdrawn entirely from 30 June 2021. The replacement patent box is very similar in most respects, but has a simplified system for companies with profits of under £1m and restrictions on certain other aspects of the scheme.

Only companies can benefit from Patent Box; it is not available to entities which do not pay corporation tax. There are no restrictions on the size of company that can qualify, so the smallest company with one patent can qualify in the same way as the large pharmaceutical companies.

The benefits of the Patent Box are only available to qualifying companies. A qualifying company can elect to benefit from the Patent Box (under CTA 2010 s 357A) if it is liable to UK corporation tax, it makes a profit from exploiting qualifying IP, it owns or exclusively licences qualifying IP and has undertaken qualifying development in relation to the qualifying IP.

The intention is to provide additional incentive for companies in the UK to retain and commercialise existing IP and develop new innovative products. The relief can be generous, for example, incorporating a patented item into a product (subject to anti-avoidance legislation) can qualify the income from the whole product. For example, a new patented chip in a computer, will enable the income from the whole computer to qualify for the 10% rate.

*Qualifying IP rights*

The IP rights that qualify are:

- patents granted by the UK Intellectual Property Office;
- patents not granted by the UK IPO under provisions regarding national security or public safety and the applicant has been notified that the application otherwise complies with the Patents Act 1977;
- patents granted by the European Patents Office;
- patents granted by the equivalent IP offices in certain other countries in the EEA;
- plant variety rights and data exclusivity;

- supplementary protection certificates, plant breeders' rights, community plant variety rights and marketing authorisations.

The relief extends to the worldwide patent profits derived from qualifying IP. However it does not cover other categories of intellectual property such as trademarks and copyright. If the company does not own the IP, Patent Box may still be available as the company can qualify if it holds an exclusive licence on a product. For the purposes of the Patent Box legislation an exclusive licence is one which must meet specific requirements as set out in the legislation.

*Qualifying companies*

The definition of a qualifying company requires companies to hold qualifying IP rights or hold an exclusive licence over qualifying IP at any time during an accounting period.

Where a company is a member of a group, it must also satisfy the active ownership test.

*Qualifying development*

Qualifying development in respect of an IP right is considered to be where a company has created, or significantly contributed to the creation of, the invention or it has performed a significant amount of activity to develop the invention (including developing new ways for the invention to be used) or any item or process that incorporates the invention.

Where a company is a member of a group, it may be a qualifying company if another company in the group has carried out the qualifying development.

*The calculation*

Unfortunately, the headline of 'a 10% tax rate on patents' undersells the complexity of the calculation necessary to take advantage of the regime.

The 10% rate of tax is effected by taking a deduction in the corporation tax computation for an amount calculated as follows:

$RP \times ((MR - IPR)/MR)$

Where:

RP is the relevant IP profits of the trade of the company;

MR is the rate of corporation tax; and

IPR is the special IP rate of corporation tax (currently 10%).

The calculation of RP is extensive.

The phased in benefit of the Patent Box is effected by FA 2012 Sch 2 para 8(1) and treats RP as meaning the following:

In financial year:

| | |
|---|---|
| 2013 | 60% of RP; |
| 2014 | 70% of RP; |
| 2015 | 80% of RP; and |
| 2016 | 90% of RP. |

*The relevant IP profits of the trade*

The calculation of qualifying profits (RP) is complex and involves seven steps which broadly:

- Identify the percentage of gross income earned from patents. Qualifying income includes:

  - Income from the sale of patent protected products,
  - Income from the sale of products containing a patent protected component,
  - Licence fees/royalties for granting rights over qualifying patents,
  - Notional royalty income,
  - Proceeds of sale/exclusive licencing of patent,
  - Income from infringements, damages, insurance or other compensation related to patents rights.
- Identify relevant profits (taxable profits subject to certain adjustments) and apply the percentage.
- Strip out profits not arising as a direct result of the patents:
  - Routine return – which is broadly 10% of routine costs such as general admin and sales.
  - Marketing return – this is to eliminate profit from the use of a brand.

There are two main sub-elections that can be made. These are:

(a) Streaming – this uses actual income and expenses attributable to patents rather than the standard apportionment method.

(b) The small claims election – this is a simpler method of removing a marketing royalty using a 25% reduction rather than undertaking a complex transfer pricing based exercise. This election is altered under the revised patent box scheme, instead the company treats 75% of the IP-related income as relevant IP profits.

HMRC's internal manuals provide an excellent basis for the first time computation, with a step by step approach explaining what is required of each part of the computation, with step by step guidance for every term and worked examples. The guidance starts at CIRD200000 with an index page.

*Making a claim*

Where a company has a customer relationship manager or customer coordinator they should approach them in the first instance with any specific queries on Patent Box. Companies which do not have either of these contacts should contact their regional R&D unit which deals with Patent Box claims. Their contact details are available at CIRD80350.

Businesses which may wish to make a claim will need to ensure that the relevant accounting information is captured to provide easily accessible figures for the computation of relevant IP profits. In particular, detailed sales records will be needed to identify the turnover related to products which fall into the patent box regime.

## B1. Petunia Engineering Ltd Tax computation for the year ended 30 June 2016

| | | |
|---|---|---|
| | | £ |
| Profit before tax per accounts | | 788,398 |
| *Less:* | | |
| Interest income | 3,000 | |
| Capital allowances | 101,834 | |
| Uplift on R & D: £172,689 x 130% | 224,496 | |
| | | (329,330) |
| Add: | | |
| Depreciation of equipment | 34,903 | |
| Amortisation of patents | 1,498 | |
| Donation to charity | 450 | |
| Entertaining | 847 | |

| | |
|---|---|
| | 37,698 |
| Net taxable trading profit | 496,766 |
| Non trading income - interest | 3,000 |
| Patent box deduction (see below) | (160,449) |
| Net taxable profit | 333,317 |
| Corporation tax at 20% | £66,663 |

So the patent box deduction has reduced Petunia Engineering Limited's corporation tax liability by £32,090 (£160,449 @ 20%).

The Patent box deduction is calculated as follows:

| | | | £ |
|---|---|---|---|
| **Step 1** | | | |
| Total Gross income | TI | | |
| Turnover per accounts | | | 1,491,250 |
| Exchange differences | | | 8,402 |
| Hire charges | | | 3,004 |
| Total | | | 1,502,656 |
| **Step 2** | | | |
| IP percentage of total gross income | X% | | |
| Sales of patented items | | | 844,508 |
| Hire charges | | | 3,004 |
| Relevant IP income | RIPI | | 847,512 |
| X% = RIPI/TI | | | 56.40% |
| **Step 3** | | | |
| Adjusted trading profits and apportionment | | | |
| Trading profit as above | | | 496,766 |
| Add back R & D uplift | | | 224,495 |
| R & D shortfall adjustment | | | 0 |
| Adjusted trading profits | ATP | | 721,261 |
| **R & D shortfall calculation** | | | |
| Costs in 2012 | | 149,021 | |
| 2013 | | 195,777 | |
| 2014 | | 201,664 | |
| 2015 | | 155,148 | |
| Total | | 701,610 | |
| Average | | 175,403 | |
| 2016 R & D | | 172,689 | |
| This is more than 75% of the average so no shortfall | | | |
| X% of ATP | | | 406,791 |
| **Step 4** | | | |
| Routine return amount | RRA | | |
| Head 1 – capital allowances | | | 101,834 |
| Head 2 – premises costs | | | |
| Rent | | 74,044 | |
| Light and heat | | 3,502 | |
| Rates and insurance | | 8,330 | |

| | | | |
|---|---|---|---|
| Premises repairs | | 4,250 | 90,126 |
| Head 3 – personnel costs | | | |
| Total salaries | | 203,846 | |
| Less allocated to R & D | | (148,935) | 54,911 |
| Head 4 – plant and machinery | | | 0 |
| Head 5 – professional services | | 11,341 | |
| Less : relating to patents | | (3,499) | 7,842 |
| Head 6 – misc services | | | |
| Sub-contract work (non R&D) | | 39,846 | |
| Internet services | | 4,520 | |
| Motor expenses | | 8,647 | |
| Travel and hotels | | 847 | |
| Office general expenses | | 3,776 | |
| Total expenses for RRA purposes | | | 316,046 |
| RRA is 10% of total expenses above | | | 31,605 |
| IP element of RRA (X%) | | | 17,825 |
| Qualifying residual profit | QRP | | |
| IP element of ATP | | | 406,791 |
| Less: IP element of RRA | | | (17,825) |
| QRP | | | 388,966 |

**Step 5**

| | | | |
|---|---|---|---|
| Consider small claim amount | | | |
| Condition A QRP < £1 million | | MET | |
| Small claim available | | | |
| Small claim – lower of 75% QRP | | 291,725 | |
| and | | 1,000,000 | |
| So the small claims amount would be | | | 291,725 |

However, as the company operates in a purely technical field the Marketing asset adjustment is likely to be zero, so the company would be better off with a full claim.

**Step 6**

| | |
|---|---|
| Deduct marketing assets return | 0 |

**Step 7**

| | |
|---|---|
| Does not apply | |
| Final relevant IP profit | 388,966 |

**Patent box relief**

| | | | |
|---|---|---|---|
| Main rate of corporation tax | MR | 20% | |
| Patent box rate | IPR | 10% | |
| Transitional rate (2016–17) (80% [15/16] * 9/12 + 90% * 3/12 [16/17]) | | 82.5% | |
| (MR-IPR)/MR | | 50% | |
| | | | £160,449 |

## B2. Petunia Engineering Ltd Tax computation for the year ended 30 June 2017

Step 1. Divide the income into the 'relevant IP stream' and the 'standard income stream' – essentially the same as before.

Step 2. Divide the IP income stream into sub-streams attributable to specific IP items, processes or rights.

Step 3. Allocate the trading expenses between the relevant IP income sub-streams and the standard trading income stream on a just and reasonable basis

Step 4. Deduct the expenses of each sub-stream from the sub-stream in question. Then deduct the routine return for the sub-stream of 10% of the aggregate heads of expenditure (which are similar to the previous patent box routine).

Step 5. If the small claims treatment for the marketing return is required under s. 357BNA CTA 2010 et seq. then either the company elects to deduct the notional royalty election of 25%, makes the small claims election, or makes a global streaming election.

The small claims election takes the profit attributed to each sub-streams after step 4 (A), the qualifying residual profit of the trade after step 4 (QRP), compares the result for each sub-stream to the small claims threshold (SCT) and applies a routine return of A-((A*SCT)/QRP) for each sub-stream.

A global streaming election permits the company to claim patent box relief as if it had a single stream of relevant IP-profit rather than being required to calculate it for each sub-stream.

Step 6. If a small claims election is not made the marketing asset return is then computed for each sub-stream and deducted from the sub-stream QRP. The marketing return is the notional marketing royalty, less any actual royalty paid for the IP. If the actual royalty exceeds the notional royalty, or if the notional royalty is less than 10% of QRP, then no adjustment is made to the sub-stream QRP.

Step 7. The result of the QRP less the marketing asset return for each sub-stream is then multiplied by the R&D fraction, which is the lesser of 1 and the following fraction:

[(D + S1) * 1.3] / (D + S1 + S2 + A)

D = the company's qualifying expenditure on relevant R&D undertaken by the company. This excludes expenditure by a foreign permanent establishment in respect of which an election under s.18A CTA 2009 has been made (the election makes the PE non-taxable in the UK).

S1 = the company's qualifying expenditure on relevant R&D sub-contracted to unconnected persons.

S2 = the company's qualifying expenditure on relevant R&D sub-contracted to connected persons, which is 65% of the expenditure in the period sub-contracted to connected persons, and including expenditure by a foreign permanent establishment in respect of which an election under s. 18A CTA 2009 has been made.

A = The company's qualifying expenditure on the acquisition of relevant qualifying IP rights.

The formula effectively compares 130% of the proportion of R&D incurred by the claimant company (or subcontracted to connected companies/its PE's not taxable in the UK) to the total R&D spend and takes the lower of the proportion and 1, unless the company sub-contracts the bulk of its R&D the result is likely to be 1.

Step 8. Add the results for each sub-stream together to get the total IP profit for all the sub-streams.

Step 9. Add any amounts arising in respect of earlier years before a patent was granted calculated in accordance with s. 357BN (similar to pre-grant allowances under the previous patent box regime).

Calculation:

**Step 1.** Allocate income between standard stream and relevant IP income stream:

| | *Standard* | *IP* | *Total* |
|---|---|---|---|
| Sales | 450 | 1,500 | 1,950 |

**Step 2.** Allocate income between streams.

| | *Non-trade* | *Patent A* | *Patent B* | *Patent B* | *Total* |
|---|---|---|---|---|---|
| Sales | 450 | 500 | 500 | 500 | 1,950 |

**Step 3.** Allocate trading expenses between streams

| | *Non-trade* | *Patent A* | *Patent B* | *Patent B* | *Total* |
|---|---|---|---|---|---|
| Cost of sales | (200) | (0) | (0) | (0) | (200) |
| Allowable R&D costs | (0) | (50) | (50) | (50) | (150) |
| In-house R&D | (0) | (150) | (200) | (10) | (360) |
| Sub-contracted R&D | (0) | (50) | (0) | (190) | (240) |
| Royalties | (0) | (20) | (5) | (0) | (250) |

**Step 4a.** Calculate routine return.

| | | | | | |
|---|---|---|---|---|---|
| *Expenditure* | | | | | |
| *R&D costs* | (0) | (250) | (250) | (250) | (750) |
| 10% routine return | (0) | (25) | (25) | (25) | (75) |

**Step 4b.** Deduct expenses and routine return from income for each stream

| | *Non-trade* | *Patent A* | *Patent B* | *Patent B* | *Total* |
|---|---|---|---|---|---|
| Sales | n/a | 500 | 500 | 500 | 1500 |
| Less: Cost of sales | n/a | (0) | (0) | (0) | (0) |
| Allowable R&D costs | (0) | (50) | (50) | (50) | (150) |
| 10% routine return | n/a | (25) | (25) | (25) | (75) |
| In-house R&D | n/a | (150) | (200) | (10) | (360) |
| Sub-contracted R&D | n/a | (50) | (0) | (1900) | (2400) |
| Royalties | n/a | (20) | (5) | (0) | (25) |
| Qualifying residual profit: QRP | n/a | 205 | 220 | 225 | 650 |

**Step 5.** Small claims treatment 357BN

QRP is less than the small claims threshold (of £1m for a stand-alone entity) accordingly small claims treatment is available.

| | | | | | |
|---|---|---|---|---|---|
| *Notional royalty election 75%* | n/a | 154 | 165 | 168 | 487 |
| Small claims figure election 75% QRP | | 154 | 165 | 168 | 487 |
| Global streaming election | | n/a | n/a | n/a | 487 |

As 75% of QRP is lower than the SCT (£1m) the small claims figure is 25% of the sub-stream following step 4 which means that the small claims figure gives the same result as the notional royalty election.
If 75% of the QRP was higher than the SCT, then the small claims figure would be A – (A/QRP) * SCT.

**Step 6** – if there was no small claims election

| | *Non-trade* | *Patent A* | *Patent B* | *Patent B* | *Total* |
|---|---|---|---|---|---|
| Actual royalties | n/a | (20) | (5) | (0) | (20) |
| Notional royalties | n/a | (15) | (45) | (1) | (20) |
| 10% of QRP | n/a | 13 | 13 | 13 | n/a |
| Royalty restriction | n/a | (0) | (40) | (0) | (40) |

Patent A has no restriction for royalties as the actual royalty is more than the notional royalty.
Patent B has a restriction of 40, as the notional royalty exceeds 10% of QRP and the actual royalty. The restriction is the excess of the notional royalty (45) over the actual royalty (5).

| | *Non-trade* | *Patent A* | *Patent B* | *Patent B* | *Total* |
|---|---|---|---|---|---|

Patent C has no restriction for royalties, as the notional royalty is less than 10% of the QRP.

| | *Non-trade* | *Patent A* | *Patent B* | *Patent B* | *Total* |
|---|---|---|---|---|---|
| *QRP b/f step 4* | n/a | 205 | 220 | 225 | 650 |
| Royalty restriction | n/a | (0) | (40) | (0) | (40) |
| IP profit working c/f | n/a | 205 | 180 | 225 | 610 |

**Step 7 & 8.** Apply R&D fraction & add together the results

As in this case the royalty restriction is less with step 6 than if the small claims election is made, the election should not be made.

| | | | | | |
|---|---|---|---|---|---|
| *In-house R&D* | D | (150) | (200) | (10) | (360) |
| Sub-contracted R&D – third party | S1 | (0) | (0) | (0) | (0) |
| 65% sub-contracted R&D - connected | S2 | (32) | (0) | (124) | (156) |
| Expenditure on acquisition of IP | A | (0) | (0) | (0) | (0) |
| Fraction - numerator | (D+S1) *1.3 | (195) | (260) | (13) | n/a |
| Fraction - denominator | D+S1+S2+A | (182) | (200) | (134) | n/a |
| R&D fraction | | 1* | 1* | 0.097 | n/a |
| R&D fraction applied to step 6 c/f | | 205 | 180 | 22 | n/a |

* R&D fraction is the lower of 1 and [(D+S1)*1.3 / (D+S1+S2+A)]

**Step 9.** Add amounts arising in earlier years while patents were pending.

| | |
|---|---|
| *Step 8 c/f IP profit* | 407 |
| Prior amount IP profit | 300 |
| Relevant IP profit for period | 707 |

| | |
|---|---|
| Calculate deduction | |
| MR: Corporation tax rate | 20% |
| IPR: Patent box rate | 10% |
| MR-IPR / MR | 50% |
| CT deduction available | **354** |

## Explanatory Notes

*Research and development (R&D) tax reliefs*

(1) Where *any* trader either incurs revenue expenditure on research and development related to his trade, or pays a sum to an approved scientific research association, university, college or research institute to be used for that purpose, the expenditure is deductible as a trading expense of the accounting period in which it is incurred (CTA 2009 ss 87 and 88).

(2) The special 225% (prior to 1 April 2012 200%) enhanced tax deduction for R&D revenue expenditure by small/medium-sized (SME) companies was originally introduced by FA 2000 s 69 and Sch 20. R&D relief is now covered in CTA 2009 Part 13.

Under the SME scheme losses attributable to qualifying revenue R&D expenditure may, subject to conditions, be surrendered for a tax credit equating to 14.5% (before 1 April 2014 the rate was 11%) of the loss enhanced at 225%. This gives effective relief of 32.63% (14.5% x 225%). In recent years, the rate of relief against profits has increased; whilst the effective rate for the repayable tax credit remained around 25% until April 2014.

R&D tax reliefs have been the subject of constant revision and amendment since their introduction.

Relief is available only to a claimant that is a going concern (CTA 2009 ss 1046 and 1057). A company is a going concern if the latest accounts were published on a going concern basis, and expectation of tax credits was not the only reason for adopting the going concern basis.

For pre-trading R&D expenditure, the company may elect to treat the 225% deduction as a trading loss for that pre-trading period and it will not then be treated as incurred on the first day of trading under the normal rules (CTA 2009 s 1045) (see **Example I1 explanatory note 6**).

Before 1 April 2012 the R&D credit was restricted to the total amount of the company's PAYE and Class 1 national insurance payments for the relevant accounting period. For this purpose the PAYE/NI for the tax months (to 5th of each month) ending in the accounting period would be taken. Say, for example, the year to 31 March 2012 a company spent £120,000 on R&D (on revenue account) so the R&D tax deduction at 200% (old rate) was £240,000. The PAYE/NI for the period was £21,000. In this case the maximum potential R&D tax refund would have been £30,000 (= 12.5% of £240,000) but the R&D tax credit repayment would have been restricted to £21,000. The repayment represented a trading loss of £168,000, leaving an unused loss available to carry forward of £72,000 (£240,000 less £168,000).

(3) From 1 April 2016, claims by companies which are ineligible for the small company scheme are made under a scheme called Above the Line relief (ATL). ATL gives an 11% tax credit for R&D expenditure (10% before 1 April 2015). The credit is shown as income in the accounts and then deducted as a credit from the corporation tax payable. Where a company is loss making, it may, subject to some restrictions surrender the credit net of corporation tax for a refund. Large companies previously claimed a similar uplift to the small company regime, with a 30% addition to qualifying expenditure, bringing relief to 130% overall. Below is a comparison of HMRC's examples of ATL with the old 130% scheme:

| **Profitable company** | **Old scheme** | ATL |
|---|---|---|
| | £K | £K |
| Turnover | 2,400 | 2,400 |
| R&D expenditure | (1,000) | (1,000) |
| ATL credit | | 110 |
| Other expenditure | (1,000) | (1,000) |
| Profit | 400 | 510 |
| R&D enhancement | (300) | |
| Taxable profit | 100 | 510 |
| Tax @ 20% | 20 | 102 |
| ATL credit | 0 | (110) |
| **Tax payable** | **20** | 0 |

| **Loss making company** | **Existing scheme** | ATL |
|---|---|---|
| | £K | £K |
| Turnover | 1,400 | 1,400 |
| R&D expenditure | (1,000) | (1,000) |
| ATL credit @ 10% | | 110 |
| Other expenses | (1,000) | (1,000) |
| Loss | (600) | (490) |
| R&D enhancement | (300) | |
| Tax loss c/fwd | (900) | (490) |
| ATL tax credit | | 110 |

| | |
|---|---|
| Less notional CT @ 20% | (21) |
| **Payable tax credit** | **88** |

(4) Where a large company carries out R&D on its own behalf, the qualifying rules include the same provisions as for SMEs in relation to the requirement for the expenditure not to be capital in nature and to be incurred on staffing costs, consumables, software or utility costs, and for the company to be a trading company.

A principal difference from the SME relief relates to subcontracted R&D, as it is possible the relief to be claimed by a small/medium-sized subcontractor working for the large company. There are also provisions giving the enhanced relief where a large company makes contributions to special defined bodies or individuals conducting R&D which is relevant to the trade of the company concerned.

# Question

## A.

Domo Ltd is a UK trading subsidiary of a large multinational group, which has over twenty active UK and overseas trading companies. The majority of Domo Ltd's business is carried on from the UK but it also has a branch in Norland, a country which imposes taxation at the rate of 35% on the profits or gains of companies resident there and on any profits or gains arising there for non-resident companies. Domo Ltd also has a number of trade-related investments.

The following information relates to Domo Ltd for the year ended 31 March 2017:

| | £ |
|---|---|
| *Trading income* – UK trade | 180,000 |
| – Norland branch (before deducting tax suffered in Norland) | 30,000 |
| *Investment income* | |
| Dividend received in May 2016 on a holding of 15% of the ordinary (voting) shares in Fiord Norland Ltd. | |
| (Assume for these purposes that the dividend does not fall into an exempt class and will be subject to taxation in the UK.) | |
| (after deducting 15% withholding tax) | 11,050 |
| Interest receivable on a holding of 12% of the debentures of Lake Norland Ltd | |
| (after deducting 20% withholding tax) | 12,000 |
| Dividend received in May 2016 on a holding of 8% of the ordinary shares of Valley Norland Ltd. Assume for these purposes that the dividend falls into an exempt class and will not be subject to taxation in the UK. | |
| (after deducting 15% withholding tax) | 10,200 |
| Net capital profit on land in Norland bought for £20,000 in Jan 2009, | |
| sold in March 2017 for £37,000 – Norland tax suffered £5,950 | |
| (UK indexation allowance to be taken as 25%) | 11,050 |
| Charitable donation paid to NSPCC | 5,000 |
| Dividend paid – January 2017 – final for year ended 31 March 2016 | 152,000 |

The company did not have any unrelieved amounts brought forward at 1 April 2016.

Compute the corporation tax payable by Domo Ltd for the year ended 31 March 2016 after claiming all possible reliefs.

## B.

Jones Ltd is a member of an international group of 30 companies and its only investment is a 40% holding in Shelley SA, a company resident in Ruritania. This is a country which has not agreed a double taxation agreement with the UK. In June 2016, Jones Ltd received in cash a dividend of 108,000 Ruritanian Dollars (R$), that had suffered 10% Ruritanian withholding tax. Assume for these purposes that the dividend does not fall into an exempt class and will be subject to taxation in the UK. The rate of exchange throughout the periods in question is R$1 = £1.25.

The company's resolution did not indicate the accounting period for which the dividend was paid. The Ruritanian accounts of Shelley SA for the three years to 31 October 2014, 2015 and 2016 are set out below.

**Shelley SA – trading and profit and loss account**

| | *Year ended 31.10.14* | *Year ended 31.10.15* | *Year ended 31.10.16* |
|---|---|---|---|
| | *R$* | *R$* | *R$* |
| Operating profit before tax | 205,000 | 350,000 | 400,000 |
| Unrealised exchange gain/(loss) on investments | 100,000 | (80,000) | 70,000 |
| Taxation | | | |
| Current tax | (40,000) | (60,000) | (80,000) |
| Deferred tax | (15,000) | (20,000) | (20,000) |
| (Under-)/over-provision for previous year | 10,000 | (5,000) | (5,000) |
| Profit after taxation | 260,000 | 185,000 | 365,000 |
| Unrealised exchange items transferred (to)/from non distributable capital reserve | (100,000) | 80,000 | (70,000) |
| Transfer to statutory non-distributable reserve for contingencies | (30,000) | (30,000) | (30,000) |
| Transfer to general reserve | (25,000) | (45,000) | (60,000) |
| Dividend paid in the year | – | – | (300,000) |
| Retained profit/(loss) per accounts | R$ 105,000 | R$ 190,000 | R$ (95,000) |
| Actual tax paid for the year | R$ 45,000 | R$ 65,000 | R$ 80,000 |

For its year ended 31 March 2017, Jones Ltd has adjusted trading income profits taxable of £200,000, before deducting non-trade interest payable of £150,000. It also paid a dividend of £80,000 in January 2017. There were no unrelieved amounts brought forward at 1 April 2016.

(a) Compute the foreign income assessable arising from the dividend, and

(b) Calculate the corporation tax payable by Jones Ltd for the year ended 31 March 2017.

# Answer

## A. Domo Ltd – Mainstream Corporation Tax for year ended 31 March 2017

| | | *Trading Income* | | *Loan Relationship* | *Foreign Income* | | |
|---|---|---|---|---|---|---|---|
| | *Total* | *UK* | *Norland Branch (Note 1)* | *Non-Trade Profits Lake Norland (Note 2)* | *Fiord Norland (Note 3)* | *Valley Norland (Note 4)* | *Foreign chargeable gains (Note 5)* |
| | £ | £ | £ | £ | £ | £ | £ |
| Trading profit | 210,000 | 180,000 | 30,000 | | | | |
| Debenture interest | 15,000 | | | 15,000 | | | |
| Foreign dividends | 20,000 | | | | 20,000 | 0 | |
| Chargeable gains | 12,000 | | | | | | 12,000 |
| | 257,000 | 180,000 | 30,000 | 15,000 | 20,000 | 0 | 12,000 |
| Less charitable donation relief (see **note 6**) | (5,000) | (5,000) | | | | | |
| Taxable total profits | 252,000 | 175,000 | 30,000 | 15,000 | 20,000 | 0 | 12,000 |
| Corporation tax payable @ 20% | 50,400 | 35,000 | 6,000 | 3,000 | 4,000 | 0 | 2,400 |
| Less double tax relief | (15,406) | | (6,000)* | (3,000) | (4,000)* | 0 | (2,400)* |
| * restricted to UK tax | | | | | | | |
| Corporation tax payable | 35,000 | 35,000 | 0 | 0 | 0 | 0 | 0 |
| Foreign tax unrelieved | | | | | 4,950 | 1,800 | 3,550 |
| Unrelieved foreign tax carried forward (or carried back) | | | 4,500 | | | | |

### Notes

(1) Norland branch profits foreign tax – 30,000 @ 35% = £10,500

The excess double tax of £4,500 suffered on the Norland branch income (i.e. £10,500 less £6,000 maximum offset) can be carried back for set-off against UK tax suffered on the Norland branch income of the three years to 31 March 2016, any balance being carried forward to set against UK tax suffered on future Norland branch income (Taxation (International and Other Provisions) Act 2010 (TIOPA 2010) s 73).

(2) Debentures in Lake Norland – 12,000 + (20/80) 3,000 withholding tax = £15,000

(3) Shares in Fiord Norland (holding carries at least 10% voting power):

| | £ |
|---|---|
| Dividend (net) | 11,050 |
| Withholding tax (15/85) | 1,950 |
| Franked dividend | 13,000 |
| Underlying tax (35/65) | 7,000 |
| Foreign income | 20,000 |

Foreign dividends received in the UK may not be subject to tax if they meet the conditions for exemption (see **explanatory note 7**).

As Domo Ltd is a large company, a dividend it receives will only be exempt if it falls into one of the classes for companies that are not small (Corporation Tax Act 2009 (CTA 2009) Part 9A Chapter 3). In this case the dividend does not fall into an exempt class and will be subject to UK tax, but will also be eligible for credit relief for both withholding tax and underlying tax.

The calculation of foreign income includes all foreign taxes, whether relievable or not. The maximum relievable foreign tax (known as the 'mixer cap') is 20% of the sum of the dividend plus the underlying tax, in this case £4,000.

*Unrelieved foreign tax*

The tax suffered on the Fiord Norland dividend exceeds the 20% mixer cap restriction. This excess of £4,950 cannot be relieved. (see **explanatory note 11**).

(4) Shares in Valley Norland (8% holding)

| | £ |
|---|---|
| Dividend (net) | 10,200 |
| Withholding tax (15/85) | 1,800 |
| | 12,000 |

CTA 2009 s 933 charges income dividends of a non-UK resident company to corporation tax if they are received by a UK tax resident company or an overseas branch of a UK tax resident company.

Exemptions are included, which provide exemption from UK corporation tax in Chapter 2 for small companies receiving dividends if certain conditions were met (CTA 2009 s 931B). Provided none of the anti-avoidance rules set out in CTA 2009 Part 9A s 931J apply, this dividend will fall into the exempt class for portfolio dividends set out in CTA 2009 Part 9A s 931G.

Domo Limited is a large company but the dividend from Valley Norland Ltd may still be exempt from corporation tax if it is exempt under CTA 2009 ss 931E to 931I (see **explanatory note 7**).

As the dividend is not taxable in the UK, none of the foreign tax of £1,800 will be relievable.

| | | | |
|---|---|---|---|
| (5) Chargeable gain: | Sale proceeds March 2017 | | 37,000 |
| | Cost – Jan 2009 | 20,000 | |
| | Indexation allowance 25% | 5,000 | (25,000) |
| | Net Gain | | 12,000 |

(6) Charitable donations are paid gross and relief given under qualifying charitable donations relief (CTA 2010 s 189) See **Example I1 explanatory note 11.**

## B.

### (a) *Jones Ltd – Foreign income arising from June 2016 dividend*

Jones Ltd's dividend received from Shelley SA before 10% withholding tax is grossed up as follows:

$$108{,}000 \times \frac{100}{90} = \text{R\$}120{,}000$$

The total dividend paid by Shelley SA is:

$$120{,}000 \times \frac{100}{40} = \text{R\$}300{,}000.$$

As the dividend is not paid out of a specified period (see **explanatory note 4**), it is treated as coming first out of the distributable profits of the year to 31 October 2015 (being the last accounts before June 2016 when the dividend was received) then the previous year as follows:

| | | | *Year to 31.10.15* | | | *Year to 31.10.14* |
|---|---|---|---|---|---|---|
| | | | R$ | | | R$ |
| Retained profits per accounts | | | 190,000 | | | 105,000 |
| Add transfer to general reserve | | | 45,000 | | | 25,000 |
| | | | 235,000 | | | 130,000 |
| Attributable to dividend (R$ 300,000) | | (1st) | 235,000 | (balance) | | 65,000 |
| Actual tax paid | | | 65,000 | | | 45,000 |
| Underlying tax: | | | | | R$ | |
| Year to 31.10.15 40% × | 65,000 | | | | 26,000 | |
| 31.10.14 40% × | | $\frac{65,000}{130,000}$ | × *45,000* | | 9,000 | |
| | | | | | 35,000 | |
| Dividend inclusive of withholding tax | | | | | 120,000 | |
| | | | | | 155,000 | |
| Overseas tax borne (35,000 + 12,000) | | | | | 47,000 | |
| Converted to sterling at R$1 = £1.25 = | | | | | | 58,750 |
| Dividend received R$108,000 converted at R$1 = £1.25 = | | | | | | 135,000 |
| Foreign income (including overseas tax £58,750) | | | | | | £193,750 |

However if the dividend had been declared as an interim distribution for the year ended 31 October 2016, or specified as a distribution of the profits of this later period, then it would taxed as follows:

| | | | *Year to 31.10.16* | | *Year to 31.10.15* |
|---|---|---|---|---|---|
| | | | *R$* | | |
| Retained (loss)/ profits per accounts | | | (95,000) | | 190,000 |
| Add dividend paid | | | 300,000 | | – |
| Add transfer to general reserve | | | 60,000 | | 45,000 |
| | | | 265,000 | | 235,000 |
| Attributable to dividend (R$ 300,000) | (1st) | | 265,000 | (balance) | 35,000 |
| Actual tax paid | | | 80,000 | | 65,000 |
| Underlying tax: | | | | R$ | |
| Year to 31.10.16 40% × | 80,000 | | | 32,000 | |
| 31.10.15 40% × | | $\frac{35,000}{235,000} \times 65,000$ | | 3,872 | |
| | | | | 35,872 | |
| Dividend inclusive of withholding tax | | | | 120,000 | |
| | | | | 155,872 | |
| Overseas tax borne (35,872 + 12,000) | | | | 47,872 | |
| Converted to sterling at R$1 = £1.25 = | | | | | £59,840 |
| Dividend received R$108,000 converted at R$1 = £1.25 = | | | | | £135,000 |
| Foreign income (including overseas tax £59,840) | | | | | £194,840 |

The above Example demonstrates that if the dividend had been declared as an interim dividend for the period ended 31 October 2016, rather than an unspecified period, it would have increased the amount of foreign income taxed in Jones Limited. Although the amount of foreign income in this Example should not create a significant additional UK corporation tax liability, as the overseas tax rate exceeds 30%.

## (b) *Corporation tax payable by Jones Ltd for year to 31 March 2017*

| | *Total* | *Trading Income* | *Foreign Income* |
|---|---|---|---|
| | £ | £ | £ |
| UK and foreign profits | 393,750 | 200,000 | 193,750 |
| Non-trading deficit (interest payable) | (150,000) | (150,000) | |
| Taxable total profits | 243,750 | 50,000 | 193,750 |
| Corporation tax payable @ 20% | 48,750 | 10,500 | 38,750 |
| Less double tax relief (restricted to UK tax) | (38,750) | | (38,750) |
| Mainstream corporation tax | 10,500 | 10,000 | 0 |

Assuming a distribution of profits from 2015 and 2014 the excess foreign tax suffered on the dividend from Shelley SA of £20,000 (£58,750 – £38,750) represents eligible unrelieved foreign tax (EUFT) which for dividends received after 1 July 2011 is no longer relievable (see **explanatory note 11**).

## Explanatory Notes

*Interest received*

(1) Interest received from abroad by individuals is taxed as income from foreign securities as interest income under Income Tax (Trading and Other Income) Act 2005 (ITTOIA 2005) Part 4 Chapter 2. This does not apply to companies, for whom both UK and foreign interest is taxed according to the 'loan relationships' provisions (see **Example K2**). Unless received by a financial business as trading profits, it is taxed under loan relationships non-trading profits, as shown in **part A** of the Example.

The 'loan relationships' rules provide for interest received to be brought into account on an accruals basis, rather than on the amount that arises in the period. As a result, foreign tax may be apportioned to an earlier accounting period than that in which it was suffered. Thus in **part A** of the Example, the debenture interest receivable from Lake Norland Ltd of £12,000 after 20% withholding tax may include interest accrued but not received at 31 March 2017. The withholding tax taken into account for double tax relief would include the tax suffered on the accrued amount.

*Double taxation relief*

(2) Where a company suffers tax twice on the same profits, whether they are income profits or capital profits, relief may be claimed either under the provisions of a double tax treaty (TIOPA 2010 Part 2 Chapter 1 ss 2–7) or unilaterally (TIOPA 2010 Part 2 Chapter 1 ss 8–17) for a credit against the UK tax charged. Double tax treaties specify which taxes are covered by the agreement. Most treaties are based on the OECD model agreement, but as each is separately negotiated between the respective countries, there are often points specific to the particular treaty. HMRC have issued Statement of Practice 7/91 concerning their approach to identifying relevant foreign taxes where unilateral relief applies.

(3) Double tax relief is computed on a 'source by source' basis. For each source, the relief given is at the lower of the UK tax (based on the most beneficial allocation of losses etc) and the overseas tax attributable to the income or gain.

A measure of relief is available for unrelieved foreign tax relating to *overseas branch income*. The relief enables any unused double tax relief credit to be carried back against the UK tax on the same source of foreign income for up to three years and then carried forward indefinitely against future UK tax from the same foreign source (TIOPA 2010 s 73).

A claim to relieve unused foreign tax must be made within four years after the end of the accounting period in which the amount arose (TIOPA 2010 s 77).

Clearly, if the overseas tax rate suffered on the foreign income is consistently higher than the UK rate, these rules are likely to be of little assistance.

*Relief for underlying tax and relevant profits*

(4) Normally, only direct overseas taxes are taken into account, but underlying tax on overseas *dividends* may be taken into account if the UK company controls not less than 10% of the voting power in the foreign company. Following the introduction of the UK dividend exemption on 1 July 2009, this relief will only be applicable in the minority of cases where the dividend does not qualify for an exemption.

Relief may also be claimed for underlying tax paid by other companies in a chain where the 10% control test is met at each stage in the chain and dividends are paid by one company to the other (TIOPA 2010 s 64). There are anti-avoidance provisions to prevent companies exploiting these provisions (see **explanatory note 6**).

The underlying tax is that part of the foreign tax on the relevant profits that is attributable to the dividend. The relevant profits are as follows:

(a) If the dividend is paid for a specified period, the profits of that period, or

(b) The profits of the last set of accounts ended before the dividend became payable.

If (a) or (b) applies, but the total dividend exceeds those profits, the excess is treated as coming out of earlier undistributed profits, latest first (TIOPA 2010 s 59).

Thus, in **part B** of the Example, the dividend (being for an unspecified accounting period) is treated as being paid out of the last accounting period (31 October 2015) which *ended* before it was paid in June 2016. The balance of 'unmatched' dividend is then allocated to the prior accounting period to 31 October 2014.

(5) The relevant profits are the foreign company's *distributable* profits, not profits for tax purposes (*Bowater Paper Corporation Ltd v Murgatroyd* (1970) now in TIOPA 2010 s 59(8)). This provides that the distributable profits are based on the foreign company's accounts drawn up under the law of that country. Those accounts must only include reserves, provisions for bad debts or contingencies permitted under the law of the company's home State. HMRC takes the view that:

(i) Realised gains on exchange differences are distributable profits. Unrealised exchange gains are not, unless they are in fact used for a dividend or are treated by the foreign company as distributable profits. (In **Example B**, the unrealised exchange gains on investments have been transferred to a non-distributable reserve).

(ii) Realised capital profits are also distributable profits.

(iii) Deferred tax, and any under- or over-provisions for tax in earlier years may be taken into account in computing distributable profits (but not in computing the actual rate of underlying tax).

HMRC's views on this point are set out in the International Manual at INTM164160.

*Anti-avoidance provisions*

(6) There are anti-avoidance provisions in TIOPA 2010 s 82 to prevent group companies, particularly financial companies, artificially increasing the amount of underlying tax they are entitled to by means of an avoidance scheme. The provisions limit relief for underlying tax by reference to the rate of corporation tax payable by the UK company on the dividend it receives.

There are also rules in TIOPA 2010 Part 7 to prevent banks and other financial traders getting excessive relief for foreign tax paid on overseas interest that is part of their trading profits. A number of detailed technical anti-avoidance provisions exist, targeted at schemes notified to HMRC under the Disclosure of Tax Avoidance Scheme rules (DOTAS).

*System of taxation of overseas dividends*

(7) The rules for dividends received by small companies differ from those for medium and large companies, however in each case it is likely that the great majority of dividends will be exempt from corporation tax.

*Small Companies*

The exemption for small companies is set out at CTA 2009 ss 931B and 931C. A company is small if, in the accounting period, it has less than 50 employees, and either a turnover or balance sheet total not exceeding €10 million. A company is considered together with the other members of its group for these purposes.

A dividend received by a small company will generally be exempt provided the paying company is resident in a qualifying territory. A qualifying territory is one which is party to a double taxation agreement with the UK which contains a non-discrimination provision. This definition will generally exclude tax haven locations.

*Companies that are not small*

For companies that are not small there are five exempt classes which may apply. These are set out in CTA 2009 ss 931E–931I and can be summarised as follows:

(i) distributions from controlled companies

(ii) distributions in respect of non-redeemable ordinary shares

(iii) distributions in respect of portfolio holdings

(iv) dividends derived from transactions not designed to reduce tax

(v) dividends in respect of shares accounted for as liabilities.

CTA 2009 ss 931J–931Q provide detailed rules including detailed anti-avoidance provisions in respect of artificial structures and CFCs. These anti-avoidance provisions only apply to dividends received by medium and large companies.

It is possible to elect out of the exemption in respect of a specific dividend (CTA 2009 s 931R). This may be desirable where treaty benefits would be denied if the dividend is not subject to tax in the UK.

*Treatment where double tax relief not claimed*

(8) Where no credit is claimed for the overseas tax, the foreign profits are taken into account net of the overseas tax (TIOPA 2010 s 35).

If, for example, profits, including overseas profits, were to be reduced to nil by trading losses, so that no UK tax was payable, there would be no credit available for the foreign tax. By including the foreign profits net of overseas tax, the offset of losses would be reduced, leaving the losses available to set against other profits as shown below:

| | £ |
|---|---|
| UK profits | 60,000 |
| Overseas branch profits (£50,000 less foreign tax paid £20,000) | 30,000 |
| | 90,000 |
| Trading losses (part of £130,000) | (90,000) |
| Total taxable profits | 0 |
| Losses available against other profits | 40,000 |

If the overseas branch profits had been brought into account before overseas tax, giving total profits of £110,000, no foreign tax credit would have been available since no corporation tax is payable, and the unrelieved losses would be only £20,000 instead of £40,000.

*Treatment of donations etc*

(9) Where there are qualifying charitable donations, management expenses, group relief, or other amounts which can be offset against profits of more than one description, the company is able to use them in the most advantageous manner for double tax relief (TIOPA 2010 s 52(2)). Domo Ltd in **part A** can accordingly offset the donation paid against UK profits in priority to foreign income and gains, leaving a higher amount of foreign profits to absorb double tax credits. The non-trade interest (loan relationship non-trading 'deficit') can be set against the UK trading profits rather that the overseas trading profits, as shown for Jones Ltd in **part B** of the Example.

*Later adjustments to foreign tax paid*

(10) If the amount of foreign tax payable is later adjusted, the amount of double tax relief claimed will be similarly adjusted. If an adjustment to foreign tax results in too much relief having been claimed, HMRC must be notified within one year after the adjustment (TIOPA 2010 ss 114 and 115).

## I7.1 RELIEFS FOR THE CREATIVE SECTOR

You have received the following letter from Mr Lovie, one of your Firm's wealthiest private clients.

'Broadway',
Creative Street,
London,
1 August 2016

Mr A Smith
Carter & Sons
London

Dear Andrew,

Further to our conversation I would like to obtain your advice on some potential tax reliefs. As I mentioned to you, I have been considering diversifying some of my investments. I have a long standing interest in the arts and the production of television programmes, film and theatre. I have seen recent press coverage that new tax reliefs have been introduced and that further tax reliefs may be available in the near future. Clearly the fact that there are some tax advantages available makes investment in these quite appealing as it also serves as a hobby to myself.

As I am now taking early retirement I would like to be involved in the production of these activities on a day to day basis. I have had thoughts on some dramatic productions which I could either put on stage or could screen as either a film or television series. Could I claim the tax reliefs myself for my expenditure on production or are there any other requirements. Are there restrictions on the expenditure that would qualify for relief?

My son is trying to persuade me to invest in video games and CGI animation as well. Apparently there are also reliefs available in this field that were introduced recently?

Could you please confirm whether my understanding is correct that there are tax reliefs available and if so outline what is required to qualify for said reliefs and how much relief is available.

Yours sincerely

John Lovie

# Answer

Dear Mr Lovie

Thank you for your enquiry regarding tax reliefs. You are indeed correct that there are a number of wide ranging tax reliefs for investment in the creative industry (CITR). There are six distinct reliefs in place:

1. Film Tax Relief;
2. Animation Tax Relief;
3. High-end Television Tax Relief;
4. Theatre Tax Relief; and
5. Orchestra Relief; and
6. Video Games Tax Relief.

The Government continues to attempt to encourage investment in the creative industries and is currently consulting on a proposed relief for Museum's and Art Galleries.

Film Tax Relief (FTR) was the first of these reliefs to be introduced in April 2007. Animation Tax Relief (ATR) and High-end Television Tax Relief (HTR) were introduced from April 2013. Video Games Tax Relief (VGTR) became available in April 2014 and Theatre Tax Relief (TTR) from 1 September 2014 with Orchestra Relief (OR) introduced from 1 April 2016

The principles that underpin each of these reliefs are similar as you will see as you read through each form of relief. The first thing to note is that these reliefs are only available to companies. Direct investment by you will not qualify for any form of tax relief. The tax reliefs are all corporation tax reliefs, therefore you will need to carry out all of the investment via a corporate vehicle which is liable to corporation tax. Typically the most straight forward way to do so is to incorporate a limited company which would then invest in the various qualifying activities. If you chose to operate through such a company it is worth noting that film, television, animation, video game and theatre production companies are subject to certain specific tax rules, which differ from other corporates. These govern the recognition of income and expenditure for production companies. Each production, in any of these creative areas is treated as a separate trade within the company.

The reliefs promote British productions in the main although the latest reliefs do provide relief for expenditure incurred in the European Economic Area. In order to qualify for CITR all productions (other than theatre productions) must pass a 'cultural test'. In order to gain recognition as such, the production must be certified by the British Film Institute (BFI). Broadly speaking this means that the production must be a 'British' one, whether that be a 'British' film, television programme, animation or video game.

CITR is only available on the core production costs of each production, typically this is limited to the actual preparation and production activities. Extraneous costs do not qualify.

In addition you may wish to consider the tax reliefs available for investment in these companies rather than setting up your own companies. I have included these at the end of the letter.

### Film Tax Relief *(See note 1)*

FTR was introduced by Finance Act 2006, Schedule 6 and outlined three conditions in order for a film production company (FPC) to qualify for the relief:

1. The film must be intended for theatrical release, i.e. for exhibition on a commercial basis. A significant proportion of the film's earnings must come from the theatrical release. HMRC accept that 5% of the earnings qualifies as significant.

2. The film must be a 'British' film. This is based on a certification process by the Secretary of State for Culture, Media and Sport obtained by application to the BFI.

3. Not less than 10% of the core expenditure on the film must be UK expenditure by the film production company. A special rule applies in the case of a co-production so that the 10% UK expenditure condition is applied by reference to expenditure incurred by all the co-producers.

For tax purposes each film is treated as a separate trade, with each film having its own profit and loss account. FTR is then available on the basis on an enhanced tax deduction in relation to certain expenditure on the film.

*Eligible expenditure*

The enhanced tax deduction is available calculated by reference to the amount of core expenditure that is UK expenditure. Core expenditure is limited to that incurred on pre-production, principal photography and post production. It does not include any of the distribution or marketing expenditure which does not relate to the production of the film. One of the most critical exceptions to core expenditure is on development, this is not included on core expenditure.

One of the key considerations when determining the relief is to identify any amounts which relate to development expenditure as opposed to pre-production costs. Costs which straddle both parts of production can be apportioned in a reasonable way so as to treat some of the expenditure as core expenditure which is included in calculating the relief.

In addition there is a requirement that the expenditure be incurred for use in the UK. It does not matter if the supplier of the goods or services is based outside of the UK, merely the goods or services are consumed or used in the UK. In most cases it will be clear where the goods or services are consumed or used, for example for photography services relating to multiple countries the costs would need to be reviewed and only those amounts relating to the UK will be available for the claim.

One of the more difficult areas of core expenditure to apportion is likely to be in relation to actors. For actors whose contracts specify the amount of time that they will need to spend on production and time spent on other activities, for example promoting the film, then the apportionment should be straight forward. However where an actor is on a single contract, then the apportionment will have to be carried out on a just and reasonable basis. It may be necessary to review the contract to see if there is an amount set aside for the actor's acting and an amount for the use of the actor's image rights which would not relate to the production costs of the film.

It also follows that any non-core expenditure incurred by the FPC does not qualify for FTR. For example if costs are incurred on ascertaining the viability of the production then these will not be considered to part of the production costs of the film and therefore will not be included in the FTR.

Certain costs are specifically treated as ineligible. The specific prohibitions include any form of insurance (including completion bonds), development costs, entertaining, publicity and promotion, audit fees and bank interest or charges (other than any bank charges directly connected with paying for core expenditure).

*Calculation of the FTR claim*

A FPC can claim an additional deduction in computing its taxable profits relating to the film. The deduction can be used to:

1. Reduce the amount of taxable profit generated by a film; or

2. Create or increase a loss which can be surrendered in return for a Tax Credit payable from HMRC.

The amount of the claim is the lower of:

1. 80% of the total core expenditure; or

2. The actual UK core expenditure incurred.

The FPC is entitled to claim the FTR even where the production is abandoned.

There is flat rate of relief regardless of the size of the budget of the film. The relief is provided at a rate of 100% of the qualifying expenditure If the relief results in a loss, that loss (or such part of it as relates to the amount of expenditure on which FTR is claimed) can be surrendered in return for a 25% payable tax credit.

Where the production covers more than one period of account, a claim can be made each period on the basis of interim certification that the film meets the cultural test. The calculations for each period are made on a cumulative basis and then adjusted for amounts previously claimed.

The claim itself is included in the company's corporation tax return or within one year of the filing deadline for the corporation tax return.

### Television Tax Reliefs (TTR): High-end Television Tax Relief (HTTR) and Animation Tax Relief (ATR) *(see note 2)*

ATR and HTTR were introduced by Finance Act 2013 Sch 16 and provide enhanced tax relief for expenditure on certain television and animated programmes. As with the FTR, each programme is treated as a separate trade for tax purposes. The relief has been available in respect of qualifying expenditure incurred since 1 April 2013.

There are a distinct set of technical rules for the recognition of income and expenditure. Broadly the trade is treated as commencing when the programme production either starts to incur expenditure or receive income. The trade ceases when the programme rights are sold or transferred or when the television production company stops actively exploiting the programme and does not expect any future income to arise in respect of it. Also there are specific rules for the recognition of the timing of income and expenditure where these are on long term contracts.

These rules apply to television production companies (TPC) who are actively involved in the making of TV programmes or animations which are:

1. A 'British programme';
2. Programmes intended for broadcast; and
3. At least 10% of the core expenditure is incurred on goods or services consumed or used in the UK.

As with the FTR above, the programme will need to be certified as British by application to the BFI and the conditions to be met for that certification can be found on the BFI website. Those conditions relate to the setting, characters, story, language, British culture, work carried out in the UK and nationality of key personnel and are similar (although not identical) for high-end TV and for animations.

It will generally be obvious that a production is intended for broadcast this can be on either the television or over the internet. It should be for public broadcast therefore private productions will not qualify for relief. All programmes intended for public viewing, whether on the television or via the internet, will meet the 'intended for broadcast' test.

HTTR is available to programmes which meet the following conditions:

1. A drama, documentary, or children's programme;
2. It must be of at least 30 minutes duration;
3. Have an average core expenditure of at least £1m per hour duration; and
4. Not be an excluded programme.

ATR shares the same restrictions as HTTR, except those relating to length, cost and genre. The relief includes all animations, including hand drawn illustrations, CGI or stop motion animation. If a programme has a blend of animation and other content, as long as 51% is animated then it will qualify for ATR. The conditions regarding length and cost do not apply to the relief for children's television programmes which are defined as those which can be reasonably expected to be viewed primarily by children under the age of 15.

*Exclusions*

Excluded programmes (for the purposes of both HTTR and ATR) include:

1. Advertisement and marketing;

2. News or current affairs;
3. Quiz shows, game shows or similar;
4. Competitions; or
5. Training programmes.

A children's programme is not an excluded programme if it a quiz show or competition if there are only small prizes available. Small prizes means those costing under £1,000 or under that amount in cash.

The HTTR/ATR is only available to a company that is responsible for the following aspects of the production:

1. Pre-production, principal photography, post-production and final delivery of the programme;
2. Production planning and decision making throughout the production process; and
3. Negotiate all contracts and rights relating to the production.

Unlike the FTR outlined above, there can only be one qualifying TPC per programme. Although production can be split between two companies, only one company can benefit from the HTTR/ATR which is the company most directly involved with all of the above activities (although that company can elect to stand aside in favour of the company next most directly involved and so on).

The amount of HTTR/ATR is limited to the core expenditure on the production. This relates solely to pre-production, principal photography and post-production. No HTTR/ATR is available on other non-core expenditure, such as marketing or distribution. Similarly to FTR one of the key areas to consider is the difference between the development of the production and the pre-production phase of expenditure. Development is generally viewed as anything prior to a decision being made to progress a feasible production. Pre-production might include various activities such as securing the necessary rights, developing artwork and characters as well as developing the script and securing cast members.

As outlined above in the FTR section, all of the expenditure incurred on goods or services must be for consumption or use in the UK in order for it to qualify for HTTR/ATR. Any expenditure on goods or services outside of the UK does not qualify. Similarly if there is expenditure for both UK and overseas use then the amount must be fairly apportioned with relief available only on the UK element.

A claim for HTTR/ATR can be made once a production is ready for broadcast on the basis of a final certificate that it meets the cultural test. If production spans more than one period of account, on the basis of an interim certificate that can be obtained from the BFI. If after claiming relief on the basis of an interim certificate the programme fails to get a final certificate, any relief given on an interim basis is clawed back.

The calculations for each period are made on a cumulative basis and then adjusted for amounts previously claimed.

Simply because the programme is not broadcast, or production is abandoned, does not preclude relief from being claimed – the critical test is whether it was intended to be broadcast.

*Tax relief calculation*

A TPC can claim relief restricted to the lower of:

1. 80% of the total core expenditure; or
2. The actual UK core expenditure.

This can either be used to reduce taxable profits (or generate a loss). If the TPC has no taxable profits (after applying the HTTR/ATR), then the company can claim a payable tax credit of 25%.

*Losses*

If the programme incurs a loss then there are limited uses for the loss. Until the programme/animation is complete, losses which relate to qualifying amounts can only be utilised as follows:

1. Carry forward for use against profits of the same separate trade (programme);

2. Surrender the loss for a 25% tax credit.

The claim itself is included in the company's corporation tax return or within one year of the filing deadline for the corporation tax return. The claim can still be made if the production is abandoned.

Once the programme/animation is completed the choices for using the loss are widened. Any loss of the separate trade brought forward from an earlier period is treated as if it were a loss arising in the later period and the TPC can set them losses against profits of same or earlier period or surrender them as group relief (although group relief surrender is restricted to exclude any amount attributable to the HTTR/ATR). If there are unused losses in the period that the separate trade ceases, special terminal loss provisions allow losses to be carried over to and treated as losses of another separate trade being carried on by the same company or surrendered to another group company if that company has become the TPC in relation to the programme.

## Theatre Tax Relief *(See note 3)*

TTR was introduced for expenditure incurred after 1 September 2014. Again, the common theme of each production being a separate trade also holds true for each theatrical production. The types of performances included within the remit of the relief are ballets and dramatic productions.

The legislation in CTA 2009 Part 15C outlines that a dramatic production may be a play, opera or musical but it must meet the following requirements:

1. That the actors, singers, dancers or other performers are to give their performances wholly or mainly through the playing of roles;

2. Each performance in the proposed run of performances is to be live; and

3. The presentation of live performances is the main object, or one of the main objects, of the company's activities in relation to the production.

The definition also extends to circus routines. The following performance types are excluded from the TTR:

1. Advertisement;

2. Contests or competitions;

3. Any use of wild animals;

4. Any performance principally of a sexual nature; or

5. Where recording the performance is the main motive of the production company.

Unlike the reliefs available to films, TV, animation and video games, there is no certification process involved.

Again, the relief is only available to companies. The requirements that the company be actively involved in the producing, decision making and negotiations regarding the production are the same as those for the HTTR outlined above. The following requirements must also be met, that:

1. That the production is for commercial gain and for viewing by the public; and

2. That at least 25% of the core expenditure is incurred on goods or services that are provided from within the European Economic Area.

If these requirements are met then the company is entitled to an enhanced deduction for corporation tax purposes. The relief is restricted to the lower of:

1. 80% of the total core expenditure; or

2. The actual UK core expenditure.

Core expenditure has the same meaning as for the CITRs outlined above but relates to producing the production and closing the production but not any expenditure not directly linked to the production itself.

This amount can then be used to reduce the company's taxable profits or surrendered against other income from theatrical productions. If the company makes a loss it may surrender this for a payable tax credit. For touring productions, i.e. those which put on performances at six or more different sites, companies can claim a 25% tax credit of the qualifying expenditure. For other productions the credit is limited to 20%.

## Orchestra Tax Relief *(See note 4)*

OR was introduced in Finance Act 2016 for expenditure incurred after 1 April 2016. Again, the common theme of each production being a separate trade also holds true for each orchestral production. To qualify in respect of a concert the concert must be a performed live to the paying public or for educational purposes, consist of at least 12 instrumentalists, and either none of the musical instruments to be played, or only a minority of those instruments, is electronically or directly amplified.

The following performance types are excluded from the OR:

1. If the main purpose, or one of the main purposes, of the concert is to advertise or promote any goods or services,

2. If the concert is to consist of or include a competition or contest, or

3. If the making of a relevant recording is the main object of the production company's activities in relation to the concert.

The relief is only available to companies. The company must be actively involved in putting on the concert (including employing or engaging the performers) the decision making, make an effective creative, technical and artistic contribution to the concert, or directly negotiates for, contracts for and pays for rights, goods and services in relation to the concert.. If more than one company meets these conditions only the company most directly engaged will qualify.

At least 25% of the core expenditure must be incurred in the EEA.

If these requirements are met then the company is entitled to an enhanced deduction for corporation tax purposes. The relief is restricted to the lower of:

1. 80% of the total core expenditure; or

2. The actual EEA core expenditure.

This amount can then be used to reduce the company's taxable profits or surrendered against other income from theatrical productions. If the company makes a loss it may surrender this for a payable tax credit of 25%.

## Video Game Tax Relief *(See note 5)*

As you stated, a new relief was brought in from April 2014 to cover video games. The relief is similar to the other creative reliefs outlined above. VGTR is available to companies which are designing, producing and testing video games. If the company is actively engaged in the management of the production of the video game it will be entitled to VGTR. The requirements are that:

1. The video game is British;

2. It is intended for release; and

3. That at least 25% of the core expenditure is incurred on goods or services that are provided from within the European Economic Area.

The video game must be certified as 'British'. A certificate may be obtained by application to the BFI and the conditions to be met for that certification can be found on the BFI website. Those conditions relate to the setting, characters, subject matter, language, British culture, work carried out in the UK and nationality of key personnel (although similar, the tests to be applied are different to those applicable to HTTR and ATR).

If these requirements are met then the company is entitled to an enhanced deduction for corporation tax purposes. The relief is restricted to the lower of:

1. 80% of the total core expenditure; or
2. The actual EEA core expenditure.

Core expenditure is defined as it is for the other CITR. This amount can then be used to reduce the company's taxable profits, or if the company makes a loss in it may surrender this for a payable tax credit of 25% of the qualifying expenditure. The other computational rules and procedural rules also work in the same way as for the other CITR reliefs.

It is worth noting that the development of video games may qualify for research and development tax credits as well. If the company wishes to claim these then it will not be entitled to VGTR. As it is likely that any company you looked to invest in initially would be a smaller company then the reliefs under the R&D scheme can be very generous. The relief on qualifying expenditure is given at an additional 125% of the expenditure incurred on R&D.

I trust that this gives you a better understanding of the tax reliefs available for your proposed activities. Please contact me with any further questions.

Yours sincerely

A Smith

## Explanatory Notes

*Note 1*

A film must be intended for release (CTA 2009 s 1196). It is expected that the film will be released for viewing in the UK, given that there is a requirement that the film is a 'British' film. It does not matter if the film is also released overseas or if large proportions of income arise overseas.

A qualifying British film (CTA 2009 s 1197) can be certified by the Certification Unit, BFI, 21 Stephen Street, London, W1T 1LN. There are three ways in which a film can qualify as British. It may:

- satisfy the cultural test inserted into Schedule 1 to the Films Act 1985 by SI 2006/3430 (the Films (Definition of a British Film) (No. 2) Order 2006);
- meet the terms of one of the United Kingdom's bilateral co-production treaties; or
- meet the terms of the European Convention on Cinematic Co-Production.

Core production costs are detailed in CTA 2009 s 1184 and include expenditure on pre-production, principal photography and post-production.

UK expenditure is defined by CTA 2009 s 1185, 1200. It is necessary to allocate the expenditure in an acceptable way. The key areas for consideration will be identifying items such as pre-production costs which could relate to various jurisdictions, IP costs or similar for the use of characters or trademarks which might be used for both marketing (non-allowable for FTC) and production or where post production pieces such as CGI takes place.

Ineligible costs are outlined in CTA 2009 s 1199. All non-core expenditure will be treated as ineligible for relief. The key primary costs will be items such as insurance, marketing, development and other standard disallowable expenditure (entertaining, certain legal fees etc). The eligible core expenditure is the amount of claim is outlined in CTA 2009 ss 1199, 1200.

Rates of relief are outlined in CTA 2009 ss 1200 & 1202. These amounts are included in the company's CT600 at Box 167 and 101 if additional relief is claimed or at Box 87 and 168 if a tax credit is being claimed.

The rules regarding abandonment are found at CTA 2009 ss 1212 – 1216.

FA 2015 s 29 introduced flat rate reliefs for all qualifying films regardless of expenditure (the amounts included above). Prior to 1 April 2014 there were differing relief dependent on the expenditure levels. The rate of relief was dependent on the size of the budget of the film. A film whose core expenditure is £20 million or less attracts relief at the rate of 100% of the amount claimed. Where a production was abandoned, the question of whether the film is such a limited budget film or not should be judged on the basis of the core expenditure that would have been incurred had the project been completed.

For all other films relief is given at the rate of 80% of the amount claimed. If the relief results in a loss, that loss (or such part of it as relates to the amount of expenditure on which FTR is claimed) can be surrendered in return for a 20% payable tax credit (or 25% in the case of a limited budget film).

*Note 2*

The general definitions were inserted by FA 2013 Sch 16 into Part 15A CTA 2009 ss 1216AA, 1216BA. There is a specific HMRC unit based in Manchester (Incentives and Reliefs Team) which deal with the HTTR/ATR. Excluded programmes are outlined at CTA 2009 s 1216AD.

A Television Production Company is defined at CTA 2009 s 1216AE with trading periods at CTA 2009 s 1216B and the restriction on co-production at CTA 2009 s 1216AI.

The categories of expenditure, including the definition of core and UK expenditure are found at CTA 2009 ss 1216AF – 1216AH.

Completion of a programme is defined at CTA 2009 1216AA(5).

The relief for makers of children's television programmes was introduced by FA 2015 s 30.

The qualifying expenditure requirement for HTTR was reduced from 25% to 10% by FA 2015 s 31

*Note 3*

TTR was introduced by FA 2014 into CTA 2009.

CTA 2009 ss 1217F – 1217FC define a qualifying company and the qualifying productions which are entitled to relief and the separate trade requirement is found at CTA 2009 ss 1217IA - 1217IF.

CTA 2009 ss 1217G – 1217GC outline the qualifying conditions.

The definition of qualifying expenditure is found at CTA 2009 s 1217JA and the tax credits claimable at CTA 2009 ss 1217K – 1217KC.

*Note 4*

OR was introduced into Part 15D CTA 2009 by FA 2016 Sch 8. CTA 2009 ss 1217P – 1217U outline the key conditions to be met by the company and the concert in order to qualify for relief. The separate trade requirement is at CTA 2009 ss 1217Q.

*Note 5*

VGTR was introduced into Part 15B CTA 2009 by FA 2013 Sch 17. CTA 2009 ss 1217AA – 1217AE outline the key conditions to be met by the company and the video game in order to qualify for relief. The separate trade requirement is at CTA 2009 ss 1217B – 1217BE.

Details of the available relief and associated tax credit is found at CTA 2009 ss 1217C - 1217CJ.

# Close companies

# Question

## A.

Bray Motors plc has an issued and fully paid up share capital of 10,000,000 ordinary shares of £1 each, and its shares are listed and regularly dealt in on the Stock Exchange.

The present shareholdings in the company are as follows:

| | *Shares* |
|---|---|
| John Bray (the company's founder, now retired) | 2,550,000 |
| Colin Rawson (a private investor) | 1,000,000 |
| Lawrence Jones (the company's managing director) | 600,000 |
| Globe Autos Ltd (a close company) | 470,000 |
| Alan Brooks (a private investor) | 460,000 |
| James Baker (the company's financial director) | 370,000 |
| Ace Car Hire Ltd (not a close company) | 370,000 |
| Brian Pritchard (a private investor) | 360,000 |
| Edward Hay (a private investor) | 340,000 |
| 340 private investors, none of whom own more than 20,000 shares | 3,480,000 |
| | 10,000,000 |

All the shares are beneficially owned.

None of the shareholders is related to or associated with any other shareholder.

The company owns a trade investment of 5,000 shares in Marsh Alternators Ltd, an unquoted trading company with an issued and fully paid up share capital of 100,000 ordinary shares of £1 each.

The other shares in the company are currently owned as follows:

| | *Shares* |
|---|---|
| Norman Marsh | 8,000 |
| Trustees of a settlement made by Norman Marsh for his grandchildren | 19,000 |
| Henry Simpson (Norman Marsh's cousin) | 3,000 |
| Gerald Black (no relation to any of the above) | 5,000 |
| Ellen Black (Gerald's wife) | 1,000 |
| Tom Black (Gerald's son) | 4,000 |
| Nigel Clement (Gerald Black's nephew) | 3,000 |
| Walter Metcalfe (Nigel Clement's partner in an unrelated antiques business, and sole owner of the wholly independent company Metcalfe Motors Ltd) | 3,500 |
| Richard Court (no relation to any of the above) | 3,500 |
| Keith Court (Richard's brother) | 1,000 |
| 35 other shareholders, none of whom owns more than 2,000 shares and none of whom is related to or associated with any other shareholder | 44,000 |
| | 95,000 |

All the shares are beneficially owned.

The directors of Marsh Alternators Ltd are Gerald Black and Richard Court.

Set out the reasoning as to whether the close company provisions are applicable to:

(i) Bray Motors plc

(ii) Marsh Alternators Ltd.

**B.**

Indicate the circumstances in which a close company is within the definition of a 'close investment-holding company' and state the consequences.

**C.**

Cook has held an investment generating £5,000 in dividends per annum for years, encouraged by this successful investment Cook is about to acquire shares in a publicly quoted company for £350,000 out of his own funds, giving him around a 2% equity stake. The shares currently yield a dividend of £28,000 pa and the prospects of significant capital appreciation in the future are excellent. At the end of 10 years, Cook may decide to sell some or all of the shares. It has been suggested to Cook by a friend, Dodge, that instead of buying the shares himself he should form a new investment company, Cook Ltd. Cook would subscribe for 350,000 £1 shares in Cook Ltd, which would then use the cash to buy the shares. Dodge has told Cook that he could draw out director's remuneration of up to £10,000 pa and that Cook Ltd could deduct this against the dividend income and that the balance of £18,000 would only attract a small amount of corporation tax.

State whether the advice which Cook has received from Dodge is correct.

**D.**

You have been appointed to act professionally for Morrissey Ltd, a close company which was formed a month ago and which has an issued share capital of £50,000 divided into 50,000 ordinary shares of £1 each. The funds for the set-up of the company and subscription to share capital were provided by an inheritance.

The managing director, Mr Morrissey, has only a general knowledge of corporation tax and is particularly anxious that you should explain to him:

(i) what is meant by a 'distribution';

(ii) whether the fact that it is not intended that the company should declare any dividends during the first few years of its existence, but rather to retain any profits in the business, would have any taxation effects;

(iii) whether the granting of a loan by the company to any of its shareholders would be affected by taxation;

(iv) how the company might be affected from a taxation point of view if it had to go into liquidation.

Mr Morrissey stresses to you that it should be borne in mind that the company's operations will be confined to the UK, its income will only be derived from its trading profits and from the letting of property owned by it and it is not intended that the company's issued share capital should be altered in any way nor any other shares or securities issued.

Draft the body of a letter to Mr Morrissey setting out the information requested by him.

# Answer

## A.

(i) **Bray Motors plc**, whilst controlled by five participators, is a quoted company in which 35% of the shares are held by the public and not more than 85% are held by the principal members, viz:

| *Name* | *Shares* | *Control Test* *5 largest participators* | *Public ownership Test 35%* | *Principal Members Test* *5 largest over 5% (500,000 shares)* |
|---|---|---|---|---|
| John Bray | 2,550,000 | 2,550,000 | | 2,550,000 |
| Colin Rawson | 1,000,000 | 1,000,000 | | 1,000,000 |
| Lawrence Jones (director) | 600,000 | 600,000 | | 600,000 |
| Globe Autos Ltd (close company) | 470,000 | 470,000 | 470,000 | |
| Alan Brooks | 460,000 | 460,000 | 460,000 | |
| James Baker (director) | 370,000 | | | |
| Ace Car Hire Ltd (open company) | 370,000 | | 370,000 | |
| Brian Pritchard | 360,000 | | 360,000 | |
| Edward Hay | 340,000 | | 340,000 | |
| 340 private investors | 3,480,000 | | 3,480,000 | |
| Total Shares | 10,000,000 | 5,080,000 | 5,480,000 | 4,150,000 |
| Percentage | 100% | 50.8% | 54.8% | 41.5% |

Therefore Bray Motors plc is *not* a close company.

(ii) *Marsh Alternators Ltd* is controlled by five participators together with their associates, viz:

| | | | *Holding including associates* |
|---|---|---|---|
| *5 largest holdings* | | | |
| Norman Marsh | | 8,000 | |
| Trustees of settlement for grandchildren | | 19,000 | 27,000 |
| Gerald Black | | 5,000 | |
| His wife | | 1,000 | |
| His son | | 4,000 | 10,000 |
| Nigel Clement | | 3,000 | |
| Walter Metcalfe, Nigel Clement's partner | | 3,500 | 6,500* |
| Richard Court | | 3,500 | |
| His brother | | 1,000 | 4,500 |
| Bray Motors Ltd | | | 5,000 |
| Shares held by 5 largest shareholders | 53% | | 53,000 |
| Others: | H Simpson | | 3,000 |
| | 35 other shareholders | | 44,000 |
| Shares held by other shareholders | 47% | | 47,000 |
| | | | 100,000 |

Marsh Alternators Ltd is therefore a close company.

## B.

A close company is a close investment-holding company in an accounting period *unless* throughout that period it exists wholly or mainly for one or more of the following purposes:

(i) Carrying on a trade on a commercial basis (including dealing in land, shares or securities).

(ii) Investing in land or buildings for letting to third parties (i.e. other than to persons connected with the company or their spouses or relatives).

(iii) Acting as a holding company for one or more companies each of which qualifies under **(i)** or **(ii)** **above.**

A company that makes loans to qualifying companies in the same group, or holds property or provides other services for those companies, qualifies for exclusion, as does a holding company that itself carries on a trade, or acts as the top company in a group and merely holds shares in a subsidiary that has qualifying subsidiaries (CTA 2010 s 34)).

Where a close company goes into liquidation, it is not treated as a close investment-holding company for the accounting period commencing with the winding-up if it was a qualifying company in the previous accounting period (but this may not help if the company ceased trading some time before going into liquidation – see **Example J4 explanatory note 5**).

The main consequence of being a close investment-holding company historically was that, regardless of the level of the company's profits, corporation tax was charged at the full rate, i.e. it is not entitled to the benefit of the corporation tax small profits rate, or marginal relief (CTA 2010 s 18 (b)). However, with the introduction of a single rate of corporation tax on non-ring fenced profits (the main rate) from 1 April 2015, this issue is no longer relevant.

The remaining important restriction is that interest relief on loans taken out to acquire ordinary share capital of a close company is not given if the company is a close investment-holding company or becomes such a company (ITA 2007 ss 383(2c), 392 (2a)).

## C.

Since Cook Ltd would be controlled by Cook, it would be a close investment-holding company.

As far as director's remuneration is concerned, the remuneration would have to be wholly and exclusively for the purposes of the company's business. If the only activity of the company was to hold the shares in the public company it is clear that Cook's directorship would not involve much commitment and it is unlikely that anything more than a nominal amount would be deductible as director's fees.

In the long term, the capital appreciation on the shares may lead to double taxation, if the company is liquidated when the shares are sold. The capital gain on the disposal of the shares would be charged to tax at the full corporation tax rate. (Given that Cook Ltd would only hold a 2% interest in the shares, it would not be entitled to the substantial shareholdings exemption on the disposal – see **Example K3**.) Cook could either extract the company's chargeable gain as a dividend prior to the liquidation, receiving the balance of the proceeds by way of capital distribution, or leave the gain as part of the funds paid out on the liquidation. If the company sold the shares for, say, £550,000 and, assuming indexation allowance of £50,000 for the company, with entrepreneur's relief not applying as this is not a trading company, the comparative position using anticipated long term corporation tax rate of 20% is set out below. (It is assumed that there is no retained income in the company at this point.)

### If accounting profit (reserves) paid out as dividend prior to liquidation

| | £ |
|---|---|
| Gain (£550,000 less cost £350,000) | 200,000 |

| | £ |
|---|---|
| Corporation tax @ 20% rate on capital gain of £150,000 (£200,000 less indexation) | (30,000) |
| Cash dividend (= reserves) | 170,000 |
| Cook's income for tax purposes | 170,000 |
| Tax thereon @ say 38.1% | 64,770 |
| Balance of proceeds paid out in liquidation (= share capital) (550,000 less tax and dividend amounting to 200,000) | 350,000 |
| Cost of Cook's shares in Cook Ltd | 350,000 |
| Chargeable gain | – |
| Surplus on share sale, net of tax (£550,000 – £350,000 – 30,000 – 64,770) | 105,230 |

### Note

For those with incomes over £150,000 for 2015/16 the dividend tax rate is 38.1%. The Example assumes Cook's income will be over £150,000 and this rate will apply. The actual tax due on the large dividend will depend on Cook's other income and actual tax rates in the year in which the distribution is made.

The corporation tax rate will reduce to 19% on 1 April 2017 and 17% on 1 April 2020. As the rate of corporation tax reduces the 'double taxation' cost reduces and accordingly the benefit of holding such assets via a company increase.

### If investment shares sold and company liquidated

| | £ |
|---|---|
| Sale proceeds for investment shares | 550,000 |
| Corporation tax on gain @ 20% rate | (30,000) |
| Capital distribution to Cook | 520,000 |
| Cost of Cook's shares in Cook Ltd | (350,000) |
| Chargeable gain | 170,000 |
| Capital gains tax @ 20% (assuming annual exemption already used and higher rate taxpayer) | (34,000) |
| Surplus on sale of shares net of tax (£550,000 – £350,000 – 30,000 – 34,000) | 136,000 |

### Note

There would be a financial cost to liquidate the company. See **Example J3 explanatory note 7**.

If Cook held the investment shares personally, his surplus on sale would be £160,000, calculated as follows:

| | £ |
|---|---|
| Sale proceeds | 550,000 |
| Cost of investment shares | (350,000) |
| Chargeable gain | 200,000 |
| CGT @ 20% (assuming annual exemption used elsewhere and higher rate taxpayer) | (40,000) |
| Surplus on sale | 160,000 |

This demonstrates the impact of the 'double taxation' which arises where appreciating assets are held within an (investment) company.

### D.

Thank you for your letter of 1 July asking me for information on the taxation treatment of certain matters affecting your company. The answers to the points raised by you are as follows:

(i) *Meaning of the term distribution*

The term distribution has a very wide meaning for corporation tax, and that meaning is extended in the case of companies controlled either by their directors or by five or fewer participators (broadly shareholders). Such companies are termed close companies and Morrissey Ltd falls within the definition.

Many of the provisions relating to distributions are concerned with share issues, redemptions etc, and since your company is not contemplating any changes in its share capital they will not apply. The term distribution in your case will therefore cover:

(a) Any dividends paid in cash.

(b) Any distribution of assets in a non-cash form, and any benefit provided for shareholders or their associates (such as the use of cars, provision of living accommodation, entertainment etc). Directors and employees are charged to tax on the provision of assets and benefits as employment income and the company suffers a Class 1A national insurance contributions charge of 13.8%. The expense of the provision is deductible by the company in arriving at its profits so long as it can be shown to be wholly and exclusively for the purposes of the trade.

(ii) *Effect of retaining profits rather than paying dividends*

The fact that the company does not intend to make any distributions within the first few years will not have any immediate taxation effects and will undoubtedly assist with your cash flow and working capital requirements.

Some companies are required to pay corporation tax in instalments, but only where their profits exceed a specified limit, presently £1,500,000 (which is not expected to apply in your case).

For dividends paid after 5 April 2016 the first £5,000 of dividend is effectively taxed at 0%, with the balance taxable as follows:

- for basic rate taxpayers at 7.5%
- for higher rate taxpayers 32.5%; and
- for additional rate taxpayers 38.1%.

Dividend income is treated as the very top slice of income for determining the rate of tax due on it, and the new £5,000 dividend tax allowance at 0% is treated as using up the next tranche of income – that is reducing the basic rate band or higher rate band for affected taxpayers.

If the company's profits can be retained and subsequently taken in a 'capital' form, this may prove more beneficial for tax purposes. Capital gains are currently taxed at 10% or 20% (depending upon whether you are a basic rate taxpayer or a higher or additional rate taxpayer), unless entrepreneurs' relief applies, in which case the tax rate is 10%.

Entrepreneurs' relief applies only to significant disposals of business assets, and relief is limited to the first £10 million of net gains per lifetime realised since 6 April 2008. (The limit has fluctuated since introduction.)

Entrepreneurs' relief applies only to the disposal of the whole or a substantial part of a business, and also to associated business assets. Subject to a number of conditions, gains on sales of shareholdings in personal trading companies (companies in which the seller owned a holding of at least 5% for at least a year, and in which they were an officer or director), qualify for a reduced rate of 10%. The fact that the company receives letting income and has surplus cash may, however, prevent it qualifying as a 'trading' company for entrepreneurs' relief.

A company's trading status is normally considered by reviewing all its activities and particular circumstances. To be trading any investment or non-trading activities should be no more than 20% of total activities. Therefore any substantial ownership of properties acquired with the intention of letting (other than as furnished holiday lets), is likely to disqualify the company as a trading company and therefore deny entrepreneurs' relief on a disposal. It may be borne in mind that the difference in rate between qualifying and not qualifying for entrepreneur's relief is currently 10% however, capital gains treatment at 10% or 20% is normally preferable to income tax treatment at dividend rates.

In the company's case, the opportunities for shareholders to take capital profits are relatively limited, for example, on receiving a capital sum on a liquidation (see **(iv) below**) or on selling shares back to the company on retirement (provided they have been held at least five years and certain other conditions are satisfied), in which case entrepreneurs' relief may be available. Such considerations would not usually be expected to dictate the company's dividend policy during its early years, although reduction of surplus cash balances by payment of dividend may prove to some extent beneficial in establishing trading company status.

(iii) *Loans to shareholders*

If the company makes loans to shareholders (other than loans of £15,000 or less to full-time directors or employees who do not own more than 5% of the share capital) the company will have to pay tax at a rate of 32.5% of the amount of the loan, repayable by HMRC as and when the loan is repaid by the shareholder to the company. This is a 'stand-alone' tax charge and is not deductible from the corporation tax payable on profits.

If the company should release or write off such a loan, the company can reclaim the tax paid. However, a shareholder who controls the company is connected with the company under the special rules for loans. As far as the shareholder is concerned, any amount released is taxed as if it were dividend income. For a basic rate taxpayer there is a liability of 7.5%, a higher rate tax payer suffers a rate of 32.5% and an additional rate taxpayer is taxed at 38.1%, although the first £5,000 of dividends in the tax year are taxed at 0% for all taxpayers. If the shareholder is a director or employee then they will be charged to tax under the employment-related loans provisions. This means that he will be deemed to have received extra remuneration equal to interest on the loan at the prevailing official rate (currently 3%) less any interest which he actually pays to the company (which will be computed and returned on his P11D form). This will not apply if the total loans outstanding in a tax year to that shareholder or anyone connected with him do not exceed £10,000. If the loan is one on which interest (if charged) would have been available for income tax relief, no taxable benefit arises.

You should also note that the company will have to pay Class 1A national insurance contributions at 13.8% on the deemed taxable benefit arising from the notional interest charge on non-qualifying loans. If a loan to a director-shareholder or other employee-shareholder is written off or released, HMRC will expect Class 1 national insurance contributions to be accounted for through the RTI payroll on the amount written off as if cash salary had been paid to the shareholder. However as already mentioned the Employer's Allowance of £3,000 may be available, but there would still be a primary (employee) liability at 12%, reducing to 2% on amounts over £43,000 (See **Example B1** for details of RTI.)

Where loans to employees or directors are written off or released, there is ordinarily a deemed employment benefit to the value of the write-off or release that the employer must report on the P11D for income tax purposes. Where the loan is to a shareholder, however, the amount is treated for income tax purposes as a distribution as described above instead, these rules taking precedence over the employment income provisions.

Releases and write off do not attract corporation tax relief and therefore cannot be claimed in calculating trading profits.

(iv) *Tax consequences of liquidation*

If the company goes into liquidation, the commencement of the winding-up will denote the end of an accounting period and commencement of another for corporation tax. If the company ceases trading prior to the commencement of liquidation the cessation of trading also triggers the end of a corporation tax accounting period.

The cessation will require balancing adjustments to be made in respect of capital allowances claimed and if trading losses arise in the final twelve months that are not covered by other profits of the same period, relief may be claimed against the total profits of the three previous years, latest first. Profits may arise in the final trading period in the form of chargeable gains on the disposal of assets, but it would be necessary for the contract for the disposal to be made before the cessation of trade to enable trading losses in the final accounting period to be set off against those gains. Brought forward trading losses cannot be set against other sources of income or gains.

To the extent that the company retains income and capital profits, a double tax charge will inevitably occur on liquidation. The company will have paid corporation tax at the time the profits were made, and unless they have been distributed to the shareholders as a dividend before the liquidation, the retentions will swell the amounts received by the shareholders in the winding-up. Amounts paid out to the shareholders during the liquidation will be chargeable to capital gains tax, after deducting their base value for the shares, any capital gains tax reliefs, including entrepreneurs' relief if applicable, and any available personal annual exemption. Where entrepreneurs' relief applies, the capital distribution should be made within three years of cessation of trade to ensure the conditions for relief are met.

I shall be happy to provide any additional information you require, or to discuss further with you the matters dealt with above.

## Explanatory Notes

*Definition of close company*

(1) A close company is one under the control of five or fewer participators or of participators who are directors (CTA 2010 s 439).

(2) A *participator* is a person having a share or interest in the capital or income of the company (CTA 2010 ss 454, 1068, 1069), the most common form of participator therefore being a shareholder although the legislation does not restrict the definition to a shareholder. The word 'person' includes both an individual and a company.

(3) *Control* means exercising, or able to exercise, or entitled to acquire control over, the company's affairs, and in particular, but without prejudice to the general meaning of the foregoing, possessing or entitled to acquire the greater part of the share capital, or issued share capital, or of the voting power in the company (CTA 2010 s 450(2)).

An entitlement to receive now or in the future the greater part of the income if the whole income were to be distributed, or the greater part of the assets of the company that were available for distribution among the participators on a winding-up, also denotes control.

*Participator's associates etc*

(4) In determining whether five or fewer participators (or participators who are directors) control a company, the rights of certain other persons must be regarded as those of the participator, namely:

(a) His nominee (CTA 2010 ss 451(1, 3), 1069(3)).

(b) His associates, being (CTA 2010 ss 451, 1069(3)):

(i) a business partner;

(ii) his spouse or civil partner, parent or remoter forebear, child or remoter issue, brother or sister;

(iii) trustees of any settlement made by the participator or the relatives in **4(b)(ii) above**;

(iv) where the participator has an interest in shares or obligations of the company that are in a trust or deceased's estate, the trustees and personal representatives and, if the participator is a company, any other company interested in those shares or obligations. (This provision covers, inter alia, trusts for occupational pensions and employee benevolent funds.)

(c) Any company or companies of which the participator or he and his associates have control (CTA 2010 ss 451, 1069(3)).

*Close company exclusion where public holdings are 35% or more*

(5) There is an exclusion from close company status if shares in the company carrying not less than 35% of the voting power (and not carrying a fixed rate of dividend with or without further rights to participate in profits) are *held by the public* (see **explanatory note 6** below) and such shares have within the preceding twelve months been listed on and the subject of dealings on a recognised stock exchange (CTA 2010 s 446(1, 6)). This exclusion does not, however, apply where the voting power possessed by the principal members exceeds 85%, the principal members being the five persons possessing the greatest percentage of the voting power, each owning over 5% (CTA 2010 s 449). Where there are no such five persons, because two or more possess equal percentages, all those with equal percentages are counted, e.g. two with 20% and five with 10% = seven principal members together holding 90%.

(6) Shares are regarded as held by the public if they satisfy one of the following tests (unless they are excluded by the next following paragraph):

(a) If held by a non-close company;

(b) If held on trust for an approved superannuation fund;

(c) If not held by a principal member.

Public holdings *exclude* a holding by a director or his associate or by a company under their control, or by a company associated with the company concerned, or a holding by certain funds for the benefit of past and present employees, directors or their dependants (for example occupational pension funds, employee share trusts and benevolent funds). Companies are 'associated' if, within twelve months previously, one has control of the other or both are under the control of the same person or persons (CTA 2010 s 449).

The holding of a non-close company counts as a public holding and is included in the 35% rule, but if the non-close company has one of the five largest vote carrying holdings it also counts as a principal member and is therefore included in the 85% rule.

For example, voting power in quoted company held as follows:

| | (a) | (b) |
|---|---|---|
| Two directors equally | 60% | 60% |
| Non-close company | 10% | 30% |
| Members of public (none holding over 5%) | 30% | 10% |
| | 100% | 100% |

In both cases the public holdings are 40%.

In Example (a) the principal members hold 70% and the company is accordingly *not* a close company.

In Example (b) the principal members hold 90% and the company *is* a close company.

*Other exclusions from close company status*

(7) There are certain other exclusions from close company status:

(a) a non-resident company;

(b) a registered industrial and provident society (within the meaning of CTA 2010 s 1119);

(c) a building society;

(d) a company controlled by the Crown, unless it could be treated as a close company on the ground of being under the control of persons acting independently of the Crown;

(e) a company controlled by a company which is not a close company (other than by reason of non-residence), or by two or more companies none of which is a close company, where it cannot be treated as a close company except by taking as one of the five or fewer participators requisite for its being so treated a company which is not a close company;

(f) a company which could only be close by taking as a participator entitled to receive the greater part of its assets on a winding-up, a loan creditor which is a non-close company (other than by reason of non-residence).

(CTA 2010 s 439.)

*Consequences of being a close company*

(8) Where a company is within the definition of a close company, the following provisions apply:

(a) Any benefits derived by a participator, other than an employee or a director, are regarded as distributions of profits rather than deductions from trading profits (see **Example J2**).

(b) If a close company makes a loan to a participator, the company has to pay tax at 32.5% on the amount of the loan, subject to certain exceptions (CTA 2010 s 455 – see **Example J2** and also **(e) below**).

(c) The small profits rate was not available if the company was also a close investment-holding company (CTA 2010 ss 3 and 34)).

(d) If the company transfers an asset at undervalue, the shareholders will suffer an appropriate reduction in the capital gains base cost of their shares, unless the shortfall has already been taken into account for income tax (TCGA 1992 s 125 and HMRC concession D51).

(e) Under the 'loan relationships' rules for companies (see **Example K2**), where the parties to a loan are a close company and a participator or associate of a participator, the following provisions apply:

(i) The company is denied a deduction for a loan written off if the loan is to a controlling shareholder (see **Example K2 explanatory note 7**). See **Example J2 explanatory note 11** for the treatment of individuals where loans to them have been written off.

(ii) Where the company has borrowed from a participator or his associate, or from a company controlled by a participator, or in which a participator has a 40% or greater holding, interest paid by the company more than twelve months after the period in which it would otherwise be treated as accruing cannot be deducted until it is paid, unless the participator or associate is a company that has included the interest in its profits on an accruals basis (CTA 2009 s 375).

(iii) Where the close company has borrowed from the participator or associate on a deeply discounted security (i.e. where the difference between issue price and redemption price is more than 0.5% per year or more than 15% overall), relief for the discount is not given until the security is redeemed (CTA 2009 s 409), unless the holder of the security is within the loan relationships rules, i.e. is taxed on the discount (CTA 2009 s 410).

See also **Example K8 note 4** re the apportionment of gains of non-resident companies that would have been close companies if they had been UK resident.

*Distribution – general meaning*

(9) For companies in general the term 'distribution' means (CTA 2010 s 1000):

(a) Any dividend paid by the company, including a capital dividend.

(b) Any other distribution out of the company's assets, whether in cash or not, except a repayment of capital or an amount for which new consideration is given.

(c) Any bonus issue of securities or redeemable shares issued in respect of shares or securities of the company (excluding scrip dividends – see **explanatory note 14**).

(d) Any excess of market value of benefit received where assets or liabilities are transferred to shareholders over any new consideration given (except for intra-group transfers).

(e) Where share capital (other than fully paid preference share capital) is repaid, bonus issues made at the same time or subsequently. This does not apply to non-close listed companies where the bonus issue is not redeemable share capital and takes place more than 10 years after the repayment of capital.

(f) Interest payments on securities in certain circumstances, e.g. where the interest exceeds a normal commercial rate or varies with the company's profits. This does not, however, catch interest on 'ratchet loans' (i.e. loans where the rate increases as profits deteriorate and vice versa). The legislation is intended only to apply where interest effectively represents a share in profits. The provisions are complex and are subject to anti-avoidance provisions in CTA 2010 s 1032 which prevent interest payments from one company to another being artificially turned into franked investment income in the receiving company's hands because of the distribution provisions.

(10) Distributions in a winding-up do not count as income distributions and are subject to capital gains tax (as a 'deemed' disposal of shares under TCGA 1992 s 122).

(11) The distribution provisions are relaxed in relation to demergers (see **Example K5**) and the purchase by a company of its own shares (see **Example J5**).

*Qualifying and non-qualifying distributions*

(12) Non-qualifying distributions are bonus issues of redeemable shares or securities, either issued directly or issued out of bonus redeemable shares or securities received from another company (CTA 2010 s 1136). The shareholder is liable to tax at the relevant dividend rate (0%, 7.5%, 32.5% or 38.1% depending on other income).. The company is required to notify HMRC within fourteen days after the end of the quarter in which the non-qualifying distribution is made (CTA 2010 s 1101). When the shares are redeemed the redemption is a qualifying distribution but tax paid at excess rates on the non-qualifying distribution may be set against any tax due at excess rates on the later qualifying distribution (ITTOIA 2005 s 401).

*Distribution – extended meaning for close companies*

(13) For close companies the term distribution has an extended meaning (CTA 2010 s 1000(2)). It covers the provision of benefits to participators and their associates, except those provided to directors and employees which are already assessable as employment income (see **Example B2**). The calculation of the amount of the distribution in respect of benefits to participators is made in the same way as for benefits to directors and employees (CTA 2010 s 1064(3)). For further details on directors' loans see **Example J2**. Close company liquidations are dealt with in **Example J4**.

*Scrip dividends*

(14) As indicated in note 9(c), scrip dividends, i.e. dividends taken in the form of shares rather than in cash, are not treated as distributions.

Where an individual takes a scrip dividend, he is deemed to have received dividend income equal to the 'appropriate amount in cash'. The 'appropriate amount in cash' means the amount of the cash option, unless it is substantially different from the market value of the shares, 'substantially' being interpreted by HMRC as 15% or more either way (Statement of Practice A8). If the difference is substantial, the appropriate amount in cash is the market value of the shares on the first day of dealing.

The equivalent of scrip dividends is income of a deceased's estate when such shares are issued to personal representatives. It is also income of discretionary and accumulation trusts (other than trusts in which the settlor has retained an interest), the trustees being liable to tax at 7.5% (up to £1,000) and 38.1% on income over £1,000.

Where scrip dividends are issued to a company, or a trust in which the settlor retains an interest, they are capital rather than income, with a capital gains base cost of nil.

Companies have to make separate quarterly returns of any scrip dividends issued (CTA 2010 s 1052).

*Loans written off*

(15) See **Example J2 note 11** for the treatment of individuals.

*Capital gains*

(16) For detailed notes on entrepreneurs' relief see **Example L5.**

# Question

On 1 April 2016 Wayne set up a company producing an online magazine after being made redundant from his publishing employment. The company operates from his home and he is the sole director shareholder. His friend told him to take a small salary and extract any other profits as dividends. This he duly did by setting up separate electronic banking transfers called 'salary' and 'dividend'. The company's turnover is below the VAT threshold and it has not registered for VAT.

The company did very well and on 1 July 2016 Wayne borrowed £3,600 from the company to help provide a deposit for the purchase of a new house. On 30 September Wayne borrowed a further £9,000.

In December 2016, Wayne was talking to another friend in the pub who told him that his company could pay various other bills and obtain tax relief provided he could come up with a business reason. Following this advice Wayne decided the company should pay all drinks and food costs during his weekly visits to the local pub (good source of advertising/networking with contacts), his music downloads (music improves his work performance), his February skiing holiday (fitness and health of employees is very important) etc. His friend also suggested that if he repays the loans during December 2017 and re-draws the money on 1 January 2018, he will avoid paying tax on the loan.

(a) State the taxation position resulting from the balance on the director's current/loan account with the company at 31 March 2016, and Wayne's proposal to repay the loan.

(b) Briefly highlight any potential problems that can occur with an inexperienced (in terms of running a company) directors.

(c) State what the consequences and procedure would be if it was discovered during a HMRC enquiry after the submission of the tax return for the year to 31 March 2016, Wayne had been paid £15,000 in cash for advertising a local business in the online magazine in August 2016 and had not recorded the income or loan in the company books.

(d) Calculate the tax cost of the options for dealing with a director's overdrawn loan account of £20,000 for the year ending 31 March 2017. Assume no salary or other income has already been taken during 2016/17, a normal 1100L tax code exists, it is currently the beginning of March 2017 and the director is the sole shareholder.

The official rate of interest is set at 3.25% for 2016/17.

# Answer

## (a) Tax position on directors' loans

### Tax charge under CTA s 455

The company will have to pay tax on the amount of the directors' overdrawn accounts at 31 March 2017 amounting to 32.5% × £9,600 = £3,120. The tax is payable by 1 January 2018, interest being charged from that date if the tax is not paid (CTA 2010 s 455). The tax is not payable if the loan is repaid within that time (see **explanatory notes 5 and 9**), and this is the basis of Wayne's friend's suggestion. However, where a repayment of at least £5,000 is matched by a further loan of at least £5,000 within 30 days (either side), or the further loan is anticipated at the time of the repayment the repayment is matched with the new loan rather than the old balance outstanding, and thus Wayne's plan will not relieve the tax on the loan.

The company must report the loans made during the year ended 31 March 2017 on supplementary page CT 600A on its self-assessment corporation tax return for the year. If it fails to do so, it will have made an inaccurate return and be liable to a penalty based on the potential lost revenue and the behaviour associated with the inaccuracy on the return. See **part** (c) for further details.

If the company released or wrote off the loans or any part of them, then that part released or written off would be included in the director's taxable income and taxed as if it was a distribution. The first £5,000 will be taxed at 0% and the balance at 7.5%, 32.5% or 38.1% depending on whether the dividends fall into the basic, higher or additional rate bands. Note that the first £5,000 does not reduce dividend income (or the taxable amount of the loan write off) and therefore forms part of the basic rate band or higher rate band as appropriate.

This charge takes priority over the release of loans taxed as a benefit under ITEPA 2003 s 188. HMRC believes that loan write-offs are normally employment related and hence must be treated as payments of earnings for Class 1 national insurance purposes. The s 455 charge is relevant only to tax, so although the write-off is taxed as a distribution rather than as an employment benefit, Class 1 NI contributions remain payable. Employment allowance may be available to shelter the first £2,000 of the employer (secondary) liability if not already used against NIC on pay.

If the directors repay all or part of the loans *after* the s 455 tax falls due, the company may claim repayment of the appropriate part of the tax paid (CTA 2010 s 458) using a form L2P. The tax will be due for repayment nine months after the end of the accounting period in which the loan is repaid, and the repayment will attract interest from that date (see **explanatory note 11**). If the loan is released or written off, the company may reclaim the tax in the same way as for loans repaid (see **explanatory note 12**).

### Charge on director under employment-related loans rules

Notwithstanding the operation of CTA 2010 s 455 HMRC will also apply the employment-related loans rules contained in ITEPA 2003 ss 173–191 by calculating the notional interest chargeable as a benefit.

The normal method of calculation (ITEPA 2003 s 182) is to take the average of the opening and closing overdrawn balances at the beginning and end of the tax year (or from the date the account was overdrawn to the date the loan was repaid, as the case may be), multiply by the complete months for which the loan was outstanding and divide by 12, then multiply by the official rate of interest. This gives the following result:

Average balance for period 1 July 2016 – 5 April 2017

$$\frac{3{,}600 + 12{,}600}{2} = £8{,}100$$

6,600 × 9/12 (9 months) @ 3% = £149

The 'alternative' method shows a higher amount of interest payable, i.e. £221 (see **explanatory note 2**).

## (b) Inexperienced directors

Inexperienced directors can suffer from the misconception that the company's bank account is an extension of their own, not be familiar with rules & regulations and fail to understand the importance of producing supporting paperwork. The company should have registered for PAYE, filed RTI monthly returns on or **before** any salaries or wages were paid and should have prepared payslips, dividend vouchers and board minutes (simply labelling electronic transfers is insufficient).

Under RTI salary and wages are required to be reported to HMRC before payment is made. The on or before requirement will cause problems if the company has failed to register for PAYE and or if the accountant discovers a reportable payment; for example salary credited (credit treated as payment) to the director's loan account or the payment of a personal liability.

Wayne needs professional advice about what expenses he should and should not be claiming and any implications. For example, Wayne could claim genuine business entertaining back from the company but it should be supported by records of the amounts spent on the particular occasions, the nature of the entertainment, the persons entertained and the reasons for the entertainment. He should also be made aware that the expenditure will be disallowed for corporation tax purposes.

Following the pub advice in December it appears some personal expenses have been paid via the company. Where a personal bill is paid by the company, depending upon the facts it should either be:

(1) Debited to the directors loan account,

(2) Treated as earnings for PAYE/NIC and grossed up via the payroll, or

(3) Reported on form P11D.

If the director's loan account is or becomes overdrawn, there may be s 455 tax and a taxable benefit in respect of the loan interest (see **(a) above**). If items are debited to an overdrawn loan account there is also the issue of how to clear the debt (see **(d) below**).

HMRC's normal approach to the payment of a personal liability is to consider it is earnings and taxable under PAYE. If the PAYE regulations have not been complied with correctly (failure to register, late returns and or incorrect returns) it will be necessary to make a disclosure of any inaccuracies and seek to ensure future compliance. It depends in part on the nature of the inaccuracies but in general, HMRC is likely to charge a penalty. Failure to take advice is normally 'failure to take reasonable care' but claiming personal expenditure as business on weak arguments could be deemed a deliberate understatement.

With the move to RTI, it is even more important that directors of smaller companies keep up to date with their payroll. New penalties commenced in 2014/15 for late filing of RTI returns (late being after payment has been made), and from April 2015 there is also a penalty for failure to pay over deductions on time. In outline the penalties are:

- Failure to submit RTI returns on or before payment is made – penalties commenced in October 2014 for late submission of full payment summaries. A flat penalty of £100 is charged – although the first late return in a year is not penalised. Small companies (with 9 or fewer employees) can file monthly, even if payment is made more frequently.

- Failure to pay tax on time – automatic penalties for late payment commenced in April 2015, with a rising rate of penalty according to how many late payments have been made in a tax year. Interest is also charged on late payments during the tax year.

- Error in taxpayer's documents – for 2013/14 onwards penalties under FA 2007 Sch 24 can be applied to all returns submitted under RTI, e.g. the monthly / weekly in year returns and the final RTI submission.

See **Example B1** for full details of the PAYE requirements and **Example G1** for the penalty rules.

Bookkeeping and paperwork can be a nuisance for any small business. Historically, many clients have wanted to get on with the business of making profits and leave the accountant to sort out the books at the year end. With RTI, real time record checks and the increased use of penalties this is a dangerous practice which should be discouraged, and all businesses should be encouraged to keep good basic records which are made up to date regularly.

## (c) £15,000 cash retained by Wayne & income not reflected in company books

The profits of the company would be increased by £15,000, and the tax payable adjusted accordingly.

Wayne would also be treated as having had an additional advance of £15,000 from the company on which a tax charge at 25% amounting to £3,750 would be payable to HMRC (CTA 2010 s 455). This £3,750 would be repayable by HMRC to the company following the repayment by Wayne to the company of the £15,000 irregularities (CTA 2010 s 458). The underpaid corporation tax and tax under s 455 would attract interest and penalties, with the penalty regime in FA 2007 applying. Where a corporation tax return is shown to understate the true tax liability the company is subject to a tax-related penalty, the amount of which depends on the nature of the inaccuracy:

- mistake despite reasonably care (no penalty);
- careless inaccuracy (maximum 30%, minimum 0%);
- deliberate not concealed (maximum 70%, minimum 20%); and
- deliberate and concealed (maximum 100%, minimum 30%)

The reduced rates of penalty apply where the taxpayer company discloses the inaccuracy and provides full information to HMRC about it. If the disclosure is prompted by an intervention from HMRC, a lower rate of reduction applies, so that the maximum penalty rates above are halved. **Example G1** provides a comprehensive explanation of the penalty for inaccuracy legislation.

For the purposes of computing the potential lost revenue, on which the penalty is based, no account is taken of s 455 tax which is refundable or relievable due to the loan being repaid (FA 2007 Sch 24 para 5(4)).

It is highly unlikely that HMRC would accept the behaviour as taking reasonable care, or even merely being careless, without strong supporting evidence and reasoning.Indeed HMRC states that 'deliberately withdrawing money for personal use from an incorporated business and not making any attempt to make sure it is treated correctly for tax purposes' is an example of a deliberate inaccuracy. Whether HMRC would also consider that steps have been taken to conceal the inaccuracy is debatable; Wayne does not seem to have taken any active steps to hide what he has done, so it is likely that the penalty rate demanded by HMRC will start at 70%.

The penalty can be mitigated very substantially for unprompted disclosure, co-operation and access to records, accordingly the company should provide the help and access required by HMRC.

Because of the discovery of unrecorded cash income, HMRC would likely seek to satisfy themselves that no other irregularities, extractive or otherwise, had occurred by means of an in-depth examination of the company records and of the personal finances of the directors, in the latter case satisfying themselves in particular that all personal bank/building society lodgements, asset purchases and personal and private expenditure were properly explained and accounted for.

HMRC are strictly entitled to assess Wayne on employment-related loan interest under ITEPA 2003 s 175 in respect of the advances of £15,000. In practice, HMRC does not do so where the extractions also involve liabilities to corporation tax and under s 455 with interest and penalties thereon.

## (d) Calculations of the tax cost of dealing with an overdrawn loan account of £20,000

Subject to the anti-avoidance rules – see **explanatory note 9**.

## J2.5 CORPORATION TAX COMPUTATION – DIRECTORS' AND EMPLOYEES' BENEFITS AND DIRECTORS' OVERDRAWN LOAN ACCOUNTS

*Option 1 Pay the s 455 tax*

| | |
|---|---|
| £20,000 @ 32.5% | £6,500 |

This tax will be due for payment 1 January 2016. If in due course the loan can be repaid, the tax will be refunded. The timing is slow; repayment is not until nine months after the end of the accounting period in which the loan is repaid and repayment interest does not start to run until this date is past so s 455 tax can be compared to an interest free loan to HMRC.

As the loan remains outstanding there will be an amount of tax and NIC due on the benefit in kind of the interest free loan. The income tax will fall due under self assessment on 31 January 2018, although on receipt of form P11D in June/July 2017 HMRC is likely to code out the benefit by reducing Wayne's tax code. Class 1A NIC will also be due at 13.8% on the benefit in kind amount, and although the amount is small, the penalty for failing to file form P11D(b) by 19 July is a minimum of £100.

*Option 2 Declare a bonus*

Gross pay required to clear an overdrawn loan account of £20,000 is £25,150*.

| | £ |
|---|---|
| Income tax on gross (25,150 – 11,000) * 20% | 2,830 |
| Employee NIC on gross (25,150 – 5,824) * 12% | 2,319 |
| Employers NIC on gross** (25,150 * 13.8%) | 3,471 |
| Corporation tax relief (£22,872 + £471) @ 20% | 4,669 |
| Net tax cost of bonus payment (2,830+2,319+3,471–4,669) | 3,951 |

*PAYE calculated using 2016/17 rates.

** Employment allowance reduces Employer NIC by £3,000 for 2016/17.

If the bonus is provided in the accounts and paid (made available / credited to director's loan account) within nine months after the year end (i.e. by 1 January 2018) it can still be deducted against the company's taxable profits for the year ending 31 March 2017. However the PAYE payment would be delayed until the 19th (or 22) following the month of payment. Therefore if the bonus was provided now and paid 1 December 2017 the s 455 tax charge is avoided, the corporation tax relief for the bonus would be given against the corporation tax due 1 January 2018 and the PAYE would be due 19 January 2018. This does mean the loan is outstanding for a further eight months and hence there will be an additional amount of tax and NIC due on the benefit in kind of the interest free loan. This benefit could be reduced slightly (without changing the PAYE due date) if the employer qualified for quarterly payment of PAYE by paying the bonus on 6 October 2017.

Note that if the company has another employee subject to NIC, even if paid below the primary threshold (i.e. paid between the lower earnings limit of £112 per week but less than £155 per week) then the employment allowance of £3,000 can be claimed reducing the above cost significantly.

*Option 3 Write the loan off*

| | £ |
|---|---|
| Loan write off | 20,000 |
| Tax liability on the director (20,000 – 11,000 - 5,000) * 7.5% | 300 |
| Employee NIC on write off (20,000 – 155) * 12% | 2,381* |
| Employers NIC on write off (20,000) * 13.8% | 2,760** |
| Corporation tax relief on employers NIC (2,760 * 20%) | 552 |
| Net tax cost of loan write off | 4,889 |

* Using 2016/17 tax rates.

** Employment allowance may reduce Employer NIC by £3,000 for 2016/17 if there is another employee subject to NIC as explained above.

Loans written off are treated as a dividend. The personal allowance would be available to set against the dividend, giving a taxable dividend in 2016/17 of £9,000 (based on personal allowance of £11,000), with the first £5,000 taxable at Nil, and the balance at 7.5% for a tax charge of £300.

The waiver creates an employee's NIC liability of £2,381. This sum will need to be paid by the director or will create a new debit to the loan account. In 2017/2018 no payments on account of income tax will be required as the income tax liability is less than £1,000. .

The waiver can be before 31 March 2017 to avoid the need to report an overdrawn loan account (although ensure the employees NIC is settled) or within nine months of the year end, 1 January 2018 to avoid the s 455 tax liability. Depending upon the exact dates there will be an amount of tax and NIC due on the benefit in kind of the interest free loan.

It should be borne in mind that directors have a duty to protect the company's creditors (especially insolvent companies) and this should be considered before waiving any sums due to the company.

*Option 4 Declare a dividend*

| | £ |
|---|---|
| Dividend | 20,000 |
| Tax liability on the director (20,000 – 11,000 - 5,000) * 7.5% | 300 |
| Net tax cost of a dividend | 300 |

A company can only declare a dividend if it can meet the requirements of the Companies Act 2006. This includes sufficient justified accumulated profits (after corporation tax) to cover the dividend. The company should also follow the procedures set out in CA 2006 and prepare the necessary supporting documentation.

The dividend will give rise to a tax charge of £300 in this example. See **part (a)**.

The dividend would need to be before 31 March 2017 to avoid the need to report an overdrawn loan account in the statutory accounts or within nine months of the year end, 1 January 2018 to avoid the s 455 tax liability. Note that the fact that the loan was overdrawn should be disclosed in the related party transactions note and the supplementary pages to the tax return. Depending upon the exact dates there may be an amount of tax and NIC due on the benefit in kind of the interest free loan.

If the ability exists it would be advisable to change the company's dividend policy such that dividends are declared before funds are withdrawn by the director/shareholder. The issues of overdrawn loan accounts and benefits in kind are then avoided. Where the dividend is intended to clear an overdrawn loan account the dividend should be credited directly against the loan in the books, rather than paid out and the loan repaid in cash, as the latter approach can result in the repayment being ignored for s.455 purposes under one or more of the anti-avoidance provisions against bed-and-breakfasting loans see 9(d) below.

The dividend option has been included for completeness; however in some circumstances it is not available (e.g. insufficient reserves). Which of the above options is then preferable depends upon the exact circumstances of the company and director.

## Explanatory Notes

*Benefit charge on interest-free or cheap loans*

(1) Where a company makes a loan either interest-free or at a rate below the 'official rate' to an employee or to a director (or to their relatives, meaning spouse, parents and remoter forebears, children and remoter

issue, brothers and sisters, and the spouses of any of these relatives) the benefit is charged to tax under ITEPA 2003 ss 173–191 on the shortfall of the interest charged compared with the official rate. The official rate is normally set in advance for the whole of the tax year: The average rate for 2016/17 is 3%.

There is no tax charge on loans made to employees on commercial terms by employers who lend or supply goods and services on credit to the general public. No employment-related loan charge arises if the loan is a qualifying loan, i.e., where the interest on the loan (irrespective of whether it is actually paid) would qualify for income tax relief (for example, a loan taken out to buy shares in a close company or a loan used for trading purposes – see **Example A1 explanatory note 13**) (ITEPA 2003 s 178). Nor is there any charge if the total of all non-qualifying loans to any person or those connected with him do not exceed £10,000 at any time in the tax year (ITEPA 2003 s 180). If there are qualifying loans and non-qualifying loans, there is no charge on the non-qualifying loans if they do not exceed £10,000 in total at any time in the tax year. Although the average balance on the loan is £8,100, the balance during the year was £12,600 so the de minimis does not apply.

If the loan is for a qualifying purpose for interest relief (see **Example A1 explanatory note 13**), the tax relief due on the interest paid reduces the tax chargeable.

(2) The normal method of calculation of the beneficial loan interest is shown in **part (a)** of the Example. An employee may elect for the interest to be calculated using the alternative method. The alternative method may also be used if the officer so requires (ITEPA 2003 s 183). The time limit for the employee or officer to make such an election is one year from 31 January following the relevant tax year. To calculate the interest under the alternative method, the amounts outstanding for each day in the tax year for which the interest rate is the same are added together, divided by 365 (or 366 in the case of a leap year) and multiplied by the official rate. The amounts arrived at for each rate are then added together. The interest for Wayne on the alternative method is therefore calculated as follows:

| | | | |
|---|---|---|---|
| 01.07.2016 – 30.09.2016 | 3,600 × 92 days | = | 331,200 |
| 01.10.2016 – 05.04.2017 | 12,600 × 187 days | = | 2,356,200 |
| | | | 2,687,400 |

$$\frac{2{,}687{,}400}{365} \times 3.0\ \% = £221$$

(3) Employers must show the cash equivalents of employment-related loans on Forms P11D, a copy of the P11D being given to employees (see **Example B1**). Where there are several loans, the loans are not aggregated to calculate the benefits. Employers who are close companies may, however, elect to aggregate non-qualifying employment-related loans in the same currency that are outstanding at the same time in the tax year (ITEPA 2003 s 187).

*Class 1A NIC charge on taxable benefits*

(4) Employer's Class 1A national insurance contributions are chargeable on all taxable benefits in kind provided to P11D employees and directors (except for certain childcare benefits and apart from those already subject to the normal Class 1 charge, such as loans written off, readily convertible assets and the payment of personal bills). The Class 1A national insurance contributions charge is based on cash equivalents calculated under the taxable benefits provisions. See **Example H1** for details.

*Loans by close companies to participators*

(5) If a close company makes a loan or advances any money to a participator, there are tax implications for the company under CTA 2010 s 455, as indicated in **part (a)** of the Example. These are, in addition to the employment-related loans, rules where the participator is a director or employee. A loan is treated as made where the participator incurs a debt to the close company, or to a third party who assigns the debt to the close company. The provisions of CTA 2010 s 455 do not apply to:

(a) a loan made in the ordinary course of a money lending business;

(b) a debt for goods or services unless more than six months' credit or a longer credit period than normal is given; and

(c) a loan of up to £15,000 to a full-time employee/director owning not more than 5% of the ordinary share capital.

As indicated in **part (a)** of the Example, under self-assessment, loans to participators are reported on the supplementary CT 600A with the corporation tax return CT 600, which must be submitted within twelve months from the end of the company's accounting period.

The 32.5% tax charge on the loan is due nine months and one day after the end of the accounting period in which the loan is made (CTA 2010 s 455), and interest is charged from that date if the tax is not paid on time. Tax is not payable if the whole of the loan is repaid within the nine month period. Companies show the tax on s 455 loans in their tax returns as part of the total tax due, but can claim an offsetting deduction if the loan has (in whole or part) been repaid before the return is filed.

*Repayment of loans after tax paid*

(6) When all or part of the loan is repaid after the tax has been paid, the company may claim repayment of the appropriate amount of tax, the time limit for the claim being six years after the end of the accounting period in which the loan is repaid (CTA 2010 s 458). However, this tax is not repayable until nine months after the end of the accounting period in which the loan is repaid and interest on the repayment runs from that date (ICTA 1988 s 826(4)).

(7) Thus in **part (a)** of the Example, if the director repaid the loans on or before 1 January 2018 the company would not have to pay tax on the loans under s 455. If the loans were repaid in (say) February 2018, i.e., in the accounting period ended 31 March 2018, the company should have paid the tax by 1 January 2017 (interest being charged from that date if it had not) and would not be entitled to repayment until 1 January 2019, interest on the tax repayable running from that date.

*Loans written off*

(8) If a loan or overdrawing by a participator is written off by a company, the effect on both the lender and the borrower needs to be considered.

As far as the lender company is concerned, writing off loans is normally allowable under the 'loan relationships' rules unless the parties are connected, the 'connected' test does not apply to *all* participators, only to controlling shareholders (see **Example K2** for the detailed provisions). The company may recover the tax paid on loans written off in the same way as for loans repaid (CTA 2010 s 455).

The release of a loan due to a 'non-connected' company gives rise to a taxable credit in the borrower's books, except where the release is part of a relevant compromise or arrangement (CTA 2009 s 358). A released debt for expenditure previously deducted against the borrower's trading profits produces a taxable receipt under CTA 2009 s 94. (This debt would fall outside the loan relationship regime as it represents an amount due for the supply of goods and services and not the lending of money (CTA 2009 s 302).

For close companies, the treatment for a shareholder of loans written off (including a shareholder who is a director or employee) is as indicated in **part (a)** of the Example. Thus s 455 loans written off are treated as effectively being taxed in the same way as dividends, but (in the opinion of HMRC) nevertheless subject to Class 1 national insurance contributions if the shareholder is an employee or director. HMRC won this argument in *Stewart Fraser Ltd* (2011). This case involved the regular release of loans to a director/shareholder who was unable to draw dividends due to a dispute with a minority shareholder. The circumstances were slightly unusual and the company's evidence was thin. It may be possible to avoid liability to NIC if it can be established that the write off was made for a reason that is not employment related. For example, on the death of the individual or as a result of fraud.

If the write-off of the loan is not caught by the close company rules for loans to shareholders, and it has been obtained by reason of the borrower's employment then whether the employee is a P11D employee or not, and whether or not the loan is at a rate of interest below the 'official rate', the director or employee is treated as having received an equivalent amount of remuneration at that time (which also attracts Class 1 national insurance contributions). This does not apply to loans written off on death. Nor does it apply if the write-off occurs after the employee has left, except for P11D employees. Any such loan write-off on termination of the employment cannot benefit from the £30,000 exemption under ITEPA 2003 s 403 because it is already taxable under the benefits code.

*Anti-avoidance*

(9) From 20 March 2013 the s 455 charge above was extended to counter avoidance in the following areas:

(a) Avoidance using partnerships – this widens the definition of a participator to include all partnerships. For example, an individual (X) owns 100% of the shares in a close company (C Ltd). X & C Ltd set up an LLP with themselves as partners. C Ltd makes a loan to the LLP. Unless one of the exceptions in CTA 2010 Chapter 3 applies, C Ltd has made a loan to an LLP in which there is an individual partner who is also a participator in the close company and so the loan is chargeable to s 455 tax.

(b) Avoidance using trusts – this widens the definition of a participator to include trustees and actual or potential beneficiaries.

(c) Extraction of value/other benefits – the new s 464 A applies if a close company is (at any time) party to tax avoidance arrangements which result in any non-taxable benefit (directly or indirectly) being conferred on an individual who is a participator or an associate of a participator in the company. For example, an individual (X) is a participator in C Ltd. X & C Ltd are partners in a partnership. Under the partnership agreement 80% of profits are allocated to C Ltd. However C Ltd leaves its profits undrawn and X draws on them.

(d) Bed & breakfasting – a s 455 charge can be avoided if the loan is repaid (or written off) within nine months of the end of the accounting period during which it was advanced. A new rule has been introduced to deny relief for repayments of more than £5,000 that are withdrawn within 30 days either side of the repayment. In addition, relief is denied if the amount outstanding exceeds £15,000 and at the time of repayment there are arrangements or intentions to redraw an amount at a future date. There is an exception to this rule were the repayment gives rise to a charge to income tax, e.g. the loan is cleared by declaring a dividend or salary or waiving, so the considerations in part(d) where a bonus or dividend are considered would not trigger the anti-avoidance rules, and would result in the loan being treated as repaid on the relevant date.

Also see **Example N5** for the general anti-abuse rule introduced from 1 April 2013.

*Irregular extraction of company funds*

(10) Extractive irregularities are not treated as additional remuneration. They are not subject to tax on the directors. Instead, the directors are accountable to the company for their repayment; corporation tax then being payable on the additional profit if the extractions arise from suppressed income or overstated expenses. Tax at 32.5% is also payable by the company pending repayment by the directors to the company of the amounts extracted. Since interest and penalties are calculated on both the corporation tax and the s 455 liabilities which arise out of the same irregularities, the interest and penalty cost is that much greater than in the case of identical irregularities by sole traders and partners.

The first-tier tribunal upheld s 455 assessments in the case of *Powerlaunch Ltd v HMRC* TC01426. In this case, HMRC formed the opinion that a company had under declared its profits. They issued discovery assessments to collect the corporation tax and also s 455 on the basis that the under declared takings had been loaned or advanced to the company's director.

*Unpaid PAYE*

(11) Where a debit balance has arisen on a director's loan account and a net bonus is voted through the accounts regard should be had to *R V CIR ex parte McVeigh* (1996) STC 91. In this case, HMRC sought to collect unpaid PAYE on bonuses from one of the directors personally under reg 49(5) Income Tax (Employments) Regulations 1993 SI 1993 No 744. The director appealed on the basis that the bonuses had been credited to his current account net of tax, although the company had failed to pay the tax over. It was held that

deduction could only be made at the time of payment. Payment was made in round sum amounts some time before the bonus amounts were recorded and thus at the time payment was made no deduction was suffered. The entries showing net pay and recoding tax and NIC deducted were found to be merely accounting entries. The appeal was therefore dismissed.

The case was brought under the previous PAYE regulations. These were replaced by similar regulations in SI 2003 No 2682. What were known as reg 42 and reg 49 determinations are replaced by regs 72 and 80–82 of the new regulations. These regulations can create a personal liability on a director in respect of PAYE which should have been deducted.

*Personal liability notices*

(12) HMRC may issue a personal liability notice' (PLN) on any director of a company when the company has failed to pay national insurance contributions within the time allowed (so not necessarily under circumstances of insolvency) where that failure to pay appears to be due to the fraud or neglect of individuals who were at the time of the failure to pay, officers of the company (Social Security Administration Act 1992 s 121C).

There have been a number of cases regarding PLNs including *Peter Inzani v R&C Commrs* (2006) STC SCD 279 and *Stephen Roberts & Alan Martin V R&C Commrs* (2011) UK FTT 268. In *O'Rorke V R&C Commrs* TC01675 the company went into liquidation owing a large amount of NIC. The taxpayer appealed against the PLN and said that his addiction which affected his behaviour should be taken into account when deciding whether he had been negligent in carrying out his duties. Both parties submitted evidence on whether the test of 'neglect' in s 121C was objective or subjective. The first-tier tribunal said that s 121C is a penal measure and as such the tribunal should be careful in how the legislation is construed. Thus the tribunal decided to follow some of the matter quoted in Hansard and found the test to be a subjective test which must take into account the state of mind of the officer concerned. The appeal was accordingly allowed.

*HMRC toolkit*

(13) HMRC publish a toolkit to assist with 'directors' loan accounts' which may be a useful and vital tool for small practitioners who wish to show they have taken 'reasonable care' (see **Example G1**). The toolkit focuses on errors HMRC officers find commonly occur. It takes the form of a checklist followed by explanation and further sources of guidance.

Using the toolkit does not supplant the taxpayer's obligation to ensure that their corporation tax returns are complete and accord with the Taxes Acts. Indeed HMRC comment that their 'application to specific cases will depend on the law at the relevant time and on the precise facts', and 'it is not a comprehensive statement of all risks that may arise in any particular return'.

# Question

Tank Engines Ltd trades as a manufacturer of toy train and railway sets, and draws up accounts to 31 March each year. It has a dormant subsidiary company, Toby Ltd. There are no other associated companies. Following a successful advertising campaign, the company is making substantial profits and expects that its profits for the current year to 31 March 2017 will be around £1,200,000. (Its total asset value at the year-end is expected to be around £6,000,000.)

Mr Thomas (aged 52) is the company's managing director and owns 800 of the company's 1,000 £1 ordinary shares. The other 200 shares are held by the trustees of an accumulation and maintenance trust set up for the benefit of Mr Thomas's children, Annie and Clarabel.

Following this year's exceptional trading performance, Mr Thomas wishes to extract £200,000 for himself either as a bonus or dividend. He already draws a monthly salary of £4,000. Mr Thomas is a member of the company's pension scheme (which he joined 20 years ago).

Mr Thomas also plans a £50,000 bonus for each of his other directors, Mr Gordon and Mr James. Both directors have intimated that they would like a small shareholding in Tank Engines Ltd as they have both worked for the company for over 10 years and would welcome a sense of proprietorship. Mr Thomas is agreeable to this provided they take no more than 5% of the company's total shareholding.

Mr Thomas also wishes to pass some income to his wife, who does not work for the company and has little personal income. He realises that he cannot pay her a significant salary and therefore wishes the company to issue her with sufficient non-voting preference shares to provide her with an annual dividend of £10,000.

Mr Thomas has asked you to comment on his proposals at a meeting before the company's year end on 31 March 2017. Prepare a detailed briefing paper for Mr Thomas to consider at the meeting.

# Answer

## Mr Thomas – Bonus v dividend

(1) The decision to take £200,000 either as a bonus or dividend depends on a number of factors. A key consideration is usually the combined tax and national insurance (NIC) cost for each option

As Mr Thomas draws a salary of £48,000 per annum, he is a higher-rate taxpayer and above the upper earnings limit for NIC purposes(43,000 for 2016/17). Thus he will only be liable for the additional 2% charge on any bonus. Employer's NIC would be paid on the bonus at the rate of 13.8%.

(2) A comparison between the *bonus v dividend* routes shows the following:

| | *Bonus* | *Dividend* |
|---|---|---|
| | £ | £ |
| Profits to be extracted | 200,000 | 200,000 |
| Less: Employers NIC (200,000 * 13.8/113.8) | (24,253) | (0) |
| Corporation tax @ 20% (200,000 * 20%) | 0 | (40,000) |
| Bonus / dividend payment | 175,747 | 160,000 |
| Loss of personal allowance (11,000 @ 40% HR) | (4,400) | (4,400) |
| Less: tax & NIC on bonus / dividend | | |
| Dividend £5,000 nil rate | | (0) |
| Higher rate: 102,000 @ 40% / 97,000 @ 32.5% | (40,800) | (31,525) |
| Additional rate: 73,747 @ 45% / 58,000 @ 38.1% | (33,186) | (22,098) |
| NIC: 175,747 @ 2% / Not applicable | (3,515) | (0) |
| Net cash in hand after tax | 94,846 | 101,977 |

**Workings assuming Mr Thomas' only other income for the year is salary of £48,000**

| | *No bonus* | *Bonus* | *Dividend* |
|---|---|---|---|
| Salary | 48,000 | 48,000 | 48,000 |
| Bonus | | 175,747 | |
| Dividend | | | 175,000 |
| Total income | 48,000 | 223,747 | 223,000 |
| Less Personal allowance | 11,000 | 0 | 0 |
| Taxable income | 37,000 | 223,747 | 223,000 |
| Income taxable at: | | | |
| Basic rate | 32,000 | 32,000 | 32,000 |
| Higher rate 40% on salary | 5,000 | 15,000 | 15,000 |
| Higher rate 40% on bonus | | 102,000 | |
| Zero percent rate on dividend | | | 5,000* |
| Higher rate 32.5% on dividend | | | 97,000 |
| Additional rate 45% on bonus | | 73,747 | |
| Additional rate 38.1% on dividend | | | 58,000 |

Extraction of the profits by dividend rather than bonus would leave Mr Thomas with (101,977 – 93,846 =) £8,131 additional cash.

* the £5,000 dividend covered by the dividend allowance uses up higher rate band, so only £97,000 of the higher rate band rather than £102,000 remains available after the £48,000 salary is taken into account.

(3) PAYE is deducted at the time of the bonus payment. If the bonus was paid in March 2017, the PAYE tax would be due by 19 April 2017 (or 22 April if paid electronically). In the case of a dividend, the tax would be paid in accordance with Mr Thomas's self-assessment payment position. Assuming Mr Thomas's only income for the previous year was his salary, the dividend upper rate tax on a dividend paid in March 2017 would not fall due until 31 January 2018. However at the same time he would be required to make a payment on account of his following year's tax liability. Payments on account are normally due in two instalments (31 January and 31 July) each equal to half of the previous year's liability. If the dividend was one off, his following year's liability may be met in full under PAYE and the amount of the payment on account could be reduced. However if dividends are to become a regular form of profit extraction the payment on account may be due and hence the initial time delay would not be so significant in future years. The corporation tax on the profits out of which the dividend is to be paid would not be due until 31 December 2017. A dividend would thus also offer a small cash flow saving.

If the bonus is provided in the accounts and paid (or made available) within nine months after the year end (i.e. by 31 December 2017), it can be deducted against the company's taxable profits for the year ended 31 March 2017. However the PAYE payment would be delayed until the 19th (22nd) following the month of payment.

If payment of the dividend was delayed until after 6 April 2017, payment of the higher and additional rate tax due thereon would be delayed one year until 31 January 2019.

(4) Pension contributions may be made based on the lesser of the cumulative lifetime limit remaining (1,000,000 for 2016/17) or the annual limit (£40,000 for 2016/2017 although carry forward of unused relief from the three preceding tax years may also be available). Payments in excess of these limits attract an annual allowance charge at the taxpayer's marginal rate. If contributions are paid by an employer, they will be tax-deductible provided they are expended wholly and exclusively for the purpose of the trade. Where contributions are paid by an individual rather than an employer, tax relief is also restricted with reference to the greater of £3,600 or 100% of earnings. Pensions tax relief is restricted from 2016/17 for very high income individuals (broadly those with income in excess of £150,000) by means of a taper which could reduce the annual allowance to a minimum of £10,000.depending on the levels of Mr Thomas's other income. Note that for this purpose, any employer contribution is treated as income for the income test.

(5) Other factors to consider would include the following:

(i) The fact that dividends are payable pro-rata to shareholding to all shareholders may not provide a fair basis for rewarding the 'working' shareholder, Mr Thomas. If, for example, a dividend of £200,000 was declared, 20% would be received by the trustees of the accumulation and maintenance trust, leaving Mr Thomas with only £160,000. As an alternative, a dividend of £250,000 could be proposed, with the trustees of the accumulation and maintenance trust waiving their entitlement to the trust's dividend of £50,000 (20% × £250,000) before it becomes payable, but waiver of dividends may be perceived as a form of avoidance, and could give rise to an HMRC enquiry. A less provocative method to achieve the desired goal than repeated dividend waivers would be for the trust shares to be re-designated as 'B' shares which would permit a differential rate dividend to be declared without need for dividend waivers, under any method however the trustees would have to approve the change and would do so only if the effect was to benefit the beneficiaries of the trust.

(ii) Share valuations – while dividend payments may influence *minority* share valuations for capital tax purposes, they would not usually be a factor in determining *controlling* shareholding valuations, which tend to be based on earnings and/or net asset values.

(iii) For NIC purposes earnings are defined as 'including any remuneration or profit derived from an employment.' (SSCBA 1992 s 3) Such a wide definition can cover dividends if they are paid as a substitute for salary or bonuses. The Government has indicated that it would not normally consider the imposition of national insurance on dividends although, 'schemes' that seek to convert remuneration to dividends are very likely to face challenges. The case of *HMRC v PA Holdings* [2011] EWCA Civ 1414 was found to tax substance (PA decided that its employees should receive a bonus) over form (payment of dividend). Another similar case where distributions were found to be remuneration is *Manthorpe Building Projects Ltd* TC1778. Mr Thomas therefore needs to proceed with considerable care and:

- Ensure any dividends declared are not a reward for his employment.
- Review whether a waiver by the trustees is beneficial. If sufficient funds exist, are there any IHT or other advantages in allowing 20% of the dividend declared to be paid to the trust effectively passing wealth to the next generation (the beneficiaries are his children).

(iv) Consideration should also be given to the general anti-abuse rule see **Example N5.**

(6) The dividend route gives a saving in post-tax funds, but it is less flexible and may cause difficulties with the amounts payable to each party especially once Mr Gordon and Mr James become shareholders in the future. The non-monetary factors must be explained fully to Mr Thomas.

## Mr Gordon and Mr James – bonus

(7) The net cost to the company of paying £100,000 out as bonuses (£50,000 each) before 6 April 2016 to Mr Gordon and Mr James would be:

| | £ |
|---|---|
| Bonuses (50,000 × 2) | 100,000 |
| Employer's NIC @ 13.8% | 13,800 |
| Gross cost | 113,800 |
| Corporation tax relief @ 20% | (22,760) |
| Net cost | 91,040 |

The bonuses would rank for tax relief if paid during the year ended 31 March 2017 or if provided in the accounts to 31 March 2017 and paid within nine months of the year-end.

Mr Gordon and Mr James have expressed an interest in receiving a shareholding (see below). Although issues with regard to all shares ranking evenly (as discussed above), future payments of 'bonuses' via dividends may be more tax efficient.

## Mr Gordon and Mr James – shares in Tank Engines Ltd

(8) Any issue or transfer of shares in the company to Mr Gordon and Mr James would be regarded as obtained by virtue of their employment. Each director would have an amount of employment income equal to the difference between the market value of the shares less the amount they paid for them. In this instance, the market value of the shares would be based on the value of a very small minority holding and hence would be heavily discounted. Assume that, based on its past maintainable earnings, Tank Engines Ltd is worth £4,000,000. A shareholding of (say) 2½% might be valued at (say) £25,000 (i.e. £4,000,000 × 2½% × 25% (75% discount)). Each director would have to pay around £25,000 for his shares in order to eliminate any taxable benefit.

If the shares constitute 'readily convertible assets' (i.e. where there are trading arrangements in existence enabling the director, or likely to enable him, to obtain cash for his shares now or at a future date), any tax due on a transfer at a discount to market value would be payable through the PAYE system (ITEPA 2003 s 696) and NICs would also be chargeable (see **explanatory notes** 7 and 8). If the shares are not readily convertible assets, no NICs would be due and the tax would be payable via the self-assessment return. In practice an unlisted company is unlikely to have shares which are readily convertible assets, however it is possible in some cases, for example if the controlling shareholder has issued a standing offer to buy-back shares to the other shareholders.

In addition, the company would have to complete HMRC's employment related securities spreadsheet and submit it to HMRC Employee Shares & Securities Unit before 7 July 2017. To access it the employer must register for the employment related securities service via PAYE online. https://www.gov.uk/topic/business-tax/employment-related-securities.

(9) Consideration should be given to granting share options under the enterprise management incentive (EMI) scheme. This would enable the directors to be granted options to acquire shares exercisable at any time (within ten years). No income tax (or NIC) charge arises if the option enables the shares to be acquired at an amount equal to their market value at the date the option is *granted*. The total initial market value of the shares (based on the value at the date of the grant) held under EMI options granted by the company cannot exceed £3 million at the date of any grant (see **Example N1** for details). Tank Engines Ltd will therefore not have any difficulty in meeting this requirement. Tank Engines Ltd should also satisfy the various qualifying conditions for establishing an EMI scheme. It is an independent (non-controlled) company and carries on a qualifying manufacturing trade. The balance sheet total of its gross assets is well within the maximum permissible amount. The EMI scheme is much more attractive than an approved company share option plan as it gives complete flexibility with regard to the timing of the exercise of the options, and the procedure enabling the value of shares to be agreed with HMRC Shares & Assets Valuation (promptly) at the time of the grant gives certainty of tax treatment. EMI share option agreements must be notified to HMRC within 92 days of the option grant. The clear disadvantage of granting options rather than awarding shares is that the two directors have no ownership interest until they exercise their options (and cannot be paid dividends), but this also means that they will have no shares to be bought back if they leave the company before they exercise.

EMI options need not be granted at full market value, but if the exercise price is discounted so that the directors can buy shares at low cost the discount is subject to income tax at exercise. Whether the exercise price is set at or below market value, the company should be able to claim a corporation tax deduction for any discount to current (rather than initial) market value when the options are exercised.

There will generally be a capital gains tax charge when the employee disposes of his shares. To qualify for entrepreneur's relief the individual normally needs to hold a 5% stake in a company. However, in recognition that companies often, as in this example, wish to give a smaller stake in the company through EMI, entrepreneurs relief has been extended to EMI shares, making EMI options even more attractive. See **Examples L5** and **N1**.

## Providing a dividend income of £10,000 for Mrs Thomas

(10) As a 75% plus controlling shareholder, Mr Thomas could arrange for Tank Engines Ltd to issue non-voting preference shares carrying the relevant dividend coupon to give Mrs Thomas a dividend of £10,000. However, following the case of *Young v Pearce* (1996) (see **Example A2 part (b)(iii)**), it is likely that such arrangements would be treated as a settlement by Mr Thomas in favour of his wife. This would mean that the dividend income on the shares would be taxed on Mr Thomas as settlor (ITTOIA 2005 ss 624–626).

(11) If, however, shares which carried substantive rights (such as voting rights and an entitlement to capital surpluses on a winding up, as well as dividend income) were issued or transferred to Mrs Thomas, this may escape the settlement provisions, since the shares would be an outright gift which carried other significant rights apart from a right to income (s 626).

Mr Thomas could transfer part of his existing (ordinary) shareholding to his wife. Alternatively, he could arrange for the company to create another class of ordinary shares (but carrying virtually the same rights as the existing ordinary shares). This would provide greater flexibility with regard to future dividends, for example enabling dividends to be declared on the new class of shares. Mr Thomas could provide the necessary funds to enable his wife to subscribe for the new class of shares, although this would involve injecting capital in a non-distributable form.

(12) Over a number of years, HMRC sought to apply the settlements legislation in ITTOIA 2005 s 624 to dividends paid to the spouse of the main earner in certain circumstances. The case of *Jones v Garnett* (the Arctic Systems case) confirmed that the inter-spouse exemption applied in the case of company ordinary shares – although the settlements legislation is still in point in all other cases.

In the *Arctic Systems* case, HMRC targeted the situation where profits derived principally from the work of the main earner, and where the main earner took remuneration at less than the market rate, thereby allowing funds to accumulate, to be paid subsequently as dividend, resulting in income being transferred to the other spouse in proportion to shareholding. The House of Lords decided that the shares benefitted from the outright gift exemption, meaning that although a settlement had been created, it was not caught by s 624.

## Explanatory Notes

*Bonus v dividend*

(1) The detailed comparisons between bonus and dividend payments are set out in **notes 1** to **6** of the example. Even if substantial dividends are being contemplated, it is recommended that a basic level of remuneration is paid to acquire state pension credits, and access to some other benefits. The National Minimum Wage Act 1998 does not require payment of minimum wage to a director unless the director has an 'explicit' contract of employment with the company – that is he has taken the trouble to create a formal contract of employment. If he does have an explicit contract he would fall within the minimum wage rules (from 2016/17 National Living Wage) and must pay himself at least £7.20 per hour. Dividends are disregarded for minimum wage purposes. Similarly, benefits in kind are ignored, except living accommodation, subject to a limit. Regular remuneration and a formal contract of employment also provides the basis for any redundancy entitlement, and assists with mortgage applications etc. Where the director may wish to take parental leave, statutory payments (the cost of which is borne by the state) may also be available. For employees aged under 25 reduced NMW hourly rates of £6.70 (age 21-24) or £5.40 (18–20) apply.

(2) The overall tax/NI cost is substantially less for a dividend than for paying bonus at all rates of corporation tax. This difference has increased year on year due to the successive reductions in the rate of corporation tax but reduced in 2016/17 due to the introduction of the new dividend taxation rules.

While accrued bonus is tax-deductible if paid within nine months of the year end, pension contributions cannot be deducted if they are accrued. If a combination of bonus and pension is considered, it must be considered well before the year end, and the company must pay the contribution before the year end.

(3) For shareholders paying tax at the basic rate, and liable to additional employees' NIC at the main rate of 12%, separate calculations are required in each case to determine whether a bonus or dividend should be paid, although the comments in **note 1** regarding payment of a basic level of remuneration are likely to be particularly appropriate.

*Pension contributions*

(4) The annual allowance for pension contributions is £40,000 for 2016/17 although this is reduced for people with income (including the pension contribution) of over £150,000 to a minimum of £10,000. Contributions paid in a pension input period (PIP see **Example A6**) in excess of the annual allowance attract an annual allowance charge (F(No 3)A 2011 s 66) at the taxpayer's marginal rate of tax.

There is limited scope to carry forward unused annual allowances (FA 2004 new s 227A). If the individual **was a member** of a registered pension scheme in the previous tax year, any unused allowance for that year may be carried forward. The carry forward can be for up to three years. Unused relief is calculated as £40,000 less the amount paid in the PIP ending in the relevant tax year. HMRC have confirmed that if no premium was paid in the earlier year the full annual limit can be carried forward, provided that the individual was a member of a scheme during the year.

Brought forward amounts are used up on the basis of the oldest amounts first. See **Example A6** for further details.

If Mr Thomas agreed to take £190,000 via a dividend and £10,000 as a pension contribution, the situation would be:

| | *Dividend £200,000* | *Dividend £190,000 Pension £10,000* |
|---|---|---|
| Profit | 200,000 | 190,000 |
| Corporation tax @ 20% | (40,000) | (38,000) |
| Dividend | 160,000 | 152,000 |
| Loss of personal allowance | (4,400) | (4,400) |
| Dividend 0% band of £5,000 | 0 | 0 |
| Dividend income tax 97,000 @ 32.5% | (31,525) | (31,525) |
| Excess @ 38.1% | (22,098) | (17,374) |
| Net cash available | 101,977 | 98,701 |
| Contribution to pension fund | | 10,000 |
| Value received | 101,977 | 108,701 |
| Tax borne | 98,023 | 91,299 |

The reduction in current year taxes would be £6,724, but the pension will be subject to PAYE when drawn (although perhaps at a lower rate, and no NICs will be due as the law currently stands). To be tax-deductible for Tank Engines Ltd, the pension contribution, as other remuneration or costs, must be expended wholly and exclusively for the purpose of the trade. HMRC guidance specifically states that the contribution is looked at in the context of the overall remuneration package, not a stand-alone amount. The proportion of pension contribution to other remuneration is not considered for this purpose.

The normal situation is that contributions will be tax-deductible, unless there is an identifiable non-trade purpose. As Tank Engines Ltd is a profitable trading company, and paying this remuneration out of profit, there should be no objection from HMRC, in spite of the tax saving arising from the salary (bonus) sacrifice.

Rules exist to remove the tax and NIC advantages of employers paying pension contributions into their employees' family members' pensions as part of their employees' remuneration package. For example if Tank Engines Ltd wished to make pension contributions to a pension for Mrs Thomas as part of Mr Thomas's remuneration package (on the basis Mrs Thomas does not work for the company and hence cannot justify a remuneration package in her own right).

*Dividend waivers*

(5) To be effective for income tax purposes, dividend waivers must be made before the dividend becomes due and payable. For this purpose, an interim dividend does not become due and payable until it is actually paid – the directors could rescind the dividend at any time before it is paid. However, a final dividend becomes payable at the company's annual general meeting when it is declared, unless the resolution specifies a later date (*Hurll v CIR* (1922); *Potel v CIR* (1970)).

(6) A dividend waiver would only be treated as a settlement for income tax purposes where the necessary element of bounty was present (*CIR v Plummer* (1979)). HMRC would argue that 'bounty' would have been conferred if the company's distributable profits could not have supported the dividend without the waiver, i.e. where the waiver enables one or more shareholders to receive a greater dividend than would otherwise be the case. In such cases, HMRC would only apply the settlements legislation where dividends are waived to increase the dividend payable to the settlor's spouse, children or the trustees of an accumulation and maintenance trust for the settlor's children (ITTOIA 2005 s 624). There is no transfer of value for inheritance tax purposes, provided a dividend waiver is made within twelve months before the right to the dividend accrues (IHTA 1984 s 15). The detailed inheritance tax provisions are in the companion to this book, **Tolley's Taxwise II 2016/17**.

If dividends are waived by non-employee shareholders so that large sums can be paid to those working in the business in lieu of bonuses, regard should be had to *HMRC v PA Holdings* [2011] EWCA Civ 1414. Also see **answer 5 (iii)** regarding NIC on dividends where part of a scheme to convert remuneration to dividends.

*Giving shares to employees*

(7) Except for shares acquired under HMRC-approved schemes (as to which see **Example N1**), a tax charge arises on shares given to employees unless full market value is paid for them. The taxable amount is the market value of the shares less the amount (if any) paid for them and this is chargeable under the normal 'money's worth' provisions of ITEPA 2003 s 62, although as it is not a payment in cash it is not chargeable through PAYE unless the shares are readily convertible assets. Since it is chargeable under s 62, it is outside the 'cash equivalents' benefits charging provisions for P11D employees and directors. The employer is, however, required under SI 2003/2682 reg 85 and ITEPA 2003 s 421J to make a return before 7 July after the end of the tax year. Employees need to report the relevant details in their tax returns. Gifts of shares in an employer company that are not readily convertible assets are not chargeable to either Class 1 or Class 1A national insurance contributions (SI 2001/1004 reg 40 and Sch 3 Part IX para 2).

(8) Unquoted shares are unlikely to be readily convertible assets unless there are arrangements which exist or might in future exist enabling them to be realised in cash. This might be the case where there is a planned sale or flotation of the company or where an employee share trust is available to buy the shares. The wide subjective nature of the definition can be difficult to apply.

(9) The provisions of Chapter 2 of Part 7 of ITEPA may be relevant. These impose tax charges where shares issued or transferred to employees are subject to restrictions that depress the value. The lifting of any such restriction in the future may give rise to a 'chargeable event' and an income tax charge. These rules would not apply if the shares were acquired by the employee for their unrestricted market value, or if the employee and employer elected at the time of acquisition to pay tax as if the restrictions did not apply.

# Question

The Steamdriven Computer Co Ltd has faced a declining market in recent years. It is expected to make a net *unadjusted* trading loss, including interest income, of £17,750 in the six months ending on 31 March 2016. Results for the previous three years (*before* any adjustments for tax purposes) have been as follows:

| | *Trading Profits* | *Bank Interest receivable* |
|---|---|---|
| | £ | £ |
| Year ended 30 September 2014 | 11,200 | – |
| Year ended 30 September 2015 | 3,000 | – |
| Year ended 30 September 2016 | 4,000 | 400 |

The projected balance sheet at 31 March 2017 on a going concern basis is as follows:

| | | |
|---|---|---|
| *Fixed assets* | £ | £ |
| Office premises (at valuation) | | 120,000 |
| Fixed plant and machinery | 12,000 | |
| *Less*: Depreciation | (2,400) | 9,600 |
| | | 129,600 |
| *Current assets* | | |
| Trading stock | 39,000 | |
| Cash | 500 | |
| | 39,500 | |
| *Less*: Creditors (excluding any corporation tax of year to 30 September 2016, which will be discharged by loss claim) | (4,000) | |
| *Net current assets* | | 35,500 |
| Total assets | | 165,100 |
| Financed by: | | |
| Share capital | | 10,000 |
| Retained profits | | 130,100 |
| | | 140,100 |
| 10% Debenture interest | | 25,000 |
| | | 165,100 |

The projected profit and loss account for the six months to 31 March 2017, again on a going concern basis, is as follows:

| | | |
|---|---|---|
| | £ | £ |
| Sales | | 91,000 |
| Opening stock | 42,000 | |
| Purchases | 60,000 | |
| *Less*: Closing stock | (39,000) | (63,000) |
| Gross profit | | 28,000 |
| *Less*: Staff and administrative costs | 42,200 | |
| Depreciation | 600 | |
| Debenture interest | 1,250 | |

| | £ | £ |
|---|---|---|
| Bank interest | (200) | (43,850) |
| Net loss | | (15,850) |

Mr Ludd, who owns 99.9% of the company's issued share capital, proposes that the company should sell all of its assets on 31 March 2017 for cash to an unconnected third party for a total amount of £143,000, attributable as follows:

| | £ |
|---|---|
| Goodwill | – |
| Office premises | 107,000 |
| Plant and machinery | 2,000 |
| Trading stock | 34,000 |
| | 143,000 |

Immediately after the assets are sold, the company would cease trading and the liquidation of the company would commence. The company would pay all of its liabilities at cessation and the liquidator would distribute the balance of cash to its shareholders shortly afterwards. Mr Ludd is unsure whether the cash should be distributed before or after 6 April 2017.

The company is expected to receive any repayments of corporation tax, including any arising out of its trading loss, by 7 June 2017. It is estimated that these amounts will just be sufficient to cover the liquidator's fees so that no further cash will be distributed to the company's shareholders.

The following information is also available:

(i) The 10% Debenture was issued in March 2005 to finance the company's trading activities. Interest is payable and has always been paid half yearly on 30 September and 31 March. The interest has been deducted in arriving at the profit figure shown.

(ii) All of the plant and machinery was acquired on 1 April 2015. The company has claimed maximum writing-down allowances (but no other allowances) in respect of this expenditure.

(iii) In computing depreciation for accounts purposes, the company uses a straight-line basis of 10% per annum and applies the same depreciation rate to all of the plant and machinery.

(iv) The company has no associated companies and has not paid dividends for several years.

(v) The disposal of the office will give rise to a nil gain/nil loss position for capital gains purposes.

(vi) Mr Ludd inherited his shares in the company in March 1982, when they had a probate value of £10,000.

(vii) Mr Ludd, who is single and aged 56, will have total income of £60,000 in 2016/17 and around £10,000 in 2017/18. He plans to retain all of his existing capital assets (except his shares in the company) for the foreseeable future.

Assume that all staff and administrative expenses are fully allowable.

On the basis of the estimated figures:

(a) Compute the final corporation tax liabilities of the company in respect of the periods commencing 1 October 2013 and ending 31 March 2017.

(b) Compute the total amount which should be repaid to the company by HMRC on 7 June 2017.

(c) Advise Mr Ludd as to which method of distributing cash by the company is preferable.

# Answer

## A. Final corporation tax liabilities for periods from 1 October 2013 to 31 March 2017

| | *Year to 30.09.14* | *Year to 30.09.15* | *Year to 30.09.16* | *6 mths to 31.03.17* |
|---|---|---|---|---|
| | £ | £ | £ | £ |
| Profit per accounts | 11,200 | 3,000 | 4,000 | |
| *Add*: depreciation (see workings) | 0 | 1,200 | 1,200 | |
| *Less*: capital allowances (see workings) | 0 | (2,160) | (1,771) | |
| Trading income | 11,200 | 2,040 | 3,429 | – |
| Loan relationships | | | | |
| Bank interest | 0 | 0 | 400 | 200 |
| Total profits | 11,200 | 2,040 | 3,429 | 200 |
| *Less:* loss relief under CTA 2010 s 37 (totalling £17,269) | (11,200) | (2,040) | (3,829) | (200) |
| Taxable profits | – | – | – | – |
| Unrelieved loss (26,420 per workings – 17,269) | | | | £9,151 |

Debenture interest is treated as a trading expense (see **note 4**).

*Workings*

### Capital allowances computation:

| | | £ |
|---|---|---|
| Additions 1 April 2015 | | 12,000 |
| Yr to 30.09.15 | WDA 18% | (2,160) |
| | | 9,840 |
| Yr to 30.09.16 | WDA 18% | (1,771) |
| | | 8,069 |
| 6 mths to 31.03.17 | Sale proceeds | (2,000) |
| | Balancing allowance | 6,069 |

### Loss to 31 March 2017:

| | £ |
|---|---|
| Net loss per accounts | (15,850) |
| Depreciation | 600 |
| Bank interest | (200) |
| Capital allowances | (6,069) |
| Loss on sale of stock (39,000 – 34,000) | (5,000) |
| Loss available for relief under CTA 2010 S37 | (26,420) |

**Depreciation:**

Cumulative figure of £2,400 on balance sheet represents £1,200 per annum on a straight-line basis from 1 April 2015 to 31 March 2017.

## B. Amount repayable to company on 7 June 2017

No tax is payable for the six months to 31 March 2017. Tax for the year to 30 September 2016 is normally payable 1 July 2017. However this is after the loss claim and repayment and hence no tax will be paid. Interest on the repayment for the years to 30 September 2015 and 30 September 2014 runs from 1 January 2018 (the payment date for the loss period). Since the repayment is made on 7 June 2017, it does not attract any interest.

| | |
|---|---|
| The repayment will therefore be: | £ |
| Year to 30 September 2014 | |
| 11,200 @ 20% | 2,240 |
| Year to 30 September 2015 | |
| 2,040 @ 20% | 408 |
| Total | 2,648 |

| | |
|---|---|
| The losses also save tax from being payable: | |
| Year to 30 September 2016 | |
| 3,829 @ 20% | 766 |
| Six months to 30 March 2017 | |
| 200 @ 20% | 40 |
| Total | 806 |

## C. Advice to Mr Ludd on how cash should be distributed

If all the cash is distributed before 6 April 2017, Mr Ludd will have a chargeable gain in 2016/17 as follows.

| | |
|---|---|
| Available funds in company: | £ |
| Proceeds of sale of assets | 143,000 |
| Add cash in hand | 500 |
| *Less*: amounts used to pay creditors and debenture holders (4,000 + 25,000) | (29,000) |
| Distributable to shareholders | 114,500 |
| Mr Ludd's share of distributions (99.9%) | 114,386 |
| Cost of shares March 1982 | (10,000) |
| Gain before entrepreneur's relief and annual exemption | 104,386 |
| Annual exemption | (11,100) |
| | 93,286 |
| Taxable @ 10% | 9,329 |

For entrepreneur's relief to apply, the distribution has to be within three years of the cessation of trade. If entrepreneur's relief did not apply the advantage to delaying the distribution would be obtaining the 10% CGT rate on the amount of gain up to Mr Ludd's unused basic rate band in the 2017/18 tax year plus the timing delay in payment being due one year later.

# Explanatory Notes

*Chargeable accounting periods*

(1) CTA 2009 ss 10 and 12 provide that a chargeable accounting period ends on the earliest of the following (see **Example I3 explanatory note 2(C)**):

Twelve months from its commencement

An accounting date of the company

Cessation of trading

Immediately before the commencement of a winding-up.

*Trading losses*

(2) Trading losses carried forward are only available against future profits of the *same trade* (CTA 2010 s 45). If any chargeable gains had arisen in the liquidation period, therefore, the losses could not have been set against them. Trading losses are extinguished on the cessation of trade. However, under CTA 2009 s 196 any post-cessation trading receipts arising in the liquidation can be deemed to arise on the last day of trade and accordingly be offset against the loss that would otherwise be eliminated . Trading losses may normally be carried back only 12 months (CTA 2010 s 37) but on a cessation this period is extended to three years (CTA 2010 s 39). The trading loss available for carry back is the loss arising in the last 12 months of trading. The three-year carry back is measured from the beginning of each loss making accounting period. This can have the effect of giving relief against profits which may have been earned more than four years prior to the cessation of trade.

*Interest on overpaid tax*

(3) For detailed notes on the dates from which interest runs when tax is repaid following loss claims, see **Example I4 explanatory note 6**.

Interest on underpaid and overpaid tax is taken into account in calculating taxable profits. If interest on overpaid tax is received or receivable by a company in liquidation in its final accounting period, however, the interest will not be included in taxable profits if it does not exceed £2,000 (CTA 2010 s 633). The actual tax repayments in this Example did not attract any interest.

*Loan interest payable*

(4) Interest on a loan for the purposes of the trade is deducted on an accruals basis in arriving at the trading profit. For detailed notes see **Example K2**.

*Close investment-holding companies*

(5) For periods prior to 1 April 2017 where a company is a close investment-holding company, it is liable to tax at the full corporation tax rate, no matter how small its profits are (CTA 2010 s 34). (For detailed notes see **Example I7**.) If the company was not close before liquidation, it will not become close as a result of the liquidation.

Companies that are trading or property investment companies are excluded from the definition of close investment-holding company, but clearly there was a potential problem when a company goes into liquidation following the cessation of its trade. CTA 2010 s 34(5) provides that a company that is wound up will not be treated as a close investment-holding company in the accounting period commencing with the winding-up if it was outside the definition in the previous accounting period. But the cessation of a trade itself triggers the end of an accounting period, and there will often be an interval between that cessation and the passing of the winding-up resolution, in which case the company in liquidation will not be helped by this provision. The provision was helpful however when a company's trade had been continued by a receiver or administrator up to the date of the winding-up resolution, or when a company had let properties and the lettings continued after the cessation of the trade, enabling the company to escape close investment-holding company status in the period leading up to the winding-up resolution.

*Liquidation distributions*

(6) Once a liquidation has commenced, sums can only actually be paid to shareholders by the liquidator as a capital distribution payment in respect of their shares. Any surplus over the cost of the shares is subject to capital gains tax, after taking into account available reliefs and exemptions, including entrepreneurs' relief and the annual exemption, as shown in the Example.

Any distributions before the commencement of the liquidation are taxed as income dividends, see **Example J2** for detailed consideration of the recent changes to dividend taxation.

The life time limit for entrepreneur's relief is £10M. It is available providing the shares in the trading company (or holding company of a trading group) had been held throughout a period of one year ending with the date on which the company ceases to be a trading company or a member of a trading group and that date is within the period of three years ending with the date of disposal and the individual was:

- an officer or employee of the company: and
- owned at least 5% of the share capital and that holding enables the individual to exercise at least 5% of the voting rights.

For an additional rate taxpayer, a comparison of the tax burdens at the maximum amount attracting entrepreneur's relief (ignoring CGT annual exemption) follows:

| | *No entrepreneurs' relief* | *Entrepreneurs' relief* | *Dividend* |
|---|---|---|---|
| Distribution available | 10,000,000 | 10,000,000 | 10,000,000 |
| Capital gain/income | 10,000,000 | 10,000,000 | 10,000,000 |
| Tax rate | 20% | 10% | 38.1% |
| Tax | 2,000,000 | 1,000,000 | 3,810,000 |

The capital gains rate for gains on shares not qualifying for Entrepreneur's relief is 20%. The dividend example above ignores the £5,000 dividend nil rate band,

(7) In the case of a formal liquidation CTA 2010 s 1030 provides that distributions received in respect of share capital are treated as capital receipts. If instead application is made for the company to be struck off under Companies Act 2006 s 1003, this provision would not apply. Instead SI 2012/266 reg 18 applies which sets a limit on the total amount being distributed for capital treatment to apply. If the total being distributed (i.e. to all shareholders) is no more than £25,000 then the receipt is treated as capital in their hands. If the distribution is in excess of this amount the entire amount is treated as income, and taxed as an income distribution. In looking at the £25,000 limit, HMRC will also take into account distributions made in anticipation of the striking off, so this limits the opportunity to pay dividends to reduce the distribution on striking off to below £25,000. Thus, the striking off route is really only of interest to shareholders with very low sums available to distribution. Note also that if the shareholder is a basic rate taxpayer, an income distribution may be preferable to a capital distribution if their CGT annual exemption is not available. The procedure for voluntary striking-off is in the Companies Act 2006 ss 1003 to 1011.

Those with more substantial amounts to distribute will therefore be forced to choose liquidation in order to access CGT treatment and avail themselves of entrepreneur's relief. Current costs quoted for a small solvent company with a single shareholder and bank account but no other assets are £3,000 to £5,000.

If a company returns share capital without going through the process of a formal winding up, this is technically under company law an unauthorised distribution and as such *Bona Vacantia* or Crown property. However, in practice, the Treasury Solicitor's policy is not to pursue return of share capital after a striking off; there was previously a financial limit to this policy, but it has now been removed. Repayment of non-distributable reserves remains an unauthorised distribution and should be avoided by performing a capital reduction under CA 2006 prior to striking off.

*Disincorporation relief*

(8) FA 2013 ss 57 to 60, introduced a temporary relief for disincorporations between 1 April 2013 and 31 March 2018. This has been introduced following recommendations by the Office of Tax Simplification to remove the tax barriers when a small company's shareholders want to transfer the business to a sole trader or partnership. The relief avoids an immediate capital gains tax charge on the disposal of assets and goodwill by adjusting the transfer value (which would normally be market value). Only small companies will potentially qualify as the relief is only available if the market value of the total assets of the company does not exceed £100,000.

The transfer value depends on the type of assets being transferred, their creation and corporate tax treatment. The intention is that the reduced value is such that no corporation tax is payable by the company on transfer; the relief does not affect the shareholders at the time of winding up. CTA 2009 s 849A specifies disposal value is treated as the lower of market value and another value (eg cost, tax written down, nil) depending upon circumstances.

The relief is not applicable to Steamdriven Computer Co Ltd as the business is ceasing.

*Administrations and Voluntary Arrangements*

(9) Under the Insolvency Act 1986, Administrations and Voluntary Arrangements may be used (among other purposes) to obtain a more advantageous realisation of a company's assets than would occur on a winding-up. HMRC have a unit to handle voluntary arrangements, known as the Voluntary Arrangements Service.

When a company goes into administration, this marks the start of a new accounting period. Thereafter, the normal rules apply so that an accounting period ends on cessation of trade or the normal accounting date. The date when a company comes out of administration will represent the end of an accounting period (CTA 2009 s 10(1)(j)). Liabilities for corporation tax, PAYE/NIC and other taxes arising in the course of an administration are payable as an expense of the process.

A Voluntary Arrangement may be agreed, based on 'a proposal to the company and its creditors for a composition in satisfaction of its debts or a scheme of arrangement of its affairs'. A compromise in satisfaction of debts would constitute a release of each debt to the extent specified by the terms of the Voluntary Arrangement, but the debtor does not have to treat the amount released as a taxable receipt (CTA 2009 ss 94 and 322) and the creditor may claim a deduction for the release of the debt provided that the parties are not connected (see **Example K2 explanatory note 6**).

The definition of 'statutory insolvency arrangement' is found in CTA 2010 Sch 1 para 701(3). A statutory insolvency arrangement is an arrangement under British insolvency laws or the Companies Act, or a corresponding arrangement in countries outside the United Kingdom.

# Question

## A.

Fitzwilliam Ltd is an unquoted trading company in which 80% of the share capital is owned by members of one family. The remaining shares are currently owned by Hilton, who is not related in any way to the other shareholders.

Hilton, a longstanding employee, now wishes to retire from work and to dispose of all or part of his shareholding. The other members do not have funds which they could use to purchase his shares, but the company has sufficient funds and distributable reserves to purchase at least part of his shareholding.

Consider whether capital or income tax treatment would apply to the purchase of shares from Hilton by the company in 2016/17 together with the respective tax implications.

## B.

You act as tax adviser for Bliss Ltd (which operates a successful marriage bureau) and its managing director, Mr Crippen. The company has made tax-adjusted trading profits in excess of £250,000 pa over the previous five years. It has now built up a substantial reserve of cash, since its policy has been not to pay out any dividends. The company has not made any chargeable gains in recent years and has always made up its accounts to 30 April. Mr Crippen informs you that he and Mr Bluebeard, his fellow shareholder, are in serious disagreement about the future strategy of the company and that this is having a very harmful effect on the running of the business. It has therefore been decided that Mr Bluebeard should no longer be involved in the management of the company and that the company will purchase all of his shares from him.

Further relevant information is as follows:

(a) Mr Bluebeard is 64 years old and has worked in the company as a full-time director since it was incorporated on 1 January 1990, when he acquired 30% of the ordinary shares at par for £50,000. The company has agreed to buy the shares back at their market value of £662,000 on 7 April 2016.

(b) All of Bliss Ltd's assets are in use for the purposes of its trade.

(c) Mr Bluebeard, who is single, has a private income of £55,000 pa and has made no capital disposals in 2016/17.

Set out the amounts and dates of payment of the tax liabilities which would be incurred by both Bliss Ltd and Mr Bluebeard in respect of the share purchase, on the assumption that:

(i) the purchase does not qualify for the special treatment in CTA 2010 ss 1033–1063,

(ii) the purchase does qualify for the special treatment.

# Answer

## A.

Fitzwilliam Ltd – consideration of whether capital or income tax treatment would apply to the share buy back and the respective tax implications.

### Treatment of share purchase as capital gains disposal

(1) Under the provisions of CTA 2010 ss 1033–1063, the purchase of its own shares by an *unquoted* trading company will not be treated as a distribution for tax purposes but as a capital gains tax disposal by the shareholder providing certain conditions are satisfied, as follows:

- (a) Hilton must be resident and ordinarily resident in the UK.
- (b) He must have owned his shares for at least five years.
- (c) The company must either acquire the whole of Hilton's shareholding or his holding must be 'substantially reduced', which means that the holding *after* the purchase as a fraction of the reduced share capital must not exceed 3/4 of the corresponding fraction before the purchase. In Hilton's case this means that he must not be left with more than 15% of the reduced share capital.
- (d) The purchase must be made wholly or mainly to benefit the company's trade and not to enable Hilton to participate in profits without receiving a dividend or for tax avoidance reasons.
- (e) The purchase must not be part of a scheme or arrangement under which, although Hilton's shareholding is initially substantially reduced, his interest at a later stage will be such as to breach the 'substantially reduced' requirement.

(2) The company may apply for a pre-transaction clearance from HMRC to confirm that HMRC agrees that the conditions for capital treatment will be met such that the proposed purchase will not be treated as a distribution. It is also usual to apply for clearance under ITA 2007 s 701 (transactions in securities).

(3) Within 60 days of paying for the shares the company must provide details to the company's tax office.

(4) If the purchase is treated as a disposal for capital gains tax, it may be possible to reduce any gain if the conditions for entrepreneur's relief are met and by the annual exemption of £11,100 unless Hilton has already used these reliefs. Assuming entrepreneur's relief is available any balance will be taxable at 10%.

HMRC is currently consulting on simplifying the above rules.

### Treatment of share purchase as income distribution

(5) If the purchase does not satisfy the requirements in 1 above, the excess of the price paid by the company over the amount originally subscribed for the shares will be treated as a distribution. Hilton will be liable, if applicable, at the dividend rates (0%, 7.5%, 32.5% and 38.1%). For capital gains purposes, Hilton would effectively be regarded as having disposed of his shares for the amount originally subscribed for them, since the price he receives will be reduced by the net distribution amount on which he pays income tax. Assuming the base cost of the shares was equal to their subscription price, there would be no capital gain and no allowable loss. Care should be taken if there has been a reorganisation of the share capital of Fitzwilliam Ltd.

Hilton should also be wary of a new Targeted Anti-Avoidance Rule ["TAAR"] introduced in FA 2016 to combat 'phoenix' scenario's which may result in his disposal being taxed as a distribution if, within 2 years of the sale, he carries on any trade or other similar activity previously carried on by the company.

## B.

Amounts and dates of payment of tax liabilities which would be incurred by Bliss Ltd and Mr Bluebeard in respect of the share purchase

### (i) If the purchase does not satisfy the provisions of CTA 2010 ss 1033–1063

| | | |
|---|---|---|
| | | £ |
| Payment received 7 April | | 662,000 |
| Amount subscribed for shares | | (50,000) |
| Taxed as a dividend | | 612,000 |
| Taxable | | |
| 5,000 @ 0% | 0 | |
| 90,000 @ 32.5% (£150K – £55K – 5K) | 29,250 | |
| 517,000 @ 38.1% | 196,977 | |
| 612,000 | | |
| Tax payable on dividend | | 226,227 |
| Loss of personal allowance 11,000 @ 40% | | 4,400 |
| Total tax payable | | 230,627 |

As shown above, the excess of the payment by Bliss Ltd over the amount subscribed for the shares is treated as a distribution.

Mr Bluebeard is regarded as having received dividend income of £612,000 on 7 April 2016. This will form part of his taxable income for 2016/17. Also, his income is now above £122,000 so he will not be entitled to a personal allowance. Relief for the personal allowance would normally be given via his PAYE code and hence it has been included above as extra tax due. The tax will be payable with his balancing payment under self-assessment on 31 January 2018.

He will also be treated as having disposed of his shares for capital gains tax purposes, the position being:

| | |
|---|---|
| | £ |
| Disposal proceeds April 2016 (£662,000 less £612,000 charged as income) | 50,000 |
| Cost January 1990 | (50,000) |
| | Nil |

No gain or loss therefore arises.

### (ii) If the purchase does satisfy the provisions of CTA 2010 ss 1033–1063

Bliss Ltd will be treated as having bought the shares from Mr Bluebeard for £662,000. The purchase will not result in a tax liability for the company.

Assuming all the conditions for entrepreneur's relief are met and neither this relief nor the annual capital gains tax exempt amount have been used elsewhere, Mr Bluebeard will be liable to capital gains tax for 2016/17 on:

| | |
|---|---|
| | £ |
| Sale proceeds 7 April 2016 | 662,000 |
| Cost January 1990 | (50,000) |
| | 612,000 |
| Annual exemption | (11,100) |

| | |
|---|---|
| Chargeable gains for 2016/17 | 600,900 |
| Capital gains tax thereon @ 10% | £60,090 |

Due for payment 31 January 2018

## Explanatory Notes

*Purchase of own shares by unquoted company*

(1) The provisions of CTA 2010 ss 1033–1063 enable the purchase by an unquoted trading company of its own shares to be effectively treated as a disposal by the shareholder subject to capital gains tax rather than the receipt of a distribution attracting an income tax liability provided certain conditions are met. For HMRC guidance see CTM17500 onwards and CTM17570 for capital treatment.

(2) Where an unquoted trading company or the unquoted holding company of a trading group (75% subsidiaries) buys back its own shares (or redeems them or makes a payment for them in a reduction of capital) in order to benefit a trade (excluding dealing in shares, securities, land or futures), the transaction will *not* be treated as a distribution (attracting dividend income upper rate tax where appropriate). Instead, there is a disposal for capital gains tax. (Where there is an arrangement the main purpose of which is simply to get undistributed profits into a shareholder's hands without incurring the 'distribution' tax liabilities, capital gains treatment will be denied.) For HMRC's view as to whether a purchase is for the benefit of the trade see SP 2/82.

(3) In order for the transaction to be treated as a capital gains tax disposal and not a distribution the very detailed requirements of the legislation must be complied with. These are broadly as follows:

(i) The company must be an unquoted trading company or holding company of a trading group (companies on the Alternative Investment Market being treated as unquoted). The company does not qualify if its trade is dealing in shares, securities, land or futures.

(ii) The shareholder must be resident and ordinarily resident in the UK.

(iii) The shares must normally have been owned by the shareholder for at least five years but where the shares are in an estate (or have been inherited) the period is reduced to three years, and ownership by the deceased (and the estate) counts towards the three years. If during the five years the shares had been transferred to the shareholder by his spouse with whom he still lives, the spouse's ownership is treated as the shareholder's ownership.

(iv) The shareholder must either dispose of his entire interest in the company or his interest must be 'substantially reduced'. This means that the fraction he owns of the (reduced) issued share capital immediately after the purchase must not exceed 75% of the corresponding fraction he owned immediately before the purchase and also that he would not be entitled to more than 75% of the share he was previously entitled to of the company's distributable profits. HMRC have indicated that a purchase would rarely be regarded as for the benefit of a company's trade unless virtually the whole of the shareholder's interest was disposed of. Furthermore, in order to ensure the 'trade benefit' test is satisfied, any existing directorship with the company must be severed and a director cannot continue to act for the company in a consultancy capacity. The 75% rule would permit a purchase to be made in stages, or a small number of shares to be retained for sentimental reasons.

(v) The shareholder must not immediately after the purchase be connected with the company (ie be able to control it, or be in possession of more than 30% of the voting power, share capital, combined share capital and loan capital etc).

(vi) There are provisions dealing with cases where the company is a member of a group, and interests held by associates after the purchase have to be taken into account. Associates include husband or wife, civil partners, minor children, trustees of a settlement created by the shareholder and a wide range of other relationships.

(vii) The capital gains treatment is not applied if there are arrangements under which certain of the tests could cease to be satisfied.

(viii) The company must send a return to HMRC within 60 days after the purchase stating that the payment has not been treated as a distribution.

(4) The redemption, repayment or purchase of its own shares by an unquoted trading company or unquoted holding company of a trading group is also not treated as a distribution where the payment (net of any capital gains tax arising) is used to pay inheritance tax charged on a death, but only where the inheritance tax cannot otherwise be paid without undue hardship and is paid within two years of the death.

(5) A company may apply for clearance under CTA 2010 s 1044, before a transaction is undertaken.

(6) If the above provisions do *not* apply, then part of a payment for the purchase by a company of its own shares will be treated as a dividend income distribution. The amount of the distribution is the excess of the payment over the amount originally subscribed for the shares (even though the vendor may not be the original subscriber) (CTA 2010 s 1000(1) B(a)).

(7) Insofar as the company is concerned, the purchase of the shares must be covered by the proceeds of a new issue or by a transfer from distributable reserves (although any premium on the redemption must be taken from reserves). Any legal costs and other expenditure incurred by a company in purchasing its own shares will not be allowable against the company's profits.

*Capital gains and entrepreneur's relief*

(8) Where entrepreneurs' relief is validly claimed, a 10% tax rate applies. Entrepreneurs' relief is available on up to £10M of gains (TCGA 1992 s 169N(3)). The limit operates as a lifetime limit (see **Example L4**).

For gains not qualifying for entrepreneurs' relief, the gain is added to the individual's income for the relevant year and amounts within the basic rate band are taxed at 10% whilst gains in the higher rates are taxed at 20%, except for gains on residential property which are taxed at 18% and 28% respectively.

Given that a buy-back of shares which is treated as a distribution is taxed at either 32.5% or 38.1% for higher or additional rate taxpayers respectively, many shareholders will wish to ensure that their sale back to the company is structured as a capital gains transaction within CTA 2010 s 1033 so far as this is practicable.

*Stamp Duty*

Stamp duty is normally payable on a purchase of own shares at the rate of 0.5% where the consideration exceeds £1,000. Stamp duty is always rounded up to the nearest £5 (never rounded down). Where the consideration is below this limit the company can sign the certificate on the Companies House form (SH03), otherwise the form needs to be stamped before it is delivered to Companies House. See **Example M1 answer B** for more details on stamp duty. The company law requirements on a purchase of own shares are set out in Chapter 4 of the Companies Act 2006 (s 690 onwards). The act requires the company to follow procedures, deliver documents and pay fees to Companies House within certain time limits.

# Groups of companies and international aspects

# Question

## A.

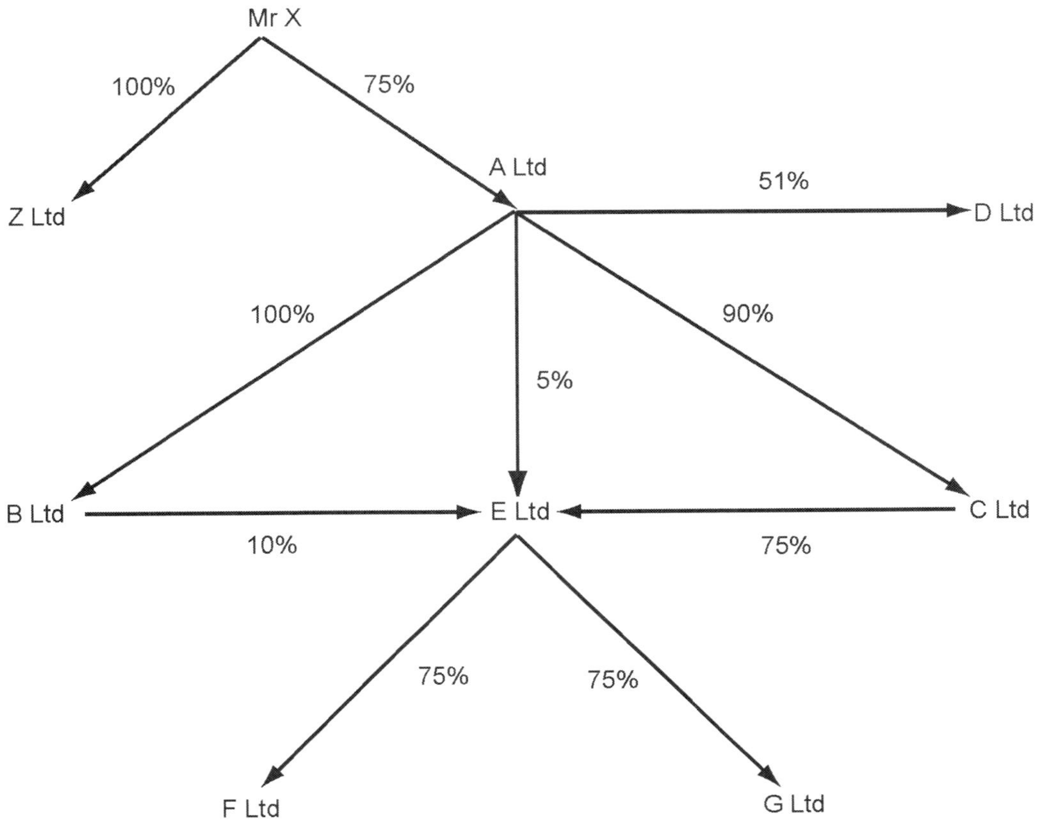


This diagram outlines ownership of various companies. They are resident in the United Kingdom and none deals in shares. The remaining 10% shares of E Ltd are owned by unconnected parties.

From the diagram above calculate the percentage ownership in each case and explain the relationship for taxation purposes amongst the companies and the taxation position in regard to:

(i) deduction of tax from payments passing between them;

(ii) assets transferred for the purposes of capital gains.

## B.

The directors of Spitch Ltd, the parent company of a trading group, intend that the company should purchase an interest in Wick Ltd, a manufacturing company, in the autumn of 2016. The proposal is that Spitch Ltd will acquire either 70% or 80% of the issued share capital of Wick Ltd.

Wick Ltd has accumulated unrelieved trading losses brought forward, and it is expected that the company will continue to incur losses for the next few years.

It is intended that, after the purchase, freehold property owned by Wick Ltd, which is surplus to that company's requirements, will be transferred to Spitch Ltd at market valuation (which is substantially above cost) and used subsequently by Spitch Ltd for the purpose of its trade.

Draft a memorandum in note form of the taxation consequences (including stamp duty taxes) of the proposals.

# Answer

## A. Relationship for tax purposes among group of companies

D Ltd is a 51% subsidiary of A Ltd.
B Ltd is a 100% subsidiary of A Ltd.
C Ltd is a 90% subsidiary of A Ltd.
E Ltd is owned as follows:

| | |
|---|---|
| Directly by A Ltd | 5.0% |
| Through B Ltd 100% × 10% | 10.0% |
| Through C Ltd 90% × 75% | 67.5% |
| | 82.5% |

Therefore E Ltd is the 82.5% subsidiary of A Ltd.

F Ltd and G Ltd are each 75% owned by E Ltd, who in turn is 82.5% owned by A Ltd, therefore F Ltd and G Ltd are 75% × 82.5% = 61.875% subsidiaries of A Ltd.

Mr X controls:

| | |
|---|---|
| 100% of Z Ltd | |
| 75% of A Ltd | |
| Through A Ltd – | |
| 75% of 51% | = 38.25% of D Ltd |
| 75% of 100% | = 75% of B Ltd |
| 75% of 90% | = 67.5% of C Ltd |
| 75% of 82.5% | = 61.875% of E Ltd |
| 75% of 61.875% | = 46.4% of F Ltd and G Ltd |

### (i) *Taxation position in relation to deduction of tax from intra group payments*

As all the companies in the group are UK-resident, tax will not be deducted from any payments of interest and patent royalties between them. (For any non-UK tax resident companies tax would have to be deducted based on the rates outlined in the Double Taxation Agreement in place between the UK and the country of residence of the other company.) Tax is still required to be deducted from some payments in other circumstances, although there are now very few payments to which this applies. For the detailed provisions see **Example I6 explanatory note 8.**

### (ii) *Taxation position in relation to assets transferred for the purposes of capital gains*

Assets transferred between connected persons (including group companies) are normally deemed to be transferred at open market value for capital gains purposes (Taxation of Chargeable Gains Act 1992 (TCGA 1992) ss 17 – 18). Assets are, however, transferred on a no loss/no gain basis in a group of companies which have a UK-resident parent company and UK-resident subsidiaries and also any UK resident sub-subsidiaries, provided that:

- each parent company owns more than 75% of the subsidiary, which in turn owns more than 75% of its subsidiary, and
- each company of those 75% subsidiaries that is an 'effective 51% subsidiary', ie a company where the parent company is entitled to more than 50% of any profits available for distribution to equity shareholders and more than 50% of the assets available to equity shareholders on a winding-up (TCGA 1992 s 170).

A company is a 75% subsidiary of another company if the other company owns, directly or indirectly, not less than 75% of its ordinary share capital (CTA 2010 s 1154).

A non-UK resident parent or subsidiary company can be included in establishing the required group relationship for chargeable gains purposes. A non-UK resident company can also be the principal company of the chargeable gains group. (Previously the chargeable gains group could only comprise UK-resident companies and required a UK-resident principal company at the 'top' of the group ownership structure.) However, despite the removal of the UK residence requirement, companies can only benefit from the reliefs if they are UK-resident or regarding assets that would be chargeable to UK corporation tax under TCGA 1992 s 10B (ie capital assets that have been used or will be used for the purposes of a UK trade carried on by a non-resident through a permanent establishment). For example, the no gain no loss transfer rule under TCGA 1992 s 171(1) (dealt with below) would only operate on a transfer between UK-resident companies or in relation to assets used for the purposes of a UK permanent establishment trade carried on by a non-resident company (TCGA 1992 s 171(1) and (1A)). Finance Act (No 2) 2005 (F(No 2)A) 2005 ss 51–65 introduced reliefs facilitating the formation of a Societas Europaeas by merger on or after 1 April 2005, with the reliefs intended to apply as if they arose for UK resident companies, or non-UK resident companies with UK permanent establishments.

The inclusion of sub-subsidiaries means that the group relationship between a parent and a sub-subsidiary can be less than 75% (ie the ownership of the sub subsidiary could be as low as 56.25% with the legislation permitting no gain/no loss transfers to still apply).

In this Example B Ltd, C Ltd and E Ltd are all 75% subsidiaries of A Ltd, with F Ltd and G Ltd, 75% subsidiaries of E Ltd. All these companies are also effective 51% subsidiaries of A Ltd. Hence, aside from D Limited, all of the companies controlled by A Ltd form a 75% group for chargeable gains purposes.

Where TCGA 1992 s 171(1) applies to a transfer of assets between group companies, the transferee takes over the base cost of the transferor, inclusive of any indexation allowance due at the date of transfer, but not so as to create or increase a loss when the transferee disposes of the asset (TCGA 1992 s 56). The rule about indexation allowance not creating or increasing a loss does not apply to indexation allowance already incorporated into base cost as a result of no gain/no loss transfers made before 30 November 1993 (TCGA 1992 s 55(7) and (8)).

For disposals on or after 6 April 1988, an irrevocable election under TCGA 1992 s 35 may be made for all assets that were owned on 31 March 1982 to be treated as acquired at their market value on that date. Where the election is made, indexation allowance is given on that 31 March 1982 value. Where the election is not made, the asset is still treated as acquired at its 31 March 1982 value in calculating the gain or loss on disposal unless using original cost (or 6 April 1965 value for assets acquired before that date) would give a lower gain or lower loss. (For most taxpayers, the time limit for making the election will have expired.) Indexation allowance in this event is always given on the higher of 31 March 1982 value and cost (or 6 April 1965 value if that value is used to calculate the gain or loss under the pre-31 March 1982 rules) (TCGA 1992 ss 35 and 55).

Where an asset acquired before 31 March 1982 is transferred on or after 6 April 1988 to another group company, then when the acquiring company disposes of the asset outside the group, the indexation allowance is still calculated using the 31 March 1982 value where this is beneficial, but the indexation allowance included in the base cost on the intra-group transfer is excluded from the allowable cost on the eventual disposal (TCGA 1992 s 55). If the intra-group transfer was made before 30 November 1993, indexation allowance up to the date of the transfer may be used to create or increase an allowable loss when the transferee company disposes of the asset, as indicated above.

Unless a 31 March 1982 rebasing election had been made, however, the value of the asset on the intra-group transfer would be its original cost plus indexation allowance to the date of the transfer. On a subsequent disposal outside the group, the transferee company is treated as holding the asset on 31 March 1982 (TCGA 1992 Sch 3 para 1) and can use the 31 March 1982 value of the asset with full indexation based thereon. The transferee company would therefore do two computations, using the deemed acquisition cost (as adjusted for indexation) and 31 March 1982 value, and take the lower gain or lower loss. In practice, this intermediate step would usually be ignored as 31 March 1982 value will normally give a lower gain or loss – the transferee company will simply calculate the gain by reference to 31 March 1982 value with full indexation from March 1982 to date.

**Example:**

| | £ |
|---|---|
| Asset cost 1980 | 100,000 |
| 31.3.82 value | 120,000 |
| Irrevocable election for 31 March 1982 value not made. | |
| Transferred intra-group May 1989 when asset valued at | 170,000 |
| Deemed to be transferred at cost of £100,000 plus indexation allowance of 44.8% calculated on 31.3.82 value of £120,000 = £53,760, giving | 153,760 |
| Sold April 2016 by transferee company for | 500,000 |

Assume indexation allowance from March 1982 to April 2016 – 261.4%.

The position on sale is as follows (based on 31.3.82 value since using cost would clearly give a higher gain):

| | £ | £ |
|---|---|---|
| Sale proceeds April 2016 | | 500,000 |
| Value at 31 March 1982 | 120,000 | |
| Indexation allowance 261.4% × £120,000 31.3.82 value | 313,680 | 433,680 |
| Gain | | £66,320 |

If the sale proceeds had been £110,000, then the indexation allowance of £53,760 accrued up to the time of the intra-group transfer in May 1989 would be allowed as part of the cost in computing the allowable loss, but the lower loss would in fact be arrived at by using the 31 March 1982 value as follows:

| | *Using cost* | *Using 31.3.82 value* |
|---|---|---|
| | £ | £ |
| Sale proceeds | 110,000 | 110,000 |
| Deemed cost | (153,760) | |
| 31.3.82 value | | (120,000) |
| Giving loss of | (43,760) | (10,000) |
| Allowable loss would therefore be | | £10,000 |

The provisions of TCGA 1992 s 171 deeming intra-group transfers to be on a no loss/no gain basis do not apply where there is a share for share exchange between group companies (TCGA 1992 s 171(3)). However, from 1 April 2002, the disposal may be eligible for the substantial shareholdings exemption (SSE) in TCGA 1992 s 192A and Sch 7AC (introduced by Finance Act 2002 (FA 2002)), even though the disposal is to a fellow group company. Where the share for share exchange rules disapply TCGA 1992 s 171, the transferor's chargeable gains position is protected by the SSE (assuming all the relevant conditions are met) since TCGA 1992 Sch 7AC para 4(1)(b) also overrides the application of the capital gains 'no disposal' treatment under the reorganisation provisions of TCGA 1992 s 127. Thus the transferor's base cost for the new 'replacement' shares is market value (and *not* the original cost of the 'transferred' company's shares).

Where the SSE is not available (for example, where the transfer occurred before 1 April 2002 or where the transfer does not satisfy all the relevant SSE conditions), the transferor company is treated as acquiring the replacement shares at the original cost of the shares for which they were exchanged (TCGA 1992 ss 127 and 135), and the transferee company is treated as acquiring the transferred shares at market value (TCGA 1992 s 17(1)). This, of course, assumes that HMRC accepts that the share exchange was motivated by bona fide commercial reasons, for which clearance may be obtained in advance under TCGA 1992 s 138, if appropriate. Nor do the no gain/no loss rules apply if shares are exchanged for a new issue of loan notes which constitute qualifying corporate bonds. The provisions of TCGA 1992 s 116 require the gain or loss at the time of such an exchange to be calculated and held over until the bonds are disposed of (see **Example L7 explanatory note 4**), but the exchange is not treated as a disposal of the shares (TCGA 1992 s 116(10)). For TCGA 1992 s 171 to apply there must be both a disposal and an acquisition (TCGA 1992 s 171(1) – see Revenue's Tax Bulletin December 1996). Once again, as noted above, the SSE can override the 'no disposal' rule in appropriate cases (TCGA 1992 Sch 7AC para 4(1)(a)).

There are anti-avoidance provisions where a company leaves a group within six years after acquiring an asset from another group company on a no loss/no gain basis (TCGA 1992 s 179), these are commonly called 'de-grouping charges'.

There are wide-ranging anti-avoidance provisions in TCGA 1992 ss 177A, 184A–184H and Sch 7A to eliminate the benefit of 'capital loss' buying or 'capital gain' buying. The provisions effectively prevent group companies deriving a tax benefit by bringing together gains and losses that have accrued while the relevant assets were in unrelated ownership.

## B. Taxation consequences of proposal for Spitch Ltd to acquire 70% or 80% of issued share capital of Wick Ltd

(1) Unless Spitch Ltd acquires at least 75% of the share capital of Wick Ltd it will not be able to take advantage of either the group relief provisions for trading losses or the group chargeable gains provisions.

(2) If Spitch Ltd acquires 75% or more of Wick Ltd's share capital and is entitled to 75% of Wick Ltd's profits and 75% of its assets on a winding-up, the trading losses of Wick Ltd arising after the acquisition will be able to be transferred to Spitch Ltd under the group relief provisions, providing Spitch Ltd has sufficient profits in the relevant corresponding accounting period to cover the losses it wishes to claim.

(3) Similarly, 75% share capital ownership and entitlement to more than 50% of profits and of assets on a winding-up will enable Spitch Ltd to acquire by transfer the freehold property from Wick Ltd on a no loss/no gain basis for capital gains purposes (TCGA 1992 s 171). This will also enable any capital losses realised by Wick Ltd or Spitch Ltd after the takeover to be offset against capital gains made by the other company provided a joint election is made under TCGA 1992 s 171B. This election was changed slightly from 21 July 2009 by Finance Act 2009 (FA 2009) and enables a 75% group member disposing of a chargeable asset to transfer a gain or loss arising to a fellow 75% group member provided that prior to the disposal, TCGA 1992 s 171(1) would have applied to a disposal of the asset from the one group company to the other immediately prior to the gain or loss accruing. For corporation tax purposes, the effect of the election to transfer the gain or loss from company A to company B is that the gain or loss is treated as accruing to company B at the time that it would have accrued to company A and company B will record the chargeable gains computation on its tax return even though the actual disposal is made by company A.

(4) A similar 'tax neutral' basis applies for intangible fixed assets transferred between group companies under the intangible fixed assets regime (Corporation Tax Act 2009 (CTA 2009) s 775). For these purposes, the 'group' definition is based on 75% ownership of subsidiaries and is very closely modelled on the one used for capital gains purposes (see CTA 2009 ss 764–773). These rules enable intangible fixed assets, such as goodwill, intellectual property etc. acquired by the *group* after 31 March 2002 to be transferred at their original cost to the group company, irrespective of the actual consideration passing between the companies (and recorded in their accounts).

(5) Assets normally pass between group members in a 75% ownership relationship without attracting stamp duty. However group asset transfers for stamp duty are subject to increasingly complicated anti-tax avoidance clawback provisions. The current rules are set out in Finance Act 2003 (FA 2003) s 62 and Sch 7 for stamp duty land tax but the arrangements were first set out in FA 1930 s 42 for stamp duty remaining applicable to share transfers.

The stamp duty 'group' requirements are satisfied where the parent company (directly or indirectly) holds at least 75% of the ordinary share capital (as well as *at least* 75% of the profits available for distribution to equity holders and assets available on a winding up). Anti-avoidance rules were introduced in Finance Act 1967 (FA 1967) s 27 which prevented stamp duty intra-group transfer relief being given in certain specified cases, such as where there were arrangements for the transferee company to leave the group at the date of the intra-group transfer. Furthermore, for transfers after 15 April 2003, a stamp duty de-grouping charge applied where land was transferred (or a lease had been granted or surrendered) and the transferee company left the group within three years after the transfer. In effect, the stamp duty relief obtained on the intra-group transfer is clawed back (FA 2002 s 111 and FA 2003 s 126). Note that the claw-back avoidance device of dropping property into a subsidiary and then selling the *parent* company of that subsidiary has also been blocked.

(6) As far as Wick Ltd's brought forward trading losses are concerned, it will not be possible for these to be carried forward for use against trading profits subsequently made by Wick Ltd, unless the change of ownership is unaffected by the 'blocking' provisions of CTA 2010 s 673.

(7) Where there is a change in ownership of a company, CTA 2010 s 674(2) prevents trading losses being carried forward to a period after the change, and s 674(1) prevents losses being carried back to a period before the change, if either:

(a) within a period of three years during which a change of ownership occurs there is also a major change in the nature or conduct of the trade; or

(b) the change in ownership occurs after the scale of activities of a company has become small or negligible and before any considerable revival.

(8) Although a major change in the nature or conduct of the trade is widely defined and includes a major change in the types of property dealt in, the services or facilities provided, or customers and outlets, it is sometimes possible to steer clear of the three year rule in 7(a) by keeping the trade ticking over at its current level for three years and not making any significant changes in customers, outlets etc during that time. But there is no three-year time limit for 7(b) and so if Wick Ltd's scale of activities has already sunk to a low level, a revival at any time would bring the provisions of CTA 2010 ss 673(2) and 673(3) into effect.

(9) For small profits rate purposes, the relevant upper and lower limits are divided by the number of associated companies. Spitch Ltd and Wick Ltd will be associated companies for this purpose, since Spitch Ltd will control Wick Ltd. The companies are treated as associated from the time when 'arrangements' are in place for the acquisition of Wick Ltd.

## Explanatory Notes

*Statutory provisions relating to groups*

(1) The main provisions relating to groups of companies and the required group relationships are as follows:

| | | |
|---|---|---|
| Group relief for losses etc | 75% groups | (CTA 2010 ss 97 to 188) |
| Group capital gains | 75% groups | (including 75% sub-subsidiaries)<br>(TCGA 1992 ss 170 to 184) |
| Group intangible fixed assets | 75% groups | (including 75% sub-subsidiaries)<br>(CTA 2009 ss 764–799) |
| Group stamp duty land tax relief | 75% groups | FA 2003 Sch 7 |
| Group stamp duty relief | 75% groups | FA 1930 s 42 |

*Change in ownership of a company*

(2) There are various anti-avoidance provisions that apply when there is a change in ownership of a company coupled with a major change in the nature or conduct of the trade or business, as follows:

*CTA 2010*

| | |
|---|---|
| ss 710 | Avoiding payment of corporation tax (see **explanatory note 6**) |
| ss 674(2) and 674(1) | Carrying trading losses forward and back (see **part B note** (7)) |
| s 682 | Carrying excess management expenses etc forward (see **explanatory note 4**) |
| *TCGA 1992* | |
| ss 177A, 184A–184H & Sch 7A | Set-off of pre-entry losses and use of pre-entry gains when a company joins a group (see **Example K1**) |

The rules for deciding whether a change of ownership has occurred are in CTA 2010 ss 719 to 725, which provides that true economic ownership is taken into account. Revenue Statement of Practice SP 10/91 indicates their interpretation of 'a major change in the nature or conduct of a trade or business'.

*Change in ownership of company with investment business*

(3) Provisions similar to those in CTA 2010 s 673 outlined in **note** (7) of **part B** to the Example apply to companies with investment business (for accounting periods beginning before 1 April 2004, investment companies only comprised those companies whose business consists wholly or mainly of making investments and whose income is mainly derived therefrom – CTA 2009 s 1218). Unrelieved management expenses, interest and charges of a company with investment business and, from 1 April 2002, unrelieved non-trading losses on intangible fixed assets, may not be carried forward where, within the six years beginning three years before the change of ownership, there is:

- a major change in the nature or conduct of the business; or
- the business revives at any time, after having become small or negligible; or
- after the change there is a significant increase in the company's capital.

Similarly, unrelieved management expenses, interest etc of an acquired company with investment business cannot be used to reduce capital gains arising on the disposal of an asset routed through that company by a member of the purchasing group. This restriction only applies to disposals within the three years following the takeover of the company with investment business (CTA 2010 ss 677–684).

*Schemes to avoid corporation tax liabilities*

(4) CTA 2010 s 710 contains provisions to counteract schemes under which a company's trading assets are transferred to another group company prior to the sale of the company and the new owners strip the company of the remaining cash assets, leaving the company unable to pay its corporation tax. (Such action may result in criminal proceedings on the basis that it may involve conspiracy to defraud HMRC.)

Corporation tax liabilities arising before the sale of the company may in prescribed circumstances be collected from the previous owners. There are also provisions in CTA 2010 s 713 which enable unpaid corporation tax liabilities arising after a sale to be collected from the previous owners if it could reasonably have been inferred at the time of the sale that the tax liabilities were unlikely to be met. HMRC have specific powers in CTA 2010 s 728 to obtain information re changes in ownership. From 17 July 2013 the Finance Act 2013 Sch 43 introduced a General Anti Abuse Rule.

*Capital gains*

(5) **Part B** of the Example indicates that Wick Ltd is still incurring losses. If it transfers its freehold property to Spitch Ltd *before* it becomes its 75% subsidiary, a chargeable gain will arise, but trading losses of the *same accounting period* will be able to be set off against the gain, and the cost of the property to Spitch Ltd will be the higher market value at the time of transfer. This would enable some of the Wick Ltd current trading losses to be utilised more quickly and put Spitch Ltd in a better position on a future sale of the property.

Had the property been standing at a loss at the time of the intra-group transfer, the loss could not be used to offset a capital gain made by Spitch Ltd after the transfer. For details see **Example K1**.

(6) See **Example L10 part (2)** and **explanatory notes 1** and **2** for further notes on the capital gains position on intra-group no gain no loss transfers, including a potential problem where the transfer was made between 31 March 1982 and 5 April 1988.

*Cross references*

(7) For detailed notes on group relief and on management expenses see **Example K2**. Other examples deal in detail with the computation of the various reliefs. See **Example K1** for group capital gains (including the election for group companies to be *deemed* to have transferred assets between them and the provisions of TCGA 1992 ss 178–180 where a company leaves a group within six years of acquiring an asset from another group company). The group aspects of rollover relief for replacement of business assets are dealt with in **Example L9 explanatory note 9**.

# Question

## A.

You have received the following letter from Mr Wilkins, Finance Director of Systems Holdings plc, one of your major clients.

Systems House
97 Commercial Road
Birmingham
21 July 2016

J S Lower Esq
Carter, Sons & Co
Chartered Accountants
19 South Street
Birmingham

Dear Mr Lower,

### Group Borrowings

The above matter was discussed at our last Board Meeting. I have been asked by the Board to prepare a report on current and future borrowing requirements of the group. The report will include a section on taxation, covering the occasions on which income tax has to be deducted at source from interest, the deductibility of interest for corporation tax purposes and the reliefs available for a loss attributable to interest payments. It would be helpful if you could provide an analysis of these tax aspects to enable me to draft the tax section of the report.

As you know, we have a number of trading and investment companies in our group all based in the United Kingdom. Our current financing comes mainly from three sources:

(1) overdrafts and short, medium and long-term loans from United Kingdom banks;

(2) short, medium and long-term loans from other United Kingdom based institutions;

(3) intra-group loans.

It is envisaged that the same sources will supply the necessary funds in future.

I should be grateful if you would let me have your comments on the taxation implications as soon as possible.

Yours sincerely,

T.M. Wilkins

Finance Director

Reply to Mr Wilkins setting out, with reference to the relevant legislation, the taxation implications of the above.

## B.

Baikal Ltd, a UK-resident company which is an unlisted company that is not a close company, has been engaged in the manufacture of agricultural equipment since the company was incorporated in 1956. It owns 60% of the share capital of Ladoga Ltd, another UK resident company, but is not connected with any other company.

## K2.2 TREATMENT OF 'LOAN RELATIONSHIPS'

In the summer of 2016, the directors of Baikal Ltd wish to borrow funds to expand the trade and are considering the methods shown below.

(1) A mixture of long-term loans and overdrafts from UK banks.

(2) An issue of debentures, of which 70% would be taken up by a UK merchant bank and 30% by the directors. The debentures would be redeemable in 2017.

(3) A loan for two years from Ladoga Ltd, which has surplus funds.

(4) A loan by a director. This would be repayable in eleven months' time.

Indicate how interest on each of the above types of borrowing would be relieved for corporation tax, also indicating the extent to which income tax is deductible at source.

# Answer

## A.

Carter, Sons & Co
Chartered Accountants
19 South Street
Birmingham
11 August 2016

T M Wilkins Esq
Finance Director
Systems Holdings plc
Systems House
97 Commercial Road
Birmingham

Dear Mr Wilkins,

### Group Borrowings

In reply to your letter of 21 July 2016, the treatment of interest for corporation tax purposes is part of wider provisions in Corporation Tax Act 2009 (CTA 2009) Part 5 ss 292–476 and Sch 2 paras 53–71 dealing with a company's 'loan relationships'. The term 'loan relationships' essentially means all 'money debts' (for the lending of money), except where it relates to trading transactions for goods and services. The provisions cover not only interest payable and receivable but also capital gains and losses on loans and other related transactions. The basic rules are as follows:

(1) *Deductibility of interest for corporation tax purposes*

The trading companies in your group deduct interest payable from their trading profits (CTA 2009 s 297(1) and (3)). In general, the deductions are arrived at on an accruals basis rather than on the basis of the payments made. As all of your borrowings are from UK based companies or institutions the accruals basis will be used for all of your borrowings.

The group's companies with investment business aggregate all non-trading interest receivable and payable (and also any profits and losses on the disposal of loans). They are taxed on the net credits as non-trading profits (CTA 2009 s 299(1)), on a similar basis to any trade related interest, which is also usually taxable on an accruals basis. If there is an overall loss (a non-trading deficit), the rules set out in (3) below apply.

For both trading and non-trading loans, the amounts allowable include any associated loan expenses, including incidental costs of raising the loan finance, or even of attempting to raise them even if unsuccessful (CTA 2009 s 329(1) and (2)).

As far as intra-group payments are concerned, they are treated in the same way as other payments, providing the amounts have been fully taken into account (under the UK loan relationships rules) on the accruals basis by both the borrower and lender.

Although small and medium sized group companies are exempt under TIOPA 2010 s 166 from transfer pricing (medium sized groups may become subject to transfer pricing legislation if HMRC notify them), CTA 2009 s 444 requires loan relationship transactions between group companies (which include between UK companies and between UK and non-UK resident companies) to be set on 'independent terms'. Therefore the basic principle of the loan relationships legislation is that *all* transactions involving connected persons must be on an arm's length basis.

An adjustment is required where a transaction departs from that which would have been achieved if each party had separately negotiated independent terms, and therefore conferred a tax advantage. Loan interest therefore needs to comply with transfer pricing legislation to be deductible.

Taxation (International and Other Provisions) Act 2010 (TIOPA 2010) Part 7 contains provisions designed to potentially restrict group interest deductions in the UK (commonly referred to as the 'Debt Cap'). The original legislation was enacted in Finance Act 2009 (FA 2009) and included in TIOPA 2010 under the Tax Law Rewrite project. These rules affect only large groups, ie groups in which any member has 250 or more employees or less than 250 employees if both the member's turnover exceeds €50 million and the gross balance sheet exceeds €43 million.

If the group is large, the 'Debt Cap' applies where the sum of the net debt of each group company with a UK tax presence (calculated on an entity-by-entity basis, excluding companies with debt of less than £3 million) exceeds 75% of the worldwide gross debt of the group. In such a case detailed calculations must be performed to calculate any restriction. As your group is a UK group, the UK debt will be the same as the worldwide debt and therefore although we expect to perform calculations and submit returns under the debt cap rules, no net disallowance should result.

(2) *Deduction of income tax at source*

Interest may be either short interest or annual interest. Short interest is interest on loans for a fixed period of less than twelve months, and it includes overdraft interest, since overdrafts are usually repayable on demand and are accounted for as short term liabilities. Annual interest is interest payable on loans capable of exceeding twelve months.

Income tax is never deducted at source from short interest, nor from annual interest paid to banks. As far as other annual interest is concerned, companies do not have to deduct tax from interest payments made after 1 April 2001, where they reasonably believe the recipient company to be a UK corporation tax payer, ie where the lender is either a UK-resident company or a UK permanent establishment of a non-resident company Income Tax Act 2007 (ITA 2007) ss 930–938. This will, of course, include interest paid to other UK-resident group members. As you are entirely a UK group there is no need to consider any withholding tax on interest paid. Additionally, companies have not had to deduct tax from interest paid after 1 October 2002 to local authorities or certain tax-exempt bodies including pension funds (ITA 2007 s 936).

Following the changes outlined above, the distinction between short and annual interest only remains important for interest paid to non-UK resident lenders, non-corporate lending institutions other than local authorities and exempt bodies, or individuals. In such cases, UK basic rate tax must still be deducted at source from annual interest but not from short interest. Where any such interest is paid, all companies should deduct 20% income tax therefrom and account for it to HMRC (ITA 2007 s 901). The tax is accounted for on Form CT 61 within 14 days after each calendar quarter end, ie by 14 April, 14 July, 14 October and 14 January, and also within 14 days after the end of the company's accounting period if it does not coincide with one of the calendar quarter ends (ITA 2007 ss 946–950). If payment to HMRC is not made on the due dates, interest is payable thereon.

(3) *Reliefs available for a loss attributable to interest payments etc*

Interest that has been deducted by trading companies in arriving at trading income as indicated above will be incorporated within any trading loss the company makes, and the normal reliefs for trading losses may be claimed. These are that the loss may be the subject of a group relief claim (see below), and any part of the loss not included in such a claim may be set against *any* profits (including chargeable gains) of the same accounting period, then against any profits of the previous year (CTA 2010 s 37). Any remaining balance may be carried forward to set against later trading income from the same trade (CTA 2010 s 45).

As far as companies with investment business are concerned, any interest losses will be incorporated within an overall non-trading deficit on loans (see (1) above). Under CTA 2009 Part 5 Ch 16 ss 456–463, relief for all or part of the deficit may be claimed against any other profits (including capital gains) of the deficit period (CTA 2009 s 459), or by way of group relief (see below), or against loan relationship profits of the previous year (CTA 2009 s 463(1)). Any part of the deficit for which relief is not claimed as indicated above will be carried forward to set against the *total* non-trading profits (including capital gains) of later accounting periods. A claim may, however, be made for all or part of any carried forward amount not to be set against the non-trading profits of the accounting period immediately following the deficit period (CTA 2009 s 458). Such a claim may be desirable in order to maximise taxable overseas income and its corresponding double tax relief.

Where losses that are attributable to interest payments arise in groups of companies (in which there is a minimum 75% parent/subsidiaries relationship), they may be surrendered to other companies in the group who have profits available in the corresponding accounting period to cover the amount surrendered (Corporation Tax Act 2010 (CTA 2010) Part 5 ss 98–110). The available amount may be split between two or more companies in the group.

If a loan between companies in your group was written off, under CTA 2009 s 354 no relief would be available to the lender. Conversely the borrower would not have to bring any credit into account (CTA 2009 s 358).

(4) *Documenting transfer pricing policies*

Under corporation tax self-assessment, it is necessary to keep and maintain adequate records to support a correct and complete return. In relation to transfer pricing with connected companies, the documentation must demonstrate that carefully considered arm's length transfer pricing policies were adopted and applied. The payment of interest between group companies should therefore be reviewed together with any other group transactions as part of a transfer pricing exercise. From 1 January 2017 the deduction of interest by UK companies paid to certain hybrid entities will be disallowed. For example if there is a deduction in the UK but no taxable inclusion in the overseas territory then the UK amount would be disallowed. Also Finance Act 2016 has brought in a cap of 30% of EBITDA for interest deductions for group borrowing from 2017. If you decide to pursue this route then we would have to look at the circumstances of the arrangements to advise you further. In addition there is currently ongoing consultation on implementing group ratios. This would be based on the external net interest to EBITDA ratio for the worldwide group. If implemented this would replace the current Worldwide Debt Cap rules.

I would like to be able to advise you further on these proposals but at the moment we are still awaiting further guidance from HMRC but I will avail you of the information as soon as it is available.

It will be seen from the foregoing that the tax treatment of interest is fairly complex, particularly in relation to non-trading interest and where losses are involved. If there are any points on which you would like further information or which you would like to discuss with me, please let me know.

Yours sincerely,

J S Lower

## B. Baikal Ltd – treatment of interest paid

(1) Interest on overdrafts and long-term loans from UK banks is paid gross and deducted as a trading expense in arriving at the trading profit, the amount allowable being arrived at on the accruals basis.

(2) Interest paid on the debentures is paid gross to the merchant bank as the bank is a UK-resident company. The interest paid to the directors is subject to deduction of tax, with the tax being accounted for on the normal quarterly basis. The gross amount of the interest is allowed on the accruals basis in arriving at the trading profit.

(3) Interest on the loan from the subsidiary company, Ladoga Ltd, is paid gross and deducted from trading profits on the accruals basis as in 1 and 2.

(4) Since the loan from the director is for less than a year, it is 'short' interest and tax is not deducted at source. The interest is allowed as a trading expense on an accruals basis.

## Explanatory Notes

*Loan relationships rules*

(1) The provisions of CTA 2009 Part 5 (ss 292–476) and Sch 2 paras 53–71 deal with profits, gains and losses (including exchange gains and losses (CTA 2009 s 328)) on a company's 'loan relationships', which essentially means all money debt (both UK and foreign), except where it relates to trading transactions for goods and services. The provisions therefore cover both simple debts and securities such as government stocks and corporate bonds. Where a company has guaranteed a debt, however, a payment under the guarantee is outside the loan relationships rules (see **Example L10**). Interest may not be deducted from profits other than under the loan relationships rules (CTA 2009 s 295). Certain interest is, however, treated as a distribution rather than as interest and such interest is outside these rules (CTA 2009 s 465). For notes on such interest see **Example J1 explanatory note 1.**

Shares are not loan relationships (CTA 2009 s 303(4)). Building society permanent interest bearing shares (PIBS) are excluded from the definition of shares, and are therefore within the loan relationships rules for all purposes. (For individuals and trusts, PIBS are an exempt asset for capital gains tax as they are treated as a qualifying corporate bond in their hands (Taxation of Chargeable Gains Act 1992 (TCGA 1992) s 117(A1), (4), (5)).)

Non-resident companies who have UK income that does not arise through a UK permanent establishment pay *income tax* on that income (see **Example K9**). The loan relationships provisions only apply for corporation tax. The income tax provisions for interest paid and received are dealt with in the income tax examples.

References in the following notes are to the CTA 2009 provisions unless otherwise stated.

(2) A company's income profits include not only interest payable and receivable but also profits and losses on the disposal of loans and fees and expenses incurred. Guarantee fees incurred in connection with loan relationships are considered by HMRC to be allowable where the loan would not be granted without the guarantee being given (as is frequently the case). The basic rules are subject to various special provisions, particularly in relation to unit trusts, investment trusts and insurance companies. There are also special rules for stock market transactions such as manufactured payments and stock 'repos' (sales and repurchases of stock).

Under s 328 foreign exchange gains and losses on loan relationships are brought within the loan relationships rules.

*Authorised accounting methods*

(3) Traditionally there were two statutory authorised accounting methods for bringing amounts of interest into the corporation tax computation – the 'accruals basis', and the 'mark to market' basis under which amounts are brought into account in each period at fair value. The 'mark to market' basis was repealed for accounting periods beginning on or after 1 January 2005 (Finance Act 1996 (FA 1996) s 85).

For accounting period beginning on or after 1 January 2005, the 'accruals basis' was the method used to account for interest in tax computations. The 'accruals basis' means that adjustments are made so that the taxed amounts are either those receivable or payable in the period, rather than those which are received or paid. Where the accruals basis is used, interest that has been capitalised in the company's accounts is still deducted as it accrues (s 320).

However accounts prepared for tax purposes must be prepared in accordance with UK GAAP, or in accordance with IFRS, which was made the full equivalent of UK GAAP by FA 2004. The trend is for UK GAAP to align with IFRS. The new terminology is amortised cost (which is broadly equivalent to accruals) and fair value (which is broadly equivalent to mark to market). For the vast majority of loans on standard terms by commercial providers of finance, the amortised cost (or accruals method) will continue to be used. There are special rules for derivatives (Part 7), and a special regime for securitisation companies (CTA 2010 Part 13 Ch4 ss 623–625).

*Bringing amounts into account*

(4) Amounts that relate to a trade are brought into account in calculating the profits of a trade (s 297). See **Example I5** for details of the relief available for trading losses. Non-trading profits and losses, including foreign exchange gains and losses, are aggregated. An overall non-trading profit is charged to corporation tax as income (s 299). If there is an overall loss (a 'non-trading deficit'), relief is available similar to that available for trading losses. The reliefs for deficits are outlined in **part A** of the Example. For detailed notes see **Example K2.**

Except for moneylending businesses such as banks, the amounts brought into the computation of trading profits comprise interest payable on loans for the purposes of the trade and expenses relating thereto. The non-trading amounts for non-moneylending businesses comprise interest payable on loans re investments, such as the purchase of shares in an associate/subsidiary or let property (other than qualifying furnished holiday lettings, for which the interest is treated as relating to the trade – see **Example D2**), interest receivable, expenses relating to non-trading loans, and any profits and losses on the disposal of loans.

In the case of indexed gilts held for non-trading purposes, taxable income is reduced each year by the index increase (or increased if the index decreases) (s 400). Other indexed securities (except those linked to a share index – see **Explanatory note 5**) are treated in the same way as other loan stock.

Some companies may be neither trading companies nor companies with investment business (for example housing associations). Such companies were previously only able to get relief for interest in restricted circumstances. They are now entitled to relief under the provisions for non-trading profits and losses.

*Financial instruments*

(5) There are a number of provisions clarifying the treatment of certain financial instruments, and extensive technical anti-avoidance provisions.

(a) Derivative contracts – CTA 2009 Part 7 ss 570–710 set out the rules for derivative contracts which are options, futures and contracts for differences, as disclosed in accounts prepared according to relevant accounting standards.

'Debits' and 'credits' (all revenue gains and losses recognised by accounting standards) are treated in one of two ways: if the company entered into the contract for trading purposes, they are income or expenses of the trade; if entered into for non-trading purposes, they are within the loan relationship rules. Where derivatives are embedded in a host loan contract, and split into separate contracts in accordance with accounting standards, s 415 provides that the host contract is taxed under loan relationship rules, while the derivative contracts are taxed under the derivative rules (s 585). Special rules for embedded derivatives are in ss 639–673.

(b) Securitisation companies regime – SI 2006/3296 'The Taxation of Securitisation Companies Regulations 2006' defines securitisation companies, and sets out the basis of taxation for those securitisation companies that elect to use it. Securitisation companies typically involve financial assets generating an income stream, matched by liabilities by which these assets were acquired. For example, a batch of commercial property mortgages generating rents receivable may be transferred to a securitisation company, which funds the purchase price by issuing marketable bonds, allowing the transferor company to raise further borrowings for further productive assets. The margin between the income receivable and the costs of funding the borrowings may be very fine.

Under IFRS, there is a danger of mismatch if the financial assets are valued at fair value, while the corresponding funding liabilities are valued at amortised cost. This might produce unpredictable tax liabilities which the company would have no means of paying out of its narrow margin. The regulations are intended to ensure that a major source of finance is not destabilised.

The effect of the regulations is to tax only the retained profits (as defined) of the company, avoiding the potential fluctuations in fair value arising from application of accounting standards, particularly IAS 39.

**Treasury stock**

Schedule 2 para 69 provides that the income to be taken into account in respect of holdings of 5.5% Treasury Stock 2008/2012 shall be confined to the interest, unless the stock is held as an integral part of the trade.

*Loss of money lent*

(6) Writing off or releasing debts covered by the loan relationships provisions are allowable for tax purposes (except for loans between connected persons – see **Explanatory note** 7). Any subsequent recoveries must be brought into account. If the borrower is a company, that company is required to bring a credit into account for the amount released, unless the release is part of a compromise or arrangement with creditors (for notes on such arrangements see **Example J4 explanatory note** 8). The loan relationships rules effectively extend to all companies the treatment that previously applied only to moneylending companies.

(7) Special rules apply where the parties to a loan relationship are connected in an accounting period. A person (including a company) is connected with a company only if they are able to secure that the company's affairs are conducted in accordance with their wishes, by reason of their shareholding, voting power, or rights under the company's Articles etc in the accounting period (s 466).

(a) Where a company lender writes off or releases a loan to a connected person, a deduction is not allowed (s 354). If the borrower is a company, that company does not have to bring a credit into account (s 358). See **Example J1** for further points relating to close company loans, including the income tax treatment of the release of loans made to close company participators.

(b) The rules in respect of late paid interest were amended by FA 2009.

The pre-FA 2009 rules (amendments are in FA 2009 Sch 20).

Relief is available for interest on an accruals basis if the loan is from any company and that company is taxable in its own country by reason of domicile, residence or place of management and the UK has a double tax treaty with that country which includes a non-discrimination article (in practice this means an accruals basis deduction is available on most overseas corporate loans to the UK).

The post-FA 2009 rules

Interest paid more than twelve months after the period in which it would otherwise be treated as accruing cannot be deducted until it is paid, unless the other party to the transaction is a company that has brought the full amount into account on the accruals basis under the loan relationships rules (s 373). This 'late interest' rule applied where one of the parties had control of the other (s 374 as defined in s 466 – see above), or where one had a major (ie 40%) interest in the other (s 377), or in most cases where the loan was made by trustees of a retirement benefits scheme (s 378). These provisions also extended to cover loans to *close* companies where the lender was a participator, associate of a participator, or a company in which that participator had a major interest (s 375).

(c) The rules which disallow deductions for certain discounted securities until payment are similar to the late paid interest rules. They are also relaxed by FA 2009.

The post-FA 2009 rules (amendments are in FA 2009 Sch 20).

Relief is available for discount on an accruals basis if the loan is from any company and that company is taxable in its own country by reason of domicile, residence or place of management and the UK has a double tax treaty with that country which includes a non-discrimination article (in practice this means an accruals basis deduction is available on most overseas corporate loans to the UK).

The pre-FA 2009 rules

Relief to the borrower for discount accruing on deeply discounted securities was only allowed if the lender was taxed on the amount accrued. Otherwise relief was given when the security was redeemed (s 407). This rule broadly operated where one of the companies controls or has a major interest in the other during the relevant period (using the s 466 definition of control for this purpose). For close company borrowers, relief was given only at redemption even if the participator who made the loan was a company except where the lender was within the loan relationships rules (s 409 – see **Example J3 explanatory note 8(e)(iii)**). Securities are discounted securities where the difference between issue price and redemption price was more than 0.5% per year or more than 15% overall (ITTOIA 2005 s 430).

*Groups of companies*

(8) Prior to F(2)A 2005 changes transfers of loan relationships between companies in a 75% group were ignored, however it is now necessary to treat the transfer as being at the notional carrying value (s 340).

*Anti-avoidance provisions*

(9) There are anti-avoidance provisions covering transactions not at arm's length (s 444, although for large companies and by HMRC direction, TIOPA 2010 Part 4 transfer pricing provisions will take priority) and loans for unallowable purposes (s 441). See also **Example K1 explanatory note 4** for the provisions dealing with losses on change of ownership of a company with investment business.

Finance Act 2013 Sch 43 introduced a General Anti Abuse Rule which covers all aspects of corporation tax. Any transactions entered into after 17 July 2013 is potentially covered by the GAAR.

*Short interest*

(10) The meaning and treatment of short interest is outlined in **part a** of the Example. Where statutory interest is payable on late paid commercial debts, HMRC regard it as short interest, so that tax is not deducted at source. As interest on a money debt it will be taken into account by companies under the loan relationships rules (see Revenue Tax Bulletin August 1999).

*Deduction of tax from interest payments*

(11) The ITA 2007 s 933 provisions re paying interest gross between UK companies from 1 April 2001 are dealt with in **Example I3 explanatory note 8**. For the detailed treatment of the way tax deducted from other interest is accounted for see **Example I3**.

*Transfer pricing*

(12) See **Example K7 note 13** for the FA 2004 changes for more details on transfer pricing.

*Alternative finance arrangements*

(13) Certain finance arrangements are structured so as to avoid giving rise to the receipt or payment of interest, principally for reasons of observance of Islamic law. These arrangements often involve contracts of agency, partnership, co-ownership or rent, which can have an effect similar to that of conventional financial products.

Provisions in CTA 2009 (originally the Finance Acts of 2005, 2006 and 2007) provide that the alternative finance arrangements covered shall be treated in the same way for tax as equivalent conventional products.

The products include savings products, asset finance, and Islamic bonds. These are brought within the loan relationship rules for all purposes, in the same way as their conventional counterparts are.

This provides certainty on the tax treatment of the products, facilitating their use, and removing disadvantages facing institutions trading in the UK financial markets.

# Question

The Fabian Group manufactures and sells pharmaceutical products and develops potential drugs, making up accounts to 31 December each year. All companies in the group pay tax at the main rate (currently 20%) and there are no brought forward trading or capital losses.

The corporate structure of the Fabian Group shown below (indicating the relevant percentage of ordinary share capital and voting rights held for each holding) has remained the same for many years.

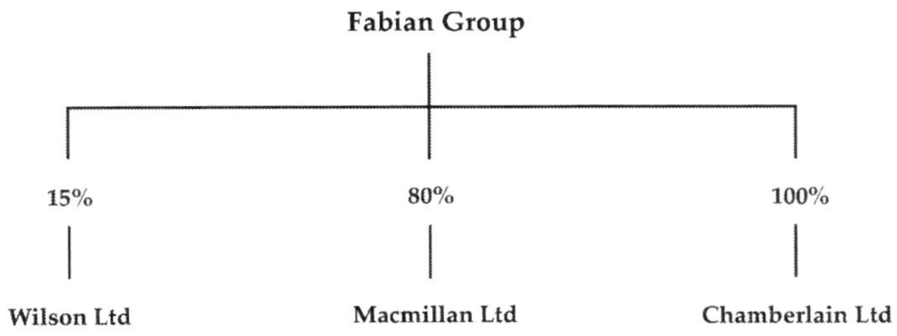


All the above companies carry on pharmaceutical trades except Chamberlain Ltd, which specialises in the development of herbal remedies. The remaining 85% of Wilson Ltd's ordinary share capital is held by Leviosa Spa, a listed Italian resident company. 20% of Macmillan Ltd is owned by Heath plc.

The group is currently considering an offer to sell the entire share capital of Chamberlain Ltd to Pitt plc. Chamberlain Ltd was incorporated as a subsidiary of Fabian (Holdings) Ltd in 1975 with 100,000 £1 ordinary shares (issued at par). It is estimated that Chamberlain Ltd's shares were worth about £500,000 at 31 March 1982. At that date, the value of Chamberlain Ltd's goodwill was £300,000. Chamberlain Ltd has never acquired capital assets from other members of the group.

The sale of Chamberlain Ltd is likely to take place on 31 December 2016 with legal Heads of Agreement for a share sale to be finalised some weeks earlier. The expected sale consideration is £4 million. The current balance sheet value of Chamberlain Ltd's net assets is around £1.5 million, which effectively places around £2.5 million on the value of Chamberlain Ltd's goodwill, patents and other intellectual property.

However, Pitt plc have just indicated that they would now prefer to buy Chamberlain Ltd's trade and assets (including goodwill) and would be willing to pay an additional £200,000 (ie total consideration of £4,200,000) to secure this deal structure. Mr Gladstone, the finance director of Fabian (Holdings) Ltd, still believes, however, that the disposal should proceed as a sale of the entire share capital of Chamberlain Ltd.

As tax adviser to the Fabian Group, you have been asked by Mr Gladstone to prepare a brief memorandum for him, indicating the most advantageous method of sale for the group. He has also requested that the memorandum explain why the purchaser is likely to prefer to buy the trade and assets from Chamberlain Ltd. (Assume that the rise in the retail prices index from March 1982 to December 2016 is 250%.)

# Answer

**To:** Mr Gladstone – Finance Director, Fabian (Holdings) Ltd

**From:** Disraeli

**Re:** Sale of Chamberlain Ltd

**Date:** 31 October 2016

(1) *Introduction*

You have asked me to consider the most advantageous method of structuring the sale of the business carried on by Chamberlain Ltd. The basic choice is whether the deal should be structured as a sale of the group's 100% shareholding in Chamberlain Ltd or a disposal of Chamberlain Ltd's trade and assets (including goodwill etc).

(2) *Recommendation*

In my view, for the reasons given below, the group should sell the shares in Chamberlain Ltd for £4 million and should not accept Pitt plc's current proposal for the group to sell Chamberlain Ltd's trade and assets (including goodwill) for £4.2 million.

(3) *Substantial shareholdings exemption (SSE)*

Taxation of Chargeable Gains Act 1992 (TCGA 1992) Sch 7AC provides a valuable capital gains exemption for *companies* that sell their substantial shareholdings in trading companies – this is known as the substantial shareholdings exemption (SSE). For these purposes, substantial means at least 10% of the ordinary share capital (and other economic rights such as at least a 10% entitlement in profits available for distribution) (Sch 7AC para 8).

Based on my understanding of Chamberlain Ltd's and the group's activities etc, the proposed sale of Chamberlain Ltd's shares should qualify for the SSE. This avoids a potential tax liability on a share sale of £535,500, calculated as follows:

| | £ |
|---|---|
| Sale proceeds (estimated) | 4,000,000 |
| *Less*: 31 March 1982 value | (500,000) |
| Indexation (March 1982 to date) £500,000 × 250% | (1,250,000) |
| Capital gain | 2,250,000 |
| Corporation tax thereon at 20% | 450,000 |
| Net proceeds (£4,000,000 less tax above) | 3,550,000 |

On the basis that the SSE is available, the group should expect to receive the £4 million without a tax charge. There are no other tax charges to consider as Chamberlain Ltd has not received any chargeable assets by way of intra-group transfer within the previous six years.

It is clearly important to ensure that the relevant conditions for obtaining the SSE will be satisfied (TCGA 1992 Sch 7AC). Briefly, these are:

(a) The investing company (ie Fabian (Holdings) Ltd) must be a sole trading company or a member of a trading group throughout the 'qualifying period' which *begins* at the start of the relevant twelve-month 'substantial shareholding' period (see **(b) below**) and *ends* when the substantial shareholding is sold. It must also be a sole trading company or trading group member immediately after the disposal.

(b) The relevant shareholding investment must qualify as a 'substantial shareholding' held *throughout* a twelve-month period starting not more than two years before the shares are disposed of. (It is possible to 'look through' any no gain/no loss transfer (such as an intra-group transfer) and include the *transferor's* period of ownership for the purpose of satisfying this test.)

(c) The company in which the shares are held (i.e. Chamberlain Ltd) must be a qualifying trading company or qualifying holding company of a trading group throughout the 'qualifying period' defined in **(a) above** and immediately after the disposal.

(4) *Trading group requirement*

For the purpose of the above rules, a trading company or trading group is one whose activities do *not* to any 'substantial' extent include *non-trading* activities. Based on my understanding of the group's activities, I do not see any particular difficulty here. Taken together, all the activities of the group relate to trading. Although the shareholding in Wilson Ltd might appear to be treated as an investment activity, it should qualify as a 'trading' activity under the special rules for joint venture companies (TCGA 1992 Sch 7AC para 23). Broadly, these provisions enable the corporate shareholder of a trading joint venture company to be treated as carrying on an appropriate part of the joint venture company's trading activity. This beneficial treatment is only available where the relevant shareholding is at least 10% *and* at least 75% of the shares in the joint venture company are held by five or fewer persons (irrespective of their tax residence status), which is the case in relation to the group's holding in Wilson Ltd.

(5) *Pitt plc's preference for an asset-based deal*

Given that the value placed on Chamberlain Ltd includes a substantial premium for its goodwill and related intellectual property, I suspect that Pitt Ltd is keen to benefit from the tax reliefs available for post-31 March 2002 purchases of intangible fixed assets.

Broadly, under the intangible fixed assets regime (Corporation Tax Act 2009 (CTA 2009) Part 8), Pitt plc would obtain a tax 'write-off' on the £2.7 million (£2.5 million plus additional £0.2 million) it would pay for Chamberlain Ltd's goodwill and intellectual property, subject to the constituent parts of that goodwill qualifying for a deduction. In order to claim the relief Pitt would have to identify the various elements of the goodwill. Assets which are limited to goodwill, customer information, business relationships, unregistered trademarks and licences do not qualify for a deduction. The value of this tax relief would depend on the timing of the amortisation of the goodwill/intellectual property in Pitt plc's accounts. For example, if such assets were written off over five years, the value of Pitt plc's tax relief is likely to be £113,400 each year (being £540,000 at 21%), some £567,000 in total (before discounting for the timing of the related cash flow). Furthermore, the purchase of such assets would be free of stamp duty, whereas Pitt plc would be liable to stamp duty at 0.5% on the entire amount paid for the shares in Chamberlain Ltd.

Clearly, an asset deal would be very attractive to Pitt plc and would provide them with a significant financial advantage, even allowing for their proposed 'sweetener' payment of £200,000. On the other hand, an asset deal would be expensive for Chamberlain Ltd. At the very least, Chamberlain Ltd would incur a tax charge on the sale of its goodwill/ intellectual property of £384,300 calculated as follows:

| | £ |
|---|---|
| Sale proceeds (estimated) | 2,700,000 |
| *Less*: 31 March 1982 value | (300,000) |
| Indexation (March 1982 to date) £300,000 × 250% | (750,000) |
| Capital gain | 1,650,000 |
| Corporation tax thereon at 20% | 330,000 |

In addition, it is likely that Chamberlain Ltd would incur further tax liabilities, for example due to a clawback of capital allowances and profit on the sale of its trading stock.

As the group would be able to sell the *shares* in Chamberlain Ltd on a tax-free basis, this remains the best deal structure. This would also be sensible from a commercial viewpoint since all pre-sale contingent risks and liabilities associated with Chamberlain Ltd's business and tax affairs would, in effect, be assumed by Pitt plc (subject to the negotiated warranties and indemnities). Under an asset-based deal, these risks would generally remain with the group.

## Explanatory Notes

*Substantial shareholdings exemption (SSE)*

(1) Schedule 7AC TCGA 1992 provides an important capital gains exemption enabling companies to sell their shareholdings in qualifying companies (where they hold a substantial interest) on a tax-free basis. Similarly, as the gains are not chargeable, where the relevant conditions are met, no tax recognition is given for capital losses realised in such cases. The substantial shareholdings exemption (SSE) is not restricted to shareholdings in UK-resident companies and applies equally to gains arising on the sale of non-resident subsidiaries and other eligible investments. The government's main policy objective was to increase the UK's attractiveness as a location for multinational groups, since the SSE enables them to restructure and sell their subsidiaries without triggering a tax charge.

(2) Companies wishing to rely on the substantial shareholdings exemption (SSE) must pay careful attention to the numerous qualifying conditions and various anti-avoidance provisions in TCGA 1992 Sch 7AC. The main conditions are stated in paras 7–9, 18 and 19 of the Schedule, which are summarised in **note 3** of the Example.

*Trading company and trading group requirements*

(3) It will be seen from **note 3** in the Example that both the investing company/group and the company being sold must satisfy the strict 'trading company/group' definitions laid down in the legislation. This means that, in the case of a parent company selling its sole subsidiary, it must be 'a company carrying on trading activities whose activities do not include to a substantial extent activities other than trading activities' (TCGA 1992 Sch 7AC para 20). A company is treated as carrying on trading activities if it is undertaking them on in the course of, or for the purposes of, its trade. This also includes an intended acquisition of a significant interest in the share capital of a trading company/group (from a third party). Activities carried out for the purposes of preparing to trade also count.

In practice, HMRC apply a 20% 'benchmark' for determining whether a company has a *substantial* level of non-trading activities. Where a company has 'non-trading' activities or investments, HMRC may look at a range of possible measures depending on the facts of the particular case, such as contribution to profits, assets employed, expenses and management time.

(4) A 'trading group' is defined in much the same way as a sole trading company (TCGA 1992 Sch 7AC para 21). The definition of 'group' follows TCGA 1992 s 170 (see **Example K1 part A**), except that the qualifying holding requirement is 51% (as opposed to 75%).

A trading group is one where, taking all the activities of the group together, it carries on trading activities, ignoring any insubstantial non-trading activities. The legislation requires all the activities of the group to be taken together. This ensures that any intra-group transactions are effectively ignored. For example, property leased to another 51% group member is not regarded as an investment/non-trading activity.

The special rule for joint venture companies referred to in **note 4** of the Example is covered by Sch 7AC paras 23 and 24.

*Interaction of SSE with other exemptions*

(5) The SSE takes priority over the normal capital gains reorganisation provisions, such as TCGA 1992 s 127. This means that the normal 'no disposal' treatment is not applied, and that, for example, the SSE applies (where the relevant conditions are met) on a share-for-share exchange. This is particularly helpful if the shares received on the exchange do not qualify for SSE (for example, they represent a holding of less than 10%). The new shares would be treated as being acquired for market value at the date of sale, so the benefits

of the SSE would be 'locked-in' at that point (Sch 7AC para 4). On the other hand, corporate no gain no loss transfers (such as intra-group disposals under TCGA 1992 s 171 or corporate reconstruction transfers under TCGA 1992 s 139) take priority over the SSE (Sch 7AC para 6).

*Secondary SSE*

(6) Where the vendor company satisfies the conditions for the main SSE referred to above, and owns an 'asset related to shares' (ie options over or securities convertible into such shares), any gain arising on such a related asset is tax-exempt (Sch 7AC para 2). Sch 7AC para 3 also permits relief to be claimed in circumstances where the trading company/holding company requirement is not satisfied at the time of sale but would have been met at any time in the previous two years.

*Anti-avoidance*

(7) A special anti-avoidance rule is contained in Sch 7AC para 5 to prevent the SSE being abused in certain prescribed cases. Following Finance Act 2013 Sch 43, all transactions should be considered in the light of the General Anti Abuse Rule.

*Intangible fixed assets regime*

(8) Before 1 April 2002, the capital cost of most intangible fixed assets did not attract any tax relief against trading profits, although capital allowances were available on patents and know-how. From that date, a new regime applies for companies in respect of goodwill, intellectual property and other intangible assets, including fishing and agricultural quotas. From 8 July 2015 a restriction on certain 'relevant assets' was implemented into CTA 2009. The relevant assets no longer qualifying for deduction if purchased after that date include goodwill, information regarding customers, business relationships, unregistered trademarks and licences. For the treatment of computer software see **Example C8 explanatory note 6**.

*Scope of the intangible fixed assets regime*

(9) As indicated in **explanatory note 8**, the intangible fixed assets regime in CTA 2009 Part 8 applies from the 1 April 2002 'commencement date'. However, the transitional provisions are designed to ensure that only intangible fixed assets which were acquired from an unrelated third party or internally created after 31 March 2002 qualify for relief under the regime. Special rules apply where the intangible fixed assets were owned before 1 April 2002 but additional expenditure is incurred on them after that date.

The effect of the 1 April 2002 commencement date is that intangible fixed assets held on 1 April 2002 (or acquired from a related party who held them on that date), known as 'old regime' assets, continue to give rise to capital gains on their subsequent sale. For example, if a company that started trading in 1990 sells its trading goodwill, this will generate a capital gain (with indexation relief).

The related party provisions are in CTA 2009 ss 834–851. Companies are related where one controls the other or the same person controls both. In the case of a close company, a person will be related to the company if the person is a participator or associate of a participator in that company.

(10) In broad terms, companies can generally obtain tax relief for intangible fixed assets purchased (other than from related persons) or created from 1 April 2002 onwards, referred to as 'new regime' assets. This means that expenditure on patents, trade marks, copyrights, know-how, licences, brands, names, logos, customer lists, designs, commercial formats etc now qualifies for tax relief. With effect for acquisitions on or after 8 July 2015, (unless there was an unconditional obligation to enter into the acquisition before this date), relief is no longer available for acquisitions of goodwill and customer related intangible asset acquisitions. These rules only apply for corporation tax purposes and thus to UK-resident companies and UK permanent establishments. (The existing capital gains tax rules continue to apply to individuals.)

(11) The tax relief for intangible assets will be given against trading profits for trading companies, property income for property businesses or as non-trading amounts (CTA 2009 ss 745–753). However, debits arising on disposals of goodwill and customer related intangibles taking place on or after 8 July 2015 will be treated as non-trading debits. If there is a non-trading loss, relief may be claimed within two years after the end of the accounting period to set the loss against the total profits of the same period. Any loss not relieved in that way and not surrendered by way of group relief will be carried forward to set against later non-trading profits (CTA 2009 s 753).

*Alignment with accounting treatment*

(12) The intangible assets rules follow the increasing trend of aligning the tax treatment with that adopted in the accounts. The timing of the tax relief for new regime assets therefore follows the rules in Financial Reporting Standard (FRS) 102, s. 19 (for accounting periods ending before 1 January 2015 the equivalent was FRS 10), which deals with goodwill and other intangibles, including intellectual property. FRS 102, s. 19 requires such assets to be amortised or written off against profits based on the useful working life of the asset. Under FRS 102, s. 19, goodwill and intangibles are not permitted to have an indefinite life. Where the useful economic life cannot be reliably estimated, it cannot exceed 5 years. An appropriate goodwill 'write-off' may also be made where its value has been 'impaired'. Thus overall these rules provide the advantage of tax-deductible amortisation and 'impairment review' write-downs where none existed before. It should be noted that for companies adopting International Financial Reporting Standards (IFRS), International Accounting Standard 38 (IAS 38) prohibits the amortisation of goodwill, although impairment reviews are permissible under IAS 36.

The accounting treatment adopted will therefore influence the timing of the tax relief for purchased goodwill or intellectual property, being based on the amount amortised in the accounts, as illustrated in **note 5** of the Example (CTA 2009 ss 726–729). However, as an alternative, companies may elect to claim tax relief at the rate of 4% of the goodwill/ intellectual property cost per year (CTA 2009 s 730).

Where the accounting treatment does not properly reflect generally accepted accounting practice (GAAP), it will be replaced for tax purposes by a treatment that accords with that practice. This is most likely to apply to UK permanent establishments of companies incorporated outside the UK, since they are not required to comply with UK GAAP. However, for accounting periods beginning on or after 1 January 2005, accounts drawn up in accordance with IFRS, whether those adopted by the European Commission or full IFRS, will be accepted as the equivalent of UK GAAP. (Finance Act 2004 (FA 2004) s 50.)

*Profits on sale of intangible fixed assets and 'income' rollover relief*

(13) Any profits on the sale of goodwill and other intangible property will be treated as income rather than capital gains (CTA 2009 ss 720–721). However, the tax can be deferred under an 'income' style rollover relief, provided the proceeds are reinvested into other new regime intangible fixed assets within the normal 'reinvestment window' starting one year before and ending three years after the gain arises (CTA 2009 ss 754–763).

The rollover relief for intangible fixed assets is modelled on the existing capital gains rollover relief, and is extended to cover intangible fixed assets transactions by 75% group members (CTA 2009 s 777). Profits arising on the disposal of such assets are deferred to the extent that the proceeds are reinvested in intangible fixed assets. The relief is reduced where only part of the proceeds are reinvested. The base cost of the 'replacement' intangible fixed asset is reduced by the original profit. Thus, as the relief reduces the base cost for tax deduction purposes, there will be a mismatch with the accounting treatment. Separate computations will be required to calculate the tax deduction for each period and keep track of the post-rollover relief base cost applying for tax purposes.

There is a special rule (CTA 2009 s 778) designed to give some neutrality between asset and share-based acquisitions. In such cases, profits on intangible fixed assets may be rolled over against any new regime intangible fixed assets *owned by an acquired 75% subsidiary* (CTA 2009 s 765). The broad effect of this special rule is therefore to look through the shareholding investment in the 75% subsidiary to its underlying *new regime* intangible fixed assets. The profits will be deducted from the carrying values of the relevant intangible fixed assets owned by the subsidiary at the date of its acquisition.

Under transitional rules, capital gains on old regime goodwill and fishing and agricultural quotas will qualify for the rollover relief when reinvested into new regime intangible fixed assets (CTA 2009 s 898). Under further transitional rules in TCGA 1992 s 156ZA, old regime goodwill and quotas disposed of on or after 1 April 2002 may be rolled over under the capital gains rules against certain pre-1 April 2002 acquisitions of goodwill or quota or under the intangibles rules or partly under the capital gains rules and partly under the intangibles rules.

*Treatment of groups*

(14) Intra-group transfers of new regime assets are made on a no gain/no loss ('tax-neutral') basis in broadly the same way as the capital gains rule in TCGA 1992 s 171 (CTA 2009 s 775). The same 75% group definition also applies (CTA 2009 ss 764–773).

(15) An income-based degrouping charge applies if new regime intangible fixed assets are transferred on a tax-neutral basis between group companies and the transferee company leaves the group within six years, still owning the transferred asset (CTA 2009 ss 780–794). The mechanics of the intangible fixed assets degrouping charge and the related exemptions are identical to those used for group capital gains purposes. Thus, for example, the degrouping charge can be rolled over or reallocated within the group (see **Example K1 part (d)** for detailed coverage of the capital gains rules).

*Treatment of royalties etc*

(16) The intangible fixed assets regime applies equally to payments made for the use of both old and new regime intangible fixed assets. Hence, royalties payable and receivable are taxed on the amount reflected in the accounts. Special transitional rules ignore any royalties previously recognised for tax purposes (see **Example I1 explanatory note 4**).

# Question

Fred Nietz, the managing director of Chase Ltd, has approached your firm for advice.

Chase Ltd, a UK company that has been trading for 30 years making up accounts annually to 31 March, is a subsidiary of a large UK-resident trading company. The present market conditions have hit Chase Ltd particularly hard and it is essential that substantial investment of £250,000 in new machinery be made. The directors of the parent company are unwilling to authorise this expenditure and instead propose to sell the company.

Fred and his colleagues are interested in acquiring the business of Chase Ltd and have arranged the necessary finance for the acquisition and for the new machinery.

Chase Ltd has unrelieved trading losses of £200,000 and a property worth £440,000 which was acquired from the parent company in October 2009 at its cost price of £220,000 when its market value was £370,000. The parent company had bought the property in February 1993. Assume indexation from February 1993 to October 2009 was 45.0%.

Write a memorandum to the Tax Partner, outlining the tax matters to be considered in effecting the buy-out either:

(a) through a direct purchase of the shares held by the parent company, or

(b) by forming a new company which would acquire the trade and assets of Chase Ltd,

and indicating any income tax points that should be brought to the attention of Fred Nietz and his colleagues.

# Answer

1 June 2016

**To:** Tax Partner
**From:** Alan White

## Chase Ltd – Proposed management buy-out

I have considered the proposed buy-out of Chase Ltd by Fred Nietz, managing director, and his colleagues and outline below the tax matters to be considered.

## Acquisition by direct purchase of shares held by parent company

(1) The parent company would almost certainly favour a sale of the shares in Chase Ltd, since any capital gain should be entirely exempt under the substantial shareholdings exemption (SSE) rules in Taxation of Chargeable Gains Act 1992 (TCGA 1992) Sch 7AC. (The explanatory notes set out the criteria that the each of the companies will need to meet to obtain the SSE.) Furthermore, the parent company would not have any balancing charge on the sale of the assets, and any contingent commercial and tax liabilities will effectively be assumed by the purchaser. The latter is subject to any limitations imposed by warranties and indemnities under the share sale agreement, but these are often restricted in management buy-out situations as managers are assumed to be aware of the company's previous commercial and financial obligations and possibly its tax compliance history (see **2(c) below**).

On the other hand, the parent company might consider an asset sale if this would facilitate the acquisition, provided there were no material tax costs. For example, the trading losses brought forward are available against any balancing charges. Also, the proceeds could be paid up to the parent as a 'tax exempt' dividend or, alternatively, loaned by Chase Ltd (which would of course in those circumstances still be a group member) to other group companies. The transfer pricing implications of such loans would, of course, require further consideration.

(2) A share purchase/sale has several disadvantages for the buy-out team:

(a) It may be more difficult to raise finance for the purchase of the shares than it would be for the purchase of machinery, for example through hire purchase.

(b) There would be a crystallisation of the held-over gain on the property acquired from the parent company in October 2009 (the de-grouping charge), as Chase Ltd is leaving the group with the property within six years of the acquisition. Chase Ltd would be deemed to have made a gain of (£370,000 – £220,000) = £150,000 less indexation allowance of 45%, (ie £99,000) = £51,000, in October 2009. The gain would be regarded as arising at the beginning of Chase Ltd's accounting period in which the shares were purchased (likely to be in the accounting year commencing 1 April 2015).

Such de-grouping gains can be allocated to the parent company or any of its 75% subsidiaries by making a TCGA 1992 s 179A election. This would enable the gain to be sheltered by any capital losses either arising in the same year or losses brought forward from previous years in those companies. Alternatively it can be rolled over under the business assets rollover rules – either against qualifying expenditure in the parent company's group (under TCGA 1992 s 179B) or within Chase Ltd itself (for example, to the extent that the new machinery qualified as *fixed* plant or machinery). The replacement qualifying assets must be purchased within the normal reinvestment period beginning one year before and ending three years after the gain occurs. (Note that post-31 March 2002 acquisitions of goodwill do not count as a qualifying business asset for capital gains regime rollover relief.)

If the gain (and hence the liability) remains within Chase Ltd, it would be necessary to ensure that the purchase price of the shares was reduced to take account of this tax charge. The gain cannot be reduced by brought forward trading losses, but if the trading losses were still being made, the losses of the same accounting period could be offset against it.

However, it should be noted that the 6-year de-grouping period will expire shortly given that the original group transfer was in October 2009. Therefore, if commercially possible, it may be worth considering a small delay in the transaction as this will extinguish the capital gains tax liability arising on the de-grouping charge.

(c) There may be other tax or financial liabilities of which Fred Nietz is not aware, because of decisions taken at parent company level and because of statutory non-compliance or HMRC making an enquiry under corporation tax self-assessment, which may extend to earlier years.

Whilst the buy-out team should seek to obtain suitable warranties and indemnities from the parent company as part of the agreement to purchase, these are often restricted (for the reasons outlined in 1 above). Furthermore, the transaction is inevitably far more complicated, costly in legal fees and time-consuming.

(d) There is a possibility that the brought forward losses plus any further losses not relieved against other profits may be forfeited because of the provisions of Corporation Tax Act 2010 (CTA 2010) s 673 (the change in trade and ownership provisions). This section prevents losses being carried forward following a change of ownership if either:

(i) Within a period of three years there is both a change of ownership and also a major change in the nature or conduct of the trade, or

(ii) The change in ownership occurs after the scale of activities of a company has become small or negligible and before any considerable revival.

In the particular circumstances of this buy-out, Fred Nietz and his colleagues could argue a strong case against the application of s 673, since it appears unlikely that the trade has sunk to a negligible level. Furthermore, the injection of new machinery should be held not to constitute a major change in the nature or conduct of the trade, particularly having regard to SP10/91, under which HMRC confirm that the section will not be applied to investment necessary to keep pace with new technology etc. HMRC apply this particular section very strictly to ensure losses are only available where a trade is being continued on a similar basis, and, therefore the carry forward losses may be vulnerable to forfeiture. If any enhanced payment is sought for the trading losses (as part of the share price), the payment for them should be deferred until the time when the future loss offsets are effectively agreed by HMRC. A non statutory clearance to HMRC clarifying the position of the trading losses brought forward should be considered to give the requisite comfort.

If the trade and assets were purchased instead of the shares, there would, however, be no possibility at all of the losses being carried forward because Chase Limited would cease trading on the transfer of its trade to the new company.

FA 2014 introduced a relation to the rules where a new holding company is inserted above the loss-making company, however there are strict requirements which would not be met in either scenario of the direct acquisition by the existing parent company or the insertion of a newco with different shareholdings from Chase Ltd.

## Acquisition by forming new company to acquire trade and assets of Chase Ltd

(1) This method will probably be the preferred method for the buy-out team because it is more straightforward and does not have the disadvantages of the share purchase as set out earlier.

(2) The stamp duty land tax on the chargeable assets purchased may, however, be more expensive than a share purchase. (Shares only attract stamp duty at 0.5% and would effectively be based on the *net* value of the company (ie reduced by debt).) If the consideration (which includes assumed liabilities) allocated to land and property assets, such as property (£440,000) and fixed plant, exceeds £500,000, stamp duty land tax

will be levied at 4%. Chargeable consideration between £250,000 and £500,000 attracts stamp duty land tax of 3%. Stock and moveable plant should not attract a stamp tax charge. Goodwill and intellectual property transfers (such as trade marks, patents, etc) are specifically exempt from stamp duty.

(3) The buy-out team would be able to claim capital allowances on the plant transferred, as well as on the new purchases. They should review the plant transferred to them and consider whether the lifetime of the assets is less than 8 years and whether a short lifetime election under Capital Allowances Act 2001 (CAA 2001) s 86 should be made. The current writing down allowance for qualifying plant and machinery is 18% pa. Furthermore, the annual investment allowance (AIA) may be available, which provides 100% relief for the first £200,000 of qualifying additions.

(4) The sale of assets as far as the parent company is concerned may be more difficult to achieve, bearing in mind that a 'share sale' of Chase Ltd is exempt from tax under the SSE rules noted above. However, the following points may be relevant in trying to negotiate an 'asset deal':

(a) Although there would be a balancing charge on the disposal of the assets on which capital allowances had been claimed, this could be offset by the brought forward trading losses of £200,000; if not used before sale, these losses may have to be discounted on a share sale because of the provisions of CTA 2010 s 673 mentioned above. If a profit still remained, the tax thereon would be at a maximum rate of 20% if it occurred in the year to 31 March 2017 %).

(b) There would be a capital gain on the disposal of the property but part of this will crystallise in any event on a share sale (under the degrouping rules) and would have to be taken into account in the price for the shares. There may be the possibility of rolling over the gain (on a direct disposal) against other acquisitions of the group. Alternatively, the property could be retained and leased to the new company formed by the purchasers.

(c) The parent company should be able to extract the book profit on the sale of the assets (less any corporation tax thereon) by way of a tax-exempt dividend. The overall tax arising on the sale may therefore be minimal if the balancing charge on the assets can be mitigated by the brought forward trading losses and the property gain can be rolled over.

(d) If a trade and assets sale is considered then the parties must be aware of the VAT implications. The Transfer of a Going Concern (TOGC) rules are mandatory rules and may impose a VAT liability on the sale. If the TOGC requirements are satisfied then VAT need not be charged.

Overall, the parent company is likely to seek to sell the shares in Chase Ltd because of the SSE exemption and the much greater commercial protection. In practice, it would only accept the sale of Chase Ltd's trade and assets if it can be structured on a broadly 'tax-neutral' basis.

## Other considerations

If the parent company sold Chase Ltd to an outside party, it could be involved in significant redundancy payments and potential union problems unless the staff were taken over under the Transfer of Undertakings (Protection of Employment) ['TUPE'] rules. If the staff are transferred under TUPE, which is likely in an asset sale, both seller and buyer are vulnerable to unfair dismissal and other staff claims. This favours a share sale unless indemnities are obtained from the buyer.

## Income tax points to be brought to the attention of Fred Nietz and his colleagues

(1) It appears that the new venture, whether through Chase Ltd or a new company, will be a close company. Fred Nietz and his colleagues should therefore be able to obtain interest relief on money borrowed to buy their shares or lent to the company for the company to buy the assets, providing they either each own more than 5% of the share capital, or own some share capital and work full-time in the management of the company (Income Tax Act 2007 (ITA 2007) s 383).

Funds provided as share capital will be locked into the company, whereas money provided on loan can be withdrawn when the company is able to repay it. If money is borrowed to lend to the company, interest relief is restricted if the loan is repaid by the company without a corresponding reduction in the loan to the buyout team.

(2) HMRC take the view that where employees buy out the company or business for which they previously used to work, they do so in pursuance of an opportunity offered to them as employees of that company or of a new company formed to take over the business. There is a contrary argument that where a new company is formed to purchase the target company or its assets and trade, the management buy-out team acquire the shares in the new company as founders.

Clearly, the risk exists that HMRC will look for any 'benefit' derived from the managers' employment. This would arise where the parent company has sold the company or business to the management team below an arm's length price. There are likely to be practical difficulties in demonstrating that a commercial price has been paid by the management team in the absence of comparable bids for the company from third parties. A discount may be appropriate on a management buy-out if the deal can be completed quickly and with fewer warranties (see above).

Many buy-out teams typically form a new company to acquire the shares or trade and assets, as this is more efficient for financing and facilitates bank and institutional lending and investment. If management acquire their shares in the new company on preferential terms (for example, compared with shares issued to institutions etc), it may be argued that an employment income charge arises.

This is a notoriously difficult area in practice. Under self-assessment, appropriate disclosure is required (to avoid any accusation of being careless). A fully justified case should be disclosed on the return where no taxable amount is being reported.

(3) If a new company is formed, and at some future date the shares are disposed of at a loss, the capital loss may be available to be set off against income of the year of disposal or the previous year (or both years, if the loss is large enough) (ITA 2007 s 131). This relief is only available where shares have been subscribed for and so would not be available if the management team directly purchased the existing shares in Chase Ltd from the parent company.

(4) Whether the existing shares are purchased or new shares subscribed for, any new capital could be raised from non-working shareholders through the enterprise investment scheme. On an assets purchase, all the share capital put up by non-working shareholders would qualify whereas only new capital would qualify on a share purchase (but see **explanatory note 4**).

If the management team formed a new company to acquire the *shares* in Chase Ltd, then the non-working shareholders could subscribe for shares in the new company and obtain enterprise investment relief, provided that all qualifying conditions were met and the trade and assets of Chase Ltd were hived-up to the new company on acquisition (under CTA 2010 Part 22 Chapter 1 ss 938–953 and TCGA 1992 s 171).

For EIS shares in a close company, it is not possible to get tax relief on interest paid on a loan to buy the shares. Another possible source of funding is a venture capital trust (see **explanatory note 4**).

## Explanatory Notes

*Different forms of management buy-out*

(1) The example describes the features of two of the main forms of management buy-outs.

Although a direct purchase of Chase Ltd's shares is contemplated here by the management team, it is more common for the acquisition to be made by a new company formed by the management team. This makes for easier and more efficient financing. Bank borrowing etc is through the new company, which can be repaid out of the post-acquisition cash flows of the acquired trade. If the managers borrowed personally to finance the acquisition, they would have to pay tax on monies taken out to finance the repayment of the bank borrowing.

A third possibility where the buy-out team already owns shares in the company is to utilise the provisions enabling a company to purchase its own shares without the payment being treated as a distribution. The provisions are covered in **Example J5**. Yet another variation is for assets to be hived down into a new company, using the reorganisation provisions of CTA 2010 Part 22 Ch 1 ss 938–953, and for the shares in the new company to be sold to the buy-out team.

*Substantial shareholdings exemption*

(2) From 1 April 2002, groups can sell their trading subsidiaries (or indeed any shareholding investment in a trading company in which they hold at least 10% of the equity) free of tax under the substantial shareholdings exemption (SSE) rules. This means that they will invariably be seeking to structure their 'business' disposals as a sale of shares.

*Entrepreneurs' relief*

(3) The management team are likely to want to ensure that they meet the relevant conditions to allow them the potential to benefit from entrepreneurs' relief, to the extent that they have not already utilised it, on an exit (eg a trade sale of the business or the company buying back their shareholding on retirement). Entrepreneurs' relief was introduced from 6 April 2008 to provide a tax rate of 10% (an effective rate of 10% prior to 23 June 2010) on certain 'qualifying business disposals'. Entrepreneur's relief only applies to the first £10 million of qualifying lifetime gains. The company's activities should be regularly reviewed to ensure that no investment activities are started which could jeopardise the shareholders' entrepreneurs' relief (see **Example M1** for the detailed provisions).

*Sources of finance*

(4) Financing a buy-out can be a major problem. It may be helped by the provisions of the enterprise investment scheme linked with the provisions enabling a company to buy its own shares. This means that the company may buy back an investor's shares after the five-year period has elapsed, but it is not possible for guaranteed exit arrangements to be provided at the outset (ITA 2007 s 177).

A newly formed company may qualify under the enterprise investment scheme (EIS) rules where it is formed to buy the trade and assets *or* the shares in Chase Ltd. (HMRC normally accepts that the share subscription proceeds were applied for trading purposes if the trade and assets of Chase Ltd were transferred to the new company on acquisition – see below.) The management team could not, however, obtain any EIS relief as they would be 'connected' with Chase Ltd and the new company under ITA 2007 s 166.

Bank borrowing and any institutional finance may be conveniently structured through a new company, which then makes the acquisition.

A direct purchase of the existing shares in Chase Ltd would not qualify for EIS relief but the subsequent issue of new shares (for new assets and new working capital) should attract relief.

Another possible source of funding is from a venture capital trust. HMRC commented in their Tax Bulletin of August 1995 on the circumstances in which such a trust may provide funding for a management buyout. Even where the buyout company acquires shares in the existing company rather than its assets, HMRC will accept that shares issued by the buyout company to the venture capital trust will be a qualifying holding if the trade of the acquired company is hived up to the buyout company as soon as possible after the buyout.

For details of the enterprise investment scheme and venture capital trusts see **Example N7**.

*Other points*

(5) See the Revenue's Statement of Practice 10/91 for their interpretation of a 'major change in the nature or conduct of a trade'.

# Question

Plato Ltd owns 100% of Socrates Ltd and 100% of Aristotle Ltd. All companies are UK-resident, and each company carries on a different trade associated with the chemical industry.

The shareholding in Plato Ltd is held equally by three families, each of which has a different view as to how the group could be more effectively controlled and managed. Owing to the differing views of the families, it is clear that the companies in the group could be better managed by each of the families taking control of one particular trade currently carried on by the companies in the group.

This objective may be achieved through a reorganisation at the end of December 2016 by either:

(i) Plato Ltd distributing the shares in the subsidiary companies directly to the family shareholders interested in gaining control of that particular company's trade, or

(ii) Plato Ltd transferring the shares in the subsidiary companies to new companies especially formed for that purpose. These new companies would then issue shares to the respective shareholders of Plato Ltd.

Under either alternative, the shares held in Plato Ltd by the families who are to acquire Socrates Ltd and Aristotle Ltd will be cancelled, leaving the members of the third family as the only shareholders in Plato Ltd.

State what reliefs (if any) are available to the shareholders of Plato Ltd if the proposals at **(i)** or **(ii) above** were implemented and what conditions must be satisfied for those reliefs to apply.

Comment on any other tax implications.

# Answer

## (a) Reliefs available to shareholders of Plato Ltd and conditions to be satisfied for those reliefs to apply

There are various tax problems associated with a company break-up such as that planned for Plato Ltd, and some of the problems are dealt with under the demerger provisions of Corporation Tax Act 2010 (CTA 2010) Part 23 Chapter 5 ss 1073–1099, as follows:

(1) Distributions that are exempt distributions as defined are not treated as income in the hands of the shareholders. An exempt distribution is defined as (CTA 2010 s 1076):

   (a) a distribution consisting of the transfer by a company to all or any of its members of shares in one or more companies that are its 75% subsidiaries; and

   (b) the conditions set out in CTA 2010 ss 1081 and 1082 are met in respect of the distribution; and

   (c) if the company making the transfer is a 75% subsidiary of another company, there are further conditions set out in CTA 2010 s 1085 to be met in respect of the distribution.

(2) Both the distribution of the subsidiaries' shares directly to the individual shareholders as proposed in Plato Ltd's alternative (i) and the transfer of the subsidiaries' shares to the relevant new companies as proposed in alternative (ii) would come within the definition of exempt distributions (CTA 2010 s 1073). The distributing company will often be a holding company distributing one or more trades or shares in 75% subsidiaries. In some cases, a singleton trading company may distribute one or more of its trading divisions via a demerger distribution. The shares in the new companies would be issued to the requisite family shareholder groups in Plato Ltd. Since the distributions would be exempt distributions, there would be no income tax implications for the shareholders.

(3) An exempt distribution under part (a) of the definition is also not treated as a capital distribution for capital gains purposes, but as a company reorganisation under the provisions of Taxation of Chargeable Gains Act 1992 (TCGA 1992) ss 126–131 (for companies TCGA 1992 s 192). This covers the distribution of the subsidiaries' shares in alternative (i), so that no capital gains tax consequences should arise for the shareholders as a result of the demerger. Under the second alternative, the issue of shares in the new companies in exchange for the Plato Ltd shares should not be treated as a CGT disposal under the shareholder reconstruction provisions in TCGA 1992 s 136 (reconstruction involving issue of securities) – the shareholders would effectively retain their existing base cost and would have a potential chargeable gain on the future disposal of the new shares.

(4) As far as corporate gains are concerned, Plato Ltd will make a capital gains disposal when it distributes its 100% holdings in Socrates Ltd and Aristotle Ltd. From 1 April 2002, it is important to note that the substantial shareholdings exemption (SSE) could apply to the disposal of a qualifying shareholding (see **Example K3 explanatory notes 1** to 7). However, where the disposal falls to be dealt with under the TCGA 1992 s 139 corporate capital gains reconstruction relief provisions (which provide for 'no gain/no loss' treatment), these will prevail over the SSE (TCGA 1992 Sch 7AC para 6(1)(a)). The SSE should be available to exempt any gain arising on the direct 'demerger' disposal of the shares to the individual shareholders under alternative (i) as this would not rank for s 139 relief. This is because one of the pre-conditions for s 139 relief is that the disposal is to another *UK-resident company* (or of an asset which is to be used in a UK permanent establishment trade carried on by a non-resident). Alternative (ii) should meet this requirement as the transfer of the shares in the 100% subsidiaries (treated as the transfer of a business for TCGA 1992 s 139 purposes) is to the relevant two new *companies*. Thus, under this route, the shares in the subsidiaries should be transferred on a no gain/no loss basis (ie at their indexed base cost) under s 139 and not under the SSE provisions.

(5) The provisions in TCGA 1992 s 179 for the crystallisation of capital gains on a company leaving a group do not apply when a company ceases to be a member of a group as a result of an exempt demerger

distribution. There will therefore be no charge on Aristotle Ltd and Socrates Ltd when they leave the group under either alternative (i) or (ii), in respect of any assets that have been transferred to them on a no gain no loss basis by any group company within the previous six years. Similarly, a 'de-grouping charge' under the intangible fixed assets provisions (see **Example K3 explanatory note 15**) will not apply to an exempt distribution (Corporation Tax Act 2009 (CTA 2009) s 787).

In order for the above treatment to apply the following conditions (CTA 2010 ss 1081 and 1082) must be satisfied:

(i) All the companies concerned must be UK-resident at the time of the distribution.

(ii) The distributing company must be a trading company or member of a trading group and each subsidiary must be either a trading company or the holding company of a trading group.

(iii) The shares transferred by the distributing company and, where relevant, issued by the transferee company, must be non-redeemable and must constitute all or substantially all (considered by HMRC to mean around 90% or more) of the ordinary share capital, and confer all or substantially all of the voting power in the company concerned.

(iv) The distributing company must remain a trading company or member of a trading group unless the demerger involves two or more 75% subsidiaries and the parent company is wound up without there being any net assets available for distribution (other than to cover liquidation costs and any negligible share capital remaining – Revenue concession C11).

(v) Where a trade is transferred the distributing company must not retain more than a minor interest in the trade (which HMRC interpret as around 10% or less).

(vi) The only or main activity of any transferee company must be to carry on the trade or hold the shares transferred to it.

(vii) The distribution must be wholly or mainly to benefit some or all of the trading activities previously carried on by a single company or group and subsequently by two or more companies or groups.

(viii) The distribution must not be part of a tax avoidance scheme, or a scheme to enable other persons to obtain control of one of the companies, or a scheme for the purpose of the cessation or sale of a trade. Where a payment other than a bona fide commercial payment is made to the shareholders within five years after an exempt distribution it is treated as miscellaneous income in their hands, the paying company may not deduct it for corporation tax and the 'demerger' capital gains reliefs (such as protection from the TCGA 1992 s 179 de-grouping charge but not the general TCGA 1992 ss 136 and 139 reconstruction reliefs) are withdrawn.

It appears, from the information available, that either of the alternatives proposed by Plato Ltd would satisfy the required conditions, but there is provision for advance clearance of a demerger transaction and it is obviously sensible for the clearance to be obtained. Furthermore, the shareholder capital gains tax relief under TCGA 1992 s 136 and the company reconstruction capital gains relief under TCGA 1992 s 139 are dependent on the transaction being for bona fide commercial purposes, for which advance clearance can be sought under TCGA 1992 s 138 and s 139(5) respectively. (A statutory clearance is not required for SSE disposals under TCGA 1992 Sch 7AC.)

The demerger provisions do not provide relief for all the tax consequences of a demerger. Under both routes, the anti-avoidance rules that prevent the carry forward of trading losses or shadow ACT on a change of control may be triggered if there is a major change in the nature or conduct of the trades (CTA 2010 s 673 previously Income and Corporations Taxes Act 1988 (ICTA 1988) s 768 and shadow ACT rules in SI 1999/358 reg 16). HMRC has, however, indicated in Statement of Practice 13/80 that these matters will be given sympathetic treatment. Plato Ltd's disposal of the shares in the subsidiaries to the shareholders under the first alternative should be exempt under the SSE provisions (as indicated above).

Stamp duties must always be considered when structuring a demerger. A direct demerger distribution to shareholders (first alternative) should not give rise to any stamp duty or stamp duty land tax liability. An indirect demerger distribution by a holding or 'stand-alone' company should obtain relief under Finance Act 2003 (FA 2003) Sch 7 para 8, restricting the tax to 0.5% on the dutiable assets transferred. This relief is particularly beneficial if chargeable assets (such as property) are being transferred as a demerger distribution of a trade (where the shareholdings are being split). Goodwill was exempted from charge with effect from 23 April 2002. Since alternative (ii) involves the transfer of shares which only attract a 0.5% stamp duty charge, there would be no need to rely on the FA 2003 Sch 7 para 8 transfer of undertaking relief in this case.

There is the possibility of problems occurring under both alternatives by reason of Income Tax Act 2007 (ITA 2007) s 684 (cancellation of tax advantage from transactions in securities). A clearance procedure is, however, available (s 701).

## Explanatory Notes

*Aim of demerger provisions*

(1) The aim of the demerger legislation, according to the then Chancellor, was to enable businesses grouped inefficiently under a single company umbrella to be run more dynamically and effectively by being demerged and being allowed to pursue their separate ways under independent management. It is accordingly not aimed at situations where the objective is for a company to be liquidated or sold.

*Company reconstructions*

(2) The shareholder and company reconstruction reliefs in TCGA 1992 ss 136 and 139 respectively both require a 'scheme of reconstruction'.

Under the statutory rules, of TCGA 1992 Sch 5AA a scheme of reconstruction contains the following key elements:

- Only the ordinary shareholders of the relevant business must receive ordinary shares under the scheme, ie no one else must be entitled to receive new shares.
- The proportionate interests of the shareholders before and after the reconstruction must remain the same.
- The business previously carried on by the 'original' company or companies must be carried on by one or more successor companies *unless* the scheme is carried out under a compromise or arrangement under Companies Act 2006 Part 26. Companies Act 2006 s 834(5) defines a 'scheme of reconstruction' as being that given in TCGA 1992 Sch 5AA.

*Other statutory demerger routes*

(3) A further type of statutory demerger covered by the 'exempt distribution' provisions involves the transfer of a trade or trades to one or more new companies in consideration of the transferee company/companies issuing shares to all or any of the distributing company's shareholders. Such a demerger would normally be covered by the TCGA 1992 s 139 corporate reconstruction provisions, so that the relevant assets such as 'old regime' goodwill (see **Example K3 explanatory notes 9** and **13**) and property would be transferred on a no gain no loss basis (see **note (4)** in the Example). A similar 'tax neutral' treatment applies to the transfer of goodwill under the intangible fixed assets regime in CTA 2009 Part 8 (CTA 2009 s 818).

It is possible to have a variant of this basic transaction. CTA 2010 s 1082 (3) and (4) enables the demerger distribution of the trade and assets to be made by a *75% subsidiary company* to the new company (although this would not qualify for the FA 2003 Schs 7–8 stamp duty reduction). Where the subsidiary makes a demerger distribution of the trade and assets, this must be followed by a further demerger distribution by the parent company of that subsidiary company's shares (their value would invariably be minimal due to the prior demerger distribution).

It should be noted that it is not possible to transfer the trade and assets directly to the shareholders, although, as seen in alternative (i) in the Example, this is permissible for a transfer of shares in a 75% subsidiary. The general thrust of the demerger rules requires the trades and underlying assets to remain in the corporate sector.

Where a demerger proceeds as a transfer of a trade and assets, the distributing company will be treated as ceasing to carry on the relevant trade, with the normal tax consequences, such as the forfeiture of brought forward trading losses and the potential crystallisation of balancing charges on the transfer of plant. These particular adverse effects could be eliminated if the transfer of the trade fell within the scope of the CTA 2010 Part 22 Ch 1 corporate trade succession provisions, which require, amongst other things, that there is 75% common ownership at shareholder level before and after the transfer.

*Non-statutory demerger using Insolvency Act 1986 s 110*

(4) It is possible to demerge businesses or 75% subsidiaries without using the statutory demerger provisions in 2010 Part 23 Chapter 5 ss 1073–1099. This route would involve winding up the relevant company, with the liquidator then distributing the businesses or subsidiaries under the procedure laid down in s 110 of the Insolvency Act 1986. These are often known as 'non-statutory' demergers and may be used where it is not possible to satisfy a particular condition in the statutory demerger code, for example where an investment business (such as property letting, which is not a trade) is being demerged by way of a partition between different groups of shareholders. It is necessary for the transfers (which are generally for no consideration other than the assumption of liabilities) to take place in the course of a winding up to prevent the shareholders from suffering an income tax charge under the distribution provisions (CTA 2010 Part 23 Chapter 2 s 1000). The shareholders' and corporate capital gains reconstruction reliefs under TCGA 1992 ss 136 and 139 should also apply here.

*Demergers and trusts*

(5) Although, as indicated in the example, demergers usually have neither income tax nor capital gains tax consequences for shareholders, there are particular problems for trustees. For details see **Example L7 explanatory note 3**.

## K6.1 TAXATION INDEMNITIES AND WARRANTIES WHEN PURCHASING THE SHARE CAPITAL OF A COMPANY

# Question

Harrison Group Ltd is considering making an offer for the whole of the ordinary share capital of Jayes Ltd (a close company making electrical components).

The finance director of Harrison Group Ltd has asked you to write a memorandum indicating the various taxation indemnities and warranties which should be incorporated in the purchasing agreement.

Draft a reply to the finance director, explaining the thinking behind the inclusion of these aspects in the agreement, the meaning of each of the terms, their purpose and significance.

Incorporate into your reply five areas that you consider should be the subject of a tax warranty and five areas that would be dealt with by a deed of indemnity.

# Answer

## Memorandum to the finance director of the Harrison Group Ltd (Harrison) in connection with the possible offer for the whole of the ordinary share capital of Jayes Ltd (Jayes)

Since Harrison proposes to acquire the share capital of Jayes as distinct from purchasing its assets on a going concern basis and continuing the trade, any actual or contingent liabilities and potential claims against Jayes will not be affected by the sale of shares. Harrison will effectively take over the history of Jayes and all of the liabilities that arise as a part of that.

In the event of claims (of whatever nature) arising against Jayes, Harrison will be affected in that the price which it is proposing to pay for the Jayes shares may, with the benefit of hindsight, be thought excessive. The nature, seriousness and size of any claim could also affect the continuing operating conditions for Jayes.

The currently known liabilities and defined contingent liabilities will be taken into account in fixing the purchase price for the shares. However, it is the future, as yet unknown, claims in respect of which care has to be exercised in a transaction of this sort.

Such claims are not limited to taxation matters and can arise, for example, through product guarantees, breach of trade descriptions, property liabilities (such as contaminated land), employee matters (such as for asbestosis) and so on. Together with those relating to taxation, these items will be the subject of a series of indemnities and warranties in the purchase agreement. The objective of the warranties and indemnities is to ensure that Harrison, as the new owner of the shares, is protected against claims which are made against Jayes that relate to the period before the shares were acquired.

It should be remembered that the value of the indemnities and warranties is only as good as the ability of the vendors of the shares to make payment in the event of a claim in addition to the considerable professional costs which are usually involved. The vendor may therefore take out appropriate insurance to cover the potential liability (although it can be relatively costly). This arrangement would be beneficial to Harrison as it would have the comfort of knowing that in the event of a potential claim arising and successfully proved, the funds will be available. If the vendor refuses to take out insurance cover, Harrison may insist on a proportion of the sale proceeds being retained for a period (for example a year) to meet any potential liabilities. (There is a view that most problems surface after the first audit by the purchaser's auditors.)

There is usually a de minimis provision in the purchase agreement so that insignificant claims are not raised, and an overall ceiling on the liability of the vendors which is normally no greater than the price paid to them for their shares.

The indemnities and warranties in the purchase agreement will be drafted to be as wide and comprehensive as possible. There will be a blanket tax indemnity covering diminution in the value of the Jayes shares as a result of any unprovided tax liability arising from the period prior to the purchase of the shares.

Having said that, it is usual in the purchase agreement to set out specific points on which indemnities and warranties are given.

*Defining the terms:*

*The deed of indemnity* (also known as the 'tax covenant') is an undertaking to compensate for loss or expense flowing from the matters contained in the deed.

*A warranty* is something contractually guaranteed, breach of which justifies a claim for damages but from which loss will not necessarily flow such that no claim will arise under the deed of indemnity.

Drawing attention to the matters which Harrison wishes to cover by warranties does, however, minimise the risk of a claim eventually arising, since the vendor of the shares is alerted to possible areas where a loss may arise. Most vendors will take the opportunity to take any appropriate corrective action before the sale. They would invariably make appropriate disclosure to Harrison (in the 'letter of disclosure'). Harrison is then deemed to take that point into account in negotiating the purchase with no claim then arising under the warranties for any future loss flowing from that point. It will normally be difficult for the 'disclosure' to protect the vendor against any liability under the deed of indemnity.

*Typical tax areas to be dealt with by the deed of indemnity are:*

(1) That there is no liability for corporation tax (including tax payable under Corporation Tax Act 2010 (CTA 2010) Part 10 Chapter 3 s 455 (loans to participators)) for periods of account ended prior to the share sale, beyond that provided in the accounts.

(2) That there is no liability for PAYE, NIC (or tax deductions from subcontractors, if appropriate) for periods of account ended prior to the share sale, beyond that provided in the accounts. This would include any PAYE liabilities arising due under employee share schemes.

(3) That there is no liability for VAT for periods of account ended prior to the share sale, beyond that provided in the accounts.

(4) That, except as provided in the accounts for the latest period ended before the share sale, no liability arises under Income Tax Act 2007 (ITA 2007) Part 15 and in particular Chapter 3 s 874 and Chapter 6 ss 898–905 (accounting for income tax on company payments which are not distributions, such as interest payments, patent royalty payments and other similar company payments).

(5) That the company has not caused any diminution of its assets which is such that an apportionment of that diminution could be made amongst its participators for inheritance tax purposes, with the liability to pay falling on the company (Inheritance Tax Act 1984 (IHTA 1984) s 94).

The share sale will inevitably not coincide with the last available accounts. The indemnity will have to be extended to cover the period from those last accounts to the date of completion of the share sale but will not apply to tax liabilities arising on transactions in the ordinary course of the business since the accounts date (other than interest, penalties, or a surcharge). Many standard 'deeds of indemnity' explicitly specify that certain tax 'anti-avoidance' provisions and capital asset disposals are *not* made in the ordinary course of business. Alternatively, if completion accounts are being drawn up, the deed of indemnity will be aligned to cover liabilities not provided for in the completion accounts.

*Typical areas covered by the warranties will be:*

(1) That there has been proper compliance with PAYE, NIC (and subcontractors tax deduction if appropriate) regulations. (If not, a liability may arise which is not covered by the creditors in the accounts.)

(2) That the accounts, tax computations and returns submitted to HMRC have been correct and that no tax enquiries or investigations are outstanding between the company and HMRC and especially those regarding the last prepared accounts prior to the share sale. Additionally where relevant the warranties should include confirmation that all pre-Corporation Tax Self-Assessment returns and computations including have been agreed. The warranties should also state that all disclosures to HMRC which should have been made as part of the tax returns have been made, and that there are no outstanding appeals or other matters.

That the correct tax has been paid by the due date. Where the company is paying tax in instalments, that tax has been paid in the appropriate instalments and there are no circumstances which could give rise to penalties for deliberately failing to pay instalments.

That no requests have been received for tax information or inspection visits from HMRC made under Finance Act 2008 (FA 2008) Sch 36 'Information & Inspection Powers' during the previous year.

(3) That the VAT regulations have been properly complied with and that no dispute exists with HMRC as to the rate and incidence of output tax and the eligibility to claim input tax (again, a liability not provided in the accounts may arise).

(4) That the base value for capital gains purposes of any assets appearing in the accounts is not less than the figure in the balance sheet. (It will be if there has been business assets rollover relief, giving a potentially higher tax liability than the commercial profit on sale.)

(5) That there is no potential capital gains liability arising from the investment of asset proceeds in wasting assets and thus having given rise to capital gains holdover relief, the tax on which will become payable at the latest ten years from the earlier sale unless replaced by rollover relief.

# Question

Chiltern Tools (UK) Ltd is a small company resident in the UK. It holds:

(a) 80% of the ordinary shares in Paradise Measuring (West Indies) Ltd, which is resident in a Caribbean country with which there is no double tax treaty. (HMRC have agreed that control is not exercised from the UK so as to make it a UK resident company.)

(b) 100% of Chiltern Tools (Europe) Ltd which is UK resident. This company is primarily engaged in retail distribution world-wide of precision scientific measuring instruments. The parent company charges rent and management charges to the subsidiary.

The stock-in-trade of each company is manufactured in various countries. Each company finds its own markets but various transactions take place between them. In the year to 31 August 2015, Chiltern Tools (UK) Ltd bought 8,000 items from Paradise for sale in UK markets.

The amount paid by Chiltern was based on the ultimate selling price of the items in the UK, which ranged between £75 and £200, subject to an agreed deduction to reflect Chiltern's profit margin.

Chiltern's corporation tax computation and return for the year ended 31 August 2015 was submitted in July 2016 reflecting the above purchases from Paradise without any further adjustment.

In December 2016, HMRC opened an enquiry into the return for the year ended 31 August 2015 and queried the basis on which the transfer price of the items purchased from Paradise had been determined.

(a) State whether each company is within the scope of the transfer pricing rules, and outline their tax obligations.

(b) Detail the procedure for HMRC's enquiry and the specific information which Chiltern requires to satisfy HMRC's queries.

(c) State how Chiltern may obtain greater certainty on the acceptability of the transfer pricing used on its future transactions with Paradise.

(d) Explain how HMRC could extend its enquiries to earlier periods if they felt that non-commercial transfer pricing was operated by the two companies in those years.

# Answer

## (a)

Under the provisions of Taxation (International & Other Provisions) Act 2010 (TIOPA 2010) s 166 small and medium-sized companies are exempt from transfer pricing rules in respect of transactions with related businesses that are based in the UK or in any country with which the UK has a double taxation treaty containing a suitable non-discrimination article. As there is no such treaty between the UK and the Caribbean country in which Paradise Measuring (West Indies) Ltd ('Paradise') is resident, the UK transfer pricing rules apply to Chiltern Tools (UK) Ltd's ('Chiltern UK') transactions with Paradise.

In determining whether a company qualifies for the small or medium status, all connected companies (including 'linked' and 'partnership' enterprises – see **explanatory note 5**) must be aggregated. Provided that the companies are not large when aggregated, Chiltern Tools (Europe) Ltd ('Chiltern Europe') will also not be caught by transfer pricing rules in respect of transactions with its parent company. Chiltern Europe will be caught by the transfer pricing rules in respect of any transactions it may enter into with Paradise in the future.

However, the standard rule that expenses are only deductible from taxable profit, if expended wholly and exclusively (Corporation Tax Act 2009 (CTA 2009) s 54) for the purposes of the trade will apply to both UK companies.

Chiltern UK must declare its taxable profit after making any adjustments necessary to bring its transactions with Paradise onto an arm's length basis to the extent that it has enjoyed a UK tax advantage. If the group qualifies as small, each UK tax resident company will tick the box on page one of the company tax return Form CT600 disclosing that it qualifies for the SME exemption for transfer pricing. In the event that its taxable profits would be reduced by a compensating adjustment under transfer pricing legislation, it would be able to irrevocably waive the SME exemption (TIOPA 2010 s 167(2)).

## (b) HMRC enquiry procedure and specific information required to satisfy HMRC

HMRC have the right to make an enquiry into the company's tax return without giving any reason. A notice must normally be issued by HMRC, indicating their intention to enquire into the return, within the 12-month period following the filing date (for returns submitted on time). However, for a company that is a member of a small group, this is shortened to twelve months from the date when the return was delivered to HMRC (for accounting periods ended after 31 March 2008) (Finance Act 1998 (FA 1998) Sch 18 para 24). The enquiry can extend to anything contained in the return.

Transfer pricing enquiries into company tax returns are subject to the standard rules of FA 1998 Sch 18. The normal rules regarding the opening, closing and conduct of enquiries apply. This includes the deadline or 'enquiry window' for such an enquiry. In Chiltern's case, the enquiry is specifically in relation to its application of the transfer pricing provisions of Part 4 of TIOPA 2010 (given that Chiltern UK has direct control of Paradise – see TIOPA 2010 s 147(1) and s 157(2)).

For the period ending in 2015, the determination of an arm's length transfer price is based on 'OECD Transfer Pricing Guidelines for Multinational Enterprises and Tax Administrations' and Chiltern UK is required to show that the amount paid for the items purchased from Paradise is justifiable on this basis. Given that no adjustment was made in the return, the amount paid to Paradise must be an arm's length price and not giving rise to a UK tax advantage. A UK tax advantage would only occur if the amount actually paid exceeded the arm's length price, reducing Chiltern's UK taxable profits. (HMRC could also attack the transaction under CTA 2009 s 54 on the grounds that the excess amount was not laid out wholly and exclusively for the purposes of the trade – although in practice this is rare.)

A vital part of Chiltern's defence is to demonstrate that a reasonable and honest attempt has been made to apply a commercially justifiable arm's length price and, furthermore, good quality documentation has been prepared and retained to support this. Chiltern UK should have the following information to support the transfer pricing policy with regard to its purchases from Paradise:

- Full details of the nature of the transactions between the two companies, showing the terms, amounts, unit prices and payment terms. Transactions of the same or similar nature can be aggregated.
- The transfer pricing methodology used, demonstrating how an arm's length transfer price was arrived at. As Chiltern is primarily acting as distributor, the Resale Price Method could easily be applied by the parties in this case. For each line item, the ultimate UK sale price would be taken, reduced by an appropriate 'gross margin' for Chiltern UK.

If Chiltern UK adds little value to the product, the gross margin would be determined by its selling and other costs, stock and bad debt risks, and its expected profit. Chiltern UK's gross profit margins earned on similar items purchased from third party suppliers would be useful here. If Chiltern had 'third party' comparable information for similar transactions undertaken by competitors and gross profit margins for similar distributorships, this would give additional support. However, care should be taken to ensure that the third party comparable information is either truly comparable to the transaction between Chiltern UK and Paradise or that reasonable adjustments can be made to the data so as to be a useful benchmark for the pricing between the connected parties.

HMRC would expect the 'connected' companies to have used their commercial knowledge and judgement to apply an arm's length transfer pricing policy on their transactions. The documentary evidence should indicate that a considered effort was made to satisfy the arm's length requirements of Part 4 of TIOPA 2010.

Obviously, there may be a range of prices which may be reasonably justifiable. HMRC may disagree that the price charged for certain items meets the arm's length standard. However, transactions between the same connected companies may be evaluated together to determine whether a UK tax advantage arises. If an adjustment is conceded, HMRC would do this as part of its 'closure notice' procedure, inviting Chiltern to amend its return on completion of its enquiry. Provided that the company has prepared appropriate documentation that supports its filing position, then Chiltern UK should be able to show that it has neither been careless nor has it deliberately prepared an inaccurate return and thus it should not be liable to a penalty under Finance Act 2007 (FA 2007) Sch 24 para 1. (See **Examples G2** and **I2** regarding the imposition of penalties by HMRC.)

However, an additional tax charge and an interest charge on the late payment of tax would arise. It will also be necessary to consider whether a corresponding adjustment is required by Paradise, if permissible under its own domestic tax rules.

### *Base Erosion and Profit Shifting*

Following on from the high profile initiatives of the OECD and G20 there have been a number of pieces of legislation introduced to tackle perceived weaknesses in the corporate tax arena. In FA 2015, Diverted Profits Tax was introduced (see **Example K8**). In 2016 we have seen the introduction of limits on the deductibility of interest in hybrid arrangements and a cap of 30% of EBITDA deductibility on intra group borrowing. In 2017 there will be further transfer pricing requirements introduced including country by country reporting and the requirement to maintain master file and local file transfer pricing information. (See explanatory note 15).

## (c) Obtaining greater certainty on the acceptability of transfer prices set on future transactions

Chiltern UK could apply to HMRC for an advance pricing agreement (APA) under Part 5 of TIOPA 2010. The APA would cover the transfer pricing basis to be used on its future transactions with Paradise. Provided the transfer prices are set in accordance with the APA, they are treated as satisfying the arm's length standard in Part 4 of TIOPA 2010 and will be accepted by HMRC while the APA remains in force. This therefore provides Chiltern UK with certainty about its transfer pricing position before it files its return.

In practice, the company would approach HMRC Policy International to discuss how an APA would apply to the relevant transactions. Chiltern UK's formal application to HMRC would then deal with the transfer pricing basis which would be applied to the purchases from Paradise so as to satisfy the arm's length requirements of the legislation, the issues on which clarification is sought from HMRC and Chiltern UK's understanding about how they should be implemented.

HMRC can revoke an APA from a particular time or where the company fails to comply with one of the conditions laid down in the APA, such as the requirement to provide information and reports.

Companies considering applying for an APA need to bear in mind that the process is designed to offer assistance in resolving complex transfer pricing issues (see HMRC's International Tax manual at INTM469020). HMRC's policy is that entering into APAs on less complex matters is not a sensible use of its resources in the absence of significant doubt as to the manner in which the arm's length principle should be applied. It may therefore decline to accept applications that do not satisfy those criteria. Depending on the complexity of Chiltern UK's submitted fact pattern, HMRC will decide whether to participate in the APA process with the Group. The fact that Chiltern UK is a small company will not affect whether HMRC's consider an application for an advanced transfer pricing agreement.

### (d) Statutory powers of HMRC to extend their enquiries to earlier years

If the results of HMRC's enquiry in (a) revealed significant problems, they may raise discovery assessments under Taxes Management Act 1970 (TMA 1970) s 29 (FA 1998 Sch 18).

HMRC's 'discovery' powers enable them to raise estimated assessments on companies where they believe tax to be understated, and the onus is then on the taxpayer company to dispute the assessment through the appeal procedure.

In practice, many Officers raise a transfer pricing enquiry in one year and then try to 'roll back' their conclusions to the previous four (previously six) years on the basis of discovery. It is possible for HMRC to go back more than four years in cases of negligent conduct or fraud (in which case HMRC can go back six and 20 years respectively).

HMRC should not, however, extrapolate conclusions about the arm's length price drawn from its current enquiry into other years where the economic and commercial factors in previous years are very different from the year under enquiry. If HMRC still has concerns about the transfer pricing in previous years then it may seek to open enquiries into those years too. For international transactions involving parties in states with which the UK has a double tax agreement, any resolution must be defensible in front of both competent authorities as taxpayers may seek to avoid double taxation under the terms of the relevant double tax treaty.

## Explanatory Notes

(1) The UK's transfer pricing regulations are set out in Part 4 of TIOPA 2010 (previously Income and Corporation Taxes Act 1988, ICTA 1988 Sch 28AA introduced by FA 1998 s 108(2)). TIOPA 2010 has effect for corporation tax purposes for accounting periods ending on or after 1 April 2010.

The transfer pricing legislation applies where a provision is made between two connected entities by the means of a transaction, or series of transactions (including arrangements, understandings and mutual practices whether or not they are or are intended to be legally enforceable). A provision includes transactions in goods and services as well as the making available of intellectual property, financing facilities and guarantee arrangements, to mention a few. Businesses are connected if one business is in a position to directly or indirectly participate in the management, control or capital of the other, or if the same person participates in the management, control or capital of a number of businesses. The rules will also apply to businesses which are under the control of a number of 'major participants'. A major participant is defined as one who has at least 50% of the holdings of the enterprise.

The regulations equally apply to transactions between two UK entities and between a UK resident and a non-UK resident entity. Transactions between a joint venture enterprise controlled by two participants (each having at least a 40% interest) are also caught.

The basic principle of the transfer pricing legislation is that all transactions involving connected persons must use arm's length prices. An adjustment to the potentially advantaged person's taxable profits or losses (TIOPA 2010 s 155) is required where any part of the arrangements involving a transaction or series of transactions departs from the arm's length standard and confers a tax advantage (ie where the price charged gives a lower taxable profit or a higher allowable loss than would have resulted if an arm's length price had been used). An arm's length price requires business to be undertaken on terms and conditions which independent parties would have adopted.

If the actual provision (ie terms of the contract) made between the 'connected' parties creates a tax advantage (when compared with the arm's length provision), the enterprise must compute its profits for corporation tax using arm's length prices (TIOPA 2010 s 147(3)). Any difference giving rise to a tax advantage should be corrected by making an appropriate adjustment in the tax return. It is not necessary for any actual contractual arrangements to be adjusted, other than to the advantaged party's tax return. There is no provision to adjust a disadvantaged party's tax return, ie to reduce taxable profits or increase tax losses.

The UK transfer pricing rules require taxpayers to construe the arm's length principle in accordance with the 'OECD Transfer Pricing Guidelines for Multinational Enterprises and Tax Administrations' (the OECD Guidelines).

(2) The OECD Guidelines set out five transfer pricing methods but they state a preference for using the three transactional methods, namely:

(i) Comparable Uncontrolled Price (CUP) – using evidence of prices in similar transactions between independent parties dealing at arm's length;

(ii) Resale Price Method – applying a discount from the end selling price of the goods to determine the transfer pricing;

(iii) Cost-plus approach – applying an arm's length mark-up to the value added costs of the selling party to identify the transfer price (with bought-in goods and services on which no risk is taken or value added being recharged at cost as disbursements incurred on behalf of the other company).

Evidence of prices on comparable transactions between unconnected buyers and sellers is often hard to come by. The companies may have no near competitors selling similar products. Even where there are similar transactions the question is complicated by such matters as the terms of the transaction, after sales service, warranties, discounts etc. Often the information will be unavailable because it is confidential to the parties concerned. Whilst CUP is the preferred method in most cases, the difficulty of obtaining reliable information available in the public domain makes it difficult to apply the CUP method in practice.

The discounted resale price approach has the advantage of starting from the actual price at which the goods are sold, but the determination of an appropriate discount (known as a gross margin) can be difficult because different accounting approaches between entities can impact on the gross margins they report and because they may bear risks, or perform functions, to a different extent.

The cost-plus approach is similarly fraught with all sorts of difficulties relating to the manner in which the companies operate their allocation of central and other costs, and the identification of the value added nature of those costs.

(3) As mentioned above, the transfer pricing rules apply to all forms of provision, including non-trading and financial transactions. Thus, where a UK-resident company makes an interest-free loan to a non-resident subsidiary, the loan would be the provision and a commercial rate of interest would have to be charged on the loan. However, where a UK subsidiary pays excessive interest on a loan from an overseas group company, the excess interest is disallowed. (Interest may be deemed to be excessive not simply because of the rate charged but also in terms of the size of the loan, for example where the UK company is thinly capitalised.)

(4) HMRC's specialist transfer pricing team deals with large and complex cases involving multinationals. Other transfer pricing enquiries are dealt with at area level, with appropriate support.

*Documenting transfer pricing policies*

(5) Under CTSA, taxpayers must keep and maintain adequate records to support a correct and complete return. In relation to transfer pricing with connected companies etc, the documentation must demonstrate that carefully considered arm's length transfer pricing policies were adopted and applied. The precise form of the documentation would depend on the complexity of the transactions involved. The HMRC manuals suggest that whilst the exact form of a business' documentation is for it to decide, it should:

- identify the associated businesses with which the relevant transactions took place and the nature of the association;
- describe the nature of the business in the course of which the relevant transactions took place, and the property (tangible and intangible) used in that business;
- set out the contractual or other understandings between the associated businesses and the risk assumed by each party;
- describe the method used to establish an 'arm's length' result and explain why that method was chosen;
- not have to provide evidence about associations or transactions between businesses where those associations or transactions are not within the scope of UK transfer pricing rules;
- not have to provide evidence related to each relevant transaction, but may provide aggregated evidence related to a class of similar transactions;
- not have to create new evidence in relation to transactions that occur after evidence has been created in relation to transactions that are similar and for which there have been no material changes in the circumstances for determining an 'arm's length' result;
- not have to commission the production of evidence from a professional adviser if the business is able to produce appropriate evidence itself;
- choose to explain its general commercial and management strategy, or that of the group of businesses of which it is a member, as well as the current and forecast business and technological environment, competitive conditions, and regulatory framework;
- choose to make documentation in relation to relevant transactions available to HMRC before the tax return in which those transactions are reflected is due to be made.

To reduce or eliminate the administrative burden, most small and medium-sized businesses will largely be exempt from the transfer pricing rules. The adjectives 'small' and 'medium-sized' are defined using EU criteria. These definitions apply to an employee headcount ceiling and a financial ceiling to a business or, where that business is part of a group, to the group. The thresholds are set out in the Annex to the Commission Recommendation 2003/361/EC of 6 May 2003.

A small business is one with fewer than 50 employees and either an annual turnover or a balance sheet asset total not exceeding €10,000,000.

A medium-sized business is one with fewer than 250 employees and either an annual turnover not exceeding €50,000,000 or a balance sheet asset total not exceeding €43,000,000.

The thresholds are applied on a group-wide basis and the definition of a group is widely drawn to include 'linked and partnership enterprises'.

Small and medium-sized businesses benefit from the transfer pricing exemption in respect of transactions with related businesses which are based in the UK or in any country with which the UK has a double taxation treaty containing a suitable non-discrimination article. Tax treaties drafted on the OECD model contain such a clause, but each treaty must be checked individually.

Notwithstanding the exemption, HMRC have power to require transfer pricing adjustments to be made in exceptional cases involving medium-sized businesses. Such an instruction will only be issued where the amount of tax involved is 'significant'. There is no equivalent power for HMRC to issue a similar notice to a small business.

(6) The documentation should exist at the latest by the time the corporation tax return is made. It is not necessary to prepare fresh documentation for each return period, provided the original information supports a correct and complete return. If significant transactions are not documented, the taxpayer may be exposed to penalties under FA 2007 Sch 24 para 1.

(7) The normal self-assessment rules for retaining records apply (see **Example I2 explanatory note 10** for corporation tax).

*Use of Advance Pricing Agreements*

(8) As noted in **part (b)** of the Example, Advance Pricing Agreements (APAs) under Part 5 of TIOPA 2010 can be used to achieve greater certainty about the transfer pricing policies used in transactions between connected companies. APAs are particularly useful for very complex transactions where there are considerable difficulties or doubts in determining the method by which the arm's length principle should be applied. An APA is likely to be much more efficient than a retrospective examination of transfer pricing policies.

An APA is a binding written agreement between the company and HMRC for determining the transfer pricing method before the return is submitted. HMRC's detailed policy and procedures relating to applications for APAs are originally set out in SP 2/10. Provided the terms of the APA are complied with, it will be binding on HMRC and the company for the period covered by the APA. The company is expected to propose the initial term for the APA over which the relevant transfer pricing method(s) will remain appropriate – this is expected to be between three and five years. The APA will apply to accounting periods beginning after the application has been made, but may also be effective for a period which has ended before agreement has been reached.

(9) An APA may be used to determine:

(a) transfer pricing between separate companies where issues arise as to the determination of the arm's length provision under the legislation;

(b) transfer pricing between parts of the same company operating in different countries where it is necessary to determine the taxable income arising in each country, as follows:

- The attribution of income to a UK permanent establishment (where there is no double tax treaty).
- The attribution of income arising outside the UK within a UK-resident company (where there is no double tax treaty).
- Income attributable to any permanent establishment where a double tax treaty is in force.

(10) A 'bilateral APA' enables the transfer pricing basis to be agreed by the UK HMRC and the relevant overseas tax authority and is therefore preferred. This can only be obtained where there is a double tax treaty between the UK and the relevant overseas country which contains a mutual agreement procedure (see **explanatory note 12**).

UK companies providing the same service or facility (for example, licensing know-how or brand names) in several countries may wish to seek APAs with the various overseas tax administrations using a so-called multilateral APA. There is no formal mechanism for negotiating multilateral APAs and this will strictly represent a series of bilateral APAs. In some cases, whilst the arrangements may appear to be the same, there can be individual variations requiring a different transfer pricing basis to be adopted. Multilateral APAs are especially useful for allocating the profits of a global activity or operation carried out in various UK and overseas permanent establishments so as to avoid double taxation.

(11) A 'unilateral APA' only provides agreement with HMRC on the UK tax treatment of transfer pricing. It does not necessarily provide an agreed basis with the overseas tax jurisdiction and may therefore give rise to double taxation. A UK company would, however, choose a unilateral APA where it considers the 'bilateral APA' process to be unnecessarily long or complicated or there is no double tax treaty with a mutual agreement procedure.

It should be noted that HMRC only intend to enter into APAs to resolve difficult transfer pricing problems which involve significant doubt and may decline applications where the transfer pricing can be readily established (such as where reliable market comparables exist). Consequently, Chiltern Tools (UK) Ltd may not be successful in obtaining an APA on its UK distributorship of precision tools as there should be comparable 'benchmark' transactions within the industry etc.

Once the policies have been agreed by HMRC, then provided the relevant transactions are priced in accordance with the APA, they will be accepted by HMRC as satisfying the arm's length requirement.

An APA is nullified if the taxpayer fraudulently or negligently provides false or misleading information when negotiating an APA and a penalty of up to £10,000 can also be imposed (TIOPA 2010 s 227).

*Procedures for corresponding transfer pricing adjustments*

(12) Transfer pricing adjustments in one country clearly could have consequences in relation to tax charged in the other country, and consequently transfer pricing is one of the matters dealt with in double taxation agreements. The OECD model agreement and various guidelines provide for a profits adjustment where transfers between associated enterprises result in profits that are not at arm's length. Countries in the European Union have established a mechanism for resolving transfer pricing disputes between member states, following the ratification by member states of the Arbitration Convention, which came into force on 1 January 1995. TIOPA 2010 s 127 requires effect to be given in the UK to agreements and decisions under the Convention. See also the HMRC Tax Bulletin of October 1996 for their transfer pricing procedures in the light of the OECD Guidelines and the Arbitration Convention and the mutual agreement procedure enabling countries with double tax treaties to consult one another to resolve transfer pricing issues and if possible to prevent any adjustments resulting in unrelievable double taxation. On 14 September 2009, the European Commission adopted a new Code of Conduct for effective implementation of the Convention. The Code aims to improve prevention of double taxation resulting from transfer pricing adjustments.

The intention is that transfer pricing should not cause double taxation of the same profits. As far as cross-border transactions are concerned, double taxation treaties already contain procedures for addressing this. For domestic transactions, a compensating reduction in the profits of one party to a transaction is allowed where there has been a transfer pricing adjustment to increase the taxable profits of the other party. The legislation provides for 'balancing payments'. These enable a business with the benefit of a compensating reduction in profits to pass the cash effect of the benefit back to the related business which suffered the disallowance.

*Payments of interest*

(13) The transfer pricing rules perform the same function as the 'thin capitalisation' rules in force in many countries to counter excessive amounts of interest being charged between parent companies and other group members funding subsidiaries with higher levels of debt than would have been available on an arm's length basis. In determining whether the interest payment is greater than that which would have been made in the absence of a special relationship or connection, the following criteria should be considered:

(a) the extent of the borrowing company's overall indebtedness;

(b) whether the loan or the amount of the loan would have been made to the borrowing company if arm's length conditions had applied; and

(c) whether the rate of interest charged and the other terms of the loan were on a commercial basis.

Interest on loans which are made between companies under common control, whether UK-resident or not, will be subject to restrictions. Where a loan exceeds the amount that would have been provided by an unconnected lender, the interest on the 'excessive' part of the borrowing is disallowed as a tax deduction. Similarly, the lending company is only taxed as if it had received an arm's length amount of interest.

The anti-avoidance provisions of TIOPA 2010 s 162 counter tax advantages derived from financing arrangements set up by parties acting in concert up to six months before a control relationship exists. This is intended to counter coordinated avoidance action by investors who (although not connected parties according to the normal definition) share control of the company. Although any of the parties concerned may be minority owners, if interest paid to any or all of them is not considered to be at an arm's length rate, relief for excessive interest can be denied.

Since late 2007 it has been possible for companies to make a unilateral agreement (known as an Advance Thin Capitalisation Agreement (ATCA)) with HMRC to agree the arm's length borrowing capacity and interest rates to apply to lending to the company from connected parties.

Historically, thin capitalisation issues were addressed through applications under Double Tax Agreements by non-resident entities. The introduction of the ATCA process has meant that it is now possible to negotiate a thin capitalisation agreement outside the treaty route. Although based on the same statutory provisions, the negotiation of APAs and ATCAs are separate processes. ATCAs are available to companies brought into transfer pricing legislation by virtue of the 'acting together' legislation set out in TIOPA 2010 s 161 referred to above.

(14) In addition to the thin capitalisation rules, financing costs may be restricted under the rules known as the 'worldwide debt cap' rules. These generally apply to accounting periods beginning on or after 1 January 2010 and are set out in Part 7 of TIOPA 2010. The rules apply to groups which are 'large' under the definitions set out in the Annex to the EC Recommendation 2003/361/EC which are explained above at **explanatory note 5**. Where the rules apply they seek to limit the amount of interest and other financing expenses of UK companies in large groups to the total external interest and finance expense of the group as a whole. Groups do not need to have an overseas presence in order for the rules to apply.

*Base Erosion and Profit Shifting*

(15) The OECD has introduced a number of action items to address the BEPS issues. The action plans covered:

The digital economy

Hybrid mismatch arrangements

Controlled foreign companies (CFC) regimes

Financial payments

Harmful tax practices

Treaty abuse

Permanent establishment (PE) status

Transfer pricing and intangibles

Transfer pricing and risks/capital

Transfer pricing and other high risk transactions

Data and methodologies

Disclosure of aggressive tax planning

Transfer pricing documentation

Dispute resolution mechanisms

A multilateral instrument

In the UK we have seen legislation to address and indeed go further than, many of these items. THE OECD's actions plan can be found on the OECD website.

# Question

The directors of your company have decided to set up a trading operation in a country outside the European Economic Area where the rate of corporation tax is 10%. They are considering two alternative approaches:

(a) To run the overseas operation as a permanent establishment of the UK company;

or

(b) To run it as a foreign-registered subsidiary of the UK company.

Prepare detailed notes on the UK taxation implications of each of the alternative proposals as a basis for a report to the directors.

# Answer

## A. UK tax implications of operating as an overseas permanent establishment compared with operating through an overseas subsidiary

### Setting up an overseas permanent establishment or an overseas subsidiary

*Introduction*

The taxation of overseas operations is undergoing a period of considerable change with further changes expected over the next few years. In addition companies are coming under increasing public scrutiny where they appear to be shifting profits into low tax jurisdictions. This has seen increased rigour in the transfer pricing arena, greater requirements to disclose tax information in country by country reporting and the introduction of limits to debt deductibility and hybrid structures. In July 2014 the EU announced changes to the Parent/Subsidiary Directive which basically annulled the tax advantage of hybrid loan relationships within the EU. This was followed in 2015 by the introduction of the Diverted Profits Tax ('DPT') which has effect for affected companies from 1 April 2015. When considering the use of overseas permanent establishments or subsidiaries it is important to ensure that these have economic substance in the country where they are to be based. Failure to do so could be seen as artificially avoided UK tax and bring the company within the scope of DPT.

Historically UK corporation tax has been levied on worldwide operations. However the current government proposes a more territorial corporation tax system to increase the UK's competitiveness in the world markets. The optional permanent establishment exemption (see below, introduced 2011) and the distribution exemption (introduced 2009) have the effect that profits earned through foreign operations potentially cannot be taxed in the UK except by reason of the Controlled Foreign Company legislation and other anti-avoidance rules.

(1) The establishment of either an overseas permanent establishment or an overseas subsidiary company will involve foreign tax being suffered on the profits, because the company will be moving from trading *with* the country concerned to trading *in* it. Overseas countries generally impose tax where business is carried on through a permanent establishment in their country. The company should confirm whether there is a double tax treaty, and the terms of the treaty, between the UK and the country that they are planning to open a permanent establishment in.

Most double tax treaties have a similar definition to the OECD model, which states that a permanent establishment includes a place of management, a branch, an office, a factory, a workshop and a mine, oil or gas well, quarry or any other place of extraction of natural resources (subject to certain exclusions). The way in which the foreign tax may be relieved is dealt with below.

### UK corporation tax liability re overseas permanent establishment

(2) If a trade is carried on through an overseas permanent establishment of a UK-resident company, the company is potentially liable to corporation tax on all of the profits made by the permanent establishment.

For accounting periods ended on or after 1 April 2000, any trading loss etc incurred by such an overseas operation can only be group 'relieved' provided it is *not* relievable against taxable overseas profits of any other company under the law of the relevant foreign jurisdiction Corporation Tax Act 2010 (CTA 2010) s 106. This would exclude, for example, any loss which is offset in a consolidated tax return or surrendered under foreign group relief provisions. Under the group relief provisions as amended by Finance Act 2000 (FA 2000), the loss can be surrendered to:

- a UK-resident holding company; or
- any UK-resident subsidiary; or

The parties are treated as connected if they fall within the transfer pricing rules at TIOPA 2010 s 148, they are therefore caught if A or B participates, directly or indirectly in the control of the other company(FA 2015 s 106). There are conditions to be met:

(1) The condition is met if at the time of making or imposing the material provision or within a time of 6 months beginning with the date of the material provision is made or imposed either:

 (a) One of the parties was directly or indirectly participating in the management, control or capital of the other; or

 (b) The same person or persons was or were directly or indirectly participating in the management, control or capital of each of the relevant parties.

(2) The condition is met f at the time of making or imposing the material provision,

 (a) one of the relevant parties was directly or indirectly participating in the management, control or capital of the other, or

 (b) the same person or persons was or were directly or indirectly participating in the management, control or capital of each of the relevant persons.

An effective tax mismatch FA 2015 s 107) arises if:

(1) expenses of the first party for which a deduction is allowable for a relevant tax and/or a reduction in income that would otherwise have been taken into account by the first party in computing its liability for a relevant tax, and

(2) the reduction in the first party's liability to a relevant tax exceeds any resulting increase in the relevant taxes payable by the second party for the corresponding accounting period and

(3) the above results are not 'exempted', and

(4) the second party does not meet 'the 80% payment test'.

Exempted payments are those that arise from certain exempted bodies, including charities, pension schemes and those exempt from tax. The 80% payment test means that the second party's taxes must increase by at least 80% of the reduction in the tax payable by the first party.

The insufficient economic substance condition (FA 2015 s 110) is met if any of three scenarios are met:

(1) If it is reasonable to assume that the transaction was designed to secure a tax reduction. Therefore if the tax benefit outweighs any financial benefit it is likely to be assumed that this condition is met; or

(2) The second test extends the first test to a series of transactions whereby securing a tax advantage appears to outweigh the commercial advantage of the transaction; or

(3) The third test applies where there is a person that is party to a transaction and it is reasonable to assume that the person's involvement in the transaction was designed to secure the tax reduction.

Section 86 of the legislation can apply where foreign companies make substantial sales through activity in the UK while avoiding the creation of a UK permanent establishment. Such arrangements are often combined with other arrangements that allow the foreign company to transfer profits associated with those sales to companies resident in territories where little or no tax is paid.

The legislation seeks to identify these cases by identifying whether economic activity takes place in the UK in connection with the supply of goods, or other property by a foreign company, but structured in a way so as to ensure that the foreign company is not carrying on a trade in the UK for CT purposes. This includes, for example, arrangements involving significant sales activity in the UK, but designed to stop short of the conclusion of contracts.

Section 86 applies where the following conditions are met:

(1) there is a company, that carries on a trade, that is not resident in the UK (the 'foreign company');

(2) another person ('the avoided PE') is carrying on an activity in the UK in connection with the supplies of goods, services or other property by the foreign company in the course of its trade. It does not matter if that person is a UK resident;

(3) the avoided PE and the foreign company are not small or medium sized enterprises, as defined by TIOPA 2010 Section 172; and

(4) it is reasonable to assume that the activity of the avoided PE or the foreign company (or both) is designed so as to ensure that the foreign company does not, for the purposes of corporation tax, carry on a trade in the UK (whether or not it is also designed to secure any commercial or other object). In practice, this means that the activity is designed so as to ensure that the foreign company does not have a UK PE.

In addition either or both of the following conditions must be met:

(1) the mismatch condition, or

(2) the tax avoidance condition.

The tax avoidance condition is met if the transactions in place are such that the main, or one of the main purposes, is to avoid UK tax. There is no legislative definition of the terms but it is likely to have the same meaning that HMRC have sought to apply elsewhere in the taxes acts.

Companies within the scope of DPT are required to notify HMRC within 3 months of falling within the regime under FA 2015 s 92.

## Explanatory Notes

*Factors affecting choice between overseas permanent establishment and overseas subsidiary*

(1) The main UK tax considerations in the choice between an overseas permanent establishment and an overseas subsidiary are explained in the Example. The UK position must be considered alongside the taxation position in the overseas country. There are also many commercial factors, such as the local 'commercial' perception of dealing with a local company rather than a permanent establishment of a UK company. In certain countries there is a legal requirement to have a local company in order to conduct business.

Following the introduction of the substantial shareholdings exemption (SSE) from 1 April 2002, UK companies may prefer operating their overseas business through a separate subsidiary, if it is likely to be sold at some stage. The SSE is available on the sale of shares in a trading subsidiary etc and the exemption is available on shareholdings in both UK and overseas resident companies (see **Example K3**). Also, there is no requirement that the subsidiary's trade is carried on in the UK. In contrast, the sale of the trade and assets (including goodwill) of an overseas permanent establishment may be subject to UK (and possibly overseas) tax. (Some protection of the UK tax base from possible exploitation of the exemption has been introduced by FA 2002 s 90, amending ICTA 1988 s 747 – see **explanatory note 6**.)

Other overseas taxes must be considered, such as indirect (VAT or sales type) taxes, property taxes (which can be expensive), employee taxes and social security.

Many overseas tax authorities have thin capitalisation and/or earnings stripping type rules which prevent excessive debt being used to finance the overseas company (to secure as much tax deductible interest as possible). From the UK company's viewpoint, it would not be efficient for interest charged on debt (fully taxed in the UK) to create surplus losses overseas.

The method of financing the overseas permanent establishment or company also requires careful consideration, for example local 'third party' borrowing is tax-efficient for a permanent establishment of the UK company (as 'interest' on internal funds from the UK head office would not be tax-deductible).

*Residence of a company*

(2) CTA 2009 s 14 provides that companies incorporated in the UK on or after 15 March 1988 are resident here, no matter where they are managed and controlled (subject to what is said in **explanatory note 6**).

(3) The following general principles have been established from case law:

(a) A company resides where its real business is carried on, ie where the central management and control is situated (*De Beers Consolidated Mines v Howe* (1906)).

(b) The place of incorporation is a factor to be considered but is not conclusive (*Calcutta Jute Mills v Nicholson* (1876)).

(c) The place where directors meet is an important indicator (*Cesena Sulphur v Nicholson* (1876)) but again it is not conclusive.

(d) Control as a shareholder does not amount to management and control (*Kodak Ltd v Clark* (1901)). (But where a parent company usurped the functions of its subsidiary company's board, or the subsidiary's board merely rubber stamped the parent company's decisions without independently considering them, HMRC would draw the conclusion that the subsidiary's residence was the same as that of the parent company.)

(e) A company may have dual residence, but this requires some substantial business operations in each country (*Bullock v Unit Construction Co Ltd* (1959)).

Where dual residence is concerned, many double tax treaties provide that the company is deemed to be resident where its place of effective management is situated. The treaty may also have a 'tie breaker' clause under which a company is held to be resident in only one of the two countries (see **explanatory note 6**).

(f) In cases where management decisions are extended and/or devolved to non-directors and third parties, the residence of those 'dictating' decisions to management are also taken into consideration when deciding the residence of the company (*Wood v Holden* (2006) and *Laerstate BV v Commrs of HMRC* (2009)). This is of particular significance when interpreting the role and influence of professional advisers or sole shareholders in management decisions.

(g) The place of effective management is considered a more accurate measure of residency to that derived from the place where the centre of top level management is located (*Smallwood v Revenue & Customs* (2008)). Effective management is decided given consideration to points (a) to (f) above, and is generally where key management and commercial decisions necessary for the conduct of the business are in substance made and given. This case was overturned by the High Court in 2009, but on the basis that there was no reason to invoke the tie breaker in the treaty.

It is worthy of note that given the increasing sophistication of communication systems, it is no longer necessary for a group of people to meet in one location to make decisions. This may have a significant impact on the incidence of dual residence and the application of effective management tie breakers.

(4) The case law provisions outlined in **explanatory note 3(A)** to **(E)** are still relevant to decide where companies incorporated abroad are resident (subject to what is said in **explanatory note 6**). If they are regarded as UK-resident and if they wish to migrate, they will have to give HMRC notice of their intention and make HMRC-approved arrangements for payment of tax under the Taxes Management Act 1970 (TMA 1970) s 109B – see SP 2/90). This will include tax on unrealised gains, except on UK assets of a permanent establishment which remains here (TCGA 1992 s 185). Deferment is possible in respect of foreign assets of a foreign trade if the company is a 75% subsidiary of a company remaining resident in the UK and the two companies so elect within two years. The parent company is then charged to tax on the net gains on the deemed disposal as and when the subsidiary disposes of the assets (within six years), or ceases to be a subsidiary (at any time) (TCGA 1992 s 187).

(5) Certain UK incorporated companies were treated as non-resident at 15 March 1988 or had applied to be so treated at that date and obtained Treasury consent subsequently. Such UK companies will not be treated

as UK-resident unless they cease business or cease to be liable to overseas tax, in which case they will be treated as UK-resident from that time. If, however, they transfer their central management and control to the UK, they will be treated as resident from the time of the transfer (CTA 2009 Sch 2 Part 5).

*Dual resident companies*

(6) Where there is a tie-breaker clause in a double tax agreement that provides for a company to be resident in another country and *not* in the UK, CTA 2009 s 18 provides that the company is non-resident for the purposes of the Corporation Tax Acts (preventing, for example, the surrender of losses by way of group relief). From 1 April 2002, these provisions are disregarded in deciding whether a company is a 'person resident in the UK' for the controlled foreign company rules dealt with in **explanatory notes 9** and **10**. This exception does not, however, apply to companies treated as not resident in the UK immediately before that date (ICTA 1988 s 747 as amended by FA 2002 s 90).

Dual resident companies that are *not* regarded as non-UK resident under a tie-breaker clause are not within CTA 2009 s 18. However, if they are *investing* companies they are subject to some specific anti-avoidance provisions, the main ones being the following:

(a) The company cannot surrender losses, non-trading deficits on loans, qualifying charitable donations relief etc under the group relief provisions (CTA 2010 s 109).

(b) Where an asset is sold to such a company by a company under the same control, the sale may not be treated as being at written down value for capital allowances (CAA 2001 s 570).

(c) An asset may not be transferred intra-group to such a company on a no loss no gain basis for capital gains purposes (TCGA 1992 s 171).

(d) Rollover relief on replacement of business assets cannot be claimed within a group where the new asset is acquired by such a company (TCGA 1992 s 175).

*Capital gains on transfer of business within EU*

(7) For businesses operating in the European Union, TCGA 1992 s 140C provides an alternative to the relief available under TCGA s 140 outlined in **note 8** of the Example. Under the EU Mergers Directive, local tax is not payable on a transfer of a business between companies resident in member states. TCGA 1992 s 140C provides for a UK-resident company to claim relief on the transfer of a non-UK trade carried on through a permanent establishment located in a country in the EU to a company in another member state in exchange for shares or securities in the other company. The transfer must be for bona fide commercial reasons and not part of tax avoidance arrangements (TCGA s 140D). Where the conditions are satisfied, the net capital gains are charged to tax, but the tax is reduced by the local tax that would have been paid in the country where the permanent establishment is located had it not been for the Mergers Directive (TCGA s 140C(5) and CTA 2010 s 122).

Under the provisions of the Distributions Directive (90/435/EEC), most EU companies do not deduct withholding tax from dividends to parent companies in other EU countries, although many countries have imposed a minimum time for the parent to have held shares in the subsidiary before this applies ('subsidiary' in this context requiring not more than 25% ownership by the 'parent'). F(No 2)A 2005 ss 51–58 introduce reliefs to facilitate the tax neutral formation of the Societas Europaeas (SE) from 1 April 2005.

Where a permanent establishment was converted into a subsidiary before 6 April 1988 and capital gains tax was deferred under the provisions of TCGA 1992 s 140, then if the deferred gain related wholly or partly to an asset acquired before 31 March 1982, and it crystallises on or after 6 April 1988, one half of the gain is exempt from tax (TCGA 1992 Sch 4 para 4). If the conversion took place on or before 31 March 1982, however, and the date when the liability would crystallise is on or after 6 April 1988, the deferred gain is wholly exempt from tax (TCGA 1992 Sch 4 para 4(5)).

*Controlled foreign companies*

(8) The controlled foreign company ('CFC') legislation of TIOPA 2010 Part 9A is aimed at preventing UK companies diverting profits to overseas tax havens or preferential tax regimes. The rules are particularly intended to counter the establishment in low tax areas of companies interposed between UK supplier and

foreign customer, or vice versa, captive finance and insurance companies, and companies established to accumulate dividends from other foreign subsidiaries. Where the low tax area is an EU country, the UK provisions may well conflict with EU law.

The CFC rules were radically changed for accounting periods starting after 31 December 2012. As there is no continuity between the old and new rules (although some similarities), only the new rules are discussed here.

A non-resident company can only be a CFC if the UK company has at least a 25% 'interest' in it. There is a legal control test based on shares and voting rights and an economic rights test based on distribution of share capital, income and assets on winding up. There is an additional 'dominant control' test which assumes control for CFC purposes where the UK company is the non-UK company's parent under FRS 2, and the notional CFC apportionment would result in more than half the CFC's chargeable profits being attributed to the parent company and all its subsidiaries (TIOPA 2010 s 371RE).

The UK 'control' definition includes joint venture 'CFC' companies where at least 40% of the shares etc are held by a UK company and at least 40% (but not more than 55%) are held by a foreign person.

(9) There are a number of entity level exemptions. These may be summarised as follows:

(a) Exempt period exemption (TIOPA 2010 s 371JA – JG)

A CFC is not brought within the CFC charging regime in the first 12 months of becoming a CFC. For example, this applies when a company is first acquired by a UK group. The exempt period exemption only applies where there is no CFC charge in the following accounting period.

(b) Excluded territories exemption (TIOPA 2010 s 371KB)

This applies where a CFC is resident in a territory listed by HMRC in 'The Controlled Foreign Companies (Excluded Territories) Regulations 2012' and all the following conditions are met:

(i) The income in certain specified categories, Categories A-D does not exceed the greater of £50,000 (proportionately reduced for short accounting periods) and ten per cent of the CFC's accounting profits;

(ii) The CFC's profits must not include IP profits of which a significant part was transferred from the UK in the previous six years;

(iii) There is no tax avoidance motive.

Categories A-D are defined in TIOPA 2010 s 371KE–371KI.

(c) Low profits exemption (TIOPA 2010 s 371VD)

This exemption applies where either the CFC's UK tax-adjusted profits or its accounting profits are either less than £50,000 in total, or £500,000 or less and not more than £50,000 of profits are non-trading income. These amounts are reduced proportionately for short accounting periods.

(d) Low profit margin exemption (TIOPA 2010 s 371MA-371MC)

The low profit margin exemption applies where a CFC's accounting profits, excluding interest costs, are no more than ten per cent of the 'relevant operating expenditure'.

(e) The tax exemption (TIOPA 2010 s 371NB)

A CFC is exempt if it is not subject to a 'lower level of taxation' in its country of residence. To determine whether this applies, the UK tax that would have been charged on the profits of the CFC calculated under UK tax principles is compared with the actual overseas tax paid. The exemption applies if overseas tax is 75 per cent or more of the notional UK tax amount. This exemption is not available where the CFC is subject to 'designer rate tax provisions' (TIOPA 2010 s 371NA-371NE).

If no entity-level exemption applies, then there are a number of profit gateway tests which may nonetheless exempt some or all of the CFC's profits. If the gateway tests apply, then profits pass the gateway (ie are potentially chargeable). The primary gateway test applies unless one of the following conditions is met:

- Condition A - The CFC does not hold assets or bear risks under a tax avoidance arrangement.
- Condition B - The CFC does not have any UK-managed assets or bear any UK-managed risks.
- Condition C - If there are any UK-managed assets or risks, these could cease to be managed in the UK without compromising the business operations or profitability of the CFC.
- Condition D - The CFC's assumed total profits consist solely of non-trading finance profits; and/or property business profits.

(TIOPA 2010 Part 9A Chapter 3.)

If profits pass through the primary gateway, the detailed profit gateway tests in Chapters 4-9 must be considered. The chapters are as follows:

- Chapter 4 – business profits.
- Chapter 5 – non-trading finance profits.
- Chapter 6 – trading finance profits.
- Chapter 7 – captive insurance companies.
- Chapter 8 – banks.
- Chapter 9 – special provisions which exempt some or all of the profit made on qualifying loans.

There are various anti-avoidance provisions throughout the CFC legislation and the complex rules need to be considered very carefully.

*Self-assessment provisions*

(10) For accounting periods ending after 30 June 1999, UK (holding) companies must 'self-assess' their corporation tax liabilities in respect of CFCs. Where the UK company pays its tax in instalments (as will often be the case) the tax relating to CFCs must also be included in the estimated tax payable.

Full details of all CFCs must be disclosed on the supplementary page CT 600B of the corporation tax return CT 600. If the CFC's profits are covered by an exemption (see below), an appropriate note is made. For each *non-exempt* CFC, the company must report its chargeable profits (less creditable tax) and the UK tax due.

Companies which *may not* be CFCs (for example, because they are not subject to a lower level of tax) but would clearly be covered by an exemption can also be shown on the return. This saves the UK company the cost of working out whether the company is, in principle, a CFC and preserves its disclosure position.

Under self-assessment, the UK corporation tax payable in respect of a non-exempt CFC is based on the UK company's share of the CFC's income profits (which must be at least 25% as indicated in **explanatory note 9**), as computed for UK corporation tax purposes. If the CFC is carrying on a trade, it is treated as though it were a UK resident carrying on a trade wholly abroad, using miscellaneous income rules. The UK corporation tax on the CFC's income is then reduced by the appropriate share of 'creditable tax', which comprises double tax relief for overseas tax, including local tax payable in the CFC's country of residence and any actual UK tax charged on any part of the CFC's profits.

To give companies greater confidence in determining their self-assessment position and liabilities in respect of CFCs, HMRC introduced a comprehensive CFC clearance system for companies and their advisers. Clearances generally apply indefinitely provided the underlying facts and the law remain the same. HMRC work to a 28-day turnaround target provided all the necessary information is included in the clearance application. Full details are given in HMRC's CFC guidance notes.

*Transfer pricing*

(11) Transactions between UK-resident and non-resident companies under common control are subject to the self-assessment transfer pricing provisions. Transactions for goods, services, financing etc between the UK company and its overseas subsidiary company must be based on arm's length prices or consideration. The UK company's tax computation and return must incorporate arm's length income and expenditure on transactions with 'connected' overseas companies (with an appropriate transfer pricing adjustment if necessary to reflect this). If the UK company fails to reflect arm's length transfer pricing on its return, it is likely to be liable to significant penalties and interest. (The UK transfer pricing legislation is based on OECD principles and most overseas jurisdictions have similar tax rules.) See **Example K7** for the detailed provisions.

The profits of an overseas permanent establishment would be fully liable to UK tax. The overseas jurisdiction would normally have powers to ensure that the profits arising in the permanent establishment are established on an arm's length basis, for example under the 'associated enterprises' article of a double tax treaty.

*Double tax relief*

(12) The calculation and application of double tax relief is dealt with in **Example I6**. However, as mentioned above most dividends required by UK companies after 1 July 2009 should be exempt from UK tax and consequently will not need to claim double tax relief on such income.

*Anti-avoidance*

(13) The interaction of rules of different jurisdictions has provided an opportunity for many tax-avoidance schemes of a technical nature, and many have been notified under the avoidance disclosure regime. Many of the CFC and DTR regulations are the subject of detailed technical anti-avoidance provisions, contained in FA 2005 and F(No 2)A 2005 and in the various provisions of the CFC rules in TIOPA 2010 Part 9A.

From 17 July 2013, the Finance Act 2013 introduced a General Anti-Abuse Rule which covers all aspects of corporation tax.

A new diverted profits tax (DVT) was introduced which applied to diverted profits arising on or after 1 April 2015. The aim of the DVT is to deter multi-national groups from undertaking aggressive tax planning methods which divert profits away from the UK artificially. It applies to transactions between group members which are both large. Where it applies it imposes a 25% tax charge on diverted profits relating to UK activity.

*International Tax Enforcement Arrangements*

(14) FA 2006 s 173 paved the way for a major strengthening in international tax enforcement arrangements. At present a number of agreements, for instance under double tax treaties, allow for the exchange of information between the UK and overseas tax jurisdictions, typically limited to direct taxes.

F(No 3)A 2011 s 87 and Sch 25 introduce legislation to enable the UK to implement the Mutual Assistance Recovery Directive (MARD) agreed by the EU in 2010. These are primary powers to introduce the Directive; further regulations will be needed to cover the detailed rules. The new Directive applies from 1 January 2012. Under this Directive EU member states can provide each other with assistance in the recovery of tax debts and duties, which includes service of documents and exchanging information in connection with the recovery of claims. The new legislation replaces and repeals the existing MARD set out in FA 2002 s 134 and Sch 39.

Following increased scrutiny on both tax evasion and on avoidance in the form of Base Erosion and Profit Shifting the UK has also signed a number of information sharing agreements with Crown dependencies such as Jersey, Guernsey, Isle of Man and the Virgin Islands. All of which are well known for their favourable tax regimes.

# Question

Bergplatz SA, a company resident in Austria for tax purposes, has decided to set up a business in the UK manufacturing plastic food containers under the name Boris. The anticipated profits of the branch are likely to be around £100,000 for the first few years.

Draft notes briefing the tax partner as to the major UK tax considerations that should be borne in mind in determining whether to operate through a permanent establishment or subsidiary company, and consider whether a European Company (SE) would be possible or advantageous.

(Comment on the specific provisions of the UK/Austria double tax agreement is not required.)

# Answer

1 June 2016

**To:** Tax partner
**From:** A D Viser

## Bergplatz SA: UK permanent establishment or subsidiary – major UK tax considerations

### Operating through UK permanent establishment

(1) As Bergplatz SA is setting up a factory in the UK, it can consider becoming a permanent establishment for UK tax purposes. Bergplatz SA will be liable to corporation tax on the permanent establishment's trading profit and on any income from property or rights used or held by the permanent establishment. It will also be liable to corporation tax on any capital gains on the disposal of property or rights held by the permanent establishment and assets situated in the UK used for the trade or by the permanent establishment (Corporation Tax Act 2009 (CTA 2009) ss 5 and 19 and Taxation of Capital Gains Act 1992 (TCGA 1992) s 10B). If there are any sources of UK income that are not connected with the permanent establishment the company will be liable to income tax at the basic rate thereon.

There will be no tax consequences when the permanent establishment makes remittances to Bergplatz.

Assuming Bergplatz SA has no UK subsidiaries, the legislation enabling UK permanent establishments of non-resident companies to take advantage of the group relief provisions for losses and the capital gains provisions for tax neutral intra-group transfers and group rollover relief on replacement of business assets is not relevant.

(2) A non-resident company is subject to corporation tax under Corporation Tax Act 2010 (CTA 2010) s 18, and must pay the full rate, currently 20% for financial year (FY) 2016 commencing 1 April 2016.

(3) Where a permanent establishment pays interest for the purposes of the trade, it is normally deductible as a trading expense (on an accruals basis) (CTA 2009 ss 296–301). The borrowing would be taken out by Bergplatz for the purpose of the UK permanent establishment's trade. In contrast any interest charged to the permanent establishment by Bergplatz SA as a result of an internal transfer of funds would not be allowable since a permanent establishment is not a separate entity. As a general rule, third party borrowing is advised in order to ensure that competent interest deductions can be made by non-banks. See **explanatory note 3**.

There will be no deduction for royalties paid by the permanent establishment to Bergplatz SA – see **explanatory note 1** for the treatment of royalty and interest payments.

(4) If the permanent establishment suffers any foreign taxes, double taxation relief may be claimed for both direct and underlying foreign tax paid other than in Bergplatz SA's home state, ie Austria (CTA 2010 ss 18 and 30).

(5) A permanent establishment of a non-resident company is outside the definition of close company in CTA 2010 s 439. Close trading companies do not, however, suffer any major tax disadvantages, so this exclusion has little practical importance.

### Operating through UK subsidiary

(6) For Boris to be set up as a UK subsidiary it must be resident in the UK. In order to be classed as UK resident Boris must either be incorporated in the UK (CTA 2009 s 14) or its place of central management and control must be in the UK. If Boris's place of incorporation and central management and control are two different places then the tie breaker clause within the double tax treaty is used to determine residence (typically this

is the place of effective management and control). Unless this applies, the subsidiary would be treated as a non-resident company and its tax treatment would be the same as that described above for a permanent establishment.

(7) If the subsidiary is regarded as UK-resident, then it will be fully liable to UK corporation tax on its worldwide (see **Example K8**) profits in the same way as any other resident company.

(8) The general right to repayment of dividend tax credits to non-residents ceased on 6 April 1999, but this does not affect tax credits repayable under some of the UK's double tax treaties (Finance Act No 2 1997 (F(No 2)A 1997) s 30(5) and (9)). Dividends paid by a UK subsidiary may continue to enjoy repayment of part of the tax credit in certain countries. However, with the lower tax credit of 10%, the amount refunded will be correspondingly reduced. Any treaty refund must be claimed direct from HMRC's Centre for Non-Residents (CNR).

(9) Interest paid by a UK subsidiary for the purposes of a trade is normally deductible as a trading expense. In order to prevent thin capitalisation, interest paid to a non-resident parent company by a UK subsidiary is not, however, deductible to the extent that it exceeds the amount that would have been paid between unconnected companies. If certainty is required an Advanced Thin Capitalisation Agreement could be sought with HMRC outlining the level of acceptable debt, interest rate and other ratios.

(10) For accounting periods commencing on or after 1 January 2010 the amount of interest deductible by a UK company may be further restricted by the debt cap provisions in TIOPA 2010 Part 7 if the group is large. See **Example K2** group borrowings for further details. HMRC's corporate finance manual CFM70000 onwards provides further information including the anti-avoidance provisions at CFM 79610.

## Converting a branch to a subsidiary

(11) If Boris is set up in the first place as a permanent establishment, it may subsequently be converted into a UK-resident subsidiary. The transfer of the trade from the non-resident parent to the UK-resident subsidiary will not have any adverse effect on the subsidiary's tax position because the acquiring company will take over the losses, capital allowances etc (CTA 2010 s 944 and s 955). Stock can be transferred at the amount paid rather than open market value, providing that amount is taken into account in the subsidiary's profit computation and an election is made by both companies under CTA 2009 s 167 within two years after the transfer.

(12) As far as capital gains are concerned, where a non-resident company transfers the whole or part of a UK permanent establishment business to a UK resident company in the same group (as defined in TCGA 1992 s 170), the chargeable assets are automatically transferred on a no loss no gain basis (TCGA 1992 s 171).

## Societas Europaeas (SE)

(13) It might be beneficial for the company to consider setting itself up as a Societas Europaeas (SE). A Societas Europaeas must have their head office in an EU member state, such as the United Kingdom or Austria. The purpose of the SE is to allow businesses operating in several member states to combine their operations into a single entity without tax cost. The resulting SE would be subject to the tax regime of the country in which its head office is registered. An SE has corporate governance obligations similar to a plc, and is required to make provision for employee participation. The minimum issued share capital for an SE is €120,000 including at least £50,000 in sterling in the UK.

It should be noted that Bergplatz SA can only group activities into an SE to the extent that the commercial bodies forming an SE have their registered offices in the EU.

## Diverted Profits Tax (DPT)

(14) If the company fails to set up a permanent establishment in the UK then it may be subject to DPT. This only applies where the company in question has either £10m of UK related sales or £1m of UK related expenses. If this was the case then the company would be liable to DPT at a rate of 25%. Due to the size of this company it is unlikely to fall within the DPT regime. See **Example K8**.

## Explanatory Notes

*Taxation of non-UK resident companies*

(1) The basis of charge to corporation tax is found in CTA 2010 ss 969–972 (previously Finance Act 2003 (FA 2003) ss 148–156) and is as follows:

(a) A non-UK resident company is to be subject to corporation tax by reference to a 'permanent establishment' in the UK.

(b) There are specific rules for quantifying the profits attributable to a permanent establishment. For this purpose, the permanent establishment must be treated as a separate enterprise dealing independently with the non-UK resident company.

(c) Mechanisms in the UK tax system for the assessment, collection and recovery of tax, as well as for interest on unpaid tax, will apply to the permanent establishment as a representative of the non-UK resident company.

A non-UK resident company, without central management and control arising in the UK, which does not carry on a trading UK business (eg property investment company) will not be subject to corporation tax, but may remain liable to income tax on any UK source profits.

(2) **What is a permanent establishment?**

Non-UK resident companies are chargeable to corporation tax if they carry on a UK trade through a permanent establishment. A non-UK resident company will have a permanent establishment in the UK if:

(a) there is a fixed place of business in the UK through which the company's business is carried on; or

(b) company business is carried on in the UK by an agent of 'independent status' acting on the company's behalf. An agent of 'independent status' is one whom has authority to conclude contracts which bind the non-UK resident company.

Some examples of a fixed place of business are:

(a) a place of management;

(b) a branch;

(c) an office;

(d) a factory or workshop;

(e) an installation or structure for the exploration of natural resources; and

(f) a building site or construction project.

However, a non-UK resident company will not be treated as having a permanent establishment if its UK activities are 'only of a preparatory or auxiliary character'. This includes:

(a) the use of facilities for the purpose of storage, display or delivery of goods or merchandise belonging to the company;

(b) the maintenance of a stock of goods or merchandise belonging to the company for the purpose of storage, display or delivery;

(c) the maintenance of a stock of goods or merchandise belonging to the company for the purpose of processing by another person; and

(d) purchasing goods or merchandise, or collecting information, for the company.

Before 2003 the UK only taxed a non-UK resident company that had a UK branch or agency: FA 2003 revised these rules introducing the wider definition, given above, of a permanent establishment. Following the change of definition, a number of non-UK resident companies, not previously subject to corporation tax, subsequently became caught by the revised regime.

In contrast to the view taken by other OECD member states, the UK does not consider that a computer server, either alone or together with websites, could in itself constitute a permanent establishment of a business. This view, as published on 11 April 2000 (press release 84/00) is taken by the UK regardless of whether the server is owned, rented or otherwise utilised by the business.

(3) **Determination of profits attributable to a permanent establishment**

Under CTA 2009 s 19 (2) and (3), the profits attributable to a permanent establishment for corporation tax purposes are:

(a) trading income arising directly or indirectly through, or from, the permanent establishment;

(b) income from property or rights used or held by the permanent establishment; and

(c) chargeable gains arising on the disposal of assets used in, or for the purposes of, the trade carried on through the permanent establishment or on the disposal of assets used or held by the permanent establishment.

However, it should be noted that the specific basis above can be overridden where there is a treaty between the UK and the non-UK resident company's home jurisdiction which contains a business profits article – Taxation (International & Other Provisions) Act 2010 (TIOPA 2010) s 6 specifies that treaty provisions take precedence over domestic law. The main assumption to be made in the determination of the relevant profits is to treat the permanent establishment as though it were a separate and distinct enterprise, engaged in the same activities under the same conditions and dealing independently with the rest of the non-UK resident company of which it is a part. This is referred to as the 'separate enterprise principle' and it reflects the wording of Article 7(2) of the OECD Model Tax Convention, incorporated into UK tax legislation in CTA 2009 Part 2 Chapter 4 ss 21–23.

In applying this principle, transactions between the permanent establishment and any other part of the non-UK resident company are deemed to take place on an arm's length basis, unless the non-UK resident company provides the permanent establishment with goods or services which it does not supply to third parties in the ordinary course of its business. In that case, the arm's length rule is not applicable and the quantum of the permanent establishment's expense is the actual cost incurred by the non-UK resident company. In addition, expenses incurred for the purposes of the permanent establishment (even if not incurred or reimbursed by the permanent establishment itself) are deductible, as long as they would have been allowable if incurred by a company resident in the UK.

Two further assumptions underlying the separate enterprise principle are that the permanent establishment is to be treated as having:

(a) the same credit rating as the non-UK resident company; and

(b) such equity and loan capital as it could reasonably be expected to have if it were an independent enterprise.

The law then prohibits deductions in arriving at taxable total profits in excess of those which would have arisen on those assumptions.

No deduction is available to a permanent establishment for royalties and similar payments made to any part of the non-UK resident company for the use of intangible assets held by the non-UK resident company (although contributions to the costs of creating such assets are allowable). It is difficult to reconcile this stipulation with the separate enterprise principle – in particular, it is unclear why a permanent establishment, which is treated for tax purposes as an independent entity, should not be allowed to deduct an arm's length charge for the use of an intangible asset. See HMRC's International Tax manual at

INTM267000 onwards. However this area is currently under active consideration as part of the 'Corporate Tax Reform: delivering a more competitive tax system', which may resolve some of these issues.

Similarly, no deduction is available for payments of interest or other financing costs by a permanent establishment to other parts of the non-UK resident company, unless they are payable in respect of borrowings by a permanent establishment in the ordinary course of a financial business such as banking or money-lending carried on by it. On the other hand, a permanent establishment should be entitled to tax relief in respect of interest incurred on its own external borrowings.

There are a number of other special rules for the permanent establishments of overseas banks.

(4) **Assessment, collection and recovery of corporation tax (CTA 2010 Part 22 Chapter 6)**

The UK representative of a non-UK resident company is required to deal with all matters connected with the payment of corporation tax (including interest on unpaid tax) as if any obligations and liabilities of the non-UK resident company were its own.

The UK representative is defined as the permanent establishment in the UK through which the non-UK resident company carries on its trade. Should the permanent establishment cease to trade in the UK, it will continue to be the non-UK resident company's UK representative in relation to the profits attributable to the permanent establishment. The UK representative is treated as a distinct and separate person from the non-UK resident company.

*Factors affecting choice of UK business medium*

(5) The main points to be taken into account are explained in the example or in **explanatory note 1** above, but see **explanatory notes 10** and **11** below re group relief and no loss/no gain transfers for capital gains purposes.

(6) For notes on the country of residence for a company see **Example K8.**

(7) Transactions between Bergplatz and a UK-resident subsidiary will be subject to the transfer pricing provisions. Similarly, transactions between Bergplatz and its UK permanent establishment must take place on an arm's length basis. For details see **Example K7.**

(8) The decision on whether to operate through a permanent establishment or subsidiary needs to take into account the taxation position in Austria. If a permanent establishment makes losses, it may be possible to offset them against the profits of Bergplatz in Austria. Permanent establishment profits, on the other hand, may suffer further tax in Austria. In contrast, the profits of an Austrian subsidiary would be insulated from tax in the UK provided the CFC rules have no impact.

(9) From a company law point of view, there is very little difference in that a UK subsidiary would be subject to the accounts and filing provisions of the Companies Acts, whilst a foreign company with a UK permanent establishment would have to register with the Registrar of Companies and supply information, including the company's accounts, on a regular basis.

*Group provisions*

(10) Where a non-resident company carries on a trade in the UK through a permanent establishment and is itself a member of a group which includes other UK-resident companies or UK permanent establishment activities, then it may participate in various 'group reliefs'. It may surrender to other UK-resident members of the group its trading losses etc attributable to its UK trading activities under CTA 2010 s 107. However, any part of a trading loss that is relievable against non-UK profits (not chargeable to UK corporation tax) for foreign tax purposes is excluded from the loss available for surrender (CTA 2010 s 107(5) and (6)). This rule applies irrespective of whether an actual foreign tax offset has been claimed – the fact that a loss is potentially relievable is sufficient. Similarly, the UK permanent establishment may claim group relief from other UK-resident members of the group against its profits which are chargeable to UK corporation tax. It is important to note that, following the relaxation in the UK residence requirement for certain group relationships, it does not matter if the non-resident company holding the UK permanent establishment is owned by another non-resident company.

(11) A UK permanent establishment can also transfer chargeable assets used in the UK trade to other 75% UK resident subsidiaries and vice versa under the no gain/no loss rule in TCGA 1992 s 171. The normal de-grouping charge under TCGA 1992 s 179 will arise if the recipient company leaves the group within six years of the intra-group transfer while still holding the asset. The UK permanent establishment can also participate in group rollover relief in respect of assets which have been or are to be used for the purposes of the UK trade under the provisions of TCGA 1992 s 175.

See **Example I6 explanatory note 3** re double tax relief in respect of foreign tax suffered by a UK permanent establishment of a non-resident company.

*Treatment of permanent establishment's income*

(12) Where interest is paid by any UK resident to a UK permanent establishment and the permanent establishment's profits are liable to UK tax, tax does not have to be deducted at source from the interest under ITA 2007 s 874, even though the permanent establishment is operated by a non-resident company.

(13) Where income is charged to income tax rather than corporation tax, for example where a non-resident company's only UK income is property income, it is not subject to the 'loan relationships' provisions of CTA 2009 and interest may be deducted where appropriate, despite the CTA 2009 s 1301A prohibition of a deduction for interest other than under the loan relationships provisions.

*Capital gains*

(14) There are various capital gains provisions relating to non-residents.

Non-residents are charged on gains if they carry on a trade through a UK permanent establishment (TCGA 1992 s 10B).

Rollover relief for replacement of business assets is available only where the replacement asset is within the charge to UK tax, ie acquired for the purpose of the UK trade (TCGA 1992 s 159). Group rollover relief may also be available (see **explanatory note 8**) and assets can be transferred to other UK-resident companies or UK permanent establishments under the no gain no loss rule in TCGA 1992 s 171.

Where an asset ceases to be a chargeable asset, either because the UK permanent establishment's business ceases, or because the asset is removed from the UK charge to tax, the asset is treated as disposed of and reacquired at market value, thus triggering a tax charge (TCGA 1992 s 25).

TCGA 1992 s 25 does not apply to the transfer of a UK permanent establishment by a non-resident company to another company under TCGA 1992 s 171 (intra-group disposal) or s 139 (company reconstruction). Nor does it apply to the transfer of a UK trade from one company resident in an EU country to another EU resident company in exchange for securities (including shares). Providing the conditions are satisfied, such transfers are made on a no loss no gain basis (TCGA 1992 s 140A).

Similarly, the provisions under TCGA 1992 s 25 do not apply to the transfer of assets to a non-resident company under TCGA 1992 s 140 and the gain so arising can be deferred in proportion to the consideration given in the form of shares and loan stock until:

(a) the shares and loan stock are disposed of; or, if earlier

(b) the date when the assets (or any part thereof) are disposed to a third party (if disposed of within six years of the transfer),

provided that the following conditions are satisfied:

(i) the trade (or part of the trade transferred) and all the assets of the trade (other than cash) must be transferred,

(ii) the shareholding in the transferring company immediately after the transfer must be at least 25% of the ordinary share capital.

*Recovery of unpaid tax from other group companies etc*

(15) There are provisions in TCGA 1992 s 190 to the effect that if a non-resident company operating through a UK permanent establishment fails to pay the corporation tax on a chargeable gain within six months after the due date, the tax may be recovered from another company in the same 51% group or from a controlling director.

There are separate provisions in CTA 2010 s 976 enabling *any* corporation tax due from a non-resident company that remains unpaid after six months to be collected from another company in the same group or (to the appropriate extent) from a member of a consortium owning the non-resident company.

*Societas Europapeas (SE)*

(16) The concept of the European company was created by Council Regulation (EC) No 2157/2001 of 8 October 2001, and made possible in the UK by SI No 2326/2004. It has been possible to set up this new legal entity since December 2004. Most of the tax provisions relating to it have effect from 1 April 2005.

The SE is intended for large organisations with operations in a number of member states. The legislation covering the formation and governance of SEs has many parallels with that of plcs, and accounting requirements are the same as a plc. The SE is required to have a minimum amount of subscribed share capital to the equivalent of at least €120,000 (including at least £50,000 in the UK). Its accounts can be kept in any currency.

An SE cannot be registered and brought into existence until either an agreement has been reached for employee involvement in company decisions, or until it is confirmed that the standard rules of the jurisdiction for employee involvement apply. It will be possible for an SE registered in one member state to move to another, unlike a plc.

It is envisaged that SEs will be formed by merger of the existing companies in different member states, by transformation of a plc into an SE, or by the formation of subsidiaries by companies registered in the EC. The commercial bodies forming an SE must have their registered offices in the EU, and a presence in more than one member state.

Finance Act (No 2) 2005 (F(No 2)A 2005) ss 51–65 amended existing tax legislation to ensure that a UK company's decision to merge with a company in another member state to form an SE is not disadvantaged or driven by tax considerations. These sections deal with chargeable gains, intangibles, loan relationships, derivative contracts, capital allowances and stamp duty reserve tax, giving certainty to the tax treatment of a number of transactions, and making them tax neutral. They are designed to allow UK businesses to take advantage of the new corporate vehicle if they so wish.

# Capital Gains Tax

# Question

(a) Give a brief outline of the basis of charge to capital gains tax, stating:

(i) the main persons chargeable to capital gains tax, the rates of tax and how it is charged;

(ii) how gains are measured;

(iii) what events trigger a charge to tax.

(b) Explain the effect of a UK-domiciled taxpayer's country of residence on his liability to capital gains tax.

(c) Explain the tax treatment of an individual who is temporarily resident outside the UK.

(d) In relation to connected persons in the context of capital gains tax:

(i) state what is meant by the term 'connected persons';

(ii) explain what special considerations apply when computing the chargeable gain or allowable loss arising on a disposal between a brother and his sister (both adults).

(e) Explain :

(i) the special capital gains tax rules which affect spouses and civil partners;

(ii) how these rules apply to other cohabiting couples.

Indicate the position in respect of the following:

(1) husband runs his business from premises owned by his wife, who does not work in the business. She acquired the premises in 1991. In May 2016 she transfers the premises to her husband and in June 2016 he sells them at a substantial gain;

(2) the facts are as above but the wife transferred the premises to the husband in March 2008;

(3) husband has been a full-time working director for twenty years of an unquoted trading company in which he owns 4% of the voting shares. His wife, who does not work in the business, has also owned 4% of the voting shares for a similar period. The couple is now considering selling their shareholding, realising a gain of about £1,000,000.

(f) Capital gains tax is assessed on chargeable gains accruing to a person on the disposal of assets:

(i) indicate which assets are exempt from capital gains tax;

(ii) explain, where an asset is disposed of under a contract, how the date of the disposal is determined;

(iii) explain how the date of a capital gains tax disposal is fixed where there is no contract.

(g) Indicate the annual exemption available for 2016/17 and how it interacts with the rules allowing taxpayers not to make returns of their capital gains.

(h) Explain the capital gains tax implications of a taxpayer's death.

# Answer

## (a) Basis of charge to capital gains tax

### (i) *Who is liable to tax?*

Individuals, personal representatives and trustees who are resident in the UK are liable to capital gains tax (TCGA 1992 s 2). This is a separate tax from tax on income. Non-residents are liable to capital gains tax on the disposal of UK residential property on or after 6 April 2015.

Companies usually pay corporation tax on gains, not capital gains tax. For details of the differences, see **Example L10**. However, where a non-natural person such as a company sells a residential property to which the annual tax on enveloped dwelling (ATED) rules apply, the gain (net of any losses of ATED-related disposals) is subject to capital gains tax at 28% (TCGA 1992 ss 2B-2F). The ATED rules apply to residential property worth more than £500,000 owned by companies, partnerships or collective investment schemes (whether or not they are resident in the UK)

Non-resident companies are also subject to a capital gains tax charge on the disposal of a UK residential property from 6 April 2015, irrespective of the value of the property (NRCGT). The ATED and NRCGT rules can therefore interact and overlap. To avoid double taxation where part of the gain could be subject to both ATED and NRCGT, the ATED related charge takes precedence.

There is an exclusion from the ATED-related capital gains tax charge if the disposal is made by an individual, personal representative or trustee where the gain accrues on the disposal of residential property:

- which is a partnership asset and the person is a member of the partnership; or
- which is held for the purposes of a collective investment scheme and the person is a participant in relation to the scheme.

If the disposal is excluded from the ATED-related gains rules it may be subject to capital gains tax under the normal rules discussed above.

For details of the ATED rules, see **Example D5**. For NRCGT see **Example F2**.

Charities are exempt from tax on gains, provided that they use the money for charitable purposes. Gains made on the disposal of investments held for the purposes of a registered pension scheme or overseas pension scheme are also exempt from tax.

Certain investment vehicles such as authorised unit trusts and investment trusts, open-ended investment companies and venture capital trusts are exempt from tax on gains made on their investment assets.

*Rates of capital gains tax for 2016/17*

| | Special rate gains; qualify Entrepreneurs' or Investors' relief | ATED related gains | Upper rate gains; corporate NRCGT | Upper rate gains; residential property or carried interest | Other gains |
|---|---|---|---|---|---|
| Gains meeting the relevant conditions | 10% | 28% | 20% | — | — |
| Gains taxed within the basic rate limit of £32,000 | | | | 18% | 10% |
| Gains taxed above the basic rate limit, plus trusts and personal representatives | | | | 28% | 20% |

The rates of capital gains tax are given in TCGA 1992 s 4 as 18% for upper rate gains and 10% for other gains subject to:

- The link to an individual's marginal rate of income tax; if income tax is chargeable at the higher rate or the dividend upper rate (or the gain exceeds the unused part of the individual's basic rate band) the rates of CGT are increased to 28% and 20%,
- A qualifying claim for special rate gains (ER or IR) reduces the rate to 10%,
- Trustees and personal representatives are charged CGT at 28% and 20%,
- The rate of tax in respect of gains under section 2B (ATED) is 28%,
- The rate of tax is 20% in respect of gains under section 14D and 188D (NRCGT).

*Upper rate gains*

FA 2016 s 82 reduced the rates of capital gains tax for individuals to 10% (gains within the basic rate) and 20% (gains above the basic rate band) with two exceptions. It's not exactly clear why these two exceptions were made but;

Carried interest - In the years up to 2016, HMRC undertook consultation and enacted new legislation on the taxation of managers of investment funds. The main thrust being what part of their "rewards" should be taxed as income (often at 47%) or capital carried interest chargeable to CGT (28%). Although a very specific business sector, the difference in the rates and its recent exposure could explain why it has been excluded from the reduction in CGT rates.

Residential property - Due to the existence of principle private residence relief, those actually paying CGT on a disposal of residential property are normally buy to lets, second homes or non-residents. With these targets in sight, high property prices and political pressure, it is again understandable why residential property was excluded.

Gains on the disposal of capital carried interest or an interest in residential property (to the extent not covered by reliefs) are therefore taxed as upper rate gains at the higher rates of 18% (within the basic rate band) and 28% (above the basic rate band plus trusts and personal representatives).

*Marginal rate of income tax*

For individuals who pay income tax at the higher, additional, dividend upper rate or dividend additional rate, the 28% / 20% rates of tax apply to taxable capital gains. For individuals who do not pay income tax at these rates, the 18% / 10% rates of CGT may be available either in whole or in part on the net chargeable gains for the year. For such individuals the applicable rate is calculated by adding taxable gains as the 'top slice' of the income tax calculation. The 18% / 10% rates apply to any gains within the unused basic rate and the 28% / 20% rates apply to any amount in excess of this band (TCGA 1992 s 4).

Where an individual's gains exceed the unused part of their basic rate band and are made up of different types of gains, the order in which the remaining basic rate band is used is:

(1) Special rate gains (ER & IR)

(2) Taxpayer's choice.

Therefore any gains qualifying for ER or IR take priority in using any remaining basic rate band. Once such gains are exhausted (or if none exist in that year) the taxpayer can choose which gains use any remaining basic rate band and are taxed at the lower rates.

*Special rate gains*

Capital gains tax on the disposal of the whole or part of a business, other associated disposals or shares qualifying for entrepreneurs' relief, are assessed at the rate of 10% regardless of the rate of income tax payable by the individual (TCGA 1992 s 169N). Similarly, gains on the disposal of qualifying shares in an unlisted trading company held by an individual and meeting the conditions for investors relief should qualify for a 10% rate of tax from 2019/20 (minimum three years holding period) onwards. For further details on both reliefs, see **Example L4**.

*What rate is applicable?*

There are now five rates of capital gains tax if you include exempt disposals (0%, 10%, 18%, 20% and 28%). For an advisor or student trying to determine which rate is applicable, consider:

(1) Who is making the disposal? (individual, trustees, personal representative or other entity),

(2) What is their residence status?

(3) What type of asset is being disposed of? (capital carried interest, interest in residential property, assets attracting a tax exemption/special treatment or other assets)

(4) Does that type of asset potentially qualify for any reliefs? (entrepreneurs', investors' or private residence reliefs etc.)

(5) For an individual, what is the taxpayer's marginal rate of tax?

### (ii) *How gains are measured*

Capital gains tax (or corporation tax on chargeable gains) is a tax on increases in value, not on cash profits. If a disposal or acquisition is made other than as a bargain at arm's length, the market value of the asset is used instead of any actual consideration (TCGA 1992 s 17). This means that the gain which has accrued during a person's ownership is charged when he disposes of the asset, even if he paid nothing for it (on a gift or inheritance) or receive nothing for it (on a gift).

Once all gains have been computed (netted off by any allowable losses either in the same tax year or brought forward from earlier years), the amount remaining chargeable is then reduced by an annual exemption (£11,100 for 2016/17) (TCGA 1992 s 3).

Companies do not qualify for an annual exemption although benefit from indexation allowance on chargeable disposals, which eliminates the gain as a result of inflation. See **Example L10** for more details.

### (iii) *Events which trigger a charge to tax*

The following events trigger a charge to tax on gains:

(1) disposal or part disposal of the chargeable asset by sale at arm's length, sale at undervalue, or gift (TCGA 1992 s 21);

(2) exchange of one asset for another;

(3) capital sums derived from an asset (TCGA 1992 s 22), for example insurance proceeds arising when an asset is damaged;

(4) creation of rights over an asset (TCGA 1992 s 21(2)(b)).

The following events do not trigger a charge to tax on gains:

(1) disposal of an asset which is exempt (see part (e) (i) below);

(2) disposal by an exempt person;

(3) gifts to charity and registered community amateur sports clubs (from 6 April 2002) (TCGA 1992 s 257; CTA 2010 s 658);

(4) disposals between spouses/civil partners (TCGA 1992 s 58) or companies within a 75% group (TCGA 1992 s 171). Strictly, such disposals are recognised by the legislation, but the proceeds are fixed so that the transfer occurs on a no-gain/no-loss basis meaning no chargeable gain (or allowable loss) arises;

(5) disposals on death (TCGA 1992 s 62);

(6) reorganisation of share capital (TCGA 1992 ss 126–140L).

In addition, many reliefs apply to reduce or defer the charge in certain circumstances.

## (b) Effect of residence on capital gains tax liability

An individual is liable to capital gains tax if he is resident in the UK (TCGA 1992 s 2). UK resident taxpayers who are domiciled in the UK are liable to tax in the UK on all gains wherever they arise. This territorial condition is modified where the individual is only temporarily non-resident in the UK (see part (c) below).

Prior to 6 April 2013 an individual was also liable to UK capital gains tax if non-resident in the UK but still ordinarily resident in the UK.

Non-residents are not generally liable to capital gains tax except:

(a) Where they carry on business in the UK through a permanent establishment. In that event they are liable to tax on gains arising on the disposal of business assets in the UK (TCGA 1992 s 10), and they are also liable if the assets are removed from the UK, or if the permanent establishment business ceases (TCGA 1992 s 25) (see **Example L9**).

(b) From 6 April 2015, non-residents are liable to capital gains tax on the disposal of UK residential property. This is explained in **Example F2**.

## (c) Temporary non-residence

Special rules apply to those who become 'temporarily' non-resident (TCGA 1992 s 10A). Someone who has been resident in the UK for any part of at least four of the previous seven tax years, and becomes not resident for less than five years, will be liable to tax on gains on assets owned before he left the UK. Note that the temporary non-residence rules were changed where the tax 'year of departure' from the UK (as defined by the legislation) is 2013/14 or later. Where the 'year of departure' was before 2013/14 the old rules apply.

Gains on the sale of assets held at the date the individual became non-resident, realised in the intervening period of non-residence will be taxed in the tax year when the person resumes UK residence. Losses realised in the intervening years will be allowed on the same basis as gains are taxed.

Gains on assets acquired while the individual was resident abroad that are realised in the period of temporary non-residence are exempt (subject to certain anti-avoidance provisions). The rules charging capital gains tax on the disposal of a UK residence by a non-resident take precedence over the temporary non-residence rules.

For further detail on the temporary non-residence rules, see **Example F1 explanatory note 24.**

## (d) Connected persons

### (i) *Connected persons in context of capital gains tax*

The term 'connected persons' for capital gains tax is defined as follows (TCGA 1992 s 286):

- a person is connected with an individual if that person is the individual's spouse/civil partner or is a close relative (ie brother, sister, ancestor, lineal descendant) or the spouse/civil partner of a relative, of the individual or of the individual's spouse/civil partner. An individual is also connected with business partners and their spouses/civil partners and relatives (except in relation to normal commercial acquisitions and disposals of partnership assets);
- if a person is trustee of a settlement, he is in that capacity connected with the settlor (if an individual) and with any person connected with the settlor (see above). The transfer of property into settlement is a transaction between connected persons, because the trustees become connected with the settlor at the time the settlement is created. After the settlor's death, the trustees are no longer connected with those who were connected with the settlor;
- companies under the same control are connected with each other and with any person controlling them.

### (ii) *Special considerations*

Adult siblings are connected persons in relation to each other. In computing the chargeable gain or allowable loss arising on a disposal between an adult brother and sister, the disposal is deemed to be at open market value (TCGA 1992 ss 17, 18).

If the disposal is by way of gift and it gives rise to a chargeable gain, and either the asset is a qualifying business asset or the gift is a transfer which is immediately chargeable to inheritance tax, a claim may be made for the gain not to be charged. Instead it is treated as reducing the acquisition cost of the donee, so that the donee's base cost is the same as the cost to the donor (TCGA 1992 ss 165, 260). This relief is not confined to connected person transactions. See **Example L9** for details.

If the disposal gives rise to an allowable loss, the loss may not be set against general gains, but only against a gain made on a later transaction with the same connected person (TCGA 1992 s 18). This is known as a 'clogged loss'.

Note that losses arising after the introduction of self-assessment are regarded as set off before earlier losses (FA 1995 s 113(2)). This may be relevant in relation to pre-1996/97 losses on transactions with connected persons, because if there was a gain on a later transaction with that person, that gain, together with other gains of the same tax year, would be eligible to be relieved by losses arising in and after 1996/97 before the earlier loss on the disposal to the connected person could be used against it.

## (e)

### Capital gains tax position of spouses and civil partners

Members of a registered civil partnership are subject to capital gains tax in the same way as married couples (Since 5 December 2005, FA 2005 s 103 as read with SI 2005/3229).

Under independent taxation all individuals are entitled to an annual exemption, which is £11,100 for 2016/17.

Where property is owned jointly by a couple who are married or in civil partnership, gains and losses are calculated according to the underlying beneficial ownership. See **Example A2 part (b)(iii)** for the different forms of joint ownership, ie as joint tenants or tenants in common.

Where a couple has a joint holding of shares in a company, and either or both also own shares individually, HMRC does not regard one person's share in the joint holding as being held in a different capacity from the individually owned shares. This is important when applying the special rules for matching disposals with acquisitions (see **part (d)** for an illustration).

So long as the married couple or civil partners are living together any transfers of chargeable assets between the two are deemed to take place for an amount of consideration which gives a result of nil (ie no-gain/no-loss). This will almost invariably mean that the transferee spouse/civil partner inherits the transferor's base cost.

The exception to this rule is where the asset is disposed of or acquired as trading stock, in which case the transfer is deemed to be at open market value (TCGA 1992 s 58).

Where the transfer between spouses/civil partners occurred prior to 6 April 2008 (and in respect of assets originally acquired between 31 March 1982 and 6 April 1998), indexation allowance had to be taken into account when determining the amount of the deemed consideration (see **Example L2, explanatory note 4**). This meant the transferee acquired the asset at the original cost plus indexation allowance to April 1998 or the date of the transfer if earlier.

When the abolition of indexation allowance was announced with effect from 6 April 2008, HMRC accepted that couples would be able to bank indexation allowance provided that the transfer between them occurred before 6 April 2008. However, the legislation would have had the effect of denying this to couples where the asset had been acquired before 1 April 1982. To remedy this, FA 2008 inserted TCGA 1992 s 35A to ensure that indexation could be banked in respect of all pre-April 1998 acquisitions (TCGA 1992 s 35A(2) provides that TCGA 1992 s 56(2) applies to the no-gain/no-loss transfer whereas, previously, it did not actually apply in such cases).

If, for example, an asset that had cost £10,000 was transferred from husband to wife in September 1993 at an indexed cost of £13,000 (ie this becomes the wife's base cost for capital gains tax), and the wife disposed of it in June 2016 for £21,000, the position would be as follows:

| | £ | £ |
|---|---|---|
| Sale proceeds June 2016 | | 21,000 |
| Cost | 10,000 | |
| Indexation allowance to September 1993 | 3,000 | |
| | | (13,000) |
| Gain | | 8,000 |

The no-gain/no-loss rule applies throughout the year of separation, but not in later years. Since the partners are connected persons up to the date of divorce or dissolution (as appropriate), transfers between them after 5 April following separation but before divorce (or dissolution) are deemed to be made at open market value (TCGA 1992 s 18 as read with TCGA 1992 s 286). However, where the assets transferred are used in the business of the transferor hold-over relief may be available (see **Example L9**).

Since 31 July 2002 HMRC has taken the view that transfers between a divorcing couple are deemed to take place for no consideration where the case goes to court and the court makes an order:

- for ancillary relief under the Matrimonial Causes Act 1973 or Civil Partnership Act 2005 which results in a transfer of assets from one partner to another; or
- formally ratifying an agreement reached by the parties dealing with the transfer of assets.

This means that a claim for holdover relief should not be restricted on the grounds that actual consideration has been given (CG67192).

Another consequence of this is that transferring ownership of the rights conferred by a life insurance policy under a court order is not for money or money's worth and no chargeable event gain can arise.

Married couples and civil partners may have between them at any time only one residence that qualifies as their main residence for relief under the rules in TCGA 1992 ss 222–226B (see **Example L8**).

## How the rules apply to other cohabiting couples

Other couples are not subject to any of the above rules. In particular, transfers between such couples can generate chargeable gains and/or losses (subject to the rules in TCGA 1992 s 17 concerning transactions otherwise than at arm's length). Each member of such a couple can have his or her own main residence.

An attempt for non-married couples to obtain the same taxing rights as married couples failed at the Special Commissioners (*Holland v CIR* [2003] STC (SCD) 43) on the basis that the difference in rules did not interfere with a couple's human rights. It remains to be seen whether the tax 'penalties' of being married are more susceptible to a similar challenge.

## Inter-spouse transfers

(1) The acquisition by the husband in May 2016 is treated as a no-gain/no-loss transfer by his wife. Therefore, her disposal proceeds are simply the same as her original acquisition cost (plus any subsequent enhancement expenditure reflected in the value of the property at the time of the transfer). Therefore, the husband is liable to capital gains tax on the difference between his net proceeds and his wife's qualifying expenditure.

(2) The facts are almost identical. However, because the transfer took place before April 2008, the wife's allowable expenditure (in her no-gain/no-loss disposal calculation) is increased by reference to the indexation between 1991 and April 1998. This additional relief increases the husband's base cost and therefore reduces the chargeable gain arising in June 2016.

(3) Shares can qualify for entrepreneurs' relief which will cover gains of up to £10m (lifetime limit). However, throughout the year before the disposal, the person making the disposal must (TCGA 1992 s 169I):

(a) have 5% or more of the shares (and voting rights) of the company; and

(b) be an officer or employee of the company.

Consequently, the wife cannot qualify for the relief. However, the husband can, provided his wife transfers her shares to him at least a year before the disposal.

## (f) Disposals

### (i) *Assets and gains exempt from capital gains tax*

Assets and gains which do not give rise to capital gains tax on disposal (and for which no relief is available for capital losses) are as follows:

(1) private motor cars (TCGA 1992 s 263) (see **explanatory note 10**);

(2) cash sterling (TCGA 1992 s 21(1)(b));

(3) foreign currency for personal expenditure and foreign currency within bank accounts (TCGA 1992 s 269 and TCGA 1992 s 252(2) respectively);

(4) gilts and qualifying corporate bonds (TCGA 1992 s 115);

(5) life policies in the hands of the original holder or beneficiaries (TCGA 1992 s 210) and compensation received for mis-sold policies, including payment protection insurance;

(6) non-life insurance policies, so long as the asset insured is not a chargeable asset for capital gains tax (TCGA 1992 s 204);

(7) chattels (ie tangible movable property) with a predictable useful life not exceeding 50 years, except where they are used in a business and capital allowances have been or could have been claimed. Plant and machinery is always regarded as having a predictable life of less than 50 years (even if it is a collector's item that is in fact much older) (TCGA 1992 ss 44, 45) (see **explanatory note 10**);

(8) decorations for valour acquired otherwise than for money or money's worth (TCGA 1992 s 268);

(9) bettings, pools and lottery winnings and winnings from games with prizes (TCGA 1992 s 51);

(10) compensation or damages:

- for personal or professional wrong or injury (TCGA 1992 s 51) (see explanatory note 14);
- for miss-sold personal pensions (FA 1996, s 148; ESC A99);
- For deprivation of foreign assets (TCGA 1992 s 268B);
- To Equitable Life policy holders (SI 2011/1502)

(11) woodlands. Sale proceeds (or insurance recoveries) relating to the timber element of woodlands managed by the occupier on a commercial basis and with a view to realisation of profits are excluded from CGT. (TCGA 1992 s 250);

(12) debts. A debt is not a chargeable asset to the original creditor unless it is a debt on a security. Therefore, no chargeable gain or allowable loss arises on disposal. (TCGA s 251);

(13) renewable obligation certificates. Where an individual disposes of a renewable obligation certificate in relation to an electricity generation system installed at their home, subject to conditions, no chargeable gain arises. (TCGA 1992 S 263AZA);

(14) cashbacks. Lump sums received by a customer as an inducement for entering into a transaction for a purchase (for example opening a new bank account) are normally considered to not derive from a chargeable asset so no gain arises. (see explanatory note 5 below) (SP4/97);

(15) National Savings Certificates and premium bonds (TCGA 1992 s 121);

(16) terminal bonus under a save as you earn (SAYE) contract (TCGA 1992 s 271(4));

(17) only or main residence, also known as the principal private residence (PPR) exemption (TCGA 1992 ss 222–226). Part of the gain may be chargeable in certain circumstances, see **Example L8;**

(18) disposals of assets that are considered by the Treasury to be of pre-eminent national, historic or scientific interest where the disposal is made to an approved body, such as a museum, to the Government as a gift to the nation or to HMRC in satisfaction of tax (TCGA 1992 s 258; FA 2012 Sch 14). Breach of any conditions imposed will nullify the exemption;

(19) gifts to charities and registered community amateur sports clubs (from 6 April 2002) (TCGA 1992 s 257; CTA 2010 s 658) (see **Example N4**).

(20) gifts of land to registered housing associations (TCGA 1992 s 259);

(21) shares in qualifying investment schemes. The relevant income tax reliefs must have been given and not withdrawn and the qualifying holding periods meet:

- enterprise investment scheme (EIS) (losses remain allowable) (TCGA 1992 s 150A);
- seed enterprise investment scheme (SEIS) (losses remain allowable) (TCGA 1992 s 150E);
- business expansion scheme (TCGA 1992 s 150);

(22) investments held through an individual savings account (ISA), junior ISA, child trust fund (acquire assets at MV at 18 or transfer to an ISA) or personal equity plan (PEP) (TCGA 1992 s 151; SI 1998/1870 reg 22);

(23) shares in a qualifying venture capital trust (VCT) See **Example N7** as older VCT's may include deferred gains (TCGA 1992 s 151A);

(24) employee shareholder shares. Gains on or after 1 September 2013 on disposal of shares which were worth up to £50,000 on acquisition are exempt. A lifetime limit of £100,000 applies to exempt gains on disposal of shares acquired under employee shareholder agreements entered into after 16 March 2016. See **Example N1 A(6)**;

(25) social investments. Gains accruing after the "relevant period" for which income tax relief under the SITR regime has been given and not withdrawn are not chargeable gains. (see **Example N7 answer c**) (TCGA s 255B);

(26) a substantial shareholdings exemption exists for companies where an interest of at least 10% is held for at least 12 months subject to conditions (TCGA 1992 Sch 7) (see **Example K3**);

(27) roll over and hold over reliefs. For details of the gains that can be rolled over or held over see **Example L9.**

## (ii) *Date of disposal*

Where an asset is disposed of under a contract, the date of disposal is the contract date, unless the contract is conditional, in which case the date of disposal is the date the condition is satisfied (TCGA 1992 s 28).

## (iii) *Date of disposal where no contract is in place*

There are a number of occasions where a disposal may take place without a written contract:

- where a gain is charged on a capital sum derived from an asset, the time of disposal is the date of receipt of that sum (TCGA 1992 s 22(2));

- if an asset is destroyed without compensation, the disposal occurs on the date of destruction (TCGA 1992 s 24(1));
- where land is acquired under a compulsory purchase order, the date of disposal is the date that the compensation is agreed. If the compensation is determined by a Tribunal, this is the date of disposal (even if the amount of compensation is varied on appeal) (TCGA 1992 s 246);
- where the asset is gifted, the date of disposal is the date on which the beneficial ownership passes to the recipient. In the case of chattels, this is the date of delivery. In the case of shares, it is when the donor has handed over the signed transfer form and the share certificate (*Re Rose (deceased); Rose and Others v IRC* [1952] 1 All ER 1217).

## (g) Annual exemption

Individuals, except those who make a claim under ITA 2007, s 809B to be taxed on the remittance basis, are entitled to an annual exempt amount. The exempt amount is £11,100 for 2016/17 (TCGA 1992 s 3).

Personal representatives are entitled to an exemption of the same amount on disposals in the tax year of death and the next two tax years (but not thereafter).

Trustees are entitled to an annual exemption of £5,550 or £11,100 if the trust is a trust for the disabled. The annual exemption is divided equally between trusts created by the same settlor in existence at any point during the tax year, subject to a minimum exempt amount of £1,110 for each trust (except for pre-7 June 1978 trusts, or pre-10 March 1981 disabled trusts) (TCGA 1992 Sch 1). No annual exemption is available to companies.

Individuals, personal representatives and trustees do not need to complete capital gains supplementary pages to the tax return if (TCGA 1992 s 3A):

- the chargeable gains for a tax year do not exceed the annual exempt amount; and
- total proceeds from chargeable disposals do not exceed four times the annual exempt amount (£44,400 for 2016/17 for individuals and personal representatives and up to £22,200 for 2016/17 for trustees)

## (h) Capital gains tax implications of a taxpayer's death

No capital gains tax charge arises on death (TCGA 1992 s 62).

If prior to his death the deceased has made losses in excess of gains in that tax year, they may be carried back and set against gains assessable in the three previous tax years, latest first. As with brought forward losses, the set-off is made only against any gains not covered by the annual exemption in the carry back years (TCGA 1992 s 62).

Following the reduction of earlier gains, tax will be refunded accordingly, with interest if appropriate. Although the repayment is calculated by reference to the tax position of the earlier year(s), interest on the repayment runs from 31 January following the tax year of death (TMA 1970, Sch 1B).

If the gains of the year of death exceed the losses of that year they are taxable in the usual way and the full annual exempt amount is available.

The personal representatives or legatees are treated as acquiring the assets at the market value at the date of death (TCGA 1992 s 62). Market value normally means open market value (TCGA 1992 s 272). Where, however, the probate value has been ascertained for inheritance tax, that value is taken as the market value for capital gains tax (TCGA 1992 s 274). Inheritance tax will not be ascertained where no tax is payable on the estate, for example because of exemptions and/or the inheritance tax nil-rate band.

When personal representatives dispose of assets at values in excess of the values at death, gains arising are charged to CGT, but the personal representatives may claim the annual exemption in respect of disposals by them in the tax year of death and in each of the two following tax years (TCGA 1992 s 3(7)).

If any losses arise, they may only be set against gains of the personal representatives and cannot be transferred to the beneficiaries. Personal representatives pay tax on gains at the rates of 28% / 20% depending upon type of gain (see above) (TCGA 1992 s 4(3)).

For inheritance tax, where land is sold within three years after death, a claim may be made by those liable to pay the tax to substitute the sale proceeds for the value at death (IHTA 1984 ss 190, 191). A similar claim is available in the fourth year after death if the property is sold at a lower value than its value at death (IHTA 1984 s 197A). Such a claim is normally relevant where land is sold at a loss. In the case of *Stonor & Mills (Dickinson's Executors) v CIR* [2001] STC (SCD) 199, no inheritance tax was payable on the estate because of the nil-rate band and exemptions. The executors sold freehold properties from the estate for significantly more than the probate value. They tried to claim under IHTA 1984 s 191 to substitute the sale proceeds for the probate value, thus increasing the capital gains tax base cost and eliminating the gains. It was held that, since no one was liable to pay any tax on the estate, no one was entitled to make a IHTA 1984 s 191 claim.

Personal representatives are allowed to treat an allowance representing the costs of obtaining probate as allowable expenditure for CGT purposes. SP 2/04 sets out HMRC's policy on this and a simplified calculation using a sliding scale. Alternatively, the personal representatives may claim a deduction for the actual costs.

If the personal representatives distribute assets to the legatees, this is not treated as a disposal for CGT purposes, as the legatee is treated as having acquired the asset at the date of death. Therefore the legatee's base cost is the market value at the date of death (TCGA 1992 s 62(4).

Within two years after a death it is possible under IHTA 1984 s 142 for the beneficiaries to legally vary the terms of the will in order to alter the way in which the deceased's assets are distributed. If a statement in the deed of variation is included which says that it is to take effect for capital gains tax, the variation is not regarded as a disposal by those originally entitled to the assets. Instead the variation is treated as having been made by the deceased at the date of death so that no capital gains tax charge arises on any increase in value between the dates of death and variation for those who give up all or part of their entitlement (TCGA 1992 s 62(6)–(9)). The beneficiary receiving the chargeable asset does so for tax purposes at the value at the date of death.

In *Marshall v Kerr* [1994] STC 638, the House of Lords decided that this deeming provision only had the effect of exempting gains on the variation itself. A trust established by a variation is treated for capital gains tax as settled by the person who made the variation, not by the deceased (TCGA 1992 s 68C).

Personal representatives can claim only or main residence relief in relation to the disposal of a residence if any persons who lived in the property both before and after the relevant death were entitled to at least 75% of the net proceeds of sale (TCGA 1992 s 225A). A specific claim for relief is required by the personal representatives.

For example, Mr X owned a house and following his death his widow and children occupied the house until it was sold by the personal representatives. Mrs X and children were entitled to over 75% of the net proceeds (proceeds less costs allowable under TCGA 1992 s 38(1)(c)). Any gain arising between date of death and the sale of the house would be exempt under the only or main residence rules.

For detailed provisions on inheritance tax and the taxation of personal representatives, see the companion to this book, **Tolley's Taxwise II 2016/17**.

## Explanatory Notes

*Scope of capital gains tax*

(1) Capital gains tax was introduced on 6 April 1965 to charge tax on gains arising on the disposal of assets on or after that date. Companies are usually charged to corporation tax on their gains rather than capital gains tax as indicated in **part (a)** of this Example (see also **Example I1 explanatory note 10**).

Technically, the charge covers all assets unless the *gain* is specifically exempt, and the assets themselves are not classified as either chargeable or exempt. It is, however, more usual and convenient to use the terms chargeable assets and exempt assets.

In general the same rules apply for calculating allowable losses as for chargeable gains (TCGA 1992 ss 15, 16). Where losses exceed gains of the same chargeable period the excess is carried forward to set against later gains. Special rules apply to losses on transactions between connected persons, as indicated in **part (d)(ii)** of this Example.

(2) Where an asset is not a chargeable asset, then neither a chargeable gain nor allowable loss can arise (TCGA 1992 ss 15, 16). All forms of property, including options, debts and intangible property, any currency other than sterling, and assets created by the person disposing of them (eg goodwill) are chargeable assets unless they are specifically exempt, either wholly or in part (TCGA 1992 s 21) or, in the case of companies, are covered by the loan relationships rules (see **Example K2**) or intangible assets rules (see **Example K3**). Special provisions apply to taxpayers other than companies in respect of the loss of money lent.

(3) The method of calculation of chargeable gains and allowable losses depends on whether or not the person disposing of the asset is a company. Companies are able to deduct indexation allowance to reflect the inflationary effects on their costs since the time of acquisition (see **Example L10**). Individuals, personal representatives and trustees are not able to deduct indexation allowance from their consideration in calculating the gain or loss arising on the disposal.

*Meaning of 'disposal'*

(4) A gift of an asset is normally treated as a disposal at open market value (TCGA 1992 ss 17, 18). See **Example L9 explanatory note 17** where the gift was made between 6 April 1980 and 13 March 1989. A disposal includes a part disposal, and where a capital sum is derived from an asset even though no asset is acquired by the person paying the capital sum. In the case of a capital sum derived from an asset, the time of disposal is the date the capital sum is received (TCGA 1992 s 22). Examples of capital sums derived from assets include insurance proceeds for loss of or damage to an asset, and compensation for surrendering rights. Where *statutory* compensation is paid, for example to business tenants under the Landlord and Tenant Act 1954, the receipt is exempt for capital gains tax (see HMRC Tax Bulletin April 1996 for the circumstances in which such an exemption will apply). Certain other compensation is exempt (see items 8 and 9 of **part (e)(i)** of this Example and **explanatory note 14**).

*Cashbacks*

(5) HMRC has stated its view on the treatment of 'cashbacks' offered as inducements to purchase goods, services or financial products (for example in connection with a mortgage or car purchase). Such payments are not regarded as deriving from an asset and are exempt from capital gains tax. An income tax liability may, however, arise if the payments are received by a business, or by an employee by reason of his employment (SP 4/97).

*Building society and other mergers, conversions etc*

(6) Payments to account holders on building society *mergers* are regarded by HMRC as being income payments and are paid net of 20% tax. Following *Foster v Williams; Horan v Williams* [1997] STC (SCD) 112, HMRC accepts that the treatment of cash payments on building society takeovers and conversions is that amounts received by depositors (and presumably by borrowers) are wholly exempt from tax, and gains on amounts received by *shareholders* are taxable. Calculations are not, however, necessary, where the payment is covered by the annual exempt amount (taking into account any other capital gains in the tax year).

Where *shares* are received in a building society conversion or takeover, there is no capital gains liability at that time and they are treated as acquired for the amount paid for them. Where they are issued free, there is no allowable cost for a future disposal (TCGA 1992 s 217).

Some mutual insurance companies have also converted into companies, and the tax treatment depends on the facts of the particular case (see HMRC Tax Bulletin April 1998). For both building society and insurance company conversions, it was possible to avoid future capital gains tax on shares issued on the conversion by transferring the shares to a PEP, but only up to 5 April 1999. Shares cannot be transferred in this way into an ISA, see **Example A5**.

Where shares are issued to the members of the mutual organisation and are then exchanged for loan notes, the capital gain is 'frozen' at the date of the exchange and deferred until the loan notes are encashed. However, the encashment of the loan notes over a period of years enables the holder to set several annual exemptions against the capital gain.

*Connected persons*

(7) All transactions between connected persons, or not at arm's length, are regarded as being made at open market value (TCGA 1992 ss 17, 18, 286). This does not apply to transactions between spouses/ civil partners, which take place on a no-gain/no-loss basis. These rules also do not apply to normal commercial transactions between business partners. HMRC accepts the value placed thereon by the partners (eg goodwill on admission of a new partner), where this is dictated by commercial terms and not because of any familial relationship between the partners.

(8) In general, market value means the price that might reasonably be expected on a sale in the open market (TCGA 1992 s 272). Quoted securities are valued at the *lower* of (a) one-quarter up from the lower of the quoted prices and (b) halfway between the lowest and highest recorded bargains (TCGA 1992 s 272(3)). Unit trust holdings are valued only at the bid price, not 'quarter up' (TCGA 1992 s 272(5)). In valuing unquoted securities it is assumed that all relevant information is available to the prospective purchaser (TCGA 1992 s 273). Where the value of an asset has been ascertained for inheritance tax on a death, that value is regarded as the market value at death for capital gains tax (TCGA 1992 s 274), and whoever acquires the asset acquires it at that value.

(9) Where a person disposes of assets on different occasions within a period of six years to one or more persons connected with him, and their value taken together is higher than their separate values, then the disposal value for each of the transactions is a proportionate part of the aggregate value. All necessary adjustments will be made to earlier tax charges (TCGA 1992 ss 19, 20). See also part (d)(ii) of this Example.

*Exemptions*

(10) The exemption for private motor cars applies to 'a mechanically propelled road vehicle constructed or adapted for the carriage of passengers, except for a vehicle of a type not commonly used as a private vehicle and unsuitable to be so used...' (TCGA 1992 s 263). It therefore covers veteran and vintage cars (except one-seater models), and is available whether or not the car is used in a business. So profits on the disposal of cars are either (a) trading profits if the seller is carrying out 'an adventure in the nature of trade' or (b) exempt. A one-seater car that is not covered by the 'cars' exemption, and also any other 'plant or machinery', would be exempt as a wasting chattel even if it was a collector's item (TCGA 1992 ss 44, 45). The chattels exemption therefore covers items such as antique clocks and watches.

(11) Prior to 6 April 2012, foreign currency within bank accounts was only exempt where the currency was acquired by the holder for the personal expenditure outside the UK of the individual or his family or dependants (including expenditure on the provision or maintenance of any residence outside of the UK). This restriction was removed with effect from 6 April 2012 (FA 2012 s 35).

(12) For details of gilt-edged securities and qualifying corporate bonds see **Example L7**.

(13) Where chattels are used in a business, and/or are non-wasting chattels, gains are exempt if the chattel is sold for £6,000 or less (TCGA 1992 s 262). For details see **Example L2 explanatory note 5**.

(14) There is a complete exemption for compensation or damages for any wrong or injury suffered by an individual in his person or in his profession or vocation (TCGA 1992 s 51(2)). HMRC considers that 'in his person' has a wide definition extending beyond physical injury, so that damages or compensation for 'distress, embarrassment, loss of reputation or dignity' such as unfair discrimination are not chargeable (see ESC D33 para 12). The same exemption applies to wrong or injury suffered in a professional capacity, such as libel or defamation.

Where compensation is for personal injury, and it is received by way of periodical payments, or where interest is payable on the compensation, such payments are income rather than capital, but they are similarly exempt from income tax (ITTOIA 2005 ss 731, 732, 751).

Strictly, any right to compensation or damages not covered by the exemption is taxable. By ESC D33, however, damages of up to £500,000 are treated as derived from any underlying assets (and therefore exempt, taxable or partly taxable depending on the extent to which the underlying asset is exempt or taxable). Under TCGA 1992 s 268B certain compensation from foreign governments for property lost or confiscated is exempt.

*Contracts*

(15) In the case of *Jerome v Kelly* [2004] STC 887, the House of Lords had to examine the effect of the contract disposal rule in TCGA 1992 s 28. Mr Jerome (J) made a disposal of land which, for the purposes of illustration, can be simplified as follows:

- in tax year 1, J signed a contract to sell the land, for delivery in tax year 3;
- in tax year 2, J assigned the land (subject to the contract for sale) to a foreign trust;
- in tax year 3, the trustees completed the sale and received the consideration.

HMRC assessed the gain on disposal on J in tax year 1. He appealed, contending that TCGA 1992 s 28 could only fix the time of disposal, but it could not change the identity of the person who made that disposal – in this case, the trustees. In the High Court, Park J agreed with this argument, and suggested that HMRC should have assessed J on his disposal to the trustees in year 2.

The Court of Appeal restored the traditional understanding of the effect of TCGA 1992 s 28. The asset was disposed of under a contract; the signing of that contract fixed not only the time of disposal, but also the identity of the seller.

The House of Lords' view was that TCGA 1992 s 28(1) was no more than a timing provision and did not deem the contract to be a disposal. Furthermore, Parliament should not be attributed as having intended to impose a liability on someone who would not be treated as having made a disposal under the scheme for taxing the disposal of assets held on trust. The House of Lords allowed the taxpayer's appeal and held that the disposal was made by the foreign trust.

Subject to further legislative changes, this may leave scope for some limited post-transaction planning in cases where there is a period between entering into a contract for disposal and the executing of the contract (completion). For example, a husband agrees a contract and then realises that his wife has unrelieved losses brought forward. The husband could transfer the land subject to the uncompleted contract. However, there may be stamp duty land tax implications to consider.

(16) However, a mere cancellation of a binding contract will not constitute a disposal and subsequent re-acquisition (*Underwood v HMRC* [2009] STC 239).

*Date of disposal*

(17) A Special Commissioner's hearing, *Smith and another v CIR* [2004] STC (SCD) 60, considered whether a contract was conditional on giving vacant possession. Mr & Mrs Smith owned a farm where they carried on their business as farmers. They received an offer and payment for the farm in 1991. However they remained in occupation until 31 October 1999. They paid rent from 1 February 1992. The letter of offer placed an obligation on the sellers 'to flit and remove from the subjects (ie farm property) at 1 February 1992 or such other date on which the sellers are entitled to take occupation of their new farm . . . '. The taxpayers tried to argue that this made the contract conditional, so the time of disposal was when the condition (the purchase of the new farm) was satisfied. The Commissioner rejected this argument.

*Upper rate gains*

(18) For discussion of what counts as residential property (and hence the gain is taxable at the higher rates) see **Example L8 explanatory note 11.**

# Question

(a) A acquired a chargeable business asset in April 1984 at a cost of £10,000. In September 1984 the value of the asset was increased by enhancement expenditure of £5,000 and the value was further increased in June 1997 by enhancement expenditure of £15,000. Show the capital gain or loss arising on the asset, assuming that the asset was sold on 10 May 2016 for (i) £50,000 or (ii) £28,000, and that no claim to roll-over or hold-over relief is available.

Without making calculations, indicate what the position would have been if the facts had related to A Ltd rather than an individual.

(b)

(i) On 1 January 1989 D purchased an antique for £2,600 and on 20 April 2016 sold it at auction for £7,200, incurring selling expenses of £720.

(ii) On 1 January 1989 E purchased a picture for £7,000 and sold it on 20 April 2016 for £4,850.

(iii) On 1 January 1996 F purchased a set of antique candlesticks for £5,400 and sold part of the set to a collector on 20 April 2013 for £2,600. On 20 April 2016 he sold the remainder to the same person for £4,600.

D, E and F are private collectors. Show the capital gains or losses arising in each case.

(c) Explain what determines wasting assets (other than short leases) for capital gains tax purposes, and state the taxation implications on the disposal of such assets.

(d) G, a property owner, acquired a 51-year lease for £60,000 on 16 March 2013. On 16 March 2017 he assigned the lease to Y for £77,000. Show the capital gain or loss arising.

(e) John Gregory owned a farmhouse which had been let to tenants for many years. On 1 January 2016 he granted an option to Jack Price, on payment of £10,000, to acquire the property for £215,000. The option could be exercised at any time between 1 January 2016 and 31 December 2016. Finding himself unable to finance the purchase, Jack sold the option to Jimmy Matthews on 30 June 2016 for £15,000. Jimmy exercised the option on 31 December 2016.

(f) C sold an investment property on 10 April 2016 for £450,000 which had cost £10,000 on 10 April 1960. The costs of purchase and sale were £185 and £9,000 respectively. The value was £15,000 at 6 April 1965 and £48,200 at 31 March 1982.

(g) H purchased a house for £44,000 on 5 January 1974 and on 5 July 1977 paid £12,000 to convert the house into two self-contained flats. On 27 April 2016 he sold the upper floor flat for £365,000 but declined an offer of £377,000 for the ground floor flat. He recognised that £377,000 was the market value, but preferred to let that flat in the expectation that the value would increase during the next few years. At no time did H live in the house. The market value of the whole at 31 March 1982 was considered to be £60,000.

Set out the taxation implications of the transactions described above.

# Answer

## (a) A – treatment of enhancement expenditure

The chargeable gain or allowable loss on the sale of the chargeable business asset for (i) £50,000 in 2016/17 is calculated as follows:

| | | |
|---|---|---|
| *Disposal - May 2016* | | £ |
| Sale proceeds | | 50,000 |
| Less: Cost April 1984 | 10,000 | |
| Enhancement expenditure September 1984 | 5,000 | |
| Enhancement expenditure June 1997 | 15,000 | (30,000) |
| Chargeable gain | | 20,000 |

It is assumed that the enhancements in 1984 and 1997 were reflected in state of the asset at the time of disposal (TCGA 1992 s 38(1)(b)).

The gain of £20,000 would be aggregated with A's other gains and losses for the tax year and then be reduced by the annual exempt amount of £11,100.

The chargeable gain or allowable loss on the sale of the chargeable business asset for (ii) £28,000 in 2016/17 is calculated as follows:

| | | |
|---|---|---|
| *Disposal - May 2016* | | £ |
| Sale proceeds | | 28,000 |
| Less: Cost April 1984 | 10,000 | |
| Enhancement expenditure September 1984 | 5,000 | |
| Enhancement expenditure June 1997 | 15,000 | (30,000) |
| Allowable loss | | (2,000) |

If the facts had related to A Ltd, indexation allowance would have been available. This would have enabled A Ltd to claim additional deductions to reflect the increase in the retail prices index between the dates of expenditure (April 1984, September 1984 and June 1997) and the date of disposal (May 2016).

Indexation allowance, however, cannot be used to create a loss. Therefore, in (i) the maximum indexation allowance would be limited in any case to £20,000. Nor can indexation allowance be used to increase a loss. Therefore, in (ii) the situation would be unchanged from that shown above for A. See **explanatory note 4** for details of how to calculate indexation allowance for companies.

Companies are not entitled to an annual exemption.

## (b) Sales of chattels

The chargeable gains or allowable losses on the sale of the chattels in scenarios (i), (ii) and (iii) is calculated as follows:

| (i) | | (ii) | | (iii) | |
|---|---|---|---|---|---|
| | £ | | £ | | |
| Sale by D (£7,200 – £720) | 6,480 | Sale by E (deemed) | 6,000 | F's two transactions are treated as one since the set has been sold to the same person | |
| Cost Jan 1989 | (2,600) | Cost Jan 1989 | (7,000) | | |
| | | | | Thus: | £ |
| Gain | 3,880 | | | 1st sale | 2,600 |
| | | | | 2nd sale | 4,600 |
| | | | | | 7,200 |
| | | | | Cost Jan 1996 | (5,400) |
| | | | | Gain | 1,800 |
| | | | | This is less than 5/3 × £1,200 = £2,000 | |
| Limited to (£7,200 – £6,000) = £1,200 × 5/3 | 2,000 | Allowable loss | (1,000) | Chargeable gain | 1,800 |

HMRC states in CG76637–CG76638 that the gain in (iii) should be apportioned between the two tax years of disposal in proportion to the sale proceeds, so (£2,600/£7,200) x £1,800 = £650 would be assessed in 2013/14 and the remaining £1,150 would be assessed in 2016/17. See **explanatory note 6**.

## (c) Wasting assets

Wasting assets are defined in TCGA 1992 s 44 as assets with a predictable useful life not exceeding 50 years, subject to the following:

(a) freehold land is never a wasting asset;

(b) plant and machinery is always treated as a wasting asset.

The cost of a wasting asset is deemed to waste away on a straight line basis over its useful life (TCGA 1992 s 46). However, if the asset has been used in a trade, profession or vocation and capital allowances have been or could have been claimed on it, the rules for straight line depreciation do not apply (TCGA 1992 s 47).

Where the wasting asset is a chattel, ie tangible movable property, then unless it is used in the business of the disposer it is not a chargeable asset for capital gains purposes, so that no chargeable gain or allowable loss can arise (TCGA 1992 s 45, as amended by Finance Act 2015 s40). Gains on business chattels are exempt if the chattel is sold for £6,000 or less. For further points on business chattels see **explanatory note 5**.

Since wasting chattels are either exempt or are business chattels to which the straight line rules do not apply, the provisions of TCGA 1992 s 46 will apply only to intangible property, such as options (see **part** (**e**) of this Example and also **explanatory note 9**). Special rules apply to short leases – see **part** (**d**) of this Example and **explanatory note 7**.

## (d) G – assignment of short lease

The chargeable gain or allowable loss on the sale of the lease is calculated as follows:

| | £ |
|---|---|
| *Disposal - March 2017* | |
| Sale proceeds | 77,000 |
| Cost March 2012 $£60{,}000 \times \frac{\text{Years unexpired on sale } 47}{\text{Years unexpired on acquisition } 51}$ | |
| Substituting percentages $£60{,}000 \times \frac{98.902}{100}$ | (59,341) |
| Chargeable gain | 17,659 |

For more details of the capital gains tax treatment of short leases, see **explanatory note 7.**

## (e) Tax implications of option transactions

### John Gregory

Since the option was exercised in a later tax year than it was granted, John Gregory will initially have been liable to tax on the option proceeds of £10,000 in 2015/16 (less the annual exempt amount if available).

The option then being exercised, the price paid for the option is incorporated with the proceeds for the farmhouse to form a single transaction. The tax originally charged will be taken into account in the amount of tax payable on the exercise of the option.

John Gregory will therefore be liable to capital gains tax on the disposal in December 2016. His proceeds are the £10,000 received on granting the option plus the £215,000 paid for the farmhouse. This will be reduced by the cost of the farmhouse plus any enhancement expenditure which is reflected in the value of the property when sold. Any capital allowances given to John will not be deducted from the cost in computing the gain (whether or not they have been withdrawn by means of a balancing charge).

### Jack Price

Since Jack Price did not exercise the option, the disposal of it is treated as a separate chargeable transaction in 2016/17. The option is a wasting asset and its cost wastes away on a straight line basis over its life, ie from 1 January 2016 to 31 December 2016. The allowable cost is restricted according to how much of that life has expired. The depreciated cost is set against the disposal proceeds of £15,000. The position is therefore as follows:

| | £ |
|---|---|
| *Disposal - June 2016* | |
| Sale proceeds | 15,000 |
| Depreciated Cost $10{,}000 \times \frac{6}{12}$ | (5,000) |
| Chargeable gain | 10,000 |

### Jimmy Matthews

Since Jimmy Matthews exercised the option, the purchase of the option and of the farmhouse will be treated as a single transaction.

## (f) C – asset acquired before 1 April 1982

The gain must be calculated using the 31 March 1982 value (TCGA 1992 s 35(2)):

| | |
|---|---|
| *Disposal - April 2016* | £ |
| Net sale proceeds (£450,000 - £9,000) | 441,000 |
| Less: 31 March 1982 value | (48,200) |
| Chargeable gain | 392,800 |

See **explanatory note 1**.

## (g) H – part disposal

The disposal of the first floor flat is a part disposal of the original asset purchased. No account is taken of the enhancement expenditure incurred in 1977 as the market value as at 31 March 1982 is the deemed cost. The chargeable gain is calculated as follows:

| | | |
|---|---|---|
| *Disposal - April 2016* | | £ |
| Sale proceeds | | 365,000 |
| | 31 March 1982 MV $£60{,}000 \times \frac{£365{,}000}{£365{,}000 + £377{,}000} =$ | (29,515) |
| Chargeable gain | | 335,485 |

# Explanatory Notes

*Introduction and application of capital gains tax legislation*

(1) Capital gains tax is primarily a tax on gains arising on the disposal of assets by individuals, trustees and personal representatives. Although, it is extended for residential property. The ATED regime applies to non-natural persons and the NRCGT regime applies to non-residents. (see **Example L1**).

Where the asset was held on 31 March 1982 the original cost is ignored and instead the cost is deemed to be the market value as at 31 March 1982 (TCGA 1992 s 35(2)).

The gains of companies are computed under capital gains principles but (other than ATED and NRCGT) are charged to corporation tax rather than capital gains tax.

For details of chargeable disposals and exempt assets, see **Example L1**.

If a disposal or acquisition is made other than as a bargain at arm's length, the market value of the asset is used instead of any actual consideration (TCGA 1992 s 17).

Once all gains have been computed (netted off by any allowable losses either in the same tax year or brought forward from earlier years), the amount remaining chargeable is then reduced by an annual exemption (£11,100 for 2016/17) (TCGA 1992 ss 2(2), 3). For the rates of capital gains tax, see **Example L1**.

Companies can still benefit from indexation allowance on chargeable disposals.

*Allowable expenditure*

(2) The allowable expenditure that may be taken into account in computing gains and losses is (TCGA 1992 s 38):

(i) cost of the asset plus incidental costs of acquisition;

(ii) enhancement expenditure, ie additional capital expenditure reflected in the state of the asset at the time of disposal;

(iii) incidental costs of disposal.

Incidental costs of acquisition or disposal are fees etc for:

- services of surveyors, valuers, auctioneers, accountants, agents or legal advisers;
- costs of transfer or conveyance (including stamp duties);
- advertising to find a seller or a buyer;
- costs of making valuations or apportionments, including expenses of ascertaining market value.

Incidental costs do not, in HMRC's view, include any costs incurred in *agreeing* a valuation (CG15260). Under self-assessment, individuals, trustees and companies may apply for a valuation check using form CG34 (CG16600). The application is made to HMRC after the transaction has completed but before the tax return is submitted. The advantage of asking for a valuation check is that any values agreed in this way will not later be challenged unless information relating to the valuation has been withheld.

*No-gain/no-loss disposals*

(3) Married couples and civil partners are taxed independently on their capital gains, with separate annual exemptions, and losses of one spouse/civil partner may not be netted off against gains of the other. Assets may, however, be transferred from one spouse/civil partner to the other on a no-gain/no-loss basis (see **Example L1**). Certain other disposals may also be made on a no-loss/no-gain basis.

*Indexation allowance*

(4) No allowance was made for the effects of inflation until 1982, when an indexation allowance was introduced for individuals, trustees and companies to reduce the gain that would otherwise arise.

The position since April 2008 is that indexation allowance is *only* available for companies. Although historic indexation allowance may still be incorporated within the base cost of assets held by individuals if they were transferred from a spouse/civil partner prior to 6 April 2008 (see **Example L1**).

Indexation allowance is calculated in relation to disposals by companies by applying to each item of expenditure the increase in the retail prices index between the month when the expenditure was incurred, or March 1982 if later, and the month of disposal of the asset.

The formula used for this calculation is:

$$\frac{RD - RI}{RI}$$

RD is the index for the month of disposal and RI is the index for the month in which the expenditure was incurred (or March 1982 if later). If the index for the month of disposal is less than that for the month the expenditure was incurred, the indexed rise on that item of expenditure is nil. The index increase is expressed as a decimal and rounded (up or down) to three decimal places (TCGA 1992 s 54).

Where a call option is exercised and settled in cash, rather than by delivery of the asset, the grantor of the option is treated as having disposal proceeds equal to the price paid by the grantee for the option, less the cash payment made by the grantor. The grantee is treated as having disposal proceeds equal to the cash received on exercise of the option less the cost of the option (the indexed cost where the grantee is a company) (TCGA 1992 s 144A).

In *Garner v Pounds Shipowners & Shipbreakers Ltd* [2000] STC 420 a company received some £400,000 for the grant of an option over land it owned, and applied £90,000 in removing a restrictive covenant over the land. Although the prospective purchaser had requested this, the option was not exercised, and the £400,000 was assessed as a gain without deducting the £90,000 of costs. The House of Lords held that this was correct: the £90,000 was a cost of improving the land which was still owned, and was neither an allowable cost nor a deduction from proceeds in the computation of the gain on the option. The obligation to obtain the release of the covenants was 'not a prerequisite of the option being exercised' and so the expenditure was not wholly and exclusively incurred by the company in providing the option.

(10) In relation to shares, the above provisions are modified to bring options within the rules for matching disposals with acquisitions. For companies, options of the same series are pooled if an acquisition is not matched with a disposal on the same day or within the next nine days, and indexation allowance will then be available. If an option is exercised, the shares acquired merge with any existing pool of shares of the same class in the same company, and the indexed cost of the option will form part of the pool cost.

For disposals by non-corporates, the matching rules are outlined in **Example L6** Part 1.

# Question

(1) Calculate the capital gains tax payable in the following circumstances all relating to the tax year 2016/17:

(i) Chloë is an additional-rate taxpayer with income of in excess of £200,000. She makes gains of £20,000 on selling a ring and realises no losses in the year;

(ii) Zoë, aged 90, has no income. In order to meet living expenses, in August 2016 she sells a family heirloom realising a gain of £20,000. She realises no losses in the year;

(iii) a discretionary trust (not settlor-interested) makes non property gains of £94,000 and losses of £1,200. The settlor had not made any other settlements.

(iv) Daniel is an employed plumber earning £25,000 pa. He makes a gain on selling a seaside property he inherited from his aunt five years ago of £20,000. Daniel has only used the property for occasional holidays and allowed friends to use it on a rent-free basis.

(2) On 10 April 2017, Leo (a higher rate taxpayer) disposes of an asset (not residential property) for £400,000, creating a chargeable gain, after the annual exemption, of £350,000. Assuming no change in the law, state how the tax will be paid if:

(i) the contract was dated 31 March 2017;

(ii) the contract was dated 6 April 2017;

(iii) the contract was dated 31 March 2017, and the consideration will be payable in four instalments of £100,000 each on 31 March 2017, 31 March 2018, 31 March 2019 and 31 March 2020.

(3) Beatrice sold her company on 30 September 2016 in a deal which gave her £1m in cash immediately, with a promise of 20% of the profits earned over the next four years, payable on 31 March 2021. The company had been set up in 1990 for £1. Set out the capital gains tax consequences if the following figures apply to the right to receive more proceeds as valued in 2016, and the amount of the further proceeds actually received:

| | 2016 *value* | *Received* |
|---|---|---|
| (i) | £200,000 | £900,000 |
| (ii) | £900,000 | £900,000 |
| (iii) | £900,000 | £200,000 |

Assume that Beatrice does not qualify for entrepreneurs' relief.

(4) What (in principle, without calculations) would the situation be if Beatrice was instead given £1m of shares in the purchasing company in 2016, with a promise of more shares to the value of 20% of the profits over the next four years, so she received further shares in 2021?

What would the situation be if the right to more consideration was in the form of loan stocks rather than shares? Would it make a difference if Beatrice continued to be employed by the company?

# Answer

## Rates of tax

(1) FA 2016 s 82 reduced the rates of capital gains, subject to exceptions for residential property and carried interest. Gains on the disposal of interests in residential property (not covered by reliefs) and capital carried interest are now taxed as upper rate gains. The 18% and 28% rates have been retained for gains on the disposal of these assets.

Capital gains for individuals are added to the individual's income for the 2016/17 tax year. To the extent that gains fall within the individual's basic rate band, they are taxed at 10% or 18% if upper rate. Gains above this threshold are taxed at 20% or 28% if upper rate (TCGA 1992 s 4).

Gains made by trustees and personal representatives are taxable at 20% or 28% if upper rate (TCGA 1992 s 4(3)).

In summary, the rates for upper rate gains and other gains for 2016/17 are:

| | *Upper rate gains; residential properties & carried interest* | *Other gains* |
|---|---|---|
| Gains taxed within the basic rate limit of £32,000 | 18% | 10% |
| Gains taxed above the basic rate limit, plus trusts and personal representatives | 28% | 20% |

Gains on assets qualifying for entrepreneurs' and investors' reliefs are taxed at 10% (TCGA 1992 s 169N), see Example L5.

The tax due on the gains made by (i) Chloë, (ii) Zoë, (iii) the discretionary trust and (iv) Daniel is:

| | | £ | £ |
|---|---|---|---|
| (i) | Gains | 20,000 | |
| | Less: annual exemption | (11,100) | |
| | | 8,900 | |
| | Capital gains tax @ 20% | | 1,780 |
| | | £ | |
| (ii) | Gains: | 20,000 | |
| | Less: Annual Exemption | (11,100) | |
| | | 8,900 | |
| | Capital gains tax @ 10% | | 890 |
| | | £ | |
| (iii) | Gains | 94,000 | |
| | Less: current year losses | (1,200) | |
| | Less: annual exemption | (5,550) | |
| | | 87,250 | |
| | Capital gains tax @ 20% | | 17,450 |
| (iv) | Gains | 20,000 | |
| | Less: annual exemption | (11,100) | |

| | £ | £ |
|---|---|---|
| | 8,900 | |
| Capital gains tax @ 18% | | 1,602 |

## Payment of tax, including payment by instalments

(2) Where a disposal is made under contract, the disposal is deemed to occur on the date on which the contract is agreed (or, if later, becomes unconditional) (TCGA 1992 s 28). The timing of the actual conveyance is not relevant.

The tax is paid on the various scenarios as follows:

(i) disposal on 31 March 2017 — the disposal occurs in the 2016/17 tax year. Capital gains tax is payable by 31 January 2018 (see **Example G2** for details of the payment of tax, interest and penalties under self-assessment). Capital gains tax has no effect on payments on account for the following year, which are only based on income tax liabilities;

(ii) disposal on 6 April 2017 — the disposal occurs in the 2017/18 tax year. Capital gains tax is payable by 31 January 2019. A delay of 6 days in executing the contract delays payment of the tax by 12 months;

(iii) disposal on 31 March 2017 with payment of consideration by instalment — ordinarily, the tax payable would be £350,000 @ 20% = £70,000, which would be due on 31 January 2018. However, by that date, Leo would have received only £100,000 of the proceeds. Since the instalments are payable over a four-year period, Leo may opt to pay the tax by such instalments as HMRC allow (see **explanatory note 3**) (TCGA 1992 s 280). Interest is charged only on instalments paid late. HMRC's practice is to set the instalments at 50% of the consideration received to date, although the taxpayer may be able to negotiate better terms depending on the circumstances (CG14910). Otherwise it is likely in this example that the instalments will be £50,000 due on 31 January 2018 (the normal due date) and the balance of £20,000 on 31 March 2018 when the second instalment is paid.

## Earn-outs

(3) The earn-out deal is treated as two separate disposals. The 'right to more' is valued and forms part of the proceeds for the first disposal, and this value is then the base cost for the second disposal, see explanatory note 6.

The three scenarios produce the following gains and losses:

| | *(i)* | *(ii)* | *(iii)* |
|---|---|---|---|
| | *£'000s* | *£'000s* | *£'000s* |
| 2016/17 | | | |
| Proceeds: £1m cash plus right to future profits | 1,200 | 1,900 | 1,900 |
| The initial cost is ignored as negligible, therefore the chargeable gain in 2016/17 is | 1,200 | 1,900 | 1,900 |
| | £'000s | £'000s | £'000s |
| 2020/21 | | | |
| Proceeds: cash received | 900 | 900 | 200 |
| Cost | (200) | (900) | (900) |
| Chargeable gain/(allowable loss) | 700 | Nil | (700) |
| Total chargeable | 1,900 | 1,900 | see below |

Under TCGA 1992 s 279A, Beatrice could make an election in respect of the 2020/21 disposal to treat the loss of £700,000 as realised instead in 2016/17. This would have the effect of reducing the gain of that year to £1,200,000. It would ensure that Beatrice is not prejudiced by her over-optimistic valuation of the earn-out right (on which she paid tax up-front). The election is complicated if there are other reliefs which have already been used against the gain in the earlier year. See **explanatory notes** 7 and 8.

(4) If Beatrice was given shares in 2016/17 plus a right to more shares in the future based on profits, she would be treated as receiving two different securities, unless she elected to be treated as making a full disposal in 2016/17. The transaction would be a 'share-for-share exchange' within TCGA 1992 s 135. Strictly, the base cost should be split between the actual shares received and the deemed securities, so that the cost of the 'more shares' relates to the amount allocated to the deemed securities. In this case, the cost is insignificant, so this is not important.

If the right to more was in the form of a right to qualifying corporate bonds (QCBs), it would again in theory be necessary to value that right so that the base cost could be split between the shares and the deemed securities. When the QCBs are issued in satisfaction of the deemed securities, a gain must be calculated on the basis of the value of the loan stock at that time, and the gain will be attached to the loan stock and charged at disposal. In this case, because the cost is insignificant, the 'frozen gain' on issue of the loan stocks will simply be equal to their value.

For more on share-for-share exchange and QCBs, see **Example L7**.

See **explanatory note** 9 for the implications of Beatrice continuing to be an employee.

## Explanatory Notes

*Rates of tax – individuals*

(1) Individual taxpayers pay capital gains tax at four rates. Gains are added to the individual's income for the tax year. Gains within the basic rate band are taxed at 10% or 18% (upper rate), gains above the threshold of the basic rate band are taxed at 20% or 28% (upper rate) (TCGA 1992 s 4). Gains on assets qualifying for entrepreneurs' (ER) and investors' (IR) reliefs are known as special rate gains and subject to qualifying conditions and limits taxed at 10% (see Example L5) (TCGA 1992 s 169N).

Where more than one rate of tax is payable:

- The unused basic rate band is used by special rate gains (ER & IR) in priority to any other gains. This limits or eliminates access to the lower rates of CGT where those reliefs are due. Once the special rate gains are exhausted (or if none exist in a year) the taxpayer can choose which gains use any remaining basic rate band.
- Any losses and the annual exempt amount can be offset against gains in the most beneficial manner. This allows the maximum relief to be claimed and a taxpayer would normally choose to offset such reliefs in the order:
  - Upper rate gains (residential property / carried interest) (18%, 28%).
  - Other gains (10%, 20%)
  - Special rate gains (ER and IR) (10%)

Personal allowances cannot be set against chargeable gains.

*Rates of tax etc – trustees and personal representatives*

(2) The capital gains tax rate for all trusts and for personal representatives is 20% or 28% depending on whether an upper rate asset (residential property or carried interest) (TCGA 1992 s 4(3)). The taxation of trusts and estates is dealt with in detail in the companion to this book, **Tolley's Taxwise II 2016/17**.

*Payment by instalments*

(3) Where the consideration, or part of the consideration, is payable over a period exceeding 18 months from the date of disposal then the taxpayer can opt to pay the capital gains tax by such instalments as HMRC allows over a period not exceeding eight years and ending not later than the time of the last instalment (TCGA 1992 s 280). No specific provision is made for interest on overdue tax, so interest would be payable on any instalment that was paid late. HMRC's practice is illustrated in **part** (2)(**iii**) above.

Capital gains tax may also be paid by instalments on certain gifts where gains on the gifts cannot be deferred under the hold-over relief provisions. The gifts concerned are gifts of land, or a controlling holding of shares or securities in a company, or minority holdings of shares or securities in a company that is not quoted on a recognised stock exchange. Companies whose shares are traded on the Alternative Investment Market (AIM) are treated as unquoted. Tax may be paid by 10 annual instalments. Interest is, however, charged on the full amount outstanding, the interest being added to each instalment (TCGA 1992 s 281).

(4) For a further illustration of the instalment option and for the detailed provisions of hold-over relief, see **Example L9**.

(5) Where consideration is due after the time of disposal, provision is made for a gain to be adjusted if part of the consideration becomes irrecoverable (TCGA 1992 s 48). It was held by the Court of Appeal in *Goodbrand v Loffland and Bros North Sea Inc* [1998] STC 930 that where the consideration was in foreign currency (in this case US dollars) payable by instalments over several years, what is now TCGA 1992 s 48 did not cover a loss arising as a result of the sterling equivalent of the consideration being much lower than expected because of exchange rate fluctuations.

In effect, the company made a chargeable gain based on the sterling equivalent of the contract price, as calculated on the date of the contract; it then made a separate loss on realisation of the contract debt (an exempt asset, not being a 'debt on a security') in later years.

*Earn-outs*

(6) An 'earn-out' is the usual expression used to describe the type of deal in **part** (3) above, which involves 'contingent variable' consideration. This is dealt with in accordance with the decision in the case *Marren v Ingles* [1980] STC 500:

- the initial disposal is treated as a sale for consideration in two parts – the 'right to more' has to be valued as at the date of the contract (ie building in estimates of the likelihood of receiving something, the likely amounts, and the timing);
- the receipt of further consideration is a further disposal for capital gains tax – the base cost of the 'right to more' is the value brought into account on the first disposal, and the 'more' is the proceeds.

This can have unfortunate results. The most basic problem is the difficulty of valuing the contingent right, which is by its nature speculative. Strictly, the value of the earn-out right does not constitute 'consideration receivable by instalments', so there is not a clear right to payment of tax by instalments, but this may be negotiated with the HMRC officer, as the situation is very similar to the receipt of fixed instalments and may cause the same hardship. Nevertheless, if a high value is placed on the earn-out right, it may create a cash-flow difficulty for the vendor.

If an over-optimistic value is placed on the 'right to more', it is possible to pay extra capital gains tax on the first disposal and then incur a loss on the second. Where the loss arose before 10 April 2003 this could not be offset against the gain in the earlier year. Instead, under general principles, the loss could only be utilised against current year gains or carried forward to set against future gains.

(7) Finance Act 2003 introduced a significant relief to reduce the disadvantage of overvaluing the earn-out right. Where the 'second disposal' takes place on or after 10 April 2003, it is possible to elect for a loss on the second disposal to be treated as if it had been realised in the same year as the first disposal, so allowing offset against the gain on that first disposal. The rules, in TCGA 1992 ss 279A-279D, are very complicated, because they determine the interaction between this loss and gains, other losses of the year of the first disposal, losses brought forward and relieved in that year, and all the other details of capital gains tax. The essence of the relief is that the loss on the second disposal will reduce the gain on the first disposal, so that

it will be charged to tax as if exactly the right value (without any discounting for time) was placed on the earn-out right at the time of the first disposal. It should be noted that this special loss carry-back relief is only available to individuals and trustee vendors (not companies).

(8) Where the 'right to more' is only a right to securities (of a variable amount) in the purchaser, the first and second disposals are treated as 'share-for-share exchanges' (provided the normal rules in TCGA 1992 s 135 are met). It is recommended that advance clearance is obtained on this point. The 'right to more' is treated as if it were a security itself. This is not available if there is any possibility that the further consideration could be taken in cash.

The first disposal still requires a valuation of the 'right to more', because the original cost has to be split between the immediate consideration (whether shares or cash) and the deemed security. The portion of the cost which is allocated to the deemed security is then carried forward and transferred to the shares which are issued in satisfaction of the earn-out right.

Prior to 10 April 2003 it was necessary to elect for 'security treatment'. This tax treatment is now automatic unless the vendor elects for it not to apply under TCGA 1992 s 138A. It is most likely to be beneficial.

If the vendor continues to work for the company, entrepreneurs' relief might continue to be made available (see **Example L5** for further details).

If the earn-out right is eventually exchanged for qualifying corporate bonds (QCBs), a charge to capital gains tax is calculated at that point and attached to the bonds (as described in **Example L7 explanatory note** 3). Even if the eventual consideration will be exempt QCBs, the deemed security is not a QCB and is regarded as chargeable to capital gains tax.

*Employment-related securities*

(9) The complex employment-related securities regime in ITEPA 2003 Part 7 created some uncertainties in relation to the tax treatment of earn-outs satisfied by loan notes and/or shares in the acquirer. Where the right is obtained by reason of employment or prospective employment, the receipt of the earn-out loan notes or shares would be subject to an income tax charge and, where appropriate, national insurance contributions.

HMRC has confirmed in ERSM110920 that where an earn-out fully represents consideration for sale of the target company's shares (as it will normally do) the income tax charges above will not apply. However, where all or part of an earn-out relates to value provided to an employee as a reward for services over a performance period, this remuneration element would constitute taxable earnings.

HMRC has issued guidance in ERSM110940 on the key factors for determining whether an earn-out is further sale consideration rather than remuneration. Where the earn-out is a mixture it is necessary to make a just and reasonable apportionment.

*Loss on unquoted shares in trading company*

(10) Where an individual makes a loss on the disposal of shares he may be able to claim income tax relief under ITA 2007 s 131 instead of relief against capital gains. This income tax relief is available if the loss is made on shares:

- on which enterprise investment scheme (EIS) income tax relief has been claimed (see **Example N7**); or
- which were subscribed for in money or money's worth in an unquoted qualifying trading company (see below).

The relief does not apply to shares acquired some other way, for example by transfer from another shareholder, unless the transferor subscribed for the shares and the transfer is a lifetime transfer to his or her spouse/civil partner (ITA 2007 s 135).

As it it possible to obtain income tax relief on the loss arising on the sale of shares which did not qualify for EIS income tax relief, it is possible (provided the conditions below are met) to qualify for ITA 2007 s 131 relief even if the individual is connected with the company, or where the share subscription exceeded the EIS subscription limit (see **Example N7**).

Relief may be claimed against the net total income of the tax year in which the disposal is made or the previous year (or both, if the loss is large enough). Relief for the capital loss takes priority over a claim under ITA 2007 ss 64 or 72 in respect of an income loss (ITA 2007 s 133). The tax saving flowing from carrying back the loss against an earlier year's income is computed by reference to the tax position of the earlier year, but the claim is given effect in the tax year of loss (see **Example G3**).

The time limit for the claim is one year from 31 January following the tax year of loss (ITA 2007 s 132).

The rules for identifying which shares have been disposed of depend on the shares which have been sold. Usually the normal share matching rules apply (see **Example L9**). However, if the shareholding includes EIS shares, the matching rules are the same as those that apply under the EIS rules (ITA 2007 s 148 as read with ITA 2007 s 246). EIS is covered in detail in **Example N7**.

A disposal does not qualify for relief under these provisions unless it is (ITA 2007 s 131(3)):

(a) at arm's length for full consideration;

(b) a distribution in a winding up (or when the disposal occurs on the dissolution of a company without a distribution being made);

(c) a disposal under TCGA 1992 s 24(1) where an assets has been lost or destroyed; or

(d) a deemed disposal under TCGA 1992 s 24(2) where the shares have become of negligible value.

In relation to (d), in cases where the claim is considered not contentious, HMRC may accept a loss claim of less than £100,000 without referring the case to Shares Valuation specialists if the company is UK registered, is not quoted and is either in liquidation or has ceased trading (see CG13131).

# Question

(a) Explain how relief is given for capital losses in respect of UK-domiciled individuals.

(b) Explain how the loss relief is used in the following situations:

(i) in 2016/17, Abigail has realised a £15,000 loss and a gain of £20,000;

(ii) Brenda has £15,000 unused losses brought forward from an earlier year. In 2016/17, she makes a disposal of an asset, realising a gain of £20,000.

(c) Show the treatment of the following gains and losses for a taxpayer who had no losses brought forward at 6 April 2014:

| | *Gains* | *Losses* | *Annual exemption* |
|---|---|---|---|
| | £ | £ | £ |
| 2014/15 | 3,000 | 6,000 | 11,000 |
| 2015/16 | 7,200 | 1,000 | 11,100 |
| 2016/17 | 20,000 | 1,000 | 11,100 |

(d) What would the position in 2016/17 have been if the losses in 2014/15 had been £20,000?

# Answer

## (a) Relief for capital losses – UK-domiciled individuals

In general, allowable losses are calculated in precisely the same way as chargeable gains (TCGA 1992 s 16(1)). So, for example, supposing an individual bought a second home for £500,000 (plus associated costs of £30,000) in year 1 and sold it in year 2 realising sale proceeds of £500,000 (but incurring sale costs of £10,000), the individual would have an allowable loss of £40,000. As outlined below there are certain exceptions to this rule.

### Exception to the basic rule

Loss relief is restricted in respect of chattels sold for less than £6,000 but costing more than that. In such cases, the loss is calculated as if the disposal proceeds were £6,000 (so that the loss is limited to the amount by which the acquisition costs exceed £6,000) (TCGA 1992 s 262(3)).

### How loss relief is given

Losses are relieved by deducting them from any gains arising in the same tax year (TCGA 1992 s 2(2)(a)).

For the purposes of entrepreneurs' relief, gains and losses with respect to the qualifying disposal must be aggregated. As such, losses on disposal of assets qualifying for entrepreneurs' relief are first offset against gains from the disposal of the business. Excess and other losses are offset against other gains in the same year. For a discussion of entrepreneurs' and investors' reliefs, see **Example L5**.

Where the individual has capital gains which are taxed at different rates, the losses can be set off against gains in the most tax efficient way (TCGA 1992 s 4B). This means that the losses can be allocated against gains taxable at the highest rates of tax first.

If there are net gains for the year, then no further calculations are made even if the gains (without the benefit of the loss relief) fall within the annual exemption.

If, however, the total losses exceed the total gains, then the excess is carried forward to be available for set off against gains in future years. These losses are set off against gains until such time as the losses are fully utilised. However, losses brought forward from earlier tax years are utilised only so far as is necessary to reduce a person's gains to the annual exempt amount (TCGA 1992 s 2(2)(b)). The individual does not have a choice on whether to use the brought forward losses as they must be used against future gains at the first opportunity (whilst preserving the annual exempt amount) (TCGA 1992 s 3(5A)). However, as above, the brought forward losses can be set against gains taxable at higher rates of tax in preference to gains taxable at lower rates (TCGA 1992 s 4B).

Losses are generally not carried back. However, unrelieved losses arising in the year of a taxpayer's death may be carried back up to three years (TCGA 1992 s 62(2)), see **Example L1**. In addition, where the value of an earn-out must be ascertained under the *Marren v Ingles* [1980] STC 500 principle, losses on the actual disposal of the earn-out can now be related back to the year of the original disposal (TCGA 1992 ss 279A–279D), see **Example L3**, explanatory notes 6-8.

### Restriction on use of losses

In relation to disposals which took place on or after 6 December 2006, there is an anti-avoidance rule which prevents taxpayers from realising losses artificially and claiming relief thereon (TCGA 1992 s 16A).

The rule means that a loss ceases to be an 'allowable loss' (and is therefore unavailable to be set off against capital gains) if it arises as a result of any arrangement for which the main purpose or one of the main purposes is to secure a tax advantage (widely defined) (CG15835).

The difficulty with these rules is that they are broadly drafted and will catch almost every loss ever realised. HMRC's guidance appears in the Capital Gains Manual.

## (b) Allocation of loss relief

### (i) Abigail

Abigail must use her entire loss even though this will take her net gains to £5,000 (ie below the annual exemption) (TCGA 1992 s 2(2)(a)).

### (ii) Brenda

Brenda must reduce the gain by £8,900 so as to match the net figure to her annual exemption of £11,100 (TCGA 1992 s 2(2)(b)). Brenda will have no capital gains tax to pay for the year and her losses carried forward will be reduced to £6,100.

## (c) Treatment of losses brought forward

The chargeable gains for the three tax years is as follows:

| | | |
|---|---|---|
| *2014/15* | Net losses for the year carried forward (£3,000 - £6,000) | (£3,000) |
| *2015/16* | Net gains for the year of £6,200 are covered by the annual exemption, leaving losses carried forward as before | (£3,000) |
| | | £ |
| *2016/17* | Gains (£20,000 – £1,000) | 19,000 |
| | *Less*: losses brought forward | (3,000) |
| | | 16,000 |
| | *Less*: annual exempt amount | (11,100) |
| | Chargeable gains | 4,900 |

## (d) Losses brought forward limited to annual exemption

If losses in 2014/15 had been £20,000, ie £14,000 higher:

| | | |
|---|---|---|
| *2014/15* | Net losses for the year carried forward (£3,000 - £20,000) | (£17,000) |
| *2015/16* | Net gains for the year of £6,200 are covered by the annual exemption, leaving losses carried forward as before | (£17,000) |
| | | £ |
| *2016/17* | Gains (£20,000 – £1,000) | 19,000 |
| | *Less*: losses brought forward | (7,900) |
| | | 11,100 |
| | *Less*: annual exemption | (11,100) |
| | Chargeable gains | Nil |
| | | |
| | Losses available to carry forward | £ |
| | Brought forward | 17,000 |
| | Used in 2016/17 | (7,900) |
| | Carried forward to future years | 9,100 |

# Question

(a) Brown makes a gain of £1,700,000 on the sale of 100% of the shares in an unquoted trading company on 15 July 2016. He has no other gains or losses in the year.

Calculate the capital gains tax due.

(b) Cooper is a farmer with 100 acres of land. If she sells 10 acres, could she qualify for entrepreneurs' relief?

(c) Kennedy is a beneficiary of the Sunshine Trust. The trustees own a factory which has been occupied and used for the purposes of Kennedy's manufacturing business. Kennedy is considering retirement and the sale of the business. Advise the trustees on the extent to which they might qualify for entrepreneurs' relief on the disposal of the factory and, if they might qualify, explain which timing conditions need to be satisfied.

(d)

(i) Eagle, a higher rate taxpayer, sold the shares of her personal company on 1 June 2016 realising a gain of £250,000. The company used premises which Eagle owned personally which were sold at the same time at a gain of £500,000. Is Eagle entitled to entrepreneurs' relief on the disposal of the premises?

(ii) Assume the same facts as (i) but, in addition, Eagle receives an earn-out on the sale of the shares. This is to be settled in cash. The earn-out right is valued at £100,000 on 1 June 2016. Eagle receives £250,000 under the earn-out on 25 March 2018. Assume the premises fully qualify for entrepreneurs' relief.

What is the capital gains tax payable in 2016/17 and 2017/18. Assume the annual exemption in 2017/18 is £11,100.

(e) Identify which of the following disposals qualify for entrepreneurs' relief:

(i) Mr Osborne has held 4% of the ordinary share capital of a trading company for two years. He had originally acquired 10% of the shareholding but transferred 6% to his wife to reduce exposure to higher rate tax. He retires from the business and sells his shares realising a capital gain of £400,000. Osborne's wife sells the shares at the same time realising a gain of £600,000;

(ii) Cameron has held 6% of the ordinary share capital of a trading company for two years. He retires from the business and sells his shares realising a capital gain of £400,000. Six months before the disposal, his voting rights increased from 4% to 6%;

(iii) Cable owns a manufacturing business. It operates two factories. On 19 September 2016, Cable closes down and sells one factory (realising a gain of £250,000) and transfers production to the other site. However, on 25 January 2017, Cable receives an offer for the business which he accepts, realising a gain of £500,000, and retires;

(iv) Gauke was granted an EMI option on 1 May 2015 in respect of 2% of the shares in Thatcher Limited, a trading company. On 31 October 2016 the entire share capital of Thatcher Limited is sold with Gauke exercising his option the previous day. Gauke's sale proceeds are £50,000. The market value of his shares at grant (both restricted and unrestricted) was £10,000. The exercise price was also £10,000.

(f) Briefly describe investors' relief including:

(i) Qualifying shares,

(ii) Potentially qualifying shares,

(iii) Excluded shares,

(iv) Who does the relief apply to?

(v) The matching rules,

(vi) Disqualification,

(vii) Relevant employee,

(viii) Claims for relief.

# Answer

## (a) Brown – calculating the relief

The capital gains tax due on the sale of unquoted shares in a trading company in 2016/17 is:

| | £ |
|---|---|
| Capital gain | 1,700,000 |
| Less: annual exemption | (11,100) |
| | 1,688,900 |
| Capital gains tax at 10% | £168,899 |

Capital gains tax is payable at 10% as the disposal qualifies for entrepreneurs' relief (TCGA 1992 s 169I(2)(c)). The tax is due by 31 January 2018.

## (b) Cooper – disposal of part of farm

Cooper will not generally be entitled to entrepreneurs' relief on the disposal of a number of fields. The key test will be whether or not she has disposed of a part of her business and the case law suggests that selling a number of fields represents merely a disposal of some assets used in the business (TCGA 1992 s 169I(2)(a)). See **explanatory note 13**.

A different result may emerge if it can be shown that the fields disposed of represented an identifiable part of the business. For example, were those fields dedicated to crops and sold so that Cooper could focus on, say, cattle production?

## (c) Kennedy – trust business assets disposal

Trustees' disposals of assets might qualify for entrepreneurs' relief. The first hurdle is to ensure that Kennedy is a qualifying beneficiary under TCGA 1992 s 169J(3).

This requires Kennedy to have an interest in possession in the trust (or the part of the trust which includes the factory) and not be merely a member of the class of discretionary beneficiaries under TCGA 1992 s 169J(3).

Secondly, that interest in possession must not be a fixed interest. However, it can be a defeasible interest.

If that condition is satisfied, the trustees must take care to satisfy the timing requirements.

First Kennedy must have carried on the business throughout a full year ending no more than three years before the date on which the factory is to be sold (TCGA 1992 s 169J(5)(a)).

Secondly, Kennedy must cease to carry on the business during or at the end of that three-year period (TCGA 1992 s 169J(5)(b)).'

## (d) Eagle – associated disposal

### (i) *Sale of premises on 1 June 2016*

Under TCGA 1992 s 169K, there are three conditions to establish entitlement to entrepreneurs' relief in respect of associated disposals:

- the principal disposal must be a material disposal of business assets – being shares (or securities) in the individual's personal company or an interest in a partnership;

- the disposal must be part of the individual's withdrawal from participation in the business carried on by the company or partnership;
- the asset on which the relief is claimed must have been used in the business throughout the year ending with the earlier of the material disposal or the cessation of the business.

However, it is also necessary to consider the various ways in which the relief can be restricted under TCGA 1992 s 169P (see **explanatory note 20**).

### First condition – material disposal of business assets

Eagle sold the shares in her personal company on 1 June 2016. Given that the company is a personal trading company, this disposal would be a 'material disposal' of business assets if it qualified as a personal trading company throughout the year from 2 June 2015 to 1 June 2016 (TCGA 1992 s 169I(6)).

Alternatively, the disposal of shares would be a material disposal of business assets if the company so qualified throughout a year ending on any date between 2 June 2013 and 1 June 2016 (TCGA 1992 s 169I(7)).

Finance Act 2015 introduced a further condition, that in order to benefit from the associated disposal rules, the material disposal must be of a minimum of 5% of the shares in the company, or of at least 5% of the partnership assets if the material disposal is related to a partnership. This change takes effect for disposal on or after 18 March 2015 (FA 2015 s 41, amending TCGA 1992 s 169K). FA 2016 s 83 relaxed the 2015 changes in a number of commercial situations backdated to 18 March 2015. This includes the minimum size (5%) may not apply if the claimant is disposing of all their interest in the partnership or shareholding.

The meaning of 'personal company' is discussed in **explanatory note 22.**

### Second condition – withdrawal of participation

Secondly, the share disposal must have been part of Eagle's withdrawal of participation in the company's business. Whilst the legislation appears to be restrictive, the practice of HMRC is to interpret this condition very broadly (see CG63995).

### Third condition – use of the asset

It is stated in the question that the premises were used for the company's trade. In order for the sale of the premises to qualify for entrepreneurs' relief as an associated disposal, the company must have so used the premises throughout the year ending with the disposal of the shares (or, if the business ceased before that date, the year ending with the cessation).

If the property has not been in business use throughout the entire period of ownership, then the relief is available but is restricted to the period used in the business, see explanatory note 20 (TCGA 1992 s 169P).

(ii) *2016/17*

The capital gains tax due is:

| | |
|---|---|
| Gains: | £ |
| Shares | 250,000 |
| Earn-out right | 100,000 |
| Premises | 500,000 |
| | 850,000 |
| Less: annual exemption | (11,100) |
| | 838,900 |

| | |
|---|---|
| Capital gains tax at 10% | £83,890 |

*2017/18*

The capital gains tax due is:

| | £ |
|---|---|
| Earn-out proceeds | 250,000 |
| Less: base cost | (100,000) |
| | 150,000 |
| Less: annual exemption | (11,100) |
| | 138,900 |
| Capital gains tax at 20% | £27,780 |

Eagle does not meet the personal company shareholder requirement after 1 June 2016 and so cannot meet the requirements of entrepreneurs' relief. In calculating the capital gains tax due it is assumed that Eagle is a higher rate or additional rate taxpayer in both tax years.

(e)

## (i) *Mr Osborne – 4% shareholding; Mrs Osborne – 6% shareholding*

As Mr Osborne holds only 4% of the ordinary share capital, it is not his personal company and therefore entrepreneurs' relief is not available (TCGA 1992 s 169I(6)(a)).

Mrs Osborne's ownership would qualify for relief if (TCGA 1992 s 169I(6)):

- she acquired the shares more than a year before the date of disposal; and
- she is for that year an employee or officer (full or part-time).

The meaning of 'personal company' is discussed in **explanatory note 22.**

## (ii) *Cameron – 6% shareholding*

The company was not Cameron's personal company for the year before the disposal because for some of that year he held less than 5% of the voting rights (TCGA 1992 s 169I(6)(a)).

The meaning of 'personal company' is discussed in **explanatory note 22.**

## (iii) *Cable – two factories*

The disposal of the first factory does not on its own qualify for entrepreneurs' relief as it appears, based on the facts in the question, that there has been not been a disposal of the whole or part of the business (TCGA 1992 s 169I(2)(a). It is important to make enquiries to establish whether or not the factory can be considered to be a separate distinct part of the business. See CG64020, CG64021, CG64030 and CG64035 for HMRC's view.

It is important to note that it is not possible for the sale of the factory to be considered an 'associated disposal' as only those disposing of an interest in a partnership or shares in their personal company can qualify. The conditions in TCGA 1992 s 169K preclude claims from sole traders. This is because sole traders who make a material disposal of the whole or part of their business can obtain entrepreneurs' relief on later disposals of business assets retained under TCGA 1992 s 169I(4) (ie where the business has ceased and business assets are sold within three years of cessation).

### (iv) *Gauke – EMI option*

For disposals which take place on or after 6 April 2013, there is an exception to the general rule under TCGA 1992 s 169I(6) which requires a trading company to be the personal company of the individual making the disposal for it to qualify for entrepreneurs' relief.

Where an employee has EMI share option rights in a trading company, the 12 month qualifying period is measured from the date of grant of the option and not the exercise date, so long as the EMI shares were acquired on or after 6 April 2013 (TCGA 1992 s 169I(7A)-(7E)). It is not necessary for the option holder to have an interest of at least 5% of the ordinary shares and votes. Therefore, entrepreneurs' relief is available on the disposal by Gauke.

Note that where the EMI shares were acquired during the 2012/13 tax year transitional rules apply under FA 2013 Sch 24 para 6 (see CG64052).

For the meaning of 'trading company' for the purposes of entrepreneurs' relief, see **explanatory note 12.**

## (f) Investors' relief (IR)

Although introduced as an extension of entrepreneurs' relief (ER), investors' relief is a separate relief. It applies a 10% CGT rate to qualifying gains up to a separate lifetime limit of £10 million. As for ER, qualifying gains are taxed at 10% regardless of an individual's marginal rate of tax. There is no minimum percentage shareholding (ER = 5%) but shares have to be subscribed for and held for three years (ER = one year). All references are to TCGA 1992 unless otherwise stated.

### (i) *(i) Qualifying shares*

The conditions for qualifying shares are set out in a list in section 169VB (2) (a) to (h). All conditions must be met. Broadly, subject to disqualification a qualifying share is:

(a) Subscribed for by the investor,

(b) Held continuously by the investor for the relevant time,

(c) Issued after 17 March 2016,

(d) Not quoted at the time of subscription,

(e) An ordinary share (at issue and the relevant time),

(f) In a trading company or the holding company of a trading group (throughout shareholding period),

(g) One where the investor (or person connected to them) is not a relevant employee at any time in the relevant period,

(h) Held for at least three years.

With regard to (h), shares issued between 17 March 2016 and 5 April 2016 have to be held until 6 April 2019 to qualify, i.e. three years and a few extra days.

### (ii) *Potentially qualifying shares*

A potentially qualifying share meets all the tests (a) to (g) above but doesn't meet (h) as it hasn't yet been held for the necessary three year holding period. Potentially qualifying shares become qualifying shares as soon as the three years are reached (provided on or after 6 April 2019).

### (iii) *Excluded shares*

Excluded shares are defined as shares that are not qualifying shares or potentially qualifying shares. They are shares that can never qualify for relief. For example, shares purchased before 17 March 2016.

Shares that have been disqualified are also treated as excluded shares. The disqualification rules (Schedule 7ZB) override the definitions at (i) & (ii) above.

### (iv) *Who does the relief apply to?*

The relief applies to individuals who subscribe for shares alone or jointly (with another individual) and trustees.

In the case of trusts, further conditions apply which are set out in section 169VH. The amount of investors' relief available is attributed to and deducted from a qualifying beneficiary's own individual lifetime limit. Where there is more than one eligible beneficiary section 169VI can, in applicable circumstances, reduce the investors' relief available.

### (v) *The matching rules*

Where only some of the shares in the holding are qualifying shares, only that portion will qualify when IR is claimed (s 169VD).

> For example, Jack owned 5,000 qualifying shares and 10,000 excluded shares. On disposal of all shares only 5,000 / 15,000 (a third) of the gain will qualify for IR.

Where a part disposal occurs and IR is claimed, the qualifying shares are deemed to be sold first (s 169VD (4)).

> So if Jack only sold 7,500 shares, it would be made up of 5,000 qualifying shares and 2,500 excluded shares. Therefore, the fraction of the gain qualifying for IR becomes 5,000/7,500 (two thirds). Jack's remaining 7,500 shares would all be excluded shares.

If a claim for IR is not made, excluded shares are deemed to be sold first (s 169VG).

> Continuing the above example, Jack's gain on selling 7,500 shares is £11,000 and he makes no other capital gains during the year. He could therefore choose not to claim IR, use his annual exemption to cover the gain and his shareholding carried forward would consist of 5,000 qualifying shares and 2,500 exempt shares (hence saving the IR for a later disposal).

Where a disposal occurs at a time the holding includes potentially qualifying shares the objective of the legislation is to preserve the maximum future investors' relief. The matching rules are divided into two:

Where a claim is made to IR (s 169VF) – the disposal is matched:

(1) Qualifying shares,

(2) Excluded shares,

(3) Potentially qualifying shares – LIFO basis (Last In First Out or shares acquired later are deemed to be sold first).

> For example, Chloe has 1,000 qualifying shares, 2,000 excluded shares and 3,000 potentially qualifying shares. She sells 3,500 shares and claims IR. The gain qualifying for IR is 1,000/3,500. The shares sold are the 1,000 qualifying shares, 2,000 excluded shares and 500 of the potentially qualifying shares. Therefore the shares carried forward to a future disposal are the remaining 2,500 potentially qualifying shares. If these shares are held for the required three years they may become qualifying shares in the future.

Where a claim is not made for IR (s 169VG) – the disposal is matched:

(1) Excluded shares,

(2) Potentially qualifying shares – LIFO basis,

(3) Qualifying shares.

Continuing with Chloe above, assume she didn't claim IR (gain below annual exemption or loss made during the year). The shares sold become the 2,000 excluded shares and 1,500 of the potentially qualifying shares. The shares carried forward are then the 1,000 qualifying shares plus 1,500 potentially qualifying shares. The 1,000 shares already qualify and the 1,500 could become qualifying if held for the required three years.

### (vi) *Disqualification*

Briefly, if an investor receives value of £1,000 (cumulative limit, ignored if "arrangements" exist) at any time starting one year before and usually (shares issued before 5.4.16 have a few extra days) ending three years after the shares are issued except defined qualifying payments (Sch 7ZB (4) the shares are disqualified. Where shares are disqualified they become excluded shares. (Schedule 7ZB).

### (vii) *Relevant employee*

Generally, a person who at any time (in relevant period) is (or is connected to) an officer or employee of the issuing company (or connected company) is a relevant employee. This means they are unable to qualify for IR. However, this relief is aimed at professional investors such as business angels. Such individuals often invest funds PLUS provide expertise to promote the business's success. Section 169 VW therefore includes exclusions from being a relevant employee where a person becomes:

- An unremunerated director of the company or connected company,
- An employee of the company at least 180 days after the share issue, provided (at the time of share issue) there was no reasonable prospect the person would become an employee.

An unremunerated director must never have been involved with the issuing company before their investment and they must not receive disqualifying payments. Disqualifying payments are anything not specifically allowed at section 169VX (2) (a) to (f). The list (a) to (f) sets out six allowable payments which include reimbursement of traveling expenses (wholly, exclusively and necessarily) and dividends which do not exceed the normal return.

### (viii) *Claims for relief*

Investors' relief must be claimed. In the case of:

- An individual - by that individual personally.
- A joint holding – either or both of the individuals can choose to claim personally.
- A trust – jointly by the trustees and eligible beneficiary (or more than one, all those eligible beneficiaries).

The time limit is the first anniversary of the 31 January following the tax year in which the disposal is made (s 169VM).

# Explanatory Notes

*Introduction*

(1) Entrepreneurs' relief was introduced on 6 April 2008 and is largely based on the old rules for retirement relief. Indeed, some retirement relief cases are again relevant.

*The key elements of entrepreneurs' relief*

(2) Where entrepreneurs' relief is validly claimed, a 10% tax rate applies to qualifying gains which arise on or after 23 June 2010 (TCGA 1992 s 169N(3)). Prior to that date the gain was reduced by 4/9ths and subject to capital gains tax at 18%.

(3) Entrepreneurs' relief is available on up to £10m of gains (TCGA 1992 s 169N(4)). That amount operates as a lifetime limit. Previous limits are:

- £5m 23 June 2010 to 5 April 2011.
- £2m 6 April 2010 to 22 June 2010.
- £1m 6 April 2008 to 5 April 2010.

(4) Claims for relief must be made by the second 31 January following the end of the tax year in which the qualifying disposal was made (TCGA 1992 s 169M(3)). Therefore, for a disposal which occurs in 2016/17, the claim for entrepreneurs' relief must be made by 31 January 2019.

*Qualifying for entrepreneurs' relief*

(5) There are, broadly, three types of disposal qualifying for entrepreneurs' relief:

(a) 'material disposals of business assets' (TCGA 1992 s 169I);

(b) disposals of 'trust business assets' (TCGA 1992 s 169J);

(c) associated disposals (TCGA 1992 s 169K).

*Material disposals of business assets*

(6) A material disposal of business assets is (TCGA 1992 s 169I(1)):

- a disposal by an individual;
- of business assets (as defined);
- which is material (as defined).

(7) A disposal is of business assets if it is a disposal of (TCGA 1992 s 169I(2)):

- the whole or part of a business;
- an asset or assets in use for the purposes of the business at the time at which the business ceases to be carried on;
- an interest or interests in such assets;
- one or more assets consisting of shares in or securities of a company; or
- interests in such shares or securities.

(8) Where the disposal is of the whole or part of the business, the disposal is material if the business had been owned throughout the year ending with the date of the disposal (TCGA 1992 s 169I(3)). Entrepreneurs' relief is only given in respect of relevant business assets, ie assets used in the business of the individual or partnership (not assets held as investments) (TCGA 1992 s 169L).

(9) Where the disposal is of assets (or interests in such), the disposal is material if (TCGA 1992 s 169I(4)):

(a) the business had been owned throughout the year ending with the date on which the business ceased; and

(b) the disposal takes place within three years of that cessation.

Again, entrepreneurs' relief is only given in respect of relevant business assets, ie assets used in the business of the individual or partnership (not assets held as investments) (TCGA 1992 s 169L). However, with effect for disposals on or after 3 December 2014, relief is no longer available on the disposal of goodwill or other customer related assets to a close company which is related to the disposer. This affects goodwill on incorporation, on which the disposer faces either a full CGT charge or seeking relief under TCGA 1992 ss 162 or 165. (These reliefs are covered in **Examples L9** and **N3**). A partner who retires at the point that the firm is sold to a close company will retain the benefit of entrepreneurs' relief on his share of the gain on disposal of goodwill.(FA 2015 s 42, introducing new TCGA 1992 s 169LA.)

(10) Where the disposal is of shares or securities (or interests in such), the disposal is material if conditions (a) or (b) are met (TCGA 1992 s 169I(6), (7)):

(a) throughout the year ending with the disposal:

– the company is the individual's personal company (see **explanatory note 22**);

– the company is a trading company or the holding company of a trading group; (see **explanatory note 12**) and

– the individual is an officer or employee of the company (or, if the company is a member of a trading group, of one or more companies within the group).

(b) the disposal occurs within three years of the following two dates and the three conditions in (a) above are met throughout the year ending with the date on which either:

- the company ceases to be a trading company without continuing to be or becoming a member of a trading group; or

- the company ceases to be a member of a trading group without continuing to be or becoming a trading company.

(11) For disposals on or after 6 April 2013, where the shares sold are relevant EMI shares then it is possible to qualify for entrepreneurs' relief even though the interest is less than 5% and the shares have been held for less than 12 months. Qualification is possible under either TCGA 1992 s 169I(7A) or TCGA 1992 s 169I(7B). Neither of these requires that the issuing company be the individual's personal company. Instead it is necessary for the date of grant of the option in respect of the relevant EMI shares to have been more than 12 months prior to the date of disposal and that the issuing company is a trading company or the holding company of a trading group. The individual must have also been an officer or employee of the company for the 12 months prior to the disposal.

'Relevant EMI shares' are shares acquired by the individual on or after 6 April 2013 within 10 years of grant under a qualifying EMI scheme. If there has been a 'disqualifying event' prior to the exercise of the shares and the exercise does not occur within 90 days of that event, the EMI shares are not relevant for the purposes of this rule (TCGA 1992 s 169I(7C)-(7E)).

Care needs to be taken where there has been a share reorganisation. For full commentary see Simon's Taxes C3.1302.

Note that where the EMI shares were acquired during the 2012/13 tax year transitional rules apply for entreprenuers' relief under FA 2013 Sch 24 para 6 (see CG64052).

(12) The meaning of 'trading company' for the purposes of entrepreneurs' relief is taken from TCGA 1992 s 165A (TCGA 1992 s 169S(5)). It means a company carrying on trading activities whose activities do not include to a substantial extent activities other than trading activities. HMRC intreprets 'substantial' as meaning more than 20% (see CG64090).

Finance Act 2015 s 43 changes the definition of a trading company or holding company of a trading group to require the trade to be carried on in the company's own right, and holding companies of similarly defined trading companies. This excluded (from 18 March 2015) disposals of shares in joint venture and similar companies from qualifying for relief. (FA 2015 s 43, amending TCGA 1992 s 169S). However, FA 2016 s 85 reversed some of the 2015 changes to activities carried on by a joint venture to be treated as carried on by a company where effective interest in the joint venture is 5% or more. New definitions of trading company and trading group are set out in TCGA 1992 schedule 7ZA.

*Part disposals of business assets*

(13) The requirement for there to be a disposal of a business or part of a business is reminiscent of the retirement relief rules. This was an issue that arose in a number of High Court cases – in particular *Purves v Harrison* [2001] STC 567; *Barrett v Powell* [1998] STC 283; *Wase v Bourke* [1996] STC 18; *Jarmin v Rawlings* [1994] STC 1005; *Pepper v Daffurn* [1993] STC 466; *Atkinson v Dancer*; *Mannion v Johnst* [1988] STC 758 (these two cases were heard together) and *McGregor v Adcock* [1977] STC 206. See CG64020, CG64021, CG64030 and CG64035 for HMRC's view on these cases.

A case concerning the sale of part of a business for the purposes of entreprenuers' relief was heard in 2011. In *M Gilbert v HMRC* [2011] UKFTT 705 (TC), the taxpayer was a food broker acting for nine suppliers. He sold the part of the business relating to one supplier as a going concern and continued with the other eight. The sale included goodwill, trademarks and a customer database. Mr Gilbert was successful but the case illustrates the difficulties in determining whether the disposal is 'part of a business'.

(14) The key point is that there is a difference between a business and a mere asset used in the business.

*Interests in a partnership*

(15) The statute (TCGA 1992 s 169I(8)) ensures that in the context of partnerships:

- disposals of interests in assets used for the purposes of an individual's business on entering into a partnership which will carry on the business is to be treated as a part disposal of the business;
- similarly, disposals by individuals of the whole or part of the individual's interest in a partnership's assets will be treated as a disposal of the whole or part of the business carried on by the partnership;
- at any time when a business is carried on by a partnership it is treated as owned by each individual who, at the time, is a member of the partnership.

See also CG64040.

*Disposals of trust business assets*

(16) Trustees are treated as making disposals of trust business assets if the following conditions are met (TCGA 1992 s 169J(1)-(2)):

- the disposal is of assets that are settled property which are:
  - shares in or securities of a company; or
  - assets (or interests in assets) used or previously used for the purposes of a business.
- an individual is a 'qualifying beneficiary' (see below).

In the case of a disposal of shares or securities, throughout a period of one year at some point within three years before the disposal (TCGA 1992 s 169J(4)):

- the company is the personal company of the 'qualifying beneficiary';
- the company is either a trading company or a holding company of a trading group; and
- the 'qualifying beneficiary' is an officer or employee of the company (or, if the company is a member of a trading group of companies, of one or companies within the trading group).

In the case of a disposal of assets (TCGA 1992 s 169J(5)):

- the assets are used for the purposes of the business carried on by the qualifying beneficiary throughout a one-year period ending during the three years before the disposal; and
- the 'qualifying beneficiary' ceases to carry on the business on the date of disposal or within the three previous years.

(17) Again the statute provides that businesses carried on by the qualifying beneficiary can include businesses carried on in a partnership of which the qualifying beneficiary is a partner. Cessations of businesses by a qualifying beneficiary include the qualifying beneficiary ceasing to be a member of the partnership or the partnership ceasing to carry on the business (TCGA 1992 s 169J(6)).

(18) To be a 'qualifying beneficiary', an individual must have an interest in possession (other than for a fixed term) in the whole of the settled property or a part of it which consists of or includes the disposed assets (TCGA 1992 s 169J(3)).

*Associated disposals*

(19) The third route to entrepreneurs' relief arises if there is an 'associated' disposal of an asset (TCGA 1992 s 169K). That arises if:

- an individual makes a material disposal of business assets consisting of either:
  - the whole or part of the individual's interest in the assets of a partnership;
  - shares in or securities of a company; or
  - interests in such shares or securities.
- that disposal is made as part of the individual's withdrawal from participation of the business (which in the case of a disposal of company shares or securities can be carried on by a company which is a member of the same trading group as the company concerned) (see CG63995); and
- the asset(s) subject to the associated disposal are in use for the purposes of the business throughout the year ending with the earlier of:
  - the date of the material disposal of business assets; and
  - the cessation of the partnership or company's business.

(20) Relief for an associated disposal is restricted where the use of the asset in the business (TCGA 1992 s 169P):

- has been for only part of the period of ownership;
- has been only partly used;
- the individual has only been involved in the business for part of the period of ownership;

or

- has been dependent upon the payment of rent.

Rent paid prior to 6 April 2008 is ignored (FA 2008 Sch 3 para 6).

*Business*

(21) Although the statute refers to business assets, the term 'business' is narrowly defined to cover only trades, professions or vocations (as defined in the Income Tax Acts). Furthermore, the activity has to be conducted on a commercial basis and with a view to the realisation of profits (TCGA 1992 s 169S(1)). Therefore, hobby farms, for example, will not qualify.

*Personal company*

(22) For a company to be his personal company, an individual must hold 5% or more of both the ordinary share capital and the voting rights in the company (TCGA 1992 s 169S(3)).

It is not possible to aggregate shareholdings of connected parties. Thus, suppose a husband and wife owned 4% each of a trading company, neither would qualify for entrepreneurs' relief in respect of that shareholding. One would have to transfer a minimum 1% shareholding to the other at least a year before the earlier of the cessation of the business or the disposal of the shares. For entrepreneurs' relief to be available in respect of the combined shareholding then one spouse would have to transfer the entire shareholding to the other at least a year before the earlier of the cessation of the business or the disposal of the shares.

*Deferred gains*

(23) Where gains which could have been subject to entrepreneurs' relief are instead re-invested in either EIS shares or an investment under the Social Investment Tax Relief (SITR) scheme, the relief would normally be lost as the subsequent disposal (when the original gains re-surface) would not be a qualifying disposal, as it is unlikely to meet the qualifying conditions. For qualifying disposals (that is, those which attract relief) on or after 3 December 2014, which are re-invested in either EIS or SITR the original gain will eventually re-surface with an entitlement to entrepreneurs' relief. (Finance Act 2015, s 44 introducing new TCGA 1992 ss 169T to 169V).

*Investors' relief*

(24) Provisions exist that deal with acquisitions and reorganisations (TCGA 1992 s 169VI onwards). Where conditions are met, it is potentially possible to exchange old qualifying shares for new qualifying shares. Where the new holding will not qualify, it is possible to elect to crystallise the gain and use any available tax relief at that point.

The rules on subscription are given in TCGA 1992 s 169VP. They include clauses on the subscription being "wholly for cash", fully paid, a purpose test (issued for genuine commercial reasons, not as part of a scheme or arrangement the main purpose or one of the main purposes of which is the avoidance of tax) and a bargain at arm's length. This section also contains a useful relaxation on the subscription requirements by allowing transfers to a spouse or civil partner.

# Question

(1) Explain the share identification rules with effect from 6 April 2008 for the purposes of capital gains tax. Identify the exceptions to the general rule and briefly explain the extent to which the pre-2008 rules remain relevant.

(2) Jeremy sold 5,500 shares in Penny Pincher plc (a quoted company) on 15 August 2016 for £41,250, his previous dealings in the shares having been as follows:

| | | | | |
|---|---|---|---|---|
| 10 November 1986 | bought | 3,000 | shares for | £6,100 |
| 16 July 1988 | bought | 1,000 | | £3,060 |
| 25 May 1990 | sold | 2,000 | | £9,125 |
| 15 July 2013 | bought | 3,500 | | £14,210 |
| 25 March 2014 | bought | 500 | | £2,675 |
| 30 March 2014 | sold | 2,000 | | £12,700 |
| 15 June 2016 | bought | 3,000 | | £18,000 |

Calculate his chargeable gains on the disposal on 15 August 2016. Jeremy is not and has never been an employee of the company.

(3) Pickles had the following dealings in the shares of Chutney plc:

| | | | | |
|---|---|---|---|---|
| 10 May 1983 | bought | 2,000 | shares for | £8,000 |
| 14 July 1983 | bought | 1,000 | | £5,300 |
| 18 October 1984 | bought | 500 | | £2,300 |
| 21 February 1985 | bought | 500 | | £2,250 |
| 13 June 1996 | sold | 2,500 | | £16,500 |
| 17 July 2014 | bought | 1,000 | | £9,500 |
| 19 September 2016 | sold | 2,000 | | £17,700 |

(a) calculate the gain or loss on the September 2016 disposal;

(b) state how the computation would be affected if Pickles bought another 1,000 Chutney plc shares for £8,950 later in September 2016.

(4) In July 1983 Kevin bought 2,000 ordinary shares in Collins plc for £12,000. Collins plc made a scrip issue of one ordinary share for every four held in December 1985 and a further scrip issue of one for one in May 2005. In July 2016 Kevin sold 2,500 of his shares for £20,840.

Calculate the chargeable gain or allowable loss arising.

(5) On 27 June 2016 Julian sold 5,000 quoted ordinary shares in Verdon plc for £31,250. The history of his holding being as follows:

| | | £ |
|---|---|---|
| March 1979 | Bought 4,500 shares for | 3,520 |
| September 1980 | Bought 1,500 shares for | 3,050 |
| November 1982 | Bought 2,000 shares for | 4,130 |
| July 1989 | Bought 2,400 shares for | 12,000 |
| March 1994 | Sold 1,000 shares for | 3,500 |

| | |
|---|---|
| April 2010 | Received a 1 for 2 scrip issue |
| May 2014 | Rights offer of 1 for 5 at £2 a share. One half of the rights sold nil paid for proceeds of £2.50 a share and other half of rights shares taken up. Ex rights price was £4.80 a share. |

The market value of the shares in issue at 31 March 1982 was £2.10 per share.

Calculate the chargeable gain or allowable loss arising on the sale of the rights shares in May 2014 and the 5,000 shares in June 2016.

# Answer

## (1) Introduction to share pooling and identification

Share pooling and identification provisions are required to provide a set of rules that determine how gains (and losses) are to be calculated when part-disposals of shareholdings are made. Without prescriptive rules, it would be possible to argue that shares acquired on a particular acquisition have been disposed of so as to minimise the gain arising (or to maximise the loss arising or to ensure that the annual exemption is not unduly wasted).

### Example

Suppose Byron acquires 500 shares in Fairfax plc for £1 each on 1 May 2016 and a further 200 shares for £1.50 each on 13 May 2016.

If Byron then sells 350 shares for £1,000, without special rules, it would be arguable that either:

(a) Byron sold 350 of the shares originally acquired on 1 May 2016 (realising a gain of £650);

(b) Byron sold the shares acquired on 13 May 2016 plus 150 of the shares acquired on 1 May 2016 (realising a gain of £550); or

(c) some combination of the two.

### Summary of the operation of the rules

Different rules apply for corporation tax. The rules below relate only to capital gains tax.

Until 5 April 2008, different rules applied to the identification of shares and other securities depending on when the securities were acquired.

From 6 April 2008, however, shares and securities are pooled so as to form a single asset which increases or decreases as and when individual shares are acquired or disposed of (TCGA 1992 s 104).

Thus, applying the facts of the above example:

Byron is treated as holding an asset (containing 700 shares) with a base cost of £800 ((500 shares × £1) + (200 shares × £1.50)).

So, when the 350 shares are sold, Byron will be treated as making a gain of £1,000 – (£800 × 350/700 = £400) = £600. Byron's remaining shareholding of 350 shares will have a base cost of £400 (£800 - £400).

### When share identification rules apply

The share identification rules apply whenever a taxpayer acquires (TCGA 1992 s 104(1)):

- shares of the same class;
- in the same capacity.

Thus, if a father owns shares for himself and also as trustee for his infant daughter, the two holdings are not treated as the same for the share identification rules.

Similarly, different classes of shares are kept separate (even if the underlying rights are the same).

This rule is subject to the following exceptions:

- shares acquired and disposed of on the same day (TCGA 1992 s 105(1)) – these shares are matched to each other so far as is possible;
- shares acquired under a tax-advantaged share scheme (TCGA 1992 s 105A) if an election is made;
- shares acquired in the 30-day period following the disposal (TCGA 1992 s 106A(5)). This rule was introduced to prevent 'bed and breakfast transactions' in which taxpayers made disposals on one day only to reacquire the shares the next (at negligible net cost) to create a loss or to take advantage of the annual exemption by increasing the shares' base cost.

In addition, TCGA 1992 s 105(2) provides a fall back option for shares disposed of yet not covered by any of the above. Given the introduction of the 30-day rule in FA 1998, it is highly unlikely that this rule will be applied in practice. However, where it does, it ensures that earlier acquisitions are matched to disposals before any later acquisitions.

### Other assets subject to the rules

The matching rules discussed above do not apply only to shares. They apply also to company securities and any other asset which might be dealt in without identification of the particular assets involved. For example, suppose Max and Dan were to buy a house jointly and then Max subsequently bought Dan's share. If Max were then to sell a share of his interest to John, the share identification rules would be in point. Another example would be milk quota.

### Exception to the matching rules

Not all shares and securities use the matching rules discussed above. Different matching rules apply to:

- shares which have benefitted from tax relief (whether income tax or capital gains tax) under the enterprise investment scheme (EIS), venture capital trusts (VCT), seed enterprise investment scheme (SEIS), community investment tax relief (CITR), see **Example N7 explanatory notes 20** and **27**;
- shares which qualify or potentially qualify for investors relief. The objective of the identification rules for these shares is to preserve the maximum potential investors' relief. The identification rules for such shares are in TCGA 1992 sections 169VD to 169 VG. See **Example L5**.
- 'relevant securities'(TCGA 1992 s 106A), such as those within the accrued income scheme rules, see **Example A5**, and qualifying corporate bonds, see **Example L7 explanatory note 3**.

Also, if the shares were acquired under an approved share scheme, it is possible to make an election under TCGA 1992 s 105A for these shares to be treated as a separate transaction to other shares of the same class in the same company which were acquired or disposed on the same day (CG56460 - CG56467).

### Relevance of pre-2008 rules

The pre-2008 rules continue to be relevant because the pools formed on 6 April 2008 (made up of shares owned before that date) acquire their base costs from the shares not previously deemed to have been disposed of.

The key differences between the pre-2008 rules and the rules which apply to disposals from 6 April 2008 are that, pre-2008:

- shares acquired after 5 April 1998 were not pooled;
- shares acquired pre-31 March 1982 formed a pool separate from those acquired between 31 March 1982 and 5 April 1998;
- shares acquired pre-6 April 1965 were also kept in a separate pool.

## (2) Jeremy

Before calculating the chargeable gain or allowable loss on the August 2016, it is necessary to build up the TCGA 1992 s 104 pool.

Although the disposal in May 1990 took place before the rules changed on 6 April 2008, to simplify matters the pool can be reconstructed (for the purposes of the August 2016 disposal) as if the post-April 2008 rules were always in existence.

As far as the sale on 15 August 2016 is concerned, the position is therefore as follows:

TCGA 1992 s 104 pool

| | | *Shares* | *Cost* |
|---|---|---|---|
| | | | £ |
| November 1986 | Bought | 3,000 | 6,100 |
| July 1988 | Bought | 1,000 | 3,060 |
| | | 4,000 | 9,160 |
| May 1990 (2,000/4,000 x £9,160) | Sold | (2,000) | (4,580) |
| | | 2,000 | 4,580 |
| July 2013 | Bought | 3,500 | 14,210 |
| March 2014 | Bought | 500 | 2,675 |
| | | 6,000 | 21,465 |
| March 2014 (2,000/6,000 x £21,465) | Sold | (2,000) | (7,155) |
| | | 4,000 | 14,310 |
| June 2016 | Bought | 3,000 | 18,000 |
| | | 7,000 | 32,310 |
| August 2016 (5,500/7,000 x £32,310) | Sold | (5,500) | (25,386) |
| Pool values carried forward | | 1,500 | 6,924 |

The chargeable gain is calculated as follows:

| | |
|---|---|
| *Disposal - August 2016* | £ |
| Sale proceeds | 41,250 |
| Less: cost (see above) | (25,386) |
| Chargeable gain | 15,864 |

## (3) Pickles

(a) Before calculating the chargeable gain or allowable loss on the September 2016 disposal, it is necessary to build up the TCGA 1992 s 104 pool.

Although the disposal in July 1996 took place before the rules changed on 6 April 2008, to simplify matters the pool can be reconstructed (for the purposes of the September 2016 disposal) as if the post-April 2008 were always in existence.

As far as the sale on 19 September 2016 is concerned, the position is therefore as follows:

TCGA 1992 s 104 pool

| | | Shares | Cost |
|---|---|---|---|
| | | | £ |
| May 1983 | Bought | 2,000 | 8,000 |
| July 1983 | Bought | 1,000 | 5,300 |
| October 1984 | Bought | 500 | 2,300 |
| February 1985 | Bought | 500 | 2,250 |
| | | 4,000 | 17,850 |
| June 1996 (2,500/4,000 x £17,850) | Sold | (2,500) | (11,156) |
| | | 1,500 | 6,694 |
| July 2014 | Bought | 1,000 | 9,500 |
| | | 2,500 | 16,194 |
| September 2016 (2,000/2,500 x £16,194) | Sold | (2,000) | (12,955) |
| Pool values carried forward | | 500 | 3,239 |

The chargeable gain is calculated as follows:

| | |
|---|---|
| Disposal - September 2016 | £ |
| Sale proceeds | 17,700 |
| Less: cost (see above) | (12,955) |
| Chargeable gain | 4,745 |

(b) If Pickles had purchased a further 1,000 shares in Chutney plc in September 2016 following the disposal earlier that month this would mean that the 19 September 2016 disposal of 2,000 shares would be matched as follows:

(i) with the 1,000 shares of the same class in the next 30 days (TCGA 1992 s 106A(5));

(ii) with 1,000 shares of the same class in the TCGA 1992 s 104 pool.

Therefore, for capital gains tax purposes, he would have made two disposals and the chargeable gains and allowable losses would have to be calculated separately.

The disposal of the 1,000 shares purchased later in September 2016 would give rise to an allowable loss of £100, ie proceeds of £8,850 (£17,700/2) less costs of £8,950.

The disposal of the remaining 1,000 shares would come from the TCGA 1992 s 104 pool and give rise to a gain of £2,372, ie proceeds of £8,850 less costs of £6,478 (1,000/2,500 x £16,194). Therefore the overall chargeable gains in the year would be £2,272 before the annual exempt amount, being the gain of £2,372 less the loss of £100.

This would leave a balance of 1,500 shares in the TCGA 1992 s 104 pool with an associated base cost of £9,716 (£16,194 - £6,478).

## (4) Kevin

Kevin's shares would be pooled as follows:

| | | *Number of shares* | *Cost* |
|---|---|---|---|
| | | | £ |
| July 1983 | Bought | 2,000 | 12,000 |
| December 1985 (1 for 4) | Scrip | 500 | - |
| | | 2,500 | |
| May 2005 (1 for 1) | Scrip | 2,500 | - |
| | | 5,000 | 12,000 |
| July 2016 (2,500/5,000 x £12,000) | Sold | (2,500) | (6,000) |
| Pool values carried forward | | 2,500 | 6,000 |

The chargeable gain is calculated as follows:

| | |
|---|---|
| Disposal - July 2016 | £ |
| Sale proceeds | 20,840 |
| Less: cost (see above) | (6,000) |
| Chargeable gain | 14,840 |

## (5) Julian

Before calculating the chargeable gain or allowable loss on the May 2014 and June 2016 disposals, it is necessary to build up the TCGA 1992 s 104 pool.

Although the disposal in March 1994 took place before the rules changed on 6 April 2008, to simplify matters the pool can be reconstructed (for the purposes of the 2014 and 2016 disposals) as if the post-April 2008 were always in existence.

The TCGA 1992 s 104 pool is as follows:

| TCGA 1992 s 104 *pool* | | *Shares* | *Cost (or market value at 31 Mar 1982)* |
|---|---|---|---|
| | | | £ |
| Mar 1979 | bought | 4,500 | |
| Sept 1980 | bought | 1,500 | |
| | | 6,000 | 12,600 |
| Nov 1982 | bought | 2,000 | 4,130 |
| Jul 1989 | bought | 2,400 | 12,000 |
| | | 10,400 | 28,730 |
| Mar 1994 (1,000/10,400 x £28,730) | sold | (1,000) | (2,763) |
| | | 9,400 | 25,967 |
| April 2010 (1 for 2) | scrip | 4,700 | – |
| | | 14,100 | 25,967 |
| May 2014 (1 for 5) (50% taken up @ £2 per share) | rights | 1,410 | 2,820 |
| May 2014 (50% sold - 'small' proceeds) | sold | | (3,525) |
| | | 15,510 | 25,262 |

| | | | |
|---|---|---|---|
| June 2016 (5,000/15,510 x £25,262) | sold | (5,000) | (8,144) |
| Pool values carried forward | | 10,510 | 17,118 |

In order to calculate the chargeable gain or allowable loss on the sale of the rights nil paid, the market value of the shares retained plus the proceeds received needs to be found. This can be shown as:

| | £ |
|---|---|
| 15,510 shares @ market value of £4.80 each | 74,448 |
| 1,410 rights shares worth £2.50 each nil paid | 3,525 |
| | 77,973 |

The proceeds of the rights nil paid are £3,525. As this figure is less than 5% of the market value of the shares retained (£77,973 x 5% = £3,899), the proceeds are 'small' (see IR 164). Therefore, Julian has the choice of whether to treat the sale of rights nil paid as a part disposal or take the automatic treatment under TCGA 1992 s 122 and instead deduct the proceeds of £3,525 from the cost.

In the answer, Julian has taken the automatic treatment under TCGA 1992 s 122.

The chargeable gain or allowable loss on the sale of 5,000 shares in June 2016 is as follows:

| | £ |
|---|---|
| Disposal - June 2016 | |
| Sale proceeds | 31,250 |
| Less cost (see above) | (8,144) |
| Gain | 23,106 |

## Explanatory Notes

*Corporate shareholders*

(1) The calculation and treatment of chargeable gains and allowable losses of corporate shareholders differs in some respects from that for other shareholders. The question only deals with the position for non-corporate shareholders. The position of corporate shareholders is dealt with in **Example L10**.

*Matching rules - further points*

(2) As discussed in part (1) of the answer, the matching rules apply to shares in the same company of the same class acquired in the same capacity (TCGA 1992 s 104(1)). This means that shares held by trustees or personal representatives are not identified with shares owned personally. It does not, however, in the view of HMRC, treat shares held jointly by individuals (eg spouses) as held in a different capacity from shares held by them separately.

Where shares are held in a new individual savings account (NISA) they are regarded as held in a different capacity from other shares held. NISAs are covered in detail in **Example A5**.

(3) The 30-day rule is included in the matching rules to prevent 'bed and breakfast' transactions, where shares are sold and bought back on the following day in order either to use the capital gains exemption or to produce losses to reduce chargeable gains. However, it is still possible to 'bed and breakfast' with a spouse or civil partner, ie one spouse or civil partner disposes of shares and the other spouse/civil partner purchases shares of the same class in the same company on the open market (not directly from the other spouse).

In the case of *Davies v Hicks* [2005] STC 850, the 30-day rule was successfully used to avoid an exit charge by a trust which was about to become non-resident in the UK. The trustees sold their shareholding shortly before ceasing to be UK resident and reacquired shares of the same class in the same company after becoming non-resident in the UK within 30 days of the original disposal. Using the matching rules, the disposal of shares was matched with the shares subsequently acquired and so a considerable gain was eliminated. The non-resident trustees consequently acquired the original base cost of the shares.

This was blocked with effect from 22 March 2006. The 30-day rule no longer applies in respect of any acquisition by a person who is not UK resident (and not treated as resident under a tax treaty) (TCGA 1992 s 106A(5A)).

Tax Bulletin 52 (April 2001) contains a review of HMRC's understanding of the identification rules, and comments on a number of published planning schemes which make use of the 'bed and breakfasting' rule (although bear in mind it was written prior to the change of law of 22 March 2006). HMRC does not believe that the identification of 'same day share transactions' overrides the many provisions of TCGA 1992 which trigger a gain or loss by deeming a 'disposal and immediate reacquisition' of an asset.

Tax Bulletin 54 (August 2001) included further examples of how HMRC resolves the difficult interaction of share identification and inter-spouse disposals (now also relevant for civil partners). Note that this was written prior to the abolition of taper relief in April 2008.

*Quoted shares and securities*

(4) For tax purposes, shares and securities are 'quoted' or 'listed' if they are listed on a recognised stock exchange. A 'recognised stock exchange' is defined as a market designated as such by an order by HMRC and these stock exchanges can be based in the UK or abroad (ITA 2007 s 1005). For a list of which stock exchanges are 'recognised', see www.gov.uk/guidance/recognised-stock-exchanges.

Securities on the Alternative Investment Market (AIM) are unquoted (CG50255).

*Unit trusts, investment trusts and open-ended investment companies (OEICs)*

(5) Authorised unit trusts and investment trusts are exempt from tax on their gains (TCGA 1992 s 100).

Disposals by those who invest in such trusts are usually chargeable to capital gains tax in the normal way. Where the investment is through monthly savings schemes each monthly contribution must be identified as a separate purchase for the matching rules. Similarly, if the investor holds accumulation units then the automatic reinvestment in new units is treated as a separate purchase.

Open-ended investment companies (OEICs) are collective investment schemes. The shares in OEICs may be continuously created or redeemed, depending on investor demand. Essentially, they are treated in the same way as unit trusts, and existing unit trusts may convert into OEICs if they wish.

*Stock lending, repos, etc*

(6) In line with the Government's intention to maintain the competitiveness of the UK in world financial markets, there are various special rules designed to facilitate stock market transactions such as stock lending, manufactured payments and 'repos' (ie sale and repurchase transactions where the repurchase price is fixed, fluctuations in market value being borne by the original holder) (ITA 2007 ss 601–614; ITA 2007 ss 614ZA–61ZD; ITA 2007 ss 653–655; TCGA 1992 ss 263A–263I). See **Tolley's Capital Gains Tax 2016/17** Chapter 62.26–61.27.

*Reorganisation of share capital*

(7) A reorganisation of a company's capital is not treated as a disposal of the original shares or acquisition of a new holding. The new shares stand in the shoes of the old as regards acquisition date and cost (TCGA 1992 ss 126–131).

If the shareholder receives any cash from the company on the reorganisation, that cash is regarded as a capital distribution and is usually treated as a part disposal of the original holding unless the amount received is small (see **explanatory note 8**).

*Capital distributions*

(8) Where a company makes a capital distribution it is treated as a disposal of an interest in the shares and a chargeable gain or allowable loss arises accordingly, unless the distribution is regarded as 'small' (TCGA 1992 s 122).

HMRC will accept a distribution as small if it is either not more than 5% of the value of the shares or not more than £3,000, and it will consider on their merits cases where the taxpayer wants an amount to be treated as small even though it exceeds both these limits (RI 164).

Where the capital distribution is small then instead of being treated as a part disposal it is regarded as reducing the base cost of the holding. HMRC will not, however, object if someone wants to treat the receipt as a part disposal, which may be to their advantage if a gain would be covered by the annual exemption, or if a loss would reduce an existing chargeable gain. A small capital distribution must be treated as a part disposal if it exceeds the allowable expenditure (ie the base cost of the shares), or if the allowable expenditure is nil (as is the case with demutualisation shares). Where there is allowable expenditure that is less than the 'small' capital distribution, the amount chargeable may be reduced by that expenditure, leaving the holding with no allowable cost for future disposals.

Some companies return capital to shareholders by linking the payment to a consolidation of the shares in order to avoid a reduction in earnings per share. The cash received in such instances represents a capital distribution that is subject to the rules outlined above. Other companies have merely paid special dividends to shareholders, such dividends being treated as income and having no capital gains consequences.

Previously, some companies carried out a reorganisation of share capital into 'ordinary shares' and 'B shares', followed by a purchase of the B shares through a broker or redemption of the B shares by the company. Although this seemed a transparent scheme to circumvent the treatment of a purchase of own shares as a dividend, it was allowed until 5 April 2015. From 6 April 2015, FA 2015 s 19 removes the choice between taxation as income or capital by adding ITTOIA 2005 s 396A.

*Scrip dividend options*

(9) Where scrip shares are offered by a UK resident company as an alternative to a cash dividend, the capital gains tax cost for an individual, personal representatives, or trustees of a discretionary trust (other than one in which the settlor retains an interest) is the 'appropriate amount in cash'. That means the amount of the cash option, unless it is substantially different from the market value of the shares (TCGA 1992 s 142). 'Substantially' is defined as 15% or more either way (ITTOIA 2005 s 412).

For shares acquired on or after 6 April 1998, scrip option shares are treated as a separate, free-standing acquisition.

Where scrip option shares are issued to a corporate shareholder or to a discretionary trust in which the settlor retains an interest, they are capital rather than income, with a capital gains base cost of nil (because the 'income' treatment in ITTOIA 2005, s 410 only applies where an individual is beneficially entitled to the shares, or when the shares are issued to personal representatives or trustees of discretionary trusts – see **Example J1 explanatory note 6**). This means that the whole of their value will be reflected in a capital gain on disposal, with no cost.

The position of life interest trusts is not explicitly clear under the legislation. SP 4/94 explains that HMRC's position is that it is up to the trustees, taking into account trust law and the position of the particular trust, to decide whether the scrip shares constitute capital or income. HMRC will not seek to challenge what the trustees have done if they have treated the scrip dividend in one of the following ways:

(a) the scrip dividend belongs to the income beneficiary;

(b) the scrip dividend belongs to the trust capital; or

(c) the scrip dividend is added to capital, but the income beneficiary is compensated for the loss of the cash dividend he would have had.

The effect of alternative (a) would be that the trustees would be treated as holding the shares as bare trustees, the beneficiary thus being treated as having acquired the shares directly. Under alternatives (b) and (c) the treatment would be the same as for a corporate shareholder, ie there would be no income tax implications and the shares would be treated as acquired at nil cost for capital gains tax. Different provisions apply to Scottish life interest trusts (see SP 4/94).

Some companies have replaced scrip dividend options with dividend reinvestment plans (DRIPs), under which shareholders may use their dividends to acquire shares bought on the stock market by the company on their behalf. Such schemes avoid the reduction in value of existing shares caused by issuing scrip dividend shares. Shareholders taking DRIPs have higher costs than for scrip dividends, because they have to pay brokers' fees and stamp duty reserve tax. Since the abolition of the repayable tax credit in April 1999, and the treatment of scrip dividend options as market purchases from April 1998, DRIPs are now taxed in exactly the same way as scrip dividend options (income tax on the cash dividend forgone, and a purchase of shares for CGT at the same amount).

*Part sale of rights*

(10) **Part** (5) of this Example illustrates the treatment of a rights issue where the shareholder sells some of the rights nil paid and takes up the balance. The value of the unsold holding at the time of the sale includes the 'nil paid' value of the rights retained as well as the ex rights value of the existing shares.

Rights shares are sometimes issued partly paid. In that event, the unpaid amount is added both to the sale proceeds when the shares are sold and to the cost (TCGA 1992 s 128).

*Negligible value*

(11) See **Example L10 explanatory note 8** for the treatment of shares that have become of negligible value.

*Stamp duty and stamp duty reserve tax*

(12) Disposals of shares and securities are subject to stamp duty or stamp duty reserve tax. See **Example M1** for details.

*Disposals before 6 April 2008*

(13) For the purposes of calculating the chargeable gains and allowable losses on disposals made before 6 April 2008, shares of the same class in the same company were subject to a pooling system, except for certain pre-6 April 1965 acquisitions. There were two separate pools for each class of shares:

- one relating to shares acquired between 6 April 1965 and 5 April 1982, referred to in the legislation as the 1982 holding (TCGA 1992 s 109) but referred to in this book as the pre-1982 pool; and
- one relating to shares acquired between 6 April 1982 and 5 April 1998, referred to in the legislation as the TCGA 1992 s 104 holding but referred to in this book as the post-1982 pool.

Shares acquired under an employee share scheme and subject to restrictions were treated as shares of a different class from unrestricted shares until the restrictions are lifted (TCGA 1992 s 104(4)).

Shares acquired on or after 6 April 1998, except for scrip and rights shares, were not pooled until 6 April 2008. Previously, they were treated as separate, free-standing assets (TCGA 1992 s 104).

The way in which the legislation developed (which may still be relevant if a share history has to be reconstructed from a list of transactions) was as follows:

(a) *6 April 1965 to 5 April 1982*

Shares of the same class held in the same capacity in the same company were pooled, ie treated as a single asset, growing with purchases and diminishing with sales, so that an average price was used as the cost of disposals.

The pool excluded shares already owned on 6 April 1965, but in respect of quoted shares the taxpayer could make an election (under what is now TCGA 1992 Sch 2 para 4) to include them in the pool at their quoted price on that day. Two pooling elections could be made, one in respect of all 6 April 1965 holdings of fixed interest securities and preference shares, and the other in respect of all other quoted securities held on that day. If such pooling elections were not made, the shares were dealt with as separate, free-standing assets according to the date they were acquired.

(b) *6 April 1982 to 5 April 1985*

Indexation allowance was introduced, but because it was subject to various restrictions, shares acquired between 6 April 1981 and 6 April 1985 were treated as separate free-standing assets.

(c) *6 April 1985 to 5 April 1998*

Following the removal of the original restrictions on indexation, the shares referred to in (b) were merged to form the post-1982 pool, except for shares acquired between 6 April 1981 and 5 April 1982, which were merged with the pre-1982 pool.

No shares were added to the pre-1982 pool, other than as a result of scrip or rights issues or as a result of a pooling election after 5 April 1985 to include pre-6 April 1965 shares in it.

From 6 April 1988 a 'rebasing' election could be made to use only 31 March 1982 value, and ignore original costs, for virtually all assets held on that day.

(d) *6 April 1998 to 5 April 2008*

Shares acquired on or after 6 April 1998 were treated as separate, free-standing assets, except for scrip and rights shares.

(e) *6 April 2008 onwards*

All shares are pooled in a single pool.

(14) Indexation allowance is not given to non-corporate shareholders on any acquisitions on or after 6 April 1998 and no further indexation allowance is given after April 1998 on earlier acquisitions (TCGA 1992 s 110A).

Although indexation has been abolished, it remains relevant where there were pre-5 April 2008 transfers at no-gain/no-loss where the disposal proceeds were deemed to equal the base cost plus indexation (see **Example L6**). An example of when this is relevant is where there was a transfer of shares from a husband to his wife in, say, March 2008 and he had acquired the shares prior to 5 April 1998. The wife's base cost is deemed to be the husband's original base cost plus the indexation allowance to 5 April 1998. It is necessary to obtain details of previous spousal transfers when constructing the TCGA 1992 s 104 pool.

(15) Until 5 April 2008, taper relief was given on post 5 April 1998 disposals instead of indexation allowance. Under these rules, the gain was tapered based on:

- whether the shares qualified as business assets or not; and
- the number of complete years the shares had been owned, with an extra year added for shares acquired before 17 March 1998.

The pre- and post-1982 pools were regarded as single assets, with the post-1982 pool treated as acquired when it first came into being (TCGA 1992 s 106A), so that, providing this was before 17 March 1998, acquisitions between 17 March 1998 and 5 April 1998 still counted for the extra year's taper relief.

(16) Disposals of shares between 6 April 1998 and 5 April 2008 of the same class in the same company held by non-corporate shareholders in the same capacity were matched with acquisitions as follows (CG50564):

(a) acquisitions on the same day as the disposal;

(b) acquisitions within 30 days after the disposal, earliest first (but see notes below);

(c) previous acquisitions after 5 April 1998, latest first;

(d) post-1982 pool;

(e) pre-1982 pool;

(f) pre-6 April 1965 acquisitions not included in the pre-1982 pool, latest first;

(g) acquisitions more than 30 days after disposal, earliest first.

For disposals of shares prior to 6 April 2008, chargeable gains and allowable losses were calculated as follows:

(17) There were two pool values, one which represented the actual qualifying expenditure and the other which represented the expenditure plus indexation allowance (although note that no further indexation was added after April 1998).

To arrive at the initial figures for shares already on hand at 6 April 1985, indexation allowance was calculated on each separate acquisition from the month of purchase to April 1985, and the indexed pool of expenditure at 6 April 1985 was the total qualifying expenditure plus the total of all the calculated indexation allowances.

Where a post-1982 pool first came into being after the April 1985 date, the unindexed pool value and the indexed pool value were initially the same amount.

Every time there was an 'operative event' on the holding (ie an event which resulted in the qualifying expenditure being reduced or increased), then before dealing with that event, the indexed pool value had to be increased by:

$$\frac{RE - RL}{RL}$$

RE is the retail prices index for the month in which the event occurs and RL is the retail prices index for the month when the last event occurred (or the month the pool was created if there have been no previous acquisitions or disposals).

The first operative event after 5 April 1998 was the last occasion on which the indexation adjustment was made, indexation being given only up to April 1998. Thereafter the unindexed and indexed pool figures were adjusted only for disposals and for scrip and rights issues. It was necessary to identify separately the cost and indexed cost, because indexation could not create or increase a loss.

The index increase was expressed as a decimal (and unlike the normal indexation allowance calculation, there was no stipulation for this to be rounded to three decimal places). HMRC did not usually object if rounded figures from published indexation tables were used. If RL exceeded RE the indexed rise was nil and the indexed pool value remained the same.

After the index adjustment was made to the indexed pool, the new expenditure was then added to both pool values.

Where a disposal occurred, a proportionate deduction was made from both pools, the indexation allowance on the disposal being the difference between the two pool values.

If a receipt was not treated as a disposal (eg on a capital distribution or sale of rights), the amount received was deducted from both pool values.

(18) Where a company issued partly paid shares, the subsequent calls qualified for any available indexation allowance from the date the shares were issued, unless they were paid more than 12 months later, in which case they qualified from the date they were paid.

This did not apply where the shares were already fully paid, but were sold with the price payable by instalments. This was the case with privatisation issues, which qualified for indexation allowance on the full purchase price from the date of issue even if sold when some instalments had not been paid, provided any unpaid instalments were added to the disposal proceeds in the computation on the sale. Any privatisation issue vouchers that were used to reduce bills were deducted from the allowable cost. Any free shares acquired later were added to the holding and treated as acquired at market value on the first day of dealing.

(19) As discussed in **explanatory note 5** above, disposals of units by investors are usually chargeable to capital gains tax in the normal way. Those who invested in unit and investment trusts through monthly savings schemes prior to April 1998 could simplify the post-1982 pool calculations by being treated as if they had made a single annual investment in the seventh month of the trust's accounting year.

(20) As covered in **explanatory note 7**, a reorganisation of a company's capital (eg by scrip or rights issue) is not treated as a disposal of the original shares or acquisition of a new holding. The new shares stand in the shoes of the old as regards acquisition date and cost, but for indexation purposes any payment for rights shares was regarded as incurred on the date when it was actually incurred and not when the original shares were acquired (TCGA 1992 ss 126–131), so that indexation allowance was not given on rights shares acquired after 5 April 1998. On the other hand, when such rights shares formed part of pre-6 April 1998 acquisitions and the shares did not constitute business assets, for disposals before 6 April 2008 their cost was taken into account in computing the gain eligible for the extra year's taper relief.

(21) **Explanatory note 8** explains that where a company makes a capital distribution it is treated as a disposal of an interest in the shares and a chargeable gain or allowable loss arises accordingly, unless the distribution is regarded as 'small' (TCGA 1992 s 122).

If the 'small' capital distribution related to a pre-1982 pool or to pre-6 April 1965 shares, the legislation provided that the original cost of the holding (or 31 March 1982 value where appropriate) was indexed from March 1982 and the reduction from base cost was indexed from the date the capital sum was received (TCGA 1992 s 57). These adjustments were not necessary, however, if the pre-1982 pool was maintained in the same way as the post-1982 pool.

(22) As discussed in **explanatory note 9**, in most cases where scrip shares are offered by a UK resident company as an alternative to a cash dividend, the capital gains tax cost is the 'appropriate amount in cash'. That means the amount of the cash option, unless it is substantially different from the market value of the shares (TCGA 1992 s 142).

For shares acquired before 6 April 1998, the the purchase was treated in the same way as a purchase of rights shares, ie the shares increased existing holdings proportionately, and the deemed cost attracted indexation allowance from the month of issue. This did not apply to a 'bare trust', ie where someone was absolutely entitled as against the trustees (or would have been but for being an infant or a person under a disability). For bare trusts, the scrip shares were treated as acquired for the 'appropriate amount in cash' by the beneficiary directly, so that they were not treated as an addition to an existing holding.

(23) As mentioned in **explanatory note 10**, rights shares are sometimes issued partly paid and where this is the case the unpaid amount is added both to the sale proceeds when the shares are sold and to the cost (TCGA 1992 s 128).

For the purposes of indexation allowance, the unpaid amount was indexed from the date of acquisition of the rights shares unless it was due more than 12 months later, in which case it was indexed from the payment date. Therefore, if partly paid shares were sold more than 12 months before the balance was due, the balance did not qualify for indexation allowance even though it was included in the allowable expenditure.

# Question

(1) On 1 May 1981 Larkin purchased 6,000 ordinary shares in Maine plc at a price of £2 each. On 1 November 1981 there was a scrip issue of 1 for 2. The market value of the shares at 31 March 1982 was £1.30 each, giving a value of £11,700 for the 9,000 shares held at 31 March 1982.

On 1 March 2016 there was an offer of £0.50 cash plus two ordinary shares of Street plc for each Maine plc share held.

The offer was accepted and following acceptance Street plc's shares were quoted at £2.50 each.

Calculate the chargeable gain, and show the position if Larkin then disposes of the Street plc holding in December 2016 for £49,500.

(2) Pamela bought 2,000 shares in Fielding plc for £3,300 in February 1984. In November 1986 Fielding plc made a rights issue of 1 preference share for every 10 ordinary shares held, at £1.20 each. Pamela took up her rights in full. The opening market values on the first day of dealing ex rights were £2 for the ordinary shares and £1.40 for the preference shares. The ordinary shares were sold for £8,000 in September 2016.

Calculate the capital gain or allowable loss on the disposal of the ordinary shares.

(3) Victoria owned 20,000 shares in Forum Follies plc which she purchased in May 1998 for £50,000. In November 2015 Exciting Enterprises plc acquired all the share capital of Forum Follies plc. Under the terms of the takeover shareholders in Forum Follies received 3 ordinary shares and 1 preference share in Exciting Enterprises plc plus £1 cash for every 2 shares previously held in Forum Follies plc. Immediately after the takeover the ordinary shares in Exciting Enterprises were quoted at £3 each and the preference shares at £1.50 each. Victoria then sold the preference shares, receiving £15,000, in June 2016.

Calculate Victoria's gains for 2015/16 and 2016/17.

(4) On 31 March 2002, Neville bought 10,000 ordinary shares in Bateman plc at a cost of 310p per share. On 10 January 2004 a demerger took place in which shareholders received 1 Newbee plc ordinary share for each Bateman plc share. First day prices were Bateman plc ordinary 630p, Newbee plc ordinary 625p. On 15 June 2016 Neville sold his Newbee plc shares for £65,000. He retained his holding of Bateman plc shares.

Show the treatment of the demerger and of the sale of the Newbee plc shares.

(5) Michael Stewart received £250,000 on 10 July 2016 from Big plc when that company repaid all its issued 9% loan stock at par. Mr Stewart had received the loan stock (which is a qualifying corporate bond) in June 2008 in exchange for his 100,000 shares of £1 each in Small Ltd when Big plc acquired Small Ltd. Mr Stewart had acquired his shares in Small Ltd for £125,000 in November 1983. The shares were worth £250,000 in June 2008.

Show Mr Stewart's tax position at the time of the takeover and at the time of the repayment of the loan stock.

(6) Alex acquired shares in his employer's company (a quoted trading company) as follows:

| | | *Number of shares* |
|---|---|---|
| June 2007 | Free shares from SIP | 650 |
| June 2008 | Free shares from SIP | 560 |
| June 2009 | Free shares from SIP | 500 |
| June 2010 | Free shares from SIP | 400 |
| June 2011 | Free shares from SIP | 500 |

| | | *Number of shares* |
|---|---|---|
| June 2012 | Free shares from SIP | 450 |
| June 2013 | Free shares from SIP | 550 |
| June 2014 | Free shares from SIP | 600 |
| June 2015 | Free shares from SIP | 500 |
| June 2016 | Free shares from SIP | 550 |

| | | *Number of shares* | *Grant price £* |
|---|---|---|---|
| August 2007 | Exercised SAYE options | 1,000 | 4,100 |
| August 2011 | Exercised SAYE options | 1,500 | 9,000 |
| August 2015 | Exercised SAYE options | 800 | 3,500 |

None of the free shares from the SIP exceed the maximum value at the time the shares were awarded (ITEPA 2003 Sch 2, para 35).

Alex is forbidden by the terms of the plan to withdraw each allocation of shares within the SIP until five years after the allocation date.

The company's SAYE-related share option scheme enabled Alex to buy shares in 2007, 2011 and 2015. The value shown in the table above is the cost of exercising the options (ie the cost set at the date of grant).

On 21 January 2017 Alex withdrew 3,000 shares from the SIP and sold them on the same day. The market value of the shares on 21 January 2017 was £7.50 each.

Set out the capital gains tax position of Alex.

(7) In what circumstances will an investment by an individual constitute a 'qualifying corporate bond'?

# Answer

## (1) Larkin – takeover

### Maine plc

As noted in the question, Larkin held 9,000 ordinary shares in Maine plc on 31 March 1982. Under the rules which have been in place since April 2008, any assets held at that date are rebased using the market value on that date (TCGA 1992 s 35). The question gives the market value of the 9,000 shares as £11,700 on 31 March 1982.

In order to calculate the capital gain which arises to Larkin in 2016/17, it is first necessary to establish the total consideration received:

| | £ |
|---|---|
| 18,000 Street plc shares (2 for 1) @ £2.50 | 45,000 |
| Cash (50p per share for 9,000 shares) | 4,500 |
| Total value received | 49,500 |

On a takeover, it is the cash element which is immediately chargeable, with 'share for share' exchange rules ensuring that no gain arises where shares in an old company are exchanged for shares in the new company (TCGA 1992 s 135).

However, the cash element received is low enough to mean that the 'small' part disposal rules need to be considered. As discussed in **Example L6** explanatory note 8, this is in point if the cash proceeds are £3,000 or less than 5% of the total consideration received (TCGA 1992 s 122; IR 164). Since the cash received of £4,500 exceeds £3,000 and also exceeds 5% of the total value received (£2,475), a part disposal is triggered as follows:

*Takeover - March 2016*

| | £ |
|---|---|
| Cash proceeds | 4,500 |
| Less: market value 1982 (£11,700 x £4,500/£49,500) | (1,064) |
| Chargeable gain in 2015/16 | 3,436 |

| | £ |
|---|---|
| Disposal - December 2016 | |
| Sale proceeds | 49,500 |
| Less: market value 1982 (£11,700 - £1,064) | (10,636) |
| Chargeable gain in 2016/17 | 38,864 |

## (2) Pamela and Fielding plc – rights shares of a different class

Where rights shares of a different class are acquired, the respective pool values are then split according to the ex rights values of the different classes of shares on the first day that prices are quoted, as follows:

| | £ |
|---|---|
| 10 ordinary shares @ £2 | 20.00 |
| 1 preference share @ £1.40 | 1.40 |
| | 21.40 |

The TCGA 1992 s 104 pool values are split in those proportions, ie 0.93458 (ie £20/£21.40) to the ordinary shares and 0.06542 (ie £1.40/£21.40) to the preference shares.

| *Fielding plc - ordinary shares* | | *Shares* | *Cost* |
|---|---|---|---|
| | | | £ |
| February 1984 | bought | 2,000 | 3,300 |
| November 1986 (1 for 10) | rights | 200 | 240 |
| | | 2,200 | 3,540 |
| Exclude re pref (£3,540 x 0.06542) | | (200) | (232) |
| | | 2,000 | 3,308 |
| September 2016 | sold | (2,000) | (3,308) |
| | | Nil | Nil |

| Fielding plc - preference shares | | Shares | Cost |
|---|---|---|---|
| | | | £ |
| November 1986 | rights | 200 | 232 |

The chargeable gain or allowable loss on the sale of the ordinary shares in 2016 is calculated as follows:

| | £ |
|---|---|
| Proceeds | 8,000 |
| Less: cost | (3,308) |
| Chargeable gain | 4,692 |

## (3) Victoria: takeover

The value received by Victoria on the takeover of Forum Follies plc by Exciting Enterprises plc in 2015/16 is:

| | *Shares* | *Market value* | *Cost* |
|---|---|---|---|
| | | £ | £ |
| New ordinary shares (3 for 2) @ £3 | 30,000 | 90,000 | 39,130 |
| New preference shares (1 for 2) @ £1.50 | 10,000 | 15,000 | 6,522 |
| Cash (£1 for every 2 shares) | | 10,000 | 4,348 |
| | | 115,000 | 50,000 |

The base cost of the original shares of £50,000 is split 90:15:10 (as shown in the table above). For example, the base cost of the Exciting Enterprises ordinary shares is calculated as £50,000 x £90,000/£115,000.

The TCGA 1992 s 104 pool is updated for the takeover as follows:

| Forum Follies plc | Bought | Shares | Cost |
|---|---|---|---|
| | | | £ |
| May 1998 - bought | | 20,000 | 50,000 |
| November 2015 - takeover | | (20,000) | |
| Cost of part disposal (cash - see above) | | | (4,348) |
| | | | |
| Cost of new ordinary shares (see above) | | | (39,130) |
| Cost of new preference shares (see above) | | | (6,522) |
| | | Nil | Nil |

| Exciting Enterprises ordinary shares | Shares | Base cost |
|---|---|---|
| | | £ |
| November 2015 takeover of Forum Follies plc | 30,000 | 39,130 |

| Exciting Enterprises preference shares | Shares | Base cost |
|---|---|---|
| | | £ |
| November 2015 takeover of Forum Follies | 10,000 | 6,522 |

Since the cash of £10,000 exceeds 5% of the total value of the takeover £115,000 (£5,750), it is treated as a part disposal of the Forum Follies plc holding for capital gains tax purposes.

The chargeable gains or allowable losses on receipt of cash on the 2015/16 takeover and the sale of the preference shares in 2016/17 is calculated as follows:

| | 2015/16 Cash - takeover | 2016/17 Sale - pref shares |
|---|---|---|
| | £ | £ |
| Proceeds | 10,000 | 15,000 |
| Less: cost | (4,348) | (6,522) |
| Chargeable gain | 5,652 | 8,478 |

## (4) Neville – demerger of Bateman plc and Newbee plc

In relation to shareholdings held by individuals, a demerger is treated in a similar way to a scrip issue of a different class. There are special rules for trusts, see **explanatory note 2**.

Since there is no cash element there is no immediate disposal which is subject to capital gains tax in 2003/04 at the time of the demerger.

The Bateman plc shares cost Neville 310p each in 2002, giving a base cost of £31,000. The base cost of the holding is split according to first day prices, as follows:

$$\text{Bateman plc} \frac{£31,000 \times 630p}{(630p + 625p)} = £15,562$$

$$\text{Newbee plc} \frac{£31,000 \times 625p}{(630p + 625p)} = £15,438$$

The TCGA 1992 s 104 pool is updated for the demerger as follows:

| *Bateman plc* | | *Shares* | *Base cost* |
|---|---|---|---|
| | | | £ |
| March 2002 | bought | 10,000 | 31,000 |
| January 2004 (see above) | demerger | | (15,438) |
| | | 10,000 | 15,562 |

| Newbee plc | | Shares | Base cost |
|---|---|---|---|
| | | | £ |
| January 2004 (from Bateman plc) | demerger | 10,000 | 15,438 |
| June 2016 | sold | (10,000) | (15,438) |
| | | Nil | Nil |

The chargeable gain or allowable loss on the sale of the Newbee shares is calculated as follows:

| | £ |
|---|---|
| Proceeds | 65,000 |
| Less: cost | (15,438) |
| Chargeable gain | 49,562 |

## (5) Michael Stewart – loan stock

There is no chargeable gain or allowable loss when shares are exchanged for qualifying corporate bonds (QCBs) (TCGA 1992 s 116).

However, as QCBs are not subject to capital gains tax on redemption (TCGA 1992 s 115), the gain is calculated at the time of the takeover but is 'frozen' and is only chargeable on disposal or redemption of the QCB (TCGA 1992 s 116).

The gain which is 'frozen' in June 2008 is:

| | £ |
|---|---|
| Deemed proceeds (market value shares at June 2008) | 250,000 |
| Less: cost | (125,000) |
| 'Frozen' gain | 125,000 |

On the repayment of the loan stock on 10 July 2016 the 'frozen' gain crystallises, so that there is a chargeable gain in 2016/17 of £125,000.

## (6) Alex - sale of shares acquired via share schemes

Shares held within a SIP are not treated as acquired until they are withdrawn from the plan. The acquisition cost of the shares is the market value at the date of withdrawal (TCGA 1992 Sch 7D para 5).

Under the share matching rules, disposals are matched firstly with shares of the same class in the same company acquired on the same day, then with shares acquired in the next 30 days and finally with shares from the TCGA 1992 s 104 pool. See **Example L6**.

As noted in the question, Alex is not allowed to withdraw shares from the SIP until five years have elapsed (earlier withdrawal would lead to an income tax charge). Therefore he can only withdraw shares from the SIP which were awarded in June 2007 to June 2011 (a total of 2,610 shares). The disposal is first matched with these shares as they

The TCGA 1992 s 104 pool is updated for the takeover as follows:

| Forum Follies plc | Bought | Shares | Cost |
|---|---|---|---|
| | | | £ |
| May 1998 - bought | | 20,000 | 50,000 |
| November 2015 - takeover | | (20,000) | |
| Cost of part disposal (cash - see above) | | | (4,348) |
| | | | |
| Cost of new ordinary shares (see above) | | | (39,130) |
| Cost of new preference shares (see above) | | | (6,522) |
| | | Nil | Nil |

| Exciting Enterprises ordinary shares | Shares | Base cost |
|---|---|---|
| | | £ |
| November 2015 takeover of Forum Follies plc | 30,000 | 39,130 |

| Exciting Enterprises preference shares | Shares | Base cost |
|---|---|---|
| | | £ |
| November 2015 takeover of Forum Follies | 10,000 | 6,522 |

Since the cash of £10,000 exceeds 5% of the total value of the takeover £115,000 (£5,750), it is treated as a part disposal of the Forum Follies plc holding for capital gains tax purposes.

The chargeable gains or allowable losses on receipt of cash on the 2015/16 takeover and the sale of the preference shares in 2016/17 is calculated as follows:

| | 2015/16 Cash - takeover | 2016/17 Sale - pref shares |
|---|---|---|
| | £ | £ |
| Proceeds | 10,000 | 15,000 |
| Less: cost | (4,348) | (6,522) |
| Chargeable gain | 5,652 | 8,478 |

## (4) Neville – demerger of Bateman plc and Newbee plc

In relation to shareholdings held by individuals, a demerger is treated in a similar way to a scrip issue of a different class. There are special rules for trusts, see **explanatory note 2.**

Since there is no cash element there is no immediate disposal which is subject to capital gains tax in 2003/04 at the time of the demerger.

The Bateman plc shares cost Neville 310p each in 2002, giving a base cost of £31,000. The base cost of the holding is split according to first day prices, as follows:

$$\text{Bateman plc}\frac{£31,000 \times 630p}{(630p + 625p)} = £15,562$$

$$\text{Newbee plc}\frac{£31,000 \times 625p}{(630p + 625p)} = £15,438$$

The TCGA 1992 s 104 pool is updated for the demerger as follows:

| *Bateman plc* | | *Shares* | *Base cost* £ |
|---|---|---|---|
| March 2002 | bought | 10,000 | 31,000 |
| January 2004 (see above) | demerger | | (15,438) |
| | | 10,000 | 15,562 |

| Newbee plc | | Shares | Base cost £ |
|---|---|---|---|
| January 2004 (from Bateman plc) | demerger | 10,000 | 15,438 |
| June 2016 | sold | (10,000) | (15,438) |
| | | Nil | Nil |

The chargeable gain or allowable loss on the sale of the Newbee shares is calculated as follows:

| | £ |
|---|---|
| Proceeds | 65,000 |
| Less: cost | (15,438) |
| Chargeable gain | 49,562 |

## (5) Michael Stewart – loan stock

There is no chargeable gain or allowable loss when shares are exchanged for qualifying corporate bonds (QCBs) (TCGA 1992 s 116).

However, as QCBs are not subject to capital gains tax on redemption (TCGA 1992 s 115), the gain is calculated at the time of the takeover but is 'frozen' and is only chargeable on disposal or redemption of the QCB (TCGA 1992 s 116).

The gain which is 'frozen' in June 2008 is:

| | £ |
|---|---|
| Deemed proceeds (market value shares at June 2008) | 250,000 |
| Less: cost | (125,000) |
| 'Frozen' gain | 125,000 |

On the repayment of the loan stock on 10 July 2016 the 'frozen' gain crystallises, so that there is a chargeable gain in 2016/17 of £125,000.

## (6) Alex - sale of shares acquired via share schemes

Shares held within a SIP are not treated as acquired until they are withdrawn from the plan. The acquisition cost of the shares is the market value at the date of withdrawal (TCGA 1992 Sch 7D para 5).

Under the share matching rules, disposals are matched firstly with shares of the same class in the same company acquired on the same day, then with shares acquired in the next 30 days and finally with shares from the TCGA 1992 s 104 pool. See **Example L6**.

As noted in the question, Alex is not allowed to withdraw shares from the SIP until five years have elapsed (earlier withdrawal would lead to an income tax charge). Therefore he can only withdraw shares from the SIP which were awarded in June 2007 to June 2011 (a total of 2,610 shares). The disposal is first matched with these shares as they are treated as being acquired on the same day (TCGA 1992 s 105(1)). The balance of the 3,000 shares sold must therefore be from the SAYE scheme under the TCGA 1992 s 104 pool.

There is no need for Alex to make an election under TCGA 1992 s 105A as there were no other shares of the same class in the same company acquired on 21 January 2017 (see explanatory note 4).

The TCGA 1992 s 104 pool in respect of Alex's holding up to the January 2017 disposal is therefore:

| | | *Shares* | *Cost £* |
|---|---|---|---|
| August 2007 | Exercised SAYE options | 1,000 | 4,100 |
| August 2011 | Exercised SAYE options | 1,500 | 9,000 |
| August 2015 | Exercised SAYE options | 800 | 3,500 |
| | | 3,300 | 16,600 |
| January 2017 (390/3,300 x £16,600) | Sold | (390) | (1,962) |
| Pool values carried forward | | 2,910 | 14,638 |

The chargeable gains or allowable losses on the sale of shares by Alex in January 2017 is calculated as follows:

| | *SIP shares* | *TCGA 1992 s 104 pool shares* |
|---|---|---|
| | £ | £ |
| Proceeds | 19,575 | 2,925 |
| Less: cost | (19,575) | (1,962) |
| Chargeable gain | Nil | 963 |

Assuming Alex has no other chargeable gains in the year, the gain of £963 will be covered by his annual exempt amount. Therefore there is no need to consider the entrepreneurs' relief position.

Leaving shares in a SIP until disposal is usually good planning as because the base cost is the market value when the shares are withdrawn from the plan and they are treated as acquired when they are withdrawn it means a sale can take place on the same day and there will be no chargeable gain.

## (7) Qualifying corporate bonds

Qualifying corporate bonds (QCBs) are defined in TCGA 1992 s 117 as sterling loan stock purchased or issued on commercial terms after 13 March 1984, including bonds that are convertible into other qualifying corporate bonds but excluding bonds that are convertible into shares or other kinds of securities and securities linked to a share index.

The interest bearing stocks that are outside the definition, therefore, are:

- those denominated in a foreign currency;
- those that are convertible into shares or linked to a share index;
- those which represent a non-commercial loan; or
- bonds purchased before 14 March 1984.

QCBs are exempt from the charge to CGT (TCGA 1992 s 115). Profits on some QCBs (those which fall into the deeply discounted security rules in ITTOIA 2005, s 427) are chargeable to income tax, see **Example A5 explanatory note 14**. However on most other QCBs an income tax accrued income scheme charge has to be calculated on disposal instead, see **Example A5**, answer (b).

Loan stock which is a 'debt on a security' and which is not a QCB is a chargeable asset for CGT, and will give rise to gains and losses in the normal way. Loan stock which is a 'simple debt' may not be chargeable to CGT. Various points on non-exempt loan stocks are set out in **explanatory notes 11** and **12**.

## Explanatory Notes

*Takeovers*

(1) Where shares or debentures in a new company are received in exchange for shares or debentures held in a company which has been taken over, the takeover is treated as if the two companies were the same company and the exchange were a reorganisation of its capital (TCGA 1992 s 135). This is known as a 'share for share' exchange or 'paper for paper' treatment.

Any cash received is therefore treated as a capital distribution as explained in **Example L6 explanatory note** 7. The part disposal proceeds in Larkin's case in **part (1)** of this Example is accordingly £4,500 and the gain is calculated by reference to the ratio that the cash bears to the cash plus market value of the shares received in exchange for the original shares (TCGA 1992 s 129). Since the cash is more than £3,000 and more than 5% of the value received, it is not 'small' and is not therefore treated as reducing the base cost of the holding (TCGA 1992 s 122; IR 164), although HMRC has indicated that it will consider a higher figure as 'small' if the taxpayer can argue that it should be treated as 'small' in the circumstances.

See **Example L3 explanatory notes 6-8** for consideration of 'earn-out' elements in a paper-for-paper takeover.

See **part (5)** of this Example for the position where part of a takeover package takes the form of qualifying corporate bonds and see **explanatory note 3** below for further comments.

*Demergers*

(2) Demergers that are 'exempt distributions' normally do not have either income tax or capital gains tax consequences for the shareholders, (see **Example K5**). The capital gains tax treatment is shown in **part (4)** of this Example. Effectively the demerger is treated like a scrip issue of a different class of shares, the base cost values of the shares being split between the demerged holdings according to market values on the first day that prices are quoted after the demerger.

Demergers can cause problems for trusts. In relation to the demerger of ICI and Zeneca, it was held in the case of *Sinclair v Lee* [1993] 3 All ER 926 that the demerger represented a capitalisation by ICI of part of its distributable profits and thus the Zeneca shares were a capital distribution in the hands of the trustees.

This is not necessarily the case for all demergers. Where shares in a 75% subsidiary are distributed direct to the shareholders (a 'direct demerger'), the HMRC view is that although the shares are exempt from income tax under the 'exempt distribution' rules, they are nonetheless income of the trust, because under company law they are a dividend paid out of accumulated profits. The treatment then differs according to whether the trust is a discretionary trust or a life interest trust (CG33921). The tax consequences for trusts of the different types of demerger are dealt with in the companion to this volume, **Tolley's Taxwise II 2016/17**, at **Example F8 (B)**.

*Reorganisations: qualifying corporate bonds*

(3) For details of the rules relating to QCBs, see **explanatory note** 5.

Sometimes on a reorganisation of share capital or on a takeover, QCBs may be converted into, or exchanged for, shares or vice versa. If QCBs are exchanged for shares, the normal reorganisation provisions dealt with in **explanatory note 1** above do not apply, and the shares are deemed to be acquired at their market value at the date of the exchange. If shares are exchanged for QCBs, the shares are treated as disposed of for their market value immediately *before* the exchange, the gain or loss at that date is calculated and is then 'frozen'. The frozen gain or loss is crystallised on the disposal of the QCBs (or part thereof), as illustrated in **part (5)** of this Example (TCGA 1992 s 116).

The same applies where a security changes its status from non-qualifying corporate bond (non-QCB) to a QCB. The frozen gain or loss does not crystallise on a transfer between spouses, or intra-group transfers made by companies, instead it is 'inherited' by the person acquiring the bonds, so that it will crystallise on disposal by that person (TCGA 1992 s 116(11). Where a frozen gain crystallises, it is possible for an individual to defer it again by subscribing for shares in a qualifying unquoted trading company under the enterprise investment scheme provisions (see **Example N7**).

Where the original shares qualify for entrepreneurs' relief and the reorganisation takes place after 22 June 2010, the individual or trustees receiving consideration in the form of QCBs must choose whether to pay tax on the disposal with the benefit of entrepreneurs' relief or to postpone the gain and lose the benefit of the relief. An election for entrepreneurs' relief on the reorganisation under TCGA 1992 s 169R means that the rules 'freezing' the gain do not apply, meaning the gain is chargeable in the tax year in which the reorganisation takes place, but only suffers tax at the entrepreneurs' relief rate of 10%.

For companies, under the rules for 'loan relationships', any gain or loss arising on the disposal of QCBs in exchange for shares on or after 1 April 1996 is brought into account in calculating income. Where shares are exchanged for QCBs before 1 April 1996, the 'frozen' gain or loss treatment applies, with the frozen gain or loss on the shares being brought in as a *chargeable* gain or loss when the bonds are disposed of (TCGA 1992 s 116(16)).

If the QCBs fall in value, the effect of the 'frozen gain' treatment may be that the taxpayer is charged on a gain even though in fact he has made a loss. This problem can be overcome by giving the bonds to a charity. The frozen gain will not then crystallise, nor are there any tax consequences for the charity when it disposes of the bonds (TCGA 1992 s 257; RI 23). However it is worth considering the rules on tainted charity donations to ensure the gift to charity is not caught (ITA 2007 ss 809ZH-809ZR).

If a frozen gain on QCBs has not crystallised by the time the taxpayer dies, the gain escapes tax (TCGA 1992 s 116(11). It is not chargeable on the personal representatives, nor on any beneficiary. If, however, there is a frozen gain accruing to the personal representatives themselves, the gain crystallises on disposal (but not on transfer to a beneficiary, the crystallisation in those circumstances being further deferred until the beneficiary disposes of the loan stock).

For individuals, trustees and personal representatives, where there are multiple acquisitions of the same QCBs matching rules are necessary to decide which frozen gain crystallises on a disposal. Disposals of QCBs are matched with (TCGA 1992 ss 104(3), 106A):

(a) acquisitions in the next 30 days (first-in first-out basis);

(b) acquisitions up to the date of disposal (last-in first-out basis).

For companies, the matching rules for disposals of QCBs are covered in explanatory note 6 below.

*Qualifying corporate bonds*

(4) Most interest bearing stocks issued by UK companies come within the definition of QCBs. Before FA 1996, both individual and company investors were exempt from tax on gains (and could not normally claim relief for losses) on QCBs and government stocks. For corporate investors, then subject to the special provision below, all profits and gains on a company's 'loan relationships' are brought into account along with interest payable and interest receivable in arriving at the company's income profits. For the detailed provisions see **Example K2**. The *chargeable gains* exemption still applies and is extended as far as companies are concerned to any securities that would previously have been outside the definition of qualifying corporate bond, subject to what is said below (TCGA 1992 s 117(A1)).

A company's gains and losses on the disposal of convertible securities and securities linked to a share index are still dealt with under the chargeable gains rules (such securities being outside the definition of qualifying corporate bond and therefore within the corporation tax charge on gains).

The exemption from CGT for investors other than companies still applies, so that there are neither chargeable gains nor allowable losses on government securities and QCBs (TCGA 1992 s 115).

*Non-exempt loan stock*

(5) Where interest bearing stocks do not qualify as QCBs (ie they are non-QCBs), these assets are chargeable for capital gains purposes.

For individuals, trustees and personal representatives the matching rules for QCBs also apply to non-QCBs (see explanatory note 3 above) (TCGA 1992 ss 104(3), 106A).

For companies, the matching rules for disposals of QCBs and non-QCBs are also the same, but are different from the rules which apply to non-corporates. The normal pooling provisions for companies do not apply. Instead each acquisition on or after 6 April 1982 is treated as a separate asset (TCGA 1992 s 108). If a rebasing election has been made to treat all assets owned on 31 March 1982 as acquired at the market value on that date, all securities of the same class in the same company owned on that date are regarded as a single asset. Even if the rebasing election has not been made, the same treatment applies for quoted securities if an election was made for acquisitions before 6 April 1965 to be pooled with later acquisitions (TCGA 1992 s 109). If there has been neither a rebasing election nor an election to pool pre-6 April 1965 quoted securities, those securities are treated as separate assets.

In summary, disposals of QCBs and non-QCBs by corporates are matched in the following order:

- those acquired in the previous 12 months on a first in first out basis;
- earlier acquisitions since 5 April 1982, on a last in first out basis;
- the pool of acquisitions from 6 April 1965 to 5 April 1982 (treated as a single asset under a rebasing election);
- non-pooled pre 6 April 1965 acquisitions, last-in first-out.

However, where, under a single bargain, a company acquires securities for delivery on a particular date and disposes of them for delivery at a later date under contango arrangements, the disposal is matched with the acquisition and no other disposal may be matched with that acquisition (TCGA 1992 s 108(7)).

No indexation allowance is available if the disposed of within the nine days after the date they were acquired (TCGA 1992 s 54(2)).

Where securities held by companies are dealt with under the loan relationships provisions, there are no special rules for matching disposals with acquisitions and any consistent basis adopted for accounting purposes is acceptable.

*Choice of QCBs and non-QCBs on takeover*

(6) Due to the different treatment of takeovers where QCBs and non-QCBs are received in exchange for shares, close attention has to be paid to the following choice:

- exchange shares for QCBs - calculate the gain at the date of exchange, 'freezing' it until the disposal of the QCB; or
- exchange shares for non-QCBs - no disposal at the date of exchange; a gain is only calculated on the disposal of the bonds.

If the individual are considering the QCB route careful attention will need to be paid to the entrepreneurs' relief position.

The non-QCB route is preferable if the loan stocks become worthless, because the gain is never charged and the loss is allowable.

As can be seen in the case of *Weston v Garnett* [2005] STC 1134, it is important that the loan note is really a QCB. In this case the loan notes were found to be non-QCBs as they carried the right (albeit indirectly) to be converted into shares.

*Unusual loan stocks*

(7) Corporate financiers often design unfamiliar financial instruments with which to carry out transactions. The terms of the instrument need to be compared carefully with the legislation to determine the correct tax treatment.

For example, a 'special stock unit' with a set redemption date and premium was issued as part of the Royal Bank of Scotland takeover of National Westminster Bank in 2000. This was treated as a share; it was chargeable if the shareholder sold it, but the premium on redemption would be charged to income tax as a dividend.

An index-linked government stock is exempt from CGT, but an index-linked stock issued by a company is an 'excluded indexed security' rather than a 'deeply discounted security'. It is therefore chargeable to capital gains tax rather than to income tax.

Some building societies have issued permanent interest bearing shares (PIBS), which are treated as QCBs for the purposes of capital gains tax, and are therefore exempt in the hands of an individual or trustee. For corporation tax purposes, PIBS are within the loan relationship rules and the chargeable gains rules do not apply. For more on the loan relationships rules, see **Example K2**.

*Shares acquired under HMRC tax-advantaged schemes*

(8) Unless they are subject to any special restrictions, shares acquired under save as you earn (SAYE) and discretionary share option schemes are treated in the same way as other acquisitions. They are regarded as acquired on the date the option is exercised for the amount paid for them, plus the amount, if any, paid for the option.

SIP shares are treated as acquired at market value on the date they are withdrawn from the plan (TCGA 1992 Sch 7D para 5) and there is no income tax liability as long as they have remained within it for at least five years (ITEPA 2003 ss 505-506). Therefore, if they are disposed of immediately after withdrawal no capital gains tax liability arises, as shown in part (6) of this Example.

The rules for matching disposals of shares with acquisitions are dealt with in **Example L6**. All acquisitions of shares of the same class in the same company on one day are normally treated as being a single asset (TCGA 1992 s 105). This rule is varied for shares acquired by employees from 6 April 2002 under an tax-advantaged share option scheme (TCGA 1992 ss 105A, 105B) (see **Example N1** for details of such schemes). Where some of the same day acquisitions are from a tax-advantaged share option scheme they may have a lower capital gains cost than the other acquisitions, which would reduce the average cost of any shares disposed of, and if there was a part disposal of the holding the capital gain would be correspondingly higher.

In respect of scheme shares acquired from 6 April 2002 on the same day as other shares, the taxpayer may make a written election, on or before the first anniversary of 31 January following the end of the tax year in which he first makes a disposal of any of the same day acquisitions. For example, the deadline would be 31 January 2019 in respect of a disposal in 2016/17. The effect of the election is that the scheme shares and the other shares treated as two separate assets and the non-scheme shares are treated as being subject to disposal first. This is likely to reduce immediate gains on a part disposal, although the remaining shares would have a lower capital gains tax cost.

# Question

(1) Show the capital gains position in the following instances:

(a) Miss Fielding sold a freehold house in Southampton on 28 March 2017 for net proceeds of £752,220. She had bought the house for £15,000 on 1 October 1971 and immediately occupied it as her sole residence; between 1 October 1973 and 1 April 1987 the house was let while she was employed in Suffolk, where she lived in rented accommodation. She resumed occupation of the house on 1 April 1987 but moved to a different permanent residence on 27 March 1999, the house then being let until the date of sale. The value of the house at 31 March 1982 was £70,000.

For 2016/17 Miss Fielding's only taxable income consisted of a pension of £25,000. Calculate the capital gains tax payable.

(b) Galsworthy bought a freehold house on 1 April 1989 for £27,000 including expenses of purchase. He lived in the house until 30 September 2010 when he took a job as a caretaker and had to live on his employer's premises. He therefore let the house until he sold it on 30 June 2016 for £352,100 after deducting expenses of sale, his employer moving him to a branch in another part of the country so that he could not resume residence.

(c) On 1 January 1972 Hardy purchased for £4,000 a flat which he used as his only residence. On 30 June 1976 he purchased a house which became his main residence and from that date his widowed mother occupied the flat free of any consideration. His mother vacated the flat on 31 March 1987 and he let it continuously at a commercial rent from that date until he sold it for £240,000 on 30 September 2016. The value on 31 March 1982 was £26,000.

(d) On 30 June 2016 Compton sold a freehold house in Hampshire for net proceeds of £973,260. He had bought the house for £70,800 on 1 October 1981 and the history of his ownership is summarised below:

| | |
|---|---|
| 1.10.81 | Occupied house as sole residence. |
| 1.04.82 | House let on taking up employment abroad. He returned to England on 1 January 1984, but started his own business in Liverpool and lived in rented accommodation, continuing to let his own house. |
| 1.07.88 | Resumed occupation of own house on ceasing business. |
| 1.01.90 | Moved to Sussex and purchased a house which became his main residence from this date, the Hampshire house being let until it was sold. |

The market value of the Hampshire house was £90,000 on 31 March 1982.

(e) Harold married Georgina on 6 April 2000. Both had been married before, and both owned houses. Harold had bought his house in April 1988, and lived in it with his first wife, who died in 1995. Georgina and her first husband bought their house in June 1992, but divorced in 2000, after the husband had moved out in January 1997. The house was subject to an order along the lines of *Mesher v Mesher*, which provided that it would be held on trust for Georgina and her former husband until their children reached the age of 18 (in October 2016), when it would be sold, and the proceeds divided equally.

Harold moved into Georgina's house in April 2000, and they have lived there ever since, during which time Harold's own house has been let out. In October 2016, they sold both houses, and bought a third. The gain on Harold's house was £400,000; the gain on Georgina's house was £200,000, of which her share was £100,000. Harold had kept his own house in his own name.

(f) Stanley's father died in 1995, and Stanley decided to provide a home for his mother. He bought a house for £160,000 and placed it into a trust in which his mother had a life interest, with reversion to Stanley on her death. In 2003, the trustees sold the first house for £260,000, and bought another for the same sum. In 2016, Stanley's mother died, when the second house was worth £440,000. It will be sold as soon as possible and the proceeds returned to Stanley.

(g) Gordon sold his house for £500,000 on 30 September 2016. He bought it for £220,000 in April 2006. He has always used 20% of his house exclusively for business purposes, and has made claims for income tax relief for that proportion of the running costs (including council tax and mortgage interest).

(h) On 31 January 2003, James transferred a house to the trustees of a discretionary trust and claimed to hold over the gain of £200,000 that would otherwise accrue. The beneficiaries of the trust are his children, Gemma and Sue. The terms of the settlement permit the trustees to allow certain persons to occupy the house. The trustees allow Gemma to do so, and she occupies the house as her only residence on 31 January 2003.

On 31 August 2016, Gemma vacates the house. The trustees then sell the property on 30 September 2016 giving rise to a gain (including the held-over gain) of £250,000.

(i) Fiona sells her main residence at a gain of £400,000 in July 2016. It has been lived in by Fiona throughout her period of ownership as her only or main residence but she also teaches typing and administrative skills to students who lodge in the property whilst undergoing tuition. It has been agreed that 30% of the property has been used for teaching, 7.5% has been used as the students' lodgings and 62.5% has been used as the residence of the owner. Ignore any entrepreneurs' relief that may be due.

(2) In addition to his London house (which he has owned and occupied since 1998) Nash has just bought a house in the country. Nash has stated that it is his intention in approximately five years to give his London house to his nephew and then live solely in his new house in the country. He now divides his time equally between the two houses and expects this arrangement to continue until he gives his London house to his nephew. The London house is currently worth about 20% more than he paid for it. Nash has a substantial part of his income charged at the 45% additional tax rate and regularly makes gains in excess of the annual exempt limit. Advise Nash what he should do.

# Answer

## (1)

### (a) Miss Fielding

For the purposes of apportioning the only or main residence relief (also referred to as principal private residence (PPR) relief), periods of occupation prior to 31 March 1982 are ignored (TCGA 1992 s 223(7)). The property was owned and occupied from 31 March 1982 as follows:

| *Period* | *Ownership (years)* | *Occupation (years)* | |
|---|---|---|---|
| 31.3.82–31.3.87 | 5 | 4 | Let while working away (resided in the property before and after) (TCGA 1992 s 223(3)(c)) |
| 1.4.87–27.3.99 | 12 | 12 | Owner occupied |
| 28.3.99–28.9.15 | 16.5 | - | Let |
| 29.9.15–28.3.17 | 1.5 | 1.5 | Last 18 months (TCGA 1992 s 223(2)(a)) |
| Total | 35 | 17.5 | |

For discussion of the deemed occupation of the property, see **explanatory note 4**.

The chargeable gain is calculated as follows:

| Disposal – March 2017 | | £ |
|---|---|---|
| Proceeds | | 752,220 |
| 31 March 1982 value | | (70,000) |
| Gain | | 682,220 |
| *Less*: exempt proportion (17.5 years/35 years × £682,220) | | (341,110) |
| | | 341,110 |
| *Less*: residential lettings exemption | | |
| Lower of £40,000 and exempt gain of £341,110 | | (301,100) |
| Chargeable gain | | 301,100 |
| Less annual exemption | | (11,100) |
| Taxable gain | | 290,010 |
| 18,000 @ 18%* | 3,240 | |
| 272,010 @ 28% | 76,163 | |
| Total capital gains tax payable | | 79,403 |

*(32,000 – (25,000-11,000)) = 18,000

For discussion of the residential lettings exemption (also known as lettings relief), see **explanatory note 8**.

Gains on the disposal of residential property were excluded from the general reduction in capital gains tax rates for 2016/17 onwards (made by FA 2016 s 82). Gains on the disposal of an interest in residential property are now known as upper rate gains and taxed at 18% to the extent they fall within an individual's basic rate band or 28% for higher rate taxpayers and trusts and personal representatives. See explanatory note 11 for the meaning of an interest in a residential property.

### (b) Galsworthy

There is no chargeable gain on the disposal. Galsworthy occupied the house from the date of purchase until September 2010 and from that date he moved out of the property and into job-related accommodation.

Galsworthy is treated as occupying the property between September 2010 and the date of sale on the basis that he lived in job-related accommodation and he intended to reoccupy his property as his main residence at some point in the future (TCGA 1992 s 222(8)). Whilst his intention was to return, he did not do so as his employer required him to move again to another part of the country. This does not change the fact that the period from September 2010 to June 2016 qualifies as occupation. For more on job-related accommodation, see **explanatory note 5**.

Even if Galsworthy had not intended to resume residence at some later date almost all of the period of absence would still have counted as deemed occupation, because Galsworthy would qualify for the four years of absence while required by one's employment to live elsewhere plus the last 18 months of ownership. This would give total deemed occupation of five and a half years. A later period of actual residence is not necessary for an employment-related absence. Periods of absence are explained in **explanatory note 4**.

(c) **Hardy**

For the purposes of apportioning the only or main residence relief, periods of occupation prior to 31 March 1982 are ignored (TCGA 1992 s 223(7)). The property was occupied from 31 March 1982 as follows:

| *Period* | *Ownership (years)* | *Occupation (years)* | |
|---|---|---|---|
| 31.3.82–31.3.87 | 5 | 5 | Occupied by dependent relative (TCGA 1992, s 226) |
| 1.4.87–29.3.15 | 28 | – | Let |
| 30.3.15–30.9.16 | 1.5 | 1.5 | Last 18 months (TCGA 1992 s 223(2)(a)) |
| Total | 34.5 | 6.5 | |

Where the owner's dependent relative occupies a property rent-free as his sole residence then this is treated as qualifying occupation for the owner for the purposes of only or main residence relief. However, this treatment is only available where the relative occupied the property on or before 5 April 1988 (TCGA 1992 s 226). For further information, see **explanatory note 6.**

The chargeable gain is calculated as follows:

| | | | |
|---|---|---|---|
| Disposal – September 2016 | | | £ |
| Proceeds | | | 240,000 |
| Less: 31 March 1982 value | | | (26,000) |
| | | | 214,000 |
| Less: | exempt proportion (6.5 years/34.5 years × £214,000) | | (40,319) |
| | Letting exemption – lower of | | 172,478 |
| | Exempt gain, and | 40,319 | |
| | Maximum | 40,000 | (40,000) |
| Chargeable gain | | | 133,681 |

The exemption for the let period is the smaller of £40,000 and the amount exempt through *qualifying* occupation (see **explanatory note 8**). HMRC's previous view was that occupation by a dependent relative did not qualify as occupation for the purposes of letting relief. However, HMRC has since changed its view and now considers occupation by a dependent relative is qualifying occupation (CG64716).

(d) **Compton**

For the purposes of apportioning the only or main residence relief, periods of occupation prior to 31 March 1982 are ignored (TCGA 1992 s 223(7)). The property was occupied from 31 March 1982 as follows:

| *Period of ownership* | | *Actual or deemed owner occupation* | | *Notes* |
|---|---|---|---|---|
| Yrs | Mths | Yrs | Mths | |

| | Period of ownership | | Actual or deemed owner occupation | | Notes |
|---|---|---|---|---|---|
| 31.4.82–31.12.83 | 1 | 9 | 1 | 9 | Let while working abroad (resided in the property before and after) (TCGA 1992 s 223(3)(b)) |
| 1.1.84–30.6.88 | 4 | 6 | 4 | 6 | Let while working in UK (resided in the property before and after) (TCGA 1992 s 223(3)(c),(d)) |
| 1.7.88–31.12.99 | 11 | 6 | 11 | 6 | Actual occupation |
| 1.1.00–31.12.14 | 15 | | | | Let |
| 1.1.15–30.6.16 | 1 | 6 | 1 | 6 | Last 18 months (TCGA 1992 s 223(2)(a)) |
| | 32 | 27 | 17 | 27 | |

The total period of ownership is 34 years three months and the period of occupation is nineteen years three months.

The whole period between 1 January 1984 and 30 June 1988 is deemed occupation as Compton occupied the property as his main residence both at some point before and after these dates. Four years qualifies under TCGA 1992 s 223(3)(c) (working elsewhere in the UK) and six months qualifies under TCGA 1992 s 223(3)(d) (absence for any reason).

The chargeable gain is calculated as follows:

| | £ |
|---|---|
| Disposal – June 2016 | |
| Proceeds | 973,260 |
| Less: 31 March 1982 value | (90,000) |
| Gain | 883,260 |
| Less: exempt proportion 19.25 years/34.25 years × £883,260 | (496,431) |
| | 386,829 |
| Less: residential lettings exemption | (40,000) |
| Chargeable gain | 346,829 |

For discussion of the residential lettings exemption, see **explanatory note 8**.

(e) **Harold and Georgina**

Married couples or those in civil partnership can only have one main residence between them (TCGA 1992 s 222(6)(a)).

Since April 2000 the main residence for both Harold and Georgina has been Georgina's house. Since Harold let out his house during this period it is not a 'residence' and so the rules on more than one residence do not need to be considered. However, Harold's house was his main residence between the date of purchase in April 1988 and April 2000 (12 years).

Harold's property was occupied from 31 March 1982 as follows:

| *Period* | *Ownership (years)* | *Occupation (years)* | |
|---|---|---|---|
| April 1988 – Apr 2000 | 12 | 12 | Actual occupation |

| *Period* | *Owner-ship (years)* | *Occu-pation (years)* | |
|---|---|---|---|
| Apr 2000 – Apr 2015 | 15 | - | Let |
| Apr 2015 – Oct 2016 | 1.5 | 1.5 | Last 18 months (TCGA 1992 s 223(2)(a)) |
| Total | 29.5 | 13.5 | |

The chargeable gain for Harold is calculated as follows:

| | |
|---|---|
| Disposal – October 2016 | £ |
| Gain | 400,000 |
| Less: exempt proportion (13.5 years/29.5 years × £400,000) | (183,051) |
| | 216,949 |
| Less: lettings exemption | (40,000) |
| Chargeable gain | 176,949 |

For discussion of the residential lettings exemption, see **explanatory note 8**.

The *Mesher* order results in a transfer into trust. Any gain on this transfer is normally covered by TCGA 1992 s 225. The sale of Georgina's house is therefore exempt from CGT, because the house has been occupied throughout as the only or main residence by a beneficiary of the trust (Georgina and the children) and there has been no previous transfer subject to hold-over relief (see part (h) below). The shares of the proceeds paid out to both Georgina and her former husband are exempt from CGT. The trustees must claim the relief.

(f) **Stanley**

The sale in 2003 is exempt under TCGA 1992, s 225, as the property was occupied by the life tenant of the trust for the entire period of ownership. The trust is one in which the settlor retains an interest (as Stanley is entitled to the reversion), but this means only that Stanley is assessable on any gains that would normally be assessed on the trustees. As the trustees would not be assessed on a gain on the disposal of the house, neither is Stanley.

The reversion to settlor on the death of the life tenant is exempt from inheritance tax (IHTA 1984 s 54) (because her interest was created before 22 March 2006), so the return to his own estate does not create an inheritance tax charge for Stanley. However, TCGA 1992 s 73 provides that the normal 'uplift to probate value' does not apply on such a reversion to settlor, so the base cost of the second house to Stanley is the trustees' deemed cost of £260,000, not the current market value of £440,000.

On the eventual sale the gain of £180,000, subject to selling costs, is realised by Stanley.

(g) **Gordon**

Where part of a residence is used exclusively for business purposes, the only or main residence relief applies to the non-business proportion only (TCGA 1992 s 224(1)).

The property has been Gordon's main residence for the entire period of ownership, but the relief is prorated so that the business portion of the gain is chargeable.

The chargeable gain is calculated as follows:

| | |
|---|---|
| *Disposal – September 2016* | £ |
| Proceeds | 500,000 |
| Less: cost | (220,000) |

| *Disposal – September 2016* | £ |
|---|---|
| Gain | 280,000 |
| Less: exempt proportion (80% × £280,000) | (224,000) |
| Chargeable gain | 56,000 |

If the business use of the property had not been exclusive, ie the room(s) had been used for private purposes at weekends or in the evenings, full only or main residence relief would have been available.

(h) **James**

Anti-avoidance legislation was introduced from 10 December 2003 to prevent exploitation of the interaction between only or main residence relief and hold-over relief to avoid CGT in situations where there would be an immediate charge to inheritance tax, ie on a transfer into a trust (TCGA 1992 s 226A). For more details on hold-over relief (also known as gift relief), see **Example L9**.

Therefore because the trustees' allowable expenditure was reduced as a result of the claim to hold-over relief, they cannot cover the whole gain by only or main residence relief. But because the gift relief related to a transfer before 10 December 2003 transitional rules apply (FA 2004 Sch 22, para 8).

31.1.03 to 9.12.03 = 313 days

31.1.03 to 30.9.16 = 4,992 days

Entitlement to only or main residence relief:

313/4,992 × £250,000 = £15,675

Only or main residence relief is not available in respect of the 4,992 days from 10 December 2003 to September 2016. The transitional rules specifically prevent any period on or after 10 December 2003 from qualifying for relief as part of the final 18 months' exemption.

(i) **Fiona**

Where part of a residence is used exclusively for business purposes, the only or main residence relief applies to the non-business proportion only (TCGA 1992 s 224(1)).

The property has been Fiona's main residence for the entire period of ownership, but the relief is prorated so that the business portion of the gain is chargeable.

The chargeable gain is calculated as follows:

| *Disposal – July 2016* | £ |
|---|---|
| Gain | 400,000 |
| Less: exempt proportion (62.5% × £400,000) | (250,000) |
| | 150,000 |
| Less: residential lettings exemption | (30,000) |
| Chargeable gain | 120,000 |

Under the provisions in TCGA 1992 s 223(4) residential lettings relief is available where the gain is not fully exempted by the only or main residence relief and at least part of the remaining gain relates to a period when the property was let. The amount available for relief is limited to the lower of:

(a) the amount of only or main residence relief available;

(b) the portion of the gain which relates to the letting; and

(c) £40,000.

In Fiona's case, the relief is limited to the proportion of the gain which relates to the letting (£7.5% x £400,000).

The residential lettings exemption is discussed further in **explanatory note 8**.

(2)

**Nash**

Based on the facts in the question, it appears that Nash will have two 'residences' once he has bought the country property. Therefore he needs to elect which of these two properties is his main residence qualifying for exemption from CGT (TCGA 1992 s 222(5)). The election must be made within two years from the date that he has a second residence available to him (Griffin v Craig-Harvey [1994] STC 54). The election can subsequently be varied, and any variation will take effect not earlier than two years before HMRC is notified that Nash wishes to vary the election (TCGA 1992 s 222(5)(a); CG64510). The gift to the nephew of the London house will be treated for CGT as a sale at open market value (TCGA 1992 s 17). If Nash elects for the London house to be his main residence for the purposes of only or main residence relief, then no chargeable gain or allowable loss will arise when he disposes of it by way of the gift to his nephew.

On the basis that the election is in favour of the London property, which is likely as the asset is pregnant with gain, this means that the country property is not the main residence for that period and so, should Nash sell the country property, at least part of the gain will be chargeable (or part of the loss will be allowable). However, Nash would be best advised to vary the main residence election prior to the disposal of the London property and back-date it for 18 months as the last 18 months of ownership automatically qualify as deemed occupation. This should mean he will only have three and a half years where the country property does not qualify as the main residence.

On the disposal of the London house the country property will automatically become the main residence, unless Nash were to acquire a new residence.

If, on the other hand, Nash were to elect for the country property to be his main residence, then no chargeable gain or allowable loss would arise on any eventual disposal. However, a proportion of the gain on the London house would become chargeable on the gift to the nephew. The last 18 months' of ownership will, however, always be counted as a qualifying period of residence, which will make the chargeable fraction quite small (perhaps 3.5/23 if the five-year timeframe is accurate).

It is also worth ensuring that the country house is treated as Nash's main residence for some period in the period of ownership (theoretically as little as one day – though see **explanatory note 2**). This will ensure that the last 18 months' of ownership will qualify for the exemption.

## Explanatory Notes

*Meaning of 'residence'*

(1) Capital gains tax relief is available on the sale of a dwelling house that has been the taxpayer's only or main residence. The meaning of dwelling house is considered in **explanatory note 10**.

A residence is more than just owning a property. HMRC considers the ordinary meaning of residence to be "the dwelling in which that person habitually lives: in other words, his or her home" (CG64427).

It is the quality of the occupation that matters rather than the quantity, although the taxpayer may have difficulties in convincing HMRC that a short period of occupation has the degree of permanence to make it a period of residence. In *Goodwin v Curtis* [1998] STC 475 the Court of Appeal decided that a short period of occupation of a property while it was up for sale did not constitute residence, even though it was accepted that there was no trading motive. It was held that the General Commissioners were entitled to conclude that the occupation did not have a sufficient degree of permanence to have the quality necessary for residence.

In *David Morgan v HMRC* [2013] TC 02596 a taxpayer was successful in a claim to PRR where he had only lived at the property for a few weeks before deciding to let it out because his girlfriend left him. The tribunal found it a finely balanced case but took the girlfriends name on the mortgage deeds as intent.

*More than one residence*

(2) The gain on the disposal of an individual's only or main residence is exempt from tax, wholly or in part (TCGA 1992 s 222). Where an individual has two or more residences he may *elect* (within two years of having more than one residence) which is to be his exempt residence for CGT and this need not be the residence which is in fact his main residence (TCGA 1992 s 222(5); CG64485). It must, however, be or have been his *residence* throughout the period during which it is the nominated main residence. An investment property in which he had never lived would not qualify. See **explanatory note 1**. If no election is made the matter is determined by the facts of the case (CG64545).

If householders realise losses rather than gains when selling properties which have been their only or main residence, such losses are not allowable losses unless and to the extent that there is a non-exempt period of ownership.

Following *Griffin v Craig-Harvey* [1994] STC 54, an election must be made within two years of a taxpayer acquiring more than one residence. If this time limit is missed, the right to make an election would revive if a taxpayer had a change of residence, or acquired a third residence, but the period covered by the election would only date from the time that the new or additional property was used as a residence if the time limit had previously expired. Tax advisers should, therefore, advise and assist clients so that they make elections within the two-year period.

Note that it has since been suggested that *Griffin v Craig-Harvey* was wrongly decided (see 'Playing the chance card www.taxation.co.uk/taxation/Articles/2008/01/23/213521/playing-chance-card' *Taxation*, 24 January 2008). If this view is correct it would mean that elections might be made at any time backdated (if necessary) by up to two years whether or not one was owned during the initial two-year period. However, as this would mean overturning a precedent, it is almost certain that HMRC would challenge the treatment and so may be worth considering only when there is no other means of re-opening the election period.

The provisions enabling a main residence election to be varied with retrospective effect for two years could be beneficial to someone who has had two residences for some years and plans to sell the one that is not the elected main residence. An election could be made for the property that is to be sold to be the main residence with effect from two years before the date HMRC was notified of the change. A further election could then be made shortly after the first election reverting back to the original main residence, again with retrospective effect for two years (CG64510). The effect would be to obtain the exemption for the last 18 months' of ownership of the property that is being sold (see **explanatory note 4**), and possibly the extra lettings exemption as well (see **explanatory note 8**), at the cost of only a short period in respect of the original main residence.

An election is not required where someone owns a residence and has a second residence that he neither owns nor leases (eg accommodation with relatives, or a hotel room). A tenancy of a property would, however, need to be taken into account even if the right of occupation had no capital value (CG64536). Note that there is a concessionary relaxation of the two-year deadline where the interest in the second residence (or all the other residences except one) is negligible and the individual is unaware an election could be made (ESC D21).

From 6 April 2015 it is not possible for a person to elect for a property to be his main residence if he is not resident for tax purposes in the country where the property is situated unless he spends at least 90 days in the property within the tax year. This restriction has been introduced to re-inforce the new regime under which non-residents are taxable on the disposal of UK situs residential property with effect from the same date. However, it also restricts the ability of UK resident taxpayers to elect for foreign properties to be their main residence. If the taxpayer's spouse is resident in the property then an election is possible without the need for the taxpayer to meet the occupation requirement. (FA 2015 Sch 8 introducing new TCGA 1992 ss 222A to 222C).

(3) For a married couple or civil partners living together, there can be only one main residence for both. If they own two or more residences between them (either jointly or separately) the main residence election must be made by both (TCGA 1992 s 222(6)). If only one member of the couple is the property owner, only that

person would make the election. If on marriage/registration of a civil partnership each owned a residence, the two year period for electing which was the main residence would start at the date of marriage/registration.

No election is necessary in the case of Harold and Georgina in **part** (e) of this Example, because Harold does not live in his house following his marriage (meaning that after the marriage the property is not used as a residence by Harold).

When one spouse/civil partner inherits the only or main residence on the other's death, then although the survivor's acquisition value for capital gains is the market value at death, the period of ownership of the other (since 31 March 1982), and therefore any non-residence during that period, may be taken into account to compute any chargeable gain on disposal by the survivor (TCGA 1992 s 222(7)). Where there is a transfer of the whole or part of an individual's interest in a dwelling house or part of a dwelling house which is their only or main residence to the individual's spouse/civil partner, the transferee is deemed to have acquired his or her interest in the property on the date that the transferor's interest was acquired. Furthermore, when calculating the transferee partner's entitlement to private residence relief the two individuals are taken to be the same individual during the period that the transferor legally held the property. Occupation by either partner, therefore, counts for only or main residence relief. Where neither occupied the property the provision is disadvantageous as the transfer (even if on death) will not wash out the period of non-residence.

*Periods of absence*

(4) There a number of periods where the property is not occupied as a residence by the owner but which are deemed to be periods of occupation. Most of these deeming provisions are covered by statute but there is one that HMRC applies by concession.

To deal with the concessionary treatment first, when the property is first purchased but there is a delay in occupying the property the period of absence can be treated as occupation where:

- the owner buys land on which the dwelling-house is to be built; or
- the owner alters or decorates the dwelling-house before moving in.

The period before occupation is deemed occupation so long as the period between acquisition and actual occupation is 12 months or less (up to 24 months if HMRC is satisfied there is a good reason for delay) (ESC D49).

There are a number of statutory provisions to deem the property to be occupied by the owner during a period of absence. All of these provisions only apply provided the property has been the individual's only or main residence at some time during his total period of ownership (whether before or after 31 March 1982) (TCGA 1992 s 223(3A)). These are:

(a) up to three years for any reason (TCGA 1992 s 223(3)(a));

(b) any absence throughout which the individual is employed abroad (TCGA 1992, s 223(3)(b));

(c) up to four years during which the individual is prevented from living in the house because of the distance from his place of work or because his employer requires him to live elsewhere (or the individual is the spouse or civil partner of someone in this situation). 'Place of work' covers both employment and self-employment (TCGA 1992 s 223(3)(c), (d));

(d) the last 18 months of ownership (TCGA 1992 s 223(1)). This applies to disposals made on or after 6 April 2014. Disposals made prior to this date benefited from deemed occupation for the last 36 months of ownership. Where the individual disposing of the property is disabled or in long-term care the final period of deemed occupation remains 36 months (TCGA 1992 s 225E).

In order for the period of absence in (a) to (c) to qualify as deemed occupation, the property must become the individual's only or main residence again at some point in the future (not necessarily immediately after) and during the period of absence the individual had no other only or main residence which qualified for relief (TCGA 1992 s 223(3B)). For the purposes of (b) and (c) if the individual is prevented from reoccupying the property because of the situation of the individual's place of work or the terms of his *employment* require him to work elsewhere this still qualifies as deemed occupation (TCGA 1992 s 223(3B)(b)).

If someone is to occupy rented accommodation while away, then the rented property would be treated as a residence (see **explanatory note 1**). However, HMRC might be prepared to accept a main residence election for the owned property, so that the rules for allowable periods of absence could apply.

For the purposes of apportioning the only or main residence relief, periods of occupation prior to 31 March 1982 are ignored (TCGA 1992 s 223(7)).

*Job-related accommodation*

(5) If a person who lives in job-related accommodation (eg caretaker, like Galsworthy in **part (b)** of this Example) owns a house that he intends in due course to occupy as his only or main residence, he is regarded as being in occupation of his house during the time he lives in the job-related accommodation (TCGA 1992 s 222(8)). This provision also applies to self-employed people living in job-related accommodation.

Job-related accommodation is defined in TCGA 1992 s 222(8A)–(8D) and is explained in CG64555.

*Residence occupied by a dependent relative*

(6) The exemption for owner-occupied property extends to a residence occupied *rent free* by a dependent relative as his sole residence. However, to qualify for relief, the relative must have occupied the property before 6 April 1988 (TCGA 1992 s 226). The exemption is not available where a dependent relative first occupies a property on or after 6 April 1988.

If there are periods of absence by the dependent relative, the same rules apply as outlined in **explanatory note 4**. However, if the property ceases to be the sole residence of the dependant after 6 April 1988, subsequent periods of occupation by that or any other relative do not qualify for relief.

The legislation defines a dependent relative in TCGA 1992 s 226(6) but imposes no income restriction, so that the relative need not be financially dependent on the owner of the residence. HMRC does not regard payments of council tax by the relative or payments towards the upkeep of the property as breaching the 'rent free' requirement providing the owner is not left with a surplus over his outgoings (ESC D20).

*Divorce and separation*

(7) When spouses or civil partners separate, the matrimonial home ceases to be the main residence of the party who leaves it. Therefore, his share of any calculated gain on a subsequent sale chargeable to the extent that it relates to the period of absence, subject to any available exemptions or reliefs.

The last 18 months of ownership always count as a period of occupation, even if a new qualifying main residence has been acquired. However, relief is available for absences exceeding the final 18-month period, if:

(a) the property is eventually transferred to the spouse/civil partner remaining in it as part of the financial settlement; and

(b) an election for a new qualifying residence has not been made by the individual moving out in the meantime (TCGA 1992 s 225B).

A better arrangement for CGT purposes might be to use a *Mesher* order, as illustrated in **part (e)**. However, after 22 March 2006, such an arrangement can give rise to an inheritance tax charge.

If the disposal occurs more than 18 months after an individual leaves it, part of the gain is chargeable, but only in the proportion that the excess period over 18 months bears to the total period of ownership since 31 March 1982 (taking into account any available annual exemption).

*Residential lettings exemption*

(8) There is a further relief for owner-occupiers who at any time during their period of ownership have let all or part of the property as residential accommodation. The gain attributable to the letting is reduced by the lower of (TCGA 1992 s 223(4); SP 14/80):

(a) an amount equal to the part of the total gain that is exempt because of the owner occupation;

(b) £40,000;

(c) the gain arising by reason of the letting.

In a simple case, where the whole property has only been used as the only or main residence, or, apart from the times it has been the individual's only or main residence, has been let as residential accommodation, then the gain remaining after deducting only or main residence relief will be the gain arising by reason of the letting. However, if part of the property has been used exclusively for the purpose of a trade, the gain remaining after deducting only or main residence relief will not only be due to the letting. In such a case, TCGA 1992 s 223(4) can only relieve part of the gain remaining after private residence relief has been deducted.

The relief is illustrated in **parts (a), (c), (d), (e)** and **(i)** of this Example.

This relief in relation to letting residential accommodation also applies where a residence is occupied under the terms of a settlement. In addition, since 2007 HMRC has accepted that lettings relief is due where the residential property rented out has been occupied by a dependent relative prior to 6 April 1988 as the only or main residence of a dependent relative so as to qualify for TCGA 1992 s 226 dependent relatives' relief.

'Residential letting' is not defined in the legislation. HMRC took the view that the letting must have some degree of permanence, but it lost a case on the point in the Court of Appeal (*Owen v Elliott* [1990] STC 469), where it was decided that the exemption was available to the owners of a small private hotel who occupied the whole of the property during the winter months, with one or two guests, but moved to an annexe during the summer.

The exemption can be claimed only if the property qualifies as the CGT exempt residence for at least part of the period of ownership, so it cannot be claimed on a property which, although the taxpayer lives in it sometimes, has never been his only or main residence for CGT. Subject to that, it can be claimed where all of the property has been let for part of the period of ownership, or part of the property has been let for all or part of the period of ownership.

*Land associated with the dwelling house*

(9) The only or main residence exemption includes land that is for 'occupation and enjoyment with the residence as its garden or grounds up to the permitted area' (TCGA 1992 s 222(1)(b)). The 'permitted area' being (inclusive of the site of the house) up to half a hectare, which is approximately one and a quarter acres. However, a larger area may be considered a permitted area if it is in-keeping with the size and character of the house. The HMRC guidance can be found in CG64800 onwards.

In the case of *Longson v Baker* [2001] STC 6, the Inspector had originally allowed an area of just over one hectare for CGT relief as being 'reasonably required' for a person who bought a house for its stables and riding opportunities. However, the taxpayer tried to claim in court that seven and a half hectares were reasonably required for this purpose. The taxpayer's appeal was dismissed. The High Court judge stated that 'reasonably required' was an objective test of the amount of land that would be reasonably required for the enjoyment of the specific property, and the taxpayer's subjective liking for horses was irrelevant. This suggests that the Inspector may have been too generous in allowing more than the minimum.

The only or main residence exemption applies even if some of the land is sold separately. But the land must satisfy the conditions *at the time of disposal*, so that in *Varty v Lynes* [1976] STC 508 it was held that land sold *after* the sale of the house did not qualify since it did not form part of the residence at that time.

*employment* require him to work elsewhere this still qualifies as deemed occuption (TCGA 1992 s 223(3B)(b)).

If someone is to occupy rented accommodation while away, then the rented property would be treated as a residence (see **explanatory note 1**). However, HMRC might be prepared to accept a main residence election for the owned property, so that the rules for allowable periods of absence could apply.

For the purposes of apportioning the only or main residence relief, periods of occupation prior to 31 March 1982 are ignored (TCGA 1992 s 223(7)).

*Job-related accommodation*

(5) If a person who lives in job-related accommodation (eg caretaker, like Galsworthy in **part (b)** of this Example) owns a house that he intends in due course to occupy as his only or main residence, he is regarded as being in occupation of his house during the time he lives in the job-related accommodation (TCGA 1992 s 222(8)). This provision also applies to self-employed people living in job-related accommodation.

Job-related accommodation is defined in TCGA 1992 s 222(8A)–(8D) and is explained in CG64555.

*Residence occupied by a dependent relative*

(6) The exemption for owner-occupied property extends to a residence occupied *rent free* by a dependent relative as his sole residence. However, to qualify for relief, the relative must have occupied the property before 6 April 1988 (TCGA 1992 s 226). The exemption is not available where a dependent relative first occupies a property on or after 6 April 1988.

If there are periods of absence by the dependent relative, the same rules apply as outlined in **explanatory note 4**. However, if the property ceases to be the sole residence of the dependant after 6 April 1988, subsequent periods of occupation by that or any other relative do not qualify for relief.

The legislation defines a dependent relative in TCGA 1992 s 226(6) but imposes no income restriction, so that the relative need not be financially dependent on the owner of the residence. HMRC does not regard payments of council tax by the relative or payments towards the upkeep of the property as breaching the 'rent free' requirement providing the owner is not left with a surplus over his outgoings (ESC D20).

*Divorce and separation*

(7) When spouses or civil partners separate, the matrimonial home ceases to be the main residence of the party who leaves it. Therefore, his share of any calculated gain on a subsequent sale chargeable to the extent that it relates to the period of absence, subject to any available exemptions or reliefs.

The last 18 months of ownership always count as a period of occupation, even if a new qualifying main residence has been acquired. However, relief is available for absences exceeding the final 18-month period, if:

(a) the property is eventually transferred to the spouse/civil partner remaining in it as part of the financial settlement; and

(b) an election for a new qualifying residence has not been made by the individual moving out in the meantime (TCGA 1992 s 225B).

A better arrangement for CGT purposes might be to use a *Mesher* order, as illustrated in **part (e)**. However, after 22 March 2006, such an arrangement can give rise to an inheritance tax charge.

If the disposal occurs more than 18 months after an individual leaves it, part of the gain is chargeable, but only in the proportion that the excess period over 18 months bears to the total period of ownership since 31 March 1982 (taking into account any available annual exemption).

*Residential lettings exemption*

(8) There is a further relief for owner-occupiers who at any time during their period of ownership have let all or part of the property as residential accommodation. The gain attributable to the letting is reduced by the lower of (TCGA 1992 s 223(4); SP 14/80):

(a) an amount equal to the part of the total gain that is exempt because of the owner occupation;

(b) £40,000;

(c) the gain arising by reason of the letting.

In a simple case, where the whole property has only been used as the only or main residence, or, apart from the times it has been the individual's only or main residence, has been let as residential accommodation, then the gain remaining after deducting only or main residence relief will be the gain arising by reason of the letting. However, if part of the property has been used exclusively for the purpose of a trade, the gain remaining after deducting only or main residence relief will not only be due to the letting. In such a case, TCGA 1992 s 223(4) can only relieve part of the gain remaining after private residence relief has been deducted.

The relief is illustrated in **parts (a), (c), (d), (e)** and **(i)** of this Example.

This relief in relation to letting residential accommodation also applies where a residence is occupied under the terms of a settlement. In addition, since 2007 HMRC has accepted that lettings relief is due where the residential property rented out has been occupied by a dependent relative prior to 6 April 1988 as the only or main residence of a dependent relative so as to qualify for TCGA 1992 s 226 dependent relatives' relief.

'Residential letting' is not defined in the legislation. HMRC took the view that the letting must have some degree of permanence, but it lost a case on the point in the Court of Appeal (*Owen v Elliott* [1990] STC 469), where it was decided that the exemption was available to the owners of a small private hotel who occupied the whole of the property during the winter months, with one or two guests, but moved to an annexe during the summer.

The exemption can be claimed only if the property qualifies as the CGT exempt residence for at least part of the period of ownership, so it cannot be claimed on a property which, although the taxpayer lives in it sometimes, has never been his only or main residence for CGT. Subject to that, it can be claimed where all of the property has been let for part of the period of ownership, or part of the property has been let for all or part of the period of ownership.

*Land associated with the dwelling house*

(9) The only or main residence exemption includes land that is for 'occupation and enjoyment with the residence as its garden or grounds up to the permitted area' (TCGA 1992 s 222(1)(b)). The 'permitted area' being (inclusive of the site of the house) up to half a hectare, which is approximately one and a quarter acres. However, a larger area may be considered a permitted area if it is in-keeping with the size and character of the house. The HMRC guidance can be found in CG64800 onwards.

In the case of *Longson v Baker* [2001] STC 6, the Inspector had originally allowed an area of just over one hectare for CGT relief as being 'reasonably required' for a person who bought a house for its stables and riding opportunities. However, the taxpayer tried to claim in court that seven and a half hectares were reasonably required for this purpose. The taxpayer's appeal was dismissed. The High Court judge stated that 'reasonably required' was an objective test of the amount of land that would be reasonably required for the enjoyment of the specific property, and the taxpayer's subjective liking for horses was irrelevant. This suggests that the Inspector may have been too generous in allowing more than the minimum.

The only or main residence exemption applies even if some of the land is sold separately. But the land must satisfy the conditions *at the time of disposal*, so that in *Varty v Lynes* [1976] STC 508 it was held that land sold *after* the sale of the house did not qualify since it did not form part of the residence at that time.

*Meaning of 'dwelling house'*

(10) There have been several cases on what constitutes a dwelling house.

In *Batey v Wakefield* [1980] STC 572 a caretaker's bungalow physically separate from the main house was included within the exemption. In *Markey v Sanders* [1987] STC 256 the court held that for a group of buildings to be treated as a single residence they must be capable of being regarded as a single building, so a large, separate staff bungalow some distance from the main house did not qualify. But in *Williams v Merrylees* [1987] STC 445 a staff lodge even further away from the house than the *Markey v Sanders* bungalow was held to be part of a single entity and included within the private residence exemption. The High Court in the case of *Lewis v Rook* [1990] STC 23 similarly held that a gardener's cottage some distance away from the house occupied by the elderly woman owner was part of the main residence, but this was overruled in the Court of Appeal ([1992] STC 171). The HMRC guidance can be found in CG64230 onwards.

*Disposal of residential property*

(11) FA 2016 s 82 reduced the rates of capital gains tax with two exclusions. One of the exclusions being a disposal of residential property. Any gain not covered by reliefs (e.g. principal private residence or letting relief) on the disposal of residential property (worldwide) is taxed at 18% (to the extent the gain falls within the basic rate band) or 28% (above the basic rate band plus trusts and personal representatives).

The FA 2016 rules on residential property build (and interact) with the rules introduced in 2015 for non-resident CGT. Residential property gains are defined (TCGA 1992 s 4BB) as either:

(1) A disposal of a UK residential property interest (as defined in schedule B1) or

(2) A disposal of a non-UK residential property interest (as defined in schedule BA1).

In summary, a residential property interest is (schedules B1 (2) & BA1 (2)):

- Land which has at any time in the relevant ownership period consisted of or included a dwelling, or
- Land under a contract for an off-plan purchase; a contract including a building (or part) which will be constructed or adapted for use as a dwelling.

A dwelling is widely defined as:

- A building used or suitable to be used as a dwelling (sch B1 s 4 (1a)),
- A building in the process of being constructed or adapted for use as a dwelling (sch B1 s 4 (1b)),
- Land which at any time, is used or intended to be used, occupied or enjoyed with a dwelling as a garden or grounds (including any building or structure on such land) (sch B1 s 4 (2)),
- A dwelling not used for a purpose set out in sub-paragraph (3) (sch B1 s 4 (3)). For example, residential accommodation for school pupils is excluded from the definition of a dwelling. The full list of buildings not treated as residential property is given Example F2 explanatory note 11.

*Part use for business*

(12) Where part of a residence is used exclusively for business purposes, the provisions for exempting all or part of the gain relating to the only or main residence (including the exemption for the last 18 months of ownership) do not apply to the business proportion of the gain (TCGA 1992 s 224(1)). However, roll-over relief is available on the business proportion if the property is replaced. See **Example L9**.

Note that these rules do not prevent only or main residence relief where a person cares for an adult under a local authority placement scheme. Although the contract with the local authority may require the carer to set aside one or more rooms exclusively for the use of the adult in care, as long as the disposal takes place on or after 9 December 2009 CGT relief will not be denied (TCGA 1992 s 225D).

*Relocation of employee*

(13) There may be times where an employee needs to relocate and so sells his home either to the employer or to a relocation company, with a right to share in any profits when the employer or relocation company later sells the home. In these circumstances, the employee is exempt from CGT on the gain to the same extent as he was exempt on the original sale (to the employer/relocation company), providing the later sale occurs within three years (TCGA 1992 s 225C).

See **Example B2 explanatory note 7** for the income tax position in relation to employee relocation

*Intention to resell at a profit*

(14) Only or main residence relief does not apply if the property was acquired with the intention of reselling at a profit. If expenditure has been incurred on the property wholly or partly to make a gain on sale, an appropriate part of the gain is chargeable (TCGA 1992 s 224(3)).

This provision is widely drawn and HMRC confirms that if the house was genuinely acquired and used as a residence and the conditions for relief are met, relief will not be restricted. The anti-avoidance rule will be applied when the primary purpose of the acquisition was an early disposal at a profit (CG65210). For an indication of when this anti-avoidance rule might be applied, see CG65240 and follow the links to other pages in the manual.

A series of profitable sales may in exceptional circumstances be challenged as trading. This was the case in *Kirkby v Hughes* [1993] STC 76, where a builder bought and sold three houses that he had renovated while living in them. See **Example B6** for the criteria for deciding when a trade is being carried on.

*Restriction of private residence relief where holdover relief is claimed*

(15) Anti-avoidance legislation was introduced from 10 December 2003 to prevent exploitation of the interaction between only or main residence relief and hold-over relief to avoid CGT in situations where there would be an immediate charge to inheritance tax, ie on a transfer into a trust (TCGA 1992 s 226A). For more details on hold-over relief, see **Example L9.**

Where the base cost of a property is reduced by an earlier hold-over relief claim under TCGA 1992 s 260 (whenever made), no only or main residence relief can be claimed on a subsequent disposal after 9 December 2003. The rules only apply where the gain is affected by an earlier hold-over relief claim. Transitional rules permit a claim for private residence relief for disposals after 10 December 2003 in respect of the period before this date on a time apportioned basis (FA 2004 Sch 22, para 8). Therefore, in **part (h)** of the Example, had the trustees triggered a disposal for CGT on say 1 January 2004 they would have suffered the disallowance of relief for only 22 days. If the holdover claim is withdrawn in respect of an earlier disposal, it is treated as if it had never been made (TCGA 1992 s 226A(6)).

To avoid this, the settlor could refrain from claiming hold-over relief on the transfer into the trust, although this would mean an immediate CGT liability. Only or main residence relief may then apply to any subsequent gains during the period in which the property was a beneficiary's main residence. If the property does not show any significant taxable gain on the date of settlement it may be worth the settlor paying CGT on this transfer if that enables subsequent gains to be sheltered by only or main residence relief.

*Trustees of settlements*

(16) For disposals on or after 10 December 2003 it is necessary for trustees to make a claim for only or main residence relief when they dispose of property which has been occupied by a beneficiary under the settlement as that person's qualifying residence (TCGA 1992 s 225).

Note that the fact the relief is not automatic for trustees means that trustees will be able to claim loss relief on properties used by beneficiaries as their only or main residence in situations where the beneficiaries would not be able to claim relief if the properties were held directly.

# Question

(a) Murray Ltd purchased a freehold building for £40,000 in June 1982 for use in the hotel trade and sold it in October 1986 for £60,000. At the same time, the company acquired another hotel for £56,000, claiming roll-over relief appropriately. The new hotel was sold in January 2017 for £300,000. Assume the retail price index in January 2017 is 265.0. Calculate:

(i) the chargeable gains arising as a result of these transactions;

(ii) the chargeable gains that would have arisen if the freehold building had been acquired in 1972 instead of in June 1982, the market value being £54,000 at 31 March 1982, and all other particulars remaining the same. From 6 April 1985 to 5 April 1988, gains on pre-March 1982 purchases were calculated using original cost, with the company having the right to elect to calculate indexation allowance on the March 1982 value.

(b) Your client, Medway Ltd, a trading company, has been offered £1,500,000 for a freehold factory it is considering disposing of in October 2016. It acquired the factory in October 1943 for £40,000 and it had been valued for insurance purposes at £136,000 in April 1965 and £380,000 in March 1982. The factory site does not have any development value. The company has not made a 31 March 1982 rebasing election.

(1) Compute the chargeable gain which will arise if Medway Ltd disposes of the factory (assuming indexation allowance from March 1982 to October 2016 to be 240%).

(2) Indicate to the company the capital gains consequences of each of the following alternative courses of action it is considering taking following the sale, and give any advice you consider to be relevant:

(i) acquiring a larger freehold factory in 2017 for £1,600,000;

(ii) acquiring a smaller freehold factory in 2017 for £900,000 and using the remainder of the proceeds as working capital;

(iii) using the proceeds to pay a premium of £1,600,000 for a 40-year lease of a new factory (it is possible that a freehold warehouse will be bought in about five years' time for an estimated cost of £1,480,000);

(iv) acquiring a 40-year lease of a new factory for a yearly rental of £56,000 and a nil premium and loaning the sale proceeds to Newtown Ltd (a subsidiary in which Medway Ltd holds between 70% and 80% of the ordinary share capital) to be used by Newtown Ltd to acquire a freehold shop costing £1,520,000;'

(v) acquiring a new lease for a nil premium (as in (iv) above) and investing the proceeds in working capital. A 100% subsidiary, Parkland Ltd, that was acquired by Medway Ltd in 1985, will dispose of a holding of shares (to which the substantial shareholding exemption does not apply) giving rise to an allowable loss for capital gains purposes of £40,000. Medway Ltd wishes to set the loss of Parkland Ltd against its chargeable gain.

(c) On 30 April 2016 Rochester disposed of his property in Darke Road, comprising a house and workshop in the garden, for £225,150. He purchased the property on 1 May 1975 for £5,000 and its value at 31 March 1982 was £58,000. Throughout his period of ownership the house was his principal private residence and the workshop was used for his printing business (20% of the property relates to the workshop).

On 20 May 2015 Rochester had purchased a house, with a workshop annexe, in Howells Road for £250,000 (15% of the property relates to the workshop). Both the house and workshop were kept empty until 30 April 2016 when his family and the printing business occupied the premises.

Calculate the chargeable gain arising, assuming that Rochester claims rollover relief on the gain on the workshop.

(d) On 1 March 2005 Fordwich, aged 57, acquired a 25% shareholding in a trading company. Of the company's chargeable assets, 85% are chargeable business assets. He gave 5% of the shares to his son on 1 May 2016, and the gain arising before taking any available reliefs into account was £80,000.

Show how much of the gain, if any, is chargeable to capital gains tax assuming all available reliefs are claimed.

(e) Quincey invested £35,000 in April 1987 in unquoted shares in his friend's trading company (the shares representing a 4% holding). On 5 July 2016 Quincey sold the shares to his sister for £55,000. She agreed to pay the purchase price in ten equal annual instalments commencing July 2016. The market value in July 2016 was £85,000. Quincey has made other chargeable disposals in 2016/17 which used the annual exemption, and he has no allowable losses brought forward.

Show the capital gain arising and state how this may be treated.

(f) In January 2017 Harry transfers a painting to a discretionary trust and claims hold-over relief. The asset was bought in March 2002 for £200,000 and was worth £500,000 at the date of transfer. Harry does not have an interest in the settlement at the date of transfer.

The asset is sold by the trustees in March 2017 for £502,000. The trustees also dispose of another asset realising a loss of £275,000.

(i) Calculate the trustees' capital gain;

(ii) Explain what the consequences would be if Harry acquired an interest in the settlement in May 2017.

# Answer

## (a) Murray Ltd – roll-over relief

*(i)*

Assuming no other acquisitions of business assets within the roll-over period, the amount of the gain rolled over from the disposal in October 1986 is calculated as follows:

| | £ | £ |
|---|---|---|
| *Disposal - October 1986* | £ | £ |
| Sale proceeds | | 60,000 |
| Less: cost (June 1982) | 40,000 | |
| Indexation allowance $\frac{98.45 - 81.85}{81.85} = 20.281\%$ | 8,112 | |
| | | (48,112) |
| | | 11,888 |
| Less: roll-over relief (balancing figure) | | (7,888) |
| Chargeable gain (£60,000 proceeds less £56,000 reinvested) | | 4,000 |

The base cost of the hotel purchased in October 1986 is £48,112 (cost of £56,000 less gain rolled over of £7,888).

Assuming no other acquisitions of business assets within the roll-over period, the chargeable gain arising on the disposal in January 2017 is calculated as follows:

| | £ | £ |
|---|---|---|
| *Disposal - January 2017* | £ | £ |
| Sale proceeds | | 300,000 |
| Less: base cost (see above) | 48,112 | |
| Indexation allowance $\frac{265 - 98.45}{98.45} = 169.17\%$ | 81,391 | |
| | | (129,503) |
| Chargeable gain | | 170,497 |

The gains on the two assets are therefore £4,000 on the October 1986 disposal and £170,497 on the January 2017 disposal. For a discussion of roll-over relief, see explanatory note 1-4.

*(ii)*

If the original hotel had been bought in June 1972, the calculation of the gain that could be rolled over would be revised as follows:

| | £ |
|---|---|
| *Disposal - Oct 1986* | £ |
| Sale proceeds | 60,000 |
| Less: cost (June 1972) | (40,000) |
| Unindexed gain | 20,000 |

| | | £ |
|---|---|---|
| *Disposal - Oct 1986* | | |
| *Less*: Indexation allowance on election for 31 March 1982 value (£54,000) | | |
| Indexation allowance $\frac{98.45 - 79.44}{79.44} = 23.93\%$ | | (12,922) |
| | | 7,078 |
| *Less*: roll-over relief (balancing figure) | | (3,078) |
| Chargeable gain (£60,000 proceeds less £56,000 reinvested) | | 4,000 |

The base cost of the hotel purchased in October 1986 is £54,461 (cost of £56,000 less gain rolled over of £1,539). Only half of the rolled over gain is deducted from the base cost as the asset was owned on 31 March 1982 and the replacement of business assets took place on or before 6 April 1988. This is known as 'halving relief', see **explanatory note 10.**

Assuming no other acquisitions of business assets within roll-over period, the chargeable gain arising on the disposal in January 2017 is calculated as follows:

| *Disposal - January 2017* | £ | £ |
|---|---|---|
| Sale proceeds | | 300,000 |
| Less: base cost (see above) | 54,461 | |
| Indexation allowance $\frac{265 - 98.45}{98.45} = 169.17\%$ | 92,132 | |
| | | (146,593) |
| Chargeable gain (assuming no other acquisitions of business assets within rollover period) | | 153,407 |

The gains on the two assets are therefore £4,000 on the October 1986 disposal and £153,407 on the January 2017 disposal.

## (b) Medway Ltd – alternatives for deferring gains

(1)

The chargeable gain which would arise on the disposal of the factory in October 2016 is calculated as follows:

| *Disposal - October 2016* | | *Cost* | *Market value 31.3.82* |
|---|---|---|---|
| | | £ | £ |
| Sale proceeds | | 1,500,000 | 1,500,000 |
| Less: cost (October 1943) | | (40,000) | |
| Less: market value 31 March 1982 | | | (380,000) |
| | | 1,460,000 | 1,120,000 |
| Indexation allowance (on 31 March 1982 value) £380,000 x 240%* | | (912,000) | (912,000) |
| Overall gain | | 548,000 | 208,000 |
| Time proportion | | | |
| 6 April 1965 – October 2016 | $\frac{51.5}{71.5} = 0.720$ | 394,560 | |
| 6 April 1945** – October 2016 | | | |

| *Disposal - October 2016* | *Cost* | *Market value 31.3.82* |
|---|---|---|
| | £ | £ |
| Chargeable gain | | 208,000 |

* Assumed figure given in Example

** Earliest date for time apportionment

If a general 31 March 1982 rebasing election had been made the gain would have been the same, ie £8,000. The election for 6 April 1965 value would clearly give a higher gain than 31 March 1982 value, so it is not considered. Companies still benefit from indexation allowance.

*(2)*

(i) If a larger freehold factory were acquired in 2017 for £1,600,000, the gain of £208,000 need not be charged and could instead be rolled over to reduce the base cost of the new factory for capital gains purposes to £1,392,000 (£1,600,000 – £208,000).

(ii) If a smaller freehold factory were acquired for £900,000 in 2017, with the remainder of the proceeds used as working capital, then the whole of the gain would be realised and included in the profit for corporation tax purposes. This is because the amount of the proceeds from the factory which were not reinvested exceeds the gain of £208,000.

The rolled over gain would thus be reduced to nil giving a base cost for the replacement factory of £900,000.

(iii) The 40-year lease of a new factory is a depreciating asset (ie an asset with a life 60 years or less at the time of acquisition, see **explanatory note 5**). Therefore, instead of rolling over the gain on the old factory, it would be frozen and the gain would crystallise on the earliest of (TCGA 1992 s 154):

(A) date of disposal of the leasehold factory;

(B) date on which the leasehold factory ceased to be used for the purposes of the trade; and

(C) 10 years from the date of acquisition of the leasehold factory.

However, if Medway Ltd were to acquire another asset which qualified for roll-over relief but was not a depreciating asset (such as the freehold warehouse) at or before the time that the gain crystallises, the frozen gain could be rolled over into the new asset (ie the third asset). The deferred gain would then reduce the base cost of this third asset for capital gains tax purposes (TCGA 1992 s 154(4)).

(iv) If the proceeds were not used by Medway Ltd to acquire qualifying assets but were instead loaned to its subsidiary Newtown Ltd, which in turn used the loan to acquire a freehold shop costing £1,520,000, the tax treatment would depend on how much of Newtown's ordinary share capital is owned by Medway.

If Medway owns 75% or more of Newtown's ordinary share capital then Medway's chargeable gain could be rolled over against Newtown's acquisition, so that Newtown's base cost would be £1,312,000 (£1,520,000 – £208,000). This is because Medway and Newtown are members of the same capital gains group (TCGA 1992 ss 170, 175).

If Medway does not own 75% of Newtown's share capital then roll-over relief would not be available and the gain of £208,000 would be immediately taxable (subject to the acquisition of qualifying assets by Medway within three years after the sale of its factory, in which event roll-over relief could be claimed).

(v) Since the requisite 75% or more parent/subsidiary relationship exists between Medway and Parkland, they form a group for capital gains purposes (TCGA 1992 s 170).

Parkland could therefore transfer the shareholding to Medway on a no-gain/no-loss basis under TCGA 1992 s 171 and Medway could then make the disposal outside the group, so that Medway would be able to set the loss arising of £40,000 against the chargeable gain of £208,000 on the sale of the factory, provided Medway disposes of the shareholding before the end of the accounting period in which it disposes of the factory.

However, there is no need for Parkland to actually transfer the shares to Medway. TCGA 1992 s 171A provides that Parkland may make the disposal of the shareholding and the two companies may elect for the loss to be transferred by Parkland to Medway. The election must be made within two years after the end of the accounting period in which the asset was sold outside the group. See **Example K1 explanatory note 3(B)** for more detailed comments.

Additional points to note in relation to the various alternatives are as follows:

(1) Roll-over relief has the effect of reducing the base cost of the replacement asset, so that when the replacement is sold, indexation allowance is effectively forfeited on the rolled over amount for the intervening period (TCGA 1992 s 152). This does not apply where gains are frozen as a result of acquiring depreciating assets, because the capital gains cost of the replacement is unaltered (TCGA 1992 s 154). On the other hand, the maximum deferral time is 10 years, so the point when tax becomes payable may be much sooner. If the depreciating asset is a lease, the cost of the lease will be depreciated once the unexpired life is 50 years or less, reducing the indexation allowance accordingly if there is a disposal of the lease.

(2) If alternative (iv) were adopted (with Medway owning 75% or more of Newtown's share capital), then a larger gain would be charged on Newtown when it disposed of the shop. Since Newtown is not a wholly-owned subsidiary a compensating financial adjustment would need to be made between the companies in respect of any additional tax arising.

(3) As it is possible for companies in the same capital gains group to elect to reallocate chargeable gains or allowable loss under TCGA 1992 s 171A (see (v) above), it is possible to choose which of the companies in the group will pay the tax. If one company has a lower marginal corporation tax rate, then this would give a further advantage.

## (c) Rochester – business use of private residence

The chargeable gain is calculated as follows:

| | | |
|---|---|---|
| *Disposal - April 2016* | £ | £ |
| Sale proceeds | | 225,150 |
| Less: 31 March 1982 value | | (58,000) |
| Gain | | 167,150 |
| *Less*: only or main residence relief (£167,150 x 80%) | | (133,720) |
| | | 33,430 |
| Less: roll-over relief | | |
| Proceeds relating to old workshop (£225,150 x 20%) | 45,030 | |
| Less: amount reinvested in new workshop (£250,000 x 15%) | (37,500) | |
| Amount not reinvested | 7,530 | |
| Rolled over gain (balancing figure) | | (25,900) |
| Chargeable gain (amount not reinvested) | | 7,530 |

It is assumed that the workshops are used exclusively for business purposes. See **Example L7 explanatory note 11** for a discussion of the implications for only or main residence relief.

It seems likely from the facts in the question that the workshop and house are treated, both on the old property and on the new, as a single asset. If this is the case, the base cost of the new house for capital gains tax purposes will be £224,100 (£250,000 - £25,900).

If the new workshop could be regarded as a separate asset which cost £37,500 (£250,000 x 15%), that separate asset would have a base cost of £11,600 (£37,500 – £25,900). The rest of the house would have a base cost of £212,500 (£250,000 - £37,500).

## (d) Fordwich – gift of shares to son

It is assumed from the question that Fordwich receives no consideration from his son on the gift of the shares. As Fordwich is connected to his son, the disposal takes place at market value for the purposes of capital gains tax (TCGA 1992 s 18). Therefore, in theory, Fordwich has tax to pay but no proceeds from which to pay it.

However, as the shares are in a trading company the disposal qualifies for business asset gift relief (TCGA 1992 s 165). This is also called hold-over relief or gift relief. It means that, depending on the circumstances, all or part of the gain can be deferred so that the transferee pays the tax on the eventual sale.

Where the disposal consists of shares there may be a restriction to the relief under TCGA 1992 Sch 7 para 7. The restriction applies where the company owns chargeable assets which are not business assets and either:

- the transferor holds at least 25% of the voting rights of the company at any time in the period of 12 months prior to the disposal; or
- the company is the transferor's personal company (ie a company in which the transferor holds not less than 5% of the voting rights) at any time in the period of 12 months prior to the disposal.

Therefore the gain that Fordwich can hold-over is restricted as he holds 25% of the voting rights.

In this case, 15% of the company's chargeable assets are held for non-business purposes, therefore only 85% of Fordwich's gain will qualify for hold-over relief.

Therefore, where less than 5% of the voting rights are held by the transferor, no restriction would apply. However if the level of non-business assets meant that the company would not be regarded as a trading company then hold-over relief would not be available at all (TCGA 1992 s 165A). It is unlikely that 15% of chargeable non-business assets is sufficient, on its own, to indicate the company is not trading; further information would be required about the importance of the non-business assets to the operations of the company. See CG66941 as read with CG17953p.

The chargeable gains is calculated as follows:

| | |
|---|---|
| *Disposal - May 2016* | £ |
| Gain before reliefs | 80,000 |
| Less: hold-over relief (£80,000 x 85%) | (68,000) |
| Chargeable gain | 12,000 |

The son's base cost of the shares would be the market value at the date of gift, less the £68,000 held-over.

## (e) Quincey – sale of shares at undervalue, payment by instalments

Quincey's sister is a connected person, therefore the sale is deemed to be at open market value (TCGA 1992 s 18).

The gain before any reliefs is calculated as follows:

| | |
|---|---|
| *Disposal - July 2016* | £ |
| Deemed sale proceeds | 85,000 |
| Less: cost (April 1987) | (35,000) |
| Gain before reliefs | 50,000 |

The actual profit made by Quincey is £20,000 (£55,000 consideration less £35,000 cost). Therefore £30,000 of the gain relates to the 'gift' element of the deemed consideration.

Quincey and his sister may jointly claim for the 'gift' element of the gain, ie £30,000, to be held-over and treated as reducing the sister's base cost of the shares. If the annual exemption is not available and tax is due, there are two alternative provisions enabling the tax on this gain to be paid by instalments.

Since part of the consideration is due more than 18 months after the date of disposal, Quincey may opt to pay the tax by such instalments as HMRC allows over a maximum of eight years (TCGA 1992 s 280). Interest will be charged only on instalments paid late.

Alternatively, he may elect to pay the tax by 10 annual instalments, but with interest on the full amount outstanding being added to each instalment. Furthermore, if the shares were later disposed of for valuable consideration (whether by the sister or by someone else) the full amount of tax outstanding at that time would be payable immediately (TCGA 1992 s 281).

Having said this, given the small amount of tax that would be due on a gain of £20,000 (even if Quincey is subject to capital gains tax at the higher rate of 20%), it may be simpler to pay all the tax on the normal due date.

## (f) Trustees' capital gain

(i)

Assuming Harry has no beneficial interest in the settlement, the trustees' capital gains tax position is:

| | | |
|---|---|---|
| *Disposal - March 2017* | £ | £ |
| Sales proceeds | | 502,000 |
| *Less*: trustees' base cost | | |
| MV January 2017 | 500,000 | |
| *Less*: gain held-over | (300,000) | |
| | | (200,000) |
| Chargeable gain | | 302,000 |

Harry can claim to hold-over the gain when he gifts the painting into the discretionary trust (TCGA 1992 s 260). The entire amount of the gain that would otherwise accrue, £300,000 (deemed proceeds of £500,000 less cost of £200,000) can be held over. The disposal from Harry to the trustees takes place at market value as they are connected persons (TCGA 1992 s 18).

The trustees can set the current year capital loss of £275,000 against the gain, leaving net chargeable gains for the year of £27,000.

(ii)

The position is different if Harry were to have an interest in the settlement. This is because hold-over relief is not available for gifts to settlor-interested trusts from 10 December 2003 (TCGA 1992 s 169B). This rule applies where the trust is settlor interested at the date of the gift or within the claw-back period (see **explanatory note 26**).

Although Harry originally benefited from the hold-over claim on the transfer of the painting in 2016/17, the gain falls back into charge in the 2017/18 tax year (the year he acquired an interest in the settlement under TCGA 1992 s 169C) as follows:

| | £ |
|---|---|
| Market value (January 2017) | 500,000 |
| *Less*: cost | (200,000) |
| Chargeable gain | 300,000 |

Again, at the time of the disposal by the trustees in March 2017 the capital gains calculation is as in (i) above, however the trustees' gain is recomputed in 2017/18 once Harry obtains an interest in the settlement.

| | £ |
|---|---|
| Proceeds | 502,000 |
| Less: trustees' base cost (MV Jan 2017) | (500,000) |
| Chargeable gain | 2,000 |

The trustees must set the current year capital loss of £275,000 against the gain, reducing the net chargeable gains for the year to nil. The excess losses of £273,000 (£275,000 - £2,000) would be carried forward and any tax that the trustees had paid on the original calculation of the gain (£27,000 see (i) above) would be repaid.

## Explanatory Notes

*Assets qualifying for roll-over relief*

(1) Traders may claim roll-over relief for business assets under TCGA 1992 s 152 when both the assets subject to disposal and those acquired are within any of the following classes (TCGA 1992 s 155):

- land, buildings and fixed plant and machinery ('fixed' is considered to mean fixed on a permanent or semi-permanent basis to the premises) used for the purposes of the trade;
- ships, aircraft, hovercraft, satellites, space stations and spacecraft;
- goodwill;*
- milk and potato quotas* (see explanatory note 11);
- ewe and suckler cow premium quotas;*
- fish quota;*
- payment entitlements under the single payment scheme or the basic payment scheme (the latter applies where the disposal or acquisition of this asset takes place on or after 20 December 2013 as the single payment scheme ceased in 2014);*
- lloyd's syndicate rights.

* Since 1 April 2002 these assets have been dealt with for companies under the intangible assets rules, see **explanatory note 15**. Roll-over relief is therefore more limited for corporate traders than for unincorporated traders.

See also explanatory **note 13** regarding roll-over relief for compulsorily purchased land.

It is also possible to holdover a gain under TCGA 1992 s 154 where the replacement asset is a wasting or a depreciating one (see explanatory note 5).

The acquisition must be made within one year before or three years after the disposal (TCGA 1992 s 152(3)). The fact that the replacement may be acquired up to one year before the disposal does not, however, permit a gain on the sale of part of an asset within 12 months after its acquisition to be rolled over against the acquisition cost (*Watton v Tippett* [1997] STC 893).

HMRC has discretion to extend the time limits for reinvestment, and would probably exercise its discretion where there was a firm intention to acquire qualifying assets within the stipulated period but the taxpayer was prevented from doing so by circumstances beyond his control (CG60640). However, as shown in *R v CIR ex p Barnett* [2004] STC 763, the discretion to allow a late claim is solely in the hands of HMRC, with no right of appeal.

The disposal and acquisition do not have to be within the same class of asset, and the replacement asset need not be used in the same trade where one person carries on two or more trades either successively or at the same time. HMRC regards two trades as having been carried on successively if there is an interval between them which does not exceed three years (SP 8/81). Disposals during the interval qualify for relief, appropriately adjusted for the period of non-business use. Gains may be rolled over by reference 'to acquisitions during the interval, providing the assets acquired are not used or leased for any purpose during that time and are brought into use in the successor trade on its commencement.

The relief is not confined to a single disposal and a single acquisition. The gain on one asset could be rolled over against several replacement assets, or gains on several assets could be rolled over against a single replacement. ESC D22 provides that capital expenditure on improvements to existing qualifying assets may be treated as expenditure on new assets. The initial cultivation costs of short rotation coppice (net of any woodland grants) count as improvement expenditure under this heading, as would the acquisition of the freehold of a factory which had been leased by the trader.

To prevent abuse of this concession, and other non-statutory HMRC practice relating to deferring gains, TCGA 1992 ss 284A–284B were introduced in relation to disposals which take place after 8 March 1999. They provide that where a gain has been deferred under a concession first published before 9 March 1999 (or a later replacement concession with substantially the same effect) then if, on disposal, the person making the disposal seeks to avoid bringing the gain into charge he is treated as having made a chargeable gain equal to the deferred gain in the tax year or company accounting period in which the disposal takes place. The person on whom the charge arises could be the same taxpayer or another taxpayer to whom the asset had been transferred with the benefit of capital gains deferral.

*Reinvesting the proceeds*

(2) To get full roll-over relief, the full amount of the proceeds must be reinvested. Where only part of the proceeds is reinvested, the chargeable gain is deemed to be reinvested last (TCGA 1992 s 153).

This means that if the amount paid for the replacement asset is less than the sale proceeds for the old asset, the difference represents a realised gain, in respect of which relief is not available. If the difference exceeds the chargeable gain then roll-over relief is not available at all.

Where several disposals take place at the same time but the total proceeds are not fully reinvested, the disposals in respect of which relief is claimed may be chosen so as to maximise the benefit of the claim (CG60770).

For example if two assets were sold for a total of £200,000, being £130,000 and £70,000 respectively, showing total gains of £70,000 (£25,000 and £45,000 respectively) and replacement assets were acquired costing £120,000, roll-over relief could be claimed in respect of the second asset, deferring £35,000 of the gain and leaving a chargeable gain on the second asset of £10,000 (being proceeds of £130,000 less £120,000 reinvested). This is the case even though, when looked at in the round, the total amount not reinvested is £80,000 (£200,000 less £120,000) and this is more than the total gains of £70,000.

The relief is available if a gain arises on a gift of a qualifying asset, providing the deemed proceeds (which are the market value of the asset at the date of disposal under TCGA 1992 s 17) are matched by reinvestment in qualifying assets.

*Affect on the base cost of the newly acquired asset*

(3) The rolled over gain on the disposal is deducted from the cost of the new asset(s).

Indexation allowance is available for companies up to the date of disposal (see part (a) of this Example).

For individuals, indexation allowance is not available.

The effect of the roll-over relief is to give a lower base cost for the replacement asset(s), which means that indexation allowance is effectively forfeited for companies on the rolled over amount for the intervening period to the time the replacement asset is sold.

(4) If, exceptionally, the gain on a qualifying asset acquired before 6 April 1965 is arrived at by using time apportionment rather than 6 April 1965 value or 31 March 1982 value, and the full proceeds are not reinvested in qualifying replacement assets, the whole of the non-reinvested gain would not be chargeable because it would be restricted by time apportionment (TCGA 1992 s 153(1)).

If, for example, in **part (b)1**, of the Example the time apportioned gain had been the lowest gain, and £100,000 of the proceeds of sale had not been reinvested, only 51½/71½ × £100,000 = £72,028 would be immediately chargeable and the remainder of the chargeable gain would be rolled over.

*Roll-over into depreciating assets*

(5) A depreciating asset is either a wasting asset (ie has a useful life of 50 years or less), or an asset which will become a wasting asset within the next 10 years. If the replacement asset is a depreciating asset, the gain cannot be deducted from the acquisition cost, instead the gain is 'frozen' and it will crystallise on the earlier of (TCGA 1992 s 154):

(i) the date of disposal of the replacement asset;

(ii) the date on which the replacement asset ceases to be used for the purposes of the trade; and

(iii) 10 years from the date of acquisition of the replacement asset.

If, however, another qualifying non-depreciating asset is purchased not later than the earliest of the three dates, the gain may instead be deducted from that purchase (TCGA 1992 s 154(4)). The rules are illustrated in **part (b) 2(iii)** of this Example.

*Roll-over relief claims*

(6) Under TCGA 1992 s 153A, provisional claims for roll-over relief may be made in tax returns before reinvestment takes place, the provisional claims being replaced by actual claims when the conditions for relief are satisfied.

If the reinvestment does not take place, the provisional claim ceases to have effect three years from 31 January following the tax year of disposal, or four years from the end of the accounting period of disposal for companies, and all necessary adjustments will then be made to earlier tax calculations.

Where the gain has been frozen following reinvestment a depreciating asset and a non-depreciating qualifying asset is later purchased (which could be up to 13 years after the disposal giving rise to the gain that has been held over), the trader should make a claim for roll-over relief under TCGA 1992 s 152. HMRC will treat the claim in relation to the depreciating asset as having been withdrawn (CG60370).

*Death of taxpayer*

(7) If a taxpayer dies before a rolled over gain crystallises, the gain escapes tax as a result of the death. This is also the case where a gain has been frozen via reinvestment in a depreciating asset (ESC D45).

*Groups of companies*

(8) Where two or more companies form a 75% group (parent company and subsidiaries in which the parent owns 75% or more of the ordinary share capital), all the trades in the group are treated as a single trade

for roll-over relief (TCGA 1992 ss 170, 175). Relief may be claimed no matter which group company makes the disposals and which the acquisitions. A non-trading company that holds assets for trading companies in its group is included in these provisions under TCGA 1992 s 175(2B).

Disposals from one group company to another are made on a no-gain/no-loss basis, as indicated in **part (b) 2(v)** of this Example (TCGA 1992 s 171). Roll-over relief is denied where the replacement asset is acquired on a no-gain/no-loss basis (TCGA 1992 s 175(2C)). These provisions would prevent Medway Ltd in **part (b)** of this Example avoiding the gain on the disposal of the factory by acquiring a qualifying business asset from Parkland Ltd on a no-gain/no-loss basis. To obtain the relief, a new asset must be brought into the group.

For detailed notes on the group capital gains provisions see **Example K1**. See also explanatory note 13 to this Example re compulsorily purchased land.

*Assets owned personally and used by company*

(9) Roll-over relief is also available on the disposal and replacement of an asset owned personally and used in the owner's partnership or personal trading company (ie a trading company in which he owns 5% or more of the voting rights) (TCGA 1992 s 157). The payment of rent does not affect the position.

Where personally-owned assets are used in a personal company, the old and new assets must be acquired by the same individual, and used by the same personal company (and not for example by a new company following the liquidation of the first company) (CG61250). If the personal company is a holding company, use of an asset by a subsidiary does not qualify, because the subsidiary does not qualify as a personal company.

*Effect of 31 March 1982 rebasing provisions on rolled over gains*

(10) If a qualifying asset was disposed of at a gain before 31 March 1982 and a replacement asset was acquired before that date against which the gain was rolled over, the effect of the rebasing provisions is that the rolled over gain escapes tax, because it is not taken into account in arriving at the 31 March 1982 value of the replacement asset.

The same result would not occur if the pre-31 March 1982 disposal had produced a gain which was frozen on reinvestment in a depreciating asset (as distinct from being rolled over), but it is provided by TCGA 1992 Sch 4 para 4(5) that any such gain also escapes tax (see below in last paragraph of this explanatory note).

If a qualifying asset acquired pre-31 March 1982 is disposed of on or after 6 April 1988, the 31 March 1982 value may be used to calculate the gain to be rolled over.

But if a roll-over occurred after 31 March 1982 and before 6 April 1988 (as in **part (a)(ii)** of this Example), then only the cost of the asset and not the March 1982 value was deducted in calculating the gain (despite the indexation allowance being calculated on the March 1982 value). In these circumstances, any increase in value at 31 March 1982 of the asset giving rise to the deferred gain forms part of the deferred amount, since the gain has not been reduced by the increase in value up to 31 March 1982.

It is accordingly provided in TCGA 1992 Sch 4 that a claim may be made two years after the end of the company's accounting period in which the relevant event occurs for only one half of any deferred amount to be charged to tax in these circumstances. This is possible where the deferred amount is attributable directly or indirectly, in whole or in part, to a gain on the disposal before 6 April 1988 of an asset acquired before 31 March 1982. This is known as halving relief.

Halving relief was withdrawn for individuals, trusts and estates from 5 April 2008 with no further claims possible after that date. The claim under TCGA 1992 Sch 4 is still available to companies and this applies in the following situations:

(a) under the following provisions, where the deduction made in the base cost of a replacement asset acquired after 31 March 1982 and before 6 April 1988 is halved:

(i) where a replacement asset is acquired after receipt of compensation or insurance money (TCGA 1992 s 23(4), (5));

(ii) where a replacement asset is acquired on the disposal of a business asset, as in this Example (see part **(a)(ii)**) (TCGA 1992 s 152);

(iii) where shares are acquired on transfer of a business to a company (TCGA 1992 s 162);

(iv) where a gain is held over on a business asset acquired by gift (TCGA 1992 s 165);

(v) Where replacement land is acquired on compulsory acquisition of other land (TCGA 1992 s 247);

(vi) where a gain is held over on an asset acquired by gift under the former general gifts relief (FA 1980 s 79).

(b) under the following provisions, where gains that have been postponed on a disposal before 6 April 1988 are halved when they crystallise (or, in the case of the first four items, possibly exempted altogether, as indicated in the last paragraph of this explanatory note):

(i) where securities are acquired in exchange for a business acquired by a non-resident company (TCGA 1992 s 140);

(ii) where gilts are acquired on compulsory acquisition of shares (TCGA 1992 s 134);

(iii) where a depreciating asset is acquired on compulsory acquisition of land (TCGA 1992 ss 247, 248(3));

(iv) where a depreciating asset is acquired as replacement for a business asset, as in part **(b) 2(iii)** of this Example (TCGA 1992 s 154);

(v) where there is a reorganisation involving the acquisition of qualifying corporate bonds (TCGA 1992 s 116(10), (11)).

Where a gain (or loss) would otherwise crystallise on or after 6 April 1988 in relation to any of the items (i) to (iv) above, and it is directly attributable to the disposal of an asset on or before 31 March 1982, then it is not brought into account at all (TCGA 1992 Sch 4 para 4(5)).

*Milk quota*

(11) Milk quota was introduced in 1984. HMRC considers that the quota is a separate asset from the land to which it relates (CG77820). See **explanatory note 15** for the treatment of milk quota in the hands of companies from 1 April 2002.

*Capital allowances*

(12) The reduction of the base values of assets for capital gains tax does not affect the income tax figures. Capital allowances would still be available, for example, on the amount of £1,600,000 (less the cost of the land) paid for the freehold factory in **part (b) 2(i)** of this Example, whereas the base figure for capital gains tax is £1,392,000. In **part (b) 2(iii)**, Medway would be able to claim a deduction against its profit each year for the part of the £1,600,000 premium that was assessed on the landlord as extra rent. For details see **Example D3 part (h)** and explanatory note 14 of that Example.

*Roll-over relief and compulsory purchase*

(13) Although roll-over relief is not normally available on investment property (except for furnished holiday lettings, see **Example D2 explanatory note 25**), TCGA 1992 s 247 allows relief to be claimed where property is disposed of under a compulsory purchase order, and a replacement is acquired within one year before and three years after the disposal.

The relief is not available if the replacement property is the taxpayer's capital gains tax exempt dwelling at any time within six years after acquisition (TCGA 1992 s 248).

Companies in a 75% group can claim this relief if one company makes the disposal and another company acquires the replacement (TCGA 1992 s 247(5A)). 'Compulsory purchase' includes purchase of the freehold by a tenant exercising his right to buy (CG61940).

Where part of a holding of land is compulsorily purchased, small proceeds may be treated as reducing the capital gains cost of the holding rather than being treated as a part disposal (TCGA 1992 s 243). 'Small' is not defined but is taken by HMRC to mean not more than 5% (RI 164).

*Roll-over relief and grants towards replacement assets*

(14) Where a grant is received towards the cost of an asset, it is generally required to be deducted from the expenditure allowable for capital gains tax (TCGA 1992 s 50).

The case of *Wardhaugh v Penrith Rugby Union Football Club* [2002] STC 776 considered whether this had any effect on a roll-over relief claim. The club sold some land for £315,000, realising a gain of £204,000. It bought a new clubhouse for £600,000 and received a grant of £409,000 from the Sports Council towards this expenditure. HMRC argued that the grant should reduce the expenditure on the new asset to £191,000 for rollover purposes, which would leave £124,000 of the gain in charge to tax. The High Court held that TCGA 1992 s 50 operates only in calculating the gain on a disposal, and is independent of TCGA 1992 s 152 which restricts roll-over relief for partial reinvestment. Accordingly, the full gain could be held over against the expenditure of £600,000. This has the surprising effect of establishing a negative cost for the asset (as it would be reduced by the rollover claim and by the TCGA 1992 s 50 deduction). HMRC appealed this decision, but the appeal was dismissed in June 2003.

*Rules for intangible fixed assets*

(15) Companies normally receive deductions from revenue profits for the cost of goodwill and fish and agricultural quotas purchased (from 1 April 2002). Accordingly, goodwill and quotas purchased from that date cease to be a qualifying assets for roll-over relief for companies (unless acquired from related parties) and the sale of such goodwill and quota is subject to taxation as a trading profit. There is a separate roll-over relief for that trading profit where the proceeds are used to buy other intangible assets: this operates in a similar way to capital gains roll-over, but is independent of it, and there is no interaction between the two reliefs (CTA 2009 ss 754–763).

There was a transitional period during which a disposal on or after 1 April 2002 of goodwill or quota acquired before 1 April 2002 could be rolled over:

- under the capital gains rules against a purchase of goodwill or quota before 1 April 2002, and within the 12 months before the sale (ie the normal reinvestment time limit), which means that claims will normally have ceased to be possible after 31 March 2003;
- under the intangible assets rules (see **Example K3**); or
- partly under the capital gains rules and partly under the intangible assets rules (TCGA 1992 ss 156ZA-156ZB; CTA 2009 ss 898-900).

Apart from this transitional provision, capital gains cannot be rolled over against the purchase of intangible assets, and gains on intangible assets cannot be rolled over against property within the capital gains roll-over classes.

Goodwill and quotas purchased by a sole trader or partnership remain chargeable assets for capital

For the detailed provisions of the intangible assets legislation see **Example K3**.

*Gifts and disposals to connected persons*

(16) A gift of a chargeable asset is regarded as a disposal at open market value (except for transfers between spouses/civil partners) (TCGA 1992 s 17), and the chargeable gain or allowable loss is computed in the usual way.

Where the parties are connected persons, then not only gifts but all transactions between them are deemed to be at market value (except for transactions between spouses and civil partners who are living together) (TCGA 1992 s 18 as read with TCGA 1992 s 286). For detailed notes on connected persons and how market value is arrived at see **Example L1**. See also **Example I7 explanatory note 8(d)** for the effect of a transfer at an undervalue by a close company.

*Hold-over relief on pre-14 April 1989 gifts*

(17) Before FA 1989, where a gain arose on a gift, a claim could be made to hold-over the gain and reduce the base cost of the asset in the hands of the donee if (FA 1980 s 79):

(a) the gift was made by an individual or trustees; and

(b) the donee was either an individual who was resident or ordinarily resident in the UK, or trustees who on a subsequent disposal would be liable to UK capital gains tax.

The relief applied to gifts from and to individuals after 5 April 1980, and was extended to include gifts to trustees after 5 April 1981 and to gifts by trustees after 5 April 1982. This general gifts relief was abolished by FA 1989 for disposals on or after 14 March 1989, but assets may still be owned against which such gains have been held-over.

(18) For disposals on or after 14 March 1989 more restricted hold-over relief provisions are now contained in TCGA 1992 ss 165, 260.

Company donors do not qualify for hold-over relief, but the donee of a TCGA 1992 s 165 gift may be a company (except for gifts of shares).

*Hold-over relief for gifts of business assets*

(19) TCGA 1992 s 165 broadly provides for individuals to claim to hold-over gains on gifts of certain assets and reduce the base cost of asset in the hands of the donee by the amount held-over. The assets which qualify for relief are:

(a) assets used in the donor's business or in his personal trading company (ie a company in which he holds not less than 5% of the voting rights), or used by a company in a trading group of which the holding company is the donor's personal trading company;

(b) farmland and buildings that would qualify for inheritance tax agricultural property relief (broadly all farming land providing certain conditions as to length of ownership and occupation are satisfied, including farmland held as an investment providing it has been owned for seven years and occupied for agriculture throughout that period) or let on a Farm Business Tenancy (TCGA 1992 Sch 7, paras 1, 3; CG66960);

(c) shares or securities in unquoted trading companies, or unquoted holding companies of trading groups (shares on the Alternative Investment Market qualify for relief);

(d) shares or securities in the donor's personal trading company or personal holding company of a trading group.

A gift of shares or securities to a company does not qualify for hold-over relief (TCGA 1992 s 165(3)(ba)).

Where agricultural property has development value, the gain qualifying for relief under (b) is not restricted to the agricultural value, even though inheritance tax agricultural property relief is so restricted (CG66962).

It should be noted that heading (d) enables relief to be claimed on a gift out of a 5% holding of shares in a *quoted* company. A holding of *any* size qualifies for relief under (c). If the holding (of quoted or unquoted shares) is 5% or more, however, relief is restricted to the business assets proportion of the gain (TCGA 1992 Sch 7, para 7). In **part** (e) of the Example, Quincey owns only 4% of the shares, so his relief is not restricted. In **part (d)** of the Example, the relief is restricted, because Fordwich owns 25% of the shares in his company.

Relief under TCGA 1992, s 165 is also available for disposals by trustees, heading (a) above being amended so as to relate to assets used in a trade carried on by the trustees or a life tenant and heading (d) relating to holdings in quoted companies where the trustees carry at least 25% of the voting power (TCGA 1992 Sch 7, para 2). Any shares or securities in unquoted trading companies, or unquoted holding companies of trading groups, qualify for hold-over relief on disposal by trustees.

Claims for TCGA 1992 s 165 relief are made jointly by the donor and donee, unless the *donees* are trustees, in which case the claim is made by the donor alone (TCGA 1992 s 165(1)(b)).

*Hold-over relief on gifts of non-business assets*

(20) TCGA 1992 s 260 provides for holdover relief on gains on the following gifts by individuals or trustees:

(a) certain gifts of heritage property (works of art, historic buildings etc);

(b) gifts to funds for the maintenance of heritage property;

(c) gifts to political parties;

(d) gifts that are immediately chargeable to inheritance tax, or would be apart from the annual exemption. This mainly covers gifts to trusts and close companies.

As with claims for relief under TCGA 1992 s 165, claims for relief are made by the donor and donee jointly, unless the *donees* are trustees, in which case the claim is made by the donor alone (TCGA 1992 s 260(1)(c)).

*Effect of hold-over relief on inheritance tax*

(21) For both TCGA 1992 ss 165, 260, any inheritance tax payable on the gift is deductible in arriving at the chargeable gain on a later disposal (but not so as to create a loss) (TCGA 1992 s 165(10); TCGA 1992 s 260(7)). This applies even where inheritance tax is payable at some later time, for example because the donor dies within seven years. All necessary adjustments will be made to the earlier computation.

However, if a gift does not qualify for hold-over relief and capital gains tax is payable, there is no direct inheritance tax relief for the capital gains tax paid if the gift becomes chargeable to inheritance tax because of the donor's death within seven years (although the capital gains tax paid has reduced the wealth of the donor and therefore the amount liable to inheritance tax on his death). The detailed inheritance tax provisions are in the companion to this book, **Tolley's Taxwise II 2016/17.**

*Assets disposed of at an undervalue*

(22) Hold-over relief under both TCGA 1992 ss 165, 260 is also available where assets are not given outright but are disposed of for less than their value. If the actual consideration is greater than the original cost of the assets, so that the donor has in fact realised some of the gain in cash, then the chargeable gain which may be held over is restricted by the excess of the actual proceeds over cost, as shown in **part (e)** of the Example.

*Effect of non-residence*

(23) Hold-over relief is not available if the donee is not resident in the UK, or would not be chargeable to tax on a gain as a result of being regarded as non-resident under a double tax treaty (TCGA 1992 ss 166, 261). Relief under TCGA 1992 s 165 is not available if the donee is a foreign-controlled company (TCGA 1992 s 167).

The held-over gain is charged to tax if the donee becomes not resident in the UK within six years after the end of the tax year in which the gift was made (TCGA 1992 s 168).

*Gifts relief claims*

(24) No specific time limit is stipulated for the hold-over relief claims, so that the normal time limit of four years from the end of the tax year in which the transfer occurred will apply (TMA 1970 s 43).

HMRC has stated that in most circumstances it will not be necessary to agree market values at the time of a claim. Establishing the market value at the date of the gift can normally be deferred until the donee disposes of the asset (SP 8/92). There is a standard claim form for holdover claims. The form is included in HMRC Helpsheet HS295. Under self-assessment the claim is separate from the return, although it will often be sent in with the return.

*Paying tax by instalments*

(25) Where hold-over relief is not available, or does not cover the full amount of the gain, any tax arising may be paid by 10 annual instalments if the asset is:

- land;
- controlling holding of shares or securities in a company; or
- a minority holding of shares or securities in an unquoted company.

Interest is charged on the full amount outstanding and is added to each instalment (TCGA 1992 s 281).

The other instalment option, outlined in **part (e)** of this Example, is only available where the consideration is payable by instalments over a period of more than 18 months (see **Example L3** explanatory note 3 for details).

*FA 2004 restriction of hold-over relief to settlor-interested trusts*

(26) Prior to 10 December 2003, hold-over relief was often used to restart the taper relief clock to avoid apportionment provisions (taper relief was abolished from 6 April 2008), as part of an inheritance tax avoidance arrangement and to use tax reliefs within a trust (eg other losses or entitlement to main residence relief) to eliminate a chargeable gain.

As shown in **part (f)** above, hold-over relief is no longer available where the trust is settlor-interested either at the date of the gift or any time before the sixth anniversary of the start of the tax year following the one in which the disposal was made (the claw-back period) (TCGA 1992 ss 169B, 260(1)). This applies to gifts under both TCGA 1992 ss 165 260.

For the hold-over claim to fail, the following conditions must be satisfied (TCGA 1992 ss 169B-169G):

(a) the disposal must be to a trust;

(b) the disposal can be from a trust to a trust or from an individual to a trust and either:

  (i) the trust is settlor interested or there is an arrangement (which is widely defined) under which an interest could be acquired by the settlor; or

  (ii) the trust is one which benefits an individual who in the past (at any point) has made a hold-over claim in respect of which that asset thereby now has a reduced base cost.

Interest is widely defined at TCGA 1992 s 169F and includes where either the settlor or spouse/civil partner (TCGA 1992 s 169F(4)) obtains a benefit directly or indirectly from such property. TCGA 1992 s 169(5) provides that an interest of a settlor (or spouse/civil partner) can be ignored in limited circumstances involving the death of particular parties.

**Point (b)** above is intended to prevent the rules being avoided using a chain of transfers, eg Connor settles assets on trust A from which he is excluded (claiming hold-over relief) which then transfers the asset to trust B from which he is not excluded.

The claw-back provisions provide that a chargeable gain arises equal to the held-over gain at the time the settlement becomes a settlor-interested settlement (TCGA 1992 s 169C). The trustees' allowable expenditure is increased by the amount of the held-over gain.

There are limited exclusions from these rules for certain disabled trusts and historic buildings (TCGA 1992 s 169D).

# Question

(1)

(a) Outline the principal differences between the tax treatment of capital gains made by individuals and those made by companies.

(b) Kaput Ltd owns a 100% subsidiary, a 60% subsidiary and a 40% stake in a consortium company. All the companies are UK resident. Comment on the implications of these shareholdings for the taxation of Kaput Ltd's capital gains, including the implications of transactions between the companies.

(2) Fancy Trading Ltd has a UK subsidiary, Plain Trading Ltd, in which it holds 80% of the issued share capital. Both companies make up accounts annually to 31 December.

On 30 May 2016 Plain Trading Ltd sold 10,000 50p ordinary shares in Twisty Ltd, a non-quoted company, for £60,000. This holding was less than 5% of the total shares in issue. It had acquired the shares in May 1986 from Fancy Trading Ltd for £1.50 each. Fancy Trading Ltd had acquired the shares at par in January 1980, and they were valued at £1.55 each on 31 March 1982.

Show the capital gains position on the sale in May 2016 and indicate what the position would have been if the proceeds had been only £6,000.

The following indexed rises may be used:

March 1982 – May 1986: 23.2%

March 1982 – May 2016: 255.7%

# Answer

## (1)

### (a) *Principal differences between the tax treatment of capital gains made by individuals and companies*

(i) Individuals are charged separately to capital gains tax (CGT) on gains, while companies treat chargeable gains as another source of taxable total profits.

For individuals there is a special 10% rate of CGT for disposals qualifying for entrepreneurs' relief, within a lifetime limit of £10m. For non-entrepreneurs' relief gains that do not arise on residential property, individuals are subject to a tax rate of 10% for gains to the extent that taxable income has not utilised the basic rate band and at 20% thereafter, capital gains on residential property are taxed at 18% within the basic rate band and 28% thereafter. Individuals may also qualify for Investors relief which also results in relevant gains being subject to a 10% rate of CGT. Further details are given in **Example L3**.

(ii) Individuals enjoy an annual exemption for capital gains (£11,100 for 2016/17), but companies do not.

(iii) Companies are entitled to indexation allowance to reflect the effect of inflation between:

the latest of:

- the acquisition date, or
- 31 March 1982,

  and
- the date of disposal.

Individuals are not entitled to indexation allowance.

(iv) For assets held before 31 March 1982, individuals are required to treat the assets as having been acquired on that date for the then market value. Companies may opt into this treatment (either globally or on an asset-by-asset basis). If they do not, two sets of calculations are necessary. Where the two calculations yield two gains or two losses, the lower of the two gains or losses is used. Where one calculation gives a gain and another a loss, then the disposal is deemed to be for neither a gain nor a loss. For companies, a third option applies in respect of assets owned before 6 April 1965. They can be rebased to that date or have time-apportionment of gains reflecting the period of ownership after 6 April 1965 (but with any period of ownership before 6 April 1945 completely ignored).

(v) For CGT, all shares and securities of the same class, held by a taxpayer in the same capacity, are pooled in a single pool (subject to some limited exceptions such as for acquisitions on the same day as the disposal and the 'anti bed and breakfasting' next 40 day first in first out, rule – see **Example L6**). For companies, different pools operate for shares acquired before 1 April 1982 and before 6 April 1965 (except where a rebasing election has been made).

(vi) Many CGT reliefs and exemptions are not relevant to companies (e.g. only or main residence, incorporation relief, entrepreneurs' relief, gift hold-over relief).

(vii) Where an individual is an officer or employee of the company (or a company within the group) in which he or she has a security holding then part or all of a gain may be taxed as income under the employment-related securities rules.

(viii) There is no 'exit charge' when an individual becomes non-UK resident, but a company becoming non-UK resident is deemed to dispose of all its chargeable assets at their market value on the date it becomes non-resident (unless the assets remain within the charge to corporation tax through being used by a UK permanent establishment of the company).

(ix) The tax treatment of loan stocks and foreign currencies is different for companies. Under the 'loan relationships' provisions, most loan stocks and currency exchange differences are dealt with for companies as income (loan relationship credits). Individuals and trustees would pay:

- income tax on the whole profit on a 'deeply discounted security';
- CGT on some loan stocks which are non-qualifying corporate bonds (non-QCBs) (e.g. stocks redeemable in a foreign currency);
- income tax on accrued income on disposal of most qualifying corporate bonds (QCBs);
- CGT on exchange profits on foreign currency assets including funds within foreign currency bank accounts (but foreign currency liabilities are outside the scope of CGT).

For the detailed corporation tax provisions on loan relationships see **Example K2**.

(x) For acquisitions on or after 1 April 2002 from unrelated parties, goodwill, intellectual property, and fishing and agricultural quotas are not chargeable assets for companies. Gains and losses on such assets are taken into account under the 'intangible assets' provisions, subject to exclusions for certain types of intangible asset introduced in FA 2016. For the details see **Example K3**.

(xi) For disposals on or after 1 April 2002, companies are exempt from tax on the disposal of a substantial shareholding (broadly 10% of ordinary share capital held for 12 months) in a trading company. For details see **Example K3**.

(xii) Companies are subject to a number of specific anti-avoidance measures (referred to by HMRC as targeted anti-avoidance rules or TAARs). These measures were intended to prevent companies avoiding tax through the creation and subsequent use of capital losses. For example the following measures were designed to target a specific area of concern:

(1) The contrived creation of capital losses (where the companies/groups concerned do not actually suffer a capital loss) – the legislation disallows losses that arise in the course of arrangements where the realisation of a tax advantage is a main or the main purpose of the arrangements.

(2) The buying of capital gains and losses – the provisions were introduced to counter schemes created to circumvent the existing capital gains and loss buying anti-avoidance rules on a change in the ownership of a company and a main or the main purpose for the change in ownership is to secure a tax advantage.

(3) Tax avoidance schemes seeking to (a) turn an income receipt into a capital receipt which can be offset by a capital loss; or (b) use capital losses to obtain a deduction against income.

Individuals, trustees and personal representatives, are also subject to a comprehensive targeted anti-avoidance rule covering all taxpayers at TCGA 1992 s 16A.

From 17 July 2013, FA 2013 Sch 43 introduced a General Anti Abuse Rule which covers all aspects of corporation and income tax. See **Example N5**.

(xiii) Companies are not 'natural persons' and so are subject to the Annual Tax on Enveloped Dwellings ["ATED"] regime, where a property within the ATED regime is disposed of by the company an ATED-related gains charge on the gain at 28% may be levied (subject to various exemptions).

*(b)*

Kaput Ltd and its 100% subsidiary are a group for capital gains purposes. This means that any assets chargeable to tax on gains are transferred between them on a 'no loss no gain' basis (see **explanatory note 1**), and a gain on the disposal of a business asset by one can be rolled over against the acquisition of a qualifying asset by the other (see **Example L9**).

Kaput Ltd and its 60% subsidiary do not qualify for the above treatment (this is because Kaput's holding in the subsidiary falls short of the 75% required for the two companies to qualify as a group for the purposes of taking advantage of the favourable CGT group provisions). The 60% holding that Kaput Ltd has in its subsidiary does, however, mean that the two companies are connected persons in relation to each other as the subsidiary is under the control of Kaput Ltd due to holding more than 50%. This means that (i) transactions between them are routinely taxed at open market value; and (ii) a loss on a disposal by one to the other can only be offset against gains on disposals to the same person.

Kaput Ltd's stake in the consortium company is only 40% meaning that it is not in control of the consortium company. This means that it is not connected with the consortium company. As such whilst a transaction which is not at arm's length would have to be adjusted to market value (in accordance with the general CGT rule where transactions which are not on third party terms take place), where there are losses on disposals by one to the other these losses should be allowed against other gains (see **explanatory note 5**).

## (2) No gain no loss transfers – disposal of shares in Twisty Ltd 30 May 2016

Plain Trading Ltd will be treated as having acquired the shares in Twisty Ltd at their cost to Fancy Trading Ltd, i.e. £5,000 (10,000 × £0.50) plus indexation allowance to May 1986 of 23.2% × £5,000 = £1,160, giving a total acquisition cost of £6,160. (Although an election could have been made to base the indexation allowance on the intra-group transfer on the 31 March 1982 value of £15,500, this would not usually have been done, since as the law then stood, it would not have affected the calculation when the asset was transferred outside the group.)

The position on the sale on 30 May 2016 is as follows:

| | | *Using cost* | | *Using 31.3.82 value* |
|---|---|---|---|---|
| | | £ | | £ |
| Sale proceeds | | 60,000 | | 60,000 |
| Deemed value on intra-group transfer May 1986 | 6,160 | | | |
| *Less*: indexation allowance included therein | 1,160 | | | |
| | 5,000 | | | |
| 31.3.82 value – 10,000 @ £1.55 | | | 15,500 | |
| Indexation allowance on 31.3.82 value 255.7% × £15,500 | 39,633 | 44,633 | 39,633 | 55,133 |
| | | 15,367 | | 4,867 |
| Chargeable gain is the lower of the two, i.e. | | | | 4,867 |

### If the sale proceeds had been £6,000

Although indexation allowance cannot normally create or increase a loss on a disposal on or after 30 November 1993, this does not apply to the indexation allowance up to the time of the intra-group transfer in May 1986. It is not clear, however, whether HMRC would be prepared to allow the calculation to be based on the 31 March 1982 value of £15,500, giving indexation allowance of 23.2% of £15,500 = £3,596, since the election to use 31 March 1982 value on such a transfer had to be made within two years from the end of the relevant accounting period (i.e. by 31 December 1988) or within such further period as HMRC allows. If HMRC did allow this, the proceeds of £6,000 would be compared with an indexed cost of £8,596, giving an allowable loss of £2,596. If they will not allow 31 March 1982 value to be used to calculate the indexation allowance, only 23.2% × £5,000, i.e. £1,160, could be added to the cost of £5,000, making £6,160, and the allowable loss would be £160 (being less than the loss using 31 March 1982 value of £15,500).

## Explanatory Notes

*No gain no loss disposals*

(1) References in this Example are to TCGA 1992 unless otherwise stated. Section 56 provides that on a disposal which would be treated as a 'no gain, no loss' disposal under the normal rules, an unindexed gain equal to any available indexation allowance is deemed to arise, thus giving a net result of no gain/no loss. Examples of where these provisions apply for companies are as follows:

(a) Transfers on company reconstructions (s 139).

(b) Transfers within a 75% group of companies (s 171).

If, however, there is a loss when the asset is eventually disposed of, for corporation tax, it is reduced by any indexation allowance added at the time of the no gain/no loss transfer (s 56(3)). This does not apply if the transfer was made before 30 November 1993, indexation allowance up to the time of such a transfer being available as part of an allowable loss (s 56).

This is an important point to spot as the on-going entitlement to 'banked' indexation allowance can be significant and is particularly alien to those who are not familiar with the old indexation allowance rules for individuals.

In **part (2)** of the Example, Plain Trading Ltd is treated as acquiring the shares in Twisty Ltd at their cost to Fancy Trading Ltd in 1980 plus indexation allowance from 1982 to the time of the intra-group transfer in May 1986. This can create a loss as it occurred before November 1993.

(2) The rebasing provisions of s 35 enable gains and losses on assets acquired before 31 March 1982 to be calculated using 31 March 1982 value. Where an asset owned on 31 March 1982 was transferred before 6 April 1988 under specified no gain/no loss provisions, and is then disposed of on or after 6 April 1988, Sch 3 para 1 provides that the eventual transferor is treated as having owned the asset on 31 March 1982. The gain or loss on that eventual disposal is therefore computed using either 31 March 1982 value or original cost whichever shows the lower gain or loss (unless a general 31 March 1982 rebasing election has been made). In making the calculation based on cost, indexation allowance can be given on 31 March 1982 value, but in order to prevent double counting the indexation allowance included in the acquisition cost has to be excluded (s 55(5) and (6)).

In **part (2)** of the Example, therefore, the calculation based on cost excludes the indexation allowance made on the intra-group transfer from Fancy Trading Ltd to Plain Trading Ltd.

The provisions to prevent double counting would also apply if the original acquisition by the first person had been before 31 March 1982 and the no gain/no loss transfer had been after 5 April 1988. For an illustration see **Example K1 part A**.

There is a problem as indicated in **part (2)** of the Example where intra-group transfers took place between 31 March 1982 and 5 April 1988. Up to 31 March 1985 indexation allowance was based on cost, and from 1 April 1985 to 5 April 1988 it could be based on 31 March 1982 value only if an appropriate election was made. Although 'rolled up indexation' on a no gain/no loss transfer between those dates may be treated as part of cost under s 56, it has never been clarified whether the indexation calculation can be made using the 31 March 1982 value where that would be beneficial to the taxpayer.

The main instances to which these provisions apply are those in (a), (b) and (c) of **explanatory note 1**, i.e. transfers on company reconstructions, within a 75% group and between spouses/civil partners.

For 75% groups of companies, the general 31 March 1982 rebasing election is made by the principal company in the group, and it applies to all group companies (subject to provisions to deal with companies joining and leaving the group – see **Example K4**) (Sch 3 para 8 and Sch 3 para 9).

*Corporate shareholders – share matching rules*

(3) Disposals of securities are matched with acquisitions as follows, except for scrip and rights shares (including scrip dividend options – see **Example L6 explanatory note 13**), which are treated as acquired when the original shares were acquired, and loan stock (see **Example L7 explanatory note 4**):

(a) Acquisitions on the same day as the disposal, s 105 (1)(b).

(b) For disposals before 5 December 2005: where the company owns 2% or more of the issued shares of a particular class, acquisitions in the previous month (latest first) then acquisitions in the following month (earliest first).

(c) Where (b) does not apply, acquisitions within the previous nine days (and no indexation allowance is available on the disposal), s107(3).

(d) The post-1982 pool, s 107(7).

(e) The pre-1982 pool s 107(7) and (9).

(f) Pre 6 April 1965 acquisitions that are not included in the pre-1982 pool, latest first, s 107(7) and (9).

(g) Acquisitions after disposal (other than those taken into account in (b)), earliest first, s 105(2).

The rules outlined above (except (b) and the scrip dividend option rules) applied to unincorporated shareholders as well as companies before 6 April 1998. The introduction of taper relief in FA 1998 led to different share identification rules for individuals, trustees and personal representatives between 6 April 1998 and 5 April 2008. With the abolition of taper relief in FA 2008 and other significant changes to the CGT rules for individuals, trustees and personal representatives (such as the complete phasing out of any deduction for indexation relief) the share identification rules for individuals changed again as outlined in **part 1(a)(v)** of the Example.

The abolition of rule (b) with effect from 5 December 2005 was a consequence of the introduction of the specific anti-avoidance rules referred to in **part 1(a)(xii)** of the Example. On the basis that artificial losses do not now qualify as allowable losses, the anti-bed and breakfasting provision previously found in s 106 was thought no longer necessary.

*Capital gains provisions for groups of companies*

(4) The capital gains treatment of groups of companies is dealt with in more detail in **Example K1**. See also **Example L9 part (b)** for rollover relief aspects.

*Transactions not at arm's length*

(5) It is necessary to use market value as the deemed proceeds for such transactions (s 17) but the restriction on the offset of losses in s 18 only applies to persons connected within s 286.

# Indirect Taxes: Stamp taxes and VAT

# Question

## A.

Briefly describe when a liability will arise to:

(a) stamp duty;

(b) stamp duty reserve tax.

## B.

A wealthy client, Mr Argenton, has been involved in a number of transactions during the year ended 5 April 2017:

| | |
|---|---|
| 8 May 2016 | He purchased the total issued share capital of a company from Mr Copperfield; the consideration was a £1 nominal cash payment together with the release of a loan of £50,000 which Mr Argenton had originally made to Mr Copperfield. |
| 9 September 2016 | As trustee of a family settlement, he arranged for the transfer of trust shares having a value of £75,000 to his eldest daughter. The transfer was made upon his daughter reaching the age of 25 and was in accordance with the terms of the settlement. |
| 15 January 2017 | Mr Argenton subscribed in cash for £250,000 nominal value 5-year convertible loan stock 8%. The issue was by his wholly owned investment company. |
| 20 March 2017 | Mr Argenton had previously loaned £250,000, interest free, to a friend's property development company. As part of a reconstruction scheme for that company, he agreed to receive 2,500,000 10p shares issued by the company in satisfaction of the debt. |

Provide Mr Argenton with a memorandum that sets out the stamp duty liabilities of each transaction.

## C.

(a) Explain what is meant by the process known as 'adjudication' in relation to stamp duty, indicating when it is used, the consequences that flow from it and the remedies available to a dissatisfied taxpayer.

(b) Brown Ltd is the parent company of a diverse group. As part of an exercise to rationalise the group investment structure, all shareholdings in both group and non-group companies are being transferred to Brown Ltd.

The following transactions took place on 31 December 2016:

(i) Blue Ltd, a wholly owned subsidiary, transferred its shares in Black Ltd (its own wholly owned subsidiary) to Brown Ltd for £50,000.

(ii) Brown Ltd owned 70% of Colourless Ltd, which in turn owned all the capital of Rainbow Ltd. All shares in Rainbow Ltd were transferred to Brown Ltd for £100,000. (The remaining 30% of Colourless Ltd was not owned by the group.)

(iii) Rainbow Ltd contracted to sell 200 shares in Indigo plc, a quoted company, to Brown Ltd for £3,000. Before the contract was completed, Brown Ltd transferred its beneficial interest in the shares to a third party for £2,900 on 21 January 2017.

Outline the stamp duty and stamp duty reserve tax consequences of these transactions.

# Answer

## A.

### (a) *Stamp Duty*

Stamp duty is a duty on documents completed in the UK relating to UK transactions involving shares and marketable securities. No duty arises on transactions which are carried out orally (FA 1999 ss 112–113 and Schs 13–16).

If an instrument that is liable to be stamped is not so stamped, it cannot be used as evidence in civil proceedings. Therefore, a failure to have a document properly stamped could lead to legal problems in the case of a dispute. A company secretary will not register a transfer of shares or securities if the document has not been properly stamped.

Although stamp duty is not directly enforceable, interest and penalties can be levied for a failure to ensure that documents are properly stamped. (The interest and penalty rules are set out at **explanatory note 2**.)

The administration and collection of stamp duty is the responsibility of HM Revenue and Customs (Stamp Taxes).

The Stamp Act 1891 s 5(a) requires that full details of the facts and circumstances relating to an instrument are provided in order to allow the correct stamp duty to be calculated. Failure to do so can lead to a fine of up to £3,000.

Duties can be 'ad valorem' which means that the duty will be a percentage of the consideration passing. Alternatively, duties can be 'fixed'. (Most fixed duties have, however, now been abolished with the exception of a limited number of cases relating to pre-SDLT land transactions.)

Some instruments – most notably instruments which transfer shares by way of a gift where no consideration is payable – are not stampable, provided that the appropriate exemption certificate is completed. These instruments are listed in SI 1987/516.

Stamp duty depends upon the heading under which a transaction falls, ie:

| | | |
|---|---|---|
| (1) | Share and convertible loan stock transactions (including purchase by a company of its own shares, takeovers, mergers, demergers, and schemes of reconstruction and amalgamation, except where there is no real change in ownership) | ½% |
| (2) | Shares converted into depositary receipts or put into duty free clearance systems (see **part (b)**) | 1½% |
| (3) | Most bearer instruments (excluding those in foreign currency – but see **part (b)**) | 1½% |

Ad valorem duty is calculated as a strict percentage, and then rounded up to the nearest multiple of £5 (FA 1999 s 112). Duty is not chargeable on a transfer of stock or marketable securities where the consideration for the sale is not more than £1,000 (FA 1999 Sch 13 para 1).

Stamp duty is not payable when a company issues new shares to its shareholders, for example on the initial creation of the company or when new shares are subscribed for.

Where shares are repurchased by a company, ad valorem duty at a rate of 0.5% is payable on the Form SH03 delivered to the Registrar of Companies. No duty is payable, however, if the shares were held on an overseas branch register unless the Form SH03 is executed in the UK.

The consideration payable by the purchaser to the vendor will usually be in the form of cash. However 'consideration' can take other forms such as other shares and marketable securities, the release of debt or liability or a dividend in specie.

Therefore stamp duty cannot be avoided by the purchaser paying for the new shares in non-cash form. Effectively the value of the non-cash assets offered in exchange for the shares is treated as consideration and is subjected to ad valorem stamp duty.

Sometimes the consideration for a transfer of shares may be uncertain at the time of the transaction. The stamp duty payable depends on how the deal is structured. If the contingent amount is fixed then that amount is also subject to stamp duty. The same rule applies if a variable amount has a maximum limit; stamp duty is then payable on the maximum amount. However, if a variable amount only has a minimum limit then stamp duty is only payable on the minimum amount. If a variable amount has no maximum or minimum limit then no ad valorem duty is payable in relation to the potential extra consideration.

If shares are exchanged, then two share transfers will be executed. Both will be liable for ad valorem duty. Each will be liable to stamp duty by reference to the value of the shares transferred by the other document.

In both cases, the transaction may be documented as a sale of the higher value shares. The transfer of the higher value shares will be liable to ad valorem duty but the transfer of the shares in consideration will not. To qualify as a sale of the higher value shares, there must be a cash element to the sale which is more than nominal.

There is an exemption from stamp duty where shares pass between two companies in a group. A group is where one company owns 75% of the shares of another, or both are under the 75% ownership of another company. This is sometimes referred to as 'stamp duty group relief' (FA 1930 s 42). The instrument of transfer must be adjudicated (see **C below**). The exemption does not apply if, at the time the instrument is executed, arrangements are in existence which mean that any other person can gain control of the transferee company (FA 1967 s 27).

There are special exemptions from duty for financial intermediaries trading in UK securities and in connection with stock lending and sale and repurchase arrangements (FA 1986 ss 80A to 80D). Exemption also applies where a mutual insurance company transfers its business to a conventional company (FA 1997 s 96), and to transfers of units in unit trusts or shares in open-ended investment companies (FA 1999 Sch 19), although the latter are now charged to stamp duty reserve tax (see **(b) below**).

A stamp duty exemption applies to instruments executed on or after 28 April 2014 relating to shares or marketable securities admitted to trading on a growth market recognised as such by HMRC but not listed on any market. (A similar stamp duty reserve tax exemption applies to any agreement to transfer securities made on or after 28 April 2014.)

A stamp duty (and stamp duty reserve tax) exemption also applies where the trustees of a tax-advantaged share incentive plan transfer shares to the employees as partnership shares or dividend shares (FA 2001 s 95 – see **Example N1 part (3)**).

## (b) *Stamp Duty Reserve Tax*

Stamp duty reserve tax (SDRT) is charged under the provisions of FA 1986 ss 86–99 on transactions in *chargeable securities* (broadly, stocks, shares, loan capital, and units under a unit trust scheme (as to which see below) (FA 1986 s 99)) which are not charged to stamp duty, for example, sales of renounceable letters of allotment. The rate of tax is ½%. Transactions under the paperless system for transferring securities (CREST), are subject to SDRT on the agreement to transfer, rather than stamp duty (FA 1996 s 186). Stamp duty continues to be charged on securities transferred outside the CREST system. SDRT does not apply to gilt edged stocks, traded options and futures, non-convertible loan stocks, foreign securities not on a UK register, depositary interests in foreign securities, purchases by a charity, transfers of units in foreign unit trusts, and the issue of new securities. See also **part (a)** for the exemption for shares transferred to employees under share incentive plans.

There are special exemptions for financial intermediaries (FA 1986 ss 88, 88B, and 89AA) which apply to transactions on a regulated market or multilateral trading facility (both as defined in the EU Markets in Financial Instruments Directive) or on a recognised foreign exchange or recognised foreign options exchange. If a person who has qualified for exemption then transfers securities to a fellow group member, the normal exemption on intra-group transfers does not apply and SDRT is payable (FA 1986 s 92). There are also exemptions for exchanges of securities between associated companies (FA 1930 s 42, FA 1986 s 88).

An anti-avoidance measure charges SDRT at ½% on transfers of foreign currency bearer shares and of sterling or foreign currency bearer loan stock that is convertible or equity related. The charge does not apply if the securities are listed on a recognised stock exchange and the transfer is not made as part of a takeover (FA 1986 s 90).

SDRT also applied to surrenders before 30 March 2014 of units in a unit trust and shares in open-ended investment companies (OEICs). The rate was ½%, but this could be reduced where within the same or following calendar month similar units are issued. This charge has now been abolished.

Liability to SDRT arises at the date of the agreement (or, if the agreement is conditional, the date the condition is satisfied) (FA 1986 s 87). For transactions via an exchange (in particular CREST transactions), the tax is payable on a date agreed with HMRC (or if there is no agreed date, the fourteenth day after the transaction). For other transactions the due date is the seventh day of the month following the date of the transaction and the person liable to pay the tax (ie the broker, dealer or purchaser) must give notice of the charge to HMRC on or before that date. If stamp duty is paid after reserve tax has been paid, the reserve tax is refunded (plus interest on refunds over £25, the interest being free of income tax).

SDRT also applies to securities converted into depositary receipts or put into a duty free clearing system, and the rate of tax on these transactions is 1½% (FA 1986 ss 93–97). For options entered into on or after 25 November 2015 and exercised on or after 16 March 2016, where securities are deposited with a depositary receipt issuer or clearance service following the exercise of an option, the 1½% rate applies to the higher of the consideration or the market value on the date of transfer. The charge extends to the issue or transfer into a depositary receipt or clearance system of foreign currency bearer instruments that would otherwise be exempt from duty, unless they are subscribed for cash and carry a right to a dividend at a fixed rate or are loan capital. The tax is only payable, however, to the extent that it exceeds any ad valorem stamp duty on the transaction, and where the ad valorem duty exceeds the amount of reserve tax, no reserve tax is payable. Clearing systems may elect to pay stamp duty or SDRT in the normal way on their transactions, and in that event the 1½% charge when securities are put into the system does not apply (FA 1986 s 97A). Following the decision of the European Court of Justice in *HSBC Holdings plc and Vidacos Nominees Ltd v Revenue and Customs Comrs ECJ*, [2010] STC 58; [2009] All ER (D) 03 (Oct), which ruled that the charge on the issue of securities into a clearance service in the EU is contrary to EU law, HMRC will not collect the SDRT charge when new securities are issued into such a clearance service or into a depositary receipt system in the EU. Where the securities are subsequently transferred into a clearing system or depositary receipts system outside the EU, that transfer will not, however, be exempt from the charge (FA 1986 s 97C).

## B. Memorandum for Mr Argenton

8 May 2016
The true consideration for the purchase of the company's share capital is £1 plus the loan of £50,000 = £50,001. The rate of stamp duty on shares is ½% rounded up to the nearest £5. Accordingly the duty payable is £255.
If the shares are actually worth less than £50,001 then the transfer may be submitted for adjudication and duty paid at the above rate on the actual value of the shares (FA 1980 s 102(2)).

9 September 2016
The trustees are transferring property in accordance with the trust deed. That transaction is exempt from duty in accordance with the Stamp Duty (Exempt Instruments) Regulations 1987 (SI 1987/516) – Category F. No duty is payable providing the appropriate certificates are signed.

15 January 2017
Mr Argenton is not liable to stamp duty on the issue of loan stock because it is specifically exempt under FA 1986 s 79(2). (That section also exempts the *transfer* of loan stock unless it carries a right either of conversion into shares or to more than a commercial rate of return, but see **part A(b)** re the charge to SDRT on the transfer of certain bearer loan stock.)

20 March 2017
No liability arose on the granting of the loan, and the issue of new shares to Mr Argenton in satisfaction of the debt is also exempt from duty. (The exemption from duty on issues of shares does not apply where they are issued as consideration for a sale. Nor does it apply to bearer shares – FA 1963 s 60.)

## C.

### (a) *Adjudication*

Adjudication is the process whereby HMRC (Stamp Taxes) assess the amount of stamp duty, if any, payable on a document, including adjudication as to the amount of any penalty payable for late stamping (as to which see **explanatory note 12**). Additionally, if after adjudication an unstamped or insufficiently stamped document is not duly stamped within 30 days, a penalty of up to £300 may be charged.

Adjudication may be voluntary or compulsory. Any person may ask HMRC to adjudicate as to whether a document is chargeable to stamp duty, and if so, to state the duty payable. If HMRC decide that no stamp duty is payable the document will be stamped to that effect. Once stamped a document is admissible in evidence (Stamp Act 1891 s 12).

Adjudication may be required where consideration needs to be established in order to determine the duty payable, eg where shares are issued as consideration for a transaction.

If a taxpayer is dissatisfied with the decision of HMRC he may appeal against it. Appeals must be made within 30 days and the duty plus any interest or penalty must be paid first. Appeals relating to late stamping penalties go first to the First-tier Tribunal and other appeals to the High Court.

### (b) *Transactions by Brown Ltd group of companies*

(i) Providing the documents are submitted for adjudication, the transfer by Blue Ltd to Brown Ltd of shares in Black Ltd will be exempt from stamp duty as Blue Ltd is a wholly owned subsidiary of Brown Ltd (FA 1930 s 42).

(ii) Stamp duty of ½% of £100,000, ie £500 will be payable as Brown Ltd owns only 70% of Colourless Ltd.

(iii) The agreement to sell shares in Indigo plc is not itself dutiable, and therefore the transfer of the beneficial interest in that contract by Brown Ltd will avoid stamp duty but not SDRT. This will be charged on Brown Ltd, ie ½% × £3,000 = £15.

The actual share transfer will be between Rainbow Ltd and the third party and that document will attract stamp duty of £15, ie ½% × £2,900 = £14.50, rounded up to nearest multiple of £5.

# Explanatory Notes

*Adjudication*

(4) The process of adjudication is outlined in **part C(a)** of the Example. Where a document bears an adjudication stamp this is normally conclusive evidence of stamping.

Section 12 of the Stamp Act 1891 provides for HMRC to 'adjudicate' on any executed instrument if requested to do so. HMRC can be asked to adjudicate on a number of points such as:

(a) whether the instrument is stampable;

(b) the amount of duty;

(c) whether a late stamping penalty is payable;

(d) what penalty is correct and appropriate.

If HMRC decides that an instrument is not chargeable to stamp duty, then it will be stamped to show this. Otherwise it will be stamped with the amount adjudicated and the relevant amount should be paid as appropriate. Adjudication is the only way to formally determine the amount of stamp duty due. Adjudication is compulsory for certain instruments, such as transfers of shares to charities, specifically exempt transfers (eg, intra group transfers) and transfers in satisfaction of a debt.

If a person is unhappy with the adjudication, he has 30 days to bring an appeal. However, an appeal can only be brought on payment of the stamp duty plus any penalty in conformity with HMRC's decision and any interest that would be payable following the adjudication.

*Interest and penalties*

(5) Penalties for stamp duty and SDRT may apply where documents are submitted late for stamping (SA 1891 s 15B). There are separate interest and penalty provisions in relation to bearer instruments.

If documents are not presented for stamping within 30 days, the penalty for documents presented up to one-year late is £300 or 10% of the duty if lower. For documents submitted outside the one year period but not more than two years late the penalty is 20% of the amount of the duty. For documents submitted more than two years late the penalty is 30% of the amount of the duty. For delays of one year or more, HMRC may impose a penalty at a higher rate if there is evidence that the failure to submit documents for stamping was deliberate (but subject to an overall limit of the amount of the duty).The penalties are subject to mitigation where there is a reasonable excuse. For documents executed abroad the 30 days and one-year periods run from the date the document is brought into the UK. There is a penalty of up to £300, or up to £3,000 in cases of fraud, for administrative offences.

Interest is chargeable where a document liable to ad valorem duty is not stamped within 30 days of execution. The interest is rounded down to a multiple of £5, and is not chargeable if it amounts to £25 or less. For documents executed abroad, the interest runs from 30 days after execution, not the date the document is brought into the UK. Where stamp duty or late stamping penalties have been overpaid, interest is payable on repayments amounting to £25 or more from 30 days after execution or from the date of payment of the duty or penalty if later. The rates of interest are, from 29 September 2009, 3% on underpayments and 0.5% on overpayments.

Executing a document outside the UK does not delay payment if it relates to UK shares, because the transaction is caught by SDRT (FA 1986 s 86(4)), even if made outside the UK between non-resident parties.

Interest is charged on overdue SDRT at the rate applicable under the cross-tax interest regime (FA 2009 s 103) from the date on which the tax becomes due and payable (see **part A(b)**). The cross-tax penalty for failure to make a return under FA 2009 Sch 55 applies to an SDRT notice of liability and the penalty for failure to make payments on time under FA 2009 Sch 56 also applies to SDRT. Interest is payable on repayments from the payment date at the rate applicable under the cross-tax interest regime.

# Question

## A.

Giles operates a bed and breakfast business, and has come to you to seek advice about his VAT. He provides you with the following information from his last four VAT returns, covering the year ended 31 December 2016:

| | £ |
|---|---|
| Total outputs (All standard rated; amount net of VAT) | 112,488 |
| Input tax recovered | 2,940 |

You ascertain that Giles also received bank interest on his business account of £123.75 in the year. Giles expects his VAT inclusive turnover to increase by around 15% in the coming year. He estimates that his input tax recovery will increase by around 5% as a result of additional costs.

The current flat rate for hotels and guest houses is 10.5%.

Perform calculations based on the VAT rate of 20% to see whether Giles would benefit from operating the flat rate scheme, and state whether he is permitted to join the scheme. Outline any further information you will need before concluding your advice to Giles on the flat rate scheme.

## B.

Andrew (a sole trader) runs a building business which is in cash flow difficulty. Andrew's bank manager has suggested that he move to cash accounting for VAT, and Andrew is somewhat dismayed to hear that you may not have advised him properly on his VAT accounting scheme; at present Andrew accounts for VAT on an invoice basis.

Andrew's turnover in the last year was £275,328, and his last balance sheet was as follows:

| | | |
|---|---|---|
| Tangible fixed assets: Van & tools | | 20,105 |
| Current assets | | |
| Stock of building materials | 4,244 | |
| Work in progress | 722 | |
| Trade debtors | 4,825 | |
| Prepayments | 628 | |
| | 10,419 | |
| Current liabilities | | |
| Trade creditors (supplier accounts) | 43,881 | |
| Other accruals | 2,476 | |
| Cash in advance from customers | 12,500 | |
| Bank overdraft | 28,754 | |
| | 87,611 | |
| Net current liabilities | | (77,192) |
| Net liabilities | | (57,087) |

| | | |
|---|---|---|
| Capital account b/f | | 1,077 |
| Loss for the year | (43,825) | |
| Drawings | (14,339) | |
| | | (58,164) |
| Capital account c/f | | (57,087) |

Write to Andrew explaining what the effect would be of changing to the cash accounting scheme for VAT.

C.

Alison's bookkeeping is poor and she constantly struggles to prepare her VAT returns on time and has recently heard of the annual accounting scheme on an HMRC Business Advice Open Day. She is keen to move to annual VAT returns to lighten the bookkeeping load. Her annual turnover (net of VAT) is around £125,000. Describe the scheme and advise whether this is appropriate for Alison.

# Answer

## A.

### Flat rate scheme computations: year ended 31 December 2016

If Giles had been operating the flat rate scheme during the last year, the calculations would have been:

| | |
|---|---|
| Outputs net of VAT | 112,488 |
| VAT at 20% | 22,498 |
| Turnover inclusive of VAT — flat rate scheme supplies | 134,986 |
| | |
| Flat rate scheme tax at 10.5% | 14,174 |
| | |
| 'Normal' output tax | 22,498 |
| Input tax recovery | 2,940 |
| Net VAT on returns | 19,558 |
| | |
| Potential saving on flat rate scheme | 5,384 |

So there is ample benefit in operating the flat rate scheme, and subject to the conditions being met, on the face of it, Giles should apply to join the scheme.

Turning to the forthcoming year, if Giles' net turnover increases by 15% this would bring it to £129,361, which is still within the threshold for the flat rate scheme, so he would be free to join on the basis of future turnover. The fact that his input tax recovery would increase by a lesser amount indicates that the growth in the business will not undermine the VAT savings we have identified. Note that bank interest is not included in the flat rate supplies, following the appeal in *Thexton Training Limited TC0919*.

In advising Giles, we would need to check the following in order to finalise our recommendations:

(a) That Giles has not previously operated the scheme and left within the last 12 months;

(b) Whether Giles is involved in any other businesses which are registered for VAT and might be regarded as associated businesses; if this is the case, he may need to seek permission to join the scheme (see **explanatory note 1**);

(c) Whether Giles has any buy to let property investments, as the rental from these would be regarded as a business receipt and would be included within the flat rate turnover. For example, an annual gross rental income of £6,000 would mean that Giles would have to pay a further 10.5% × £6,000 = £630. This would erode the benefits of the scheme, and we should therefore check whether Giles has any rental income. (See **explanatory note 5**.)

## B.

Dear Andrew

In response to your query about cash accounting for VAT, I can explain the impact on your business of the scheme as follows.

Your annual turnover is well within the limit of the scheme, so you would be entitled to operate cash accounting if you wished to do so; there is no application form to complete, nor do you need to notify HMRC, you just commence using the scheme from the start of a VAT period. However, the scheme will not be beneficial to you at all. It might help you to understand the difference between the scheme and the method you use if I take the two aspects of VAT accounting separately.

*VAT on sales (outputs)*

You currently account for VAT on an invoice basis – this means that when you issue an invoice to a customer you are obliged to include the VAT shown on the invoice on your VAT return, even if you have not been paid for the work. However, your business tends to have very few outstanding bills from customers, as it is your practice to draw stage payments from customers for any large jobs, and often to receive advance payments before work is undertaken. Under your current accounting system, you are required to account for VAT on these payments as you receive them, so there would be very little VAT cash flow advantage in moving to cash accounting, as most of your turnover is already accounted for on a cash basis. For example, at your last accounting date, the money owed to you by customers was only £4,825, meaning that moving to cash accounting would only save you paying the VAT on this amount – around £800. At the same time, you were holding customers' money to the value of £12,500, all of which was already VAT paid.

*VAT on purchases (inputs)*

At present you recover the VAT on your purchases of building materials and overheads on an invoice basis. This means that as the bills arrive, you are entitled to recover VAT on them based on the date of the invoice. Moving to cash accounting would mean that you can only recover VAT as you pay the bills, which you will be aware is some considerable time after they arrive; so the effect of moving to cash accounting would be to prevent you from recovering VAT on your purchases for quite some time. For example, at your last accounting date, you owed trade suppliers £43,881, which would mean that up to £7,314 of VAT that you had recovered at that point would have been delayed until payment of the invoices concerned.

*Summary*

I hope you agree that your best option is to remain on invoice accounting for VAT. Had you been operating cash accounting at your last accounting date, you would have been around £6,500 worse off as a result. Should things change, and the cash accounting scheme becomes beneficial for you, we shall advise you at that point to make the change, and explain what you would need to do during the change over period.

As a separate tip, an acceptable method of delaying the payment of VAT on those sales invoices you raise to customers before receiving payment is to describe the document as either an 'application for payment' or a 'request for payment' ie not a tax invoice. The document will still record the amount of VAT that is payable by the customer but the tax will not be included on your VAT return until payment has been received. At this point, a sales invoice can then be raised to your customer.

Finally, please let me know if any of your unpaid sales invoices are overdue for payment by six months or more, and are unlikely to ever be paid by the customer. If this situation applies, we can discuss how to reclaim this tax on your VAT return through what are known as the bad debt relief rules.

C.

Joining the annual accounting scheme may seem tempting for businesses which struggle to complete their VAT returns on time. However, there are some pitfalls to be aware of.

To use the scheme, a taxpayer must meet the following conditions:

(a) make interim payments by a date notified by HMRC;

(b) make interim payments by electronic means;

(c) send the annual VAT return and balancing payment by the due date;

(d) inform the local VAT Business Advice centre immediately if there is a significant change in the business.

To be eligible a business must:

(a) have reasonable grounds for believing that the value of its annual taxable supplies excluding VAT will not exceed £1,350,000;

(b) not have ceased to operate annual accounting scheme in the previous 12 months; or

(c) not be a member of a VAT group registration or a divisional registration.

HMRC will notify the business of the due date for the return, which will usually be based on a 12 month period beginning on the first day of the VAT return period in which the business makes its application to join the scheme. The due date for the return will be 2 months after the end of the annual period, although if a shorter first annual period is implemented which is for 4 months or less, the return for this first shorter period will be due one month after the end of the period

Nine interim payments are due, each payment being 10% of the expected VAT liability, and one interim payment is due on the last day of the 4th, 5th, 6th, 7th, 8th, 9th, 10th, 11th and 12th month of the period. The final balancing payment is due on the last day of the 14th month. However, a business may apply to have only 3 interim payments instead of 9, and if this request is approved, the business will pay 25% of the estimated tax on the last day of the 4th, 7th and 10th month, with the balancing payment due on the last day of the 14th month.

The main concern about Alison is that if her bookkeeping is so poor that quarterly VAT returns are delayed, it is unlikely that she will keep on top of her records sufficiently throughout the year to prepare a VAT return for a whole year within two months. Unless she can get some help with her accounting records, it is likely that after one year on the annual accounting scheme she will be in a worse position than she is now, and having to spend out on urgent assistance to meet her VAT deadline. We may be able to recommend alternative bookkeeping procedures, or indeed as her VAT exclusive turnover is below £150,000 it may be better to recommend the flat rate scheme. In order to explore this option further, we would need more information about recent VAT returns prepared by the business.

The main advantage of the business using the annual accounting scheme is that it means only one VAT return a year can be submitted or paid late, compared to four. This reduces the risk of the business incurring penalties from HMRC through the default surcharge system, where a penalty could be charged that is equal to 15% of the tax unpaid by the due date.

## Explanatory Notes

*VAT Flat rate scheme*

(1) The optional VAT flat-rate scheme is available to all businesses with a VAT exclusive annual taxable turnover of up to £150,000 in the next year – that is the first year of operating the scheme. The turnover for this purpose includes standard rated, reduced rate and zero rated sales, but not exempt business supplies. Supplies which are outside the scope of VAT are not included in the calculation.

Once they have joined the scheme, businesses are permitted to remain in it unless their total VAT inclusive turnover has exceeded £230,000 in a year. This limit includes exempt sales and those that are outside the scope of VAT. If the increase beyond £230,000 was due to a one-off source of income that will not be repeated, then a business can stay in the scheme with the agreement of HMRC if it expects its total VAT inclusive turnover in the next 12 months to be £191,500 or less.

It is not possible to join the flat rate scheme if:

– the business had previously been within the scheme and left during the previous 12 months;

– the business is or has been registered for VAT as the division of a larger business, or as part of a group, or is eligible to do so;

– the business uses one of the margin schemes for second-hand goods, art, antiques and collectibles, the Tour Operators' Margin Scheme, or the Capital Goods Scheme;

- the VAT registered person has been convicted of a VAT offence or charged a penalty for VAT evasion in the last year; or
- the business is 'closely associated' with another business, in which case permission to join the scheme may be given by HMRC.

Closely associated for this purpose means:

- one business is under the dominant influence of another;
- two businesses are closely bound by financial, economic and organisational links; or
- one company has the right to give directions to another;
- in practice your company habitually complies with the directions of another. The test here is a test of the commercial reality rather than of the legal form.

Where an association has ceased within the previous two years, HMRC will give permission if they consider that this would not pose a risk to revenue.

An application to join the flat rate scheme can be made at registration or later. If later, the taxpayer normally applies to join the scheme from the beginning of the next VAT period. HMRC may by concession allow the taxpayer to join from the beginning of the current VAT period provided the return has not already been submitted. However retrospective applications in respect of VAT returns already submitted are not normally allowed. This was the case in *Anycom Ltd* (TC1496) where the taxpayer's adviser in 2009 asked to backdate use of the flat rate scheme to 2005. The application was denied.

HMRC's guidance on the flat rate scheme, and application form to join are in Notice 733.

(2) The purpose of the scheme is to reduce the burden of accounting for VAT on each transaction by providing a simple calculation for the net output tax for each VAT period. The flat rate percentage appropriate to the business is applied to the VAT inclusive turnover to provide the net amount payable for the VAT accounting period; this amount is intended to reflect the output tax net of an allowance for input tax recovery. Thus in Part A of the example, the VAT payable is calculated at 10.5% of the flat rate turnover for the year. No input tax recovery is permitted, except in respect of fixed assets purchased for the business which cost more than £2,000 inclusive of VAT. If VAT is separately reclaimed on any items, when sold the output tax is calculated and accounted for in the normal way in addition to the flat rate result for the period.

For example, if a van on which input tax had been recovered under the flat rate scheme was sold for £4,000 plus VAT of £800, the £4,800 would be excluded from the flat rate turnover for the period, and the £800 added to the flat rate VAT calculated and declared in box 1 on the VAT return.

The appropriate flat rate for the business can be selected from HMRC's website, where there is also a calculation tool to allow businesses to check whether they would benefit from the scheme. Obviously it is crucial to select the correct rate for the business, and if the choice is not obvious the reasons for choosing the rate should be documented. If on a check it is discovered that a business is using an incorrect rate, an alternative higher rate will not normally be imposed retrospectively on the business, unless HMRC believes that the choice of rate was unreasonable.

(3) Businesses operating the flat rate scheme must still issue tax invoices to their VAT registered customers showing VAT at the full standard or reduced rates as appropriate, but need not record all the details of the invoices issued; thus customers of those operating the scheme are normally unaware of this, and their input tax recovery is not affected. The main benefit in accounting terms is the absence of a requirement to record gross and net details of purchase invoices received; any accounting records would be necessary for direct tax purposes, but for VAT purposes purchase invoice details are irrelevant.

(4) Accounts are prepared from the VAT inclusive information recorded in the accounting records, and the VAT flat rate amounts accounted for on the VAT returns are an allowable deduction for direct tax purposes. For limited companies this amount should be deducted from turnover in order to comply with the requirements of the Companies Acts, but for unincorporated businesses this can be shown as an expense item, and recorded as such on the self assessment return. No attempt should be made to calculate the VAT 'profit' for

accounting purposes, although some analysis of this may be desirable to check that the business is still benefiting from the use of the Flat rate scheme where the decision was close.

(5) Care is needed when advising on the flat rate scheme as it is a requirement to include all business income in the flat rate turnover, and this can lead to the business paying more VAT than might be expected. A business which makes exempt supplies must include those supplies in the flat rate turnover, and will therefore pay VAT at the relevant flat rate on those supplies. However, as a result of a first tier tribunal decision in February 2011, most businesses will not now have to include interest received on business bank accounts. (Thexton Training Ltd TC00919).

Rent received by the VAT registered person would be included in the flat rate turnover, and this can significantly undermine, if not reverse the decision regarding the financial benefit of the scheme. Where the VAT registration is in the name of a single individual, gross rental income on properties owned by that individual should be included in the flat rate turnover. If the properties are owned in the name of a couple, then this is regarded as a separate entity for VAT purposes, and the rental income would not affect the flat rate result. Most damaging might be the sale of a property as an exempt supply which could significantly distort the flat rate results. In such a case the option to tax might be exercised to protect the trader's interests in the case of a commercial property; alternatively, it would be advisable to withdraw from the scheme before the sale.

(6) The advice to Giles is based upon his normal input tax recovery rates, which are very low. This is often the case with unlicensed hotel premises, and as the flat rate reflects the recovery rates across the sector, joining the scheme will normally be beneficial. However, if Giles were to undertake significant property repairs, or redecoration and refitting of the rooms, including the purchase of new furniture he might be well advised to either delay his application to join the scheme, or to leave the scheme in order to recover the related input tax; in general this type of expenditure would not qualify under the £2,000 rule, as building and redecoration work are 'services' supplied to him and thus not eligible for VAT recovery.

*Cash accounting scheme*

(7) The cash accounting scheme allows businesses to account for VAT as transactions are paid rather than according to the tax point of the transaction. This is often a benefit to businesses, as the output tax is only paid over to HMRC when the cash has been received from customers. Thus the business does not have to finance the VAT element of debtors in advance of being paid.

Smaller businesses often do not have much trade credit, so although input tax recovery can be delayed by using cash accounting, this will not normally outweigh the benefit of the delay in accounting for output tax.

(8) Businesses can operate cash accounting for VAT provided they anticipate that their VAT exclusive turnover in the next 12 months will not exceed £1,350,000. This limit excludes exempt supplies, but includes taxable supplies at all rates. There is no application form, nor does the business need to notify HMRC that it is using cash accounting, although businesses must only change VAT accounting methods from the start of a VAT accounting period. However, a business cannot use cash accounting if it is behind with VAT returns or VAT payments, or if the registered person has been convicted of a VAT offence or charged a penalty for VAT evasion in the last year.

Once operating cash accounting, a business may continue to do so until the VAT exclusive taxable supplies in the last 12 months reach £1.6 million, at which point it must move to normal tax point accounting. Changing accounting methods will often require careful segregation of the supplies made before and after the date of change to ensure that the VAT is correctly accounted for, and those supporting clients may need to provide specific help with this.

(9) Cash accounting cannot be used for the following types of transactions:

- lease purchase, hire purchase, conditional sales or credit sales;
- imports of goods and acquisitions of goods from the EU;
- removals of goods from a Customs warehouse or free zone;
- invoices issued which are not due for payment within 6 months; and

- invoices issued in advance of the supply.

For all of these transactions, the normal VAT accounting rules should be used.

(10) Andrew is in the unusual position of financing his business from trade creditors and a bank overdraft. As the creditors (which will largely bear recoverable input tax) are very significant, and there are almost no trade debtors, moving to cash accounting will slow down VAT input tax recovery, while providing minimal benefits in slowing down output tax payments, so cash accounting would not be beneficial to his business.

*Annual accounting scheme*

(11) Businesses are eligible to use the annual accounting scheme if they anticipate that their VAT exclusive turnover in the next 12 months will not exceed £1,350,000. This excludes exempt supplies, but includes taxable supplies at all rates. Businesses are not eligible to join the scheme if they are behind with VAT payments.

Once using the annual accounting scheme a business may continue to do so until the VAT exclusive taxable supplies in the last 12 months reaches £1.6 million, at which point it must move to normal tax point accounting from the end of the VAT year.

# Question

John is an agricultural fencing contractor who has sought your help with his accounts. He has not previously had a professional adviser, and has prepared his accounts and tax and VAT returns unassisted for around 7 years. However, he is concerned that he is getting in a muddle with his VAT and has therefore sought your help. You ascertain the following information from your initial discussions with John.

(a) He has submitted two estimated VAT returns for the June 2013 and June 2014 quarters. He did this because he was very busy at the time the returns were due and was concerned not to incur penalties for late submission of returns, so he estimated the amounts and submitted the returns within the required deadline. He has not corrected the returns as he is not sure how to do this.

(b) He runs both a tractor and Landrover on the business. The Landrover is classed as a car for VAT purposes. He recovers VAT input tax on fuel for the Landrover when on business journeys but not when he occasionally uses it privately.

(c) He accounts for VAT on his sales as he raises the invoices. One customer has failed to pay him for work done during the last 4 years – with VAT of £700 on the invoice, which was due for payment in May 2015.

During your examination of his books and records you establish the following:

(d) John has reclaimed VAT of £2,700 on the purchase of a second hand Landrover in August 2014. His old Landrover was given in part exchange but no VAT was accounted for on the proceeds.

(e) John has failed to account for VAT on the part exchange value of a tractor in January 2013. The VAT amounts to £700.

(f) The net value of VAT overstated on the estimated June 2013 return is £1,426; the net value of VAT understated on the June 2014 return is £943.

(g) The total VAT recovered on fuel for the Landrover since January 2013 is £1,593.91. The VAT inclusive quarterly fuel scale charges applicable to the Landrover are:

| | |
|---|---|
| 1 May 2012 | £583 |
| 1 May 2013 | £590 |
| 1 May 2014 | £548 |
| 1 May 2015 | £468 |
| 1 May 2016 | £408 |

You have also identified a further £373.48 of VAT on fuel which was not recovered as it was incurred on private journeys.

All errors are to be corrected on the December 2016 return (if appropriate). Prepare a computation of the necessary adjustments, and state how you would put matters right.

# Answer

(a) The net error on the June 2013 return is an overstatement of VAT of £1,426. When corrected, this error cannot incur a penalty as it is in HMRC's favour. No interest would be payable in respect of the correction.

The net error on the June 2014 return is an underpayment of VAT of £943. It is necessary to consider what category the inaccuracy falls into:

- an inaccuracy despite reasonable care;
- an inaccuracy which is careless;
- an inaccuracy which is deliberate; or
- an inaccuracy which is deliberate and concealed.

The correct categorisation will enable us to decide what rate of penalty is likely to apply to the inaccuracy. In this case, when John submitted the estimated return he knew that it was incorrect, so the inaccuracy was deliberate, but he took no steps to conceal this fact – nor has he done so since. In this case, the maximum penalty prescribed by FA 2007 Sch 29 is 70% or £660.10, but if John makes a disclosure of the inaccuracy which is unprompted, this can be reduced to as low as 20% of the potential lost revenue (£943), ie £188.60. Note that submitting estimated VAT returns can be specifically permitted by HMRC. See the internal VAT manuals at VATAC2000.

It is important to ensure that we disclose the inaccuracy clearly to minimise John's exposure to penalties. Deliberate inaccuracies must be corrected on form VAT 652, which will achieve the necessary elements of HMRC's tests of 'telling and helping' which count towards the maximum reduction for disclosure, the third aspect being 'allowing' which means providing HMRC with access to the records (if they request it) to check that the error has been properly corrected.

(b) John should either recover all VAT on fuel and pay a fuel scale charge, or recover none of the VAT on fuel purchases. It is possible to decide from year to year which option is preferable, and it might be worth carrying out some analysis to establish this, but from the figures given, we can draw the following conclusions:

| | | |
|---|---|---|
| Input tax recovered – January 2013 to September 2016 | | £1,486.69 |
| Output tax due – Fuel scale charge | | |
| March, June 2013 at 20% | 194.33 | |
| September, December 2013 at 20% | 196.66 | |
| March, June 2014 at 20% | 196.66 | |
| September, December 2014 at 20% | 182.66 | |
| March, June 2015 at 20% | 182.66 | |
| September 2015 at 20% | 156.00 | |
| March, June 2016 at 20% | 156.00 | |
| September 2016 | 68.00 | |
| | | 1,332.97 |
| Net VAT recovery if fuel scale charge applied | | 153.752 |

However, although there is an adjustment of £1,332.97 in HMRC's favour to correct, from this we can deduct the VAT on fuel which was not initially recovered as it was incurred on private journeys, so the adjustment is reduced to £1,332.97 – £373.48 = £959.49. The net benefit of recovering VAT on fuel during the four year period is £153.75 + £373.48 = £527.23.

We also need to consider whether the inaccuracies arose after John had taken reasonable care, or whether they were careless. As the treatment of VAT on road fuel is quite complex, and the mistake John has made is very common, we may tend to view the inaccuracy as non-culpable. However, if the mistakes were held to be careless by HMRC a penalty of 30% would apply unless a full disclosure is made. In view of the fact that we already need to make a disclosure in respect of **part (a)** above, we may decide to make a protective disclosure of the inaccuracy in order to eliminate any risk of a penalty.

(c) John can recover £700 in VAT bad debt relief on the current VAT return – this is not the correction of a previous error, although he could have claimed this on the December 2015 return when the invoice was more than six months overdue for payment. A condition of reclaiming this VAT is that John must write off the debt in his accounting records. There is no requirement for him to notify his customer of this action.

(d) As the Landrover is classed as a car, no input tax should be recovered on the purchase of the vehicle if it is available for private use. This is clearly the case with John's vehicle so the error must be corrected. Once again, the nature of the inaccuracy must be determined for the purposes of the penalty regime. In this case, it is likely that the inaccuracy arose despite reasonable care. We would have to decide whether we believed that John's understanding of VAT would include the distinction between a car and a van – particularly in the case of a Landrover for which either classification can apply. If we believe that John applied reasonable care in his decision to recover the input tax on the vehicle then there is no penalty applying to the error. However, the amount of VAT involved indicates the vehicle was second hand and it may be that there was no valid VAT receipt, in which case the allegation of reasonable care is more suspect. We may therefore decide to make a protective disclosure to reduce the potential penalty from 30% (or £810) to a minimum of 0%. **Part (a)** above gives details of the disclosure required. The treatment of the old Landrover disposed of is correct. There is no VAT on the sale of a second hand car in these circumstances.

(e) John has omitted to declare output tax of £700 on the part exchange value of the tractor. This must now be corrected on the next return. Once again, the nature of the inaccuracy must be determined for the purposes of the penalty regime. If the mistake was held to be careless by HMRC a penalty of 30% would apply unless a full disclosure is made. In view of the fact that we already need to make a disclosure in respect of **part (a)** above, we may decide to make a protective disclosure of the inaccuracy in order to eliminate any risk of a penalty.

The total value of errors to correct on the December 2016 return is as follows:

| | | |
|---|---|---|
| (a) | June 2013 return | (1,426.00) |
| | June 2014 return – corrected separately as deliberate (see **explanatory note 1**) | |
| (b) | Fuel scale charges | 1,332.97 |
| | Additional input tax recovery | (373.48) |
| (c) | Not an error | |
| (d) | VAT on Landrover | 2,700.00 |
| (e) | VAT on part exchange of tractor | 700.00 |
| | Net errors for correction | 2,933.49 |

As the net value of errors to be corrected on the December 2016 return is less than £10,000, they can simply be corrected on the return. All of the adjustments listed above, plus the VAT bad debt relief should be included on the December 2016 VAT return. In addition, the inaccuracies identified above for disclosure – that is the estimated return showing an understatement of VAT and the omitted fuel scale charges and recovery of VAT on the purchase of the Landrover – will also be disclosed in a separate letter to HMRC, or by completion of form VAT 652. **Explanatory note 2** details why this is the preferred method of correcting these errors.

The deliberate inaccuracy on the June 2014 VAT return must be disclosed to HMRC by submitting form VAT 652. This will effectively count as an error notification and satisfy the 'telling' and 'helping' aspects of disclosure for the purposes of the penalty legislation.

## Explanatory Notes

*Correcting VAT errors*

(1) Net errors of up to £10,000 can be corrected on the next VAT return. If the errors due for correction exceed this amount, it may still be possible to correct them on the return if the net value does not exceed the lower of 1% of the amount in box 6 on the return and £50,000.

Where the net errors exceed these limits, it will be necessary to notify them to HMRC on form VAT 652, which sets out the inaccuracies on a period by period basis.

Deliberate inaccuracies must be notified to HMRC on form VAT 652, with details of how they arose. On submission of the form it is likely that in addition to an assessment of the VAT due, and potential penalties, HMRC will also raise an assessment for default interest. Default interest is not a penalty but is classed as commercial restitution to reflect the fact that VAT owed by a business was not paid to HMRC at the correct time.

(2) Errors separately disclosed, and subject to an assessment (usually those corrected by the use of form VAT 652) attract default interest. It is for this reason that careless inaccuracies are better dealt with by correcting the next VAT return if they are within the financial limits described in **explanatory note 1** as they will not attract default interest if corrected on the return. Where a disclosure of a careless error is necessary, this is best done by sending a separate letter of disclosure or by completing form VAT 652 indicating that the errors have already been corrected on a return, as by eliminating the need for an assessment, default interest cannot apply.

(3) The other occasion when default interest would not apply to an underpayment of tax notified to HMRC on form VAT 652 is if the error(s) has produced no net loss of tax to the exchequer. For example, an input tax error could avoid interest if the VAT in question can be reclaimed by another business. It is up to the taxpayer to identify relevant situations when interest is not appropriate at the time the VAT 652 is submitted.

HMRC's guidance on correcting VAT errors is in Notice 700/45. HMRC also have three toolkits on VAT covering input and output tax and partial exemption.

*VAT on fuel for private use*

(4) It is a common misconception that VAT on road fuel purchased for motor cars can be apportioned between business and private use; this is not the case. A VAT registered business has a simple choice – to either recover all of the VAT on fuel and pay the fuel scale charge each VAT accounting period, or recover no VAT at all on fuel. It is also possible to apportion the VAT on road fuel between business and private journeys, based on a detailed mileage record of both business and private journeys. As there is no indication that John has such a detailed log, this option is not presently available to him, but should be considered in respect of advice for the future, although the administrative burden that this presents is often a barrier for small businesses.

It is not a complex task for the adviser to explain to each client whether VAT recovery on fuel is worthwhile for his business. As VAT fuel scale charges are now linked to the $CO_2$ emissions of the vehicle, this is the only information that is needed.

For example, if Fred has a car emitting 198 g/km of $CO_2$, the quarterly gross fuel scale charge is that for the 195g/km band = £388; so if Fred spends more than £388 per quarter of fuel he will be better off recovering his VAT and paying the fuel scale charge, and if he spends less than this per quarter he would be better off not recovering VAT on fuel. Although the volatility of fuel prices can make this prediction tricky, most businesses will know which side of the line they fall. An important point to note is that the decision to not reclaim VAT on road fuel applies to all fuel bought by the business, including fuel relevant to commercial vehicles. It is not possible to claim VAT on some vehicles but not others.

As John has only recovered some of the VAT on his fuel purchases, and is better off with VAT recovery even on the amount he has already recovered, he will now need to account for the fuel scale charges less the additional VAT he can recover – assuming that he is in possession of the VAT receipts.

*Time limits for correcting errors*

(5) The time limit for correcting VAT errors (and indeed the time limit for raising assessments) is four years (since 31 March 2010). As the correction of John's errors is to be done on the December 2015 return, only errors since 1 January 2013 are to be included.

*Input tax recovery on cars and vans*

(6) No input tax recovery is allowed on cars which are available for private use. This can be a difficult question of fact, but the Tribunal has been persuaded when a car is insured for business use only or if there is some other physical restriction on private use. A statement and evidence to the effect that a car is not and would not be used privately is not sufficient, nor is evidence that the car is unsuitable for private use, as in the case of a car fitted with loudspeakers during an election campaign.

A van, however, is subject to VAT recovery, and in the case of double cab pick-ups, they qualify as a van when the payload exceeds 1 tonne, after allowing for a hard top at 45kg (if fitted). Landrovers can be classified as a car or a van, depending on the specification.

It is worth noting that HMRC's manual (at CH81145 Example 2) on penalties classifies an error in recovering VAT on an estate car (by a shopkeeper) as 'at least careless', clearly bidding up the penalty implications of such a mistake, so you should be ready to dispute this allegation if you believe it to be unreasonable in the case of your client.

*Penalties for inaccuracies*

(7) For inaccuracies on returns the penalty regime in FA 2007 Sch 24 applies. Full details of the rules and the impact of disclosure on the rate of penalty are given in **Example G2**.

The key aspect in deciding whether an inaccuracy occurs despite reasonable care is that this depends on the circumstances and abilities of the taxpayer concerned. So a large company with a tax department would have a higher standard of reasonable care than a sole trader without professional assistance. However, there is a requirement that when someone is not sure about the correct treatment of an item they should seek advice, either from a professional adviser or from HMRC. Where John has made mistakes, it is important to assess whether he knew that the issue was a complex one and failed to seek help, or whether he was oblivious to the potential complexities of the particular issue. His failure to seek help for a problem he knew about would be viewed as a failure to take reasonable care, but his lack of knowledge that a problem even existed would probably amount to reasonable care within his capabilities and resources.

# Question

(a) Explain the operation of the standard method of input tax apportionment including the annual adjustment.

(b) Juliet Ltd is partially exempt. Details of transactions and VAT in respect of the four quarters ended 30 April 2016 are as follows (all figures are expressed in £):

| | *Qtr to 31.07.15* | *Qtr to 31.10.15* | *Qtr to 31.01.16* | *Qtr to 30.04.16* | *Total y/e 30.04.16* |
|---|---|---|---|---|---|
| Taxable supplies | 99,200 | 88,040 | 95,480 | 100,440 | 383,160 |
| Exempt supplies | 12,400 | 17,360 | 9,920 | 18,600 | 58,280 |
| Total | 111,600 | 105,400 | 105,400 | 119,040 | 441,440 |
| | | | | | |
| Input tax attributable to: | | | | | |
| Taxable supplies only | 7,000 | 8,500 | 9,000 | 7,750 | 32,250 |
| Exempt supplies only | 3,000 | 1,500 | 1,700 | 2,800 | 9,000 |
| Both taxable and exempt supplies | 1,500 | 1,800 | 1,450 | 900 | 5,650 |
| Total input tax | 11,500 | 11,800 | 12,150 | 11,450 | 46,900 |

Calculate the VAT recovery for each quarter and the annual adjustment for the year ended 30 April 2016, and state when it would be made.

(c) Show how Juliet's input tax recovery would have differed if the company had adopted the simplified method of dealing with input tax, and the company's annual adjustment percentage for the year ended 30 April 2015 was 85%.

# Answer

(a) Using the standard method, input tax incurred is analysed into;

- Taxable input tax (relating wholly to making taxable supplies).
- Exempt input tax (input tax relating to the making of exempt supplies).
- Non-attributable input tax (the balance), also known as residual input tax.

In determining how much of the non-attributable input tax is available for recovery, the following fraction is computed for each quarter, and for the VAT year as a whole when performing the annual adjustment:

$$\frac{\text{Taxable supplies (excluding VAT)}}{\text{Total supplies (excluding VAT)}}$$

The values of supplies used in the calculation must exclude self-supplies, incidental income such as bank interest received, proceeds from the sale of capital goods and land and buildings (unless property investment is the core activity of the business).

This fraction is then expressed as a percentage and for businesses where the non-attributable input tax is under £400,000 per month on average, the percentage is rounded up to the next whole number. For larger businesses where the non-attributable input tax is more than £400,000 per month on average, the percentage calculated is rounded to two decimal places.

The percentage is applied to the residual input tax to arrive at the recoverable amount.

At the end of the VAT year (which will be either March, April or May depending on the stagger group and the end of March for a business on monthly VAT returns) the recoverable percentage is recalculated for the whole year and applied to the total residual input tax to arrive at the recoverable amount for the year. Any difference between this amount and the amount recovered during the year is payable or repayable on either the last VAT return of the year or the subsequent return (the business can choose which of the two returns is used).

If the total exempt input tax (including the proportion of residual input tax not claimed) for the period is less than certain limits, then all of the input tax can be reclaimed under what is known as the de minimis limits. There are three different de minimis limits, and a business will qualify as de minimis if it meets any of the three tests:

- exempt input tax is less than £1,875 per quarter or £7,500 per annum and also less than 50% of the total input tax;
- total input tax is less than £1,875 per quarter or £7,500 per annum and exempt supplies are less than 50% of total supplies – known as new Test 1;
- total input tax less input tax directly attributable to taxable supplies is less than £1,875 per quarter or £7,500 per annum and exempt supplies are less than 50% of total supplies – known as new Test 2.

(b)

| | *Qtr to 31.07.15* | *Qtr to 31.10.15* | *Qtr to 31.01.16* | *Qtr to 30.04.16* | *Total y/e 30.04.16* |
|---|---|---|---|---|---|
| Taxable supplies | 99,200 | 88,040 | 95,480 | 100,440 | 383,160 |
| Total supplies | 111,600 | 105,400 | 105,400 | 119,040 | 441,440 |
| Percentage | 88.88% | 83.53% | 90.59% | 84.38% | 86.80% |
| Rounded percentage | 89% | 84% | 91% | 85% | 87% |
| Residual input tax | 1,500 | 1,800 | 1,450 | 900 | 5,650 |
| Recoverable – taxable | 1,335 | 1,512 | 1,320 | 765 | 4,916 |
| Difference – exempt | N/A* | 288 | 130 | N/A | N/A |
| Wholly exempt input tax | N/A* | 1,500 | 1,700 | N/A | N/A |
| Total exempt input tax | | 1,788 | 1,830 | | |
| | | De minimis | De minimis | | |
| Taxable input tax | 7,000 | 8,500 | 9,000 | 7,750 | 32,250 |
| Recovered quarterly | 8,335 | 11,800 | 12,150 | 8,515 | |
| Recoverable (annual) | | | | | 37,166 |
| Less total recovered | | | | | 40,800 |
| Annual adjustment (payment to HMRC) | | | | | 3,634 |

* Wholly exempt input tax already exceeds de minimis amount – see **explanatory note 2**.

The amounts shown in each column will have been recovered on each quarterly return as submitted, with Juliet Ltd being de minimis in the October 2015 and January 2016 quarters. In these two quarters, the exempt input tax is both less than £1,875 and less than 50% of the total input tax, the first of the three de minimis tests. The exempt input tax comprises input tax directly relevant to exempt supplies plus the proportion of residual input tax that is attributable to exempt supplies.

However, the company is not de minimis for the entire year, as the wholly exempt input tax alone is more than the annual de minimis limit of £7,500, so there will be an annual adjustment which will claw back the excessive input tax recovery. This can be accounted for on either the April 2016 or July 2016 quarter (see **explanatory note 6**). As it is a payment to HMRC it is likely that the company will delay the adjustment until the July quarter for cash flow purposes. Note that the annual adjustment entry is not the correction of an error, so the rules about the maximum adjustment which can be made on a VAT return do not apply.

(c) If Juliet Ltd had adopted the simplified method of the partial exemption standard method, this would mean applying the annual adjustment percentage relevant to the year ended 30 April 2015 (ie 85%) to the following four VAT quarters up to 30 April 2016:

| | *Qtr to 31.07.15* | *Qtr to 31.10.15* | *Qtr to 31.01.16* | *Qtr to 30.04.16* |
|---|---|---|---|---|
| Provisional recovery % | 85% | 85% | 85% | 85% |
| Residual input tax | 1,500 | 1,800 | 1,450 | 900 |
| Recoverable – taxable | 1,275 | 1,530 | 1,233 | 765 |
| Difference – exempt | N/A* | 270 | 217 | N/A* |
| Wholly exempt input tax | N/A* | 1,500 | 1,700 | N/A* |
| Total exempt input tax | | 1,770 | 1,917 | |
| | | De minimis | | |

| | *Qtr to 31.07.15* | *Qtr to 31.10.15* | *Qtr to 31.01.16* | *Qtr to 30.04.16* |
|---|---|---|---|---|
| Taxable input tax | 7,000 | 8,500 | 9,000 | 7,750 |
| Recovered (quarterly) | 8,275 | 11,800 | 10,233 | 8,515 |

* Wholly exempt input tax already exceeds de minimis amount – see **explanatory note 2**.

| | |
|---|---|
| Calculation of annual adjustment | |
| Taxable supplies | 383,160 |
| Total supplies | 441,440 |
| Percentage | 86.80% |
| Rounded percentage | 87% |
| Residual input tax | 5,650 |
| Recoverable – taxable | 4,916 |
| Taxable input tax | 32,250 |
| Recoverable (annual) | 37,166 |
| Less total recovered | 38,823 |
| Annual adjustment (payment to HMRC) | 1,657 |

So using the simplified method, which applies the previous year's recoverable percentage to each quarter and then computes a revised annual adjustment at the end of the year, will result in a slightly lower recovery during the year followed therefore by a lower annual adjustment. Note that if the company had not been de minimis in the October 2015 quarter, the annual adjustment would have produced an additional recovery from HMRC as the recoverable percentage has increased from 85% to 87% from 2015 to 2016.

## Explanatory Notes

*Partial exemption – basis of input tax recovery*

(1) A VAT registered business which makes some taxable and some exempt supplies is known as partially exempt. The underlying principle of input tax recovery for partially exempt businesses is that VAT must not be recovered in relation to exempt supplies. The business may, under EU law, use any fair and reasonable method to arrive at the calculation of exempt input tax, but in the UK we have two alternative methods. The standard method may be used by any business without prior permission, and the details of the method are set out in **part (a)** of the Example. Larger businesses may be subject to the standard method over-ride, an anti avoidance measure which is explained in **explanatory note 4**.

Whatever method is used to calculate recoverable VAT on a period by period basis, the business must recompute the recoverable amounts on an annual basis at the end of its VAT year and make an adjustment on either the return for the last period of the year or the return for the first period of the subsequent year. (See **explanatory note 6**).

*De minimis*

(2) Businesses may treat themselves as fully taxable if the exempt input tax as calculated (after computing the apportioned amount) is less than £625 per month on average, and less than 50% of the total input tax. For quarterly returns this means that the exempt input tax needs to be below £1,875, and for the annual adjustment calculation the limit is £7,500.

De minimis calculations were not required in **part (b)** of the Example for quarters ended July 2015 and April 2016 as the directly attributable exempt input tax already exceeds the quarterly limit. Similarly, Juliet Ltd cannot be de minimis for the year as a whole as the directly attributable exempt input tax is £9,000 ie already greater than £7,500.

Simplified rules apply to the calculation of the de minimis limits which are intended to save businesses from computing a full apportionment each period. If a business passes either of the following tests in a VAT period, or the other test explained above, it can treat itself as de minimis for that period:

- Test 1: the total input tax incurred in the period is no more than £625 per month on average, and the value of exempt supplies is no more than 50% of all supplies, or

- Test 2: the total input tax incurred less the input tax directly attributable to taxable supplies is no more than £625 per month on average and the value of exempt supplies is no more than 50% of the value of all supplies.

So in the case of Juliet Ltd we could consider the two additional tests as follows:

| | *Qtr to 31.07.15* | *Qtr to 31.10.15* | *Qtr to 31.01.16* | *Qtr to 30.04.16* | *Total y/e 30.04.16* |
|---|---|---|---|---|---|
| Test 1 | | | | | |
| Total input tax | 11,500 | 11,800 | 12,150 | 11,450 | 46,900 |
| Limit for test 1 | 1,875 | 1,875 | 1,875 | 1,875 | 7,500 |
| | Test 1 failed in all quarters and for the year | | | | |
| Test 2 | | | | | |
| Total input tax | 11,500 | 11,800 | 12,150 | 11,450 | 46,900 |
| Less: Taxable supplies only | 7,000 | 8,500 | 9,000 | 7,750 | 32,250 |
| | 4,500 | 3,300 | 3,150 | 3,700 | 14,650 |
| Limit for test 2 | 1,875 | 1,875 | 1,875 | 1,875 | 7,500 |
| | Test 2 failed in all quarters and for the year | | | | |

The failure of tests 1 and 2 does not prevent Juliet from applying the old de minimis test on a quarterly basis – and indeed from recovering all of the VAT incurred in the two quarters as shown in **part (b)** of the answer.

The simplification also introduced a new annual test from the same date, so that if a business is de minimis in one year, it may treat itself as de minimis in the following year and merely compute an annual test to check whether any of the three tests (tests 1 and 2 and the old test) are satisfied for the year, and if not to repay the appropriate amount of input tax based on a full partial exemption apportionment. The annual test can only be used by businesses which do not expect to incur total input tax of more than £1 million in the partial exemption year.

The annual test does not apply to Juliet Ltd, as the company was not de minimis in the previous year.

*Special methods*

(3) Businesses may alternatively choose to use a special method, which is any other method of calculating recoverable input tax that is not the standard method, provided that method produces a fair and reasonable result. A business needs written approval from HMRC to use a special method, and is also required to include a statement that the method produces a fair and reasonable result in terms of input tax recovery. Although HMRC still issue letters of approval for special methods, the authority can also backdate withdrawal of an approved method if it is subsequently found not to produce a fair and reasonable result, based on the false statement made at the time approval for the method was requested. This puts businesses using special methods in an unenviable position, and those businesses adopting a new special method will need to consider their chosen method very carefully.

Special methods can include floor area splits, document or transaction counts, number of persons engaged in each activity or time analysis, and the recovery percentage is calculated to two decimal places. Retail businesses are not generally authorised to use floor area as a special method because large areas of the shop are often used for both taxable and exempt activities eg as in the case of an optician.

When HMRC find that a business is using an inappropriate special method but under circumstances where retrospective withdrawal is not appropriate, they can impose a new method by issuing a direction. The new method must then be applied from the date specified. However, this power is only used when HMRC have not been able to negotiate and agree an alternative method with the business concerned. HMRC or the business concerned may issue a special method override notice which is intended to deal with failings in a special method until a new method can be agreed. If issued by the business, HMRC will have to approve its use before the override can be adopted.

*Standard method override*

(4) This anti-avoidance measure requires partly exempt businesses to override the standard method of apportioning residual input tax where 'the result does not reflect the use made of the purchases, including cases of deliberate abuse'. A separate rule applies to businesses using a 'special method' to apportion their input tax.

Under the rule, businesses are required to adjust the input tax deductible under the standard method at the end of their VAT year if that amount is *substantially* different from an attribution based on the use of purchases.

'Substantially' is defined as:

- £50,000 or more; or
- 50% or more of the value of the residual input tax, but not less than £25,000.

This means that where the amount of residual input tax is less than £50,000 businesses can rely purely on the standard method with one exception: businesses that are defined as group undertakings by the Companies Act 2006 will have to follow the new rule where the residual input tax is greater than £25,000.

A business that has to apply the adjustment must, at the VAT year-end, calculate the difference between the input tax deductible under the standard method and that deductible according to use. This difference is the adjustment required to be made on the VAT return that follows the year-end (ie the same VAT return as that for the annual adjustment).

The override will only apply where the standard method fails to provide a fair and reasonable deduction of input tax, when compared to the extent to which purchases are used to make taxable supplies. Examples of when the standard method may not provide a fair and reasonable result are:

(a) where purchases are incurred in one tax year, but used in a different tax year in which the proportion of deductible VAT is very different; or

(b) where purchases are not used in proportion to the values of taxable and exempt supplies made;

(c) purchases are made in one period or tax year in setting up a new area of business which will significantly affect the relative values of taxable and exempt supplies in future tax years when the purchases are to be used;

(d) exceptionally high value transactions are undertaken which do not consume inputs to an extent significantly greater than transactions of lower value; and

(e) the pattern of business is such that the inputs are simply not consumed in proportion to the values of outputs.

All tax avoidance schemes which exploit the standard method in order to deduct more input tax than relates to taxable supplies are likely to trigger the partial exemption override.

Example: XYZ Ltd uses the standard method to apportion residual input tax. Using this method, deductible input tax for the four VAT quarters to 30 April 2016 was calculated as:

| | |
|---|---|
| 31 July 2015 | 58,500 |
| 31 October 2015 | 62,150 |
| 31 January 2016 | 74,224 |
| 30 April 2016 | 49,367 |
| | 244,241 |

At the VAT year end a calculation of deductible input tax based on the results of the whole year is performed. The company's results for the year ended 30 April 2016 are as follows:

| | |
|---|---|
| Input tax relating wholly to taxable supplies | 125,000 |
| Input tax relating wholly to exempt supplies | 75,000 |
| Residual input tax | 150,000 |
| Total input tax | 350,000 |

| | |
|---|---|
| Taxable supplies made in the year | 3,350,000 |
| Includes: machine sold in year (exc. VAT) | 200,000 |
| Single transaction consuming little or no inputs | 2,000,000 |
| Exempt supplies made in the year | 1,500,000 |

In calculating the annual adjustment, the value of the machine sold must be excluded from both the numerator and denominator in the fraction, so the annual adjustment (and recoverable VAT for the year) are calculated as follows:

$$\frac{\pounds 3,350,000 - \pounds 200,000}{\pounds 3,350,000 + \pounds 1,500,000 - \pounds 200,000} = 67.74\%$$

This is rounded to 68%, so the recoverable VAT is 68% × £150,000 = £102,000 +125,000 = £227,000. The annual adjustment is a payment due of £17,241.

However, XYZ Limited has incurred residual input tax of £150,000, which exceeds the £50,000 threshold applying to the standard method over-ride; we also know that there was a high value taxable transaction which consumed little or no inputs. We might therefore suspect that the input tax recovery has been distorted by this very high value taxable supply.

To perform the standard method over-ride, the business must calculate VAT recovery on the basis of use, and check whether the difference is substantial. In this Example all supplies other than the high value taxable transaction consume purchases in proportion to their values. Accordingly a fair and reasonable attribution can be achieved by excluding the high value transaction from a calculation based on the standard method.

So the recoverable percentage of non-attributable input tax becomes:

$$\frac{\pounds 3,350,000 - \pounds 200,000 - \pounds 2,000,000}{\pounds 3,350,000 + \pounds 1,500,000 - \pounds 200,000 - \pounds 2,000,000} = 43.39\%$$

This is rounded to 44%, so the recoverable input tax becomes 44% × £150,000 + £125,000 = £191,000. The difference from the unadjusted amount of £227,000 is £36,000. This difference is substantial if it exceeds £50,000 or 50% of the residual input tax and £25,000. £36,000 does not meet either of these criteria, so no over-ride adjustment is necessary.

*Simplification – provisional recovery rate*

(5) Recent efforts to simplify partial exemption calculations for smaller businesses have led to a number of developments. Probably the most important of these is the use of a provisional recovery rate. This allows a business to recover residual input tax during a partial exemption year based on the recovery rate for the preceding VAT year (to March, April or May depending on the stagger group or March in the case of a business that submits monthly VAT returns). The de minimis limits can still be checked on a quarter by quarter basis, using the provisional recovery rate, but at the end of the year a final recovery percentage is calculated in the same way as the normal annual recovery rate for the purposes of the annual adjustment. The difference is reclaimed or repaid as usual, and the new recovery rate becomes the provisional rate for the following year. If the business was de minimis in the previous year, this cannot be carried across – but see the subsequent changes to the de minimis calculations described in **explanatory note 2**.

Businesses which choose to use the provisional recovery rate to recover VAT must use this method consistently throughout a VAT year, and not change from one method to another. However, there is no requirement to notify HMRC that this method is in use.

*Early annual adjustment*

(6) Businesses may also bring forward their annual adjustment to the fourth VAT return of the VAT year instead of including it on 'quarter 5'. So in **part (b)** of the answer, Juliet Ltd is permitted to account for the annual adjustment in relation to the VAT year ended 30 April 2016 on either the return for the period ended 31 July 2016 (known as the default position) or to bring it forward and include it on the return for the period to 30 April 2016. In Juliet Ltd's case as the adjustment is a payment due to HMRC, delaying the adjustment until the July return will provide cash flow benefits. Accelerating the annual adjustment calculation so that it is carried out as soon as possible after the end of the tax year is particularly useful to businesses wishing to apply the provisional recovery rate in the following partial exemption year (see **explanatory note 5**).

# Planning and special situations

# Question

(A) Outline the provisions relating to the acquisition of shares by employees and directors and the special rules relating to the following worker participation plans:

(1) SAYE share option schemes;

(2) company share option plans (CSOP schemes);

(3) share incentive plans (SIP);

(4) enterprise management incentives (EMI plans);

(5) corporation tax relief on employee shares;

(6) employee shareholder rules;

(7) employee ownership trusts.

Disregard the impact of the rules in Part 7A of ITEPA 2003 on employment income paid via third parties.

(B) Jack Lumber was offered the job of managing director of Trefellows Ltd, a private company controlled by the Palin family. When he was appointed, they allowed him to subscribe in cash for 5% of the company's ordinary shares for £50,000, which was agreed with HMRC to be the unrestricted open market value of a holding of that size. In order to incentivise Jack to grow the business, the other shareholders later agreed with him that, if the business was sold within three years for more than £5 million, his share of the proceeds would be 10%. The business was sold 18 months later for £7 million and Jack duly received £700,000.

Outline the tax consequences of the various steps in the story.

# Answer

## A1. Acquisitions of shares and other employment-related securities by employees and directors

The legislation relating to the acquisition of securities by employees and directors is complex and wide-ranging.

The basic principle is that, when an employer gives an employee an incentive reward, it is classed as taxable income. This is as true for share-based rewards as it is for cash payments. However, there are several sets of rules that allow for certain tax advantages if conditions are met, such as treating employee gains on employer shares as capital rather than income profits (possibly taxed at only 10% where entrepreneurs' relief applies), and deferring tax charges until disposal of the shares, or even exempting gains completely. There are also detailed rules for taxing share and security transactions that do not benefit from tax advantages.

HMRC used to approve certain of these employee share schemes in advance, but employers now simply have to register them with HMRC and self-certify in the case of schemes with tax advantages (with the official checking done later) and they are generally referred to as 'tax-advantaged' schemes or plans. There are tax advantages in the following sets of rules:

- the enterprise management incentive (EMI);
- the share incentive plan (SIP, now known as a 'Schedule 2 SIP' plans);
- the Save As You Earn plan (SAYE, now known as 'Schedule 3 SAYE' option schemes);
- the company share option plan (CSOP, now known as 'Schedule 4 CSOP' schemes); and
- employee shareholder arrangements (ES).

There are very detailed statutory provisions that must be satisfied for each plan.

The costs of establishing tax-advantaged employee share plans are allowable deductions for corporation tax as are the incidental costs of running all types of employee share plans. Further corporation tax implications are considered below under **Corporation tax relief on employee shares.**

The legislation is found mainly in Part 7 of Income Tax (Earnings and Pensions) Act 2003 (ITEPA 2003), which includes numerous anti-avoidance provisions, but some of the associated capital gains exemptions are found in TCGA 1992.

Except in relation to the tax-advantaged plans and EMI, the legislation applies to 'securities' rather than just to shares. The definition of securities for these purposes in ITEPA 2003 s 420(1) is wide-ranging, including debentures, loan stock and other securities issued by companies, warrants, options (other than options over securities) as well as a range of other financial instruments, including government and local authority loan stock, and units in collective investment schemes. An award of restricted stock units, which is in reality a bonus scheme that determines the value of a cash bonus by reference to the performance of a real share that the employee never owns, is statutorily treated as a securities option with effect from 6 April 2016.

The tax-advantaged plans mainly deal only with 'ordinary shares' as defined in ITA 2007 s 989, although this does not apply to ES shares. The legislation applies where the securities have been acquired by reason of employment. It deems this to be the case where employees or directors acquire shares (or other securities) made available by their employing company or a person connected with their employer unless it can be demonstrated that the acquisition was made from an individual by reason of personal or family relationships or the securities were acquired in the open market on the same terms as are available to independent third parties (eg, shares are purchased by the employee independently on the Stock Market having made his own arrangements to do so). The employment by reason of which the individual acquires his shares includes prospective employment or any employment that terminated in the previous seven years. Where someone acquires securities by reason of the employment of another person, ITEPA 2003 Part 7 applies and the latter individual will be subject to the charges so arising as if he had acquired the securities or associated benefit himself.

The main provisions of the current tax-advantaged plans, EMI and other relevant legislation are as follows.

## Reporting requirements

Under all the tax-advantaged plans, employers are now required to register the plans online and provide annual returns to HMRC using the specified online forms. Paper returns could be used for reporting employee shares and securities transactions in 2013-14 or earlier tax years, but not for later years. Detailed information must also be provided when chargeable events occur in relation to employment-related securities. Penalties apply if the company fails to comply, unless the employer has a reasonable excuse (eg, HMRC's systems rejected or lost a valid submission). Employees must similarly ensure that appropriate details are included in their tax returns (see below under **Self-assessment**).

The legislation in ITEPA 2003 Part 7 now requires registration and self-certification by employers, by 6 July following the fiscal year, of *all* share schemes and all acquisitions by a director/employee of shares and securities by reason of employment (including past and prospective employments (s 421B)). Thus acquisition of an initial subscriber share by a company formation agent is not reportable, but generally all subsequent transfers of shares or an issue of new shares will be reportable if the shareholder is or will be a director or employee including those who are founding members of a company. The report should be made online to HMRC using an end-of-year template (42) from https://www.gov.uk/government/publications/share-schemes-employment-related-securities-42.

Where a notice to file was received for 2013-14 or earlier years, there was a potential penalty under TMA 1970 s 98 (to be awarded by a tribunal, rather than automatically applied by HMRC) not exceeding £300 for failure to file by the due date, which could be increased by up to £60 per day for continued failure. In addition, a penalty of £300 per reportable event could be imposed by way of penalty proceedings, with further penalties not exceeding £60 per day.

From 6 April 2014, ss 421JA–421JF provide for a new annual reporting regime in respect of all reportable events. Returns and accompanying information are required every year from the point at which the first reportable event occurs, they must be made electronically (unless HMRC gives explicit for another channel to be used) and they must be made on or before 6 July after the end of each tax year. Late returns, in the absence of a reasonable excuse, will incur an automatic initial £100 penalty, plus £300 if delivery is more than three months late, and a further £300 if over six months late. Once a return is nine months late, HMRC can begin to levy £10 per day of continuing failure to file. Inaccurate returns made carelessly or deliberately are subject to a penalty of up to £5,000. All penalty notices may be appealed to the first-tier tribunal.

An event is not reportable if it can be ascertained that the transfer was made by an individual connected with the employer company and the right or opportunity was made available in the normal course of the domestic, family or personal relationships of that person (s 421B(3)). If there is no element of remuneration, certain other events are also disregarded. An example is where a flat management company is incorporated and a new unrestricted share is issued to each of the residents, some of whom are directors. If the shares are restricted, the transaction must be reported in the annual 42 return, although a provision to the effect that they must be sold to another resident on sale of the flat does not count as a restriction in HMRC's view, so no reports are required.

There are some further specific circumstances where HMRC have indicated that they will not require a report. Although HMRC's guidance in the Employment Related Securities Manual (ERSM) still refers to Form 42, which was used when paper returns were required for 2013/14 and earlier, the guidance in that manual is still useful for the purposes of completing the online report. For example, ERSM140070 states that a report may not be required in respect of shares acquired by employees or directors purchased on the open market independently of the company where the company is quoted on a recognised stock exchange. Shares acquired in a company listed on a recognised stock exchange in connection with a bonus issue, rights issue or dividend reinvestment plan may also be exempt where the right is offered to all shareholders.

## Securities that are 'readily convertible assets'

Where employment-related securities are acquired by employees other than under tax-advantaged plans, or are subject to a tax charge under the rules of such a plan, employers must account for income tax and Class 1 national insurance contributions under the 'notional pay' provisions of PAYE if the securities are 'readily convertible assets' ('RCAs'), ie, they may be sold on a recognised Stock Exchange, or arrangements exist, or are likely to come into existence, for them to be traded (see **Example B1 explanatory note 12**), or they are deemed to be RCAs because they are securities that are not deductible for corporation tax purposes (see below), for example, shares in a subsidiary of an unlisted company. It should be noted that shares that are not RCAs may be deemed to be so by virtue of s 698(3) ITEPA 2003.

These provisions apply to shares acquired directly and through the exercise of unapproved options that were granted on or after 27 November 1996 (5 December 1996 for NIC purposes). They also apply where there is a chargeable event arising where a securities option is assigned or released, or a restriction attached to the securities is lifted or varied or the securities are sold when still subject to such restriction (unless certain elections have been entered into – these are discussed in more detail in the restricted securities section below), or securities are converted into other forms of security (see below). The national insurance legislation for options granted on or after 6 April 1999 deems the taxable gain to be earnings for Class 1 contributions purposes when the unapproved options are exercised, although there is no provision deeming the exercise to constitute a payment of those earnings. (See **Example H1 explanatory note 14** for the optional treatment of the employee paying the employer's secondary Class 1 liability.) The tax provisions relating to convertible shares and shares liable to forfeiture are mirrored for national insurance purposes for shares or interests in shares acquired on or after 9 April 1998. If shares are not readily convertible assets, neither Class 1 nor Class 1A national insurance contributions are payable and any income tax arising should be paid under the self-assessment system.

Shares and other securities that would not otherwise be readily convertible assets are treated as such (except for the purposes of the share incentive plan rules) unless they are shares that attract a corporation tax deduction under the provisions at (5) **below**. PAYE and national insurance extend to chargeable events within these provisions. Where the chargeable event takes the form of a receipt of money, or of an asset that is a readily convertible asset, PAYE and NICs apply regardless of whether or not the securities subject to the plan are themselves readily convertible assets. The employer must account for PAYE and Class 1 NICs even if the employee receives no cash, and the employee must reimburse the employer, either from other remuneration or by reimbursement. Until 5 April 2014, this had to happen within 90 days of the notional payment, but from 2014-15 onwards the deadline was extended to 90 days after the end of the tax year. If the employee does not make good within the deadline, the PAYE tax is deemed by ITEPA 2003 s 222 to itself constitute a benefit in kind, not cancelled out by later reimbursement of the PAYE.

Where a NIC liability is likely to arise on the exercise of an unapproved share option, or on chargeable events in respect of restricted or convertible securities within Part 7 of ITEPA 2003 (see below), the employer and employee can jointly elect, subject to certain conditions, that the employee will bear any employer NIC liability that arises (SSCBA 1992 Schedule 1 para 3B). Any such cost for the employee is deductible from the proceeds for income tax purposes. Note, though, that an election under ITEPA 2003 s 431 made at the time of acquisition to disapply restrictions takes the taxable gain outside the scope of Part 7 of ITEPA, which means that no election to transfer the NIC liability is then possible, as the value of the securities is taxed as a simple payment of general earnings, not under Part 7.

## Directors or employees with a 'material interest'

Under all tax-advantaged employee share plans, employees or directors with a material interest in the company could not previously participate if the company was a close company (see **Example J1**), but FA 2013 Sch 2 removed this bar for SIP and SAYE schemes from 17 July 2013, in the process automatically removing the limitation from any old scheme rules. Limits still apply for EMI and CSOPs, and shares given to employees in consideration of their signing an employee shareholder agreement cannot qualify as ES shares if the recipient holds a material interest. 'Material interest' is determined for EMI and CSOP purposes by the percentage of the company's ordinary share capital owned or controlled by the employee and his or her associates. Associates are normally close relatives, but also include trustees of trusts under which the employee might benefit. Shares held by a trust set up for the benefit of employees will, however, usually be ignored in determining whether an employee has a material interest (although they might not be ignored and might trigger PAYE and NIC liabilities under the Part 7A rules introduced by FA 2011 where they are earmarked by the trustees outside a tax-advantaged scheme). Employees are treated as having control of any shares that they have the right to acquire, other than those that are yet to be acquired under a qualifying option.

The relevant percentages are more than 30% for EMI plans and CSOPs. The limit for EMI plans applies to all companies, but the CSOP limit applies just to close companies. Employee benefit trusts (EBTs) do not constitute a tax-advantaged plan (though may be used in conjunction with one). However, there is a 5% material interest test for inheritance tax purposes where a close company is the settlor, but this is only important if the amount of any benefit received by an individual with a material interest is not subject to income tax and therefore not already exempt from IHT.

The relevant percentage for ES purposes is 25%. If the company is not close, this refers to the voting power, but if close it also refers to the share of assets on a winding up (ITEPA 2003 s 226D and TCGA 1992 s 236D).

## Restrictions on sale etc

Shares issued under tax-advantaged share option plans may be subject to a restriction in the company's articles of association requiring employees to sell them when they leave their employment, thus enabling companies to retain some control over holdings of their shares. Employee-controlled companies may use a class of shares of which the majority is held by directors or employees and gives them control of the company.

## Securities options

The right to acquire shares (or other securities) is a securities option. A securities option is not itself regarded as a security for tax purposes (ITEPA 2003 s 420(5)(e) and (8)) except where certain tax avoidance schemes are used.

Favourable tax treatment is given under ITEPA 2003 Part 7:

- Chapter 7 and Sch 3 for tax-advantaged SAYE plans; and
- Chapter 8 and Sch 4 for tax-advantaged CSOP schemes; and
- Chapter 9 and Sch 5 for enterprise management incentives (EMI).

Where the option is not granted under a tax-advantaged plan, an income tax charge arises at exercise on the difference between the open market value of the securities acquired at the time of exercising the right and the cost of acquiring them, including any amount paid for the option (ITEPA 2003 s 479). As indicated above, PAYE and national insurance contributions must be collected through payroll if the securities are readily convertible assets. An award of restricted stock units, which is in reality a bonus scheme that determines the value of a cash bonus and could be seen as a simple payment of earnings, is treated as a securities option with effect from 6 April 2016, rather than an arrangement for paying earnings, so tax charges will arise when it matures rather than when it is granted (ITEPA 2003, s 418(1A), inserted by FA 2016, s 17).

Where a right to acquire securities other than under a tax-advantaged plan is assigned or released, an income tax charge arises on the consideration received less the cost of acquisition of the rights. A charge to income tax also arises when any benefit is received or gain is realised because the option holder allows the option to lapse, or grants someone else an option over the securities. As indicated above, income tax and national insurance contributions will be charged through the payroll if the securities are readily convertible assets.

These income tax charges apply on the exercise, chargeable assignment or release of the option by any associated person and not just by the employee (ie, the person by reason of whose employment the option was granted). 'Associated persons' include the person to whom the option was granted (if not the employee), persons connected with the employee (or with the grantee) and members of the same household as the employee (or grantee).

A tax charge also arises on the amount or market value of any benefit received, in money or money's worth, by the employee (or an associated person) in connection with the option, which might include, for example, sums received for varying the option or as compensation for its cancellation.

Whatever the reason for a tax charge, any amount paid for the option itself is deductible in determining the taxable amount. Expenses incurred in connection with the exercise, assignment, release or receipt of benefit are also deductible, however notional costs of sale of the underlying securities are not deductible for income tax purposes.

For capital gains tax, the amount taxed as income on exercise of an unapproved employee share option counts as part of the cost of acquisition of the securities (as does anything paid for the option itself). The price paid to exercise an option will usually constitute the CGT base cost of the shares for the future in SAYE and CSOP schemes in accordance with the rules of those plans, but shares acquired under EMI options are taxed under the same principle as unapproved options.

For the purposes of the above provisions, no income tax liability arises on the *grant* of an option, unless exceptionally the option is granted at a discount under a CSOP scheme (which is unlikely, as CSOP options will not qualify as such if they are priced at a level manifestly less than market value).

## Partly-paid securities

If securities are issued at a price equal to the current unrestricted market value, with the price being paid by agreed instalments, no charge will arise under the general income tax charging provisions since full market value is being paid, and this will apply even though the market value has increased by the time the securities are paid for, unless the arrangement is being entered into for tax avoidance purposes. Any growth in value of the securities should be liable only to capital gains tax, provided that none of the other charging provisions of ITEPA Part 7 or Part 7A are in point.

A director or an employee who subscribes for securities other than under the tax advantaged plans where the capital is not called immediately is, however, regarded for P11D purposes (but not for CTA 2010 s 455 purposes) as having received an interest-free loan equal to the deferred instalments, with a taxable benefit in kind based on the taxable cheap loan rules in Part 3, Chapter 7, unless the total of all taxable cheap loans outstanding from that director or employee in the tax year, including the deferred instalments, does not exceed £10,000. Fully-paid shares sold to employees on deferred terms will give rise to a similar benefit in kind but a s 455 loan may also be created. If those shares are sold by a third party (private companies could not ordinarily hold their own shares after a purchase of own shares before company law was changed on 1 April 2013), a taxable benefit is likely to arise under Part 7A.

However, tax relief under ITA 2007 s 392 to offset the 'benefits code' charge on the notional loan is available to individuals who acquire securities in a close company (that is not a close investment holding company) and who either hold a material interest in the ordinary share capital, or work for the majority of their time in the management or control of that (or an associated) company. However, this relief will not apply to the Part 7A charge.

The loan is regarded for Part 7 as being repaid as and when the instalments are paid. Any amount written off is taxed as employment income at that time (however if at the outset there is an intention to write off the amount outstanding, HMRC will treat the securities as having been acquired at a discount, and company law will not permit the new shares to be issued for a price below their nominal value); any amount so charged is deductible for capital gains tax purposes when the securities are disposed of (ITEPA 2003 ss 446Q–446W).

There are a number of non-tax legal (eg, Companies Act and Financial Services & Markets Act) and accounting issues (eg, FRS20) associated with the offer of any securities to employees and these should be considered carefully when implementing any plan.

## Anti-avoidance rules

Various anti-avoidance provisions apply to employment-related securities. These do not apply in relation to shares that comply with the provisions of tax-advantaged plans, but it is important to note that EMI plans are not regarded as tax-advantaged plans for this purpose. Advantages gained not just by the employee but by 'associated persons' are brought fully within the charge to tax. 'Associated persons' include the person who acquired the securities (if not the employee), persons connected with the employee (or with the person who acquired the securities) and members of the same household as the employee (or person who acquired the securities). There are exemptions from some of the rules below where the securities are acquired under a public offer, or are shares in an employee-controlled company or where the event in question affects all the company's shares of the same class and the majority of them are held by outside shareholders; these exceptions apply in respect of restricted securities, convertible securities and post-acquisition benefits.

The then Paymaster General announced on 2 December 2004 that share-related avoidance schemes discovered after that date could be blocked with retrospective effect going back to that date. This threat was carried out in Finance Act 2006 with changes being made to ITEPA 2003 s 420 that took effect from 2 December 2004.

In the March 2010 Budget, the Treasury announced that it would be launching a consultation into the taxation of employment-related securities which deliver returns from what they describe as 'geared growth arrangements'. The aim of the consultation was to develop proposals that employment income from employment-related securities should be subject to income tax and NIC, but this plan was supplanted by a new focus under FA 2011 on employment income paid via third parties, which take a different approach. The resulting Part 7A of ITEPA 2003 is aimed at taxing reward, recognition and loans made available to employees via third parties such as trustees, or employers acting as their own trustees. Geared growth plans that do not involve such third parties would seem to be unaffected.

In the Emergency Budget of 22 June 2010, the Government announced its intention to examine whether the introduction of a general anti-avoidance rule would be appropriate with regard to unapproved transactions entered into by individual and corporate taxpayers which have mitigated their tax liabilities. A GAAR structured as a general anti-abuse rule eventually took effect for tax under Finance Act 2013, and for NIC purposes under National Insurance Contributions Act 2014.

## Restricted securities

If employment-related securities have certain restrictions or conditions attached to them, including risk of forfeiture (meaning a requirement to dispose of the securities for less than their market value), their actual market value (AMV) on acquisition will be less than their true initial unrestricted market value (IUMV), which reduces the charge to income tax on acquisition if the award of shares is treated as a payment of earnings. To counter this, further chargeable events subject to income tax are deemed to occur when the restrictions are lifted, or varied, or when the securities are disposed of while still subject to any of the applicable restrictions, since this could be a method of giving the employee a gain that would otherwise be a capital gain. The charge is calculated using a formula that is designed to subject to income tax the proportionate effect the restriction had on the value of the securities at the time it was lifted, charging a proportion of the value of the securities at the relevant time to income tax, whether or not there has been growth in their value. For example, if voting and dividend restrictions result in AMV being lower than IUMV by 20% at acquisition, then at the later date when those restrictions lift, 20% of the value of the shares at that time will be treated as income.

In cases where the risk of forfeiture of the securities will lift within five years, the normal income tax charge on acquisition is removed, but income tax is still chargeable when the risk of forfeiture is lifted/varied, etc.

There is no charge once seven years have expired after the relevant employment ceases and no charge on death.

For securities acquired on or after 16 April 2003 the rules may be summarised as below, but before that date, the rules were different.

Whilst the new rules might be said to be broadly comparable with the old, they can result in very different amounts being taxed at different times. They can also result in tax charges arising when the restrictions lift or are varied but there is no market for the securities on which funds could be realised to meet that liability (often known as a 'dry' tax charge, where no cash has been realised to pay the tax).

To avoid such issues, the employee and employer can together enter into an election to disapply, for tax and national insurance purposes, the effect of all or any of the restrictions attaching to the securities (ITEPA s 431). Hence if all restrictions are disapplied, on acquisition of the securities the employee would be charged to income tax (as general earnings, rather than under Part 7) on the difference between the IUMV of the securities (rather than their 'restricted' AMV) and the cost of acquisition (ie, the charge arises as if unrestricted securities were given or sold to the employee, with an earnings-based charge on any discount). The effect is to charge amounts earlier than would otherwise be the case, possibly by reference to a lower market value if the value of the securities is rising. However, the election is irrevocable, and if share values fall rather than rise, with the result that the employee never realises a gain, there is no possibility of tax and NIC being refunded. Valid elections in such cases take the form of an agreement between employer and employee, in a form approved by HMRC, made within 14 days after acquisition or a chargeable event; there is no requirement that they be submitted to HMRC or that the approval of HMRC be sought, although evidence of the election must be retained for future reference. One such election possibility is to waive the exemption on acquisition (for securities subject to early forfeiture) in order to limit the potential charge on a subsequent chargeable event; this was not possible under the old rules. As noted above, if all restrictions are deemed disapplied for tax and NI purposes, no election under SSCBA 1992 Schedule 1 para 3B is possible, so the employer must bear all secondary NIC costs.

Any amount charged to income tax forms part of the acquisition cost of the securities for capital gains tax purposes. Where the securities are held in trust until such time as the risk of forfeiture or other restriction is removed, they are usually treated as acquired at that time, rather than any earlier time, though this does depend on the exact terms of the agreement. The CGT base cost is irrelevant for shares acquired under the ES regime before 17 March 2016 and held until their sale (or other disposal after the employment has ceased), as no CGT charge should then arise, unless the employee holds ES shares worth more than £50,000 at the time of acquisition, as shares acquired in exchange for entering into an ES agreement before 17 March 2016 below that level of holding are exempt from CGT (see TCGA 1992 ss 236B to 235G). Those ES shares acquired by entering into an ES agreement after 16 March 2016 are free of CGT on first disposal up to a chargeable gain of £100,000, the new limit having been imposed by FA 2016, s 88.

### Convertible securities

Where securities are convertible into securities of a different class or description, or may become convertible if conditions are met, any income tax due on acquisition is computed by reference to what their market value would be without the conversion right. When they are converted, or on any other chargeable event (which could be a disposal, a release of the conversion right or a receipt of a benefit), the value of the conversion right is taxed at that time at its then value, with a deduction allowed for anything payable by the employee for the conversion itself. These provisions have applied since 1 September 2003 and, except for the way tax is charged on acquisition, apply to all securities from that date regardless of when they were acquired. (ITEPA 2003 ss 435–444 and FA 2003 Sch 22 para 4.)

The previous rules were different.

Amounts charged to income tax form part of the acquisition cost of the securities for capital gains tax purposes, although this will be irrelevant for shares acquired under the ES regime before 17 March 2016, or later ES acquisitions where the gain on first disposal is no more than £100,000.

### Post-acquisition benefits

Tax is chargeable on the amount or market value of any special benefit received in connection with employment-related securities. Apart from the extension of the charge to benefits received by associated persons, the rules that have applied since 16 April 2003 are fairly similar to the old rules (ITEPA 2003 ss 447–450). HMRC have stated that they will not normally argue that this provision should be used to tax dividends from employment-related securities as employment income, although the possibility exists that they will indeed do so where an avoidance scheme involving dividends has been used. In *PA Holdings Ltd v Commrs of HMRC* [2011] EWCA Civ 1414, HMRC argued instead, successfully, that dividends from shares in special purpose companies were simply bonuses that had been dressed up as dividends by a series of artificial steps.

### Securities with artificially depressed market value

If the market value at the time of acquisition of employment-related securities is depressed by 10% or more by means of non-commercial transactions, the reduction in value is charged to income tax as employment income. This also applies in conjunction with the rules above for restricted securities and convertible securities to prevent the reduction of tax charges on chargeable events under those rules. In addition, in the case of restricted securities only, if any such non-commercial transaction has occurred in the previous seven years, a charge arises on 5 April in the relevant tax year as if the restrictions had been lifted on that date. For national insurance purposes, the taxable amount is treated as earnings, but there is no provision deeming a payment to take place.

### Securities with artificially enhanced market value

Where in any tax year the market value of employment-related shares is enhanced by 10% or more by means of non-commercial transactions, the increase in value is charged to income tax as employment income on 5 April in that year or, if earlier, on disposal. For national insurance purposes, these provisions give rise to deemed earnings, but again the NIC legislation lacks a provision deeming payment to take place.

Where an employee acquires a share that increases in value in the ordinary course of events (eg, it becomes entitled under the terms of its issue and under the company's articles of association to a greater share of the value of the company, perhaps because a profit hurdle has been crossed), this rule is of no relevance.

### Securities disposed of for more than market value

When employment-related securities are disposed of for more than their market value, the excess is chargeable to income tax rather than capital gains tax. (ITEPA 2003 ss 446X–446Z).

### Priority allocations in public offers

Where shares are offered to the public, a priority allocation is often made to employees and directors. Where there is no price advantage, a benefit will not be deemed to arise because of the right to shares in priority to other persons so long as the shares that may be allocated do not exceed 10% of those being offered, all directors and employees entitled to an allocation are entitled on similar terms (albeit at different levels), and those entitled are not restricted wholly or mainly to persons who are directors or whose remuneration exceeds a particular level (ITEPA 2003 Part 7 Chapter 10).

Where employees are offered a discount compared with the price paid by the public, the employees will pay income tax on the discount, but the benefit of the priority allocation will still escape tax. The employee's base cost for capital gains tax is the amount paid plus the discount that was charged to tax.

## Tax-advantaged employee share plans

More detailed points on the various tax-advantaged employee share plans are as follows:

(1) **SAYE share option schemes**

The legislative requirements of SAYE share option schemes are set out in ITEPA 2003 ss 516–520 and Sch 3 and they are now known as 'Schedule 3 SAYE option schemes'. Income tax is chargeable neither when Schedule 3 SAYE option is granted nor on exercise where the exercise price of the option is paid out of the proceeds of a linked SAYE scheme. The purpose of the scheme must be to provide benefits to employees and directors in the form of share options and it may not offer a cash alternative as an alternative to the options.

The SAYE contributions themselves are saved with a building society or a bank by way of a deduction from net pay. The present maximum monthly contribution is £500 (£250 until 5 April 2014) and the scheme minimum contribution may not be set above £10 (and the SAYE savings contract may have a minimum of £5). There is no tax relief on the contributions, but any interest and bonuses (paid on savings at a set rate) received from the SAYE savings contract are tax-free (although the rate is currently zero on three- and five-year contracts). This applies whether or not the employee exercises the option to take up the shares.

The employee is given the option to buy shares after either three or five years, at a price which must not normally be less than 80% of the market value of the shares at the time the option is granted. The total price to be paid must not exceed the proceeds of the SAYE contract. The scheme must be available to all directors and employees within a qualifying period of not more than five years' service and it must not have features that discourage eligible employees from participating or which exclude part-time employees. If an employee dies before completing the contract, his personal representatives may exercise the option within 12 months after the date of death. If an employee dies within six months of the bonus date, the option remains exercisable until the expiry of 12 months from the bonus date.

Schedule 3 limits the choices for employers in respect of leavers, permitting certain relaxations only in defined circumstances.

If employees leave before they have held the option for three years, options must lapse, unless the termination is due to injury, disability, redundancy, retirement, a relevant transfer of the business under the TUPE Regulations 2006, or the employer company being sold out of the group. In such cases, options must lapse no later than six months after the termination date and no later than six months after the maturity of the SAYE savings contract. The scheme rules may also permit exercise within three years of grant where the employment transfers with the business to a third party without TUPE regulations applying, but the time limit for exercise must be no more than six months after the old employment ends or no more than six months after leaving because of injury, disability, etc as outlined above, and any gain is then subject to income tax, except in the case of certain cash takeovers. In the case of such takeovers, the individual may exercise a CSOP or SAYE share option before the end of the normal holding period without a charge to income tax – this relaxation was introduced in Finance Act 2013 Part 2 Sch 2.

If employees leave after the options have been held for at least three years, the scheme rules may cause the options to lapse immediately or up to six months from the termination date, provided that is also no more than six months after the bonus date of the savings contract.

An employee who has been transferred to an associated company that is not participating in the scheme may nonetheless be permitted by the scheme rules to exercise the option within six months after the date his savings contract matures, or, if he leaves because of injury, disability, redundancy or retirement, within six months of leaving.

Regardless of the treatment of the option, the SAYE contract itself may be continued by an employee after he leaves, by arrangement with the savings body, so that the benefit of receiving tax-free interest and bonuses (when bonus rates are higher than 0%) at the end of the contract is retained. Payments will then be made direct to the savings body.

(2) **Company share option plan (CSOP) schemes**

Under the provisions of ITEPA ss 521–526 and Sch 4, shares acquired by employees under a *company share option plan*, now known as a 'Schedule 4 CSOP' after FA 2014, do not attract an income tax charge when the option is granted, unless the price to be paid for the shares under the option plus the price paid for the option itself is less than the market value (meaning the unrestricted value if the shares are restricted, which became possible from 17 July 2013) of a similar quantity of shares at the time the right to acquire is granted. In that event an income tax charge arises on the difference in the year the option is granted, the amount charged to income tax then forms part of the cost of the shares for capital gains tax when the option is exercised (TCGA 1992 s 120(6)). However under a Schedule 4 CSOP, an option cannot be granted with an exercise price that is 'manifestly less' than the market value of the underlying shares at the date of grant (ITEPA 2003 Sch 4 para 22(1)(b)).

There is also no income tax charge when the option is exercised unless the plan has by then been determined by HMRC no longer to be a Schedule 4 CSOP (the equivalent before 6 April 2014 was having its approval withdrawn) and the options are exercised between three and ten years after the date they were granted. This is so even if the employee to whom the option was granted has left the employment by the time of exercise (see further below).

The shares over which CSOP options may be granted must be fully-paid and not redeemable, although they can be subject to restrictions (prior to Finance Act 2013 only certain restrictions were allowed). They must also be shares of a class listed on a recognised stock exchange or in a company which is not under the control of another company. Options could also be granted to employees of shares in subsidiaries of listed companies until ITEPA 2003 Sch 4 para 17 was changed with effect from 24 September 2010. The change removed the possibility of using shares in companies whose share value could be manipulated artificially to the benefit of option holders.

Approved options may be exercised prior to the third anniversary of grant, but if this is done, then for income tax purposes, the option is treated as an unapproved securities option (as described above), with income tax (PAYE, and national insurance if the shares are readily convertible assets) arising on the gain on exercise of the option. This is also the case if the plan has been determined by HMRC to no longer be a Schedule 4 CSOP.

Employees who leave because of injury, disability, redundancy or retirement will be allowed to exercise the option within the initial three-year period without a charge to income tax, where the CSOP rules specifically permit this and where the CSOP option is exercised within six months of the termination date. This period is extended to at least 12 months where the plan permits exercise after the employee's death. Following changes made by Schedule 2 to Finance Act 2013, if the scheme rules are written accordingly, early exercise of options is also allowed, within six months of the relevant date, for employees who cease to be in qualifying employment because their employer company was a constituent company in a group scheme, but has ceased to be controlled by the scheme organiser as a result of a general offer that has become unconditional, or because the court sanctions a compromise under Companies Act 2006 that results in a change of control. From 6 April 2014, this also extends to a change of control as a result of a non-UK company reorganisation arrangement that becomes binding on the shareholders. In certain circumstances, the scheme rules may now permit the exercise of a CSOP option within 20 days before or after a relevant event, one of which is the making of a general offer for the employer company or group. Option exercises under this rule will be void if the offer is not made within the 20 days permitted.

For directors to participate they must be full-time working directors (ie working at least 25 hours per week), but part-time employees do qualify. The value (as at the date of the grant of the option) of shares over which a person holds CSOP options must not exceed £30,000, measured at the date of grant and based on the unrestricted market value.

ITEPA 2003 Sch 3 Part 7 and Sch 4 Part 6 permit participants in a SAYE scheme or CSOP scheme to exchange existing share options for options over shares in a company that takes over the employer company, so long as an election is made within six months and certain conditions are met. In the case of certain cash takeovers, the individual may exercise a CSOP or SAYE share option before the end of the normal holding period without a charge to income tax – this relaxation was introduced in Part 2 of Sch 2 to Finance Act 2013.

(3) **Share incentive plans (SIPs)**

Under ITEPA 2003 s 488 and Sch 2 an employer can introduce a plan that enables the company to give shares to its employees and obtain a tax deduction for the market value of those shares in the accounting period in which the shares are awarded. Furthermore, the plan enables an employee to buy shares in his employing company out of his gross income (ie, such that taxable income is reduced and tax is saved) provided the conditions set out in the relevant legislation are met and the plan has received HMRC approval (pre-6 April 2014) or has been suitably self-certified and continues to meet the requirements (post-5 April 2014).

Such plans were previously referred to as 'all employee share ownership plans'. They are now commonly known as share incentive plans or SIPs, and after 6 April 2014 formally known as 'Schedule 2 SIPs'. A SIP must be made available to all employees who are eligible and liable to UK tax on employment income. An employee does not have to accept an offer to join the plan. The plan must not contain features that discourage participation (eg, loss of other rights for joining). All employees must participate on similar terms, although those terms may vary by reference to remuneration, length of service, hours worked or performance targets, but not so as to give preferential treatment to directors or higher paid employees. Certain events disqualify the SIP (see, eg, ITEPA 2003, Sch 2 para 85A, inserted by FA 2016, Sch 3 para 2) with the aim of enforcing the principle that preferential shares in a SIP cannot be issued to select employees.

The plan may contain a qualifying period for participation but this must not exceed 18 months for free and partnership shares where there is no accumulation period, or six months for partnership shares where there is an accumulation period. Where an employee within a group works for more than one group company, employment with any group company can count towards the qualifying period. An employee must not receive shares under another SIP from the same or a connected company in the same year, except, where a group restructures and the employee transfers to another company within the group. Then the employee, subject to one overall limit, may receive shares under SIPs run by both companies. Until 17 July 2013, there was a bar on participation in a SIP by any employee with a material interest in the employing company. This restriction was removed by Part 3 of Sch 2 to Finance Act 2013.

The shares available under the plan can be of four types, all of which are held in a UK resident trust established for the purpose in accordance with the SIP legislation (known as a 'SIP trust'):

(a) *Free shares*

An employee can be given shares worth up to £3,600 in a tax year (£3,000 before 6 April 2014), valued as at the date of the award. The gifted shares are held within a SIP trust and no tax liability arises on the award while the shares are so held. Free shares must normally be kept in the SIP trust for a stipulated period, which may be not less than three nor more than five years. If an employee ceases employment, the shares are removed from the SIP trust and the SIP may provide for such shares to be forfeited if this occurs within three years of the date of their award. A partial tax charge may arise if the shares are removed from the trust after three years, but before they have been held for five years. However, after five years the shares may be removed from the trust without tax charges and with the then-current value as the CGT base cost.

(b) *Partnership shares*

An employee may be given the opportunity to buy shares (known as partnership shares) by way of a salary deduction. The maximum deduction is 10% of salary as defined by the SIP (excluding benefits in kind) subject to a limit of £1,800 in a tax year (£1,500 before 6 April 2014), with a minimum deduction which may be set at a level no higher than £10. The deduction reduces gross salary before PAYE/national insurance is applied. Although that does not reduce earnings for pension and tax credit purposes, HMRC have issued guidance in leaflet IR177 on the effect any such reduction in national insurance payments might have on benefits as well as the employee's entitlement to statutory sick pay (SSP), statutory maternity pay (SMP), the state pension and any means-tested benefits or tax credits, and requires employers to include relevant warnings in the scheme documentation given to employees invited to participate. It is unlikely that anyone earning so little that their regular earnings do not even reach the lower earnings limit (ie, the qualifying minimum for SSP) will opt in to buying partnership shares through a SIP, but reducing pay by £150 per month could reduce SMP entitlement for the first six weeks, when higher rate SMP is payable, by £33.75 per week. The money deducted from salary must either be used to buy shares in the company establishing the SIP (or its parent company as set out in the SIP) within 30 days, or accumulated for up to one year, and then used within 30 days of the end of the accumulation period to acquire the shares. The price may be set by reference to three different formulae. If the employee leaves during the accumulation period, the amount deducted in that period (net of PAYE/NI) is returned to him. The employee may withdraw the shares from the plan at any time (although this may result in an income tax charge as indicated below).

(c) *Matching shares*

An employer can offer up to two 'matching shares' for each partnership share purchased, in effect permitting shares to be bought with a discount of up to 66.6% to current market value. The matching shares are awarded at nil cost. They must be awarded on the same day and on the same basis as the partnership shares and be of the same class. They are held in the SIP trust on the same terms as free shares and may be made forfeitable within a three-year period from the date of award in the event that employment is terminated (save for an excepted reason) or in the event that partnership shares are withdrawn.

(d) *Dividend shares*

The SIP may provide, or may provide for an employee to elect, for dividends or a proportion of dividends to be automatically reinvested and used to purchase further SIP shares whilst the shares on which the dividends were paid are held in the SIP trust. Before FA 2013, Sch 2 was passed, the reinvestment was subject to a maximum of £1,500 per tax year. This limit was then removed, to recognize the fact that many SIP shares have been accumulated over ten years or more and that dividends can now be substantial. Reinvested dividends do not carry a tax credit. The shares purchased must have the same rights as the shares on which the dividend is paid and are not subject to forfeiture but may be subject to a holding period of three years and, from 6 April 2014 may be subject to provision requiring the employee to offer the shares for sale, provided the employee will receive at least the value of the dividends used to buy the shares or, if lower, the market value at the time of sale (ITEPA 2003 Sch 2, para 65(2)(3)). Such shares must be acquired within 30 days of the payment of the dividend. Any dividend so invested is not liable to higher rate tax as long as the reinvested shares are held in the SIP trust, which must be for a period of at least three years. If the shares are withdrawn within that period, eg, on leaving employment, the trustee must give the employee the relevant details and extra tax may be payable by the recipient under self-assessment if he is a higher or additional rate taxpayer (after taking into account a tax credit at the rate in force when the shares are taken out of the SIP trust). The taxable value will ordinarily be the value of the dividends reinvested to buy the shares in question, but if the employee was required to offer the shares for sale and the requirements of para 65(3) were met, the value will then generally be the market value of the shares if lower than the dividends reinvested.

*General provisions*

The shares used in the SIP must be ordinary shares that are fully paid up and not redeemable. They can be listed, or shares in a company not controlled by another company, or shares in a company that is under the control of a company listed on a recognised stock exchange and is not close (or would not be close if a UK company). The shares may be subject to certain limited restrictions such as pre-emption, risk of forfeiture on termination of employment or on voting rights, subject to the detailed provisions of the legislation aimed at ensuring no manipulation of the value or selection of particular employees who might benefit disproportionately. The shares must not be in a service company. The plan could also be disqualified if certain specified events happen, such as an alteration being made to a key feature of the plan without HMRC's prior approval. Under changes made by FA 2010 s 42, disqualification may also follow where the value of shares in the SIP trust is materially affected by alterations to the rights attaching to any other share capital of the company. FA 2014 also inserted a new Part 10 into Schedule 2, setting out rules for notification of SIPs, annual returns and

HMRC enquiries, which may now result, where the SIP does not meet or has not met the full requirements, in notification that a SIP is no longer a 'Schedule 2 SIP' from a specified date, meaning that no new SIP shares may be awarded and that the employer may be liable to a penalty that is geared to twice the employees' tax and NIC savings from the plan.

*Tax provisions*

No tax charge arises on the acquisition of the shares under the terms of the SIP (and, as noted above, payroll deductions used to buy partnership shares are tax-deductible). An income tax charge (and a Class 1 national insurance charge if the shares are readily convertible assets) can, however, arise if free, partnership or matching shares are removed from the plan within three years, based on the value of the shares on the date of removal. Where shares are withdrawn from the SIP trust between three and five years, the charge is on the lower of the value on removal and, for free and matching shares, the value at the date of the original acquisition of the shares under the plan, and for partnership shares the amount of partnership share money used to acquire the shares (ie, recapturing the relief given for the payroll deductions). Dividend shares removed from a plan within three years are taxable as dividend income as indicated above, usually based on the original dividends reinvested.

No tax arises on the death of the employee, or on withdrawal after five years, when the shares are free of both income and capital gains tax provided that the shares are not held for any period after withdrawal from the SIP trust. Furthermore, no tax charge arises if the shares cease to be subject to the SIP because of injury or disability, redundancy, transfer under the Transfer of Undertakings (Protection of Employment) Regulations, change of control of the employing company or retirement. The individual may also withdraw SIP shares from the plan before the end of the normal holding period without a charge to income tax if that withdrawal relates to a cash takeover meeting certain requirements – this relaxation was introduced in Part 2 of Sch 2 to Finance Act 2013.

As far as capital gains tax is concerned, there is no liability if the shares are kept in the SIP trust until disposed of. If they are removed and held for a period before disposal, the base cost will be the value at the date of removal and the capital gain will be based on the increase in value after they are withdrawn. Partnership or dividend shares transferred to employees under the SIP are exempt from stamp duty and stamp duty reserve tax (see **Example M1 part A(b)** and (**c**)).

*Capital gains tax rollover relief (TCGA 1992 s 236A and Sch 7C)*

Where existing shareholders (other than companies) transfer ownership of shares they hold in an unquoted company to a Schedule 2 SIP that holds (either immediately or within twelve months after the transfer) 10% of the company's shares, gains arising on the shares transferred may be treated as reducing the acquisition cost of replacement chargeable assets acquired within six months after the disposal (unless the chargeable assets are shares on which enterprise investment scheme income tax relief is given (see **Example N7**) and subject to some special provisions relating to dwelling houses).

(4) **Enterprise management incentives (EMI)**

A further share option plan is known as the enterprise management incentive (EMI) plan (ITEPA 2003 ss 527–541 and Sch 5, and (until 5 April 2016, when it was repealed by FA 2016, Sch 3, para 9) TCGA 1992 Sch 7D Part 4, together making up the 'EMI Code'). The plan enables employees to be awarded qualifying share options over shares worth up to £250,000 each (£120,000 for options granted prior to 16 June 2012 and £100,000 if granted prior to 6 April 2008, all values measured assuming the shares were unrestricted) in a qualifying company (this limit is reduced by the value at grant of any shares under subsisting CSOP options). Subject to the EMI limits on individuals and in total (see below), each employee may be awarded a different amount without restriction. The grant and exercise of the option is tax- and NIC-free, except to the extent, if any, that the exercise price of an EMI option is less than the value of the underlying shares at the time the option was granted. In such a case, the element of that discount on grant is subject to income tax (and national insurance if the shares are readily convertible assets) on exercise of the option. When the shares are sold, the excess of the proceeds over the price paid to acquire the shares (plus any amount charged to income tax) is a chargeable gain for CGT purposes.

In order to qualify, the EMI must satisfy the detailed requirements of the legislation. These include:

(a) The employing company must be one that would qualify under the EMI Code at the time of granting the option as having gross assets less than £30 million, the company/group must be independent and have only qualifying subsidiaries (as defined in the EMI Code) and undertake a trade that is not excluded under ITEPA Sch 5 paras 16 to 23, the rules being similar to the rules for the Enterprise Investment Scheme (EIS) (see **Example N7**). There is also a limit of 250 on the number of full-time equivalent employees (calculated on a just and reasonable basis) of the qualifying company/group at the time of grant.

From their introduction in 2000, the rules also required a company granting qualifying EMI options to carry on a qualifying trade 'wholly or mainly' in the UK, but this contravened the EU Treaty, so after 16 December 2010 a company granting EMI options is required instead to have a 'permanent establishment' in the UK, which means that EU-based companies can benefit their UK employees, assuming no overseas tax hurdles exist.

(b) The maximum value of shares in respect of which unexercised EMI options exist at any particular grant date must not exceed £3 million (measured at the date of each grant and on the basis of their unrestricted market value).

(c) The option must be granted for commercial reasons to recruit or retain an employee and not for tax avoidance purposes.

(d) The individual must work at least 25 hours per week for the company (or if less, 75% of his working time – in both employment and self-employment if applicable) and must not, with associates, have a material interest in the company (ie 30% or more of the ordinary share capital). The Government has consulted on relaxing the working hours rule for academics who are involved in the development of new products in qualifying companies while continuing with their teaching commitments, but nothing was changed to that effect.

(e) An employee may not hold unexercised qualifying options in respect of shares with a total value of more than £250,000 when the options were granted (the value of any restricted shares being taken as uplifted to IUMV rather than AMV). Once that limit is reached, any further options granted within three years of the date of the last qualifying option are not qualifying options, regardless of whether the earlier options have then been exercised or released. Any unexercised options under Schedule 2 CSOPs (see **para (2)**) count towards the limit.

(f) The general requirements relating to the option must be met, eg, notice must be given to HMRC within 92 days of the grant of the option in the online form specified, together with a declaration that the information is complete and correct and that the employee is an eligible employee.

If a disqualifying event occurs after an EMI option has been granted, but before it is exercised, the holder of the option has 90 days (40 days before 17 July 2013) from the date of the event in which to exercise the option without losing the EMI tax benefits. If the option is exercised after that time, then income tax is charged under ITEPA 2003 Part 7 Chapter 5 s 476 on the difference between the market value of the shares on the date of exercise and their market value immediately before the disqualifying event (s 532).

Disqualifying events include (s 533):

- the company becoming a 51% subsidiary, or under the control of another company,
- the company ceasing to meet the trading activities test,
- the employee ceasing to be an eligible employee,
- a variation in the terms of the option so that the market value of the shares is increased,
- an alteration to the share capital that affects the value of the shares to which the option relates without prior HMRC approval,
- certain conversions of shares into shares of a different class,

- the company having qualified on the basis that it was preparing to trade, but not doing so within two years of the grant of the option.

(5) **Corporation tax relief on employee shares**

Companies were once encouraged to promote employee share ownership through a trust set up for this purpose known as a qualifying employee share ownership trust (QUEST). Payments made by the employer to set up the trust and to acquire shares to distribute to its employees obtained corporation tax relief so long as certain stringent conditions were met. These trusts were expensive to operate and have now been abolished, to be replaced with less restrictive arrangements.

In general now, under the terms of CTA 2009 Part 12 an employer will receive corporation tax relief of an amount equal to the difference between the market value of the shares at the time the employee exercises a share option and the price the employee pays. The relief is given in the accounting period in which the option is exercised and the shares acquired. The relief applies to CSOP, SAYE and EMI options (which are tax-free) and unapproved options or outright share acquisitions, or charges arising in connection with restricted or convertible shares, where the employee is subject to income tax.

The shares must be ordinary shares, and the company either a listed company, under the control of a listed company, or a stand-alone company (or the holding company of a group). From 24 September 2010, an anti-avoidance measure in FA 2010 s 39 barred the use in CSOP option grants from that date onwards of shares in a company under the control of a listed company, because some companies had been manipulating the values artificially to give employees guaranteed gains that were subject to CGT rather than income tax.

Shares for a SIP have always given a corporation tax deduction as set out above. Relief is not, however, permitted in respect of shares forfeited back to the trust and in respect of which relief has already been given, and FA 2010 s 42 included another anti-avoidance measure that barred a deduction under CTA 2009 s 989 for payments made by an employer from 24 March 2010 onwards pursuant to tax avoidance arrangements. This change was aimed at preventing employers using SIP trusts to gain a corporate tax deduction without giving their employees any real value in the shares held by the SIP.

(6) **Employee Shareholders**

From 1 September 2013, FA 2013 Sch 23 created a new tax-advantaged scheme which allows companies to give employees shares worth at least £2,000 in return for reduced employee rights. The aim was to remove some employment rights, seen as a burden on business, while compensating those employees who agreed to surrender the rights by offering tax exemptions in respect of the shares awarded to them.

A new 'Employee Shareholder' employment status was created by the Growth & Infrastructure Act 2013. The employee surrenders the relevant rights under a formal agreement with the company. Under the tax scheme, a company offers shares to employees in exchange for giving up rights, such as the right (in certain specified circumstances) to claim unfair dismissal, or statutory redundancy payments, or to request flexible working arrangements.

The key benefits claimed for 'Employee Shareholder' status include:

- Up to £2,000 worth of shares may be awarded to the employee shareholder tax-free, and a further £48,000 may be awarded subject to income tax and national insurance. The legislation deems the Employee Shareholder to have paid £2,000 for the shares. The employee must not be required to pay anything for the shares or the relief would be denied.

- The Employee Shareholder's gains on the eventual disposal, or transfer of ES shares worth up to £50,000 on acquisition, are generally exempt from capital gains tax and income tax, provided they were acquired before 17 March 2016, and any first-time disposal is to an arm's length third party or, once the employment has terminated, to the former employing company. As noted above, the tax-free gain was capped at £100,000 by FA 2016 for ES shares acquired after 16 March 2016.

- The company enjoys a corporation tax deduction equivalent to the total value of the shares granted to the employee at the time of issue.

(7) **Employee ownership trusts**

FA 2014 introduced a new tax relief for certain employee trusts as an incentive for individual (but not corporate) shareholders to sell their companies into a vehicle controlled by and for the benefit of all of the company's employees, on a permanent basis.

Shareholders who sell a controlling interest in ordinary shares in a trading company, or the holding company of a trading group, to a qualifying employee ownership trust (EOT) can do so without paying capital gains tax. There is a no-gain-no-loss disposal – TCGA 1992, ss 236H–236U. It is a requirement that the trust acquires more than 50% of the ordinary shares in the company and controls it, with more than 50% of the votes, a right to more than 50% of the profits available for distribution and a right to more than 50% of the net assets on a winding up, at the end of the year. The terms of the trust must be such that any benefit provided to employees must be on the same terms. The vendor shareholders may retain a small interest but there must be a sufficient change in ownership before the CGT exemption becomes available, which may be a problem in small companies with relatively few employees in comparison with a number of shareholders who would benefit from the exemption. In summary, CGT relief is denied where, in broad terms, the ratio of participators (ie, those who benefit from the exemption) to employees is greater than 40%. The company's payments to fund an EOT do not benefit from a statutory corporation tax deduction, so in practice funding is mainly by way of dividend (ie, out of after-tax profits) and sometimes by way of a bank loan, with the employer making contributions or paying dividends to the trust from time to time to enable it to make loan repayments. Since the trust is a participator, loans by the employer are generally not made. Employer contributions to the trust are deductible only to the extent that they are used by the trustees to pay interest on the borrowings or to pay employee bonuses.

A company controlled by an EOT is permitted to pay certain qualifying bonus payments of up to £3,600 per employee in a tax year free of income tax, although NIC liability still arises (ITEPA 2003, Part 4, Chapter 10A). All employees must benefit on a similar basis, the bonus may not consist of regular salary or wages, the company must meet the trading requirement throughout the qualifying period and no salary sacrifice arrangements may be in place which convert ordinary pay into the tax-free bonus. The qualifying conditions are such that directors or other officeholders may not make up more than 40% of the eligible workforce. Former employees can benefit from such bonuses provided payment is made within 12 months after cessation of the employment.

The EOT cannot create sub-trusts or make loans to beneficiaries, and there may be no provisions in any agreement or instrument affecting the company's constitution or management or its shares or securities whereby the control conditions can cease to be met without the consent of the trustees.

The key features of an EOT are that it meets participation and equality requirements. All eligible employees should benefit and should do so on the same terms if there is ever a distribution from the trust. Only employees with less than 12 months' continuous employment may be excluded from benefit, and distributions may be varied according to the level of remuneration, length of service or hours worked of the various employees. The legislation provides expressly that an EOT-controlled company may also operate a SIP, SAYE option plan CSOP or EMI scheme and, subject to conditions, the trustees may supply shares for such a share plan provided they retain a controlling interest.

Because the CGT exemption for vendor shareholders is unlimited, a sale to an EOT may be of most interest to shareholders who do not benefit from entrepreneurs' relief or whose shares exceed the £10 million lifetime limit for that relief. Bearing in minding the non-deductibility of capital payments to the EOT, and the consequent funding problems (ie, the trustees have to borrow, with little security, to buy the shares, and fund the repayments by taking dividends from the company's post-tax profits), few shareholders to date have benefited from the CGT exemption.

## B. Capital gains tax

Shares acquired under SAYE or CSOP schemes are regarded for capital gains tax as acquired at the price paid (plus the amount, if any, paid for the option), and when they are disposed of, any gain is accordingly chargeable (subject to any available allowances and any unused annual exemption). For SAYE schemes and SIPs, shares can be transferred free of capital gains tax within 90 days of emerging from the scheme, or within 90 days after the end of the three-year period, if earlier, into an Individual Savings Account (ISA) up to the annual ISA limit. Any income and gains within the ISA will then be tax-free (see **Example A5**). There is no similar provision for EMI shares. Shares acquired under SAYE schemes and SIPs may be transferred into personal pension schemes and tax relief obtained thereon (see **Example A6 explanatory notes**) subject to the normal limits. For the interaction of the employee share scheme provisions with the capital gains tax rules for matching disposals with acquisitions, including special rules where shares under SAYE share option schemes, company share option plans and enterprise management incentive schemes are acquired on the same day as other shares, see **Example L7 explanatory notes 6 to 8**.

CGT is unlikely currently to be relevant to Employee Shareholder shares, which should be wholly exempt provided the initial award was worth no more than £50,000 and the acquisition was made before 17 March 2016 (but equally cannot generate capital losses if the company fails).

## C. Self-assessment

Details of taxable events in relation to employee share plans, employment-related securities and related benefits must be shown in tax returns (in the Share Schemes section) and any tax due must be included in the self-assessment. Where securities have been taxed as notional pay under PAYE (see above), the relevant amounts will be included in the pay figures in the Employment pages of the return, but they must also be included in the SA101 additional information (Ai) pages (where required). The detailed provisions are outlined in Additional Information Notes.

Employees who are not sent tax returns must notify HMRC by 5 October after the end of the tax year if they have income or gains that have not been fully taxed (see **Example G1 note 5**). If the only untaxed amounts relate to securities or share options and the total tax due is less than £3,000, employees may ask to have the tax collected through their PAYE codings, provided any extra PAYE due will not more than double the normal liability or result in more than half of the income being deducted. When the extra tax due is £3,000 or more tax returns must be completed. Employers do not have to give details of taxable amounts on Forms P11D, but since the scheme rules require them to give details to HMRC, they should be able to provide the relevant figures.

As noted above a return of all employment-related securities and options issued, transferred, or disposed of, outside tax-advantaged schemes is required for each fiscal year normally using the latest digital version of the Form 42. The return will be made by the employer by 6 July following the fiscal year or by the person from whom the securities or option was acquired (ITEPA 2003 s 421L). Separate and distinct submissions are required for each HMRC tax-advantaged share scheme, as well as EMI.

## D. Jack Lumber

When Jack subscribes for the ordinary shares, he pays full open market value. The shares are clearly employment-related securities, but no tax charge should arise at that point, even if there are certain typical restrictions in the company's articles of association, such as pre-emption rights in favour of the controlling family, because he has paid full price.

However, when the shareholders agree with him that his entitlement on an eventual sale of the business for more than £5 million will be 10% of the proceeds, they effectively increase the value of his shares. If Jack was able to sell the shares in the open market, all other things being equal, they would have at least doubled in value as a result of the change.

HMRC might therefore seek to tax Jack on the uplift in value under ITEPA 2003 s 446L at the end of the tax year. The valuation would be a matter of opinion, based on the share rights granted by the articles to an open market purchaser, and would have to be agreed with HMRC's Shares & Assets Valuation office.

However, the shares are sold after 18 months and Jack receives £700,000 under his agreement with the other shareholders. The open market value of those shares, without the benefit of the special agreement, would probably be only his 5% pro rata share of the total proceeds, so this is a disposal for more than market value. Jack's excess profit on the disposal (after deducting his expenses of sale) would be charged to income tax under ITEPA 2003 s 446Y. As the shares are clearly readily convertible because of the sale agreement, PAYE would be due under ITEPA 2003 s 698 and NI would be due under SI 2001/1004 Reg 22(7).

# Question

## A.

Explain the rules that deem remuneration to be liable to PAYE and national insurance contributions where services are provided via an intermediary and the managed service company anti-avoidance legislation does not apply. Set out who is liable to pay the tax, the relieving provisions to mitigate double tax liabilities and the restrictions on the use of any loss created.

## B.

Outline the reporting requirements for those involved in intermediary arrangements with particular reference to employment agencies and businesses, personal service companies and umbrella employment companies.

## C.

Margaret Johnson, a design engineer, provides her services to a manufacturing client, working full-time as the manager of the R&D function, via M J Engineering Ltd, a company founded and owned equally by Margaret and her partner John Allen, who are also its only directors. (Margaret and John live together as husband and wife.) They decide on pension and remuneration policy and deal with the day-to-day administration and banking transactions, but employ accountants to calculate PAYE, and to prepare accounts at the year end. M J Engineering Ltd has always made up its accounts to 31 December each year. The latest accounts, before taking into account personal services adjustments, include:

| | | *Yr ended 31 Dec 2016* | | *Yr ended 31 Dec 2017* |
|---|---|---|---|---|
| | £ | £ | £ | £ |
| Turnover | | 46,000 | | 57,000 |
| *Less*: Salary – John Allen (administrator) | 7,210 | | 7,900 | |
| Travelling between home and client R&D office | 4,100 | | 4,280 | |
| Travelling on other business | 1,240 | | 3,006 | |
| Training and courses | 450 | | 1,060 | |
| Use of home as office | 620 | | 380 | |
| Telephone, internet and sundries | 950 | | 1,234 | |
| Bank and professional costs | 1,710 | | 1,670 | |
| Capital allowances – computers | 1,240 | | 410 | |
| Director's salary – Margaret Johnson | 6,000 | | 8,260 | |
| National insurance Class 1 on deemed payment, Class 1A on benefits | 1,900 | | 1,950 | |
| Pension payments | 5,000 | | 5,000 | |
| | | 30,420 | | 35,150 |
| Profit for year | | 15,580 | | 21,850 |

On 5 May 2016 M J Engineering Ltd declared a dividend of £10,800.

M J Engineering Ltd had paid PAYE/NI on a deemed payment plus employer's NI of £16,200 for the year 2015/16 in April 2016. The resulting loss had been carried back to the accounting year ended 31 December 2015. No dividend was paid in 2015/16. The deemed payment, net of employee's tax and NI, for 2015/16 was £9,910.

In the tax year 2016/17 M J Engineering Ltd received £49,371 (net of VAT) from clients in respect of work done by Margaret. In performing her duties she had travelled in 2016/17 13,600 miles in her own car and was paid 45p per mile mileage allowance by M J Engineering Ltd. Margaret's P11D for 2016/17 shows:

| | £ | |
|---|---|---|
| Use of home as office | 380 | |
| Excess mileage allowance (3,600* miles @ 20p per mile) | 720 | |
| Home telephone (bill in name of employee) | 700 | (one half re business) |
| Private medical insurance | 400 | |
| | 2,200 | |

* See **Example B2 explanatory note 20** authorised rates are 10,000 miles @ 45p; additional miles @ 25p

M J Engineering Ltd had paid a pension contribution for Margaret of £3,000 on 6 December in each year. The use of Margaret's home as an office has been agreed as an allowable expense against her employment income. She keeps itemised bills to support the claim that half of her home telephone bill represents business calls.

Assume that PAYE tax has been applied to Margaret's salary and taxable benefits, subject to her personal allowance of £11,000.

As the management of the company is clearly provided by the couple, and not by a service provider, the Managed Service Company rules of ITEPA 2003 Part 2 Chapter 9 do not apply.

Compute the amount liable to PAYE/NI for Margaret Johnson in the name of M J Engineering Ltd for 2016/17, together with amounts liable to corporation tax. Set out the amount of dividend taxable on Margaret for 2016/17 if the appropriate election is made.

# Answer

## A. Provision of personal services through an intermediary when legislation applies

Where an individual (known as 'the worker') *personally* provides services, or has an obligation personally to perform services, for another person (known as 'the client') and the contractual arrangements are with one or more third parties (known as the 'intermediary') through which the services are provided, in such a way that if the services of the worker had been provided directly to the client the worker would be an employee or, from 6 April 2013, office-holder of the client, then the legislation in ITEPA 2003 Part 2 Chapter 8 applies. The legislation also applies if the client is an individual who is not in business (eg, provision of care to an older person directly, and provision of services by domestic workers such as nannies or butlers). It does not normally apply to any contract where the worker does not directly or indirectly have any interest in the intermediary (eg, a non-connected employee of the intermediary).

This legislation does not apply to provision of services through managed service companies.

### Home-to-work travel expenses

With effect from 6 April 2016, each client assignment for a contract that falls within IR35 is treated as a separate employment, so the location at which the worker is based and attends regularly will be treated as a permanent workplace under ITEPA 2003, s 338. Any expenses paid by the IR35 intermediary in respect of travel between home and the deemed permanent workplace are simply treated as earnings for PAYE and NIC purposes. Travel to temporary locations (eg, a site visit, a meeting elsewhere, or a training centre) is unaffected by the rule change, as is travel to provide services in domestic premises and travel in roles that are travelling appointments (eg, travelling sales, district nursing services, or meter reading). Expenses paid for these journeys are now tax- and NIC-exempt.

### Deemed payment

Where the personal services legislation applies, a deemed payment of employment income is calculated for the work done by the worker for the client and compared with actual salary and non-cash benefits from the intermediary (net of VAT and net of allowable expenses). Any shortfall of actual salary and benefits is treated as a single payment, made on the last day of the tax year, liable to tax as employment income and to Class 1 national insurance contributions. The PAYE tax and NIC are payable by the intermediary by 19 April following the end of the tax year. Employer NICs on actual salary payments are eligible for employment allowance of up to £3,000 for 2016/17 onwards (the allowance was £2,000 from April 2014, but is now not available to companies with only one paid employee who is also a director, on the grounds that they do not create additional employment). The company cannot claim employment allowance in respect of any amount of deemed payment under IR35 or Class 1A NICs. The deemed payment should be included in an FPS on or before 5 April, as an estimated figure. It may be corrected by the submission of an EYU before 31 January after the end of the tax year. The amounts are included on the worker's P60 and therefore appear on the worker's personal tax return on the employment pages. The deemed payment, together with employer's Class 1 national insurance thereon, becomes a deduction from trading income for the intermediary in the period of account in which the last day of the tax year falls. The deemed payment is not included as income for tax credits.

### Effect on dividend payments

In so far as the deemed payment, net of PAYE and employee's national insurance, is paid out as a dividend, the intermediary company may make a claim, by 31 January following the tax year in which the dividend is paid, for the dividend to be treated as covered by the deemed payment and not therefore liable to income tax. Such dividends would however count as income for tax credits. Dividends are still disregarded in this way after the introduction of the new dividend tax in April 2016, which is intended as a deterrent to those who incorporate for tax reasons.

## Trading losses

If the deduction of the deemed payment gives rise to a loss in a trade and the intermediary is a company, then normal loss rules apply, ie the loss may be carried back one year under CTA 2010 s 37, or carried forward, and can be used in a terminal loss claim.

If the intermediary is a partnership, then the deduction can only reduce the trading profits to nil – it cannot create a loss. Any excess is unrelieved. Furthermore, in computing the trading income of a partnership the maximum deduction for expenses relating to actual earnings is restricted to the amount deductible in computing the deemed payment (including the 5% of relevant earnings deduction – see below).

## Amounts taken into account

The earnings taken into account in computing the deemed payment are the total amounts of the cash and non-cash benefits received in the tax year by the intermediary in respect of engagements to which the personal services legislation applies for that worker. The amount includes any sub-contractor's tax deducted but excludes any VAT. The exclusion of VAT applies even if the flat-rate scheme is used. Irrecoverable VAT relating to allowable expenses met by the intermediary would be allowable as part of the expenses in the same way as if the intermediary was not VAT-registered.

## Computation of deemed payment

To compute the deemed payment the following formula is used:

| | | | £ |
|---|---|---|---|
| Amounts received from relevant engagements by the intermediary | | | X |
| *Less*: 5% deduction for unspecified expenses of the company | | | (X) |
| | | | X |
| Add: any other payments or benefits received by the worker (or family) in respect of relevant engagements from anyone other than the IR35 company, not otherwise chargeable as employment income of the worker, but which would be so chargeable if the worker had been an employee of the client | | | X |
| Sub-total: income | | | X |
| *Less*: | Expenses paid by the intermediary that would have been deductible against employment income if paid by the worker (as an employee or office-holder of the client). This includes reimbursed business expenses but no longer includes travel to a deemed permanent workplace* | X | |
| | Capital allowances that could have been claimed by the worker | X | |
| | Pension contributions paid to a registered scheme by the intermediary for the worker | X | |
| | Employer's Class 1 national insurance paid and Class 1A or 1B national insurance payable in respect of the worker (net of employment allowance set against Class 1 only) | X | |
| Sub-total: allowable expenses | | | (X) |
| Net income for IR35 purposes | | | X |
| Deduct amounts actually received by the worker from the intermediary in the tax year (which do not represent items for which a deduction has already been given above): | | | |
| Taxable actual salary | | X | |
| Taxable benefits in kind, home-to-work travel costs (in PAYE) and exempt mileage allowances | | X | |
| *Less*: income already taxed or tax-free | | | (X) |
| Maximum deduction from trading income | | | X |

* FA 2016, s 18 denies a deduction for commuting expenses between home and a deemed permanent workplace, with effect from 6 April 2016, to any worker operating through an IR35 intermediary that is not a managed service company (the MSC rules already deal with such expenses).

The amount computed is the deemed payment plus employer's Class 1 national insurance contributions (note that there is no employment allowance in this calculation). If the employer's NI nil band of £8,060 (for 2016/17) has already been used for the worker then the deemed payment will be:

| | £ |
|---|---|
| Deemed payment including employer's NIC (as above) | X |
| *Less*: 13.8/113.8 × deemed payment including employer's NIC* | (X) |
| Deemed payment to enter on worker's payroll record and FPS | X |

* If the nil band has not been fully used any excess is deducted from this amount first, and if the worker is under 21, no netting down is required, as the 0% secondary Class 1 NIC rate applies here. The under-25 apprentice rate is unlikely to apply because an apprentice must be apprenticed to an employer under an apprenticeship agreement, which is highly unlikely to be possible in an IR35 company.

There is a spreadsheet template to calculate deemed payments (albeit only for full-year operations) at https://www.gov.uk/ir35-what-to-do-if-it-applies.

### More than one intermediary

If more than one intermediary exists, then all intermediaries have a joint and several liability for the PAYE/NI in so far as the intermediary has received any payment or benefit for the worker. However, the relevant earnings may be reduced by any amount included as relevant earnings by subsequent intermediaries to prevent double counting, leaving the prime liability with the last intermediary in the chain.

### Benefits received directly from client

If the worker receives benefits or other amounts directly from the client (eg, provision of a company car by client to worker) then the deemed payment is increased by that amount without a 5% deduction.

### Common control

Where the intermediary company and the client company are 'associated' by virtue of both being under the control of the worker, or of the worker and others, the IR35 rules do not apply to that engagement, so a shareholder-director of a holding company does not fall into IR35 simply because he works for a subsidiary and is paid dividends from the holding company that are partly derived from the management charges it levies on the subsidiary.

## B. Reporting requirements

A worker supplied through an agency will normally be treated as an employee of the agency if he is not already employed by a personal service company (PSC), an umbrella company or some other employer and he is subject to supervision, direction or control as to the manner of carrying out the work that he is required to do.

Such workers are technically self-employed but are deemed employees of the agency for PAYE and NIC purposes. When paying wages, the agency must operate the same deductions as would apply to employees and report the earnings under the RTI system.

Where a worker supplied through an agency is not subject to supervision, direction or control as to the manner of carrying out the work, the agency can pay him gross as a self-employed worker. Where a worker supplies his services through a PSC, under a contract between the PSC and the agency, he is already an employee of the PSC, so the agency cannot treat him as its own employee and can also make a gross payment, albeit to the PSC rather than the worker.

However, the payment in either case must be reported quarterly to HMRC within 30 days of the end of the tax quarter (ie, by 5 August 2016 in respect of the quarter ended on 5 July 2016). HMRC supplies a standard template of the required information and all reports must be made online. There are escalating penalties for failure to make reports (£250 for the first offence, £500 for the second and £1000 for subsequent failures).

Where there is a chain of intermediaries, gross payment must be reported only by the intermediary that has the contract with the end-user or client.

In a typical situation where an agency supplies to a client a worker who is already employed by an umbrella company, the umbrella company should operate PAYE/NI and report under RTI, but the agency nevertheless has to report the gross payment that it makes to the umbrella employer for the worker's services. If the umbrella company fails to operate PAYE and HMRC cannot enforce payment against it, the agency will be liable for any underpayment.

A PSC supplying its sole employee-director directly to a client is not classed as an intermediary for these reporting purposes and need not make quarterly reports. However, if an agency sources a worker who is employed by his own PSC, the agency cannot operate PAYE (because it is paying a company, not an individual) so it must report the gross payments. If the PSC has more than one employee, or it subcontracts work to another company or self-employed individual, it thereby becomes an intermediary and must make reports if it contracts directly with a client for the supply of the worker's services.

## C. M J Engineering Ltd

### Computation of deemed payment for 2016/17 for Margaret Johnson

| | | | £ |
|---|---|---|---|
| Amounts received | | | 49,371 |
| *Less*: 5% allowance | | | 2,468 |
| | | | 46,903 |
| *Less*: Expenses – Use of home as office | | 380 | |
| Business use of telephone | | 350 | |
| Pension contribution for M Johnson | | 3,000 | |
| Employer's NI for M Johnson | | | |
| Class 1 ((8,260 + 350* + 4,280†) – 8,112) | @ 13.8% | 659 | |
| Less: employment allowance | | (659) | |
| Class 1A (on medical insurance 400) | @ 13.8% | 55 | |
| Salary + taxable commuting expenses† | | 12,540 | |
| Taxable benefits and exempt mileage allowances (400 + 350 + 1,840‡) | | 2,590 | |
| | | | (18,915) |
| Excess amount | | | 27,988 |
| *Less*: Employer's Class 1 NIC therein (13.8/113.8 × £27,988) | | | 3,394 |
| Deemed payment | | | 24,594 |

* Re private element of home telephone bills – no NI on business mileage allowance since permitted NI rate for 2016/17 is 45p per mile regardless of miles travelled.

† Home to deemed permanent workplace travel expenses are now classed as earnings for PAYE and NIC purposes.

‡ Mileage paid: 13,600 × 45p = £6,120. £4,280 taxable under PAYE as commuting cost (9,510 miles @ 45p), balance of 4,090 business miles wholly exempt (less than 10,000 miles), so £1,840 deductible here.

### PAYE/NI liability on deemed payment in name of Margaret Johnson

| | |
|---|---|
| Actual salary | 8,260 |
| Taxable commuting expenses | 4,280 |
| Taxable benefits (400 + 350)* | 750 |
| Deemed payment | 24,594 |
| | 37,884 |

| | |
|---|---|
| *Less*: Personal allowance | (11,000) |
| Total taxable earnings | 26,884 |

* The P11D was wrong to include the excess mileage allowance of £720 as a benefit: allowable business mileage was below 10,000 for the year after treating the commuting mileage correctly as subject to PAYE and NIC.

Margaret's personal allowance has already been used up on salary and benefits of (8,260 + 4,280 + 750) £13,290, leaving £29,710 of basic rate band available. Employee's and employer's NI (less employment allowance) has already been charged on excess of salary (£8,260), commuting mileage (£4,280) and benefits (£350 home telephone) of £12,890, which is over the earnings threshold (£8,112 employer and £8,060 employee), so that the employee's and employer's NI rates payable are 12% (up to the upper earnings limit of £43,000) plus 2% on the excess and 13.8% respectively.

| | | |
|---|---|---|
| | | £ |
| Tax on deemed payment: | | |
| 24,594 @ 20% | | 4,919 |
| NI on deemed payment: | | |
| Employee | 24,594 @ 12% | 2,951 |
| Employer (no EA on deemed payment) | 24,594 @ 13.8% | 3,394 |
| Payable by M J Engineering Ltd by 19 April 2016 | | 11,264 |

Amounts liable to corporation tax:

| | *Year to 31.12.16* £ | *Year to 31.12.17* £ |
|---|---|---|
| Profit per accounts | 15,580 | 21,850 |
| *Less*: Personal services (inc deemed NI) | (16,200) | (27,988) |
| Loss for year carried back | (620) | |
| Loss for year carried forward | | (6,138) |

Taxable dividend 2016/17:

| | | | *Margaret Johnson* £ | *John Allen* £ |
|---|---|---|---|---|
| Dividend (50% × £10,800)* | | | 5,400 | 5,400 |
| Deemed payment – 2016/17 (excluding employer's NI) | | 24,594 | | |
| *Less*: Tax | 4,919 | | | |
| Employee's NI | 2,951 | 7,870 | | |
| Net | | 16,724 | | |
| Brought forward from 2015/16 | | 9,910 | | |
| | | 26,634 | | |
| Offset after claim for relief – | | | | |
| Worker | | (5,400) | (5,400) | |
| Others | | (5,400) | | (5,400) |
| | | | Nil | Nil |
| Available to offset future dividends | | 15,834 | | |

* The dividend nil rate on up to £5,000 is irrelevant if MJ Engineering Ltd makes a claim within the ITSA time limit under ITEPA 2003, s 58 to set the deemed payment off against the relevant distributions: all of the dividends paid in this example will be reduced to a taxable value of nil by a claim.

# Explanatory Notes

These notes refer to the personal services legislation of ITEPA 2003 ss 48–61 only, and do not cover the managed service companies legislation in ITEPA 2003 ss 61A–61J.

*Liability under personal services legislation*

**Companies**

(1) The legislation only applies to workers who have, together with associates, a material interest in the intermediary company or who receive or could receive payments or benefits from the intermediary company which are not employment income but could reasonably be taken to represent remuneration for services charged to the client by the intermediary.

Material interest means the beneficial ownership or ability, alone or with associates, to control more than 5% of the ordinary share capital, or the right to receive more than 5% of any distributions, or in a close company the right to more than 5% of assets on a winding up. For this purpose the worker does not need any holding in his own name for the holdings of associates to be included. An associate is any relative or business partner. Relative means husband or wife, civil partner, parent or remoter forebear, child or remoter issue, brother or sister. A man and a woman living together as husband and wife are deemed married and are therefore associates. The interests of the associates of business partners are included with their own interest. Trustees of settlements made by the taxpayer or any relative are also included. A company is connected with another person if that person has (together with associates) control of the company.

With effect from 6 April 2007, this (IR35) legislation has applied only to personal service companies/ partnerships that are not considered managed service companies, that is they are not involved with a managed service company service provider. In this case the company was founded by the individuals who actively control it, and its administration is either performed or delegated by them. It has its own bank account and PAYE registration, and no unconnected shareholders. These are all strong indicators that the company's activity is not caught by the managed service company legislation. If it were, any payment drawn from the company that was not already earnings would be deemed to be earnings, with a deduction for expenses only to the extent that those expenses would have been deductible if the worker had been directly employed by the client (eg, travel and subsistence expenses where the notional employee would have been at a temporary workplace).

The IR35 legislation applied to composite companies and managed personal service companies for tax purposes until 5 April 2007 (and for NI purposes until 5 August 2007, although HMRC appears to have made no such distinction in practice), but because employment status must be ascertained on a case-by-case basis, it was difficult to enforce, and there was a perception of poor compliance. To make it easier to counter such structures that primarily avoid NI, managed service company legislation was introduced that bypasses the need to look at individual contracts.

Because of an official perception that IR35 is widely ignored and is impossible to police, the government announced in the July 2015 Budget a consultation on reform of IR35, mooting the possibility of making engagers responsible for operating PAYE and NIC on payments in respect of workers who are under supervision, direction or control by the client, with the client ultimately responsible for any underpayments. A consultation paper issued in mid-2016 suggested that the new rules will be restricted to PSCs under contract to (including via agencies) public sector bodies and will apply from 6 April 2017. The need for major systems changes in public sector client, agencies and HMRC may mean implementation is delayed to April 2018.

### Partnerships

(2) Again the legislation applies to any worker whose payments or benefits from the partnership represent the amount charged for the worker's services to the client. Otherwise a partner is only caught by the legislation if one of the following tests is satisfied:

— the worker (together with his/her relatives) is entitled to 60% or more of the profits of the partnership, or

— most of the profits of the partnership arise from the provision of personal services to a single client (including the client's associates), or

— the profit share of the worker is based on the income generated by that worker in the provision of personal services.

### Individuals

(3) The legislation can apply where the intermediary is an individual (but the worker cannot be an intermediary for himself). This only applies if the amount receivable by the worker from the intermediary can reasonably be taken to represent remuneration for services provided by the worker to the client.

*Classification as an employee*

(4) The legislation only applies if the worker would have been an employee or office-holder of the client if the services had been provided directly to the client (the office-holder element was added by FA 2013 s 22 from 6 April 2013). See **Examples B6** and **G5 part (e)** for detailed notes on the points relevant to determine status as an employee. There have been several cases specifically on the issue of whether the personal service company legislation applies, and most contain discussion on employment status. Readers are referred to *PCG v IRC* [2002] STC 165, *Hewlett Packard v O'Murphy* [2002] IRLR 4 EAT, *FS Consulting Ltd v McCaul* [2002] STC (SCD) 138, *Lime-IT Ltd v Justin* [2002] SpC 342, *Synaptek Ltd v Young* [2003] STC 543, *Future Online Ltd v Faulds* (2004) Sp C 406, *Dragonfly Consultancy Ltd v Commissioners for HMRC* [2008] EWHC 2113 (Ch) (in which HMRC succeeded) and *Novasoft Ltd* [2010] TC00456 (in which the taxpayer succeeded).

It should be noted that in the case of *Cable and Wireless v Muscat* in October 2005, an individual working through an employment agency, also using a service company, was held to be an employee of the supposed 'client', and entitled to employee rights. The facts were unusual, in that Mr Muscat had been employed by the company (ie, the client) and had been forced to switch first into working through a service company to reduce employment costs, and then into working for the service company through an agency, and the court was able to find that his original employment had never actually terminated (so there was no deemed employment, just a real, uninterrupted employment).

Agency workers are not generally within IR35. Unless they are deliberately hired as direct employees of the agency, they generally work under contracts for services, and the mutuality of obligations necessary for a contract of employment do not exist (because there cannot be three parties in a master-servant relationship). Recognising this, tax and NI legislation deems them to be employees of the agency and thereby brings their earnings into PAYE (ITEPA Part 2 Chapter 7) and Class 1 national insurance (Social Security (Categorisation of Earners) Regs 1978, SI 1978/1689) unless they are subject to no right of supervision, direction or control by the end user client as to the manner of carrying out the work. IR35 is therefore mainly irrelevant to agency workers and its operation is specifically excluded for cases within the agency rules. Since the worker is deemed an employee subject to PAYE throughout the contractual relationship, there is no need for a deemed payment at the end of the tax year. In the case of *James v Greenwich BC* [2008] EWCA Civ 35 in February 2008, the Court of Appeal refused to imply a contract directly between an agency worker and the end user client in place of the agency contract. A contract of employment was to be implied only if the agency contract was shown to be a sham.

An exception to the general rule about agency workers not being under employment contracts may be seen in the case of *McMeechan v Secretary of State for Employment* [1997] ICR 549 where an agency worker claimed unpaid wages from the Redundancy Fund after his agency ceased trading through insolvency. He was able to show that the last assignment had been carried out under a short-term contract of employment with the agency, which entitled him to claim the single week's unpaid wages for that work, but the court did not rule that he had been employed throughout his period with that agency.

Note that many employment agencies operate a parallel 'umbrella company', which employs their temporary workers under permanent 'overarching' or umbrella contracts of employment. In such cases, the agency workers *are* employees subject to PAYE and NICs, so there is no need to deem an employment. IR35 should be irrelevant here unless the worker owns the agency that sells his services to end user clients.

In contrast, IR35 is relevant where a PSC finds work through an agency but the worker would be classed as an employee if the corporate wrapper was removed. The agency must pay a PSC gross – PAYE can only be deducted from payments to individuals – but if the worker would be classed as an employee in the absence of the PSC in the contractual relationship (ie, there is supervision, direction or control as to the manner of working and the job is not in one of the excluded categories), the PSC must apply the IR35 rules at the end of the tax year.

*Exclusions*

(5) The legislation does not apply to non-resident entertainers or sportsmen, who are subject to deduction of tax under ITA 2007 s 966.

(6) If the worker would not be liable to tax on UK employment income if directly employed by the client, eg, the worker is non-resident and the services are provided outside the UK, then the legislation does not apply. However, if the worker is resident in the UK, the services are provided in the UK and the client carries on business in the UK, the intermediary is treated as carrying on business in the UK wherever actually resident. See Tax Bulletin 64 (April 2003) for more detail on the service company legislation and international issues.

*Managed service companies*

(7) where an individual's services are provided through a managed service company (eg, a composite company or managed personal service company) in which he or she takes very little part in the management, the managed service company provider is responsible for applying PAYE and NI regulations to all remuneration.

*Expenses*

(8) The deductions allowable are those met by the intermediary that would have been deductible from the taxable earnings of the worker if he or she had been employed by the client and met the expenses from his or her earnings. They include all items deductible under Chapters 1 to 5 of Part 5 of ITEPA 2003 (eg expenses incurred wholly, exclusively and necessarily, allowable travel expenses (bearing in mind that the client site is now treated as a permanent workplace for workers supplied by a PSC under a contract that falls within IR35), professional fees, employees' liabilities and indemnity insurance, agency fees paid by entertainers and fixed allowances). They specifically include amounts originally met by the worker but reimbursed by the intermediary (ITEPA 2003 s 54(3)) and, where the intermediary provides a vehicle which is chargeable as a benefit in kind on the worker, approved mileage allowances which the worker could have claimed if he or she had been employed by the client and used his or her own car for business (ITEPA 2003 s 54(4)). The benefit in kind itself (representing the private use of the car) would be deductible as part of the taxable salary and benefits provided by the intermediary to the worker. If the worker uses his own car in reality (as in this Example) ITEPA 2003 s 54(7) preserves the relief for the approved mileage allowances by allowing the exempt amounts to be included in the amounts deducted as salary or benefits.

No deduction is allowed for training costs borne by the intermediary, as no claim is generally possible for such costs under Chapters 1 to 5 of Part 5 of ITEPA 2003. Work-related training is tax-free if funded by the employer, but the IR35 rules look at the hypothetical situation where the worker is engaged directly by the end-user, who would not be funding the training. Most employees cannot claim a s 336 deduction for training costs they bear personally (but see, e.g., *Commissioners for Her Majesty's Revenue and Customs v Banerjee* [2010] EWCA 843 (Ch) for an exception to this general position).

(9) Because all contracts undertaken by the worker for the intermediary relate to his/her employment with the intermediary, this means that most client premises will on basic principles be temporary workplaces (see **Example B6 explanatory note 6**) and therefore travelling costs will be allowed from the worker's home to that temporary workplace, but only provided it would be a temporary workplace if he had been directly

employed. Since a director or employee of the client would not be able to claim a deduction for the expenses of travel between home and work, other than for a visit to a temporary workplace (eg, attending a meeting at a different office), the same rule applies to IR35 workers. Each engagement of an intermediary worker is treated as a separate employment (ITEPA 2003, s 339A), which may mean that the worker has to treat travel to the client premises as travel to a permanent workplace. Where the personal service company does not fall within IR35 (ie, the worker is in effect a self-employed person trading inside a corporate wrapper, not subject to supervision, direction or control as to the manner of working and therefore not in disguised employment), the director of the PSC should be able to claim the costs of travel between his normal base (possibly his home) and all client premises, provided he expects to be at that workplace for no more than 24 months.

*Capital allowances*

(10) Only capital allowances claimable by a worker can be deducted, ie, those claimable under CAA 2001 s 262, being plant and machinery necessarily provided for use in the performance of the duties. It is likely that Margaret's computer, whilst helping her to better perform her duties, would fail this test and no deduction would be allowed.

*Employees of the intermediary*

(11) No deductions are allowed for salaries or other administrative costs in computing deemed pay. This does not prevent a deduction from trading profits for companies. However, the fact that a worker takes on an employee and is able to send that employee to carry out work under the contract will usually mean that IR35 cannot apply, since the ability to send a substitute should mean that the worker cannot be in disguised employment.

If the employee provides relevant services to the client, but does not have a material interest, etc, in the company then the amount charged to the client is excluded from the computation of deemed pay. If an invoice is rendered for the services of more than one individual, the amount must be apportioned between the individuals and only the earnings of an individual (with a material interest, etc) are taken into account.

*Dividends*

(12) To prevent double taxation, dividends may be offset by net deemed payments if a claim is made by the intermediary company by 31 January following the tax year in which the dividend is paid. The relief is given primarily against distributions of the current year and then distributions of subsequent tax years, with relief firstly against the dividends paid to the worker and then against other dividends paid for that year. The reduction of the distribution by a claim made under ITEPA 2003, s 58 means that the amount is no longer taxable as a dividend under ITA 2007, so the dividend tax rates (0%, 7.5%, 32.5% and 38.1%) are irrelevant.

*Actual pay*

(13) The deduction for actual pay is the payments or benefits received in a tax year by the worker from that intermediary which are chargeable as employment income. Consequently any payments made after 5 April 2016 cannot be deducted in 2015/16, even if the amount relates to earnings in that year which have been charged to tax as a deemed payment. Instead the amount will be deducted as actual pay in the year of payment. This could result in actual pay in a subsequent year exceeding the computed deemed payment. There is no relief for the excess. Care should be taken to distribute any amount charged as a deemed payment by way of dividend, with an appropriate claim for relief being made.

*Employment allowance*

(14) Employment allowance (EA) became available from 6 April 2014 to set against employer's secondary Class 1 liability of up to £2,000 per employer per year for most private sector businesses. It was increased to £3,000 from 6 April 2016. It may not be used against any deemed payment under the IR35 rules, although it is available against secondary Class 1 liabilities on actual salary payments in the year, provided the company is not run by a sole director who is the only paid earner. If the only paid earner is the sole director, no EA is due for 2016/17 onwards. HMRC believes the second and subsequent earners must be paid enough to trigger a liability for secondary Class 1 NICs, but that is not what the law says. NICA 2014, s 2(4A) disqualifies a company from claiming EA if all the payments of earnings in relation to which the company

is the secondary contributor in the year are made to just one earner, and that earner is a director each time payment is made. A company is the secondary contributor in relation to any payment of earnings, not just those over the earnings threshold in an earnings period, so any payment to a second employee or office-holder in the year, even if it is to a casual employee working a single shift, means that the disqualification rule cannot apply. Employment allowance does not apply to Class 1A or Class 1B employer contributions in respect of P11D benefits or PAYE Settlement Agreements.

*Computation of deemed payment other than at 5 April*

(15) If a worker ceases to be connected with an intermediary during the tax year, then the deemed payment is treated as paid immediately before that event (and the deduction for the payment is based on the day before the event occurred). For partnerships this applies when a partner (or employee) ceases to hold that position. For companies it applies if the worker ceases to be a member (shareholder), director or employee. Thus if a worker resigns as a director during the tax year, a computation of the deemed payment is due to that date, with payment of the relevant PAYE/NICs. All receipts, expenses, etc to the end of the tax year will be included in the computation, even though the payment is regarded as made at the earlier date (and the company's deduction will be based on that date). A similar provision applies where a company ceases to trade, the computation being prepared at the date of cessation with a deduction in the final accounting period.

*Accounting year-end*

(16) As **part b** of the Example shows, the deemed payment deduction from income can occur in a different accounting period from that in which the earnings arise and are charged to tax. To prevent losses arising that can only be carried forward, and which might never be relieved, it is advisable to use a 5 April year-end for any intermediary caught by these rules.

*HMRC opinions*

(17) It is possible to get an opinion from HMRC as to whether a particular contract is caught by the IR35 provisions. The email address is ir35@hmrc.gov.uk. The postal address is HMRC IR35 Customer Service Unit, Ground Floor North, Princess House, Cliftonville Road, Northampton, NN1 5AE, although this may change at any time with HMRC allocating work frequently and unpredictably to new offices anywhere in the country. There is also a dedicated helpline for IR35 matters 0300 123 2326, and a dedicated part of HMRC website at https://www.gov.uk/ir35-find-out-if-it-applies, including a deemed payment calculator (and updated address details). HMRC once published guidance on the business entity tests and the risk-based approach they use in judging whether a contract is likely to be within the scope of IR35, but the tests were withdrawn as they did not work as intended – see https://www.gov.uk/guidance/ir35-enquiry-by-hm-revenue-and-customs. It should be noted that the guidance is HMRC's view and is not necessarily accepted by others.

# Question

## A

Edzell was the sole proprietor of an aircraft maintenance business until he transferred it as a going concern to a limited company on 30 April 2016. Edzell set up the company, with himself as the sole director, on 6 April 2016.

Since founding the business in 2000 Edzell has always made up accounts to 5 April in each year.

The profits, as adjusted for income tax purposes but before capital allowances, have been calculated as £48,753 for the year to 5 April 2016 and £3,340 for the final period to 30 April 2016.

The written down values of plant and machinery for capital allowances purposes after allowances for the year ended 5 April 2015 were as follows:

| | £ |
|---|---|
| Plant and equipment pool | 3,506 |
| Motor car | 5,925 |

Subsequent plant and machinery additions have comprised a new testing machine at a cost of £2,700 on 16 June 2015 and a new aircraft tractor at a cost of £13,181 on 31 March 2016.

Edzell has always declared business use of the car at 90%, based on reasonable apportionment.

The maximum capital allowances have always been claimed as early as possible.

A freehold aircraft hangar, originally built in 1980 was acquired second-hand in 2000 at a cost of £30,000.

The market values of the assets at the time of the transfer of the business to the company were:

| | £ |
|---|---|
| Goodwill | 97,500 |
| Freehold aircraft hangar | 80,800 |
| Plant and equipment (not including any fixed plant) | 20,000 |
| Motor car | 5,000 |
| Net current assets including debtors of £15,000 (but excluding cash) | 12,700 |
| | 216,000 |

Edzell has never made any payment for goodwill. No other asset except the aircraft hangar was transferred at a market value greater than cost, and none of the plant and equipment cost more than £6,000.

For capital allowances purposes, both Edzell and the company have elected to transfer the assets at their written down value.

The transfer was satisfied by the issue to Edzell of all of the authorised share capital of 100,000 ordinary shares of £1 each of Famosa Ltd (a company formed specifically for the purpose of the transfer) and the payment to him of £60,000 cash.

(a) Show Edzell's capital allowances and taxable profits for his last two accounting periods as a sole trader and comment on what the position would have been if Edzell had made up a final account from 6 April 2015 to 30 April 2016.

(b) Calculate Edzell's chargeable gain arising on the transfer of the business to Famosa Ltd and the capital gains tax base value of his shares in Famosa Ltd.

(c) State the effect on both Edzell and Famosa Ltd, had the election to transfer the assets for capital allowances purposes at their written down value not been made.

(d) State the national insurance consequences of transferring the business to the company.

## B

Jefford has recently received a substantial legacy and is planning to buy an established hotel in a seaside resort. His wife will help him in running the business. He is expecting modest profits at the outset but hopes that his plans for the business will enable it rapidly to become highly successful.

He is not sure whether to operate the business as a sole trader/partnership or as a limited company.

Prepare illustrations to compare the tax payable if the business is operated as a partnership / company if:

(i) Profits of £100,000, salaries of the personal allowance plus the basic rate of income tax and the balance of profits retained in the company

(ii) Profits of £40,000, salaries of the personal allowance and balance taken as a dividend,

(iii) Profits of £30,000, salary of NIC threshold, balance dividend and only one shareholder / sole trader.

# Answer

## A (a) Edzell's capital allowances computation and taxable profits for final two accounting periods

### Capital allowances computation

| | | *Plant pool* | *Motor car (10% private)* | | *Total allow-ances* |
|---|---|---|---|---|---|
| | £ | £ | £ | | £ |
| WDV at 6.4.15 | | 3,506 | 5,925 | | |
| *2015/16 (6.4.15 – 5.4.16)* | | | | | |
| Additions: | | | | | |
| New testing machine | 2,700 | | | | |
| New aircraft tractor | 13,181 | | | | |
| | 15,881 | | | | |
| AIA | (15,881) | – | | | 15,881 |
| WDA 18% | | (631) | (1,067) | (90% = 960) | 1,591 |
| | | 2,875 | 4,858 | | 17,472 |
| *2016/17 (6.4.16 – 30.4.16)* | | | | | |
| Deemed transfer at tax written down value (see **explanatory note 9**) | | 2,875 | 4,858 | | NIL |

### Taxable profits

| | | £ |
|---|---|---|
| 2015/16 | 48,753 less capital allowances 17,472 | 31,281 |
| 2016/17 | (capital allowances nil) | 3,340 |

If Edzell had made up a final account from 6 April 2015 to 30 April 2016, capital allowances would be computed for that period of account. Since it is the period of discontinuance of Edzell's trade, neither AIA nor writing down allowances would have been available and the computation would have been as follows:

| | *Plant* | *Motor car* | *Total allowances* |
|---|---|---|---|
| | £ | £ | £ |
| *6.4.15 – 30.4.16* | | | |
| WDV at 6.4.15 | 3,506 | 5,925 | |
| Additions: | | | |
| New testing machine | 2,700 | | |
| New aircraft tractor | 13,181 | | |
| | 19,387 | | |
| Deemed transfer at tax written down value | 19,387 | 5,925 | – |

The taxable profit of the final period would have been increased by £17,472 in respect of the capital allowances that would no longer have been given and the written down values transferred to the company would have been increased by £16,512 on the plant pool and £1,067 in respect of the motor car, a total of £17,579. This is £107 more than the capital allowances that have been claimed, because the capital allowances on the car were restricted by that amount in respect of the private use proportion. They will not be restricted in the company's computation, but Edzell will be taxed on the benefit of private use of the car under the employment income rules.

The taxable profits would be then be as follows (see **explanatory note 10**):

| | | |
|---|---|---|
| 2015/16 | 365/390 × (48,753 + 3,340 =) 52,093 | £48,754 |
| 2016/17 | 25/390 × 52,093 | £3,339 |

## (b) Edzell's chargeable gain on transfer of business to Famosa Ltd

| | *Goodwill* | *Aircraft hangar* |
|---|---|---|
| | £ | £ |
| Market value on transfer to company | 97,500 | 80,800 |
| Cost | 0 | (30,000) |
| Chargeable gains before relief | 97,500 | 50,800 |

| | |
|---|---|
| Total gains as above | 148,300 |
| *Less*: rolled over against base cost of shares in Famosa Ltd (see **explanatory note 1**) | 107,106 |
| Chargeable gain 2016/17 (subject to annual exemption) | 41,194 |

As a disposal to a related party after 3 December 2014, entrepreneurs' relief is not available on the gain on the goodwill but it should be available on the aircraft hangar. See **Example L4**.

The remaining assets do not attract a capital gains liability, since none is transferred at a value in excess of cost (and there would not have been any capital gains in any event, since both the motor car and the items of plant and equipment each valued at less than £6,000 are exempt).

The capital gains tax base value of the shares in Famosa Ltd is 156,000 – 107,106 = £48,894.

## (c) If the election to transfer assets at written down value for capital allowances purposes had not been made

As Famosa Ltd gives full 'market value' consideration, this would determine the disposal proceeds for plant and machinery allowance purposes (CAA 2001 s 61). Famosa Ltd would therefore be deemed to have acquired the assets at market value. This would result in balancing charges on Edzell as follows:

| | *Plant* | *Motor car* | |
|---|---|---|---|
| WDV | 10,569 | 4,444 | |
| Market value 30.4.16 (but not exceeding cost) | 20,000 | 5,000 | |
| Balancing charges | £9,431 | £556 | × 90% = £500 |
| Giving an increase in 2016/17 taxable profits of £9,931 | | | |

## (d) Edzell's national insurance position

As a sole trader, Edzell will have been liable to pay flat rate Class 2 contributions of £2.80 for 2015/16. He will also have been liable to pay Class 4 contributions of 9% of his profits between £8,060 and £42,385. In addition, contributions have been payable at 2% on profits above the upper profits limit. This gave him a national insurance liability for 2015/16 of Class 2 £145.60 + Class 4 £2,089.89 = £2,235.49.

The national insurance position (using 2016/17 rates) if the business is transferred to the company is as follows. As a company director Edzell will be liable to pay Class 1 employee's contributions at the rate of 12% on his earnings between £8,060 and £43,000 per year, with an uncapped 2% charge on any earnings in excess of £43,000 per year. (As a director, he has an annual earnings period – see **Example H1 part (d)**.) In addition, the company, as his employer, will have to pay contributions at 13.8% on remuneration exceeding £8,112 per year, with no upper ceiling on the earnings on which contributions are payable. Furthermore, most taxable benefits in kind (including company cars, private fuel, living accommodation) also attract company Class 1A national insurance contributions at the rate of 13.8%. The company's contributions will, however, be allowable expenses against the profit for corporation tax.

From 6 April 2014, employment allowance is available to set against an employer's secondary class 1 liability of up to £2,000 per employer per tax year. For 2016/17 the allowance increased to £3,000 pa but is not available to companies where there is only one employee who is a director (but two paid directors is acceptable).

Edzell will be able to control how much of the profit is left in the company and how much to draw as remuneration. In relation to Famosa Ltd, for the financial year to 31 March 2017 profits will be taxed at the rate of corporation tax at 20%. This will reduce to 19% from 1 April 2017.

Since there is no upper limit for the employer's contributions, it is not possible to work out an overall maximum of national insurance contributions. But if Edzell had no other income and drew remuneration in 2016/17 of £43,000 to cover the basic rate band and personal allowance (and taking the position as if he had been employed for the full year for simplicity), the position would be:

| | £ | £ |
|---|---|---|
| Employee's contributions | | |
| (£43,000 – £8,060) × 12% | | 4,193 |
| Employer's contributions | | |
| (£43,000 – £8,112) × 13.8% | 4,815 | |
| *Less*: corporation tax relief @ 20% | (963) | 3,852 |
| Net national insurance cost | | £8,045 |
| Compared with the liability of a self-employed person earning £43,000 (class 4 + class 2) | | £3,290 |

Clearly there is a much higher national insurance liability operating through a company than as a sole trader. A slightly greater range of state benefits is, however, available to Edzell as an employee, particularly jobseeker's allowance if the business fails.

The national insurance disadvantage of operating through the company could be reduced for 2016/17 if Edzell drew a lower salary and received higher dividends, on which national insurance contributions are not payable.

## (e) 2016/17 comparison tax payable as partnership or company with a basic rate band salary

| | | | *Partners* | | *Company director* |
|---|---|---|---|---|---|
| | | | £ | | £ |
| Profits/remuneration | | | 100,000 | 43,000 × 2 | 86,000 |
| Personal allowances | | | (22,000) | | (22,000) |
| Taxable income | | | 78,000 | | 64,000 |
| | 64,000 | @ 20% | 12,800 | | 12,800 |
| | 14,000 | @ 40% | 5,600 | | |
| | 78,000 | | 18,400 | | |
| Class 2 NI | | | 291 | | |
| Class 4 NI | | | 6,569 | Employees' NI | 8,386 |
| Total personal tax and NI | | | 25,260 | | 21,186 |

| | | |
|---|---|---|
| **Company's tax and NI** | | |
| Profits | 100,000 | |
| *Less*: Directors' remuneration | (86,000) | |
| Company's NI thereon @ 13.8% on (86,000–16,224) | (9,629) | 9,629 |
| Employment Allowance (2 directors) | 3,000 | (3,000) |
| Taxable profits | 7,371 | |
| Tax thereon @ 20% | (1,474) | 1,474 |
| | 5,897 | |

| | *Partners* | *Directors* |
|---|---|---|
| | £ | £ |
| tax | 18,400 | 12,800 |
| NI contributions | 6,860 | 15,015 |
| Corporation tax | — | 1,474 |
| Total tax and NI liabilities | 25,260 | 29,289 |

The partnership shows an overall tax/NIC saving of £4,029 compared to the limited company (although the Jeffords will still have £5,897 retained after-tax profits in the company as well). However, any further increase in profits would be subject to 42% in the partnership (up to £200,000) against 20% in the company. Thus, if profits increased by £12,000, the tax liability for the partnership would rise by £5,020 (= £12,000 @ 42%), whereas tax for the company would only increase by £2,400 (12,000 @ 20%) and for 2016/17 the Jeffords would pay only no tax to extract up to £10,000 of the extra net profit as a dividend (£5,000 dividend each at the nil rate). Dividends in excess of this amount would be taxed at 32.5%.

The rate differential between the main corporation rate and the higher rate of income tax is 20% in 2016/17 (40% – 20%) and could increase to 25% or 40% for those liable at 45% or 60% marginal rate. These rates and the differential only apply when the extra profits are retained within the company.

For items with private usage, such as cars, the disallowance of private expenditure in the unincorporated business may be more advantageous than benefits in kind charges applicable to companies, depending on individual circumstances, although the proprietors may wish to retain the cars outside the company and charge a mileage rate for business journeys. Business miles would not be very high in the chosen business venture, probably including only trips to cash and carry and occasional other journeys. For businesses with very high mileage there is a significant trade-off between gaining full tax relief for motoring costs and the very high tax charges on the benefit in kind.

For 2016/17, there would be no further tax to pay on the company retentions of £5,897 if they were paid out as dividends as these would fall within the dividend nil rate band for each recipient.

**2017/18 comparison tax payable as partnership or company with personal allowance salaries**

| | | *Partners* | | | *Company director* |
|---|---|---|---|---|---|
| | | £ | | | £ |
| Profits/remuneration | | 40,000 | 11,000 | × 2 | 22,000 |
| Dividends (14,000 as below) | | | | | 14,400 |
| Personal allowances | | (22,000) | | | (22,000) |
| Taxable income | | 18,000 | | | 14,000 |
| | 18,000 @ 20% | 3,600 | | | |
| | | | 10,000 | @ 0% | — |
| | | | 4,400 | @ 7.5% | 330 |
| Class 2 NI | | 291 | Employees' NI (11,000 – 8,060) | | |
| Class 4 NI (20,000 – 8,060) @ 9% × 2 | | 2,149 | @ 12% × 2 | | 706 |
| Total personal tax and NI | | 6,040 | | | 1,036 |
| **Company's tax and NI** | | | | | |
| Profits | | | | 40,000 | |
| *Less*: Directors' remuneration | | | | (22,000) | |
| Company's NI thereon @ 13.8% on (11,000 – 8,112) × 2 | | | | (797) | 797 |
| Employment allowance | | | | 797 | (797) |
| Taxable profits | | | | 18,000 | |
| Tax thereon @ 20% | | | | (3,600) | 3,600 |
| Profits paid out as dividend | | | | 14,400 | |
| Total tax and NI liabilities | | £6,040 | | | £4,636 |
| Saving through company format | | £1,404 | | | |

**2016/17 comparison tax payable as a sole trader or company with a salary equal to NIC threshold**

| | *Personal Allowance* | *NIC threshold* |
|---|---|---|
| | £ | £ |
| Profit | 30,000 | 30,000 |
| Less salary | (11,000) | (8,060) |
| Less employers NIC | (399) | |
| Employment allowance | | |
| | 18,601 | 21,940 |
| Corporation tax @ 20% | (3,720) | (4,388) |
| Dividend | 14,881 | 17,552 |
| Employees NIC | (352) | |
| Dividend tax | 741 | 741 |
| Net to shareholder | 25,787 | 24,891 |
| Difference | (104) | |

For 2016/17 the personal allowance is £11,000 whereas the employee's NIC threshold is £8,060.. Employment allowance could reduce the employer's NIC by up to £3,000 pa but in this case it is assumed that we have a single employee who is a director, so no employment allowance would be available. Note that unused personal allowances can now be used by dividend income which is taxable within the basic rate band at 7.5%; previously any personal allowance covering dividend income would have been wasted as the tax credit was not repayable (the tax credit has been abolished in 2016/17 as part of the modernisation of the taxation of dividend income).. The payment of a higher salary is often preferred by taxpayers so that it provides a regular income, but the absence of employment allowance for single director companies may now undermine that decision.

## *Other considerations*

(1) Sole traders and partners are fully liable for the debts of the business and can ultimately be made bankrupt. The liability of company shareholders is limited to the amount, if any, unpaid on their shares. This protection is not, however, as valuable as it seems because lenders, landlords and sometimes suppliers often require directors to give personal guarantees. There are also major compliance requirements for companies under the Companies Acts. Companies whose turnover is not more than £5.6 million (and balance sheet total of not more than £2.8 million) need not have their accounts audited (although many banks may still insist on it), but there are administration costs in filing annual accounts and returns and keeping minutes of meetings. It is possible to form a limited liability partnership, which will broadly give partners the same protection as members of limited companies, although it will also involve similar accounts and filing requirements (see **Example C12 part (b)** for details).

(2) Life as a sole trader is often perceived as simpler and easier to exit if for some reason the taxpayer wishes to cease. For example, the business not be as successful as planned or there is a wish to return to the security and structure offered by the world of employment. HMRC have also introduced a simplification of small businesses accounting (non-corporate) including allowing a form of cash accounting and/or flat-rate deductions. Where a partnership is formed a partnership agreement should be drawn up.

(3) Certain social security benefits, in particular statutory maternity pay and jobseeker's allowance are not available to the self-employed (plus before 2016 earnings-related retirement pension) and the newly self-employed may be able to claim JSA in the two years after they cease to be employees if they are out of work. The self-employed may, however, be able to claim maternity allowance, which is equivalent to lower rate SMP for those women with a full Class 2 record.

(4) More generous loss reliefs are available to individuals than to companies in the early years of a new business (see **Example E2**). A business may start as a sole trader and later when proved successful incorporate. (see **Example I2 explanatory note 18**). Historically it has been difficult to go the other way around, ie disincorporation, but a temporary relief has been introduced – see **Example J4**.

(5) Businesses with high business mileage in a car may obtain more generous relief via self-employment if they can claim a high business use percentage of total car costs. In comparison company cars have seen a significant increase in the taxation of benefits in kind such that they are often avoided.

(6) Following the introduction of the 10% (basic rate) and 20% (higher/additional rate taxpayers) flat rates for capital gains and 10% rate with entrepreneur's relief, the differential in capital gains tax cost between companies and unincorporated businesses narrowed. Provided the conditions for entrepreneur's relief are observed, reinvested profits that have been taxed at 20% can under certain circumstances be extracted at the capital gains rate of 20%, or 10% if entrepreneur's relief applies or basic rate band is available. This could theoretically give an extraction rate of (100% – corporation tax at 20%) × (100% – CGT at 20%, or 10%) = 64% or 72%. Profits of unincorporated businesses would be taxed at 32%, 42% or 47% before being reinvested, but there is no further tax on these profits at extraction, giving an extraction rate of 68%, 58% or 53%. Profits in the band £100,000 to £122,000 (2016/17) suffer 62% tax giving an extraction rate on that band of income of 38%. See **Example J4** for details of a TAAR introduced in 2016/17 to minimise opportunities to reduce income tax in this way.

Because a company is likely to have higher compliance costs, and will have higher NI costs (assuming employer NICs exceed the available employment allowance), any differential in the extraction rate is unlikely to be the deciding factor on its own.

(7) Some family companies have in the past paid remuneration at around the national insurance threshold, either just below to avoid paying national insurance at all or just above, hoping to protect entitlement to contributory benefits. Benefits can now be protected without paying any contributions, since there is a 'nil' band of contributions on earnings between £112 and £155 a week. This is only possible if the family members are directors without a contract of employment, because it is necessary for family companies to comply with the National Minimum Wage Act 1998 (see **Example J3 explanatory note 1**). At the post-October 2016 minimum rate of £7.20 per hour for a person aged 25 and over, a weekly wage of £100 represents just under 14 working hours. BERR (a forerunner of the current BIS) confirmed that proprietorial directors will only be subject to the minimum wage rules if they have an *explicit* contract of employment with the company. If they are engaged in normal work in their capacity as a director, they will not fall within these regulations, since the regulations do not apply to those who are no more than office holders of the company. See HMRC's Tax Bulletin of December 2000 for further comments.

(8) Although payment of salaries may involve higher NI contributions than apply to sole trader profits, salary payments can facilitate use of rate bands and allowances between years of fluctuating profits. Furthermore, the PAYE is paid regularly, and removes the wide swings of the payment on account system that causes difficulties to sole traders. However, the burden of regular online reporting under RTI should also be borne in mind. For low paid directors it is often simplest to make an annual payment of salary and register the PAYE scheme as an annual scheme. This avoids the necessity to make a return or nil return every month under RTI.

(9) CIS deductions suffered by a company can be set monthly or quarterly against its PAYE liability, or the deductions it has collected from payments to its own subcontractors, while those of sole traders can only be recovered through the annual SA process.

(10) The settlements legislation applies to partnerships as well as to companies and it should be borne in mind that the settlements legislation is still in force notwithstanding the specific facts of the Arctic Systems case. It is important to be able to demonstrate the reality of Mrs Jefford's involvement in the business to counter any challenge that the partnership or shareholding constitutes a settlement. See **Example A2** for more detailed information on HMRC's approach to settlements between spouses and civil partners.

(11) The rules for pension contributions differ for incorporated and unincorporated businesses. A company can make employer pension contributions that do not attract NI liability, but a sole trader, partner or LLP member must pay Class 2 and Class 4 liability before making pension contributions. Although an employee also suffers Class 1 liability before paying a pension contribution, a shareholder-director can ensure that only employer pension contributions are paid.

(12) Generally speaking, a company which has only directors as employees is not subject to the auto enrolment rules, unless more than one director has a contract of employment. Payment of an employee other than a director at a rate exceeding £10,000 triggers the auto enrolment responsibilities (depending on the age of the employee) and the company would then need to arrange a suitable scheme, make deductions from the employee's pay and pay contributions itself. See **Example A6** for more detail on auto enrolment.

# Explanatory Notes

*Rollover relief under TCGA 1992 s 162 on transfer of business to company*

(1) Where a business is transferred to a company as a going concern, together with all assets of the business other than cash, wholly in exchange for shares in the company, the chargeable gains arising on the assets transferred are deducted from the cost of the shares.

Partial relief is available where the consideration is only partly satisfied by shares in the new company, using the fraction:

$$\frac{\text{Value of shares in new company}}{\text{Value of whole consideration received in exchange for the business}} \times \text{Chargeable gains on assets transferred}$$

(TCGA 1992 s 162)

The relief under s 162 is automatic and a claim is not necessary. Certain reliefs take priority over relief under s 162, such as rollover relief for replacement assets under s 152, because the relief is given by reducing the *consideration* for a disposal. But s 162 relief cannot be ignored where, for example, gains would be covered by the annual exemption. To avoid the problem, the appropriate part of the consideration equal to available reliefs and exemptions could be left on director's loan account, so that a gain would be immediately realised.

Where gains have been held over following the acquisition of a depreciating asset (see **Example L8**), those gains will crystallise when the depreciating asset is transferred to the company, but technically they do not arise on the disposal of the asset and cannot therefore be deferred under s 162.

The total market value of assets transferred by Edzell to Famosa Ltd in the Example was:

| | £ |
|---|---|
| Goodwill | 97,500 |
| Freehold aircraft hangar | 80,800 |
| Plant and equipment | 20,000 |
| Motor car | 5,000 |
| Net current assets including debtors of £15,000 (but excluding cash) | 12,700 |
| | £216,000 |

The chargeable gain can therefore be rolled over against the base cost of the shares in the proportion:

$$\frac{\text{156,000 (consideration received as shares)}}{\text{216,000 (total consideration)}}$$

| | |
|---|---|
| which is $\frac{156}{216} \times £\,148{,}300$ | £107,106 |

Stamp duty land tax is chargeable on the market value of the land and buildings transferred under the sale of business agreement:

| | |
|---|---|
| Freehold aircraft hangar | £80,800 |

However, because the premises are business premises, the rate of tax is 0% where the consideration given for the hangar is £150,000 or less (FA 2003 s 55).

*Electing under TCGA 1992 s 162A to disapply s 162 relief*

(2) The incorporation of a business can adversely affect the proprietor's entrepreneur's relief. Under s 162, the gains are rolled over and the proprietor's entrepreneur's relief clock is reset to start afresh (in relation to the shares). No entrepreneur's relief 'credit' is given for the pre-incorporation holding period of the property, goodwill etc. If a sale of the shares were to arise within the 12 months waiting period for qualification for entrepreneurs' relief, the gain would be taxable at the full CGT rate.

The TCGA 1992 s 162A election can recapture relief 'lost' on incorporation by removing the automatic application of s 162 relief to the various gains. The gains thus become chargeable and may qualify for entrepreneur's relief, provided the assets had been owned for one year and the other qualifying conditions had been met. If the rolled over assets were to be owned for less than one year, or if other qualifying conditions on shareholdings or employment/office-holding could not be met, this election may be considered. Goodwill is normally excluded from qualifying for entrepreneurs' relief on related party transfers after 3 December 2014. Calculations would normally be required in each case to determine whether a s 162A election would be beneficial.

Where the shares acquired on incorporation are sold by the end of the tax year *following* the tax year of the incorporation, the s 162A election must be made by the 31 January after the end of that *following* year (the normal time limit for amending a self-assessment return), ie by 31 January 2018 for a 2015/16 disposal. In all other cases (ie where the shares are still retained at the end of the tax year following the tax year of incorporation) the time limit is extended by a further year (to 31 January 2019 for a 2015/16 disposal).

*Retaining some assets and claiming gifts holdover relief under TCGA 1992 s 165 on others*

(3) The gain on the aircraft hangar could have been avoided if it had been retained by Edzell personally and let to the company. If there was a gain when the hangar was finally disposed, for entrepreneur's relief, charging rent (after 5 April 2008) will cause relief to be restricted (TCGA 1992 s 169P (4)(d)). As the loss of relief would result in a CGT charge rising from 10% or 20% after annual allowance, while rent would be liable to income tax at 20% or 40% or even 45% subject to personal allowances, calculations would have to be carried out on a case by case basis depending on the ownership of the property and the owners' marginal tax rates.

If the hangar was not transferred, Edzell would have a chargeable gain on the goodwill, since the relief under s 162, described in **explanatory note 1** where assets are transferred to the company is only available where the *whole assets* of the business (other than cash) are transferred.

Even in that case, however, the gain on the goodwill could be deferred if Edzell assigned the goodwill to the company under the business gifts holdover relief provisions of TCGA 1992 s 165 for any unused part of his capital gains tax annual exemption. This relief is not affected by his retaining the premises.

(A holdover election under TCGA 1992 s 165 is not available on the transfer of shares in an unquoted trading company etc to a company, although this will rarely be relevant on a business incorporation.)

Thus, if Edzell had not used his capital gains tax exemption of £11,100, he could sell the goodwill for £11,100, which would be immediately chargeable and not available for rollover. This would give him a credit of that amount to his director's account with the company and would be an exempt gain for him as follows:

| | £ |
|---|---|
| Deemed sale proceeds | 97,500 |
| Cost | 0 |
| | 97,500 |
| *Less*: Gain immediately chargeable, being excess of actual proceeds over cost value (£11,100 – 0 = £11,100), leaving a gain covered by the annual exemption | 11,100 |
| Gain held over | 86,400 |

The company would have a base cost of £11,100 as follows:

| | | |
|---|---|---|
| Market value on acquisition | | 97,500 |
| *Less:* | Heldover gain | (86,400) |
| Being: | Paid to Edzell | £11,100 |

Under this arrangement, Edzell is only credited in the accounts of the company with £11,100, and the company's capital gains cost is the same amount, rather than the market value of £97,500. The company will be entitled to indexation allowance on the amount of £11,100 (indexation allowance applying only to corporate taxpayers).

Entrepreneur's relief is not available on the gains held over under TCGA 1992 s 165 since the relief is only given on chargeable gains. It is important to note that the individual proprietor's or partner's entrepreneur's relief clock starts again based on the date the shares were acquired (or if later, when the company starts to trade). The consequential loss of the qualifying period should be taken into account when an incorporation is being considered, particularly if there is a strong likelihood of the business being sold within the next year.

Where gifts holdover relief is claimed, HMRC require the shares to be subscribed for separately from the document for the transfer of the gifted assets.

*Alternative strategy of selling goodwill at its market value*

(4) Before 3 December 2014, it was common for the sole trader's goodwill to qualify for entrepreneur's relief as an associated disposal. Hence it was often sold to the company for its fair market value at a relatively low tax cost with no stamp duty. This would enable a further 'credit' to be booked to the proprietor's loan account. The loan account was then withdrawn possibly over a number of years enabling reduced salary / dividends. Following the reduction of the rates of capital gains tax for 2016/17, this once again becomes a possibility. The business owner will have to be able to finance the liability to capital gains tax at 20% after his annual exempt amount– in this example that would be £17,280 at 20%. However, this then provides the owner with a substantial loan account on which interest might be charged. The changes to the treatment of interest income in 2016/17 would permit interest to be paid to utilise first any available personal allowance (after taking into account the salary), and then the savings starting rate band of £5,000 at 0%, followed by the Savings nil rate band, which is equivalent to the personal savings allowance of either £1,000 for basic rate taxpayers and £500 for higher rate taxpayers. This provides a very low tax method of extracting funds, provided the rate of interest charged is reasonable in the circumstances. Dividends of £5,000 could be paid in addition, providing further tax free extraction.

*Tax relief for amount paid for goodwill*

(5) Goodwill is included in the 'intangible fixed assets' provisions in of CTA 2009 Part 8 (see **Example K2**). Under GAAP, profits and losses on such assets are taken into account in calculating income profits, and provision is made for goodwill to be amortised in the accounts. On the incorporation of a business, where the unincorporated business held the goodwill at 1 April 2002, the company would not be entitled to any tax relief for the subsequent amortisation of the purchased goodwill in the company's books, as it would be acquired from a 'related party' (CTA 2009 s 882). For an incorporation before 3 December 2014, it was possible for an acquiring company to obtain tax relief on the amount paid for sole trade/partnership goodwill to the extent that the goodwill arose, or was acquired by the sole trade/partnership from an unrelated third party, after 31 March 2002. The relief was normally based on the amount written off in the accounts each year.

For all acquisitions on or after 8 July 2015, F(No2)A 2015 s 32 disallows corporation tax deductions, such as amortisation and impairment debits, for goodwill (and certain other intangible assets linked to customers). Plus any on disposal any loss will be classified as a non-trading debit. A non-trading debit is not available to relieve against general trading income (assets sold at a profit will continue to be fully taxable).

For relevant **incorporations** on or after 3 December 2014, corporation tax relief is calculated when the assets (goodwill and certain customer related intangible assets) are disposed of rather than at the time the expenditure is incurred (FA 2015 s 26). Therefore no corporation tax relief for amortisation or impairment debits was given until disposal. There was an exception in respect of goodwill that had been acquired from a third party until these rules were superseded by the changes from 8 July 2015 above. Since the implementation of FRS102 if the goodwill can be split into elements of non-customer related intangible assets, relief may again be available.

The change from 3 December 2014 is specific to incorporations between related parties. The change from 8 July 2015 relates to **any** acquisition of goodwill etc. Both changes did not affect incorporations / acquisitions made (or already subject to a binding contract) before the dates above. Those qualifying before the dates above will continue to obtain corporation tax relief for amortisation and impairment as calculated according to GAAP / CTA 2009 s 730 principles.

*Share premium account*

(6) The Example illustrates that, when a business is transferred to a limited company as a going concern, wholly or partly for consideration to be satisfied by shares in the company, it will usually not be possible to issue *a number* of shares corresponding exactly with that part of the consideration to be satisfied in shares, since the final value of the business will not be known until after the event. Thus in this Example the part of the consideration of £216,000 to be satisfied by shares is £156,000 (MV assets £216,000 less cash received £60,000) and the nominal value of the shares allotted is £100,000.

The remaining £56,000 will be dealt with in the accounts of the company through a share premium account. For tax purposes, because the incorporation involves an acquisition from a connected person, the shares will be deemed to have a value equal to the value of the business acquired, less the £60,000 of cash consideration. In this case, they would be deemed to be worth £156,000, whether £2 of share capital or £100,000 of nominal value is issued.

*Income tax basis periods*

(7) Since Edzell has always made up accounts to 5 April, his basis periods coincide with his accounting periods and there is no overlap relief. Had his annual accounts been made up to another date, any overlap relief would have been deducted from the assessable profit of the last *tax year* (see **Example E3 explanatory note** 5). If, instead of making up a final 25-day account to 30 April 2016 as in the Example, he had made up accounts for the period from 6 April 2015 to 30 April 2016, then under the change of accounting date rules in ITTOIA 2005 s 216, the accounting date would normally have been treated as having changed in 2015/16 with the basis period for that year being 12 months to the new date, ie 12 months to 30 April 2015. A change of accounting date is not, however, effective if the taxpayer does not notify the change to HMRC. The profits of the last period of account (calculated *after* capital allowances, which because of the transfer to the company would in this case be nil, as indicated in the Example) would therefore have been time-apportioned as to 365/390 to 2015/16 and 25/390 to 2016/17. Any available overlap relief would have been deducted from the 2016/17 profit, and if it created a loss the normal loss reliefs would have been available.

*Capital allowances and election to transfer at written down value*

(8) The capital allowances basis periods are the same as the income tax basis periods. If the final account had been made up for the period 6 April 2015 to 30 April 2016, then as indicated in the comments in **part (a)** of the Example, this would result in no first year or writing down allowances or AIA being available in the final period (CAA 2001 ss 46, 55 and 65). Where the final accounting period to cessation includes significant capital expenditure, it may be beneficial to draw up accounts to an earlier date prior to cessation (or, as in this Example, not to extend the normal accounting period to include a short final period) to enable annual investment allowance etc to be claimed. Alternatively, it may be possible to crystallise a large balancing allowance on cessation by selling the pooled plant (including the newly acquired items) at less than the tax written down value (and not making an election to transfer at tax written down value) (s 61). This treatment would not apply to non-pooled assets, such as expensive cars (s 79) and short life assets (s 88).

Where the consideration allocated to plant exceeds its tax written down value, a balancing charge would arise. This can be avoided as shown in the Example by an election under CAA 2001 ss 266 and 267 where the purchaser and the seller are connected persons. A written notice to HMRC is required not later than two years after the transfer date, the election being made by both parties. The company assumes the written down values of the assets, which are treated as sold in the period to the date of transfer at an amount that gives neither a balancing allowance nor a balancing charge.

The annual investment allowance (AIA) is not available to the company on assets acquired from Edzell because it is controlled by Edzell and AIA is therefore blocked by CAA 2001 ss 214 and 217 (connected persons etc).

*Relief for trading losses*

(9) If there had been unrelieved trading losses, Edzell could have obtained relief in respect of them against income from the company under ITA 2007 s 86 (see **Example E3 explanatory note** 7). An alternative way of relieving brought forward losses may arise if no election is made to transfer assets at written down value for capital allowances, so that they would be transferred at market value. If this gave rise to balancing charges (such as those indicated in **part** (**c**) of the Example), the result would be to increase the profits against which the losses could be set.

*Value added tax*

(10) Since the business is to be transferred as a going concern, the effect for value added tax purposes is that the transfer will not be treated as a supply of goods or services and no VAT will be payable on the assets transferred (assuming that the option to tax in respect of the building had not been exercised by Edzell, or Famosa Ltd had also made the election before the transfer). Famosa Ltd will accordingly have no input tax to reclaim.

HMRC VAT registration unit must be notified within thirty days of the transfer, and at the same time Edzell and Famosa Ltd may jointly apply for Edzell's VAT registration number to be re-allocated to the company if this is desired. Edzell's personal registration will then be cancelled and the company will stand in his shoes for VAT purposes. Note that it is not possible for Famosa to delay registration until reaching the VAT registration threshold, as the going concern provisions deem Edzell's supplies to have been made by the company from the date of the transfer of the business. If Famosa takes over Edzell's VAT registration number, it must also keep his records; the company would be liable for any VAT errors made by Edzell within the last four years, and for any unpaid output tax in respect of Edzell's supplies. If Famosa does not take over the VAT registration, Edzell will keep the records, but must make necessary information available to Famosa. HMRC is empowered to disclose to Famosa information that it holds from prior to transfer to allow Famosa to fulfil its VAT obligations.

# Question

## A.

(a) Fred, who is a married man born 8 October 1932, has the following income in 2016/17:

| | £ |
|---|---|
| State pension | 8,670 |
| Occupational pension (no tax deducted under PAYE) | 3,035 |
| Building society interest | 2,100 |
| Dividends | 3,100 |

He paid £1,600 net to a charity under a gift aid declaration. Show the amount of income tax payable by Fred for 2016/17.

(b) State the value of the donation to the charity.

(c) Set out the differing ways in which tax efficient donations may be made to charities.

## B.

(a) The Blackhills Rugby Club registered as a Community Amateur Sports Club (CASC) from 1 April 2002. Its income and expenditure in the year ended 31 March 2017 comprise:

| | | | £ | |
|---|---|---|---|---|
| Income: | Membership fees | | 9,800 | |
| | Donations under gift aid (including tax) | | 6,000 | |
| | Bar takings – members | 18,600 | | |
| | – non-members | 5,400 | 24,000 | |
| | Letting of club house | | 2,600 | |
| | Building society interest | | 200 | 42,600 |
| Expenditure: | Purchases for bar | | 12,600 | |
| | Expenses of running club house | | 8,400 | |
| | Maintaining pitches | | 4,800 | |
| | Travelling costs of teams | | 8,100 | |
| | Costs of members' 'night out' | | 4,800 | |
| | Other costs of running club | | 1,900 | 40,600 |
| Net surplus of income over expenditure | | | | 2,000 |

Compute any amounts liable to corporation tax for the year ended 31 March 2017, assuming appropriate claims for relief are made.

(b) Show the effect on **part (a)** if Blackhills Rugby Club had sold part of its land in the year to 31 March 2017 for £200,000, resulting in a gain of £63,000.

(c) John has income of £106,000 in 2016/17 and was a member of Blackhills Rugby Club during the year. He pays a membership fee of £50 per year and has made a further donation to the club of £50 under gift aid. Set out the effect on John's tax liability in 2016/17.

# Answer

## A.

### (a) *Fred – Income tax payable 2016/17*

| | | | *Income* |
|---|---|---|---|
| | | | £ |
| State pension | | | 8,670 |
| Occupational pension | | | 3,035 |
| Building society interest | | | 2,100 |
| Dividends | | | 3,100 |
| | | | 16,905 |
| Personal allowance | | | 11,000 |
| Taxable income | | | 5,905 |
| Income tax thereon: | | | |
| On non-savings income | | | |
| (8,670 + 3,035 – 11,000) | 745 | @ 20% | 141 |
| Savings starting rate income | 2,100 | @ 0% | 0 |
| Dividends | 3,100 | @ 0% | 0 |
| | 5,905 | | 141 |
| Tax retained on gift aid payment | | | 400 |
| Tax payable | | | 259 |

Married couple's allowance although available, has not been claimed as this would otherwise increase the tax payable to cover the tax retained on the gift aid donation. See **explanatory note 1**.

Surplus married couple's allowance is available for transfer to his wife in the full amount, producing a tax saving of £836.

### (b)

Qualifying donations made to charities are grossed up for the basic rate of income tax (ITA 2007 s 414), so the gross value of the donation depends on the basic rate of tax, which is 20% for 2016/17.

### (c) *Tax-efficient giving to charity*

#### Gifts to charity by individuals

Where an individual wishes to make a donation to a charity, tax relief can be obtained provided certain steps are taken. The gift can be made in a number of ways:

(i) Payroll giving.

(ii) Direct gift to charity with an appropriate declaration (gift aid).

(iii) Gift of stocks and shares or land and buildings.

A company can also make tax allowable gifts to a charity, including gifts of stocks and shares or land and buildings, without completing a 'gift aid' declaration. Tax relief is given on the amount of the gift by a company – there is no grossing up. This is called charitable donations relief.

## Payroll giving

Employees can authorise their employer to deduct an amount from their pay to be given to charity (ITEPA 2003 Part 12 ss 713–715). This reduces their pay for tax and tax credit purposes (but not for national insurance contributions). Tax relief is therefore given at the employee's highest marginal rate on the donation. The payroll deduction is passed to an HMRC approved payroll giving agency, who will pay the amount to the nominated charity (after deducting an administration fee, typically 5%). Voluntary payments to the agency by the employer to cover running costs are allowed against the employer's taxable profits (CTA 2009 s 72).

## Gift aid donations by individuals (ITA 2007 Part 8 Chapter 2 ss 413–446)

A gift to charity by an individual qualifies for relief at the payer's highest tax rate if a gift aid declaration is made, providing the donor is within the scope of UK tax, ie a UK resident, or a Crown employee serving overseas, or a non-resident making the payment out of income or capital gains chargeable to UK tax. The gross gift is also deductible in computing income for tax credits.

The declaration can be made for the specific gift, or for all gifts to that charity, and can be made in writing, orally, or by electronic means. Declarations may also be given in relation to donations made prior to the date of the declaration. Charities receiving oral donations need only obtain the name and address of the donor. The charity must, however, then keep a full record of the declaration, retaining a copy for inspection by HMRC. A written declaration must contain (SI 2000/2074):

- the donor's name and home address;
- the charity's name;
- a declaration that the donation is to be treated as a gift aid declaration;
- a note explaining that the donor must pay income tax or capital gains tax equal to the tax deducted from the donation;
- date of declaration;
- donor's signature.

A written record of an oral donation needs to contain the same information as a written declaration (except the donor's signature) and must in addition state that the donor may cancel the declaration within 30 days. Such a cancellation would be retrospective. Donors may cancel a declaration at any time, and all subsequent donations are not then gift aid payments.

Payments under a gift aid donation are treated as being net of basic rate tax. The charity can recover the tax deducted providing it can show an audit trail between the gift and the donor. This can be a cheque, standing order, direct debit or by physical evidence of cash giving, eg an envelope.

Higher rate relief is obtained by increasing the basic rate band by the gift plus the tax thereon. The tax on a cash gift of £4,000 is 20/80 × 4,000 = £1,000, giving a gross gift of £5,000. The basic rate band would be (32,000 + 5,000 =) £37,000. The rate of tax saved depends on the rate payable on the top slice of the taxpayer's income. For illustrations of the various marginal rates see **Example A4 part** (C). The basic rate band is not extended when computing top slicing relief on life policy gains (see **Example A5**).

Where necessary, personal allowances are restricted to ensure that sufficient tax is paid to cover the tax on the donations, as illustrated in **part** (a) of the Example. If there is still insufficient tax, HMRC will issue an assessment to recover the shortfall.

In computing the tax that has been charged on the donor's income, notional tax on life policy gains is excluded, but the tax taken into account is before deducting relief for married couple's allowance or relief for maintenance payments (see **Example A1 explanatory note 1**). Any unused married couple's allowance can be surrendered to the spouse. If the couple were not within the scope of married couples allowance they might make a claim for marriage allowance, transferring £1,100 of personal allowance to the wife and thus increasing the tax charge by £220, thereby covering the tax retained on the gift aid payment.

With income tax rates of 45% and even 60% for those whose personal allowances are withdrawn, and potentially higher rates still for those affected by the high income child benefit charge, the carry back of gift aid donations permits income taxed at high marginal rates to be relieved by subsequent gifts. The abatement of personal allowances occurs at net adjusted income of £100,000, after deducting losses, the gross amount of gift aid donations and the gross amount of pension contributions made. The personal allowance is then be reduced by half of the excess over £100,000 until it has been removed completely, giving an effective marginal rate of 60%. For details of the high income child benefit charge see **Example A2**.

The carry back election is explained in detail at **explanatory note 8**.

### Benefits from charities

A charity may make a token gesture to show its appreciation for a donation. The maximum benefits that a donor can receive are set out in ITA 2007 ss 418 and 419 and CTA 2010 s 197:

| Aggregate donations in tax year | Maximum aggregate value of benefits |
|---|---|
| £ | |
| 0 – 100 | 25% of aggregate donations |
| 101 – 1,000 | £25 |
| 1,001 – 10,000 | 5% of aggregate donations |
| 10,001 + | £2,500 but no more than 5% of the donation |

The provision of free or reduced price admission for the donor (or family) to the property of a heritage or wildlife conservation charity (such as the National Trust) is disregarded provided the right applies for at least one year or the gift is at least 10% more than the normal admission price (ITA 2007 s 420).

### Tainted charity donations

To counter perceived abuses of the charities' exemptions involving benefits provided to substantial donors, anti-avoidance legislation exists to deny relief to the donor if they received a benefit from the charity or a connected party in connection with a donation. The onus is on the donor to disallow his own tax relief if the donation and the benefit received in connection with it breach the rules. There is no particular impact on the charity recipients.

The legislation is in Chapter 8 'Tainted Charity Donations' ITA 2007 and CTA 2010 Part 21B.

### Charitable donations by companies (CTA 2010 Part 6 ss 189–217)

Companies may make tax-efficient charitable donations in a similar way to individuals, although they are not required to make gift aid declarations. The limits for benefits associated with a charitable gift are applied to companies in a consistent manner with those for individuals. Company donations will not be relieved if they are conditional or the company or a connected person receives one or more benefits from the donation and their value exceeds the relevant limits in CTA 2010 s 197 (as outlined above). Companies do not deduct tax from charitable donations, including covenanted payments. Tax relief is obtained under qualifying charitable donations relief or as a trading expense against taxable profits for corporation tax (see **Example I1 explanatory note 11**).

### Gifts of shares or land and buildings

Under CTA 2010 Part 6 Chapter 3 and ITA 2007 Part 8 Chapter 3, tax relief is available for gifts to charity by individuals or companies of shares or securities listed or dealt in on a recognised stock exchange (which includes shares on the Alternative Investment Market), units in authorised unit trusts, shares in open-ended investment companies and interests in offshore funds and gifts of a freehold or leasehold interest in UK land. The relief is equal to the market value of the security or land on the date of disposal plus costs, less any consideration received. This relief is in addition to the capital gains relief (TCGA 1992 ss 256 and 257), which treats the disposal as giving rise to neither gain nor loss. An individual deducts the relief from his total income, saving tax at his top tax rate (see **Example A4(C)**), and a company deducts qualifying charitable donations relief against profits (see **Example I1 explanatory note 11**).

Finance Act 2010 s 31 introduced anti-avoidance legislation by inserting s 438A in to ITA 2007 and including Sch 7 to amended ITA 2007 Part 8 Chapter 3 s 437. This legislation was introduced following a number of marketed tax avoidance scheme and is designed to prevent gift aid tax relief from being exploited. The legislation restricts the acquisition value taken into account when the shares or land were acquired in the four years preceding the date of the gift and the acquisition was part of a tax avoidance scheme.

Gifts of shares or land and buildings do not reduce income for tax credit purposes.

### Gifts in kind by traders

See **Example I1 explanatory note 4** for the allowance of salary payments for employees seconded to charity and business gifts to charity of trading stock and plant and machinery.

### Tax-efficient giving

An individual who wishes to give to charity needs to consider the tax implications of the gift. If they have quoted securities pregnant with gains, then a gift of the securities will not give rise to a capital gains liability (saving up tax thereon up to 20%) and in addition will attract relief at his highest marginal income tax rate, However they would, of course, no longer have the asset nor any significant benefit therefrom, following their gift.

Alternatively, for cash gifts if the individual can get his employer company to make a corporate donation themselves rather than via payroll giving, then the amount is paid out of funds that have not borne national insurance contributions.

For regular giving an indefinite gift aid declaration should be made to the charity. All gifts should be recorded and entered on the individual's tax return, so that the charity may recover the basic rate tax and the donor may obtain higher rate tax relief if appropriate. For one-off cash gifts the charity should be able to provide a gift aid declaration in the form of an envelope into which the gift is placed. Donors should maintain a record of the gift and report it on their tax return.

## B.

### (a) *Blackhills Rugby Club – corporation tax liability year ended 31 March 2017*

As Blackhills Rugby Club is a registered Community Amateur Sports Club (CASC) under CTA 2010 Part 13 Chapter 9 ss 658–667 (as amended by FA 2010 Sch 6), its income is exempt from corporation tax as follows, the exempt amount being restricted to the extent that its expenditure of £40,600 includes non-qualifying expenditure (see **explanatory note 10**):

| | £ |
|---|---|
| Trading income (exempt limit £30,000 – mutual trading with own members ignored) | 5,400 |
| Property income (exempt limit £20,000) | 2,600 |
| Gift aid income | 6,000 |
| Building society interest | 200 |
| | 14,200 |
| *Less*: Restriction re non-qualifying expenditure on members' night out | |

| | £ |
|---|---|
| $14{,}200 \times \frac{4{,}800}{42{,}600}$ | 1,600 |
| Exempt income | 12,600 |

Corporation tax is not payable on membership fees, so the only chargeable profits are the proportionate amount of non-qualifying expenditure of £1,600 and tax thereon at 20% is £320.

## (b) *Effect on (a) of sale of land with gain of £63,000*

The realised gain of £63,000 from the sale of land made by Blackhills Rugby Club has been used for qualifying purposes. This amount would be added to the amount on which the exemption is claimed in **(a) above**, but the restriction of the exemption because of the non-qualifying expenditure would increase to:

$$\frac{(14{,}200 + 63{,}000 = )\ 77{,}200}{(42{,}600 + 63{,}000 = )\ 105{,}600} \times 4{,}800 = £3{,}509$$

The chargeable amount of £3,509 would be taxed at 20%, resulting in a tax charge of £702. The effect of the land sale is an increase of £382 in the corporation tax liability if the proceeds of the land sale are used for qualifying purposes. If the proceeds of the chargeable gain on the land had been used for non-qualifying purposes, then the gain would be subject to corporation tax on the chargeable gain and increase the liability by £12,600.

## (c) *Tax treatment of John in respect of payments to Blackhills Rugby Club*

Membership fees cannot be treated as gifts for gift aid, so John will only be eligible for tax relief on £63, being £50 gift aid payment plus basic rate tax retained of £13. This will reduce John's net adjusted income, saving tax at 40% plus 20% to reflect the reduced abatement of personal allowance. So the tax saving is £63 @ 60% = £38, less tax retained £13 = £25.

# Explanatory Notes

*Paying sufficient tax to cover tax on gift aid payments*

(1) A taxpayer may offset allowances and reliefs against income of different descriptions in the most advantageous way unless the legislation provides otherwise (ITA 2007 s 25). See **Example A4 explanatory note 5**.

A taxpayer is entitled to retain the basic rate income tax deducted from gift aid payments providing he pays at least that much tax. Fred in **part (a)** of the Example must therefore have £400 of tax chargeable. Income tax or capital gains tax charged in the year can be used to cover that amount. If, however, the tax charged would otherwise be lower than the tax retained, personal allowances are restricted to keep a sufficient amount in charge (ITA 2007 ss 423–425).

If Fred had not made a gift aid payment, he would have claimed married couple's allowance as follows:

| | £ |
|---|---|
| Tax as at **85.2** above | 141 |
| *Less*: MCA (8,355 @ 10%) restricted to | 141 |
| Tax due | 0 |

(2) The tax available for offsetting tax relief under the enterprise investment scheme or venture capital trust scheme, or foreign tax credits, is after the deduction of the tax deemed to be retained on charitable payments.

(3) If, after restricting personal allowances to nil, insufficient tax has been paid, then in computing the amount of the excess to be assessed, the tax charged does not include notional tax (on non-qualifying distributions, scrip dividends and life policy gains) and tax at the basic rate on patent royalties and other annual payments.

*Settlor-interested trusts*

(4) Where a trust is caught by the anti-avoidance legislation in ITTOIA 2005 Part 5 Chapter 5, the trust income is deemed to be that of the settlor in certain circumstances. If such a trust gives money to a charity, ITTOIA 2005 s 628 provides that the amount taxable on the settlor is reduced by the amount (plus tax) given to the charity. The rate of tax recoverable by the charity depends on the tax payable by the trust. A charge on a settlor is also prevented where an interest free loan is made to a charity (ITTOIA 2005 s 620).

For detailed notes on the taxation of trusts see the companion to this book, **Tolley's Taxwise II 2016/17.**

*Exemption for trading activities*

(5) Where a charity carries on a trade as part of its charitable purpose (for instance, employing beneficiaries of the charity in producing goods) any profits will usually be exempt from tax. Profits are apportioned between those generated by the primary purpose of the charity, and those generated by other activities.

Where trading is to raise funds, the profits are taxable unless the turnover does not exceed £5,000 or, if greater, the lower of £50,000 and 25% of the charity's gross income (FA 2000 s 46; now ITA 2007 s 526 in respect of charitable trusts).

ITA 2007 s 529 exempts from tax the profits of fundraising events which are exempt for VAT purposes under Group 12 of VATA 1994 Sch 9. Essentially the events must be organised by the charity or qualifying body and must meet the qualifying conditions for VAT purposes, which include a restriction of no more than 15 events in one location in one year.

*Trading subsidiaries*

(6) If the trading activities are likely to exceed the above limits, it is advisable to set up a wholly owned trading subsidiary, which will be liable to corporation tax on its profits. Any charitable donations to the charity parent will, however, be deductible under charitable donations relief. (This arrangement effectively converts trading profits which would fall to be taxed in the hands of the charity into tax exempt investment income (see CTA 2010 s 473)). A donation made by a wholly owned trading subsidiary to its charity parent can be treated as paid in an accounting period falling wholly or partly within the nine months before the payment was made (CTA 2010 s 199). Note that the donation back to the charity is treated as a distribution in the company's accounts for company law purposes, so there must be sufficient distributable profits to cover it.

*Gift aid donations and carry back*

(7) Where an individual makes a gift aid donation before 31 January in the tax year and before the tax return for the previous tax year has been filed, an election may be made to deem the donation to be made in the previous tax year. In 2016/17 the highest rate of income tax is 45%, with an effective marginal band of 60% tax where personal allowances are abated at relevant net income of £100,000 or more. Plus a high marginal rate can also occur where the high income child benefit charge applies; see **Example A2**. The carry back of gift aid donations may allow taxpayers affected by high marginal rates of tax to reduce the impact of loss of their personal allowances/child benefit for the preceding tax year.

The carry back is not effective for tax credit purposes. The gift aid payment will still be deducted from the tax credits income on a current year basis. This is *not* treated as a claim affecting the earlier year under TMA 1970 Sch 1B but as a payment of the earlier year. The tax liability of the earlier year is reduced accordingly, as well as the payments on account for the current year.

For example a taxpayer who was a higher rate taxpayer in 2016/17 makes a gift aid payment of £800 on 31 Ma 2016. This is included, by election, in his 2015/16 tax return filed on 30 September 2016. The effect on his tax liability and payments will be:

| | £ |
|---|---|
| Reduction in 2015/16 higher rate tax | |
| 800 × 100/80 = 1,000 @ (40 – 20)% | 200 |
| Reduction in 2015/16 payment on account | 100 |
| Saving on payment due 31 January 2017 | 300 |
| Saving on payment due 31 July 2017 | 100 |
| Additional amount due 31 January 2018 (being savings in payments on account) | 200 |

*Amateur sports clubs*

(8) Under CTA 2010 Part 13 Chapter 9, tax exemptions are available to registered community amateur sports clubs (CASCs) similar to those available for charities. In order to register as a CASC, a club must be open to the whole community without discrimination, have reasonable membership fees, be organised on an amateur basis and have as its main purpose the provision of facilities for and promotion of participation in one or more eligible sports. It must also satisfy the location condition (the club must be established in an EEA member state) and the management condition (the managers must be fit and proper persons). The rules are slightly amended by FA 2013 s 46 to tighten the conditions for eligibility.

The club is required to be non-profit making, providing ordinary benefits for its members and their guests and using surplus funds for the purposes of the club. On dissolution any surplus must be paid to another CASC or eligible sports ruling body or a charity. Ordinary benefits are:

– provision of sporting facilities;

– provision and maintenance of sports equipment;

– provision of suitably qualified coaches or coaching courses;

– insurance and medical cover;

– reimbursement of travel expenses of players and officials for away matches;

– post-match refreshments for players and match officials;

– sale of food and drink associated with the sporting activities.

The club may pay staff, who may be members of the CASC, on an arm's length basis.

Once registered, a club is exempt from tax on trading income (before expenses) not exceeding £30,000, property income (before expenses) not exceeding £20,000, interest and gift aid income, and capital gains, providing in each case the whole of the income or gains as the case may be is applied for qualifying purposes (ie providing facilities for, and promoting participation in, one or more eligible sports, as designated by statutory instrument) and claims for the exemptions are made.

If expenditure is incurred for non-qualifying purposes, the total amount of exempt income and gains is reduced by the proportion of non-qualifying expenditure to total income and gains. The effect on exempt income is illustrated in **part B(a)** of the Example, where the cost of the members' night out is non-qualifying expenditure, as its main purpose is not that of providing facilities for participating in sport, resulting in part of the exempt income becoming chargeable income. Where there are exempt gains, as in **part B(b)** the non-exempt amount is increased.

(9) Registered CASCs are treated as charities for gift aid payments by individuals, and can recover the basic rate tax on donations but not membership fees. The reliefs for gifts of shares and land and buildings (see **part**

**a** of the Example) and business gifts of stock or plant (see **Example I1 explanatory note 4**) also apply, as do the capital gains tax and inheritance tax charitable gifts exemptions. Finance Act 2014 introduced restrictions on tax relief for donors where the donor benefits as a result of the gift. This essentially mirrors the restricted relief for tainted charity donations (see **part (c)** of the answer).

(10) If a CASC ceases to hold an asset for qualifying purposes (without disposing of it), or ceases to be registered, the club will be treated as having disposed of and reacquired the asset at market value. The resultant gain will be chargeable to corporation tax.

# Question

(a) Your notes of a meeting with new clients Mr Powell and Mrs Powell, both aged 48, include the following points:

(i) Your new clients have two children aged 15 and 19 (both in full time education – no income).

(ii) Mr Powell owns 60% of the share capital of P Transport Ltd, the remainder being held by Mrs Powell. The company was formed four years ago, and specialises in continental transport and storage. Its profits for the year ending 31 March 2017 are expected to amount to £330,000 after remuneration of:

| | *Mr Powell* | *Mrs Powell* |
|---|---|---|
| | £ | £ |
| Salary | 22,000 | 3,000 |
| Bonus (to be paid August 2017) | 38,000 | – |
| | 60,000 | 3,000 |

Both Mr and Mrs Powell work full time in the business. Mr Powell is the director and Mrs Powell is the business's book-keeper and also the company secretary. The business is estimated to be worth £1,500,000 as a going concern. Although the company normally has a small credit balance at the bank, it has overdraft facilities of £100,000.

P Transport Ltd anticipates needing additional storage facilities in the near future. A suitable site in the area would cost in the region of £160,000 and the required building would cost £500,000. Bank finance would be available for this project.

Your clients have suggested that the new building could be owned either:

- by the company for its own use, or
- by Mr and Mrs Powell personally, but let to the company, or
- by a self-administered pension fund, again let to the company.

(iii) Mr Powell has a retirement annuity policy with an annual premium of £2,000. He does not have any life assurance cover.

(iv) Mr and Mrs Powell have a joint building society account containing £2,000, a house in joint names worth £440,000 (with a £75,000 mortgage) and no other assets except a director's account with the company to which Mr Powell's bonuses have always been credited and which currently stands at £60,000 owing to Mr Powell.

(v) Both Mr and Mrs Powell have made wills leaving their estate to the other or, if there is no surviving spouse, equally to their children.

They have changed their adviser because they are unhappy with the lack of tax planning advice they have been receiving.

Prepare, giving reasons for the points chosen, a memorandum of tax planning points to discuss with Mr and Mrs Powell.

# Answer

## Possible tax planning points for the Powells

### (i) *Their Children*

**Both**

Could they be paid by the company for legitimate services rendered in holidays, weekends etc? Watch compliance with PAYE and employment regulations. For 2015/16 onwards there is no employer's NIC for employees under 21. Could the amount be enhanced by the company making pension contributions for them?

**Elder aged 19**

See below for possible transfer of shares to the elder child.

**Younger aged 15**

Any income produced on funds provided by parents (but not capital gains in a bare trust) would be taxed on the parent, not on the child, until the child reaches age 18 or marries before that date (ITTOIA 2005 s 629). This is subject to a de minimis exemption whereby each parent can provide funds to produce income of up to £100 per annum. This de minimis exemption is only available if the child's total income from that parent does not exceed that amount. It does not cover the first slice of a larger sum.

If money is being provided by the parents for savings, invest in sources that do not produce income, eg investment bonds , or are not liable to income tax, such as national savings children's bonds. Share transfers could be made , which would be effective for inheritance tax, but income from dividends would for the time being be treated as the parents' income. Premiums of up to £270 per annum may be paid by the parents for a qualifying friendly society policy for the child without breaching the parental settlement rules.

Parents can provide the funds for investment in a junior ISA, without the income being taxable on them. Annual contributions to a junior ISA are limited to £4,080. (See **Example A5**).

(See **Example A2 part** (c)(ii) for notes on bare trusts.)

### (ii) *Shareholdings in P Transport Ltd*

Any transfer of shares by Mr or Mrs Powell should take into account the following:

(i) They need to retain control of the company between them if they are to continue to qualify for 50% business property relief for inheritance tax purposes on any property owned by them and rented to the company. The shares themselves qualify for 100% business property relief, no matter how small the holding.

(ii) For capital gains tax, any chargeable gains on the transfer of shares could be held over by the use of business assets gifts holdover relief (TCGA 1992 s 165 – see **Example L9**), or by use of deferral relief under the Enterprise Investment Scheme (EIS) if suitable investments are made (TCGA 1992 Sch 5B – see **Example N7**). Their shareholdings should not, however, fall below the required level for the gifts relief (which is not less than 5% of the voting power). This could give rise to capital gains tax on a subsequent sale after all such relief has been used (see **Example L9**).

(iii) As P Transport Ltd is an unquoted trading company, the shares in the company should qualify for entrepreneur's relief up to the lifetime limit of £10 million of gains per individual (see **Example L5**).

Any buildings owned by Mr and Mrs Powell and used for the purposes of the business would also be eligible, but no relief will be available if they are let to the business at a full market rent. Entrepreneurs' relief has to be claimed, but gift relief could be claimed without using any entrepreneurs' relief. Provided that both Mr and Mrs Powell work in the business and have a shareholding of at least 5%, both can claim entrepreneur's relief, making two £10 million lifetime allowances available.

(iv) Mr and Mrs Powell need to be aware of HMRC's possible reaction on transfer of shares to children, and its interaction with the anti-avoidance legislation in ITTOIA 2005 Part 5 Chapter 5 (see Tax Bulletin 64, this was issued in 2003, but no more recent definitive HMRC guidance is available). This legislation applies if the purpose of the transfer is to divert income to another and tax is saved. For the rules to apply the transfer must be:

- bounteous, or
- not commercial, or
- not at arm's length, or
- in the case of a gift between spouses wholly or substantially a right to income.

The provisions are unlikely to apply in this case if the gift of shares to a child is part of a strategy of involving the child in the business with a view to eventual succession to the company, provided that no dividend waivers occur to increase the income on the child's shares, and the shares are given absolutely. Although HMRC lost the *Arctic Systems* case (*Jones v Garnett* [2007] 4 All ER 857) in respect of husband and wife ordinary shares with rights to capital, the legislation is still fully effective for other situations. Income shifting legislation was proposed in 2009/10 but none has yet been enacted. The only official line issued since that time is that the issue remains 'under review' while the settlement legislation remains in place and should be considered. Subject to the above, share transfers to the children will ensure that future growth is in the hands of the next generation, that dividends are at once treated as the income of the elder child and in three years' time will be treated as that of the younger child, and that the children are given some incentive within the business.

A return of the issue of shares in connection with employment is normally required under the employment related securities rules by 6 July following the tax year in which it is made. HMRC guidance makes it clear that the return is not required in the cases of transfers arising through personal or family relationships, and cites the example of the shares being transferred to children working in the business as an illustration of this.

Transfers now rather than later will avoid any risk that the current 100% business property relief for inheritance tax is reduced by subsequent legislation, and if the shares cease to qualify for business property relief, the seven year period during which a transfer is only potentially exempt will have begun that much sooner. On the other hand, lifetime transfers are subject to capital gains tax and although the gains may be deferred by making a holdover election they would not arise at all if the shares were still held when the parents died. However, providing each child holds at least 5% of the nominal value of the company's share capital and of the voting rights, and is an employee of the company, entrepreneur's relief should be available, resulting in an effective rate of tax of 10%. Failing this, gains will be taxed at a fixed rate of 10% or 20% (depending upon whether the disposer is a basic (10%) or higher/additional rate taxpayer (20%)), and their own annual exemptions (£11,100 for 2016/17) will still be available. Note that provided full business property relief under IHT legislation remains available, there would be no charge either to capital gains tax or inheritance tax if the shares were held by Mr & Mrs Powell until death.

From April 2016 the changes to the taxation of dividend income, and in particular the dividend nil rate band of of £5,000 a year provides further opportunity for planning by transferring shares to the children, utilising their personal allowances and dividend nil rate band, and even the basic rate band where the dividend is only taxable at 7.5%.

A shareholding by a self-administered pension fund could also be considered, subject to the same considerations and also depending upon what other involvement the fund is to have with the company (since HMRC imposes limits on the fund's participation in company shares/loans back). Furthermore the trustees of the fund may not be happy with a holding of unquoted shares which they may find difficult to realise. For further comments on self-administered schemes see (e) **below**.

### (iii) *Profits of P Transport Ltd*

If profits could be sensibly reduced tax would be saved on the reduction at the current rate of corporation tax, 20%. (See (iv) and (v) below for ways in which profits might be reduced, in addition to the possibility of paying increased remuneration.)

### (iv) *Remuneration to Mr and Mrs Powell*

Although charged in arriving at the company's taxable profits in the accounting periods to which they relate, any bonuses to Mr and Mrs Powell are taxed on them in the tax years when they are received. The August 2017 bonus of £38,000 would therefore be taxed on Mr Powell in 2017/18, and the bonus paid to him in 2016/17, if any, would be taxed in 2016/17. For the purpose of the calculations which follow it has been assumed that a similar bonus was paid in August 2016. Care must be taken if total income in 2017/18 is likely to be near to £100,000 to ensure that the restriction of personal allowances does not apply, otherwise a marginal income tax rate of 60% could apply to the top slice of income.

The couple should also be aware that if the recipient of the higher net income (after deducting the gross amount of gift aid payments and pension contributions) has income in excess of £60,000, they will face a tax charge to claw back the child benefit payments in respect of the younger child. Where the higher net income is between £50,000 and £60,000 there is a partial claw back. This may influence some of the considerations below; for example, if both had net income of just below £50,000, no high income child benefit charge would apply.

#### Increasing Mrs Powell's remuneration

Since Mrs Powell works full time in the company and is also its company secretary, a substantial increase in her remuneration could be justified. If her earnings were substantially increased and Mr Powell's correspondingly reduced, then higher rate tax would be saved. The saving in higher rate tax would, however, be partly offset by increased employee's national insurance contributions at 12% since Mr Powell is only paying contributions of 2% on his earnings above £43,000 for 2016/17, whereas his wife would pay contributions at 12% on the extra remuneration above £8,060. (Employer's contributions are at 13.8% on earnings above £8,112.) Increased remuneration could be used to support a personal pension contribution or the alternative possibility of the company starting a self-administered pension scheme or making an employer contribution direct to the employee's personal pension policy.

It is necessary to justify the services provided by her in order to substantiate her level of remuneration. She may consider drawing sufficient to fully utilise her personal allowance; as an officer of the company she is not subject to the national minimum wage legislation unless she has a formal contract of employment.

#### Paying dividends instead of remuneration

The company could consider paying dividends. In 2016/17 the dividends would be taxable at Mr and Mrs Powell's respective dividend rates of 7.5%,32½% (38.1% does not apply as it is assumed that both of their incomes for 2016/17 are below £150,000) unless substantially increased remuneration were paid to Mrs Powell in 2016/17. Assuming that Mr Powell was taking remuneration of £43,000 or more and thus paying national insurance contributions of 2% on his earnings above £43,000 as an employee, the comparative position for him in 2016/17, using a profit figure of £1,000 and a marginal tax rate of 40% for illustration, would be:

| | | £ | £ |
|---|---|---|---|
| Paying extra remuneration: | Company profit | | 1,000 |
| | Remuneration | 879 | |
| | Employer's national insurance 13.8% | 121 | 1,000 |
| | Total taxable profits | | – |

| | | | |
|---|---|---|---|
| | Gross remuneration | | 879 |
| | Income tax at 40% | 352 | |
| | Employee's NIC @ 2% | 18 | 370 |
| | Net of tax amount | | £509 |

| | | |
|---|---|---|
| | | £ |
| Paying dividend: | Company profit | 1,000 |
| | Corporation tax at 20% | 200 |
| | Dividend to shareholders | 800 |
| | Income tax at 32½% | 260 |
| | Net of tax amount | 540 |

For 2015/16 it may therefore be more tax efficient for Mr Powell to receive additional dividends, although other considerations should be borne in mind. See **Example J3 explanatory note 2.**

Any dividends paid would be taxed separately on each of Mr and Mrs Powell, so the amount saved through paying dividends instead of remuneration to Mrs Powell would be the employer's and employee's national insurance contributions plus the saving in Mr Powell's higher rate liability unless her revised income exceeded the basic rate threshold. Mrs Powell would receive a net of tax dividend of £760 out of £1,000 company profits (£1,000 x 80% less tax of 7.5%).

The payment of dividends would normally affect the value of the company's shares, but where a company is closely controlled by the family, other bases of valuation would also be considered, such as assets or earnings.

## (v) *Acquisition of new storage facilities*

There are no tax allowances for the purchase of the land or the construction of the building, although fixtures forming part of the building would be available for capital allowances, and if energy efficient technologies are fitted there may be 100% FYA's available in addition to the £200,000 annual investment allowance. Mr and Mrs Powell could acquire the building personally and obtain the same allowances, firstly against rental income and then other income of the tax year of purchase and then the following tax year (ITA 2007 s 120) although the sideways set-off would be subject to the cap on loss relief (See Example E1). If they acquired the building and let it to the company, inheritance tax business property relief of 50% would be available on an eventual transfer of ownership, so long as between them they continued to control the company. The charging of rent would reduce or remove entitlement to entrepreneur's relief in respect of the building.

The rental income arising is currently free of NI contributions, and is normally taxed on joint ownership by husband and wife as 50/50 unless an election is made for taxation to be on actual ownership. Payment of the rental income will reduce the company's total profits and provide an income stream to Mr and Mrs Powell. This could provide an alternative to taking dividends.

If eventually a capital gain arises, although companies are still entitled to indexation, the CGT regime for individuals at a flat rate of 10% or 20% (dependent on whether the disposer is a basic or higher rate taxpayer and the asset is not residential property) and individual annual exemptions is likely to prove more effective than routing a gain through the company, where it will be subject to corporation tax before the remaining funds can be extracted subject to CGT net of reliefs.

### Acquisition through self-administered pension fund

Purchase by a self-administered pension fund could also be considered. The contributions to the fund from company profits would be allowable in calculating the company's corporation tax, provided they are accepted as incurred wholly and exclusively for the purposes of the trade. Furthermore, the rent paid to the pension fund by the company would be allowable in computing company profits but not taxable in the pension fund so long as the fund was a registered pension scheme. The ability of the pension fund to acquire the land effectively gives tax relief on the land purchase, since the pension fund first has to be put in funds out of pre-tax company profits.

The amount that the fund may borrow is limited to 50% of the fund value for new loans (from 6 April 2006). The maximum annual tax relief for pension contributions is £40,000 from 2014/15 (see **Example A6** for previous allowances and the restricted limit for additional rate taxpayers from 2016/17; if Mr & Mrs Powell crystallise their money purchase pensions, the limit falls to £10,000). There is a limited scope to carry forward unused annual allowances. If the property could not be purchased outright by the pension fund, consideration could be given to an initial joint purchase (between the pension fund and directors personally) and then in specie pension contributions in future years to transfer further percentage shares in the property within the annual allowances available to each of them. This would be more expensive in terms of fees (the property would need to be valued each year to determine what percentage could be transferred) and stamp duty land tax would be due on the subsequent disposals/contributions.

The fund could take out appropriate life assurance cover on Mr and/or Mrs Powell in order to provide a capital sum with which to pay death in service benefits to the dependants in the event of the death of one or the other whilst they were still working for the company, although attention would need to be paid to their lifetime allowance. This could be an important consideration in view of the present lack of life cover. The restrictions on personal term assurance in FA 2007 Sch 18 do not affect employer contributions to group pension schemes.

One difficulty of purchasing property through a self-administered pension fund is the need to provide liquid funds to acquire an annuity on retirement. This has historically been minimised by deferring the purchase of an annuity until an age not later than 75 (since April 2011 the requirement to annuitise by age 75 has been removed) and paying the pension from the income produced by the scheme assets until that age. In addition, it might be that the children will have joined the firm and become members of the pension fund. From their contributions liquid funds could be available to purchase the annuities for Mr and Mrs Powell, so that the need to sell the property at a later date is removed. Anti-avoidance legislation exists to ensure that Mr and Mrs Powell cannot make excessive contributions to provide funds to be inherited by the children. The Taxation of Pensions Act 2014 changes implemented in 2015 offering more flexibility to over-55s about drawing pensions may affect the Powells' thinking.

Employer contributions to self-invested personal pension schemes may also be used to provide funds for those schemes to acquire an interest in commercial, non-residential, property, within limits, and possibly with mortgage funding.

### (vi) *Pension provision for Mr and Mrs Powell*

Registered pension schemes operate under the rules in FA 2004 Part 4, FA 2005 Part 5 and related regulations.

See **(v) above** for the possibility of the company starting a self-administered pension scheme or the Powells starting self-invested personal pensions to provide pensions for them.

Mr Powell already has a retirement annuity policy but neither Mr nor Mrs Powell has a registered individual pension plan. Contributions could be made personally or the company could contract direct with their schemes. Points to consider are as follows.

If Mrs Powell's remuneration is increased as suggested in **(iv) above**, any increased remuneration could be used to support an individual pension contribution of £3,600, or 100% of her earnings (subject to the annual allowance available) in 2016/17, if greater. Individuals who make contributions within the limits will obtain tax relief. Basic rate relief is normally given by deduction of tax at source and any higher rate relief claimed upon their tax return.

Mr Powell may make a personal contribution to an individual registered pension scheme of up to 100% (subject to his annual allowance minus £2,000 RAP) of his gross earnings by 5 April 2016, possibly by drawing out the balance on his director's loan account to fund it. The contributions will be paid net, but will attract higher rate tax relief. See **Example A6**.

Alternatively, or in addition, contributions could be made by the company directly into their individual schemes (assuming the schemes allow employer contributions). The company will obtain tax relief on the amount contributed but if this exceeds the individual's annual allowance available an annual allowance charge arises on the taxpayer at his marginal rate. The annual allowance available will be the current year's allowance (normally £40,000) plus any unused relief brought forward, less any contributions paid personally. See **Example A6** for more information. A deduction is only available against profits if paid wholly and exclusively for the benefit of the trade (see below).

Unlike salary, employer pension contributions do not involve the payment of PAYE or NI contributions, and unlike dividends they are under certain circumstances (see below) deductible for corporation tax. If £30,000 was available to pay a bonus for Mr Powell before 5 April 2017, to reduce corporation tax for the year ending 31 March 2017 by £6,000 (£30,000 @ 20%), the relative tax implications of salary and employer pension contribution would be:

| | *Salary* | *Pension contribution* |
|---|---|---|
| Salary/pension | 26,362 | 30,000 |
| Employer NIC @ 13.8% | 3,638 | nil |
| Cost to company | 30,000 | 30,000 |
| Income tax @ 40% | 10,545 | |
| Employee NIC @ 2% | 527 | |
| Cash available | 15,290 | |
| Payroll taxes cost | (14,710) | nil |
| Corporation tax saving @ 20% | 6,000 | 6,000 |
| Total tax (cost)/saving | (8,710) | 6,000 |

If Mr Powell is not in need of funds, he may well find a pension contribution of £30,000, at a cash cost of £24,000 (£30,000 – £6,000), extremely attractive. Should he die early, his fund could be passed tax-free to his family, and even if he has funds available after he reaches age 75, the family should be able to draw them as a taxable pension in due course, without suffering inheritance tax.

The pension contribution must be paid by the year-end, whereas an accrued bonus may be paid up to nine months after the year-end, to obtain a tax deduction.

Based on the above, for 2016/17, Mr Powell may be tempted to reduce his salary, increase dividends and consider pension contributions.

*Corporation tax relief for pension contributions*

Pension contributions paid by businesses are deductible only if expended wholly and exclusively for the purposes of the employer's trade. However, HMRC guidance specifies that it is the remuneration package in total that is considered for the wholly and exclusively test, and that the proportion of pension contributions to salary will not be relevant in the case of ordinary employees.

In the past there has been no objection to salaries at any level paid to owner-directors out of annual profits of their company, and no indication has been made that this attitude will change. Indeed, it would be hard to reconcile (for example) the IR35 rules with any limitation on payment of annual profits as remuneration.

HMRC has published in its Business Income Manual in BIM46001: Specific Deductions: Registered Pension Schemes guidance on deductibility of contributions in various circumstances, and the following paragraphs summarise the key points of this guidance.

Pension contributions, if tax deductible, are deductible only in the period they are paid, unless spread forward by tax law (which occurs if there is an increase of over 210% in contributions and the increase exceeds £500,000, see **Example A6**). If the accounts charge is different to the contribution paid, the computation must be adjusted to make it reflect the amount paid.

Contributions to registered pension schemes will always be treated as revenue expenditure, not capital expenditure.

Contributions to registered pension schemes forming part of a normal remuneration package will be tax deductible. The contribution is looked at in the context of the overall remuneration package, not a stand-alone amount. The proportion of pension contribution to other remuneration is not considered for this purpose, so salary sacrifice schemes for ordinary employees should not jeopardise the tax deduction. The annual contribution limits must be borne in mind, and individuals who are able to sacrifice a material amount of salary may be controlling directors, in which case the circumstances will be scrutinised separately.

The normal situation is that contributions will be tax deductible, except if there is an identifiable non-trade purpose, or a contribution of exceptional size.

One example would be a contribution made as part of arrangements for going out of business. It will be important to demonstrate that payments made towards cessation of a business are for the purposes of the trade. The guidance clearly specifies that payments made to fund shortfalls in company schemes under Pensions Act 1995 s 75 arise from obligations of the trade, and if made after cessation of trade are deductible as post-cessation expenses. If such a payment is made in the accounting period following cessation of trade, it will be treated as an expense of the final trading period.

The main focus of HMRC scrutiny is likely to be on directors, who are also controlling shareholders, or employees who are close relatives or friends (not defined) of the business proprietors or controlling directors.

If their total remuneration package (of which contributions are part) is similar to that of unconnected employees in genuinely similar work, then the contributions will be accepted as wholly and exclusively for the purposes of the trade. If not, the existing guidelines on amounts purporting to be remuneration of directors in BIM47105 will be followed, seeking to disallow all or some of the contribution.

There is case law that sets out some useful considerations to be borne in mind when deciding whether any item of expenditure is wholly and exclusively for the purposes of the trade. The following principles come from the judgement of Millett LJ *in Vodafone Cellular & Others v Shaw* (1996):

> 'To find out whether the payment was made for the purposes of the taxpayer's trade it is necessary to discover the taxpayer's object in making the payment. The general rule is that establishing the object behind making the payment involves an inquiry into the taxpayer's subjective intentions at the time of the payment.
>
> The "purposes of the trade" means "to serve the purposes of the trade".
>
> The "purposes of the trade" are not the same as "the purposes of the taxpayer".
>
> The "purposes of the trade" does not mean "for the benefit of the taxpayer".
>
> The "purpose for making the payment" is not the same as "the effect of the payment".'

### (vii) *Personal investment*

The company apparently has adequate cash resources taking into account its overdraft limit. The withdrawal of the £60,000 standing to the credit of Mr Powell's loan account would involve the company paying additional bank interest, but this would be tax relievable against its corporate profits, and Mr and Mrs Powell could personally use the £60,000 for tax-efficient investment, including utilising available personal pension contribution and ISA limits. (see **example A5**.)

For 2015/16 onwards, there is a starting rate of tax for savings of £5,000 at 0%, and in 2016/17 there is a savings nil rate band of £1,000 for basic rate taxpayers and £500 for higher rate taxpayers. It is unlikely that Mr Powell would be able to benefit from this starting rate, but Mrs Powell may be able to if she was a basic rate taxpayer and her non-savings income excluding dividends was below £16,000. In any event, the payment of interest on Mr Powell's director's loan account is a possibility provided his income remains within the higher rate band. This would provide additional deductible profits for the company and £500 of tax free income for Mr Powell. With no tax relief available for mortgage interest on house purchase loans, it may also be sensible to consider reducing the house mortgage.

### (viii) *Wills*

Leaving their estates to the other and failing that to the children ensures that no inheritance tax is payable on the first death (IHTA 1984 s 18), subject to any chargeable transfers within the seven years before death. FA 2008 s 10 provides for a claim to be made to transfer the unused portion of the nil-rate band of the first spouse to die to that of the surviving spouse, or civil partner, so that the nil-rate band, currently £325,000, will not be wasted.

A survivorship clause is recommended, denying the entitlement of the surviving spouse unless he/she survives the other by a stipulated period not exceeding six months (IHTA 1984 s 92). There is no point in the survivor inheriting the estate of the other in the unfortunate event of deaths in quick succession.

In considering both the wills and the proposed lifetime transfer of shares in P Transport Ltd for the benefit of the children, it is important to emphasise to the clients the practical dangers if a surviving parent were left with only a minority interest in their own company.

Care should also be taken to determine the possible source of any bequest to a discretionary fund or child on the first death. If that legacy were to include shares then a specific bequest is advisable to ensure that the relevant business property relief is given in full against that bequest. If the gift were to be part of residue with the balance to the spouse then the provisions in IHTA 1984 s 39A would apply to restrict the available relief.

It is likely that the residential enhancement to the nil rate band to be introduced from April 2017 will not apply to Mr and Mrs Powell, as the relief is tapered on gross estates of more than £2 million, and this would include the value of the shares in P Transport Ltd, even though they are likely to attract business property relief.

For detailed notes on inheritance tax see the companion to this book **Tolley's Taxwise II 2016/17**.

## (ix) *Pre-owned assets*

Although not immediately of concern to Mr and Mrs Powell, they should be made aware of the income tax implications of inheritance tax planning involving the gift of property and the subsequent use or enjoyment of that property by the donor. The provisions are contained in FA 2004 Sch 15.

A free-standing income tax charge applies to the benefit of using a property, chattel or intangible asset that was formerly owned by the taxpayer. A similar charge applies to the use of such property at low cost or to the use of such assets purchased with funds provided by the taxpayer.

The income tax charge does not apply:

(i) To property given away before 18 March 1986 (FA 2004 Sch 15 paras 3(2), 6(2) and 8(2)).

(ii) If the property was transferred to a spouse or civil partner (or to a former spouse/civil partner under a Court Order) (Sch 15 para 10(1)(c)). This also applied where the property is held in trust and the spouse/civil partner or former spouse/civil partner has an interest in possession (Sch 15 para 10(1)(d)).

(iii) If the property remains within the estate of the former owner for inheritance tax, or the 'Gift with Reservation' rules apply, then the income tax charge does not apply (Sch 15 para 11).

(iv) If the property was sold by the taxpayer at an arm's length price (Sch 15 para 10(1)(a)).

(v) Where the assets of an estate have been redirected by a deed of variation (IHTA 1984 ss 142–147) then the deed of variation applies to the asset from date of death for the pre-owned asset rules (Sch 15 para 16).

(vi) To property transferred into an interest in possession trust prior to 22 March 2006 for the benefit of the former owner. This is excluded from the income tax charge because the property remains in the estate of the donor for inheritance tax purposes. However the exemption ceases when the interest in possession comes to an end (Sch 15 para 10).

(vii) Where the gift is of property and the former owner has given part of their interest to someone with whom they share occupation or the former owner needs to move back into the gifted property following changes in circumstances (Sch 15 para 11(1)). These rules are the same as gift with reservation rules for inheritance tax.

(viii) Where the gift was in money and the gift had been made at least seven years before the donor first had use or enjoyment of the property acquired with the funds (Sch 15 para 10(2)(c)).

(ix) If the disposal was an outright gift covered by an annual exemption, small gifts exemption or was for the maintenance of the family (Sch 15 para 10(1)(d) and (e)).

(x) To the use of property that has been used in a commercial equity release scheme.

The pre-owned asset charge does not apply in any fiscal year:

(a) Where the former owner is not resident in the UK, or

(b) Where the former owner is resident in the UK but domiciled elsewhere for inheritance tax purposes, the charge then applies only to UK property, or

(c) Where the former owner was previously domiciled outside the UK for inheritance tax purposes the charge does not apply to property disposed of before becoming domiciled in the UK (Sch 15 para 12).

The income tax charge applies to the use of land or enjoyment of land, chattels and intangible assets. For the charge to apply to land the taxpayer must occupy the land (wholly or with others) and either the disposal condition, or the contribution condition must apply (Sch 15 para 3(1)).

Occupation is a very wide term and could even include usage for storage or sole possession of the means of access linked with occasional use of the property. Incidental usage is not considered to be occupation. This could include:

- Stays not exceeding two weeks each year (one month if the owner is present and it is the owner's residence).
- Social visits that do not include overnight stays.
- Domestic visits eg babysitting the owner's children.
- Temporary stays eg for convalescence after medical treatment or to look after the owner whilst they are convalescing.

However if the property is a holiday home which is only used on an occasional basis by the owner then even occasional visits by the donor could be deemed to be occupational.

The disposal condition is that after 17 March 1986 the taxpayer owned the relevant property or property the disposal of which has directly or indirectly funded the relevant property and has disposed of all or part of that interest otherwise than by an excluded transaction (see above).

The contribution condition is that the taxpayer has since 17 March 1986 contributed directly or indirectly to the purchase of the relevant property otherwise than by an excluded transaction. The charge for land is calculated by taking the appropriate rental value less any amount that the chargeable person is legally obliged to pay the owner of the relevant land in the period in respect of its occupation. The appropriate rental value is:

$R \times \frac{DV}{V}$ where

R is the rent that might reasonably be expected to be obtained on a year-to-year letting where the tenant pays all rates, charges and council taxes and the landlord bears the cost of repairs, maintenance and insurance.

DV is the contribution that can reasonably be attributed to the cost of the relevant property. If the property, or a property that this property replaced, was previously owned by the taxpayer, its value on valuation date. If the taxpayer only owned, or disposed of, a part of the land, the relevant proportion of its value.

See also companion book, **Tolley's Taxwise II 2016/17**, for inheritance tax provisions.

# Question

## Q1

Write a memorandum for colleagues summarising important points to bear in mind when designing tax planning solutions for high net worth clients to ensure they do not fall foul of HMRC's anti-avoidance strategy, including in particular points to watch in considering possible application of the general anti-abuse rule (GAAR), the regime for disclosure of tax avoidance scheme (DOTAS) and the rules about HMRC issuing an accelerated payment notice (APN). Outline how HMRC tries to guide taxpayers away from tax schemes, help them to unwind unsuccessful arrangements and force them to pay disputed tax and NICs.

## Q2

Outline the main requirements of the professional bodies' joint document on Professional Conduct in Relation to Taxation.

# Answer

## A1 Points to bear in mind regarding HMRC's anti-avoidance strategy, particularly the GAAR

### *(i) What type of arrangement is of concern?*

The types of transaction which are likely to be of interest to HMRC in reviewing tax avoidance include:

- transactions or arrangements that have no economic substance or which produce tax consequences that are not commensurate with the change in the taxpayer's (or group of related taxpayers') economic position;
- transactions or arrangements bearing little or no pre-tax profit which rely wholly or substantially on an anticipated tax reduction for significant post-tax profit;
- transactions or arrangements that result in a mismatch between:
  - the legal form or accounting treatment and economic substance;
  - the tax treatment for different parties or entities; or
  - the tax treatment in different jurisdictions,
- transactions or arrangements with little or no business, commercial or non-tax driver;
- transactions or arrangements involving contrived, artificial, transitory, pre-ordained or commercially unnecessary steps or transactions;
- transactions or arrangements where the income, gains, expenditure or losses falling within the UK tax net are not proportionate to the economic activity taking place or the value added in the UK;
- transactions or arrangements designed to sidestep the effect of tax provisions which target particular transactions or arrangements to give them a particular tax result.

The general anti-abuse rule (GAAR) does not include a definition of tax avoidance - it targets tax arrangements which have a main purpose (with or without other main purposes) of the obtaining of a tax advantage. However, its UK-wide impact is restricted only to arrangements which are 'abusive' (Finance Act 2013 s 206(1)), although the Scottish GAAR, which currently relates principally to property transactions, is wider, targeting 'avoidance' rather than the more serious 'abuse'. A tax advantage specifically includes a tax relief or increase in a tax relief, a tax repayment or increased repayment, the avoidance of or reduction in an assessment or charge to tax (or a possible charge to tax), the deferral of a tax charge or bringing forward of a tax repayment or the avoidance of an obligation to deduct or account for tax.

The above interpretations also apply in considering what HMRC might see as avoidance of liability to National Insurance Contributions.

The first point to bear in mind in designing tax planning solutions is therefore that any solution that could appear to be predominantly tax-motivated and which falls within the list above has an increased chance of triggering an HMRC enquiry.

If a person simply takes up available tax reliefs by taking the actions that the Government aims to encourage by offering tax incentives, this is not usually seen as avoidance. Likewise, a choice to enter into the more tax-efficient option where there are two equivalent ways of achieving the same business result (such as a decision to lease or buy an asset) is not of itself seen as avoidance, although HMRC will often seek to characterise anything with a hint of tax saving possibility as 'avoidance' (eg, the choice of whether to provide services through an unincorporated business or a one-man company, which can lead to lower tax and NIC liabilities if income is taken by way of dividend, or the choice of a trader whose turnover is below the VAT threshold whether to register voluntarily for VAT because the flat rate scheme confers a marginal advantage).

## *(ii) HMRC anti-avoidance strategy*

The published HMRC anti-avoidance strategy (operated through its Counter-Avoidance Directorate) has several main themes: making tax law robust, sharing HMRC's views on what constitutes avoidance, improving HMRC's knowledge about avoidance and optimising its operational response to avoidance.

### Tax law changes

HMRC aims to prevent and close down avoidance by legislation. This includes legislation which has immediate effect from the date of announcement, which can be at any time of year.

### HMRC's views

HMRC also periodically publishes 'Spotlights' on avoidance, setting out its view about particular types of arrangement which it sees as avoidance which is technically unsound (and thus not needing any change in the law). It is likely systematically to challenge any use of arrangements that have featured in 'Spotlights'. This means that although HMRC's view may not prove to be right, use of the arrangement will come at the additional cost of dealing with their challenge.

It is therefore worth regularly checking HMRC announcements to ensure that the tax law in point for any tax planning solution has not changed by an unscheduled announcement and that it is not similar in character to anything mentioned in 'Spotlights'.

### HMRC's knowledge about avoidance

In addition to internal monitoring and collation of what officers have identified as possible avoidance, HMRC gathers information via the Disclosure of Tax Avoidance Schemes (DOTAS) regime (see FA 2004, Part 7). That regime applies to arrangements the main benefit (or one of the main benefits) of which is to enable a person to obtain an advantage in relation to any of the taxes covered. It requires full details of a tax arrangement to be submitted to HMRC if it carries certain 'hallmarks' (or meets certain descriptions in the case of SDLT and IHT) and the adviser plans to offer it, or any element within it, to more than one client or potential client. A tight time limit applies in that the report to HMRC has to be made within 5 days of making the scheme available. Disclosure does not necessarily mean that HMRC will see the arrangement as avoidance or that they will even ask any questions, but there are significant penalties for non-compliance with the DOTAS regime.

Once a scheme or arrangement has been notified, HMRC will issue a scheme reference number, which must be passed on to the client for inclusion on his first tax return affected by the arrangement. Depending on the nature of the arrangement, this may result in a raised risk of challenge from HMRC. Advisers have to make a quarterly return to HMRC of the clients to whom they have issued scheme reference numbers. The DOTAS regime applies to Income Tax, Corporation Tax, Capital Gains Tax, Stamp Duty Land Tax, Inheritance Tax and National Insurance Contributions.

There is a separate disclosure regime for VAT. This is different, in that it requires disclosure of the use of listed schemes.

### Challenging schemes

HMRC challenges schemes by opening enquiries into taxpayers' returns and, after establishing the facts, issuing closure notices that deny the claimed tax advantage, or issuing determinations or notices setting out any unpaid liabilities. Taxpayers may appeal to the tribunal against such assessments.

Because HMRC faces a large number of cases arising from marketed schemes in which the facts are often subtly different, and each dispute may take years to resolve, it does not have the resources to litigate every case. Instead, it usually drives a sample or test case through the courts while, at the same time, using the ongoing litigation as a lever to persuade other taxpayers in similar schemes to abandon their claims to tax savings and settle any unpaid tax, sometimes offering a 'settlement' or 'resolution' opportunity on marginally favourable terms as an alternative to lengthy and costly litigation.

The diversity of planning arrangements has made it difficult for HMRC to challenge many of them, but it now has the power to enforce collection of any disputed tax and contributions in advance of a final decision. Before FA 2014, there was no incentive for taxpayers and scheme promoters to expedite cases because HMRC could not collect the claimed amounts while they were subject to appeal. In particular, SSAA 1992, s 117A specifically instructs county courts to adjourn NIC arrears cases automatically where an appeal against a notice of decision is unresolved, meaning that HMRC could only collect the arrears once it had litigated the case successfully and any tribunal or higher court appeal had been settled. Some scheme promoters have been known to use HMRC's inability to litigate quickly as a selling point for their product, with the worst outcome purportedly expected to be that the taxpayer might have to pay the tax due many years in the future, perhaps with some statutory interest charges.

FA 2014, Pt 4 took steps to address this state of affairs for tax purposes by instituting a new regime of follower notices (FNs) and accelerated payment notices (APNs). In summary, where a taxpayer has used an avoidance scheme that has been defeated in the courts, or that is a DOTAS-registered scheme subject to an enquiry or appeal, HMRC now has the power to require payment of the disputed amounts irrespective of whether the enquiry has been concluded or the appeal decided. In effect, the taxpayer has to deposit the disputed tax with HMRC while the dispute is pursued, which provides a serious financial disincentive to taxpayers who to date have simply paid nothing while deferring any arguments as HMRC slowly built its case against the scheme or schemes in question.

While most of these new rules began to take effect from Royal Assent to FA 2014, equivalent rules for NIC purposes, suitably adjusted to reflect the differences between the tax and NIC regimes, required separate primary legislation, which eventually followed in NICA 2015 on 12 February 2015, although apart from the regulation-making powers the relevant sections only took effect two months later on 12 April 2015.

The rules affect all outstanding disputes, whether or not the scheme or schemes in question predated the DOTAS regime introduced by FA 2004.

### Follower notices (FNs)

In outline, HMRC is now empowered to issue a FN in respect of schemes where the application of a judicial ruling in favour of HMRC in another taxpayer's case would deny the tax advantage claimed by the taxpayer in his return. FA 2014, s 204 provides that a FN can be issued to taxpayers where:

- there is an open tax enquiry or tax appeal in relation to a relevant tax;
- a tax advantage arises from the tax arrangement;
- there is, in HMRC's opinion, a relevant judicial ruling in favour of HMRC in another taxpayer's case that has become final; and
- no previous FN has been given to the taxpayer by reference to the same tax advantage.

Whether a judicial ruling is relevant is determined by FA 2014 s 205, and the content of a FN is set by FA 2014, s 206. It is not yet clear how tightly or loosely HMRC will attempt to compare schemes in dispute with schemes that have been examined by the tribunals and higher courts. HMRC has claimed success in 80% of court challenges to schemes in recent years, although this does not necessarily mean that 80% of schemes have been defeated, since many of them involve the use of employee benefit trusts and HMRC has won and lost in EBT cases, as they come in various shapes and sizes, so it remains to be seen whether follower notices will be of wide relevance.

Where a decision thought to be final is in fact reopened because the taxpayer in question is granted leave to appeal out of time, FA 2014, s 216 provides that HMRC must suspend any FN issued pending a final outcome. If the original case on which the FN is based is decided on a basis that shows it not to be relevant to the current case, the FN ceases to have effect once the suspension ends.

The taxpayer is permitted, within 90 days of the issue of the FN, to make written representations to HMRC objecting to the notice, but while HMRC must consider any such representations it is entitled to reject them and there is no further right of appeal. The only grounds for objection are that the conditions of issue under FA 2014, s 204 were not met, that the judicial ruling specified in the notice was not relevant to the arrangements in question (such as where the scheme under challenge was a variant of a scheme that has been litigated), or that the notice was not given in time (ie, within 12 months of the date of the judicial ruling on which HMRC seeks to rely or, if later, the day the return or claim in dispute was received by HMRC, or the day the tax appeal was made).

Where a notice is based on a judicial ruling made before 17 July 2014, the date of Royal Assent to FA 2014, HMRC's window for issuing the notice is 24 months from Royal Assent or, if later, 12 months from the date of submission of the relevant disputed return or claim.

The taxpayer is required to take 'corrective action' by amending the relevant return or claim to remove the denied tax advantage, or to enter into a written agreement with HMRC to relinquish the denied advantage. These actions must be taken within 90 days of the issue of the FN or, if representations are made about the validity or accuracy of the notice, within the same 90-day period or, if later, within 30 days from the date on which the taxpayer is notified of HMRC's determination in response to the representations. The taxpayer is liable to pay a 50% penalty (mitigable to 10% for cooperation) if the necessary corrective action is not taken.

## Accelerated payment notices (APNs)

While a FN can be used to enforce the amendment of a return to show the correct liability, it does not alone enforce payment by a taxpayer of a disputed amount, especially if there is an outstanding appeal against an assessment or amended self-assessment. HMRC has therefore also been empowered to serve accelerated payment notices (APNs) on many avoidance scheme users, requiring them to pay any disputed amounts, generally within 90 days of the issue of the notice. Tax collected is regarded as a payment on account of the ultimate liability and is refundable if the scheme user, or a user of the same scheme, establishes in court that the scheme succeeded. A court challenge to HMRC's original assessments is not ruled out, but the taxpayer is required to pay any disputed taxes on account until those assessments are withdrawn or finalised.

The APN and FN elements to the anti-avoidance regime are separate but related. APNs apply to schemes required to be registered under DOTAS (the Disclosure of Tax Avoidance Schemes) rules and can be issued if:

- there is an open enquiry or an open appeal;
- there is a tax advantage arising from the particular tax arrangement; and
- either:
  - HMRC has issued a FN;
  - the arrangement was registered under DOTAS, in which case the taxpayer should have included a Scheme Reference Number (SRN) on the tax return or will have otherwise notified HMRC of a SRN; or
  - a GAAR counteraction notice has been given in respect of the arrangement.

No right of appeal against an APN is available to taxpayers. HMRC will contact the taxpayer before an APN is issued and the taxpayer may, within 90 days of issue, make written representations to argue that the conditions for issuing the APN were not met, or dispute the amount of the payment demanded, but while HMRC must 'consider' any such representations, it can reject them.

Where the APN is issued while a tax enquiry is open, the taxpayer must pay on account the disputed tax specified in the notice, within 90 days of the date of issue or, if the taxpayer has made representations to challenge the validity or accuracy of the notice, 30 days after the issue of HMRC's determination in response to the representations, if that is later than the original 90-day deadline.

Penalties will be applied for failure to comply with an APN: initially, 5% of the tax due if the amount levied by the APN is not paid within 90 days of its issue or, if later, 30 days after HMRC's determination of the taxpayer's representations challenging the accuracy of the figure. A further 5% penalty will be added if the amount remains unpaid after five months, and an additional 5% penalty for failure to pay within eleven months.

Provisions on the withdrawal, modification or suspension of APNs and on their application to partners and partnerships are contained in FA 2014, ss 227-228 and Sch 32 respectively.

A judicial review of the APN rules in mid-2015 was reported as *Rowe, Worrall v CIR* [2015] EWHC 2293, which was a lead case for a group of investors who had participated in a film production arrangement that had not yet reached the First-tier Tribunal. As noted above, there is no right of appeal against an APN that meets the stated conditions and is correctly calculated, so the only legal challenge open to affected taxpayers is by way of judicial review proceedings, which could result in HMRC actions or the law being struck down in the event of a breach of natural justice, ultra vires actions, a breach of legitimate expectation, irrational official actions or incompatibility with human rights, including retrospection and proportionality. The High Court dismissed the appeal on all grounds.

However, in January 2016, it was reported that HMRC had withdrawn some 2,000 APNs issued in March 2015 because the conditions for their issue had not been satisfied. The case in question involved IR35 Manx partnerships dating as far back as 2004 that had not needed to be notified under the DOTAS regime but had been so notified as a precautionary measure by promoters who were concerned about the potential penalties for failure to notify. HMRC apologised for its technically incorrect actions. The fact that the scheme had been notified and that a SRN had been issued was insufficient to meet one of the conditions for the use by HMRC of an APN.

In June 2016 it was also reported that HMRC had decided to withdraw hundreds more APNs issued to taxpayers involved in EBT arrangements that were technically not notifiable schemes, rather than await the outcome of a further judicial review application.

It is also known that HMRC's rush to issue APNs led it to overlook the conditions in a number of other cases. For example, it has been reported that a taxpayer first discovered that the arrangement he had been using had been challenged when he was visited by a debt collector seeking to enforce an APN. The APN was withdrawn by HMRC when it was pointed out that the taxpayer had not received a notice of assessment before the time of issue of the APN, so there could have been no open appeal that would fulfil one of the preconditions for the issue.

### *(iii) GAAR*

The general anti-abuse rule (GAAR) was introduced in Finance Act 2013 Part 5. It applies to Income Tax, Corporation Tax, Capital Gains Tax, Petroleum Revenue Tax, Inheritance Tax, Stamp Duty Land Tax and the annual tax on enveloped dwellings. It is also to applied to National Insurance by means of National Insurance Contributions Act 2014 s 10, which treats NICs as tax for this purpose.

The GAAR applies to tax arrangements for which it would be reasonable to conclude that the obtaining of a tax advantage was the main purpose or one of the main purposes of the arrangements and. If those arrangements are 'abusive' provides for the tax advantages arising from them to be countered by adjustments made either though the self-assessment process or by means of assessment, amendment or disallowance of a claim by HMRC.

The stated intention of Parliament in connection with the GAAR is that it not intended to apply to legitimate tax planning. The legislation therefore focuses only on abusive arrangements, defined as those which, if entered into or carried out, cannot reasonably be regarded as a reasonable course of action in relation to the relevant tax provisions, having regard to all the circumstances. The circumstances considered include whether the result of the arrangements is consistent with any principles underlying the relevant tax law, whether the arrangements include any contrived or abnormal steps and whether the arrangements are intended to exploit any shortcomings in the tax statute.

HMRC's guidance on the GAAR shows that straightforward decisions between two courses of action both envisaged by Parliament but with different tax outcomes are not caught, nor is a course of action which is widely accepted and long-established as normal conduct on the part of individuals or business.

HMRC cannot take action under the GAAR without referring the case to the GAAR Advisory Panel, made up of (non-HMRC) individuals experienced in tax matters whose function is to advise HMRC on the 'reasonableness' of the arrangements.

It follows from the above that most ordinary tax planning arrangements should be outside the scope of the GAAR, but arrangements including particularly novel structures or arrangements that the client finds difficult to understand may be at risk.

### *(iv) Purpose/motive tests*

A common approach in anti-avoidance legislation, including DOTAS and the GAAR, is for the legislation to depend on applying a test that looks at the main purpose of the transaction or arrangement or the motive of the taxpayer to see whether that purpose or motive is to obtain a beneficial tax result, often called a 'tax advantage', which can be a lower tax bill, a higher repayment, a timing advantage or even a get-out from an obligation to deduct and account for tax, eg under PAYE or the Construction Industry Scheme.

If the predominant outcome of a particular arrangement is a beneficial tax result, HMRC are likely to assume that such a result was either a main purpose of the arrangement or that the taxpayer's motive in entering into the arrangement was to gain that beneficial tax result, unless there is evidence to the contrary.

HMRC do not see the mere existence of a commercial or other non-tax purpose as enough to prevent that the tax purpose being a main purpose, but obviously the more significant or more numerous the non-tax reasons for the course of action taken, the less likely it is that the arrangement will fall foul of a motive or purpose test.

It is therefore important to establish all the reasons associated with the course of action taken by the client, which has incorporated the tax planning. Where the client is a company, it is helpful to have those non-tax reasons clearly set out in Board minutes or in option evaluation papers submitted to the Board.

### *(v) Summary of points to bear in mind*

- Is the area of tax in question subject of a recently announced change in the law?
- Has the tax planning in question featured on HMRC's Spotlight pages? If so, and HMRC's reasoning does not seem sound, what is the client's attitude to the increased risk of HMRC challenge and consequent increased cost?
- Does the tax planning in question come within the DOTAS regime? If so, a report needs to be made, within 5 days of first offering to a client, to HMRC who will issue a scheme reference number. That scheme reference number then needs to be included in the client's tax return for the first period affected by the arrangement in question. Again it is worth ascertaining the client's attitude to the increased risk of HMRC challenge and consequent increased cost.
- Is the tax planning solution likely to come within the scope of the GAAR? If it features novel structures or arrangements that need a good deal of explanation to the client, it will be worth considering whether HMRC would question the 'reasonableness' of the course of action proposed.
- What non-tax reasons are associated with the planning in question? Contemporaneous evidence of non-tax reasons for the course of action undertaken can be an effective defence against any HMRC challenge that an arrangement represents tax avoidance.

## A2 PCRT

The joint professional bodies' statement on Professional Conduct in Relation to Taxation ('PCRT') sets out the fundamental principles of behaviour and ethical standards for tax professionals, which are:

- Integrity
- Objectivity
- Professional competence and due care
- Confidentiality
- Professional behaviour

In relation to tax planning, PCRT reminds members of the professional bodies that tax planning is legal and taxpayers are entitled to enter into transactions that reduce tax or to take interpretations of legislation that HMRC may not agree with. If HMRC wishes to challenge a particular transaction or interpretation, it may amend the return or issue an assessment accordingly. The client may then appeal against HMRC's decision through the tax tribunals and courts if necessary, with the associated costs. Ultimately only the courts can determine whether a particular piece of tax planning is legally effective or not. However, a member should always advise the client that there may be wider reputational issues in such circumstances.

Tax avoidance has become a subject of public debate, raising ethical challenges. Members are warned that involvement in certain arrangements could subject them and their clients to greater compliance requirements, scrutiny or investigation, as well as criticism from the media, government and other stakeholders, and difficulties in obtaining professional indemnity insurance cover, because claims against advisers after the failure in the courts of a number of schemes have caused insurers to re-assess whether they will offer cover to firms that market or implement avoidance schemes.

'Avoidance' is not defined in the tax legislation, and judges have to attempt to discern the intention of Parliament, relying on or providing interpretations in case law. The varying perceptions of different stakeholders makes conflict with HMRC and coverage in the media unpredictable.

This does not only affect the perception of clients trying to save tax. When giving tax advice, members must also consider the potential negative impact of their actions on the public perception of the integrity of the members themselves and the tax profession more generally.

A member is required to act with professional competence and due care within the scope of his engagement letter. A member should understand his client's expectations around tax advice or tax planning, and ensure that engagement letters reflect the member's role and responsibilities, including limitations in or amendments to that role, and should make the client aware of any uncertainties and risks in the planning.

A member does not have to advise on or recommend tax planning which he does not consider to be appropriate or otherwise does not align with his own business principles and ethics. However, in this situation the member may need to ensure that the advice he does not wish to give is outside the scope of his engagement. If the member may owe a legal duty of care to the client to advise in this area, the member should ensure that he complies with this by, for example, advising the client that there are opportunities that the client could undertake, even though the member is unwilling to assist, and recommending that the client seeks alternative advice. Any such discussions should be well documented by the member.

Ultimately it is the client's decision as to what planning is appropriate, having received advice, and taking into account their own broader commercial objectives and ethical stance. It is advisable to ensure that the basis for recommended tax planning is clearly identified in documentation.

Where a client advises a member that he intends to proceed with a tax planning arrangement without taking full advice from him on the relevant issues or despite the advice the member has given, the member should warn the client of the potential risks of proceeding without full advice and ensure that the restriction in the scope of the member's advice is recorded in writing.

Where a client wishes to pursue a claim for a tax advantage which the member feels has no sustainable basis the member should consider whether he can continue to act, bearing in mind the fundamental requirements of PCRT and the fact that the client's tax affairs may become irregular if the claim is pursued.

A member should keep sufficient appropriate records of discussions and advice and when dealing with irregularities the member should:

- Give the client appropriate advice.
- If necessary, so long as he continues to act for the client, seek to persuade the client to behave correctly.
- Take care not to appear to be assisting a client to plan or commit any criminal offence or to conceal any offence which has been committed.
- In appropriate situations, or where in doubt, discuss the client's situation with a colleague or an independent third party (having due regard to client confidentiality).
- Resign from the appointment if necessary.
- Consider AML obligations.
- Consider whether insurers should be notified.

If Counsel's opinion is sought on the planning the member should consider including the question as to whether in Counsel's view the GAAR could apply to the transaction, as well as bearing in mind that any legal opinion provided will be based on the assumptions stated in the instructions for the opinion, and on execution of the arrangement exactly as stated. HMRC and the courts will not be constrained by these assumptions.

A member must never be knowingly involved in tax evasion. It is acceptable to act for clients who need help in rectifying their affairs, but members must demonstrate the highest levels of integrity in doing so, and comply with the general law, including anti-money laundering rules.

A member should also ensure that he is aware of the scope and potential application of the GAAR. He should put appropriate measures in place commensurate with the size of his practice or business and the extent to which he is involved in areas where the GAAR will need to be considered. Measures which may be considered include:

- Training.
- Technical briefing or guidance material linking to and potentially supplementing HMRC's GAAR Guidance.
- Protocols to ensure the quality and consistency of treatment. If a member is unsure or does not have the expertise to advise he may wish to seek specialist input or refer the client to a specialist adviser.
- Raising awareness with clients or internally in the business, especially for those whose affairs may be more complex or who may undertake planning with other advisers.
- Caveat advice to explain that the GAAR is new with no precedent (or little precedent as some precedents begin to emerge) and given this uncertainty the member cannot guarantee that it will not be applied.
- Covering letters for returns might refer to the GAAR for clients whose affairs may be more complex or who may undertake planning with other advisers.
- Updating knowledge materials to ensure that they refer to the GAAR where appropriate.
- Reviewing any existing offerings which might be affected by the GAAR.
- Monitoring output of the GAAR panel.

## Explanatory Notes

(1) FA 2013 Sch 21 introduced a new general anti-abuse rule ('GAAR') which is intended to counteract the 'tax advantages' arising from 'tax arrangements' which are 'abusive'. The rule applies to tax arrangements entered into on or after 17 July 2013 (the date of Royal Assent to the Finance Act 2013) or 13 March 2014 for NIC schemes (the date of Royal Assent to the NIC Act 2014). It is important to note that HMRC must first have approval from an independent panel before they can use the GAAR provisions. The GAAR applies to a range of taxes including income tax, corporation tax and capital gains tax.

Arrangements are '*tax arrangements*' if, having regard to all the circumstances, it would be reasonable to conclude that the obtaining of a tax advantage was the main purpose, or one of the main purposes, of the arrangements. For this purpose, *'arrangements'* include any agreement, understanding, scheme, transaction or series of transactions, whether or not legally enforceable.

Tax arrangements are *'abusive'* if entering into them or carrying them out cannot reasonably be regarded as a reasonable course of action in relation to the relevant tax provisions, having regard to all the circumstances. Those circumstances include:

- whether the substantive results of the arrangements are consistent with any express or implied principles on which the provisions are based and their policy objectives;
- whether the means of achieving the results of the arrangements involve one or more contrived or abnormal steps; and
- whether the arrangements are intended to exploit any shortcomings in the provisions.

Where the tax arrangements form part of other arrangements regard must be had to those other arrangements (but see the commencement rules above where the other arrangements were entered into before 17 July 2013).

The legislation gives the following non-exhaustive examples of what might indicate that tax arrangements are abusive.

- The arrangements result in taxable income, profits or gains significantly less than the economic amount.
- The arrangements result in a tax deduction or loss significantly greater than the economic amount.
- The arrangements result in a claim for repayment or crediting of tax, including foreign tax, that has not been, and is unlikely to be, paid.

The legislation also gives an example of what might indicate that arrangements are not abusive: the arrangements accord with established practice accepted by HMRC.

A '*tax advantage*' includes relief or increased relief from tax, repayment or increased repayment of tax, avoidance or reduction of a charge or assessment to tax, avoidance of a possible assessment to tax or of an obligation to deduct or account for tax, deferral of a payment of tax, and advancement of a repayment tax.

The GAAR operates by counteracting the tax advantage under the tax arrangements by HMRC or the taxpayer making adjustments that are just and reasonable. Adjustments can be made by assessment, modification of an assessment, amendment or disallowance of a claim or otherwise. An adjustment can impose a tax liability where there would not otherwise be one or can increase an existing liability. Adjustments may be made in respect of the tax in question or any other tax to which the GAAR applies. Adjustments have effect for all tax purposes. The normal time limits for making assessments etc apply to the making of GAAR adjustments. The counteraction (the tax assessment) will not always be the maximum possible amount of tax, but must take into account reasonable decisions by the taxpayer if the arrangements are held to be abusive by the GAAR panel.

HMRC must follow the legislative procedures before making an adjustment under the GAAR. If HMRC does utilise the GAAR to amend a taxpayer's tax position then the taxpayer should be entitled to make amendments to his tax return as if the arrangements had not taken place.

Consequential adjustments can be made for any period and may affect any person, whether or not a party to the tax arrangements. Adjustments are made on a just and reasonable basis but cannot increase a person's liability to any tax. HMRC must notify the person who made the claim of any adjustments made in writing. Consequential adjustments can be made by assessment, modification of an assessment, amendment of a claim or otherwise. There are no time limits for making such an adjustment.

The procedure for claims made outside a return in TMA 1970 Sch 1A applies to claims for consequential adjustments for income tax, capital gains tax and corporation tax purposes. See FA 2013 s 207(6) for the procedure rules for other taxes.

In any court or Tribunal proceedings in connection with the GAAR, HMRC must show both that the tax arrangements are abusive and that the adjustments made to counteract the tax advantage are just and reasonable.

In making a decision in connection with the GAAR a court or Tribunal must take into account any HMRC guidance on the GAAR which was approved by the GAAR Advisory Panel at the time the tax arrangements were entered into and also any opinion of the sub-panel about the arrangements in question.

The GAAR can override any priority rule in tax legislation, ie any rule to the effect that particular provisions have effect to the exclusion of, or otherwise in priority to, anything else.

The GAAR is supported by detailed guidance, issued and regularly updated by HMRC and approved by the GAAR panel. HMRC is required by statute to issue guidance and obtain approval of the guidance before issuing it. The current version of the Guidance falls into parts A, B and C, which are published as a single document. These are accompanied by detailed examples of the application of the GAAR in part D. Part E of the guidance deals with the administrative process. This guidance can be accessed at https://www.gov.uk/government/publications/tax-avoidance-general-anti-abuse-rules.

Advisers should be aware of the guidance to the GAAR, as it provides context for the intention of the legislation and how it will be used by HMRC, the courts and the GAAR panel. It makes clear that basic tax planning, and even some quite sophisticated schemes are still acceptable, and that the limit of acceptable tax planning is when it becomes "abusive" as defined above. The examples provide a wealth of insight into not only permitted tax planning and that which is considered abusive, but also the methodology to be adopted when applying the GAAR to a particular situation.

Practical experience of the GAAR is very limited and it is understood that not a single case has yet been referred to the GAAR Panel.

During summer 2015 a consultation was launched regarding the detail of introducing a GAAR penalty regime as well as measures to strengthen the GAAR further. A penalty of up to 60%, based on the value of the counteraction adjustment, was legislated in FA 2016, Schedule 18, for taxpayers who are defeated in a dispute about a scheme after having been formally warned about the possibility of the scheme's failure and their ensuing liabilities.

## Scottish GAAR

(2) The Scottish GAAR (operated by Revenue Scotland under a statutory duty under section 3(2)(d) of the Revenue Scotland and Tax Powers Act 2014 to protect the revenue against tax evasion and tax avoidance) – and the proposed Welsh GAAR, yet to be legislated –currently relate only to devolved taxes such as the Scottish land & buildings transaction tax and Scottish landfill tax. They are anti-avoidance rules rather than anti-abuse rules, and therefore of slightly wider scope than the UK GAAR.

Revenue Scotland is empowered to counteract any tax avoidance arrangements relating to the devolved taxes which it considers artificial. The principal rule providing for counteraction is the Scottish General Anti-Avoidance Rule (or 'Scottish GAAR') which is set out in Part 5 of the RSTPA 2014.

The Scottish GAAR looks for two conditions to be met:

- Is entering into or carrying out the arrangement a reasonable course of action in relation to the tax legislation in question?
- Does the tax avoidance arrangement lack economic or commercial substance?

Arrangements that are not artificial as defined by RSTPA 2014 are not liable to counteraction under the Scottish GAAR.

The Scottish GAAR is intended to operate in tandem with Targeted Anti-Avoidance Rules (TAARs) contained in devolved tax legislation (the LBTT(S)A 2013 and LT(S)A 2014 ) and the 'Ramsay principle' of purposive statutory interpretation applied by the Scottish courts and tribunals (see *Aberdeen Asset Management v HMRC* [2013] CSIH 84). The Scottish GAAR is therefore inconsistent with the doctrine in *Ayrshire Pullman Motor Services v IRC* [1929] 14 TC 754, a case in which Lord Clyde observed that 'no man in this country is under the smallest obligation, moral or other, so to arrange his legal relations to his business or to his property as to enable the Inland Revenue to put the largest possible shovel into his stores'. Until the recent change of judicial attitude to avoidance schemes, a taxpayer was 'entitled to be astute to prevent, so far as he honestly [could], the depletion of his means by the Revenue.' In the 1949 case of *Lord Vestey's Executors & Vestey v CIR*, Lord Normand held that 'tax avoidance is an evil, but it would be the beginning of much greater evils if the courts were to overstretch the language of the statute in order to subject to taxation people of whom they disapproved.' Times have changed.

In relation to LBTT, the Scottish GAAR allows for counteraction measures to be taken in a wider range of circumstances than is the case for UK Stamp Duty Land Tax (SDLT). The Scottish GAAR is therefore wider than the anti-avoidance provisions of sections 75A to 75C of the Finance Act 2003 and the UK GAAR in Part 5 of Finance Act 2013.

The Scottish GAAR provisions have potential effect in relation to all tax avoidance arrangements entered into on or after 1 April 2015, unless actions were taken before that date relating to the post-1 April 2015 arrangements that support the view that those later arrangements were not artificial.

# Question

(a) Explain the tax reliefs available to encourage venture capital investment in small and medium sized entities (SMEs);

(b) Compare and contrast the seed enterprise investment scheme with the enterprise investment scheme;

(c) Summarise the key aspects of the relief available for qualifying investments in disadvantaged communities.

# Answer

## (a) Venture capital investment schemes

There are three tax-favoured schemes to encourage venture capital investment. These are the venture capital trust scheme (VCTs), the enterprise investment scheme (EIS) and the seed enterprise investment scheme (SEIS).

There has been a longstanding concern about a funding gap for SMEs in the UK. Following the Wilson Committee in the late 1970s, the Thatcher government first introduced tax incentives to encourage an increase in equity venture capital for such businesses. This was the business start up scheme which developed into the business expansion scheme (BES). However, as a result of perceived abuses of the BES, various restrictions and limitations were introduced into that scheme which have carried over into later tax-favoured schemes.

The BES was replaced in the early 1990s by the EIS. The EIS provides an income tax relief, an exemption from capital gains tax (CGT) on sale, CGT or income tax relief for a loss on disposal and deferral of CGT.

In addition, the alignment of CGT rates with income tax rates in 1988 had caused a concern that the high levels of CGT exacerbated the funding gap for SMEs by reducing the capital being reinvested. This concern led to a reinvestment relief being introduced which was a CGT-only relief. In 1998, reinvestment relief was merged into the EIS and created the confusing two strand nature of EIS relief (income tax relief/CGT exemption as mentioned earlier and CGT deferral-only relief).

Whilst the above reliefs were focused on individual entities, in the early 1990s it was believed that investors should be given a tax break to invest in a pooled fund of such investments, a unit trust of venture capital investments, and so VCTs were introduced.

The tax reliefs available under the EIS and for VCTs have changed considerably over time. This has created a number of legacy and transitional issues and, for instance, older VCTs may still have deferred gains (which could even qualify for entrepreneurs' relief on disposal in some circumstances). Many government reviews, refocusing of reliefs and research projects have added to the changes and made the reliefs more complex. European Union state aid concerns have added to this mix, and thankfully, occasionally, some simplifications and relaxations to the various rules have been introduced.

The outcome of this history is that VCT investors are not considered to be motivated to invest by mitigating CGT, only by reducing income tax, and so VCTs now only provide an income tax credit of 30% of the amount subscribed. Conversely, EIS investment is considered to be heavily motivated by CGT and so extensive CGT reliefs are included in the current relief as well as a 30% income tax credit. A concern over the unattractiveness of investing in small scale start-ups led to the introduction in April 2012 of the SEIS. This has a higher level of tax reliefs than EIS (including a 50% income tax relief) but is more restrictive.

## (b) SEIS v EIS

The key differences between SEIS and EIS (with income tax relief) are set out in the following table:

| | *SEIS* | *EIS* |
|---|---|---|
| *Maximum investment (individual)* | £100,000 per annum (ITA 2007 s 257AB(2)(b)) | £1m per annum (ITA 2007 s 158(2)(b)) |
| *Maximum investment (company)* | £150,000 (total) (ITA 2007 s 257DL) | £5m from all schemes in any 12 month period (ITA 2007 s 173A(1)); £12m (total) for all companies except for knowledge-intensive companies where the limit is £20m (total) (ITA 2007 ss 173AA, 173AB) * |

| | *SEIS* | *EIS* |
|---|---|---|
| *Maximum age (company)* | Less than two years old; company must not have previously carried on a trade (ITA 2007 s 257HF) | Less than seven years old when it receives its first relevant investment (10 years if it is a knowledge-intensive company) although there is no time limit where the issuing company receives follow-on funding from the initial EIS investment (ITA 2007 s 175A) * |
| *Rate of income tax relief* | 50% (ITA 2007 s 257AB) | 30% (ITA 2007 s 158) |
| *Directors* | Paid directors not excluded (ITA 2007 s 257BA) | Paid directors excluded, subject to carve-outs for directors whose entitlement to remuneration does not start until after the acquisition of shares (ITA 2007 ss 166-169) |
| *Number of employees (full-time equivalent)* | Fewer than 25 (ITA 2007 s 257DJ) | Fewer than 250 (ITA 2007 s 186A); Fewer than 500 if it is a knowledge-intensive company * |
| *Gross assets* | £200,000 before (ITA 2007 s 257DI) | £15m before and £16m after investment (ITA 2007 s 186) |
| *Use of money* | Must be used within three years (ITA 2007 s 257CC); | Must be used for the purpose of the qualifying trade within two years (ITA 2007 s 175(3)) |
| *Trading* | Company must use 70% of money for qualifying trade before claim for approval (and tax relief) can be made (ITA 2007 ss 257EB-257ED) | Company must have traded or carried on qualifying R&D for four months before a claim for approval (ITA 2007 ss 176, 179) |
| *Subsidiaries* | Can have subsidiaries, subject to conditions (ITA 2007 ss 257DM-257DN, 257HJ; ITA 2007 s 191) | Can have subsidiaries, subject to conditions (ITA 2007 ss 187-191) |
| *CGT reliefs* | The amount subscribed can be set against capital gains made as follows (TCGA 1992 Sch 5BB para 1):<br>2012/13; 100%<br>2013/14 onwards: 50% | Capital gains can be deferred (TCGA 1992 Sch 5B) |

For the definition of knowledge-intensive companies, see **explanatory note 5**.

It should not be assumed that SEIS is definitely a better option than EIS and both reliefs should be carefully considered where both could apply.

As a general rule, EIS is likely to be preferable where:

- a company is expected to grow rapidly and so quickly have further financing requirements;
- CGT deferral is required and either the investor has a substantial interest in the company (see explanatory note 31) or the gain exceeds £100,000; or
- the individual has insufficient income to benefit from the 50% income tax relief and 30% relief is sufficient.

As EIS relief is actually two reliefs rolled into one (the income tax/CGT exemption and the CGT deferral relief) there are differing but often overlapping conditions and requirements applying to each one. SEIS relief is much simpler in this respect with the CGT rules for both the exemption on disposal and the reinvestment relief mirroring the income tax relief conditions.

The company cannot have raised finance under the EIS or VCT provisions before raising finance under SEIS (ITA 2007 s 257DK). However once finance has been raised under SEIS, further finance may be raised by way of the EIS or VCT. For SEIS shares issued before 6 April 2016 the company is required to have spent 70% of the monies raised from the SEIS share issue before raising further money under the EIS or VCT (ITA 2007 s 173B, 292B).

Paid directors are *not* prevented from investing under the SEIS (ITA 2007 s 257BA). However, should the same investors wish to proceed to make further investments under SEIS then restrictions apply (ITA 2007 ss 257BA–257BF). If further investment under the EIS is likely, then the company may wish to consider issuing all the shares under the EIS rather than the SEIS.

## (c) Investments in disadvantaged communities

### *Community investment tax relief*

Community investment tax relief (CITR) applies where an individual or company makes an investment in a community development finance institution (CDFI) accredited under the scheme (ITA 2007 s 334; CTA 2010 s 219). The CDFI must use its funds to finance small businesses and social enterprises working in or for disadvantaged communities (ITA 2007 s 340; CTA 2010 s 219(1)(a)). The investment may be by loan or by subscription for shares or securities in the CDFI (ITA 2007 s 344; CTA 2010 s 225). The relevant conditions have to be satisfied for five years from the date of investment (ITA 2007 s 359; CTA 2010 s 242).

A loan must be for at least five years, but the amount can be advanced over the first 18 months. The loan must not have been made under terms which allow repayments in the first two years following the investment date and repayments exceeding 25% of the loan by the end of the third year, 50% by the end of the fourth year and 75% at the end of the fifth year. There cannot be any pre-arranged protection against risk other than normal commercial banking conditions (ITA 2007 s 345; CTA 2010 s 226).

The amount eligible for relief in the year of investment ('the invested amount') is the average balance of the loan outstanding over the first 12 months. For the second year it is the average balance outstanding between 12 and 24 months, and for the remaining three years the lower of the average balance outstanding for the investment year or for the 18 to 24-month period. Thus in the fourth year it is the lower of the average balance for the periods 36–48 months or 18–24 months (ITA 2007 s 337; CTA 2010 222).

A subscription for shares or securities must be fully paid in cash, with no rights of redemption within five years. Again there cannot be any pre-arranged protection against loss (ITA 2007 s 346-347, 349; CTA 2010 s 227-228, 230).

The investor requires a tax relief certificate to make a claim (ITA 2007 ss 335, 348; CTA 2010 ss 220, 229). The investor must not control the CDFI, or if a partnership, be a partner in the CDFI (ITA 2007 s 350; CTA 2010 s 231). Investments must be held by investors in their own names for their own beneficial interest and not as part of a scheme or arrangement to avoid tax (ITA 2007 ss 351, 353; CTA 2010 ss 232, 235).

For individuals, income tax relief is given for five tax years commencing in the tax year in which the investment is made. The relief in each year is 5% of the invested amount (see above for the rules for loans) (ITA 2007 s 335). The income tax relief is a step 6 tax reducer under the ITA 2007 s 23 income tax calculation and is deducted from the income tax liability (ITA 2007 s 335). Relief is limited to such an amount as reduces the investor's tax liability to nil (before deducting tax suffered at source, eg via PAYE); a repayment cannot be generated (ITA 2007 s 29). The relief is deducted from the investor's tax liability after any VCT/EIS/SEIS/social investments income tax relief (ITA 2007 s 27). Sufficient tax must, however, be left in charge to cover gift aid payments.

Tax relief for companies is available for the accounting period in which the investment is made and the accounting periods in which the next four anniversaries of the investment date fall. The relief in each period is 5% of the invested amount (CTA 2010 s 220). Relief is given after corporate venturing relief but before double tax relief and cannot generate a tax repayment (FA 1998 Sch 18, para 8). For periods before 1 April 2015, relief was given after any marginal small companies' rate relief.

For investments made on or after 1 April 2013 (companies) or 6 April 2013 (individuals), if the investor cannot obtain full income tax or corporation tax relief as the tax liability is not sufficient for full set off, the excess can be carried forward. The relief carried forward is set off as soon as it is possible to do so (ITA 2007 s 335A; CTA 2010 s 220A).

For investments made on or after 1 April 2013, for companies the total amount of corporation tax relief in any three-year period cannot exceed the EU State aid de minimis limits of €200,000 (CTA 2010 s 220B). When deciding whether this limit is breached, relief under CITR is considered plus any other de minimis State aid claimed in that period.

The CDFI must have accreditation at each anniversary, otherwise relief is not available for that year/period (ITA 2007 s 356; CTA 2010 s 219(1)(a)).

A disposal after the death of the individual investor does not cause the withdrawal of relief (ITA 2007 s 372(3). In all other circumstances the disposal of a loan (or part thereof) within the five-year period causes withdrawal of relief granted on the whole amount, unless it is a permitted disposal (ITA 2007 s 360; CTA 2010 s 243).

Permitted disposals include (ITA 2007 s 360(2); CTA 2010 s 243(2)):

- the repayment of the loan by the CDFI;
- a negligible value or total loss claim under TCGA 1992 s 24; or
- loss of the CDFI's accreditation.

In the case of the repayment of the loan and loss of accreditation this is because the withdrawal of relief in these situations is dealt with elsewhere (see the discussion of the loss of accreditation above) (ITA 2007 s 362; CTA 2010 s 245).

The disposal of shares or securities within five years will also cause all the relief to be withdrawn unless it is (ITA 2007 s 361; CTA 2010 s 244):

- after the death of the investor;
- a permitted disposal (as for loans); or
- a sale at arm's length for full consideration.

In the case of a permitted disposal or a bargain at arm's length, the relief granted will be reduced by 5% of the sale proceeds for each year of claim (ITA 2007 s 361(3)-(3H); CTA 2010 s 244(3)-(3H)). A sale for more than the subscription amount would therefore result in full withdrawal of relief granted.

Relief is also withdrawn if the investor receives value (other than an insignificant amount) in the six years commencing one year before the investment date (ITA 2007 s 363-370; CTA 2010 s 246-253). 'Value' is exhaustively defined but it does not include a dividend on shares providing it does not exceed a normal return.

### *Social investments tax relief*

Although not limited to disadvantaged communities, social investments tax relief (SITR) could be used to invest in such areas (ITA 2007 s 257K). SITR applies where an individual makes an investment in a 'social enterprise'. A social enterprise is defined as (ITA 2007 s 257J):

- a community interest company;
- a community benefit society (defined in ITA 2007 s 257JB) that is not a charity;
- a charity; or
- an accredited social impact contractor (defined in ITA 2007 257JD).

The individual can receive income tax relief at 30% on the subscription for new shares or qualifying debt instruments in the social enterprise. The limit on investment for income tax relief is £1m per tax year (ITA 2007 s 257JA). Relief is available in relation to subscriptions made between 6 April 2014 and 5 April 2019 (ITA 2007 s 257K). If the subscription is also entitled to relief under the EIS, SEIS or CITR regimes then SITR is not available in addition to those reliefs (ITA 2007 s 257K(3)).

The individual receives the income tax relief via a deduction from his tax liability at step 6 of the income tax calculation in ITA 2007 s 23 (ITA 2007 s 257JA(3)).

In line with other risk finance schemes, the income tax relief is withdrawn if:

- the asset is subject to disposal (apart from to a spouse/civil partner) (ITA 2007 s 257R);
- value is received by the investor (ITA 2007 ss 257Q-257QI);
- shares are repaid, redeemed or repurchased by the social enterprise (ITA 2007 ss 257QJ-257QP, 257QR);

- the social enterprise acquires an existing trade or trading assets which had been previously carried by anyone other than a qualifying subsidiary (ie a 51% subsidiary) (ITA 2007 s 257QQ);
- relief is subsequently found not to have been due (ie the qualifying conditions are not met throughout the period, eg the investor becomes employed by or otherwise connected with the social enterprise) (ITA 2007 s 257QS).

Any income tax relief clawed back is done via an assessment in relation to the tax year in which the relief was originally claimed (ITA 2007 s 257S).

Any gains on the disposal of qualifying investments in a social enterprise are not chargeable to CGT as long as the asset has been held for three years. Losses on disposal are allowable for CGT purposes but must be reduced by any income tax relief which has been given and not withdrawn (TCGA 1992 s 255B). In order to determine which assets are subject to disposal, the normal matching rules do not apply (TCGA 1992 s 255B(6)). Instead the assets are matched in the following order (TCGA 1992 s 255B(4) as read with ITA 2007 s 257TA):

- investments acquired earlier rather than later (ie first-in/first-out);
- investments on which neither SITR income tax relief nor CGT deferral relief (see below) is attributable;
- investments on which SITR CGT deferral relief but not income tax relief is attributable;
- investments on which SITR income tax relief but not CGT deferral relief is attributable;
- investments on which both SITR income tax relief and CGT deferral relief are attributable.

CGT deferral relief is also available on a qualifying investment in a social enterprise by a UK resident. All or part of the gains on the disposal of any asset can be deferred. Unlike EIS deferral relief, in order to defer the gain the investment must qualify for SITR income tax relief. The SITR investment can be made at any point from one year before the disposal to three years afterwards, however the gain must arise between 6 April 2014 and 5 April 2019 (TCGA 1992 Sch 8B para 1). The deferred gain falls back into charge when the asset is subject to disposal (including cancellation, redemption or repayment) or the social enterprise stops meeting the conditions for income tax relief.

In many cases the qualifying conditions for the social enterprise are modelled on the existing conditions for other risk finance schemes. These are:

- the qualifying investment must be subscribed for wholly in cash and must be fully paid up (ITA 2007 s 257LA);
- there must be no pre-arranged exit for the investor (ITA 2007 s 257LB);
- there cannot be any pre-arranged protection against risk other than normal commercial banking conditions (ITA 2007 s 257LC);
- there must be no linked loans (ITA 2007 s 257LD);
- the main purpose or one of the main purposes must not be tax avoidance (ITA 2007 s 257LE);
- the investor must not be connected to the company, ie be an employee or interested in more than 30% of the ordinary share capital/loan capital of the social enterprise. It is possible for the investor to be a paid director of the social enterprise as long as the remuneration is reasonable. This condition is closely modelled on the EIS 'connection with the company' condition (ITA 2007 ss 257LF-257LG)
- as for CITR, the total amount of investment in the social enterprise in any three year period cannot exceed the EU State aid de minimis limits of €200,000. When deciding whether this limit is breached, relief under SITR is considered plus any other de minimis State aid claimed in that period. The legislation provides a calculation for the social enterprise to use to check the maximum is not exceeded (ITA 2007 s 257MA);
- the gross assets of the social enterprise must not exceed £15m before investment and £16m afterwards (ITA 2007 s 257MC);

- if the social enterprise is a company it must be unquoted and no arrangements can exist for it to become quoted (ITA 2007 s 257MD);
- the social enterprise must not be under the control of a company and any subsidiary must be qualifying (ITA 2007 s 257ME-257MG);
- the social enterprise must carry on a trade which does not consist of excluded activities as defined in ITA 2007 ss 257MP-257MT (ITA 2007 s 257MJ);
- the money raised via the investment must be used for the qualifying activity (or preparation to carry on a qualifying activity) for which it was raised within 28 months (ITA 2007 ss 257ML-257MM).

However there are important differences from conditions which apply to other risk capital schemes. These include:

- SITR can be claimed on investment in debt instruments as well as shares (so long as the debt instrument is unsecured and the rate of return is commercially reasonable) (ITA 2007 s 257L);
- the qualifying activity of the social enterprise should be related to the objectives of the enterprise (especially if it is a charity), rather than just being any qualifying activity;
- lending money generally is an excluded activity, but there is an exception if the lending is to a social enterprise (ITA 2007 s 257MQ);
- the limit on staff is 500 full-time equivalent employees (rather than the lower limits for EIS and SEIS) (ITA 2007 s 257MH);
- the social enterprise and any 90% subsidiaries of the social enterprise must not be members of a partnership (ITA 2007 s 257MI).

As the relief is fairly new, the HMRC guidance is particularly important so that investors and social enterprises understand how HMRC interprets the legislation. At the time of writing, the guidance can be found at https://www.gov.uk/topic/business-tax/investment-schemes with the SITR guidance to be found towards the bottom of the landing page.

## Explanatory Notes

The EIS rules are contained in ITA 2007 ss 156–257 (income tax) and TCGA 1992 ss 150A–150C, Sch 5B (CGT). The rules for VCTs are in ITA 2007 ss 258–332 (income tax) and TCGA 1992 ss 151A-151B (CGT). The SEIS rules are contained in ITA 2007 ss 257A–257HJ (income tax) and TCGA 1992 ss 150E-150G, Sch 5BB (CGT).

(1) The provisions for the SEIS, EIS and VCTs require investment in qualifying unquoted trading companies, the first two being by direct subscription in the company and the third by acquiring shares in a VCT, which is a quoted company which invests in qualifying unquoted trading companies. Shares on the Alternative Investment Market (AIM) are regarded as unquoted shares for these provisions.

(2) Income tax relief under all three schemes is available to non-residents, but relief is given only against UK tax liabilities. EIS capital gains deferral relief is only available to UK residents (TCGA 1992 Sch 5B, para 1).

(3) The respective definitions of a qualifying company are broadly the same for each of the three reliefs, and in each case the definitions exclude companies with the following activities:

- dealing in land or property development;
- leasing;
- banking or insurance;
- providing legal or accountancy services;
- farming, market gardening, forestry or timber production;

- hotels or nursing/residential care homes;
- shipbuilding and the production of coal and steel; and
- wholesale or retail distribution.

(EIS: ITA 2007 ss 192–199; VCT: ITA 2007 ss 303–310; SEIS: ITA 2007 s 257HF as read with ITA 2007 ss 192–199)

This is not an exhaustive list. See the legislation for the full list of excluded activities.

For EIS and VCT investments, the total gross assets of the target company (and, where relevant, other companies in the same group) must not exceed £15 million immediately before the issue of the shares, nor £16 million immediately afterwards (EIS: ITA 2007 s 186; VCT: ITA 2007 s 297). The limit for SEIS relief is much lower; the gross assets must be not be more than £200,000 before the shares are issued (ITA 2007 s 257DI).

In relation to groups of companies, a parent company qualifies providing the group's activities as a whole are qualifying activities (EIS: ITA 2007 s 181(2); VCT: ITA 2007 s 290(1); SEIS: ITA 2007 s 257DA(2)). The test does not have to be satisfied by each group company. A subsidiary company can be a qualifying subsidiary if it is a 51% subsidiary except for property management or research and development subsidiaries which have to be 90% owned (EIS: ITA 2007 ss 187-191; VCT: ITA 2007 ss 298-299, 301-302; SEIS: ITA 2007 ss 257DM-257DN, 257HJ as read with ITA 2007 s 191).

The trade can be carried out by a 90% subsidiary of the qualifying investee company, or by a 100% subsidiary of a 90% subsidiary (EIS: ITA 2007 s 190; VCT: ITA 2007 s 301; SEIS: ITA 2007 ss 257DM-257DN, 257HJ as read with ITA 2007 s 191).

Note that, from the date of investment, provisions allow relevant intangible assets (intellectual property created by the SEIS, EIS, VCT target company) to be transferred between qualifying group companies. (EIS: ITA 2007 s 195(2); VCT: ITA 2007 s 306(2); SEIS: ITA 2007 s 257HF as read with ITA 2007 s 195(2)).

(4) Further restrictions are required by EU state aid rules for risk capital.

*Number of employees restriction*

The investee companies or groups may have no more than 250 full-time equivalent employees at the date of share issue (EIS: ITA 2007 s 186A; VCT: ITA 2007 s 297A). For SEIS investments, this is reduced to no more than 25 full-time equivalent employees (ITA 2007 s 257DJ). For shares issued on or after 18 November 2015, the limit is increased to no more than 500 full-time equivalent employees if the company is a knowledge-intensive company seeking EIS or VCT funding (see **explanatory note** 5).

*Value of funds restriction*

Companies may receive no more than £5 million annually from investment via VCT, EIS, SEIS and SITR (EIS: ITA 2007 s 173A; VCT: ITA 2007 s 292A). The limit is assessed each time shares are issued, looking back at the total investment in the 12 months ending with the date the shares are issued. As well as including investments in the issuing company, any investment made in 51% subsidiaries must be included (even if the investment was received prior to the date it became a subsidiary) and any investment made in a trade which is later transferred into the issuing company.

There is also a lifetime limit on the total investment a company can raise via VCT, EIS, SEIS and SITR (collectively referred to as 'risk finance investments'), which is £20m for knowledge-intensive companies and £12m for all other companies (EIS: ITA 2007 ss 173AA, 173AB; VCT: ITA 2007 ss 292AA, 292AB). This applies to shares issued on or after 18 November 2015. See **explanatory note** 5 for the definition of knowledge-intensive companies.

In the case of SEIS, in order to comply with EU state aid requirements that the investment be within the de minimis limits, the maximum investment that the company can receive from SEIS (and any other state aid) in the three years to the date of the latest SEIS share issue, must not exceed £150,000 (ITA 2007 s 257DL).

For EIS, at the time of the issue of the shares there must not be any arrangements for the company to become quoted, or to become a subsidiary of a quoted company (ITA 2007 s 184). The VCT provisions allow a VCT to continue to include shares in a company that becomes quoted in its qualifying holdings for a period of five years (ITA 2007 s 295).

A clearance procedure is available to enable companies to obtain *provisional* approval from HMRC that their shares qualify for EIS or SEIS relief using form EIS/SEIS(AA) https://www.gov.uk/government/publications/enterprise-investment-scheme-advance-assurance-application-eisseisaa. In the case of EIS investment, after four months of trading companies can apply on form EIS1 for formal clearance https://www.gov.uk/government/publications/enterprise-investment-scheme-compliance-statement-eis1.
Once formal clearance is given by HMRC, forms EIS3 are issued for investors to claim their income tax relief. Where the investment is via the SEIS, the company can apply for formal clearance using form SEIS1 when at least 70% of the investment has been spent on qualifying activities https://www.gov.uk/government/publications/seed-enterprise-investment-scheme-compliance-statement-seis1. Assuming this is successful, forms SEIS3 can be issued to investors.

*Enterprises in difficulty*

For shares issued on or after 6 April 2011, no company is permitted to qualify under the EIS, SEIS or VCT legislation if it is regarded as an 'enterprise in difficulty' under EU law (see 2004/C 244/02 http://eur-lex.europa.eu/LexUriServ/LexUriServ.do?uri=OJ:C:2004:244:0002:0017:EN:PDF at section 2.1) (EIS: ITA 2007 s 180B; VCT: ITA 2007 s 286B; SEIS: ITA 2007 s 257DE).

*Permanent establishment*

The previous rules for both EIS and VCTs required that there was a qualifying trade in the UK. For shares issued on or after 6 April 2011, this was replaced by a requirement that the company issuing the shares must have a permanent establishment in the UK (EIS: ITA 2007 s 180A; VCT: ITA 2007 s 286A). Again, this condition was incorporated into the SEIS rules (ITA 2007 s 257DD).

For the meaning of permanent establishment, see **Example K9, explanatory note 2**.

*Permitted maximum age requirement*

For shares issued on or after 18 November 2015 the company must be less than seven years old when it receives its first EIS or VCT venture capital investment (10 years if it is a knowledge-intensive company, see **explanatory note 5**).

Having said this, there is no time limit where the issuing company receives (EIS: ITA 2007 s 175A; VCT: ITA 2007 ss 280C, 294A):

(A) follow-on funding after the initial investment;

(B) an investment (or the total of such funding in a 30 day period) is more than 50% of the turnover of the company / group averaged over the previous five years and the funds are employed in launching a new product or entering a new geographical market; or

(C) condition B above was met in the past and the company raises follow-on funding for the same qualifying activity.

For investments made via SEIS the company must be less than two years old and must not have previously carried on a trade (ITA 2007 s 257HF).

(5) A company is a knowledge-intensive company if, at the date of the share issue, it meets (EIS: ITA 2007 s 252A; VCT: ITA 2007 s 331A):

- one or both of the operating costs conditions; and

- both of the innovation conditions; and/or
- at least 20% of the full-time equivalent employees are skilled employees (ie employees with relevant higher education qualifications who are directly engaged in research, development or innovation activities).

The operating costs conditions are that either (i) in any of the last three years at least 15% of the relevant operating costs are spent on research, development or innovation, or (ii) that in each of the last three years at least 10% of those operating costs were spent on those activities. The operating costs of the parent and qualifying subsidiaries are aggregated for the purposes of this test.

The innovation conditions are that the company or the group is engaged in the creation of intellectual property and that the utilisation/exploitation of the intellectual property is expected to form a greater part of the business of the company/group within 10 years.

## Guaranteed exit arrangements, guaranteed loans and share buy-backs

(6) EIS and SEIS tax relief is denied where there are arrangements at the time of an individual's investment that protect or guarantee the investment, or set up disposal arrangements for the benefit of the investor (EIS: ITA 2007 s 177; SEIS: ITA 2007 s 257CD).

Similarly, loans or securities that are guaranteed are excluded from a VCT's qualifying holdings (ITA 2007 s 264), and at least 15% of the total investment in any company must be ordinary, non-preferential shares (ITA 2007 s 274). The VCT shares must be acquired for bona fide commercial purposes and not as part of a scheme or arrangement whose purpose is tax avoidance (ITA 2007 s 261(3)).

For shares issued on or after 6 April 2014, no VCT income tax relief is available where the investment is either (ITA 2007 s 264A):

- linked to a VCT share buy-back; or
- made within six months of a disposal of shares in the same VCT.

## Income tax reliefs

(7) The EIS gives income tax relief at 30% on shares *subscribed* for up to £1 million. The relief is withdrawn if the shares are not held for at least three years unless this occurs through the death of the holder (ITA 2007 ss 158, 159, 208, 256).

An investment into a VCT gives income tax relief at the rate of 30% on shares *subscribed* for up to £200,000 (ITA 2007 s 263). In addition, dividends on VCT shares *acquired* not exceeding £200,000 are exempt from tax (ITTOIA 2005 s 709-710). To prevent the income tax relief being clawed back, the shares in the VCT must be held for at least five years (ITA 2007 s 266).

An investment for shares in an SEIS qualifying company gives income tax relief at a rate of 50% on a subscription of up to £100,000. The shares must be held for three years to avoid a clawback of the income tax relief (ITA 2007 ss 257AB, 257AC, 257F). Again, there is no clawback of relief on death of the investor (ITA 2007 s 257GC).

In the case of income tax relief available with all three schemes, the relief is a tax reducer deducted at step 6 of the ITA 2007 s 23 calculation (ie the relief is deducted from the total tax liability before taking account of tax already paid at source). A tax refund cannot be generated by the income tax relief if the venture capital relief exceeds the tax otherwise due. The UK income tax liability can only be reduced to nil and repayment cannot be generated (ITA 2007 s 29). However, if all income tax relief cannot be used it is possible to carry back a specified amount of the EIS and SEIS investment to the previous tax year (subject to the limit for relief in the previous year) so that, for income tax purposes, the relief is given in the earlier year (EIS: ITA 2007 s 158; SEIS: ITA 2007 s 257AB). Due to a quirk of the legislation, the relief carried back is given by reference to the tax payable for the earlier year, but it will be *given effect* in relation to the later tax year (TMA 1970 Sch 1B – see **Example G2**).

There is no ability to carry back a VCT investment.

Where the investor is entitled to claim income tax relief under more than one scheme in the same year, the VCT tax relief is deducted in priority followed by EIS relief and then SEIS relief (ITA 2007 s 27).

### Shares acquired by subscription or otherwise

(8) The difference between subscribing for shares and acquiring them in some other way, for example by purchase from another shareholder or as a gift, should be noted.

The income tax relief for EIS, SEIS and VCT shares and capital gains deferral relief for EIS and SEIS apply to shares *subscribed for*, and the capital gains exemption only applies to shares on which income tax relief was given. Income tax relief is regarded as having been given even if the individual's income tax liability was insufficient to enable him to benefit from the full income tax reduction available.

The VCT dividend exemptions apply to shares *acquired* up to the £200,000 limit in any year for the very practical reason that the investor puts money into the VCT rather than the investee companies. (ITTOIA 2005 ss 709-710).

VCM74060 looks at the meaning of 'subscription'. The fact that this page in the manual relates to income tax relief on disposals of certain unquoted shares at a loss does not matter, as the text applies equally to all three venture capital schemes. It states that the shares must be issued by the company for money or money's worth and not acquired from another person. It also discusses the meaning of 'issue' following *National Westminster Bank plc v CIR* [1994] STC 580.

### Claims

(9) The claim by the investor for EIS/SEIS tax relief may be included in tax returns or amendments to returns if the EIS3/SEIS3 certificate is received in time (see **explanatory note 4** for details of when the certificate can be issued). Otherwise claims are made on the form incorporated in the certificate and submitted to the investor's tax office. The overall time limit for claiming the relief is five years from 31 January following the tax year in which the shares are issued (EIS: ITA 2007 s 202; SEIS: ITA 2007 s 257EA).

Claims for VCT relief may similarly be made in tax returns (early claims may be made in advance of the submission of the return once the qualifying shares have been issued) although the time limit for making the claim is four years from the end of the tax year in which the investment is made (TMA 1970 s 43). The VCT normally sends the certificate to the investor following the issue of the shares but the investor can request one from the VCT if it is not supplied automatically (SI 1995/1979, reg 9; VCM51050).

EIS, SEIS and VCT certificates should be retained as part of the taxpayer's records.

## *Further points relating to EIS shares*

*Conditions for income tax relief*

(10) EIS income tax relief is given where a 'qualifying individual' subscribes for 'eligible shares' in a qualifying company carrying on, or intending to carry on, a qualifying business activity, as outlined in **explanatory note 3** above (ITA 2007 s 157). The subscription must be wholly in cash and all the shares must be issued to raise money for a qualifying business activity (ITA 2007 ss 173, 174). All money raised needs to be used for the qualifying activity within 24 months of the issue of the shares or of the commencement of the trade (ITA 2007 s 175)

A qualifying individual is one who is not *connected* with the company (connected broadly meaning having 30% or more control, or being or having been a director or employee) (ITA 2007 ss 166-171). If the investor already holds shares in the company, these must be founder shares or as a result of earlier venture capital investment (ITA 2007, s 164A). The investor may, however, become a paid director after the shares are issued. The connected persons rules do not apply to the EIS deferral relief (see **explanatory notes 15-17**).

Eligible shares are new ordinary shares which do not carry any preferential rights to assets on winding up or any present or future right to be redeemed (ITA 2007 s 173). It is possible for the ordinary shares to have preferential rights to dividends but these preferential rights must *not be* of the type listed in ITA 2007 s 173(2A).

If any of the requirements for a 'qualifying individual' or 'qualifying company' are breached during a 'relevant period' – broadly, in the three years after the issue of the shares or commencement of trading if later – the relief is withdrawn (ITA 2007 ss 159, 163, 180A-185, 187-188).

The relief is subject to detailed anti-avoidance provisions, including the 'guaranteed exit' provisions in **explanatory note 6.** If the anti-avoidance provisions apply and income tax relief has already been granted, it will be withdrawn and interest will be charged from 31 January following the end of the tax year in which the relief was claimed (ie the original due date for the tax) (ITA 2007 ss 234, 239).

*Minimum subscription*

(11) There is no longer a minimum amount of investment that must be made in the EIS company. For investments made prior to 6 April 2012, the minimum subscription in any one company was £500.

*Carry back to previous year*

(12) As discussed in **explanatory note 7**, a claim may be made to carry back amounts invested for relief in the previous tax year (ITA 2007 s 158).

Prior to 6 April 2009 there were more complex rules governing carry backs, which in particular limited relief to a maximum carry-back of £50,000. A carry back was also only possible in respect of half the amount invested in the first half of the tax year (ie from 6 April to 5 October).

*Withdrawal of income tax relief*

(13) Income tax relief is not available (or if already given, is withdrawn) if an individual is or becomes connected with the company within the two years before or three years after the shares were issued or trading commenced if later (ITA 2007 ss 163, 256).

There are provisions for withdrawing relief if value is received from the company within the period of one year before the shares are issued (or trading commenced, if later) and three years after that date (ITA 2007 ss 213-224 as read with ITA 2007 ss 159, 256). The legislation allows receipts of 'insignificant value' to be ignored (ITA 2007 s 214). Amounts not exceeding £1,000 will normally be regarded as insignificant (ITA 2007 s 215; VCM15050).

The amount of the relief withdrawn where value (other than an insignificant amount) is received, is equal to the EIS tax rate at the time the relief was claimed on the lower of (ITA 2007 s 213; VCM15040):

- the value received; and
- the amount on which relief was given

The EIS tax rate is the rate of income tax relief. For subscriptions since 6 April 2011 the EIS tax rate has been 30% (ITA 2007 s 158). For subscriptions prior to that date, the EIS tax rate was 20%.

'Value received' includes the repayment of loans that had been made to the company before the shares were subscribed for, provision of benefits, purchase of own shares by the company or from other shareholders, purchase of assets for more than market value or sale of assets for less than market value (ITA 2007 s 216). For details of the amount of the value which is treated as received in these circumstances, see VCM15060. It does not, however, include the receipt of dividends which do not exceed a normal return on the investment or the payment of reasonable remuneration where the investor is a director (ITA 2007 s 216(8)). If a shareholder waives a dividend, thus increasing the dividend of an EIS shareholder, that waiver will cause the EIS shareholder to have received value in excess of a normal return.

The cessation of trade will trigger a withdrawal of relief, unless the company also commences winding up at the time of the cessation, or as promptly as the circumstances permit, and the winding up is for bona fide commercial reasons and not for tax avoidance purposes (ITA 2007 ss 181-182, 189, 234). Similarly, the appointment of an Administrative Receiver does not cause the relief to be lost, providing this is done for bona fide commercial reasons and not for tax avoidance purposes.

Income tax relief is also withdrawn if the shares are disposed of within three years of the date of issue or of the date trading commenced if later (ITA 2007 s 209 as read with ITA 2007 ss 159, 256).

Where shares are sold at arm's length, the clawback of income tax relief is restricted to the lower of (ITA 2007 s 209(3)):

- the relief originally given; and
- the sale proceeds multiplied by the EIS tax rate (see above).

If the disposal is not at arm's length, the relief is withdrawn completely (ITA 2007 s 209(2)).

(14) Where income tax relief is withdrawn this is via an assessment for the tax year for which the relief was originally given (ITA 2007 s 235). See **Example G2 explanatory note 16** for the issue of assessments outside the self-assessment system. Interest on overdue tax runs from 31 January following the end of the tax year in which the relief was claimed (ie the original due date for the tax) (ITA 2007 ss 234, 239).

*Capital gains deferral relief*

(15) All or part of the gains on the disposal of any assets may be deferred by a *subscription* for qualifying EIS shares (TCGA 1992 Sch 5B paras 1(1)-(2)). The amount of the gain that can be deferred is the lower of (TCGA 1992 Sch 5B para 2):

- the gain;
- the amount used to subscribe for the EIS shares;
- a specific amount claimed (in this way the individual can ensure that the annual exemption is preserved).

There is no limit on the amount of the gain that may be deferred under the EIS, although the conditions below must be met). The period during which the shares must be issued is between one year before and three years after the gain arises (TCGA 1992 Sch 5B para 1(3)).

In order for deferral relief to be available (TCGA 1992 Sch 5B paras 1, 19):

- the individual must be UK resident (see **Example F1**);
- the shares must be eligible shares (see **explanatory note 10**) in a qualifying company (see **explanatory notes 1, 3-4**)
- the subscription for the shares must be wholly in cash;
- the issue is for a bona fide commercial purpose and not be part of arrangements where the main purpose or one of the main purposes is to avoid tax;
- the shares must be issued to raise money for a qualifying business activity (see **explanatory note 3**);

- the money must be used for the qualifying business activity for which it was raised within 12 months; and

- the total inward investment in the company under tax-incentivised schemes must not exceed £5 million in the last rolling 12 month period).

Deferral relief is not available where there are guaranteed exit arrangements (see **explanatory note 6**) (TCGA 1992 Sch 5B para 11).

(16) Deferred gains become chargeable on the disposal of the shares, other than to a spouse/civil partner (the gain or loss on the disposal itself being dealt with separately, **see explanatory notes 18-21**). Deferred gains also become chargeable if the investor becomes non-resident within three years of acquiring the shares. Deferred gains are not triggered if the investor (or spouse to whom the shares have been transferred) dies (TCGA 1992 Sch 5B para 3). EIS deferred gains are triggered if the shares cease to be eligible shares, or the company ceases to qualify within three years. Shares are treated as ceasing to be eligible shares if the investor receives value (other than an insignificant amount) from the company within one year before and three years after the shares are issued (or trading commenced, if later) (TCGA 1992 Sch 5B paras 13–15). Unlike the income tax provisions (see **explanatory note 13**), where a deferred gain is triggered because an individual receives value (other than an insignificant amount) from a company, the *whole* of the deferred gain is brought into charge, regardless of how much value is received (TCGA 1992 Sch 5B paras 13–15; VCM23300).

When deferred gains are triggered, further deferral is possible into a new subscription for qualifying EIS shares.

(17) The entrepreneurs' relief (see **Example L5**) position depends on when the original gain arose. The treatment is different depending whether the gain deferred arose:

- pre-6 April 2008;

- between 6 April 2008 and 22 June 2010;

- between 23 June 2010 and 3 December 2014;

- on or after 4 December 2014.

Pre-6 April 2008 gains which have been reinvested in EIS shares, which would have attracted entrepreneurs' relief had the relief existed at that time, will attract entrepreneurs' relief when the gain crystallises (eg on disposal of the EIS shares) (FA 2008 Sch 3 para 8(4)(a).

Where the original gain arose between 6 April 2008 and 22 June 2010, entrepreneurs' relief applied before the deferral relief so the original gain has already benefited from entrepreneurs' relief (CG64135). See the 'Expect the unexpected' http://www.taxation.co.uk/taxation/Articles/2010/08/25/265141/expect-unexpected article by Kevin Slevin in Taxation magazine (25 August 2010).

Where the original gain arose between 23 June 2010 and 3 December 2014 and the disposal qualified for entrepreneurs' relief, the individual had a choice to make. He could claim entrepreneurs' relief and pay the tax or not claim the entrepreneurs' relief, defer the gain and lose the benefit of entrepreneurs' relief when the gain crystallises. See 'The prohibition era' http://www.taxation.co.uk/taxation/Articles/2010/09/15/265151/prohibition-era article by Kevin Slevin in Taxation magazine (15 September 2010).

Where the original gain arises on or after 4 December 2014 and the disposal qualifies for entrepreneurs' relief the individual no longer has to choose between entrepreneurs' relief and EIS deferral relief. The gain frozen via the EIS deferral claim will qualify for entrepreneurs' relief when it crystallises on disposal of the EIS shares. However the gain must crystallise in the hands of the individual who made the original disposal and so the EIS shares must not have been transferred to a spouse or civil partner (TCGA 1992, s 169U).

*Capital gains exemption on disposal of shares*

(18) Gains on disposal of EIS shares *subscribed* for up to the £1 million limit per year (as distinct from deferred gains held over by reference to those subscriptions/acquisitions) are exempt, but only after the shares have been held for three years. However, losses on the disposal of EIS shares are allowable (TCGA 1992 s 150A).

(19) Where gains are chargeable, they are eligible for deferral in the same way as any other gains (see **explanatory note 15**).

(20) If the disposal results in a loss, the loss is allowable whether the disposal is within or outside of the three year period, but in calculating a loss, the allowable cost is reduced by the amount of EIS income tax relief that has been given and not withdrawn (see **explanatory note 13**) (TCGA 1992 s 150A). A loss may be relieved either against chargeable gains, including deferred gains triggered by the disposal (see **explanatory note 16**), or against income. The conditions for relief for the loss against income are discussed in **Example L3 explanatory note 10**).

(21) Where shares have been acquired at different times and some or all of the shares attract EIS relief, the normal capital gains tax identification and pooling rules do not apply.

Instead, disposals are matched with shares acquired earlier rather than later (ie, a first-in/first-out basis). Where shares were acquired on the same day, disposals are identified with acquisitions in the following order (TCGA 1992 s 150A(4); ITA 2007, s 246(2), (3)):

- shares to which neither EIS or SEIS income tax relief, EIS capital gains deferral relief nor SEIS capital gains tax reinvestment relief is attributable;
- shares to which SEIS income tax relief or SEIS capital gains tax reinvestment relief is attributable;
- shares to which EIS deferral relief but not income tax relief is attributable;
- shares to which EIS income tax relief but not deferral relief is attributable;
- shares to which both EIS income tax relief and deferral relief are attributable.

## *Further points relating to VCT shares*

*Qualifying holdings for VCTs*

(22) To be eligible for VCT relief an investor needs to be aged 18 or over (ITA 2007 s 261(3)(b)).

A VCT is a quoted company which (ITA 2007 s 274):

- derives its income wholly or mainly from investments in shares and securities;
- does not retain more than 15% of its income from investments in shares and securities;
- has at least 70% of its investments in shares or securities which are 'qualifying holdings' (of which 70% of those are in 'eligible shares');
- does not have an investment in any one company which exceeds 15% of the VCT's total investments;
- does not invest in companies which have exceeded the maximum total inward investment under risk finance investment schemes (see **explanatory note 4**).
- does not exceed the maximum age requirement (see **explanatory note 4**); and

- does not breach the 'no business acquisition' condition (this prevents the VCT from investing in a company which goes on to use the money to acquire an existing trade and it applies to investments made on or after 18 November 2015).

The 70% qualifying holdings rule is relaxed on disposals of holdings (ITA 2007 s 280A). Effectively, the qualifying holdings are allowed to fall below 70% for six months after disposal, without loss of VCT income tax relief to investors. For six months after disposal the VCT is treated as if it continued to hold the holding disposed of, and the money received from the holding is excluded from the company's assets for the same period. Furthermore, under SI 1995/1979, regs 8A-8J, approval will not be withdrawn in the event that conditions are breached as a result of events outside the company's control (VCM54360).

The requirements for a 'qualifying holding' are referenced in ITA 2007 s 286(3). Many of these conditions are the same as for a company to qualify for EIS and have been mentioned in the explanatory notes above, including the need for the company to have a permanent establishment in the UK, not be in financial difficulties, carry out a qualifying activity, be an unquoted trading company, meet limits as to gross assets and full-time equivalent employees (ITA 2007 ss 286A-310). The company must use the money for qualifying activities (see **explanatory note 3**) within two years of the issue of the shares to the VCT or the commencement of trade if later (ITA 2007 s 293). The anti-avoidance provisions in relation to guaranteed loans and share buy-backs are discussed in **explanatory note 6** above.

The definition of eligible shares for the purposes of ITA 2007 s 274 depends when the shares were issued (ITA 2007 s 285). The meaning changed on 6 April 2011. This is discussed in VCM54150.

*Capital gains exemption for the VCT*

(23) VCTs are exempt from tax on their capital gains and any losses are not allowable (TCGA 1992 s 100). There are anti-avoidance provisions to prevent the exemption being exploited by means of intra-group transfers, or by transferring a company's business to a VCT or to a company that later becomes a VCT (TCGA 1992 ss 101A–101C).

*Withdrawal of income tax relief*

(24) The income tax relief will be withdrawn if:

- any of the shares in the VCT are subject to disposal within five years of their issue (other than to the holder's spouse/civil partner, or after the holder's death) (ITA 2007 s 266);
- the VCT loses its qualifying status within the five year period (ITA 2007 s 268).

Where shares are acquired from a spouse/civil partner, there is no withdrawal of income tax relief and the spouse/civil partner is treated as if he had subscribed for the shares (ITA 2007 s 267).

As with EIS relief, the legislation provides for relief to be withdrawn by an assessment to tax for the tax year in which the relief was originally claimed (ITA 2007 ss 269–270).

*Investors' capital gains exemption*

(25) The capital gains exemption on the disposal of VCT shares applies to shares acquired up to the £200,000 limit in any year, whether acquired by subscription or otherwise. There is no minimum period for which the shares must be held. Any losses are not allowable (TCGA 1992 s 151A).

(26) The normal share matching rules to not apply to disposals of VCT shares. Disposals are matched first with any shares acquired before the trust became a VCT (TCGA 1992 s 151A(5)). Next disposals are matched with shares acquired earlier rather than later (ie a first-in/first-out basis) (TCGA 1992 s 151A(4)(a)).

Where shares were acquired on the same day, shares above the £200,000 relief limit are deemed to have been sold before those within the limit (ie, chargeable shares are sold before exempt shares) (TCGA 1992 s 151A(4)(b)).

If a VCT loses its qualifying status, shares eligible for the CGT exemption are treated as disposed of at market value (any gain being covered by the exemption) and immediately reacquired at that same value (TCGA 1992 s 151B(6)-(7)). They are then brought within the normal capital gains rules for matching disposals with acquisitions.

*Capital gains deferral relief prior to 6 April 2004*

(27) VCT investment attracted CGT relief on reinvested gains until 5 April 2004. The rules were similar to the EIS relief set out at **explanatory notes 15–17** above except the VCT shares needed to have been issued within the period of one year before to one year after the date on which the gain arose. Any gain so deferred will be triggered if the VCT loses its approval. Although these rules were abolished some time ago, it is possible that investors still retain shares in VCTs which have deferred gains attached which will crystallise on disposal or where value is received by the investor (TCGA 1992 Sch 5C).

## *Further points relating to SEIS shares*

(28) SEIS came into effect on 6 April 2012. Originally the scheme was to be available until 5 April 2017, but FA 2014 s 54 removed the sunset clause.

(29) There are three aspects to SEIS relief to consider:

(a) SEIS income tax relief – this provides a 50% tax reduction on subscription for up to £100,000 on qualifying shares in a qualifying company. The income tax relief is set against the taxpayer's income tax liability in the tax year in which the shares are issued (see **explanatory note** 7). There are carry back provisions which enables up to the full amount to be treated as subscribed in the previous year (ITA 2007 s 257AB);

(b) SEIS CGT relief – this provides relief from CGT on a disposal of shares which qualified for income tax relief, provided they are held for three years. Losses are allowable, although there is an adjustment to the amount of the loss to take into account any income tax relief which has been given and not withdrawn (TCGA 1992 s 150E); and

(c) SEIS CGT reinvestment relief – this provides for a 50% reduction in the capital gain chargeable on the disposal of *any* asset to the extent that the *gain* is reinvested in the subscription in qualifying shares in a qualifying company (on which SEIS income tax relief is available) (TCGA 1992 Sch 5BB; VCM45010). This reinvestment relief is available at the 50% rate for tax years 2013/14 onwards (FA 2014 s 55). A 100% reduction was available for reinvestment made in the 2012/13 tax year.

(30) Income tax relief and CGT relief on disposal go hand in hand and form two parts of the same relief. Reinvestment relief is a separate strand of relief that can be claimed along with the other two, but does not have to be. For reinvestment relief to be available, SEIS income tax relief has to be available and claimed (TCGA 1992 Sch 5BB, para 1(3)). This is different to EIS where deferral relief can be claimed even if income tax relief is not available because, for example, the connection tests are breached.

(31) Many of the conditions which must be met for SEIS income tax relief to be claimed are covered in answer (b) and are discussed in **explanatory notes 3, 4, 6, 8, 9.**

However, it is worth noting the condition relating to the investor's financial interest in the SEIS company (known as having a 'substantial interest') in more detail. The substantial interest condition for SEIS mirrors the capital connection condition for EIS income tax relief (ITA 2007 s 170).

SEIS income tax relief is not available if, at any point from the date of incorporation to three years after issue of the shares, the individual is entitled to more than 30% of (ITA 2007 s 257BF):

- the ordinary share capital of the company/subsidiary company;
- the issued share capital of the company/subsidiary company;

- the voting power in the company/subsidiary company;
- the assets eligible for distribution to equity holders on winding up of the company/subsidiary (or in any other circumstances).

If the individual has control of the company or any subsidiary company this is also taken to be a substantial interest (ITA 2007 s 257BF(6)). The meaning of control is discussed in VCM32030.

Both the individual's holdings and those of his associates must be taken into account when deciding whether the 30% threshold is breached (ITA 2007 s 257BF(7)). The meaning of associate for these purposes is discussed in VCM32020.

If the only reason why the individual has a substantial interest in the company is because it has issued only 'subscriber shares' and has not yet taken any steps to begin trading then the legislation does not deem a substantial interest to arise (ITA 2007 s 257BF(5)). Subscriber shares are those issued as part of registering the company with Companies House.

# Question

Convey commenced to practise on 1 May 1977.

In 1981 he took Sing into partnership, the balance sheet immediately after the admission being:

| | £ | £ | | £ | £ |
|---|---|---|---|---|---|
| Capital accounts: | | | Fixed assets: | | |
| Convey | 10,000 | | Premises – at cost | | 7,500 |
| Sing | 4,000 | | | | |
| | | 14,000 | | | |
| Current liabilities: | | | Current assets: | | |
| Creditors | 2,000 | | Work in progress | 4,500 | |
| Bank overdraft | 4,000 | | Debtors | 8,000 | |
| | | 6,000 | | | 12,500 |
| | | 20,000 | | | 20,000 |

It was agreed that the premises, which had been acquired by Convey some time earlier, be vested in both partners, that the profit sharing ratio be two-thirds to Convey and one-third to Sing, and that they should contribute capital as agreed from time to time.

No payments or adjustments were made for goodwill or increase in value of premises on the admission of Sing, although it was acknowledged at that time that should Convey have sought a payment from Sing, the premises were worth £20,000 and the goodwill £10,000.

In April 1993 it was decided to introduce goodwill into the accounts and a value of £75,000 was agreed. The book value of the premises was not disturbed. The value of goodwill on 31 March 1982 is agreed at £30,000, the value of the premises on that day being £20,000.

From 1 May 1994 the profit sharing ratio was altered to give equal shares to Convey and Sing. Although no accounting adjustments were made, the partners acknowledged that the premises were worth £97,500, and the goodwill £99,000 at the time.

In anticipation of the retirement of Convey, a longstanding employee, Dance, was admitted to the partnership from 1 May 2006 as an equal partner. It was agreed that at that stage no payment or accounting adjustments should be made for goodwill and premises.

Convey retired from the business on 30 April 2016, which was his 65th birthday .

Sing and Dance remained as equal partners.

It was agreed that the terms of Convey's retirement should reflect an appropriate amount for his share in the premises and goodwill, the values of which assets were acknowledged as being £420,000 each, the accounts however still showing the premises as having cost £7,500, with £75,000 included for goodwill on the basis of the 1993 valuation, the values in the accounts not having been disturbed.

The profits of the firm have generally increased over time and the relevant tax adjusted profits have been:

| | | £ |
|---|---|---|
| Year ended 30 April | 1997 (after capital allowances of £20,000) | 150,000 |
| | 1998 (after capital allowances of £22,000) | 168,000 |
| | 2010 (after capital allowances of £18,000) | 140,000 |
| | 2011 (after capital allowances of £25,000) | 171,000 |

| | £ |
|---|---|
| 2012 (after capital allowances of £33,000) | 130,000 |
| 2013 (after capital allowances of £20,000) | 202,000 |
| 2014 (after capital allowances of £30,000) | 255,000 |
| 2015 (after capital allowances of £20,000) | 280,000 |
| 2016 (after capital allowances of £50,000) | 450,000 |

The retail prices index for the relevant months was March 1982 79.44, April 1993 140.6, April 1994 144.2, April 1998 162.6.

In September 1988, the partners made general 31 March 1982 rebasing elections in respect of partnership chargeable assets.

Show the taxation implications arising from the above assuming that Convey, on his retirement, in order to reflect the full value of the premises and goodwill, received in addition to the balance on his capital account either:

(a) £280,000 cash;

(b) an annuity of £46,000 per annum (having an estimated capital value of £280,000) in consideration of his past services in the partnership; or

(c) a reduced annuity of £34,500 per annum plus a lump sum of £70,000.

# Answer

## Capital gains liabilities

Note that the references to SP D12 in the answer refer to the version as updated in September 2015, rather than the version in place at the time of these events.

### (i) *1981 admission of Sing to the partnership*

As no payment was made for the chargeable assets of the partnership and the assets were not revalued in 1981, the disposal is deemed to take place at an amount which produces neither a gain nor a loss (SP D12 para 4.2). Therefore there is no chargeable gain arising to Convey on admitting Sing to the partnership. See **explanatory notes 1** and **4**.

### (ii) *April 1993 revaluation of goodwill*

There is no disposal in April 1993. All that has happened is that a value for the goodwill has been included in the accounts. There was no change in profit sharing ratio. See **explanatory notes 2** and **4**.

### (iii) *May 1994 change in profit sharing ratio*

Convey disposes of a one-sixth share to Sing as his share goes from two-thirds down to one-half.

The premises has not been revalued and therefore the fractional disposal occurs at a no gain/no loss value (SP D12 para 4.2).

The share of goodwill is deemed to be disposed of at the revaluation figure from 1993, because two-thirds of that will have been credited to Convey's capital account (SP D12 para 6.2). Before the change Convey's share of the 31 March 1982 market value is £20,000 and Sing's is £10,000.

The gain on the disposal of goodwill by Convey is as follows:

| | | £ |
|---|---|---|
| Proceeds of one-sixth share (£75,000/6) | | 12,500 |
| Less: market value 31.3.82 (£30,000/6) | | (5,000) |
| | Indexation: Mar 82–Apr 94 $(\frac{144.2 - 79.44}{79.44}) = 81.5\%$ | (4,075) |
| Chargeable gain | | 3,425 |

Indexation allowance is available as the disposals occurred before 6 April 2008. See **explanatory note 6**.

Convey's base cost of goodwill is reduced to £15,000 (£20,000 less £5,000) and Sing's base cost of £10,000 is increased by the deemed proceeds of £12,500.

### (iv) *May 2006 admission of Dance to the partnership*

On admitting Dance to the partnership on 1 May 2006, Convey and Sing each dispose of a one-sixth share of goodwill and premises to him as their shares go from one-half to one third.

The disposal of the premises takes place on a no gain/no loss basis, since there has been no earlier revaluation and no payment by Dance to the partners (SP D12 para 4.2). This means that the deemed proceeds are equal to the cost plus indexation allowance.

Due to the earlier revaluation of goodwill, each of Convey and Sing has deemed disposal proceeds of £12,500, being amounts in their capital accounts not now represented by their share in goodwill (SP D12 para 6.2).

Their capital gains indexed base costs of their current shares of the assets are as follows:

| | *Goodwill – Convey* | *Goodwill – Sing* | *Premises – each* |
|---|---|---|---|
| | £ | £ | £ |
| Base cost (Market value 31.3.82) | 15,000 | 10,000 | 10,000 |
| Indexation to April 1998 $(\frac{162.6 - 79.44}{79.44}) = 104.7\%$ | 15,705 | 10,470 | 10,470 |
| April 1994 (Change in profit sharing ratio) | | 12,500 | |
| Indexation to April 1998 $(\frac{162.6 - 144.2}{144.2}) = 12.8\%$ | | 1,600 | |
| Indexed cost | 30,705 | 34,570 | 20,470 |
| | £ | £ | £ |
| Deemed proceeds | 12,500 | 12,500 | 6,823 |
| Less: cost (one third of half share) | (10,235) | (11,523) | (6,823) |
| Capital gains | 2,265 | 977 | Nil |

The gains shown would have been reduced by business asset taper relief which applied to disposals made between April 1998 and April 2008. The amount of taper relief depended on whether the asset was a business asset or not and how long the asset had been held.

Indexation allowance is available as the disposals occurred before 6 April 2008. See **explanatory note 6**.

After the transaction, the partners' capital gains base costs (excluding indexation for Convey and Sing) are as follows:

| | | | *Goodwill* | | *Premises* |
|---|---|---|---|---|---|
| | | | £ | | £ |
| Convey | (March 1982) | (15,000 – 5,000) | 10,000 | (10,000 – 3,333) | 6,667 |
| Sing | (March 1982) | (10,000 – 3,333) | 6,667 | (10,000 – 3,333) | 6,667 |
| | (April 1994) | (12,500 – 4,167) | 8,333 | | |
| Dance | (May 2006) | (12,500 + 12,500) | 25,000 | (6,823 + 6,823) | 13,646 |

On disposals after 5 April 2008, no indexation allowance is available to the partners, but as far as the disposals by Dance are concerned, the indexation allowance within his base cost for the premises needs to be identified in the event of a disposal at a loss (see **explanatory note 6**).

## (v) *April 2016 retirement of Convey*

### (a) Cash settlement

Under this scenario, Convey receives no annuity, only a cash payment of £280,000 on retiring from the partnership.

The capital gains tax treatment of the payment is:

| | | *Goodwill* | *Premises* |
|---|---|---|---|
| | | £ | £ |
| Disposal proceeds | | 140,000 | 140,000 |
| Base cost for capital gains tax (**see (iv)**) | | (10,000) | (6,667) |
| Gains | | 130,000 | 133,333 |
| | | | £ |
| Total gains on goodwill and premises | | | 263,333 |
| Less: | annual exemption | | (11,100) |
| Chargeable gain | | | 252,233 |
| Capital gains tax @ 10% | | £25,223 | |

The proceeds of £280,000 are split on pro rata basis to the agreed market values (of £420,000 each). The balance sheet values are not disturbed.

Tax is due at 10% on the assumption that entrepreneurs' relief applies. See **explanatory note 8**.

The capital gains tax base costs of goodwill and premises for Sing and Dance will each be increased by £70,000 (ie £70,000 on each of the two assets for each of the two partners, total £280,000), being the amount paid to Convey to acquire his share of the assets.

### (b) Annuity

Under this scenario Convey receives no cash payout and instead receives £46,000 each year as an annuity from the partnership.

In this situation his capital gains tax position would be as follows:

| | *Goodwill* | *Premises* |
|---|---|---|
| | £ | £ |
| Deemed disposal proceeds | 10,000 | 6,667 |
| Base cost (see above) | (10,000) | (6,667) |
| No gain/no loss | Nil | Nil |

As the annuity is less than the 'reasonable amount' and is not a lump sum equivalent or a purchased life annuity then no capital gains tax is due on the capitalised value of the annuity. Since the goodwill and the premises are subject to disposal but a capital gain cannot arise, the disposal must take place for an amount that gives neither a gain nor a loss. See **explanatory note 9**.

The capital gains tax base costs of goodwill and premises for each of Sing and Dance will be increased by half (ie their share) of £10,000 and £6,667 respectively.

The annuity itself is not chargeable to capital gains tax (see **explanatory note 9**) but it will be assessed to income tax in the hands of Convey, and allowed as a deduction from income for Sing and Dance, on which they will obtain relief at their marginal rate of tax (see 'Income tax implications of retirement of Convey' note (b) below).

### (c) Annuity plus lump sum

Under this scenario Convey receives a cash payment of £70,000 and £34,500 each year as an annuity from the partnership.

In this situation his capital gains tax position would be as follows:

| | *Goodwill* | *Premises* |
|---|---|---|
| | £ | £ |
| Disposal proceeds (split pro rata) | 35,000 | 35,000 |
| Base cost (see above) | (10,000) | (6,667) |
| Gains | 25,000 | 28,333 |

| | |
|---|---|
| | £ |
| Total gains on goodwill and premises | 53,333 |
| *Less:* annual exemption | (11,100) |
| Chargeable gains | 42,233 |
| Capital gains tax @ 10% | £4,223 |

Tax is due at 10% on the assumption that entrepreneurs' relief applies. See **explanatory note 8.**

The capitalised amount of the annuity is not subject to capital gains tax as the annuity plus one-ninth of the lump sum is less than the 'reasonable amount'. See **explanatory note 10.**

The capital gains tax base costs of premises and goodwill for each of Sing and Dance will be increased by half (ie their share) of £35,000 in each case.

## Income tax implications of retirement of Convey

(a) The retirement of Convey on 30 April 2016 will not affect the calculation of the taxable profits of Sing and Dance.

The amount taxable on Convey is his share of the profits (net of capital allowances) for the year ended 30 April 2016 less overlap relief for the period 1 May 1996 to 5 April 1997 (calculated on profits *before* capital allowances), ie:

| | |
|---|---|
| | £ |
| ⅓ × £450,000 | 150,000 |
| Less: overlap profits 340/365 × (½ × (150,000 + 20,000)) | (79,178) |
| | 70,822 |

(b) In scenario (b), the receipt of the annuity of £46,000 per annum would be taxable as pension income in the hands of Convey from 2016/17 onwards.

The payment of £46,000 per annum would be an annual payment for Sing and Dance and could be deducted from their income in the year of payment. It would be paid net of basic rate tax, so would be disallowed in computing trading profits (PM31110). The gross amount paid in the *tax year* (not the accounting period) must be shown in the annual partnership statement, divided between the partners in the way profits are shared in the tax year. Each partner will show his share in his own self-assessment tax return (PM31120). See **explanatory note 12.**

(c) The annuity of £34,500 would be treated in the same way as under (b) above.

# Explanatory Notes

*Partnership capital gains*

(1) The rules relating to partnership capital gains are contained in TCGA 1992 ss 59, 59A and 286(4), supplemented by SP D12 originally issued on 17 January 1975. The statement has been updated, most recently in September 2015. The latest version was updated following recommendations by the Office of Tax Simplification and contains a new paragraph on the treatment of capital contributions by partners to the partnership (paragraph 5) and a new paragraph to cover capital gains tax reliefs in relation to partnership gains (paragraph 14).

The position is very complex and there are areas where the approach to be taken is not clear. This is particularly so in relation to the integration of the 31 March 1982 indexation provisions with the 1975 statement. It is considered that the approach taken in this Example reflects the views expressed in the practice statements.

(2) Any charge to capital gains tax arises in the hands of each individual partner, not the partnership, each partner being deemed to own a proportionate part of the partnership's chargeable assets, being his share under the partnership agreement. The amount of the partner's capital/current account is irrelevant and it is helpful in understanding the capital gains tax aspects of partnerships to remember that a partner's capital/current account arises in one of three ways:

(i) cash (or other assets) introduced;

(ii) profits are retained;

(iii) assets are revalued, the capital account being credited with the partner's share of the surplus (or debited with his share of the deficit).

If capital is withdrawn, it will comprise a mixture of those three items.

Clearly there is no capital gains tax on withdrawals up to the amount introduced, nor on the withdrawal of retained profits. If, however, amounts are realised (as distinct from the capital account becoming overdrawn) in excess of these two items, they must reflect an upward revaluation of assets or, by implication, a payment for goodwill.

In order for capital gains tax to arise there must be a disposal, and a mere revaluation with a credit to the partners' capital accounts in the profit sharing ratio does not constitute a disposal. A subsequent withdrawal of the capital account on retirement, however, would do so, the liability on revaluation then crystallising.

It will also crystallise on (i) the admission of a new partner or (ii) a change in profit sharing ratio, since the capital/current account of the partner whose share is being reduced then includes an amount over and above the value of his new share in the chargeable asset concerned – tantamount to his having made a disposal, his capital account containing the proceeds.

(3) In relation to partnership assets, a partner is not connected with his fellow partners if the transaction is a bona fide commercial arrangement (TCGA 1992 s 286(4)). This means that unless the partners are otherwise connected, eg father and son (and even then if the same transaction could be expected to have been made were they not so connected), HMRC will accept whatever valuation is placed upon a transaction by the partners and will not substitute market value under TCGA 1992 s 18 (SP D12 para 8; CG27800). In the same way, no charge to inheritance tax will arise (IHTA 1984 s 10; PM60420). Furthermore it renders the hold-over relief for business gifts in TCGA 1992 s 165 unnecessary in these situations.

(4) Therefore, on the admission of a partner or a change in profit sharing ratio, no charge to capital gains tax will arise unless:

- there is or has been a revaluation of assets with a corresponding adjustment in the capital/current accounts; or
- payment is made for assets.

The reason is that on the admission of a partner, any cash he pays into the partnership will not constitute a disposal for capital gains tax purposes on the part of the existing partners if it is credited to the incoming partner's capital account. Unless he pays the existing partners for a share in the goodwill (or other chargeable assets), it will be treated as a disposal by the existing partners to the incoming partner for a consideration of such amount that neither chargeable gain nor allowable loss arises for capital gains purposes (ie a no gain/no loss disposal). The future ownership of each chargeable asset then being in the future capital profit sharing ratio.

*Bringing goodwill into the accounts*

(5) On the introduction of goodwill into the accounts in 1993 the accounting entries will have been:

| | *Goodwill (Asset Account)* | *Capital Accounts* Convey (2/3rds) | Sing (1/3rd) |
|---|---|---|---|
| Valuation | £75,000 | £50,000 | £25,000 |

Upon the profit sharing ratio being altered in 1994 this is tantamount to saying that Convey has disposed of (2/3rds – 1/2 =) 1/6th of the goodwill to Sing. But his capital account still contains the credit of £50,000, so this is equivalent to his having realised £12,500 of chargeable gains – that is £50,000 credited to capital account less £37,500 which is the value of his half share of the goodwill after the change in profit sharing ratio.

The same applies on the introduction of Dance, this time both Convey and Sing making disposals. The calculations are as follows:

| | *Convey* £ | *Sing* £ | *Dance* £ |
|---|---|---|---|
| Amount originally credited to capital account in 1993 | 50,000 | 25,000 | – |
| *At 1 May 1994* | | | |
| Disposal on change in profit sharing ratio | (12,500) | | |
| Deemed cost of acquisition for Sing | | 12,500 | |
| | 37,500 | 37,500 | |
| *At 1 May 2006* | | | |
| Deemed cost of acquisition for Dance | | | 25,000 |
| Disposal by Convey and Sing (since these amounts remain in their capital accounts) | (12,500) | (12,500) | |
| New share of goodwill in accounts is deemed to be | 25,000 | 25,000 | 25,000 |

*Effect of rebasing to 31 March 1982 values*

(6) Following the rebasing provisions of FA 1988 (as applied to partners by SP 1/89), for disposals on and after 6 April 1988 partners were able to take advantage of using the market value at 31 March 1982 in computing gains provided the asset had been held on that date. This effectively meant that on 6 April 1988 they are deemed to hold their then shares of partnership assets acquired before 31 March 1982 at either original cost or 31 March 1982 value, whichever shows the lower gain or loss on a disposal, or, as with Convey and Sing, where a general rebasing election has been made, at 31 March 1982 value in any event.

Where any no gain/no loss disposals (see **explanatory note 4**) take place on or after 6 April 1988 they are deemed to be for such consideration as gives a nil result after taking any available indexation allowance into account.

If no gain/no loss changes in partnership sharing ratios occurred between 6 April 1985 and 5 April 1988 inclusive, the no gain/no loss provisions operated *before* taking indexation allowance into account, so that allowable losses would have been created on such changes. In these circumstances, indexation allowance on disposals on and after 6 April 1988, although computed on 31 March 1982 value if appropriate, is calculated from the date when the indexation allowance was given on the no gain/no loss disposal.

For disposals on or after 30 November 1993, indexation allowance cannot be used to create or increase a loss, but can be used to reduce a profit (to nil if appropriate). Accordingly the no gain/no loss provisions still apply after taking any available indexation allowance into account, but the base value carried forward must be divided into cost and indexation allowance and in so far as a disposal results in a loss, indexation allowance will be reduced by the amount of loss. Therefore a loss can only arise based upon cost (including indexation allowance for any pre-30 November 1993 transactions) or market value on 31 March 1982 as appropriate.

The modernisation of capital gains tax which took place for disposals on or after 6 April 2008 abolished the cost option on all assets owned before March 1982 (for individuals and trustees, but not companies). This means that the base cost of all assets held on 31 March 1982 is the market value at that date, whether an election was made or not. This will not affect any subsequent disposal by the partnership in this Example as they had already made an election for this treatment in any case. HMRC confirmed that the post-April 2008 practice is consistent with SP 1/89 in Revenue & Customs Brief 09/09 webarchive.nationalarchives.gov.uk/+/hmrc.gov.uk/briefs/cgt/brief0909.htm.

(7) Indexation allowance for individuals and trustees is no longer available for disposals after 5 April 2008, however, the provisions described above affect the earlier disposals in the Example, and thus affect the cost of assets transferred between the partners. No indexation allowance can apply in respect of any disposals after 5 April 2008, whatever the result.

*Entrepreneurs' relief*

(8) Entrepreneurs' relief is available in respect of the disposal of a partners' share in his business, and thus will apply to Convey's sale in 2016/17 (TCGA 1992 s 169I).

The maximum amount of gain which can attract relief is £10 million in the disposer's lifetime (TCGA 1992 s 169N.

A gain qualifying for entrepreneurs' relief is subject to a separate 10% tax rate (TCGA 1992 s 169N). This relief is discussed in detail in **Example L5**.

*Annuity to retiring partner*

(9) Where an annuity is paid on the retirement of a partner by reason of age or ill health, then capital gains tax is not chargeable on the capitalised value provided the payment is in reasonable recognition of past service and is not a lump sum equivalent or a purchased life annuity (SP D12 para 9; CG28400).

A 'reasonable amount' is regarded as being the appropriate fraction of the retiring partner's average taxable profits *before* capital allowances or charges of the best three of the last seven years in which the partner was required to devote substantially the whole of his time to acting as a partner. The appropriate fraction depends on the complete years of service to the partnership (or a predecessor firm prior to merger) as follows:

| *Complete years* | *Fraction* |
|---|---|
| 1–5 | 1/60 per year |
| 6 | 8/60 |
| 7 | 16/60 |
| 8 | 24/60 |
| 9 | 32/60 |
| 10 or more | 2/3 |

Taking the table from the question above and adding back the capital allowances, this gives partnership profits as follows:

| | | £ | *Convey's profit share* |
|---|---|---|---|
| Year ended 30 April | 2010 (before capital allowances of £18,000) | 158,000 | One-third |
| | 2011 (before capital allowances of £25,000) | 196,000 | One-third |
| | 2012 (before capital allowances of £33,000) | 163,000 | One-third |
| | 2013 (before capital allowances of £20,000) | 222,000 | One-third |
| | 2014 (before capital allowances of £30,000) | 285,000 | One-third |
| | 2015 (before capital allowances of £20,000) | 300,000 | One-third |
| | 2016 (before capital allowances of £50,000) | 500,000 | One-third |

Convey's best three out of the last seven shares of profit in this Example are as follows:

| | | £ |
|---|---|---|
| 2014/15 | ⅓ x £285,000 | 95,000 |
| 2015/16 | ⅓ x £300,000 | 100,000 |
| 2016/17 | (⅓ x £500,000) - £79,178 overlap | 87,489 |
| | | 282,489 |

Average profits ⅓ x £282,489 = £94,163.

Maximum annuity which can be disregarded in computing capital gains (SP D12) is:

⅔ x £94,163 = £62,775.

*Lump sums and purchased annuities*

(10) Where a lump sum is paid (or an annuity is *purchased* in addition to the provision of an annuity from the partnership), the whole of the capitalised value of the *annuity from the partnership* plus the lump sum is treated as a payment for chargeable assets.

The capitalised value of the annuity from the partnership does not increase the capital gains tax base cost of those partners paying the annuity – they are after all getting relief for income tax at their marginal rates on such payments (see **explanatory note 12**).

If, however, the sum of the annuity from the partnership plus 1/9th of the lump sum or purchased annuity amounts to less than the 'reasonable amount' defined in **explanatory note 9**, the *capitalised value of the annuity* from the partnership is not chargeable to capital gains tax, but the *lump sum or cost of the purchased annuity* remains so (SP 1/79; CG28420; PM31130).

Note that for income tax purposes a purchased annuity is treated as savings income (ITA 2007 s 18(3)(b)) but a partnership annuity is treated as pension income.

(11) The 'reasonable amount' per **explanatory note 9** is £62,775. This is compared with:

| | | |
|---|---|---|
| *Scheme (b)* | Annuity | £46,000 |
| | | £ |
| *Scheme (c)* | Annuity | 34,500 |
| | 1/9th × £70,000 | 7,778 |
| | | 42,278 |

Since in each case the amount is less than £62,775 the capitalised value of the annuity is not chargeable to capital gains tax, but the lump sum in scheme (c) represents part of the disposal proceeds and is brought into the capital gains tax computation as indicated at **part (v)(c)** of the answer.

*Tax position of partners paying the annuity*

(12) Partnership annuities are annual payments as far as the paying partners are concerned and they are not deductible from trading profits (PM31110). They are allocated to partners in profit sharing ratios, and the amount deductible from income is the amount paid in the tax year (ITA 2007 s 448). Although see PM31120 for a discussion of situations where income tax relief might not be available.

Purchased annuities must be paid subject to PAYE under real time information (RTI), but PAYE does not apply to annuities paid by the partnership, although tax must still be withheld under ITA 2007 s 900 (PM31110).

(13) If the partners pay a 'reasonable annuity' and continue to do so, there is no gain for the retiring partner, and there is symmetrical income tax treatment for those paying and receiving. If, instead, the other partners purchase an annuity on the date of retirement, then there will be a gain for the retiring partner by reference to the purchase price, and the cost will be added to the other partners' base costs.

There is a disadvantage if the partners commence to pay an annuity and then replace it at a later date by buying an annuity. It is likely that the right to receive the annuity is a chargeable asset, and the disposal of it in consideration for the amount paid for the purchased life annuity would give rise to a capital gains tax charge; but the other partners would not at that time acquire any asset, so the cost to them would obtain no tax relief at all.

*Limited liability partnerships (LLPs)*

(14) LLPs can be formed under the Limited Liability Partnerships Act 2000. For the detailed provisions, see **Example C13 explanatory notes 3–8**. As indicated in that Example, if an LLP goes into formal liquidation it will be treated as a company from that time, and the partners' shares in the LLP will then be chargeable assets in their own right.

SP D12 makes it clear that a LLP will be treated for capital gains tax purposes as a 'normal' partnership (that is the partners will be assessed on their shares of the underlying assets and the LLP will be 'transparent') as long as the LLP is within TCGA 1992, s 59A(1) (carrying on a trade or business and not in liquidation).

*Goodwill*

(15) It is common for partners gradually to increase their share of partnership goodwill over a number of years. It would be open for HMRC to argue that 'shares of goodwill' are 'fungible assets' subject to the share identification rules in TCGA 1992 s 104(3). SP D12 states that HMRC will not take this view, but will regard a share of partnership goodwill as a single asset that is successively enhanced. This makes the computations much easier.

# INDEX

References are to page numbers

**B**

## E

**F**

## S

## T